A HISTORY OF THE CRUSADES

Kenneth M. Setton, GENERAL EDITOR

A HISTORY OF THE CRUSADES

Kenneth M. Setton, GENERAL EDITOR

Volume III

THE FOURTEENTH
AND FIFTEENTH CENTURIES

Bertrandon de la Brocquière offering to Philip the Good of Burgundy a translation of the Koran, at the Abbey of Pothière during a siege of Mussy-l'Evêque.
From the manuscript *Avis directif pour faire le passage d'Outremer*,
in the collections of the Bibliothèque nationale

A HISTORY OF

THE

CRUSADES

KENNETH M. SETTON

GENERAL EDITOR

Volume III

THE FOURTEENTH
AND FIFTEENTH CENTURIES

EDITED BY

HARRY W. HAZARD

THE UNIVERSITY OF WISCONSIN PRESS

Published 1975
The University of Wisconsin Press
Box 1379, Madison, Wisconsin 53701

The University of Wisconsin Press, Ltd.
70 Great Russell St., London

First printing

Printed in the United States of America
For LC CIP information see the colophon

ISBN 0-299-06670-3

Dulcem patriam revidere

CONTENTS

MAPS

*Maps compiled by Harry W. Hazard and executed by the
Cartographic Laboratory of the University of Wisconsin, Madison*

FOREWORD

Almost twenty years have now passed since the appearance of the first volume of this *History of the Crusades* (1955). In the Foreword to that volume I cited the maxim attributed to Augustus, which Petrarch once quoted to his friend Boccaccio: Whatever is being done well enough, is being done soon enough (*Epp. seniles,* XVI [XVII], 2). Since seven years elapsed before the second volume was published (1962), I have never been under the illusion that we were doing our task soon enough. I can only hope that we have done it well enough. Now, after another dozen years, we present the third volume to our readers, but I am glad to say that the fourth volume has also gone to the press.

Volume III, as its title indicates, deals with the period of the later Crusades. The fourteenth century witnessed the two Smyrniote Crusades (1344–1347), the sack of Alexandria (1365), the anti-Bulgarian and anti-Turkish expedition of Amadeo VI of Savoy (1366–1367), the Barbary Crusade (1390), and the Christian defeat at Nicopolis (1396). The fourteenth century closed with the anti-Turkish expedition of the doughty marshal Boucicault in defense of Constantinople (1399–1400), and the following century opened with his harassment of the Mamluk coast of Syria (1403). After Boucicault most Christian expeditions against the Moslems were directed against the Ottoman Turks; they were primarily defensive, to stem the Turkish advance into Christian territory.

The hope of rewinning the Holy Land had largely passed by the fifteenth century, although it remained the ideal of propagandists at the Curia Romana. The fall of Constantinople in 1453 was a blow to eastern Christendom from which recovery was to prove impossible. Pius II's crusading efforts died with him at Ancona (1464), and little came of the crusading dreams of visionaries at the court of Burgundy in the time of Philip the Good (1419–1467). The Conciliar movement had distracted the papacy; the anti-Hussite Crusades helped spend the military resources of the Germans. Nevertheless, the fifteenth century was marked by the Hungarian expeditions which John Hunyadi and Matthias Corvinus led against the Turks. If the Christians were defeated at Varna (1444), they repulsed the Turks at Belgrade (1456). If the Mamluks reduced Cyprus to a tributary state

xiii

with the humiliation of king James (1426), the Venetians later acquired the island and held it for more than eighty years (1489–1571). Early in the sixteenth century Selim I's destruction of the Mamluk power in Egypt (1517) made the Turks masters of the eastern Mediterranean littoral. The Hospitallers had to surrender Rhodes on the first day of the new year 1523, but Malta held out against the Turks in 1565, and the naval forces of Christendom were victorious at Lepanto in 1571.

Although Dr. Hazard and I had once hoped to carry the *Crusades* down to the Venetian surrender of Crete to the Turks in 1669, time and circumstance have moderated our ambition. Our plans have changed somewhat—inevitably so—in the twenty years that have passed since the appearance of the first volume. Volume IV will deal primarily with the art and architecture of the crusader states; Volume V, with political and economic institutions, agricultural conditions, crusading propaganda, western missions, religious minorities, and social history. Volume VI will be an atlas and gazetteer of crusading history.

KENNETH M. SETTON

The Institute for Advanced Study
Princeton, New Jersey
October 10, 1974

PREFACE

Having devoted nearly a quarter of a century to this series of volumes on the crusades, and having known for at least a decade that eventually this preface would be required of me, I nevertheless have accumulated no philosophical profundities to share with the reader, merely some deeply felt apologies and regrets, gratitude and hopes.

Apologies for the inordinate delays in producing this and its companion volume, now in press, are due both to the readers who have—we trust—been impatiently awaiting their appearance, and to the contributors, many of whom have conscientiously revised chapters submitted in the 'fifties and 'sixties to take into account subsequent research. Regrets parallel the apologies, for the inexorable passage of time has claimed the lives of four of our contributors—Sir Harry Luke and Professors Ettore Rossi, Mustafa Ziada, and Edgar Johnson—so that we have had to prepare their chapters for publication without the benefit of their advice, in rueful awareness that we could never duplicate their specialized knowledge. I can only hope that such footnotes and bibliographical additions as I have supplied, and such modifications as I have had to make in their original manuscripts, would have met with their approval.

Gratitude, of course, is due primarily to our other contributors, not only for revising their chapters but for their forbearance with editorial exigencies and suggestions. Many others have helped, over the years, and our deep appreciation is here acknowledged, to Mrs. Jean T. Carver for extensive impeccable typing, to Mrs. Margaret T. Setton and Dr. David L. Gassman for meticulous proof-reading, to Mrs. Mary Maraniss of the University of Wisconsin Press for equally meticulous preparation of the manuscript for the printer, to Professor Randall T. Sale and his staff for the maps which embellish these pages, to the anonymous printers who have cheerfully incorporated countless revisions and corrections, and not least to the ever-helpful director of the Press, Thompson Webb, Jr.

As for our hopes, without which the effort of assembling and editing such collaborative works as this would be intolerable, they will surprise no one: the hope that this third volume is as generously received as its two predecessors, and stands up as well over the years; the hope that volume IV will appear shortly, and that volumes V and

VI will follow with all deliberate speed; the hope that perusal of the
series will prove profitable, not only in supplying information presented from varied points of view, but in providing occasion for
contemplation of a world in upheaval, so different from our own and
yet so inescapably similar.

HARRY W. HAZARD

The Institute for Advanced Study
Princeton, New Jersey
October 25, 1974

A NOTE
ON TRANSLITERATION
AND NOMENCLATURE

One of the obvious problems to be solved by the editors of such a work as this, intended both for general readers and for scholars in many different disciplines, is how to render the names of persons and places, and a few other terms, originating in languages and scripts unfamiliar to the English-speaking reader and, indeed, to most readers whose native languages are European. In the present volume, and presumably in the entire work, these comprise principally Arabic, Turkish, Persian, and Armenian, none of which was normally written in our Latin alphabet until its adoption by Turkey in 1928. The analogous problem of Byzantine Greek names and terms has been handled by using the familiar Latin equivalents, Anglicized Greek, or, occasionally, Greek type, as has seemed appropriate in each instance, but a broader approach is desirable for the other languages under consideration.

The somewhat contradictory criteria applied are ease of recognition and readability on the one hand and scientific accuracy and consistency on the other. It has proved possible to reconcile these, and to standardize the great variety of forms in which identical names have been submitted to us by different contributors, through constant consultation with specialists in each language, research in the sources, and adherence to systems conforming to the requirements of each language.

Of these, Arabic presents the fewest difficulties, since the script in which it is written is admirably suited to the classical language. The basic system used, with minor variants, by all English-speaking scholars was restudied and found entirely satisfactory, with the slight modifications noted. The chief alternative system, in which every Arabic consonant is represented by a single Latin character (t for th, ḫ for kh, ḏ for dh, š for sh, ġ for gh) was rejected for several reasons, needless proliferation of diacritical marks to bother the eye and multiply occasions for error, absence of strong countervailing arguments, and, most decisively, the natural tendency of non-specialists to adopt these spellings but omit the diacritical marks. The use of single letters in this manner leads to undesirable results, but the spellings adopted for the present work may be thus treated with confidence by any writer not requiring the discriminations which the remaining diacritical marks indicate.

The letters used for Arabic consonants, in the order of the Arabic alphabet, are these: ', b, t, th, j, ḥ, kh, d, dh, r, z, s, sh, ṣ, ḍ, ṭ, ẓ, ', gh, f, q, k, l, m, n, h, w, y. The vowels are a, i, u, lengthened as ā, ī, ū, with the *alif bi-ṣūrati-l-yā'* distinguished as â; initial ' is omitted, but terminal macrons are retained. Diphthongs are *au* and *ai*, not *aw* and *ay,* as being both philologically preferable and visually less misleading. The same considerations lead to the omission of *l* of *al-* before a duplicated consonant (Nūr-ad-Dīn rather than Nūr-al-Dīn). As in this example, hyphens are used to link words composing a single name (as also 'Abd-Allāh), with weak initial vowels elided (as Abū-l-Ḥasan). Normally *al-* (meaning "the") is not capitalized; *ibn-* is not when it means literally "son of," but is otherwise (as Ibn-Khaldūn).

Some readers may be disconcerted to find the prophet called "Mohammed" and his followers "Moslems," but this can readily be justified. These spellings are valid English proper names, derived from Arabic originals which would be correctly transliterated "Muhammad" and "Muslimūn" or "Muslimīn." The best criterion for deciding whether to use the Anglicized spellings or the accurate transliterations is the treatment accorded the third of this cluster of names, that of the religion "Islam." Where this is transliterated "Islām," with a macron over the *a,* it should be accompanied by "Muslim" and "Muḥammad," but where the macron is omitted, consistency and common sense require "Moslem" and "Mohammed," and it is the latter triad which have been considered appropriate in this work. All namesakes of the prophet, however, have had their names duly transliterated "Muḥammad," to correspond with names of other Arabs who are not individually so familiar to westerners as to be better recognized in Anglicized forms.

All names of other Arabs, and of non-Arabs with Arabic names, have been systematically transliterated, with the single exception of Ṣalāḥ-ad-Dīn, whom it would have been pedantic to call that rather than Saladin. For places held, in the crusading era or now, by Arabs, the Arabic names appear either in the text or in the gazetteer, where some additional ones are also included to broaden the usefulness of this feature.

Large numbers of names of persons and groups, however, custom-arily found in Arabicized spellings because they were written in Arabic script, have been restored to their underlying identity when-ever this is ascertainable. For example, Arabic "Saljūq" misrepresents four of the six component phonemes: *s* is correct, *a* replaces Turkish *e*, for which Arabic script provides no equivalent, *l* is correct, *j* replaces the non-Arabic *ch*, *ū* substitutes a non-Turkish long *u* for the original *ü*, and *q* as distinguished from *k* is non-existent in Turkish; this quadruple rectification yields "Selchük" as the name of the eponymous leader, and "Selchükid"—on the model of 'Abbāsid and Timurid—for the dynasty and the people.

It might be thought that as Turkish is now written in a well-conceived modified Latin alphabet, there would be no reason to alter this, and this presumption is substantially valid. For the same reasons as apply to Arabic, *ch* has been preferred above *ç*, *sh* above *ş*, and *gh* above *ğ*, with *kh* in a few instances given as a preferred alternate of *h*, from which it is not distinguished in modern Turkish. No long vowels have been indicated, as being functionless survivals. Two other changes have been made in the interest of the English-speaking reader, and should be remembered by those using map sheets and standard reference works: *c* (pronounced dj) has been changed to *j*, so that one is not visually led to imagine that the Turkish name for the Tigris—Dijle/Dicle—rhymes with "tickle," and what the eminent lexicographer H. C. Hony terms "that abomination the undotted ı" has, after the model of *The Encyclopaedia of Islām*, been written i̇.

Spellings, modified as above indicated, have usually been founded on those of the Turkish edition, *İslâm Ansiklopedisi*, hampered by occasional inconsistencies within that work. All names of Turks appear thus emended, and Turkish equivalents of almost all places within or near modern Turkey appear in the gazetteer.

In addition to *kh*, Middle Turkish utilized a few other phonemes not common in modern Turkish: *zh* (modern *j*), *dh*, *ng*, and *ä* (modern *e*); the first three of these will be used as needed, while the last-mentioned may be assumed to underlie every medieval Turkish name now spelled with *e*. Plaintive eyebrows may be raised at our exclusion of *q*, but this was in Middle Turkish only the alternate spelling used when the sound *k* was combined with back instead of front vowels, and its elimination by the Turks is commendable.

Persian names have been transliterated like Arabic with certain modifications, chiefly use of the additional vowels *e* and *o* and replacing *ḍ* and *dh* with *ẓ* and *z̲*, so that Arabic "Ādharbaijān" becomes Persian "Āz̲erbaijān," more accurate as well as more recognizable. Omission of the definite article from personal names was considered but eventually disapproved.

Armenian presented great difficulties: the absence of an authoritative reference source for spelling names, the lack of agreement on transliteration, and the sound-shift by which classical and eastern Armenian *b, d, g* became western Armenian *p, t, k* and—incredible as it may seem to the unwary—*vice versa;* similar reciprocal interchanges involved *ts* and *dz,* and *ch* and *j.* The following alphabet represents western Armenian letters, with eastern variants in parentheses: a, p (b), k (g), t (d), e, z, ē, î, ṭ, zh, i, l, kh, dz (ts), g (k), h, ts (dz), gh, j (ch), m, y, n, sh, o, ch̲, b (p), ch (j), ṛ, s, v̰, d (t), r, t̲s̲, u or v, p̣, ḳ, ō, f. Many spellings are based on the Armenian texts in the *Recueil des historiens des croisades.*

In standardizing names of groups, the correct root forms in the respective languages have been identified, with the ending "-id" for dynasties and their peoples but "-ite" for sects, and with plural either identical with singular (as Kirghiz) or plus "-s" (Khazars) or "-es" (Uzes). In cases where this sounded hopelessly awkward, it was abandoned (Muwaḥḥids, not Muwaḥḥidids or Muwaḥḥidites, and certainly not Almohads, which is, however, cross-referenced).

The use of place names is explained in the note preceding the gazetteer, but may be summarized by saying that in general the most familiar correct form is used in the text and maps, normally an English version of the name by which the place was known to Europeans during the crusades. Variant forms are given and identified in the gazetteer.

Despite conscientious efforts to perfect the nomenclature, errors will probably be detected by specialists; they are to be blamed on me and not on individual contributors or editorial colleagues, for I have been accorded a free hand. Justifiable suggestions for improvements will be welcomed, and used to bring succeeding volumes nearer that elusive goal, impeccability in nomenclature.

HARRY W. HAZARD

[Princeton, New Jersey, 1962]

Reprinted from Volume I, with minor modifications.

ABBREVIATIONS

AOL   *Archives de l'Orient latin*, 2 vols., Société de l'Orient latin, Paris, 1881–1884.

CSHB   *Corpus scriptorum historiae byzantinae*, ed. B. G. Niebuhr, I. Becker, and others, 50 vols., Bonn, 1828–1897.

Dipl.   *Diplomatari de l'Orient català*, ed. Antoni Rubió i Lluch, Barcelona, 1947.

Malta   Royal Malta Library, Archives of the Order of St. John of Jerusalem.

MGH, SS.   *Monumenta Germaniae historica: Scriptores*, ed. G. H. Pertz, T. Mommsen, and others, 32 vols., Reichsinstitut für ältere deutsche Geschichtskunde, Hanover and elsewhere, 1826–1934.

PG   *Patrologiae graecae cursus completus* . . . , ed. J. P. Migne, 167 vols., Paris, 1857–1876.

PL   *Patrologiae latinae cursus completus* . . . , ed. J. P. Migne, 221 vols., Paris, 1841–1864.

RHC, Arm.   *Recueil des historiens des croisades: Documents arméniens*, ed. E. Dulaurier and others, 2 vols., Académie des inscriptions et belles-lettres, Paris, 1869–1906, reprinted 1967.

RHE   *Revue d' histoire ecclésiastique*, Louvain, 1900-date.

RHGF   *Recueil des historiens des Gaules et de la France*, ed. Martin Bouquet [1685–1754] and others, 24 vols. in fol., Académie des inscriptions et belles-lettres, Paris, 1738–1904.

RISS   *Rerum italicarum scriptores* . . . , ed. L. A. Muratori [1672–1750], 25 vols. in 28, Milan, 1723–1751; new edition by G. Carducci and V. Fiorini, 34 vols. in 109 fasc., Città di Castello and Bologna, 1900–1935.

ROL   *Revue de l'Orient latin*, 12 vols., Société de l'Orient latin, Paris, 1893–1911.

RTA   *Deutsche Reichstagsakten*, vols. 8–9, Akademie der Wissenschaften, Munich, 1867–1868, reprinted Göttingen.

U.B.   *Urkundliche Beiträge zur Geschichte des Hussitenkrieges* . . . , ed. František Palacký, 2 vols., Prague, 1873, reprinted Osnabruck, 1966.

Volume III

THE FOURTEENTH
AND FIFTEENTH CENTURIES

1. Western Europe

I

THE CRUSADE IN THE FOURTEENTH CENTURY

The historiography of the crusades has undergone considerable emendation in recent times, and many accepted ideas have had to be revised. One of the most notable among these altered conceptions is that of the limits of the Age of the Crusades. The older historians considered the crusades as a movement coterminous with the life of the Latin kingdom of Jerusalem, at least in regard to the closing date of this tragic confrontation between two large sections of medieval humanity. According to the old school of thought, the crusades suddenly began in 1095 with Urban II's famous declarations at Clermont in Auvergne, and ended equally suddenly in 1291 with the termination of Latin dominion in the Holy Land when Acre and the remaining Christian outposts fell into the hands of the Baḥrī Mamluk sultan al-Ashraf Khalīl.[1] This is the cataclysmic viewpoint of the Age of the Crusades, which has been repudiated in the light of modern researches in this field.

Here we are concerned only with the closing chapters in the history of the movement, and this volume will, it is hoped, show beyond doubt that the fall of Acre did not spell the end of the crusades. When the last vestiges of the Latin kingdom in Palestine disappeared before the irresistible advance of Islamic forces, its crown was transferred to the Lusignan dynasty in Cyprus,[2] and the Hospitallers, who had been its staunch defenders, moved the center of their crusading activities from Syria to the island of Rhodes,[3] which they wrested from Byzantium after a short sojourn in Cyprus.

The deadly blow which the Christians had sustained at Acre seems to have awakened western Christendom to the stark reality of their precarious position in the Levant. To the contemporary mind, the collapse of Acre in 1291 was comparable to Saladin's storming of

1. See volume II of this work, pp. 595–598, 754.
2. See below, chapter X.
3. See below, chapter VIII.

3

Jerusalem in 1187. Toward the end of the thirteenth century, the crusading spirit had been slumbering throughout Europe. Now the time was ripe for action, but the calamities and humiliations which had befallen the Christian hosts in the past indicated the need for better organization and a greater measure of harmony in the future. Thus the crusade in the fourteenth century passed through two distinct stages. The first was that of propaganda, consisting mainly of literary works by numerous thinkers and pious travelers who planned the *passagium* and advised the leaders on the elements of a successful campaign. The second comprised positive action in a series of expeditions conducted against the Moslem states in the Near East. The first phase occupied roughly the first half of the century, while the second followed as a natural corollary to propagandist efforts on behalf of the crusading cause. In a number of cases we find that propagandists also took part in some of the memorable crusading campaigns of the later Middle Ages.

In regard to the crusading terrain, the fourteenth century presented a broader arena. In 1096, when Godfrey of Bouillon embarked with the blessing of pope Urban II on his momentous journey to the Near East, the medieval world was still very limited in dimensions. Beyond the confines of Egypt and the Fertile Crescent, if we except certain areas on the western shores of India, the rest of the globe was enveloped in the thick mist of oblivion.[4] It was not until the age of the later crusades that the clouds began to lift and the imagination came to perceive the alien regions of Central Asia and the Far East. This immense growth in the size of the known world was, in part, a by-product of the later crusades. Even though the movement lacked the full vigor and the spectacular achievements of the early crusades, its later history brought forth results of a more enduring value for mankind. It is true that the traditional scene of action remained as before in the Levant, and the eyes of all Christians remained fixed on the land of promise, but the crusading mind traveled much farther into limitless Cathay with the adventurers and missionaries who opened up the eastern route to Khanbaliq ("Cambaluc," Peking) in the heart of Asia. The idea of collaboration with the Mongols, who had become a growing factor in world politics and who shared with the Christians an abhorrence for the Moslem Mamluks, was regarded as basic to the foreign policy of the papacy and its

---

4. For a full discussion, see John Kirtland Wright, *The Geographical Lore of the Time of the Crusades* (New York, 1925), and a more recent work by I. de Rachewiltz, *Papal Envoys to the Great Khans* (Stanford, 1971).

associates in western Europe, and was reiterated by the propagandists for the crusade in the later medieval period.[5]

Thus the field of crusading activities during the fourteenth century included not only Europe and the Levant but also the Mongol world with its sweeping vistas far beyond the frontiers of the Near East. Though the face of the Respublica Christiana in Europe was changing, and crusading ideas were being submerged in the tumult which accompanied the rise of the new nations and the continuous decline of the old order, certain events helped to resuscitate the moribund cause throughout the decades under review. The fall of Acre in 1291, like the loss of Jerusalem in 1187 and the collapse of Constantinople in 1453, brought home to Christians in Europe a feeling of dismay and aroused in them a spirit of defensive, if not offensive, crusading. The occasional presence of wandering kings from the Near Eastern Christian states served their western coreligionists in Europe as another reminder of the sad fate of fellow Christians beyond the sea. The western peregrinations of Peter I de Lusignan (whom Philip of Mézières described as the *athleta Christi*) between 1362 and 1365 preceded the sack of Alexandria in the latter year. King Leon VI of Cilician Armenia spent his closing days as a refugee in Europe until he died in Paris in November 1393, hardly three years before the crusade of Nicopolis. It was after the rout of the united forces of Europe outside the walls of Nicopolis that emperor Manuel II Palaeologus undertook his "mendicant pilgrimage" to the west between 1399 and 1401, in order to persuade the pope and the kings of France and England to send military aid for the relief of his beleaguered city of Constantinople.[6] Even after the downfall of Byzantium and the flight of the Palaeologi to the Morea, an imperial pretender, Thomas Palaeologus, would take refuge in Rome in 1461. By then, however, the opportunity for major crusading conquests would be gone beyond recall.

During the fourteenth century, propagandists for holy war included even more potent elements than the solitary royal figures from the Near East who moved from court to court in Europe without any direct contact with the people of western Christendom. The innumerable wandering knights of the dislocated military-religious orders and the dwindling Latin principalities in the Levant did much to renew the crusading zeal which, though weakening, had

5. See below, chapter XV.
6. See below, chapter III.

never been extinguished. Men of the sword and men of the pen together with a stream of pilgrims returning from Jerusalem helped to rekindle enthusiasm for the cause by word of mouth and by the written letter. Indeed, it would be idle to attempt to make a full list of the late medieval propagandists and to outline their life and work. The fourteenth century in particular is marked by an avalanche of literary propaganda covering almost all the countries of Europe.

That propaganda was inaugurated by an eye-witness of the fighting which had taken place within Acre in 1291, one Thaddeus of Naples. He wrote a tract of considerable interest under the title of *Hystoria de desolacione . . . tocius Terre Sancte . . .*[7] shortly after he had been forced out of Acre with the rest of its Christian inhabitants. He describes himself as "Magister Neapolitanus" and presents his work in the form of an *Epistola* addressed to the whole of Christendom. He describes the siege and the storming of the city in a style designed to arouse the feelings of all Catholics for the revival of the crusading movement against the enemies of the cross. He exhorts all the princes of Europe to abstain from their local squabbles and join their forces and efforts into one united body under the leadership of the church militant in order to save the Holy Land, which he calls "our heritage."

Thaddeus was a contemporary of pope Nicholas IV (1288–1292), whose pontificate was an important landmark in the history of propaganda for the crusade. Nicholas grouped around himself at the Roman curia a number of men devoted to the cause, two of whom are worthy of special mention. Charles II of Anjou, king of Naples, who had inherited his father's claim to the crown of the kingdom of Jerusalem, was naturally interested in the affairs of the east; he was also a papal vassal and as such collaborated with Nicholas IV in his project of a *passagium generale.* The second advisor to Nicholas was a Franciscan friar named Fidenzio of Padua, who had just returned from a special mission to the east before the Moslem conquest of Acre. He drew up his recommendations in his *Liber recuperationis Terre Sancte.*[8] He favors a maritime blockade of the Mamluk empire, and he states that certain points on the coast of Cilician Armenia would provide a fine base for military operations against Syria and Palestine. His book deals with the routes as well as with numerous details concerning the fleet and the land forces and other items of interest to the pilgrim and the crusader. Perhaps the most vulnerable

7. Ed. Paul Riant (Geneva, [1873]).
8. Ed. G. Golubovich, *Biblioteca bio-bibliografica della Terra Santa e dell' Oriente francescano,* 1st ser., II (Quaracchi, 1913), 1–60.

point in his memorandum is that he wrote it when Acre was still in Christian hands, and so considerable modification had to be introduced in his plans to cope with the new situation. On the whole, the reign of Nicholas IV witnessed the birth of an epoch of intense literary and diplomatic propaganda for the crusade.

During the same period, a new departure in propagandist literature appeared in the work of Raymond Lull, a Catalan born in 1232. A poet, a philosopher, and a prolific author of several hundred books and treatises of the most varied nature, Lull was also one of the most active figures of his time. Like Roger Bacon, he was one of the early pioneers of the principle of the unity of human knowledge, which he exemplified in his *Arbor scientiae*. Like Frederick II, he was one of the earliest orientalists, mastering the Arabic tongue and even composing Arabic poetry; and like him, too, he was a crusader who believed in the ways of peace rather than the ways of war for a permanent settlement of the causes of difference between east and west. Whereas Frederick II resorted to diplomacy, Raymond Lull became the great exponent of religious missionary work among the followers of Mohammed. It is here that Lull's real contribution rests, though he was not without a precursor in this field. Around the middle of the twelfth century, Peter the Venerable, abbot of Cluny, after a visitation tour of the Cluniac houses in the Iberian peninsula which brought him into direct contact with Moslems, had formulated a new thesis for relations with the enemies of the cross. His treatise, entitled *Contra sectam Saracenorum*,[9] makes it clear that he wished Christians to approach Moslems "not with arms as the crusaders do, but with reason, not with hatred but with love," for, in so doing, they might win them over to Christ and save their souls from perdition. His work was a counterfoil to that of his great contemporary, Bernard of Clairvaux, whose vehement appeal to arms is found in his treatise *De laude novae militiae.*[10]

Peter paved the way for Raymond Lull, the great apostle of missionary work among Moslems. Though he did, like most of the authors of his time, start by promoting a new plan for a crusade, in the *Liber de fine*,[11] which he wrote at an early stage in his career, Lull afterward gave up this plan and embraced the idea of converting Moslems to Christianity, instead of destroying their bodies and the

9. In Migne, *PL,* CLXXXIX, as "Adversus sectam sive haeresim Saracenorum," and trans. J. Thomä, *Zwei Bücher gegen den Muhammedanismus* (Leipzig, 1906). On Peter, see James Kritzeck, *Peter the Venerable and Islam* (Princeton, 1964).

10. In Migne, *PL,* CLXXXII–CLXXXV; also several other editions and translations.

11. Ed. A. Gottron in *Ramon Lulls Kreuzzugsideen* (Abhandlungen zur mittleren und neueren Geschichte, vol. XXXIX; Berlin, 1912).

souls therewith. In order to achieve his aim, he bought a Moorish slave who was a good enough scholar to teach him Arabic and thus enable him to preach the Christian doctrine and attempt to refute Islam in the countries beyond the sea. Thrice he crossed the western Mediterranean to the sultanate of Tunisia, where he engaged himself in perilous discussions with the shaikhs of Islam. During his first and second trips, he was able to formulate the terms of his debate with them in his treatise called *Disputatio Raymundi Christiani et Hamar Saraceni*,[12] but he was deported by the lenient Moslem governor after a period of captivity. In his third crossing, after a relatively peaceful stay among the Moslems of Tunis, he sallied into Bugia on the Algerian coast, where he earned his much desired crown of martyrdom. At the age of eighty-three, in the year 1315 or 1316, he stood in the middle of the town market to preach his faith, but the fury of the fanatic Berbers led them to stone him to death on the beach, where his body was picked up by a Genoese ship and taken for interment in the cathedral of Palma on the island of Majorca.

Contemporary with the movements identified with Nicholas IV on the one hand and Raymond Lull on the other, there arose a royal center of propaganda at the court of Philip IV the Fair, king of France (1285–1314). Philip's reign was one of great moment in the annals of France, of the papacy, and of Europe in general. He had visions of amalgamating France and the empire under his own sovereignty. He disgraced Boniface VIII and succeeded in drawing the papacy to France, at Avignon, with immeasurable consequences. He even dreamt of the creation of a new eastern empire, including Byzantium together with the Holy Land and the whole of the Mamluk sultanate of Egypt, under the rule of one of his sons. Such visions of world hegemony in the age of the crusades were bound to direct the king's attention to the possibilities accruing from the leadership of the movement of holy war. The crusade, which was a basic element in papal foreign policy, eventually became one of the chief factors in the effort to impose the supremacy of the Roman see over Europe. Thus Philip undoubtedly wanted to follow the example of the pontiff and, by espousing the international cause, place himself at the head of the Christian commonwealth. His advisors and courtiers naturally echoed the royal aspirations in their propagandist writings. They included two great jurists, Peter Dubois and William of Nogaret, as well as four men of action—Jacques de Molay, grand master of the Templars, Fulk of Villaret, master of the Hospitallers,

---

12. Ed. I. Salzinger, *Opera omnia,* 10 vols. (Mainz, 1721–1740), IV; cf. A. Gottron, *L'Edició maguntina de Ramón Lull* (Barcelona, 1915).

Henry II de Lusignan, king of Cyprus, and Benedict Zaccaria, Genoese admiral.

The work which best represents the ideas and policies prevailing at Philip's court is Peter Dubois's treatise entitled *De recuperatione Terre Sancte*,[13] which he wrote under the auspices of the French king and dedicated in 1307 to Edward I of England, known for his crusading enthusiasm. Dubois's treatise is one of the most remarkable documents of its kind produced during this period. Written by a man of law, it deals systematically with all the contemporary problems arising from the projects of crusade and offers all the solutions in line with the royal policy. Dissensions in Europe should be completely eradicated, and the unwilling states brought to reason by force. Discords must be submitted for final settlement by a European tribunal of arbitration composed of three ecclesiastical dignitaries and three laymen known to be inaccessible to corruption. Trade with the recalcitrant members of European society should be banned, and their citizens transported to colonize Palestine. The right of appeal to the pope should remain, but the papacy, according to his conception, must be deprived of its independence and dispossessed of its landed heritage. The popes must be settled in France, and the whole of the church hierarchy should return to the life of poverty exemplified in its early history. The administration of church fiefs should be entrusted to the king of France, and the revenues of the Templars and Hospitallers should be confiscated and used for financing the crusade. In fact, these two orders should be united into a single organization whose sole business would be crusading. The routes to the east could be selected according to the position and exigencies of each country. The empire must adopt a hereditary regime with a French prince on its throne. The government of the Holy Land, after its reconquest, should be arranged on a military basis with a *dux belli* and a body of centurions and cohorts of twelve warriors in every town. Each state should have its special hostels prepared for the reception and accommodation of its own subjects. The eastern Christians and all heretical sects must be persuaded to join the Roman church. Missionary work should be undertaken by competent persons conversant with the languages of the Orient. The priories of the Templars and Hospitallers should be utilized for the institution of schools where these languages would be taught. The crown of Egypt and "Babylon" would be conferred upon Philip's second son, Philip

13. Ed. C. V. Langlois (Collection de textes pour servir à l'étude et l'enseignement d'histoire, IX; Paris, 1891); trans. W. I. Brandt, *The Recovery of the Holy Land* (Columbia University Records of Civilization, no. 51, New York, 1956).

(V), who would organize an eastern empire with French leanings. This curious medley of ideas, both feasible and unfeasible, provides the keynotes to the project formulated by Peter Dubois under the auspices of a royal master to whom the crusade appears to have been a means rather than an end in itself.

Perhaps the most practical propositions were those which came from a Latin resident in the Levant, Marino Sanudo Torsello, who was related to an important Venetian dynasty settled in the Archipelago. He wrote a monumental work which he called *Liber secretorum fidelium crucis;*[14] he submitted its first redaction to pope Clement V in 1309 and the second to king Charles IV of France in 1323. As one who had traveled far and wide in the Levant, he had managed to collect more data and original material about the countries of that part of the world than any of his Latin contemporaries. His conception of a successful crusade is based on economic principles above all other considerations. The chief source of Mamluk superiority is trade. The western maritime powers send their ships to the trade emporia of Egypt and Syria for the purchase of goods imported from India and the Far East. By this means they enrich the sultans with Christian money which they employ in fighting the Christians in Palestine. Furthermore, some of the Christian states themselves perfidiously supply the enemy with war material from European markets and with slaves from Kaffa and elsewhere, destined to feed the Mamluk ranks with warriors. Past experience has taught Christians the hopelessness of depending solely on armed expeditions for the recovery of the Holy Land. In order to defeat the Mamluks, the Christians must first drain their foes' economic resources and stop their slave trade with the Tatars. Therefore, a general ban on trade with the Islamic states in the Near East should be declared by the papacy on pain of excommunication and interdict. Next, a maritime blockade should be enforced on the Moslem shores of Egypt and Syria. Special galleys should stand by to guard the waters of the Levant against intrusion and intercept any Moslem craft attempting to reach the western world. If this blockade were rigorously sustained over a period of three years, the Mamluk sultans would be completely crippled, and their resources of men and material dried up. It is only then that the Christians might conduct their crusade with assured success for the recapture and retention of the Holy Land.

In reality, the examples mentioned represent only a fraction of

14. Ed. J. Bongars in *Gesta dei per Francos*... (2 vols. in 1, Hanover, 1611); partial trans. by A. Stewart for Palestine Pilgrims' Text Society (London, 1896).

the vast propagandist literature originating from the pens of theorists, ideologists, and pilgrims of various nations in the west during
the fourteenth century. In the meantime, the idea of an alliance with
the Mongols for joint action against Islam, formulated in the age of
Innocent IV (1243–1254) and Louis IX (1226–1270), continued to
haunt the imagination of western potentates even after the decline of
the crusade. During this period the most striking efforts to convert
the Mongols to Christianity are exemplified by the heroic careers of
John of Monte Corvino and his worthy contemporary Odoric of
Pordenone, whose lives and activities are landmarks in Far Eastern
missionary history. Settled at Khanbaliq after extensive peregrinations in Asia, John of Monte Corvino became the original founder of
the Catholic church in Cathay. He might have passed unnoticed by
the west had one of his letters not accidentally reached pope Clement V. In 1304, he is said to have baptized five thousand souls at
what is now Peking, and built two churches. He may have translated
the New Testament and the Psalter into the Mongol language, which
he had mastered, though this remains to be proved. It was probably
in the second decade of the century that Odoric joined him at
Khanbaliq after one of the longest journeys on record in the Middle
Ages. Odoric took the route to China by way of Constantinople,
Tabriz, Baghdad, Hormuz, then by sea to Malabar, Ceylon, and
Madras, whence he attained Sumatra and Java in the East Indies,
finally reaching Zaitun (probably Tsinkiang) and Khanbaliq. He
returned to Avignon in 1330 completely exhausted, to die at Udine
in the following year. In the meantime John, who had been elected
bishop of Sultaniyeh and the Far East, had died in 1328. When
James of Florence was murdered at an unknown place in the heart of
China in 1362, it may be said that Catholic Christianity had come to
an end in those remote regions, though the idea of joint action with
the Mongols never died, but lay dormant in the western mind until
Christopher Columbus revived it by his westward journey to India,
only to discover the New World and give history a new orientation.[15]

While the propagandists were busy stirring up the medieval mind
for the crusade, a number of leading men decided to take positive
action. Thus a series of minor preludes led the way to the greater
campaigns of the second half of the fourteenth century. Apart from
some abortive attempts against the Byzantine empire, the first expedition to come within the category of holy warfare at this time was

15. See below, chapters XV and XVIII.

the Aegean crusade, which resulted in the capture of Smyrna in 1344.[16] After prolonged negotiations between the Roman see and Venice, pope Clement VI in a memorandum dated August 1343 proclaimed the formation of a Holy League to suppress Turkish aggression. The constituent members of the League agreed among themselves on raising a fleet of twenty galleys to intercept Turkish movements in the Archipelago; Venice was ready to provide six, the pope four, king Hugh IV of Cyprus four, and the Hospitallers six. Clement VI finally nominated Henry of Asti, the Latin patriarch of Constantinople, as head of the coalition fleet and Martin Zaccaria, the Genoese former lord of Chios, as commander of his naval squadron. Venice appointed Peter Zeno admiral of the Venetian galleys. They met at Negroponte and were joined by the remaining ships from Cyprus and Rhodes, now the seat of the Hospitallers, under their master Hélion of Villeneuve. The joint fleet then sailed toward Anatolia and took the city of Smyrna by surprise, though the citadel was held by Umur Pasha, emir of Aydin. Their armies made a triumphant entry into the city on October 28, 1344. It would remain in the hands of the Christians until the whole of Asia Minor was seized by the invincible hordes of Timur after the battle of Ankara in 1402.

The crusade of Humbert II of Viennois was the natural continuation to the success of the Holy League in the Aegean. Meager as it may seem, the capture of Smyrna was hailed by the pontiff as the beginning of the end of the sorrows and humiliation of the Latins in the Near East. Processions were ordained to commemorate the victory in the streets of Avignon. The pope urged the kings of England and France, Edward III Plantagenet and Philip VI of Valois, to desist from the Hundred Years' War and unite their forces against their common enemy. He wrote the doge of Venice a congratulatory message to induce him to persist in his struggle against the Turks. In brief, western Europe seemed astir, and another Godfrey of Bouillon was expected to emerge on the scene of events and lead the Christian hosts to a crushing victory over the forces of Islam.

It was at this moment that Humbert II, dauphin of Viennois, a very unhappy man, took to the idea of the crusade. The death of his only son and heir had left him inconsolable, and he had resolved to drown his grief in fighting the Moors in Spain and to atone for his past disaffection with ecclesiastics by serving the Roman see. As soon as the news of the fall of Smyrna reached the west in December

16. See Paul Lemerle, *L'Émirat d'Aydin, Byzance et l'occident* (Bibliothèque byzantine, Études, II; Paris, 1957), pp. 180–203, and cf. below, pp. 294–295.

1344, he decided to deflect his project from Spain and continue the Aegean campaign under the auspices of the pope. After renouncing his feudal rights over the Dauphiné, which would ultimately go to the French crown, he offered to equip five galleys with twelve bannerets, three hundred knights, and a thousand arbalesters. In return, he requested that the pope grant him the high command of the crusade, allow him the proceeds of the usual tithes, and recognize his suzerainty over all the conquered territories. With some reluctance, Clement VI and his cardinals approved these terms on condition that Humbert should remain in the east for three years with some hundred men-at-arms. Finally the "Captain-General of the Crusade against the Turks and the Unfaithful to the Holy Church of Rome," as Humbert was styled, sailed from Marseilles in September 1345 and disembarked at Genoa, to cross Lombardy to Venice and, after weeks of negotiation, resume his voyage. He was urged by the pope to proceed, if possible, to the Genoese colony of Kaffa across the Black Sea, and to help in its relief from the Tatars, who were besieging the whole of the Crimea.

When Humbert reached the Aegean, he allowed himself to become involved in the futile diplomatic and military broils of the Genoese with the members of the League and the Latins of the Orient to such an extent that he suffered some losses at the hands of the Genoese in the waters of Negroponte. Afterwards, he seems to have scored some minor successes over Turkish mariners on the high sea and later at Smyrna. But until the summer of 1347, he neither attained the Black Sea nor achieved any substantial victories over the enemies of his faith. Meanwhile his wife died, and her death completed the tragedy of his private life. In despair, he suddenly decided to relinquish all his plans and retire to France, where he became a Dominican friar. The pope absolved him from his previous obligations and, in 1351, even granted him the honorary title of Latin patriarch of Alexandria. On January 24, 1354, he was nominated bishop of Paris, but he died at Clermont at the age of forty-three before reaching his new see. To the end, he preferred to retain the semblance of his old titles and subscribed himself "the late dauphin of Viennois."

The highwater mark in the history of the Levantine crusade in later medieval times was reached during the reign of Peter I de Lusignan, Latin king of Cyprus (1359–1369). Since the extermination of the crusader states in the Holy Land, Cyprus had become one of the chief bulwarks of western Christianity in the eastern Mediterranean. It was therefore natural that its Latin monarchs should do everything in their power to enhance the cause of holy war against their dangerous Moslem neighbors. Thus the island, which became an important trade emporium for the Latins, also turned out to be a key point in crusading activities. As a beginning, the Lusignan kings conducted several minor attacks on some of the coastal towns of Mamluk Syria and Turkish Anatolia. Peter managed indeed to capture the city of Adalia and some other smaller settlements on the southern coast of Asia Minor, but these successes proved to be merely modest forerunners to the sack of Alexandria in 1365.[17]

Peter's closest associates in the forthcoming fray were Peter [de] Thomas and Philip of Mézières, two of the outstanding figures in the propaganda for the crusade. Peter Thomas became Latin patriarch of Constantinople and apostolic legate for the east in 1364. Thenceforth he devoted himself to the twofold task of converting the Orthodox Greeks to the Roman creed and promoting the cause of holy war against Moslems in the Levant. Realizing the tenacity of the Greeks in matters of faith, he found it more advantageous to dwell in Cyprus with a king who shared his aspirations and with his disciple Philip of Mézières.

When these three champions of the crusade assembled in Cyprus, war with the Moslems became a foregone conclusion. Peter's occupation of Adalia in 1361 only whetted the king's appetite for further and greater victories against the Moslems in other fields. In order to ensure the success of his *passagium generale,* the king embarked on a European tour to implore the sovereigns of western Christendom for manpower and materiel. He sailed from Famagusta in the company of the patriarch Peter Thomas and his chancellor Philip of Mézières on October 24, 1362. After a short halt at Rhodes, where he was encouraged by the Hospitallers and their master Roger de Pins, he landed with his suite at Venice on December 5, 1362. He had a royal reception in the commune and obtained promises from the doge Lorenzo Celsi to supply the crusade with indispensable galleys. The king then led a triumphant journey through the north Italian towns of Mestre, Padua, Verona, Milan, Pavia, and Genoa, where he spent more than a month to reconcile the Genoese and win their sympathy and maritime aid for his project. Then he proceeded to Avignon, the seat of pope Urban V, where he successfully carried out some important negotiations under papal auspices with the French king John II the Good, who promised full support to the august visitor. The pope then officially declared the crusade on April 14 and appointed cardinal Elias Talleyrand of Perigord apostolic legate for

17. On Peter I and the sack of Alexandria see also below, pp. 353–357.

the campaign, while the two kings took the cross from Urban's hands. Thence Peter traversed almost the whole of the European continent in search of recruits and material aid from its various potentates and great feudatories. He followed a rather circuitous route across France, Flanders, Brabant, Germany, and back to Paris to discuss concrete details with John II, then traveled around Brittany and Normandy until he sailed from the port of Calais to England. He was received with honor at Smithfield by Edward III, who paid all his expenses during his stay in England and presented him with a good ship named Catherine, costing 12,000 francs.

Afterward, Peter spent Christmas of 1363 in Paris and went to meet the Black Prince in Aquitaine, where the news of the death of king John in April 1364 forced his return to the French capital to attend the royal funeral. He had to renew negotiations with John's successor, Charles V the Wise, who was more restrained in his promises than his late father. After assisting in the coronation ceremony at the cathedral of Rheims, the train of the Cypriote monarch again penetrated Central Europe and won more adherents to the cause, notably at the courts of margrave Frederick III of Meissen, duke Rudolph II of Saxony, and even the Holy Roman emperor Charles IV at Prague, in addition to the kings of Hungary and Poland. Jousts, tournaments, and all manner of festivities were held in his honor everywhere. Cracow was probably the farthest point that he attained eastward. Finally, his entry into Venice was registered on November 11, 1364, and soon afterward he and his chivalry boarded the Venetian fleet prepared for the occasion.

While the king thus journeyed throughout Europe, diplomatic action was conducted by the papal curia in other fields. Cardinal Talleyrand had died, so Urban V appointed Peter Thomas as his successor in the crusade. The new legate and Philip of Mézières were the chief instigators in papal activities. Letters were sealed by the pontiff inviting all the sovereigns of Europe to join the crusade, and papal bulls were issued at Avignon to grant the usual privileges together with plenary indulgences to all crusaders. Men of many nations had already been waiting at Venice before the king's arrival, and a number of small companies are said to have sailed from Otranto and Genoa, though the Genoese contribution was much more modest than that of the Venetians in this campaign. All the forces were ordered to converge in the waters of Rhodes, and the king and his retinue finally set sail from Venice on June 27, 1365. Their ultimate objective was guarded as a close secret within the limited circle of his most trusted advisors. He feared the perfidy of the Venetians, who he suspected might betray the destination of the crusade to the enemy in exchange for trade privileges.

The joint fleet which was convened at Rhodes from Cyprus, Venice, and elsewhere between June and October 1365 totaled about 165 vessels, including transports, galleys, and all manner of sea-craft. In the end, the various contingents went aboard their respective ships on Saturday, October 4, 1365, in readiness for their unknown destination. The waters of Rhodes rang with their war cries, and the captains were ordered to sail parallel to the southern coast of Anatolia. Off the little island of Crambusa, the aim of the campaign was announced and the fleet was ordered to turn south in the direction of the city of Alexandria, which they sighted on Thursday, October 9.

Alexandria was undoubtedly one of the most important seaports not only in the Mamluk empire but in the whole of the Mediterranean basin. Its remarkable hostels and bazaars abounded in all manner of merchandise. Its markets surged with tradesmen from the east and the west, for here was the center of exchange of the staples and goods of all nations. The immense revenues levied by the sultan from these vast transactions filled his coffers with the money necessary for the purchase of the implements of war and the slaves used in fighting the Christians, more especially since the breakdown of the European maritime blockade. Peter's decision to capture Alexandria and use it as a base for further conquests to disable Egypt was regarded as wise, and the times were propitious for the campaign. Ibn-'Arrām, governor of the city, was absent on a pilgrimage to Mecca. The reigning sultan Sha'bān was a small boy of eleven, and his guardian prince Yelbogha abused the wide powers with which he was entrusted. The Mamluk battalions were torn asunder into factions without an overall leader. Yet it would be wrong to assume that Alexandria was in no position to withstand attacks. The city was strongly fortified with double walls and a series of invulnerable towers. Its arsenal was full of war materiel, even though the number of regular troops was depleted. The unexpected collapse of the defense was due to other unforeseen causes.

When Peter made a forced landing, after some opposition which his men crushed with little difficulty, the crusaders began to attack the Green Gate on October 10. They soon saw the futility of their endeavors, since the upper walls were heavily guarded in that area. Later in the day, however, they discovered that the section of the walls overlooking the Custom-House Gate was completely undefended. That gate opened from the inside to the Custom-House, which was locked by the customs officer Ibn-Ghurāb to prevent theft of the goods stored therein. Meanwhile, a great tower barred access from the part of the wall above the Green Gate to that above the Custom-House Gate. That gap in the defense provided the attackers with their sole opportunity, which they seized immediately by burning the undefended gate while others employed ladders to mount the wall. The bewildered Egyptians watched the assault and then hastened toward the land gates to save their lives. These are the main data on which William of Machaut[18] and an-Nuwairī al-Iskandarī, [19] the two historians and eye-witnesses of the crusade from the opposing camps, are in full agreement.

For the rest of the story, we have to rely on the Egyptian annalist—that is, from the occupation of the city on October 10 to its evacuation on October 16. The havoc that followed the appearance of the Christian knights within the walls was indescribable. Masses of inhabitants thronged the narrow circuitous lanes with their light treasures, pushing toward the Rosetta Gate in the east and the southern land gates. The miserable fate of those who lagged behind was sealed, for they were either killed or carried into captivity. The trade storehouses were pillaged, and what could not be carried away was destroyed. Public buildings and emptied warehouses were set aflame. The sack of the city was completed systematically, and in that short span of time the "Queen of the Mediterranean" was left in a state of irreparable wreckage; even the Coptic churches of their fellow Christians of the east were looted. The harmless beasts of burden were put to the sword after the conveyance of the booty, and their bodies were collected and burnt only later by the Moslems on reëntering the city. When all their havoc was accomplished, the looters took to their ships in groups, deserting their posts in the city, much to the disgust of such dedicated leaders of the crusade as the king and his two consultants, Peter Thomas and Philip of Mézières. At this juncture the vanguard of the troops from Cairo, alleged to be some hundred thousand strong, appeared in the outskirts of the city.

In the end, after some futile negotiations between Yelbogha's emissaries and the king on board one of his galleys, the Christian fleet sailed back home laden with booty and without releasing the

18. Ed. Louis de Mas Latrie as *La Prise d'Alexandrie ou chronique du roi Pierre Ier de Lusignan* (Société de l'Orient latin, série historique, no. 1; Geneva, 1877).

19. Or, as he describes himself, "al-Iskandarānī." Excerpts ed. É. Combe, in Farouk University, Faculty of Arts, *Bulletin (Majallat Kulliyat al-ādāb)*, III (Alexandria, 1946), 99–110, 119–129. The full text of an-Nuwairī's "Kitāb al-ilmām" dealing with the crusade from the Egyptian side has been published by the present writer in 6 vols., in the *Da'iratu'l-Ma'arif-il-'Osmania* (new series, Hyderabad, 1968–1973).

Moslem captives. There ensued a series of minor incidents during the next four years. Prolonged negotiations were interrupted by Cypriote raids on the Syrian and Egyptian shores to force a written peace treaty out of the sultan's hands. But Yelbogha was only playing for time while Egypt was diligently importing timber from Syria to construct a fleet for retaliation on Cyprus. The Egyptians never forgot the calamity which had befallen them at Alexandria, and the Cypriotes were doomed to pay a heavy price for their untoward adventure.[20] Peter Thomas died at Famagusta in 1366; his disciple Philip of Mézières did not return to Cyprus after the assassination of Peter I in 1369. He later became tutor to the French crown prince Charles (VI).

Perhaps the main immediate result of the sack of Alexandria was the promotion of another crusade which took place in a totally different region. As soon as the tidings of the triumph achieved at Alexandria were circulated in the west, a wave of excitement swept the European courts for the continuation of the work so auspiciously reinaugurated by Cyprus. Pope Urban V at Avignon was overjoyed, while Charles V of France delegated John d'Olivier to inform Peter de Lusignan that his hosts would soon join the Cypriotes in a final effort to rout the Moslems and return the Holy Land to the Latins. Bertrand du Guesclin renewed his crusading vow, and Florimont of Lesparre actually reached Cyprus with a band of followers for the purpose of aiding the king in his strife. Still more important was the project of count Amadeo VI of Savoy, who had previously taken the cross with king Peter from Urban's hands at Avignon. As he was preparing to sail to Cyprus, the Venetians told him, allegedly, that peace had been concluded with Egypt. In any event, he directed the new expedition toward Byzantium to fight the Turks and Bulgars. Amadeo was motivated to take up arms in the Balkans by his relationship with John V Palaeologus, his cousin.

In January 1366 the count began his preparations for what was intended to be a *passagium generale*. In addition to his own feudal militia, he recruited great numbers of mercenaries from Italy, Germany, France, and England. His fleet, totaling fifteen galleys, was to sail in three squadrons from Venice, Genoa, and Marseilles, with Coron in the southern Morea as their rendezvous, whence concerted action would begin according to a preconceived plan. The count himself sailed from the lagoons of Venice on June 11, 1366, and all the galleys reunited at Coron on July 19. After settling a local dispute

20. See below, pp. 371–375.

between Angelo, the Latin archbishop of Patras, and Marie of Bourbon, the titular empress of Constantinople, Amadeo's ships proceeded toward their first objective, Gallipoli, across the Aegean by way of Negroponte. Gallipoli had been the earliest European prey to Ottoman aggression when in 1354 it was wrested by sultan Orkhan from emperor John VI Cantacuzenus; thenceforth that peninsula had become the chief landing place for the Asian troops on European soil and a magnificent base for military operations in the Balkans. It was in August that the crusaders landed there and took the town of Gallipoli by surprise. After the Moslem garrison fled from the invaders, Amadeo appointed Aimon Michel captain of the citadel and entrusted James of Lucerne with the governorship of the town. He left the German company with them as a garrison and set sail for Constantinople.

On his arrival in September, Amadeo discovered that his imperial cousin had been detained at Vidin because the Bulgarians would not permit him safe passage through their territory. This proved fatal to the campaign against the Turks, since Amadeo pursued the Bulgarians to regain John V's freedom instead of purging the Balkans of Moslem contingents. The count, wisely avoiding the treacherous land route to the heart of Bulgaria, sailed through the Bosporus and northward on the Black Sea until he landed at a small place named Sozopolis. His men took it by storm, together with a few other Bulgarian coastal towns including Mesembria, until they finally laid siege to the fortified city of Varna. Realizing the impregnability of its walls and towers, however, he decided to send a group of envoys to negotiate the liberation of John V. An agreement was reached whereby the emperor was freed and the siege of Varna was raised. The campaign lasted from October till December and the smaller towns were ceded to the Greeks against the payment of a sum which helped Amadeo to meet his liabilities to the mercenaries, soon to be disbanded after their year's term of service. At the same time, Amadeo tried hard to persuade John to accede to the principle of the reunion of the eastern church with Rome, but his efforts were foiled by the Greeks, who hated the Latins. In the end, the party sailed from Pera on June 4, 1367, and reached Venice on July 31. The count visited Urban V, now in Rome, and ultimately regained Turin, his capital.

A lull in crusading activities followed the indecisive campaigns of Peter de Lusignan and Amadeo of Savoy. Toward the beginning of the last decade of the fourteenth century, the center of crusading gravity was moving slightly to the west, where in France the "good duke" of Bourbon, Louis II of Clermont, was persuaded by the Genoese to lead a joint crusade with them in North Africa. Genoese trade had been suffering considerably at the hands of Saracen corsairs in the western Mediterranean, and some drastic measures had to be taken to save their merchant fleet from imminent dangers of piracy. The Ḥafṣid kings of Tunisia encouraged the Moorish pirates, whose chief nest was the strong town of Mahdia, known in the French sources as the "Cité d'Auffrique"; and the Genoese therefore decided to launch a great campaign against it. On the other hand, Louis of Bourbon was fascinated by the idea of marching in the steps of the great St. Louis by conducting a crusade against the city of Tunis. A compromise was reached in 1390 by the allied parties. The Genoese republic provided the fleet with its equipment and manpower, while the duke recruited an army of fifteen thousand, comprising nobles, knights, men-at-arms, and squires. The Avignonese pope Clement VII granted plenary absolution from sins to all those who joined the crusade, and the French king issued royal ordinances empowering Louis to carry out the enterprise. Gentlemen from France, England, Hainault, and Flanders hastened to enlist under the ducal banner. John Centurione Oltramarino was appointed admiral of the fleet and was accompanied by one thousand arbalesters and two thousand men-at-arms in addition to four thousand mariners from Genoa. The French embarked from Marseilles, and the foreign contingents took to the sea from Genoa. After an uneasy voyage, the ships reassembled at the islet of Conigliera, sixteen leagues off the African coast, and within reasonable reach of Mahdia. They halted at that island for nine days for recuperation and for consideration of their tactics. This delay gave the Tunisians time to muster their forces for the coming battle and to reinforce the city garrison.

The landing of the Christians took place without interruption just outside Mahdia. Then they remained in a continuous state of war for nearly two months of the merciless African summer. On the whole, the city garrison assumed a strictly defensive attitude, while the joint armies of the kingdoms of Tunisia, Bugia, and Tlemsen unremittingly harassed the Christians from outside without allowing themselves to be drawn into an open or decisive battle with them. Though prodigies of valor were allegedly displayed and all manner of war machinery was used, the issue remained undecided until the Genoese secretly began to treat with the enemies in favor of their trade interests. A truce was concluded for ten years, during which the Moslems were bound to abstain from all acts of piracy on the high seas. Aḥmad, the ruler of Tunisia, also promised to pay an annual tribute for fifteen years to the Genoese for retaining Mahdia in Moslem hands, and further, to pay an immediate war indemnity of 25,000 ducats, to be shared between the duke and the commune. Both sides were exhausted, and the Christian council of war approved the treaty, with the duke insisting that he should be the last to board a galley. The armies reached Europe in October 1390. The Genoese had achieved their aims, and the crusaders had unwittingly helped in the fulfillment of the Genoese aspirations. In other words, the duke and his contingents proved to be a cat's-paw for the clever Genoese merchants, and the Barbary crusade failed to accomplish its original purpose as a holy war.[21]

The pious propagandists and earnest crusaders had again suffered disillusionment, and their spiritual agonies were voiced in the works of Philip of Mézières, who had retired in 1380 to the convent of the Celestines in Paris, to devote himself to crusade propaganda until his death in 1405. The period between the campaign of 1390 and the crusade of Nicopolis in 1396 represents the peak of Philip's prolific output in the field of propagandist literature. It was then indeed that his project of a New Militia found its fullest expression in several new tracts, notably in his unpublished epistle to Richard II dated 1395. [22] The importance of this document lies in the fact that it was semi-official, since it was submitted by order of Charles VI of France to the English king. In its nine "materes," or chapters, he preached peace between the two monarchs and the unity of their armies with the New Militia in order to serve effectively the cause of the crusade. Although the proposition was not discountenanced in either of the two courts, its supporters had to turn elsewhere for a leader of the new movement, and this they found in rich Burgundy. Its duke Philip II the Bold wanted his son, John of Nevers, to be knighted in the field of honor fighting the "infidels" and, moreover, to earn much prestige for his duchy by leading the crusade.

The time was ripe for war in the east. Alarming news had reached the west about the advance of the Ottoman Turks even beyond the confines of the Byzantine empire. King Sigismund of Hungary sent John of Kanizsay, the archbishop of Gran, to solicit help at the French court in 1395. The response to the call for a crusade was widespread among the French nobility, particularly in Burgundy.

21. On Louis of Bourbon's crusade see also below, pp. 481–483. Apparently neither the indemnity nor the tribute was ever paid.
22. British Museum, MS. 20, B VI.

John (le Meingre) Boucicault, marshal of France, the admiral John of Vienne, Enguerrand of Coucy, Philip and Henry of Bar, Guy and William of Trémolay, and many other nobles of distinction took the cross and came with followers, feudal retainers, and mercenary troops to join the movement. Elaborate preparations for this Hungarian voyage were undertaken everywhere, especially in Burgundy, where nothing was overlooked and no expense spared, according to Froissart's report.[23] Benedict XIII, the Avignonese pope, issued a series of bulls in the course of 1395 to release John of Nevers, now recognized as head of the Franco-Burgundian contingents, from certain vows and to grant him and all his followers the usual plenary absolution from sins on the occasion of the crusade. Still earlier, the Roman pope, Boniface IX, had already declared the holy war in the countries adhering to his obedience in east Central Europe in 1394. The Great Schism of the church in the west did not affect the unanimity of all parties in regard to this crusade.

The news spread far and wide in the western states, and auxiliary armies began to form in Germany and elsewhere. The German crusaders were led by the palsgrave Rupert II (Ruprecht Pipan), the count of Katzenellenbogen,[24] count Hermann II of Cilly, and burgrave John III of Nuremberg. Although it was formerly believed that a large English contingent participated in the crusade, the contemporary sources do not justify this view.[25] A few Englishmen did take part, and similarly small numbers of volunteers and mercenaries were raised from Spain and the Italian communes. But the main bulk of the army accompanied Sigismund from Hungary, and detachments of no mean size also came from the eastern European countries of Bohemia, Poland, and, above all, Wallachia. The total numbers of the combined forces have been estimated at anywhere from ten to a hundred thousand strong.[26]

---

23. Ed. J. M. Kervyn de Lettenhove, 25 vols. (Brussels, 1870–1877); also numerous other editions and translations, including abridged version of Thomas Johnes's text as revised by H. P. Dunster, in Everyman's Library (London and New York, 1906), p. 540. Cf. the account of J. Delaville Le Roulx, *La France en Orient au XIVᵉ siècle: Expéditions du Maréchal Boucicaut* (Paris, 1886), pp. 211–299.

24. Alois Brauner, *Die Schlacht bei Nikopolis, 1396* (Breslau, 1876), p. 10, identifies him as John III, of three contemporaries who held this title.

25. See C. L. Tipton, "The English at Nicopolis," *Speculum,* XXXVII (1962), 528–540.

26. The units of the crusading army have been estimated as follows: French and Burgundians, 10,000; Germans, 6,000; English, 1,000; Hungarians, 60,000; Wallachians, 10,000; with the other 13,000 comprising Bohemian, Polish, Spanish, and Italian volunteers, and mercenaries; A. S. Atiya, *The Crusade of Nicopolis* (London, 1934), pp. 66–67, 184, notes, and *idem, The Crusade in the Later Middle Ages* (London, 1938), p. 440, note 7. But cf. R. Rosetti, "Notes on the Battle of Nicopolis," *Slavonic and East European Review,* XV (1937), 636, estimating each side's strength at 10,000 to 20,000.

The Franco-Burgundian forces started from Dijon in April 1396 and pursued the route along the Danube. Their general rendezvous with the other contingents was Buda, where all the leaders held a council of war with Sigismund to consider future plans and tactics. This must have taken place in late July or early August 1396. Sigismund suggested the adoption of defensive tactics, which he knew from experience to be more effective in dealing with the Turks. His advice was rejected outright by the western generals, who, according to Froissart, had come "to conquer the whole of Turkey and to march into the empire of Persia, . . . the kingdom of Syria, and the Holy Land."

The united armies thus moved south as far as Orsova and crossed the Danube at the Iron Gate. From that point, the real campaign began with several minor successes. The crusaders seized the towns of Vidin and Rahova in Bulgaria, and evidently they did not discriminate between the Turkish garrisons and the original Orthodox Christian natives. Their victorious march south of the Danube, marked by atrocities, met its first check at the strong city of Nicopolis, which they reached on September 10. Nicopolis was built on a fortified hill overlooking the Danube to the north and a vast plain to the south. It was surrounded by double walls and invulnerable towers, and was impossible for the crusaders to take by storm, so they decided to lay siege to it. Although the Venetians had agreed to provide naval support for the crusade, their flotilla never came near Nicopolis. The grand master Philibert of Naillac, however, did appear with a contingent of Hospitallers. The siege lasted fifteen days. During that period, no constructive measures were taken to face future emergencies; the besiegers wasted the time in gambling, orgies, and debauchery.

The position on the Turkish side stood in complete contrast to that of the Christian camp. Sultan Bayazid I, called "the Thunderbolt" (Yîldîrîm), was besieging Constantinople when the news of the advent of the crusaders was communicated to him from Nicopolis. He raised the siege immediately and mustered all his Asian and European troops for the relief of Nicopolis, which he reached on September 24 with an army about the size of the crusaders'.[27] But although the two camps were numerically almost equal, the Turks were far superior to the Christians in discipline, unified action, tactics, and unflagging leadership.

---

27. The Turks have been estimated to have had a 34,000-man vanguard of infantry, 30,000 cavalry in the "main battle," and 40,000 more cavalry in the rear guard and the sultan's bodyguard; Atiya, *Nicopolis,* pp. 68–69, 185, note, and *Later Middle Ages,* p. 446, note 3. But see preceding note for smaller estimate.

In the first instance, Sigismund urged the French and foreign contingents to remain in the rear for the decisive blow in the forthcoming battle, but these protested vigorously against a plan which would in their opinion deprive them of the honor of leading a victory. Sigismund pleaded that the Hungarians were more conversant with Turkish methods of war, and that he wanted to plant the Wallachians in the van rather than leave them in the rear on account of their doubtful allegiance, but his plea was without avail. On Monday, September 25, the French and allied legions occupied the main battle in the van for the first assault, while the greater masses of the Hungarians, Wallachians, and other eastern European contingents were stationed in the rear. Whereas the Christians occupied the plains, the Ottomans arranged their lines on a southern hill in a very strong position. Bayazid placed his irregular light cavalry (akinjis) on the hillside facing the Christians with a thick field of long, pointed stakes behind them. Next above stood the foot-archers (janissaries and azabs). The French and allied contingents galloped uphill with their heavy shire horses and had no difficulty in routing the mounted Turkish vanguard. The survivors fled right and left to regroup their formations behind the archers in readiness to resume hostilities. Confronted by the stakes and exposed to Turkish arrows, the Christian front lines had to dismount and pull the stakes in order to reach the Ottoman bowmen for hand-to-hand fighting. With considerable effort and some losses, they achieved their purpose and inflicted heavy slaughter on the Turks, who fled for their lives toward the hilltop pursued by the Christians. On attaining the summit completely exhausted, the latter, to their horror, saw Bayazid's picked cavalry (sipahis), together with his vassal Serbs under Stephen Lazarevich, several thousand strong, hidden behind the skyline. Thus the pursuers became the pursued and the slaughter was reversed even more fiercely, while the survivors were carried into captivity.

The position of the Hungarians and Wallachians had become desperate even before the Turks descended on the plain. The stampede of the riderless horses discarded before the field of stakes was taken in the rear as a sign of discomfiture, and the Wallachians started to withdraw. Confusion followed in the Hungarian lines as a consequence, though Sigismund and his loyal feudatories continued to fight as hard and as long as was humanly possible. In the end, he had to take to flight with some of his leading men, the grand master of Rhodes, and the burgrave of Nuremberg. They boarded a small boat and floated down the Danube to the Black Sea, whence they returned in Venetian galleys to their respective homes by way of

Constantinople, Rhodes, and Ragusa. The rest of their men, apart from the few who managed to save themselves by hurried flight through the neighboring woods, were either killed or imprisoned.

Later, Bayazid was startled when he realized his own losses, estimated at "thirty thousand," and his wrath was demonstrated in the treatment of the three thousand Christian prisoners on the morrow of the day of the battle. Stripped of their clothes and tied together with ropes, the captives were led before the sultan in groups to be decapitated in cold blood. Bayazid discovered among them a certain James of Helly, whom he had previously employed in his eastern campaigns and who knew Turkish. It was through his mediation that the French and Burgundian nobility escaped the rank and file's grim fate; their lives were spared for the heavy ransom of 200,000 gold florins. Among others, these included John of Nevers, Enguerrand of Coucy, Guy of Trémolay, and Philip of Artois, count of Eu. Young men under twenty were spared for sale in the slave markets of the Levant or presentation to other Moslem potentates. The news of the complete discomfiture of the crusaders overwhelmed European society with deep grief, which was alleviated only slightly by the return of the few noble captives after the payment of their heavy ransom.

The downfall of the western chivalry on the field of Nicopolis marked the end of any hope that the Ottoman empire could be destroyed by Christendom, and Turkey was accepted as a European power. Though the road to the Hungarian plains was open before the Turks after Sigismund's disaster and flight, Bayazid preferred to consolidate his Balkan possessions and bide his time for further expansion. Meanwhile, the crusade had become an anachronism. Only a few revered its memory and continued to work hard at resuscitating the moribund movement. After the defeat of 1396, Philip of Mézières, in his retreat in the convent of the Celestines in Paris, composed yet another of his famous epistles, which he entitled *Epistre lamentable et consolatoire* and presented to the duke of Burgundy.[28] In it, he enumerates the causes of the calamity and prescribes remedies for healing the wounds of Christendom, which lacked the four virtues of good governance—Order, Discipline, Obedience, and Justice. In their stead, the three daughters of Lucifer—Vanity, Covetousness, and Luxury—ruled the whole society. The "Nova Militia Passionis" is termed the only hope for the eradication of these vices and for redeeming the honor of (western) Christendom. Philip extols the principles of his new organization, representing the *summa*

---

28. Extracts in vol. XVI of Froissart's *Chroniques,* ed. Kervyn de Lettenhove.

perfectio, to ensure victory for his three "estates" of kings, nobility, and bourgeoisie, equivalent to the classes of commanders, cavalry, and infantry in the forthcoming campaigns against "miscreants." Again, Philip preaches peace and goodwill among all Christians of the west, and he advises the duke of Burgundy, the kings of France and England, and all good Catholics to join forces to avenge their humiliation in the east and restore the birthplace of Christ to Rome. But Philip of Mézières was, to use his own words, an old dreamer—a voice from the past in a world of change. The crusade of Nicopolis was the last serious attempt by western Europe at united offensive action of the traditional kind in the history of the holy war against Islam.

2. Central Europe

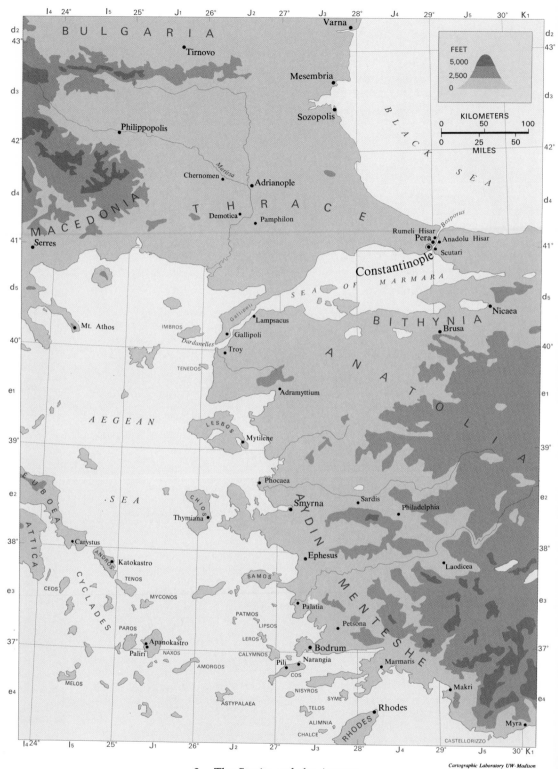

3. The Straits and the Aegean

Cartographic Laboratory UW-Madison

II

BYZANTIUM AND THE CRUSADES, 1261–1354

From the first the Byzantine empire had been intimately connected with the movement of the western crusades to the Holy Land. It had perhaps even been the appeals of Alexius I Comnenus for aid against the Selchükid Turks that had put into the head of pope

The principal Greek historians for the period 1261–1453, of primary importance for the Byzantine aspect of the later crusades, are George Pachymeres, *De Michaele et Andronico Palaeologis libri XIII* (ed. I. Bekker, *CSHB,* 2 vols., Bonn, 1835); Nicephorus Gregoraṣ, *Byzantina historia* (ed. L. Schopen and I. Bekker, *CSHB,* 3 vols., Bonn, 1829–1855); John Cantacuzenus, *Historiarum libri IV* (ed. L. Schopen, *CSHB,* 3 vols., Bonn, 1828–1832); George Sphrantzes, *Annales* (ed. I. Bekker, *CSHB,* Bonn, 1838, and ed. J. B. Papadopulos, 2 vols., Leipzig, 1935–1954) [while his *Chronicon minus* is accepted as authentic, the *Chronicon maius* is disputed, and has been termed a later compilation by Macarius Melissenus]; Laonicus Chalcocondylas, *De origine ac rebus Turcorum* (ed. I. Bekker, *CSHB,* Bonn, 1843, and ed. E. Darkó, *Historiarum demonstrationes,* 2 vols. in 3, Budapest, 1922–1927); and Ducas, *Historia byzantina* (ed. I. Bekker, *CSHB,* Bonn, 1834, and ed. V. Grecu, *Istorija turco-bizantină 1341–1462,* Bucharest, 1958). All of these are also published in Migne, *Patrologia graeca (PG).* Further source material is cited in F. J. Dölger, *Regesten der Kaiserurkunden des oströmischen Reiches . . . ,* parts 3–5 (Munich and Berlin, 1932–1965).

Very little has been written specifically on Byzantine attitudes toward the later western crusades; see V. Laurent, "L'Idée de guerre sainte et la tradition byzantine," *Revue historique du sud-est européen,* XXIII (1946), 71–98; P. Lemerle, "Byzance et la croisade," *Relazioni del X Congresso Internazionale di Scienze Storiche,* III (Florence, 1955), 595 ff.; and J. Bouquet's brief "Byzance et les dernières offensives de l'Occident contre Islam," *Congrès de l'Ordre International Constantinien* (Zurich, 1961), pp. 1–15.

Western sources and monographs, on the other hand, which touch on the Byzantine involvement in the later period are extremely numerous; only a few can be cited here. First we note the general works by A. S. Atiya, *The Crusade in the Later Middle Ages* (London, 1938), covering the entire movement but emphasizing the western and Arab sides; J. Delaville Le Roulx, *La France en Orient au XIVe siècle* (Paris, 1886); N. Iorga, *Philippe de Mézières (1327–1405) et la croisade au XIVe siècle* (Paris, 1896); A. Luttrell, "The Crusade in the Fourteenth Century," in J. Hale *et al.,* eds., *Europe in the Later Middle Ages* (London, 1965), pp. 122–154; and P. Lemerle, *L'Émirat d'Aydin, Byzance et l'Occident* (Paris, 1957). Other works touching on various of the later crusades and Byzantium are D. Geanakoplos, *Emperor Michael Palaeologus and the West 1258–1282* (Cambridge, Mass., 1959); U. Bosch, *Kaiser Andronikos III. Palaiologos* (Amsterdam, 1965); and E. Dade, *Versuche zur Wiedererrichtung der lateinischen Herrschaft in Konstantinopel im Rahmen der abendländischen Politik, 1261 bis etwa 1310* (Jena, 1938); also G. Bratianu, "Notes sur le projet de mariage entre l'empereur Michel IX Paléologue et Cathérine de Courtenay

Urban II the idea of launching the First Crusade.[1] The armies of this initial expedition and of the Second Crusade, as well as portions of

(1288–95)," *Revue historique du sud-est européen,* I (1924), 59–63; and C. Marinescu, "Tentatives de mariage de deux fils d'Andronic II Paléologue avec des princesses latines," *ibid.,* 139–140. On Charles of Valois's plans see Delaville Le Roulx, *La France en Orient,* pp. 40–47, and H. Moranvillé, "Les Projets de Charles de Valois sur l'empire de Constantinople," *Bibliothèque de l'École des chartes,* LI (1890), 63–86. Other modern works dealing in part with the subject are M. Viller, "La Question de l'union des églises entre grecs et latins depuis le concile de Lyon jusqu'à celui de Florence (1274–1438)," *Revue d'histoire ecclésiastique,* XVI (1921), 260–305, 515–532, and XVIII (1922), 20–60; J. Gill, *The Council of Florence* (Cambridge, 1959); O. Halecki, *Un Empereur de Byzance à Rome, 1355–1375* (Warsaw, 1930); J. Smet, *The Life of Saint Peter Thomas by Philippe de Mézières* (Rome, 1954); and F. J. Boehlke, Jr., *Pierre de Thomas: Scholar, Diplomat, and Crusader* (Philadelphia, 1966). On the crusade of Peter I of Cyprus and the Byzantine reaction, see Iorga, *Philippe de Mézières,* and on Amadeo VI of Savoy, see K. Kerofilas, *Amadeo VI di Savoia nell' impero bizantino* (Rome, 1926), P. L. Datta, *Spedizione in Oriente di Amedeo VI* (Turin, 1826), and E. L. Cox, *The Green Count of Savoy: Amadeus VI . . .* (Princeton, 1967). On the battle of Kossovo and Byzantium, see H. Grégoire, "L'Opinion byzantine et la bataille de Kossovo," *Byzantion,* VI (1931), 247 ff., and on Nicopolis, besides A. S. Atiya, *The Crusade of Nicopolis* (London, 1934), and G. Ostrogorsky, *History of the Byzantine State* (Oxford, 1956), which is useful for the entire period, see R. Rosetti, "The Battle of Nicopolis (1396)," *Slavonic Review,* XV (1937), 629 ff., and G. Kling, *Die Schlacht bei Nikopolis im Jahre 1396* (Berlin, 1906). For the entire later period, see E. Pears, *The Destruction of the Greek Empire and the Story of the Capture of Constantinople by the Turks* (London, 1903); M. Silberschmidt, *Das orientalische Problem zur Zeit der Entstehung des türkischen Reiches nach venezianischen Quellen* (Leipzig, 1923); A. Grunzweig, "Philippe le Bon et Constantinople," *Byzantion,* XXIV (1954), 47–61; A. G. Mompherratos, *Diplomatic Activities of Manuel II . . .* [in Greek] (Athens, 1913); and J. W. Barker, *Manuel II Palaeologus (1391–1425): A Study in Late Byzantine Statesmanship* (New Brunswick, 1969). For Boucicault's expeditions, see especially *Livre des faits du Maréchal Boucicaut,* ed. J. F. Michaud and B. Poujoulat, in *Nouvelle collection des mémoires pour servir à l'histoire de France,* II (Paris, 1836), 205–232. For a collection of articles on the fall of Constantinople, including appeals to the west for a crusade, see *Le Cinq-centième anniversaire de la prise de Constantinople (L'Hellénisme contemporain,* 2nd ser., VII; Athens, 1953); also the articles in Greek and French by R. Guilland on Constantine XI, such as "Les Appels de Constantin XI Paléologue à Rome et à Venise," *Byzantinoslavica,* XIV (1953), 226–244; see also S. Runciman, *The Fall of Constantinople, 1453* (Cambridge, 1965). On Humbert's crusade, see U. Chévalier, *La Croisade du dauphin Humbert II* (Paris, 1920). Other works of importance are J. Gay, *Le Pape Clément VI et les affaires d'Orient* (Paris, 1904), and W. Miller, *The Latins in the Levant* (London, 1908); for Catalan designs on Constantinople in the 15th century, see especially F. Cerone, "La Politica orientale di Alfonso di Aragona," *Archivio storico per le province napoletane,* XXVII (1902), 3–93, 380–456, 555–634, 774–852, and XXVIII (1903), 154–212, and for documents, A. Rubió i Lluch, *Diplomatari de l'Orient català* (Barcelona, 1947). There are some pages of interest in G. Schlumberger, *Byzance et croisades* (Paris, 1927), and F. Thiriet, *La Romanie vénitienne au moyen âge . . .* (Paris, 1959); finally, for general source material, see N. Iorga, *Notes et extraits pour servir à l'histoire des croisades au XVe siècle* (6 vols., Paris and Bucharest, 1899–1916); the propagandistic account of William Adam ("Brocardus"), *Directorium ad passagium faciendum,* in *RHC, Arm.,* II (1906), 367 ff.; and Marino Sanudo "Torsello," *Istoria del regno di Romania,* ed. C. Hopf in *Chroniques gréco-romanes* (Berlin, 1873), and Sanudo's *Secreta fidelium crucis,* in J. Bongars, *Gesta Dei per Francos,* II (Hanover, 1611), 1–281.

1. See P. Charanis, "Aims of the Medieval Crusades and how they were viewed from Byzantium," *Church History,* XXI (1952), 123–134. This covers the first crusades.

the Third, all passed through Constantinople. And indeed, in 1204, western leaders of the Fourth Crusade, instead of going to Jerusalem, had diverted their forces and attacked and captured Constantinople itself. Thereafter, all the way to 1453, Byzantium, willing or not, would remain in one way or another inexorably bound to all western crusading movements.

In 1261, after more than a half century of Latin occupation, Constantinople was reconquered for the Greeks by Michael VIII Palaeologus.[2] After this date the original purpose of the early crusades was somewhat altered. For though the primary goal of subsequent expeditions still remained Jerusalem, the term "crusade" began also to be applied to western projects to reconquer Constantinople and restore the Latin empire. Such a perversion of the original crusading ideal was justified even for the more religious-minded westerners on the grounds that the city of Constantine had now fallen into the hands of "Greek schismatics," in effect semi-infidels. By this criterion a crusade against Christian Constantinople became either a worthy goal in itself or—as crusader-propagandists of the fourteenth century came to emphasize—a preliminary step to uniting eastern and western Christendom so that, with the greatest possible force, the "holy war" could be carried to the Moslems in Jerusalem.

After 1261 western leaders of the crusading movement, with some notable exceptions, were not unduly troubled by the need for finding an ideology for their expeditions. To the politician of the west, be he prince or pope, the crusade all too often became merely a political or military effort of which the primary goal was the aggrandizement of the leader himself or of the institution he represented. The old religious zeal of the west, the contagious piety so important in launching the First Crusade, had now conspicuously diminished. The crusades had become secularized.

Among the Byzantines what might perhaps be considered protocrusades, expeditions to recapture Syria and Palestine, had been conducted as early as the seventh century by their emperor Heraclius and in the tenth century by Nicephorus Phocas and John Tsimisces. Nevertheless, despite these "holy" wars, the ideology of a crusade in the western sense of the word, as an expedition preached by the church to recover the Holy Sepulcher, with remission of sins promised to the expedition's participants, was totally alien, indeed almost incomprehensible, to the Byzantines.[3] It does not have to be noted

---

2. See volume II of this work, pp. 228–232.

3. See V. Laurent, "L'Idée de guerre sainte," pp. 71–98; Lemerle, "Byzance et la croisade," pp. 595 ff.; and A. Vasiliev, *History of the Byzantine Empire* (Madison, Wis., 1958), especially pp. 389–400. P. Alphandéry and A. Dupont, *La Chrétienté et l'idée de*

that in these tenth-century Byzantine expeditions to Syria and Palestine, the Greek soldiers did not wear the cross as a badge, nor did they term their wars "crusades."[4] Rather, behind their expeditions was not so much the concept of freeing the Holy Land from "the pollution of the infidel" as the desire to restore to the authority of the basileus certain lost areas of the *Basileia*, the sacred empire, in particular Syria and Palestine.

The Byzantine lack of appreciation for the religious aspect of western crusading ideology may already be seen during the First Crusade. Even the usually astute Anna Comnena demonstrated a certain lack of insight when she viewed all the western knights merely as predatory, bent only on looting the empire. Nor does the sophisticated emperor Alexius I seem truly to have appreciated the extent of the genuine piety in crusader motivations. He was, to be sure, amazed at the masses of westerners who left home and family to take the cross. But he always suspected that the motive of self-aggrandizement, the personal ambition of the leaders, was at the bottom of all crusading ventures, despite the outpouring of pious fervor that manifested itself on the surface. Alexius's worst fears of Latin motivations were confirmed by the aggressive actions of Bohemond—fears transmitted to his grandson, Manuel I, and from him to all subsequent Greek emperors. By Manuel's time (1143–1180) there was greater reason for the Byzantine suspicion of the crusading movement. For during the Second Crusade (1147) Louis VII of France had contemplated taking Constantinople, and similarly in 1185 the late Manuel's archenemy, the German emperor Frederick I Barbarossa, encamped before the walls of the capital, had pondered whether to assault the city. After the Fourth Crusade in 1204, with its unparalleled looting of Constantinople and enforced Greek conversion to "Catholicism," Byzantine suspicions and fears of the Latins had became so ineradicably a part of their psychology that nothing thereafter seemed able to assuage them.

Accordingly, from the time of the Greek recovery of Constantinople by Michael VIII in 1261 until the final fall of the city in 1453,

---

croisade: Les premiers croisades (Paris, 1959), is of little help on the Byzantine side. See also S. Runciman, "The Byzantine Provincial Peoples and the Crusade," *Relazioni del X Congresso Internazionale di Scienze Storiche,* III (1955), 621–624.

4. Possibly the first, or one of the first, Byzantine uses of the western term crusade is in Nicetas Choniates (*staurophoroi*: bearers of the cross), referring to the western knights of the First Crusade coming to Constantinople. This term is not used during the 9th- and 10th-century Byzantine campaigns in Syria and Palestine, and the Greek church, though it blessed the Greek armies and was anxious for the recovery of the holy places and holy relics, did not promise any special rewards such as remission of sins to the expedition's participants.

whenever the Byzantines heard of western plans for a new crusade they at once assumed a negative, defensive posture. With few exceptions most Byzantines paid no heed at all to the idealism, the pious words of pope Gregory X (1271–1276) or of certain enlightened western crusader-propagandists like Humbert of Romans (d. 1277) and Marino Sanudo Torsello (d. 1334). Almost pathologically the mentality of the Byzantine man on the street came to be deeply conditioned by the conviction that the crusades were merely organized expeditions of bandits aimed at the resubjugation of Byzantium. Whatever their guise might be—whether an overt attempt to restore the Latin empire, a crusade to take Smyrna, or plans to attack Egypt—all mass movements to the east on the part of western arms and men were for the Byzantines suspect and potentially terrifying.

The history of Byzantium's connection with the later crusades may be divided into three major phases. The first, from 1261 to 1331, the death of prince Philip of Taranto, grandson of Charles I of Anjou and heir to his aspirations, was dominated by the attempts of western claimants to restore the Latin empire. In the second phase, extending from 1331 to the battle of Nicopolis in 1396, western expeditions to the east were motivated both by papal fears and by the commercial interests of Venice, whose eastern trade and colonies were increasingly threatened by the advance of the Ottoman Turks. Hence arose the dual aim of clearing the Aegean of Turkish pirates and establishing a Latin beachhead in Asia Minor—considerations leading to the remarkable western-Byzantine coalition of 1334 and the crusade to Smyrna in 1344. Byzantium was, to be sure, not directly involved in all these expeditions, and never really responded positively to appeals for a crusade, although a change in the situation had effected a partial alteration of the Byzantine attitude. With the end, in 1331, of overt western attempts to restore the Latin empire of Constantinople, some Greeks began to realize that their own fate might well depend on whatever results western arms might be able to achieve against their oppressors, the Ottoman Turks. The once mighty Byzantine empire had by then become in large part merely an onlooker, one which gazed as if mesmerized yet was almost powerless to do anything about events directly affecting its own destiny. In the third phase, from 1396 to 1453, the overwhelming problem which cast everything else into the shade was the ever-growing threat of the Ottoman Turks, who had almost completely encircled Constantinople and who, if Constantinople should fall, would even menace the west. Growing increasingly fearful of the Turks, the leaders of Latin

Christendom launched or helped to launch two major expeditions to aid the Byzantines: the luckless crusade of Nicopolis in 1396,[5] and the essentially Polish-Hungarian crusade of Varna in 1444.[6]

The Byzantine point of view in connection with the crusading expeditions from 1261 to 1453 has not hitherto been dealt with systematically. Though any direct Byzantine involvement in these events is usually difficult to ascertain, it was, nevertheless, often greater than appears on the surface. Indeed, if one judges strictly from the Byzantine viewpoint, all three phases from 1261 to 1453 may be characterized as a Byzantine struggle for survival—in the first, to preserve Greek independence in the face of threats from western pretenders to the throne of Constantinople, and in the two subsequent phases, to protect the empire against the advancing Ottoman Turks.

Byzantine statesmen from Michael VIII to 1453 realized that Byzantium had become too weak to stand alone and must therefore secure allies from the only source that could provide effectual help, the west, in particular its leader the pope. At the same time the Byzantines understood that from him no aid would be forthcoming unless they were willing to pay his price, ecclesiastical union, entailing subordination of the Greek church to Rome. Hence, as we shall see, in all three periods a basic, sometimes the most significant, factor was the repeated proposals of the Byzantine emperors to the popes and western rulers for union of the churches. And it is this factor, with its accompanying and often complex diplomatic negotiations, that seems always to be intertwined with, at times even to predominate in, the history of Byzantium's involvement in the later crusades.

The majority of the Byzantine populace, however, remained so deeply hostile to the Latins that any attempt at union, for whatever reason, was rejected out of hand. It was not only the persistent fear of a possible new Latin invasion that aroused the Greeks against ecclesiastical union, but even more, it would seem, the belief that union meant the dilution of the purity of the Orthodox faith and thus, through this beginning of a process of Latinization, the loss of their identity as a people. Paradoxically, as the medieval Greeks became weaker and weaker politically and militarily, more than ever they clung tenaciously to their religion, believing that loss of the Orthodox faith would bring with it the destruction of the empire itself. By 1400, in fact, certain segments of the populace, especially

5. See above, pp. 21–25.
6. A chapter on the crusade of Varna is planned for volume V of this work, in preparation.

among the lower classes, came to prefer as the lesser of two evils the possibility of Turkish occupation to a renewed Latin domination. In any discussion of Byzantium and the later crusades, therefore, many complex factors must be considered: political, social, economic, and religious. In the final analysis, however, it is the last-mentioned factor, the question of accepting or rejecting union with Rome, that always seems to lie near the surface, and gives an element of continuity to the total picture.

The reign of Michael VIII Palaeologus (1261–1282),[7] which opens the first phase of Byzantium's involvement in the later crusades, is in a sense the prototype for all east-west relations up to 1453. It was he who established that pattern of imperial diplomacy, so often to recur, of offering religious union to the papacy in exchange for support in thwarting the designs of external enemies against Constantinople. Almost immediately upon recovering Constantinople in 1261 Michael had to face the problem of western attempts to restore the Latin empire, often through the launching of a new crusade. For in conquering Constantinople Michael had not only ended Latin rule but had, at the same time, terminated papal jurisdiction over the Greek church, a control which at least technically the popes had exercised since 1204. From 1261 onward it was the aim of almost all popes to seek by one means or another the return of the "schismatic" Greeks to the "bosom of the Roman church," an aim which many western ecclesiastics believed could best be accomplished through the medium of a new crusade.

The immediate reaction of pope Urban IV, on hearing of the Greek recovery of Constantinople,[8] was to look to the preservation of the remaining Latin possessions in Achaea, Negroponte, and the Aegean islands, while at the same time taking measures to secure western support for the dethroned Latin emperor Baldwin II. To this end Urban commanded the preaching of a crusade in France, Poland, and Aragon—a crusade whose stated goal was not, as before, the Holy Land, but the recovery of Constantinople.[9] Urban's directive is significant because it is the first in history to order the preaching of a crusade specifically against the Greeks. Though, to be sure, in 1204 Innocent III had finally sanctioned the conquest of Constantinople by the western armies of the Fourth Crusade, his earlier, more

---

7. On Michael's relations with the west, especially the papacy, see Geanakoplos, *Emperor Michael*.

8. *Ibid.*, chap. V.

9. *Ibid.*, pp. 139–142.

immediate reaction had been to excommunicate the Latin troops. Now, however, in the time of Michael VIII we see pope Urban justifying a crusade against Constantinople not only on the grounds that the "schismatic" Greeks had again fallen away from Rome, but—as the pope wrote to Louis IX urging him to join the anti-Byzantine expedition—because "if the Greeks seize all of Romania, the way to Jerusalem will be barred."[10] In a subsequent letter sent to bishop Henry of Utrecht, Urban was in fact to proclaim that he would promise "to all who personally [assist in the restoration of the Latin empire] the remission of sins, the same privileges granted to those aiding the Holy Land."[11]

To preserve the Latin territorial possessions in the east and restore Latin rule over Constantinople, Urban now took a very active part in forming a coalition consisting of the Latin princes of the Morea (the Peloponnesus), the dethroned emperor Baldwin II, and the Venetians of Negroponte. In May 1262 and subsequently in July of the same year, these parties, the pope among them, signed at Viterbo an agreement prescribing joint action against Michael in the Morea.[12] But their efforts bore little fruit; the Greco-Latin struggle over the Morea was to last almost until 1453.

Urban's plan to launch a crusade against Constantinople never really got off the ground. The most respected ruler of the west, the French king Louis IX, was not disposed to fight a Christian emperor, even a Greek "schismatic," believing that all military efforts should instead be directed to recovering Jerusalem.[13] But a more basic deterrent to a crusade against Constantinople was the preoccupation of the papacy itself with its struggle against the Hohenstaufen heirs of Frederick II, notably Frederick's illegitimate son Manfred, king of Sicily. Urban therefore shifted the focus of his attention from a Byzantine crusade to a crusade against the papacy's more immediate antagonist, Manfred;[14] for the next seven years almost all papal political maneuvers would be motivated by the desire to crush the Hohenstaufen.

From the first, Michael VIII was aware of the powerful western enemies his capture of Constantinople would evoke. Hence directly after his recovery of the city, he sent two envoys to the pope bearing

10. *Ibid.*, p. 142.
11. J. Guiraud, ed., *Les Registres d'Urbain IV (1261–1264)*, II (Paris, 1901), no. 577, pp. 292–293 (dated 1264).
12. *Ibid.*, II, 47–48, and cf. II, 292–293.
13. R. Sternfeld, *Ludwigs des heiligen Kreuzzug nach Tunis, 1270* (Berlin, 1896), p. 308, and Dade, *Versuche*, p. 11.
14. W. Norden, *Das Papsttum und Byzanz* (Berlin, 1903), p. 431, and Geanakoplos, *Emperor Michael*, pp. 143 ff.

letters promising to establish ecclesiastical union with Rome if the pope would recognize his possession of Constantinople.[15] Neglecting no diplomatic opportunity, Michael also made overtures to Manfred, offering an alliance against the papacy. When negotiations with Manfred proved futile,[16] Michael redoubled his efforts vis-à-vis the pope, even proposing, in addition to union, his aid for a crusade to recover Jerusalem, an astute maneuver because at that time Urban was himself promoting the launching of a crusade against the Greeks.[17] Realizing the papacy's power, Michael indicated in his letter to the pope his readiness to subject all the eastern patriarchs to Rome.[18] Fearful of Manfred's increasing power in Sicily, Urban on his side seized upon Michael's offers of union. But soon the appearance in Italy of the new papal champion Charles I of Anjou, to combat the Hohenstaufen, swung the pope again away from Palaeologus, and Urban announced his intention to reëstablish the Latin empire as soon as Manfred was defeated.[19]

With the death of Manfred in 1266 at the battle of Benevento and the execution at Naples in 1268 of the only surviving legitimate successor of Frederick II, the young Conradin, Byzantine relations with the Latin west entered a more critical period. The new master of southern Italy and Sicily, Charles of Anjou, the shrewd, energetic, and intensely ambitious brother of Louis IX, now became captive to the old Norman-Hohenstaufen dreams of conquering Constantinople. Thus almost immediately after his enthronement Charles began to muster a tremendous coalition of forces against Michael Palaeologus, a coalition including Michael's Latin enemies, many of the Italian communes, Byzantium's Slavic neighbors, and, finally, even the Venetians, who hoped to displace their rivals the Genoese in the lucrative Byzantine trade. Arranging a diplomatic marriage between his son Philip and Isabel, the heiress of William of Villehardouin, prince of Achaea, Charles in 1267 signed the treaty of Viterbo, the terms of which purported to give Charles and Philip legal title to Byzantium and called for Charles to attack Constantinople and restore the Latin empire.[20]

15. *Ibid.*, pp. 140–141, quoting Pachymeres, *De Michaele . . .* , II, 36 (*CSHB*, I, 168–169).

16. Pachymeres, III, 7 (*CSHB*, I, 181, 183).

17. Guiraud, *Registres d'Urbain IV*, II, no. 577, pp. 292–293; Geanakoplos, *Emperor Michael*, p. 176.

18. Guiraud, *Registres d'Urbain IV*, II, 357.

19. Geanakoplos, *Emperor Michael*, p. 184 and pp. 164–165, notes 14, 16.

20. Treaty printed in G. del Giudice, *Codice diplomatico del regno di Carlo I e II d'Angiò*, II (Naples, 1863), 30 ff. See also J. Longnon, "Le Rattachement de la principauté de Morée au royaume de Sicile en 1267," *Journal des savants*, 1942, 134–143; Geanakoplos, *Emperor Michael*, pp. 197 ff.

One very important figure was still lacking in Charles's alliance, the pope. As spiritual head of Christendom his sanction was indispensable if Charles's expedition was to be blessed as a crusade. Moreover, as the pope was Charles's direct feudal overlord for Sicily, his approval was all the more necessary for a Greek campaign. For the next fifteen years Charles and Michael were to pit their formidable diplomatic talents against each other, each in the aim of winning the papacy to his side. Michael VIII continued his policy of holding out the bait of union to the popes. Under Urban's successor Clement IV, moreover, he again brought up the question of a crusade to the Holy Land. But this time Michael offered to participate personally in the expedition as well as to enlist the support of the strategically situated Christian king of Cilician Armenia, Heṭoum I. He assured the pope that with the participation of the Greeks, Latins, and Armenians, the Mamluks of Egypt were sure to be defeated. In exchange Michael asked the pope to provide him with guarantees that Byzantium would not be attacked by Latins while he himself was away on the crusade.[21] The negotiations between emperor and pope, which had progressed far, were suddenly brought to a halt in 1268 by the death of Clement.

Clement's demise removed the chief obstacle to Charles's plans for a Greek expedition, and the Angevin monarch now began anew to muster his forces. Michael, however, agilely responded by sending appeals to the brother of Charles, Louis IX of France. Realizing Louis's unfaltering desire to lead a crusade to the Holy Land, Michael shrewdly pointed out to the French king that an attack upon Constantinople by Charles would adversely affect Louis's own plans for a crusade. "If the forces of both Charles and Michael are set at war with each other," Michael told the king, "neither can contribute to the security of your own expedition." Envoys from Michael appeared before Louis's camp in Tunisia during the latter's ill-starred crusade in North Africa in 1270, bearing splendid gifts and hoping to enter into direct negotiations. Before anything could be discussed Louis succumbed to the plague and Michael once again had to face an unrestrained Charles of Anjou.[22] Only an act of fate, a storm

21. E. Jordan, ed., *Les Registres de Clément IV (1265–1268)* (Paris, 1893; repr. 1945), no. 1201, p. 404; A. L. Tăutu, ed., *Acta Urbani IV, Clementis IV, Gregorii X (1261–1276)* (Vatican City, 1953), no. 25, pp. 71–72.

22. Jordan, *Registres de Clément IV,* no. 1201, p. 404. Also L. Bréhier, "Une Ambassade byzantine au camp de Saint Louis devant Tunis," *Mélanges offerts à M. Nicolas Iorga* (Paris, 1933), p. 140; Pachymeres, V, 9 (*CSHB,* I, 362–364); O. Raynaldus (Rinaldi), *Annales ecclesiastici,* ad ann. 1270, no. 33; Geanakoplos, *Emperor Michael,* pp. 224–227. See also volume II of this work, pp. 509–518.

which shattered Charles's fleet off Trapani in Sicily, now spared Michael's capital from invasion.[23]

Charles, though disappointed, was undaunted and immediately began to rebuild his fleet and refurbish his alliances. But he was again frustrated when in 1271, after a papal interregnum of three years, Gregory X was elevated to the papal throne. Strong-willed, pious, and able, Gregory had himself long been consumed by a desire to recover Jerusalem from the Moslems, and he tended to view everything else as subordinate to this aim. Not only would good relations with Byzantium, as he saw it, be beneficial to Christendom, but, more important, only with Greek support could Jerusalem be retaken and maintained.[24] To halt Angevin designs against Byzantium Gregory now even pushed Charles into making a truce with Michael.

The negotiations taking place between Michael and Gregory culminated in 1274 in the celebrated Council of Lyons, at which religious union was signed by the pope and Michael's envoys, headed by his grand logothete George Acropolites.[25] We omit discussion of the theological aspects of the council in order to examine its implications for the crusade. As far as Michael was concerned, Lyons was primarily an act of political expediency entered into in the aim of saving his throne and empire. For Gregory, on the other hand, perhaps the only truly sincere actor in the drama transpiring at Lyons, now that the two churches of east and west were finally united, it was only natural to expect that both would join in a great crusade to overwhelm the Moslems and restore Jerusalem to the Christians.

As has already been emphasized, the underlying religious motives for a crusade were not grasped by the Byzantines. Thus Michael, fearing a repetition of the Latin conquest of 1204 if massed western armies should again appear in the east, demanded that Gregory assure the integrity of his empire. Michael's surprising confidence in the pope's intentions therefore seems to have been based on what he believed to be Gregory's power and authority, on the pope's sincerity of motive, and, no less important, on the belief that Gregory would personally lead the crusade through the Byzantine territories.

23. Geanakoplos, *Emperor Michael,* pp. 227–228; William of Nangis, "Gesta Philippi tertii francorum regis," in *RHGF,* XX, 480.

24. V. Laurent, "La Croisade et la question d'Orient sous le pontificat de Grégoire X (1271–1276)," *Revue historique de sud-est européen,* XXII (1945), 105–137, and his "Grégoire X (1271–1276) et la projet d'une ligue antiturque," *Échos d'Orient,* XXXVII (1938), 257–273.

25. On Lyons, see Geanakoplos, *Emperor Michael,* pp. 258–276, and volume II of this work, p. 584.

But all was for naught. The union of the two churches was accomplished only on paper. Most Greeks insisted that, since the four eastern patriarchs had been unrepresented at Lyons and since no later council had pronounced it ecumenical, Lyons was nothing but a "robber council." Thus for them the act of union subscribed to by pope and emperor was invalid. Far more basic than this legal technicality, however, was the deep-seated emotional aversion of the Greeks for anything Latin. Near civil war resulted upon the return of Michael's envoys to Constantinople. Violently rejecting the results of Lyons, the Byzantine populace believed that effective union with the Latins would corrupt the purity of their faith. Worse, they insisted that if the faith were corrupted, Constantinople, the city "guarded by God," would itself be doomed because of the loss of divine favor. The unionist patriarch John Beccus acutely reflected this feeling when he wrote, "Men, women, the old and the young consider the peace [with the west] a war and the union a separation."[26] Even the idea of a cöoperative effort by Greeks and Latins to recover Jerusalem was derided by the people. The Virgin, the protectress of Constantinople, would never, the Byzantines believed, sanction an expedition against territories rightfully belonging to themselves if it were launched in alliance with Latin "heretics."

Yet in courting the pope Michael had at least achieved his immediate aim. The act of union proclaimed at Lyons acted as a powerful brake to the aspirations of Charles of Anjou. With the Greeks again apparently reconciled to the Roman church, any expedition Charles launched against Byzantium would not be regarded as a true crusade. Rather, in the eyes of Gregory at least, it would be a fratricidal war between two "Catholic princes," a war which, instead of promoting a crusade against the Moslems, would actually weaken the Christians. With Byzantium in effect now a kind of papal protectorate, Charles, as a vassal of the pope, could hardly contravene Gregory's orders to desist.[27]

Negotiations moved forward regarding the question of a crusade. Shortly after the signing of union at Lyons the papal legate to Constantinople, Bernard Ayglier, abbot of Monte Cassino, returned to Rome with a report that Byzantine ambassadors charged with discussion of the crusade would soon follow.[28] The imperial envoys,

26. Pachymeres, V, 23; V, 14; VI, 23 f.; III, 11; VI, 24 (*CSHB,* I, 401 ff., 379 ff., 482 ff., 192–193, 489 ff.).

27. Geanokoplos, *Emperor Michael,* chap. XII. On Charles's career see also S. Runciman, *The Sicilian Vespers* (Cambridge, 1958).

28. Geanakoplos, *Emperor Michael,* pp. 285–286.

George Metochites, archdeacon of Constantinople, and the grand intendant Theodore, met in 1276 with Gregory, probably first in southern France and later at Lausanne, where they witnessed the western emperor Rudolph of Hapsburg taking the cross.[29] Already at Lyons Gregory had proclaimed that the arms of both the eastern and the western emperors would crush Islam, and Michael in turn had promised that Byzantium would contribute provisions, revenues, troops, and whatever else was necessary for the *passagium* to the Holy Land. Undoubtedly Michael had at first suggested the general idea of a crusade as an inducement to curry favor with Gregory. Now, however, his envoys came forward with a striking new proposal: that the Latin crusaders, instead of crossing by sea, should proceed by land across the Balkans to Constantinople and thence through Asia Minor.[30] Apparently Michael had in mind a repetition of what had been achieved by his predecessor Alexius I: reconquest from the Turks, by means of the crusader armies, of the former Byzantine territories in Anatolia. Execution of such a plan would not only restore Asia Minor to Byzantine rule and avert the danger of the Turks in general, but at the same time serve to thwart the growing menace of the Mamluks of Egypt, who were now penetrating Cilician Armenia.

According to Metochites' report, pope Gregory seemed favorable to the plan. Impressed by Michael's plea for the recovery of "the hallowed Christian cities of Asia Minor," Gregory agreed that the land route would avoid for the western armies the hardship and danger of a long sea voyage as well as providing a strong base of operations from which to take and maintain Jerusalem. Moreover, the grave problem of finding enough ships to transport the western armies across the Mediterranean would be solved.

To insure complete accord on the plan, pope and emperor, it is interesting to note, were to meet personally for discussions either at Brindisi on the Adriatic or at Avlona in northwest Epirus.[31] But the death of Gregory in January 1276 removed the possibility of a united Christendom opposing the Turkish advance in Asia Minor. Not that such a joint venture would easily have succeeded. The

29. M. H. Laurent, *Le Bienheureux Innocent V (Pierre de Tarentaise) et son temps* (Studi e testi, 129; Vatican City, 1947), pp. 269, 440.

30. See report of Metochites in V. Laurent, "Le Rapport de Georges Métochite, aprocrisiaire de Michel VIII Paléologue auprès du pape Grégoire X (1275–1276)," *Revue historique du sud-est européen*, XXIII (1946), 233–247, and V. Laurent, "Grégoire X"; cf. Geanakoplos, *Emperor Michael*, pp. 287–289.

31. M. H. Laurent, *Le B. Innocent V*, pp. 439–440; Geanakoplos, *Emperor Michael*, pp. 288–289.

mutual distrust of Latins and Greeks, the probable unwillingness of Latin leaders to relinquish territories taken by their arms, the constant temptation for the crusaders to seize Constantinople for themselves, and finally the ill-will, if not overt hostility, of the Byzantine population to the entire expedition—all these factors would have seriously hampered the success of any such joint action, and perhaps even resulted in war between Greeks and Latins.

Under the new pope, Innocent V, the plan for a land expedition through Anatolia was abandoned. Apparently Michael VIII had confidence only in Gregory, or the new pope may have distrusted the Greeks. Moreover, the western leaders may have believed that a sea route was more practicable.[32] Nevertheless, negotiations for some kind of joint expedition were continued by Michael and Innocent. Now, however, Michael raised many questions as to the participation and attitude of western rulers. He also sought to clarify the question of the future of Egypt, since Michael himself was then in alliance with the Mamluk sultan Baybars. To these complex political factors was added the question of how the union of Lyons was to be implemented in the Byzantine areas. This was a particularly touchy matter since Charles of Anjou was continuously pressing the pope to unleash him against Michael on the grounds that the emperor was reneging on or lax in fulfilling his promises to implement the union.[33]

Several popes succeeded Innocent, and with all of them Michael exchanged numerous embassies. In 1277, however, he encountered a really intransigent pontiff, Nicholas III. While expressly forbidding Charles to attack Constantinople, Nicholas demanded that Michael, in accordance with papal stipulations, impose on his empire complete uniformity of (Latin) dogma and liturgical custom. To this end the pope sought to dispatch a cardinal-legate to Constantinople and even to demand from each Greek ecclesiastic a personal oath of submission to Rome.[34] Meanwhile Charles, impatient at all the years of

32. Actually the land route was no longer practicable for the west, especially as Adalia, on the southern Anatolian coast, had been in Turkish hands since 1207. Thus after 1204 Cyprus was considered even more precious than Constantinople. But when Michael VIII reigned, Constantinople was again considered necessary for a crusade to Jerusalem. See V. Laurent, "La Croisade et la question," p. 133, and his "Grégoire X," pp. 265–267; also the 13th-century theoretician Fidenzio of Padua, *Liber de recuperatione Terrae Sanctae,* in G. Golubovich, ed., *Biblioteca bio-bibliografica della Terra Santa e dell' Oriente francescano,* II (Quaracchi, 1913), 51. M. H. Laurent, *Le B. Innocent V,* p. 273, does not think Gregory was well informed as to the risks involved on the land route.

33. M. H. Laurent, *Le B. Innocent V,* pp. 256–286. Pachymeres, V, 26 (*CSHB,* I, 410) describes Charles as pressing the pope against Michael.

34. E. Van Moé, "L'Envoi de nonces à Constantinople par les papes Innocent V et Jean

waiting, launched a premature attack across the Adriatic against the Byzantine town of Berat in Albania, presumably with the ultimate aim of driving along the Via Egnatia to the Byzantine capital itself. At Berat Michael was, however, able to achieve a stunning military victory over Charles.[35]

Still not daunted, Charles, at the death of Nicholas III, was able at long last to arrange for the elevation in 1281 of a pontiff favorable to his political aspirations, Martin IV. Soon after his enthronement Martin, repudiating the union of Lyons, excommunicated Michael and "urged" Charles to lead a crusade against "the Greek schismatics."[36] The death knell of the Byzantine empire seemed about to sound, for in addition to the papacy Charles's many allies now included the powerful Venetian fleet. But Michael was equal to the challenge. For some time he had been pursuing a diplomatic policy of allying himself with the pro-Hohenstaufen, anti-Angevin elements in Sicily, and also with king Peter III of Aragon, son-in-law of Manfred. Michael poured Greek gold into the coffers of the Aragonese king and at the same time subsidized the Hohenstaufen party in Sicily. Finally, on Easter Monday, March 30, 1282, a dramatic event, the Sicilian Vespers, occurred, the Sicilians rising in revolt against the hated Angevin rule. They were joined shortly by the forces of Peter of Aragon, and soon Charles's troops were completely expelled from the island.

In this celebrated event the fine hand of Michael, even if active only behind the scenes, undoubtedly played a significant role.[37] Thus Michael VIII Palaeologus, largely through his diplomatic genius, saved his empire from Charles I of Anjou, whose plans constituted, in the entire period from 1261 to 1453, the most serious attempt to reëstablish Latin rule over Byzantium. Charles's preparations received considerable publicity in Constantinople and did a good deal to embitter the Byzantine attitude toward the west. More than ever the Greeks came to believe that any military succor coming from the west would ultimately be directed against Constantinople. Moreover,

---

XXI," *Mélanges d'archéologie et d'histoire,* XLVII (1930), 48 ff.; V. Grumel, "Les Ambassades pontificales à Byzance après le IIe concile de Lyon (1274–1280)," *Échos d'Orient,* XXIII (1924), 437–447; J. Gay and S. Witte, eds., *Les Registres de Nicolas III (1277–1280),* part 1 (Paris, 1898), pp. 76–86; Geanakoplos, *Emperor Michael,* pp. 305–324.

35. *Ibid.,* pp. 329–334.

36. Bull of excommunication in Raynaldus, *Annales ecclesiastici,* ad ann. 1281, no. 25, and F. Olivier-Martin, ed., *Les Registres de Martin IV (1281–1285)* (Paris, 1901–1935), p. 100, no. 69, and p. 115, no. 78.

37. On Michael's role in the Sicilian Vespers, see Geanakoplos, *Emperor Michael,* pp. 344–367 and the bibliography cited there.

after Michael's attempt to ram the union of Lyons down the throats of the Byzantines, the latter became even more certain that a western crusade would bring with it the attempted conversion of the Greeks to Catholicism—the final result of which would be the Latinization of the Greek people. The Greek rabble, significantly, had shouted to Michael's legate on his return from Lyons: *"Efrangepses!"* ("You have [through accepting union] become a Frank!").[38] For the Latins, on the other hand, the memory of the Byzantine disavowal of the union of Lyons undoubtedly served to increase western suspicions of the Greeks, and thus the next two centuries, as we shall see, would witness failure after failure on the Latin side to provide Byzantium with any effective aid against the Turks.

Under Michael's son and successor Andronicus II Palaeologus (1282–1328) there was, as might be expected, a violent reaction in Byzantium against what appeared to be the pro-western orientation of Michael. No longer endangered by the threat of an Angevin crusade, Andronicus, reflecting popular sentiment, now reverted to a policy of overt anti-Latinism. The Greek churches were purified of "contamination" from association with the Latins, and it was the turn of Michael's adherents to be incarcerated, while the former anti-unionists returned to power from exile or imprisonment.[39] All that remained of the eight years of attempted communion with Rome was a growing Greek hatred of the Latins, which increased the more as subsequent popes excommunicated the Greeks[40] and accorded favor to a series of French pretenders who began to claim the Byzantine throne. Indeed, the popes of the late thirteenth century and the Avignonese popes of the early fourteenth continued the policy of Martin IV. In place of a precarious entente with the Greeks, they generally preferred a military effort at restoration of the Latin empire, their French orientation making them automatically partisans of the Valois claimants to the throne of the Latin empire of Constantinople.

One pope, however, Nicholas IV (1288–1292), did seek a peaceful solution to the problem—through a diplomatic marriage which, if we can believe a western source, he himself proposed between Catherine

---

38. Report of Metochites in M. H. Laurent, *Le B. Innocent V,* p. 424, note 23.

39. Nicephorus Gregoras, VI, I (*CSHB,* I, 160). The anti-union reaction was not complete: see Pachymeres, *De Andronico . . . ,* I, 7 (*CSHB,* II, 22–23), emphasizing a celebration attended by Greeks and Latins in which only some of the Greeks gave candles to the Latins.

40. Clement V, the first Avignonese pope, excommunicated Andronicus II in 1307, and actually awarded the crusaders going against Byzantium the indulgences of an expedition to the Holy Land (Raynaldus, *Annales ecclesiastici,* ad ann. 1306, no. 25; ad ann. 1307, nos. 6–7).

of Courtenay, the titular empress of the Latin throne, and the Greek heir-apparent, young Michael (IX) Palaeologus.[41] Andronicus II, on his side, riding the current of anti-Latinism, was at first uncertain of what policy to follow with respect to the pope,[42] although one Byzantine source implies that the initiative was his.[43] In any event, he showed interest when he realized the possibility, through this marriage, of warding off a western threat to Constantinople in the person of a princess who, as granddaughter to the last Latin emperor, Baldwin II, had fallen heir to his claim to the Latin throne at the death in 1283 of her father Philip. The negotiations collapsed, however, the overpowering anti-unionist sentiment in Constantinople making it impossible for Andronicus to fulfill the papal condition for the marriage—recognition of the pope's supremacy over the Greek church. Soon thereafter, in 1295, Michael IX married Rita ("Maria Xenia"), a sister of king Heṭoum II of Cilician Armenia, thereby foreclosing this opportunity to achieve a solution to the political disagreement between east and west.[44] Thereafter Andronicus, occupied with Byzantine internal affairs, remained largely indifferent to western developments until later, when the danger from the west once again became pressing.

As for Catherine, a succeeding pope, Boniface VIII, reverting to Martin IV's aggressive policy toward Constantinople, sought to marry her to a powerful western prince able to arouse Europe to a crusade against Byzantium. Indeed, according to one modern authority it was following a suggestion originally contained in a memoir (composed c. 1300) of the French legist and propagandist Peter Dubois, that in 1301 a marriage was concluded between Catherine and Charles of Valois, brother of the French king, Philip IV the Fair, thus giving Charles a claim to the Latin empire of Constantinople.[45] Dubois in another work, De recuperatione Terre Sancte, advised king Philip that on the return of the French "crusading" armies from recapturing Jerusalem they should, under Charles of Valois, stop on the way

---

41. See Bratianu, "Notes sur le projet," pp. 59–63, and Marinescu, "Tentatives de mariage," pp. 139–140.

42. In 1284 Andronicus II himself married Yolanda ("Irene"), daughter of William VII, marquis of Montferrat, so as to do away with the Montferratine claims to the Byzantine throne. Nicephorus Gregoras, VI, 2 (CSHB, I, 167–168) says that the pope withheld his approval.

43. Ibid., VI, 8 (CSHB, I, 193), however, implies that the initiative was taken by the "king of Italy," Catherine's father. He says that the negotiations failed because of the excessive demands made by the westerners ("dia ta hyper to prosekon zetemata").

44. Ibid., VI, 8 (CSHB, I, 193 ff.); cf. Bratianu, "Notes sur le projet," pp. 59 ff.; Marinescu, "Tentatives de mariage," pp. 139–140.

45. Dubois was ostensibly discussing how Philip IV could acquire universal domination. On all this see Delaville Le Roulx, La France en Orient, pp. 48 ff. On the memoir, see E.

and capture Constantinople from its unlawful ruler "Palerlog" [Andronicus II].[46] The might of France was to be thrown into the balance behind western designs against Byzantium.

Two western protagonists now arose to revive the old aspirations of Charles I of Anjou. Their support came from France and the Angevin kingdom of Naples. Philip of Taranto, the son of Charles II of Anjou, king of Naples, held Angevin territory in Epirus and claimed suzerainty over Latin Greece. In alliance with the Catholic Albanians Philip carried on minor military operations in the Balkans but accomplished little. More significant was the activity of Charles of Valois,[47] brother of Philip IV and husband of Catherine of Courtenay, who in 1306 entered into alliance with Venice, the enemy of Andronicus and of his Genoese allies. Venice could not resist the temptation to revert to its aggressive anti-Byzantine policy of 1204, especially in view of the fact that after 1261 Michael VIII had bestowed upon the Genoese most of the old Venetian privileges in the Byzantine empire. In June 1307 Charles of Valois prevailed upon pope Clement V, the first of the Avignonese popes, to support the projected undertaking by excommunicating Andronicus II and even offering to the "crusaders" who would combat Byzantium the same indulgences accorded to crusaders going to Jerusalem.[48] The anti-Byzantine alliance being organized won the adherence of Naples and of the Serbs under king Stephen Urosh II Milutin. Charles was even able to number among his supporters certain Byzantine nobles,[49] a circumstance revealing the degree of internal disorganization in Byzantium at this time.

Only a few years before, the famous Catalan Grand Company had appeared in the east.[50] A small but reckless and powerful group of adventurers from Catalonia and Aragon who had fought in the long war which culminated in the Sicilian Vespers, they had been deprived

---

Boutaric, *La France sous Philippe le Bel* (Paris, 1861), pp. 411–413; it is apparently still unpublished.

46. English trans. by W. I. Brandt, *The Recovery of the Holy Land* (Columbia University Records of Civilization, no. 51; New York, 1956), p. 172.

47. On Charles of Valois's plans, see Delaville Le Roulx, *La France en Orient*, pp. 40–47; Moranvillé, "Les Projets," pp. 63–86; and J. Petit, *Charles de Valois, 1270–1325* (Paris, 1900), pp. 114 ff. Cf. Ostrogorsky, *Byzantine State*, pp. 440–441.

48. Raynaldus, ad ann. 1306, nos. 2–5; ad ann. 1307, nos. 6–7: letter of Clement V to archbishop Reginald of Ravenna; cf. Viller, "La Question de l'union," *Revue d'histoire ecclésiastique*, XVI, 270, note 2. See also Bouquet, "Byzance et les dernières offensives," p. 5.

49. Ostrogorsky, *Byzantine State*, p. 441: the governor of Thessalonica and the commander of Sardis.

50. See below, pp. 167–171.

of employment with the signing of peace in 1302 at Caltabellotta between the Sicilian Aragonese and the Neapolitan Angevins. They then made their way to the east, where they offered their services to Andronicus. Most of the provinces of Byzantine Asia Minor had already been overrun by the advancing Ottoman Turks; the Ottoman peril to the remnant of Asia Minor had brought Byzantine affairs to a grave crisis, once again necessitating reorientation of Byzantine policy toward the west. Hence Byzantium's interest in any new Latin plans for a crusade.

The Mongol invasion of the mid-thirteenth century had stirred up the entire Near East. As a result several nomadic Turkish tribes had been pushed into Asia Minor, where they came into collision with the Selchükid principalities of the area or, farther west, with the Byzantine territory in Anatolia. The old Byzantine system of border defense utilizing the so-called *akritai* (border-defenders) had fallen into decay, in large part because of Michael VIII's preoccupation with the western danger. Michael's removal, in 1261, of the Byzantine administrative center from Nicaea to Constantinople had itself served to reduce the Byzantine powers of resistance in Asia Minor.[51] After Michael's death in 1282 the meagerness of the funds in the imperial coffers brought about a further reduction of Byzantine military forces. Finally, the internal factor of the loosening ties between the central government and the provinces, or what has been termed the growing "feudalization" during the Palaeologian period, also hastened the decay of the Greek military freeholdings on the Anatolian frontier. These combined financial, social, and political considerations helped to undermine the Byzantine system of administration and defense in the east, the result being that by 1300 almost all Asia Minor had succumbed to the Turkish flood. Only a few Greek fortresses on the Aegean seacoast remained, along with the several Selchükid principalities.

At this critical juncture the leader of the Catalan Grand Company, Roger de Flor, offered his services to Byzantium against the Ottoman Turks in Bithynia. With the acceptance of the proposal by emperor Andronicus in 1303, the Catalans proceeded to defeat the Turks in several campaigns in Asia Minor. But emboldened by their success and disgruntled by the irregularity of their pay, the arrogant Catalans began to pillage Byzantine territory around Constantinople. Rela-

51. G. Arnakes, *The First Ottomans* (in Greek; Athens, 1947). Pachymeres, *De Michaele . . .*, II, 28 (*CSHB*, I, 149) quotes the Byzantine writer Senacherim as seeing the supplanting of Nicaea by Constantinople as the chief cause of the weakening of the eastern frontiers.

tions between Greeks and Catalans grew increasingly tense until 1305, when suddenly Roger was assassinated in the palace of the imperial prince, Michael IX.[52] Open warfare now broke out, with the Catalans plundering a wide range of Byzantine territory and even sacking the monasteries of Mount Athos.[53]

It was in this period of acute distress for Byzantium that Charles of Valois reached an agreement against Andronicus with representatives of the Catalan Grand Company. In 1308 Charles's plenipotentiary, Theobald of Cépoy,[54] arrived in Euboea with Venetian vessels, whence he proceeded to Cassandrea, in Macedonia, in order to receive an oath of fealty from the Catalan Grand Company.[55] But the Catalans, indifferent to Charles's plans, did not implement the alliance. Instead, after ravaging Thessaly, they unexpectedly moved on to the weakened Burgundian duchy of Athens. On March 15, 1311, in a notable battle at the Cephissus river, they annihilated the numerically superior forces of the Frankish nobles. Thenceforth Frankish power in Thebes and Athens was replaced by Catalan; the principality they established at Athens and Thebes was to endure for over seventy years.[56]

The withdrawal of the Catalans to Frankish Greece not only brought relief to Byzantium but left high and dry the aggressive plans of Charles of Valois.[57] Meanwhile, the legal claim of the Valois to the crown of Constantinople had, on the death early in 1308 of Charles's wife, Catherine of Courtenay, passed to her daughter Catherine of Valois. In 1313 the latter, though still a child, was married to Philip of Taranto, who thereupon formulated more intensive plans for the conquest of Constantinople.[58] Indeed, with the death of king Philip IV of France in 1314, and of his brother Charles of Valois in

52. Sources are Nicephorus Gregoras, VII, 3 (CSHB, I, 220 ff.) and Pachymeres, De Andronico . . . , V, 12 (CSHB, II, 393 ff.) for the Byzantine viewpoint. The Catalan Raymond Muntaner participated in the expedition (Crònica, ed. K. F. W. Lanz, Stuttgart, 1844; new ed. by "E. B.," Barcelona, 1927–1951, 9 vols. in 2; trans. J. A. C. Buchon in Chroniques étrangères relatives aux expéditions françaises pendant le XIIIᵉ siècle, Paris, 1875). There is a large literature on this; see Ostrogorsky, Byzantine State, p. 439.

53. Vasiliev, Byzantine Empire, p. 606. No wonder the Byzantines feared the crusades: a few thousand trained Catalan troops could keep their formerly great empire in a state of anxiety and ruin. See below, pp. 167–169.

54. J. Petit, "Un Capitaine du règne de Philippe le Bel, Thibaut de Chépoy," Le Moyen âge, ser. 2, I (1897), 231–236, and his Charles de Valois, pp. 114 ff.

55. Ostrogorsky, Byzantine State, p. 441.

56. K. M. Setton, Catalan Domination of Athens (Cambridge, Mass., 1948); A. Rubió i Lluch, Diplomatari de l'Orient català (Barcelona, 1947). See below, chapters VI and VII.

57. Moranvillé, "Les Projets," pp. 63 ff.

58. L. de Mas-Latrie, Commerce et expéditions militaires de la France (Collection de documents inédits, Paris, 1880), pp. 62–78. For letters on the projected expedition to Constantinople, see Viller, "La Question de l'union," RHE, XVI, 270.

1325, Philip of Taranto remained as the only prince interested in a crusade to recover the Latin throne of Constantinople. In 1318 Philip allied himself with the Angevin king of Hungary, Charles Robert, and, in 1320, bought certain rights in the principality of Achaea. He even secured papal support to call upon Frederick II, king of Sicily and a papal vassal, for help against Byzantium.

But Philip of Taranto's projects, though supported by the power of France and Naples, did not advance beyond the preparatory stage. The political and internal conditions of the west were simply not right for such an expedition. Thus the schemes of both Charles of Valois and Philip—pale imitations, one might say, of those of their more able predecessor Charles I of Anjou—eventually disappeared like smoke. Even avaricious but realistic Venice had in 1310 signed a ten-year non-aggression pact with Andronicus II.[59] Never again, in fact, was Venice to attempt to revive the now hopeless schemes of the Fourth Crusade. And in 1324 Venice, her traditional interest in the restoration of the Latin empire shelved, went so far as to inform Andronicus that the western princes had no intention of attacking the imperial city.[60]

As for the papacy, its attempt to return to the policy of Innocent III had become anachronistic and could not be implemented in this century of "décroisades." Indeed, the only westerners who now seemed eager to go to the east were merchants and mercenaries. This marked the end of any really serious attempt at western restoration of the Latin empire, though an occasional pretender to the Latin throne of Constantinople was not lacking even as late as 1494, when the French king Charles VIII would launch his fateful invasion of Italy, with Constantinople his probable ultimate objective.[61]

Despite the end of the ambitious designs of Charles of Valois and Philip of Taranto, sporadic but abortive attempts to use force against Byzantium continued to be made from time to time. Thus, in 1323 Andronicus learned that a French fleet in the service of pope John XXII and under the command of Amalric of Narbonne was on the point of setting sail for Constantinople.[62] Alarmed by what he

59. On all this, see Ostrogorsky, *Byzantine State,* p. 442.

60. See Bouquet, "Byzance et les derniers offensives." But note, however, the Venetian Marino Sanudo Torsello's plans for coöperation between Byzantium and Venice for a crusade to recover Jerusalem, in his *Secreta fidelium crucis,* ed. Bongars, II, 281; cf. especially Sanudo's letters (dated 1324 and 1326) to Andronicus II on church union and the crusade (II, 299, 301).

61. See M. Gilmore, *World of Humanism* (New York, 1952), p. 151.

62. L. Bréhier, in *Cambridge Medieval History* (1927 ed.), IV, 614, and C. Diehl *et al., L'Europe orientale de 1081 à 1453* (Paris, 1945), p. 223.

pope as his envoy the Genoese bishop of Kaffa in the Crimea, in order to assuage John's hostility by reopening the *pourparlers* for religious union.[63] In view of the calamities and dangers to his empire, it is not surprising that Andronicus felt he could not maintain to the end his uncompromising attitude toward the Latins of the earlier part of his reign. The pope's immediate reaction to Andronicus's *démarche* is not known, but several years later Andronicus made still another proposal. For, in 1326 (or 1327?), despite the categorical statement of Venice as to the cessation of western aggressive designs on Byzantium, king Charles IV the Fair of France had himself taken the cross. And it was this event, leading Andronicus to believe that French forces would soon be directed at Constantinople, which evoked the Greek emperor's new initiative. As his envoy the Greek emperor in 1327 sent to Paris a noble Genoese, Simon Doria,[64] who in diplomatic terms affirmed "the emperor's desire to live in peace with all Christians" and especially with the French ruler—in other words proposing a treaty of non-aggression together with a plan to seek union of the churches. At Paris and Avignon this was exaggeratedly interpreted as a promise of ecclesiastical union.[65]

In the same year, acting in accord with pope John XXII, the French monarch, Charles IV, sent to Constantinople as his envoy a Dominican professor of the Sorbonne, Benedict Asinago of Como, with full powers to conclude a union of the churches.[66] When Benedict arrived in Constantinople, however, he found the capital torn by dissension, a virtual civil war having broken out between the old emperor Andronicus II and his young grandson Andronicus (III). Neither of the two antagonists wished to risk his position with the people by entering into negotiations with the papal envoy regarding union. Benedict's mission was therefore over before it had even begun and he returned empty-handed to France. A western monk, Philip Incontri, then living in Pera, across from Constantinople, explains in the following manner the reason for the reluctance of Andronicus II to deal with Benedict:[67] "The emperor, fearing that

63. Simon Doria (see below) may be the "bishop of Kaffa" sent by Andronicus, rather than Jerome, listed by C. Eubel, *Hierarchia catholica medii aevi . . .*, I (2nd ed., Münster, 1913; repr. 1960), 154, as elevated in 1322 and dead by 1324.

64. Bouquet, "Byzance et les dernières offensives," p. 6. The bishop of Leon, García of Ayerbe, expressing his opinion on the crusades to Charles IV of France, said that the crusaders should go by land and envisage a Tatar alliance; they should first conquer the Greeks and then turn on the Moslems (Delaville Le Roulx, *La France en Orient*, p. 83).

65. Bouquet, *op. cit.,* p. 6, and cf. Diehl, *L'Europe orientale*, p. 223.

66. Bouquet, *loc. cit.*

67. See Thomas Kaeppeli, "Deux nouveaux ouvrages de Frère Philippe Incontri de Péra," in *Archivium Fratrum Praedicatorum,* XXIII (1953), 172–173.

the Greeks of Constantinople would rise against him and deliver the empire to his grandson, Andronicus III, pretended . . . that his envoy [to the west] had imperfectly understood and had not in fact reported his exact words."[68] The implication in this statement seems to be that Andronicus II had previously made some kind of secret commitment regarding religious union to the pope and the French king, from which he was now seeking to back away.

As the report of Benedict states, Andronicus protested that the present time was inappropriate for realization of the union "because of the suspicions that our people generally have [for the Latins]" ("propter suspicionem quam haberet generaliter populus noster.").[69] To justify his conduct, Andronicus wrote to the French king explaining the state of affairs in Byzantium and enclosing a letter of apology.[70] The result was that pope John, after hearing the report of his emissary Benedict of Como, abandoned his plans for religious union.[71] The French king himself died the following year (1328). Fate had again intervened to relieve Byzantium of another enemy seeking to conquer the empire under the guise of a crusade. This episode, though inconclusive, is significant because it shows that once more the west had given in to the illusion that the "conversion" of the Greek emperor would *ipso facto* guarantee that of his subjects.

The difficulties experienced by the pope in raising an army in the west—despite the several claims to the Latin throne of Constantinople—were due in great part to the internal political situation of the west. France and England were preoccupied with the quarrel which would culminate in the Hundred Years' War. Emperor Louis IV the Bavarian had withdrawn Germany from papal influence, while the papacy itself, in exile at Avignon, was unable to control even Italy. Venice and Genoa, the only two powers that could in any way be counted on, were more interested in assuring their profits than in undertaking a hazardous expedition of conquest.[72] Moreover, the competition between Venetians and Genoese in the east was often encouraged by the Byzantine emperor himself when it served his purposes. Merchants of the two cities even trafficked with the Turks

68. Also H. Omont, "Projet de réunion des églises grecque et latine sous Charles le Bel en 1327," *Bibliothèque de l'École des chartes,* LIII (1892), 254–257.

69. *Ibid.,* p. 255.

70. Andronicus wrote two letters: Omont, "Lettres d'Andronique II au pape," *ibid.,* LXVII (1906), 587.

71. A curious passage in Cantacuzenus, II, 4 (*CSHB,* I, 335, line 16) relates that in 1328 the Germans sent an envoy to emperor Andronicus II asking monetary aid on the basis of an old alliance.

72. W. Heyd, *Histoire du commerce du Levant au moyen-âge* (trans. Furcy Raynaud, 2 vols., Leipzig, 1885, repr. 1923, 1936, Amsterdam, 1967), *passim.*

in defiance of papal fulminations against the practice, and western knights, for the sake of adventure, not infrequently became mercenaries of the Turkish sultans. Finally, though the Venetians and Genoese were repeatedly able to put into battle against each other thirty to forty galleys, when called upon to fight the Turks they could contribute only three or four vessels for the service of Christendom. The "ecumenical" spirit of the earlier Middle Ages—a crusade presumably for the benefit of the west as a whole—seems to have almost completely evaporated.

In Byzantium, meanwhile, Andronicus II had been deposed by his grandson, who in 1328 assumed the imperial throne as Andronicus III. Once in power the latter reached a decision to continue the policy of friendliness to the Latins characteristic of the latter part of his grandfather's reign, and especially to reëstablish friendly relations with the papacy—relations which had not really been cordial since 1281, the failure of the union of Lyons. Andronicus's policy was dictated by his preoccupation with the Turks, whose progress in Asia Minor during the reigns of Michael VIII and especially Andronicus II had become increasingly disastrous for Byzantium. Another factor affecting Andronicus's decision may well have been the influence of his second wife, Anna of Savoy, who as a Latin princess had formed a pro-unionist party in Constantinople.

In the same year (1327) that the shadow of Charles IV of France was cast over Constantinople, efforts had been initiated in the west to form a league against the Turks which would bring together those Latin powers with vital interests in the Levant.[73] The Turks, in order to attack the coastal Byzantine cities of Asia Minor more successfully, had taken to piracy and were now harassing both the Greek and the Latin possessions in the Aegean and Mediterranean seas. To protect the Latin crusader states in the east in the face of this danger, the pope and especially Venice sought to form a union to fight off the Turks. This proposal for an anti-Turkish front was implemented in Rhodes on September 6, 1332,[74] an agreement being signed by a representative of the Hospitallers of Rhodes and by Peter da Canale, the plenipotentiary of Venice, who found himself, in a complete reversal of Byzantine policy, also the representative of emperor Andronicus III.[75] The event is especially meaningful because it was the first time since before the Fourth Crusade that Byzantium had

73. Lemerle, *L'Émirat d'Aydin*, p. 54.
74. *Ibid.*, p. 92.
75. *Diplomatarium veneto-levantinum (1300–1454)*, ed. G. M. Thomas, I (Venice, 1880; repr. New York, 1965), no. 116, pp. 225–229.

become associated with any west European project for a great coalition, such as had long constituted its gravest danger. The realization had apparently finally dawned on at least a few Byzantines that the primary threat to Byzantium's existence lay not so much in the west but rather in the farther advance of the Turks.

The terms of the treaty were as follows: the Greek emperor—and this is extraordinary in view of the precarious state of Byzantine finances—was to furnish ten galleys for a period of five years; Venice was to provide six, the Hospitallers four. The fleet was to assemble at the port of Negroponte on April 15 of the following year (1333), and the commander was to be a Venetian.[76] But the coalition was not ready to take action until May of 1334, at which time the several signatories were joined by three more powers, king Hugh IV of Cyprus, king Philip VI of France, and the pope, John XXII, whose role had actually been decisive behind the scenes during earlier negotiations.[77] According to the anti-Latin Byzantine historian, Nicephorus Gregoras, the emperor felt compelled to join the coalition after receiving a menacing embassy from the western powers calling upon him to join his forces to theirs under penalty of being considered an enemy. The same author notes that Andronicus had to press his subjects hard to collect the gold required to equip a fleet of twenty ships.[78] Yet in the spring of 1335 when the fleet was in readiness the Latins, because of problems arising among themselves, defected.[79]

Nevertheless, some naval operations, resulting in occasional debarkations in Asia Minor, did take place, with the result that for some months a certain protection was afforded to the Christian population, both Greek and Latin, of the Aegean area, along with greater security of navigation.[80] One of the more important achievements of the enterprise was the destruction in the gulf of Adrammyttium of the Turkish fleet under Yahshi. The return of the allied fleets to their home ports, however, was not followed by the reconstitution of the expedition, since on December 4, 1334, pope John XXII died.[81] For some time events in the west, especially the

76. *Ibid.*

77. Lemerle, *loc. cit.;* cf. Delaville Le Roulx, *La France en Orient,* pp. 97 ff., which gives different figures for negotiations at Avignon. The famous *Directorium ad passagium faciendum* of William Adam (ascribed to "Brocardus"; see below) was written as a guidebook for the king of France on the expedition.

78. Nicephorus Gregoras, XI, 1 (*CSHB,* I, 524).

79. *Ibid.* (I, 523–525): "Thoryvous kai tarachas hoi Latinoi cholethentes apraktoi kai pseutheis peri tas eppaggelias ephanesan."

80. Lemerle, *L'Émirat d'Aydin,* p. 98.

81. Delaville Le Roulx, *La France en Orient,* p. 100.

hostility between France and England, prevented either power from joining a common naval front against the Turks. The final result was the dissolution of the coalition and the resumption of Turkish piratical activity in the Aegean.[82]

With respect to the crusade, it should be noted that in this period the idea of a crusading expedition against the Greeks was gradually giving way in the west to the idea of a common Greco-Latin enterprise against the Turks menacing the Christian eastern possessions, both Greek and Latin. As we shall see, this attitude would be the prelude to the concept of saving Constantinople and the Balkans from the Turks by means of a crusade. The reasons for this significant change are to be found, as we have seen, in the awareness of the many difficulties involved in reëstablishing the Latin empire of Constantinople, and, more especially, in the growing realization that perhaps more could be accomplished against the Turks through the collaboration of east and west on a plane of friendship and alliance. With respect to the last point, the influence of certain western theoreticians and promoters of a crusade was significant; in general they tended to discourage overt Latin aggression against the Greeks and to emphasize rather the importance of acquiring a knowledge of the east, its language, and its people. For this purpose missionaries were to be sent to the east.[83]

Nevertheless, some of the most important crusader theoreticians— like William Adam and especially Raymond Lull—though accepting the need for collaboration with the Greeks, insisted that the Greeks first must be converted to Catholicism, by force if necessary. William Adam even suggested a kind of "brain-washing" of the Greeks, by sending one child from each Greek family to the west to be raised in the Latin faith. Later, Peter Dubois recommended that noble, educated Latin girls go to the east to do charity work in hospitals, the most comely to marry leading Greeks (clerics in particular!) in order ultimately to convert the entire east to the Catholic faith.[84]

82. On these matters Atiya, *The Crusade in the Later Middle Ages,* has been corrected by Lemerle, *L'Émirat d'Aydin,* p. 100, note 1.

83. Especially Golubovich, *Biblioteca bio-bibliografica.*

84. On all these see Geanakoplos, *Byzantine East and Latin West* (Oxford, 1966), p. 2. It should be noted that scholars now agree that the *Directorium ad passagium faciendum* was not written by "Brocardus." According to Ch. Kohler, he never existed; see "Documents relatifs à Guillaume Adam archevêque de Sultaniyeh . . . ," *Revue de l'Orient latin,* X (1903–1904), 16–56, especially p. 17, and his "Quel est l'auteur du *Directorium ad passagium faciendum?" ibid.,* XII (1909), 104–111. But not all scholars agree that it should be attributed to William Adam; see F. Pall, in *Revue historique du sud-est européen,* XIX (1942), 27–29 (of offprint), and cf. below, p. 543, where it is attributed to "William Adam or (more probably) Raymond Étienne." It is referred to hereafter, however, as the work of

In 1333, Andronicus III had entrusted to two Dominicans returning from a mission to the Mongols a message for pope John XXII.[85]
Andronicus's letter was received favorably by the pope, who thereupon wrote to the principal dignitaries of the Greek empire, seeking
to open negotiations for union through his envoy, the Genoese
Pisani. The two Dominicans had returned to Constantinople with
instructions from the pope, directing them to hold public discussions
with the Greek clergy. But the mission of the papal ambassadors was
rendered ineffective because of the intervention of the scholar Nicephorus Gregoras, who in an eloquent and lengthy speech argued
against putting trust in the words of the Latin envoys. As Gregoras
himself put it in his history: "In 1334 there came to Byzantium two
bishops from the pope to discuss the peace and unity of the
churches. When the people of Constantinople saw them they became
excited. The patriarch and the bishops, ignorant of Latin, called
upon Gregoras [who knew Latin] to talk with them. I, however, not
considering their proposal worthy of attention, decided not to waste
my time. However, to satisfy the patriarch and bishops, I got them
together and gave a long speech explaining why they should pay no
heed to them. . . ."[86] As the result of Gregoras's intervention, the
negotiations came to nothing.

In 1335, in order to demonstrate his good will and at the same
time not lose the possibility of future western help, Andronicus III
consented to participate in a new crusade to recover the Holy Land,
being organized under the leadership of the new pope Benedict XII
and Philip VI, king of France. Philip's intentions regarding a crusade
were probably more sincere than had been those of his uncle Philip
IV the Fair.[87] For where Philip IV had used the crusade as a façade
to gain other ends for the crown—church tithes, destruction of the
Templars, and, probably, the conquest of Byzantium through his
brother Charles of Valois—Philip VI seems to have desired a *passagium* (a full-scale crusade) to the Holy Land at least in part for
religious reasons.[88] Pope John XXII, impressed by Philip's apparent
zeal, had promulgated two bulls which gave the king the right to levy
the tithe on church property for a period of two years. In 1333 the
privilege was renewed for six years. Thus for this crusade all the

---

William Adam. On Lull, see S. Cirac Estopañán, "Ramon Lull y la union con los Bizantinos:
Bizancio y España," *Cuadernos de historia Jerónimo Zurita,* III (Saragossa, 1954).

85. On earlier messages from this pope to the Mongols, see below, p. 543.

86. Nicephorus Gregoras, X, 8 (*CSHB,* I, 501 ff.).

87. S. Runciman, *A History of the Crusades,* III (Cambridge, 1954), 1440.

88. Delaville Le Roulx, *La France en Orient,* p. 86.

resources of the church—revenues from tithes, church benefices, and indulgences—were put at the service of the French king.

Already in 1331 Philip had written to Venice to ascertain the conditions under which the Venetians would be willing to participate. But Venice took six months to answer. In fact it was less the Holy Land that interested Venice than her commerce in the Aegean, which was now endangered by the raids of the Turks in the area. In order to have a plan for the crusade Philip had asked for the drawing up of memoranda setting forth a definite program.[89] Among the propaganda writings produced was a detailed, carefully worked out scheme submitted by William Adam (erroneously ascribed to one Brocardus), who had lived in Lesser Armenia (Cilicia), and whose primary aim was the achievement of a religious union of the Armenians with Rome. William Adam's scheme was grandiose and interests us here primarily for what he had to say about Byzantium and the crusade. In his eyes an essential preliminary for the success of any western crusade to the Holy Land was the conquest and conversion of Byzantium.[90]

In 1339 Andronicus, growing more and more fearful of the Turkish advance, which by 1338 had reached the Bosporus across from Constantinople, sent a secret mission to pope Benedict XII. The embassy's aim was to secure western aid for a joint crusade against the Turks. It was the turn of the Greeks to take the initiative for a joint Greco-Latin expedition. Andronicus's envoys were the Venetian Stephen Dandolo and one of the most famous of Byzantine humanists, Barlaam, the Calabrian monk and *hegoumenos* of the monastery of the Savior in Constantinople. Arriving in Avignon the envoys eloquently pleaded the cause of Byzantium before the pope.[91]

In his plea Barlaam, the chief envoy, proposed two main points: the convocation of a general council at which the question of religious union would be discussed, and the organization of a crusade not only to recapture the Holy Land but to deliver the Christian towns of Asia Minor from the Turks. Andronicus's tactics are clear: he sought from the beginning to allay the deep anti-Latin fear of the Byzantine populace through the convocation of an ecumenical council—a council in which all the patriarchs would appear and open discussion would be held. Moreover, through the organization of a

89. *Ibid.,* pp. 86–87, and Lemerle, *L'Émirat d'Aydin,* pp. 90–91; Bouquet, "Byzance et les dernières offensives," p. 8.

90. *Directorium ad passagium faciendum,* in *RHC, Arm.,* II, 367 ff. Cf. Marino Sanudo's plan for Byzantine-Venetian coöperation for a crusade to Jerusalem, in his *Secreta fidelium crucis* (see above, note 60).

91. Gay, *Clément VI,* pp. 49–50.

crusade he envisaged, following the precedent of Alexius I and the plans of Michael VIII, the recovery of Byzantine provinces of Asia Minor from the Turks. Most important in his proposals was his insistence on discussions to be entered into before the consummation of union, a point directly contrary to papal policy, which insisted on the conclusion of union first and then discussion. These points, which were made in two speeches to the pope and the assembled cardinals of the curia, deserve at least to be summarized because Barlaam here states more clearly than anyone else the difficulties lurking in the minds of the Byzantines with respect to religious union. As he put it to the pope:[92] "The emperor does not dare to manifest publicly that he desires union with you. If he did declare this, a great number of princes and men of the people, in the fear that he would renew the experience of Michael Palaeologus, would seek an occasion to put him to death."

As Barlaam realized only too well, the problem for the emperor was, in accordance with papal demands, to find the means to promise union and to begin its execution without at the same time irritating his subjects. For they did not want to hear even the suggestion of a Latin rapprochement.[93] Thus on behalf of the emperor, Barlaam proposed a formula that might without violence lead the Greeks to union and at the same time show the pope their sincerity. It was the suggestion of a general council to be held in the east. As he said,

You have two means peacefully to realize the union. You can either convince the scholars, who in their turn will convince the people, or persuade both people and learned men at the same time. To convince the learned men is easy, since both they and you seek only the truth. But when the scholars return home they will be able to do absolutely nothing with the people. Some men will arise who, either from jealousy or from vainglory, and perhaps believing they act rightly, will teach all exactly the opposite of what you will have defined. They will say to the Greeks, "Do not let yourselves be seduced by these men who have sold themselves for gold and are swelled up with pride; let them say what they wish, do not change anything of your faith." And they will listen to them. . . . To persuade therefore both the people and the learned men together there is only one way: a general council to be held in the east. For the Greeks admit that all that has been determined in a general council conforms to the faith. You will object, saying that already at Lyons a council to treat of union was held. But no one of the Greeks will accept that the Council of Lyons was ecumenical unless another council declares it so. The Greeks present at Lyons had been delegated neither by the four patriarchs who govern the eastern church nor by the people, but by the emperor alone, who, without seeking to gain their consent, wanted to

92. *PG,* CLI, cols. 1341 ff.; cf. Viller, "La Question de l'union," *RHE,* XVIII, 21–24.

93. Pears, *Destruction of the Greek Empire,* pp. 69–70, says that on his arrival at Avignon Barlaam pointed out that the Turks had seized four metropolitan sees and suggested that, as a condition for religious union, the Turks be expelled from Asia Minor.

achieve union by force. Therefore send legates to the four patriarchs; under their presidency a general council will be held which will make union. And all of us who will have been present at this council will say to the people, "Here is what the Holy General Council has decreed. It is your duty to observe its decisions." And all will submit.[94]

At this point Barlaam added a crucial stipulation—that no such council could take place until the Latins first aided the Greeks to evict the Turk from the towns of Asia Minor. But the provision was flatly rejected by Benedict XII and his cardinals, who insisted that it was not proper to put in question an article of the faith which had already been defined.[95] Curiously enough, Gregoras was later to turn the same phrase against the Latins. Barlaam had not been given full authority to negotiate for the emperor, and in effect spoke in his own name. Andronicus III, in fact, afraid of public reaction in Constantinople to such a report, had dispatched him secretly to Avignon. Benedict and the curia argued every point raised by Barlaam, upholding the papal principle of conversion first, then military assistance. Despite the intense interest generated, the interview in the end produced only vague promises, and no concrete results came about.

Nevertheless, though his proposals were not accepted, Barlaam's speech remains of the utmost significance for understanding Byzantine psychology with respect to union. Having lived for long periods in both east and west, and being possessed of an equally good knowledge of both Latin and Greek, he was supremely qualified to assess the fears and hopes of each side. His program reflected accurately not only the political realities of the situation, but more important, the Greek attitude and complaints against the Latins, which sometimes they themselves perhaps did not fully understand, emotional as they had become in their psychology of a dominated people. As he put it so well: "The Greeks feel they have been wronged and it is up to you to offer a concession to them first." But Barlaam's words fell on deaf ears. He was too far ahead of his time—ahead of the Greeks because he realized that in order to save their empire, they had to overcome their deep prejudices and unite with the Latins to repulse the common enemy, the Turk. He was ahead of the Latins as well, since the west would not really begin to interest itself in the fate of the east until the Turks had approached so close as to begin to threaten the western European territories.

94. *PG,* CLI, cols. 1332 ff.; Viller, "La Question de l'union," *RHE,* XVIII, 22–23; also C. Giannelli, "Un Projetto di Barlaam per l'unione delle chiese," *Misc. Giovanni Mercati,* III (Studi e testi, 123; Vatican City, 1946), 171 and note 22.

95. Viller, *op. cit., RHE,* XVIII, 23, quoting Nicephorus Gregoras, X, 8 (*CSHB,* I, 501); *PG,* CXLVIII, col. 717.

In the end the discussions failed, and Barlaam and his companion returned empty-handed to Byzantium. In his *pourparlers* Barlaam had emphasized that the Greeks, if they learned of the papal refusal to attend a general council, would accuse the Latins of being afraid of the truth.[96] And exactly as he had foreseen, the Greeks, especially Gregoras, turned against the pope his refusal to meet at a common council. Indeed, only a few decades later the influential Nilus Cabasilas, Greek metropolitan of Thessalonica, in his works *On the Causes of the Division of the Church* and *On the Primacy of the Pope,* would insist that one of the two basic causes for the schism was this very refusal of the pope to submit controversial doctrine to the judgment of a general council.[97]

For several years following Andronicus's death in 1341 Byzantium was again the scene of civil war, this time between the usurper John Cantacuzenus and the widow of Andronicus III, the Latin empress Anna of Savoy, who sought to protect the rights of her minor son John V. If we can believe the testimony of Anna's bitter enemy, the emperor-historian Cantacuzenus, Anna during this civil strife (on October 21, 1343) dispatched to pope Clement VI an ambassador, the Latin Philip of St. Germain, bearing letters from her and from her minister the grand duke Alexius Apocaucus.[98] Expressing her devotion and that of her son to the Roman church, she asked the pope's mercy (*elaion*) for the "heresies" of the Greeks and pleaded for the dispatch of a fleet and army to defend Constantinople from the usurper John Cantacuzenus. The latter adds in his history that she affirmed to the pope that after the defeat of Cantacuzenus negotiations for religious union could openly (*phaneros*) be entered into. Clement responded favorably to her advances without however promising support other than in general terms.[99] Whether Anna at this time envisaged the launching of a full-scale "crusade" on her own behalf is doubtful; rather, in the Byzantine tradition, she too seems to have intended the dispatch of mercenary troops.[100]

96. Viller, *op. cit., RHE,* XVIII, 24.
97. PG, CXLIX, cols. 684 ff. Cf. L. Petit, "Les Évêques de Thessalonique," *Échos d'Orient,* V (1901), 94.
98. Not all scholars agree that she sent letters to the pope; Iorga, "Latins et grecs d'Orient et l'établissement des Turcs en Europe (1342–1362)," *Byzantinische Zeitschrift,* XV (1906), 183, accepts that she did.
99. Cantacuzenus, III, 87 (*CSHB,* II, 539–540); see Lemerle, *L'Émirat d'Aydin,* p. 183, for careful analysis.
100. There is a question here of "false" letters written by Anna's minister Apocaucus against the regent Cantacuzenus and borne secretly to Clement VI by a certain *praipositos* (Lemerle, *L'Émirat d'Aydin,* p. 183, note 1).

Whether or not we accept Cantacuzenus's statement that Anna had no scruples whatever in making promises to the pope, her sending an envoy to the pope seems only logical, given her hard-pressed situation. From Clement's correspondence with Anna, we may sense the illusions that were entertained at Avignon regarding the Greeks. Even before Anna's approach to the pope she had sent still another ambassador to Venice, seeking military aid against the Turks. Responding to her letter on May 12, 1343, the senate declared that Venice would do its best to aid her and that in fact a new anti-Turkish league composed of Cyprus, the Hospitallers, and king Robert of Naples was then in process of formation under the auspices of the pope. Anna's envoy also asked that Venice intervene with Stephen Dushan, ruler of the Serbs, to enlist his aid against Cantacuzenus. Again Venice reacted favorably, the senate designating a Venetian, Marino Venier, to accomplish the mission. [101]

Meanwhile Clement VI, reacting to Anna's proposals for religious union in exchange for aid against Cantacuzenus, sent out a series of individual letters, all looking toward the end of the schism. One was dispatched to Anna's crafty minister, Apocaucus, another to all the Greek bishops, still others to the monks of Mount Athos, to the commune of Pera, to the Venetian bailie in Constantinople, and finally to the Franciscan and Dominican convents in Pera. All were invited to aid the apostolic delegate in the task set before him. [102] On October 27, 1343, Clement wrote again to Apocaucus, announcing to him that he was looking forward to the end of schism and that the Catholic confessor who was to be chosen by Apocaucus himself would have the power in the name of the pope to remit all of his (Apocaucus's) sins [103] —as if this "concession" mentioned by the pope would have been a spur to Apocaucus, who was, if anything, even wilier than other Byzantines of the period! A few days later, on November 15, 1343, the pope also wrote to Demetrius Palaeologus, a relative of the emperor, encouraging his zeal in favor of the Roman faith. In this case, however, the pope prudently charged the Genoese podestà, the Dominican abbot, and the commune of Pera to work on

---

101. *Ibid.*, pp. 182–183. On August 8, 1343, Clement VI announced to Venice the formation of a new league—to include the Hospitallers, Cyprus, and himself—and requested Venice to contribute five or six galleys (a total of twenty ships were to meet at Negroponte but Euboea, Melos, and Paros were to furnish their own contingents). The Byzantine emperor rallied to this later; the league was to last three years. Meanwhile Genoa, Pisa, and Aragon loaned vessels to the pope (see Iorga, *Philippe de Mézières*, p. 40).

102. Lemerle, *L'Émirat d'Aydin*, p. 183.

103. E. Déprez, ed., *Clément VI (1342–1352): Lettres closes, patentes et curiales se rapportant à la France . . .* , fasc. 1 (Paris, 1901), no. 493, and cf. nos. 467, 491.

Demetrius in order to keep him well disposed to the question of union. [104]

Evidence indicates that Clement was sincere in his desire for union with the eastern church. Thus in the letters he wrote to the titular Latin patriarch of Constantinople, Henry of Asti, then in residence at Negroponte, to the Dominicans of Pera, and even to the Venetian and Genoese colonies of Constantinople, the pope urged them to exert every effort to prepare for the union. [105] His unionist enthusiasm notwithstanding, Clement nevertheless demonstrated precisely the same point of view as his papal predecessors in his insistence that the sending of military aid to Constantinople must be contingent on the eastern church's prior abjuration of the schism.

In the same year (1343), and probably even before receiving the appeal contained in Anna's letter, Clement authorized the preaching throughout western Europe of a crusade against the Turks. [106] For this purpose he made plans for the reorganization of the old naval league which had been formed in 1334 at the instance of pope John XXII. This was the first step in the initiation of the famous crusade against the important Turkish-held port of Smyrna in Asia Minor. For such an enterprise it would have been logical for Clement to seek adhesion to the coalition by Byzantium, that is, by its regent Anna of Savoy. [107] It is clear, however, that Byzantium took no active part in the expedition that was soon launched. Actually the aim of the campaign was twofold: to crush the growing menace of the Selchükid principality of Aydin, of which Smyrna was the chief port, and to suppress the resurgent Turkish piracy in the Aegean, for which Smyrna was the primary base. At the head of the papal galleys Clement placed the Genoese lord Martin Zaccaria. From the Byzantine view this was an affront, since he hated the Byzantines, who had expelled him in 1329 from his possession of Chios. [108] As supreme commander of the entire expeditionary force, however, the pope appointed the patriarch Henry of Asti, [109] who had strict orders not to permit the deflection of the expedition to any other objective.

104. *Ibid.*, nos. 522–523; cf. Lemerle, *L'Émirat d'Aydin*, p. 183, note 2.

105. See Lemerle, *loc. cit.*, and Cantacuzenus, *loc. cit.*

106. A papal bull authorizing contributions for a crusade was launched on September 30, 1343 (Iorga, "Latins et grecs," p. 189; *Philippe de Mézières*, pp. 40 ff.).

107. In 1343, during negotiations with Anna, the Dominican Philip Incontri of Pera (Kaepelli, "Deux nouveaux ouvrages," pp. 172–173) wrote the pope that the crusading forces being prepared for Smyrna should make a demonstration before Constantinople and that the recalcitrant people would then obey Anna.

108. Iorga considers his appointment a mistake ("Latins et grecs," pp. 190–191).

109. Lemerle, *L'Émirat d'Aydin*, p. 187. Iorga ("Latins et grecs," pp. 192 ff.) errs in

John Cantacuzenus was the ally of the Selchükid emir of Aydin, Umur Pasha, and it was therefore to the interest of Anna and her court at Constantinople to spur Clement in every way possible to a crusade against Smyrna. [110] We shall not enter here into the complexities of the campaign against Smyrna. In a preliminary naval battle the Turks are supposed to have lost as many as fifty ships. [111] Martin Zaccaria, the papal naval commander, who hated Cantacuzenus, would have liked to use the papal galleys in the reoccupation of Chios, which he contended could be used to advantage as a base against Smyrna. The pope, however, refused his suggestion, not only because it was contrary to the original plans but more especially on the grounds that it would compromise the hope for reunion of the Greeks with Rome and might even push the Greeks into an alliance with the Turks.

The crusading expedition to Smyrna had been long and secretly prepared, and the Turks of Umur were taken by surprise. Cantacuzenus had gotten wind of the expedition, but the letter he wrote from Demotica to his ally Umur apprising him of the western advance came too late. [112] His letter reveals that in the Greek east, in any case, the preparations of the west for the crusade were known. The expedition remained purely Latin, however, there being no record that Byzantine ships—those of Anna—participated. [113] Cantacuzenus of course was considered an enemy by the Latins. After some fighting, the western fleet finally took the port area of Smyrna, and the town itself, but the Turks continued for many years to hold a fort situated high on a nearby hill, commanding the city. [114] Thus the crusade was not yet over, for the crusaders in the city, who were under pressure from the Turks in the fort, had to be relieved, and an

preferring Peter Thomas, on whom see the biography by Philip of Mézières edited by Smet, and the studies by Iorga and Boehlke cited in the bibliographical note.

110. On Byzantium and the league of 1343, see Iorga, *Philippe de Mézières*, p. 40, notes 6, 7; Raynaldus, *Annales ecclesiastici*, ad ann. 1344, no. 2; and Heyd, *Histoire du commerce*, I, 383. For works on the crusade to Smyrna, see Gay, *Clément VI;* Iorga, "Latins et grecs," pp. 179–222; Chevalier, *La Croisade du dauphin Humbert II;* Iorga, *Philippe de Mézières*, pp. 33–62; Delaville Le Roulx, *La France en Orient*, pp. 103–110; C. Faure, "Le Dauphin Humbert II à Venise et en Orient (1345–1347)," *Mélanges d'archéologie et d'histoire*, XXVII (1907), 509–562; Lemerle, *L'Émirat d'Aydin*, pp. 187 ff. Also see B. T. Goryanov, "An Anonymous Unpublished Byzantine Chronicle of the Fourteenth Century" [in Russian], *Vizantiiskii Vremennik*, II (1949), 276–293.

111. Atiya, *Crusade in the Later Middle Ages*, p. 293. On these events cf. Nicephorus Gregoras, XIII, 13 (*CSHB*, II, 689), and Cantacuzenus, III, 68 (*CSHB*, II, 420–423).

112. Lemerle, *L'Émirat d'Aydin*, p. 186.

113. Although the absence of affirmative evidence cannot be considered conclusive proof of Byzantine non-participation, other considerations make such participation improbable.

114. Atiya, *op. cit.*, pp. 294–298.

adequate permanent garrison installed. Moreover, the pope had additional plans in mind; he intended, it seems, to strengthen the league by securing more troops. At the same time he sought to assist the Genoese in defending their colony of Kaffa in the Crimea, which was being invested by the Tatars.

At this critical juncture for the Latin states in the east, there came onto the scene a man who was to remain at the center of events for some years, the western noble Humbert II, dauphin of Viennois. He was imbued with the old crusading spirit and fervor but was incompetent as a military commander, a fact which was to result in the ultimate failure of the crusade. Humbert had taken the cross at Avignon and had been named by the pope captain-general of the apostolic see and chief of the army of the Christians against the Turks. [115] Recent scholarship has shown that a supposed victory on his part over the Turks at the Greek island of Lesbos in full winter at the start of February 1346 is mere legend. [116] At any rate, in June of 1346 he finally arrived before Smyrna. Regarding the events which followed, western accounts differ remarkably and Byzantine sources offer little help. [117] We shall concentrate here only on those events which involved or had a direct influence on the Byzantines. After leaving Smyrna, having accomplished nothing, and while spending the winter of 1346–1347 at Rhodes, Humbert wrote to Clement at Avignon. In his response the pope made the very firm point that, despite Humbert's request for papal permission to intervene on behalf of Anna against Cantacuzenus, he did not feel it to be proper, certainly not until the treaty with the Turks had been concluded. [118] Clement's remark reveals his sensitivity to the delicate power balance in the east, especially his desire to keep on good terms with both sides so as not to destroy any prospect for union.

The commander of the Venetian fleet in the crusade of Humbert, Nicholas Pisani, had in the meantime gone with a companion to the court of Constantinople in an attempt to persuade the empress Anna

115. Lemerle, *L'Émirat d'Aydin,* p. 194, note 3, remarks that on these events Atiya (*op. cit.,* pp. 303–318) is insufficiently critical. Humbert sought command of this crusade, offering troops and 1,000 arbalesters (Iorga, *Philippe de Mézières,* p. 45, note 3).

116. Lemerle, *L'Émirat d'Aydin,* pp. 195–196, on the basis of *Storie pistoresi,* ed. S. A. Barbi, in Muratori, *RISS,* XI, pt. 5 (Bologna, 1627; rev. ed. 1907–1927); cf. C. Faure, "Le Dauphin Humbert II," p. 529.

117. Lemerle uses here a new Turkish source on Umur, the Düstūrnāme of Enveri, published as *Le Destān d'Umūr Pacha,* ed. and trans. I. Mélikoff-Sayar (Bibliothèque byzantine, documents, no. 2; Paris, 1954).

118. Lemerle, *L'Émirat d'Aydin,* pp. 199–201, note 1: the pope instructed Humbert to lie off Constantinople and not to interfere in the civil war between Cantacuzenus and Anna.

to cede, temporarily, to the crusader forces the adjacent island of Chios as a base of operations against the Turks. [119] Evidently the tension between the Greeks of Anna's party and the Latins had slackened somewhat and the possibility of an anti-Turkish entente between east and west had grown stronger. Clement's letter to Anna, [120] dated June 15, 1346, seems in any case to give this impression. Any such possibility was, however, quashed by the Genoese, who coveted Chios in the interests of their own trade. And so the Genoese in the same year dispatched a fleet to Chios and seized it from the Greeks for themselves. The Greeks, as well as the Venetians and the other western powers involved in Humbert's expedition, were angered. [121]

It is noteworthy that while Humbert was in the east he made attempts to treat with the Greeks personally on the problem of ecclesiastical union. The talks appear to have been of little consequence, however. And soon afterward, irritated by the constant bickering of his Latin allies, Humbert sought and received permission from the pope to retire from the crusading expedition. [122] This ended any actual or potential connection of Byzantium with the ill-fated crusade. Nevertheless, Humbert's interest in the Greek east seems to have been long-lasting, for on his return to France in the summer of 1347 (he entered a Dominican convent) he set up scholarships at the University of Paris, many of which he reserved for young men belonging by birth to Greece and the Holy Land. These men were to teach Greek in the Dominican convents of France and do missionary work in the east. [123] Despite his keen interest in the Levant, however, Humbert was out of step with his age. A genuine idealist, he would have been more at home in the crusades of the late eleventh and early twelfth centuries. His inability to act independently and the lack of scruple exhibited by the Italian cities of Venice and Genoa brought his crusading efforts to nothing. Nevertheless, he is one of the first examples of a western layman who, as a result of personal contact with the east, encouraged the study of Greek in a Latin university and who took a special interest in missionary activity. With respect to the problem of the crusade, though, the whole expedition of Humbert was futile; its primary

119. Atiya, *op. cit.,* p. 311.
120. Letter of Clement commending the crusaders to Anna: see Gay, *Clément VI,* pp. 70–71, and Atiya, *op. cit.,* pp. 311–312.
121. Nicephorus Gregoras, XV, 6 (*CSHB,* II, 765–767; *PG,* CXLVIII, col. 1005); Cantacuzenus, III, 95 (*CSHB,* II, 582–583; *PG,* CLIII, col. 1269).
122. Iorga, "Latins et grecs," pp. 202–204.
123. Atiya, *op. cit.,* p. 317.

importance lay in its indication that the pope and the western church were finally ready to regard an expedition to Asia Minor as a genuine crusade. The attention of the west had thus definitely shifted from the Mamluk Turks of Egypt and Syria to the Ottomans and other Turks of Asia Minor. For the Byzantines the expedition was important because as a result of it they had lost Chios and Phocaea to the Genoese. Nevertheless, since the Greeks were the principal victims of the Turks in that area, prospects were now brighter for the formation of a joint Byzantine-Latin front against the Turks. From such a coalition the Byzantines would naturally derive the chief profit.

After a prolonged civil war John Cantacuzenus was finally able to crush the party of Anna and on February 3, 1347, to return victorious to Constantinople. He then established himself and young John V as co-emperors. The civil war, so destructive to the Byzantine state territorially, economically, and morally, was temporarily ended. During the conflict Cantacuzenus had taken an action which at the time did not seem fraught with real danger for the Greeks. In the winter of 1344–1345 John Cantacuzenus, after obtaining the approval of his close friend and ally Umur, emir of Aydin, had sought an alliance with his former enemy Orkhan, the Ottoman emir of Bithynia. This new alliance Cantacuzenus sealed with the marriage of his daughter Theodora to the sexagenarian Orkhan. It was Orkhan's assistance that helped to produce his triumph over the Latin-oriented party of Anna. But it is important to note that as a result of the new alliance between Orkhan and Cantacuzenus the Ottomans, as Cantacuzenus's mercenaries, were now for the first time brought across the Dardanelles into Europe. [124]

Cantacuzenus was nonetheless worried over the reaction of the pope and the western rulers to his alliance with the Ottomans. Indeed, after his triumphal entrance into Constantinople he confided his apprehensions to Bartholomew of Rome, former vicar of the Latin patriarch, who had previously been sent by Humbert to Anna. Evidence is to be found in two letters sent by Bartholomew at this time or soon after to pope Clement VI and Humbert, from which it may be inferred that Cantacuzenus informed him that he intended not only to reëstablish the union of the churches but even to fight on the side of the papacy against the Turks. [125] But Cantacuzenus was a Byzantine in the convoluted diplomatic tradition of Michael VIII, and so he at the same time continued to maintain his relationship

124. Ostrogorsky, *Byzantine State,* pp. 463–464.
125. Cantacuzenus, IV, 2 (*CSHB,* III, 12–20); cf. Lemerle, *L'Émirat d'Aydin,* p. 224.

with Orkhan, which was of use to him in his conflict against the Serbs.

Our knowledge of the negotiations between John VI Cantacuzenus and Clement was formerly derived only from John's own history, which is certainly biased and often chronologically confused. But information from documents published recently enables us to see the drift of Cantacuzenus's negotiations with the papacy. In meetings held in Constantinople (September 1 to October 9, 1347) before the emperor, between Bartholomew of Rome and John's three ambassadors—the protovestiarius George Spanopulus, the official Nicholas Sigerus, and the Latin knight from Auvergne, Francis du Pertuis— Cantacuzenus recognized "the primacy and universality of the Roman church" and engaged himself to observe toward Rome the same obedience as the king of France. [126] So what the Greek emperor had so long feared might now come to pass. Cantacuzenus would, according to this affirmation, be regarded as simply another ruler subservient (like those of the west) to the pope. In order to end the schism he proposed the calling of a council to be held in a maritime city situated halfway between Constantinople and Avignon. [127] While requesting that the pope intervene with the Serbian ruler Stephen Dushan, who had "unjustly" occupied Greek territories, Cantacuzenus offered to participate personally in a crusade against the Turks, [128] evidently even against his own ally, the emir of Aydin. In another letter (March 5, 1348), John repeated his earlier offers and for a crusade proposed to furnish either four thousand men or fifteen to twenty thousand, depending on whether the west at this time envisaged only a *parvum passagium* with a limited objective or a full-scale crusade (*generale et magnum sanctum passagium*). [129]

Clement quickly acknowledged reception of Cantacuzenus's embassy, but, well informed as to the situation in the east, he was apparently suspicious of Cantacuzenus's motives and thus gave only a vague answer to his proposals. Indeed, a considerable period was to elapse before Clement in turn dispatched representatives to Constantinople, with instructions to begin negotiations for union. What is important in all these complex negotiations is that Cantacuzenus had made a secret, solemn commitment to fight in person with all his forces against the Turks, even against his old ally Umur, the emir of Aydin.

126. R. J. Loenertz, "Ambassadeurs grecs auprès du pape Clément VI (1348)," *Orientalia Christiana periodica*, XIX (1953), 180–184; cf. Lemerle, *L'Émirat d'Aydin*, p. 225.

127. Loenertz, *loc. cit.;* also Pears, *Destruction of the Greek Empire*, p. 83.

128. Cantacuzenus, IV, 9 (*CSHB*, III, 53–62).

129. Loenertz, *op. cit.*, pp. 178–196; cf. Gay, *Clément VI*, pp. 104 ff.

More important from the papal side, Clement reacted favorably to the suggestion for the calling of a council. This was the first time in centuries that a pope had agreed to this condition of the Greeks. The way was now open not only for a full-scale east-west crusade to eject the common enemy from Asia Minor but, no less significant, for the holding of an ecumenical council which could finally and irrevocably unite the long-separated churches. Once more, however, the time was not propitious. The disruptive situation in the east, the turmoil in France and England of the Hundred Years' War, and the perennial internal troubles of Italy, not to speak of the devastation sown throughout all of Europe in 1348 by the Black Death—at least one third of the entire population of Byzantium and the west perished of plague—conspired to delay any such coöperation. Negotiations, nevertheless, continued between the papacy and Byzantium, to be terminated only in 1352 with the death of Clement. [130]

For the west, all that remained of the complex campaigns and negotiations connected with the crusade to Smyrna was the Latin occupation of the port. The Greeks, on the other hand, who had technically stood aloof, gained little or nothing. Indeed, they had lost the important island of Chios, and Phocaea as well. Nevertheless, later in the fourteenth century, the famous Byzantine scholar and statesman Demetrius Cydones, seeking to emphasize to his countrymen the advantages of a new Greco-Latin alliance, would point back to the Latin possession of Smyrna as an example of the efficacy of Latin military intervention in the east. [131]

A direct result of the Latin possession of Smyrna was an embassy sent to the pope in 1352, shortly before Clement's death, by the Greek inhabitants of the Anatolian city of Philadelphia. In this embassy, which was received by Clement's successor Innocent VI, the Greeks sought succor from the pope against the persecutions of the Turkish emirates, which had now completely encircled their city. Papal sponsorship of the expedition at Smyrna must have made a considerable impression on the population of Philadelphia. For in exchange for papal protection the Philadelphians sought to place themselves and their city, in perpetuity, under the hegemony of the pope "in all that concerns temporal affairs (*ad temporalia*)," that is, to become "vassals" of the pope but without abandoning their

130. Gay, *Clément VI*, pp. 107 ff.; Lemerle, *L'Émirat d'Aydin*, pp. 226 ff.

131. When Cydones later urged the Byzantines to accept the aid of Amadeo VI of Savoy, he reminded them of the effectiveness of Latin aid at Smyrna (*PG*, CLIV, col. 981; Loenertz, *Les Recueils de lettres de Démétrius Cydones*, Vatican City, 1947, pp. 111–112). Cydones says the Greeks reaped the profit (*kerdos*) of the Latin sacrifices in the taking of Smyrna.

Orthodox faith. Innocent VI, with rather unwarranted severity, wrote back to Philadelphia emphasizing his demand that its people should first abandon the schism and recognize the primacy of the Roman church "in order to avoid eternal punishment, which is something much graver than the peril of the Turk." Once this was done, he affirmed, God would imbue them with enough strength so that one man alone could triumph over a thousand Turks. After abjuration of the schism let them (the Philadelphians) send new envoys, after which the pope in turn would dispatch Latin theologians to instruct them, and perhaps one day he could also aid them to secure victory. [132] The pope's answer seems to us today rather callous in view of the near-desperate situation of the city. In any event, this dramatic plea of Greek citizens to the pope from a city in far-off Asia Minor, though in itself not of much importance, enables us to see with great clarity the dilemma of the Greeks—desperate in their need for military aid but at the same time unwilling to accept the western demand to relinquish their traditional faith, a faith which to them was their mark of identity. How much more severe the punishment of God would be, they must have thought, were they voluntarily to give up the purity of their own faith in exchange for papal aid.

The installation of Cantacuzenus on the Byzantine throne, [133] besides ending the civil war, had still another result: it confirmed the triumph of the hesychastic movement. Hesychasm, which emphasized a kind of spiritual union of man and God already in this life, had been flourishing mainly among the monks of Mount Athos, and at the council in 1356 it was proclaimed as official Orthodox doctrine. The entire empire had been drawn into the religious discussion over hesychasm. One side, the anti-hesychasts, are sometimes viewed as representing the Latinophile outlook; [134] Barlaam was their spokesman, while Gregoras had come forward as the leader of the hesychastic, pro-nationalist outlook. In contrast to Michael VIII, who was considered sympathetic to the Latins, Andronicus II and John VI may be considered as proponents of the Orthodox, more conservative outlook.

This period of struggle between rival claimants to the Byzantine throne permitted the rise to power of the Serbian ruler Stephen Dushan. Assuming the imperial title itself—he styled himself "emper-

---

132. On the exchange of letters, see Lemerle, *L'Émirat d'Aydin,* pp. 236–237.

133. Cantacuzenus evidently used German mercenaries (I, 20; *CSHB,* I, 98).

134. Not always justifiably, as the division between pro-Latin and anti-Latin did not invariably correspond to the beliefs for and against hesychasm; see, for example, J. Meyendorff, *A Study of Gregory Palomas,* trans. George Lawrence (London, 1964), p. 16.

or of the Serbs and Greeks"—Stephen conquered almost the whole of Macedonia (except Thessalonica), Albania, Epirus, Thessaly, and other areas. At the end Dushan had control of more than half of the old Byzantine territories. [135] He lacked Constantinople, but for its capture he needed a fleet. Nevertheless, despite all his blandishments in their direction the Venetians, whose fleet he coveted, did not intend to see the weak Byzantine empire replaced with a strong Serbian power.

Conditions in other spheres also worsened for Byzantium. At sea the Genoese, as we have seen, had recaptured Chios in 1346, and the Byzantine naval power, which had revived under Andronicus III and been further strengthened by Cantacuzenus at heavy cost, was destroyed. Hemmed in at sea between Venice and Genoa, two enemies constantly at war in Greek waters, Byzantium had now sunk to a pitiful state, while on land she was defeated and humiliated by the Ottomans and the Serbs. Even worse was the economic status of the empire: Byzantine trade was ruined (most of it being usurped by the Genoese of Galata), the population was in no position to pay taxes, agriculture was in a state of ruin, and the value of the hyperper (*hyperpyron*) itself was diminishing daily. The depths to which the Byzantine state had sunk are almost unbelievable.

In the dissolution of the Byzantine empire in this last century of its life the effects of the constant Venetian-Genoese wars should not be underestimated. Ensconced in Galata, across from Constantinople, the Genoese, formerly the allies of Michael VIII Palaeologus, were able to interfere frequently in Byzantine affairs, especially when their extensive trading privileges were affected. But this brought them into constant collision with their rivals, the Venetians, who controlled Modon and Coron in the Morea, Euboea, and especially the islands of the southern Aegean. Of course the antagonists in this intense commercial rivalry took no note of the weakening effect it had on Byzantium and of the opportunity it offered the Turks. All was subordinate to the profits that could be extracted from the corpse of Byzantium. Cantacuzenus struggled against the Genoese as the more dangerous of the two rivals, but the empire could not free itself from the Genoese yoke. [136] A war broke out over Genoese attempts to block the passage of foreign—especially Venetian—vessels through the Dardanelles and Bosporus into the Black Sea, particu-

135. Ostrogorsky, *Byzantine State,* pp. 466 ff. In 1354 Dushan sent to Avignon offering his submission to Rome if the pope would name him captain-general against the Turks; nothing came of this (Iorga, "Latins et grecs," p. 217).

136. Ostrogorsky, *Byzantine State,* p. 471. Cantacuzenus had converted the Byzantine part of the Morea into a semi-autonomous despotate.

larly to the port of Kaffa. Aragon, Venice, Genoa, and indirectly Orkhan were all involved, the only result being the further humiliation of Byzantium and a Byzantine promise to cede to Venice the island of Tenedos.

All this was rendered even more complicated by the renewal of the civil war between John VI Cantacuzenus and the legitimate emperor, his son-in-law John V Palaeologus. Sentiment in Constantinople began to favor the legitimate dynasty, especially after the advance of the Ottoman Turks across the Dardanelles and their seizure of Gallipoli. The population of Constantinople was seized by panic and the position of the usurper Cantacuzenus became untenable. The prominent scholar-statesman of the period Demetrius Cydones testifies that lamentations resounded throughout Constantinople as the citizens wailed, "Are not all of us within the walls caught as if in the net of the barbarians?" [137] John V, meanwhile, to secure Genoese support, had promised them the Greek island of Lesbos, and in November 1354, with Genoese help, the partisans of John V were able to force their way into Constantinople. Compelled to abdicate, John Cantacuzenus entered a monastery and thenceforth took no further part in politics, spending his last years writing his famous history and theological tracts defending hesychasm. The Byzantine empire seemed on the verge of complete collapse.

137. *PG,* CLIV, col. 1013.

III

BYZANTIUM AND THE
CRUSADES, 1354–1453

With the retirement of John VI Cantacuzenus in 1354, John V Palaeologus ruled alone. He did not underestimate the gravity of the situation, and like his predecessor, soon after his accession made an attempt to save the empire by the usual device of seeking western aid. Half-Latin himself, and inspired by his mother Anna of Savoy with what seems to have been a certain devotion to the Latin church, he set to work to bring about religious union. On December 15, 1355, one year after his accession, he sent Innocent VI at Avignon a very detailed but surprisingly naive letter containing a series of astounding proposals for the effecting of union.[1] To begin with, he requested the pope to aid in the defense of Constantinople by sending five galleys and fifteen transport vessels with a thousand foot soldiers and five hundred horsemen. All these were to be placed under the command of the emperor, but their expenses for six months were to be borne by the pope. In exchange John committed himself to some remarkable concessions. He pledged to convert his subjects within six months to the faith of Rome. To convince the pope that he would carry out the terms promised, he offered remarkably far-reaching guarantees, more than the direst need of any empire could justify on the part of its ruler. First of all John promised to receive the papal legates with respect and accord them the authority to appoint to ecclesiastical benefices in Constantinople whomever they wished. To disseminate a knowledge of Latin culture the papal ambassadors would be permitted to found colleges in Constantinople for the teaching of Latin.[2] John even promised to send his second

For bibliography, see preceding chapter.

1. See Halecki, *Un Empereur de Byzance*, pp. 17 ff. and 31 ff., who probably over-emphasizes the significance of negotiations with the pope under Cantacuzenus (Gay, *Clément VI*, pp. 111 ff. is more reserved); see also Viller, "La Question de l'union," *RHE*, XVIII, 26 ff. On John's letter to the pope, see Halecki, *loc. cit.*

2. During the Latin occupation of Constantinople the Latin emperor had sought to found a Latin college in Constantinople, but the papacy and especially the University of Paris had blocked it. But events had so changed that crusader theoreticians like Raymond Lull and

son Manuel, then a child of seven, to the papal court to be educated by the pope in the Latin faith. The emperor went so far as to pledge that, should these promises for some reason not be fulfilled, he would himself abdicate the throne. In that case control of the empire would be left to the papal ward, Manuel, or if he were still a minor, to the pope.[3]

Not surprisingly, Innocent replied enthusiastically to this astonishing letter. No less understandably, he apparently had some reservations about the seriousness of the proposals, for in his reply he made no reference to anything specific; rather, in general but warm terms, he praised the imperial sentiments. At the same time he wrote letters to the Byzantine patriarch Callistus and to the principal Greek bishops, while dispatching two nuncios to Constantinople, one of them the famous Carmelite Peter Thomas.[4] Though the pope himself was guarded in his approach, news of the proposals was received in other western quarters with distrust mixed with gratification. Characteristically, Philip of Mézières, a propagandist for the crusade in the court of king Peter of Cyprus, wrote, "The news of John V's desire for conversion was very difficult to believe, because it had been so long that the Greeks were separated from the church, and because in previous negotiations they had so often deceived the Roman church."[5]

Wishing nevertheless to capitalize on the opportunity offered, Innocent made overtures to Venice, Genoa, the king of Cyprus, and the Hospitallers of Rhodes in order to secure ships to send to Constantinople, but he failed in his efforts. No one would furnish the contingents requested; papal plans were also set back by the hostilities of the Venetian-Hungarian war. As for the Byzantine emperor, seeing no help forthcoming from Rome, he was obliged to write to Innocent that he was in no position to win the Greek populace over to his policy,[6] since their inherent suspicions were now magnified by the west's failure to send military aid. Negotiations for union were ended for several years.

Yet the case for Greco-Latin rapprochement found its defenders also in the west. And the thought planted in the mind of the pope by

---

William Adam now sought to "Latinize" the Greeks, forcibly or otherwise, by compelling many to learn Latin (Geanakoplos, *Byzantine East and Latin West*, p. 2, note 3, and p. 103, note 74).

3. Halecki, *op. cit.*, pp. 31 ff.

4. Iorga, *Philippe de Mézières*, pp. 137–138; at Constantinople Peter Thomas instructed John in the Catholic faith.

5. Smet, *Life of Saint Peter Thomas*, p. 74.

6. Iorga, *loc. cit.*

young John V bore fruit in the pope's dispatch again to Constantinople, in 1361, of the Latin archbishop of Crete, Peter Thomas, to look more carefully into the question of a possible union. Peter had lived for years in the east and, experienced in its problems, was a most suitable person to entrust with the delicate task of converting the Greeks to Catholicism.[7]

John V listened patiently to the arguments of the papal nuncio and showed signs of willingness to accept the creed of Rome. According to Philip of Mézières, John was even ready to depose the incumbent anti-unionist patriarch of Constantinople, Callistus, and replace him with a Catholic ("patriarcham Graecum perfidum, et unitatis Ecclesiae inimicum promisit deponi et unum alium Catholicum eligi debere").[8] In spite of the favorable motives of both pope and emperor the mission seems to have come to nothing. Though it was clearer than ever that any efforts to obtain western aid could succeed only as a result of papal influence, the difficulty was that, as a consequence of its experience at Lyons, the papacy always demanded as a precondition that military aid follow the Greek abjuration of schism. On their side, the Greeks, reversing these conditions, insisted that aid should be sent before conversion as a sign of papal good faith. An impasse accordingly resulted in which each side waited for the first long step to be taken by the other. Of course what blocked even an initial advance was the suspicion underlying the attitude of each side. Contributory too was the rapid succession of popes, each one having to assess the situation anew for himself before he would act. There was also a misunderstanding in the west regarding the efficacy of imperial power. For in the west, where the Byzantine emperor was—erroneously—believed to have complete power over church and state (Caesaropapism, that is), the fact that he was unable, as we have seen, to force union on his recalcitrant clergy and people was usually misinterpreted as insincerity on his part.[9] Barlaam's words quoted above are especially appropriate here.

In the mid-fourteenth century, under the shadow of the Ottoman

---

7. Another example besides Peter Thomas, who died in 1396 as titular Latin patriarch of Constantinople, is his predecessor Paul of Smyrna; also the archbishop of Thebes, Simon Atumano. See G. Mercati, *Simone Atumano arcivescovo di Tebe* (Studi e testi, 30; Rome, 1916); K. M. Setton, "The Byzantine Background to the Italian Renaissance," *Proceedings of the American Philosophical Society*, C (1956), 51; and G. Fedalto, *Simone Atumano, monaco di studio, arcivescovo latino di Tebe (secolo XIV)* (Brescia, 1968).

8. Philip of Mézières, *Vita S. Petri Thomasii*, p. 616 (Acta Sanctorum, III [Paris, 1863], 605 ff.); Atiya, *op. cit.*, p. 132.

9. Geanakoplos, "Church and State in the Byzantine Empire and the Problem of Caesaropapism," in his *Byzantine East and Latin West*, pp. 57 ff., and "The Council of Florence and the Problem of Union . . . ," *ibid.*, p. 94, note 41.

advance, two parties emerged in Byzantium with different views as to the source of succor against the Turks. The overwhelming majority of the masses and the clergy, always steadfastly Orthodox, were against any rapprochement with the Latins. The opposing party, the chief spokesman of which was the grand logothete, the scholar Demetrius Cydones, looked to the west as the only effective source for aid against the Turks. In this view the Christians of both east and west should unite in a common front against the "infidel" Turk.[10] For the salvation of the state they were willing, though reluctantly, to pay the price of ecclesiastical subordination to Rome, the *sine qua non* of such an alliance.

The Orthodox party, however, had other ideas. It envisioned a pan-Orthodox coalition of the Balkan Slavic states against the Turks, a proposal which came to have no little appeal to many at this time. The policy came to the fore in 1355 when a preparatory meeting of Orthodox clergy sat at Constantinople and drew up provisions for an Orthodox league. For a time John V himself was, or seemed to be (perhaps owing to popular pressure), interested in the proposal. He even married his son Andronicus to a Bulgar princess in order to strengthen the ties between the two Orthodox states.[11] But so desperate had John now become that, in the same year, he wrote his famous letter to Rome with its sensational proposals. His ardor for a pan-Balkan alliance cooled, though patriarch Callistus of Constantinople continued the negotiations with the Slavic churches. In 1363 he even visited Serres, then under Serbian control, where he made an attempt to persuade the Serbian prelates of the great benefits to be derived from such an alliance, but died before he accomplished this. Under his successor-patriarch the effort was carried on, with the suggestion for the participation of Russia in the proposed alliance.[12]

The influential Demetrius Cydones, however, grand logothete of the empire and intellectually sympathetic toward the Latins, severely criticized the movement for a pan-Orthodox confederation. Emphasizing the futility of such an alliance, he pointed out the weakness and fickleness of the Slavic states as well as their traditional hostility toward Byzantium.[13] Nevertheless, the project did not die until the

10. See D. Cydones, "De subsidio Latinorum" and "De non reddendo Callipoli," in *PG*, CLIV, cols. 961–1008 and 1009–1036. D. Zakythinos discusses his views in *La Grèce et les Balkans* (Athens, 1946), pp. 52–56.

11. On this pan-Orthodox union see Zakythinos, *Byzantion, State and Community* [in Greek] (Athens, 1951), pp. 140–141.

12. Nicephorus Gregoras, XXXVII, 16 (*CSHB*, III, 537); cf. Ostrogorsky, *Byzantine State*, p. 479.

13. Cydones, *PG*, CLIV, cols. 973, 976.

battle of Kossovo in 1389 and the capture of Tirnovo in 1393, when both the Serbian and the Bulgarian states fell irrevocably under the hegemony of the Ottomans. The destruction of these two states ended any hopes for a Balkan Orthodox alignment against the Turk.

Following in the steps of Innocent VI and his predecessor Clement VI, the new pope Urban V worked toward the formation of a Greco-Latin coalition against the Turks. In 1363, at papal urging, Louis I of Hungary and the Serbs united in an attempt to capture the Turkish-controlled fortress of Adrianople in Thrace. The Greeks seem to have held aloof from this expedition, which, because of the large number of forces involved (some say twenty thousand men), has sometimes been termed a crusade. One modern historian believes that had the Greeks been able to overcome their fear of Turkish reprisals and participated, the Turkish threat might have been completely destroyed.[14] At any rate, the campaign ended in a surprise attack and a massacre of the Christians by the Turks.

By this time opinion in the west had changed direction; an expedition against the Turks was no longer viewed as merely the prelude to a crusade to the Holy Land but, because of the increasing Turkish danger to Europe, in itself constituted the crusade. Western Europe had finally begun to realize that a Christian Constantinople, even though Greek, was necessary for the defense of all Christendom. Thus in 1363 pope Urban V preached a crusade against the Ottomans to take place under the leadership of Peter I, king of Cyprus. Although not specifically planned to relieve Constantinople—it aimed ultimately at conquering Palestine by attacking Egypt[15] —this expedition was important as representing the first support, however indirect, given by the west to Byzantium.

Evidence indicates that the pope appealed strongly to emperor John V to participate in the expedition. John's initial reaction was, however, one of fear of retaliation from the Turks, and he was therefore reluctant to join. But upon hearing of the vast preparations being made and the size of the forces involved he changed his mind. Accordingly, he wrote to Urban that as soon as the Turks were expelled from Thrace he would join the crusade, meaning of course that once the westerners had aided the Greeks to recover Thrace he would join in ousting the Turks from Asia Minor and the Holy Land. From John V's viewpoint, with the objective of the expedition Egypt instead of Thrace or Asia Minor, his hope of profit from the crusade

---

14. H. Gibbons, *The Foundation of the Ottoman Empire* (Oxford, 1916), pp. 22–23.
15. Peter de Lusignan's crusade was the last with Jerusalem as its aim.

was shattered, and he offered no help to Peter.[16] But that John entertained hopes of deflecting the aim of the crusade from Alexandria to Asia Minor is indicated by the appearance at Avignon, in 1365, of a Latinophile friend of Demetrius Cydones, John Lascaris Calopherus, with instructions to that end.[17]

Peter I de Lusignan, king of Cyprus, was a fiery paladin who had, in 1361, taken from the Turks the city of Adalia, situated in Asia Minor across from Cyprus.[18] To defend this new possession and simultaneously to loosen the Moslem stranglehold around his kingdom, which since the fall of Acre constituted the most advanced western outpost in the east, Peter had gone to Avignon to meet Urban V and the king of France, John II the Good. It was not unduly difficult to persuade them to provide support, given the precarious position of Cyprus, the most important Latin base in the east, and on March 31, 1363, a full-fledged crusade (*passagium generale*) was proclaimed with the French king as captain-general.[19] But there was the difficult problem of persuading the western princes and knights to participate. The pope wrote everywhere, to all the Catholic rulers of the west, and, for reasons of propaganda, the king of Cyprus himself undertook a great tour across France, England, Germany, and even Poland. Despite the cordiality of his reception on all sides almost nothing concrete resulted. Only the king of Hungary, Louis I, and the count of Savoy, Amadeo VI, showed any willingness to follow.[20] Peter, who had no particular interest in Byzantium, left for the east before the arrival of these potential allies. In 1365 his forces sacked the rich port of Alexandria, and raided other coastal cities of the Levant. But the crusaders withdrew from Alexandria when the main Egyptian army approached, and in the long run little was accomplished. In 1370 a truce was signed with the sultan to maintain in effect the status quo as it was before the expedition to Alexandria.[21]

With the appearance of Amadeo VI, count of Savoy, however, Byzantium became more closely involved with the crusade. Amadeo, called the Green Count (*Conte Verde*), was the cousin of John V through John's mother, Anna of Savoy. John's initial lack of enthu-

---

16. Iorga, *Philippe de Mézières*, pp. 280–283, saying that a few Greeks (John Lascaris Calopherus and John Angelus) joined Peter's army. Most Greeks showed no interest.

17. G. Mercati, "Per l'epistolario di Demetrio Cidone," *Studi bizantini e neoellenici*, III (1931), 215–216.

18. On Peter I, see below, pp. 352–360.

19. Raynaldus, *Annales ecclesiastici*, ad ann. 1363, no. 4.

20. Iorga, *Philippe de Mézières*, pp. 172–204.

21. Atiya, *Crusade in the Later Middle Ages*, pp. 345–378.

siasm for the expedition gave way to readiness to participate when he heard of the magnitude of the preparations, which seemed to guarantee results. It seemed possible that he could even redirect the crusade to aid Constantinople. Accordingly, in 1364 he sent as his envoy to Urban the Genoese Michael Malaspina, offering the aid of Byzantine forces for the projected crusade to the Holy Land. He prescribed, however, that the Turks first be ejected from Thrace. As we have seen, this was his way of emphasizing the need to alleviate the pressure on Constantinople. The pope responded prudently, in his reply including a pledge that Michael VIII had much earlier demanded from pope Gregory X: namely, that while the Byzantine emperor was away on the crusade the western crusaders would promise to do no damage to his empire.[22] For the pope evidently realized that even as late as a century and a half after 1204 the Greeks still feared a repetition of that catastrophic event. The aims of John V seemed finally about to be realized.

But the pope on his side had further demands to make. In February 1366 Urban wrote to John V promising to induce count Amadeo ("consanguineus tuus"), as well as king Peter of Cyprus and king Louis of Hungary, to come to the rescue of Byzantium if John would renounce the schism and submit to Rome in full sincerity ("in sinceritate cordium"). Louis meanwhile wrote to Urban that he had promised to send aid to John V, but Urban wrote him to postpone his crusade until the union of the churches had been accomplished.[23] So even Louis thenceforth insisted on the papal principle of first union, then assistance.

Byzantine diplomacy was in the meantime not inactive. In the spring of 1366 John V, alarmed at the Turkish capture of Adrianople and Philippopolis, decided to go to Hungary to appeal personally for aid and remove Louis's scruples about aiding a "schismatic." Entering a foreign country, a Byzantine emperor thus went for the first time not at the head of an army but almost as a beggar seeking help. There was, however, little profit to either the Byzantine or the Hungarian side; the demeanor of both men was cold.[24] According to

22. P. Lecacheux, ed., *Lettres secrètes et curiales du pape Urbain V* (Paris, 1902), p. 211, no. 305; see also K. Kerofilas, *Amedeo VI,* and Cox, *The Green Count of Savoy: Amadeus VI.*

23. See A. Theiner and F. Miklosich, eds., *Monumenta spectantia ad unionem ecclesiarum graecae et romanae,* II (Vienna, 1872), 74–75; cf. Halecki, *Un Empereur de Byzance,* p. 129; and Norden, *Papsttum und Byzanz,* p. 703. But the events are not clear. On January 25, 1366, the pope had sent another letter to the emperor announcing that a combined expedition (of Cyprus and Hungary) would attack the Turks (Raynaldus, ad ann. 1366, no. 2). Cf. Iorga, *Philippe de Mézières,* p. 331, notes 7–9.

24. Halecki, *Un Empereur de Byzance,* pp. 129, 134.

the contemporary source, John offended Louis by his arrogance, refusing to doff his hat to the king. In any case, Louis of Hungary did not join the campaign, and later even became hostile to Byzantium.

On his way home from Hungary John encountered a new difficulty. Arriving in Hungarian-occupied Vidin, he was forced to interrupt his journey, as the Bulgars would not permit him to pass.[25] It was only the exertions of his cousin Amadeo that enabled him to return safely home. The Green Count was on his way to the east to join the crusade of Peter I of Cyprus when he was—falsely—informed by the Venetians, who usually opposed new crusades because of the resultant damage to their eastern trade, that a treaty of peace had been signed between Cyprus and Egypt. Thereupon Amadeo, perhaps at the suggestion of the pope, sailed with his troops and ships to Constantinople. With no more than 1,800 men he attacked and took Gallipoli, which he promptly handed over to the Byzantines. Then, leaving some of his forces to strengthen the garrison at Gallipoli, he proceeded to Constantinople, where he was welcomed with great joy by the populace. Learning of the plight of his unhappy cousin, he left a garrison to guard Constantinople and sailed along the Black Sea coast seizing Bulgarian cities.[26] At Varna, which he besieged, he forced the release of his cousin on December 21, 1366, and then lifted the siege.

An agreement was then reached between Amadeo and John. For the sum of 15,000 florins Amadeo handed over to the emperor the cities he had taken in Bulgaria, including Mesembria and Sozopolis. During his stay with the emperor in Constantinople the recurrent problem of ecclesiastical union was discussed, and Amadeo, a forceful personality, succeeded in persuading John that the emperor should go personally to Rome to seek aid.[27] An interested participant in the discussions was Paul of Smyrna, the Latin patriarch of Constantinople, who, according to one Greek source not previously used, had brought to the emperor letters from the pope concerning union.[28]

25. Iorga, *Geschichte des osmanischen Reiches,* I (Gotha, 1908), 224, note 2, and 230; and Ostrogorsky, *Byzantine State,* p. 479. Several authors, however, believe (probably erroneously) that John V was actually seized by the Bulgars, (Delaville Le Roulx, *La France en Orient,* p. 152, following P. Datta, *Spedizione*).

26. For Amadeo's motives in aiding Byzantium, see Delaville Le Roulx, *La France en Orient,* pp. 141–142, and Atiya, *op. cit.,* pp. 380–381. On Amadeo's expedition, see *Chroniques de Savoye,* in *Historiae patriae monumenta,* III: *Scriptores,* I (Turin, 1840), cols. 5–382; cf. Datta, *Spedizione,* and M. Canale, *Della Spedizione in Oriente di Amadeo di Savoia* (Genoa, 1887).

27. *Chroniques de Savoye,* p. 314; Delaville Le Roulx, *La France en Orient,* pp. 156–157; Ostrogorsky, *Byzantine State,* p. 480.

28. *Synodicae constitutiones* [in Greek], 58, in *PG,* CLII, cols. 1410–1412.

The conversations held at this time and the new western proposal for union are reported in a letter of the patriarch of Constantinople, Philotheus, which he addressed to the Greek bishop of Ochrida: "Most blessed bishop of Prima Justiniana [Ochrida], and of all Bulgaria: The cousin of my emperor, the count of Savoy, having come to Constantinople with ships and having with him a western bishop, Paul, conveyed the letters of the pope to the emperor concerning the unity and peace of the churches, that is, of ours and that of the Latins. The . . . emperor showed the letters to me and to the most holy patriarchs of Alexandria and Jerusalem and then to the members of the holy synod, the most holy bishops. After assembling, we unanimously voted to hold an ecumenical council, according to the example of the other seven ecumenical councils." Philotheus's letter goes on to say that all the eastern patriarchs were instructing their subordinate bishops to come to the council in order to uphold the faith. The council was to be held in June of 1369. He continues: "We have thus agreed with the representatives of the pope. If in the council our faith is proved by the holy scriptures to be stronger than that of the Latins, they shall come over to us and confess as we do."[29] The information provided by this letter is significant because it indicates that the papal emissary as well as Amadeo and the emperor had all finally agreed with the Greek clergy that an ecumenical council should be held—the date was even set—in which once and for all doctrinal differences would be resolved.

Whether the pope, as seems likely, rejected his envoy Paul's agreement as exceeding the authority delegated to him we are in no position to judge. At any rate, despite the fixing of a date, the council was apparently not convoked, and henceforth the Greek clergy would take no further part in the negotiations. Moreover, the Greek clergy now took a position in opposition to John's projected journey to the west. John himself became reluctant to leave because of the worsening condition of his empire. We probably need not accept the report of the *Chronicles of Savoy* that count Amadeo, in order to force the ecclesiastical submission of the emperor to Rome, abducted and held as hostages the Greek patriarch and four Greek noblemen.[30] In the chronicles it is also affirmed that, just before this, the patriarch had warned Amadeo that the emperor could not possibly go to Rome because the populace would depose him.[31]

Two Greek ambassadors now accompanied Amadeo to the west, and it was understood in Constantinople that as soon as they re-

29. *Ibid., loc. cit.,* dated *c.* 1366.
30. *Chroniques de Savoye,* pp. 318–319; cf. Atiya, *op. cit.,* pp. 395–396.
31. *Chroniques de Savoye,* pp. 316–317; Atiya, *loc. cit.*

turned John V would depart for Italy. But John's trip was delayed. On June 4, 1367, Amadeo and the two Greek envoys left Byzantium from Pera, the Byzantine envoys not returning until over a year later, on September 20, 1368. The letters from the pope were then read publicly in the Hippodrome.[32] Thus ended the crusade of Amadeo, the Green Count. It was an expedition of a kind the Byzantines would have welcomed more often. For though it was not decisive in results, it was at least helpful. Most important, it showed that coöperation and understanding between crusaders and Byzantines was possible if the Byzantines could be made to realize that, as in the case of the mild and unambitious Amadeo, not every western leader intended to carve out a state for himself in the east.

In 1369 John himself finally undertook his journey to the west. At the request of the pope his trip was facilitated by both Venice and Genoa. With him John took many high state dignitaries, but, revealingly, not a single ecclesiastic accompanied him. In Rome John met the pope, who had himself come down from Avignon, and in October of 1369 John presented his confession of faith, abjured the schism, and attended mass at St. Peter's with the pope and the cardinals. This act of submission to the Roman church, dramatic as it was, was nonetheless only a personal, individual act and could not really be binding on his Greek subjects. Urban did, however, write at once to the Greek clergy and urge them to follow John's example.[33]

While John was renouncing his Orthodox faith in Rome, the anti-unionist patriarch Philotheus was taking measures in Constantinople to strengthen the cause of Orthodoxy. He issued hortatory letters not only to all the Orthodox within the empire but also to those of Syria, Egypt, and Balkan Slavic territories, and even Russia. The pope, on his side, issued an encyclical announcing the great news of John's conversion to the princes of Europe. Jubilant, the pope loaded the emperor with presents and encouraged John to negotiate with English mercenaries then in Italy for service in Byzantium.

The way finally seemed open for collaboration between John V and the western powers for a joint crusade. It had already been foreseen that Amadeo's expedition would be only the forerunner of

---

32. S. Lampros and K. Amantos, "Brachea Chronika" [in Greek], *Mnemeia tes Hellinekes historias,* I (1932), no. 47, pp. 25–30, and Atiya, *op. cit.,* p. 396. Cf. P. Charanis, "Les 'Brachea Chronika' comme source historique," *Byzantion,* XIII (1938), 339, note 6. Strangely, the best 15th-century Greek historians omit mention of John's trip to Buda and even of Amadeo's expedition.

33. A. Vasiliev, "Il Viaggio dell' imperatore bizantino Giovanni V Paleologo in Italia," *Studi bizantini e neoellenici,* III (1931), 151–193. Cf. Ostrogorsky, *Byzantine State,* p. 480, and Halecki, *Un Empereur de Byzance,* p. 205.

a vast expedition to follow John's conversion. And now pope Urban V preached a new crusade.[34] At the start of 1370 he wrote to Venice, Genoa, and Savoy not only informing them of John's abjuration but exhorting them to prepare a new expedition. Moreover, he requested queen Joanna of Naples to accord free passage to the troops of the various nations that John V, "the Catholic prince," was to lead against the Turks.[35] Despite all the papal exhortations there was as usual little response from the west, since the Hundred Years' War had started again after a brief pause. To cap it all the pope himself died shortly thereafter.

John V did not at once return to Constantinople but proceeded to France with money borrowed from the Venetians. Later, unable to pay his debt, he was actually imprisoned in Venice, as an "insolvent debtor."[36] How low the might of Byzantium had fallen! He was freed only through the efforts of his son Manuel, who raised the necessary sums. In October 1371 John was once again back in Constantinople, his exertions having accomplished nothing except to induce him to renounce his own faith. In these hopeless circumstances he could not, understandably, attempt to persuade his countrymen to accept the union of the churches. There was in fact an Orthodox reaction in Constantinople. Yet John's conversion does not seem to have aroused the intensity of feeling that Michael VIII's signing of the union at Lyons had done a century before. This may reflect the engrossment of the clergy of Constantinople in the last stage of the hesychastic controversy. No doubt constant harping on the theme of religious union, together with the actual Turkish inroads, played some part as well.

The new pope, Gregory XI, however, did not mean to lose this opportunity for converting the Greeks to Catholicism, so in 1373 he organized a congress at Thebes to plan a crusade; to it he invited the titular Latin emperor, the Venetians, the Genoese, the Hospitallers of Rhodes, the vicar of the duchy of Athens, the kings of Cyprus, Hungary, and Sicily, and—most important for us—the Byzantine emperor. Despite these grandiose preparations, nothing seems to have been accomplished. Louis of Hungary, whose participation was indispensable, was involved in a dynastic conflict of his own, and

---

34. Raynaldus, ad ann. 1369, no. 4; cf. Pears, *Destruction of the Greek Empire*, p. 92.

35. Lecacheux, *Lettres secrètes d'Urbain V*, no. 3040, p. 524.

36. F. Dölger proves this in his "Johannes VII., Kaiser der Rhomäer," *Byzantinische Zeitschrift,* XXXI (1931), 22, note 2, in contrast to Halecki, *op. cit.,* pp. 335 ff., who considers it legend; cf. Ostrogorsky, *Byzantine State*, p. 481, and R. J. Loenertz, "Jean V Paléologue à Venise (1370–1371)," *Revue des études byzantines*, XVI (1958), 217–232.

Venice and Genoa, instead of fighting the Turks, had provoked a new war between themselves.[37] In 1374 Gregory dispatched four legates to Constantinople, to promote conversions.

John V's envoys vainly scoured Europe for help, extracting only vague promises from king Charles V of France. Abandoned by everyone and realizing that he could no longer effectively resist the Turk, John, cut off from the rest of Europe by a large strip of Turkish territory, with no fleet and almost no army, took the supremely humiliating step of acknowledging himself the vassal of the Turks. To Murad I, the Ottoman sultan, he even handed over his favorite son Manuel as a hostage for his conduct. Later Manuel and his nephew John VII actually had to assist the Turks in besieging the last Greek stronghold remaining in Asia Minor, Philadelphia,[38] the inhabitants of which only a few years before had, as we have seen, vainly pleaded for protection from the pope.

In both east and west events forced the abandonment of any further attempts at a crusade—the renewal of the Hundred Years' War between France and England and especially the conflict that erupted between Venice and Genoa over possession of the island of Tenedos at the mouth of the Dardanelles. In Byzantium itself, as if things were not bad enough, a new civil war broke out between John V and one of his sons, Andronicus (IV), and later between John and his grandson John (VII). In view of these new preoccupations Byzantine hopes for a crusade had to be put off. A glimmer of hope for succor appeared however in 1388, when pope Urban VI sent to the east two armed galleys for the defense of Constantinople. The pope even issued indulgences as for a crusade.[39] But once again nothing came of this.

In 1382 a compromise, arranged at Turin through the mediation of count Amadeo VI of Savoy, finally settled the Veneto-Genoese war over Tenedos.[40] But the Turks continued to advance, Thessalonica even falling temporarily to them in 1387. With the battle of Kossovo in 1389 and the capture of Tirnovo in 1393 the fate of the Slavic

---

37. See Halecki, *op. cit.,* pp. 289–319, who does not believe that the congress was ever actually convened. Incidentally, the Genoese of Pera refused to break their treaty with the Turks to enter into the league being formed by the pope (Délaville Le Roulx, *La France en Orient,* p. 159).

38. On this, see Barker, *Manuel II Palaeologus,* pp. 22, 79.

39. On the complex Italian rivalries, see Delaville Le Roulx, especially on Venice's tergiversations. At one point Manuel, discouraged, even offered to hand Constantinople over to Venice to defend, under certain conditions (Heyd, *Histoire du commerce,* II, 264).

40. On the Tenedos war, see F. Thiriet, "Venise et l'occupation de Ténédos au XIVe siècle," *Mélanges d'archéologie et d'histoire,* LXV (1953), 219–245.

nations of the Balkans was sealed.[41]   The last center of Slavic resistance had been crushed and the Turks now cast their shadow rapidly over all the Balkans.

The civil war between John V and his grandson John VII continued. The grandson was supported by the Turks, who hoped thereby to take the first step toward the occupation of Constantinople. John V's turbulent reign, spanning—with interruptions—half a century, at last came to an end in 1391. Luckily for Byzantium his able son Manuel II, at the news of his father's death, was able to escape from the Turkish camp where he was still held hostage and to reach Constantinople to assume the imperial throne. But Manuel's empire was now but a shadow of its former self, consisting only of the city of Constantinople, Thessalonica, and the outlying despotate of the Morea, which, though itself prosperous enough, was distant and unable to communicate with the capital except by sea.

The tremendous Ottoman successes in the Balkans made a great impression on the west. With the Ottoman crossing of the Danube, Hungary was directly threatened, and the Latin principalities in Greece also began to feel the pressure of the Turks.[42] Until this time Byzantine appeals for western aid, as well as papal admonitions to western princes, had generally fallen on deaf ears. But at last the west was shocked enough to feel that drastic, concerted measures were imperative. King Sigismund of Hungary in particular, fearing for the safety of his country, was spurred into action. And so in 1393–1394 Hungary, which had long shown scant concern for Christian solidarity, sought to assemble a great Christian army to oppose the Turkish advance. Sigismund's appeal was answered by the chivalry of several western nations, by German, French, and Burgundian knights;[43] by the Burgundians, especially, the old chivalric ideal of a crusade was still held in esteem. Even usually aloof Venice joined the coalition, sending a small fleet to patrol the Dardanelles and keep open the line of communications between Byzantium and the crusading forces assembling in Hungary.[44]

Sigismund could not have overlooked the strategic importance of

41. On Kossovo, see H. Grégoire, "L'Opinion byzantine et la bataille de Kossovo," *Byzantion*, VI, 247 ff., and Ostrogorsky, *Byzantine State*, p. 486.

42. See below, pp. 245–247.

43. See especially R. Rosetti, "The Battle of Nicopolis (1396)," *Slavonic Review*, XV (1937), 629 ff. Cf. Atiya, *Crusade in the Later Middle Ages*, pp. 435–436; Ostrogorsky, *Byzantine State*, p. 490; and above, pp. 21–25.

44. Venice, to protect her interests, was then preparing to send an embassy to Bayazid to reconcile him with Byzantium, a fact which provoked a protest from Sigismund (document

Constantinople and the possibility of securing assistance from the nation most threatened by the Turks. The Greek emperor Manuel, however, was caught on the horns of a dilemma. To be sure, Byzantium's rescue from the Turk might be forthcoming from this expedition if it were to turn out successfully. But in the event of failure, encircled as his capital was by Turkish territory on all sides, he would have to risk the severe retaliation of the Turks, who in fact only a short time before had begun a blockade, though not systematic, of Constantinople. Despite this pitfall, Manuel, with the best interests of his empire at heart, courageously prepared to coöperate as best he could with the crusaders without arousing Turkish suspicions. According to the Greek historian Ducas, it was in fact Manuel whose appeals for aid to the pope, the king of France, and the king of Hungary had originally aroused Europe to organize this crusade. The passage of Ducas is vague (he does not even give a date), and the Hungarian chroniclers, perhaps more correctly, ascribe instigation of the crusade rather to Sigismund.[45] Whatever the truth of Ducas's assertion, we know that Hungarian envoys had been in Brusa, attempting to negotiate with the Turks, and it is not improbable that on their return to Hungary they stopped in Constantinople and discussed a possible alliance with the Greeks.[46] Moreover, in May 1395 a Greek envoy of the emperor was in France, and although we are not certain of the specific aim of his mission, it is most probable that the projected crusade was under discussion. Greek embassies to the west in this period were frequent, but it is difficult to assign any specific significance to each one with respect to imperial policy toward the crusade. At any rate, whatever Manuel's actual role in the launching of this western expedition, known to history as the Crusade of Nicopolis, it seems correct at least to affirm that during this period the Byzantines, mindful of their extreme weakness, showed no little indecision for fear of severe Turkish retaliation.

A congress of states interested in stopping the Turkish advance convened at Venice in the spring of 1395, where Greek envoys had been present since December of the previous year. We do know that Manuel's representatives participated in the negotiations. Manuel in fact undertook to equip ten galleys and to pay the salary of the crews for a month, Sigismund for three months. For this purpose

---

ed. S. S. Ljubić in *Monumenta spectantia historiam Slavorum meridionalium*, IV [*Listine . . .* , 1358–1403; Zagreb, 1874], 360–361).

45. Ducas, I, 13 (*PG,* CLVII, col. 813). Cf. "Sphrantzes," I, 14 (ed. Papadopulos, p. 64). Atiya, *The Crusade of Nicopolis,* pp. 34–36, Ostrogorsky, *Byzantine State,* p. 490, and Vasiliev, *Byzantine Empire,* p. 630, seem to think Sigismund began the crusade.

46. See Atiya, *Crusade of Nicopolis,* p. 35, and p. 173, note 1.

30,000 ducats were given by Manuel to the imperial envoy Manuel Philanthropenus.[47] Meanwhile, Manuel seems to have entered into a league with the Christian outposts of the Aegean, the Genoese of the islands of Lesbos and Chios, and also the Knights Hospitaller of Rhodes.[48] Manuel's actions reveal his desperation and willingness to risk all to save his empire. There is an interesting passage in the *Chronicon maius* ascribed to George Sphrantzes, a work which has been shown probably to be a later compilation by Macarius Melissenus and therefore to be used with extreme caution. It states that on Sigismund's arrival at the city of Nicopolis in Bulgaria, he sent a messenger secretly to Manuel to inform him "to be ready to destroy the enemy of the faith. . . . As the thirsty land receives the shower, the Greeks joyfully received the envoy and secretly made preparations for war."[49]

The ensuing battle of Nicopolis (September 25, 1396), which had apparently held such great promise, ended in complete failure, the motley western host being completely routed by sultan Bayazid and his Turks. The reason for the western failure lies primarily in the lack of coöperation between the Hungarian and French troops.[50] Sigismund himself escaped capture by flight, and with Philibert of Naillac, the grand master of the Hospitallers, went by sea to Constantinople on vessels which had been mere onlookers at the battle; thence, by way of the Aegean and Adriatic seas, he finally arrived home. His passage through the Dardanelles was made to the accompaniment of piteous cries of Christian captives lined up by Bayazid along the shore to humiliate him.[51]

According to Jean Froissart, the French chronicler of the Hundred Years' War, Manuel II Palaeologus played the role of informer to Bayazid regarding the movement of the western crusaders. But his testimony is probably false, irritated as he was at the deaths of so

47. Delaville Le Roulx, *La France en Orient*, p. 243.

48. Silberschmidt, *Das orientalische Problem*, p. 119, and A. Mompherratos, *Diplomatic Activities of Manuel II* [in Greek].

49. I, 14 (ed. Papadopulos, p. 64; *CSHB*, p. 59). On the authenticity of the *Chronicon maius*, see Ostrogorsky, *Byzantine State*, p. 417, note 2, and R. J. Loenertz, "Autour du Chronicon maius attribué à Georges Phrantzès," in *Miscellanea Giovanni Mercati*, III (Studi e testi, 123; Vatican City, 1946), 273–311.

50. Kling, *Die Schlacht bei Nikopolis;* Rosetti, "The Battle of Nicopolis," pp. 629 ff.

51. Report of the Bavarian John Schiltberger, *Reisebuch*, ed. V. Langmantel (Tübingen, 1885), p. 7. Barker, *Manuel II Palaeologus*, pp. 482 ff., quotes a letter of Sigismund to Philibert of Naillac, showing that Sigismund conferred with Manuel in Constantinople after the battle (first published by H. V. Sauerland as "Ein Brief des Königs Sigismund von Ungarn an . . . Philibert von Naillac," *Neues Archiv der Gesellschaft für ältere deutsche Geschichtskunde*, XXI [1896], 565–566). In this letter, dated November 11, 1396, Sigismund mentions a league including Manuel, the Genoese of Pera, and the Hospitallers.

many western knights, and, in the "best" western tradition, looking for a Greek scapegoat. Another western historian lays the blame on a letter of Manuel which was intercepted. Still other historians consider John Galeazzo Visconti, duke of Milan, a possible traitor, for he had reason to be hostile to the French, who had kept him from attaining his goals against the Genoese.[52] That Manuel, a genuine Byzantine patriot, was a traitor is very hard to believe, in view of the fact that nothing would have augured better for the safety of his empire than a successful crusade.

After the catastrophe at Nicopolis the situation worsened even further for Byzantium. For, according to the *Chronicon maius,* the Turks had discovered the secret alliance of Manuel and the western crusaders, and therefore resumed their blockade of Constantinople both on land and sea "for a long period of time."[53] Turkish armies also crossed the isthmus of Corinth and defeated Theodore, the Byzantine despot of the Morea, temporarily occupying the lower city of Athens, plundering and devastating everything in their path. [54] The plight of Constantinople seemed hopeless; the capture of the blockaded capital seemed imminent.

In the west the reaction to the debacle of Nicopolis—which is often taken to be the last great crusade of the medieval period—was one of utter dismay. The wholesale massacre of so many members of prominent noble houses made it virtually impossible to rouse the nobles again for common action in defense of the east. Crusading expeditions were, more than ever, considered in the west to be expensive and futile schemes. Eastern Europe and Hungary were therefore left alone to cope with the Turks as best they could.[55]

But the impression the defeat at Nicopolis made on the Byzantine mind was even graver. As we have seen, the *Chronicon maius* affirms that Bayazid, having discovered Manuel's negotiations with Sigismund, besieged the city by land and sea "for a long period." The

52. See Delaville Le Roulx, *La France en Orient,* p. 258.

53. "Sphrantzes," I, 14 (ed. Papadopulos, p. 65).

54. Zakythinos, *Despotat grec de Morée,* I (Paris, 1932), 156 ff.

55. Powerful Burgundy had connections with Byzantium even after Nicopolis. In 1421, duke Philip III the Good (and king Henry V of England) charged Gilbert of Lannoy with a mission to the east. In 1433 another Burgundian envoy, Bertrandon of La Broquière, went to the east, perhaps with reference to plans for a crusade. And in 1442, when the small flotilla of Geoffrey of Thoisy sailed to the east, an envoy of John VIII Palaeologus appeared at the Burgundian court to seek aid against the Turks. The Burgundian *Chronicle of Wavrin* (ed. and trans. Wm. and E. L. C. P. Hardy as *Recueil des chroniques...* [Rerum brittanicarum medii aevi scriptores, nos. 39, 40; 8 vols., London, 1864–1891]) affirms that Waleran and John of Wavrin had gone to Constantinople to aid the Greeks before the battle of Varna (1444). Also it is stated in the *Annales veneti* of Stefano Magno that 300 Burgundian

people within the city, according to Ducas, were so discouraged that many lost their courage and even began to show a tendency to betray their country to the Turks. Emperor Manuel now clutched at any straw, sending envoys to beg assistance at practically every court of the west. Bearing fresh appeals, his ambassadors appeared not only before the pope, the doge of Venice, and the kings of France, England, and Aragon,[56] but even before Basil I of Muscovy.[57] From some of these rulers Manuel collected money; from France in particular he had the hope of securing men-at-arms.[58] According to the French chronicler of St. Denis, Charles VI of France was particularly flattered because "it was the first time the ancient emperor of the world had appealed for help to such a remote country."[59] Charles, to be sure, refused to allow his brother Louis, the duke of Orleans, to go personally to aid the east, but implementing his pledge, he sent to Constantinople twelve hundred well-trained mercenaries, men who had little feeling for a crusade but were eager for booty. These were put under the command of marshal Boucicault, the valiant, chivalric survivor of Nicopolis, whose career and personality, especially his sincere lack of desire for personal aggrandizement, remind one of Amadeo VI of Savoy.[60] It is of interest that at this time Charles VI refused to buy the claim to the empire of Constantinople offered to him by Manuel's nephew and rival John VII, who wanted in exchange a castle in France and an annual income.[61]

Meanwhile pope Boniface IX had responded favorably to Manuel's pleas and in April 1398, and again in March 1399, preached a holy war against the "infidels." We can hardly describe this as a crusade,[62] for the western princes, discouraged and wholly occupied

---

soldiers went in 1445 to aid the despot Constantine in the Morea. See C. Marinescu, "Philippe le Bon duc de Bourgogne," in *Actes du VIe Congrès International d'Études Byzantines,* I (Paris, 1950), 152–162.

56. On Manuel's diplomacy see Delaville Le Roulx, *La France en Orient,* pp. 355–358. Cf. Ducas, I, 13 (*PG,* CLVII, col. 813).

57. *Nikonovskaya letopis,* in *Polnoe sobranie russkikh letopisei (Complete Collection of Russian Annals),* XI (1897), 168, as cited in A. Vasiliev, *Byzantine Empire,* II (1961), 632.

58. Delaville Le Roulx, *La France en Orient,* p. 363.

59. *Chronique de religieux de St. Dénis,* ed. Bellaguet, II, 562.

60. On Boucicault's expedition to Constantinople, see especially *Livre des faits du maréchal Boucicaut,* II, 205–232. Cf. Delaville Le Roulx, *La France en Orient,* pp. 359–375.

61. In 1397 Manuel sent his brother to Paris to appeal for aid, as Manuel mentions in his funeral oration on Theodore, referring to his brother's trip to England, France, and Italy (S. Lampros, "John Palaeologus . . ." [in Greek], *Neos Hellenomnemon,* X [1913], 248 ff.). Theodore Cantacuzenus, called "an uncle of the emperor," in 1398 went to ask aid of the king of France (Iorga, *Philippe de Mézières,* pp. 504–505).

62. Atiya, *Crusade in the Later Middle Ages,* p. 465.

with their own affairs, would not respond to the pope's appeal. Manuel's request to Moscow for help was supported by a patriarchal appeal as well. Though the Greek embassy was favorably received in Moscow, the Russian ruler, like most of the westerners, was not disposed to send men but only money, "granting alms," as he put it, "to those who are in such need and misery besieged by the Turks."[63]

Bayazid attempted to oppose the approach of marshal Boucicault and his French troops through the Dardanelles to Constantinople.[64] But Boucicault managed to reach the capital safely, to the great joy of the populace. Leaving his lieutenant John of Châteaumorand to protect the capital, Boucicault, together with Manuel and his Greek troops, made a number of attacks on the Turkish-held Asiatic coast of the Marmara and Bosporus areas, extending their patrols even into the Black Sea. But despite the considerable moral stimulus afforded the Greeks, the modest allied forces were insufficient to alter the situation radically. Boucicault therefore decided to return to France, but only after persuading his good friend Manuel to accompany him in order to lend the weight of his prestige to a new, personal attempt to induce the western rulers to take more decisive steps in his favor.

Leaving his son John in Constantinople to rule in his stead, and in the company of Boucicault, Manuel set out, on December 10, 1399, on his celebrated journey to the west.[65] His first stop was Venice, where he was magnificently received and where, like his successor John VIII, he probably viewed in St. Mark's the rich loot taken two centuries before, in 1204, from the altar of Hagia Sophia. Everywhere Manuel was paid honors and accorded lavish receptions, his bearing and noble demeanor deeply impressing all the westerners with whom he came in contact. In Paris he even participated in theological disputations with theologians of the university. In Paris also, perhaps at Boucicault's initiative, it seems to have been suggested that Manuel do homage to king Charles VI, as his vassal, and thereby receive the right at feudal law to French military aid; the

63. See note 57 above, *loc. cit.*

64. The Gattilusi, Genoese rulers of Lesbos, kept Bayazid informed as to Boucicault's movements (Delaville Le Roulx, *La France en Orient*, p. 365).

65. On Manuel's journey, see especially A. Vasiliev, "The Journey of the Byzantine Emperor Manuel II Palaeologus in Western Europe (1399–1402)" [in Russian], *Journal of the Ministry of Public Instruction*, n.s., XXXIX (1912), 47–78, 260–304; M. Jugie, "Le Voyage de l'empereur Manuel Paléologue en Occident (1399–1403), *Échos d'Orient*, XV (1912), 322–332; H. Luke, "Visitors from the East to the Plantagenet and Lancastrian Kings," *Nineteenth Century*, CVIII (1930), 760–769; and Barker, *Manuel II Palaeologus*, pp. 167–199. On John of Châteaumorand, see G. Schlumberger, *Byzance et Croisades: Pages médiévales* (Paris, 1927), pp. 84–147.

Venetians, Genoese, and Hospitallers of Rhodes are supposed to have seconded this proposal. But Charles does not seem to have acceded to this remarkable suggestion of a non-Latin emperor's swearing allegiance to a western king.[66]

Manuel was momentarily moved enough by the king of England's easy promises to write that "The king gives us help in warriors, marksmen, money, and vessels to carry the troops where we need."[67] But Manuel spoke too soon, for Henry IV was too busy consolidating his recently acquired throne to be of any real help. One Englishman, Adam of Usk, however, moved by the incongruity of Manuel's noble demeanor and his tragic plight, wrote, "How cruel it is that this great Christian prince from the distant East has been compelled by threats of the infidel . . . to supplicate for help against them. My God, where art thou, ancient glory of Rome!"[68] But Manuel's efforts accomplished little except to secure for him many vague, ultimately unfulfilled promises.[69]

After more than two years abroad Manuel was suddenly recalled home by the wonderful news of the annihilation of the Ottoman armies of Bayazid by Timur Lenk (the Lame) at the battle of Ankara on July 28, 1402.[70] This critical battle, which struck down Ottoman power and led to dynastic discord among Bayazid's sons, was to prolong the life of Byzantium for another half-century. Utter confusion reigned among the Ottomans, and for two decades they were unable to reorganize their forces to resume the attack on the Byzantines.

The Byzantines on their part, however, were unable to take full advantage of the unexpected respite afforded, in order to prepare a new crusade in collaboration with the west, which was at this time wholly distracted by the Great Schism in the Latin church. France, in particular, the traditional home of the crusaders, was rent by civil war. Moreover, Manuel's successes in promoting intrigues among the rivals to the Ottoman throne seem to have slaked whatever thirst he

66. Delaville Le Roulx, *La France en Orient,* 377–378; note the suggestion that Manuel hand the empire over to Charles, provided Manuel gets aid to guard the city.

67. *Lettres de Manuel Paléologue,* ed. E. Legrand, I (Paris, 1893), 52.

68. Adam of Usk, *Chronicon,* ed. E. M. Thompson (London, 1904), p. 57.

69. Almost the only real subsidy Manuel received was 3,000 marks from Richard II of England, which Richard had raised earlier to aid Constantinople (Delaville Le Roulx, *La France en Orient,* p. 382).

70. G. Roloff, "Die Schlacht bei Angora," *Historische Zeitschrift,* CLXI (1940), 244 ff. D. Cantemir, trans. N. Tindal, *History of the Growth and Decay of the Othman Empire* (London, 1734–1735), and Giorgio Stella, *Annales genuenses (RISS,* XVII), p. 1194, affirm that Manuel was in contact with Timur as a potential ally against the Turks, which is quite possible.

may have had for religious union with the Roman church. Consequently, from 1402 to 1417 he took no important action in the west.[71] Nor did he even send a special representative to the opening session of the Council of Pisa, although his trusted envoy-at-large, John Chrysoloras, was in the area; when Manuel II learned in 1409 that his Cretan-born friend Peter Philarges, who had been a professor at the University of Paris, and later archbishop of Milan,[72] had been chosen pope (Alexander V), he wrote him that he was sending John to Pisa.[73]

Manuel meanwhile recovered Thessalonica from the Turks, as well as a few other areas on the Aegean and Black seas. He also took measures to strengthen his empire internally. He went to Mistra, the capital of the Byzantine Morea, and rebuilt the Hexamilion, the wall across the isthmus of Corinth. The Greek forces in the Morea continued their long-lasting campaign against the Latins of the area, to be climaxed, ironically just before the fall of Constantinople in 1453, with the Byzantine seizure of practically all the Morea.[74]

Manuel wrote unceasingly to the princes of the west imploring aid—men, money, anything that could be spared. Thus he addressed two letters to the kings of Aragon, Martin I (1395–1410) and Ferdinand I (1412–1416). In the first, which was delivered by the famous Byzantine humanist Manuel Chrysoloras, the emperor wrote that at Martin's request he was sending some precious relics, and begged him to send to Constantinople the money collected in Spain to aid the Greek empire. In the second, Manuel appealed to Ferdinand to implement his previous promises to come to the aid of the despotate of the Morea against the Turks.[75]

More work must be done in the archives of western Europe before we know the full story of Manuel's many negotiations with the Latin rulers. One item that has usually been overlooked is the apparent intention of Alexander V to launch a crusade to save his compatriots in the east from the Turks. Evidence indicates that he at once sent a

---

71. L. Bréhier, in *Cambridge Medieval History* (1927 ed.), IV, 619.

72. Geanakoplos, *Byzantine East and Latin West,* pp. 153–154. Alexander V was the conciliar rival to the Roman pope Gregory XII (1406–1415) and the Avignonese Benedict XIII (1394–1423); his successor was John XXIII (1410–1415).

73. Letter in H. Simonsfeld, "Analekten zur Papst- und Konziliengeschichte im 14. und 15. Jahrhundert," *Abhandlungen der philosoph.-histor. Classe der bayer. Akad. der Wissen.,* XX (1893), 45–46.

74. Zakythinos, *Despotat grec de Morée,* I, 180 ff.

75. C. Marinescu, "Manuel II Paléologue et les rois d'Aragon," *Bull. de la section hist. de l'Acad. roumaine,* XI (1924), 194–195, 198–199. On Manuel's career, see Berger de Xivrey, "Mémoire sur la vie . . . de l'empereur Manuel Paléologue," *Mémoires de l'Académie des inscriptions et belles-lettres,* XIX-2 (Paris, 1853), 1–201, and Barker, *Manuel II Palaeologus,* with particular reference to these letters on pp. 183, 333–334.

deputation to Constantinople to discuss the question of union, a project always connected for the papacy, as we have seen, with the question of military aid to Byzantium.[76] But his disputed pontificate of less than a year was too brief to produce genuine results, though if any pope could have aided Constantinople in this it was he.

It should be noted that in the course of Manuel's many attempts to secure aid from the west he tried as much as possible to avoid the question of religious union. In Paris, to be sure, he debated publicly the question of the procession of the Holy Spirit from the Son (the *filioque*) with the most celebrated French theologians and acquitted himself well. But Manuel knew the dangers inherent in a proposal of union and preferred not to antagonize the west further by futile negotiation. If we can believe the account of the *Chronicon maius,* Manuel on his deathbed warned his son and successor, John VIII, not to consider the union as anything but a weapon against the Turks. "Always keep the light burning for union but never bring it to a conclusion. Propose a council, open negotiations, but protract them interminably. The pride of the Latins and the obstinacy of the Greeks will never agree. By wishing to achieve union you will only widen the schism."[77] Whether or not these words were actually uttered, they seem to characterize well the policy followed by Manuel toward the west.

With the accession of sultan Murad II the Byzantine breathing space was over and a period of Ottoman aggressiveness began. On June 8, 1422, Murad laid siege to Constantinople,[78] but his lack of a fleet and artillery saved the city. The last phase of the Byzantine death struggle had begun. In 1423, the Turks broke into southern Greece and destroyed the Hexamilion wall. The entire Morea was now devastated. Thessalonica was threatened in the summer of 1423. The despot Andronicus finally handed it over to Venice, which promised to defend the city while respecting the rights and customs of the people. After seven years of Venetian rule, however, the Turks under Murad seized Thessalonica in 1430.[79]

76. Sermon of John Gerson before the king of France, 1409, *Opera omnia,* II (Antwerp, 1706), col. 144: "[Petrus] . . . jam commisit legationem." F. Dölger, *Regesten,* part V, ad ann. 1409, p. 97, no. 3326. See Barker, *Manuel II Palaeologus,* p. 269, on Manuel's idea of a Christian league against the Turks after Ankara.

77. "Sphrantzes," II, 13 (ed. Papadopulos, p. 178). On its authenticity see above, note 49.

78. Account of the siege by John Cananus, in *PG,* CLVI, cols. 68–81. At this time pope Martin V, to aid Byzantium and negotiate union, sent the Franciscan Antonio of Massa as his legate to Constantinople (Barker, *Manuel II Palaeologus,* p. 327).

79. K. Mertzios, *Mnemeia Makedonikes historias* [in Greek] (Salonika, 1947), pp. 34 ff.; P. Lemerle, "La Domination vénitienne à Thessalonique," *Fontes Ambrosiani,* XXVI (=

Once the Turkish menace was renewed, Manuel II almost inevitably turned again to the papacy for aid. Thus in 1417, he sent to pope Martin V an embassy headed by Manuel Chrysoloras which appeared at the Council of Constance. And again with Murad II's siege of Constantinople in 1422, Manuel sent to the west his son and heir, the future John VIII. Accompanying the latter as interpreter was the emperor's secretary, the Italian humanist Francis Filelfo. The two visited successively Venice, Milan, and Hungary in order to negotiate for union and military aid.[80] Manuel was at the same time in contact with the western emperor Sigismund, who was one of the promoters of the Council of Constance.[81]

The new pope elected at this council, Martin V, was strongly in favor of union with the Greeks, and he made a series of conciliatory proposals that he thought would induce them to accept union. He even suggested that an ecumenical council take place in Italy, and, in 1423, went so far as to offer a large sum to the emperor to defray the expenses of the Greeks who would appear at the council. Showing an unexpected willingness to compromise, the pope, in 1425, authorized Latin-Greek mixed marriages, nominated a cardinal as his legate to Constantinople, and granted indulgences to anyone who would go east to aid Byzantium.[82] These concessions fitted in well with the terms the Greek east had long been demanding, especially the convocation of an ecumenical council. Nevertheless, the thought of concluding a religious union with Rome was probably far from Manuel's mind. He knew the temper of the Greeks regarding union and of course the attitude of the Turk, and therefore had to temporize.

In 1425 Manuel II died, a broken man suffering from epilepsy. His successor was his son John VIII, whose brothers Constantine and Theodore, ruling in the Black Sea area and the Morea, were virtually independent rulers. The dismembered empire was now nothing but a ruin.

Misc. G. Galbiati, III, Milan, 1951); G. Tsaras, ed., *Hioannou Anagnostou Diegesis peri tes teleutaias haloseos tes Thessalonikes* [in Greek] (Salonika, 1957).

80. C. Marinescu, "Deux empereurs byzantins en Occident: Manuel II et Jean VIII Paléologue," *Comptes-rendus de l'Académie des inscriptions et belles-lettres* (Paris), 1957, pp. 23–35.

81. On Sigismund see below, chapter XVII. On unionist matters then see also R. Loenertz, "Les Dominicains byzantins Théodore et André Chrysobergès et les négotiations pour l'union des églises grecques et latines de 1415 à 1430," *Archivum Fratrum Praedicatorum,* IX (1939), 12–15. S. Syropulus, *Vera historia unionis non verae inter Graecos et Latinos* (The Hague, 1660), pp. 8–9, refers to Sigismund's offer to make John his heir to the Holy Roman empire in return for healing the schism (cf. Barker, *Manuel Palaeologus,* p. 372).

82. Bréhier, in *Cambridge Medieval History* (1927 ed.), IV, 619. By now Manuel's power was so weak that he had to acknowledge himself tributary to the sultan.

Sentiment for an ecumenical council was inevitably growing in both east and west as a solution to more than the narrowly theological problem. After persistent papal refusal of a general council with the Greeks, the papacy finally, beginning with the pontificate of Martin V and especially that of his successor, Eugenius IV, more or less accepted the conditions insisted upon by the Greek clergy and people. At this point a new phase in the ecclesiastical relations of east and west may be said to have begun. Certain popes, to be sure, had earlier seemed to lean toward calling such a council, but they never gave it full support until their bitter enemies, the western conciliarists—who of course favored a council—forced the papacy's hand. For over a century many Greeks had insisted that an ecumenical council was the sole means of ending the schism between east and west: Barlaam perhaps the first,[83] then Nicephorus Gregoras, John Cantacuzenus, Joseph Bryennius, and others.[84] Even earlier than this, late in the thirteenth century, the Latin Humbert of Romans, who had himself lived in the east and knew intimately the Greek psychology, had proposed to the pope the calling of an ecumenical council in the east as the only solution.[85] With the decline of papal prestige in the west as a result of the Great Schism and of the increasing emphasis in responsible western quarters on the theory of a council's supremacy over the pope, the Greeks found support for their thesis. The popes were thus induced to view the Greek proposals in a more favorable light. One qualification was made, however, in acceding to the Greek demands—namely, that the council be held somewhere in the west, instead of in the east as the Greeks had been demanding.

But the situation between east and west had become very complex, in fact three-cornered. For besides the holy see and the Greeks, there was also involved the rival of the papacy, the conciliarist party sitting in council at Basel. The Byzantine emperor was now in the advantageous position of being courted by both pope Eugenius IV and the fathers of Basel,[86] each side trying to outbid the other in offering concessions to the Greeks—military aid for the capital and the payment of all expenses for the journey of the Greek delegation to the west. The emperor exchanged a series of embassies with both

83. Giannelli, "Un Projetto di Barlaam Calabro," p. 171.

84. See Viller, "La Question de l'union," *RHE*, XVIII, 20 ff., for these.

85. Mansi, *Concilia*, XXIV, col. 128. Quoted in Viller, *op. cit., RHE*, XVIII, 23, note 1: "Papa in Graeciam deberet descendere, si spes esset probabilis quod propter hoc reuniretur ovile."

86. On the preliminaries to Florence, see Geanakoplos, *Byzantine East and Latin West*, chap. 3, and especially the monograph of Gill, *Council of Florence*, with full bibliography.

parties, the Greeks for a time still insisting on the convocation of the council in beleaguered Constantinople. One of the western ambassadors, the pope's legate Christopher Garatoni, sent to Constantinople in 1434, in fact accepted the proposal to hold the council in the imperial capital, but the Council of Basel, through its envoy John of Ragusa, refused to agree to this.[87] Both western envoys returned again to Constantinople in order to bring back the Greek envoys, the tenor of whose instructions from the Greek emperor was to extract the broadest possible concessions. At Basel violence had in the meantime broken out over the choice of a site for the council—whether it should be held at Avignon, Florence, or Udine.

After some complex maneuvering—for a time it seemed that the Greeks would never make up their minds—the emperor finally chose to go to the papal rendezvous of Ferrara rather than to the cities selected by the conciliarists. Why did the Greeks prefer the papacy when their own tradition seems essentially conciliar in nature? One reason was the Greek insistence on the presence of the pope at the council, a prescription the fulfillment of which was unlikely at Basel. Then, geographically, the Greeks preferred the papal choice of Ferrara as the site for the council rather than more distant Basel, Avignon, or Savona. Moreover, the Greeks were more familiar with the traditional papal prestige than with the new phenomenon of western conciliarism, and indeed conciliarism as a movement soon proved to be ephemeral. Finally, we must not overlook the role of the Greek emperor himself; despite his somewhat decreasing power over the Greek church, in comparison with the rising power of the patriarch, he was still of great influence, and doubtless preferred to negotiate with a single absolute authority rather than the factious fathers at Basel.[88] According to the Greek historian Sylvester Syropulus, a factor which contributed to John's decision to go to the pope was his expectation of military aid from his colleague, the western emperor Sigismund, but Sigismund died at about this time. It is an irony of history that the Greek preference for the pope over the conciliarists was a major factor in the subsequent triumph of the pope over the western conciliarist movement.[89]

On November 24, 1437, the huge Byzantine delegation of seven hundred ecclesiastics and laymen, including emperor, patriarchs, and papal representatives, set out for Venice. At Venice, according to

87. John's report is found in E. Cecconi, *Studi storici* (Florence, 1869), pp. 487 ff., and that of Garatoni, *ibid.,* p. DLXXVII.
88. Geanakoplos, *Byzantine East and Latin West,* pp. 92–94.
89. Cf. Gill, *Council of Florence,* p. 411.

Syropulus's intimate account, the Greeks became emotional when they saw exhibited before them at St. Mark's the treasures of their cathedral of Hagia Sophia.[90] We need not discuss the questions of protocol which immediately arose between pope and patriarch and pope and emperor over the problems of kissing the pope's foot or the question of precedence in the seating in the cathderal.[91] Nor is this the place to discuss the complex theological and liturgical questions that were debated for over one and one-half years. We should note briefly, however, that on the most basic doctrinal question, that of the *filioque,* Greek conservatism opposed what might be termed the more flexible western attitude toward the problem of development in the doctrine and institution of the church. The Greeks insisted on absolute adherence to the doctrine and traditions of the first seven ecumenical councils, while the Latins equally insisted on the correctness of their addition to the original creed, the *filioque* clause. The fundamental anxiety of the Greeks, as Syropulus clearly implies, prejudiced as he is against the Latins, was the sometimes unconscious Greek fear of Latinization. As one Greek bishop at Florence insisted, "I prefer to die rather than ever to become Latinized."[92] This is one of the basic reasons why the Greeks, despite the clear implication that Constantinople would fall to the Turks without western aid, so intransigently opposed the western innovation to the creed. They feared not only that this would lead to loss of the independence of their church but that from this it would be a short step to political subjugation as well.[93] As Bryennius had said at the beginning of the fifteenth century to the Greeks of Constantinople, "Let no one be deceived by delusive hopes that Italian allied troops will come to save us. If they pretend to rise to defend us they will take arms only to destroy our city, our faith, and our name."[94]

Some Greeks, especially among the upper classes (and possibly under the influence of Greek translations of Latin scholastic works, especially of Thomas Aquinas), were ready to accept union as a lesser evil than Islamization. On the other hand some anti-unionists had become so extreme in their fear of Latin penetration that they openly declared their preference for the "turban of the Turk to the tiara of the pope." The supposedly enlightened humanist Petrarch

90. Syropulus, *Vera historia,* pp. 80 ff., especially p. 87.

91. See Geanakoplos, *Byzantine East and Latin West,* pp. 95–96.

92. *Acta graeca,* ed. J. Gill (Rome, 1953), p. 400.

93. On this problem of Latinization see Geanakoplos, *Byzantine East and Latin West,* pp. 104–107, especially notes 81 and 84.

94. Quoted, *ibid.,* p. 106.

himself had said in 1366, "The Turks are our enemies but the Greeks are schismatics and worse than enemies. They hate us in their guts."[95]   And John Gerson, chancellor of the University of Paris, in an address to the king of France delivered shortly after the Council of Pisa (1409), had affirmed that the Greeks "prefer the Turks to the Latins."[96]

This Greek feeling of ethnic difference from the Latins had of course already been manifested even before the eleventh century. But the movement of the crusades with the accompanying western aggressions against the Greeks had transformed it into a sharp hostility, even an implacable hatred for the Latins. Thus the question of the *filioque,* so bitterly debated at Florence, may be said in one sense to have masked the underlying antagonism of Greeks and Latins for each other. To many Orthodox, submission to papal authority meant the prelude to assimilation by the Latins. As George Scholarius, only a few years later, was in effect to say to those Greeks who inclined toward the west, "By accepting the union you will submit yourselves to shame and the Latin church, and God's punishment through the Turks will not be averted."[97]

As the deliberations proceeded the Greek emperor took special care that the theological discussions would not push into the background the plan for a crusade to save Constantinople. The pope on his part pledged to preach a crusade for Constantinople's defense, to maintain a permanent force of three hundred men as a guard at Constantinople, and to supply galleys in the event of a siege. In the meantime, after long, repetitious, and heated arguments, the Greeks, influenced by the ever-deteriorating military situation of Constantinople and the persuasiveness of the emperor and the pope, surrendered. The pope won on all the major points at issue, though the important question of papal supremacy was solved by a kind of compromise, a marvelously ambiguous definition proposed by the Greek unionist Bessarion to the effect that while the universal authority of the pope was recognized in his capacity as the "vicar of Christ," at the same time the "rights and privileges of the eastern patriarchs were reserved."[98]

95. Ducas, 37 (*CSHB,* p. 264); Petrarch, *Lettere senili,* ed. G. Fracassetti, I (Florence, 1869), 422–424.

96. A. Galitzin, *Sermon inédit de Jean Gerson sur le retour des grecs a l'unité* (Paris, 1859), p. 29; cf. Manuel Calecas, IV (*PG,* CLII, col. 239).

97. A. Demetrakopoulos, *Historia schismatis quod intercedit inter ecclesiam occidentalem et orientalem* (Leipzig, 1867), pp. 163 ff. Cf. Geanakoplos, *Greek Scholars in Venice* (Cambridge, 1962), p. 77, and I. Ševčenko, "Intellectual Repercussions of the Council of Florence," *Church History,* XXIV (1955), 294, quoting Ubertino Puscolo.

98. *Acta graeca,* ed. Gill, p. 464 (Mansi, *Concilia,* XXXIA, col. 1032); Syropulus, *Vera*

At the council the Greeks had finally been able to debate openly with the Latins and Mark of Ephesus, the most obdurate, to bring his objections into the open. It seemed that at last after centuries of schism and so many false starts regarding union, Christendom was once more to be united and would now be able to devote itself to the long-wished-for crusade against the Turk. But the people of Constantinople, on whom in the last analysis the success of union depended, had yet to make themselves heard.

When the delegates sailed into the Golden Horn the city was in an uproar against them. Ducas tells us that the population of the capital greeted them with insults and cries of betrayal of the Orthodox faith.[99] The people based their opposition to union on the belief that the Greek representatives had signed only under duress, that the military aid agreed to by the pope, like previous promises, would be ineffectual—as one person rather logically emphasized, "If the pope has been unable to aid the Latin states in the east how can the Latin princes aid Constantinople?"[100] —and, finally, on the conviction that the Byzantine people themselves would suffer the "judgment of God" if the purity of the faith were altered. The Greek legates, on their part, maintained that they had been coerced into signing the document of union. A veritable rebellion broke out led by the monks, especially Mark of Ephesus, who for many became the hero of the hour, the focus of anti-Latin resistance. On his side were ranged the monks of Constantinople and Mount Athos, all of whom refused to communicate with the unionists. The expected crusade from the west did not materialize and the tremendous exertions of the Greek politicians to save Constantinople by bowing to Rome were a failure.[101]

The direct effect of the council on the question of the crusade was minimal. Before the council began its actual discussions the Greek emperor had insisted on postponement of deliberations until the expected arrival of the western lay princes or their representatives. For him overriding all other considerations was the defense of Constantinople and therefore, more forcefully than ever, he adhered to the old Byzantine principle of aid first and ecclesiastical union later. It was a matter of profound disillusionment for John, however,

---

historia, pp. 293 ff.; cf. Geanakoplos, "Edward Gibbon and Byzantine Ecclesiastical History," *Church History,* XXXV (1966), 179, and *Byzantine East and Latin West,* p. 108.

99. Ducas, 31 (*CSHB,* p. 216).

100. Geanakoplos, *Byzantine East and Latin West,* p. 111, notes 113 and 109.

101. "Sphrantzes," II, 13 (ed. Papadopulos, pp. 178–180); Ducas, 37 (*CSHB,* pp. 259–260); Marcus Eugenicus (Mark of Ephesus), ed. L. Petit in *Patrologia orientalis,* XVII (1923), 456.

that in the end, except for duke Philip of Burgundy, no secular prince sent representatives to Florence. That no considerable aid could be expected even from Burgundy must have been evident to the emperor from the attitude of the Burgundian envoys, who on their arrival approached the pope and in the prescribed papal protocol kissed his right knee, while completely ignoring the Greek emperor. John was so chagrined that he refused to continue at the council unless he was properly saluted. [102]

In the meantime Murad II, who had been watching the Florentine negotiations with more than a little interest, was told by the Greek emperor that the *pourparlers* were purely religious in character. We may be sure, however, that the sultan fully understood the political implications involved. Pope Eugenius attempted to implement his promise to aid Byzantium by issuing bulls directing the preaching of a crusade, by imposing a tithe upon the whole church to be paid as quickly as possible, and by assigning part of his own income for the raising of an army and fleet.[103] But the western powers were still in no position to lend aid. France and England were at each other's throats in the very climax of the Hundred Years' War, there was strife over the succession to the western imperial throne, and the selfishness of the Italian mercantile states remained stronger than ever.

The only nations to respond to the papal appeal for a crusade were the Balkan peoples who now found themselves directly in the path of the Ottoman advance: the Poles, the Rumanians, and especially the Hungarians. [104] Advancing against the Turks the voivode of Transylvania, John (Corvinus) Hunyadi, managed to secure some minor victories. And soon, after making considerable preparations, a motley force of some twenty to twenty-five thousand men was assembled in southern Hungary under three rulers, king Vladislav III of Poland and Hungary, the voivode Hunyadi, and the Serbian ruler George Brankovich. Advancing, the allied army managed to defeat the Turks in 1444 on the heights above Nish in Serbia. On June 12 of the same year, however, a truce of ten years was signed at Adrianople between Hungary and sultan Murad II, apparently without the knowledge of the papal legate cardinal Julian Cesarini. Upon being apprised of the treaty cardinal Cesarini, who was then with the crusading army, absolved king Vladislav of his oath to the "infidel." By September of 1444 the crusading army was again on the march.

---

102. Syropulus, *Vera historia*, pp. 175–177; cf. *Acta graeca* (ed. Gill), pp. 212–213.

103. Gill, *Council of Florence*, pp. 328–329.

104. Atiya, *Crusade in the Later Middle Ages*, p. 467; Gill, *Council of Florence*, pp. 332–333.

Intending to follow the Black Sea coastline to Constantinople and expecting promised Venetian naval aid, which did not arrive, the army was weakened by the defection of the Serbian ruler Brankovich, who was evidently satisfied by the ten-year agreement. The Turks, enraged by the breaking of the pact, in turn moved rapidly against the Christians and on November 10, 1444, annihilated the crusading armies at the famous battle of Varna. [105]

The defeat at Varna meant the beginning of the end for Constantinople as well as for the Latin union with the Greeks, for there was little chance that any pope for many years could again mount such a large crusading expedition. The Turks had shattered the last Christian attempt at concerted action against them, the result being that Constantinople was more than ever exposed to attack. The Balkan Christians were in despair, and the Byzantine emperor had even to welcome the victorious Murad back with congratulations and gifts.[106]

Before the battle of Varna the Greek emperor had learned of the treaty signed between Murad and the Hungarian crusaders, probably through the Italian archaeologist Cyriac of Ancona, who was then traveling in the area. The emperor had evidently even been convinced by Cyriac that the Greeks should at least indirectly intervene in the campaign. [107] John himself seems to have gone, in strictest secrecy, to Mistra, in the despotate of Morea; thence, before the battle of Varna, he probably sent a letter to king Vladislav in which he appealed to him not to disappoint the hopes of the east by making peace with the Turks and abandoning the plans for a proposed crusade, thus leaving the Greeks in a very risky position. [108] Though

105. On the confused sequence of events of the Varna crusade, see also letters of the humanist Cyriac of Ancona, in F. Pall, "Ciriaco d'Ancona e la crociata contro i Turchi," *Bull. de la section hist. de l'Acad. roumaine*, XX (1938), 9–68, and Pall, "Autour de la croisade de Varna," *ibid.*, XXII (1941), 144 ff.; O. Halecki, *The Crusade of Varna* (New York, 1943), pp. 25–26; F. Pall, "Un Moment décisif de l'histoire du sud-est européen: la croisade de Varna," *Balcania,* VII (1944), 102 ff.; and F. Babinger, "Von Amurath zu Amurath: Vor- und Nachspiel der Schlacht bei Varna," *Oriens,* III (1950), 229 ff.

106. On the battle of Varna there is a poem written in Greek by Zoticus, a Greek witness to the battle; see K. Krumbacher, *Geschichte der byzantinischen Literatur* (2nd ed., Munich, 1897; repr. New York, 1958), p. 832; and N. G. Svoronos, "To peri tes maches tes Varnes poiema" [in Greek], *Athena,* XLVIII, 163–183; cf. A. Turyn, *Byzantine Ms. Tradition of Euripides,* pp. 390–391. Text in G. Moravcsik, *Görög Költemény a Varnai Csatáról* (Budapest, 1935); see especially p. 24, lines 140 ff.

107. See above, note 105.

108. See Ostrogorsky, *Byzantine State,* p. 503, note 1, on the question of whether a peace treaty was signed. Ubertino Puscolo, a contemporary Italian living in Constantinople, says the grand admiral of Constantinople, Lucas Notaras, believed Vladislav's crusaders were more interested in conquering Byzantine lands than in liberating the Greeks (Puscolo, *Constantinopolis,* ed. A. Ellissen, I, 464–491, 518–520, in *Analekten der mittel- und neugriechischen Literatur,* III [Leipzig, 1857]; cf. Halecki, *Crusade of Varna,* pp. 26 ff.).

the authenticity of this letter has recently been cast into doubt, it seems clear that if John VIII had in fact planned to aid the crusading armies he could have best done so from the Morea rather than from Constantinople, which was then tightly encircled by Turkish territory.

Without awaiting the crusaders' arrival, the Greek military forces had moved from the Morea, attacking the Turks and gaining several successes. Byzantine hopes in Constantinople were raised by the arrival of an allied crusader-fleet of twenty-four Venetian, papal, and Burgundian ships mobilized in the summer of 1444 and joined by two Byzantine galleys but not including the ships promised by the duke of Milan and king Alfonso V of Aragon. The fleet remained for about a year and then sailed back to the west, leaving behind only the Burgundian ships to defend the city.[109] It is curious how little reference there is in the Greek polemical literature of the time to the campaign at Varna. Perhaps the Greek anti-unionists did not wish to emphasize the papal efforts or were so immersed in their own squabbles that they thought the Latins, as usual, would provide little aid. [110]

Hunyadi made one more desperate attempt to come to the aid of Constantinople, but he was defeated at the (second) battle of Kossovo in October 1448, largely because of the treachery of the Wallachians, who went over to the Turks. But it was not only the hostility of the Byzantine people to religious union which militated against more western aid for Constantinople. Effective coöperation on the part of the western states themselves was difficult, as we have seen, because of their conflicting interests and the ambitions of western monarchs.

Some justification for the suspicions of the Byzantines as to the motives of the Latins, so often expressed in the polemical and historical literature of the period, is clearly seen in the aspirations of king Alfonso V of Aragon and Naples. In regard to Byzantium, this most powerful prince of the Mediterranean was motivated by the same aggressive designs as were his Norman predecessors in Sicily. True, his aim was to wage a vast campaign in the east against the Turks, but it was not to aid the Greeks but rather to reëstablish the old Latin empire with himself as emperor. [111] His grandiose schemes were never realized, but they deprived the humanist pope, Nicholas

109. Grunzeweig, "Philippe le Bon et Constantinople," pp. 47–61.
110. Bertrandon of La Broquière, the traveler who visited the east in 1432, opined (ed. T. Wright, p. 366) that it would be easy to defeat the Turks, but that the Greeks, having suffered long from crusaders, soldiers, merchants, and clergy, could not trust the Latins.
111. Cerone, "La Politica orientale di Alfonso di Aragona."

V, who was sympathetic to the Greeks, of some much-needed resources just before and after Constantinople's conquest. [112] After
the Slavic-western alliance had been defeated at Varna, the anti-
unionist Greeks could point the finger of scorn at the Greek unionists and ask how much western help was really worth.

The disaster and disappointment of Kossovo hastened the end of
emperor John VIII, who died October 31, 1448. He was succeeded
by his younger brother Constantine, despot of the Morea, who had
managed to aggrandize the Greek territory in the Morea at the
expense of the Latins and even to win several battles against the
Turks. But Constantine XI, a worthy successor to his original namesake, had the misfortune of being opposed by a terrible adversary,
the youthful sultan Mehmed II, whose obsession it had become to
seize at any price the imperial city of Constantinople. It is not our
intention to narrate the details of what was to be the most famous
siege in history. We shall concentrate rather on the western attempts
to aid beleaguered Constantinople within the framework of crusading
ideology.

Constantine, realizing the religious sensitivity of his subjects, followed a moderate policy and at first avoided coming openly into
contact with the west. Thus, under Greek anti-unionist pressure, he
tolerated the deposition, or rather removal from his throne, of the
unionist patriarch Gregory II Mammas in 1451. [113] But after 1451,
when Mehmed succeeded the more pacific sultan Murad, Constantine
felt he could no longer continue his isolation from the west. In the
spring of the same year Constantine sent a special envoy to Rome,
but the papal answer was as much discouraging as cynical: "Now
pursuing political projects, you are willing to apply for the holy
union but know that a bad intention is punished by destruction from
God." [114] The climate of opinion in Constantinople turned violently
against any support for union. Conflict broke out in the streets,
placards were posted everywhere by the new leaders of the anti-

112. C. Marinescu, "Le Pape Nicolas V et son attitude envers l'empire byzantin," *Bull. de
l'Institut archéologique bulgarien,* IX (1935), 331 ff. Also R. Guilland, "Ai pros ten dysin
ekklesis Konstantinou" [in Greek], XI, *Epeteris hetaireias Byzantinon spoudon,* XXII
(1952), 60 ff.

113. It has been shown that the synod supposedly convoked in 1450–1451 is only a
fiction; see *Religious and Ethical Encyclopedia* [in Greek], (Athens, 1964), IV, 735. Also
cf. *Tusculum Lexicon,* ed. W. Buchwald, S. Hollweg, and O. Prinz (Munich, 1963), citing the
date 1451.

114. Letter in G. Hofmann *et al.,* eds., *Concilium florentinum: Documenta . . . ,* ser. A,
III (Rome, 1953), 135–138.

unionists, and the fiery George Scholarius proclaimed the "judgment of God" if the people accepted the union. [115]

Meanwhile the pope, increasingly disturbed at the reception of the union in Constantinople, declared that military aid depended on acceptance of two terms: official recognition of papal supremacy, and restoration of the deposed unionist patriarch Gregory. He said nothing about dogmatic questions, which he considered either too ticklish or, more probably, now of secondary importance. Constantine, not without reason, hesitated to accept the papal terms and instead tried to convince other western princes to intervene in order to rescue Constantinople. He appealed successively to practically all western rulers, to the doge of Venice Francis Foscari, whose daughter he had negotiated to marry (Constantine broke off the attempt because of the opposition of his Greek subjects), to the duke of Milan Francis Sforza, to the French king Charles VII, to the duke of Burgundy Philip the Good, to the German emperor Frederick III, to the king of Aragon and Naples Alfonso V, to the government of Genoa, and to the king of Hungary Ladislas (László V). But the results again were only some kind letters expressing sympathy. [116] Finally Constantine, anxiously observing Mehmed's massing of troops around his capital, yielded to the pope and requested the dispatch of a capable legate who could make the union acceptable to the Greek clergy. The pope sent Isidore, former metropolitan of Kiev, and a Greek himself, who entered into negotiations with the anti-unionists, lavished promises and made threats, and ended by winning over part of the higher clergy. Among those who sided with Isidore were a circle of intellectuals including humanists like John Argyropulus, Michael Apostolius, and the learned monk Isaac, all of whom later became important for the dissemination of Greek learning to Renaissance Italy.[117] According to the historian Ducas a number of Greek priests joined the pro-unionist party. [118] A part of the population, until then opposed to union, now also followed the example of the emperor. This is interesting because the union of 1452 is generally portrayed as lacking all popular support—a view evidently not corroborated by the sources. Submission of this group was aided by a promise of future revision of the terms of union. When pressed by the reproaches of the uncompromising anti-unionists, the new unionists, who were generally motivated only by expe-

115. Gill, *Council of Florence,* pp. 383 ff.; Pears, *Destruction of the Greek Empire,* p. 204.

116. R. Guilland, "Ai pros ten dysin ekklesis Konstantinou," pp. 60–74.

117. Geanakoplos, *Greek Scholars in Venice,* pp. 78–79.

118. Ducas, 36 (*CSHB,* p. 253).

diency, answered, "Wait until God shall have delivered the city from the great dragon who seeks to devour us. Then you will see whether we are truly reconciled with the Azymites [Latins]."[119] Others in Constantinople said that they preferred to hand over the city to the Latins, who at least believed in Christ and the Blessed Virgin Mary. To these the grand admiral Lucas Notaras gave answer with his now famous words: "Better to see in the city the Turkish turban than the Latin tiara."[120]

At the eleventh hour several western monarchs seemed to conclude that they might do something more to aid Byzantium than write sympathetic letters to its emperor. Thus it is known that emperor Frederick III of Germany in 1453 sent to sultan Mehmed II a bombastic letter in the form of an ultimatum, ordering Mehmed to leave Constantinople, which he had already begun to besiege. [121] And in 1453 Hunyadi and Ladislas V of Hungary sent a letter to the pope indicating that they were now ready to take part in a crusade against the Turks.[122]

Venice at this critical hour in Byzantium's history finally broke off relations with the Turks. She made some attempt to coöperate with the pope and openly with the Greeks by arming a small fleet which she intended to send to Constantinople. But when it was ready it came too late to be of any use. In the hope that Mehmed II would not harass its colony at Galata, Genoa made no effort to aid the Greeks, though the Genoese lord of Lesbos, John Giustiniani, in contrast, made a personal contribution to Constantinople's defense of a 700-man force, two ships, and finally his own life. [123] The only official contingent of papal-financed troops that actually participated in the defense of Constantinople seems to have been the 200 archers from Crete that went to Constantinople with the papal legate cardinal Isidore.[124]

When Isidore arrived at Constantinople on October 26, 1452,

119. Ducas, 36 (*CSHB*, p. 256). Scholarius, ed. L. Petit, X. A. Siderides, and M. Jugie, *Oeuvres complètes* (8 vols., Paris, 1928–1936), III, 173, 177, 184; Puscolo, *Constantinopolis,* III, 654 f., 668 f., 723, 729 ff.

120. Ducas, 37 (*CSHB*, p. 264).

121. Gill, *Council of Florence,* p. 382; Guilland, "Ai pros ten dysin ekklesis Konstantinou," pp. 60 ff.

122. On Hunyadi and Ladislas, see R. Guilland, "Les Appels de Constantin XI Paléologue à Rome et à Venise," *Byzantinoslavica,* XIV (1953), 226–244.

123. On the actions of the Greek emperor and Giustiniani see, in *Le Cinq-centième anniversaire,* G. Kolias, "Constantin Paléologue, le dernier défenseur de Constantinople," pp. 41–54; and K. Amantos, "La Prise de Constantinople," pp. 9–22; also D. Zakythinos, "Ideological Conflicts in Besieged Constantinople" [in Greek] *Nea Hestia,* XLVIII (1950), 749–799.

124. Gill, *Council of Florence,* p. 383. On Cretans who aided in the siege of 1453 see M.

Mehmed was already preparing for the siege. Isidore's presence and propaganda disconcerted the anti-unionists and they rushed to the cell to which their leader George Scholarius had retired, to ask his advice. His answer, put in writing, was that they should depend on help only from God, not the Franks. What the anti-unionists had tried to prevent now came to pass. On December 12, 1452, a solemn liturgy celebrating the union was held in Hagia Sophia, before the officials and the people, with the reading of the Florentine decree of union and the commemoration of the pope and the (exiled) unionist patriarch Gregory in the diptychs. [125] Scholarius and others took no part in the ceremony. This act produced an explosion of fanaticism and agitation among the population of the city, so much so in fact that all or most of the Greeks deserted their cathedral, refusing to attend any further services there as if it were polluted. [126] They then rushed to Scholarius's cell to seek his reaction, only to see a placard he had put there: "Oh miserable Romans . . . why have you abandoned the truth and why . . . have you trusted in the Italians? In losing your faith you will lose your city." On the day of the proclamation of union many worshipers in the cathedral refused to take the *antidoron* (holy bread) as a sign of disapproval. Scholarius's manifesto was posted everywhere in the city, and a riot followed. The devout Orthodox besought aid from the Virgin against the Turks, recalling how in centuries past she had saved them from the Persians, the Arabs, and the Slavs. [127]

It would seem that Scholarius and his circle preferred to surrender to the Turks while remaining faithful to Orthodoxy, rather than to defend the city with Latin help. And prophecies were quoted which predicted the inevitability of the city's fall. But Constantine had other ideas as to his duty and honor. Thus while the Turks besieged Constantinople, the emperor had to face almost a kind of fifth column which undermined the defense of the city by spreading defeatism. [128] Leonard of Chios, the Catholic archbishop of Myti-

---

Manousakas, "Les Derniers défenseurs Crétois de Constantinople d'après les documents vénitiens," *Actes des XL. Byz. Kongress 1958* (Munich, 1960), pp. 331 ff.; these Cretans were inspired by Greek patriotism. Also see N. Tomadakes, *On the Capture of Constantinople* [in Greek] (Athens, 1953), p. 145, note 2, and R. Browning, "A Note on the Capture of Constantinople," *Byzantion*, XXII (1952), 379–386; cf. Gill, *Council of Florence*, p. 383.

125. The failure at Varna was evidently the turning point for John VIII, who adopted a moderate attitude to the anti-unionists though keeping Gregory on the patriarchal throne.

126. Ducas, 36 (*CSHB*, pp. 252–253).

127. Ducas, 36 (*CSHB*, pp. 253–254).

128. Ducas, *loc. cit.;* cf. K. N. Sathas, ed., *Mesaionike bibliotheke*, VII (Paris, 1894), v; Scholarius, IV, 217.

lene, who took part in the city's defense, informs us that during the
siege the people of Constantinople were divided into two opposed
camps, those who followed the emperor, and the partisans of Scholarius, who refused to fight the Turks. [129] But Constantine continued
the hopeless struggle, steadfastly opposing the Turks until the last
moment of the siege. Abandoned by western Europe and even by a
part of his own people, Constantine fought bravely in the streets
until his death, as the Turks poured through the gates of the last
bastion of the thousand-year-old empire. The empire had finally
fallen and the crescent banner now waved above Constantinople's
walls.

In the centuries-long duel between Christendom and Islam, the fall
of Constantinople may in one sense be taken as marking the end of
the great movement of the medieval crusades. It is in fact evidence of
the inflexible persistence of the original crusading ideal. For instead
of saving eastern Christendom from the Moslems, the western crusades, despite repeated expressions of immense concern, did virtually
nothing to help avert the final destruction of the eastern Christians'
principal bastion, Constantinople. Despite centuries of ecclesiastical
and political negotiations, of ambitious plans partially fulfilled or
more often completely rejected, the Greek and Latin halves of
Christendom were never able to coöperate successfully with each
other. And it is this lack of coöperation, based essentially on an
inability or even a refusal to understand each other's needs and
mentality, that was in large part responsible for the failure of the
crusading movement to respond effectively to the Turkish threat.
For in the last analysis, though the popes in the latter part of the
fourteenth century were able, finally, to transmute the original
purpose of the crusade from reconquering the Holy Land to rescuing
Constantinople from the Turk, most westerners were unable to
accept this shift in emphasis. Nor, on the Byzantine side, were the
Greeks as a whole willing to believe that the west would come to save
them except to reimpose Latin hegemony in the guise of a new
crusade. If, as many western leaders must increasingly have come to
think, the Christian Greeks themselves would rather see in Constantinople the Turkish turban than the Latin tiara, why should they
launch a crusade to save Byzantium?

129. Leonard of Chios, *Historia,* in *PG,* CLIX, col. 926.

IV

THE MOREA, 1311–1364

By the two treaties of Viterbo (May 1267) Charles I of Anjou had obtained the legal basis for the predominance of his house in the affairs of the remaining Latin states in Greece. The death of William of Villehardouin in 1278 without a male heir had left Charles prince of Achaea. King of Sicily and claimant to the throne of Jerusalem, Charles was also king of Albania, and this mountainous land at the western end of the Via Egnatia, together with the flourishing principality of the Villehardouins, was the base for the great *Drang nach Osten* whose aim had been the recapture first of Constantinople and later of Jerusalem. The Sicilian Vespers had, however, ruined these plans and involved the Angevins in a long war with the Aragonese in Sicily.

To a considerable extent this and the succeeding chapter are based on published sources already cited in the opening note to chapter VII of volume II of this work, pp. 235–236. Of these sources, we cite here those that are indispensable for chapters IV and V, together with a number of works bearing directly or indirectly on the Morea and Latin Greece in the fourteenth and fifteenth centuries. We also cite certain periodical articles based on research in Mediterranean archives and presenting new evidence or interpretations. Most of the publications mentioned in this note appear in the extensive bibliography to chapter IX, "The Latins in Greece and the Aegean from the Fourth Crusade to the End of the Middle Ages," by K. M. Setton, in *The Cambridge Medieval History*, IV-I (1966 ed.), 908–938.

For the connections of the principality of Achaea with the kingdom of Naples see the documents in Ch. Perrat and J. Longnon, eds., *Actes relatifs à la principauté de Morée 1289–1300* (Paris, 1967, Collection de documents inédits sur l'histoire de France, 8° ser., vol. 6); these charters were copied from the Angevin registers of Naples before their destruction in 1943. The *Chronicle of the Morea* is a most valuable source despite numerous errors of fact. The French version is cited in the edition of Longnon, *Livre de la conqueste de la princée de l'Amorée: Chronique de Morée (1204–1305)* (Paris, 1911); the Greek version in that of J. Schmitt, *The Chronicle of Morea: To chronikon tou Moreōs* (London, 1904); and the Aragonese in that of A. Morel-Fatio, *Libro de los fechos et conquistas del principado de la Morea* ... (Geneva, 1885). The Greek version has been translated by H. Lurier, *Crusaders as Conquerors: The Chronicle of Morea* (New York and London, 1964; [Columbia University] Records of Civilization: Sources and Studies, LXIX). On the question of the original chronicle and the relationship of the versions to one another see, besides Lurier's introduction, especially D. Jacoby, "Quelques considérations sur les versions de la 'Chronique de Morée'," *Journal des savants*, July–September 1968, pp. 133–189, and the articles of G. Spadaro, "Studi introduttivi alla Cronaca di Morea," *Siculorum gymnasium*, n.s., XII (1959), 125–152, XIII (1960), 133–176, and XIV (1961), 1–70; also cf. review by P. Topping in *Speculum,* XL (1965), 737–742, and A. Luttrell, "Greek Histories Translated

Charles II of Anjou had been willing that Isabel of Villehardouin, William's elder daughter, should rule Achaea as his vassal following her marriage in 1289 to her second husband, Florent of Hainault. But the restoration of the Morea to the Villehardouins was "by pure liberality and special grace," and on the pretext that she had not sought his permission to marry her third husband, Philip of Savoy,

---

and Compiled for Juan Fernández de Heredia . . . ," *Speculum,* XXXV (1960), 406 and note 36.

The code of feudal Achaea was edited by G. Recoura, *Les Assises de Romanie* (Bibliothèque de l'École des hautes études, fasc. 258; Paris, 1930), English translation with commentary by Topping, *Feudal Institutions as Revealed in the Assizes of Romania, the Law Code of Frankish Greece* (Translations and Reprints from the Original Sources of History, 3rd ser., vol. III; Philadelphia, 1949). For all questions concerning the Assizes and the feudal law of the Latin states see above all Jacoby, *La Féodalité en Grèce médiévale: Les "Assises de Romanie": Sources, application et diffusion* (Paris and The Hague, 1971; École pratique des hautes études, VIe sect., Documents et recherches . . . , X). C. Hopf, *Chroniques gréco-romanes inédites ou peu connues* (Berlin, 1873) contains chronicle sources and documents on the principality of Achaea; its genealogical tables badly need correction and revision. Of the many works of J. A. C. Buchon on Frankish Greece, the *Nouvelles recherches historiques sur la principauté française de Morée et ses hautes baronnies* (2 vols., Paris, 1843 [1845 in some copies]) has greatest value for the present chapters. The sources on the Acciajuoli in Greece are cited in Setton, *Catalan Domination of Athens 1311-1388* (Cambridge, Mass., 1948), pp. 66-68.

Valuable documents or summaries thereof relating to Achaea from 1311 to 1432, especially to its external relations, are to be found in the following editions: R. Predelli and P. Bosmin, *I Libri commemoriali della republica di Venezia: Regesti* (8 vols., Venice, 1876-1914); C. N. Sathas, *Documents inédits relatifs à l'histoire de la Grèce au moyen âge* (9 vols., Paris, 1880-1890); O. Raynaldus (Rinaldi), *Annales ecclesiastici ab anno 1198* (15 vols., Lucca, 1747-1756); N. Iorga, *Notes et extraits pour servir à l'histoire des croisades au XVe siecle* (6 vols., Paris and Bucharest, 1899-1916); A. Rubió i Lluch, *Diplomatari de l'Orient català (1301-1409)* (Barcelona, 1947); and in the monumental series, *Lettres des papes du XIVe siècle* (Paris, 1900 ff., 3rd ser. of the *Bibliothèque des Écoles françaises d'Athènes et de Rome).* On this series, and on other editions of papal correspondence, see Setton in *Catalan Domination,* pp. 273-274, and *Cambridge Medieval History* IV-I (1966 ed.), 911.

Byzantine historians relevant to the present chapters are Nicephorus Gregoras, *Historia byzantina,* ed. L. Schopen and I. Bekker (*CSHB,* 3 vols., Bonn, 1829-1855); John Cantacuzenus, *Historiarum libri IV,* ed. Schopen (*CSHB,* 3 vols., Bonn, 1828-1832); Laonicus Chalcocondylas, *Historiarum demonstrationes,* ed. E. Darkó (2 vols. in 3, Budapest, 1922-1927); Ducas, *Historia byzantina* (ed. I. Bekker, *CSHB,* Bonn, 1834; ed. V. Grecu as *Historia turcobyzantina (1341-1462)* [Scriptores byzantini, I; Bucharest, 1958]); and George Sphrantzes, *Memorii, 1401-1477,* ed. Grecu (Scriptores byzantini, V; Bucharest, 1966).

Among secondary works, that of Ch. Du Cange still must be consulted on the affairs of Achaea: *Histoire de l'empire de Constantinople sous les empereurs français* . . . (Paris, 1657; 2nd edition, ed. J. A. C. Buchon, 2 vols., Paris, 1826). The massive work of Hopf, "Geschichte Griechenlands vom Beginn des Mittelalters bis auf unsere Zeit," in J. S. Ersch and J. G. Gruber, eds., *Allgemeine Encycklopädie der Wissenschaften und Künste,* vols. LXXXV and LXXXVI (Leipzig, 1867-1868; repr. New York, 1960), has considerable value for the history of the principality, especially because of its numerous citations from the now-destroyed Angevin registers; Hopf's statements and references must, however, be closely checked whenever possible. Important later accounts are W. Miller, *The Latins in the*

Charles in 1304 declared Isabel and her third consort deposed. In reality Charles was acting to put his second son Philip, prince of Taranto, into actual possession of the Morea. Already in 1294 he had transferred to this son his rights as suzerain over the principality of Achaea, the duchies of Athens and of the Archipelago, the kingdom of Albania, and the province of Vlachia (Thessaly). Philip's marriage

Levant: A History of Frankish Greece (1204–1566) (London, 1908; 2nd ed., in Greek, by Sp. P. Lampros, 2 vols., Athens, 1909–1910), and J. Longnon, L'Empire latin de Constantinople et la principauté de Morée (Paris, 1949). A. Bon, La Morée franque: Recherches historiques, topographiques et archéologiques sur la principauté d'Achaïe (1205–1430) (Paris, 1968) is especially valuable for topography and the monuments.

For Catalan-Achaean relations see Setton, Catalan Domination, passim, and R. J. Loenertz, O. P., "Athènes et Néopatras: Regestes et notices pour servir à l'histoire des duchés catalans (1311–1394)," Archivum Fratrum Praedicatorum, XXV (1955), 100–212, 428–431. On Latin Patras consult E. Gerland, Neue Quellen zur Geschichte des lateinischen Erzbistums Patras (Leipzig, 1903). For Byzantine-Achaean contacts see D. A. Zakythinos, Le Despotat grec de Morée, vol. I, Histoire politique (Paris, 1932), and vol. II, Vie et institutions (Athens, 1953); also Loenertz, "Pour l'histoire du Péloponèse au XIVe siècle (1382–1404)," Études byzantines (later Revue des études byzantines), I (1943), 152–196. On the Knights Hospitaller of Rhodes and Achaea, and on the manner in which the Navarrese entered the principality, see Loenertz, "Hospitaliers et Navarrais en Grèce 1376–1383: Regestes et documents," Orientalia Christiana periodica, XXII (1956), 319–360. Further on the Hospitallers and the defense of Greece, see Luttrell, "Intrigues, Schism, and Violence among the Hospitallers of Rhodes: 1377–1384," Speculum, XLI (1966), 30–48, and his articles cited therein, and in chapter VIII, below. In addition see his "Aldobrando Baroncelli in Greece: 1378–1382," Orientalia Christiana periodica, XXXVI (1970), 273–300. Two articles by R. Cessi deal with the claim of Amadeo of Savoy, lord of Pinerolo, to Achaea and with the relation of the dispute over Argos thereto: "Amedeo di Acaia e la rivendicazione dei domini sabaudi in Oriente," Nuovo archivio veneto, XXXVII (1919), 5–64, and "Venezia e l'acquisto di Nauplia ed Argo," ibid., XXX (1915), 147–173 (reprinted in Cessi, Politica ed economia di Venezia nel trecento: Saggi [Rome, 1952], 249–273). See also Luttrell, "The Latins of Argos and Nauplia: 1311–1394," Papers of the British School at Rome, XXXIV (n.s., XXI; 1966), 34–55.

The following are important works which touch on the affairs of the principality as part of much larger subjects: R. Caggese, Roberto d'Angiò e i suoi tempi (2 vols., Florence, 1922–1930); G. M. Monti, Nuovi studi angioini (Trani, 1937); and É. G. Léonard, La Jeunesse de Jeanne Ire, reine de Naples, comtesse de Provence (2 vols., Monaco and Paris, 1932), continued by Le Règne de Louis de Tarente (1936). A fourth volume intended to complete Léonard's masterly dissertation has not been published; for a condensation of it, as well as of the preceding volumes, see his Les Angevins de Naples (Paris, 1954).

For the trade of the Morea there are notices in W. Heyd, Histoire du commerce du Levant au moyen-âge (trans. Furcy Raynaud, 2 vols., Leipzig, 1885–1886, repr. 1923, 1936, 1967), and F. Thiriet, La Romanie vénitienne au moyen-âge: Le développement et l'exploitation du domaine colonial vénitien (XIIe-XVe siècles) (Paris, 1959, Bibliothèque des Écoles françaises d'Athènes et de Rome, fasc. 193). Pertinent archival sources are inventoried in idem, Régestes des délibérations du sénat de Venise concernant la Romanie (3 vols., Paris and The Hague, 1958–1961; École pratique des hautes études, VIe sect., Documents et recherches . . . , I–II, IV), and B. Krekić, Dubrovnik (Raguse) et le Levant au moyen âge (Paris and The Hague, 1961; in the same series, no. V). On the society and rural economy of Achaea see the materials in Documents sur le régime des terres dans la principauté de Morée au XIVe siècle, ed. Longnon and Topping (Paris and The Hague, 1968; in the same series, no. IX), and the following studies: Topping, "Le Régime agraire dans le Péloponnèse latin au

to princess Thamar of Epirus in the same year had given him an important foothold in that state. The titular Latin empress of Constantinople, Catherine of Courtenay, may have had higher rank than Philip in the heraldic lists, but he was a kind of viceroy who had large authority, direct or indirect, over the Greek lands not held by emperor Andronicus II. It is not surprising that the Morea was not the major preoccupation of a ruler who bore the exalted title "despot of Romania and lord of the kingdom of Albania," and who also had important responsibilities in the Angevin kingdom of Naples.[1]

In 1306 Philip made his only visit to the Morea in order to direct a campaign against the Byzantines of Mistra. Some notable successes on this occasion were followed by an unsuccessful invasion of the despotate of Epirus. During the period when he was formally prince of Achaea (1307–1313), Philip, like his father and grandfather when they held the same title, resorted to the unsatisfactory practice of ruling the Morea through bailies. In 1309, with the aim of anticipating any claims to Achaea that Mahaut of Hainault, the daughter of Isabel of Villehardouin by Florent, might make, he arranged her betrothal to his eldest son, Charles of Taranto. Two years later Isabel, still considering the principality of her fathers as hers to dispose of, willed her rights to Mahaut. Isabel's act was in itself ineffectual, but her hopes were to be partially realized in 1313.

On March 15, 1311, on a Boeotian battlefield near the Cephissus river and the classical Chaeronea, the soldiers of fortune of the Catalan Grand Company, with the aid of Turkish allies, completely destroyed one of the finest armies ever assembled in Frankish Greece, captained by the headstrong Walter I [V] of Brienne, last French duke of Athens. The victors organized a state which was to last about three-quarters of a century, drawing its dukes from the Catalan houses of Sicily and Aragon. The Catalans' triumph spread fear throughout Frankish Greece. The Briennist fiefs of Argos and Nauplia were threatened. The allies of Brienne, notably Achaea, the

---

XIVᵉ siècle," *L'Hellénisme contemporain,* 2nd ser., X (1956), 255–295; Longnon, "La Vie rurale dans la Grèce franque," *Journal des savants,* 1965, pp. 343–357; and Jacoby, "Les Archontes grecs et la féodalité en Morée franque," *Travaux et mémoires,* II (Paris, 1967, Centre de recherche d'histoire et civilisation byzantines), 421–481.

1. The real basis of Philip of Taranto's power and influence was the large and privileged territory of Tarentum, which Charles II had reconstituted for his favorite son from the Norman-Swabian principality of that name. It consisted of many lands scattered through Lucania and Apulia; in it Philip had the rarely given authority of the *merum et mixtum imperium.* See Léonard, *La Jeunesse de Jeanne Iʳᵉ,* pp. 126 ff. On events in the Morea before 1311, including the Angevin diplomatic maneuvers, see volume II of this work, chapter VII.

duchy of the Archipelago, and the marquisate of Bodonitsa, having lost their finest chivalry in the disaster at the Boeotian Cephissus, feared that the offensive power of the Catalans would soon be turned against them. Venice was anxious for the security of the important colony of her citizens at Negroponte, in Euboea. The Neapolitan Angevins were naturally disturbed by the extension of Aragonese power into central Greece.

King Philip IV of France and pope Clement V were forced to reconsider plans for the recovery of Constantinople and the revival of the crusade against the Moslems, now that they were deprived of the French duchy of Athens as a base. All the popes of the Avignonese line were to show themselves consistently hostile to the Catalans of Greece, whose suzerains they regarded as usurpers of the papal fief of Sicily, bestowed by an earlier French pope, Urban IV, upon Charles I of Anjou. Writing from Vienne on May 2, 1312, Clement V warned the Catalans to abandon "certain conventions and pacts" that they had entered into "with the enemies of the Catholic faith" against prince Philip of Taranto, under pain of excommunication. On the same day Clement wrote to Fulk of Villaret, the master of the Hospitallers, to urge him to coöperate with the prince of Taranto in a campaign to expel the Catalans from Athens. But the knights, only recently established in Rhodes and striving to extend their sway over the neighboring islands and coast, declined to enter into hostilities with the redoubtable Company.[2]

Philip the Fair's interest in the crusade, however insincere, and his position as head of the house of France, made it natural for him to intervene in the troubled affairs of the Frankish states of Greece. Thus in 1312 and 1313 he promoted several political marriages which directly or indirectly affected these states and which it was hoped would enable them to present a solid front to the Catalan danger and finally to achieve the reconquest of Constantinople. The recapture of the great city was a precondition of Philip's own assumption of the cross.

With the death of Catherine of Courtenay early in 1308, her rights to the Latin empire had passed to her daughter Catherine, whose father was Philip's brother, Charles of Valois—"fils de roi, frère de roi, père de roi, et jamais roi." Charles favored a match between his daughter and Philip of Taranto in order to combine the prince of Taranto's real authority in the Balkan peninsula with Catherine's claims to the empire. The Angevin prince was free to

2. On Fulk and the Hospitallers, see below, pp. 283–288. On the Catalan duchies, see below, chapter VI.

consider such a match, since in 1309 he had repudiated his wife Thamar on grounds of flagrant adultery, and after a short imprisonment the beauteous Epirote princess had died. But an obstacle to the match remained. Catherine of Valois had been affianced from infancy to duke Hugh V of Burgundy, whose mother, Agnes of France, widow of duke Robert II, could not be persuaded to break the engagement. So the child-empress—Catherine was not yet twelve— was made to declare before witnesses on September 30, 1312, that she did not consider the duke strong enough to "undertake the needs of the empire;" she preferred as her husband the "prince of Taranto, son of the king of Sicily." Thereupon Hugh V, whose health was always precarious, gave up his fiancée, and five matches were arranged involving the houses of France, Naples, and Burgundy, and the princely line of the Villehardouins.

Philip of Taranto married Catherine of Valois at Fontainebleau on July 29, 1313. He had to agree that his child-bride's maternal lands of Courtenay and other estates in France, Flanders, and Hainault be ceded to Joan of Burgundy, Hugh V's sister, and that Mahaut of Hainault receive the principality of Achaea. Hugh V was betrothed to another Joan, daughter of Philip IV's second son, the later king Philip V the Tall. Joan of Burgundy became the wife of Catherine's half-brother Philip of Valois, the future king Philip VI of France, bringing to him as her marriage portion the Courtenay lands. Hugh V's brother Louis married Mahaut, also (probably) on July 29, 1313, thereby obtaining the principality of Achaea. Hugh gave up to Louis the rights to the Latin kingdom of Thessalonica which the last Latin emperor, Baldwin II, had given in 1266 to the grandfather of Hugh and Louis, Hugh IV. Louis in return renounced all claims to his parents' inheritance, for the benefit of Hugh V. Finally, Philip of Taranto's eldest son, Charles, who for four years had been the fiancé of Mahaut, was, in compensation, betrothed to Joan of Valois, the younger sister of the Latin empress.

The return of the Morea to the Villehardouin family was hedged about with restrictions typical of Angevin calculations. If Louis died childless before Mahaut, she would have only the usufruct of the land during her lifetime. She had to promise not to marry in the future without the prince of Taranto's consent, even as her mother had promised his father not to marry against the latter's wishes. After her death the principality would in any case revert to the house of Burgundy, whether or not she left children by another marriage. Philip the Fair's distrust of the prince of Taranto is revealed in the obligation he imposed on the latter to obtain the approval of the pope for the cession of the Morea to Mahaut and for certain related arrangements; if Philip of Taranto violated these conventions, he was liable to excommunication and interdict. Likewise, he was required to obtain the approval of his brother Robert the Wise, king of Naples.

The new prince of Achaea did homage to Philip of Taranto for his principality and pledged his assistance in the campaign to recover Constantinople. In an act issued at St. Denis in October 1314, Philip the Fair defined the military service that Louis would owe his suzerain if he succeeded in conquering Thessalonica. Louis's proxies had arrived in the Morea a year earlier to take possession of the peninsula in his name and Mahaut's.

Nothing seemed less likely, following the elaborate arrangements of 1313–1314 under the high auspices of the king of France, than that when Louis of Burgundy should arrive in the Morea he would have to engage in a violent conflict with a determined claimant to the coveted title prince of Achaea. Unfortunately for him, his preparations for his departure from Burgundy and Hugh V's premature death (May 1315) delayed his arrival in Greece until early in 1316. The summer before, the infante Ferdinand of Majorca had landed at Glarentsa to claim the principality.

The adventurous infante, younger son of king James I of Majorca, had already figured in the turbulent politics of the Near East when he served briefly as commander of the Catalan Grand Company in 1307 in the name of his cousin, king Frederick II of the island of Sicily (Trinacria). His claim to the Morea derived from his marriage to Isabel of Sabran, the daughter of Margaret of Villehardouin, who was the younger daughter of prince William, and was known as the lady of Akova from the Arcadian barony of that name.[3] Soon after the death of her sister Isabel in 1311, Margaret had visited the court of king Robert of Naples to ask for the cession of the Morea, or at least one-fifth of the principality. Her claim, however, was a tenuous one, if only because Charles II had in 1289 granted the principality expressly to Isabel of Villehardouin and the heirs of her body; thus Mahaut of Hainault had rights in it superior to those of her aunt. In reality the Angevin suzerains of the Morea disposed of the land in any way that suited their tortuous diplomacy, and as we have noted they saw fit in 1313 to cede it to Mahaut and Louis of Burgundy in

3. Isabel was Margaret's only child, her daughter by her first husband, Isnard of Sabran (d. 1297), an important feudatory of the Angevin kingdom of Naples.

order to facilitate the match between Philip of Taranto and Catherine of Valois.

Having been rebuffed by the Angevins, the lady of Akova had looked about for a champion to sustain her pretensions. None was likelier and more willing than the landless infante of Majorca, who accepted Margaret's offer of her daughter's hand; nor was his cousin of Sicily averse to the prospect of the further extension of Aragonese-Catalan influence in Greece at the expense of the Angevins. The marriage was solemnized at Messina in February 1314. Isabel of Sabran brought to her husband virtually all her mother's possessions and claims, including the barony of Akova and whatever rights she may have had to the principality of Achaea, or at least to one-fifth thereof. When Margaret returned to the Morea, however, in the early summer of 1314, the leading feudatories severely reproached her for giving her daughter to a Catalan, and they proceeded to confiscate the barony of Akova and her personal property. Nicholas le Maure, acting as bailie for Louis of Burgundy, arrested Margaret and imprisoned her in the great castle of Clermont in Elis. There, in February or March 1315, the unlucky princess died. Her jailers had naturally refused the repeated demands of the infante Ferdinand for the restitution of his mother-in-law's possessions.

To help his cousin in the impending contest with the Angevins and Burgundians for the possession of the Morea, Frederick of Sicily lent Ferdinand military assistance and accepted his homage for the principality. He also wrote to the Venetian doge, John Soranzo, on April 28, 1315, to commend his cousin to the republic and to inform its government that Ferdinand had sworn not to harm its possessions in Greece. Early in 1315 Ferdinand was finally ready to invade the Morea with a force of five hundred mounted troops and a much larger number of infantry. But he was further delayed by the birth on April 5 of a son (who was to become the ill-fated last king of Majorca, James II), and by the death of his young wife thirty-two days later, both events occurring at Catania. Isabel willed the fief of Akova and her claim to Achaea to her son, and in the event of his death to her husband. Ferdinand entrusted the baby to the famous chronicler, Raymond Muntaner, to take to his mother, the queen-dowager Esclarmonde, at Perpignan. Then he set sail for the Morea from Messina about the end of June.

Landing near Glarentsa, Ferdinand was at first checked by the defending forces but rallied to rout them. The burgesses of the port city promptly recognized him as their legitimate lord. On August 17, 1315, the infante wrote to king James II of Aragon to report his capture of the city and his subjugation of "almost the entire principality." More accurately, he was master of the rich plain of Elis, including Andravida, the capital of the Frankish state. He called himself "lord of the Morea" and minted coins bearing his name at Glarentsa, the rarest of all the *tournois* of Achaea.

It was only at the end of November 1315 that the legitimate prince of Achaea, Louis of Burgundy, arrived at Venice on his way to the Morea. The new situation caused by the infante's usurpation no doubt prompted him to seek more Venetian aid, at least in ships and money, than his earlier plans had called for.[4] According to the Aragonese version of the *Chronicle of the Morea* princess Mahaut preceded her husband to Achaea, going directly from Marseilles to Port-de-Jonc in southwestern Messenia—the "Port of the Rushes" of the Franks, better known under the celebrated name of Navarino. She led a thousand Burgundians, while Louis was to follow with the main force. The bailie, Nicholas le Maure, came to receive her when he learnt of her arrival, and the count of Cephalonia, the baron of Chalandritsa, and others who had taken Ferdinand's side declared themselves her lieges and were pardoned.[5] The infante reacted to these defections by capturing and garrisoning Chalandritsa and demanding that archbishop Renier surrender Patras. On being refused he at once attacked the city, but failed to capture it. Soon afterward, on February 22, 1316, according to the Aragonese Chronicle, there occurred at a place called Picotin, near Palaeopolis (the ancient Elis),[6] a hard battle between the princess's troops and the Catalans. The latter were victorious, and among the fallen was Gilbert Sanudo, brother of duke William I of the Archipelago.[7]

4. Hopf cites a document of the Misti del Senato (State Archives of Venice) which evidently refers to this Venetian assistance ("Geschichte Griechenlands . . . ," in Ersch and Gruber, LXXXV [1867], 400; repr. 1960, I, 334).

5. The chief exception was the baron of Nivelet, who remained loyal to Ferdinand. According to the lengthy document composed sometime during the reign of James II of Majorca (1324–1349) and usually referred to as the *Declaratio summaria,* concerning the Achaean venture of the infante Ferdinand, his early success gained for him the allegiance of the count of Cephalonia, the bishop of Olena, and even Le Maure, the bailie. The text of this recital, surviving only in Du Cange's copy, is in Du Cange, *Histoire de l'empire de Constantinople,* ed. Buchon, II, 383–392, and in Buchon, *Recherches historiques sur la principauté française de Morée* (2 vols., Paris, 1845), I, 442–450.

6. S. N. Dragoumis connected Picotin with the village of Boukhioti in the vicinity of Palaeopolis (*Chronikon Moreos toponymika, topographika, historika* [Athens, 1921], pp. 260–261); this identification is not convincing. Picotin is mentioned again in a document of 1361 (cf. below, p. 138).

7. There is a reference to the infante's victory in a letter from Nicholas Doria to James II of Aragon dated at Genoa, May 5, 1316 (published in Rubió i Lluch, *Diplomatari de l'Orient català,* pp. 99–100). This confirmation of an event otherwise mentioned only in the Aragonese Chronicle helps to establish the general authenticity of that chronicle's account

It would appear that Louis and his forces arrived in Greek waters about the time of the battle of Picotin. Messengers sent by the princess urged them to hasten their landing in the Morea in order to prevent the infante from exploiting his victory. On hearing of Louis's arrival, the infante dispatched a galley to Majorca to obtain reinforcements from his brother, king Sancho, and sent a second galley to Attica to request aid from the Catalan Company. Louis failed in an attempt on the castle of Chalandritsa, despite the use of a machine against the tower. He then visited Patras to rest his troops and while there was advised by the archbishop to seek aid from the Byzantine governor at Mistra, Cantacuzenus. From Chalandritsa the infante started on his way to Glarentsa, where he could safely have waited for the reinforcements; these would have given him equality with the Burgundian forces. This strategy was urged upon him by his counselors, especially since the arrival of a numerous force of Greeks from Mistra had given Louis a large superiority in numbers. Louis was now pressing the enemy and anxious to engage him before he reached Glarentsa. But the proud infante told his counselors "that he was the son of a king and that it did not please God that he should flee the camp to avoid a battle."

The fateful clash took place at Manolada in the Elian plain northeast of Glarentsa, on July 5, 1316. In the first collision the infante broke through the line led by count John (Orsini) of Cephalonia, for whom he had a great hatred, not only because he had violated the oath of fealty so recently sworn by him but also because he had mistreated the infante's late mother-in-law, the lady of Akova.[8] But Louis, leading the second line of the Burgundians, broke the Catalan attack, and in the ensuing melee the infante was thrown to the ground and killed, despite Louis's orders that his person be unharmed. The baron of Nivelet was taken prisoner and executed as a traitor. The infante's forces had gone into battle already demoralized, and many of them virtually deserted by fleeing to Glarentsa while the fighting was in progress.[9] The Catalan triumph of 1311 in Boeotia was not to be repeated on the field of Manolada

of the infante Ferdinand's Achaean venture, though it confuses personal names and errs in chronology.

8. Margaret of Villehardouin's second husband was Richard Orsini, count of Cephalonia (d. 1304), the father of John. On Richard's death Margaret had to bring suit in the high court of Achaea against her stepson to try to recover Richard's personal property.

9. Hopf, citing the Misti del Senato, points out that Ferdinand's relations with Venice were bad at the very time his military position had been weakened; his men had harassed Venetian merchantmen. Rubió i Lluch searched in vain in the Venetian archives for the document cited by Hopf, as he reports in "Contribució a la biografía de l'infant Ferran de Mallorca," *Estudis universitaris catalans*, VII (Barcelona, 1913), 314, note 2.

in 1316. The counterpart to Walter of Brienne was not another French prince but the infante of Majorca, whose severed head was displayed before the gates of Glarentsa on the morrow of his defeat.

The troops sent by the Catalans of Athens had arrived at Vostitsa on the Gulf of Corinth on the eve of the battle at Manolada, but they turned back when they learnt of Ferdinand's death. A few days after the battle ten ships bearing reinforcements from Majorca arrived in Glarentsa harbor. Part of the Aragonese-Catalan forces in the city insisted on holding the place against Louis, in the name of the infante's son James as prince of the Morea. Though they had the support of the new arrivals from Majorca, the faction which favored surrender to Louis prevailed, thanks in part to a liberal flow of Burgundian money into their leaders' purses.

Only four weeks after Manolada, and before the negotiations for the surrender of Glarentsa had been completed, the young prince of Achaea—he was scarcely eighteen—was dead. The French version of the *Chronicle of the Morea* states that he was stricken by a fatal malady, but a pro-Catalan source[10] charges that he was poisoned by the sinister count John of Cephalonia. Louis's death made Mahaut, at twenty-two, a widow for the second time.[11] She was hardly more than the nominal ruler of a principality that was on the point of dissolution, caused by invasion and civil conflict. She had to face powerful external enemies in the Catalans of Athens and the Byzantines of Mistra, the latter having aided Louis only in order to prevent an Aragonese-Catalan conquest of the Morea.

Mahaut's weakness was revealed when she proved unable to answer an appeal for military aid from the barons of Euboea, one of her vassal states, who were fighting an invasion by the Catalan Company. She could only urge doge John Soranzo, in a letter from Andravida dated March 28, 1317, to send aid to expel the invaders from the island and to order the Venetian bailie there (Michael Morosini) not to make any peace or accord with them. The republic responded by sending twenty galleys to Negroponte under a new bailie, Francis Dandolo. This action was decisive. The Catalans, although now led by their great vicar-general Don Alfonso Fadrique, withdrew from the island, except for Carystus at its southern end. [12] But if the Catalans yielded to Venetian pressure in respect to Eu-

10. The so-called *Declaratio summaria* (see note 5, above).
11. She had been left a child-widow by the death of duke Guy II de la Roche of Athens in 1308.
12. On Don Alfonso's career see below, chapter VI.

boea, they felt under no obligation to desist from aggression upon Mahaut's principality, which they were still raiding in 1321.

The Angevins were not minded to allow Mahaut to enjoy, without interference, the life usufruct of Achaea that she was entitled to by the will of Louis of Burgundy. To bring her land under direct Angevin rule, and at the same time to provide his youngest brother, John of Gravina, with a fine appanage, king Robert of "Sicily" (Naples) made it known to Mahaut through certain Moreote vassals that he wished her to marry John. When the princess refused, the king dispatched two high officials to Achaea to bring her to Naples. Here Robert arbitrarily assumed her consent to the marriage, and in July 1317 instructed Philip of Taranto, the immediate suzerain of Achaea, not to dispose of the principality in any manner, since it was now the possession of their brother. Mahaut adamantly refused to submit to a third political marriage. Robert then enlisted the aid of pope John XXII in the effort to persuade the princess to accept the proffered match. According to the Aragonese Chronicle, confirmed by Giovanni Villani, Robert acted to prevent Mahaut from escaping to France from Rome, to which she had been allowed to make a pilgrimage. In the end the princess's resistance was worn down so far that she consented under oath to a complicated convention with Robert which amounted to a surrender of her claims if she did not marry his brother (June 13, 1318). The king promptly communicated this agreement to the feudatories of Achaea and sent Frederick Trogisio as his bailie in the land.

Even now the Angevins' hold on the unfortunate principality was not uncontested. Duke Odo IV of Burgundy, who had succeeded Hugh V, asserted his own claim to it as the heir of their brother Louis. He enjoyed the diplomatic backing of his father-in-law, king Philip V of France, whose daughter Joan was married to Odo after the death of her first fiancé, Hugh V. It is not likely that Odo ever contemplated an expedition to the distant Morea; after twice protesting the Angevins' "usurpation" to the pope he agreed to sell his rights to Achaea and the kingdom of Thessalonica to Louis, count of Clermont and later first duke of Bourbon, for 40,000 livres (April 14, 1320). However, at this juncture Philip of Taranto intervened effectively to satisfy the Burgundian claims by negotiating their purchase for the same sum of 40,000 livres, from which 5,500 livres was deducted as repayment of a loan made by Baldwin II, the last Latin emperor of Constantinople, to Odo's grandfather, Hugh IV.

This settlement was undoubtedly facilitated by the marriage in May 1321 of prince Philip of Taranto's eldest surviving son by

Thamar, the despot Philip, to Beatrice, the daughter of count Louis I of Clermont. Furthermore, the prince of Taranto quickly found the money for the transaction at the French court. In 1313 Philip the Fair had promised to provide the Angevin with five hundred men, to be maintained for a year, to help him recapture Constantinople, whose repossession was regarded as a step "preparatory and very necessary" for the *passage d'outremer* to recover the Holy Land. Philip V had renewed this agreement in 1319. But it was further agreed in September 1321 that Philip of Taranto should receive this aid in the form of 70,000 livres, that he should buy the Burgundian claims[13] with part of the sum, and that the principality should be the perpetual and proper inheritance of Catherine of Valois and of her direct heirs by prince Philip.

The last act in the contest of wills between the king of Naples and the refractory Villehardouin princess took place in Avignon, where Robert resided from 1319 to 1324 and to which Mahaut was now brought (1321). Pope John XXII once more ignored her plea to invalidate the match with John of Gravina, bidding her to accept him as her husband. Mahaut now revealed that this was impossible, inasmuch as she had been secretly married for some time to a Burgundian knight, Hugh of Lapalisse, who had very probably gone to the Morea among the troops accompanying prince Louis. The admission played into Robert's hands. Both Mahaut and her mother had on various occasions pledged themselves not to remarry without the consent of their Angevin overlords. These pledges were invoked against Mahaut and she was declared forfeit of the principality. Robert now arranged its assignment to John of Gravina, who paid their brother Philip, according to the Aragonese Chronicle, either 40,000 florins or 10,000 gold ounces, a sum which we may take to be the equivalent of that paid by the prince of Taranto to Odo of Burgundy. In an impressive ceremony at the papal court on January 5, 1322, the king invested Philip with the much-disputed principality, and the latter in turn accepted the homage of his younger brother for it.[14]

Any possibility that Mahaut might return to the Morea and upset

13. To the Morea only, the kingdom of Thessalonica being excluded.

14. We have the act of January 5, 1322, in a summary by C. Minieri-Riccio of the original in the Angevin archives: "Genealogia di Carlo II d' Angiò," *Archivio storico per le province napoletane,* VII (1882), 481–484.

G. M. Monti, in his *Nuovi studi angioini,* pp. 606–629, published for the first time eight documents issued by Robert of Anjou at Avignon in 1321 concerning the claims to Achaea by his brothers and Odo of Burgundy and the plans to reconquer the parts of the Morea which were then in Byzantine hands. John of Gravina was to head the campaign by virtue of a special appointment as vicar-general.

the Angevins' rule was forestalled by her confinement in the Castel dell' Uovo at Naples. Robert even manufactured grounds for her arrest and imprisonment by charging her with being the accomplice of Hugh of Lapalisse in a plot against his life. This conspiracy, which is reported by Villani, supposedly occurred in September of 1322. In 1324 Mahaut's cousin, count William I of Hainault, in vain offered Robert the sum of 100,000 livres for her release. The next year king Charles IV of France made an unsuccessful plea on her behalf. In 1328 the unfortunate woman was removed to Aversa, where she died three years later, only thirty-eight years old. The last princess of the Villehardouins remains a pathetic figure in the often violent annals of Frankish Greece, where women of high birth had repeatedly to play important roles in public life and were pawns in the diplomacy of political marriages.

In the meantime the feebleness of the Frankish Morea was being revealed by the alarming inroads of the Greeks of Mistra. The imperial governor was the capable Andronicus Palaeologus Asen, nephew of emperor Andronicus II and son of the deposed Bulgarian tsar, John III Asen. His term of service from 1316 to about 1323 contrasts with the shorter terms of the Angevin bailies.[15] With the aid of liberal bribes to their castellans, Asen in his campaign of 1320 captured the vital Arcadian strongholds of Akova or Matagrifon, Karytaina, and St. George. At St. George the Franks, led by the bailie Trogisio, were badly ambushed (September 9, 1320); the commander of the Teutonic Knights lost his life, and bishop James of Olena and the grand constable of Achaea, Bartholomew II Ghisi, were among the many captured. Asen promptly freed the bishop (whose ear had been cut off in the battle) on account of his rank; but he took Ghisi to Constantinople, where this leading magnate, who was a triarch of Euboea and lord of the islands of Tenos and Myconos, remained a prisoner for several years until freed through Venetian intervention. Asen's campaign is narrated in the Aragonese Chronicle, and is supplemented by the report in the French version that he captured Polyphengos,[16] a castle southwest of Corinth, also during 1320. It was Asen's victories that led many Frankish settlers of Arcadia, perhaps mainly the offspring of Greek mothers, to go over to the Orthodox church. In a letter dated October 1, 1322, John XXII called on Nicholas, the titular Latin patriarch of Constan-

15. On the dates of Asen's service see Zakythinos, *Le Despotat grec de Morée,* II, 64.
16. A site corresponding to the ancient Phlious. One of the Byzantine "short chronicles" mentions the capture of Akova, Karytaina, and St. George under the year 6829 (1320–1321 A.D.). See Loenertz, "Pour l'histoire du Péloponèse," p. 154.

tinople, and on William Frangipani, archbishop of Patras, to take energetic measures against the converts.

In the desperate situation resulting from the Byzantine successes, the barons looked around for a better protector than the Neapolitan Angevins and decided to offer the principality to the Venetians. We learn from two documents of June 1321, addressed to the doge, John Soranzo, that John of Les Vaux, grand preceptor of the Hospital in "Romania," along with James, bishop of Olena, and the chancellor Benjamin, sent Peter Gradenigo, prior of the Franciscans in "Romania," as their agent to Venice, and instructed him to acquaint the signoria with the plight of the barons, "whose lord seems not to care much for them," and to offer the principality together with the suzerainty of Negroponte to the republic. The Venetians hesitated to accept the thorny gift. They had shown themselves favorable to Mahaut's claims, interceding with the pope on at least one occasion. This attitude was no doubt one cause for hesitation, since Mahaut was not yet, in the summer of 1321, entirely the prisoner of her Angevin hosts.

The reduced principality, whose direct rule John of Gravina assumed in 1322, consisted mainly of the western and northern coastal areas of the Morea. Excluding the Venetian way-stations of Modon and Coron in the extreme southwest, the Frankish holdings covered— to use the ancient names—the provinces of Messenia, Triphylia, Elis, Achaea, Corinthia, and the Argolid; of the last, Argos and Nauplia were enfeoffed to the Enghien family by the Briennist claimants to the duchy of Athens. With the loss to the Byzantines of Akova and Karytaina in 1320, there now remained only three of the original twelve baronies—Patras, Vostitsa, and Chalandritsa, neighboring fiefs in the district of ancient Achaea.

Patras, with its fine port and fertile lands, was a flourishing ecclesiastical barony virtually independent of the prince of Achaea and acknowledging the pope as suzerain. In this period it was ably governed by the Franciscan William Frangipani (1317–1337), of a distinguished Roman family. He and his successors were generally on good terms with Venice, whose government allowed the archbishops to travel on its merchantmen and to import arms. In return the republic was secure in its commercial interests in Patras and enjoyed considerable political influence, thanks in part to the Venetian origin of some of the cathedral canons. But the archbishops consistently obeyed the papal direction in matters of church discipline and the propagation of the faith, and Frangipani followed John XXII's bidding in supporting Walter II [VI] of Brienne's unsuccessful campaign in 1331–1332 to reconquer his father's duchy from the Catalans. Venice had compacted with the excommunicated masters of that state and had rejected the papal entreaties to assist Walter. Frangipani twice pronounced excommunication against the Catalans, in 1332 and 1335.

The port of Vostitsa (the classical Aegium) was the seat of another flourishing barony. Nicholas of Martoni, the notary and pilgrim from Carinola, near Capua, who touched there in 1395, describes it as an opulent town with a fine castle. The founding family of Charpigny became extinct in the male line early in the fourteenth century. According to the Aragonese *Chronicle of the Morea* (par. 624), Louis of Burgundy married the heiress to one of his knights, Dreux of Charny, to whom he also gave the fief of the traitorous lord of Nivelet. The baronies of Vostitsa and Nivelet were later bought from Guillemette of Charny by Marie of Bourbon, who in turn sold them to Nerio Acciajuoli in 1363.[17]

The fief of Chalandritsa was in the hinterland of Patras, and the founding family of Dramelay or Trémolay of Burgundy was represented in the early fourteenth century by Nicholas of Trémolay.[18] We have seen how he finally remained loyal to Louis of Burgundy in the struggle with the infante Ferdinand; but he died just before the battle fought at Picotin, whereupon Louis granted the barony to two of his knights, the brothers Othon and Aimon of Rans. When Othon died Aimon decided to return to his homeland, even as a more famous Burgundian, Othon de la Roche, conqueror and "Great

17. Cf. page 140, below. On the basis of the Angevin registers Hopf stated that the Nivelet widow Beatrice was married to the Catalan Bertrand Galcelm or Ganselmi in 1316 (in Ersch and Gruber, LXXXV [1867], 406B and note 80; repr. 1960, I, 340B). It may be doubted, however, if Galcelm thereby entered the feudal aristocracy of the Morea as lord of Nivelet. In any case it is certain that Vostitsa and Nivelet were united in the hands of the Charny family in the middle decades of the fourteenth century (see Du Cange, ed. Buchon, II, 224, 264–265).

18. The genealogy of the family of Trémolay or Dramelay, like that of many of the Frankish lines of the Morea, is imperfectly known. Hopf shows "Audebert de la Trémouille" as the founder of the family and the father of Guy, who was bailie in 1282–1285 (*Chroniques gréco-romanes*, p. 472). It is unlikely that the two men's lives spanned a century. A "G." of Dramelay is mentioned in a document in 1209; he is very probably the grandfather of the bailie. (Cf. Jean Longnon, "Problèmes de l'histoire de la principauté de Morée," in *Journal des savants*, 1946, p. 86, and *L'Empire latin*, p. 261; he also corrects Trémouille to Dramelay or Trémolay.) As for Nicholas of Trémolay, Longnon calls him simply the last baron of this family (*ibid.*, p. 315), but it is not clear whether he belonged in the main line. Hopf gives him no place in it. There is an interesting mention of Nicholas and his treason in the eighteenth chapter of the *Assizes of Romania;* it would appear from it that Aimon of Rans was related to him. Since Nicholas is here mentioned only as lord of a fief (Mitopoli) within the barony of Chalandritsa, it is possible that he did not hold the entire barony, as the Aragonese Chronicle assumes.

Lord" of Athens, had done a century before. Aimon sold Chalandritsa to Martin Zaccaria of the famous Genoese family, a nephew
(or less probably a grandson) of the great Benedict Zaccaria. Martin
was already co-seigneur (1314–1329) of the rich island of Chios,
which Benedict had seized from the faltering Byzantine state in
1304. He so distinguished himself against the Turkish pirates, providing valuable protection to Latin merchants and travelers, that Philip
of Taranto and the empress Catherine bestowed upon him the
exalted but empty title "king and despot of Asia Minor" (1325). His
"kingdom" was made up of a number of large and small islands off
the Asian coast, including, besides Chios, Samos and Cos. Martin
promised his Angevin suzerains five hundred horsemen to help in the
recovery of Constantinople. He became a still more important feudatory of the Morea in 1327 through his marriage to Jacqueline de la
Roche, who was the heiress of Damala in the Argolid (near the
ancient Troezen), a fief belonging to a cadet branch of the Athenian
La Roche family. Damala was in a sense a fourth original barony,
inasmuch as the La Roches had held the "conquest" fief of Veligosti
jointly with Damala and continued to use the title lord of Veligosti
after this place had fallen to the Greeks.[19]

It is a striking fact that in a little over a century since the
establishment of the principality all the original French baronial
families had become extinct in the male lines. Not enough of the
followers of Louis of Burgundy remained in the Morea to reinforce
the French element to any significant degree. Italian families like the
Venetian Ghisi, the Genoese Zaccarias, and shortly the Florentine
Acciajuoli entered the aristocracy of the fourteenth-century Morea
through marriage to the French heiresses or by receiving grants of
lands. We must not overlook, however, the two important French
families of Aulnay and Le Maure (or Le Noir), who settled in the
Morea in the second half of the thirteenth century. When the
conquest of Constantinople by the Greeks in 1261 made him a
refugee, Vilain I of Aulnay received from his cousin William of
Villehardouin the important fief of Arcadia (the ancient Cyparissia)
in Messenia, which was formed out of the princely domain. In John
of Gravina's time the fief was in the possession of Erard II of Aulnay
and his sister Agnes. With Agnes's marriage to Stephen le Maure, the
son of Louis of Burgundy's bailie, half of Messenian Arcadia was
merged with the barony of St.-Sauveur, the fief of the Le Maure
family, likewise in Messenia. Another Messenian barony, Molines,

19. The town of Veligosti was the medieval successor to Megalopolis, though not located
on the same site.

was at this time held by Janni Misito, the castellan of Kalamata, whose name seems to show a Greek origin. At all periods in the history of the principality there were Greek landowners (the *archontes* of the *Chronicle of the Morea*) who accepted Frankish rule and retained their estates. The Misito family remained important fief-holders in the Kalamata area until nearly the end of the fourteenth century.

Outside of the Morea the authority of the prince of Achaea as suzerain was now much diminished as compared with his position before the Catalan triumph of 1311. The powerful Company of course ignored the Angevins' claims to suzerainty over Athens. The marquis of Bodonitsa and the triarchs of Euboea continued technically to be the vassals of the principality throughout the fourteenth century, but we have seen how Mahaut was unable to help the Euboeans against the Catalans, while the Angevins themselves were hardly more effective as suzerains. Like Patras, Bodonitsa and Negroponte came to depend more and more on the great merchant republic of the Adriatic, although Venice might choose to refer a dispute involving the two to the Angevin bailie of Achaea, as happened in the time of the marquis Nicholas I Giorgio or Zorzi (1335–1345). Bodonitsa, however, did not escape Catalan pressure altogether: in the reign of Nicholas I's son Francis I (1358–1382), and probably as early as the father's rule, the small border state had to pay an annual tribute of four equipped horses to Catalan Athens.

Over the duchy of the Archipelago the princes of Achaea enjoyed a real suzerainty, as is proved by the substantial aid in men and arms which the island dukes provided to Mahaut and Louis and again to John of Gravina. The aid to Mahaut led to savage reprisals by the Catalan Company against the population of Melos, an event recalling the brutal enslavement of the Melians by Athens during the Peloponnesian war. When Venice protested to the Company's suzerain, king Frederick II of Sicily, he replied with legal exactness that the republic's remonstrance was groundless because the island duchy was vassal only to the principality of Achaea.

The question of the suzerainty of Achaea over the strategically situated county of Cephalonia and Zante was at this time complicated by Angevin designs on the expiring despotate of Epirus. Count Nicholas Orsini (1317–1323), however, upset these plans in 1318 by murdering the despot Thomas, who was his uncle. He married Thomas's widow, Anna Palaeologina, and further to ingratiate himself with his subjects he adopted the Greeks' religion and made some use of their language. When king Robert of Naples and Philip of

Taranto ordered him to do homage in 1319, an act by which he would have admitted Angevin suzerainty over both his island domain and the despotate, he boldly defied them. His career was fittingly cut short by assassination at the hands of his own brother, John II. The new ruler also ignored Philip of Taranto's claims to the despotate and even threatened Corfu and the other holdings comprising the Angevin "despotate of Romania."

The troubled situation in Epirus helped to hasten the preparation of the important expedition of John of Gravina and Philip of Taranto to the Morea and Epirus—an expedition which might even, it was hoped, result in the recovery of Constantinople for the titular empress, Catherine of Valois, and her Neapolitan consort. In May 1323 the two brothers formally pledged mutual assistance; each agreed to contribute two hundred knights, five hundred foot, and ten ships to a joint armament. The Angevin registers revealed that throughout the years 1322 to 1324 large amounts of money and provisions flowed from Naples to the Morea. A new bailie, Perronet de Villamastray, went out from Naples in November 1322, and he in turn was replaced by an able French knight, Nicholas of Joinville (1323–1325), a great-grandson of the biographer of St. Louis. The titular duke of Athens, Walter II [VI] of Brienne, was eager to ally himself with the Angevins in the hope of regaining his father's duchy, but financial difficulties in his Italian fiefs kept him at home. The efforts which king Robert of Naples himself made to persuade Venice to join the expedition failed; that most commercial of states was not on sufficiently bad terms with the Catalans and the Greeks to go to war to help a powerful Angevin prince replace the weak Andronicus II on the throne of the *basileis*.

The fine armament led by John of Gravina finally set sail from Brindisi in January of 1325. It stopped at Cephalonia and Zante and easily occupied those islands. The Orsini dynasty was declared deposed, but count John II was secure in his mainland domain, having shut himself up in the fortress of Arta. The invading force went on to land at the chief port of the Morea, Glarentsa. Here the assembled barons of the principality, on this rare occasion of a personal visit of a prince of the house of Anjou, did homage and swore fealty to John of Gravina. The duke of Naxos, Nicholas, was present with a contingent to assist his superior lord. The Aragonese Chronicle also mentions the presence of archbishop William Frangipani of Patras and of the Euboean lords Peter dalle Carceri and Bartholomew Ghisi, the latter only recently released from his captivity in Constantinople.

4. Frankish Greece

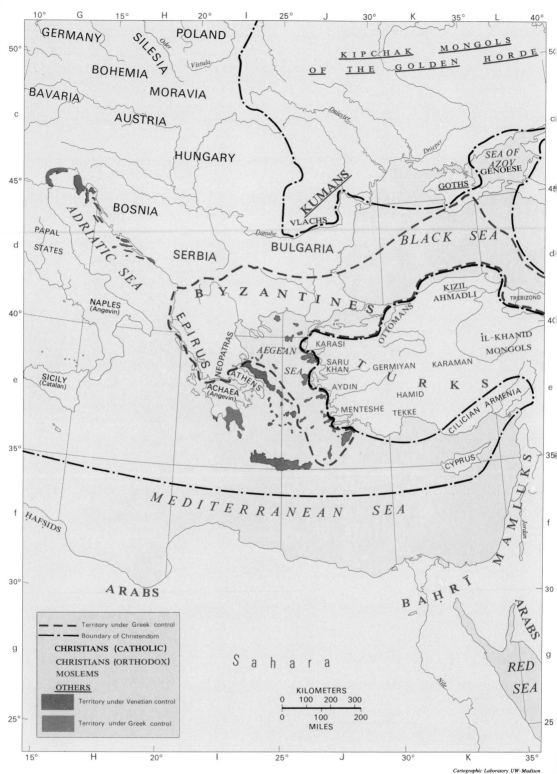

GERMANY

SILESIA

POLAND

BOHEMIA

MORAVIA

BAVARIA

AUSTRIA

Oder

Vistula

KIPCHAK   MONGOLS

OF   THE   GOLDEN   HORDE

HUNGARY

Dniester

Dnieper

SEA OF
AZOV
GENOESE

BOSNIA

KUMANS

GOTHS

ADRIATIC SEA

PAPAL
STATES

SERBIA

VLACHS

Danube

BULGARIA

BLACK   SEA

TREBIZOND

NAPLES
(Angevin)

B Y Z A N T I N E S

KIZIL
AHMADLI

EPIRUS

NEOPATRAS

AEGEAN

KARASI

OTTOMANS

İL-KHANID
MONGOLS

SICILY
(Catalan)

SEA

SARU
KHAN

GERMIYAN

KARAMAN

T U R K S

ATHENS

ACHAEA
(Angevin)

AYDIN

HAMID

CILICIAN ARMENIA

MENTESHE

TEKKE

CYPRUS

M E D I T E R R A N E A N   S E A

HAFSIDS

MAMLUKS

Jordan

A R A B S

BAHRĪ

ARABS

Territory under Greek control

Boundary of Christendom

CHRISTIANS (CATHOLIC)

CHRISTIANS (ORTHODOX)

MOSLEMS

S a h a r a

RED
SEA

OTHERS

Nile

Territory under Venetian control

Territory under Greek control

KILOMETERS

0   100   200   300

0   100   200

MILES

Cartographic Laboratory UW-Madison

5. The Levant in 1300

The Greeks had securely garrisoned the castles on the frontier between the principality and the despotate of Mistra. The Frankish
forces advanced to attack the Arcadian fortress of Karytaina, one of
the strongest military points of the Morea. While they were concentrated there, the Byzantines made damaging raids on the Frankish
lands. The defenders of the fortress held out successfully until the
cold weather set in, forcing John of Gravina to return to Glarentsa
for the winter. In the spring of 1326 he departed for Naples, never to
return to his Greek domains. Although the warlike duke of Naxos,
whom he left in command of his army, defeated the Byzantine forces
in a hard battle fought below the castle of St. Omer in Elis, this was
not a decisive setback to the Greeks.[20]

The costly expedition of the prince of the Morea was an almost
total failure; even the islands of Cephalonia and Zante soon returned
to the rule of the Orsini house. For Achaea the most permanent
result of the enterprise was the introduction into the ranks of its
nobility of the famous Florentine commercial and banking family of
the Acciajuoli, which was destined to play a leading role in the affairs
of Latin Greece for more than a century. John of Gravina borrowed
heavily from the Acciajuoli in order to prepare his expedition; while
it lasted they sent great quantities of provisions to the Morea. They
received payment in the form of two fiefs in Elis, Lichina and
Mandria. Other Italians to whom Gravina was in debt were also given
estates in the Morea. One of these was a Diego Tolomei of Siena,
who received lands at Mandria and an estate called Speroni. Thus did
the "Italianizing" of the Achaean landholding class make further
progress, at the expense of the waning French element.

While John of Gravina filled various important posts in Italy in the
service of king Robert, the Morea was governed by four bailies in the
years 1325–1332; of these the most notable was the archbishop of
Patras, William Frangipani, who was the first cleric appointed to the
position (1329–1331). It was necessary to import grain from Apulia
throughout these years to provision the fortresses of the principality.
We hear of the bailies deciding minor feudal cases and of Frangipani
mediating a dispute involving Stephen le Maure and the Venetians.

In August 1331 young Walter of Brienne left Brindisi with a large

---

20. Caggese, in his *Roberto d' Angiò*, devotes several pages to the military and diplomatic
preparations for John of Gravina's campaign (II, 312–317); his account is based on the
Angevin registers of Naples, destroyed in 1943. Once the expedition had arrived in Greece
the enthusiasm for it quickly evaporated, for lack either of an organic plan of action or of
the necessary means. Many Neapolitan sailors and crossbowmen, having no desire to risk
their lives in distant parts, left the expedition before reaching their term of voluntary
service, but having first collected their pay (*ibid.,* II, 317).

force in an attempt to regain his father's duchy of Athens from the Catalans. His successes at Leucas and in Epirus are described elsewhere, as is his inability to bring the Catalans to battle. He spent some months in Patras, which seems to have served as his headquarters, before returning to Brindisi in the late summer of 1332, never to set foot in Greece again. His son by Beatrice of Taranto died an infant in Greece in 1332, so he was succeeded as titular duke of Athens by two sons of his sister Isabel, Sohier (1356–1364) and Louis (1381–1387/90) of Enghien; their brother Guy inherited Walter's lordship of Argos and Nauplia.[21]

During Walter of Brienne's absence in Greece Philip I of Taranto died in Naples on December 26, 1331. He had tried ineffectually for over a generation to play a large role in the affairs of the Balkan peninsula. His sons by Thamar of Epirus having predeceased him, it was his eldest son by Catherine of Valois, Robert, who succeeded to his lands and titles, including the suzerainty over Achaea, under the tutelage of his mother. But John of Gravina refused to do homage for Achaea to a mere nephew and a female guardian, and it required king Robert's intervention as the superior suzerain to end the family dispute. By the compromise reached on December 17, 1332, John agreed to exchange the principality of Achaea for the duchy of Durazzo and the lordship of the "kingdom of Albania," plus a payment of 5,000 gold ounces to compensate him for the greater value Achaea represented as compared with the somewhat shadowy realm in Albania. The money was, not surprisingly, advanced to Catherine by the Acciajuoli. Pope John XXII confirmed the settlement in January 1333.

Robert of Taranto was technically prince of Achaea from 1333 to 1364, but the empress Catherine as his regent and guardian was in reality princess till her death in 1346. Catherine promptly sent a bailie to take possession of the principality on her behalf. But neither he nor his successor could impose his authority effectively upon the greater lords. The increasing independence of the archbishops of Patras has already been noticed. When the great William Frangipani died in 1337, Catherine's third bailie, Bertrand of Les Baux, a member of the highest Neapolitan nobility, occupied various lands of the archbishopric and laid siege to Patras, in an effort to bring the ecclesiastical state under the suzerainty of the empress. Pope Bene-

---

21. Guy's daughter Marie, lady of Argos and Nauplia (1377–1388), was to cede this fief to the Venetians in 1388. Sohier's son Walter (1364–1381) was a namesake of Isabel's husband, Walter of Enghien, count of Conversano. On Walter of Brienne see below, chapter VI.

dict XII had to remind Catherine that Patras was a fief of the holy see, and when Bertrand continued his attacks he directed the bishops of Coron and Olena to lay all Achaea under an interdict.

Catherine decided to go to Greece to deal with the situation in person. Hers was no hasty visit. Her sons Robert, Louis, and Philip accompanied her. She had three hundred men-at-arms, and she took provisions for the castles of the principality. Above all she had as her close adviser and factotum one of the most astute Italians of the Trecento in the person of Nicholas Acciajuoli (1310–1365). Nicholas began with great advantages as a member of the Acciajuoli house and son of a chamberlain and privy councillor of king Robert. But his own ability, driving ambition, capacity for intrigue, and personal charm mainly account for his extraordinary rise to the position of grand seneschal of the kingdom of Naples and arbiter of its destiny during much of the turbulent reign of Joanna I. Buchon exaggerated in ascribing to the twenty-two-year-old Nicholas the leading role in the negotiations over the Morea between Catherine and John of Gravina in 1332, but the young man impressed Catherine favorably and won her confidence and kept it until her death.[22] She made him administrator of the affairs of her young sons and put him in charge of their education. In 1334 he replaced the company of the Acciajuoli as holder of the fiefs of Mandria and Lichina in Elis. From Diego Tolomei he acquired the fief of Speroni and his possessions at Mandria. In 1335 king Robert conferred knighthood on him and appointed him master of the household and guardian of prince Louis. Between 1336 and 1338 Catherine and her eldest son Robert granted Nicholas several more fiefs in the principality as a reward for his "immense and fruitful services." In further appreciation they reduced the customary service, notwithstanding, they admitted, that the lands and rights ought to carry greater feudal service to accord with their annual value, and that the customs of the principality prohibited diminution in the service and revenues of fiefs. Nicholas's suzerains went even further and gave him the right to exchange, sell, or mortgage his fiefs freely, provided that they did not fall into the hands of possessors unable to perform military service for them, like ecclesiastics.

It was, then, as a privileged liege feudatory of Achaea that Nicholas Acciajuoli joined his suzerains on November 15, 1338, at Brindisi to embark for Glarentsa; his entourage included twenty-five mounted

22. Following L. Tanfani (*Niccola Acciaiuoli* [Florence, 1863], p. 24), É. G. Léonard, in his *Boccace et Naples* (Paris, 1944), pp. 16–17, rightly rejects the gossip, which is reflected in one of Boccaccio's Bucolics and reported by Giovanni Villani, that Nicholas was Catherine's lover.

men. On September 28 he had made a remarkable will, much of which was concerned with the building of a Carthusian monastery (Certosa) near Florence where he planned to have an imposing tomb with a statue of himself in knightly armor. "No vainglory and no vanity push me to this, but a zeal full of love of God and for the world." With these words the late bourgeois, who had been made a knight only three years earlier at the age of twenty-five, tried to disarm the criticism of his associates and friends. Once more the empress had set aside the feudal customs of Achaea to accommodate her protégé: by an act dated July 15, 1338, she approved the arrangement whereby the revenues of Nicholas's Moreote estates, in case he died leaving only minor heirs, would go to the building of his mausoleum until his children reached their majority. As it turned out, the Certosa of the Val d'Ema was completed within Nicholas's lifetime, having been built in part from the spoils of a Greece which was a profitable colonial area for the Italian merchants and financiers of the fourteenth century. Writing to his father on October 8, 1338, Nicholas expressed the hope that for every denier expended in Achaea he would receive ten; the actual return on his Peloponnesian investment was probably a profitable one though surely not as spectacular as that.

Once in the Morea Catherine asserted her authority in order to end her bailie's attempted subjection of Patras. It can scarcely be doubted that the close financial ties between the Acciajuoli house and the papacy were a factor determining Nicholas's advice to the empress to restrain Bertrand of Les Baux and acknowledge the archbishop's dependence on the papacy. Catherine also realized she must have the pope on her side to help her stop the incessant and damaging raids of the Turks on the coasts of the principality. She and Nicholas spent two and a half years in the Morea in a concerted effort, in which money was not spared, to exact obedience from feudatories and to restore the defenses of the principality against the Turks, Catalans, and Greeks. Nicholas at his own expense built a fortress in "the barony which is called the vale of Calamy" for the defense of northern Messenia against incursions from Mistra. Among grants which he received while in Greece were this barony and the castle of Piada in the Argolid, near Epidaurus. The king of Naples confirmed the old and the new concessions in an act of April 27, 1342, which lists all the estates and gives their annual value in gold ounces.[23] For his extensive possessions Nicholas is held to the

23. Buchon, *Nouvelles recherches,* II, 109–114. Robert is here acting, as on previous occasions, in his capacity of higher suzerain over Achaea: "racione et potestate majoris dominii quod nobis competere noscitur in principatu jam dicto" (*ibid.,* p. 112).

service of one knight and fourteen squires, "according to the usage and custom of the principality." But earlier custom had exacted much more than such light service: the host of barons, lieges, men of simple homage, and sergeants mentioned in the *Chronicle of the Morea* and the *Assizes of Romania* was now replaced by a smaller number of great lords—some of whom were often absentees like the Acciajuoli—and above all by hired troops. From the document just cited we also learn that in the decade 1332–1342 the Acciajuoli had advanced to John of Gravina and Catherine of Valois 40,000 gold ounces altogether for the purchase of the principality of Achaea and for its maintenance and defense, of which sum 3,000 ounces were still outstanding. To appreciate the size of these expenditures we may recall that John of Gravina had purchased the principality for 10,000 gold ounces from his brother Philip.

We should consider at this point, at least briefly, the question of a relationship between Catherine of Valois and the two fundamental sources for the history and institutions of the principality of Achaea, the *Chronicle of the Morea* and the *Assizes of Romania.* It has been argued that the lost prototype of the Chronicle was composed in Italian about 1325 and that the French version—which alludes to the empress as still living—was prepared for her at the end of her residence in Greece. It has been further suggested that Nicholas Acciajuoli interested himself in the production of the French *Chronicle of the Morea.*[24] However, a recent and thorough comparative analysis of the principal versions of the Chronicle has led to different findings which are much more persuasive than the above hypotheses. It is very likely that the original text of the Chronicle was composed in French about the beginning of the fourteenth century, and served as the basis for a shorter French version made about 1320–1324. In turn, this prose version was recopied with interpolations between 1341 and 1346. It was this copy that was rendered into Greek "political" verses for recital before an audience of Greek landholders of the principality. The author of the Greek version belonged to this milieu and perhaps even to the Roman church, for his invectives against the Byzantine and Epirote Greeks are more violent than those of the French version. Finally, it has been shown that the basic text incorporated in the Aragonese version of the *Chronicle of the Morea* was first composed in French in the Morea during 1377–1381 and

---

24. See Longnon, *L'Empire latin,* pp. 317, 325. Longnon also conjectures that Boccaccio may have been referring to the French Chronicle when he described Nicholas as writing "in French of the deeds of the knights of the Holy Expedition." However, Léonard has shown that the allusion is to a lost "Golden Book" of the "Ordre du Saint-Esprit au Droit Désir" known to have been composed by Nicholas (*Boccace et Naples,* p. 116).

drew liberally from both the French and the Greek versions, besides adding valuable information from other sources, especially for events of the fourteenth century.[25]

The connection of the empress Catherine with the law code of feudal Achaea—familiar under the modern title *Assizes of Romania*—is even more tenuous than that with the Chronicle. The view that the Assizes were officially recorded under the auspices of the Angevin rulers of the principality about 1320[26] must be abandoned. Far from having an official character, the Assizes were a private collection of the customs of the principality made by an unknown legist who wrote in French, about the middle of the fourteenth century. The law he recorded had evolved progressively in the thirteenth and early fourteenth centuries. It had been partly recorded in a set of assizes that existed in the princely chancery about 1275. From this and other written texts, as well as from unrecorded customs, the author of the Assizes made his final redaction. Although never officially sanctioned in Achaea, the Assizes answered the needs of the feudality of Latin Greece as a whole. They have reached us in a Venetian translation probably made in Negroponte in the late fourteenth century. By permitting their application in its own colonies, the Venetian government assured their survival long after the end of the principality of Achaea.[27]

The empress Catherine and her party returned to Naples in June 1341. Events were quickly to show that nothing short of continuous residence of the ruling family could maintain the Angevin authority in the Morea. In fact, even while the empress was still in Greece Robert the Wise had to write (December 24, 1340) to the prelates and barons of the principality to exhort them to be loyal to his sister-in-law and nephews, since he had learned that archbishop Roger of Patras and the bishop of Olena, with Philip of Jonvelle (the lord of Vostitsa) and other conspirators, had leagued with the Greeks.

This letter helps to confirm the report in the memoirs of John VI Cantacuzenus of the negotiations in 1341 between himself and a

---

25. See Jacoby, "Quelques considérations sur les versions de la 'Chronique de Morée'," *Journal des savants,* July–September 1968, pp. 133–189.

26. Cf. Recoura, *Les Assises de Romanie,* pp. xiii, 44–46; Longnon, *L'Empire latin,* p. 318; Monti, *Nuovi studi angioini,* pp. 630–634.

27. See Jacoby, *La Féodalité en Grèce médiévale, passim.* Jacoby shows that the document of November 21, 1342, issued by Robert of Naples has been wrongly used to prove the existence of the Assizes by this date and to connect Catherine and her son Robert with them (*ibid.,* p. 82).

party of Achaean notables. In the years immediately preceding, Andronicus III and Cantacuzenus, then the grand domestic, had succeeded in recovering Epirus, Acarnania, and Aetolia for the empire—one of the last glorious achievements of Byzantine policy, which the earlier Palaeologi and the Nicaean emperors had vainly attempted. The boy despot, Nicephorus II, was deposed, but he managed later to escape to the court of Catherine of Valois at Patras. With Angevin encouragement and material aid a serious revolt was organized against the central authority, centering in the inland fortresses of Arta and Rogoi and in Thomokastron on the coast. Nicephorus himself crossed over to Thomokastron with an Angevin naval contingent. In the spring of 1340 the emperor and Cantacuzenus reappeared in western Greece to press the siege of the rebel strongholds already begun by subordinate commanders. Thanks in large part to Cantacuzenus's persuasive diplomacy, all three places surrendered in the course of the year. In a meeting with the envoy of the Thomokastron rebels—a certain Richard, the Frankish tutor of Nicephorus—Cantacuzenus argued that the defenders were greatly deceived if they hoped to recover their independence with the aid of the Angevins, who if victorious would only enslave their allies. He also promised to give one of his daughters in marriage to Nicephorus and to rear him as his own son.

With the surrender of Thomokastron the emperor's authority was reëstablished in the despotate, and the titular empress of Constantinople had lost a battle in the unending contest between the Latins and Byzantium for control of the Balkan peninsula. The Achaean feudatories and troops that took part in the defense of Thomokastron returned to the Morea much impressed by Cantacuzenus, and supported a movement to offer the principality to him. An embassy composed of bishop Andrew of Coron and John Siderus visited the grand domestic in his camp at Demotica in Thrace and announced the desire of the leading men to place themselves under the emperor, provided that they could hold their estates and pay the same dues as those to the prince. It was revealed to Cantacuzenus by letter that the Moreote nobles had planned to go over to the empire while Andronicus III was still living, but that the news of his death (which occurred on June 15, 1341) had upset their plans. Cantacuzenus told the envoys that since it was already autumn he could not take his army beyond the frontiers, but that he would appear in the Morea the following spring. In the meantime, he was sending a familiar of his, Jacob Vroulas, back with them to the Morea to act for him in preparing the change to imperial control.

At about the same time, in a council summoned to discuss how to
meet the Serbian danger, Cantacuzenus expressed high hopes for the
restoration of the empire, in words which anticipate the "great idea"
of modern Greek political leaders. "For if, God willing," he quoted
himself as saying, "we should gain control over the Latins dwelling in
the Peloponnesus, the Catalans who live in Attica and Boeotia would
have to yield to us whether willingly or through force. When this is
done and the hegemony of the Romans extends unbroken from the
Peloponnesus to Byzantium as it did in former times, we can envisage
that it would not be a difficult task to exact retribution from the
Serbs and the other neighboring barbarian peoples for the injuries
which they have been inflicting upon us for so long." All the hopes
and plans of the Byzantines, however, were shattered by the outbreak of the disastrous civil war of 1341—1347 and by the spectacular expansion of the Serbian state under Stephen Dushan as far as the
Gulf of Corinth.

The failure of the overture to the Greek emperor led the barons of
Achaea to turn to a distant Latin ruler who had a connection with
the land—James II of Majorca, the son of the unlucky infante
Ferdinand. The pressing Turkish peril and the neglect of the principality by Catherine and her sons, now involved in the murderous
politics of the reign of Robert's granddaughter, Joanna of Naples
(1343—1382), justified the search for a better protector. According
to a document seen by Du Cange, the barons met at Roviata in Elis
in October 1344, and approved an act which was conveyed to James
probably by Erard III le Maure (Mavro), baron of Arcadia and St.-
Sauveur. By it they notified him that he was the "legitimate" heir to
the principality inasmuch as his mother Isabel was the daughter of
Margaret of Villehardouin, the younger daughter of prince William;
on his arrival in the Morea they would acknowledge him as their
rightful lord. The seals of Roger, archbishop of Patras, of fifteen
barons and knights, and of eight squires authenticated the document.

A few years before, about 1338, a memorandum had been prepared which set forth in greater detail the purported rights of James
II.[28] According to it William of Villehardouin had named Margaret
and her children as his heirs after his older daughter Isabel, in case

28. This document has survived in Du Cange's copy and was thrice printed by Buchon;
see also the reprinting of it in the *Diplomatari de l'Orient català*, pp. 222–224, where Rubió
i Lluch argues for the date *c.* 1338; Hopf adopted the date 1338. William Miller (*Latins in
the Levant,* pp. 275–276) and Jean Longnon (*L'Empire latin,* p. 326) make no distinction
between the act at Roviata (seen by Du Cange) and the earlier memoir, although Du Cange
refers expressly to two documents (*Histoire de l'empire de Constantinople,* ed. Buchon, II,
224–225).

the latter died childless. As it happened, the document alleged, not only did Isabel's daughter, Mahaut, die a prisoner of the Angevins without leaving issue, but while being conducted to the Castel dell' Uovo she exclaimed that she was being unjustly imprisoned and that she was leaving whatever she possessed as of right to James of Majorca. The memorandum of course chose to ignore the fact that by her third husband, Philip of Savoy, princess Isabel had had another daughter, Margaret, who was still living. In its closing section it furnishes several interesting details about the principality. We are told that Peter dalle Carceri and Bartholomew Ghisi are among its vassals and that between them they control the island of Negroponte (Euboea), said to be as large as Majorca. Nicholas Sanudo of the Archipelago is also a vassal of Achaea *de jure et de facto.* Walter of Brienne holds Argos and Nauplia under fealty to Robert of Taranto. The Catalan Company, however, ignores the suzerainty of Achaea. Whoever should hold the entire principality of Achaea would have under him one thousand baronies and knights' fees, each of them worth 300 pounds of Barcelona annually. After deducting the expenses for the maintenance of the castles, the prince would have left 100,000 florins. These figures are exaggerated, unless they are meant to refer to the principality at its largest extent, before the establishment of the despotate of Mistra, with the addition perhaps of the lands of its vassal states.

The offer to James II of Majorca came to nothing. His conflict with the kingdom of Aragon, which cost him his kingdom and his life, removed any possibility that he might have gone to the Morea to make good his claim. His only recorded action as "prince of Achaea" was to appoint Erard III le Maure hereditary marshal of the principality and to grant him all the lands which had belonged to Nicholas Ghisi, formerly constable of Achaea; this is known to us from an act drawn up in Montpellier on November 24, 1345. With the failure of the overtures to Cantacuzenus and James a state of anarchy became almost normal in the Frankish Morea, except in the ecclesiastical fief of Patras, whose independence reached its height under archbishop Reginald (1351–1357).

Robert of Taranto was never to revisit the Morea after living there in his early youth with his mother. The Aragonese version of the *Chronicle of the Morea* mentions his coming of age soon after the family's return to Italy and his performance of homage for the principalities of Taranto and Achaea before his uncle, king Robert.[29]

29. *Libro de los fechos,* ed. Morel-Fatio, par. 675. Robert was born in 1326 (Léonard, *La*

Upon the death of Catherine of Valois in October 1346, he became prince regnant of Achaea and took the title emperor of Constantinople. For several months preceding his mother's death he had occupied the exalted position of vicar-general of the kingdom of Naples, but he had failed ingloriously.[30] Having lost out to his brother Louis in the competition for the hand of the young widowed queen Joanna of Naples, Robert married Marie, daughter of duke Louis of Bourbon and widow of Guy de Lusignan, the oldest son of king Hugh IV of Cyprus, in September 1347. The Aragonese Chronicle (paragraphs 676, 677) reports that he sent four bailies to Achaea before he was taken prisoner by his cousin, Louis I the Great of Hungary, on the latter's invasion of the kingdom of Naples. Since Bertrand of Les Baux had a second bailliage in Morea in 1341–1344,[31] Robert's appointees probably belong to the years 1344–1348. He was to spend four years as a captive in Hungary (1348–1352).

Pope Clement VI, always a strong protector of the Italian Angevins, showed great solicitude for Robert and his fellow-prisoners (his brother Philip and two sons of John of Gravina). Among other measures he sent letters to the prelates, officers, lords, and bourgeois of the principality of Achaea bidding them remain loyal to their captive suzerain.[32] The Aragonese Chronicle reports that Robert's wife Marie, who had gone to Avignon, sent as bailie in 1348 an able French knight, John Delbuy, whose appointment is confirmed by the Misti del Senato. But his early death, the Chronicle continues, led the prelates and barons assembled at Glarentsa to choose as temporary bailie one of themselves, Philip of Jonvelle, the lord of Vostitsa. Envoys were sent to prince Robert in Hungary and to Marie in Avignon to announce Delbuy's demise, whereupon the empress designated archbishop Bertrand of Salerno as bailie. During the term of this prelate a Burgundian knight with several companions seized the

---

Jeunesse de Jeanne Ire, I, 178, note 1). If we assume that he came of age about 1342 it follows that he at least shared in the government of Achaea before 1346, when Catherine died. His appointment of bailies, as reported in the Aragonese Chronicle (pars. 676, 677), suggests that his role in Achaean affairs was an active one even before 1346. Hopf wrongly makes Louis the oldest son of Philip of Taranto (*Chroniques gréco-romanes*, p. 470).

30. See Léonard, *La Jeunesse de Jeanne I*^{re}, I, 595.

31. Hopf, who did not know the Aragonese Chronicle, gives 1341–1346 as the dates of Bertrand of Les Baux's second term (in Ersch and Gruber, LXXXV, 435 [repr., I, 369]; no source cited). Jules Gay, in *Le Pape Clément VI et les affaires d'Orient (1342–1352)* (Paris, 1904), p. 59, note 5, shows that Bertrand was no longer bailie after 1344. Joanna's marriage to Louis I's brother Andrew had ended with his murder in 1345.

32. Léonard, *La Jeunesse de Jeanne I*^{re}, II, 97; Gay, *Clément VI*, p. 154. The captive princes of Durazzo were Louis and Robert, whose brother Charles had been executed by Louis I during his occupation of Naples in 1348.

castle of the Messenian Arcadia in the absence of its lord, Erard III le Maure, capturing his wife and his daughter. They retained the stronghold and their prisoners for some time until Erard agreed to a ransom.

The dominating factor in the external relations of Frankish Morea during Robert's personal rule was the increasing Turkish danger. So great now was the threat to the Christian states in the eastern Mediterranean that the Avignonese popes, Clement VI (1342–1352), Innocent VI (1352–1362), and Urban V (1362–1370), labored unceasingly to build up an effective coalition to stop the piracy and raids of the Anatolian emirates *per partes maritimas Romaniae.* [33]

The "holy league" of Venice, Cyprus, and the Hospitallers of Rhodes which Clement had succeeded in forming had won a great victory when it captured the castle of the port of Smyrna from the Selchükid emir Umur Pasha of Aydin in 1344. This feat of Christian arms had aroused intense enthusiasm in the west. The pope had tried to stop the Hundred Years' War and to organize an expedition of united Christendom against the "infidels" as in the great age of the crusade. To emphasize the Turkish danger Clement had written to Philip VI of France (May 11, 1345) to urge him to strike at once against the Turks, inasmuch as they were threatening the principality of his nephew, Robert of Taranto, and unless checked might easily go on to Naples. But the exigencies of the war with England were such that Philip, who a decade earlier had displayed great zeal for the crusade, now felt that a new expedition to the Near East would deprive him of very valuable knights.

A more immediate blow to the Christian cause was the ignominious failure of the dauphin Humbert's expedition, under the auspices of the papal league, to relieve Smyrna (1346). This defeat was only partly redeemed by the naval victory at Imbros—mainly the achievement of the Hospitallers' galleys—over a large Turkish fleet (1347). That the naval resources of the Turks were not decisively weakened is shown by the great raid on the principality of Achaea by a fleet of eighty ships, based at Ephesus, which entered the Gulf of Corinth in the spring of 1349. Under papal pressure Venice, Cyprus, and Rhodes renewed the maritime league in 1350, 1353, and 1357, but the bitter commercial war between Genoa and Venice paralyzed the allied effort from the beginning.

According to Giacomo Bosio, the sixteenth-century chronicler of

---

33. For a vivid Turkish account of the "holy war" against the eastern Christians in the 1330's and 1340's, see *Le Destān d'Umūr Pacha (Düstūrnāme-i Enverī)*, ed. and trans. by Irène Mélikoff-Sayar (Paris, 1954), and P. Lemerle, *L'Émirat d'Aydin, Byzance et l'Occident: Recherches sur "La Geste d'Umur Pacha"* (Paris, 1957).

the Order of St. John of Jerusalem (the Hospitallers), pope Innocent VI in 1356 sought to induce the order to buy the principality of Achaea and thus insure that its population would be "devoted and obedient to the holy see."[34] This project lay very close to Innocent's heart; the correspondence in 1356–1357 between the pope and the master Roger de Pins, which Bosio cites, alludes repeatedly to the *negotio dell' Acaia.* James of Savoy, who laid claim to Achaea, was willing, says Bosio, to sell the principality, and the pope wanted the knights to buy it from him.[35] At the same time, Robert of Taranto had to approve the transaction. However, when the pope, early in 1357, sent the archbishop of Salerno and a knight of the Hospital to Naples to see the prince, the latter refused his consent. Thus, concludes the chronicler, the "affair of Achaea" was concluded only in the time of Juan Fernández de Heredia.[36] It is reasonable to infer from Bosio's account that Innocent wanted the Hospital to acquire Achaea in order to assure its effective defense against the Turkish raiders. But a modern historian of the Order of St. John had no warrant for asserting that Innocent planned to move the Hospitallers from Rhodes to the Morea and that the true author of this scheme was not the pope but the future grand master Heredia, who enjoyed such high influence and favor at Avignon.[37]

Although frustrated in his plan to extend the Hospitallers' sway to the Greek mainland, Innocent continued to press the Angevins to defend Achaea. On October 12, 1357, he appealed to Robert's brother, king Louis of Naples, to help the church relieve the plight of the faithful in the principality. He informed Louis that he was writing to Robert, too, and that he was sending the archbishop of Salerno to Naples to act for the holy see. From another letter of

34. *Dell' istoria della sacra religione ed illustrissima milizia di S. Gio. Gierosolimitano,* II (Rome, 1629), 91.

35. James's father, Philip of Savoy, the third husband of Isabel of Villehardouin, had continued to use the title prince of Achaea, inasmuch as the Angevins had not fully carried out the terms of the agreement of 1307 (cf. vol. II of this work, p. 268) whereby Philip relinquished the principality to Charles II of Anjou in return for the county of Alba. Philip remarried after Isabel's death, and the male descendants of this union, starting with James, styled themselves princes of Achaea until 1418.

36. Bosio, *op. cit.,* pp. 91–94. For Heredia and the Hospitallers in the Morea 1376–1381 see below, chapter V, pp. 147–149, and chapter VIII, pp. 302–303.

37. See J. Delaville Le Roulx, *Les Hospitaliers à Rhodes jusqu'à la mort de Philibert de Naillac, 1310–1421* (Paris, 1913), pp. 130–133. Delaville Le Roulx was in part misled by Karl Herquet, who believed, mistakenly, that Heredia was in Patras in 1353 and that he rather than Innocent conceived the scheme of acquiring Achaea in 1356 (*Juan Ferrandez de Heredia, Grossmeister des Johanniterordens, 1377–1396* [Mühlhausen i. Th., 1878], p. 28 and p. 37, note 1). See Luttrell, "Greek Histories Translated and Compiled for Juan Fernández de Heredia, Master of Rhodes, 1377–1396," *Speculum,* XXXV (1960), 402 and note 5, as well as chapter VIII, below.

Innocent's, written in 1359 to Nicholas Acciajuoli, we learn that the grand seneschal was at that time preparing a fleet to attack the Turks.[38] Only the year before, Nicholas had received the strategic castellany of Corinth from prince Robert; this acquisition made it imperative for him to deal seriously with the Turkish peril. However, although he strengthened the defenses of Corinth, he did not undertake any naval expedition against the Turks.

In contrast to these abortive efforts stands the victory of a Christian coalition over a Turkish fleet off the coast of Megara about the year 1359. The allies were Walter of Lor, the bailie of Achaea, Manuel Cantacuzenus, the despot of Mistra, the Venetian signoria, and the Hospitallers of Rhodes. The Venetians and the knights contributed a certain number of galleys. "They were all together at Megara and there burnt thirty-five vessels of the Turks, and the Turks fled to Thebes to Roger de Lluria." Thereupon the commanders of the land forces and the captains of the galleys, being unable to do further injury to the Turks, dispersed to their home places. Such is the brief account of this action preserved in the Aragonese *Chronicle of the Morea* (pars. 685–686). John Cantacuzenus probably refers to the same event when he reports an invasion of Boeotia against Roger de Lluria by the Peloponnesian Greeks and Latins under the command of his son, the despot Manuel.[39] In the same passage the ex-emperor mentions, certainly with exaggeration, "many victories" of the allies over the Turkish raiders. He also magnifies the degree of his son's ascendancy over the Franks of the Morea. But there is no doubt that Manuel—whose long rule (1349–1380) at Mistra was a model administration compared to the turbulent situation in the Angevin Morea—enjoyed great prestige throughout Achaea, and he may well have taken the initiative in forming the coalition which gained the victory near Megara.[40]

At best, however, this isolated victory could have given the harassed population of the Morea only temporary relief from the Anatolian raiders. Like his predecessors Clement VI and Innocent VI, pope Urban V showed much concern over the plight of the exposed Frankish principality. On August 10, 1363, he wrote to Robert of Taranto commending the newly appointed archbishop of Patras, Bartholomew, who apparently was prevented by the Turks and the "schismatic Greeks" from occupying his see. In 1364 the pontiff

38. Buchon, *Nouvelles recherches,* II, 135–136.
39. IV, 13–14 (*CSHB,* III, 89–90).
40. Various dates, as early as 1357 and as late as 1364, have been proposed for the battle near Megara. Our preference for *circa* 1359 is based in part on the probable dates for the bailliage of Walter of Lor. Cf. Loenertz, "Athènes et Néopatras . . . ," pp. 430–431.

urged Bartholomew, Peter Thomas, Latin patriarch of Constantinople, the Venetian bailie of Euboea, and the feudality of that island
to concert all measures to defend the principality. He wrote in
similar terms to the Angevin bailie and to the ecclesiastics and lords
of Achaea. These appeals did not, apparently, lead to any united
action by the Latins of Greece against the Turks. The crusade led by
Peter I of Cyprus with the zealous support of Urban V might have
brought important relief to the Latin states of Greece if directed
against the emirates of Anatolia.[41] Instead, Peter's spectacular capture and sack of Alexandria in 1365, far from liberating Jerusalem,
would only weaken the whole Christian position in the Levant and
allow the Turks to plunder and penetrate the Greek peninsula almost
at will.

Robert of Taranto had returned to Naples from his Hungarian
captivity early in 1353. As the elder brother of queen Joanna's
consort, Louis of Taranto, and as an important territorial lord, it was
natural that he should try to play a leading role in the affairs of the
kingdom of Naples, the "Regno." But he was as ineffectual now as in
the years before his captivity. If the Regno counted for something at
this time in the Italian peninsula and in Europe, it was due solely to
the statesmanship of Nicholas Acciajuoli, who had been appointed
grand seneschal in 1348. In the principality of Achaea Nicholas's
influence was still greater than before; he acted as Robert's principal
adviser in Greek matters, as he had done for Catherine of Valois, and
his services were again rewarded with large estates in the Morea. In a
letter dated February 22, 1356, which the grand seneschal addressed
to his familiar, Americo Cavalcanti, and to his favorite cousin, Jacob,
he reports that "the emperor" (i.e., Robert) has commissioned him
"to reform the principality." Nicholas needs to send out a good
bailie and wants Americo to consider the post. But he adds frankly
that "the emperor" has no money to give from Italy and that the
country is no longer as prosperous as it used to be. A few weeks later
(March 14, 1356), writing to his cousin Jacob, Nicholas reports that
he will advise Robert to appoint Adam Visconte bailie. It was
probably Visconte to whom Robert sent orders on July 10, 1356, to
enforce respect for the trading privileges of the Venetian merchants
in Achaea.[42]

41. Cf. A. S. Atiya, *The Crusade in the Later Middle Ages* (London, 1938), p. 332, note
1. See chapter X, below.

42. The texts of these letters are in Léonard, *Louis de Tarente*, pp. 574–575, 589–590;
partial text of the letter of March 14, 1356, is in Buchon, *Nouvelles recherches*, II,
124–125. Adam Visconte is probably the same person as "micer Adam, vizconte de

Early in 1358 the inhabitants of the castellany of Corinth sent a despairing plea to their prince to rescue them from impending enslavement by the Turks. Robert responded promptly by granting the entire strategic area to Nicholas Acciajuoli as a barony, with rights of high justice (April 1358). Shortly after (November 1358), at the grand seneschal's instance, Robert ordered the remission of all the dues which Nicholas's "men and vassals" in Achaea and in the castellany owed to the princely fisc. At the same time Robert ordered that measures be taken to induce the serfs who had fled from the unprotected castellany to return to their habitations. The prince further allowed Nicholas to perform all the feudal service which he owed for his Greek estates on the frontiers of the exposed barony. Archaeological evidence indicates that Nicholas spent large sums to rebuild a long stretch of the great circuit wall of Acrocorinth.

Du Cange long ago remarked on the special affection and solicitude which Robert of Taranto demonstrated for Marie of Bourbon. The prince had given repeated proof of his sentiments by granting his consort large estates and by treating her son, Hugh of Galilee, as if he were his own. He had warmly espoused Hugh's claims to the throne of Cyprus. At the time of their marriage (September 1347) Robert had assigned to Marie for her dower an annual revenue of 2,000 gold ounces from his possessions in Italy and in Corfu and Cephalonia. In 1355 he granted her for her household an annual income of 1,050 ounces from his Italian lands. In 1357 he bestowed on her the rich castellany of Kalamata, with two dependent castles and the rights of high justice. About this time Marie purchased the two important baronies of Vostitsa and Nivelet.[43] The purchase was made from Guillemette, heiress of the Charny family, and her spouse, Philip of Jonvelle; it included the castle of Phanaro on the left bank of the Alpheus a little to the east of Olympia. In 1359 Robert conferred

---

Tremblay" mentioned three times as a bailie in the Aragonese Chronicle, pars. 676, 684 (the appointment of 1356?), and 688. Difficulties arising over the commercial privileges of Venice in Achaea and the treatment of her merchants were frequent in these years. Cf. Predelli, *I Libri commemoriali*, II, 234, nos. 101, 102; and II, 249, nos. 167, 170, 171, 172; Léonard, *Louis de Tarente*, p. 496, note 7, and Hopf, in Ersch and Gruber, LXXXVI (1868; repr. 1960, II), 2. Venetian merchants had a privileged status in Robert's Italian domains, especially at Trani; the relations of the two sides were mutually profitable here (Léonard, *Louis de Tarente*, pp. 494–495).

43. These baronies are often confounded, with Nivelet being placed near Vostitsa (cf. Miller, *Latins in the Levant*, p. 148). However, from the content of the report of Nicholas of Boyano (see note 44, below) it is certain that Nivelet consisted of scattered estates in Messenia and that it was here that John I of Nivelet received compensation for the loss of his ancestral barony and castle of Geraki following the reëstablishment of the Byzantines in the southeastern Morea in 1262.

upon her and his stepson a village and the mountain of Moundritsa, situated close to Phanaro.

In the winter of 1360–1361 an emissary of Marie's, Nicholas of Boyano, made a careful inquiry into the state of her extensive domains in the Morea. The report on this mission which he addressed to her "imperial majesty, madame the empress," is a precious record of the economic and political state of the Frankish Morea in the middle of the fourteenth century.[44] In addition to the baronies of Kalamata, Vostitsa, and Nivelet, and the castle of Phanaro, Marie also held the fief of Picotin in Elis. Nicholas of Boyano mentions the production of silk, valonia, and salt on this estate. But in general the agricultural yield of Marie's estates, especially in cereals, was poor, partly because of bad weather in 1359–1360. He recommends that two villages in the barony of Nivelet should cultivate the vine instead of planting wheat. At two other places in this barony the serfs complained of having to do the *corvée* at distant points a whole day's march or more from their villages, to the neglect of their own fields and houses. Two years after the concession of Corinth to Nicholas Acciajuoli, Nicholas of Boyano finds that its villages, along with those of Basilicata (Sicyon) and the environs of Vostitsa, were still deserted because of Turkish pirates. He plans to visit the area if he can go securely by sea, and will try to rent the lands to somebody (*mello è pocu avere che perdere tutto,* he remarks). He had inventories drawn up in Greek of the Nivelet estates and intended to do the same for Vostitsa.

As striking as the report of the poverty of the country is Nicholas of Boyano's testimony to the insecurity in the principality caused by the feebleness of Angevin authority. He mentions the failure of several important vassals of the prince to provide feudal service or payments—the grand seneschal (Nicholas Acciajuoli), the count of Cephalonia (Leonard I Tocco), Centurione I Zaccaria, baron of Chalandritsa, and the lord of Arcadia (Erard III le Maure). The insubordination of Zaccaria was a scandal. He would need more than two days, Nicholas says, merely to record all of the complaints he heard about Centurione's excesses. When Nicholas sent him a command to make amends for damage done to Marie's property, Centurione "replied with bland words, acting as if he were prince William [of Villehardouin] himself come back to life." Prince Robert's own bailie was powerless to curb the insolent baron—a "tyrant," Nicholas

44. The original is in the Bibliothèque Nationale (Mss. Fr. 6537); it is published as document VIII by Jean Longnon and Peter Topping in *Documents sur le régime des terres dans la principauté de Morée au XIVe siècle.* On the dating of this document see *ibid.,* p. 144.

warned the empress, whom she must effectively curb if she and her son were ever to enjoy any real authority "in Romania." Nicholas of Boyano concludes his report with the news that Venice was arming twenty galleys for the capture of Constantinople, in order to avenge the "schismatic" emperor's mistreatment of Venetian merchants and officials. This was the hour, he urged, for prince Robert to form a league with Venice for the recovery of Marie's imperial heritage; the opportunity was the more favorable because the "signor of the Turks" was causing such devastation on land that no one dared emerge from the gates of Constantinople. This was fascinating intelligence, indeed, if accurate. One suspects, however, that Marie's humble servitor was exaggerating various reports and rumors reaching the Morea in order to flatter their imperial majesties.

Early in 1360 Nicholas Acciajuoli was in Avignon on an important mission for the Neapolitan court. Through his efforts large sums of the *cens* of the kingdom, for long in arrears, were paid into the papal coffers. A grateful Innocent VI bestowed on the grand seneschal the highest papal decoration, the Golden Rose, till then reserved only for princes. He further rewarded him by naming his kinsman, John Acciajuoli, to the vacant see of Patras (May 1360). The archbishopric was in a troubled state internally, and it was no doubt hoped that the secular authority of Nicholas Acciajuoli would help his cousin restore stability there.

John's brother Nerio went to Patras as leader of a small armed force, to enable the youthful archbishop to impose his authority.[45] This is the first appearance in Greece of the young Florentine destined to wear the ducal coronet of Athens. He was one of the two adopted sons of the great Nicholas, who had already provided lands in Italy for him in his final testament, drawn up in September 1359. Now both his adoptive father and his brother the archbishop tried to improve Nerio's prospects in Greece through a brilliant marriage. They sought for him the hand of Florence Sanudo, who was left heiress to the Archipelago when her father John I, the sixth duke, died in 1361.[46] They asked queen Joanna of Naples and Robert of Taranto, as suzerains of the Archipelago, to write on Nerio's behalf to Venice. The two rulers informed the republic that as their vassal Florence was free to dispose of her hand as soon as Robert gave his consent thereto. A firm rejoinder came that Florence was first of all a Venetian citizen and subject whose heritage would long since have

---

45. É. G. Léonard, "La Nomination de Giovanni Acciaiuoli à l'archevêché de Patras (1360)," *Mélanges offerts à M. Nicolas Iorga* (Paris, 1933), pp. 513–535.

46. For this date see Miller, *Latins in the Levant*, p. 590, note 3, and Jacoby, *La Féodalité en Grèce médiévale*, p. 301, note 8.

disappeared except for Venetian protection; since Robert provided no protection, it was the republic's matter to care for the duchess's future and security. The republic was of course determined that Florence should marry only a Venetian subject and thus continue the regime of indirect Venetian control of the Archipelago. To forestall any attempt by the Acciajuoli to kidnap Florence, the Venetian authorities of Euboea abducted her first and conveyed her to Crete. In 1364 she was married in Venice itself to her cousin Nicholas Sanudo, called Spezzabanda.

Archbishop John Acciajuoli died in 1363.[47] On November 8, 1365, the life of his famous kinsman Nicholas would end. Although he would be succeeded as grand seneschal by his eldest son Angelo, his true successor as the most influential Acciajuoli in Greece was to be his young cousin Nerio. Already in 1363–1364 Nerio had entered the ranks of the Achaean feudality by purchasing for 6,000 ducats the baronies of Vostitsa and Nivelet from Marie of Bourbon, who had at first pawned them to Nicholas. We shall have frequent occasion in the following chapter to allude to the later activities of the Acciajuoli in Greece, especially the extraordinary fortune which Nerio found there.

47. On this date see Léonard, "La Nomination de Giovanni Acciaiuoli," p. 513, note 1, and p. 531, note 3. Louis of Taranto had died in 1362, and Joanna had taken as her third husband James of Majorca (d. 1375).

V

THE MOREA, 1364–1460

Robert of Taranto, prince of Achaea and titular emperor of Constantinople, died at Naples in September 1364. A year later Nicholas Acciajuoli, for thirty years the counsellor, confidant, and main support of the prince, was also dead. A new phase in the history of the principality now began, even though the immediate connection of the small state with the Angevin dynasty of Naples continued until 1383.

From 1365 the principality steadily declined, until its last remnant was absorbed in 1432 by the expanding Greek despotate of the Morea, with its capital at Mistra. Throughout this period it was generally on the defensive in its relations with the despotate. Among the Latin states of Greece it was put in the shade by the brilliant duchy of the Florentine Acciajuoli in Athens and by the remarkable state created by Charles Tocco in the Ionian islands and Epirus. It was almost a satellite of Venice, and from the 1390's on it was tributary to the Ottoman Turks. Yet until nearly the end of its existence it was a factor in the politics of the Levant and in the waning crusading movement. Repeatedly popes and grand masters sought to establish the great military-religious organization of the Knights of St. John (Hospitallers) in the strategic peninsula of the Morea. The title prince of Achaea was hardly less coveted than that of emperor of Constantinople or king of Jerusalem. Paradoxically, in the second half of the fourteenth century the claimants to the principality founded by the Villehardouins multiplied in proportion as its territorial extent and authority over its vassal states diminished.

The death of Robert of Taranto led to a serious conflict over the succession to his Greek dominions. His surviving brother Philip II, the youngest of the sons of Philip I of Taranto, claimed Corfu and Achaea, together with the title emperor of Constantinople. However, he faced a determined counter-claimant in the person of his brother's stepson Hugh de Lusignan, titular prince of Galilee, who had the

For bibliography see preceding chapter.

141

support of his energetic mother, Marie of Bourbon. Hugh had been cheated of the throne of Cyprus, to which he was rightfully entitled by the custom of primogeniture, by his uncle, the crusading Peter I (1359–1369).[1] Marie and her son now sought compensation for this loss in the principality of Achaea. To take effective possession of the land they sent mercenary forces to the peninsula sometime in the first half of 1366.[2] In the meantime, according to the Aragonese version of the *Chronicle of the Morea,* the feudality of Achaea, including archbishop Angelo of Patras, had declared itself for Philip of Taranto. However, a certain William of Talay, captain of Port-de-Jonc (Navarino), one of the castles in Marie's Peloponnesian dower, refused to surrender this strategic place to Philip's bailie, Simon del Poggio of Perugia, and in fact imprisoned the latter when he came to treat with him. He also appealed for aid to the despot, Manuel Cantacuzenus, and Guy of Enghien, baron of Argos and Nauplia.[3] Cantacuzenus and Guy sent troops to the plain of Elis, where they did considerable damage.

At this juncture, with the loyalist forces under archbishop Angelo besieging Port-de-Jonc, there appeared a *deus ex machina* in the person of Amadeo VI of Savoy. The "Green Count" was on his way to Constantinople to rescue his cousin, emperor John V, from Bulgarian harassment. He landed at Modon on July 17, 1366, and two days later at Coron.[4] His mediation, promptly offered and accepted, brought the civil war to an end, at least temporarily. Angelo raised the siege of Port-de-Jonc, and William of Talay released Simon del Poggio. But the Bourbon-Lusignan forces remained in the southwestern Morea. At the beginning of 1369 the Venetian government wrote to Hugh to urge the dismissal of the faithless Talay, who

1. See below, pp. 351–352.

2. No doubt the payments which Peter I de Lusignan made to Marie on her dower and to Hugh in satisfaction of his claims to Cyprus were largely used up to finance the campaign in the Morea. Cf. Louis de Mas Latrie, *Histoire de l'île de Chypre,* II, 253, and Leontius Machaeras's *Chronicle* (ed. and trans. R. M. Dawkins [2 vols., Oxford, 1932]), pars. 105–108. In 1365 Marie and Hugh sent their seneschal Gurello Caracciolo to Frederick III of Sicily to seek aid (Hopf, in Ersch and Gruber, LXXXVI [1868; repr. 1960, II], 5, and note 47, citing the Palermitan archives).

3. The despoina, Isabel (or "Maria"), was a Lusignan, second cousin of Marie of Bourbon's first husband (Hugh's father), Guy of Galilee; see S. Binon, "Guy d'Arménie et Guy de Chypre: Isabelle de Lusignan à la cour de Mistra," *Mélanges Emile Boisacq* (Brussels, 1937–1938), pp. 124–142.

4. The dates appear in the records of disbursements by Amadeo while on the crusade, published by F. Bollati di Saint-Pierre, *Illustrazioni della spedizione in Oriente di Amedeo VI (Il Conte Verde)* (Biblioteca storica italiana . . . della R. Deputazione di storia patria, V [i.e. VI]; Turin, 1900), p. 43, nos. 105, 106, and cf. p. 44, no. 115, for payment to "Guillelmo de Taley, capitaneo castri de Jout . . ." (obviously William of Talay at Port-de-Jonc). On Amadeo's crusade see above, pp. 18–19, 74–77.

had been plotting the capture of Modon.[5] In the next year the unlucky prince of Galilee gave up completely the struggle to establish himself in the Morea. At Naples on March 4, 1370, he and his mother reached an agreement with Philip of Taranto whereby they renounced their claim to Achaea in return for a yearly pension of 6,000 florins. Marie's dower in the castellany of Kalamata was excepted from the agreement, and she also continued to use the title empress of Constantinople.[6]

Like his brother Robert, Philip II of Taranto was too deeply involved in Neapolitan affairs to give much attention to the principality of Achaea. Of mediocre ability, insubordinate to popes Urban V and Gregory XI as well as to queen Joanna, feuding frequently with his sister Margaret's husband, Francis of Les Baux, he was as little constructive in Italy as in Greece. He unjustly withheld properties in Italy from Marie of Bourbon, who, apparently impoverished by her Achaean venture, obtained the intervention of Urban V against her brother-in-law.[7] The practice of frequent appointments of bailies in Achaea, some of whom were not native barons, contributed nothing to the stability of the principality. According to the Aragonese Chronicle (pars. 690–704) Philip sent or appointed one special emissary and seven bailies (including Centurione I Zaccaria twice) in the Morea between 1364 and 1373. One of these, Louis of Enghien, count of Conversano, apparently used his position mainly in order to aid his brothers—John, count of Lecce, and Guy, lord of Argos and Nauplia—in an abortive attempt in 1371 to overthrow the Catalan duchy of Athens.

Philip's last bailie but one was a Genoese knight, Balthasar de Sorba. It is likely that Philip made his acquaintance during his long visit (1369–1371) at the court of Louis I the Great of Hungary, who had appointed Balthasar admiral of Dalmatia.[8] The new bailie's

---

5. Hopf, in Ersch and Gruber, LXXXVI (repr., II), 9, and notes 66–72, all citing the Misti del Senato.

6. *Ibid.*, p. 9, and note 74, citing the Angevin archives. Cf. E. Gerland, "Bericht über Carl Hopfs litterarischen Nachlass," *Byzantinische Zeitschrift*, VIII (1899), 350, note 1.

Miller and Longnon give more elaborate accounts of the conflict between Philip of Taranto and Hugh of Galilee for mastery of Achaea, using the *Vita Caroli Zeni* by Jacopo Zeno (in Muratori, *RISS,* vol. XIX, part VI [Bologna, 1940–1941]) to supplement the Aragonese Chronicle (pars. 689–702). Although the Chronicle is obviously wrong at several points, it is closer to the events it describes. Romanin, Heyd, and Hodgson have pointed out the fictionalized character of the *Vita.* There is no question, however, of Zeno's early connection with Patras as a cathedral canon; cf. *Lettres communes du Pape Urbain V 1362–1370*, ed. M. H. Laurent (vol. I, fasc. 2, Paris, 1955), no. 2207.

7. Urban wrote to Philip July 7, 1367, and November 4, 1369: *Lettres secrètes et curiales d'Urbain V* (fasc. 3, Paris, 1954), nos. 2476, 2997.

8. On Balthasar de Sorba's Hungarian service, cf. Hopf, in Ersch and Gruber, LXXXVI

arbitrary and violent acts in the Morea at the expense of Venetian citizens led to strong representations by the senate to Philip and his bailie. John Piacentini, the archbishop of Patras (1371–1375), was so harassed that he went to Venice in 1373 in order to place himself and his see under the protection of the republic. The senate seemed ready to accept the offer and also considered transferring Venetian trade from Glarentsa to Patras, when Philip's death later in the same year (November 25) removed the cause of the conflict. Patras was not to become Venetian until 1408.

As already noted, the remarkable career of Nicholas Acciajuoli came to an end with his death in November 1365. In his princely testament of September 1359 he had provided handsomely for his three surviving sons, for his two adopted sons, and for various spiritual bequests. He was buried in the Certosa near Florence, in the imposing mausoleum which he had built for himself with much care and lavish expense.

Nicholas's eldest son, Angelo, received the greater part of his vast possessions in Italy and Greece, as well as the dignities of count of Melfi and grand seneschal of the Regno. But the true successor to Nicholas Acciajuoli was the masterful diplomat Nicholas Spinelli of Giovinazzo, chancellor of the kingdom. Angelo even had difficulty keeping his titles and lands in Italy in 1366–1367.[9] Being weak in Italy he could never be influential in Greece. Although Robert of Taranto had conferred the castellany of Corinth upon Nicholas as a hereditary fief, Philip granted it to Angelo only for the latter's lifetime (November 7, 1366). Later, to be sure, while in Buda (February 26, 1371), Philip regranted Corinth to Angelo as a hereditary fief along with the title of palatine; the prince thus rewarded Angelo for his trouble and expense in accompanying him to Hungary. However, it would appear that effective possession of the strategic castellany had already passed to Angelo's cousin Nerio. From the terms of the testaments of the adoptive brothers it is clear that Angelo had long since pawned the castellany to Nerio. Neither Angelo nor his three sons ever redeemed it. Pope Gregory XI evidently regarded Nerio as an independent lord when he addressed him as *dominus civitatis Corinthiensis* in November 1372. The Corinthian barony added to that of Vostitsa made Nerio master of the northeastern Morea. In 1374 he seized Megara from the declining Catalan duchy. By 1388 he was complete master of Attica, including the Athenian Acropolis.

(repr., II), 9; on Philip in Hungary, cf. Léonard, *Angevins de Naples,* p. 430, and Buchon, *Nouvelles recherches,* I, 118.

9. Léonard, *Angevins de Naples,* p. 416.

Gregory XI's letter to Nerio was one of the invitations which the pope sent to the Latin lords in the Levant, to the Byzantine emperor, to the doges of Venice and Genoa, and to the kings of Hungary and Aragonese Sicily to attend a congress at Thebes in October 1373. There Gregory hoped to form a grand alliance against the Ottoman Turks, whose crushing victory over the Serbs at Chernomen on the Maritsa (September 26, 1371) imperiled the entire Christian position in southeastern Europe. But the project of a crusading congress was most impractical in a year, 1373, which saw Genoa attack Cyprus and Louis of Hungary declare war on Venice. Indeed, the pope himself seems tacitly to have abandoned the utopian scheme only a few months after its conception. Instead he tried to raise a small fleet of twelve ships to be stationed permanently in the Aegean Sea and the Straits in order to impede Turkish communications between Asia Minor and Thrace. Gregory asked queen Joanna and Philip of Taranto, among other rulers, to contribute galleys to the allied fleet,[10] but even this modest objective could not be realized. The pope nevertheless persisted in his efforts to persuade the monarchs of the house of Anjou—Louis of Hungary and Joanna of "Sicily" (Naples)—to contribute to the defense of the Greek empire. He emphasized that the fall of Constantinople would lead to the Turkish conquest of the entire Balkan peninsula, including Achaea and the Aegean islands, following which Hungary and Italy would be directly menaced. There could be no hope of a *passagium generale* to recover the Holy Land unless Byzantium were first saved.[11]

Like so many similar papal appeals in the fourteenth century, this was in vain. The crusading zeal of Gregory XI was an anachronism in the 1370's. He had no more loyal adherent and vassal than the much maligned queen of Naples, who was, indeed, soon to lose crown and life for supporting the French line of popes in the first years of the Great Schism. But Joanna was both unwilling and unable to give more than lip-service to the ideal of the crusade, although it was in theory the *raison d'être* of the Angevin kingdom of Naples.

On the death in 1373 of Philip II of Taranto without heirs, Joanna decided to exercise direct rule over his Greek possessions, of which she had long been suzerain. But Philip left a sister, Margaret, whose

---

10. Probably in June, if not in March, 1373: O. Halecki, *Un Empereur de Byzance à Rome* (Warsaw, 1930), p. 277, note 3; Philip seems to have promised two vessels (*ibid.,* p. 300). Halecki rightly questions whether the congress of Thebes actually met; most historians of Latin Greece assume that it did (cf. *ibid.,* chapters X–XI). Cf. also Rubió i Lluch, *Diplomatari de l'Orient català,* p. 423, note 1.

11. Letters of Gregory XI to Louis and Joanna, October 27, 1375, analyzed in Halecki, *Empereur de Byzance,* pp. 314–315.

second husband was Francis of Les Baux, duke of Andria and lord of extensive estates in Provence and southern Italy. The half-royal Les Baux were one of the greatest families of the Regno. Margaret and her husband claimed the principality of Taranto and Philip II's Greek lands and titles for themselves and their son James, the last male descendant of Philip I of Taranto. But Joanna acted decisively to put down the open rebellion of the family and deprived Francis, for the crime of *lèse-majesté*, of all of his titles and possessions (April 1374).[12]

The civil war between Joanna and the Les Baux is echoed in the Aragonese version of the *Chronicle of the Morea*. Soon after Philip II of Taranto's death the barons of the Morea sent an important embassy to Naples to examine the rights of the two sides respecting the principality of Achaea. Its members were Erard III le Maure, the lord of Messenian Arcadia, Centurione I Zaccaria, lord of Chalandritsa, John II Misito, baron of Molines, and Leonard I Tocco, one of the peers of the principality, who had been created count of Cephalonia and Zante in 1357 by Robert of Taranto and was married to a niece of Nicholas Acciajuoli. The embassy decided in favor of the queen and did homage to her as their princess after she had sworn to respect the usages and customs of the principality.

Joanna then sent Francis of San Severino, a member of the highest Neapolitan aristocracy, as her bailie in the Morea. He broke the peace of long standing between the principality and the despotate of Mistra by attacking the castle of Gardiki, which commanded the pass of Makryplagi in the border country of Messenia and Arcadia. Although he defeated a relieving force led by the despot Manuel Cantacuzenus, the fortress held out and he had to retire to Glarentsa. Venetian sources report the harassment of the republic's merchants by Francis in Achaea and by the queen's governor in Corfu. Francis also encroached on the territory of Modon and Coron. In answer to the republic's protests Joanna sent strict orders to her officials to uphold all Venetian franchises and privileges. A mixed commission was agreed on to define the boundaries between Achaea and the Venetian colony.

On March 25, 1376, Joanna of Naples married her fourth husband, Otto of Brunswick-Grubenhagen. She bestowed upon him the principality of Taranto, which she had lately confiscated from the Les

---

12. Pope Gregory XI supported Margaret's claims: cf. G. Mollat, ed., *Lettres secrètes et curiales du pape Grégoire XI (1370–1378)*, fasc. 4 (Paris, 1955), col. 1063, no. 3302; col. 1080, no. 3371; col. 1081, no. 3374. Gregory addresses James of Les Baux as *despotus Romaniae* in a letter of June 30, 1371 (*ibid.*, col. 769, no. 2251); it is possible that Philip had granted the title to his nephew.

Baux. She did not, however, as so often stated, grant him the principality of Achaea.[13] Rather, later in the year 1376 (perhaps in August) she leased the entire principality to the Knights Hospitaller for five years at an annual rent of 4,000 ducats. Thus was realized the project, which pope Innocent VI had promoted in 1356, of bringing the principality of Achaea under the control of the Order of St. John.[14] According to the Aragonese version of the *Chronicle of the Morea* queen Joanna sent the Hospitaller Daniel del Carretto, who held the commanderies of Cyprus and Genoa, to the Morea as her bailie to take possession of the principality in the name of the order.

On September 24, 1377, the famous Juan Fernández de Heredia was appointed grand master of the Hospitallers and at the end of the year himself embarked at Naples for northwest Greece.[15] It is possible that the Hospital's intervention in this region was part of a larger plan, to which the leasing of Achaea was related, to defend Greece against the Turks. The order's acquisition of the port of Vonitsa in Epirus in 1377 from Maddalena de' Buondelmonti, regent of the duchy of Leucadia, was also, apparently, related to the larger scheme. In late April 1378 Heredia was in Vonitsa. He was now near Arta, the capital of the newly constituted Albanian seigneury of Aetolia and Acarnania. In a rash attempt to take this city, however, Heredia was captured by its lord, Ghin Boua Spata, who soon sold him to the Turks. The order ransomed the grand master without great delay, for by May 20, 1379, he was in Glarentsa.[16]

It was about the time of Heredia's capture—in the spring or early summer of 1378—that his commandant in the Morea, Gaucher of La

13. Hence Otto must not be reckoned among the princes of Achaea. For this, and several other important corrections in the older accounts of the period 1376–1383, see R. J. Loenertz, "Hospitaliers et Navarrais en Grèce 1376–1383: Regestes et documents," *Orientalia Christiana periodica,* XXII (1956), 319–360.

14. Cf. p. 134, above. Loenertz deduces the date August 1376 from the document of August 24, 1381, which mentions the retrocession of the principality to the queen's officials; he assumes that if the lease had not run its course of five years this fact would have been mentioned (*loc. cit.,* pp. 329, 351). Anthony Luttrell, however, prefers the year 1377 ("The Principality of Achaea in 1377," *Byzantinische Zeitschrift,* LVII [1964], 341–342), and below, p. 302.

15. The Aragonese *Chronicle of the Morea,* compiled at Heredia's command shortly before 1393, ends with Daniel del Carretto's passage to Greece, omitting any description of the grand master's inglorious campaign in Epirus. On the date of the compilation of the Aragonese Chronicle see Jacoby, "Quelques considérations sur les versions de la 'Chronique de Morée'," *Journal des savants,* July–Sept. 1968, pp. 177–179.

16. Loenertz, *loc. cit.,* p. 331. There is no warrant for Loenertz's statement that Heredia captured Naupactus (Lepanto) and Vonitsa before marching on Arta. See Luttrell, "Aldobrando Baroncelli in Greece: 1378–1382," *Orientalia Christiana periodica,* XXXVI (1970), 280, 289. Lepanto, acquired by the Angevins in 1294, was a dependency of the principality of Achaea. The Hospitallers made payments for its defense during the time they were in the Morea (Loenertz, p. 335).

Bastide, prior of Toulouse, hired two small companies of Navarrese and Gascons to serve the order for eight months. The captains of the two companies were Mahiot of Coquerel and John de Urtubia. Two years earlier these redoubtable mercenaries had captured Durazzo, then in Albanian hands, for their employer, Louis of Évreux, brother of king Charles II of Navarre. Durazzo and the *regnum Albaniae* were the dower of Louis's consort Joanna, a granddaughter of John of Gravina and daughter of the late Marie of Anjou, sister of queen Joanna. Louis of Évreux died in 1376, following his success at Durazzo. We do not know by what route the Navarrese and Gascons reached the Morea, nor can we infer much about their activities there during the remainder of the Hospital's lease.[17]

Sometime during the first half of 1379 John de Urtubia left the Morea and the service of the Hospital and with the connivance of Nerio Acciajuoli effected the violent conquest of Thebes, the capital of the Catalan duchy of Athens. It does not appear that the knights abetted this attack, but it is significant that they did not prevent or discourage it. Following Urtubia's departure the Navarrese and Gascons remaining in Achaea were reformed into a single company under three chiefs: Mahiot of Coquerel, Peter Bordo de Saint Superan, and Berard de Varvassa. Saint Superan and Varvassa had been members of Urtubia's force. It is this new organization which we may call, conveniently if not with entire accuracy, the Navarrese Company of Achaea. It is a mistake to infer from the conquest of Boeotia by Navarrese and Gascon mercenaries that the Company of their compatriots in the Morea similarly invaded and overthrew the Angevin principality of Achaea. We know that high officials of the Order of St. John made a large payment to the company for additional, but unspecified, services, which must have been rendered in 1380 or 1381. In the spring or summer of 1381 Dominic de Alamania, lately the order's bailie in Achaea, went from Italy to the Morea in order to hand over the administration of the principality to the officials of queen Joanna.[18]

17. The payments for their service to the order are recorded in the document of August 24, 1381, by which Heredia and the convent of Rhodes approved of the accounting for the years 1378–1381 which was presented by Dominic de Alamania. Loenertz has published this document from the Malta archives, *loc. cit.,* pp. 350–355. Alamania was the bailie of the principality during much of the Hospital's stay there (Longnon and Topping, *Documents sur le régime des terres dans la principauté de Morée au XIV* siècle, p. 196 and note 5).

18. Four letters by Aldobrando Baroncelli written in 1381–1382 shed additional light on the activities and behavior of the Navarrese mercenaries during their first years in the Morea. The Hospital's officials could not restrain their aggressions, which included the seizure and plundering of estates of the Acciajuoli. See Luttrell, "Aldobrando Baroncelli in Greece," *loc. cit., passim.*

The withdrawal of the Hospital from its costly venture in the Morea barely preceded the queen's capture on September 2, 1381, by her second cousin and the pretender to her throne, Charles of Durazzo. Charles was a grandson of John of Gravina and was married to his cousin Margaret, one of the daughters of Joanna's sister Marie of Anjou. Joanna had infuriated the Italian Urban VI by her vigorous support of the French cardinals who elected Clement VII. In retaliation Urban first offered her throne to Charles (1379) and later formally invested him with the Regno as Charles III (June 1, 1381). The queen had thus been forced to adopt duke Louis of Anjou, the brother of Charles V of France, as her son and heir (June 29, 1380). But Louis's delayed invasion of Italy in 1382 came too late to save Joanna. The luckless queen—who once wrote that her only regret was that the Creator had not made her a man—was assassinated at Muro on July 22, 1382.

These events profoundly affected the Greek possessions of the Angevin dynasty. Among the immediate beneficiaries of the triumph of Charles III was the pretender to the principality of Achaea, James of Les Baux. On September 7, 1381, his banner was raised over the castle of Taranto. On January 18, 1382, the Navarrese Company concluded a treaty with the chancellor of Modon and Coron in the latter city, settling disputes over the borders of the colony and the principality in southern Messenia. Those who swore to uphold the agreement in the name of the Company were Mahiot of Coquerel, as "imperial" bailie of Achaea, and Peter Bordo de Saint Superan and Berard de Varvassa, as "imperial" captains in the principality. It is evident that James of Les Baux had conferred these titles and appointments on the chiefs of the Company in the last months of 1381 in return for their acknowledgment of him as lawful prince of Achaea and titular emperor of Constantinople. James was also acknowledged as lord in Corfu. Two acts of his of December 26, 1381, regarding fiefs of Corfiote nobles are preserved.

On March 2, 1382, James married—by proxy at Naples—Agnes of Anjou-Durazzo, another daughter of Joanna's sister Marie of Anjou. The match at first estranged the king of Naples and the prince of Taranto, now his wife's brother-in-law, but on September 16, 1382, Charles III granted the island of Corfu in perpetuity to James of Les Baux as the marriage portion of Agnes. However, the princess was already dead by February 10, 1383, and a few months later, in July, her husband James, the last titular emperor of Constantinople, followed her to the grave.

With the death of James of Les Baux the Angevin principality of Achaea was virtually at an end. Such authority as Charles III of

Naples (1381–1386) and his son Ladislas (1386–1414) enjoyed in the Morea was too shadowy to allow us to speak of a regular connection between the Greek province and the Neapolitan court. The long succession of Angevin bailies sent out from Naples now ceased. The Navarrese Company remained the only organized power in the principality of Achaea, except the archbishopric of Patras. The new arrivals did not displace certain older families, such as the Zaccarias of Chalandritsa, the Le Maures of St.-Sauveur and Messenian Arcadia, and the Misitos of Molines. But the extensive estates of the heirs of Nicholas Acciajuoli in Elis, westernmost Skorta, and Messenia passed into Navarrese hands. Their most important possessions of course were the estates and castles of the princely domain, including the coastal fortresses of Kalamata and Port-de-Jonc (Navarino) in Messenia, close to the Venetian colony of Modon and Coron. The town of Androusa, near the classical Ithome, overlooking the rich plain of Kalamata, served as their headquarters and capital. The imposing remains of its castle and aqueduct testify to its importance under Frankish and Turkish rule.

Although the Navarrese Company was the effective power in Achaea with which all interested parties had to deal, it was not so independent as to be able to scorn all claimants to the principality. It was certainly not nearly so numerous or so powerful as the Catalan Company had been immediately after its conquest of the Burgundian duchy of Athens, and even the Catalans had felt it necessary to seek the protection of the Aragonese house of Sicily and to accept their dukes therefrom.

James of Les Baux had bequeathed his rights to Achaea and to the Latin empire of Constantinople to his cousin Louis I of Anjou, the adopted son of the late queen Joanna. Louis died in September of 1384, having failed to wrest the kingdom of Naples from Charles III, but his widow, called Marie of Brittany, claimed Achaea for her seven-year-old son, Louis II. This enterprising lady thought of selling her son's rights to the Order of St. John, whose grand master never gave up the scheme of establishing the Hospitallers on the Greek mainland. Heredia promptly made contact with the Navarrese to learn on what terms they would give up the princely castles and domains to his order. A memorandum in the archives of Malta which records these conditions shows how wary and demanding the real masters of the principality were.[19] They required proof that James of Les Baux had designated Louis I and his son as his heirs along

---

19. Text in Delaville Le Roulx, *Hospitaliers à Rhodes*, p. 380; 1385 is the probable date of the document.

with certification by the pope (Clement VII) and his cardinals that Louis II was king of "Sicily." For their services to James and for protecting the principality after his death, they asked 70,000 ducats. Besides keeping the lands they already held outside the domain, they wanted a castle within it for their captain, Mahiot of Coquerel. Finally, they asked that the pope, the king of France, and Louis II of Naples should ratify any agreement adopted.

No treaty resulted from these negotiations. The money demands of the Navarrese were obviously exorbitant. In any case it would have been difficult to provide them with the proofs and ratification they demanded at a time when the power of Charles III was preponderant in Italy and the church was hopelessly divided in its allegiance to two popes. Ignoring the Navarrese Company, Marie of Brittany and Heredia concluded a contract of sale on January 24, 1387, whereby the Hospital bought her son's rights to Achaea for 20,000 gold florins. Clement VII approved the transaction.

In the meantime Mahiot of Coquerel had died (1386) and Peter Bordo de Saint Superan had assumed command of the Company. Saint Superan continued the negotiations begun under his predecessor to settle the differences between the Company and the Venetian republic. By the treaty concluded July 26, 1387, the Venetians were promised compensation for damages suffered on the entry of the Navarrese into Achaea and were assured the right of preëmption to Port-de-Jonc whenever the Company should decide to dispose of it. The Genoese had lately shown a lively interest in the strategic harbor; its acquisition by Venice's arch-enemy would have neutralized the value of her way-stations at Modon and Coron. Saint Superan's concession to Venice in this matter helped to assure him the support of the republic, which was to be demonstrated on more than one critical occasion. The treaty of 1387 undoubtedly enhanced the prestige of the Navarrese leader. It is significant that he was empowered to negotiate it by all the important men of the principality—twenty-eight religious and secular lords—including the Venetian archbishop Paul Foscari of Patras, who conscientiously looked after the interests of his mother country in the Morea.

It was also in 1387 that the crusading Louis II of Clermont, duke of Bourbon, showed an interest in the principality of Achaea. His aunt, Marie of Bourbon, appointed him her universal heir in her testament drawn up in Naples early in 1387. Although this document makes no mention of the principality—to which Marie and her son Hugh of Galilee had given up all claim in 1370—the duke's faithful servitor, John of Châteaumorand, twice visited the Morea and brought back the report that the Achaean lieges were only awaiting Louis's arrival to acknowledge him as their seigneur. Doubtless, in the fluid situation existing in Achaea in the 1380's, the actual arrival of an enterprising western prince with a plausible claim and some troops would have resulted in the quick submission of the country to him. Louis had the advantage of Venetian favor, the senate warmly commending him to Saint Superan and Nerio Acciajuoli. However, he was soon involved in preparations for the great Genoese-French expedition against the Barbary pirates in 1390, and he never set foot in Greece.

The most remarkable of the several claims to Achaea asserted at this time was that of pope Urban VI. On September 6, 1387, at Lucca he appointed archbishop Paul Foscari of Patras vicar-general and regent of the principality. The land was his to dispose of, Urban declared, inasmuch as it had devolved to Charles III on the death of James of Les Baux and had then entered the immediate possession of the holy see when the pope declared his vassal Charles forfeit in 1385. The problem of the Navarrese Company was to be neatly solved by Paul's using Saint Superan and his men to recover the parts of the principality which were in the hands of the "schismatic" Greeks of Mistra; the Navarrese would hold the new lands as fiefs of the church. There is no evidence that the archbishop of Patras tried to take the place of Saint Superan, whom he had very recently supported as chief negotiator of the treaty of July 26, 1387, with Venice. The Navarrese in any case did not need papal encouragement to attack the Greek despotate. They had a permanent invitation from the landowning caste (*archontes*) of the Byzantine province to support their rebellions against the despot, Theodore Palaeologus. The Navarrese at times hired Turkish pirates to raid the despot's lands. They were likewise at odds with Theodore's father-in-law, Nerio Acciajuoli, whose barony of Vostitsa they had seized.

Yet another claimant to the coveted principality of Achaea in the 1380's—and this the most zealous of all—was Amadeo of Savoy, lord of Pinerolo. His tenuous claim derived from his grandfather Philip, who had ruled Achaea briefly at the beginning of the century.[20] Like the other claimants he was acting to fill the vacuum left by the virtual abandonment of Achaea by the Neapolitan Angevins. His Achaean venture had the blessing of the Avignonese pope Clement VII and indirectly of the dynasty of France. This was consistent with

20. Cf. Longnon, *L'Empire latin de Constantinople,* pp. 289–291, 327, 340, and above, chapter IV, p. 107.

his position as a satellite of the French crown in the politics of northern Italy. He was also acting in full accord with his cousin, Amadeo VII of Savoy, the "Red Count," who pledged material aid and diplomatic support.

For five years (1386–1391) Amadeo conducted complex diplomatic negotiations in the west and in Greece in order to secure effective recognition as prince of Achaea and to prepare an expedition to the Morea. His protest to Heredia against Marie of Brittany's sale of her son's rights to the principality resulted in a bull by Clement VII (April 11, 1387) which in effect revoked his approval of the transaction. In his early negotiations at Venice and Avignon Amadeo employed as his unofficial agent John Lascaris Calopherus, one of the most important Byzantine converts to the Latin church and for decades a favorite of the French popes. As the son-in-law of Erard III le Maure, a leading baron of Achaea, Calopherus had a personal stake in the success of Amadeo's Greek venture. The prince showed his appreciation of his services by investing him with extensive estates in Messenia, as well as with the county of Cephalonia (July 19, 1387), where at the time Maddalena de' Buondelmonti was regent for her son Charles Tocco.[21]

Amadeo's task was greatly complicated in 1389–1391 by the seizure of Argos and its Larissa by Theodore Palaeologus. The Venetian government had purchased Nauplia and Argos—strategic places from which all the Morea could be acquired, as a senate document noted—on December 12, 1388, from the young widow Marie of Enghien, who was unable to defend them. However, the despot seized both places before the Venetians could take possession.[22] The high commissioner sent out from Venice early in 1389 succeeded in taking over Nauplia, but his demand for the surrender of Argos was met by Theodore's determined refusal. The question of the recovery of Argos made allies of Venice and the Navarrese Company, in opposition to Theodore and his father-in-law, Nerio. The republic looked upon Acciajuoli as mainly responsible for the despot's *coup de main.* Being both unable and unwilling to engage in a costly war with Theodore—who was supported in the Argos affair by his suzer-

21. This was the second time that title to this island realm was conferred on Calopherus. A Barcelonese document of 1383 (text in Rubió i Lluch, *Diplomatari de l'Orient català,* doc. DXLI, p. 590) referring to him as count of Zante and Cephalonia is cited by Loenertz ("Hospitaliers et Navarrais en Grèce 1376–1383," p. 347), who comments that the title could have been conferred on Calopherus only by James of Les Baux as prince of Achaea, perhaps to reward him for persuading the barons of Achaea to acknowledge James as prince. Cf. also David Jacoby, "Jean Lascaris Calophéros, Chypre et la Morée," *Revue des études byzantines,* XXVI (1968), 216–218.

22. Zakythinos, *Le Despotat grec du Morée,* I, 133, note 4.

ain, the sultan Bayazid—Venice hoped to use the Navarrese as troops against him. As for Amadeo, it was obviously necessary for him to be on good terms with both sides in the conflict. He not only desired Venetian transports for his expedition to the Morea but also needed the favor of Theodore and Nerio, who were powerful neighbors of the principality. On September 26, 1390, Venice agreed to transport Amadeo or his brother Louis by sea to Greece with three hundred mounted men and six hundred crossbowmen or foot-soldiers. In return Amadeo promised his support in the recovery of Argos. He made his pledge more specific in a renewal of this agreement (May 30, 1391), when he promised to take Argos by siege and to deliver it into Venetian hands.

In the meantime the Navarrese were proving their worth as allies to Venice by capturing Nerio Acciajuoli at Vostitsa on September 10, 1389, whither the ruler of Athens had gone, unsuspectingly, to discuss the question of Argos with Saint Superan. The Venetians consented (on May 22, 1390) to have Nerio freed only after he promised to obtain the surrender of Argos; among other pledges for his good faith he delivered Megara to them and his own favorite daughter Frances, the wife of Charles Tocco, as a hostage in Euboea. As matters turned out it was only in 1394 that the stubborn despot yielded the town and citadel of Argos to the Venetians, and then as a result of internal revolt in the despotate and fear of the Turks, rather than because of any pressure exerted upon him by Amadeo or Nerio. The Savoyard prince, indeed, secretly intrigued with Theodore despite his agreement with Venice, and annoyed the senate by engaging in direct negotiations with the Navarrese. His need for Venetian transports was not urgent enough to make him serve the republic's interests in respect to Argos. The negotiations with the Company resulted in the treaty of June 5, 1391, concluded at Venice. The Navarrese acknowledged Amadeo as prince and received confirmation of all the lands they held outside the domain. Amadeo agreed to pay the Company 20,000 gold ducats and to appear in the Morea in person by March of 1392. He spent the months of July and August in recruiting troops for his expedition and negotiating for aid from the Red Count.

The failure of Venice's diplomacy in Greece is evident in the cordial relations which now obtained between Amadeo and Theodore and even more in the treaty which the envoys of the prince of Achaea concluded with the lord of Athens in the palace chapel on the Acropolis on December 29, 1391. Nerio recognized Amadeo as prince of Achaea and suzerain of Athens and promised to help him *totis viribus* to conquer the principality and expel the Navarrese. He promised even to obtain the aid of the despot for the enterprise. His obligation to Venice to help her recover Argos was, however, expressly restated. Nerio's reward was to be the restitution to him of the Acciajuoli lands seized by the Navarrese, especially his own barony of Vostitsa.

The tortuous and contradictory diplomacy which Amadeo was pursuing in Greece was never put to the test. His envoys in Athens were negotiating in ignorance of the sudden accidental death of his cousin Amadeo VII on November 1, 1391. Not only was Amadeo of Achaea deprived of the material aid promised by the Red Count, but the upsetting of the political balance in northern Italy made it imperative for him to remain in his principality. Thus, although Amadeo (d. 1402) and after him his brother Louis (d. 1418) continued to use the title "prince of Achaea," neither ever went to Greece or had a lasting influence on the course of events there.

It is to Amadeo's interest in Achaea that we owe an important document prepared for him by the Navarrese in 1391. It is a list of princely and baronial fiefs held by the members of the Company, with the addition of four fiefs held by the Zaccaria family. It is somewhat less comprehensive than the feudal roll prepared for queen Joanna in 1377,[23] since it does not include the castles of the archdiocese of Patras nor those of the castellany of Corinth. It shows that the Navarrese were in firm control of the western Morea—the areas of Elis, Triphylia, and Messenia—and in addition held the strategic castle of Vostitsa on the Corinthian Gulf. The barony of Vostitsa was assigned to the vicar-general Saint Superan, who also had immediate possession of five rich fiefs on the princely domain—Glarentsa, Beauvoir (Belvedere), St. Omer, Androusa, and Kalamata. In addition, nine more baronial fiefs were held by him personally or by leading men of the Company in his name. Three of these had belonged to the late John II Misito. The list of 1391 is further valuable for the prosopography of the Company. Jacob of Cyprus and William de la Forest, who negotiated the treaty of 1387 with Venice, each held a fief. Still another fief once belonging to Misito was now held by Bertranet Mota de Salahia, a Gascon adventurer who briefly held the castle of Livadia and thus came into possession of its most precious relic, the head

---

23. Rather than for Marie of Bourbon in 1364, as Hopf and others have thought; on this correction see the articles by Luttrell in the *Byzantinische Zeitschrift,* LI (1958), 355–356, and LVII (1964), 340–345, with a revised text in the latter. Hopf first published the two lists in *Chroniques gréco-romanes,* pp. 227–230.

of St. George, sought by several kings of Aragon.[24] He was one of
the many Gascons in the Navarrese Company, which included a
number of Catalans and Sicilians as well. Among other fief-holders in
1391, Nicholas of Taranto and Le Moyne de Pollay are likewise
found in contemporary documents.

No doubt the roll of 1391 accurately records the fiefs of the
Navarrese, and these they expected to retain when Amadeo took
over the principality, except for the estates of the domain. But the
list of the higher vassals or peers of the prince which is appended to
the roll of 1391 is largely theoretical. It parallels the list of peers
given in article 43 of the *Assizes of Romania* in respect to the dukes
of Athens and the Archipelago, the triarchs of Euboea, the marquis
of Bodonitsa, the count of Cephalonia, and the ecclesiastical lord of
Patras. The peers of the Assizes had also included the lords of
Karytaina, Matagrifon (Akova), and Kalavryta—all three of which
fiefs were long since in Greek hands—and the marshal, whose office
apparently did not now exist. In their place the roll of 1391 puts the
duke of Leucadia (Leucas), the countess of Salona, and the lords of
Chalandritsa and Messenian Arcadia. Charles Tocco was of course
ruler of both Cephalonia and Leucas, but the "count of Cephalonia"
meant in a document specially intended for Amadeo could only have
been his favorite, John Lascaris Calopherus, with Tocco being confined to Leucas. Since Chalandritsa and Arcadia were now held by
one baron, Andronicus Asen Zaccaria, only he and the archbishop of
Patras would have been peers of Amadeo within the Morea, whereas
in the list of the Assizes five peers were Moreote lords. In any case,
the vicar-general of the Navarrese Company was ignored by the
outside peers as in any true sense a suzerain of theirs, and it is
impossible to say to what extent Amadeo would have made the list
of peers less theoretical if he had established himself in Achaea. As
for the first lord on this list, the duke of Athens, when Ladislas of
Naples formally bestowed this title on Nerio Acciajuoli in January
1394, he made him his direct and immediate vassal, thus eliminating
the suzerainty which the lords of Athens traditionally owed to the
princes of Achaea.[25] Ladislas had earlier (1391) conferred the office
of vicar-general of Achaea and of Lepanto on Nerio, a paper appointment which he now (1394) transferred to Nerio's brother, the
cardinal Angelo.

24. He was otherwise prominent in Latin Greece in the 1390's; cf. Rubió i Lluch's note,
Diplomatari de l'Orient català, p. 666, and K. M. Setton, "Saint George's Head," *Speculum*,
XLVIII (1973), 1–12.
25. See below, pp. 254–255.

The failure of Amadeo to appear in Greece left the Morea divided among the Navarrese, the Byzantines, the Venetians, and the Florentine Nerio Acciajuoli. But there was no security anywhere in the land with the ever-present menace of Turkish invasion and the incessant raids of Turkish and Catalan pirates. After their momentous victory at Kossovo (1389) it was apparently simply a question of time until the Ottoman armies would overrun the entire Balkan and Greek peninsulas. The conquest of Thessaly and of the Catalan principalities of Neopatras and Salona in 1393–1394 established the invaders on the Gulf of Corinth. The duchy of Athens, the Venetian colony of Negroponte, and all the Morea were in immediate peril.

Following the settlement of the conflict over Argos, Venice made a serious effort to pacify the Morea through a union of its four Christian powers.[26] The Venetians saw clearly that only military coöperation among the four states and the construction of a wall across the isthmus of Corinth—the Hexamilion—could save their own Peloponnesian colonies. Yet the ever-cautious statesmen of the lagoons were not quite serious enough. They hesitated to enter into a binding alliance that might involve them in actual conflict with the sultan. In any case common action by the Christian states of the Levant, even in the face of imminent destruction by the enemy of the faith, was always difficult to achieve. Nerio Acciajuoli became tributary to the sultan in 1393. In 1387 the despot Theodore had become the willing vassal of Murad I in order to crush his own rebellious *archontes* and gain the advantage over his Christian adversaries in the Morea. This relationship was broken early in 1394 only because Bayazid made impossible demands on his vassal—especially the surrender of Argos—thus causing Theodore's flight from his camp. And it was also in the early months of 1394 that the vicar-general of Achaea visited Bayazid to incite him against the despot and Nerio.[27]

The response to Saint Superan's invitation came the next winter. The redoubtable general Evrenos Beg, who in 1387 had raided the Morea as far as Modon and Coron, crossed the isthmus again, at the end of 1394 or the beginning of 1395. After spending a fortnight in Laconia he met the Navarrese forces at Leondari and together with them captured the fortress of Akova from the Byzantines on Cheese

---

26. Max Silberschmidt, *Das orientalische Problem zur Zeit der Entstehung des türkischen Reiches nach venezianischen Quellen (1381–1400)* (Leipzig and Berlin, 1923), pp. 89–96.

27. Silberschmidt, *op. cit.,* p. 90 and note 2. Even Venice for a moment in 1390 thought of inducing Turkish intervention against Theodore over the Argos imbroglio (Hopf, in Ersch and Gruber, LXXXVI [repr., II], 54 and note 7, citing the Misti).

Sunday (February 28, 1395). Evrenos then chose to withdraw to his Thessalian fief, while the war between the Navarrese and the Greeks continued. On June 4, 1395, Saint Superan was defeated by the Byzantine forces and taken prisoner, together with his brother-in-law, the grand constable Andronicus Asen Zaccaria. In order to restore the balance in the Morea Venice intervened to persuade Theodore to release his high-ranking prisoners (December 1395). The republic paid the despot the sum of 50,000 hyperpers as ransom, against Port-de-Jonc and Vostitsa as sureties.

It is obvious that if Nerio Acciajuoli had been living at the time of Saint Superan's capture he would have urged his son-in-law Theodore to resist the Venetian pressure to release their hated rival, who had treacherously imprisoned the ruler of Athens in 1389. But the extraordinary career of Nerio had ended on September 25, 1394, when he died at Corinth. By his eccentric will he bequeathed Athens to the church of St. Mary (the Christianized Parthenon), Boeotia to his bastard Antonio, and Megara, Basilicata (Sicyon), and his valuable Corinthian barony to his daughter Frances, the wife of Charles Tocco. To complicate matters further he commended all his lands and possessions to the protection of the Venetian signoria.

The disinherited despot of Mistra regarded Corinth as rightfully his and fought a brief war with Charles Tocco—who was supported by large Turkish forces—over its possession. Charles eventually (in 1395 or 1396) yielded Acrocorinth to his wife's brother-in-law. The great stronghold now included the impoverished town of Corinth within its extensive ramparts. But the strategic importance of the citadel was undiminished, and the Greeks rightly regarded Theodore's recovery of it as a national triumph.

It is possible that Saint Superan, during his submission to Bayazid, sought to constitute himself prince of Achaea under the sultan's suzerainty. As it turned out he did not need to apply outside Christendom to achieve his ambition. King Ladislas of Naples readily consented to make him hereditary prince of Achaea early in 1396 for the price of 3,000 ducats. The new prince, however, proved unable or unwilling to pay even this modest sum for his illustrious title. In 1404 the king of Naples was still trying to collect the amount from his successor, prince Centurione (II) Zaccaria. By bestowing the title of prince on Saint Superan, Ladislas naturally implied confirmation of his vassal and the other Navarrese in the possession of their lands, which included the estates of the Acciajuoli family. Perhaps the ruler of Naples had this situation in mind when, in an act of July 17, 1399, he confessed that he had "inadvertently" made concessions prejudicial to the grand seneschal of his realm, Robert Acciajuoli, the grandson of Nicholas.[28]

The project of fortifying the Hexamilion was revived in February of 1396 when the Venetian signoria promised to support it and also to induce the "lord vicar or prince" to coöperate. Whether owing to Venetian prompting or not Saint Superan sent envoys to Venice to offer to contribute to the undertaking. His envoys were also to submit to arbitration the perennial disputes with the colony of Modon and Coron over boundaries and refugee serfs. These differences were soon settled, and on July 10, 1396, the agreements of 1382 and 1387 between the republic and the Navarrese Company were renewed.

The Morea was spared a Turkish invasion in 1396, probably because of Bayazid's preparations to meet the Christian host advancing to Nicopolis. His crushing victory there (September 25, 1396) laid all the unconquered portions of the Balkan peninsula at his mercy. In fact 1397 was the most catastrophic year of the fourteenth century for the Latin part of the Morea. Large Turkish forces led by Timurtash Beg and Ya'qūb Pasha devastated the peninsula, climaxing their invasion with the capture and sack of Argos on June 3, 1397. The surviving population of the city was enslaved and deported to Asia Minor.[29]

In anticipation, apparently, of this great invasion, the despot Theodore had offered Corinth to the Venetian republic in return for military aid, only to have his proposal rejected by the senate (April 29, 1397). When the Turks laid siege to the citadel in the summer of 1397 Theodore in terror and desperation offered Corinth to the Order of St. John. The knights accepted, and it is probable that they took possession of Corinth before the end of 1397. In 1399–1400 the sale of the entire despotate to the order was negotiated. The grand master Philibert of Naillac hoped to acquire the entire peninsula of the Morea and to replace the half-anarchic and mutually hostile states of Achaea and Mistra with a well-organized state capable of withstanding the Turkish assaults and of serving as a base for united action of the Christian states against the common enemy. In July 1399, at the same time that the grand master accredited Eli

28. By this act Ladislas confirmed and reëstablished Robert in the lands which he had held in Naples and the Morea and had lost while remaining a faithful vassal to Ladislas during the vicissitudes of the 1380's and 1390's in the Regno. It is most unlikely that the regranting of his estates in 1399 was of any practical benefit to Robert in Achaea. (Text in Buchon, *Nouvelles recherches*, II, 214–218.)

29. On Timurtash rather than Evrenos as one of the Turkish commanders in 1397 see Loenertz, "Pour l'histoire du Péloponèse au XIVe siècle," p. 155.

of Fossat, the castellan of Corinth, to Theodore, he sent Gerard of Le Puy to the prince of Achaea.[30]

Saint Superan at first promised to lend his military strength to the order and to help complete and defend the Hexamilion (November 23, 1399). It must have been about this time, too, that he defeated a Turkish invading corps and earned the congratulations of the Roman pope Boniface IX, who conferred on him (February 15, 1400) the title "vicar and gonfalonier" of the holy see in Achaea. But no titles conferred by king or pope could turn Saint Superan into a champion of the faith. Early in 1401 we find him raiding Modon and Coron in the company of the Turks.[31] Whether this alliance was also directed against the Hospitallers is not clear. We know that the prince was on good terms with the order in the summer of 1401.[32] In the end, however, the Hospital's new venture in the Morea was no more successful than that of Heredia two decades earlier. The removal of the immediate Turkish menace to Greece as a result of Bayazid's defeat and capture by Timur at Ankara (July 28, 1402) only reinforced Theodore in the intention he had already formed of exercising his right to buy back the despotate from the order (1402–1404).[33]

In the meantime the prince and Venice had composed their differences once more. Feeling his end approaching, the aging Saint Superan asked the signoria to become the guardian of his small sons after his death. He had cause to be concerned about his family's future. In 1401 the grand constable, Andronicus Asen Zaccaria, had died, leaving four sons: Centurione, who became baron of Arcadia, Erard, Benedict, and Stephen, later the archbishop of Patras (1404–1424). In November of 1402 the prince of Achaea followed his brother-in-law to the grave. His widow, Maria Zaccaria, succeeded him as princess of Achaea and assumed the regency for their oldest son. Whether out of sentiment or necessity she appointed her nephew Centurione her vice-regent. As the head of the oldest and wealthiest baronial family left in the land Centurione thought he better deserved to rule Achaea than did the sons of his aunt's parvenu husband Saint Superan. Early in 1404 he secretly proposed to king Ladislas of Naples that he be invested with Achaea as a hereditary

30. Delaville Le Roulx, *Hospitaliers à Rhodes,* p. 277; cf. Loenertz, "Pour l'histoire du Péloponèse au XIVe siècle," p. 188.

31. Documents from the Misti of April 22 (24?) and May 6, 1401, in Sathas, *Documents inédits relatifs à l'histoire de la Grèce au moyen âge,* II, 25–26, 30.

32. Delaville Le Roulx, *Hospitaliers à Rhodes,* p. 280, note 5.

33. See below, pp. 307–309. Cf. Loenertz, "Pour l'histoire du Péloponèse au XIVe siècle," pp. 186–194.

principality in return for prompt payment of the 3,000 ducats owed by Saint Superan's heirs for the title conferred on the late prince in 1396. On April 20, 1404, the always impecunious Ladislas accepted the proposal and declared the sons of Saint Superan forfeit of the principality because they had failed to take the oath of fealty to him; simultaneously he conferred their patrimony upon Centurione and directed him to take the oath of homage in the hands of his brother Erard. Thus did Centurione II Zaccaria, through a shabby transaction, become the last prince of Frankish Achaea in succession to the Villehardouins, the Angevins of Naples, and a mercenary captain from Gascony. Of the last reigning princess of Achaea and her children, nothing is known after their dispossession.

Thanks to his own resourcefulness and to timely Venetian intervention on several occasions, Centurione prolonged the existence of the principality of Achaea for an entire generation (1404–1432). The implacable foe of the Navarrese and the Zaccarias, despot Theodore I, made a last effort to conquer the principality in 1406. Despite his alliance with Charles Tocco and Centurione's brother Stephen, he once more was cheated of his objective. His death in 1407 and the minority of his nephew and successor, Theodore II Palaeologus, the second son of emperor Manuel II, freed Centurione from any threat from Mistra for several years. But his coreligionists, the vigorous Tocco brothers of Cephalonia, Charles and Leonard, remained a grave menace to the security of Achaea throughout his reign. Leonard, who held the island of Zante from Charles as an appanage, had been enfeoffed with estates in the Morea by Saint Superan. Centurione had seized these lands early in 1404 and had been ordered by king Ladislas to surrender them to Leonard. It is not likely that the prince paid any attention to the distant monarch's injunction. Toward the end of 1407, however, Leonard seized Glarentsa, the most important city in Centurione's control.[34] The prince begged for Venetian aid to recover the port. The republic offered to intervene in return for the cession of Port-de-Jonc. Nothing came of these negotiations; however, in 1408 the youngest of the Zaccaria brothers, archbishop Stephen, harassed by Turkish attacks and financial difficulties, decided to lease Patras to Venice for five years at an annual

---

34. The capture is mentioned in a Venetian document of February 6, 1408 (Sathas, *Documents inédits*, II, 193, where 1407 should be 1408). The unpublished Greek verse "Chronicle of the Tocchi" describes the successful expedition of the Greek and Albanian forces raised by the Tocchi. It adds that Charles set out for the Morea, intending to reduce Centurione to impotence, but did not reach Glarentsa. See G. Schirò, "Struttura e contenuto della Cronaca dei Tocco," *Byzantion,* XXXII (1962), 214–215. Perhaps Leonard's occupation of Glarentsa was of brief duration.

rental of 1,000 ducats. Stephen retained his spiritual jurisdiction while the Venetian governor conducted the secular administration in the archbishop's name.

Having acquired Naupactus (Lepanto) in June 1407, Venice now controlled the two keys to the Gulf of Corinth and could protect her important commercial interests at Patras against the Turks or any Christian competitor. The republic appeased Suleiman, the ruler of European Turkey, by paying tribute for both places. The payment for Patras was made through prince Centurione, himself tributary to the Turk. The prince at first protested the Venetian lease of Patras, but his position was so precarious that he seriously considered offering his own land to the republic. Yet when his conflict with the Tocchi was renewed Centurione was so successful on land and sea that the brothers appealed to Venice to accept them as vassals. Instead the republic mediated a three-year armistice in 1414 whereby the prince of Achaea retained Glarentsa.

It was about this time that Centurione, along with other Christian princes of the Balkans, sent felicitations to Mehmed I, "the Gentleman," now the sole ruler (1413–1421) of the reunited Ottoman empire.[35] The cordial relations which emperor Manuel II enjoyed with the sultan enabled him to spend a year in the Morea (1415–1416). During this memorable visit the basileus pacified the despotate internally and erected the Hexamilion. He also—according to the historian Ducas—imposed his authority on prince Centurione and the Navarrese feudatories, so that on departing for the capital "he left behind his son Theodore as despot of all Pelopennesus."[36] The claim is exaggerated, but it almost became a reality as a result of the war between the Byzantines and Centurione in 1417–1418. In 1417 John (VIII) Palaeologus, the emperor's eldest son, captured Androusa, "the key and entrance" to the rich province of Messenia, as a Venetian chronicle describes it. The same source remarks that Centurione was always concerned to amass money and to keep only enough troops to guard his places, instead of maintaining men in the field.[37] The Byzantine forces overran Messenia and pressed

---

35. Ducas, XX (*CSHB*, pp. 97–98). Hopf probably reads too much into this passage when he states that Theodore II Palaeologus and Centurione did homage to Mehmed (in Ersch and Gruber, LXXXVI [repr., II], 76A).

36. Ducas, XX (*CSHB*, p. 102). The "Chronicle of the Tocchi" may now be adduced as evidence that Centurione and the Achaean nobles recognized Manuel as suzerain, at least for the moment. See the extract published by Schirò in *Byzantion*, XXIX–XXX (1959–1960), 228–230, especially lines 1976, 1984–1986.

37. *Cronaca dolfina*, MS. in the Museo Correr, Venice, cited by N. Iorga, *Notes et extraits pour servir à l'histoire des croisades*, I, 267, note 3.

Centurione hard in Elis, forcing him to take refuge in Glarentsa.[38]

The Greeks' brilliant successes and the devastation of Modon and Coron by Albanian forces with the despot's connivance, coupled with the fact that Centurione had earlier been negotiating with his ancestral city of Genoa over the cession of Achaea, led the Venetians to take the preventive action of occupying Port-de-Jonc. At the same time archbishop Stephen invited a Venetian garrison from Euboea to Patras to prevent the city from falling to the Greeks. Had the Venetians been allowed to remain in Patras they might have prevented the Greek reconquest. But the papacy insisted on the inalienability of church property and required the republic to withdraw in 1419. This shortsightedness resulted in the loss of the first city of the Morea to the Greeks a decade later.

In the meantime a former captain of the despot named Oliver Franco (or Francone) seized Glarentsa early in 1418, taking one of Centurione's brothers captive. To save appearances the prince gave one of his daughters to the adventurer, with Glarentsa as her dower. But neither the hand of the princess nor her rich dower could hold Franco in Greece; in 1421 he accepted Charles Tocco's offer to buy Glarentsa and left the country. In the same year the war between the despot and the prince was renewed.[39] In their extremity Centurione and Stephen sought to interest the Knights of Rhodes once more in the Morea. Perhaps Stephen hoped that the papacy would allow him to alienate his ecclesiastical barony to the great military-religious organization. Or perhaps an anti-Moslem coalition of the states of the Morea with the Hospitallers was in question, since Theodore II of Mistra was in correspondence with the order at the same time as the Zaccarias. But the reply of the Hospitallers to all three rulers (May 10, 1422) was a rather curt refusal to become involved in the affairs of the Morea at a time when they were deeply engaged against the Turkish states of Asia Minor.[40]

The anarchy now prevailing in the Morea made the government of

38. Cf. the anonymous panegyrist on Manuel II and John VIII Palaeologus, published in Sp. P. Lampros, *Palaiológeia kaì peloponnesiaká*, III (Athens, 1926), 174–175, and the introduction to that volume by K. Voyatzidis, pp. xv–xvi.

39. The "Chronicle of the Tocchi" has a somewhat different account of these events. Centurione had brought Oliver over from Apulia with a hundred men in order to defend Glarentsa. Oliver, however, betrayed the prince by seizing the fortified port and holding the princess and Centurione's brother Benedict to ransom. Centurione, who had been absent from Glarentsa, entered into an alliance with the Byzantines of Mistra, but failed to retake the city. Finally Tocco bought it in order to rid himself of a dangerous neighbor. The Byzantines then launched their own campaign to capture Glarentsa. (See Schirò's summary of this part of the chronicle in *Byzantion*, XXXII [1962], 246–250.)

40. See below, pp. 312–313.

Venice decide to acquire the entire peninsula as the only effective way of protecting its subjects and trade and of building a strong dam against the Turkish assaults that were certain to come. But nothing came of the negotiations in Venice during the winter of 1422–1423 between the signoria and envoys representing emperor Manuel, Theodore II, Centurione, Stephen, and Charles Tocco. The Venetians mediated a one-year peace and admonished the contestants to unite against the Turks. They themselves undertook to protect the land against Catalan pirates, who are mentioned in Venetian documents of the time only less frequently than Turkish raiders. Although the republic failed to annex the Morea, it strengthened and enlarged its valuable Messenian colony in 1422–1423 by acquiring the castle of Grisi midway between Modon and Coron and by purchasing Port-de-Jonc.

Murad II now ruled over the reunited Ottoman state. The expected Turkish storm burst upon the Morea in the spring of 1423 when a great host under Turakhan Beg quickly scaled the Hexamilion and proceeded to devastate the peninsula, sparing only Charles Tocco's possessions in Elis. The republic was now alarmed, and tried once again to bring together the warring dynasts of the Morea. Venice warned Tocco not to feud with Theodore or call on the Ottomans for assistance. Momentarily Centurione and the despot ceased their fighting. But in the next round of their bitter conflict Theodore succeeded in making the prince his prisoner, in June of 1424. A few months earlier, in January, archbishop Stephen had died. The power of the Zaccaria family in the Morea was virtually at an end.

The papacy again lost an opportunity to allow Venetian influence to predominate in Patras by insisting on the appointment of Pandolfo Malatesta of Pesaro as Stephen's successor, instead of a Venetian cleric. Pope Martin V thus hoped to dispose Theodore favorably to the holy see, since the despot was the husband of Pandolfo's sister Cleopa. But Theodore and his numerous brothers were only awaiting an opportunity to conquer the ecclesiastical state. First, however, Charles Tocco had to be expelled from the Morea, where he had replaced the prince of Achaea as the chief foe of the Byzantine despotate. This task was executed with dispatch in a campaign against Tocco (1427–1428) on land and sea led by emperor John VIII and Constantine (XI), the ablest of the sons of Manuel II. John VIII gained the last naval victory of Byzantium in the battle of the Echinades islands off the Acarnanian coast, in which he destroyed the superior forces of the duke of Leucadia. Charles not only surrendered his possessions in Elis, including Glarentsa, to Constantine but also gave him the hand of his niece Maddalena, the elder daughter of the late Leonard II. The turn of Patras came in 1429–1430, when town and citadel yielded successively to the Palaeologus destined to be the last emperor of Byzantium; Constantine had defied a warning from Murad II not to take the city, which paid tribute to the Turks.

It fell to Thomas Palaeologus to put an end to the principality of Achaea, now reduced to little more than the baronies of Chalandritsa and Messenian Arcadia. He besieged Centurione Zaccaria, who had been released from his imprisonment, in the castle of Chalandritsa, and forced the prince to give him his older daughter Catherine in marriage, along with all his possessions—except Arcadia—as her dower (September 1429). The marriage was celebrated at Mistra in January 1430. John Asen, Centurione's natural son, was ignored in these transactions. Centurione, it seems, continued to bear the title "prince of Achaea" until his death in 1432. Then Thomas Palaeologus not only deprived his mother-in-law of the barony of Arcadia but also confined the unfortunate woman in prison for the rest of her life.

Thus after 227 years the Morea was once more entirely under Byzantine control, except for the Venetian establishments in Messenia and the Argolid. But although there was no longer any organized Frankish power in the peninsula there must have been a number of Franks remaining in the land who were willing to join a restoration movement. It is probable that John Asen Zaccaria took refuge in Venetian territory after 1432. During sultan Murad's great invasion of the Morea in 1446 a Greek magnate in rebellion against the despots Thomas and Constantine proclaimed John Asen prince of Achaea. But the rising failed, and Thomas imprisoned the "prince" and his son in the fortress of Clermont. However, during the formidable revolt of the Albanians of the Morea, with the support of Greek rebels, against the despots Thomas and Demetrius Palaeologus in 1453–1454, John Asen Zaccaria escaped and again became a serious menace to the regime. The Venetian doge, Francis Foscari, and king Alfonso V of Naples sent congratulations to him as "prince Centurione." But as usual the fate of the Morea was decided by the sultan. Mehmed II preferred two puppet Byzantine governments in the peninsula to a Graeco-Albanian state in which the Franks might make a comeback with Venetian or Neapolitan support. Accordingly he sent the veteran Turakhan Beg to the Morea to help the despots put down the revolt. John Asen Zaccaria "Centurione" fled to Modon, whence he reached Italy, and was successively pensioned by

Alfonso, by Venice, and by pope Paul II. He was to die in Rome in 1469.

If after 1454 the revival of the Frankish principality in the Morea gave Mehmed II no concern, it was otherwise with the Greek client states there. The two despots, far from being peaceful tributaries, resumed their unseemly feuding. There was danger to Mehmed in the fact that each sought aid in the west against the other. For the remainder of the decade of the 1450's the sultan had good reason to fear a Venetian or Neapolitan attempt, with papal encouragement and material aid, to occupy the Morea. Turkish control of the strategic peninsula was necessary for Mehmed's own project of attacking Italy in due time. Therefore, the great sultan personally led campaigns in 1458 and again in 1460 that extinguished the last remnants of Byzantine sovereignty in the Morea. The definitive annexation of the peninsula by Turkey deprived the Christian west of its most valuable base for any anti-Turkish crusade.

Ironically, the Morea's importance to the crusading movement was never more succinctly expressed than on the eve of the Ottoman conquest. In a letter addressed to the citizens of Nuremberg on the opening day of one of the most futile of crusading congresses, the Assembly of Mantua (June 1, 1459), pope Pius II wrote: "The country of Peloponnesus has such advantages for the conduct of operations by land and by sea that no other eastern region offers comparable opportunities for protecting our interests and wearing down the power of the Turks."[41]

41. Iorga, *Notes et extraits*, IV, 169.

VI

THE CATALANS IN GREECE
1311–1380

When night descended on the battlefield of the Cephissus on Monday, March 15, in the year 1311, the last day of Burgundian greatness in Greece had drawn to a dark and tragic close. Never again would a Frankish duke of Athens disport himself with confident pride and rich panoply in a tournament in Greece, as had Guy II de la Roche in the famed Corinthian lists of a half dozen years before. In the marshes of the Cephissus Walter of Brienne, last Burgundian duke of Athens, had perished with, it was claimed, seven hundred knights, and the Catalan Grand Company now took over the duchy of Athens and Thebes, together with the wives of the many Frenchmen they had slain.

Extensive bibliographies of Catalan activity in the Levant in the fourteenth century, together with much related material, may be found in Kenneth M. Setton, *Catalan Domination of Athens, 1311–1388* (Cambridge, Mass., 1948), pp. 261–301, and in *The Cambridge Medieval History,* IV-1 (1966), 908–938. There is another bibliographical survey in Salvatore Tramontana, "Per la storia della 'Compagnia Catalana' in Oriente," *Nuova rivista storica,* XLVI (1962), 58–95; see also R. Ignatius Burns, S.J., "The Catalan Company and the European Powers, 1305–1311," *Speculum,* XXIX (1954), 751–771. At about the same time as the appearance of the *Catalan Domination of Athens,* which contains (pp. 286–291) a discussion of the works of the great Catalan historian Antoni Rubió i Lluch (1855–1937), the Institut d'Estudis Catalans in Barcelona published Rubió's *Diplomatari de l'Orient català,* which issued from the press at the end of the year 1947, and which forms a landmark in the historiography of the Catalans in Greece and elsewhere in the Levant in the fourteenth century. During a scholarly career of over half a century Rubió i Lluch published some forty books, articles, and monographs on his countrymen in Greece, several of which are cited below.

During the twenty-five years since *Catalan Domination* appeared, various works have added substantially to our knowledge of the Catalan states in Athens and Neopatras. Especially important have been the studies of Raymond J. Loenertz, O.P., "Athènes et Néopatras: Regestes et notices pour servir à l'histoire des duchés catalans (1311–1394)," *Archivum Fratrum Praedicatorum,* XXV (1955), 100–212, 428–431; "Athènes et Néopatras: Regestes et documents pour servir à l'histoire ecclésiastique des duchés catalans (1311–1395)," *ibid.,* XXVIII (1958), 5–91; and "Hospitaliers et Navarrais en Grèce (1376–1383): Regestes et documents," *Orientalia Christiana periodica,* XXII (1956), 319–360. Other pertinent articles by Loenertz include "Pour l'histoire du Péloponèse au XIVe siècle (1382–1404)," *Études byzantines,* I (1943), 152–196; "Généalogie des Ghisi, dynastes

The Grand Company had first been organized by Roger de Flor of Brindisi, a turncoat Templar, shortly after the twenty years' war between the houses of Anjou and Aragon over possession of the island of Sicily had finally ended in the treaty of Caltabellotta (August 31, 1302). Members of the Company had helped maintain the energetic king Frederick II upon the throne of Sicily (1296–

vénitiens dans l'Archipel (1207–1390)," *Orientalia Christiana periodica,* XXVIII (1962), 121–172, 322–335; "La Chronique brève de 1352," *ibid.,* XXIX (1963), 331–356, and XXX (1964), 39–64; "Les Querini, comtes d'Astypalée (1413–1537)," *ibid.,* XXX (1964), 385–397; "Une Page de Jérôme Zurita relative aux duchés catalans de Grèce (1386)," *Revue des études byzantines,* XIV (1956), 158–168; and "La Chronique brève moréote de 1423," in *Mélanges Eugène Tisserant,* II-1 (Studi e testi, no. 232; Vatican City, 1964), 399–439. A few of these articles, but unfortunately not those in the *Archivum Fratrum Praedicatorum* (the most important for our purpose), have recently been reprinted in R. J. Loenertz, *Byzantina et Franco-Graeca,* ed. Peter Schreiner (Rome, 1970).

Among other recent works mention must be made of Antoine Bon's important study of *La Morée franque: Recherches historiques, topographiques et archéologiques sur la princi- pauté d'Achaïe (1205–1430)* (2 vols., Paris, 1969). Jean Longnon has written a well-known account of *L'Empire latin de Constantinople et la principauté de Morée* (Paris, 1949), and D. A. Zakythinos, an equally well-known history of *Le Despotat grec de Morée* (2 vols., Paris and Athens, 1932–1953). Freddy Thiriet has published the extremely useful *Régestes des délibérations du sénat de Venise concernant la Romanie* (3 vols., Paris and The Hague, 1958–1961), as well as a very readable book on *La Romanie vénitienne au moyen-âge: Le Développement et l'exploitation du domaine colonial vénitien (XIIe–XVe siècles)* (Paris, 1959). The Catalans figure prominently in Paul Lemerle's unusual monograph on *L'Émirat d'Aydin, Byzance et l'Occident: Recherches sur "La Geste d'Umur Pacha"* (Paris, 1957). The once-perplexing problem of a Catalan duchess of Athens and some "mysterious documents" was cleared up in K. M. Setton, "Archbishop Pierre d'Ameil in Naples and the Affair of Aimon III of Geneva (1363–1364)," *Speculum,* XXVIII (1953), 643–691. Wil- helm de Vries, S.J., has given us a survey of papal efforts against schismatics and heretics in the fourteenth century, in "Die Päpste von Avignon und der christliche Osten," *Orientalia Christiana periodica,* XXX (1964), 85–128, and we may also note the monograph by F. J. Boehlke, Jr., *Pierre de Thomas: Scholar, Diplomat, and Crusader* (Philadelphia, 1966), and that by G. Fedalto, *Simone Atumano, monaco di studio, arcivescovo latino di Tebe* (Brescia, 1968). On the latter subject, cf. also K. M. Setton, "The Archbishop Simon Atumano and the Fall of Thebes to the Navarrese in 1379," *Byzantinisch-Neugriechische Jahrbücher,* XVIII (1945–1949, publ. in 1960), 105–122, which study, together with the one on Pierre d'Ameil referred to above (as well as a number of others), has just been reprinted in *Europe and the Levant in the Middle Ages and the Renaissance* (London, 1974).

Of various articles by Anthony T. Luttrell, in addition to those cited in the notes to chapter VIII, below, special attention should be called to the following: "The Principality of Achaea in 1377," *Byzantinische Zeitschrift,* LVII (1964), 340–345; "The Latins of Argos and Nauplia, 1311–1394," *Papers of the British School at Rome,* XXXIV (new series, vol. XXI, 1966), 34–55; "Malta and the Aragonese Crown (1282–1530)," *Journal of the Faculty of Arts,* Royal Malta University, III-1 (1965), 1–9, and "The House of Aragon and Malta: 1282–1412," *ibid.,* IV-2 (1970), 156–168; "John Cantacuzenus and the Catalans at Constantinople," in *Martínez Ferrando, Archivero: Miscelánea de estudios dedicados a su memoria* (1968), pp. 265–277; and "Venezia e il principato di Acaia: secolo XIV," *Studi veneziani,* X (1968), 407–414. Cf. in general F. Giunta, *Aragonesi e Catalani nel Mediter- raneo* (2 vols., Palermo, 1953–1959); C. E. Dufourcq, *L'Espagne catalane et le Maghrib aux XIIIe et XIVe siècles* (Paris, 1966); and J. A. Robson, "The Catalan Fleet and Moorish Sea-power (1337–1344)," *English Historical Review,* LXXIV (1959), 386–408. The feudal

1337), to the great humiliation of pope Boniface VIII and the Angevins in Naples. With the advent of peace they needed employment, which they found, under Roger's command, in the service of the Byzantine emperor Andronicus II Palaeologus,[1] who hoped to use their strength against the newly risen power of the Ottoman Turks in Asia Minor. In September 1303 Roger de Flor and the chief body of the Company had arrived in Constantinople, having sacked the island of Ceos on the way (August 18, 1303). The Turks in Asia Minor soon felt the heavy force of their arms and learned of their prowess. Roger was ambitious, however, and having married into the imperial family, he became, as the months passed, an object of not unwarranted suspicion in the capital. It was feared that he might prefer the part of a ruler to that of a defender of the empire. At the end of April 1305 he was murdered by the Palaeologi, but the Catalan Company, which had come to include Turks in their ranks, held much of the Gallipoli peninsula until June 1307; thereafter they moved westward rapidly, ravaging Thrace and Macedonia; by the end of August 1307 they were at Cassandrea in the Chalcidic peninsula; in the spring and summer of 1308 we find them menacing the monks of Mt. Athos; in the spring of 1309 they entered the plains of Thessaly, and a year later passed into the employ of duke Walter I of

---

world of Latin Greece is depicted in David Jacoby, "Les Archontes grecs et la féodalité en Morée franque," *Travaux et mémoires,* II (Paris, 1967), 421–481. Jacoby has also written on "La 'Compagnie catalane' et l'état catalan de Grèce: Quelques aspects de leur histoire," *Journal des savants,* 1966, pp. 78–103, and has produced the most discerning work thus far written on the "Assizes of Romania," the feudal law code of Frankish Greece, in *La Féodalité en Grèce médiévale* (Paris and The Hague, 1971). Although the Catalans in Athens, Thebes, and Neopatras lived under the "laws of Aragon and the customs of Barcelona" *(fori Aragonie vel consuetudines Barchinonie),* a knowledge of the Assizes adds much to one's understanding of the political and social conditions which obtained in the Latin states neighboring upon the Catalan duchies in Greece. On such conditions within these duchies, see Setton, "Catalan Society in Greece in the Fourteenth Century," in the dedicatory volume to the late Basil Laourdas, now in the press in Thessaloniki.

1. The account of Raymond Muntaner, who was close to Roger de Flor, makes clear that the initiative for the Company's employment by Andronicus II lay with Roger, who was fluent in Greek (*Crònica,* ch. CXCIX, ed. Karl Lanz, *Chronik des edlen En Ramon Muntaner* [Stuttgart, 1844], p. 358; ed. E. B. [Enric Bogué], 9 vols. in 2, VI [Barcelona, 1951], 20). At the time of their departure from Messina the Company consisted of 1,500 horse, some 4,000 *almogàvers* (Castilian, *almogávares*), and 1,000 other footsoldiers, all of whom were Catalans or Aragonese (ch. CCI, Lanz, p. 361; E. B., VI, 22; and cf. ch. CCIII). They were later reinforced by 300 horse and 1,000 *almogàvers* (ch. CCXI, Lanz, p. 376; E. B., VI, 41), but after the murder of Roger de Flor, the Byzantines allegedly killed so many of the Company that only 3,307 men, both horse and foot, remained (ch. CCXV, Lanz, p. 382; E. B., VI, 47). These numbers were further reduced by an encounter with the Genoese, leaving only 206 horse and 1,256 foot, according to Muntaner (ch. CCXV, CCXIX, Lanz, pp. 383, 386; E. B., VI, 48, 52), but before leaving Gallipoli the Company was joined by a Turkish force of 800 horse and 2,000 foot (ch. CCXXVIII, Lanz, p. 405; E. B., VI, 76), and more Catalans and Aragonese were subsequently added to their forces.

Athens.[2] They served him for six months against the Greek rulers of Thessaly and Epirus and against the emperor Andronicus himself; they won him lands and castles in southern Thessaly; and when his use for them was done, he sought to dismiss them, although he still owed them four months' wages. He chose from among them two hundred knights and three hundred *almogàvers;* to these he paid what he owed them, gave them lands, and enfranchised them; the others he ordered to be gone. But the Company claimed the right to hold of him, as fiefs, some strongholds which they had taken in southern Thessaly, and which they refused to give up to him, for they had nowhere else to go.

The duke of Athens and the Catalan Company spent the fall and winter of 1310–1311 in preparation for the struggle which should decide who would go and who would stay. The Company was

2. The chronology of the movements of the Catalan Company has caused much difficulty. Roger de Flor and the Company arrived in Constantinople some time in September 1303 (their arrival has often been, by error, referred to the second half of 1302): they are declared in a Venetian document dated September 27, 1319, to have sacked the island of Ceos, on their way, on August 18, 1303 (G. M. Thomas, ed., *Diplomatarium veneto-levantinum,* I [1880, repr. 1965], no. 76, p. 138, and cf. nos. 77, 79, pp. 149, 163; Rubió, *Dipl.,* doc. CXI, p. 135, and cf. doc. CXIII, pp. 137–138). The Company had more or less fixedly encamped in Gallipoli by October 1304, where they remained, after the murder of Roger de Flor (April 30, 1305), until June 1307; all the events described in Muntaner, *Crònica,* ch. CCXXX–CCXXXVI (ed. Lanz, pp. 407–423; ed. E. B., VI, 78–99), took place in June, July, and August of 1307. Rubió's *Dipl.,* docs. I-XLIV, pp. 1–55, is a most valuable and convenient assemblage of documents concerning the Company's eastern expedition and its early leaders, especially Berenguer de Entença.

The Greeks had reason to fear the Catalans. Although on October 30, 1303, king James II of Aragon wrote Berenguer de Entença and Roger de Flor, thanking them for their assistance in arranging a projected alliance with emperor Andronicus II Palaeologus (*Dipl.,* doc. IX, pp. 9–10), the intentions of Roger de Flor became not unreasonably suspect by the early summer of 1304, when his former employer king Frederick II of Sicily may have entertained the hope of conquering the Byzantine empire (*Dipl.,* doc. XI, pp. 11–12, dating from early July 1304: "Item fa a saber lo dit senyor rey Frederic . . . que ell [enten] sobra lo feit de Romania, ço es asaber de conquerirla . . ."). A letter of May 10, 1305, written by Entença from Gallipoli to Peter Gradenigo, doge of Venice, relates that "ad presens guerificamus cum domino imperatore [Andronico II Palaeologo]," and informs him briefly "de statu nostro et homicidio infideliter facto [i.e., Rogerii] de mandato eiusdem domini imperatoris per Michaelem [IX] filium eiusdem" (*I Libri commemoriali della republica di Venezia: Regesti,* lib. I, no. 240, ed. R. Predelli, I [Venice, 1876], 51; published in full in *Dipl.,* doc. XIV, pp. 15–16). The memorandum published by Heinrich Finke, *Acta aragonensia,* II (Berlin and Leipzig, 1908), no. 431, pp. 681–686, and reprinted by Rubió, *Dipl.,* doc. XV, pp. 16–19, summarily traces the history of the Company from Sicily through some of their eastern adventures until Entença was captured by Genoese assisting the emperor, and up to the point where the Catalans achieved an obscure victory over the Greeks about July 1, 1305 (on which see in general the data in Franz Dölger, *Regesten der Kaiserurkunden des oströmischen Reiches,* part 4 [Munich and Berlin, 1960], nos. 2246, 2249, 2252, 2258, 2263, 2268–2269, 2271, 2273–2274, 2277–2279, 2281–2282, 2285, pp. 38–46, and Roger Sablonier, *Krieg und Kriegertum in der Crònica des Ramon Muntaner* [Berne and Frankfurt am M., 1971]).

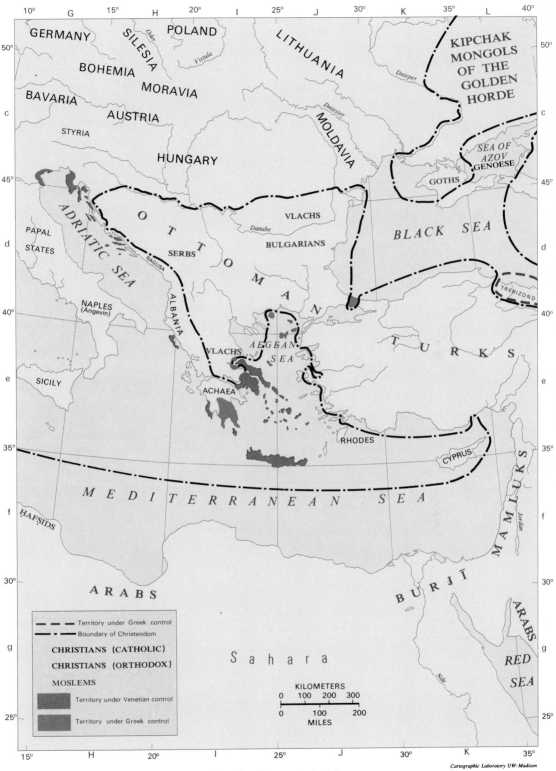

6. The Levant in 1400

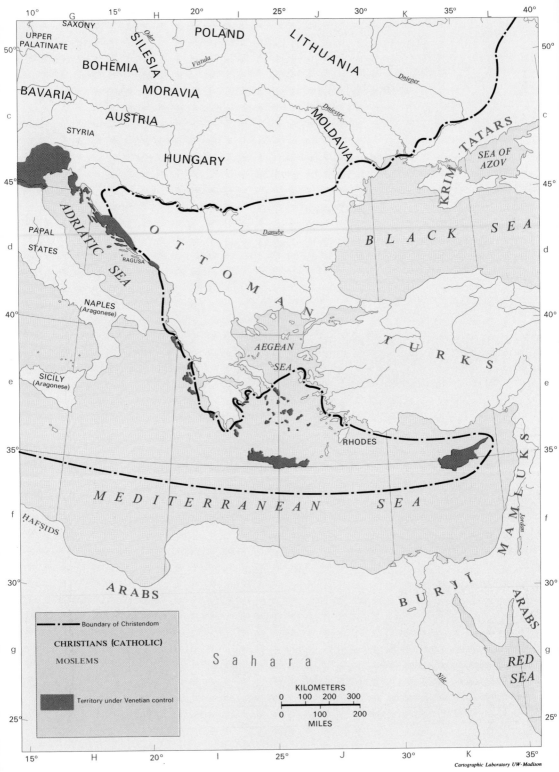

Boundary of Christendom

CHRISTIANS (CATHOLIC)

MOSLEMS

Territory under Venetian control

KILOMETERS
0 100 200 300

0 100 200
MILES

Cartographic Laboratory UW-Madison

rejoined by their five hundred fellows, who preferred the yellow banner with the red bars to the gold and azure of Brienne. Thus it came about that the Company, with their Turkish allies, met Walter and his Frankish army on the right bank of the river Cephissus, as Muntaner says, "in a beautiful plain near Thebes."[3] On the field of battle the duke of Athens and his knights, assembled from most of the Latin states in Greece, displayed the reckless courage of their class; they made a dashing attack upon the enemy; men and horses charged into prepared ditches; they piled upon one another; they sank into the bogs and marshes, covered with a treacherous sward of green; they were shot down by arrows, ridden down by horses, cut down by knives. The Frankish losses were fearful; Walter of Brienne was killed; it was a catastrophe from which there was to be no recovery.

French knights had jousted in the plains of Boeotia and Attica and feasted in great castles on the Cadmea and the Acropolis for more than a hundred years (1204–1311). All this had now come to an end. Thebes, the capital of the Athenian duchy, was immediately occupied; many of the Latin inhabitants of the duchy sought refuge on the Venetian island of Euboea (Negroponte).[4] The great castle of St. Omer (on the Cadmea), then famous for its frescoes, was taken over by the Company, and other towns and strongholds in Boeotia quickly followed. The Greek natives of the fortress town of Livadia admitted the Catalans with a "spontaneity" that bespoke no love for the French, and for this assistance some of them received the rights and privileges of "Franks" (Catalans),[5] except that, as schismatics, they were commonly denied the right to marry Frankish women. Athens was surrendered to the Catalans by the now widowed duchess of Athens, Joan of Châtillon, daughter of the constable of France. Of the Burgundian duchy of Athens and its dependencies the family of Brienne now possessed only Argos and Nauplia in the Morea, which their advocate Walter of Foucherolles held for them. Attica, like Boeotia, was now a Catalan possession, and land and vineyards and olive groves which had once been the property of Pericles and Herodes Atticus were owned by Catalan soldiers of fortune.

---

3. *Crònica,* ch. CCXL (ed. Lanz, p. 430; ed. E. B., VI, 107).

4. *Dipl.,* doc. CLXXVI, pp. 227–228, dated June 27, 1340, and referring to the fall of Thebes in 1311.

5. A half century later a letter patent of Frederick III of Sicily, then Catalan duke of Athens, recalled the events at Livadia in 1311 (*Dipl.,* doc. CCLXVIII, pp. 352–353, where the letter is misdated 1366; Loenertz, "Athenes et Néopatras," *Arch. FF. Praed.,* XXV [1955], 117, no. 63, and especially pp. 194, 199–200). The document should be dated July 29, 1362.

Muntaner has informed us, with much exaggeration,[6] that, of all the seven hundred knights who had ridden with Walter of Brienne into the battle of the Cephissus in March 1311, only two came out alive, Boniface of Verona, "lord of the third part of Negroponte, a very honorable, good man, who had always loved the Company," and Roger Deslaur, through whose efforts the Catalans had first hired out their services to Walter. The few thousand Catalans and Aragonese who took over the duchy of Athens lacked a leader of prestige and rank. They offered the perilous responsibility of governing them to Boniface of Verona, who felt obliged to reject their offer, whereupon they turned to their other important captive, Roger Deslaur. He accepted the proffered post, Muntaner relates, and received therewith the castle of Salona ("La Sola") and the widow of Thomas III of Autremencourt, whose great fief Salona had been until he lost his life on the banks of the Cephissus. Roger Deslaur seems to have proved unequal to the task of maintaining the duchy against the Catalans' Venetian enemies in Negroponte and their Frankish enemies in the Morea. The Grand Company therefore turned, with reluctance according to Marino Sanudo Torsello,[7] to king Frederick II of Sicily, who at their behest appointed as duke of Athens his second son, the infante Manfred, who was then only five years of age. The Company's acceptance of Catalan-Sicilian rule was negotiated by Roger Deslaur early in the year 1312.

An interesting document has survived, containing the articles and conventions whereby the "Corporation of the Army of Franks in Romania," as the Company was officially known, recognized the infante Manfred as their "true, legitimate, and natural lord." By the common consent and will of the individual members of the Company, duly assembled in council for this purpose, the young infante and, on his behalf, the king were to exercise all right, dominion, power, and jurisdiction over the members of the Company and their possessions; allegiance to their new prince was an obligation undertaken by them in perpetuity, and in accordance with the laws of Aragon and the customs of Barcelona. Frederick II, on behalf of his son, undertook to exercise the dominion, right of governance, and jurisdiction thus granted in strict accord with these laws and customs. The king and his son were to maintain and defend every member of the Company in such status, office, and fief *as he then held,* although they acquired in Attica and Boeotia such feudal rights

6. *Crònica,* ch. CCXL (ed. Lanz, p. 431; ed. E. B., VI, 108).

7. *Ep.* XVI, in Jacques Bongars, *Gesta Dei per Francos* (2 vols. in 1, Hanover, 1611), II, 307.

and perquisites as obtained in the kingdom of Aragon. The lord king declared, for himself and for his son, the royal intention to rule in accordance with these terms.[8] The king then sent Berenguer Estañol of Ampurias as the young duke's vicar-general, and when Estañol arrived in Piraeus with five galleys to take over his command, Roger Deslaur, who had governed the Company for a year (1311–1312), retired to his lordship of Salona and figures no more in the history of the Athenian duchy.[9]

Berenguer proved an able ruler, and under him the Catalans were able to consolidate their position in Attica and Boeotia. He protected them against the hostility of the Venetians in Negroponte, the Greeks in Thessaly and Epirus, and the Briennist retainers in Argos and Nauplia in the Morea. In 1316 Berenguer died, after prolonged illness and four years of effective service, and the Catalans elected a member of the Company, one William de Thomas, as their captain and vice-regent,[10] until the arrival in Athens of king Frederick II's natural son, Don Alfonso Fadrique of Aragon, who had been appointed vicar-general for the infante duke Manfred. On November 9, 1317, Manfred died in Trapani as a result of a fall from his horse; his younger brother became duke William [II] of Athens.[11] Appointed, therefore, as duke Manfred's vicar-general, it was as the vicar of duke William II that Alfonso Fadrique was to hold the chief post in the duchy of Athens—and after 1319 in the duchy of Neopatras—for about fourteen years (1317–1330),[12] during which period the Catalan Company in Greece enjoyed the height of their power and their security.

The organization of the new Catalan state in Greece illustrates very well the medieval theory of a contract between the ruler and his people, expressly called a contract (*capitula et conventiones*) in the first words of the document of 1312.[13] The Company remained

8. *Dipl.,* doc. LIII, pp. 67–69, and cf. doc. CXXXIII, p. 164, from Marino Sanudo Torsello, *Ep.* XVI, in Bongars, *loc cit.*

9. Muntaner, *Crònica,* ch. CCXLII (ed. Lanz, p. 433; ed. E. B., VI, 111).

10. Cf. *Dipl.,* doc. LXXXIV, p. 104, and Sp. P. Lampros, 'Έγγραφα ἀναφερόμενα εἰς τὴν μεσαιωνικὴν 'Ιστορίαν τῶν 'Αθηνῶν (Athens, 1906; hereafter cited as *Eggrapha,* vol. III of Lampros's Greek translation of Gregorovius, *Geschichte der Stadt Athen im Mittelalter,* 2nd ed.), part IV, doc. 104, pp. 355–356. Setton, *Catalan Domination,* pp. 15–17. William died August 22, 1338. Duke William I was William de la Roche (1280–1287).

12. The last clear reference to Alfonso Fadrique's tenure of the chief command in Greece comes in a Venetian document dated March 4, 1326 (*Dipl.,* doc. CXXXII, p. 163) although his authority continued for some time thereafter (cf. *Dipl.,* docs. CXXXIX, CXLI, CXLVI). His successor, Nicholas Lancia, is identified as *vicarius generalis* on April 5, 1331 (*Dipl.,* doc. CLIII, pp. 196 ff.).

13. *Dipl.,* doc. LIII, p. 67.

legal owner of the lands which they had won and now held by right of conquest, but seeking perhaps a more constitutional basis for their authority, and further protection in time of need, they had surrendered to and received back from the Catalan duke in Sicily their fiefs and offices in the Athenian duchy. The grand enfeoffment of 1312, however, whereby the duke was obliged to confirm the distribution of lands and offices which the Company had already effected among themselves, was largely theoretical, for it was they who granted the ducal domain to him rather than he who granted their fiefs to them. From the time of their early establishment in Greece the Company possessed written Articles or Statutes *(Capitula),* an actual constitution, composed in Catalan and largely based upon the Constitutions of Catalonia and the Customs of Barcelona. The text of the Statutes of the Company (*els Capítols de la Companyía*) has unfortunately not survived, although here and there a fragment appears in the documents, most notably the article prohibiting landed gifts and testamentary bequests to the church.[14] To important documents the chancellor of the Company affixed the Company's own seal, which depicted St. George slaying the dragon.[15]

The duke appointed the vicar-general, the chief executive of the duchy, who swore fealty to the duke in Sicily, and upon his arrival in Athens or Thebes took an oath before representatives of the Company to discharge the duties of his office properly, in accordance with the Statutes of the Company. The duke quickly acquired, however, the right of appointment to the chief military post in the Catalan state, that of marshal of the duchy, or after 1319, when Don Alfonso Fadrique added the duchy of Neopatras to that of Athens, marshal of the duchies. But the highest offices in the state were

14. See *Dipl.,* doc. CCXCIV, p. 382, dated June 8, 1367; note also doc. CCCXCI, pp. 476–477; and cf. doc. CDXXXIII, p. 508. (Landed property and feudal revenues were to be reserved for *gents d'armes* who could defend the state.)

15. A copy of this seal, from the collection of Count Pierre de Viry, was published by Gustave Schlumberger, "Le Sceau de la compagnie des routiers catalans à Gallipoli, en 1305," *Comptes-rendus de l'Académie des inscriptions et belles-lettres* (Paris), 1925, pp. 131–137; *Anuari de l'Institut d'estudis catalans,* VII (1921–1926), 302–304; and Gustave Schlumberger, Ferdinand Chalandon, and Adrien Blanchet, eds., *Sigillographie de l'Orient latin* (Paris, 1943), pp. 208–209. Muntaner, *Crònica,* ch. CCXXV (ed. Lanz, p. 397; ed E. B., VI, 66), relates that after Roger de Flor's death the Company had made a great seal upon which was represented *lo benauirat monsènyer sant Jordi* and bearing the inscription *Segell de la host dels francs qui regnen lo regne de Macedònia* (and for Muntaner's idea of Macedonia, see, *ibid.,* ch. CCXIV, Lanz, pp. 379–380; E. B., VI, 44–45). The copy of the seal extant bears the official title of the Company, familiar to us from papal and royal documents, *Felix Francorum exercitus in Romanie partibus* [not *finibus*] *comorans,* on which see Jacoby, "La Compagnie catalane," *Journal des savants,* 1966, pp. 80–87, 93 ff., who believes that this seal must be dated after 1312.

reserved, for the most part, for the Catalans themselves, including the office of marshal, which, whether by royal appointment or not, was apparently held for almost two generations (until 1354?) by the important family of the Novelles.

Thebes was the capital of the Athenian duchy. The Catalans in Athens conducted various local affairs as a municipal corporation with their own civil and military officers and with their own syndics, aldermen, and municipal council. The city of Neopatras was the capital of the northern duchy, within the boundaries of which were located the important castle and town of Zeitounion (in Catalan *la Citó*), the ancient Lamia. A captain presided over the city of Neopatras, and a castellan commanded the garrison in the castle. Conditions in Neopatras, owing to its semi-isolation in the north, were unique, and authority resided not only ultimately but directly in the sovereign duke in Sicily or, after 1379, in Aragon-Catalonia. The duchy of Neopatras possesses far less history than that of Athens.

It is difficult to make valid generalizations concerning the administration of the municipalities or town corporations in the two duchies—Athens, Thebes, Livadia, Siderokastron, and Neopatras—but they all belonged to the royal domain. Greeks served on the municipal councils in Athens, Livadia, and Neopatras. The Assizes and Customs of Romania, which were presumably the feudal law of Burgundian Athens, gave way in 1311 to the Customs of Barcelona, which thereafter formed the basis of public and private law in the Athenian duchy as in Catalonia, and the high court of the Frankish baronage was replaced by the court of the vicar-general, which was located in Thebes. Disputed cases were adjudicated by appeal in the royal court in Sicily. After 1355, as we shall see, the duke of Athens was also, in the person of Frederick III, the king of Sicily; this increased the ducal dignity if not the ducal power. The duke commonly nominated the veguers and castellans in the chief towns and fortresses in the Athenian duchy; and on the surface the Catalan feudatories, the municipalities, and even the clergy possessed fewer rights of private jurisdiction than had their Frankish predecessors. The royal act of appointment to or removal from office, however, was often not the royal will, and again and again in the troubled history of Catalan Athens the Sicilian royal duke had no alternative but to accept the accomplished fact with which he was firmly presented by his loyal subjects across the sea.

The Catalans had made their entrance into the Latin politics of Greece as unseemly intruders, and they were at first unpopular with almost everyone in continental Greece and the Morea—emperor Andronicus II Palaeologus and his imperial governor of Mistra (then the father of the future emperor John VI Cantacuzenus); the Greek ruler John II Ducas "Comnenus" of Thessaly and his relative, the despoina Anna of Epirus; the Frankish barons in Achaea, vassals of the absentee prince Philip I of Taranto, among them the Briennist retainers in Argos and Nauplia; the Venetian bailie in Negroponte and the Venetian feudatories in the Archipelago; as well as the pope in Avignon, the vigilant guardian of Latin legitimacy in the Levant as elsewhere. All these looked forward to the collapse of the Company of Catalan cutthroats holding sway in Boeotia and Attica. They had long to wait. The Venetians were the first to become reconciled to the Company, or at least resigned to the Catalan occupation of the Athenian duchy. Since the Catalans had long been enemies of the Genoese and, after the murder of Roger de Flor, enemies also of the Byzantine emperor, the Venetians had looked upon Catalan activities in the Levant with no particular concern from 1303 to 1309–1310, but when the Catalans finally settled in southern Thessaly and the Athenian duchy, acquired allies among the Turks, and displayed a marked penchant for piracy, the Venetians in nearby Negroponte had reason for apprehension. This change in the republic's attitude toward the Catalan Company was first markedly demonstrated in a treaty negotiated at Constantinople on November 11, 1310, between emperor Andronicus II and envoys of Peter Gradenigo, the doge of Venice, a treaty that was to last for twelve years. The Venetians undertook, among other articles of agreement, not to go into Byzantine territories held by the Company, still in Thessaly in the employ of duke Walter of Brienne, although trading rights between the empire and the republic were to be reëstablished in the territories in question after the withdrawal therefrom of the Catalans.[16]

  Although in April 1315, in connection with the Moreote expedition of the infante Ferdinand of Majorca, king Frederick II of Sicily had occasion to ask the doge, John Soranzo, for friendship and devotion from Venice,[17] the Venetians in Euboea found Frederick's subjects in Thebes and Athens rather deficient of friendship and devotion toward them. Soranzo must have been interested to learn from Mahaut of Hainault, widow of Louis of Burgundy, who had protected her claim to the principality of Achaea by his victory over Ferdinand of Majorca at Manolada in Elis (on July 5, 1316), that

16. *Dipl.*, doc. XLVI, pp. 56–58 (also in Thomas, *Diplomatarium veneto-levantinum,* I, no. 46, pp. 82 ff.).
17. *Dipl.*, doc. LXXV, pp. 92–93.

even as she wrote (in March 1317), some two thousand Catalans from the Athenian duchy were in the city of Negroponte: "We make known to your highness that, owing to the dissension which has existed between Messer Andrew Cornaro [Venetian lord of Carpathos and of a "sixth" of Euboea] and Boniface of Verona [who held Carystus and a "third" of the island] and the understanding reached between your bailie of Negroponte [Michael Morosini, 1316–1317] and Messer Andrew Cornaro, the said Messer Andrew has made peace and an accord with the Catalan Company in the duchy of Athens, and has introduced into the city of Negroponte all told more than 2,000 of the Company on horse and foot . . . ." The island and city were thus in danger of falling to the Catalans, which would be a grievous loss to Venice and a peril to Mahaut. She urged the doge to see to the removal of the Catalan force from the island, and to instruct the bailie to make neither peace nor an agreement with the intruders. She also requested the doge to direct Andrew Cornaro to break off his entente with the Company, which he already regretted. Speed was necessary to deal with this emergency, "and you know well, my lord, that those people in the Company will maintain neither faith nor honesty with you nor with us nor with anyone in the whole world."[18]

A year later, on March 17, 1318, John of Gravina, prince of Achaea through his "marriage" to the unhappy Mahaut of Hainault, wrote to Soranzo complaining of Don Alfonso Fadrique's offenses against both the Angevins and the Venetians in Negroponte.[19] On the following day both king Robert of Naples and prince Philip of Taranto, brothers of John of Gravina, sent similar letters to the doge,[20] who replied on April 13 expressing his gratitude for this interest in Venetian affairs; but even before having received the royal letters, the republic had had news from Greece concerning Don Alfonso Fadrique's activities. An envoy had already been sent to king Frederick II of Sicily, Don Alfonso's father, and the republic hoped that the king would himself put a peaceful and tranquil end to their

18. *Dipl.,* doc. LXXXVI, pp. 105–106; Louis de Mas Latrie, *Mélanges historiques,* III (Paris, 1880), no. IV, pp. 32–34 (Documents inédits sur l'histoire de France); Loenertz, *Arch. FF. Praed.,* XXV, no. 5, p. 104; Karl Hopf, "Geschichte Griechenlands . . . ," in Ersch and Gruber, *Allgemeine Encyklopädie,* LXXXV (1867), 413a (repr. New York, 1960, I, 347a), rather fanciful. Mahaut calls the Catalans "la Compagne des Castellains [Castilians!] qui sunt en ducaume de Staines [Athens]"; her letter was dated at Andravida March 28 (of 1317). Boniface of Verona died before May 8, 1318 (*Dipl.,* doc. XCIV, pp. 113–114), presumably in the late fall of 1317.

19. *Dipl.,* doc. LXXXIX, pp. 108–109.

20. *Dipl.,* docs. XC, XCI, pp. 109–110. King Robert wrote again on June 24 (*ibid.,* doc. XCVII, pp. 116–117).

problems. If it should prove otherwise, the letter ends serenely, the republic intended to do what might be pleasing to God and the honor of the state and in the interests of Robert and his brothers.[21] The signoria of Venice was much concerned with the affairs of the Catalan Company throughout the spring of 1318. In April representatives of the constable Gaucher of Châtillon and his daughter, the dowager duchess of Athens, presented a petition to the doge; they sought a large loan and ships enough to transport four or five hundred knights and a thousand or more infantry to Negroponte or to Nauplia. The doge replied that the Briennist feudatories in Argos and Nauplia were now allied with the Catalan Company, and since their own vassals were not loyal, their proposal would only entail a vain expenditure of men and money.[22]

On May 8 pope John XXII wrote the doge and republic of Venice, urging the expulsion of the Catalans from the island of Euboea, where Don Alfonso held the fortress towns of Carystus and Larmena as his wife's dowry. The pope claimed that Don Alfonso aimed at the occupation of the entire island and, which was quite true, that he had Turks in his employ; the Venetians should expel the Catalans not only from Euboea, but from the duchy of Athens also, in which business, the pope indicates, his beloved son king Robert of Naples had some interest.[23] On June 18, 1318, Don Alfonso himself wrote a letter from Athens to Francis Dandolo, the captain and bailie of Negroponte, expressing his astonishment that Catalans from the

---

21. *Dipl.*, doc. XCII, p. 111. The principality of Achaea was much threatened by the Greeks of Mistra, who in 1320 occupied the Arcadian castles of Akova or Matagrifon, near the modern Dimitsana, and Karytaina, which overlooks the valley of the Alpheus. They also seized the fortress of St. George between Mistra and Karytaina (cf. A. Morel-Fatio, ed., *Libro de los fechos* [Geneva, 1885], pars. 641–654, pp. 140–143; Jean Longnon, ed., *Chronique de Morée* [Paris, 1911], pp. 404–405, chron. table; and R. J. Loenertz, "La Chronique brève moréote de 1423," in *Mélanges Eugène Tisserant,* II-1, 403, 413–414). King Robert of Naples, who was then living in Avignon, was much concerned with the recovery of lands lost to the Greeks and with the protection of those being attacked by the Catalans and Turks. G. M. Monti, *Nuovi studi angioini* (Trani, 1937), pp. 612–629, has published eight relevant documents dated from July 18 to November 10, 1321. The Greeks had taken Matagrifon, Karytaina, and St. George, but on July 18 (1321), king Robert seemed to think that Don Alfonso Fadrique "with that dismal Company" had seized these three places (Monti, *op. cit.*, p. 626). On October 1, 1322, pope John XXII wrote the Latin patriarch Nicholas and archbishop William Frangipani of Patras, excoriating "Alfonso the captain and the other leaders ... of the Grand Company, ... walking damnably in the darkness and shadow of death," who had been attacking the principality of Achaea: the patriarch and the archbishop were to make the Grand Company call a halt to their criminal activity by the application of ecclesiastical censure (*Dipl.*, doc. CXX, pp. 148–149, misdated by Rubió i Lluch). So far, it must be admitted, this had proved a rather inefficacious weapon.

22. *Dipl.*, doc. XCIII, pp. 112–113.

23. *Dipl.*, doc. XCIV, pp. 113–114. On Don Alfonso's marriage, see below, p. 185.

Athenian duchy had been guilty of depredations against the Venetians, "with whom we have a truce and are at peace." He promised an investigation and the punishment of the offenders; he desired peace with the Venetians, of whom, however, he was clearly suspicious.[24]

An interesting report of June 26, 1318, sent to the doge of Venice by Dandolo, concludes with the news, "On June 21 at about the hour of vespers we learned from a trustworthy source that a ship of 48 oars has been armed at Athens. It is to carry two ambassadors of Don Alfonso, [chosen] from among his better people, to the [Greek] emperor, and it is to leave Athens tonight. We have also learned from the same reliable informant that another ship is being armed at Athens, which is to take [another] two ambassadors of Don Alfonso . . . with two Turkish ambassadors into Turkey. They are going to enlist a goodly number of Turks, from 1,000 to 1,500 . . . ."[25]

Diplomatic representations were made to Don Alfonso Fadrique and to his father Frederick II of the harm which Catalan corsairs and their Turkish allies were doing to Venetian commerce and of the ultimate consequences of Venetian hostility to the Catalan Company. On September 2, 1318, king Frederick II of Sicily answered the several grievances detailed by the Venetian envoy of whom the doge had written the Angevin princes; Frederick had probably warned his son to be careful some time before this, but the Sicilian archives are very fragmentary for this period. The king refused to recognize as infractions of the peace or as unjust the acts charged in most of the complaints made against his son Alfonso, and his replies to the Venetian envoys are full of Catalan enmity toward the Angevin lords of Achaea.[26] But with the Venetians the king of Sicily desired amicable relations and the settlement of differences existing between them, and he appointed envoys to treat with the doge and republic of Venice "to achieve a final peace and concord or a long truce between the republic of Venice, her citizens and subjects, and Alfonso and the Catalan Company."[27]

24. *Dipl.,* doc. XCV, pp. 114–115. Catalan piracy was unceasing, however, among the islands of the Archipelago (cf. *Dipl.,* docs. XCVI, C–CII); see W. Heyd, *Histoire du commerce du Levant,* trans. Furcy Raynaud, I (repr. 1967), 538.

25. *Dipl.,* doc. XCVIII, p. 119. Catalan sloops (*vachetae*) had been on a raid to Euboea, and a fleet (*armata*) had just attacked Cassandrea on the Thermaic Gulf.

26. *Dipl.,* doc. CIII, pp. 124–127; Thomas, *Diplomatarium veneto-levantinum,* I, no. 64, pp. 110–113; cf. Setton, *Catalan Domination,* p. 34.

27. *Dipl.,* doc. CIV, pp. 127–128; Thomas, *Diplomatarium veneto-levantinum,* I, no. 65, pp. 113–114. The Venetian conditions of peace presented to the Sicilian envoys in the early winter of 1318 and the doge's statement of terms for the envoys to take to Frederick II are

Such a peace was finally established, after detailed negotiations, on June 9, 1319, when a six months' agreement was reached, at a conference in Negroponte, between Don Alfonso and the whole Company on the one hand and on the other the bailie Francis Dandolo, his councillors, and the feudal lords of Euboea, John de Noyer of Maisy, Peter dalle Carceri, Andrew Cornaro, and Bartholomew II Ghisi. The Catalans bound themselves to disarm their trading vessels and to arm no others in the Saronic Gulf or elsewhere in places bordering upon the island of Euboea; vessels with oars they agreed to draw up on land, a plank was to be removed from the bottom of each hull, "and the tackle of the vessels themselves should be stored on the Acropolis." Such unarmed merchantmen as were then sailing from the port of Livadostro ("Rivadostia") might be maintained, for Livadostro was in the northeast corner of the Corinthian Gulf, whence the Catalans could neither harry the islands of the Archipelago nor combine in raiding sorties with their friends and allies the Turks.[28] This treaty, if strictly adhered to, must have been most detrimental to trade with Sicily, Majorca, and Barcelona. The Venetians, however, always insisted on its terms. The treaty was renewed on May 11, 1321.[29] It was renewed again at a meeting held in Thebes on April 5, 1331.[30] In all three treaties the Company held itself liable to a fine of 5,000 hyperpers for the violation of its pledges, while to the treaties of 1321 and 1331 a half dozen clauses or more were added to the specific effect that the Catalans should conclude no new alliances with the Turks and should not aid them in attacks upon the island of Euboea or the Venetian possessions in the Archipelago.[31] These agreements were renewed from time to time in the years that followed. With each decade that passed the Catalans became rather more reliable, and although relations between the Catalans in the Athenian duchy and the Venetians in Negroponte sometimes degenerated into actual warfare, at the termination of each such period of armed conflict the Venetians always insisted upon the Catalans' never maintaining armed vessels in the harbor of Piraeus.[32]

---

printed in *Dipl.*, docs. CVI, CVII, pp. 129–131, and in Thomas, *op. cit.*, I, nos. 66, 67, pp. 115–117. The doge insisted that the Catalans could not maintain vessels equipped with oars *(ligna a remis)* in the Athenian duchy (Rubió, *Dipl.*, p. 130).

28. The text of the treaty of June 9, 1319, has often been printed, most recently in Rubió's *Diplomatari*, doc. CIX, pp. 132–134.

29. *Dipl.*, doc. CXVI, pp. 141–144.

30. *Dipl.*, doc. CLIII, pp. 196–200.

31. *Dipl.*, docs. CXVI, p. 142, and CLIII, p. 198.

32. As in the interesting and instructive treaty of July 25, 1365 (*Dipl.*, doc. CCLVIII, pp.

Pope Clement V and his successors in Avignon looked with anxiety upon the machinations of Catalan kings in Barcelona and Palermo. The Briennes were a French family of distinguished ancestry, loyal Guelfs, and vassals of the Angevin princes of Achaea. Inevitably the popes sought to aid young Walter II [VI] of Brienne, son of the slain duke of Athens, to recover the rich heritage the Catalans had wrested from him in the marshes of the Cephissus. Nevertheless, if in the confused pattern of interests and events in the Levant, some place could be found to employ the Company to the advantage of the church, the curia would not be loath to do so. When the crusade was discussed at the Council of Vienne, the papal vice-chancellor proposed to the representatives of king James II of Aragon that the Catalan Company, now securely established in Thebes and Athens, should be employed in a crusading expedition to pass through Greece, subject the schismatic church to the Catholic faith, and proceed by way of Christian (Cilician) Armenia against the Moslem in the Holy Land. On November 22, 1311, his majesty was reminded of the strategic location, for the purposes of the crusade, of the Company, composed of Catalans and Aragonese, now in Greece, already the conquerors of many lands.[33] But the Catalans and Aragonese had had too long an acquaintance with papal politics, too much experience of Turkish power, too many Turkish friends, and too good a stroke of fortune in acquiring the duchy of Athens to embark on an expedition to Palestine. The problem of the Catalans in Greece had, therefore, to be met otherwise, for their activities were proving most injurious to the Angevins and to Latin ecclesiastics both in continental Greece and in the Morea.

On May 2, 1312, pope Clement V wrote from Vienne to "his beloved sons, the Catalan Company in Romania," that Philip I of Taranto, prince of Achaea, had lodged a complaint at the curia in Avignon to the effect that the Company had entered into "certain conventions and pacts" with enemies of the Catholic faith against the prince and his Moreote vassals. His holiness ordered the immediate abandonment of these conventions and pacts, warning the Company that excommunication would be the price of their refusal. He notified the Company also that he was writing to Fulk of Villaret, master

---

341–342; Sp. M. Theotokes, in Ἐπετηρὶς Ἑταιρείας Βυζαντινῶν Σπουδῶν, VIII [1931], 200–205). Cf. Setton, *Catalan Domination,* pp. 60–61.

33. *Dipl.,* doc. LII, pp. 65–66. For some Catalan crusading ideas, especially those of Raymond Lull, see A. S. Atiya, *The Crusade in the Later Middle Ages* (London, 1938), pp. 74 ff.; A. Gottron, *Ramón Lulls Kreuzzugsideen* (Berlin and Leipzig, 1912); and E. Allison Peers, *Ramon Lull, a Biography* (London, 1929), *passim.*

of the Hospital of St. John of Jerusalem, to help expel them from "Romania" if they failed to obey the apostolic admonition.[34] On the same day he wrote to Fulk to the same effect.[35] The Catalans, of course, did not desist. Fulk, however, made no effort to drive them from the Athenian duchy; he was too much occupied with the affairs of the Hospitallers on the newly acquired island of Rhodes.[36]

Conditions in Latin Greece were nearly intolerable, and complaints were continually coming to the curia. Catalan depredation had reduced the revenues of the archbishopric of Corinth;[37] the new archbishop of Thebes dared not take up residence in his see;[38] and the aged bishop of Negroponte could not return to Euboea from the Council of Vienne because of the general insecurity which the Catalan Company had caused.[39]

The pope could not but feel that the cause of Latin Christendom in Greece had been severely hurt by the advent of the Catalans, for duke Walter I [V] had been a loyal son of the church, an assiduous defender of the faith.[40] On January 14, 1314, therefore, pope Clement V had reason for his indignant letter to Nicholas, the Latin patriarch, excoriating the Catalan Company for their attacks upon churches, ecclesiastics, and their fellow Christians, and for the death of Walter, "who had been laboring in defense of the faithful . . . against the Greek schismatics."[41] On the same day the pope wrote the patriarch that he should effect the transfer of such properties as the Knights Templar had possessed in the duchy of Athens to Gaucher of Châtillon, constable of France and grandfather of the titular duke Walter II, in order that such properties might be used to defend the faithful against schismatics "and certain other characters in a certain Company."[42] Another letter bearing the same date was dispatched to king James II of Aragon—"since the greater part of the

34. *Dipl.*, doc. LVI, pp. 71–72; *Regestum Clementis Papae V* (Rome, 1885–1888), annus septimus, no. 7890, pp. 72–73.

35. *Dipl.*, doc. LVII, p. 72; *Regestum Clementis V, loc. cit.*, no. 7891, p. 73.

36. See below, pp. 283–286.

37. *Dipl.*, doc. LVIII, p. 73; *Regestum Clementis V*, annus septimus, no. 8597, p. 238, dated June 23, 1312.

38. *Dipl.*, doc. LIX, pp. 73–74; *Regestum Clementis V*, annus septimus, no. 8138, p. 125, dated July 13, 1312.

39. *Dipl.*, doc. LXII, pp. 77–78; *Regestum Clementis V*, annus octavus, no. 9153, pp. 131–132, dated 23 March, 1313.

40. Lampros, *Eggrapha*, part I, doc. 31, p. 52, dated November 11, 1309.

41. *Dipl.*, doc. LXIV, pp. 80–81; *Regestum Clementis V*, annus nonus, no. 10167, p. 45; O. Raynaldus, *Annales ecclesiastici*, ad ann. 1314, no. 9 (vol. V [1750], p. 22); Lampros, *Eggrapha*, part I, doc. 32, p. 53; and cf. *Dipl.*, doc. LXVI, p. 83, *et alibi.*

42. *Dipl.*, doc. LXIII, pp. 78–79; *Regestum Clementis V*, annus nonus, no. 10166, pp. 44–45, and cf. the letter of January 14 to Fulk of Villaret (*Dipl.*, doc. LXV, pp. 81–82; *Regestum, ibid.*, no. 10168, pp. 46–47).

Company is said to have been recruited from your kingdom"—asking his majesty to warn and to exhort the Catalans to give up the castles and the lands they had occupied.[43]   According to a seventeenth-century annalist of the kings of Aragon, king James II replied that his holiness would do well to look upon the Catalans and Aragonese in Greece as "the right arm and faithful instrument" of the holy see, which might be employed against the schismatic Greeks.[44]   Be that as it may, James II wrote twice directly to the Catalan Company, expressing a desire to recall them "to the path of righteousness," and ordering "that you desist completely from the invasion and occupation of the duchy of Athens, and withdrawing therefrom completely, that you leave it peacefully and quietly to its rightful heirs."[45]   These letters, however, were apparently nothing more than a diplomatic gesture.

Very likely the Company in Thebes and Athens took the admonitions of king James II no more seriously than he had intended, but their isolation was most serious, despite their connection with the royal house of Sicily and the able leadership of their vicar-general, Berenguer Estañol (1312–1316). On March 26, 1314, with a gesture worthy of them, they formally bestowed upon Guy de la Tour, baron of Montauban, third son of the dauphin Humbert I of Viennois (d. 1307), the erstwhile Latin kingdom of Thessalonica. Their sole claim to the kingdom, which a century before had existed briefly (1204–1224), was that their former leader Bernard (Bernat) of Rocafort had once aspired to possess it. But now they pledged their every assistance to enable Guy to acquire Thessalonica,[46]   for with pleasant memories of the Thermaic Gulf and the rich plains of Thessaly, the Catalans would have been happy to extend their sway northward. If Guy could help them to do so, he was obviously an ally worth having. But nothing came of all this, for a month before (on February 22) king Robert of Naples had made Guy de la Tour his captain-general in

43. *Dipl.*, doc. LXVI, pp. 82–83; Finke, *Acta aragonensia*, II, 749–751.

44. Pedro Abarca, *Los Anales históricos de los reyes de Aragón*, II (Salamanca, 1684), cap. 6, nos. 7–9, pp. 61ᵛ–62ᵛ, quoted in Setton, *Catalan Domination*, p. 26. Rubió i Lluch searched in vain for the text of king James's alleged reply in the Archives of the Crown of Aragon in Barcelona (*Dipl.*, p. 84, note), but it would seem to have been rather in accord, as James might have reminded the pope, with the papal vice-chancellor's own observation of the possible usefulness of the Company against the non-Catholics in the east (*Dipl.*, doc. LII, p. 66).

45. *Dipl.*, doc. LXVII, p. 84, dated February 28, 1314, and doc. LXXII, p. 90, dated March 27, 1314; cf. doc. LXXIII, p. 91. James II also wrote Philip the Fair of France of his "vehement displeasure" at the Catalan conquest and of his orders to the Catalans to abandon the duchy of Athens to its rightful heirs (*Dipl.*, doc. LXVIII, pp. 84–85).

46. *Dipl.*, doc. LXX, pp. 88–89, dated at Thebes on March 26, 1314; see also Schlumberger, Chalandon, and Blanchet, *Sigillographie de l'Orient latin*, pp. 210–211.

Lombardy, and king Robert was one of the Catalans' most determined enemies.[47]

Papal opposition to the Catalan Company continued with undiminished vigor, and on September 4, 1318, when the negotiations between the Catalan king of Sicily and the Venetians were far advanced, cardinal-bishop Nicholas of Ostia and Velletri wrote to the doge and council of Venice of the disquieting news that the curia was receiving from Greece about the Catalans.[48] On August 2, 1319, about the time the news of the Catalan-Venetian peace of June became known in Avignon, pope John XXII wrote to Walter of Foucherolles (1311–1324), Briennist advocate in Argos and Nauplia, and to the people and clergy of the Argolid diocese, urging continued loyalty to young Walter II and his mother the dowager duchess of Athens.[49] According to Karl Hopf, however, who cites a Venetian document of December 6, 1317, Don Alfonso Fadrique had already withdrawn from Negroponte and the island of Euboea, retaining only the disputed castles of Carystus and Larmena.[50] Catalan and Turkish piracy could not be checked,[51] but hostilities with the Venetians on a serious scale seem not to have been renewed after Don Alfonso's withdrawal from Negroponte, and, as we have seen, he claimed in June 1318 to be observing the "truce and peace" which the Company already had with the Venetians.

The years that followed 1318–1319 were the most secure and successful years the Catalan Company was to enjoy in Greece. Don Alfonso Fadrique was probably the most distinguished Catalan ever to take up residence in the Athenian duchy, and during the years that he was vicar-general the Catalans added the only conspicuous gains made to their Greek territories after the triumph of the original conquest itself. When he passed from the scene, their career as Conquistadors, as they called themselves, had come to an end. Don Alfonso is referred to in all documents—Catalan, Venetian, and even Angevin and papal—with the respect befitting the rank of a king's son. He is called in the Catalan-Venetian peace of 1319 "the magnifi-

47. Gregorovius (tr. Lampros), *Athens* [in Greek], II (Athens, 1904), 95–97. Guy de la Tour died in 1317; he did not go to Greece.

48. *Dipl.*, doc. CV, p. 128.

49. *Dipl.*, doc. CX, pp. 134–135, G. Mollat and G. de Lesquen, eds., *Jean XXII: Lettres communes*, II (Paris, 1905), no 9879, p. 421.

50. Hopf, in Ersch and Gruber, LXXXV, 413 (repr., I, 347), which is probably accurate, but seems to indicate that negotiations were rather more advanced than might be assumed from the documents of September 2, 1318 (cf. *ibid.*, p. 415 [repr., I, 349], and Rubió's *Dipl.*, docs. CIII, CIV, pp. 124–128).

51. Cf. *Dipl.*, docs. C, CI, pp. 121–123, dated July 16 and 26, 1318.

cent lord, Don Alfonso, son of the most excellent lord, Don Frederick, by the grace of God king of Sicily, and commander of the fortunate army of the Franks [Catalans] in the duchy of Athens and other parts of the empire of Romania."[52] At first Don Alfonso appears to have resided in Athens, presumably in the Burgundian castle on the Acropolis.[53] He was soon accepted as a friend and ally by the great Lombard magnate, Boniface of Verona, triarch of Euboea, who gave him his daughter Marulla (Maria) in marriage in 1317:

> And they [the Catalans] were very content and soon procured a wife for him [Fadrique], and gave him to wife the daughter of micer Bonifazio of Verona, to whom had been left all micer Bonifazio possessed, namely the third part of the city and of the town and of the island of Negroponte, and full thirteen castles on the mainland of the duchy of Athens [which Boniface had received as fiefs from the Burgundian duke Guy II de la Roche].[54] And so he had to wife this damsel who was the daughter of that nobleman who was, I believe, the wisest and most courteous noble ever born . . . . And by this lady En [Catalan for Don] Alfonso Federico had plenty of children and she was the best lady and the wisest there ever was in that country. And, assuredly, she is one of the most beautiful Christians of the world; I saw her in the house of her father when she was about eight years old . . . .[55]

In the late fall of 1317 (or possibly early in 1318) Boniface of Verona died, and Don Alfonso prepared to press his wife's claims by force of arms. Dispute centered especially upon the claims now put forward to, and the Catalan occupation of, the castles of Carystus and Larmena on the island of Euboea. Thomas (or Tommasaccio) of Verona, who seems, for whatever reason, to have been virtually disinherited by his father, claimed the castles of Larmena and Carystus. According to the statement of king Frederick II of Sicily, Boniface of Verona had held these castles as fiefs from John de Noyer of Maisy, and the latter had recognized Marulla's right to them and formally invested her with them, deciding against the claims of Thomas, while the latter is expressly declared to have accepted this

52. *Dipl.*, doc. CIX, p. 132; Thomas, *Diplomatarium veneto-levantinum*, I, no. 70, p. 120. Cf. Rubió, *Dipl.*, docs. LXXXIX–XCII: "nobilis Alfonsus, natus domini Frederici de Aragonia"; and cf. John XXII's letter of May 8, 1318: "nobilis vir Alfonsus, filius naturalis carissimi in Christo filii nostri Friderici Trinacrie regis illustris" (*Dipl.*, doc. XCIV, p. 113), and similar references in other documents.

53. Cf. *Dipl.*, doc. XCVIII, p. 117, dated June 26, 1318: " . . . dominus Alfonsus, qui est Athenis . . . ."

54. Cf. K. Hopf, *Storia di Karystos*, trans. G. B. Sardagna (Venice, 1856), pp. 32–34; Hopf, in Ersch and Gruber, LXXXV, 412 (repr., I, 346).

55. Muntaner, *Crònica*, ch. CCXLIII (ed. Lanz, pp. 434–435; ed. E. B., VI, 112; trans. Hakluyt Society, II, 582); this is Muntaner's last reference to the Catalans in the Athenian duchy. Cf. Rubió i Lluch, *Paquimeres i Muntaner* (Barcelona, 1927), pp. 22.

judgment.[56] Pope John XXII, however, protested that Thomas of Verona had been despoiled of his inheritance,[57] while the Venetians, who looked with fear upon the Catalan possession of Carystus and Larmena, demanded their surrender to the republic, promising somewhat ambiguously to do full right and justice to the claims of Marulla.[58] Don Alfonso kept the castles. In the years that followed, however, Thomas of Verona made peace with his brother-in-law and sister, because upon his death in February 1326 we find him possessed of Larmena and other lands and fiefs on the island of Euboea. When his sister and, conceivably, Don Alfonso sought to enter the city of Negroponte on March 1 to do homage to the triarchs Peter dalle Carceri, Beatrice de Noyer of Maisy, and Bartholomew II Ghisi for these lands and fiefs, all three refused the lady, who had come with a large armed escort, admittance to the city. The island was, they said, under the protection of Venice, and since they feared the consequences of Catalan possession of such strongholds on Euboea, the signoria would have to declare the policy to be followed.[59] But the Venetians were not minded to make concessions to the unreliable family of the Fadriques, because although major hostilities were avoided, it was well known in Venice that Catalan-Turkish piracy was an almost undiminished menace.[60] As for the castle town of Carystus, Venice would be unable to secure it from the Fadrique family until 1365–1366.

Don Alfonso Fadrique was restless and aggressive. When the young ruler of Thessaly, John II Ducas Comnenus, died childless in 1318,[61] Don Alfonso invaded his lands; his attacks were rapid and destructive, but some of his conquests were to endure for more than seventy

---

56. *Dipl.*, doc. CIII, p. 126; Thomas, *Diplomatarium veneto-levantinum*, I, no. 64, pp. 112–113.

57. *Dipl.*, doc. XCIV, pp. 113–114.

58. *Dipl.*, doc. CVI, p. 129; Thomas, I, no. 66, p. 115.

59. *Dipl.*, docs. CXXX–CXXXII, pp. 161–164, dated March 3–4, 1326; cf. Hopf, in Ersch and Gruber, LXXXV, 413, 415, 416, 425 (repr., I, 347, 349, 350, 359). Beatrice of Verona, mother of Peter dalle Carceri, had remarried John de Noyer.

60. Marino Sanudo Torsello, *Ep.* XVI (written in 1326), in Bongars, *Gesta Dei*, II, 307; cf. *Ep.* XVII (1327), in Bongars, II, 309. Note also *Ep.* V (1326), in Bongars, II, 298, in which Sanudo also dilates on the danger presented to the Greek islands by the Turks and Catalans, against whom Venetian Euboea needed especial protection. Sanudo alludes to the Turkish problem a number of times, and incidentally laments the Hospitallers' traffic with Christian pirates on the island of Rhodes (*Ep.* XXI, in Bongars, II, 314, dated February 15, 1329).

61. In May 1317 John II of Thessaly was calling himself lord of Athens as well as of his ancestral domain of Neopatras (*Regesti dei commemoriali*, lib. II, no. 41 [ed. Predelli, I, 177]). In 1318 the Greek ruling family of the "Comneni" died out in both Thessaly and Epirus with the deaths of John II and his cousin Thomas of Epirus (Nicephorus Gregoras, *Historia byzantina*, VII, 13, 3 [*CSHB*, I, 278–279], and VIII, 1 [I, 283]).

years. He seized John II's capital city of Neopatras, the castle of
Siderokastron (near the ancient Heraclea), and Loidoriki, Domokos,
and Pharsala; he was also able to occupy the castle of Zeitounion and
the town of Gardiki in Thessaly. We are fortunate to have an account
of the Catalan conquests just after 1318 from the pen of the famous
crusading publicist Marino Sanudo Torsello, who in 1325 wrote
archbishop Inghiramo Stella of Capua, chancellor of the king of
Naples, about Don Alfonso's gains to the north of the Athenian
duchy.[62] He took the title "vicar-general of the duchies of Athens
and Neopatras," and in later generations, apparently until the establishment of the Bourbon monarchy in Spain, the title duke of Athens
and Neopatras commonly remained a part of the nomenclature of
the crown of Aragon.[63] One unexpected result of Don Alfonso's
Thessalian campaign of 1318–1319 was that the inhabitants of the
city of Pteleum, at the entrance to the Gulf of Volos, offered their
city to the Venetians, and emperor Andronicus II, since he could not
protect Pteleum, assented to this acquisition by Venice of a valuable
commercial station across the narrow strait from the island of

62. Marino Sanudo Torsello, *Ep.* III (1325), in Bongars, *Gesta Dei,* II, 293, and *Dipl.,*
doc. CXXIX, pp. 159–161: "... Nova quae habeo de Romania per hominem fide dignum
et sciolum qui venit de Nigroponte sunt ista: Dicit quod Athenarum ducatus quam
plurimum est ditatus, et quod Catellani, qui dominantur ibidem, acquisiverunt, et tenent in
Blachia [Thessaly], *Lapater* [i.e., La Patria, Neopatras] et castra *Lodorichi* [Loidoriki] et
Sidero-Castri [near Heraclea], *Gitonis* [cf. the Catalan Citó, i.e., Zeitounion, Lamia],
Gardichie [Gardiki], *Donchie* [Domokos], et *Ferselle* [Pharsalus]. . . . Est etiam quidam
Graecus . . . , qui vocatur *Missilino,* qui tenet castrum *del Castri* [of which there were several
in continental Greece] et de *Liconia* [Cat. Lechonia, near Mt. Pelion] : et videtur quod iste
contraxerit parentelam cum Catellanis, eo quod tradidit sororem suam in uxorem mare-
scalco Catellanorum [Odo de Novelles]: et videtur quod fecerit ei fidelitatem, non tamen
quod in eius manibus se sic ponat. Veneti habent unum castrum iuxta mare in Blachia,
nomine *Fetenli* [Pteleum], quod de bona voluntate et sua licentia reliquit eis imperator
Graecorum, qui obtinuissent cum aliter Catellani . . . ."
Missilino, the Greek archon of Castri and Liconia, may have been the uncle or great-uncle
of Missili de Novelles, who in 1380–1381 was "senyor del castell den Estanyol" (*Dipl.,* doc.
CDLXXXIX, p. 548), but who En Estanyol (if the text is accurate), i.e., Don Estañol, was
and where his castle stood, no one knows (Loenertz, *Arch. FF. Praed.,* XXV, 186–187).
Hopf, in Ersch and Gruber, LXXXV, 315, 422 (repr., I, 249, 356), and *Chroniques
gréco-romanes,* p. 536, table 3, believed the name Missilino was a garbling of Melissenus,
whence he drew conclusions challenged by Loenertz, *op. cit.,* pp. 184–185.
In his letter to the archbishop of Capua, Sanudo dwelt at some length on the current
Albanian invasion of Thessaly, which he thought might prove a useful distraction to the
Catalans, who however learned to live with the Albanians; among the eighteen Catalan
feudatories given in the list of 1380–1381 is one count Dimitri, written "de Mitre" by the
scribe. An Albanian chieftain, this Dimitri had 1,500 horse under his command and flew the
royal banner as a born vassal of Aragon-Catalonia (*Dipl.,* doc. CDLXXXIX, p. 548, and doc.
CDLXI, p. 528, addressed to "lo comte Mitra," and see Loenertz, *op. cit.,* nos. 164, 191,
pp. 142, 148).
63. Setton, *Catalan Domination,* p. 31, note 37.

Euboea.[64]   Don Alfonso had no alternative to reluctant acquiescence. After the conquests of the Serbs and Albanians, led especially by the Serbian tsar Stephan Dushan, who in 1348 annexed Thessaly as well as Epirus to his domains, the Catalans had no chance of recovering the fortress towns of Pharsala, Domokos, Gardiki, and Liconia, which they had somehow lost.[65]

Ten or a dozen years after his conquest of Neopatras we find Don Alfonso seeking personal enfeoffment of the town and castle, a crown property. On April 15, 1328 (or 1329 or 1330), he sent a petition from Thebes, the only original Catalan document we possess from the Catalan chancery in Greece, to his cousin king Alfonso IV of Aragon, asking the latter to intercede with his father king Frederick II of Sicily to grant him the castle of Neopatras. He informed king Alfonso "that the aforesaid lord king, my father, has by his favor provided me with six castles which he has kindly given me: in the midst of the said six castles there is one castle called Neopatras, which is the center of the area and the capital of the duchy of Vlachia." He acknowledged that he had many times asked his father for Neopatras, always unsuccessfully, but he hoped that he might still attain his objective by Aragonese mediation.[66]   He failed again. Frederick II doubtless believed that he had already alienated quite enough of the royal domain. It is difficult to identify the "six castles" which Don Alfonso stated his father had given him. Until the Serbian conquest of Thessaly, Neopatras was "in the midst" of all Catalan strongholds north and west of Thebes. In any event Don Alfonso had become lord of Salona under circumstances we do not know, but possibly the fief had escheated to the Company upon the deaths, without heirs, of Roger Deslaur and his wife, the widow of Thomas III of Autremencourt. Don Alfonso probably possessed, in the north, the castles of Pharsala and Domokos, as well as Gardiki and Zeitounion east of Neopatras, and in the south he certainly held those of Loidoriki and Veteranitsa. Like Neopatras, Siderokastron was a crown property. The decade of the 1320's was the period of Don Alfonso's enjoyment of power and success. He was vicar-general

64. Heyd, *Histoire du commerce du Levant,* I, 453. According to an article in the Catalan-Venetian two years' truce of April 1331, Don Alfonso and the Company were not to molest Pteleum so long as the inhabitants remained under the dominion of the republic (*Dipl.,* doc. CLIII, p. 199, and Thomas, *Diplomatarium veneto-levantinum,* I, no. 108, p. 218).

65. Loenertz, *Arch. FF. Praed.,* XXV, no. 10, p. 105, notes that Pharsala, Domokos, and Gardiki do not occur in the documents relating to the Catalan duchies, and so must have been lost early. Liconia also does not appear in the documents.

66. *Dipl.,* doc. CXLI, p. 172: " . . . Patria, qui es cap del pahis e es cap del ducam de la Blaquia . . . ."

from 1317 to about 1330; why he was removed from office we do not know. On November 20, 1330, he was made hereditary count of Malta and Gozo in the mid-Mediterranean.[67] From his wife Marulla he had received the lordship of Aegina and the fortress city of Carystus on the island of Euboea. Marulla also gave him five sons who in after years were to play leading roles in the history of the Catalan duchy of Athens.

For twenty years young Walter II [VI] of Brienne was brought up in the hopes of winning back the Athenian duchy which his father had lost to the Catalan Company in the battle of the Cephissus. His mother Joan of Châtillon and her father the constable of France had kept his interests constantly before the pope, the king of Naples, the doge of Venice, and the king of France. Pope John XXII had continued his support of young Walter's right to the ducal coronet of Athens, and when Walter was ready at last to prosecute his claim by force of arms, the pope directed the Latin patriarch and his venerable brothers of Otranto, Corinth, and Patras to preach a crusade, with "that full forgiveness of all their sins" to those who participated, against the Catalans, "schismatics, sons of perdition, and pupils of iniquity, devoid of all reason, and detestable."[68] On July 21, 1330, king Robert of Naples granted permission to his feudatories to join Walter's projected expedition against the Catalan Company in the duchy of Athens and, with some reservations, remitted the feudal service due the royal court to those who fought with Walter.[69] On October 12 king Robert published throughout his kingdom the papal bull (of June 14) announcing the crusade.[70]

In late August 1331 Walter assembled at Brindisi an army apparently too large for his resources; it included some eight hundred French knights and five hundred Tuscan foot; to transport them to Epirus he mortgaged many of his holdings; and, like his father before him, he pledged his wife's dowry in the "business of Athens." As vicar of prince Philip of Taranto, whose daughter Beatrice he had married, Walter occupied the island of Santa Maura (Leucas), the mainland stronghold of Vonitsa, and Arta, capital of the despotate of

---

67. Cf. *Dipl.*, doc. CCCXCIII, pp. 482–485. The last document to refer to Don Alfonso as vicar-general, *praesidens in ducatu Athenarum,* is dated March 4, 1326 (*Dipl.*, doc. CXXXII, pp. 163–164).

68. *Dipl.*, docs. CL, CLII, pp. 189–191, 193–194, dated June 14, 1330. The ecclesiastical ban levied upon the Catalans did not apply to the lands such as Neopatras and Zeitounion which they had conquered from the Greeks in 1318–1319.

69. *Dipl.*, doc. CLI, pp. 191–192; G. Guerrieri, *Gualtieri VI di Brienne, duca di Atene e conte di Lecce* (Naples, 1896), p. 57.

70. *Dipl.*, doc. CLII, pp. 192–196, dated November 22, 1330.

Epirus, forcing count John II Orsini of Cephalonia to acknowledge the suzerainty of king Robert. Walter made his way across the peninsula, expecting to vindicate by victory in battle the name of Brienne in Greece. The vicar-general of the Catalan Company was Nicholas Lancia,[71] who refused to meet Walter in the open field. The months passed. Walter ravaged the countryside, but his funds were running out. No help could be expected from the Venetians; in April 1331 they had renewed their treaty with the Catalans. On February 28, 1332, in the Franciscan church of St. Nicholas in Patras, archbishop William Frangipani (1317–1337) again proclaimed the ban of excommunication against the Catalans;[72] Walter's headquarters were apparently at Patras. He found no support anywhere among the native Greeks, which does not speak badly for the years of Don Alfonso's rule. The expedition proved to be a failure, and Walter returned to Brindisi in the late summer of 1332. He had won for himself Leucas and Vonitsa, restored for years the Angevin suzerainty over Epirus, and probably made more secure his hold upon his fiefs of Argos and Nauplia in the Morea.[73]

During the years 1334 and 1335 Walter contemplated another attempt upon the duchy of Athens. He appealed to the pope, and the usual ecclesiastical fulminations were forthcoming. On August 12, 1334, John XXII repeated his excommunication of the Catalans.[74] On December 29, 1335, archbishop William Frangipani again excommunicated the leaders of the Catalan Company—duke William of Randazzo; Don Alfonso Fadrique and his sons Peter and James; Nicholas Lancia, the vicar-general of the Company; Odo de Novelles, the marshal; and more than a score of others.[75] But success depended upon Venice, and on November 4, 1335, the signoria refused, with expressions of their profound love, to help him, although they

71. A document of August 5, 1331, refers to Odo de Novelles, marshal of the Company, as *vicarius . . . in partibus Romanie (Dipl.,* doc. CLIV, p. 201). He may have been appointed to command the Company against Walter. Hopf, in Ersch and Gruber, LXXXV, 416b, 422a (repr., I, 350b, 356a), refers to Odo de Novelles as "hereditary marshal" (*Erbmarschall*) of the Athenian duchy, for which there seems to be no evidence.

72. Chas. Du Cange, *Histoire de l'empire de Constantinople,* ed. J. A. Buchon, II (Paris, 1826), 203; Hopf, in Ersch and Gruber, LXXXV, 429–430, and cf. pp. 420–421 (repr., I, 363f., cf. 354 f.).

73. Hopf, *op. cit.,* LXXXV, 430, 441 (repr., I, 364, 375). On the value of the Argolid, note Luttrell, "Latins of Argos and Nauplia," *Papers of the British School at Rome,* XXXIV (1966), 37–38.

74. G. Mollat, ed., *Jean XXII: Lettres communes,* XIII (Paris, 1933), no. 63752, p. 182; printed in full in Lampros, *Eggrapha,* part I, doc. 34, pp. 55–60, and in Rubió, *Dipl.,* doc. CLVIII, pp. 206–209, but incorrectly dated 1333 in both Lampros and Rubió.

75. Du Cange (ed. Buchon), *Constantinople,* II, 204–205; Hopf, *op. cit.,* LXXXV, 436 (repr., I, 370); and on their names, see Rubió, *Dipl.,* p. 208, note.

offered him the use of state galleys to reach Glarentsa or his lands in the Morea.[76]

Through the decade of the 1330's Walter of Brienne continued his diplomatic efforts to ensure that the doge of Venice and the papacy should not forget his claim to the Athenian duchy.[77] The archbishop of Thebes, however, the tough-minded Dominican Isnard Tacconi, whom Clement V had made titular patriarch of Antioch (in 1311) and John XXII had returned to the Theban minster in the spring of 1326,[78] entertained Ghibelline sympathies, and was hostile to Walter, who in March 1337 denounced him to the pope and requested the renewal of censure against the Catalan Company.[79] Two years later, after further inquiry, Benedict XII not only moved to gratify Walter's request, but ordered the vicars of "Constantinople" and Negroponte to cite Isnard and his vicar Gregory of Pavia, also a Dominican, to appear within six months at the curia in Avignon to face charges of having disregarded John XXII's excommunication of the Catalan invaders of the Athenian duchy, in whose presence Isnard had deliberately celebrated mass, and on whose behalf he had falsely published a declaration that the papacy had relaxed the ban of excommunication which had fallen upon them.[80] Walter of Brienne, however, never returned to Greece, although he always planned to do so. He became in after years the tyrant of Florence (1342–1343), fought at Crécy in 1346, and died a constable of France at Poitiers in September 1356. He was the last of his line.[81]

After the Brienne expedition of 1331–1332 the Catalans in Greece enjoyed a period of relative peace and prosperity. When about 1330, or possibly before, Don Alfonso Fadrique was removed from the

76. Hopf, op. cit., LXXXV, 433, 436 (repr., I, 367, 370); Dipl., docs. CLXII, CLXIII, pp. 212–214, and cf. doc. CLXV, pp. 214–215.

77. Cf. Dipl., docs. CLXV, CLXVII, pp. 214–216.

78. Dipl., docs. L, CXXXV, pp. 63, 166–167; Regestum Clementis V, annus septimus, no. 8255, pp. 158–159; Du Cange (ed. Buchon), Constantinople, II, 196.

79. Dipl., doc. CLXVII, p. 216; Lampros, Eggrapha, part I, doc. 37, pp. 67–68; J. M. Vidal, ed., Benoît XII: Lettres communes, I (Paris, 1903), no. 5214, p. 493. Walter had read an intercepted letter from archbishop Isnard to king Frederick of Sicily.

80. Vidal, Benoît XII: Lettres communes, II (Paris, 1906), no. 7420, pp. 206–207, dated March 16, 1339; Dipl., doc. CLXVIII, pp. 217–220, misdated 1338; Lampros, Eggrapha, part I, doc. 35, pp. 60–66; Loenertz, "Athènes et Néopatras," Arch. FF. Praed., XXVIII (1958), nos. 66, 70, pp. 43–44.

81. On Walter's expedition, cf. Setton, Catalan Domination, pp. 38–44. Cesare Paoli, "Nuovi documenti intorno a Gualtieri VI di Brienne, duca d'Atene e signore di Firenze," Archivio storico italiano, 3rd ser., XVI (1872), 39–52, has published a text of Walter's will dated July 18, 1347 (misdated June 18 by the editor), on which cf. Hopf, Chroniques gréco-romanes (Berlin, 1873), pp. XXIX–XXX, 537, and Luttrell, "Latins of Argos and Nauplia," p. 37.

vicariate-general, conceivably at the insistence of the Venetians as the price of their neutrality, the policy of Catalan expansion came to an end. Since his successors were less aggressive, the Venetians worked with them more easily. The Turks became a menace to the Catalans in the Athenian duchy almost as much as to the Venetians in Euboea.[82] The Venetians may have believed that the Catalan Company, without Don Alfonso, would assist them against the Turks,[83] and a Venetian document dated March 4, 1339, probably after Don Alfonso's death, seems to indicate that the Catalans were willing to assist the Venetians to maintain the naval defense of Euboea against the Turks.[84]

As the power and enterprise of the Turks grew, a change in papal policy became necessary; relations between Avignon and Sicily became slightly relaxed (although complete reconciliation would not come until 1372); and in 1339 pope Benedict XII had much fault to find with conditions in the kingdom of Naples (although the papal-Angevin entente remained firm). King Robert could not hope to restore Walter to his distant duchy, and the Turks were an increasing menace to the Angevin principality in the Morea.[85] Thus it finally came about that, shortly before his death, Benedict XII wrote from Avignon in February 1341 to Henry of Asti, Latin patriarch and bishop of Negroponte, that the Company's procurators would be received at the curia to treat of the Catalans' reception back "into the bosom of mother church."[86] In 1342 the difficult Isnard died, and the Carmelite friar Philip, formerly bishop of Salona (1332–1342), replaced him as archbishop of Thebes.[87] Benedict had planned a league of the great powers against the Turks; his successor Clement VI continued his work; and on August 31, 1343, he named the patriarch Henry of Asti papal legate in the crusade against the Turks.[88] On October 21 of the same year Clement wrote Henry directing him to undertake the reconciliation of Walter of Brienne

---

82. Cf. Marino Sanudo Torsello, *Ep.* XXI, in Bongars, *Gesta Dei,* II, 314, also in *Dipl.,* doc. CXLIV, pp. 175–176, dated February 15, 1329.

83. Cf. *Dipl.,* docs. CLXII, CLXIII, pp. 212–214. The Venetians would not at any rate give Walter of Brienne any assistance against the Catalans.

84. *Dipl.,* doc. CLXXIII, pp. 225–226, and cf. Hopf, in Ersch and Gruber, LXXXV, 438b (repr., I, 372b).

85. Setton, *Catalan Domination,* p. 47.

86. Georges Daumet, ed., *Benoît XII: Lettres closes, patentes et curiales se rapportant à la France,* fasc. II (1902), no. 810, cols. 515–516; *Dipl.,* doc. CLXXVII, pp. 228–229.

87. *Dipl.,* doc. CLXXIX, pp. 230–231, dated August 26, 1342; in 1351 Philip was transferred from the Theban archdiocese to Conza in southern Italy, and Sirellus Petri succeeded him (*ibid.,* doc. CXCVIII, p. 256).

88. *Dipl.,* doc. CLXXXI, pp. 232–234; Lampros, *Eggrapha,* part I, doc. 39, pp. 70–74; Eugène Déprez, ed., *Clément VI: Lettres closes . . . ,* fasc. 1 (1901), no. 388, cols. 162–163.

and the Catalan Company to advance the planned offensive against the Turks.[89]   After Henry's unexpected death at Smyrna in the Turkish attack of January 17, 1345, the pope gave instructions on April 1, 1345, to continue the efforts to effect peace between Walter and the Company, for it was important to the prosecution of the war against the Turks.[90] Great interests were at stake, and as the pope had written to patriarch Henry on August 31, 1343, the Turks were "thirsting after the blood of Christian people and yearning for the extinction of the Catholic faith."[91] Finally, on June 15, 1346, at the behest of Humbert II, the dauphin of Viennois, who was then in the east on the second Smyrniote crusade, pope Clement VI removed for three years, without prejudice to the rights of Walter of Brienne, the bans of excommunication and interdict laid long before upon the Catalans and their lands, provided the Catalans furnished a contingent to the army of the crusaders.[92]

The Catalan Company did not take part in the crusade, and before the expiration of the three-year period, as provided in the papal letter of suspension, the bans were automatically renewed "entirely as before." In 1354–1355, however, king Peter IV of Aragon, while seeking to get possession of the head of St. George, patron of Catalonia, which was preserved in the Catalan castle of Livadia,[93] promised the Catalan Company that he would use his full influence to have the interdict lifted.[94] On September 16, 1356, Peter IV wrote cardinal Peter de Cros, asking him to seek the removal of the interdict "for the confusion of the infidel Turks and of the schismatic Greeks, enemies of the Roman Catholic faith,"[95] and on December 3, 1358, pope Innocent VI suspended for a year the bans of excommunication and interdict,[96] but they were renewed "just as

89. *Clément VI: Lettres closes . . . ,* fasc. 1, no. 465, cols. 204–205; *Dipl.,* doc. CLXXXII, pp. 234–235.

90. *Clément VI: Lettres closes . . . ,* fasc. 2 (1925), no. 1608, cols. 482–484; *Dipl.,* doc. CLXXXIII, pp. 236–237. Rubió, *Dipl.,* p. 237, note 1, questions the date of Henry's death only because he has misdated the document; for the facts and sources, see A. S. Atiya, *Crusade in the Later Middle Ages,* pp. 295–296, and Lemerle, *L' Émirat d'Aydin,* pp. 190–194. The crusaders had taken Smyrna from Umur Pasha, emir of Aydin, on October 28, 1344 (Lemerle, *op. cit.,* pp. 186–190); they held the city until its occupation by Timur the Lame in 1402.

91. *Dipl.,* doc. CLXXXI, p. 232.

92. *Dipl.,* docs. CLXXXVIII, CLXXXIX, pp. 242–247.

93. *Dipl.,* doc. CCXIV, p. 293, dated December 1, 1354, and docs. CCXV–CCXX, pp. 293–296. On the extraordinary history of this relic, see K. M. Setton, "Saint George's Head," *Speculum,* XLVIII (1973), 1–12, reprinted in his *Europe and the Levant . . . ,* no. VII.

94. *Dipl.,* doc. CCXXI, p. 297, dated March 17, 1355.

95. *Dipl.,* doc. CCXXX, p. 304. Cardinal Peter de Cros was Clement VI's nephew (Conrad Eubel, *Hierarchia catholica medii aevi,* I [1913, repr. 1960], 19).

96. *Dipl.,* doc. CCXXXV, pp. 309–310.

before," and on December 25, 1363, they were removed again for three years by pope Urban V.[97] The Catalans had a hard time making peace with the church, and many of them abandoned Latin Catholicism for Greek Orthodoxy.

When Don Alfonso Fadrique died about 1338, Catalan relations with the Venetians in Negroponte, which had much improved since his removal from the vicariate-general of the Company in 1330, became still more friendly. Through the decade of the 1330's, too, the Catalans were anxious to preserve good relations with the Venetians to help offset Walter of Brienne's influence in Naples and Avignon. The Venetians still had occasion, however, from time to time, to complain of Catalan violence and piracy, for in March 1350 the Serenissima was distressed by an attack upon Venetian subjects in Pteleum by "members of the Company and the Albanians," and held up to opprobrium the piratical conduct of Don Alfonso's eldest son, Peter [I] Fadrique.[98]

Peter had succeeded his father about 1338 as lord of Salona, Loidoriki, Veteranitsa, Aegina, and possibly Zeitounion. His fiefs were confiscated to the crown between 1350 and 1355 for reasons, wrote king Frederick III, "which we believe are not unknown to you," but which are in fact quite unknown to us. Peter died before 1355. Nevertheless, his brother James recovered his fiefs, and thus succeeded him, as their father had wished if Peter left no heirs.[99] A third brother, John, was lord of Aegina and Salamis in 1350,[100] and a fourth, Boniface, possessed—apparently as a legacy from his mother, Marulla of Verona—the stronghold of Carystus in Euboea and certain other valuable properties in Attica which in 1359, after long residence in Sicily, he appeared in Greece to claim.[101] With the passing of the vigorous Don Alfonso, the great days of Catalan unity and strength in Greece had come to an end, but with some vicissitudes of fortune his descendants prospered after him.

---

97. *Dipl.*, doc. CCLV, pp. 338–339. The disaster of the Cephissus was never forgotten at the French-dominated curia, where the Athenian duchy was regarded as the possession *de jure* of the Briennes and their heirs, "ducatus Athenarum detentus agentibus que dicuntur Magna Societas pro interfectione Gualterii ducis . . . ," but the bans were periodically lifted from the Grand Company for a good reason.

98. *Dipl.*, doc. CXCV, p. 253.

99. Cf. *Dipl.*, doc. CCXXIII, pp. 298–299; Rosario Gregario, ed., *Opere rare edite ed inedite riguardanti la Sicilia* (2nd ed., Palermo, 1873), p. 360; *Dipl.*, doc. CCLXXII, pp. 356–357, relating to the possession of Salona, Loidoriki, and Veteranitsa by James, the second son of Don Alfonso.

100. *Dipl.*, doc. CXCVI, p. 254.

101. Cf. Setton, *Catalan Domination*, pp. 50–51.

When the infante Don Manfred, duke of Athens, died at Trapani in Sicily on November 9, 1317, his younger brother succeeded him in the ducal title as William II. Twenty years later, on the night of June 24–25, 1337, their energetic father king Frederick II of Sicily died, and by his will, dated March 29, 1334, William II's right to the duchies of Athens and Neopatras, as well as to certain possessions in Sicily, was confirmed. [102] Frederick II had provided in his will that, if William II wished to go to his dominions in Greece, his elder brother, king Peter II, was to supply him with twenty armed galleys and two hundred knights with pay. The young duke's illness and the confusion in Sicily which followed Frederick II's death prevented any such journey to Greece. On May 11, 1338, duke William II made his own will; three months later he was dead (August 22); and a younger brother, the marquis of Randazzo, became duke John II of Athens. He was the only one of Frederick II's sons with anything like the stature of their father. It is said that in 1344 he sought to raise an army of six hundred knights and four thousand *almogàvers* in Aragon for an expedition against the Turks in the Levant. In his will, dated January 9, 1348, John II of Aragon-Randazzo acknowledged the receipt from the Sicilian royal court of 17,000 ounces of gold "for our voyage to Romania," and he wished the money returned to the court if death should prevent his going to Greece.

On April 3, 1348, John of Randazzo succumbed to the Black Death; his son, Frederick I, succeeded him as duke of Athens. Blasco of Alagón, count of Mistretta and guardian of the young Frederick I, is alleged to have urged his ward to undertake an expedition to Athens in 1349, but like the plan of his father, John II, this too came to nothing, and Frederick I of Aragon-Randazzo died in his turn of the plague on July 11, 1355. Frederick I was now followed as duke of Athens and Neopatras by his nephew Frederick II, who became shortly thereafter king Frederick III of Sicily. Frederick III's rule was never strong in Sicily where he was; it could not be otherwise than weak in Athens where he was not. He prolonged his failure, however, as a sovereign over Sicily and his Greek dominions across the sea through twenty-two years (1355–1377). [103]

In 1351 the Catalans in the Levant got caught in the renewal of the commercial war between Venice and Genoa (1350–1355). King Peter

102. The text of the will has been published by Giuseppe La Mantia, *Archivio storico per la Sicilia*, II–III (1936–1937; published 1938), 13 ff., and see pp. 31–32, 35–36; Rubió, *Dipl.*, doc. CLIX, pp. 209–210.

103. For the above, see Setton, *Catalan Domination*, pp. 15–17, 184, note 27. Duke John I of Athens was John de la Roche (1263–1280).

IV of Aragon took much interest in the Greek dominions of the Sicilian branch of his family, an interest which seems to have been neither much resented nor resisted in Sicily. On June 1, 1351, therefore, Peter wrote the Aragonese and Catalans in Greece, his countrymen whom innate constancy and loyalty, he declares, bound with indissoluble ties to the crown of Aragon with a strength no distance could diminish. His majesty informed the Catalans in Thebes, Athens, and elsewhere, of revolt in his kingdom of Sardinia and Corsica; he was now at war with Genoa and in alliance with Venice; and thus did the Catalans in Greece learn that they too were at war with the Genoese. [104] On January 16, 1351, a treaty had been concluded at Perpignan—it was ratified by the doge on July 12— between the republic and the king of Aragon in order to effect the final destruction of the Genoese. Emperor John VI Cantacuzenus was forced into the alliance against the Genoese. [105] The latter gave a good account of themselves, however, and a fleet of sixty-two ships under Paganino Doria laid siege to the fortress town of Oreus, a Venetian possession in northern Euboea. Catalans of the Athenian duchy dispatched a force of three hundred horse and a large body of foot to hold Oreus against the Genoese and prevent their establishing themselves in the island. [106] After a siege of two months, from mid-August to October 1351, the Venetian fortress was saved by the arrival of aid from Venice and of a strong Aragonese fleet under the admiral Pons of Santa Pau. After this, if the Catalans in Athens and Thebes played any part in the war, record of it seems not to have survived, although we read in one document of Aragonese-Catalan crewmen from the fleet who made their way to the Athenian duchy after suffering shipwreck. [107]

On February 13, 1352, near Constantinople a major naval battle was fought when the Venetian and Aragonese fleets sighted the Genoese cruising in "Turkish waters." Both sides claimed victory in a brutal encounter, and Santa Pau wrote to Peter IV of victory over the Genoese, claiming the capture of twenty-three of their galleys, with the destruction of all aboard, and the loss of only twelve

104. *Dipl.*, doc. CXCIX, pp. 257–258.

105. Cf. Camillo Manfroni, "Le Relazioni fra Genova, l'impero bizantino e i Turchi," *Atti della Società ligure di storia patria*, XXVIII (1896–1902), 706 ff., and on the background of the Aragonese-Venetian alliance see the detailed study of Mario Brunetti, "Contributo alla storia delle relazioni veneto-genovesi dal 1348 al 1350," in the *Miscellanea di storia veneta*, 3rd ser., IX (Venice, 1916).

106. Nicephorus Gregoras, XXI, 22 (*CSHB*, III, 47 ff.), but according to a note in William Miller (tr. Sp. P. Lampros), Ἰστορία τῆς φραγκοκρατίας ἐν Ἑλλάδι, I (Athens, 1910), 430, note 1, the Genoese attacked Oropus, not Oreus.

107. *Dipl.*, doc. CCV, p. 263, dated August 20, 1352.

Aragonese ships, from which the crews of only two were lost. [108]
Nevertheless, the naval battle favored the Genoese, for when the
battered fleets of the allies withdrew from the region of the Bosporus, emperor John VI Cantacuzenus was obliged to make peace
with Paganino Doria (May 6), and on August 2 Peter IV wrote to
Cantacuzenus in distress at the news of his willingness to make peace
with the depraved Genoese, the sons of Belial. [109] With the war as
such we are not here concerned, although we may note that the
Genoese were defeated at Alghero, a Catalan city in Sardinia, on
August 29, 1354, but they captured thirty-five Venetian galleys on
November 4 at Zonklon (Navarino), not the least memorable event in
the brief reign of the hated doge Marino Falieri. On June 1, 1355,
the Venetians made peace with the Genoese. The war would be
renewed, in after years, over possession of the strategic island of
Tenedos, and would end in 1380–1381 with a Venetian victory in
the lagoons of Chioggia and in the subsequent peace of Turin, but
since the fleets of both the maritime republics were almost ruined in
the encounter, neither Venice nor Genoa was thereafter in any
condition to moderate the increasing ambition and enterprise of the
Turks.

The loss of a large number of registers from the royal archives of
the Catalan kings of Sicily from the years preceding 1355 has left a
gap of some twenty years in our knowledge of the inner history of
the Catalan states in Greece, which has been little filled by papal and
Venetian documents, and even the names of the Catalan-Sicilian
vicars-general after Nicholas Lancia and Odo de Novelles are unknown (from 1331 to 1354). King Frederick III's first known act as
duke of Athens, however, was to consult Artale of Alagón, the
imposing chief justiciar of the Sicilian kingdom, in connection with
the request made in December 1355 on behalf of James Fadrique,
second son of Don Alfonso, for royal confirmation of his right, now
that his brother Peter was dead, to the county of Salona and the
lordship of Loidoriki. [110] Peter had been dispossessed by the crown,
but apparently Artale of Alagón favored the Fadrique petition,
because James must have acquired Salona and Loidoriki at this time.
King Frederick next received an embassy from the Greek duchies
requesting the removal from office of the vicar-general Raymond
Bernardi (Ramón Bernat de Sarbou), whose failure to rule in Greece

---

108. *Dipl.,* doc. CCII, pp. 259–260; cf. docs. CCV–CCIX.
109. *Dipl.,* doc. CCIV, pp. 261–262. On the battle of the Bosporus (February 13, 1352)
and the Cantacuzene peace of May 6 with the Genoese, see Luttrell, "John Cantacuzenus
and the Catalans at Constantinople," in *Martínez Ferrando, Archivero,* pp. 265–277.
110. *Dipl.,* doc. CCXXIII, pp. 298–299.

and exact obedience from those under him was exposing the duchies, it was claimed, to extreme danger of collapse. [111] The Catalan representatives suggested, among others, that James Fadrique should be made vicar-general, which appears not to have been done.

The loss of Catalan documents in Sicily was due not only to wars and fires, but also to the failure to establish a single repository in a central capital. Material was left in Palermo, Catania, and Messina. When the series of extant Palermitan documents begins, the chronology of king Frederick III's appointments to the office of vicar-general remains still obscure, but the documents do furnish us with information about the following vicars-general and supply the following dates for their appointments: Raymond Bernardi (1354–1356); [112] Gonsalvo Ximènez of Arenós (1359 and possibly 1362–1363); [113] Matthew of Moncada, grand seneschal of the Sicilian kingdom ("Trinacria") and count of Aderno and Agosta in Sicily (1359–1361 and, officially at least, 1363–1366); [114] and the violent Peter de Pou, a Catalan resident in Thebes, who seized from James Fadrique the castles of Salona, Loidoriki, and Veteranitsa (1361–1362), and met his death in an uprising against him in Thebes (1362). [115] The powerful Roger de Lluria, who led the opposition to

111. *Dipl.*, doc. CCXXV, pp. 300–301, dated January 27, 1356.

112. *Dipl.*, docs. CCXIV, CCXXV, pp. 293, 300–301.

113. Cf. *Dipl.*, doc. CCCVII, p. 393, properly dated May 30, 1378 or 1379: An appeal for the recovery of funds having been made before the royal court in Sicily, Maria, daughter of the late Frederick III, now queen of Sicily and duchess of Athens and Neopatras, wrote the vicar-general in Greece, "quod anni [decem et] *octo vel circa* sunt elapsi, vertente questione . . . coram nobili quondam Consalvo Eximes de Arenis [sic], vestro in eodem vicariatus officio precessore . . . ." The scribal error to the effect that about eight rather than eighteen years had elapsed since Gonsalvo had considered the case misled Rubió i Lluch into misdating doc. CCCVII to May 30, 1368.

Gonsalvo was vicar-general on October 30, 1359 [. . . *penultimo Octubris XIII indictionis*], as shown by a letter of Maria dated June 7, 1378 or 1379, published by Loenertz, *Arch. FF. Praed.*, XXV, p. 202, and cf., *ibid.*, nos. 38, 42, 142–143. The Sicilian chancery began the indictional year with September 1 (as shown clearly by the royal letter in *Dipl.*, doc. CCLXXX, pp. 364–365), and so the thirteenth indiction ran from September 1, 1359, through August 31, 1360. It seems likely that Gonsalvo served again as vicar-general in 1362–1363 (Loenertz, *op. cit.*, nos. 53–55, 59, 87, and especially nos. 142–143, pp. 137, 157).

114. *Dipl.*, docs. CCXLV, CCLXXXIX, pp. 326–327, 376–377, on which note Loenertz, *Arch. FF. Praed.*, XXV, nos. 43, 49, pp. 112, 113, for Moncada's first tenure of office. For his second appointment, see *Dipl.*, docs. CCLIII, CCLIV, CCLVII, CCLXXXIX, CCXC, pp. 336–338, 340–341, 375–378, and Loenertz, *op. cit.*, nos. 66–69, 75, 83, pp. 117–118, 120, 122. Moncada's second appointment had terminated before August 3, 1366, when a royal letter officially styles Roger de Lluria vicar-general (*Dipl.*, doc. CCLXXI, p. 355). In the *Diplomatari,* doc. CCLXVII, with its reference to Moncada (pp. 350–351), should be dated 1362 (Loenertz, *op. cit.*, no. 50, p. 113).

115. Matthew of Moncada was still vicar-general on June 17, 1361 (*XVII Iunii XIIII indictionis*), when Peter de Pou advised him in certain suits involving the interests of the

Peter de Pou, was marshal of the Company before December 1354; he took over the functions and apparently usurped the title of vicar-general from 1362 to 1366. He was assisted by his brother John, and the pope was sadly aware of their dominance in the capital city of Thebes, since for a while they used Turks to maintain their position. [116] The royal court in Sicily recognized Roger's authority from some time before August of the latter year until, presumably, his death in 1369 or 1370. [117] His successor was the ineffective Matthew of Peralta, of the family of the counts of Caltabellotta in Sicily (1370–1374). [118] Finally, the grandson of the great Don Alfonso, Louis Fadrique, the "last count of Salona," was vicar-general from April 1375 to the fall of 1381.[119] He died the following year.

marshal Roger de Lluria (*Dipl.,* doc. CCLXXXIX, pp. 376–377, and cf. Loenertz, *Arch. FF. Praed.,* XXV, no. 49, p. 113), but Peter must have been himself appointed to the vicariate soon thereafter, perhaps on Moncada's recommendation. For example, a document of August 3, 1366, recalling the tragic events of early 1362, refers to the seizure of Salona, Loidoriki, and Veteranitsa, "que [castra] ... per Petrum de Putheo, *tunc vicarium dictorum ducatuum,* eiusque complices et consortes occasione guerre tunc vigentis ibidem occupata detenebantur contra iusticiam et per vim ..." (*Dipl.,* doc. CCLXXII, pp. 356–357; Loenertz, *op. cit.,* no. 52, p. 114). Peter de Pou was removed from office before May 28, 1362, when Frederick III appointed a new vicar-general (*Dipl.,* docs. CCC–CCCVI, pp. 388–393; Lampros, *Eggrapha,* part IV, nos. 1–7, pp. 233–238; and for the dating, see Loenertz, *op. cit.,* nos. 53–60, pp. 114–116).

116. Cf. Urban V's letter of June 27, 1364, to Roger and John de Lluria in Archivio Segreto Vaticano, Reg. Vat. 246, fol. 241^r: "... quod vos contagiosa familiaritate a participatione infidelium Turchorum, vestras famam et animas maculantes, ipsos in terris vestris receptatis eisque datis auxilium et favorem ..." (also in *Dipl.,* doc. CCLVI, p. 339, where by a slip the text reads "receptis," which is untranslatable, for "receptatis"). A Venetian document of July 25, 1365, refers to Roger de Lluria both as *vicarius Thebarum* and as marshal and *vicarius generalis universitatis ducatus Athenarum* (*Dipl.,* doc. CCLVIII, p. 341), and Venetian documents of August 28, 1365, and July 5, 1369—both relate to Roger's seizure of some 520 *hyperperi* from a Venetian citizen in August 1362—identify Roger as *vicarius universitatis Athenarum* (*Dipl.,* docs. CCLX, CCCXIII, pp. 344, 400). The titles are as odd as his position was irregular. On August 3, 1366, however, Frederick III addressed Roger officially as *ducatuum Athenarum et Neopatrie vicarius generalis* (*Dipl.,* doc. CCLXXI, p. 355; Lampros, *Eggrapha,* part IV, no. 89, p. 335), which shows that his appointment must have preceded this date.

117. Roger de Lluria was still the vicar-general on November 16, 1368 (*Dipl.,* doc. CCCXI, p. 397).

118. Cf. *Dipl.,* doc. CCCXXI, pp. 408–410, dated May 31, 1370, the appointment being made *ob mortem nobilis Rogerii de Lauria,* at which time a third nomination of Matthew of Moncada was annulled. Peralta was still vicar-general on January 18–19, 1374 (*Dipl.,* docs. CCCXLII, CCCXLV, pp. 430, 432). He probably did not live many months longer, and was dead before April 18, 1376, when the Venetian senate was asked to transport his two sons from Thebes to their home in Sicily (*Dipl.,* doc. CCCLXII, pp. 446–447).

119. Louis Fadrique, son of James, had obviously taken over the functions of the vicariate after the death or incapacitation of Matthew of Peralta (cf. *Dipl.,* docs. CCCXLVIII, CCCL, pp. 435–437). His commission as vicar-general is dated April 6–9, 1375 (*Dipl.,* docs. CCCLI, CCCLIII), on which cf. Loenertz, *Arch. FF. Praed.,* XXV, nos. 132, 134–135, pp. 134, 135, 157.

If the Theban uprising of 1362 caused excitement at the royal court in Sicily, it also produced a ripple at the papal court in Avignon. Here interest fastened on the money and other assets left by Peter de Pou's supporter and fellow victim Michael Oller, Catalan dean of the church of Thebes, who died intestate. Like others of his time, Oller must have found the ecclesiastical life remunerative, for in addition to other property he is said to have left cash amounting to some 5,000 or 6,000 gold *regales* Majorcan. [120] While we are under no obligation to audit accounts six centuries old, we may well wonder how much of Oller's cash and *alia bona* he had lifted from the estate of the late Sirellus Petri, archbishop of Thebes.

Pope Urban V was wondering the same thing when on November 3, 1363, he wrote the Franciscan friar Thomas, archbishop of Paros and Naxos, that his predecessor Innocent VI had learned that all the movable goods, property, and income of the late Sirellus Petri were properly reserved for the holy see. Nevertheless, the recently deceased Michael Oller, dean of the church of Thebes, and his accomplices had illegally seized Sirellus's possessions and usurped his income. Innocent VI had therefore instructed Thomas of Paros, archbishop Nicholas of Athens, and bishop Nicholas of Andros to conduct a full investigation of Sirellus's assets, which Thomas tried to do, but reported back to the curia in Avignon that he had encountered an obstacle. When in obedience to the papal mandate he had claimed Michael Oller's estate for the apostolic treasury, one Grifon of Arezzo, a canon of Coron, had intervened. Grifon represented himself as the vicar-general of Peter Thomas, now archbishop of Crete, but at the time bishop of Coron. Since May 1359 Peter Thomas had been apostolic legate *in partibus ultramarinis* (he later increased his fame by the part he played in the Alexandria crusade of 1365). [121] Grifon stated that Oller's movable goods had been especially reserved by papal letters for Peter Thomas, and he so warned the archbishops of Paros and Athens in the course of their investigation, as well as archbishop Paul of Thebes. Grifon in fact informed them all that they faced the prospect of excommunication if they acted contrary to the special commission which he held from the legate Peter. Under these circumstances, Thomas of Paros wrote the pope, he had desisted from execution of the papal mandate until he could receive further instructions from Avignon. At this point Urban could consult the legate Peter Thomas himself about Grifon's asser-

120. *Dipl.*, doc. CCLII, p. 335, dated at Barcelona August 26, 1362; king Peter IV of Aragon claimed Oller's estate for the latter's next of kin.
121. See below, pp. 297–298, 352–357.

tions, for Peter was in Avignon, having just returned from the east. The legate was unaware of any papal concession of Michael Oller's estate (and the possessions of the late Sirellus), and denied ever having authorized Grifon to claim it for him. The pope therefore directed his grace of Paros to take over and restore to the holy see the properties and revenues left by Sirellus (which were chiefly at issue), notwithstanding the alleged mandate of Grifon or of any other claimant of whatsoever rank or condition who might appear on the scene. Thomas of Paros was, if necessary, to have recourse to the secular arm, and whoever might seek to impede him exposed himself to excommunication. [122]

In the meantime, in 1362, possibly as a result of the seizure of money or property belonging to a Venetian citizen, [123] the marshal Roger de Lluria and his partisans found themselves virtually at war with Peter Gradenigo, Venetian bailie of Negroponte. Although we know little of the extent of Catalan or Venetian operations, hostilities continued until 1365. There was discord in the Catalan duchies, and Roger lacked a legal basis for his exercise of authority. He sought the assistance of the Turks, as had Don Alfonso a generation before, and early in 1363 Turks were admitted within the walls of Thebes. Paul, archbishop of Thebes (1357–1366) and later the Latin patriarch, [124] and three other notables appeared before Frederick III in Sicily, allegedly as "envoys or ambassadors sent by certain municipalities . . . of the aforesaid duchies." In July or early August 1363 they informed the royal court that Turkish troops had entered Thebes, and it was now (on August 16) that Frederick reappointed Matthew of Moncada as vicar-general to free his faithful citizens of

122. Archivio Segreto Vaticano, Reg. Vat. 246, fols. 45ᵛ–46ᵛ. On Peter Thomas's activities in 1362–1363, see Boehlke, *Pierre de Thomas*, pp. 204 ff. Peter Thomas was bishop of Coron from May 10, 1359, until his successor was elected on February 17, 1363; he held the archiepiscopal see of Crete from March 6, 1363, until his appointment to the Latin patriarchal title of Constantinople on July 5, 1364; he helped lead the Alexandria crusade of 1365, and died on January 6, 1366. Cf. Eubel, *Hierarchia catholica*, I, 212, 215, 206. Sirellus Petri, whose possessions were at issue, was a native of Ancona; he was archbishop of Thebes from May 20, 1351, until his death before May 15, 1357, when the well-known Paul of Smyrna was selected as his successor (Eubel, *op. cit.,* I, 482, and *Dipl.,* doc. CCXXXII, p. 305). Archbishop Thomas of Paros and Naxos was a Franciscan; he held the island sees from June 30, 1357, but the date of his death appears still to be unknown (Eubel, I, 358). Nicholas de Raynaldo was appointed archbishop of Athens on June 19, 1357 (Eubel, I, 115, and *Dipl.,* doc. CCXXXIII, pp. 306–307), and died before June 6, 1365 (Loenertz, *Arch. FF. Praed.,* XXVIII, nos. 137, 139–140, 142, 152, 159). Nicholas of Andros was an Augustinian; appointed bishop on July 14, 1349, he died before June 16, 1376 (Eubel, I, 89, and Loenertz, *loc. cit.,* nos. 112, 190).

123. *Dipl.,* docs. CCLX, CCCXIII, pp. 344, 400: " . . . quoddam damnum . . . ad summam yperperorum quingentorum viginti duorum . . . ."

124. Cf. *Dipl.,* docs. CCXXXII, CCLXIV, pp. 305, 347; Eubel, *op. cit.,* I, 206.

Thebes from the horrors of the infidel encampment in their midst. The delegation from Greece had apparently requested Moncada's return to the vicar's palace in Thebes. He was to proclaim an amnesty; receive into his charge the castles and fortified places on the royal domain; appoint castellans, veguers, and captains, and receive their oaths of fealty in the king's name; and collect crown revenues and proper exactions for the support of himself and his retinue, for the maintenance of royal castles, and for his various official burdens. [125] Although Moncada did not go into Greece to assume his command, he did dispatch an armed force against the doughty marshal de Lluria, whose troopers annihilated them. [126] Roger's troopers may have included his mercenary Turks, and the Turkish menace was then weighing heavily on the seraphic minds of the hierarchy in France.

Curial officials were talking constantly about the crusade, for in Avignon on March 31, 1363, king John II of France, Peter I of

---

125. *Dipl.*, doc. CCLIII, pp. 336–337; Gregorio, *Opere rare*, pp. 357–358. Roger de Lluria's contingent of Turks was said to be a menace to both town and countryside: " . . . fideles nostri tam cives quam agricolae aliique ad civitatis ipsius per tramites discurrentes tam mares quam feminae diversa gravia et abominanda flagitia patiantur . . ." (*Dipl.*, p. 336).

During his sojourn in Sicily, having obviously fled from Roger de Lluria, archbishop Paul of Thebes served Frederick III as envoy to Naples when in 1363–1364 efforts were being made to arrange peace between queen Joanna I of Naples and Frederick, *detentor insule Sicilie* (for the whole course of negotiations, see Setton, "Archbishop Pierre d'Ameil in Naples," *Speculum*, XXVIII, 643–691). Paul consulted with the then archbishop of Naples, Peter d'Ameil, concerning the possibility of arranging a marriage between Constance, *ducissa Athenarum*, and Aimon III, eldest son of count Amadeo III of Geneva. Constance was the daughter of the late John of Randazzo, duke of Athens and Neopatras from 1338 to 1348 (Setton, *op. cit.*, p. 669), and she apparently bore the courtesy title duchess of Athens. Peter d'Ameil gave some consideration to the proposal, although he was trying strenuously to marry Aimon to duchess Joanna of Durazzo, perhaps the richest heiress in Italy, niece of queen Joanna and stepdaughter of Philip II of Taranto, who then bore the title prince of Achaea. See the letters of Peter d'Ameil dated October 29, 1363 (*Dipl.*, doc. CCCXV, pp. 401–402, text incomplete, misdated 1369; Lampros, *Eggrapha*, part I, doc. 47, pp. 86–88; A. Mango, *Relazioni tra Federico III di Sicilia e Giovanna I di Napoli* [Palermo, 1915], doc. XLIII, pp. 93–96; and cf. Setton, *op. cit.*, pp. 657–659) and July 12, 1364 (*Dipl.*, doc. CCCXIV, pp. 400–401, misdated 1369; Lampros, *Eggrapha*, part I, doc. 46, pp. 85–86; not in Mango; and cf. Setton, *op. cit.*, pp. 682–683, note). The letter given by Rubió in the *Dipl.*, doc. CCCXII, pp. 398–399 (from Lampros, *Eggrapha*, part I, doc. 45, pp. 82–84), is misdated January 4, 1369; it was actually written on December 29, 1363, and sent on the following January 4 (Mango, *Relazioni*, doc. L, pp. 116–118); it concerns duchess Joanna of Durazzo, and has nothing to do with the so-called "duchess of Athens" (Setton, *op. cit.*, pp. 665–666). Cf. the summaries in Loenertz, *Arch. FF. Praed.*, XXV, nos. 70–71, 74, and *ibid.*, XXVIII, nos. 151, 154–156; on the activities of archbishop Paul in the Greek world, see K. M. Setton, "The Byzantine Background to the Italian Renaissance," *Proceedings of the American Philosophical Society*, C (1956), 45–46, reprinted in his *Europe and the Levant . . .* , no. I.

126. *Dipl.*, doc. CCXC, p. 378; Lampros, *Eggrapha*, part IV, no. 20, p. 257; Loenertz, *Arch. FF. Praed.*, XXV, no. 67, p. 117.

Cyprus, cardinal Elias Talleyrand of Perigord, and various nobles had taken the "red cross of Outremer." King John was made "rector and captain-general" of the expedition, and Talleyrand the papal legate. Urban V offered John a tithe to be levied in France, as well as unassigned and unspent gifts, fines, legacies, penances, and the like of the past twelve years and similar subsidies for the next six "to help with the vast expenses" of the projected expedition. The French hierarchy was to gather the allotted funds every six months and submit them in gold to the curia within two months of each collection, and rather elaborate precautions were supposed to be taken to see that this financial harvest was expended solely on the crusade. Papal letters went out to most of the important princes and prelates of Christendom, announcing the crusade (which was to set out on March 1, 1365), granting the crusaders the usual indulgences, and taking their possessions under the protection of the holy see.[127] Obviously marshal Roger de Lluria had not chosen a good time to admit Turks into the capital city of Thebes.

We cannot pursue here the details of Urban V's untiring efforts to help organize a crusade, but one can imagine the reaction at the curia when word reached Avignon "that in the city of Thebes and other places roundabout a profane multitude of infidel Turks are dwelling," as Urban wrote archbishop Bartholomew of Patras on June 27, 1364, "and constantly striving to attack the lands of your church of Patras and other nearby areas belonging to the faithful." Urban charged the archbishop "that fired with the love of God and with fervor for his faith you should rise up against these Turks, manfully and as powerfully as your strength allows, so that with God's right hand providing you and his other servants with valor the said Turks may be repulsed . . . , and you stepping forth as a true boxer of Christ may gain more fully thereby the reward of eternal recompense and the plenitude of our grace."[128] On the same day Urban addressed a letter of grim remonstrance to the brothers Roger and John

127. N. Iorga, *Philippe de Mézières* (Paris, 1896), pp. 158–162 (on p. 160, line 3, read 1362 for 1363), 165–172, and Boehlke, *Pierre de Thomas*, pp. 211–216; P. Lecacheux, ed., *Lettres secrètes et curiales du pape Urbain V (1362–1370) se rapportant à la France*, I, fasc. 1 (Paris, 1902), nos. 346–347, pp. 40–41. Cardinal Elias Talleyrand died in January 1364, and was replaced as legate for the crusade by Peter Thomas, who already held general legatine authority in the east.

128. Archivio Segreto Vaticano, Reg. Vat. 246, fol. 240, letter dated at Avignon on June 27, 1364. In a bull, directed *ad perpetuam rei memoriam* and dated March 21, 1364, Urban V excommunicated among various other classes of malefactors those who supplied horses, arms, iron, timber, and *alia prohibita* to the Moslems, who carried on war against the Christians (Arch. Segr. Vaticano, Reg. Vat. 246, fol. 141ᵛ, "datum et actum Avinione XII Kal. Aprilis anno secundo").

de Lluria, ordering them to dismiss their Turkish mercenaries and take up arms against them, restore to the Theban church the goods and properties they had seized, and readmit archbishop Paul to his defenseless see. [129]

The Angevin bailie of the principality of Achaea and Manuel Cantacuzenus, the despot of Mistra, together with the Venetians and the Hospitallers, employed their resources in common to combat the Turkish peril. The Turks were defeated in a naval battle off Megara, southern fortress of the Catalan duchy of Athens; they lost thirty-five ships, and looked to the walls of Thebes for safety and to the assistance of Roger de Lluria. But in the long run the defeated Turks would be a poor ally, and the indignant pope, the inimical Angevin, and the sage Venetian the wrong enemies. Roger therefore sought peace with the Venetians in Euboea, and on July 25, 1365, the senate, with some reservations, sanctioned the cessation of hostilities, and so informed their bailie in Negroponte. [130] When the Turks had departed from Thebes, and peace was thus restored with the Venetians, close relations were finally reëstablished between the rebellious Catalans in the Athenian duchy, led by the marshal Roger de Lluria, and their king and duke in distant Sicily.

On February 24, 1365, king Frederick III had directed his cousin James Fadrique and Roger de Lluria to receive his appointee Matthew of Moncada as vicar-general of the duchies of Athens and Neopatras and to help him secure possession of the royal castles of Livadia, Neopatras, and Siderokastron. Frederick now stated that he had appointed Moncada to the office for life, and he professed to believe that previous letters to this effect had been lost. [131] It seems

129. *Dipl.*, doc. CCLVI, pp. 339–340, and cf. Lecacheux, *Lettres secrètes et curiales*, I, fasc. 2 (Paris, 1906), no. 1050, p. 163.

130. *Dipl.*, doc. CCLVIII, pp. 340–341, and cf. Setton, *Catalan Domination*, pp. 60–61. Loenertz, *Arch. FF. Praed.*, XXV, nos. 68, 73, pp. 118, 119, is doubtless correct in assuming that Roger de Lluria's Turks were not an Ottoman contingent, sent to his aid by sultan Murad I, but mercenaries secured from one of the emirates of Asia Minor. The Turkish defeat off Megara, formerly put in the summer of 1364, should conceivably be dated about 1359–1360, and may explain how Roger came to hire Turks in the first place, but the chronology is uncertain (cf. Loenertz, *op. cit.*, pp. 430–431). According to the Aragonese *Chronicle of the Morea* (ed. Morel-Fatio, *Libro de los fechos* [Geneva, 1885], par. 685, p. 151), when Walter of Lor was bailie of the Angevin principality (1357–1360), he burned thirty-five Turkish ships after an encounter at Megara, his allies in the undertaking being the despot Manuel Cantacuzenus, the Venetians, and the Hospitallers, "and the Turks fled to Thebes, to Roger de Lluria, who was at that time vicar and governor of the duchy." The imperial historian John Cantacuzenus, IV, 13 (*CSHB*, III, 90, lines 3–7), alludes to the same event and also identifies Roger de Lluria by name (cf. D. M. Nicol, *The Byzantine Family of Kantakouzenos [Cantacuzenus], ca. 1100–1460* [Washington, D.C., 1968], p. 125). In any event we have seen that the papal correspondence makes it perfectly clear that there were Turks in Thebes early in 1364.

131. *Dipl.*, doc. CCLVII, pp. 340–341.

safe to assume that the Catalan feudatories had merely disregarded the royal letters of appointment. But after Roger's destruction of the advance force which Moncada had sent into Greece, the latter seems to have entertained no enthusiasm for taking up his honorific but perilous post. In a recently published letter to Moncada dated August 9, 1365, Frederick informed him that an envoy bringing a petition *(capitula)* from the Company had just described the daily harassment of the duchies by the Venetians. The king's subjects overseas complained that they were left without proper protection because of the absence of the vicar-general, and were being forced into an alliance with the doge and republic of Genoa, "and if this should take effect, which heaven forbid, quite obviously the abdication of the duchies from our sovereignty and dominion would follow. . . ." Frederick could not tolerate the prospect of losing Greece, the provincial ornament in his crown, which his predecessors had won by the clash of arms and the shedding of blood. The Catalan duchies must not perish for want of a defender. Moncada was to proceed to Greece with an adequate force within three months or Frederick would replace him with another vicar-general. [132]

Even if Roger de Lluria's government was illegal and he could not protect the Athenian duchy from Venetian depredation, there was still no way to get rid of him. There was a large work of political reorganization to be done, and since Frederick III was obliged to accept accomplished facts, some of his rebellious subjects were to be rewarded for their self-willed estrangement from the crown. A score of documents testify to the administrative activity of the year 1366. We must pass over various matters, but should note that when on August 3 king Frederick wrote marshal Roger de Lluria (concerning certain Fadrique property claims), he addressed him for the first time as vicar-general. [133] Roger's boldness had been justified by his success, for at Messina on May 14, 1367, a chancery clerk prepared another royal letter of commission that signalized his official appointment to the office he had exercised for some five years in the protection and pursuit of his own interests, and the various officials of all the municipalities of the duchies of Athens and Neopatras were informed by letters patent of his appointment as vicar-general. [134] Grants of land and privilege made to Roger in years past by John II of Randazzo and his son Frederick I, dukes of Athens from 1338 to 1355, by his majesty's late brother Louis, king of Sicily (1342–

---

132. Loenertz, *Arch. FF. Praed.*, XXV, 428–429, document dated at Messina on August 9, 1365.

133. *Dipl.*, doc. CCLXXI, pp. 355–356.

134. *Dipl.*, docs. CCLXXXVI, CCLXXXVII, pp. 370–372.

1355), and by Frederick III himself were now confirmed, [135] and the royal indulgence was formally renewed to the energetic Roger and his partisans for the many crimes of violence of which they had been guilty during the uprising at Thebes in 1362, when Peter de Pou and his wife Angelina were killed, as well as Michael Oller, then dean of the Theban minster, and a number of others, some of whom are named in the document. [136]

Roger de Lluria and his heirs were confirmed in possession of the town of Stiris in Phocis and of a stronghold called Methocya. [137] Stiris had belonged to Ermengol de Novelles, who had been adjudged a "rebel" in 1365 because of his failure to surrender the castle of Siderokastron to the vicar-general Moncada when ordered by Frederick III to do so, whereupon James Fadrique had virtuously seized the castle in the king's name and continued to hold it as his own castellany! [138] Roger had occupied Stiris in even less graceful fashion, for Ermengol had mortgaged the place for 8,000 hyperpers of gold to Bernard Desvilar, whom Roger had "wickedly slain in his own house," during the outbreak of violence at Thebes. When Desvilar's widow Beatrice married Bernard Ballester, Roger required them to surrender their rights to Stiris for a mere 2,000 hyperpers, which of course he never paid. Since he had a tyrant's grasp upon the duchies, he could thus add insult to injury, but years later, in 1381, Ballester was to secure a royal judgment against Lluria properties in the city and district of Athens. [139] By then Roger de Lluria had been dead for more than a decade. Death often came more quickly than justice in the Catalan duchies.

At the beginning of the year 1367 the free inhabitants of the duchies had assembled in their town councils to provide for the future, now that the uncertainties of rebellion and war seemed to be past. A general assembly had met at Thebes and prepared a petition for presentation to king Frederick III in Sicily. The chancellor of the Catalan Company affixed the seal of St. George to the petition, called by Rubió i Lluch the "Articles of Thebes," on January 2, and on May 18 its provisions were read to the king at Messina, and he answered them one by one. He insisted upon retaining the final right of appointment to the important castles of Livadia, Neopatras, and

135. *Dipl.,* doc. CCLXXXVIII, p. 373, dated May 16, 1367.
136. *Dipl.,* doc. CCXC, pp. 377–379, dated May 18, 1367.
137. *Dipl.,* doc. CCXCI, pp. 379–380, dated May 18, 1367.
138. *Dipl.,* docs. CCLVII, CCCXCII, CDXVIII, pp. 340–341, 480, 499, dated in 1365 and 1380.
139. *Dipl.,* doc. DCCXIII, pp. 743–744; Loenertz, *Arch. FF. Praed.,* XXV, nos. 75–76, 195, pp. 120, 149–150, 183, 185–186.

Siderokastron, and he maintained the young Louis Fadrique in possession of Siderokastron, although this was apparently not to the liking of marshal Roger de Lluria. He agreed to a (modified) renewal of the appointment, as we have seen, of Roger as vicar-general; agreed to the desired amnesty for Roger and his partisans; and agreed to the expropriation, more or less, of properties of the late Peter de Pou in favor of the marshal as compensation for the expenses he had undergone and the losses he had suffered. [140] But apparently Francis of Cremona, Roger's representative in Messina, was insistent with regard to Siderokastron, because a month later, on June 11 (1367), the king granted a life appointment to the castellany and captaincy of Siderokastron to Nicholas de Sosa, ordering young Louis Fadrique to desist from his exercise of those offices. [141] Thus did king Frederick III try to restore peace to his Greek dominions.

Following the declaration of the Articles of Thebes in 1367 there were some years of uneasy peace in the Catalan duchies, although, to be sure, in 1370–1371 the nephews of Walter II of Brienne, his sister Isabel's sons—John of Enghien, count of Lecce, Louis, count of Conversano, and Guy, lord of Argos and Nauplia—actually embarked upon a campaign against the Catalans. [142] But they failed to win Venetian support to help wrest the Athenian duchy from that "nefarious Company of Catalans who seized and still retain the aforesaid duchy against God and justice." [143] The Briennist heirs

140. *Dipl.*, doc. CCLXXXIX, pp. 374–377. The castles of Livadia and Neopatras were at the king's good pleasure *in dictarum universitatum custodia,* which meant that the town councils provided and controlled the garrisons, but the king refused to delete the saving phrase *ad beneplacitum regie maiestatis* in his grant of the custody since it would derogate from the royal dignity, and emergencies might at some time require him to appoint castellans whom he could trust to take charge of the castles. For further details concerning the petition, see Loenertz, *Arch FF. Praed.,* XXV, nos. 93, 98, pp. 125, 126.

141. *Dipl.,* doc. CCXCV, pp. 383–384.

142. A Venetian document of March 21, 1396, in Misti, Reg. 43, fol. 119[r], seems to refer to Guy of Enghien's "war" with the Catalan duchy twenty-five years before (*tempore domini Guidonis de Engino et eo habente guerram cum ducatu Athenarum . . .*). On the futile effort of the Enghien brothers to recover the Athenian duchy, see Luttrell, "Latins of Argos and Nauplia," *Papers of the British School at Rome,* XXXIV (1966), 41–42. The Enghiens of course claimed only the duchy of Athens, not that of Neopatras (as Luttrell, *op. cit.,* pp. 41, 46, inadvertently says), which the Catalans had taken from the Greeks in 1319.

143. *Dipl.,* doc. CCCXX, pp. 407–408, dated April 22, 1370, and doc. CCXVII, pp. 403–405, dated February 9, 1371 (misdated February 8, 1370, in *Dipl.* and Loenertz, *Arch. FF. Praed.,* XXV, nos. 111–112, p. 130). The latter document appears in the Archivio di Stato di Venezia, Misti, Reg. 33, fol. 91, where it is dated "MCCCLXX ind. VIIII die nono Februarii," which *more veneto* means 1371. Cf. Loenertz, *Arch. FF. Praed.,* XXVIII, no. 172, p. 65, where the year is corrected to 1371, but the day is still wrong.

were thus forced to accept a truce with the Catalans in August 1371, and a proposed marriage alliance between the Enghiens and the Llurias came to nothing. [144] The Catalans in Athens, in the meantime, who had observed with dismay the inept rule of king Frederick III in Sicily, the persistence of the Enghiens, and the ever-growing menace of the Turks, had "on many and diverse occasions" asked queen Eleanor of Aragon, wife of king Peter IV and sister of Frederick III, "that she might be willing to receive them as vassals," and in June 1370 her majesty informed her royal brother in Sicily that she was prepared to take over the Catalan duchies in Greece and would make therefor considerations totaling some 100,000 florins. [145] These negotiations, too, came to nothing, and the Catalans in Athens and Neopatras had to wait another decade before they found themselves directly under the "sacrosanct crown of Aragon."

When Roger de Lluria died near the end of the year 1369 or, very likely, at the beginning of 1370, king Frederick III appointed Matthew of Peralta vicar-general of the Catalan dominions in Greece (on May 31, 1370). [146] The last letter addressed by the king to Peralta as his vicar in Greece is dated January 18, 1374. [147] The late 1360's and the early 1370's found the royal duke of Athens seeking to strengthen his rule in the duchies by appointing Sicilians to critical posts, sometimes to the great annoyance of the Catalan colony in Thebes, or by appointing Catalans who he believed (or hoped) might prove devoted to the crown. The vicariate of Matthew of Peralta must have been welcomed by the pro-Sicilian group in the duchies. On October 28, 1370, however, the king appointed the late Roger de Lluria's chief ally William of Almenara, a Catalan, to the offices of captain and castellan of the town and castle of Livadia. Indeed, he promised Almenara a lifetime tenure of the offices if he could allay the constant strife between the barons and his other "faithful" subjects. In the meantime Almenara was to exercise authority at his majesty's good pleasure. [148] But on October 4, 1373, in the face of a mounting protest, which emanated especially from the capital city of Thebes, the king tried to remove Almenara on the grounds that continuing "dissensions and discords" were causing havoc in the

144. *Dipl.*, docs. CCCXXXI, CCCXXXII, pp. 418–419.

145. *Dipl.*, docs. CCCXXIII, CCCXXIV, pp. 411–415, especially p. 414.

146. *Dipl.*, docs. CCCXXI, CCCXXII, pp. 408–411. These documents first inform us of the death of Roger de Lluria, who has been "exercising the office" of vicar-general, and apparently disregarding his formal appointment thereto on May 14, 1367, declare the official removal from office of Matthew of Moncada.

147. *Dipl.*, doc. CCCXLII, p. 430.

148. *Dipl.*, docs. CCCXXV–CCCXXVII, pp. 415–417.

duchies, and besides, his baffled majesty wanted (he said) to observe the Articles of the Company which expressly limited tenure of the offices of veguer and captain to a period not exceeding three years. Frederick was gravely troubled, he informed Almenara, by the chaotic conditions in Greece which had brought "multifarious losses and burdens" upon his faithful subjects, and he was anxious to restore his overseas dominions to a "healthy and tranquil state." [149]   It was usually the Catalans in the duchy who insisted upon the three-year tenure of office. Citizens of lower rank resented royal appointments which tended to convert public offices into hereditary fiefs, and if they were unhappy about the intrusion of outsiders from Sicily into their affairs, they were no less opposed to the ambitions of their own more powerful compatriots.

On January 24, 1371, the young Galcerán of Peralta was confirmed in his (earlier) appointment to the castellany of Athens, [150] our first knowledge of an appointee to the command of the garrison on the Acropolis since William de Planis held the position of *castellanus et vicarius Athenarum* in 1321. [151]   On January 7, 1372, Galcerán, who was apparently a relative of the vicar-general Matthew, was confirmed in the office of veguer and captain of Athens for life, with the right to appoint a substitute every three years, "according to the Customs of Barcelona," the intention being, of course, to circumvent the Customs.[152]   Such an obvious subterfuge was bound to prove unsatisfactory, and some twenty months later, on October 4, 1373, Galcerán was officially removed from office, the same day as Almenara was ordered to give up the veguería and captaincy of Livadia, and as a result of the same "dissensions and discords" which had arisen as a result of these prolongations of tenure beyond the statutory limit of three years. [153]   The orders removing Almenara and Peralta authorized the municipal corporations of Livadia and Athens to elect their successors and submit the latters' names for royal confirmation. But nothing was done, and so on January 19–20, 1374, king Frederick III officially replaced Almenara as castellan of

149. *Dipl.,* doc. CCCXXXIX, pp. 427–428.
150. *Dipl.,* docs. CCCXXVIII, CCCXXIX, pp. 417–418.
151. *Dipl.,* doc. CXVI, p. 143. "Guielmus de Planis" looks like the founder of the fortunes of the Ses Planes family, who were still deriving an income from "certain possessions and properties belonging to the castle of Athens and to its guard, defense, and custody" as late as January 7, 1372, when the king annulled their grants extending through three generations; this was done doubtless at the behest of Galcerán de Peralta (*Dipl.,* doc. CCCXXXIV, pp. 421–422). The revenues were to be used thenceforth for the defense of the Acropolis.
152. *Dipl.,* doc. CCCXXXIII, pp. 420–421.
153. *Dipl.,* docs. CCCXXXIX, CCCXLI, pp. 427–430.

Livadia by Francis Lunel (Llunel) of Thebes, and as veguer and captain of Livadia by one Gilbert Vidal, while Peralta was supposed to be succeeded as castellan of the Acropolis by William Pujol, and as veguer and captain of Athens by one Bernard of Vich. Although the vicar-general was duly notified of all these changes in the administration of the Athenian duchy, [154] it is extremely unlikely that any one of the new appointees could enter into the office assigned to him. Peralta in Athens, like Almenara in Livadia, was a petty Pisistratus in a land which has often known tyranny; they were both formidable local figures, and the royal writ no longer ran in Greece.

In the early 1370's Frederick III of Sicily had so completely lost the confidence of the Catalan feudatories in Greece that they had several times expressed the desire to join the Crown of Aragon, and his attempts to reëstablish his rule in Greece by appointing to castellanies, captaincies, and other offices servitors presumably loyal to his interests hardly achieved even a modest success. But his position among the sovereigns of Europe seemed to be raised in 1372 when queen Joanna I of Naples renounced the Angevin claim to the Sicilian kingdom, and pope Gregory XI accepted the Sicilian branch of the house of Barcelona back into the fold of the church. [155] Thus when on November 13, 1372, most of the Christian princes of eastern Europe and the Levant, as well as the doges of Venice and Genoa, were summoned to come in person or send representatives to a congress of alliance against the Turks, scheduled to meet on October 1, 1373, Thebes was chosen as the place of assemblage, because it was "considered to be more convenient than any other place." The congress was being summoned because of the "tearful exposition" of conditions in the Balkans which his holiness had had from archbishop Francis of the Catalan see of Neopatras (1369?–1376), and the many recipients of the summonses (if, indeed, they ever received them) were told that a great multitude of Turks were extending by force of arms their perfidious and infidel sway "to the confines of the kingdom of Serbia and Albania, the principality of Achaea, and the duchy of Athens."[156] The congress apparently never took place, [157] and no union of Latin strength against the Turks was possible at this time. And if it were, the Catalans were in no position

---

154. *Dipl.,* docs. CCCXLIII–CCCXLVI, pp. 431–434.

155. *Vita Gregorii XI,* in G. Mollat, ed., *Vitae paparum Avenionensium,* I (1914), 421, and cf. Francesco de Stefano, "La Soluzione della questione siciliana (1372)," *Archivio storico per la Sicilia orientale,* XXIX (2nd ser., IX, 1933), 48–76.

156. *Dipl.,* docs. CCCXXXVI, CCCXXXVII, pp. 424, 425, and cf. Loenertz, *Arch. FF. Praed.,* XXVIII, no. 176, p. 66.

157. See O. Halecki, *Un Empereur de Byzance à Rome* (Warsaw, 1930), pp. 254–263.

to assist a Christian alliance. Toward the end of the year 1374, after the death of the vicar-general Matthew of Peralta, Nerio Acciajuoli, the Florentine lord of Corinth, seized the Catalan castle of Megara, despite its defense by Francis Lunel, whom Nerio captured and kept in prison. [158] Megara was never regained by the Catalans, and it commanded the isthmian road to Athens and to Thebes.

Even before the death of Matthew of Peralta, probably in the mid-summer of 1374, internecine strife was beginning to tear the Catalan duchies apart. Hostility and tyranny grow easily in the thin soil of Greece. In 1366, upon the death of his father James, Louis Fadrique had inherited the lordship of Zeitounion, and despite his tender years was, as we have seen, retained as castellan and captain of Siderokastron, a crown property, from which however on June 11, 1367, Frederick III had tried to remove him because he was still under age. [159] But minor though he was, Louis apparently had no intention of being removed, and maintained his hold upon Siderokastron, which he still possessed at his death in 1382. [160] Louis was soon engaged in a bitter contest with Galcerán of Peralta, who had obviously not obeyed the royal order to give up the castellany and veguería of Athens. The ancient rivalry of Athens and Thebes was reënacted as Louis received support from the latter city, as well as from Livadia.

For whatever reasons, James Fadrique had already in his lifetime ceded to his brother Boniface "all his rights and properties" in the duchy of Athens, [161] which must have included the important fiefs of Salona, Loidoriki, Veteranitsa, and Aegina, but obviously not the stronghold of Zeitounion and the castellany of Siderokastron. After the death of the ineffective vicar-general Matthew of Peralta (in 1374), Louis Fadrique and his uncle Boniface were the prime feudatories in Catalan Greece. When Megara fell to Nerio Acciajuoli, and

158. *Dipl.*, doc. CCCLIV, p. 440.

159. James Fadrique was dead before August 3, 1366, as shown by *Dipl.*, doc. CCLXXII, pp. 356–357, and a royal order of the following October 5 reveals his son Louis as in possession of Zeitounion, *castrum Citonis* (*ibid.*, doc. CCLXXXII, p. 366). Nicholas de Sosa's letter of appointment as castellan and captain of Siderokastron refers to the removal from office of Louis, who is directed "quod desistat ab officiis castellanie et capitanie . . . terre Siderocastri" (*ibid.*, doc. CCXCV, pp. 383–384, dated at Messina on June 11, 1367), although only three weeks before Frederick had informed the Catalan municipalities in Greece that he was going to leave Siderokastron in Louis's hands (*ibid.*, doc. CCLXXXIX, p. 375, dated May 18, 1367).

160. Cf. *Dipl.*, docs. CCCXCII, CDXVIII, DXXVI–DXXVIII, pp. 480, 499, 579–581.

161. *Dipl.*, doc. CCLXXII, p. 357: " . . . idem nobilis Jaymus dum viveret cesserit eidem Bonifacio omnia bona sua atque jura que habebat et habere possit in futurum in eodem ducatu Athenarum . . . ."

the threat of turmoil was hanging over them, the Catalan municipalities and other districts turned to Louis Fadrique as their governor. On April 6 and 9, 1375, Frederick III confirmed all Louis's
official acts, and formally appointed him vicar-general of the duchies
of Athens and Neopatras. [162] The ambitious Louis had been getting
on badly with his uncle Boniface. He may have challenged the
legality or propriety of the late James's cession to Boniface of the
castles of Salona, Loidoriki, Veteranitsa, and Aegina. Boniface and
his son Peter took up arms against Louis, who finally defeated his
uncle and his cousin, sending the latter out of Greece into exile and
imprisonment in Aragon. [163] Louis's father James had ceded the
castle and island of Aegina to Boniface "in a donation pure and
irrevocable . . . with all rights and appurtenances under certain pacts
and conditions," and Aegina had passed to Peter as a gift from his
father. But Louis repossessed the island, and later on a royal patent
confirmed the legality of his tenure, because Peter had "rebelled"
against him when he held the post of vicar-general. [164]

Galcerán of Peralta was a tougher opponent, however, and Louis
was finally forced to make an agreement with him in "all those pacts,
covenants, articles, affirmations, and usages [which king Peter IV of
Aragon confirmed in September 1380 after he took over the
duchies, and] which were sworn to and affirmed between the magnificent Don Louis of Aragon, the vicar, and the municipalities
[universitats] of Thebes and Livadia on the one hand and, on the
other, the noble Don Galcerán of Peralta, formerly governor [olim
regidor] of Athens, together with the said municipality of

162. *Dipl.,* docs. CCCL, CCCLI, CCCLIII, pp. 436 ff. Louis had already arranged his own
election by some sort of oligarchical acclamation.

163. As the Catalan duchies came under Aragonese sway, king Peter IV wrote Louis
Fadrique, *vicari en los ducats de Attenes e de Neopatria,* on September 30, 1379, "del fet
que'ns havets fet saber de Pere d'Aragó, vos certifficam que encontinent havem fet prendre
aquell, lo qual tendrem tant pres, fins que vos nos haiats fet saber que volrets que s'en fasa"
(*Dipl.,* doc. CCCLXXXII, p. 462; Rubió, *Los Navarros en Grecia* [Barcelona, 1886], app.,
part 2, doc. XVI, pp. 228–229), and so apparently the king intended to allow Louis to
determine his defeated rival's punishment. The fortunes of Boniface are less clear; he was
dead before September 1380 (cf. *Dipl.,* doc. CCCXII, p. 480): ". . . magnifich don Bonifaci
d'Aragon *quondam,* pare de don Pedro d'Aragon . . . ," relating to the latter's loss of Aegina.

164. *Dipl.,* doc. CDXVI, p. 498, dated September 17, 1380: " . . . dictus Petrus de
Aragonia contra vos ut tenentem locum vicarii improvide rebellavit . . . ." Cf., *ibid.,* doc.
CCCXCII, pp. 480–481. Rubió i Lluch, "La Grècia catalana . . . (1377–1379)," *Anuari de
l'Institut d'estudis catalans,* VI (1915–1920), 170–171, believes that Louis captured Peter,
and sent him as a prisoner to Aragon (cf. Setton, *Catalan Domination,* pp. 111 ff.).
Loenertz, *Arch. FF. Praed.,* XXV, nos. 130, 132, 157, pp. 134, 140, believes that Peter fled
to Aragon, where the king had him arrested (*havem fet prendre aquell,* see the preceding
note), which may be the case. For an attempt at a sketch of fourteenth-century Aeginetan
history, see Setton, *Catalan Domination,* pp. 108–110, note.

Athens . . . ."[165] It would appear, then, that young Peter Fadrique was a "rebel" only because Louis defeated him, but Galcerán of Peralta remained a loyal Catalan subject because he successfully opposed Louis, who obviously could not dislodge him from the Acropolis. Galcerán must have had the support of the Catalans in his bailiwick. Although Athens figures in numerous earlier documents, this is the first time, as Loenertz has observed, that the city and its castellan play a leading role in the political history of the Catalan duchies in Greece.

On May 8, 1381, Boniface Fadrique's widow Dulcia and his son John obtained a royal order from Peter IV of Aragon, who was by this time duke of Athens and Neopatras, for the immediate restoration of the properties they had lost as a consequence of Boniface's clash with Louis. [166] On the same day Boniface's name appeared at the head of a list of five persons to whom, posthumously or otherwise, Peter IV granted pardon for whatever offenses "before the said duchies had come under our dominion they have committed against the vicar and other officials by violating the oath and homage by which they were bound." [167] Whether Dulcia and John Fadrique ever recovered any of their castles and towers we cannot say, nor do we know anything about Salona, Loidoriki, and Veteranitsa from the time Boniface possessed them until we find Louis Fadrique identified as the "count of Salona" in 1380–1381, when his name appears first among *los nobles principals* in a list of the high ecclesiastics and chief feudatories of the Catalan duchies in Greece. [168] The harbor town of Veteranitsa (on the Gulf of Corinth) went with Salona, and so doubtless did the landing at Galaxidi. The fortress of Loidoriki also lay within the orbit of the so-called county of Salona, and Louis held it as well as, to the north, the important castle town of Zeitounion, which he had of course inherited from his father. Louis had apparently been doing well enough when about 1368 or so he married a Byzantine princess, Helena Asenina Cantacuzena, one of the three daughters of Matthew Asen Cantacuzenus, eldest son of (and briefly co-emperor with) John VI Cantacuzenus. In 1361 Matthew had gone into the Morea to settle down after a turbulent career in Constantinople, and had taken Helena with him. For some twenty years Matthew assisted his brother Manuel, despot of Mistra (1349–1380),

165. *Dipl.,* doc. CCCXCI, p. 474.
166. Cf. *Dipl.,* doc. CDLXXXIII, p. 544, but note Loenertz, *Arch. FF. Praed.,* XXV, no. 198, pp. 150–151, and p. 178.
167. *Dipl.,* doc. CDLXXXVIII, p. 547. The purpose of the pardon was to forestall the forfeiture of property to the crown for treason.
168. *Dipl.,* doc. CDLXXXIX, p. 548.

whom he succeeded as *locum tenens* until the end of 1382. Louis and Helena had one daughter, destined to a sad fate. [169] Momentous events occurred during the vicariate of Louis Fadrique (1375–1381). Catalan rule was drawing to a violent close in Athens, Thebes, and Neopatras.

King Frederick III of Sicily died in Messina on July 27, 1377; with him the male branch of the Catalan dynasty in Sicily came to an end. He had wished to leave both Sicily and the duchies of Athens and Neopatras to his fifteen-year-old daughter Maria, although the will of king Frederick II of Sicily, who had died forty years before (1337), had expressly excluded the women of his house from the royal succession. [170] King Peter IV of Aragon therefore laid claim to the island kingdom of Sicily and to the Catalan duchies in Greece. Succession struggles followed in Sicily and possibly in Greece. Maria was eventually to marry Don Martin (in November 1391), grandson of king Peter IV and son of king Martin I of Aragon, and the rival dynastic claims would thus be combined and so settled for both the royal title to Sicily and the ducal title to Athens and Neopatras. But in the meantime Peter IV and his son did not relinquish their claims to the Greek duchies. We know very little about the Catalan states in Greece during 1376 and 1377. No document has survived referring to Athens or Neopatras, and only two documents refer to the capital city of Thebes during these years. [171] The young queen Maria of Sicily ruled the duchies after a fashion from 1377 to 1379, and at

---

169. On Matthew Cantacuzenus, see Nicol, *The Byzantine Family of Kantakouzenos,* pp. 108–122; on Helena, *ibid.,* pp. 160–162; and on Louis Fadrique's daughter Maria, *ibid.,* pp. 162–163. In the Archivio di Stato di Venezia, Misti, Reg. 40, fol. 129ᵛ, one may find a resolution of the Venetian senate dated August 26, 1388 (with the wrong date in Thiriet, *Régestes,* I, no. 743, p. 179), "quod scribatur domine Hellene Cantacusini olim consorti egregii domini Don Loysii de Aragono domini Sole . . ." [i.e., of Salona]. The despot Manuel died on April 10, 1380, and was succeeded by John V's fourth son, Theodore Palaeologus, who arrived in the Morea about the end of 1382 (Loenertz, in *Mélanges Eugène Tisserant,* II, 417–420). Matthew himself died in 1383 or 1391, for which the sole evidence seems to be the obscure text of the Short Chronicle of 1391 (Nicol, *op. cit.,* p. 120).

170. For the text and a discussion of the will of Frederick II, dated March 29, 1334, see Giuseppe La Mantia, "Il Testamento di Federico II aragonese, re di Sicilia," *Archivio storico per la Sicilia,* II–III (1936–1937), 13–50. On July 15, 1357, twenty years before his death, and before the birth of his daughter Maria, king Frederick III had guaranteed the succession to the kingdom of Sicily, the duchies of Athens and Neopatras, and certain other rights and possessions to his sister Eleanor and her husband king Peter IV of Aragon in the event he should die "without legitimate offspring, male or female" (*Dipl.,* doc. CCXXXIV, p. 308).

171. *Dipl.,* docs. CCCLXIII, CCCLXIV, pp. 447–449. There is also a resolution of the Venetian senate dated April 18, 1376 (*ibid.,* doc. CCCLXII, pp. 446–447), providing for the return of the two sons of the late vicar-general Matthew of Peralta from Thebes to Sicily in Venetian ships, as noted above, note 118.

least two of her letters relating to Greek matters are extant. [172] But in 1379, despite the presumed opposition of the Sicilian faction in the Athenian duchy, king Peter IV with the loyal support of Louis Fadrique, the vicar-general, and of Galcerán of Peralta, captain and castellan of Athens, finally secured the annexation of the duchies of Athens and Neopatras to the crown of Aragon. [173] Dissension within the Athenian duchy, however, and the Florentine seizure of Megara left the Catalans ill prepared for the heavy blow which now fell upon them, delivered by the so-called Navarrese Company led by an able captain named John de Urtubia.

The Navarrese Company had fought in the war between Charles II the Bad of Navarre and Charles V the Wise of France. When the war ended in 1366, the Navarrese (reformed as a new company) entered or remained in the service of Louis of Évreux, count of Beaumont-le-Roger, the brother of Charles II of Navarre. Louis was preparing to press by force of arms the claim to the "kingdom of Albania" which he had just acquired through his marriage with the Angevin princess Joanna, duchess of Durazzo. She was a granddaughter of John of Gravina, whose campaign in the Morea in 1325–1326 had first given the Acciajuoli a foothold in the Greek peninsula, and whose exchange of the ill-gotten principality of Achaea for the kingdom of Albania and the duchy of Durazzo (in 1332) had thus given the lady Joanna her title to the Angevin lands in ancient Epirus. [174] In 1368 the kingdom of Albania, together with the city of Durazzo, had fallen to the Albanian lord Charles Topia, and Louis of Évreux was faced with no inconsiderable task if he would give effect to his right to rule over the "kingdom" he had thought to possess through his marriage to the heiress Joanna. Louis received much assistance from his royal brother of Navarre and from Charles V of France. In 1372 very active recruiting added to the numbers of the new Navarrese Company, but the chief contingents and the most important leaders were engaged in 1375 and 1376, and they passed, for the most part, directly from Navarre to Albania. Extensive preparations were made

172. *Dipl.*, doc. CCCVII, pp. 393–394, properly dated 1378 or 1379, and Loenertz, *Arch. FF. Praed.*, XXV, nos. 142–143, pp. 137, 202.

173. For details and for references to the relevant works of Rubió i Lluch, see Setton, *Catalan Domination*, pp. 99–117 and ff.; *Dipl.*, docs. CCCLXXII–CCCLXXXIII, pp. 453–464, dated at Barcelona from September 7 to 30, 1379; and cf. Loenertz, *Arch. FF. Praed.*, XXV, nos. 146–159, pp. 138–141, where no. 158 is misdated by a typographical error.

174. Gregorovius (tr. Lampros), *Athens* [in Greek], II, 127–128; W. Miller, *Latins in the Levant* (London, 1908), pp. 257–258, 260–261; Longnon, *L'Empire latin*, pp. 320–323; and on the duchess Joanna of Durazzo, cf. Setton, "Archbishop Pierre d'Ameil in Naples . . . ," *Speculum*, XXVIII, 643–691.

for the expedition, and almost a score of names of military contractors have come down to us in the enrolment lists of 1375–1376. [175] Of the details of Louis's Albanian expedition little is known, but Durazzo was apparently occupied in the midsummer of 1376. Louis died about the same time, and shortly thereafter his widow Joanna married duke Robert of Artois. Most of the Navarrese Company spent about two hard years in impoverished Durazzo (1376–1377). Anxious to return to their homes in Navarre and Gascony, and considering their allegiance to Joanna terminated by her second marriage, the leaders of the Company attempted, early in 1377, to enter the service of king Peter IV of Aragon.

King Peter wrote to the four captains of the Company on June 21, 1377, acknowledging "their wish and obligation to serve him in his wars," and accepting their offer subject to the consent of Charles II of Navarre. The leaders of the Company were Peter de la Saga, Mahiot of Coquerel, both chamberlains of the Navarrese king, and John de Urtubia and a certain Garro (or Guarro), who are designated squires. The king wrote that he would send two ships to convey them back to Spain, but that their horses should come in other transports, of which the Company was said to have a number. [176] Two days later he wrote on their behalf to the king of Navarre. [177] Of the four leaders of the Company (or rather companies) named in Peter IV's letter, all of whom appear in the enrolment lists of 1375–1376, only two were to play an important part in the history of medieval Greece, John de Urtubia as conqueror of Boeotia and Mahiot of Coquerel as bailie of James of Les Baux, titular prince of Achaea and last claimant to the Latin throne of Constantinople. Peter de la Saga and Garro seem to make no further appearance in the documents.

When the plans to serve the king of Aragon came to nothing, Urtubia and Coquerel turned for employment to the Hospitallers, who were now reorganizing their forces in the Morea, where they had leased the Achaean principality for five years from queen Joanna I of Naples, the agreement apparently being made about August 1376. [178] The affairs of the Hospital were in disorder after the grand

175. Published by Rubió i Lluch, *Los Navarros en Grecia, y el ducado catalán de Atenas en la época de su invasión* (Barcelona, 1886), part I, doc. VII, pp. 211–215, and cf. docs. I–III, V–VI. (These documents were unfortunately not reprinted in Rubió's *Diplomatari.*)

176. *Dipl.*, doc. CCCLXV, p. 449: "Als amats nostres mossen P. dela Saya e Mahiot de Cocorell, camarlenchs de nostre car frare lo rey de Navarra, e Johan d'Ortruvia e Garro, escuders." Actually there were four companies *(societates),* each under one of the military contractors named in the royal letter.

177. *Dipl.*, doc. CCCLXVI, p. 450, dated June 23, 1377. This letter expressly states that the Navarrese Company was then in Durazzo.

178. Loenertz, "Hospitaliers et Navarrais en Grèce," *Orientalia Christiana periodica,* XXII

master Juan Fernández de Heredia's unsuccessful campaign against the Albanian prince Ghin Boua Spata of Arta—Heredia was captured in the early summer of 1378, and thereafter held for a large ransom for some ten months by Boua Spata. It was apparently in the early summer of 1378 that Gaucher of La Bastide, prior of the Hospital in Toulouse and Heredia's lieutenant in the Morea, enrolled John de Urtubia's company of one hundred men-at-arms. He agreed to pay 9,000 ducats for eight months' service, 1,000 ducats for maintenance of Urtubia's high estate, and another 1,000 ducats for division among the "corporals" of Urtubia's company. Financial accounts of the Hospital show that one Peter Bordo de Saint Superan, whom the wheel of fortune was one day to make prince of Achaea, belonged to Urtubia's company. Gaucher of La Bastide also enrolled Mahiot of Coquerel with his company of fifty men for eight months, "and the said prior promised to pay him one half the price promised to Janco de Urtubia, namely 5,500 ducats for the stated period." In fact, Coquerel was finally paid more than the sum specified, because he began his service before the date called for by the contract.[179] When the eight months came to an end, early in 1379, Urtubia and his troops moved on to make history in Thebes, while Coquerel and his men remained in the Morea.

King Peter IV had disapproved of the Hospitallers' plans to enlarge their establishment in the Morea, and when Heredia, after his elevation as grand master in September 1377, had summoned commanders and knights of the order to join him in his projected "passage to Romania," the king forbade the Hospitallers in his domains, under penalty of losing their revenues, to go to Heredia.[180] Perhaps the king feared the too close proximity of the armed might of St. John to the Athenian duchy over which he had just declared

---

(1956), reg. no. 1, pp. 329–330, and cf. doc. I, art. 9, p. 351, and D. Jacoby, "Jean Lascaris Calophéros, Chypre et la Morée," *Revue des études byzantines,* XXVI (1968), 203, note 92. Joanna had succeeded Philip II of Taranto in the Achaean succession in 1373.

179. Royal Malta Library, Valletta, Archives of the Order of St. John, Cod. 321 (Lib. Bullarum, VI, for 1381–1382), fol. 204, financial accounts of the Hospital, dated at Rhodes on August 24, 1381, published by Loenertz, "Hospitaliers et Navarrais en Grèce," *Orientalia Christiana periodica,* XXII, 350–355, arts. 13 ff., 26–27, 28 ff. The accounts show the close connection between Urtubia and Nerio Acciajuoli. Cf. in general Setton, *Catalan Domination,* pp. 122–130, and on the affairs of the Hospitallers (complicated by the Great Schism), Luttrell, "Intrigue, Schism, and Violence among the Hospitallers of Rhodes, 1377–1384," *Speculum,* XLI (1966), especially pp. 33 ff. Heredia was invested with the office of grand master of the Hospitallers by pope Gregory XI on September 24, 1377, for which see Luttrell, "Interessi fiorentini nell' economia e nella politica dei Cavalieri Ospedalieri di Rodi nel Trecento," in the *Annali della Scuola normale superiore di Pisa: Lettere, storia e filosofia,* 2nd ser., XXVIII (1959), 323 and note 6.

180. *Dipl.,* docs. CCCLXVII, CCCLXVIII, pp. 450–451, dated May 10, 1378.

his rule, but his attitude was not likely to please the commanders of the Hospital in the Morea. Although Peter IV remained on friendly terms, apparently, with Heredia,[181] the Hospitallers' attitude toward the Catalans in Thebes and Athens was one of hostility, and Heredia's lieutenant in the Morea, Gaucher of La Bastide, clearly abetted the attack of the Navarrese Company under John de Urtubia upon the city of Thebes.

In the early spring of 1379 Urtubia and the so-called Navarrese or White Company, which must have included at least as many Gascons and Italians as Navarrese, set out from the Morea, conceivably from the headquarters of the Hospitallers in Navarino (St. Mary of Zonklon) or Kalamata. They made their way through the Corinthian barony of Urtubia's good friend Nerio Acciajuoli, who also held the Megarid, and launched their attack upon the city of Thebes. They proceeded obviously with the permission and presumably with the encouragement of Nerio. They came most inopportunely for Louis Fadrique, since the two years of uncertainty which had followed the death of king Frederick III had not prepared the Catalans in the Athenian duchy to withstand a powerful assault. In 1379 the Catalans no longer possessed the strength which had been theirs when they had repulsed Walter II of Brienne in 1331. Also the destruction of the castle of St. Omer on the Cadmea by the Catalans on the occasion of Brienne's expedition, for fear that he might occupy the castle and hold it against them, had made Thebes, although the capital of the southern duchy, much less easy to defend than the Acropolis, known to the Catalans as the "Castell de Cetines." Urtubia and the Navarrese Company took Thebes in a violent encounter, with ample assistance from traitors within the city, one of whom, John Conominas, "revealed himself as quite adept in securing the loss of Thebes, dealing with Messer Nerio [Acciajuoli]."[182] Whether Urtubia acted as Nerio's ally or employee remains uncertain. Barcelonese documents show clearly that the fall of Thebes was known at the royal court in Aragon by September 13, 1379.[183] Allowing three or possibly four months for the bearers of the sad tidings to make the voyage to Barcelona from the Athenian duchy,

181. Cf. *Dipl.*, doc. CCCLXXI, p. 453, dated August 2, 1379.

182. *Dipl.*, doc. CCCXCI, p. 476, lines 12–13: " . . . lo qual dit Johan se trobà esser bo en la perdua de Estives tractant ensemps ab miçer Aner . . . ." A decade later, a Barcelonese document of January 3, 1390, refers to the siege of Neopatras by Nerio Acciajuoli, ". . . la ciutat nostra de la Patria asseiat per micer Arner, enemich nostre capital . . ." (*Dipl.*, doc. DCXXVII, p. 657). For the identification of Aner or Arner, see Loenertz, *Arch. FF. Praed.*, XXV, no. 209, pp. 153, 193–194.

183. *Dipl.*, docs. CCCLXXVIII, CCCLXXX, pp. 459–461.

we may assume that Urtubia took Thebes in May or June 1379. [184] Despite treachery within the walls of Athens on the part of those who wished to see that historic city also succumb to Urtubia, the Acropolis was to remain in Catalan hands for another decade.

After the fall of Thebes to Urtubia, when the Catalan vicar-general, Louis Fadrique, was unwilling to conclude an unfavorable peace with the Navarrese, probably on a basis of the status quo, the Hospitallers sought to bring pressure upon him. On September 23, 1380, Peter IV wrote to Gaucher of La Bastide and the high command of the Hospital in the Morea: "Both by letters sent to us by the eminent Louis Fadrique of Aragon . . . and by the account of his envoy we have learned that you have often requested the same Louis and caused that he be requested to make peace with John de Urtubia and his followers, with the threat that unless he complied, you would proceed to make war upon him, his people and lands, at which we are no little astonished. For you know that the said John de Urtubia . . . with his followers, some time ago, suddenly seized and now holds the city of Thebes and has further plundered and destroyed other places and people belonging to us in the duchies. . . . Since it becomes our majesty to watch over and to defend our peoples, kingdoms, duchies and lands with courage, we require and ask of your Order that upon receipt of the present letter you desist from these threats . . . ." [185] The king threatened the confiscation of the Hospitallers' lands and revenues in his domains if they did not cease thus aiding and encouraging the Navarrese. Two weeks before this,

184. Rubió i Lluch, "Conquista de Tebas por Juan de Urtubia: Episodio de la historia de los Navarros en Grecia," *Homenaje a D. Carmelo de Echegaray: Miscelánea de estudios referentes al País Vasco* (San Sebastian, 1928), p. 389. However urgent Louis Fadrique, Peralta, Bellarbre (see below), Almenara, and other barons, and the officers of the Catalan municipalities may have felt it to inform Peter IV of Urtubia's invasion, their messengers, Bernard Ballester and Francis Ferrer, obviously had to find suitable transport to Barcelona, which may have involved difficulty in view of the turmoil into which the Navarrese had thrown the Athenian duchy.

A "short chronicle" in Codex Paris. gr. 445, fol. 126^v, published by G. T. Dennis, "The Capture of Thebes by the Navarrese," *Orientalia Christiana periodica*, XXVI (1960), 45–47, places the Navarrese seizure of Thebes "at the ninth hour of the night" on Friday, March 6, 1378. But, in 1378, March 6 fell on a Saturday (and in 1379 on a Sunday), which reveals at least one defect in the text. Cf. K. M. Setton, "The Latins in Greece and the Aegean . . . ," *Cambridge Medieval History*, IV-1 (1966), 420, note. Also, in the two documents which Loenertz (*Arch. FF. Praed.*, XXV, nos. 142–143, pp. 137, 202) has identified as belonging to the ducal rule in Greece of Maria of Sicily—dated May 30, 1378 (or 1379), and June 7, 1378 (or 1379)—there is clearly no knowledge in Catania of Urtubia's occupation of Thebes as late as June 1378 (or 1379). Taking the earlier date for the latter document (June 7, 1378), however, if Urtubia had captured Thebes on March 6 of that year, the news would have reached Catania in less than three months.

185. *Dipl.*, doc. CDXXV, p. 503.

on September 10, the king had sent two letters of similar tenor to Heredia and other commanders and officials of the Hospital. [186] There is no reason to believe that Heredia himself encouraged Urtubia in the attack upon Thebes, but it is possible that he knew it was in the offing, and he clearly did nothing to prevent it. Little is known of the career of John de Urtubia.

Of Nerio's well-known hostility to the Catalans we shall have further opportunity to speak. But Urtubia found other allies, whether by prearrangement or not, in Nicholas II dalle Carceri, lord of two "thirds" of Euboea and duke of the Archipelago, and in Francis I Giorgio, marquis of Bodonitsa. At the end of April 1381, when king Peter IV informed the Venetian bailie of Negroponte of the (second) appointment of Philip Dalmau, viscount of Rocaberti, as vicar-general of his Greek duchies, he requested Venetian aid to restrain the duke of the Archipelago, the marquis of Bodonitsa, and others from rendering assistance "to our enemies the Navarrese." [187] The Venetians, however, were fighting the Genoese in the War of Chioggia, and the attention of the statesmen of the republic was directed to their affairs in northern Italy rather than in central Greece.

The first known act of Peter IV as duke of Athens and Neopatras is dated September 7, 1379, and in it his majesty notified Romeo de Bellarbre, "castellan and captain of the castle and city of Athens," of the appointment of Philip Dalmau, viscount of Rocaberti (1342–1392), as vicar-general of the duchies of Athens and Neopatras. He directed Bellarbre to give up the Acropolis *(lo castell)* and the city to "mossén Dalmau," his friend and councillor. On the same day a similar letter was written to William of Almenara, who was still castellan and captain of Livadia. [188] Galcerán of Peralta, castellan, captain, and veguer of Athens, had fallen into Urtubia's hands while attempting either to defend or to recover Thebes. Obviously Peter already knew this, for on September 8 he wrote to Peralta as *castellá, capitá e veguer del castell e ciutat de Cetines,* addressing the letter either to him *o a son lochtinent.* Bellarbre had been holding the

186. *Dipl.,* docs. CCCXCVIII, CD, pp. 487–489: " . . . intelleximus quod Johannes d'Ortobia nacionis Navarre, qui pridem cum suis complicibus . . , civitatem de Estives invasit et gentes in ea habitantes destruxit et improvide disraubavit . . ." (p. 489).

187. *Dipl.,* doc. CDLVII, pp. 525–526, dated April 31 (*sic*), 1381. According to Stefano Magno (d. 1572), in the so-called *Annali veneti,* ed. Hopf, *Chroniques gréco-romanes,* p. 183, "In questo anno [1383] si fo morto Nicolò dale Carcere, ducha del Arcipielago et dominador de do terzi de lisola de Negroponte, havendo fato molte cose cative et desoneste contra suoi subditi. . . . [Nicolò] avea tratado cum una compagnia de Navarexi . . . per signorizar la citade de Negroponte."

188. *Dipl.,* doc. CCCLXXII, pp. 453–454.

"lieutenancy" for some time, as Peter was aware when a chancery clerk prepared the letter of the preceding day. As a legal gesture, however, Peter asked Peralta to give up the *castell e ciutat* to the newly appointed Dalmau, and stated further that "we have received a letter which you have sent us dealing with the affairs and the state of the duchies of Athens and Neopatras, asking us for aid and succor and that we should send you our vicar or lieutenant . . . , to which [letter] we reply with the full expression of our thanks for the affection and good will which you have for us and for our crown as a loyal vassal and our natural servitor."[189]

On September 30 the king wrote Peralta again; this time he referred to a letter he had received from Louis Fadrique. Indeed, he was by now very well informed of events in the duchies, for he had talked at length with Bernard Ballester and Francis Ferrer, who had come to Barcelona as messengers and envoys of the Catalan barons and municipalities in Greece. He was sending Ballester back to Greece as his royal ambassador, and his subjects overseas were to take care that Ballester should return to Barcelona promptly with some other suitable person "with full and sufficient authority to swear fealty and render homage and to have us for your natural lord." When this feudal formality was over and done with, Peter said that he would without fail send to Greece a "vicar with such force that you will be satisfied, and in the meantime you have the said noble Don Louis [Fadrique] of Aragon as vicar of the said duchies . . . ." He closed with a statement of the extreme displeasure which Peralta's capture and continued imprisonment had caused him.[190]

It is small wonder that Galcerán of Peralta and Louis Fadrique had written the king of Aragon-Catalonia, urging him to give force to his ducal claims and send help to his new dominions. Even Louis's father-in-law, Matthew Cantacuzenus, wrote him from the Morea (presumably at Louis's behest), offering him some sort of assistance against the Navarrese invasion.[191]   Letters also reached Barcelona

---

189. *Dipl.,* doc. CCCLXXIII, p. 454. Louis Fadrique had also written the king and received a similar reply (*ibid.*).

190. *Dipl.,* doc. CCCLXXXIII, pp. 463–464; Rubió i Lluch, *Los Navarros,* doc. XVII, pp. 229–230. A similar letter of the same date (September 30, 1379) was addressed to Peralta's erstwhile opponent, Louis Fadrique (*Dipl.,* doc. CCCLXXXII, pp. 462–463), and a letter of a year later, September 10, 1380, records that "Johannes de Ortubia . . . tenet captum nobilem virum Galcerandum de Peralta qui . . . velut fidelis servitor noster eandem civitatem [Thebas] defendit . . ." (*Dipl.,* doc. CD, p. 489). The last text is addressed to the grand master Heredia, states that Urtubia was demanding large sums for Peralta's release, and directly accuses the Hospital of being implicated in the seizure of Thebes.

191. *Dipl.,* doc. CCCLXXIX, p. 460, in which Peter IV answered Matthew on September 13, 1379.

from Romeo de Bellarbre in Athens, William of Almenara and the municipality of Livadia, and the dispossessed authorities of Thebes, who had taken refuge in Salona and Livadia. [192] On September 13 (1379) the king officially appointed Dalmau "our vicar, viceroy, and lieutenant in the said duchies and all the lands adjacent to them," defining in ample detail the manifold duties of his new office. [193] Until emissaries from the duchies had sworn fealty to the king, however, and until the new vicar-general could reach Greece, Louis Fadrique was to continue to hold the vicariate. Bernard Ballester and Francis Ferrer had given a good account of Louis's government.[194]

It is not clear how vigorously, if at all, king Peter IV had been prepared to press his claims to Athens and Neopatras until the Navarrese invasion threw the Catalan inhabitants of the duchies into his arms. Their view was that Peter might conceivably assist them, while Maria of Sicily obviously could not, and he certainly kept the clerks in the Aragonese chancery busy issuing scores of documents relating to Greek affairs. Many of the inhabitants of Thebes, both Frankish and Greek, had taken refuge on the Venetian island of Euboea, and on October 19, 1379, the king expressed his gratitude to the Venetian officials for this kind reception given to his distraught vassals and subjects. He asked the Venetian colonial government to continue to show them its favor and to allow them freely to return to Thebes with their wives, children, and goods when the Catalans should have regained the city. Bernard Ballester was conveying the royal letter to Negroponte, and would explain further his majesty's intentions concerning his newly acquired Greek dominions. [195]

Toward the end of the year 1380 or early in 1381 the castle of Livadia also fell to the Navarrese, who as previously at Thebes received aid from traitors within the walls. Some of the inhabitants fled to Negroponte, [196] others to Salona, whose "count," Louis

192. *Dipl.*, doc. CCCLXXXIII, p. 464, and cf. docs. CCCLXXVI, CCCLXXXII.

193. *Dipl.*, doc. CCCLXXIV, pp. 455–456, and cf. docs. CCCLXXV–CCCLXXX.

194. *Dipl.*, doc. CCCLXXXII, pp. 462–463, dated September 30, 1379; Rubió i Lluch, *Los Navarros,* doc. XVI, pp. 228–229. But in the instructions given to Ballester, who was returning to Greece as the royal ambassador, the barons and officials of the municipalities were to be asked to send the king the names of "three or four barons of his kingdom," from whom he would choose a vicar! (*Dipl.,* doc. CCCLXXXIII, p. 464, presumably dated September 30, 1379).

195. *Dipl.,* doc. CCCLXXXIV, p. 465, and note doc. CCCLXXVIII, p. 459, dated September 13, 1379, to the doge of Venice on behalf of the refugees from Thebes. The doge is said "already to know" *(iam scitis)* that Peter IV has succeeded "by just title" to the Greek duchies. Cf., *ibid.,* doc. CCCLXXX, pp. 460–461, also dated September 13, to the bailie and captain of Negroponte.

196. *Dipl.,* doc. CDLIX, p. 527, dated April 31 [*sic*], 1381.

Fadrique, was still serving as vicar-general, although Peter IV was again writing almost everyone in sight that he had appointed Dalmau to the vicariate. William of Almenara, castellan and captain of Livadia, had been treacherously slain within the citadel, and on May 8, 1381, Peter IV granted his widow Francula custody of their three children and title to his estate as long as she remained unmarried (otherwise her mother Escarlata was to take over both the children and the property) although her rights were protected as heiress to her father's apparently extensive estate. [197] On the same day Peter granted his faithful subjects who had fled from the city perpetual enjoyment of all their rights, privileges, franchises, and properties under the "Usatges de Barcelona" because of the loyalty they had shown his royal house, "and expressly so when recently *[nuper]* our enemies, the Navarrese, invaded the . . . duchies, and attacked and occupied in outrageous fashion the lands and the castle of Livadia." [198] The loyalty of the Greek notary Constantine "de Mauro Nichola" and his father Nicholas de Mauro now won them and their posterity the full franchise in the duchies *(tanquam Catholici et Franchi),* notwithstanding the fact they were Greeks and followed the Greek schismatic rite. [199] At the same time James Ferrer de la Sala, a native of Barcelona, who had proved his devotion to the royal house for more than twenty years in the Greek duchies, and had lost all his property and almost his very life in the Navarrese seizure of Livadia, now received by royal decree all the serfs, houses, lands, and vineyards of the "traitorous Greek" notary Gasco of Durazzo, who had joined the Navarrese in the grim hour of Catalan need.[200]

It was all well enough for the king in distant Aragon to make these rhetorical grants to his faithful servitors in Greece, but nothing came of them. A dozen years later, in 1393, we are informed that the Gascon Bertranet Mota (or de Salahia), who is referred to as *capitá del ducham de Athenes,* was in possession of the city of Livadia, which he had but recently taken. [201] Bertranet possessed the head of St. George, which in 1393 king John I of Aragon, like his father

197. *Dipl.,* doc. CDLXXVII, p. 538. Francula's father was the well-known Catalan baron Peter de Puigpardines.

198. *Dipl.,* doc. CDLXXVIII, p. 539, dated May 8, 1381.

199. *Dipl.,* doc. CDLXXIX, pp. 540–541, dated May 8, 1381.

200. *Dipl.,* doc. CDLXXX, pp. 541–542, also dated May 8, 1381. For *Rotari* in this text, read *notari* (Loenertz, *Orientalia Christiana periodica,* XXII, no. 32, p. 339).

201. *Dipl.,* doc. DCXXXVIII, p. 667, dated April 13, 1393. In a document dated July 28, 1400, Bertranet is referred to as "aquest Gascó qui era senyor dela Levadia . . ." (*Dipl.,* doc. DCLVI, p. 683). See Rubió i Lluch, *Dipl.,* pp. 666–667, note.

Peter IV some forty years before, was most anxious to acquire. St. George was patron of England, however, as well as of Catalonia, and Bertranet for a time apparently contemplated the sale of the relic to king Richard II of England. [202] Bertranet clearly did not regard himself as holding Livadia by warrant of the king of Aragon, nor is there any evidence that the Catalans ever regained Thebes. In any event Thebes and Livadia became Florentine possessions, and Nerio Acciajuoli left them to his son Antonio I in 1394. Since Nerio also made a bequest to Bertranet ("Baltrineto di Salai"), the connection between the latter and the Acciajuoli is obvious. Bertranet may well have been in Nerio's employ. [203] By the beginning of the year 1394, however, the Turks were overrunning central Greece. They occupied Livadia. Obviously the invasion of the Navarrese Company under John de Urtubia had meant for the Catalans the permanent loss of ancient Boeotia and of Locris, and when in 1379 Peter IV of Aragon began the last decade of Catalan rule in continental Greece, he possessed little more than the capitals of the two duchies, now the city of Athens itself and Neopatras, together with some of their dependencies, and the so-called county of Salona.

202. *Dipl.,* doc. DCXXXVIII, p. 667. Before December 1399 the head of St. George would pass into the possession of Alioto de Caupena, Catalan lord of Aegina, who seems to have received it from Bertranet (*Dipl.,* docs. DCLIII–DCLV, DCLXIX, DCXCVIII).

203. For Nerio's will, see J. A. C. Buchon, *Nouvelles recherches historiques,* II (Paris, 1845), 257, 260, and Lampros, *Eggrapha,* part III, doc. 4, pp. 149, 152, and cf. Setton, *Catalan Domination,* pp. 147, 197.

VII

THE CATALANS AND
FLORENTINES IN GREECE
1380–1462

During the last decade of Catalan rule in the Athenian duchy (1379–1388) the Aragonese chancery issued almost 250 documents relating to Greek affairs. The number attests the royal concern with such affairs, as well as the fortunate survival of the Archives of the Crown in Barcelona. As the shock of the Navarrese invasion subsided, a parliament was assembled in Athens to which were summoned the syndics, aldermen, and council of the municipal corporation. This parliament prepared a petition, dated May 20, 1380, for submission to king Peter IV, who by accepting or rejecting its terms would determine the conditions under which the chief officers and citizens of Athens would become the vassals of the crown of Aragon. Rubió i Lluch has called this important document the "Articles of Athens" (*els Capítols d'Atenes*); of the sixteen or seventeen items which it contains, only four or five relate to the common concerns of the state and the community. The remaining dozen items consist of personal requests which seem to show small understanding of the perilous condition to which the duchy of Athens had been reduced; the parliament at Athens was anxious to secure rewards from the crown for those who had proved their loyalty by resisting the Navarrese invasion.

The parliament was under the dominance of Romeo de Bellarbre, castellan and captain of Athens, and Galcerán of Peralta had become merely "our former governor" as he languished in his Theban prison. The petitioners' first request of Peter IV was that he send them a proper "official" to govern the duchies, one who could reconquer

For bibliography see preceding chapter.

225

the lands which the Navarrese had seized. Peter was to answer, when he ratified or rejected the various articles of the petition at Lerida on the following September 1, that he was sending Philip Dalmau, viscount of Rocaberti, as his vicar-general to Greece, and that Dalmau would be accompanied by forces strong enough to restore the territorial integrity of the duchies and reëstablish a peaceful life within them. When preparing their petition in May, however, the Catalans had informed the king that if he could not immediately send them the strong governor they needed, they would be pleased to have "as our official and governor of Athens the most honored Don Romeo de Bellarbre, who knows the desperate conditions in the said city and the poverty and anxiety of its people." Indeed, they had hoped it would please his majesty to give Bellarbre a lifetime appointment to the post. Peter replied that he had conferred upon Dalmau all the offices in the two duchies, both castellanies and captaincies, but he did bestow upon Bellarbre a lifetime command of the Acropolis as well as certain estates confiscated from those who had been guilty of treachery during the Navarrese invasion. Bellarbre's Greek mistress, Zoe of Megara, by whom he had had children, was granted the Catalan franchise with the customary rights of acquiring and disposing of property.[1]

The petitioners sought king Peter's approval of the agreements which we have seen made (about 1376–1377) "between the magnificent Don Louis of Aragon, the vicar [general], and the municipalities of Thebes and Livadia on the one hand and, on the other, the noble Don Galcerán of Peralta, formerly the governor of Athens, together with the said city of Athens . . . ," agreements which had established the virtual independence of Athens. But Peter realized that if the magnates had not been quarreling among themselves in the period just before the Navarrese attacks, they might have successfully defended Thebes, and so he refused the request. All divisions and dissensions of times past must cease, he said, and Dalmau must rule as vicar-general over the united duchies.

The Articles of Athens also affirmed the long dedication of the Greek notary Demetrius Rendi to the *sacra corona d'Aragó*, request-

---

1. The text of the Articles of Athens may be found in Rubió i Lluch, *Los Navarros en Grecia* (Barcelona, 1886), doc. XXXII, pp. 241–251, and in the *Diplomatari,* doc. CCCXCI, pp. 473–479. At Lerida on September 1, 1380, king Peter IV also confirmed the requests contained in the "Articles of Salona," which had been prepared on May 31, 1380, on behalf of Louis Fadrique, lord of Salona and count of Malta. The Articles of Salona are still extant (Rubió, *Los Navarros,* doc. XXXIX, pp. 256–259, and *Dipl.,* doc. CCCXCII, pp. 480–482). Cf. in general Setton, *Catalan Domination,* pp. 158–164, and Loenertz, *Arch. FF. Praed.,* XXV, nos. 167–172, 175–177, pp. 143–145, 171–172.

ing the same rights and privileges for him "as for all the other Conquistadors of the said duchies of Athens and Neopatras." The Articles as extant contain the Catalan text of king Peter's renewal of the full franchise which Frederick III had granted Rendi years before (on July 29, 1362) when Rendi, his sons, daughters, and descendants received the right to retain their Orthodox faith and at the same time to contract marriage with Latin Catholics, notwithstanding statutes which the Company had enunciated to the contrary. With the franchise went the usual right to buy, sell, alienate, and exchange at will both movable and immovable goods "just like the Frankish inhabitants of the aforesaid city [of Athens]."[2] The king now directed his officials everywhere in the duchies to "consider the true fealty and the sincere loyalty of the notary Demetrius Rendi, citizen of our city of Athens, who has persevered in service, good faith, and loyalty toward our royal majesty, and with all his power and strength has maintained and defended the said territory of the duchies . . . against our mortal enemies, and yet, as our majesty has been informed, . . . the said notary Demetrius Rendi has sustained affliction and anxiety in the castle of Megara when it was taken by our enemies." Demetrius's young brother-in-law and adopted son John Rendi shared with him all the benefits of enfranchisement, and Peter confirmed Demetrius's title to the property which the deceased Constantine Calochini had possessed in Athens, and which had reverted to the fisc upon his death. Frederick III had conferred this property on Demetrius between 1375 and 1377 after Rendi's valiant but vain defense of Megara against Nerio Acciajuoli. Finally, the king bestowed upon Demetrius and his heirs, "for all time and in perpetuity," the office of chancellor of Athens, with an annual income of forty gold *diners* payable from the city's tolls and customs duties. Just outside Athens, off a road that runs to Piraeus, the little village of Rendi still stands, preserving the name and memory of the energetic notary Demetrius. As one turns the corner into the village, a superb view of the Acropolis and the Parthenon makes it clear that what was once the Rendi family estate, conceivably Constantine Calochini's own property, is close to the center of historic Athens.

The Articles of Athens are in a rather haphazard order, and show signs of haste in compilation. After the king had made some further grants of property he was finally asked "to turn his eyes toward the noble Don Galcerán of Peralta," whom the Navarrese in Thebes were

---

2. The grant of July 29, 1362, of the franchise to Demetrius Rendi, or rather the confirmation of his Catalan citizenship, may be found in Lampros, *Eggrapha* (1906), part IV, doc. 94, pp. 342–343, and in *Dipl.,* doc. CCLXIX, pp. 353–354, misdated 1366.

holding for a higher ransom than the Catalans in Athens could pay. Peter was sadly aware of Peralta's captivity, the petitioners were told, and he had instructed Dalmau to see to his release. Also the refugees from Thebes and other places in the duchy, who had found a temporary haven in Athens, had their rights and titles to property confirmed, for they hoped to return to Thebes and resume possession of their homes when Dalmau expelled the Navarrese.

As usual in a medieval *magna carta,* the voice of the church was heard. The petitioners asked for the revocation of the statute or statutes which the Conquistadors had passed decades before "against the soul's true conscience and against the church of the Catholic faith," and which forbade the faithful to leave to the church "estates, lands, vineyards, as well as other things" or even to free serfs from their harsh bondage to the soil. It had hitherto been the Catalan practice to use property bestowed upon the church, in violation of the statutes of the Company, to maintain or extend the Acropolis fortifications, to which Peralta had given much attention. In rejecting this request, the king reminded the Catalans in Athens that their numbers were sparse, and that if they began leaving their possessions to the church, they would soon lack the men and resources necessary to defend the duchies, "for ecclesiastics are not soldiers, and they are not under the jurisdiction of the lord king." Peter said that when Dalmau arrived in Greece, he would make whatever provisions for the church were in keeping with the public interest.

The Catalans concluded their petition with a solemn request for the royal pledge to preserve in Athens "the statutes, constitutions, usages, and customs of Barcelona," and never to alienate the ducal dominions in Greece from the sacred Crown of Aragon. To these requests Peter readily gave his assent (*plau al senyor rey*). The Articles of Athens, formulated perhaps on the Acropolis on May 20, 1380, were thus confirmed or modified at Lerida on the following September 1, and Peter took an oath upon the four gospels always to observe them "in royal good faith." Thereupon bishop John Boyl of Megara and Gerard (Guerau) de Rodonella, envoys of the Catalans in Athens, solemnly swore the feudal allegiance of their principals to the king of Aragon and his successors.[3] Ten days later, on September 11, Peter wrote to Bellarbre as castellan of Athens and to the syndics, aldermen, and council of the city that bishop John Boyl and

---

3. *Dipl.,* doc. CCCXCI, pp. 473–479, and for the order in which the petitions appear in the Articles of Athens, cf. Loenertz, *Arch. FF. Praed.,* XXV, no. 167, p. 143. John Boyl and Rodonella had arrived in Lerida on August 1, 1380 (*Dipl.,* doc. CCCXC, p. 472). Five weeks after dealing with the Athenian petitions, Peter IV repeated his prohibition against selling,

Rodonella had taken the oath of fealty and done homage, formally making the Catalans in the duchies his vassals and liegemen. He exhorted them to defend the duchies, and promised that within a brief time he would send Dalmau with forces large enough to guarantee their security and chastise their enemies.[4]

The loss of Thebes rankled in the king's mind. He seems to have thought that Urtubia and the Navarrese were still somehow under the control of the Hospital, and he cautioned the grand master and his commanders against any further attacks upon his Greek dominions. Indeed, he told them that they had better set about undoing the damage they had done, and that they could start by securing the release of Galcerán of Peralta, who had been captured in a vain attempt to defend Thebes.[5] Peter had doubtless derived his knowledge of conditions in Greece from John Boyl and Rodonella, who had told him what they knew (or wanted him to know) about the loss of Thebes. They also told him who had kept faith with the Catalan cause and who had failed it. John Boyl obviously made a very favorable impression upon the king, who wrote on his behalf to Dalmau, the new vicar-general: ". . . We wish that our honored father in Christ Fra John Boyl, bishop of Megara, should receive the archbishopric of Thebes, and in fact we have written to the holy father [Urban VI] that he should remove the present incumbent [Simon Atumano] and give the archbishopric to the said bishop. In the meantime we also want the said bishop to have the movable and immovable goods which belonged to Don Oliverio Domingo, by whose work the city of Thebes was lost, and it was through no fault of his that the city and castle of Athens did not rebel . . . ." John Boyl should continue to receive, Peter said, the annual income of twenty-four gold ducats accruing from the chapel of St. Bartholomew in the palace of the castle of Athens, *la capella de sant Berthomeu del palau del castell de Cetines,* as well as the additional allotment which he had been receiving for himself and his two servitors.[6] In exchanging Megara for Thebes, John Boyl would merely be giving up one titular see for another, and until the Catalans

---

giving, or bequeathing property or rents to the church, although donations in money might be made (*ibid.,* doc. CDXXXIII, p. 508).

4. *Dipl.,* doc. CDXII, pp. 495–496.

5. *Dipl.,* docs. CCCXCVIII, CD, pp. 488, 489, dated September 10, 1380.

6. *Dipl.,* doc. CCCXCVI, pp. 486–487 (also dated September 10, 1380), and on the confiscation of Oliverio Domingo's property and that of others, whose "bens son confiscats a la cort per lo crim . . . comés en la perdició de la ciutat d'Estives," see also, *ibid.,* doc. CDXXIV, pp. 502–503. The ducal palace on the Acropolis was built into the Propylaea, and the lines of the chapel may still be seen east of the so-called Pinakotheke.

could recover the Cadmea, obviously his grace needed an income.

Urtubia had apparently had much assistance in the occupation of Thebes, for the documents name several traitors "by whose work the city was lost." John Boyl and Rodonella would seem to have come to Lerida with a proscription list, and who can say whether malice added names? In any event Peter IV wrote pope Urban VI (on September 11, 1380) accusing archbishop Simon Atumano of Thebes, one of the great scholars of the time, of complicity in the Navarrese capture of the city: "Most holy father: We are assured that owing to the machinations and efforts of the archbishop of the city of Thebes—which together with other cities, castles, and places in the duchies of Athens and Neopatras now belong to our dominion—the said city was captured by our enemies, and even now is being held by them on the advice of the archbishop himself."[7]

The king repeated his request for the transference to the Theban see of bishop John Boyl, "who has suffered many ills in his own person for the defense of Christians." In two other letters of the same date (September 11) he asked, first, that John Boyl be appointed apostolic legate in the duchies of Athens and Neopatras as well as in the neighboring provinces of Romania (which would have meant the virtual displacement of archbishop Antonio Ballester of Athens as vicar of the so-called patriarchate of Constantinople), and secondly, that the interdict be lifted from the newly acquired dominions of Aragon in Greece.[8]

Since the royal letters of early September 1380 refer more than once to John Boyl's discourse in audiences with Peter IV, we may safely assume that the lively bishop of Megara told his attentive sovereign a good deal about the monumental beauty of Athens. The talks were not lost on Peter, and when John Boyl requested a guard of ten or a dozen men-at-arms for the Acropolis, the king ordered the treasurer of Aragon to provide twelve well-equipped archers for four months, by which time (he said) he should have sent Dalmau to Greece. A proper watch was necessary on the Acropolis, "especially as the said castle is the richest jewel there is in the world and such that all the kings of Christendom could not create its equal."[9] This

7. *Dipl.*, doc. CDVI, pp. 492–493. On Simon Atumano, see Giovanni Mercati, *Se la Versione dall' ebraico del codice veneto greco VII sia di Simone Atumano, arcivescovo di Tebe: Ricerca storica con notizie e documenti sulla vita dell' Atumano* (Studi e testi, no. 30; Rome, 1916); Giorgio Fedalto, *Simone Atumano, monaco di studio, arcivescovo latino di Tebe, [nel] secolo XIV* (Brescia, 1968); and K. M. Setton, "The Byzantine Background to the Italian Renaissance," *Proceedings of the American Philosophical Society*, C (1956), 47–52, reprinted in his *Europe and the Levant . . .*, no. I. Simon Atumano was appointed archbishop of Thebes by Urban V.

8. *Dipl.*, docs. CDVI–CDVIII, pp. 493–494.

9. *Dipl.*, doc. CDIV, p. 491, dated September 11, 1380: ". . . majorment con lo dit

text, hidden for five centuries in an Aragonese archival register, is probably the first aesthetic description of the Acropolis after a millennium of silence in western sources.

As John Boyl and Rodonella conveyed the "Articles of Athens" to the king at Lerida (and swore fealty for the municipality), so Bernard Ballester presented the petitions of Louis Fadrique, as well as those of the worried citizens of Livadia and the refugees from Thebes, to whom Louis was still giving shelter in the fastness of Salona.[10] King Peter IV knew Ballester well, for he had come to Barcelona a year before, as we have seen, bringing the first official news of the Navarrese capture of Thebes, and had then served as the royal envoy to the duchies upon his return to Greece.[11] He must have received a cordial welcome, not merely because he had come to swear fealty for his principals, but because he had first organized baronial support for Peter's acquisition of the duchies. Ballester now received no niggard-ly reward "for the service which he had done us in securing for us the cession of the duchies of Athens and Neopatras," because on September 25 (1380) the king granted him 4,000 gold florins of Aragon from the revenues of the royal third of the tithe of the city of Jativa and its territory, to be paid in annual instalments of 4,000 *solidi* until Ballester had received the full amount.[12]

On April 28, 1381, the king reaffirmed the appointment of Philip Dalmau, viscount of Rocaberti, as his vicar, viceroy, and lieutenant in

---

castell sia la pus richa joya qui al mont [i.e., món] sia, e tal que entre tots los reys de cristians envides lo porien fer semblant." Cf. Gregorovius (trans. Lampros), *History of the City of Athens* [in Greek], II (1904), 194–195; Rubió i Lluch, "Significació de l'elogi de l'Acròpolis d'Atenes pel Rei Pere'l Ceremoniós," in the *Homenaje ofrecido a [D. Ramón] Menéndez Pidal* (Madrid, 1925), III, 37–56, and *Los Catalanes en Grecia* (Madrid, 1927), pp. 131–137; Setton, *Catalan Domination,* pp. 187–188. On the dispatch of the twelve archers from Catalonia to Athens, see *Dipl.,* doc. CDXXVII, p. 505, dated September 29, and docs. CDXXVIII–CDXXXI, CDXXXV, pp. 505–507, 509, dated October 5, 6, and 11, 1380.

10. *Dipl.,* doc. CCCXCII, p. 481.

11. Cf. *Dipl.,* docs. CCCLXXV, CCCLXXVI, CCCLXXXI–CCCLXXXIII, CCCLXXXV, CCCLXXXVI, pp. 457 ff., dated September, October, and November 1379. Ballester had doubtless returned to Catalonia on the same ship as John Boyl and Rodonella, arriving in Lerida on August 1, 1380.

12. *Dipl.,* doc. CDXLI, p. 513, dated February 14, 1381: ". . . e aquesta gracia li havem feta per lo servey que'ns ha fet en fernos donar los ducats de Athenes e de la Patria." Peter IV made the grant of money to Ballester on September 25, 1380, the dated text being given in the infante Don John's confirmation of July 10, 1381 (*Dipl.,* doc. DII, pp. 555–556, "datum Ilerde XXV. die Septembris anno . . . MCCCLXXX," misdated September 28 by Rubió i Lluch, *loc. cit.,* and by Loenertz, *Arch. FF. Praed.,* XXV, no. 185, p. 147). The king is also explicit in this latter document as to Ballester's service to the Aragonese crown, "ad grata et obsequiosa servitia per vos . . . Bernardum Ballistarii nobis prestita signanter ut ducatus Attenarum . Neopatrie ad nostrum dominium pervenirent" (*Dipl.,* p. 555). Note also *Dipl.,* docs. CD? ', CDLXXXV, CDXCI, pp. 500, 545, 549.

the Greek duchies and adjacent lands, and defined in some detail his manifold administrative and judicial responsibilities.[13] The chancery was kept busy, and a harassed clerk dated thirteen documents April 31 (!), including the various notifications of Dalmau's appointment sent to the Venetian bailie of Negroponte, Nerio Acciajuoli, the refugee citizens of Thebes and Livadia, the Albanian chieftain count Dimitri, Louis Fadrique, archbishop Paul Foscari of Patras, the countess palatine Maddalena of Cephalonia, the acting despot Matthew Asen Cantacuzenus of Mistra, the officials of the Hospital in the Morea, and certain other interested dignitaries.[14]

There were delays in getting Dalmau's two galleys ready, but he was dilatory himself; on August 6, 1381, Peter IV ordered him to depart immediately or incur the royal displeasure. He sailed from Barcelona before August 13.[15] On his voyage to Greece, he put in at the island of Cephalonia, where he ordered the seizure, from a ship, of various goods and merchandise belonging to Florentine merchants, whom he forced to redeem their property by a payment of 1,000 gold ducats. He gave them a note in his own hand, duly sealed, promising to restore the money "in case we should regard the Florentines as our friends and well-wishers." On May 12 the king wrote Dalmau from Valencia that the Florentines were clamoring for restitution. He stated that he did indeed regard and wished to retain the Florentines as friends and well-wishers despite the late pope Gregory XI's decree against them as excommunicates and outlaws, condemning "all Florentines to servitude and their goods to seizure."[16] Dalmau was to return the 1,000 ducats, immediately upon receipt of the royal letter, either to those from whom he had taken the money or to their authorized agents.[17] Since Nerio Acciajuoli, the *enemich capital* of Aragon in the Athenian duchy, was a Floren-

13. *Dipl.,* doc. CDLV, pp. 522–524.

14. *Dipl.,* docs. CDLVII–CDLXIX, pp. 525–533, including letters addressed to Nerio and his father-in-law Saraceno de' Saraceni of Negroponte. The king hopes, in writing to Saraceno, that he will assist Dalmau "ut cum Raynerio genero vestro se habeat amicabiliter et conservet pacem . . ." (p. 533), which also shows that Nerio had married Agnes de' Saraceni at least a decade before 1390, the date which Hopf assumed for the marriage (*Chroniques gréco-romanes* [Berlin, 1873], p. 476).

15. *Dipl.,* docs. CDXCIX, DIV, DV, pp. 553–554, 557–558.

16. On the excommunication of the Florentines and their declaration as outlaws in the "War of the Eight Saints" see Ludwig von Pastor, *Geschichte der Päpste,* I (repr. 1955), 107–108.

17. *Dipl.,* doc. DXIII, pp. 563–564. Dalmau was well received in Athens, according to a royal confirmation dated December 5, 1382, of the rights and privileges of the *universitas civitatis Athenarum* (*Dipl.,* doc. DXXXII, pp. 583–584).

tine, Rocaberti's action was perhaps not so high-handed as it might at first appear.

Although the Aragonese archives have yielded some letters addressed to Dalmau during his tenure of the vicariate in Greece, little is known of his performance as either a soldier or an administrator. He seems to have provided the king's subjects in Athens with good government. However, he accomplished little in Greece, whence he departed in the spring of 1382. At least he had made a truce with Nerio Acciajuoli, to whom on September 12 Peter IV sent an expression of his pleasure in the peace which he professed to believe had been established. He stated that he would send Dalmau back to Greece without fail the following spring, and in the meantime he asked Nerio's consideration for Raymond de Vilanova, whom the vicar-general had left behind as his lieutenant in Athens. [18] We still do not know how and when Nerio Acciajuoli acquired Thebes, and presumably Livadia, from the Navarrese, but the mercenary bands which had served under Mahiot of Coquerel and John de Urtubia seem finally to have merged into a single "Company," which is referred to in the Hospitaller financial accounts of August 1381 as the *Societas sistens in principatu [Achaye]*.[19] John de Urtubia had apparently disappeared from the scene. His former lieutenants Peter Bordo de Saint Superan and Berard de Varvassa had joined with the redoubtable Mahiot as leaders of the unified company. Toward the end of the year 1381 they recognized James of Les Baux as prince of Achaea and Latin emperor of Constantinople, and he in turn named Mahiot as his bailie and Peter Bordo and Berard as imperial captains in the principality.[20]

The Navarrese Company had quickly become one of the chief powers in the divided Morea, and during his residence in Athens Dalmau had sought an accord with the three leaders. Whereas he had made a truce (*treva*) with Nerio, Dalmau had reached some sort of alliance (*liga*) with the Navarrese. On September 12 Peter IV wrote Mahiot, Berard, and Peter Bordo, hailing the pact the vicar-general had made with them, assuring them of Dalmau's return to Greece the

18. *Dipl.*, doc. DXX, p. 575, and cf. doc. DXXXIII, p. 585: "Ramón de Vilanova, lochtinent del dit vescomte en los dits ducats . . . ."

19. Loenertz, "Hospitaliers et Navarrais en Grèce," *Orientalia Christiana periodica*, XXII (1956), no. 14, pp. 332–333, and Royal Malta Library, Archives of the Order of St. John, Cod. 321, fol. 204[r], ed. Loenertz, *ibid.*, p. 351.

20. Loenertz, *ibid.*, nos. 38, 42–43, pp. 340, 341–343, who notes that this treaty provides the first evidence of James of Les Baux's relations with the Navarrese Company, although Venetian recognition of their "imperial" titles shows that James must have so designated them at least some weeks before the date of the treaty.

following year, and recommending Raymond de Vilanova to them. [21]
It seems likely that Urtubia had died, and that Berard and Peter
Bordo had sold Thebes to Nerio, and then joined Mahiot in the
Morea to see what the future might hold. Of all this there is of course
no evidence, but it would have been impossible for Dalmau to enter
into any sort of alliance with the new Navarrese Company if any of
its leaders still held Thebes.

While Dalmau was in Greece, he had discussed with Louis Fadrique
the possibility of his son Bernaduch's marrying Louis's daughter
Maria. Just about the time of Dalmau's return to Barcelona, however,
Louis died, and the outstanding Catalan in Greece was lost to the
cause of Aragon. On November 18, king Peter sent countess Helena
Cantacuzena an expression of his distress to learn of her husband's
death and of his royal desire to preserve her honor and well-being. At
the countess's request he granted her daughter Maria the castle of
Siderokastron for her lifetime, but he added the proviso that to get
the castle, Maria must go through with the projected marriage to
Bernaduch Dalmau.[22] But Maria Fadrique did not marry the young
lord Bernaduch, and presumably she never held Siderokastron, to
which no further reference occurs in the Catalan documents.

In the late summer of 1382 the municipality of Athens sent an
emissary to Peter IV, asking royal confirmation of the privileges,
concessions, and immunities which the Catalan kings of Sicily had
granted to Athens in past decades. The emissary found the king at
Tortosa by the Ebro. He acceded to the requests on December 5,
recalling how the Catalans in Athens had always preserved the
natural tie which bound them to the fatherland.[23] There is indeed
abundant evidence of the attachment of the Catalan creoles in
Greece (and of course in Sicily) to their Iberian homeland, but they
also came to love the sunny skies and evening breezes of Athens and
Thebes. By a letter patent of April 1368, for example, addressed to
the then vicar-general Roger de Lluria and the municipalities of the
duchies, king Frederick III besought protection for one Bartholomew
de Valerio, who had been serving the crown in Sicily but now
proposed to return to Greece "and to see again the city of Thebes,
his beloved home" (*ac civitatem Thebarum eius dulcem patriam
revidere*).[24]

The emissary who brought the Athenian requests to Tortosa

---

21. *Dipl.,* doc. DXXI, p. 575.
22. *Dipl.,* doc. DXXVI, pp. 579–580, and cf. docs. DXXVII, DXXVIII, pp. 580–581.
23. *Dipl.,* docs. DXXXII, DXXXIII, pp. 583–585.
24. *Dipl.,* doc. CCXCIX, p. 387, and cf. Setton, *Catalan Domination,* pp. 87–88.

brought also a good report of Dalmau's lieutenant in Athens, Ray-mond de Vilanova, to whom the king wrote in friendly fashion on December 11 (1382), "we are confident that you will serve us well and loyally."[25] As time passed, Peter needed Vilanova's loyal service, because for one reason or another Dalmau did not get back to Greece, although on June 20, 1383, his majesty assured the officials of Athens and Neopatras as well as Vilanova and countess Helena that the vicar-general would in fact, *Deo volente,* soon be setting out to resume command in the duchies.[26]

Although there is no dearth of documents for the years 1382–1383, we are still unable to determine who held Thebes and Livadia. On December 31, 1382, the king wrote pope Urban VI that after the union of the Athenian duchy with the crown of Aragon, the intrigues of certain rebels had resulted in a monstrous defection of loyalty from the crown. He implied that this had been the reason for levying the papal interdict upon the duchy (which was certainly not the case), but now that "all the inhabitants of the duchy have of their own accord recognized the error of their ways and returned to the Aragonese obedience," the long-standing interdict was unnecessary. The king asked his holiness to remove the ban and restore his "faithful subjects" to the loving embrace of the church. The bearer of the royal letter was to be bishop John Boyl of Megara, who had returned to Catalonia and was now setting out for Rome.[27] His persistent majesty made a further attempt to have the learned Simon Atumano removed from the archiepiscopal see of Thebes, and again recommended John Boyl's nomination thereto,[28] but the request was no more successful this time than it had been two years before.[29] Probably John Boyl made a better impression on the Aragon-ese court, where he could speak Catalan, than on the curia, for he may never have learned the Italian vernacular. In any event, Simon

25. *Dipl.,* doc. DXXXIV, pp. 585–586.

26. *Dipl.,* docs. DXLVI, DXLVIII–DL, pp. 595–597. The king asked Vilanova to guard well *lo castell e ciutat de Cetines.*

27. *Dipl.,* doc. DXXXVII, p. 587: ". . . omnes dicti ducatus tanquam nostri fideles eorum recognoscentes errorem spontanei ad nostram obedienciam et dominium redierunt. . . ." The statement is simple enough, but the meaning is unclear. Loenertz, *Arch. FF. Praed.,* XXVIII, no. 216, p. 75, says "le document semble impliquer que Thèbes et Livadia sont rentrées sous la domination catalane, fait important . . . ," and the fact would indeed be important if it were true, but a royal letter of April 10, 1383 (*Dipl.,* doc. DXLIII, p. 592), certainly shows that by that date the "city and district of Thebes" had not returned to Catalan rule. In reference to this document Loenertz, *loc. cit.,* speaks of "l'interdit qui pèse sur les duchés grecs," but the text specifies the duchy of Athens, and the interdict did not fall upon that of Neopatras.

28. *Dipl.,* doc. DXXXVIII, p. 588, dated December 31, 1382.

29. Cf. *Dipl.,* docs. CCCXCVI, CDVI, CDXIII.

Atumano was then in Rome, and could defend himself before the pope, who knew him. Simon had clearly not remained in Thebes very long after the Navarrese occupation of the city, even though (as we have seen) Peter IV had accused him of acting in collusion with the invaders. But before he left, he had embarked upon his most significant work, a trilingual Bible in Latin, Greek, and Hebrew, of which a partial Greek translation of the Old Testament is still extant in Simon's own first-draft, autograph manuscript, once the possession of cardinal Bessarion and perhaps the most important contribution of Catalan Greece to the scholarship of the Italian Renaissance.[30]

By the time of John Boyl's arrival at the curia with the royal letters of December 31 (1382), Simon Atumano was a familiar figure in intellectual circles in Rome. Urban VI, to whom he dedicated his *Biblia Triglotta,* provided him, on May 29, 1383, with a letter of safe conduct for a mission to Constantinople which was envisaged as possibly lasting a year.[31] When Simon died (in or before 1387), Urban is said to have taken possession of the *Biblia,*[32] suggesting that the esteem in which he was held at the curia was too much for John Boyl to combat.

If John Boyl had secured the archiepiscopal title to Thebes, it would have done him little good. The Catalans apparently never recovered the city, although Peter IV continued to hope, and his subjects in Greece still held out their hands for further grants. The Navarrese invasion had thrown central Greece into worse turmoil than ever. Travel was difficult and more dangerous still, for the Turks had overrun Thrace and Macedonia, and were said to be assailing the Morea.[33] One could leave his home in the Kastro in the morning and be carried off into slavery in the afternoon.

30. Biblioteca Centrale Marciana, Cod. gr. VII, published by Oscar Gebhardt and Fr. Delitzsch, *Graecus venetus: Pentateuchi Proverbiorum Ruth Cantici Ecclesiastae Threnorum Danielis versio graeca.* Ex unico bibliothecae S. Marci Venetae codice . . . (Leipzig, 1875). Incidentally, to go with his Greek translation of the Old Testament, Simon also prepared for scholarly or missionary purposes a Hebrew version of the New Testament, which was, at least in part, still extant in the year 1516 (Mercati, *Simone Atumano, arcivescovo di Tebe,* pp. 12–43).

31. Mercati, *Simone Atumano,* doc. III, pp. 50–51.

32. Mercati, *op. cit.,* pp. 16–17: ". . . cum morte praeoccuparetur, papa totum [Vetus Testamentum] sibi retinuit."

33. Demetrius Cydones, *Epistulae,* XXII, 226 (written to Simon Atumano from Constantinople in 1380 or 1381), ed. R. J. Loenertz, *Démétrius Cydonès: Correspondance* (Studi e testi, no. 208; Vatican City, 1960), pp. 120–121, and first published by Mercati, *Simone Atumano,* pp. 55–56. On July 17, 1385, king Peter IV thanked Mahiot of Coquerel and Peter Bordo de Saint Superan, imperial bailie and captain in the Morea, for assisting his

In 1381–1382 a plague swept from Pera to the Morea,[34] taking many lives. Galcerán of Peralta, onetime captain and castellan of Athens, had escaped it. He had regained his freedom, but ever since his displacement by Romeo de Bellarbre he knew that, although he was young, he had no future in Greece. On April 23, 1383, Peter IV wrote Bellarbre that "we have learned that at the time [Peralta] lost the aforesaid captaincy and castellany a large amount of his property remained in the castle of Athens, which despite his numerous requests he has been unable to secure from you, to his no small prejudice and loss." The king ordered the prompt restoration of Peralta's possessions, and warned Bellarbre that he would incur the royal displeasure if Peralta was obliged again to have recourse to the crown to secure justice in this connection.[35] Peralta presumably got back his property, because at this point Bellarbre had no intention of displeasing the king. He had apparently had enough of Greece, and was himself preparing to beat a retreat. In June (1383) Peter granted Bellarbre, in recognition of past services and in expectation of future loyalty, an emolument of 20,000 or 30,000 solidi Barcelonese.[36] And so we may assume that Bellarbre went back home with his beloved Zoe of Megara and their children, for after 1383 he is no longer a part of the history of Athens.

As king Peter worried about his distant domain and would have liked to hasten the vicar-general's departure for Greece, since Athens and Neopatras were threatened with ever-increasing danger, he learned that Dalmau had become ill.[37] The delay continued for months. On April 20, 1384, however, king Peter IV wrote his son, the infante Don John, that the necessity of sending aid to the duchies was not diminishing. Indeed, they might be lost. Whoever was threatening the Greek duchies at this time, it was apparently not Nerio Acciajuoli, the king's *enemich capital.* At least it was not he if we can take at face value a royal letter of May 30 (1384) in which the king thanked Nerio for keeping the peace he had made with Dalmau and for having "defended our city of Athens." The king did emphasize, to be sure, that the vicar-general was going to Greece with "so strong a force of men-at-arms" that the duchies would have full

---

subjects in the duchy of Athens against the "daily" incursions of Greeks and Turks (*Dipl.,* doc. DLXXV, p. 613).

34. Cf. Loenertz, "La Chronique brève moréote de 1423," in *Mélanges Eugène Tisserant,* II-1 (1964), 418.

35. *Dipl.,* doc. DXLIV, p. 593.

36. *Dipl.,* docs. DXLV and DXLVII, pp. 594, 595, dated June 1 and 20 respectively and giving 30,000 and 20,000 solidi as Bellarbre's emolument.

37. *Dipl.,* docs. DLII, DLIII, p. 598, dated September 16 and October 23, 1383.

security and the good friends of Aragon such as Nerio would have cause for contentment.[38]   Rather similar letters went off to countess Helena Cantacuzena, the syndics and council of Athens, and the lieutenant Raymond de Vilanova, informing them that once the then meeting of the Corts Generals had adjourned, Dalmau would leave promptly for Greece. Vilanova's young son Albert was anxious to go to Greece to relieve him of his duties and allow him at long last to return home, but Peter wanted the father and not the son in command on the Acropolis until the vicar-general could arrive in Athens.[39]

It is at this point that Nerio Acciajuoli emerges from behind the scenes into the full light of the Athenian stage, and for the first time we get a panoramic view of his activities in a letter which James, the Dominican bishop of Argos, wrote Nerio's brother Angelo, whom Urban VI had recently created a cardinal. Since the affairs of Greece were much influenced by the turbulence in the kingdom of Naples, where Charles III of Durazzo had displaced Joanna I, the Acciajuoli were inevitably much interested in the Neapolitan scene. Bishop James wrote cardinal Angelo from Venice that "our lord [the pope] hates to death my lord count of Nola [Nicholas Orsini], to such an extent that he has deprived him of his county, and this because the said lord count has made friends with king Charles . . . ,"[40] and more to the same effect, concerning which the cardinal must have been much better informed than the good bishop. The Acciajuoli had been caught up in the shifting currents of Neapolitan politics (into which we shall not go) for more than half a century, but certainly cardinal Angelo did not lose interest in James of Argos's letter as he continued reading:

Since your excellency wants reliable news of the lord Nerio, know that by the grace of God he is very well, as are his lady [Agnes de' Saraceni] and their daughters, the despoina Bartolommea and Francesca, and a beautiful family they make! The Navarrese who are in the Morea, as I see it, have no love for him and would willingly do him damage in a big way if they could, but they do not dare show their hand. In short, they make war on the despot [Theodore I Palaeologus, Nerio's son-in-law, the husband of Bartolommea], whose affairs are going badly because all his barons are rebelling against him and are siding with the Navarrese. The lord Nerio aids the despot, but not very vigorously, and excuses

---

38. *Dipl.*, doc. DLXI, p. 603.

39. *Dipl.*, docs. DLXII–DLXIV, pp. 604–606, dated May 30, 1384, and see also docs. DLXVI, DLXVIII, pp. 606–607.

40. On Urban VI's savage struggle with the Durazzeschi, to which bishop James alludes, see Angela Valente, *Margherita di Durazzo, vicaria di Carlo III e tutrice di Re Ladislao* (Naples, 1919), especially pp. 73–85.

himself to the Navarrese on the grounds that he is not helping the despot against the Navarrese but against the despot's Greek barons who are in revolt, and this is not contrary to the articles of peace.

But I think that this cloaking of motives will hardly endure, and in my own opinion there will be war between the Navarrese on the one hand and the lord Nerio and the despot on the other. A sign of this is the fact that news has just come from Argos that the Navarrese for their part are preparing to wage heavier warfare with the despot than they can [manage at present] as soon as a new opportunity arises. The despot is also getting ready, because a hundred horse have come to him from the city of Thessalonica, where his brother [Manuel] is ruler, and the lord Nerio is collecting men-at-arms from everywhere he can, and so I do [not] doubt there will be war. The lord Nerio can raise a good 70 lances, 800 Albanian horse, and a good many foot. The despot, moreover, who is always with the lord Nerio, will also have at least 200 horse and a good many foot including Turks in his force. The Navarrese however have about 1,300 horse. Your excellency will be able to inform your brother, the lord Donato, about all this . . . .[41]

Very likely the bishop of Argos knew a good deal about Nerio Acciajuoli's intentions, but troops raised for one purpose could usually be employed for another. If not against the Navarrese, why not against the Catalans? Nerio was not only recruiting land forces. He also wanted (he said) to share in the defense of east central Greece against constant Turkish assault. He had offered the bailie, captain, and councillors of Negroponte 8,000 ducats for the lease of an armed galley for a year to guard the Greek littoral, in conjunction with the republic's "galley of Negroponte." Since a resolution of approval was passed by the senate,[42] we must assume

41. Ferd. Gregorovius, "Briefe aus der 'Corrispondenza Acciajoli' in der Laurenziana zu Florenz," *Sitzungsberichte der philos.-philol. u. hist. Classe der k. bayer. Akademie der Wissenschaften zu München,* II (1890–1891), 297–300; Gregorovius (tr. Lampros), *Athens* [in Greek], II, 640–644; *Dipl.,* doc. DLXXIV, pp. 611–613; and cf. in general Setton, *Catalan Domination,* pp. 174 ff., with sources. The reference to Angelo Acciajuoli's creation as cardinal of San Lorenzo in Damaso on December 17, 1384 (Eubel, *Hierarchia catholica,* I, 24, 42–43), helps to date the letter with some precision.

On the early years of Theodore I Palaeologus in the despotate of Mistra, see Loenertz, "Pour l'histoire du Péloponèse au XIVᵉ siècle (1382–1404)," *Études byzantines,* I (1943), 161 ff., and on the background of events in the Neapolitan kingdom, to which James of Argos refers, see especially Noël Valois, *La France et le grand schisme d'Occident* (4 vols., Paris, 1896–1902, repr. Hildesheim, 1967), II, 65 ff., 112 ff., and in brief compass, É. G. Léonard, *Les Angevins de Naples* (Paris, 1954), pp. 464–467, 474–475. A letter of king Peter IV, dated July 17, 1385, to Mahiot of Coquerel and Peter Bordo de Saint Superan makes it clear that Greeks and Turks were "daily" crossing the borders of the Athenian duchy (*Dipl.,* doc. DLXXV, p. 613, referred to above), and the letter of James of Argos shows that these Greeks and Turks were troopers of the despot Theodore. For the political and military situation in continental Greece and the Morea at this time, see George T. Dennis, *The Reign of Manuel II Palaeologus in Thessalonica, 1382–1387* (Rome, 1960), pp. 114–128.

42. Archivio di Stato di Venezia, Misti, Reg. 38, fol. 10ʳ, dated "MCCCLXXXII indict. sexta, die vigessimo Febr.," in the Venetian style, i.e., February 20, 1383.

that Nerio paid his money and got his galley. He seems to have invaded Attica by land, and probably sailed his galley into Piraeus, seizing the harbors and height of Munychia. A Venetian document of July 7, 1385, refers to "dominus Raynerius de Azaiolis, dominator Choranti et ducaminis,"[43] which clearly means that the senate now recognized Nerio as lord of the Athenian duchy as well as of the Corinthian barony. Nerio was obviously getting along very well with the Venetians, and every advance in the date of the documents seems to bring him closer to the palace built into the Propylaea. Thus when on January 15, 1387, Nerio issued a confirmatory grant of lands, he called himself "lord of the castellany of Corinth, the duchy of Athens, and their dependencies."[44] But the document was drafted in the lower city, and Nerio was finding the ascent to the Acropolis hard going.

On the Acropolis itself Raymond de Vilanova had been finding it hard going for months, and had written king Peter IV that he could no longer maintain his position "without evident peril." Vilanova was of course the lieutenant of the vicar-general Philip Dalmau, who had bound him by oath and homage personally to defend the Catalan states in Greece, but Vilanova was anxious to be released from his obligation, because he wanted to return home and apparently regarded the situation as hopeless. The king rather peremptorily ordered Dalmau publicly to release Vilanova from the bonds of oath and homage, and directed him also to notify those who held the castle and duchy of Athens to give up their commands to the person or persons who would presently be designated, for the king still intended to send "some one of our loyal subjects, a provident and discreet man, with a proper force of armed men to guard and defend the duchy, cities, towns, castles, and people . . . ."[45] When Dalmau was slow to comply with the royal commands, Peter wrote him again to do immediately as he was bid.[46] The break was coming between the king and Dalmau, who was then supporting the infante Don John against his imperious father, and when instead of obedience Dalmau allegedly offered Peter "arguments unacceptable to us," he was angrily reprimanded and now told to obey the present mandamus within eight days of its receipt.[47] On January 6, 1386, Dalmau

43. Misti, Reg. 39, fol. 110ᵛ.
44. J. A. C. Buchon, *Nouvelles recherches historiques,* II (Paris, 1845), *Florence,* doc. XL, pp. 220–221; Fr. Miklosich and Jos. Müller, *Acta et diplomata res graecas italasque illustrantia,* III (1865, repr. 1968), doc. no. 8, pp. 248–249; *Dipl.,* doc. DC, pp. 636–637.
45. *Dipl.,* doc. DLXXVII, pp. 614–615, dated September 12, 1385.
46. *Dipl.,* doc. DLXXVIII, pp. 615–616, dated September 20, 1385.
47. *Dipl.,* doc. DLXXXIV, pp. 618–619, dated December 22, 1385. Much concerned

replied courteously that he had only seen one letter from the king, which he had answered with the reminder that he had gone to Greece at the royal command and secured for his majesty the castles of Athens and Neopatras. He had employed his own resources for the honor of Aragon, and the crown still owed him 5,000 florins and the pay for twenty-five lances. He would return to Greece if his majesty so wished, but he did not deserve such treatment for the services he and his ancestors had rendered the royal house.[48] Peter responded promptly, on January 17, insisting upon the release of Vilanova from his personal commitments to Dalmau so that another commander might be sent to take over Athens and Neopatras. He did not want to send Dalmau back to Greece. He had never caused a loss to any man, however, nor would he to Dalmau, and so the latter might send someone to the court with his accounts which the royal treasurer would go over, and his just claims would be met.[49]

However much Dalmau might choose to remonstrate, the king had decided to remove him from the Greek vicariate. On June 26, 1386, his majesty wrote Raymond de Vilanova from Barcelona that "whereas for certain reasons we have revoked the concession we have made to the viscount of Rocaberti of the office of the vicariate of the duchies of Athens and Neopatras, we have recently bestowed the said office upon the young Don Bernard [Bernat] of Cornellà, who will presently have to betake himself to the . . . duchies on this account, and therefore we require that you give up to the said Bernard the castles and the city of Athens . . . , which you hold by command of the viscount of Rocaberti, [and] which he holds on our behalf . . . ." Vilanova had in fact already left Athens for Catalonia, and had turned over the Acropolis and the other castles on the royal domain to one Peter of Pau, who had thus perforce become Cornellà's lieutenant in the duchies.[50]

For whatever reason, official notifications of Cornellà's appointment were not sent out by the Catalan chancery for almost two months. At length on August 17 (1386) the king did so notify countess Helena Cantacuzena, and at the same time he chided her for seeking a husband for her daughter Maria outside the ranks of the Catalan nobility. He wrote Helena that he would send Cornellà to Greece without fail the following spring, and the men-at-arms whom the new vicar-general would bring with him would protect the

---

with the "affairs of Athens," Peter had been impatiently summoning Bernard Ballester to the court for consultation (*ibid.*, docs. DLXXIX–DLXXXII, DLXXXV).

48. *Dipl.*, doc. DLXXXVI, pp. 620–621.

49. *Dipl.*, doc. DLXXXVII, pp. 621–622.

50. *Dipl.*, doc. DXC, pp. 623–624, and cf. doc. DXCVII.

countess's lands as well as the castles of the royal domain.[51] On the same day (August 17) notices of Cornellà's appointment to the Greek vicariate were prepared in the king's name for dispatch to the lords of Argos, Lepanto, and Patras, who were told "that within a few days we shall send to the said duchies our said vicar and lieutenant with such a force of men-at-arms, both horse and foot, that you and all our friends shall have cause for satisfaction."[52] Even Cornellà's lieutenant Peter of Pau was given to understand that Cornellà was being sent to Greece "within a few days,"[53] although when the king informed the Navarrese Company in the Morea and the anxious officials of Athens and Neopatras of Cornellà's appointment, he stated (as he had to Helena) that the new vicar would set out for Greece the following spring.[54]

The extant copy of Bernard of Cornellà's commission as "vicar-general and viceroy" is dated August 18, 1386. It conferred upon him the usual jurisdiction in civil and criminal cases and all the other rights and responsibilities adhering to his new office.[55] By this time Raymond de Vilanova had returned to Barcelona, having turned over his command in Greece to Peter of Pau, who would of course surrender the cities and castles on the royal domain to Cornellà upon the latter's arrival in Athens.[56] Cornellà, however, bore the title vicar-general for less than a year (1386–1387). He never went to Greece, and "by a public instrument executed in the city of Athens on November 4, A.D. 1386," Peter of Pau selected Gerard de Rodonella, who with bishop John Boyl had presented the Articles of Athens to Peter IV a half dozen years before, to go as his emissary to Barcelona, to swear fealty and render homage to the new vicar-general, and of course to inform the royal court that Nerio Acciajuoli had laid Athens under siege. We have noted that by mid-January 1387 Nerio had occupied the lower city, a fact which Rodonella did not know as he made his way to Barcelona, in those days a voyage of about three months.

King Peter IV the Ceremonious died in the queen's palace at Barcelona on January 5, 1387, some weeks before Rodonella's ship put into the harbor. The infante Don John succeeded his father as

51. *Dipl.,* doc. DXCI, pp. 624–625.
52. *Dipl.,* doc. DXCII, pp. 625–626.
53. *Dipl.,* doc. DXCV, p. 628.
54. *Dipl.,* docs. DXCIII, DXCIV, pp. 626–627.
55. *Dipl.,* doc. DXCVI, pp. 628–630.
56. *Dipl.,* doc. DXCVII, p. 633, a letter of the king to Peter of Pau dated July 18, 1386

king of Aragon, count of Barcelona, and duke of Athens, but John's health was so poor that when Rodonella arrived in Barcelona he had to wait more than a month for an audience. As he recovered, king John gave some attention to Greek affairs. On March 3 he ordered the bailie of Jativa to pay Bernard Ballester, "citizen of Valencia and inhabitant of the duchy of Athens," 2,000 solidi still owing on his annual pension of 4,000 (which was to run until the royal grant of 4,000 gold florins, made by king Peter in September 1380, had been paid in its entirety).[57] On Monday, the 18th, John received Rodonella at Barcelona, and accepted the letter of procuration prepared at Athens the preceding November 4. Rodonella explained to his tired majesty that he had come from Athens as Peter of Pau's special emissary to learn what was to be done about the duchies, which by this time were in even greater danger than Rodonella knew. John answered that he had removed Cornellà from the vicariate-general and reappointed Philip Dalmau, the viscount of Rocaberti, his councillor and chamberlain, to whom he now directed Rodonella to swear fealty and do homage in Peter of Pau's name. Rodonella went through the feudal ceremony, pledging Peter's loyal defense of the duchies and his allegiance to the vicar-general and his sovereign.[58]

As Rodonella was getting ready to return to Greece, the royal chancery in Barcelona prepared notices of Dalmau's reappointment on April 17, 1387, one of which (as protocol required) was addressed to Nerio Acciajuoli, wherein king John informed "the lord of the castellany of Corinth" that the Catalans intended to preserve the "peace and truce" which Dalmau had negotiated with Nerio during his first tenure of office.[59] His majesty also wrote to the aldermen of Athens with words of praise and gratitude for the love and loyalty which the Catalans in Athens had exhibited toward the crown of Aragon. He told them of the reappointment of Dalmau, who would rewin the lost *viles e lochs* with a strong corps of men-at-arms and archers. He also assured his threatened subjects overseas that they were not to think he had forgotten such an illustrious part of his crown as the city of Athens and that he hoped to pay the Catalans in Athens a personal visit, to encourage by his royal presence both the Catalans and all who served him, "and those both near and far will

---

(from the Arx. Cor. Aragó, Reg. 1559, fol. 15ᵛ). Rubió i Lluch has perhaps unnecessarily altered the date of August 18, the official date of Cornellà's appointment to the vicariate, to which the letter relates. But we know that the king had already decided upon Cornellà's appointment before June 26 (cf. *Dipl.*, doc. DXC).

57. *Dipl.*, doc. DCI, p. 637, and see above, p. 231.

58. *Dipl.*, doc. DCII, pp. 638–639.

59. *Dipl.*, doc. DCIII, p. 639, and cf. Setton, *Catalan Domination*, pp. 179 ff.

know that you are our people, a special part of our crown, and that we are your king, prince, duke, and lord by divine grace."[60]

On April 17 John also notified countess Helena Cantacuzena of Dalmau's reappointment to the vicariate-general, but acknowledged that Dalmau could not immediately proceed to Greece.[61] John's letter probably made little impression on Helena, who knew that Nerio Acciajuoli had already taken the lower city of Athens, and probably suspected that Dalmau would never return to Greece. The Catalan duchies, or what was left of them, were in a sad state, as Rodonella had unquestionably lamented at some length. Nerio was moving freely about in the lower city of Athens and held the Acropolis under intermittent siege.

During these months the valiant soldier Peter of Pau, "the last of the *almogàvers* in Greece," was defending Athena's towering rock against Nerio's increasing pressure. If Rodonella ever got back to Athens carrying the king's letters of April 1387, he must have found Aragonese rule in the city confined to the citadel. Although communication between Athens and the Aragonese court had obviously become difficult, Peter managed to get letters safely through Nerio's lines. It is easy to imagine what he wrote king John when the latter replied on April 22, 1388, that "we have seen your letters in which you make known to us that Messer Nerio, the Florentine, holds our castle of Athens strongly and tightly under siege . . . ." Peter had stated that he could not hold out in the Acropolis much longer. The king had to acknowledge that he was unable to send assistance immediately but was asking countess Helena to do so. If the countess could not or would not help, however, Peter was to do what he thought best, and his majesty would certainly regard the defenders of the citadel as his good and loyal vassals.[62] King John wrote the countess at the same time. He told her of the siege (of which she must have known more than he), and reminded her that the Florentine occupation of the Acropolis would be an "irreparable loss" to Aragon. For various good reasons he could not just then send aid, but implored her to break the siege by an armed force or in any other way she could, and free Peter and those who were helping him defend the citadel. If the countess did so, John promised to turn over the Acropolis to her, and she could retain it until he had reimbursed

---

60. *Dipl.,* doc. DCVIII, pp. 642–643, dated April 26, 1387. An earlier letter to the *prohomens* of Athens, dated April 17 (*ibid.,* doc. DCIV, p. 640) "was not sent in this form," according to a marginal note in the register preserving the text (Arx. Cor. Aragó, Reg. 1675, fol. 124, ref. from Rubió i Lluch): it was too formal, too brief, and too abrupt.

61. *Dipl.,* doc. DCV, pp. 640–641.

62. *Dipl.,* doc. DCXX, p. 651.

her for all the expense she would undergo in saving it from the enemy: "We assure you that this is a matter which we hold dear to our heart, and we want it done!"[63] But the Acropolis was not strong enough to laugh a siege to scorn, for by now famine and plague had joined the opponents of Aragon.

King John might hold the defense of the Acropolis dear to his heart, but Peter of Pau and his fellow Catalans could not withstand Nerio Acciajuoli's unrelenting pressure. Only ten days after the date of John's letters to Peter and countess Helena (and long before they could have received them, if indeed they ever did), Nerio's forces entered the world's most famous citadel. The event is dated in a letter (now in the Laurentian Library in Florence) which one James of Prato, possibly a relative of Louis Aliotti of Prato, first Florentine archbishop of Athens, wrote on May 9, 1388, to Donato Acciajuoli in Florence: "Most reverend lord: May your revered Magnificence know . . . I arrived in Patras safe and sound, and here I found the news that Messer Neri and all his family are well, and on the second day of this month he took the castle of Athens. It is true that there is plague in Athens, and great loss of life, from which Messer Neri with all his family has gone away and is staying in Thebes [*Stive*]. . . ."[64] Unfortunately James of Prato did not bother to inform Donato of the fate of Peter of Pau and the Catalan garrison on the Acropolis. Whether the plucky Peter met his death in a Florentine assault or saved his life by flight or surrender, we do not know, but when dead or alive he came down from the citadel, the rule of Aragon in Attica had come to an end.[65] Nerio Acciajuoli was sailing smoothly before the wind, but he would soon strike the shoals of adversity.

The Turks had taken Thessalonica in April 1387, and were threatening the Venetian colony at Negroponte. The castellans of Coron and Modon also reported to the home government that Turkish incursions into the southern Morea were netting the invaders *animae et animalia.* On September 28, 1387, the Venetian senate decided to send an envoy to sultan Murad I (1362–1389),[66] and on October 3,

63. *Dipl.,* doc. DCXXI, p. 652.

64. Lampros, *Eggrapha,* part II, doc. 10, p. 119; *Dipl.,* doc. DCXXII, pp. 652–653.

65. Cf. Laonicus Chalcocondylas, *Historia,* II (*CSHB,* p. 69); E. Darkó, ed., *L. Chalco-candylae historiarum demonstrationes,* I (Budapest, 1922), 63: "Some [of the Catalans] returned to Italy, and some remained in Greece until they died . . . ." The brothers Roger and Antonio de Lluria are said in fact to have sought refuge in Sicily (Gerónimo Zurita, *Anales de la Corona de Aragón,* II [Saragossa, 1610], p. 403ᵛ).

66. Archivio di Stato di Venezia, Misti, Reg. 40, fol. 94ᵛ: "Quia propter nova que habentur a castellanis Coroni et Mothoni de incursionibus Turchorum factis in locis nostris predictis capiendo animas et animalia et multa alia damna et spolia inferrendo . . . ." Equally discouraging news came from Negroponte, and so choice was to be made of "unus ambaxator sufficiens ad dominum Moratum Bey. . . ."

when Daniel Cornaro was chosen for the mission, he was instructed to ask the sultan to order the return of all persons, animals, and other property seized from Venetian territory by Turks under the command of Evrenos Beg, and to receive assurance from the Ottoman government that subjects of the republic would not again suffer such captivity or loss as they had in the recent depredation of the Morea and the attack upon Euboea.[67] The Turks, however, were not merely following a policy of raid and run. They were assisting their good friend Theodore I Palaeologus against his rebellious Greek *archontes* and his Latin enemies in the Morea, including presumably the Navarrese.

The despot Theodore and his ambitious father-in-law Nerio Acciajuoli worked together, though their union may have been less close than one seemed to think in Venice. Now that he was lord of Athens, Nerio probably wanted Argos and Nauplia also, fiefs of the Athenian duchy in the old days of the French dukes. At first Nerio entertained an understandable apprehension of the Turks, which had led him to rent a Venetian galley and to share with the republic the burden of maintaining coastal defense against Turkish corsairs. But when Manuel Palaeologus, Theodore's brother, lost Thessalonica to Murad, he became a Turkish vassal, and Theodore himself now saw some advantage in acknowledging the suzerainty of the sultan in distant Adrianople so long as he could get Turkish assistance to advance his own interests in the Morea.[68]

The Morea had known little peace since the Fourth Crusade. There had been much tension under the Villehardouins, much turmoil after them. The Byzantine despots in Mistra had helped undermine the Latin hegemony, and now the arrival of the Ottoman Turks in force became a threat to Christian dominance in the peninsula. We have noted Nerio Acciajuoli's initial desire to coöperate with the Venetians to ward off Turkish attacks upon their Greek territories, and for a while Nerio stood out as a Latin champion, even winning a "remarkable victory" over the Turks, allegedly with Venetian aid.[69]

---

67. Misti, Reg. 40, fols. 95^r–96^r, and cf. F. Thiriet, ed., *Régestes des délibérations du sénat de Venise*, I (1958), nos. 735–736, pp. 177–178; Loenertz, "La Chronique brève moréote . . . ," *Mélanges Eugène Tisserant*, II-1, 420; and cf. the *Chronicon breve*, ad ann. 6896 (1388), appended to Ducas's *Historia byzantina* (*CSHB*, p. 516); and on the Turkish occupation of Thessalonica see Dennis, *The Reign of Manuel II Palaeologus in Thessalonica, 1382–1387*, pp. 151 ff.

68. Cf. Loenertz, "Pour l'histoire du Péloponèse . . . (1382–1404)," *Études byzantines*, I, 166–170.

69. Misti, Reg. 40, fol. 17^v, dated in the Venetian style "MCCCLXXXV die VI Februarii indictione nona," i.e., February 6, 1386. Nerio's victory is said to have been achieved with Negropontine help. Cf. Thiriet, *Régestes*, I, no. 707, p. 171.

After this, Nerio had other uses for his time and money (in the siege of Athens), and he preferred the conquest of territory to warfare against the Turks. Furthermore, as his son-in-law, the despot Theodore, became almost a vassal of the sultan, Nerio's own attitude toward the Turks changed. To the exasperation of the Venetian senate, he did not even pay the full wages of the crew on the galley he had rented from the republic. What is more, in a letter of July 24, 1388, the senate charged Nerio directly with being the "principal cause" of the great Turkish invasion of the preceding autumn.[70] If true, Nerio was in a dangerous business.

In 1388 Greek affairs were complicated by the death of the Venetian magnate Peter Cornaro, who had held Argos and Nauplia for some years by virtue of his marriage with the Enghien heiress Marie. The despot Theodore promptly seized both places with Turkish assistance and with Nerio's obvious encouragement. But on December 12 (1388) Marie, who was then in Venice, sold both Argos and Nauplia to the republic for (among other considerations) an annual income which she and her descendants were to receive for as long as the republic should hold the two places.[71] If the financial terms were not generous, neither was Venice in possession of Argos and Nauplia. Any Venetian court would uphold the legality of the republic's purchase, but in the Morea possession was more than nine points of the law.

Since the acquisition of the erstwhile strongholds of the Enghiens was a matter of "notable" concern to the state, the Venetian senate decided on January 26, 1389, to send a commissioner (*provisor*) on an armed galley to the Morea to make certain of their purchase.[72]

---

70. A text of July 24, 1388, shows that the *intentiones Morati erga nos* worried the Venetians constantly (Misti, Reg. 40, fol. 127ᵛ); the senate sent Nerio a letter (*ibid.*, fols. 125ᵛ–126ʳ) in which the serious charge was made that ". . . sicut a recto novimus in anno elapso fuistis potissima causa faciendi descendere Turchos et alias gentes ad damnum locorum nostrorum qui multa mala nobis et aliis intullerunt, de quo gravamur quantum plus possumus, ymo quod cedit ad maiorem turbationem nostram persensimus quod in presenti tempore conamini favere Turchis qui asseruntur descendere ad damnum locorum nostrorum, quod penitus importabile foret."

71. G. M. Thomas, ed., *Diplomatarium veneto-levantinum*, II, nos. 126–127, pp. 211–215; D. A. Zakythinos, *Le Despotat grec de Morée*, I (1932), 132–133; Setton, *Catalan Domination*, p. 190; Luttrell, "The Latins of Argos and Nauplia," *Papers of the British School at Rome*, XXXIV (1966), 47–48. The enemies of Venice are the despot Theodore and the "cruel tyrant" Nerio Acciajuoli, who must not get Argos and Nauplia (Archivio di Stato di Venezia, Secreta Consilii Rogatorum, Reg. E, fol. 46ᵛ, summarized in Thiriet, *Régestes*, I, no. 744, p. 179, dated December 12, 1388, and cf. R. Cessi, "Venezia e l'acquisto di Nauplia ed Argo," *Nuovo archivio veneto*, new ser., XXX [1915], 152). On Peter Cornaro see Luttrell, *op. cit.*, pp. 44–45.

72. Misti, Reg. 40, fol. 146ʳ; Cessi, in *Nuovo archivio veneto*, n.s., XXX, 153.

The able Perazzo Malipiero was chosen for the mission; his commission is dated February 18, and contains detailed instructions which he was to follow. The text rehearses the essential facts of Marie's sale of Argos and Nauplia, and deplores the despot Theodore's *molestia et novitas,* which indicates that he had employed force in taking both places. The castellans of Modon and Coron, also acting under senatorial instructions, had been unable to prevail upon Theodore to order the evacuation of his forces. The senate had written to him and to Nerio asserting the claims of the republic to Argos and Nauplia. Paul Foscari, the archbishop of Patras, and Peter Bordo de Saint Superan, the Navarrese commander, had both offered their assistance "to obtain the aforesaid places."[73] Since Foscari was a Venetian, and the Navarrese were notoriously hostile to the aggressive despot, obviously the republic could rely on them.

Perazzo Malipiero did succeed in taking over Nauplia, but Argos was another matter. On May 31, 1389, the senate directed Nicholas Zeno, Venetian "captain of the gulf," to proceed to Nauplia to confer with Malipiero, after which they should go together to the despot Theodore, and state "that we have fully understood the letters which he has sent us with reference to our city of Argos." They were to demand that Theodore immediately desist from his armed occupation of the city, which he was holding contrary to God and justice and his own honor. The senate was all the more disturbed because Theodore had written that he was waiting for the answer to an inquiry he had addressed to sultan Murad, and that his hands were tied until it came. The senate did not believe him; the sultan had nothing to do with it all. Inasmuch, however, as Nerio Acciajuoli was said to be the principal cause of the difficulty, the captain and Malipiero should also wait upon Nerio, remind him of the ample (and unkept) promises he had been making the republic, and admonish him to get Theodore to remove himself from Argos.[74] But the Venetians could get nowhere with Nerio, and on June 22 (1389) the senate passed a resolution that figs from Attica and currants from Corinthia were no longer to be imported into Venice or into any Venetian territories. The castellans of Modon and Coron had already stopped the export of iron and plowshares to Nerio's domains (and to those of the despot); the senate approved of their action, but

---

73. Misti, Reg. 40, fols. 157^r–158^r, by original (faulty) foliation. Cf. Thiriet, *Régestes,* I, no. 748, p. 180.

74. Misti, Reg. 41, fol. 6^v; Cessi, in *Nuovo archivio veneto,* n.s., XXX, 155; Thiriet, *Régestes,* I, no. 753, p. 181, and cf. no. 762. On August 16, 1389, the senate made various provisions for the security and governance of Nauplia (*ibid.,* no. 761, p. 183).

provided for the resumption of trade with Mistra, Corinth, and Athens when the despot gave up the city of Argos.[75]

At this point Peter Bordo de Saint Superan entered the scene, presumably as an honest broker, to try to adjudicate the issue which was dividing the Christian Morea. Since it was useless for him to approach the despot Theodore, with whom he was at armed odds, he made overtures to Nerio to confer with him at the Navarrese fortress of Vostitsa on the Gulf of Corinth. It was later said that he gave Nerio the fullest assurances of his safety, which was doubtless true, for otherwise Nerio would never have gone. He arrived at Vostitsa on September 7; discussed Argos (and related matters) with Peter Bordo for three days; and probably professed the innocence of a bystander in the whole affair. On September 10 Nerio was informed he was a prisoner. An old hand at hunting, he had fallen into a trap.[76] On September 15 Nerio's wife Agnes wrote his brother Donato from Corinth, "We must inform you that the lord messer Neri has gone to Vostitsa to talk with the vicar of the Morea and with others of the Company to bring about peace [*hordine*] for the well-being of the country and for other affairs of theirs. The vicar has had him arrested and carried off into prison, and this happened on Friday, September 10. The reason why they have detained and taken him I cannot explain to you clearly, because I do not know it. . . . I must also tell you that all the country, both the duchy [of Athens] and the castellany [of Corinth], is holding firm in loyalty to us. . . ."[77]

It is quite possible that at the time of his imprisonment Nerio was willing to see the relaxation of tensions in the Morea, for he had just undertaken the siege of Neopatras, intending to add the northern duchy to his Athenian domain. Andrew Zavall, castellan and captain of the city, notified king John as soon as he could, and the latter wrote back on January 3, 1390, asking him to hold out, because "you will soon have that succor and assistance you hope to receive

---

75. Misti, Reg. 41, fol. 16ᵛ. Cf. Gregorovius (trans. Lampros), *Athens* [in Greek], II, 238–239; Thiriet, *Régestes*, I, no. 757, p. 182; and esp. Cessi, in *Nuovo archivio veneto*, n.s., XXX, 158–159. On June 10 (1389) the senate had dismissed an ambassador from Nerio since he had had "nothing new" to say (Misti, Reg. 41, fol. 13ᵛ). In mid-June on the field of Kossovo sultan Murad I was slain by a Serb posing as a deserter, but Murad's son Bayazid I took over the Ottoman command and inflicted a crushing defeat upon the Serbs (cf. G. Ostrogorsky and M. Dinić, in the *Cambridge Medieval History*, IV-1 [1966], 373–374, 550–551). Now all the Balkans as well as Greece lay in the shadow of Turkish power.

76. Cf. Buchon, II (1845), *Florence:* doc. XLVI, pp. 241–242, 248, and Cessi, in *Nuovo archivio veneto*, n.s., XXX, 160–161.

77. F. Gregorovius, "Corrispondenza Acciajoli," *Sitzungsb. d. Akad. zu München,* II (1890), 305, and Gregorovius, trans. Lampros, *Athens,* II (1904), 649–650; Rubió i Lluch, *Diplomatari,* doc. DCXXV, pp. 655–656.

from us."[78] It was no use; Nerio would eventually get the city; but John had clearly not yet heard of Nerio's detention by the Navarrese at the time of this letter.[79]

Donato Acciajuoli had heard of it, and so had the Florentine government, which sent an envoy to Venice to try to arrange for Nerio's release. The senate rejected the first proposals,[80] and the subsequent negotiations were long drawn out. Among other concessions, Donato offered to surrender, temporarily, Athens, Thebes, and certain other places in the castellany of Corinth (but not Acrocorinth), together with merchandise "to the value of twelve to fifteen thousand ducats or thereabouts," which Nerio then had in Corinth—all as a guarantee that the republic should receive Argos.[81] The Venetians were reminded that Nerio was one of their honorary citizens, and they were informed that the despot Theodore was holding Argos "against the will of messer Nerio," which considering Nerio's plight was doubtless the truth.[82] Cardinal Angelo Acciajuoli, who had almost won the triple tiara in the conclave of late October and November 1389, appealed to the new pope, Boniface IX, and a papal embassy set out for Venice. Donato sent two more Florentine envoys to the lagoons on February 24, 1390, and other great personages were prepared to put pressure on Peter Bordo and the Navarrese Company. The doge of Genoa had offered to convey Donato and a retinue of twenty-five to Corinth and even to arrange for the transport of horses and men-at-arms.[83]

Nerio had certainly not been abandoned. From faraway Chieri in Piedmont, Amadeo of Savoy, prince of Pinerolo, wrote Donato on March 30, 1390, of his displeasure in learning of Nerio's detention "in our principality of Achaea." For the last three or four years

---

78. *Dipl.,* doc. DCXXVII, p. 657: "Entés havem que vos sots aqui en la ciutat nostra de la Patria asseiat per miçer Arner [Nerio], enemich nostre capital, lo qual sens tota rahó s'esforce damnificar aquella . . . ." King John also wrote countess Helena Cantacuzena of Salona, appealing to her to help defend Neopatras (*ibid.,* doc. DCXXVI, p. 656).

79. Cf. Loenertz, *Arch. FF. Praed.,* XXV, nos. 207–209, pp. 152–153.

80. Misti, Reg. 41, fol. 49[v], dated December 23, 1389: ". . . non possemus nos intromittere in procurando liberationem domini Nerii . . . donec haberemus ipsam nostram civitatem [Argolicensem] . . . ," and the same answer was given to bishop James of Argos, who had also gone to Venice on behalf of Nerio's wife Agnes (Buchon, II, *Florence:* doc. XLVI, p. 249).

81. Buchon, II, 238–239, 243–244.

82. Buchon, II, 241–243.

83. Buchon, II, 247–252, especially p. 249, and for the Venetian replies to the envoys dispatched by Donato on February 24 see Thiriet, *Régestes,* I, no. 771, pp. 185–186, dated March 13, 1390. Although the exhausting war over Tenedos had led in 1381 to peace between Venice and Genoa, the Venetians believed the Genoese needed constant watching. Genoese corsairs were also active in Greek waters at this time.

Amadeo had been pressing the old claims of his house to the principality; in fact he informed Donato that he had been planning "for many years . . . to reduce our principality . . . to obedience."[84] Egged on by that arch-intriguer John Lascaris Calopherus and supported by the count of Savoy, Amadeo was quite beguiled by the idea of gaining Greek recognition as the prince of Achaea. He had troubles enough at home, but he thought for a while of approaching his Genoese neighbors to help him in the Greek adventure. Eventually he turned to Venice, perhaps at the instigation of Calopherus, whom he sent to the senate to seek passage for a sizeable force to the Morea. Amadeo had already sent envoys into the Morea, and negotiated with Peter Bordo and the despot Theodore.[85]

Although the affair of Argos had drawn the Navarrese and Venetians together in their common hostility to the despot, they were unsteady allies. Nerio's captivity seemed to be serving no purpose, and was quite as embarrassing to the Venetians as to Theodore. The Florentines were seeing to that. Argos was the chief complaint the Venetians had against Nerio, then confined in the castle of Listrina near Vostitsa; any fool could see that his confinement was not helping them to get the city, and there were few fools in the Venetian senate. The despot had continued his struggle with the Navarrese, and launched attacks upon Venetian territories.[86] The senate sought a clearer understanding with the Navarrese as to Nerio's position, and on May 22, 1390, at a rendezvous two miles from Vostitsa, the castellan of Modon and Coron and the republic's high commissioners of Romania reached a preliminary agreement with Nerio himself, looking toward the recovery of his freedom and the Venetian occupation of Argos.[87]

84. Gregorovius, "Corrispondenza Acciajoli," *Sitzungsb. d. Akad. zu München,* II, 306; *idem* (trans. Lampros), *Athens* [in Greek], II, 651.

85. See in general R. Cessi, "Amedeo di Acaia e la rivendicazione dei domini sabaudi in Oriente," *Nuovo archivio veneto,* new series, XXXVII (1919), 5–64, with selections from the accounts of the "treasurer of Achaea," Archivio di Stato di Torino, Principato d'Acaia. Cf. David Jacoby, "Jean Lascaris Calophéros," *Revue des études byzantines,* XXVI (1968), 214–216.

Amadeo of Savoy, commonly known to Italian history as Amadeo of Achaea—not to be confused with Amadeo VII (1383–1391), the Red Count of Savoy, a mistake made by Zakythinos, *Le Despotat grec de Morée,* I, 135, 137, 149, 150, and Thiriet, *Régestes,* I, no. 779, pp. 187–188—died at Pinerolo on May 7, 1402, and was succeeded in his Piedmontese possessions by his brother Louis (d. 1418), last Savoyard claimant to the princely title of Achaea.

86. Thiriet, *Régestes,* I, no. 773, p. 186, dated April 23, 1390.

87. The first agreement between Nerio and the Venetians, dated May 22, 1390, has been published from the Commemoriali, book VIII, fol. 180, by L. de Mas Latrie, "Documents concernant divers pays de l'Orient latin, 1382–1413," *Bibliothèque de l'École des chartes,*

After about a year's captivity Nerio was released late in the year 1390. As stipulated, his daughter Frances was to become a hostage in his stead, committed to the care of the Venetians at Negroponte. Nerio did not have to admit the Venetians into Athens and Thebes, but he turned Megara over to them, as well as all his goods in Corinth, as a pledge that when he had regained his freedom he would prevail upon Theodore to surrender Argos, or else would join the Venetians against him. Thus peace was restored between Nerio and the republic, and when the terms thereof had finally been fulfilled, the "black bridge" at Negroponte could again be opened, and Venetians could trade again with the Athenian duchy.[88] But the peace with Nerio brought the Venetians little immediate benefit. Theodore continued to hold Argos, and now the Turks were assailing Nauplia.[89] Since Nerio was continuing to pay a heavy price for Theodore's intransigence, a rift occurred between them, and Theodore became isolated in the peninsula. At long last, however, Nerio bought him off, and on June 11, 1394, Theodore surrendered Argos to the Venetians,[90] thus concluding an ill-advised adventure which had thrown Latin Greece into turmoil and made the Ottoman Turks feel at home in the Morea.

In the meantime Amadeo of Savoy had been pursuing his dogged if

---

LVIII (1897), 98–102, and summarized by R. Predelli, ed., *Regesti dei Commemoriali,* III (Venice, 1883), no. 343, p. 206. The negotiations continued (*op. cit.,* no. 348), and four years later the despot Theodore finally agreed to give up Argos (nos. 408–411, 413). Cf. *Chronicon breve,* ad ann. 6902 (1394), appended to Ducas's *Historia byzantina* (*CSHB,* p. 516).

88. Cf. Hopf, in Ersch and Gruber, LXXXVI (1868; repr., II, 1960), 51–52. The prohibition against the export of figs and currants, *que nascantur in terris et locis domini Nerii Romanie basse et ducaminis,* passed by the Venetian senate on June 22, 1389, was renewed with heavier penalties on September 1, 1390 (Misti, Reg. 41, fol. 101ʳ; Thiriet, *Régestes,* I, no. 778, p. 187), and retained for some time thereafter. In May 1391 James, the bishop of Argos, was in Venice seeking modification and clarification of the articles of agreement obtaining between Nerio and the republic (Misti, Reg. 42, fol. 1, dated May 26, and misdated in the summary of Thiriet, I, no. 792, p. 190).

89. Misti, Reg. 41, fol. 127ʳ, dated February 21, 1391, in the Venetian style: "Cum loca nostra Neapolis Romanie, Coroni et Mothoni multum opprimantur a Turchis et quotidie dicti Turchi capiant de nostris et vadant in cursum circa loca nostra predicta, et precipue tenent locum nostrum Neapolis sub tanta obsidione," the senate took steps to send a galley to relieve the Turkish "siege" of Nauplia, for no one dared to emerge from the town (cf. Thiriet, *Régestes,* I, no. 784, p. 189).

90. Lampros, *Eggrapha,* part II, doc. 7, p. 114, a letter to Donato Acciajuoli dated at Venice on July 30, 1394. Having broken with the Turks and being pressed by the Navarrese, the despot Theodore had seen the advantage of an accord with Venice, which was reached in the treaty of Modon dated May 27, 1394, by which he ceded Argos to the republic (for the text, see Lampros, *Eggrapha,* part V, doc. 10, pp. 374–385, especially pp. 379 ff., and cf. Zakythinos, *Le Despotat grec de Morée,* I, 138–143, and Loenertz, "Pour l'histoire du Péloponnèse . . . ," *Études byzantines,* I, 172–184).

confused policy of trying to obtain the principality of Achaea. Although he seemed to veer toward Nerio and the despot Theodore, he needed Venetian transport to get his troops to Greece. On August 12, 1390, the senate flatly declared "that he could not achieve his objective without coming to an understanding with the Navarrese,"[91] and Amadeo was quite prepared to do so. Some six weeks later, in actions of September 20–26, the senate agreed to carry a Piedmontese force of three hundred mounted lancers and six hundred foot or bowmen into the Morea, and Amadeo committed himself to helping the Venetians oust the despot from Argos by force if necessary.[92] The Venetians were of course no more concerned that Amadeo should become prince of Achaea than he was that they should acquire Argos. He exchanged envoys with Peter Bordo and the Navarrese, and finally reached an accord with them which took little or no stock of Venetian interests. But he quickly abandoned the Navarrese,[93] and turned once more to the ever-ready Nerio, who had taken up residence in Athens. On December 29, 1391, Nerio met with Amadeo's envoys in the palace chapel on the Acropolis, and as the "lord of Corinth, the duchy of Athens, and Neopatras" he recognized Amadeo, prince of Achaea, as his suzerain. Nerio now promised to drive the Navarrese from the Morea, and to enlist the aid of the despot Theodore in the undertaking, although he acknowledged his own commitment to the Venetians to wrest Argos from Theodore! He asked for the "restitution" of the Acciajuoli estates in the old castellany of Corinth (the lands of the grand seneschal Nicholas), and he made a special request for Vostitsa, which Amadeo's envoys assured him he would have.[94] Fortunately perhaps for Amadeo, as he boldly faced all four cardinal points of the diplomatic compass at the same time, the death of his namesake and supporter, Amadeo VII, the Red Count of Savoy (on November 1, 1391), deflected his attention to Piedmontese and Savoyard affairs. Amadeo never got to Greece, where he had made an alliance with almost everyone except the Turks.

---

91. Misti, Reg. 41, fol. 98[v].

92. Cessi, "Amedeo di Acaia," *Nuovo archivio veneto,* n.s., XXXVII, 24–27; Predelli, *Regesti dei Commemoriali,* III, no. 352, p. 209; Thiriet, *Régestes,* I, no. 779, pp. 187–188. About this time Amadeo wrote Theodore a letter assuring him of his princely affection, to which Theodore returned a courteous response (Miklosich and Müller, *Acta et diplomata,* III, 249–250).

93. Cf. Cessi, "Amedeo di Acaia," *Nuovo archivio veneto,* n.s., XXXVII, 35–36, 40.

94. Lampros, *Eggrapha,* part VI, doc. 1, pp. 405–407, also published by Cessi, *Nuovo archivio veneto,* XXXVII, 40–42. Nerio had purchased Vostitsa, together with Nivelet, from Marie of Bourbon, princess of Achaea, and her son Hugh of Galilee in 1364 (cf. Du Cange [ed. Buchon], *Constantinople,* II, 265; Buchon, *Recherches et matériaux,* I [1840], 347).

In his pact with Amadeo, Nerio claimed possession of Neopatras. He had presumably taken it from the Catalan castellan Andrew Zavall, but he soon lost it to the Turks. Sultan Bayazid I invaded central Greece toward the end of 1393 and the beginning of 1394. He occupied Neopatras and Livadia, and seized the county of Salona together with its dependencies of Zeitounion, Loidoriki, and Veteranitsa. Nerio must have received the news with trepidation. On February 20, 1394, he wrote his brother Donato from Corinth that the Gran Turco had descended into Greece from Thessalonica, taken Salona, and sent the much-wooed Maria Fadrique, daughter of countess Helena Cantacuzena, into his harem.[95] Now Nerio would have to pay tribute to the Turk for the Athenian duchy. To pope Boniface IX the situation in central Europe and in Greece looked desperate, and so it was: his holiness shuddered to think of what the Turks had done. A crusade was proclaimed to save eastern Christendom from the direst peril.[96]

Nerio Acciajuoli had reached the pinnacle of his career and was nearing the end of his life. Like the early Catalan dukes before him, however, he held Athens only by right of conquest. He was anxious to secure a more constitutional basis for his possession of the duchy. He turned to Italy, to Rome and Naples, for the legitimization of his position. King Ladislas of Naples, the young son of Charles III of Durazzo (d. 1386), still preserved the Angevin claim to the suzerainty of Achaea, upon which the duchy of Athens rested in feudal dependence. Recalling the great services which Nerio had allegedly rendered the house of Anjou-Durazzo, and professing to regard him as having wrested "the duchy of Athens, part of our principality of Achaea, . . . from the hands of some of our rivals," king Ladislas formally bestowed upon Nerio and the legitimate (male) heirs of his body, in perpetuity, the city and duchy of Athens with all the rights and appurtenances accruing to them. Louis Aliotti, archbishop of Athens, promised on Nerio's behalf to render the royal prince of Achaea whatever feudal service adhered by custom to the ducal fief, and at Gaeta on January 11, 1394, Ladislas invested his grace of Athens, as Nerio's proxy, with the fief by placing a ring on his finger.[97] Nerio, however, had

95. Gregorovius, "Corrispondenza Acciajoli," *Sitzungsb. d. Akad. zu München,* II, 307; *idem* (tr. Lampros), *Athens* [in Greek], II, 652; *Dipl.,* doc. DCXLIV, pp. 673–674. Contrary to Gregorovius, *loc. cit.,* this letter is not an autograph, as shown by the postscript which he failed to transcribe and apparently forgot. Chalcocondylas, *Historia,* II (*CSHB,* pp. 67–69; ed. Darkó, I, 62–63), gives a detailed account of the Turkish invasion and the fall of Helena—and of "a certain priest named Strates with whom she was in love"—which may be generally accurate, but the names he gives to the characters in his drama are peculiar (on which note Hopf, in Ersch and Gruber, LXXXVI [repr., II], 62, note 83).

96. O. Raynaldus, *Annales ecclesiastici,* ad ann. 1394, vol. VII (1752), pp. 584–585.

97. Buchon, II. *Florence:* doc. XLI, pp. 223–228; *Dipl.,* doc. DCXLIII, pp. 671–673, the

no legitimate male heirs; his only son, Antonio, was the child of his mistress Maria Rendi. On the next day therefore, with cardinal Angelo's consent, Ladislas provided that the Athenian succession should pass to Donato and the latter's legitimate sons "in case the said Nerio should depart this life without leaving legitimate male heirs of his body even if legitimate daughters should survive him," [98] which excluded Bartolommea, the wife of the despot Theodore, and Frances, who had married Charles I Tocco, the duke of Leucadia (Leucas, or Santa Maura) and count palatine of Cephalonia.

As in the days of the grand seneschal Nicholas a half century before, the Acciajuoli star seemed to be in the ascendant, and on January 14 king Ladislas appointed his "dearest friend" cardinal Angelo, then the apostolic legate and bailie of the Neapolitan kingdom, as his vicar in the principality of Achaea and the city of Lepanto with full jurisdiction over matters relating "both to justice and to war."[99] The Acciajuoli family had reached its height, but now it was stricken with misfortune. Nerio died suddenly, and his brother Donato lost the Athenian succession which Ladislas had just granted him. The sad news was contained in a letter which James, the bustling bishop of Argos, wrote at Nauplia on November 2, 1394, to Donato in Florence: ". . . With extreme bitterness of heart I inform your excellency that the magnificent lord Nerio, your excellency's brother, ended his last day on the 25th of the month of September just passed. And after his death the despot [Theodore] seized all the castles of the castellany of Corinth. He is even holding the fortress [Acrocorinth] and the city of Corinth under siege. Moreover, the bastard of the aforesaid lord Nerio [Antonio Acciajuoli, later duke of Athens] and Bertranet [Mota de Salahia, who was said in 1393 to be in possession of Livadia] [100] are wholeheartedly on the despot's side, and are staying with him in the field fighting against Corinth and your other places. Unless your lordship provides quick relief, the said despot will completely occupy the whole country acquired by your house up to now."[101]

---

diploma of investiture, with its usual wording. On June 1, 1398, Louis Aliotti was transferred from Athens to the see of Volterra, near Florence and Siena (Eubel, *Hierarchia catholica,* I, 115, 536, and cf. p. 349, note 10).

98. Buchon, II, *Florence:* doc. XLII, pp. 228–231.

99. Buchon, II, *Florence:* doc. XLIV, pp. 234–236.

100. *Dipl.,* docs. DCXXXVII–DCXXXIX, pp. 666–668, letters of king John I of Aragon, dated at Valencia on April 13, 1393, on which note Loenertz, *Arch. FF. Praed.,* XXV, no. 213, p. 154.

101. The letter appears to be unknown and unpublished (Univ. of Pennsylvania Library, Lea MS. 28-II, ep. 29). Its contents, however, are well known from a similar text sent by the bishop of Argos to cardinal Angelo, which has been rather carelessly published by Gregoro-

Eight days before his death, lying ill at Corinth, Nerio dictated his will, fearing perhaps that he had achieved success at the cost of salvation. He directed that his body be buried in the Parthenon, "the church of St. Mary of Athens—likewise we leave to the church of St. Mary of Athens the city of Athens, with all its appurtenances and effects." [102] His chief thought, in these last days, seems to have been for the Parthenon, for its cathedral staff, and for the masses he wanted said for his soul. He left the church his valuable stud of brood mares, and wanted the portals of the Parthenon, once adorned with silver, to be decked out in silver again; likewise all the jewels, vestments, gold, silver, and precious stones of which the church had been stripped to help ransom him from the Navarrese "should be repurchased and restored to the said church of Athens." In addition to the twelve canons who had served in the cathedral since the Catalan era,[103] Nerio provided for twenty priests, who were to be "Latins of the Catholic faith," to serve night and day, "and celebrate masses for the salvation of our soul." He wanted the income of the church and of the brood mares to be used for the support of the twenty priests, according to the discretion of the executors of his will, as well as for the fabric and general maintenance of the Parthenon. Since obviously neither the priests nor the executors of his will could defend Athens for St. Mary, Nerio placed the church and city "under the protection and guidance of the exalted and illustrious ducal signoria of Venice." [104]

Among other bequests, Nerio left Antonio Acciajuoli, his son by Maria Rendi, the castle of Livadia and his property therein, as well as the city of Thebes. To his elder daughter Bartolommea, who had married the despot of Mistra, Theodore I Palaeologus, Nerio left only the 9,700 ducats of gold "which the despot, her husband, took from the signoria of Venice." Nerio had made the sum good; Theodore had never repaid him. But what Bartolommea got, her husband got, and so Nerio directed that she should be allowed no other claim against his estate. He clearly entertained some animus against Theo-

---

vius, "Corrispondenza Acciajoli," *Sitzungsb. d. Akad. zu München,* II, 308–309, and cf. *idem* (trans. Lampros), *Athens* [in Greek] , II, 653–654, where the transcription is still poor.

102. The text of Nerio's will, dated at Corinth on September 17, 1394, may be found in Buchon, II, *Florence:* doc. XLVIII, pp. 254–261, and Lampros, *Eggrapha,* part III, doc. 4, pp. 146–152.

103. Cf. *Dipl.,* doc. CDXIV, p. 497, a letter of king Peter IV dated at Lerida on September 12, 1380: ". . . XII canonici ecclesie sedis de Cetines . . . ." There had also been a dozen canons on the cathedral staff of Thebes in the early thirteenth century (cf. Pietro Pressutti, *I Regesti del pontefice Onorio III,* I [Rome, 1884], no. 331, p. 93, and *Regesta Honorii Papae III,* I [Rome, 1888], no. 356, p. 63).

104. Lampros, *Eggrapha,* pp. 147–148; Buchon, II, 255.

dore, and he had good reason for doing so. As for Bartolommea, she was reputed to surpass in beauty all the women of her time.[105] Obviously the Acciajuoli had done quite enough for Theodore. Nerio made his daughter Frances his chief heiress—possibly because he had had no trouble with her husband, Charles Tocco, who thus stood to gain most from the success of the Acciajuoli in Greece. Frances was to receive immediately "peaceful possession" of the castle of Megara, the Basilicata (the ancient Sicyon), and 30,000 hyperpers in money and jewels. She was in fact to receive all Nerio's lands except those which went to others by specific bequests. If she had had children by the time of his death, she was to take over these lands immediately, but in any event they were to become hers in three years. Finally, Frances was to receive Corinth if the grand seneschal Robert Acciajuoli, son of the Angelo who had mortgaged the city to Nerio, did not wish "to repay the money which he owes me."[106] Nerio's wife Agnes de' Saraceni was already dead, and so he had no need to make provision for her. Nerio had apparently already promised the despot Theodore the eventual occupancy of Corinth as part of Bartolommea's dowry, but he had in effect left the city and its towering fortress to Frances's husband, Charles Tocco of Leucadia and Cephalonia.[107] He had lived amid warfare and wealth through most of his years in Greece, and now he passed them both on to his heirs.

Nerio named seven executors of his will, including the duchess Frances, bishop James of Argos, and Matthew of Montona, his castellan of the Acropolis. Should any one of the legatees wish to deprive Frances of any of the bequests her father thus left her, Nerio directed that he be considered a "traitor, and deprived of every legacy that we have left him." He was doubtless thinking of the despot, and assumed that he would attack Corinth. Inventories of his properties were to be made, and each of the seven executors was to have one. Finally, Nerio commended his lands to the signoria of Venice, and the signoria to his executors, who should look to Venice when they needed help, and "the said executors are to do every honor to the said signoria," on whose integrity he had to rely for the protection of Frances's rights.[108]

105. Chalcocondylas, *Historia*, IV (*CSHB*, p. 208; ed. Darkò, I, 195).

106. Lampros, *Eggrapha*, pp. 150–151; Buchon, II, 258–260.

107. Cf. Chalcocondylas, *Historia*, IV (*CSHB*, pp. 207–208, 213; ed. Darkó, I, 194–195, 200). However, according to Niccolò Serra, *Storia di Zante* [1784], ed. Hopf, *Chroniques gréco-romanes*, p. 342, "Si unì poscia [Carlo de' Tocchi] in seconde nozze a Francesca figlia di Reniero o Neri Acciajuoli duca di Atene colla promessa della signoria di Corinto dopo la morte del di lei padre, il quale in fatti morendo le lasciò in eredità questa porzione de' suoi stati."

108. Lampros, *Eggrapha*, pp. 151–152; Buchon, II, 259–261.

As soon as Nerio's death was known, the despot Theodore overran Corinthia and seized all the castles in the castellany. As we have seen, bishop James of Argos sent the news from Nauplia on November 2 to Nerio's brother Donato in Florence (and to cardinal Angelo as well), reporting that Theodore was laying siege to the fortress city of Corinth, where Nerio's son Antonio and Bertranet de Salahia had taken the field with him, being "wholeheartedly on the despot's side." Charles Tocco was already in Corinth. Probably the dying Nerio had assisted in the changing of the guard. We are fortunate enough to have a contemporary description of events written by the industrious notary Nicholas of Martoni, from the small town of Carinola, near Capua, who spent February 24 and 25 (1395) in Athens on his way back from a pilgrimage to the Holy Land. Nicholas informs us, "We could not get to the city of Corinth by land because of the widespread fighting then going on between the duke of Cephalonia and the despot of the Morea, brother of the emperor of Constantinople, over the lands left by the lord Nerio, duke of Athens, who was the father-in-law of the said duke and despot. The duke had on his side a large armed force of Turks, and was allied with the lord Turk against the said despot." [109]

Nicholas and his party went on, therefore, "as far as the castle of Megara, which the said duke of Cephalonia had recently taken over on behalf of his wife, a daughter of the lord Nerio . . . , [but] which we could not enter, because the castle was under tight guard for fear of the despot of the Morea, who was trying to get it from the duke, his brother-in-law, on behalf of *his* wife, who was likewise a daughter of the said lord Nerio. . . . Sailors told us we could not get into Corinth without the greatest personal danger on account of the troops of the despot, . . . who shortly before had put the said city of Corinth under siege with a great army, about 20,000 men bearing arms, trying to acquire the city for his wife [Bartolommea] as the lord Nerio's first-born daughter. The duke, perceiving that he could not withstand the might of the despot, his brother-in-law, joined with the Turk against the despot, and so a Turkish force, about 40,000 horse, came over one night to Corinth, and suddenly fell upon the camp of the despot's troops, broke it up, scattered all his people, and captured about 3,000 of the despot's horse. The despot himself barely escaped capture. . . ." [110]

109. Léon Legrand, ed., "Relation du pèlerinage à Jérusalem de Nicolas de Martoni, notaire italien," *Revue de l'Orient latin,* III (Paris, 1895; repr. Brussels, 1964), 649 [concerning Nicholas's arrival in Athens on February 24, 1395], 652–653. In Nicholas's time Acrocorinth was itself the city of Corinth, as his account makes clear (pp. 658–659). On his description of Athens, cf. Setton, *Catalan Domination,* pp. 227–232.

110. Legrand, "Relation . . . ," in *Revue de l'Orient latin,* III, 653–657.

Although Nicholas of Martoni's account suggests that Charles Tocco was determined to hold on to his wife's Corinthian inheritance, he was finally obliged to give way. Shortly after Nicholas and his companions left Corinth, Charles Tocco offered both the Corinthian citadel and that of Megara to Venice "for a certain sum of money," as the bailie and councillors of Negroponte informed the senate in letters dated May 15 (1395). The senate distrusted him, and hesitated to accept his offer, [111] but Tocco was presumably quite willing to sell what he could not hold. Finally yielding, however, to military necessity or political expediency (or to both), he surrendered Acrocorinth to Theodore Palaeologus, who reëstablished the Greek metropolitan see, and had his statue set up by the main gate with a metrical inscription recalling his imperial descent and celebrating his prowess in wresting the city from the "western Italians." [112]

As Nerio Acciajuoli had faced the prospect of the next world, he seems to have lost his sense of the practicable in this one. St. Mary could not govern Athens, and the castellan Matthew of Montona was afraid that she was not going to protect the Acropolis. Continental Greece and the Morea were alive with Turks. Sultan Bayazid I had taken Salona, supported Theodore Palaeologus against the Venetians, and was now assisting Charles Tocco against Theodore. As the Latins diminished in numbers and strength, Montona appealed for support to Andrew Bembo, the Venetian bailie of Negroponte. He proposed that the republic take over the Acropolis, see to the fulfilment of the terms of Nerio's will, and maintain the Athenians in the possession of their rights and privileges. Bembo accepted Montona's offer, subject to the approval of the home government, and from the end of the year 1394 a Venetian garrison manned the defenses on the Acropolis. Montona had also sent one Leonard of Bologna as his envoy to Venice, and after "several months," on March 18, 1395, the senate voted to take over the city of Athens, for if it were to end up in Turkish or other hands, it might be the destruction of the rich island of Euboea. The Venetian rectors would be instructed to observe all the franchises, liberties, privileges, and rights of the Athenians, while Montona was to receive an annual pension of 400 hyperpers for life, and Leonard of Bologna 200, "from the revenues of the said city." [113]

111. Misti, Reg. 43, fol. 75^r, dated July 23, 1395. Of course Tocco promised the senate to behave himself, but he was hard to deal with (*ibid.*, fols. 78^r, 78^v, 120^r, 120^v, 123^r). Cf. Thiriet, *Régestes*, I, nos. 883, 886, 905, pp. 208, 209, 212–213.

112. Zakythinos, *Le Despotat grec de Morée*, I, 144–145; Lampros, Παλαιολόγεια καὶ Πελοποννησιακά, IV (1930), 11.

113. On August 19, 1400, the Venetian senate assigned Leonard's pension at his own

Although these provisions for Montona and Leonard did not cause serious difficulty in the senate, there was some disagreement concerning the terms under which Venice should add Athens to her Greek possessions. The motion was thus made "that the lordship of the said city of Athens be received and taken up for rule and governance by our signoria according to the form and testament of the lord Nerio Acciajuoli, but because his stud of brood mares, which have been stolen, now fails us, and from this source the said church was drawing the greater part of its revenues and the necessary expenses were to be met therefrom, and also because the times are critical, and the said city of Athens requires a larger garrison and expenditures [for defense] than if the times were peaceful, . . . let it be established that for the present there shall be assigned to the celebration of divine offices in the church of St. Mary of Athens only eight priests. . . ." [114]

The Venetians were more interested in saving Athens than Nerio's soul, and probably no new priests were added at all to the cathedral staff of the Parthenon. In any event, appointment to the governorship of Athens was not an attractive prospect, whether because of the Turkish danger or not, and on April 20 (1395) the salary for the position was raised from 60 to 70 pounds, "because all those who have been elected podestà and captains of the city of Athens have declined [to go]," [115] paying very likely the accustomed pen-

---

request to his aged father, who lived in Venice (Misti, Reg. 45, fol. 26ᵛ, text published by C. N. Sathas, *Documents inédits relatifs à l'histoire de la Grèce au moyen âge,* II [Paris, 1881], no. 224, p. 8). Matthew of Montona is not identified as a Venetian in the documents, but may have come from Montona in Istria where the republic sometimes maintained a podestà (Archivio di Stato di Venezia, Mar, Reg. 4, fol. 34ʳ, dated January 18, 1451). Very little of Montona's pension was actually paid (Sathas, II, no. 220, pp. 6–7, and see below).

114. Misti, Reg. 43, fols. 50ᵛ–51ʳ, published by F. Gregorovius, "Die erste Besitznahme Athens durch die Republik Venedig," *Sitzungsb. d. Akad. zu München,* I (1888), 152–156, especially p. 155, and *idem,* trans. Lampros, *Athens* [in Greek], II (1904), 621–624, and cf. Max Silberschmidt, *Das orientalische Problem zur Zeit der Entstehung des türkischen Reiches nach venezianischen Quellen [1381–1400]* (Leipzig and Berlin, 1923), pp. 94–95. The summary of the document in Thiriet, *Régestes,* I, no. 872, is both inadequate and inaccurate.

This motion received 11 votes of approval, 5 in opposition, with 17 (and 15) uncommitted votes (*non sinceri*). If the uncommitted votes amounted to a majority of those cast, a motion was defeated, and was not in fact resubmitted as a doubtful issue for resolution at the next meeting of the senate. Such was presumably the case here, and at any rate the register (Misti, Reg. 43, fol. 51ʳ) does not carry in the left-hand margin the upright cross which indicates senatorial approval of a motion and implies that steps were taken to put it into effect. Although Nerio's will had provided for twenty priests to say masses for his soul, the senate was apparently unwilling to maintain even eight. On the passage of a "motion" (*parte*) into a *decreto* by the senate, cf. Giuseppe Maranini, *La Costituzione di Venezia dopo la serrata del Maggior Consiglio* (Perugia, 1931), especially pp. 255–258. Votes *non sinceri* were not "abstentions"; every senator present at a given session was required by law to vote.

115. Misti, Reg. 43, fol. 52ᵛ, senatorial decision dated April 20, 1395.

alty for refusal. By July 18, however, Albano Contarini had been chosen for the post, and had accepted it.[116] He became "podestà and captain of our city of Athens" for two years with the higher annual salary of 70 pounds; he was cautioned to exercise a day-and-night vigilance lest anything untoward occur in the city and also to respect local rites and customs. If he found Athenian resources inadequate for the defense of the city, he was to have recourse to the castellans of Coron and Modon and the colonial government of Negroponte. The senate provided twenty archers or crossbowmen and two officers "for the defense and security of the said castle." [117]

For some time after the Venetians took over the Acropolis their chief concern was the Turks, on whose activities the bailie of Negroponte sent worrisome reports to the senate. Athens was threatened as well as Euboea, and the plodding efforts of Venetian envoys and officials could find no answer to the perennial question of Turkish assault. [118] It is sometimes stated that the Turks occupied the lower city of Athens in the spring or summer of 1397, but the evidence for assuming so is hardly conclusive. [119] It is of course quite possible. The Turks did take Argos on June 3, 1397, sacked and burned the city, and are said to have carried off fourteen thousand persons into slavery. [120] Meetings of the Venetian senate were sad occasions as the news kept coming throughout the spring and summer of 1398

116. Misti, Reg. 43, fol. 71^r.

117. Misti, Reg. 43, fol. 76^v, publ. by Gregorovius, *Sitzungsb. d. Akad. zu München*, I, 156–158; *idem* (tr. Lampros), *Athens*, II, 624–626; Thiriet, *Régestes*, I, no. 885, p. 208; and cf. H. Noiret, *Documents inédits . . . de la domination vénitienne en Crète* (Paris, 1892), pp. 69, 71. Albano Contarini's commission is undated; the preceding entry in the Misti, *ibid.*, fol. 76^r, is dated August 8 (1395), not July 27, as stated by Gregorovius. Contarini was succeeded as governor of Athens by Lorenzo Venier (in 1397), Ermalao Contarini (1399), and Nicholas Vitturi (1400). By July 18, 1399, Albano Contarini had been appointed podestà and captain of Nauplia, and was to take over what was left of the government of Argos (Misti, Reg. 44, fol. 115^v).

118. Misti, Reg. 43, fol. 76^r, senatorial resolution dated August 3, 1395; cf. Thiriet, *Régestes*, I, no. 896, pp. 210–211.

119. Late Turkish sources place the obviously brief (if true) occupation of the lower city of Athens both before and after the battle of Nicopolis (September 25, 1396). Since some of these sources, however, identify Timurtash Pasha as the "conqueror" of the city, and since the also late but generally reliable *Chronicon breve,* ad ann. 6905, appended to Ducas's *Historia byzantina* (CSHB, p. 516), places Timurtash Pasha's Moreote campaign in June 1397 when Argos was taken, J. H. Mordtmann, "Die erste Eroberung von Athen durch die Türken zu Ende des 14. Jahrhunderts," *Byzantinisch-Neugriechische Jahrbücher*, IV (1923), 346–350, would date the so-called first Turkish occupation of Athens in 1397. Timurtash Pasha appears as Μουρτάσης in the text of the *Chronicon breve*, which does not mention any sojourn of Turkish forces in Athens, and (more to the point) the Venetian senate seems to have known nothing about it.

120. The fall of Argos to the Turks was known in Venice by July 5 (Misti, Reg. 44, fol. 10^r): "Castellanis nostris Coroni et Mothoni scribatur qualiter displicenter audivimus casum ammissionis civitatis nostre Argolicensis . . . ," which posed a threat to Coron and Modon

that the Turks were also harassing Euboea and the Aegean islands, [121] and that a serious plague was sweeping through the Morea and through Crete, [122] the sixth great pestilence to strike the Morea and the islands since the Black Death of 1348.

The despot Theodore Palaeologus feared the Turks more than the plague. In 1397 he sold the important citadel of Corinth (which he had just taken from his Latin brother-in-law Charles Tocco) as well as some other strongholds to the Hospitallers, reserving of course the right of repurchase. [123] He believed the Hospitallers could defend Corinth better than he, but he was able to redeem the city and his other strongholds in 1404 after the battle of Ankara and the Christian pact with Suleiman, the emir of Adrianople. In the meantime, however, fear of the Turk was the mainspring of almost every political decision or social enterprise in Greece.

Venetian galleys and cogs continued their usual runs to Trebizond, Syria, and Egypt, and the usual profits were made in spices, wine, grain, sugar, silk, furs, cotton, hemp, and jewels. It was big business. The Patras trade alone amounted to some 80,000 ducats during the first eight or nine months of 1400, [124] but there was a mounting dread of the Turk. Conditions had become so bad in the Morea toward the end of the year 1399 that the despot Theodore sent a Greek monk to Venice, requesting asylum for himself and his family. The senate was willing to let bygones be bygones, and the Palaeologi could take up residence in Venice if Theodore made some amends for the losses he and his people had caused Venetian subjects in the past. [125] Now, on August 3, 1400, one Nicholas Vitturi was in

---

(cf. Thiriet, *Régestes,* I, no. 936, p. 219). See Chalcocondylas, *Historia,* II (*CSHB,* pp. 97–99), and Gregorovius (trans. Lampros), *Athens,* II, 265. The Venetians had been cautiously pressing anti-Turkish plans upon king Sigismund of Hungary and the Byzantine emperor Manuel II (Thiriet, I, nos. 931–932, p. 218). By a decree of the senate of July 27, 1399, all the remaining inhabitants of Argos were to be repatriated, if possible, and those who returned were to be exempt for five years from all service except guard duty on the walls—there were many *territoria vacua* in which they could build houses (Misti, Reg. 44, fol. 119[r]; summary in Thiriet, *Régestes,* I, no. 967, p. 224).

121. Misti, Reg. 44, fols. 43[v]–44[r], 61[v]–62[r], 67[v].

122. Misti, Reg. 44, fols. 42[v], 57[v], and cf. Loenertz, "La Chronique brève moréote de 1423," *Mélanges Eugène Tisserant,* II-1, 425, and *Chronicon breve,* ad ann. 6907 (Sept. 1398–Aug. 1399; *CSHB,* p. 517).

123. Loenertz, "Pour l'histoire du Péloponnèse . . . ," *Études byzantines,* I, 186–196, and cf. Zakythinos, *Le Despotat grec de Morée,* I, 158–160.

124. Misti, Reg. 45, fol. 33[r], senatorial resolution dated September 10, 1400: the Venetian captain of the gulf was to provide an escort of armed galleys for merchantmen (summary in Thiriet, *Régestes,* II [1959], no. 993, p. 13). A year later the goods bonded at Patras were said to be worth 60,000 to 70,000 ducats (*ibid.,* II, no. 1030, p. 21).

125. Theodore asked the senate (Misti, Reg. 44, fol. 133[v], dated December 30, 1399) "ut dignaremur sibi salvum conductum facere pro se, uxore, filiis nobilibus suis, et rebus et

Venice, preparing to set out with his family for Athens; he would go first to Negroponte, whence a galley would take him to Piraeus. [126] He was to be the last Venetian governor to reside on the Acropolis.

Although Timur the Lame and his warriors were mounting a huge offensive against the Ottomans, and sultan Bayazid was collecting reinforcements against them, the Turkish menace remained. The senate lamented the terrible razzias upon the region of Coron and Modon, [127] which took place even while the Ottoman government at Adrianople was preparing to meet Timur's onslaught. On September 20, 1401, the Venetian senate authorized Nicholas Vitturi to spend 200 hyperpers to repair the walls, [128] presumably on the defenses of the Acropolis, because such a paltry sum would hardly improve the fortifications of the lower city, where a determined enemy was about to strike.

Antonio Acciajuoli, the bastard son of Nerio and Maria Rendi, suddenly swooped down upon Athens in force. His seizure of the lower city (in part at least) and his siege of the Acropolis were known in Venice well before August 22, 1402, when the Venetian senate decided to take drastic action against him. Letters were dispatched to the colonial government of Negroponte, authorizing an increase of the cavalry force at its command "from 200 to 300 beyond the fifty for which permission was previously accorded the said government." With this force, and with the bowmen and foot soldiers which they could raise locally, the bailie and councillors of Negroponte were to strive manfully "for the recovery of our city of Athens and for the injury and destruction of Antonio Acciajuoli and of Thebes and his other possessions." They were to strengthen the Acropolis and see to the supplies of munitions and food. [129] Save Athens, destroy Thebes, remove Antonio Acciajuoli. It was all easier said than done.

Francis Bembo had the misfortune to be the bailie and captain of Negroponte at this time (1401–1402). Gathering together all the

---

bonis quibuscumque suis ita quod . . . possit cum securitate et sine aliqua molestia ad civitatem nostram Venetiarum venire . . ." (summary in Thiriet, *Régestes,* I, no. 972, p. 224). Emperor Manuel II was also thinking of a Venetian refuge (Thiriet, II, no. 978, p. 10, and N. Iorga, "Notes et extraits," *Revue de l'Orient latin,* IV [1896, repr. 1964], 228).

126. Misti, Reg. 45, fol. 25^v, text in Sathas, *Documents inédits,* II, no. 222, p. 7.

127. Sathas, II, no. 235, p. 17, dated March 1, 1401. The Venetians followed Timur's progress with close attention (Iorga, "Notes et extraits," *Revue de l'Orient latin,* IV, 238 ff., 243, 245, 248–249, 254, 266 ff., 272).

128. Sathas, II, no. 256, p. 45.

129. Sathas, II, no. 310, pp. 91–92.

forces he could, he clearly took up the cudgels before receiving additional funds and final instructions from Venice. According to Chalcocondylas, Bembo marched with six thousand men from Negroponte against Thebes while Antonio Acciajuoli, when he heard of the Venetian advance, divided his men into two bands with not more than three hundred in each, and, in an unidentified pass, he caught Bembo's troopers in ambush, closed the entrance and exit to the pass, "and many of them he killed, others he captured, and he captured those who were then in command of their territory." Thereupon he returned to the siege of Athens, where treachery now opened the gates to one whose mother was Greek. Shortly thereafter he occupied the Acropolis, "and then he was lord of Attica as well as of Boeotia." [130]

On October 7, 1402, gloomy senators gathered in the doge's palace on the Bacino to consider what they should do next, "because this new development, the capture of [Francis Bembo,] our bailie and captain of Negroponte, and of the entire force which was with him, is as hard as it can be and puts the city and island in a very dangerous position." The bad news had just come in a letter dated September 5 from the castellans of Coron and Modon. [131] Since Antonio Acciajuoli was known to work hand in glove with the Turks, [132] the senate drafted elaborate plans to meet the emergency. On October 8, however, more reassuring news reached Venice, obviously to the effect that neither Antonio nor the Turks had made or seemed to be preparing any attack upon Negroponte, and so the senate decided to "proceed in these matters with fuller deliberation than before." [133] Discussion was now revolving around the election of a *provveditore* for Negroponte. Thomas Mocenigo was chosen in due course, and set out for Modon, where the captain of the gulf was instructed to meet him, and where they could plan in full detail the defense of Negroponte. [134] By the end of the month (on October 30, 1402) the Venetian government had decided to try to negotiate "with the illustrious Antonio Acciajuoli, lord of Thebes, or with his commis-

---

130. Chalcocondylas, *Historia,* IV (*CSHB,* pp. 213–215; ed. Darkó, I, 200–201).
131. Sathas, II, no. 315, p. 101, lines 31 ff.
132. Cf. Chalcocondylas, *Historia,* IV (*CSHB,* p. 215; ed. Darkó, I, 201–202).
133. Sathas, II, no. 315, pp. 95–97, 99–100.
134. Sathas, II, p. 104. The Ottoman involvement with the hordes of Timur made some shifts likely in the axes of Levantine power, *propter mutationes et momenta que fient deinde occasione conflictus Turchorum* (*ibid.,* p. 102); Timur had overwhelmed sultan Bayazid I at Ankara in late July 1402, and the news was known in Venice before October 9 when the senate wrote the Byzantine emperor Manuel II *animo iocundanti* of the Ottoman defeat (Misti, Reg. 46, fol. 47ᵛ, and Iorga, "Notes et extraits," *Revue de l'Orient latin,* IV, 254).

sioners and procurators a peace, agreement, or truce." [135]   On the same day the senate voted Mocenigo 1,700 ducats for the large expenses he could anticipate, and directed him to confer with Antonio, with whom the republic wished to be at peace. Mocenigo was to see to the recovery of Athens and to arrange for the exchange of prisoners. If Antonio would not relax his siege of the city, the officials of Negroponte would resume the war against him. [136]   Of course it would have to be war. Words would not be enough to lift the siege of Athens, and (as events proved) even war was not enough.

Nicholas Vitturi, the podestà and captain of Athens, and Matthew of Montona, the late Nerio's onetime castellan, were finally forced to surrender the Acropolis to Antonio Acciajuoli. A later document (from the spring of 1409) says that Vitturi had defended the citadel for about seventeen months, and was under siege for most of the time. He would never have given up (we are told) had it been possible to get men and food to him. The garrison had eaten every horse but those in the Parthenon sculptures. Shortly after his withdrawal from Athens, Vitturi had died in Negroponte as a consequence of the privations he had suffered. He left his widow, a son, and a seventeen-year-old daughter "in great poverty . . . , [and] the said Antonio Acciajuoli never restored his possessions, which were of no small value." The republic had to come to their aid. [137]   Montona, whose Athenian pension of 400 hyperpers (voted him on March 18, 1394) had never been paid "except for a hundred hyperpers or thereabouts," [138]   would be invested with a fief on the island of Euboea "at the pleasure of our signoria" (on April 1, 1404), [139]   from which

135. Sathas, I (1880), no. 4, pp. 4–5; Lampros, *Eggrapha,* part V, doc. 14, pp. 392–393. On Antonio I Acciajuoli, see Giambattista Ubaldini, "Origine della famiglia delli Acciaioli," in his *Istoria della casa degli Ubaldini* (Florence, 1588), pp. 176–177, on which however cf. Setton, *Catalan Domination,* pp. 245–246.

136. Misti, Reg. 46, fol. 52[v], dated October 30, 1402. If Mocenigo and the councillors of Negroponte could get back the lower city of Athens, they were to try to learn the names of the traitors (*proditores*) who had assisted Antonio to take it. Iorga, "Notes et extraits," *Revue de l'Orient latin,* IV, 256–257, has noted this text, which he misdates November 3. Mocenigo kept the senate well informed, but obviously could not prevail upon Antonio to abandon the siege of Athens. On February 10, 1403, the senate instructed Bernard Foscarini, the new bailie and captain of Negroponte, to investigate conditions in Attica and to try once more to deal with Antonio (Misti, Reg. 46, fol. 65). The senate wished Foscarini to come to some "treuguae et sufferentiae" with Antonio for a period of some months, but by this time Antonio had probably taken the Acropolis.

137. Archivio di Stato di Venezia, Grazie, Reg. 20 [originally no. 17, Oct. 1407–Jan. 1416 according to the Venetian style], fol. 14[r] by modern enumeration [formerly fol. 31[r]], of which a small part has been published by Iorga, "Notes et extraits," *Revue de l'Orient latin,* IV, 303.

138. Sathas, II, no. 220, pp. 6–7, dated July 16, 1400.

139. Grazie, Reg. 19 [originally no. 16, March 1401–Jan. 1405 according to the Venetian style], fol. 44[r]. The document has suffered from dampness.

grant he might draw a slender living for the signal service he had rendered the republic. The precise date of Antonio Acciajuoli's occupation of the Acropolis is still unknown, but it probably came in January or February of 1403. [140]

The Venetians were determined to regain Athens in order to ensure the safety of their colony at Negroponte, and in the rapid flow of events they thought they saw their opportunity. On July 28, 1402, near Ankara, the redoubtable Bayazid I "the Thunderbolt," the victor at Nicopolis, was defeated by Timur the Lame, was captured, and died the following March in the conqueror's camp in Karamania. Constantinople was spared for another half century. Suleiman, the westernized emir in Adrianople, the eldest of Bayazid's four surviving sons, now appeared to have become the arbiter of Athens' destiny. The Venetians turned to him for help to regain the city, and Antonio Acciajuoli turned to him for support to keep what he had won. The Ottoman Turks were dismayed by the startling successes of Timur's hordes in Anatolia, "for going from one city to another," according to the historian Ducas, "they left such a wilderness where a city had been that one did not hear the barking of a single dog, the crow of a cock, or the cry of a child." [141] Now, as the maritime powers seemed to be closing their ranks, the Ottoman Turks became ready to listen to Christian overtures. At least Suleiman was willing to do so, and in 1403 he made a treaty of commerce and a pact of alliance against Timur with Venice, Genoa, the Byzantine emperor, the duke of Naxos, and the Hospitallers on the island of Rhodes, agreeing among other conditions to return Thessalonica to the Byzantines, to grant the high contracting parties the right to trade in his domains, and to give Athens back to the Venetians. [142]

As the sons of Bayazid got ready to fight among themselves, Timur turned eastward, and began preparations for an invasion not of Europe but of China. His exploits had startled the world, and knowledge of them had spread to every distant corner of Christen-

140. Peter Zeno, who was trying to conclude the Christian treaty of alliance with the emir Suleiman of Adrianople, early in 1403, reported about the same time to the Venetian government "che Antuonio Azaiuoli haveva habudo lo castelo de Sitine [Athens] e tegniva ancora i vostri prisoni [presumably including Francis Bembo, the former bailie of Negroponte] ..." (Iorga, "Notes et extraits," *Revue de l'Orient latin,* IV, 259).

141. Ducas, *Historia byzantina,* XVII (*CSHB,* pp. 76–77).

142. L. de Mas Latrie, "Commerce et expéditions militaires de la France et de Venise au moyen âge," in the *Collection de documents inédits sur l'histoire de France: Mélanges historiques,* III (Paris, 1880), no. XXII, pp. 178–182, esp. article 17, p. 181; Thomas, *Diplomatarium veneto-levantinum,* II, no. 159, p. 292; Iorga, "Notes et extraits," *Revue de l'Orient latin,* IV, 82, note 3, and 258–262, 268–269; and cf. Hopf, in Ersch and Gruber, LXXXVI (repr., II), 71a; Gregorovius (trans. Lampros), *Athens* [in Greek], II, 275–276; Wm. Miller, *Latins in the Levant* (London, 1908), p. 361.

dom. King Martin I of Aragon-Catalonia was sadly aware of Timur's destruction of Damascus (in January 1401), where there had been a colony of Catalan merchants. [143] He congratulated Manuel II upon Timur's destruction of Bayazid, the archenemy of Byzantium. [144] But king Martin looked with yearning, he wrote pope Benedict XIII, "to the confusion and final overthrow of that overweening Belial called 'Temorla' [Timurlenk], adherent of the Mohammedan sect," who had spread death and destruction everywhere before him, taken Smyrna and other strongholds from the Hospitallers with such fire and sword "that nothing of these places has remained except smoke and ashes." [145] Nevertheless, when Martin received a letter from Timur, he returned an answer in fulsome praise of the conqueror's incredible victories. [146] It was no longer necessary, however, either to fear Timur or to praise him, for on February 19, 1405, he died at Samarkand.

In the meantime Suleiman, who ruled European Turkey, had made no effort to oust Antonio Acciajuoli from Athens and to effect the restitution of the city to the Venetians. Antonio's relatives in Italy could again take pride in the possession of the Athenian duchy by one who bore their name. Angelo Acciajuoli, cardinal-bishop of Ostia and Velletri, dean of the sacred college, sent an envoy to Venice, as did Antonio himself, and the senate had much occasion to consider the problem of "our land of Athens." [147] Cardinal Angelo enlisted the aid of pope Innocent VII. King Ladislas, upon whose head Angelo had placed the crown of Naples fifteen years before, also supported Antonio's claim to the duchy which his majesty had professed to bestow upon Nerio a decade before. The Venetians were experts at diplomatic fencing, but on March 31, 1405, the Acciajuoli finally carried the day. An agreement was reached at Venice whereby Antonio was pardoned for all the losses and injuries he had inflicted upon the republic, which removed a price from his head and conceded "that Antonio should rule, have and hold and possess the land, castle, and city of Athens, in modern times called Sythines." As the ally and faithful son of the republic, Antonio was to send the church of St. Mark every Christmas a silk pallium worth not less than one hundred ducats. He promised to make the friends and foes of the republic his own, to pay for the munitions he had found on the

---

143. *Dipl.*, docs. DCLXVIII, DCXCI, pp. 693, 713.

144. *Dipl.*, doc. DCLXXVII, p. 699, dated June 27, 1403.

145. *Dipl.*, doc. DCLXXII, p. 695, dated March 5, 1403.

146. *Dipl.*, docs. DCLXXIX, DCLXXX, pp. 700–701, letters to Timur and his son dated April 1, 1404.

147. Misti, Reg. 46, fol. 120^r, dated January 29, 1404.

Acropolis when he had taken the citadel, to restore to the heirs of
Nicholas Vitturi (the former governor of Athens) the goods he had
seized from him at the time of the surrender, and to ban forever
from his domain the erstwhile Greek metropolitan Macarius, who
had preferred the Turkish crescent to the Latin cross, and who had
apparently contrived to escape from his imprisonment in Venice. The
marquis of Bodonitsa, as a citizen of the republic, was included in
the pact, the infraction of which was to carry a penalty of 10,000
ducats. [148] But Antonio Acciajuoli neither sent St. Mark his pallia
nor restored Vitturi's property, and the Venetians found him neither
a dutiful son nor a loyal friend. [149]

On July 23, 1406, for example, the senators who had gathered in
their chamber at the doge's palace condemned Antonio's occupation
of territory on the mainland opposite Negroponte which had been
guaranteed to the republic in the Turkish peace of 1403. The
motion, which was carried with only two negative and seven uncommitted votes, declared Antonio's aggression against the republic "absolutely intolerable . . . , but we are the more aggrieved considering
how benignly and courteously we have received Antonio into our
favor and made him the concession of our city of Athens forgetting
the injuries and losses he has inflicted on our subjects." [150]

Although to the Florentines the title *duca d'Atene* will always
suggest the younger Walter of Brienne, who attained to lordship over
Florence for a brief period, though never over Athens, their country-
man Antonio I Acciajuoli was for some thirty-three years the duke of
Athens (1403–1435). His was the longest rule in the medieval
history of the illustrious city; the title he commonly bore was that of
"lord of Athens, Thebes, of all the duchy and its dependencies." [151]
Antonio's long rule was comparatively prosperous and peaceful. He

148. Commemoriali, X, fols. 3–4ᵛ, summarized in Predelli, *Regesti dei Commemoriali*,
III, bk. X, no. 2, pp. 309–310; Gregorovius, *Stadt Athen*, II (Stuttgart, 1889), 273–275;
idem (tr. Lampros), *Athens* [in Greek], II, 277–279.

149. Sathas, *Documents inédits*, II, nos. 365, 382, 420, pp. 135, 148–149, 183–184;
Hopf, in Ersch and Gruber, LXXXVI (repr., II), 71–72; Miller, *Latins in the Levant*, pp.
361–362.

150. Misti, Reg. 47, fols. 60ᵛ–61ʳ. Antonio had never sent the pallia he had promised to
St. Mark's church, to which the senate obviously attached much symbolic importance (*ibid.*,
fol. 61ʳ). The first pallium was apparently presented in August 1407 (*ibid.*, fol. 131ʳ;
Sathas, II, no. 420, p. 184).

151. Buchon, *Nouvelles recherches historiques*, II (1845), *Florence:* doc. LXVIII, p. 289;
cf. doc. LXIX, p. 290, and doc. LXXI, pp. 296–297, the latter being a document of Antonio's
successor Nerio II; and note Nerio II's employment of the title *dominus Athenarum et
Thebarum* (*ibid.*, docs. LXXII and LXXIII, pp. 298–299). Iorga summarizes a text referring
to Nerio II, *qui est dominus Stives et Sithines* (i.e., of Thebes and Athens), in "Notes et
extraits," *Revue de l'Orient latin*, VIII (1900–1901), 78.

never forgot that he was a Florentine, and Florence was becoming, in competition with Genoa and Venice, a great commercial power, whose galleys were plying the waters of the eastern Mediterranean in search of some share of the wealth of the Levant. In 1406 Florence had conquered the rival city of Pisa, where Catalan merchants abounded; in 1421 she purchased from the Genoese, hard pressed in their war with the duke of Milan, the port city of Leghorn (Livorno). [152] On June 22, 1422, the Florentines instructed one of their citizens, Thomas Alderotti, to seek trading rights, "as good as those of the Venetians and the Genoese," from "the magnificent Antonio Acciajuoli, lord of Corinth in Romania." [153] Although the magnificent Antonio was not, and had never been, lord of Corinth, he was glad to acknowledge his Florentine origin and that of his family, and he granted to the most puissant signoria of Florence the same trading rights possessed in his domains by the "Venetians, Catalans, and Genoese." [154] The Venetians in Negroponte found him a good neighbor and worried about him no more. [155] In Antonio's time the Athenians appear to have suffered few misfortunes, although they must have shared in the horrified reaction of Greeks and Latins alike when in May 1423 the Turkish commander Turakhan Beg entered the Morea on a terrifying razzia, ravaging the land and attacking the cities of Mistra, Leondari, Gardiki, and Tabia. [156] But if the Turks did not strike at Attica and Boeotia that year, the plague did so, and the circle of Florentines who had gathered around Antonio was vastly relieved when by December the danger had finally passed. [157]

Antonio died of a stroke in the summer of 1435. [158] He left no son

152. G. F. Pagnini del Ventura, *Della Decima e di varie altre gravezze imposte dal comune di Firenze* (4 vols., Lucca, 1765–1766; repr. Bologna, 1967), II, 28–30, with some notice of the Catalans.

153. Buchon, II, *Florence:* doc. LXVII, pp. 287–288.

154. Buchon, II, *Florence:* doc. LXVIII, pp. 289–290; Miklosich and Müller, *Acta et diplomata,* III, 251–252, doc. dated August 7, 1422.

155. Chalcocondylas, *Historia,* IV (*CSHB,* pp. 215–216; ed. Darkó, I, 202).

156. On Turakhan Beg's Moreote campaign, see Iorga, "Notes et extraits," *Revue de l'Orient latin,* V (1897, repr. 1964), 136; Chalcocondylas, *Historia,* V (*CSHB,* pp. 238–239; ed. Darkó, II-1, 16–17); *Chronicon breve,* ad ann. 6931 (1423), appended to Ducas, *Historia byzantina* (*CSHB,* p. 518); George Sphrantzes, *Chronicon minus,* in *PG,* CLVI, 1030BC; Pseudo-Sphrantzes ("Phrantzes"), *Annales,* I, 40 (*CSHB,* pp. 117–118); Sanudo, *Vite de' duchi,* in Muratori, *RISS,* XXII, 970B, 975B, 978E; Loenertz, "La Chronique brève moréote de 1423," *Mélanges Eugène Tisserant,* II (Studi e testi, no. 232, Vatican City, 1964), 434–435.

157. Buchon, II, *Florence:* docs. LIV, LX, pp. 271–272, 280–281.

158. Chalcocondylas, *Historia,* VI (*CSHB,* p. 320; ed. Darkó, II-1, 93); George Sphrantzes, *Chronicon minus,* in *PG,* CLVI, 1044B; Pseudo-Sphrantzes, *Annales,* II, 10 (*CSHB,* p. 159); Gregorovius (tr. Lampros), *Athens* [in Greek], II, 321.

to inherit the Athenian duchy, but at best it was a difficult inheritance. In October the senate wrote the colonial government of Negroponte that if the Turks or the heirs of Antonio undertook to occupy the Acropolis, they were to do so without Venetian interference. [159] Although the lord of Athens was supposed to be a vassal of the republic, the senate was obviously unwilling to try to maintain Venetian suzerainty over Attica and Boeotia, doubtless preferring to concentrate upon the defense of Negroponte against the Turks.

Although in 1394 king Ladislas of Naples had named as Nerio's heir the latter's brother Donato Acciajuoli, we have seen that Venetian governors and Nerio's son Antonio had succeeded him in the palace on the Acropolis. Donato had died in Florence in 1400, leaving three daughters and five sons; unlike their father, four of the sons were drawn to Greece, and three of them took up residence there. The lord Antonio employed one of them, Francis (or Franco), as an envoy to Venice, [160] and gave him the castle of Sykaminon (near Oropus), which had been for some years a stronghold of the Knights Hospitaller. Francis died about September 1419, leaving his young sons Nerio and Antonio a greater heritage than he himself had ever possessed, for the childless lord Antonio had already summoned the boys and their mother Margaret Malpigli to be with him in Greece. [161] Both boys were to become dukes of Athens. When they first came to Athens (in 1413), at about three or four years of age, they were accompanied by their uncle Nerio, the third son of Donato. [162] This Nerio di Donato Acciajuoli made at least one other visit to Athens (in 1423); he is an attractive figure, more interested in falconry and hunting than in fighting, a favorite of Charles I Tocco and Frances Acciajuoli, the duke and duchess of Leucadia. [163] Two other sons of Donato found ecclesiastical careers in Greece: Antonio became bishop of Cephalonia in 1427, [164] and John became, through

159. Sathas, I, doc. 131, p. 199.

160. Hopf, in Ersch and Gruber, LXXXVI (repr., II), 72; Gregorovius (tr. Lampros), *Athens,* II, 295–296; and the document dated at Venice on March 26, 1416 (Sathas, I, no. 43, p. 52).

161. Chalcocondylas, *Historia,* VI (*CSHB,* p. 320; ed. Darkó, II-1, 93), and note Buchon, II, *Florence:* doc. LXX, pp. 292–296, dated May 21, 1421. Margaret Malpigli was then living at Sykaminon with her two young sons.

162. Buchon has published a considerable correspondence addressed to Nerio di Donato Acciajuoli (II, *Florence:* docs. LIII, LIV, LVI–LVIII, LX–LXVI, pp. 269 ff.).

163. Cf. Buchon, I, 163–166; and II, *Florence:* docs. LXII–LXVI, pp. 282–286.

164. Buchon, II, *Florence:* doc. LIX, p. 280, and cf. the letter Antonio wrote to Nerio di Donato from Athens on December 16, 1423 (*ibid.,* doc. LX, pp. 280–281). Antonio appears with the name "de Morellis" in Eubel, *Hierarchia catholica,* I, 181.

the lord Antonio's influence, archbishop of Thebes. [165] The Florentines who came to Athens were delighted with what they found. One of them, a son of one of Donato's daughters, wrote from Athens in December 1423 to Nerio di Donato, then visiting his cousin, the duchess Frances, on the island of Leucas: "Ah, you have never seen a fairer land than this nor a finer fortress"—than the Acropolis! [166]

After the lord Antonio's death, his widow Maria apparently tried to secure the Athenian duchy for herself and her Greek kinsman Chalcocondylas, father of the historian Laonicus. Maria sent Chalcocondylas, well supplied with funds, to the Ottoman court to try to persuade sultan Murad II to recognize their authority over Athens and Thebes. But the Florentine party lured Maria from the security of the Acropolis, where they installed the late Antonio's young cousin and adopted heir Nerio II as duke, driving the Chalcocondylae and their supporters from the citadel and the city. Chalcocondylas failed in his Turkish mission, which was attended by rather exciting adventures, and Nerio II married the enterprising Maria, with whom (a Venetian document suggests) he settled down "in peace and concord." [167] After three or four years on the Acropolis (1435–1439?), however, Nerio II was displaced by his younger and more energetic brother Antonio II (1439?–1441). [168] After the latter's death, Nerio returned to Athens and to his ducal authority. The intervening two or three years he had spent in Florence, [169] the only Florentine ruler of Athens to see his native city again. Nerio reoccupied for about a decade the little palace built into the Propylaea, but the Athenian duchy was now being buffeted from the south by the

165. Buchon, II, *Florence:* doc. LXI, pp. 281–282; John is unknown to Eubel, I, 482.

166. Buchon, II, *Florence:* doc. LVIII, p. 279: "Mio, tu non vedesti mai el più belo paese che questo ne la più bela forteza."

167. Sathas, III, doc. 1020, pp. 427–428, dated September 5, 1435. The sources provide different accounts of what took place in Athens: Chalcocondylas, VI (*CSHB*, pp. 320–322; ed. Darkó, II-1, 93–94); Sphrantzes, *Chronicon minus (PG*, CLVI, 1044); and the Pseudo-Sphrantzes ("Phrantzes," probably not to be trusted), *Annales,* II, 10 (*CSHB,* pp. 158–160). According to the Pseudo-Sphrantzes, the dowager duchess was called Maria, and was a member of the family of the Melisseni, but neither Sphrantzes himself nor Chalcocondylas gives her name. Cf. Hopf, in Ersch and Gruber, LXXXVI (repr., II), 91; Gregorovius (trans. Lampros), *Athens,* II, 334–336; Miller, *Latins in the Levant,* pp. 404–406; D. G. Kampouroglous, *The Chalkokondylai* [in Greek] (Athens, 1926), pp. 93–99; and Zakythinos, *Le Despotat grec de Morée,* I, 212; but all these accounts are vitiated by their authors' reliance upon "Phrantzes," a later sixteenth-century forgery by Macarius Melissenus.

168. Chalcocondylas, *Historia,* VI (*CSHB*, p. 322; ed. Darkó, II-1, 94). Cf. Hopf, in Ersch and Gruber, LXXXVI (repr., II), 113; Gregorovius (trans. Lampros), II, 336; Buchon, I, 185; Ubaldini, *op. cit.* (1588), p. 177.

169. Nerio II was still in Athens on August 6, 1437 (Buchon, II, *Florence:* doc. LXXI, p. 297), and he was still in Florence on February 24 and March 5, 1441 (*ibid.,* docs. LXXII, LXXIII, pp. 298, 299). Cf. Chalcocondylas, *loc. cit.,* p. 322.

Greek despot of Mistra, Constantine Palaeologus, and from the north
by the Turkish commander Turakhan Beg and sultan Murad II. He
paid tribute to the Turk, to the Greek, and to the Turk again. [170]

The medieval history of Greece was drawing to a close. On October
31, 1448, the tired emperor John VIII died and left the city of
Constantinople to his brother, the despot of Mistra, who was proclaimed emperor as Constantine XI on the following January 6. [171]
Murad II died about two years later (on February 5, 1451), and the
young Mehmed II the Conqueror succeeded him. Nerio II died in the
same year, and left his ducal lordship to his little son Francis and to
his second wife, the duchess Clara Zorzi (Giorgio), the daughter of
Nicholas II Zorzi of Carystus, the titular marquis of Bodonitsa. Clara
fell in love with one Bartholomew Contarini, who had come to
Athens on business; Bartholomew's father, named Priam, had been
the Venetian castellan of Nauplia. [172] Bartholomew found Greece
attractive and Clara more so; to live with her in Athens he murdered
his wife in Venice. Sultan Mehmed II intervened at the behest of the
Athenians and the retainers of the Acciajuoli, who may have
feared for the little Francis. Contarini was summoned, together with
the boy, to the Ottoman court at Adrianople, where he found
Franco Acciajuoli, son of the late duke Antonio II, who after his
father's death had become a Turkish hostage. Franco now became
the last duke of Athens, but only for a brief while (1455–1456).
When he was alleged to have murdered the wayward Clara, her
indignant lover Bartholomew remonstrated with the sultan, at whose
command Omar Pasha, son of the old warrior Turakhan Beg, occupied the lower city of Athens. Franco held out for a while on the
Acropolis. Omar offered him "the land of Boeotia and the city of
Thebes," but Athens, which the sultan had given to Franco, he was
now taking away from him: Franco might withdraw to Thebes, and
take all his possessions from the castle on the Acropolis. [173] The

---

170. Cf. Chalcocondylas, *Historia,* VI (*CSHB,* pp. 319 ff.; ed. Darkó, II-1, 91 ff.);
Chronicon breve, ad ann. 6952 (1444), appended to Ducas's *Historia byzantina* (*CSHB,* p.
519); Gregorovius (trans. Lampros), *Athens,* II, 372–374; Miller, *Latins in the Levant,* pp.
409 ff.

171. Cf. Sphrantzes, *Chronicon minus* (*PG,* CLVI, 1052B), and Pseudo-Sphrantzes, *Annales,* III, 1 (*CSHB,* p. 205); Zakythinos, *Le Despotat grec de Morée,* I, 240.

172. Chalcocondylas, *Historia,* IX (*CSHB,* p. 453; ed. Darkó, II-2 [1927], 211–212);
Hopf, in Ersch and Gruber, LXXXVI (repr., II), 128; cf. J. von Hammer-Purgstall, *Geschichte des osmanischen Reiches,* II (Pest, 1828; repr. Graz, 1963), 38.

173. Chalcocondylas, *Historia,* IX (*CSHB,* pp. 454–455; ed. Darkó, II-2, 212–213);
Gregorovius (trans. Lampros), *Athens,* II, 384–388; Miller, *Latins in the Levant,* pp.
437–438. Chalcocondylas, *loc. cit.,* says that Omar Pasha besieged the Acropolis "for a long
time."

Turks took Athens over on June 4, 1456, [174] thus bringing to a close two and a half centuries of Latin domination.

Almost four years after the Turkish occupation of Athens, Franco Acciajuoli wrote duke Francis Sforza of Milan "... that while in years gone by I was ruling the city of Athens and other lands adjoining it, as my father [Antonio II] and my uncle [Nerio II] and the founders of my house had done through the course of a hundred years and more, the sultan of the Turks [Mehmed II], moved by the wiles of jealous men and having heard of the extraordinary strength of my castle and city of Athens, decided to see it. And as soon as he had seen how impregnable it was—and that he had its equal nowhere in his dominions—he conceived a very great love for it: hence he required me to be straightway removed from possession of it and to abandon my house to him, and he gave me another city by the name of Thebes, over which my fathers had formerly ruled, although they had lost control of the city when beset by the power of the present sultan's father [Murad II]." [175]   Here is no mention of duchess Clara, and

174. Wm. Miller, "The Turkish Capture of Athens," *Essays on the Latin Orient* (Cambridge, 1921; repr. Amsterdam, 1964), pp. 160–161, and *Latins in the Levant*, p. 437. Cf. *Chronicon breve*, ad ann. 6964 (1456), appended to Ducas's *Historia byzantina* (*CSHB*, p. 520); *Historia patriarchica*, ad ann. 6964 (*CSHB*, pp. 124–125); Sphrantzes, *Chronicon minus* (*PG*, CLVI, 1065A); and the Pseudo-Sphrantzes, *Annales*, IV, 14 (*CSHB*, p. 385). On October 12–13, 1456, the colonial government of Negroponte wrote the Venetian senate of various offers of towns and castles being made to the republic (Mouchli, Damala, Lygourio, Phanari), "et de oblatione contestabilis Athenarum et aliquorum civium deinde pro castro Athenarum" (Senatus Secreta, Reg. 20, fol. 105ʳ, entry dated November 12, 1456), to which the senate returned a cautious and noncommittal answer. This text seems to suggest that the Acropolis was still in Christian hands as of October 1456, but the author of this chapter knows of no documentary source to justify the statement of Hopf, in Ersch and Gruber, LXXXVI (repr., II), 128b, that the Turks did not secure the Acropolis until 1458, in which assumption he is still being followed, as by Hans Pfeffermann, *Die Zusammenarbeit der Renaissancepäpste mit den Türken* (Berne, 1946), pp. 3, 10–11, and John N. Travlos, Πολεοδομικὴ ἐξέλιξις τῶν Ἀθηνῶν (Athens, 1960), p. 173. Travlos's book is very valuable on the architectural development of the city of Athens, but contains some unfortunate errors in dates.

175. Lampros, *Eggrapha,* part VI, doc. 2, p. 408; also published in Νέος Ἑλληνομνήμων, I (1904), 216–218. Franco's statement that as soon as sultan Mehmed II saw the "castle and city of Athens" he wanted them, may seem to support the assumption that the Turks took the Acropolis in 1458 (see the preceding note) since it was after the Turkish campaign in the Morea in the spring and summer of that year that Mehmed paid his famous visit to Athens. By this time, however, Omar Pasha had already taken the citadel. Perhaps Mehmed "saw" Athens on his way south in the spring of 1458, but Franco's letter is too vague to form a basis for precise chronology. A petition presented to the Florentine signoria on October 26, 1458, on behalf of Nerozzo Pitti and his wife Laudamia, who had been married in Athens about thirty-five years before and had continued to live there, contained their request to sell a house in Florence; they needed money, having lost everything "quod ... de mense Junii anni MCCCCLVI prout fuit voluntas Dei accidit quod ipsa civitas Athenarum fuit capta a Theucris ..." (Miller, *Essays,* pp. 160–161, referred to above). Obviously the Turks took

Franco has added a generation to his family's possession of Athens.

Franco's tenure of the lordship of Thebes was short-lived. He lived in daily peril, for the Turks apparently believed that he or his followers still entertained the hope of repossessing the Acropolis. After the Turkish campaign of 1460 which had effected the final destruction of the Byzantine despotate in the Morea, Franco was ordered to assist in a campaign against Leonard III Tocco of Leucas and Cephalonia. [176] He was well aware that his rule over Attica lay in the past, and that even his future in Boeotia could not last long. On February 10, 1460, Franco wrote Francis Sforza the letter to which reference has just been made. He offered to serve Sforza for a proper stipend, to expend 10,000 ducats of his own in the establishment of a condotta, and to betake himself immediately to his excellency in Milan. [177] But he remained in Greece through the summer of 1460, witnessing the downfall of the despots Thomas and Demetrius Palaeologus and participating in the Turkish harassment of the Tocchi, after which sultan Mehmed II sent the unfortunate Franco into the encampment of Zagan Pasha, now governor of the Morea. At the sultan's command Zagan Pasha put Franco to death, [178] and thus the rule of the Acciajuoli in Thebes, as well as in Athens, came to its tragic end.

As the sun was setting on Levantine Christendom and the Turkish shadow lengthened, Venice had to give a good deal of attention to the affairs of the petty princelings of the Aegean, where the Catalans were always conspicuous throughout much of the fifteenth century. [179] Sometime before 1399 the Catalan Alioto I (Aliot) de Caupena had acquired the island of Aegina as well as the coveted

Athens in June 1456, but we do not know how long thereafter the defenders of the Acropolis held out.

176. Almost twenty years later, in the late summer of 1479, Leonard III was to flee for his life before a Turkish armada which sailed from Avlona to his island base at Leucas (Archivio di Stato di Venezia, Senatus Secreta, Reg. 29, fols. 34ᵛ–35ʳ [44ᵛ–45ʳ]). He sought refuge in Naples.

177. Lampros, *Eggrapha,* part VI, doc. 2, pp. 407–409. (Wm. Miller, *Latins in the Levant,* p. 456, seems to have misread this document.)

178. Chalcocondylas, *Historia,* IX (*CSHB,* pp. 483–484; ed. Darkó, II-2, 237); Ubaldini, *op. cit.* (1588), pp. 178–179; Theodore Spandugino, *Tratt[at]o della casa d'Ottomano,* in Hopf, *Chroniques gréco-romanes,* pp. 329, 331–332; Cornelio Magni, *Relazione della città d' Athene* [from a letter written from Athens December 15, 1674] (Parma, 1688), pp. 20–21; Gregorovius (trans. Lampros), *Athens,* II, 402–403; Miller, *Latins in the Levant,* pp. 456–457; cf. N. Iorga, *Histoire de la vie byzantine* (Bucharest, 1934), III, 291, note 2. Of the murder of Franco Acciajuoli, Akdes Nimet, *Die türkische Prosopographie bei Laonikos Chalkokandyles* (diss. Hamburg, 1933), p. 44, observes: "Dieses Ereignis wird nur von Laonikos überliefert. Eine Kontrolle ist hier nicht möglich."

179. Setton, *Catalan Domination,* pp. 212 ff.

head of St. George, which he had apparently received from Bertranet Mota, who had held Livadia a half dozen years before. [180] The Caupenas also possessed the stronghold of Piada on the mainland just northwest of Epidaurus. Fearing the Greeks, the Albanians, and especially the Turks, the Caupenas—Alioto II and his son Antonello together with his brother Arnau—turned to Venice for protection, and in March 1425 the senate accepted them as "friends" of the republic. The Caupenas also proposed that if their house should die out, Aegina, Piada, and their other holdings should pass into Venetian hands. [181] One of the Caupenas married an adopted daughter of duke Antonio I Acciajuoli of Athens, who objected to the terms under which Venice had taken the family under her wing. [182] The Caupenas, however, got along very badly with one another, especially after the death of Alioto II in 1440, and through the years their disputes ended up for adjudication in the Venetian senate, the records of litigation constituting the sparse history of Catalan Aegina. [183] Finally, in 1451 Antonello, the last lord of Aegina, bequeathed the island to Venice, disregarding the claims of his uncle and the latter's son. [184] On August 22, 1451, Louis Morosini was appointed governor of Aegina, the first of more than thirty sons of the republic to hold the post until the Turkish seizure of the island in 1537. [185]

The Caupena lordship of Aegina was a strange last remnant of the crusade which had brought the Latins into Greece. They had almost ceased to be Catalans, and the Venetians had accepted them, but the republic looked with hostile eyes upon Catalan merchants as well as corsairs, [186] and not without reason. About the time sultan Mehmed

180. *Dipl.*, docs. DCXXXVII–DCXXXIX, pp. 666–668, dated April 13, 1393, and docs. DCLIII–DCLV, pp. 680–683, dated December 21, 1399.

181. Sathas, III, doc. 858, pp. 281–282; Iorga, in *Revue de l'Orient latin,* V, 191.

182. Sathas, I, doc. 116, pp. 178–179, dated November 6, 1425, the text of which suggests that Antonio's daughter had married Alioto II, but she had presumably married the latter's bastard son and successor in the lordship of Aegina (cf. Chalcocondylas, IV [*CSHB*, p. 215; ed. Darkó, I, 202], and Archivio di Stato di Venezia, Mar, Reg. 1, fol. 12^r, dated January 17, 1441).

183. Mar, Reg. 1, fols. 86, 225^v–226^r, and Reg. 2, fol. 86^v, dated from 1442 to 1445.

184. Mar, Reg. 4, fol. 80^v, dated August 2, 1451, by which time Antonello had been dead for at least two or three months; his uncle Arnau and cousin Alioto III continued to press their claims to Aegina before the senate, which rejected them (*loc. cit.,* and Mar, Reg. 7, fol. 21^r, dated June 12, 1461). The genealogical table of the Caupenas in Hopf's *Chroniques gréco-romanes,* p. 475, requires some rectification as to the first members of the family to become lords of Aegina, and the senate itself got the family relationships confused in the text of June 1461, where we find Antonello's uncle Arnau being identified as his brother.

185. Hopf, *Chroniques gréco-romanes,* p. 376.

186. Mar, Reg. 3, fol. 161^v, dated February 10, 1450: "... Cathellani hostes nostri . . . ." On September 28, 1450, the senate complained to the grand master of Rhodes that the

II was taking over the Morea, the inhabitants of Monemvasia accepted the rule of a Catalan pirate, Lupo de Bertagna, who seems to have been plying his dangerous trade for some years in Greek waters.[187] The Monemvasiotes soon expelled Lupo, however, and sent an embassy to pope Pius II, asking him to take over their seaboard stronghold, which he did to prevent its falling into Turkish hands.[188] But the anxious Monemvasiotes were apparently no more content with the rule of the pope than with that of the pirate, and so they accepted the sway of Venice in the forlorn hope that the republic could protect them from the Turks.[189] Moreover, as the Venetians were engaged in the occupation of the castle town of Monemvasia, the senate answered point by point a petition of the fugitive despot Thomas Palaeologus, whose family had sought safety in the Venetian-held island of Corfu. Thomas was trying to keep a foot in the castle gate, so to speak, and wanted various assurances concerning the physical safety and trading rights of his erstwhile subjects in Monemvasia. Indeed Thomas was especially anxious that the Monemvasiotes should be protected against the return of the Catalan pirate Lupo de Bertagna.[190] Thus the decade which began

preceding March a Venetian merchantman with a cargo worth 15,000 ducats had been seized by two ships from Barcelona and sold with all its cargo at Rhodes to Rhodians and Genoese (*ibid.,* Mar, Reg. 4, fol. 6^v). Constant vigilance was required against Catalan enterprise in the Levant (*ibid.,* fols. 10^v–11^r, 11^v–12^r, 13).

187. Cf. Mar, Reg. 1, fol. 122^v, dated September 14, 1452: "Quia quidam Luppus Cathellanus, qui se nutrit cum quadam sua fusta in aquis Nigropontis, intulit maximum damnum quibusdam nostris civibus auferendo de quadam griparia pannos multos non pauci valoris, mandetur ... capitaneo [culphi] quod si in hac via sua reperiret eundo vel redeundo illum Luppum procurare debeat recuperandi ab eo mercationes nostrorum ...."

188. Pius II, *Commentarii,* IV, ed. Frankfurt, 1614, pp. 103–104; Magno, *Estratti,* in Hopf, *Chroniques gréco-romanes,* pp. 203–204; Raynaldus, *Annales ecclesiastici,* ad ann. 1460, nos. 56–59, vol. XIX (1693), pp. 54–56.

On February 27, 1461, Pius II confirmed all the privileges the Monemvasiotes had previously possessed, and appointed Gentile de' Marcolfi their governor (Arch. Segr. Vaticano, Miscellanea, Arm. IX, tom. 15 [Collett. per Città, Terre, e Luoghi: Lett. M e N], fols. 150^r–155^v). On July 10 (1461) the pope appointed a Portuguese soldier, Lope de Valdaro, as "captain of the city of Monemvasia" (Reg. Vat. 516, fol. 32^r), and eleven days later, on July 21, he replaced Marcolfi as governor with Francis of St. Anatolia, abbot of the monastery of St. Nicholas of Auxerre (Reg. Vat. 516, fols. 37^v–39^r). Cf. N. Iorga, *Geschichte des osmanischen Reiches,* II (Gotha, 1909), 94–95, and Miller, *Latins in the Levant,* p. 448.

189. Magno, *Estratti,* in Hopf, *Chroniques gréco-romanes,* p. 204. According to Raynaldus, *Annales ecclesiastici,* ad ann. 1462, no. 35, vol. XIX (1693), p. 120, Monemvasia was occupied by the Turks between the period of papal and that of Venetian domination: "... at dissipata sunt ea consilia [i.e., the failure of the pope's plan to exploit Monemvasia as a beachhead for sending 10,000 German troops into the Morea] in Turcicam iterum missa Monobassia servitutem, quam deinde recuperatam a Venetis, iterumque a Turcis, quibus hactenus paret expugnatam ...."

190. Senatus Secreta, Reg. 21, fols. 103^r–104^r, dated August 12, 1462: "... et maximamente da Lupo expresse sel volesse navegar ale nostre contrade per danizar ..." (fol.

with the noble family of the Caupenas still ruling in Aegina closed with the redoubtable Lupo's almost gaining Monemvasia, the strongest fortress in all Greece.

The later fourteenth and early fifteenth centuries had marked a Hellenic upsurge, an increased ethnic awareness fostered by the Orthodox church and led by the archontic families, who filled the vacuum left by the Catalans' departure, for Florentine settlement was never comparable, despite Antonio I's efforts to attract Italians to Athens and Thebes. [191] Meanwhile, Albanians had worked their way south throughout the fourteenth century, and by its end were an important segment of the population; like the Turks, they appeared originally as mercenaries, then as invaders, and finally as settlers, primarily in Epirus and Thessaly. The impact of the Albanians exceeded that of either the Catalans or the Florentines, and rivaled that of the Turks, whose four centuries of rule erased the effects of their Latin predecessors' regimes, but not their memory. This brief but colorful chapter in Catalan history inspired a lasting sense of achievement in the conquistadors' countrymen, reflected in their literature and in the sometimes partisan but often admirable works of their historians.

The Catalans had ruled in Attica and Boeotia for three quarters of a century, and on the island of Aegina for more than half a century thereafter. The chief monuments they have left behind them are documents in the archives of Barcelona, Venice, Palermo, and the Vatican. These monuments have proved more lasting than bronze, and from them the bizarre history of Catalan domination in Athens and Thebes has in the last few generations finally been written.

103ᵛ). In the exchange of petition and response, the despot Thomas represents the Monemvasiotes as his subjects (as they had been) and the senate regards Monemvasia as a Venetian responsibility (as it was becoming). Monemvasia, or "Malvasia," was of course the source of the French *malvoisie* and the English "malmsey."

191. The learned monograph of D. G. Kampouroglous, *The Chalkokondylai* [in Greek] (Athens, 1926), makes clear that the fortunes of the Chalcocondylas family, for example, were founded shortly after the Catalan era in Athens.

VIII

THE HOSPITALLERS AT
RHODES, 1306–1421

The Order of Saint John probably originated in a hospice for pilgrims founded at Jerusalem by merchants of Amalfi in about 1070. After the First Crusade this confraternity received papal protection in a bull of 1113, and subsequently it acquired a standardized rule and developed a military character as an increasingly knightly and predominantly French-speaking order. The Hospitallers continued their charitable works and maintained hospices in Syria, where they received endowments. They were granted properties and privileges all over Latin Christendom; these were mainly intended to provide resources for their activities in Syria, but the Hospitallers did fight Moslems elsewhere, notably in Spain and Cilicia. The master, or—as he gradually came to be known—the grand master, was elected by the brethren for life and, together with the important officers of the Hospital, normally resided at the Convent, the headquarters in Syria. The duties of these officers reflected the Hospitallers' activities: the grand preceptor of the Convent acted as the master's deputy; the marshal was responsible for military affairs; the turcopolier commanded the light mercenary cavalry; the treasurer, hospitaller, and draper had charge of the finances, hospital, and clothing; and the prior of the Convent ruled the conventual church and the *frères d'office* or chaplains.

Important fragments of the Hospitallers' archives for the period to 1421 are preserved in the Archives of the Order of St. John, Royal Malta Library (cited as Malta). A number of these documents are printed in S. Pauli, *Codice diplomatico del sacro militare ordine Gerosolimitano, oggi di Malta,* II (Lucca, 1737), and a few in M. Barbaro di San Giorgio, *Storia della costituzione del sovrano militare ordine di Malta* (Rome, 1927). The Malta archive was also used in the unreliable but still much cited work of G. Bosio, *Dell' Istoria della sacra religione et ill^{ma} militia di San Giovanni Gierosolimitano,* II (2nd ed., Rome, 1629); the inferior first edition should not be used as, unfortunately, it often is. On the historiography, see A. Luttrell, "The Hospitallers' Historical Activities: (1) 1291–1400; (2) 1400–1530; (3) 1530–1630," *Annales de l'Ordre souverain militaire de Malte,* XXIV

In western Europe the Hospital became a powerful social and political institution. Its extensive possessions were organized administratively in preceptories or commanderies, each ruled by a preceptor, who generally lived in a central house, usually with a chapel and stables, and sometimes with a cemetery and a hospice. Brethren of the three grades—knights, sergeants, and chaplains—all of whom took vows of poverty, chastity, and obedience, lived according to the rules laid down in the statutes; often the community included *confratres* or corrodaries, laymen who purchased their board and lodging by a donation or annual gift. Preceptories were grouped in priories under a prior who held regular chapters, enforced discipline, and, above all, collected the preceptors' *responsiones,* the money due to the Convent. Priors and preceptors were in many ways like other lords, sitting in parliaments, exercising justice, and serving as royal officials, but often they were exempt from royal and ecclesiastical jurisdictions and taxation. Their chief duties, however, were to manage their estates to the economic advantage of the Convent and to recruit and

(1966), 126–129; XXV (1967), 145–150; XXVI (1968), 57–69. The most recent major bibliography, leading to the older works, is J. Mizzi, "A Bibliography of the Order of St. John of Jerusalem (1925–1969)," in *The Order of St. John in Malta,* ed. Malta Government and Council of Europe (Valletta, 1970), pp. 108–204. The present chapter is based on a study of all the relevant material at Malta, and of many other documents elsewhere. Though specific reference to it is not made on every page below, J. Delaville Le Roulx, *Les Hospitaliers à Rhodes jusqu'à la mort de Philibert de Naillac, 1310–1421* (Paris, 1913), should be consulted in the first instance for much of the information provided; all other information is documented in the works cited below. Delaville's book, published posthumously, contains valuable material from Malta and elsewhere, but it is not always accurate, while economic and social affairs are ignored, and the presentation and interpretation of the period as a whole now seem unsatisfactory. On the Hospital's organization, see B. Waldstein-Wartenberg, *Rechtsgeschichte des Malteserordens* (Vienna and Munich, 1969), and *Der Johanniter Orden: Der Malteser Orden; Der ritterliche Orden des hl. Johannes vom Spital zu Jerusalem: Seine Aufgaben, seine Geschichte,* ed. A. Wienand (Cologne, 1970). H. Prutz, "Die Anfänge der Hospitaliter auf Rhodos, 1310–1355," in *Sitzungsberichte der königlich bayerischen Akademie der Wissenschaften—Philosophisch-philologische und historische Klasse: Jahrgang 1908, I. Abhandlung* (Munich, 1908), 1–57, though based largely on Bosio and Pauli, is not altogether superseded. N. Iorga, "Rhodes sous les Hospitaliers," *Revue historique du sud-est européen,* VIII (1931), 32–51, 78–113, 169–187, contains valuable hypotheses, though it is wildly inaccurate.

On the Hospital's achievements and weaknesses, see A. Luttrell, "The Knights Hospitallers of Rhodes and their Achievements in the Fourteenth Century," *Revue de l'Ordre souverain militaire de Malte,* XVI (1958), 136–142; "Emmanuele Piloti and Criticism of the Knights Hospitallers of Rhodes: 1306–1444," *Annales de l'Ordre souverain militaire de Malte,* XX (1962), 11–17; and in a more general context, "The Crusade in the Fourteenth Century," *Europe in the Late Middle Ages,* ed. J. Hale *et al.* (London, 1965), pp. 122–154. The European aspects of the Hospitallers' history are not treated here, but see E. Schermerhorn, *On the Trail of the Eight-Pointed Cross: A Study of the Heritage of the Knights Hospitallers in Feudal Europe* (New York, 1940). Many of the articles by A. Luttrell cited above and in the footnotes are to be published at Padua as *Hospitaller Studies: 1291–1440.*

train new brethren. Representatives from the priories attended chapters-general at the Convent to discuss policy and amend the statutes. There was a certain distinction between Levantine and European Hospitallers, but it was seldom clear-cut, and while some resided mainly or entirely in Europe and others passed most of their careers in Syria, many served partly in the Levant and partly in the priories.

While the Hospital's influence grew in Europe, the Latins' holdings in Syria dwindled. After the loss of Jerusalem in 1187 the Convent and hospital were transferred to Acre. As the Latins were pushed back toward the coast the Hospitallers, short of manpower, immured themselves in powerful defensive positions in huge stone castles such as those at Krak des Chevaliers and Margat, which were vital to the defense of the Latin kingdom. Like the Templars, the Hospitallers provided a standing force always ready for war. Men of military prowess, disciplined and resolute, they became increasingly influential in Levantine affairs. To their lands in the principality of Antioch the Hospitallers added possessions in Cyprus and Cilician Armenia. Conducting subtle, independent, and often aggressive policies, they indulged in private wars, quarreled with the Templars, and played a prominent part in almost every crusading campaign during the decades of defeat and retreat which closed with the loss of Acre and the expulsion of the Latins from Syria in 1291.

The Hospitallers fought heroically in the defense of Acre, and only a few, including the seriously wounded master John of Villiers, escaped to Cyprus. They lost many of their best men and the last of their Syrian possessions. Abandoning neither their hospitable duties nor their ideal of recovering Jerusalem, where they had first performed them, the brethren now established their Convent and hospital at Limassol. Their future seemed uncertain and they could do little to show that they retained any useful function, but they set about the reconstruction of their strength. John of Villiers held chapters-general in 1292 and 1293, and his successor Odo de Pins another in 1294. The latter's ineffectiveness led to a plea from the Convent to the pope that a council of seven be invested with control of the Hospital, but Odo died in 1296 before he could respond to a summons from the pope, who had denounced him for his errors. William of Villaret, elected master while in France, stayed there until the Convent forced him to go to Cyprus in 1300. In that year, after delays and disagreements over plans, the Hospitallers and Templars collaborated with king Henry II of Cyprus in ineffectual raids on the Egyptian and Syrian coasts. William himself went to Ruad, an island off Tortosa defended for a few years (until 1302) mainly by the Templars. He also went twice with considerable forces to Cilician Armenia, where the Hospitallers had long held possessions, and stayed there for some time. Between 1300 and 1304 he continued the revision of the statutes, one of which, defining the powers of the admiral, emphasized the Hospital's increasingly amphibious nature.

From their insecure point of exile in Cyprus the Hospitallers faced other difficulties. They were less involved in financial operations than the Templars, but people in Europe were disillusioned with the crusading idea in general and with the military orders in particular; many envied the orders' wealth and privileges, or felt that they had betrayed their cause and misused the donations made to them. Tempting schemes for reorganizing the military orders or for confiscating their lands received considerable support. James II of Aragon, who alleged that the Hospitallers were lingering idly in the Levant, sought to secure their incomes and services for his "crusades" in Granada and Sardinia, and even threatened to seize their possessions. Henry II of Cyprus quarreled with the military orders over taxation and enforced the prohibition against their acquisition of new estates. The Hospitallers' resources in Cyprus were so slender that they were at the mercy of the kings of Naples and Aragon for the importation of food, horses, and fodder, and in 1305 Fulk of Villaret, newly elected to succeed his uncle William as master, presented to the pope a crusading scheme emphasizing the complex organizational problems of raising men, money, and ships in western Europe. In Cyprus the Hospitallers mediated in May 1306 between king Henry and his brother, Amalric de Lusignan, who had seized power.[1] With the general arrest of the Templars late in 1307 and the propaganda campaign leading to their suppression in 1312, the Hospitallers' position might have been bleak had they not embarked on the conquest of Rhodes in 1306. That island offered a prospect of independence, while effective action against the Turks and the potential usefulness of Rhodes as a crusading base served to quiet the Hospital's critics.[2]

1. See below, pp. 343–345.
2. J. Delaville Le Roulx, *Les Hospitaliers en Terre Sainte et à Chypre, 1100–1310* (Paris, 1904); J. Riley-Smith, *The Knights of St. John in Jerusalem and Cyprus, c. 1050–1310* (London, 1967). See also A. Luttrell, "The Aragonese Crown and the Knights Hospitallers of Rhodes: 1291–1350," *English Historical Review,* LXXVI (1961), 1–11; "The Hospitallers in Cyprus after 1291," *Acts of the First International Congress of Cypriot Studies* (Nicosia, 1972), pp. 161–171; "The Hospitallers' Interventions in Cilician Armenia: 1291–1375" [forthcoming].

The conquest of Rhodes was one among a number of schemes, disguised as crusades, which sought to take advantage of the Greeks' inability to withstand the assaults of the Turks. The victories of the Catalan Company in Asia Minor in 1304 showed that the Turks were not invincible, but they provided only temporary relief for the Greeks. The Genoese Benedict Zaccaria demonstrated the possibilities of establishing new Latin lordships in the Aegean by occupying the island of Chios and securing the recognition of his position there from the Byzantine emperor Andronicus II. As early as 1299 there was a papal scheme by which king Frederick II of Sicily would receive Rhodes in fief, and in 1305 Frederick sent his half-brother, the Hospitaller Sancho of Aragon, on an unsuccessful expedition to occupy certain Byzantine islands. In the same year Raymond Lull advocated the seizure of Rhodes with four galleys and its use as a base from which to enforce the prohibitions against Christian trade with the Moslems. This proposal was part of a larger scheme for an attack in Romania, justified by the theorists as a move against the "schismatic" Greeks and "infidel" Turks and as a step toward the recovery of Jerusalem; it was planned by Charles of Valois, brother of king Philip IV of France and titular Latin emperor of Constantinople, with the support of the papacy and, in theory at least, of all the major Latin Mediterranean powers except Genoa. The Hospitallers were predominantly French and, unlike many of the Italian powers which were inhibited by commercial considerations, they constituted a reliable crusading element. The attack on Rhodes, however, was not itself conceived primarily as part of a crusade against Andronicus.[3]

The Hospitallers were naturally attracted to the green and fertile island, nearly fifty miles long and some twenty miles wide, lying off the southwestern coast of Asia Minor. Northeast of Crete and northwest of Cyprus, Rhodes was not on the most direct European trade routes to Constantinople or Alexandria, but its fine harbor added to its considerable strategic importance. A forested ridge of hills down the center of the island ended in a plain at the northeastern tip, where the city of Rhodes enjoyed a fresh climate some twelve miles across the water from the mainland. The Byzantine town was a

3. R. Burns, "The Catalan Company and the European Powers, 1305–1311," *Speculum,* XXIX (1954), 751–771; P. Lemerle, *L'Émirat d'Aydin, Byzance et l'Occident* (Paris, 1957), pp. 10–26, 50–52; F. Giunta, *Aragonesi e Catalani nel Mediterraneo,* II (Palermo, 1959), 170–171. Text of 1299 in V. Salavert y Roca, *Cerdeña y la expansión mediterránea de la Corona de Aragón, 1297–1314,* II (Madrid, 1956), 44–45; for Lull's scheme see A. S. Atiya, *The Crusade in the Later Middle Ages* (London, 1938), p. 82.

miserable ruin by contrast with the enormous and splendid city of ancient times, but it was strong enough to resist a determined siege in 1306. The Venetians had established a protectorate at Rhodes in 1234, but in 1248 they were ousted and replaced by the Genoese. Thenceforth Genoese merchants frequented the island which, nominally Byzantine, was often granted by the emperor to his Genoese admirals. In 1306 the Genoese Vignolo de' Vignoli apparently claimed that the emperor had granted him Cos and Leros, islands to the north of Rhodes, as well as the *casale* or manor of Lardos on Rhodes. In fact the Turks had invaded Rhodes some years earlier, perhaps profiting from a severe earthquake there in 1303, massacring many Greek inhabitants and apparently occupying part of the island. The Greeks held one of the castles in Cos in 1306. The Venetians were also established on that island in 1302, and, probably early in 1306, they attacked the island of Nisyros between Rhodes and Cos; they even considered the acquisition of Rhodes itself. Furthermore, the Venetian Andrew Cornaro seized Carpathos (Scarpanto) and other islands between Rhodes and Crete from the Genoese, whose position in the Rhodian archipelago was being seriously weakened.[4]

On May 27, 1306, the master, Fulk of Villaret, together with the admiral, the marshal, the draper, and other brethren, met Vignolo at a secret meeting near Limassol. In a notarized arrangement for the joint conquest of the Rhodian archipelago, Vignolo transferred to the Hospital his alleged rights to Cos and Leros but retained Lardos and another *casale* of his choice on Rhodes. In the lesser islands the Hospital was to receive two parts and Vignolo one part of the rents and incomes, the collectors being appointed jointly; Vignolo was to have extensive rights as *vicarius seu justiciarius* in all the islands except Rhodes, the master reserving rights of appeal, of high justice, and of jurisdiction over the Hospitallers themselves and their servants; there was no mention of Vignolo's holding lands in fief or owing military service. On June 23 Villaret left Limassol with two galleys and four other craft carrying some thirty-five Hospitallers, six Levantine horsemen, and five hundred foot. Joined by other galleys

---

4. C. Torr, *Rhodes in Modern Times* (Cambridge, 1887), pp. 4–10; W. Heyd, *Histoire du commerce du Levant au moyen-âge,* trans. Furcy Raynaud, I (rev. ed., Leipzig, 1923), 306–307, 461, 537. The situation before 1306 is obscure; see also A. Luttrell, "Venice and the Knights Hospitallers of Rhodes in the Fourteenth Century," *Papers of the British School at Rome,* XXVI (1958), 196–197; Z. Tsirpanlis, "Pages from the Medieval History of Nisyros, 1306–1453" [in Greek], *Dodekanesiaka,* II (1967), 30–33.

supplied by certain Genoese, whose seapower was essential to the whole operation, they sailed to Castellorizzo, a small island some way east of Rhodes, and there they waited while Vignolo went ahead to spy out the situation at Rhodes. The Rhodians, however, had been forewarned by a Greek in the Hospital's service, and Vignolo was barely able to escape arrest and rejoin Villaret. Meanwhile two Hospitallers with fifty men had succeeded in surprising the castle at Cos, but were unable to defend it against the Greeks who had held it for the emperor.

A land and sea assault on Rhodes failed to secure an initial victory. On September 20 the Hospitallers captured the ruined castle of Pheraclos on the east coast but five days later were repulsed in an attack on the town of Rhodes. Faced with the prospect of a long siege, they were lucky to take the castle of Phileremos in November through the treason of a Greek; three hundred Turks with whom the Greeks had garrisoned it were massacred. Probably early in 1307, eight galleys sent by Andronicus reached Rhodes and compelled the Hospitallers to raise the siege temporarily, killing ten of the brethren but losing eighty men themselves. Meanwhile the Hospital sought aid in Cyprus, where a fleet of eight galleys and another craft was in preparation. In October the Hospital held Lindos on the southeast coast, but some twenty Greek ships lay off the city of Rhodes. The Hospitallers' prospects were poor; there was some possibility of Venetian intervention against them and they resorted to diplomacy, but in April 1308 Andronicus indignantly rejected their offer to hold Rhodes under his suzerainty and to provide three hundred men to fight against the Turks. Hoping perhaps for help from Europe, the Hospitallers maintained the siege, until by chance a Genoese ship sent by Andronicus with supplies for Rhodes was blown ashore at Famagusta in Cyprus. It was handed over to the Hospitallers, and its Rhodian captain, in order to save his life, negotiated the surrender of the town on condition that the Rhodians' lives and property be spared. This was probably in mid-1308, but the whole island was not yet subdued.[5]

5. The chronology of these events remains uncertain; contemporary sources and modern works alike have confused the question of the date of the "conquest" of Rhodes by attributing a four-year process to a single, though varying, year. The best interpretation is in Riley-Smith, *Knights of St. John,* pp. 215–216, but his sources are incomplete; see especially Delaville Le Roulx, *Hospitaliers en Terre Sainte,* pp. 272–281, and E. Baratier, *Histoire du commerce de Marseille,* II (Paris, 1951), 213–215. Historians usually follow the fifteenth-century chroniclers, who imply that the initiative in 1306 came from Vignolo, but the best source, written within less than a decade of the event, *Les Gestes des Chiprois,* ed. G. Raynaud (Geneva, 1887), pp. 319–320, states that, wishing to attack Rhodes, Villaret sent for the Genoese Boniface of Grimaldi to come to him from Famagusta.

In November 1306, having left Rhodes, Fulk of Villaret held a chapter-general at Limassol and soon after sailed for Europe; after August 1307 he frequented the papal court at Poitiers for many months. Pope Clement V excommunicated Andronicus in 1307, but thereafter failed to harness against him either the Catalans or the Venetians, whose military and naval force were essential. Other prospects for a crusade were poor, so Villaret was able to win French and papal support, apparently by a policy of calculated boasting. On September 5, 1307, Clement confirmed the Hospital in the possession of Rhodes, which he prematurely declared already to be free of Greek and Turkish resistance. During 1309 Villaret was talking, it seems, of completing the conquest of Rhodes, of the defense of Cyprus and Cilician Armenia, of an attack on Byzantium, and even of recapturing Antioch and Jerusalem within five years. The crusade or *passagium generale* was reduced to a preparatory *passagium* to be led by Villaret himself, and James II of Aragon astutely remarked that the master's real aim was to consolidate the conquest of Rhodes. The pope wrote on November 4, 1309, that the *passagium* had emptied his treasury, and he then spoke of the coming expedition as intended merely to prepare for a major crusade by defending Cyprus and "other places" in Christian hands and by preventing illegal commerce with Moslems.[6]

In November 1309 Villaret left Genoa for Naples, and it was rumored variously that he would take forty galleys and a large force to Rhodes, to Lesbos, to Crete, or to Cyprus. He reached Brindisi late in January 1310, and was reportedly due to sail for Rhodes with some twenty-six galleys, a number of them Genoese, with two or three hundred knights and three thousand foot. The Venetians, having already sent fifty mercenaries to resist the Hospitallers at Cos, now took elaborate measures to protect their Aegean colonies. Bad weather delayed Villaret at Brindisi, but he set out in the spring, accompanied by the papal legate Peter de Pleine Chassagne, bishop of Rodez. By May 13 assurances of friendship sent by Villaret from somewhere in Greek waters had reached Venice.[7] Once at Rhodes, Villaret probably completed the subjugation of the island and was

6. Riley-Smith, *Knights of St. John,* pp. 216, 220–225; and texts in H. Finke, *Acta aragonensia,* III (Berlin, 1922), 191–192, 198–200, 207–211; J. Delaville Le Roulx, *Cartulaire général de l'Ordre des Hospitaliers de S. Jean de Jérusalem, 1100–1310,* IV (Paris, 1906), nos. 4734, 4735, 4751, 4841, *et passim.*

7. Archivio di Stato di Venezia: Lettere di Collegio rectius Minor Consiglio, 1308–1310, folios 63ᵛ–64ʳ, 67ᵛ, 69ʳ–69ᵛ, 83ʳ–83ᵛ. Cf. G. Golubovich, ed., *Biblioteca bio-bibliografica della Terra Santa e dell' Oriente francescano,* III (Quaracchi, 1919), 128–131, 143–144.

distracted by events in Cyprus, where reports of the coming *passagium* had justifiably perturbed the usurper Amalric de Lusignan. Early in 1310 Amalric sent king Henry to Cilicia as a prisoner, but was himself assassinated on June 5. Hospitaller Rhodes had been a center of opposition to Amalric, and in July Henry, from Cilicia, named Villaret to act for him in Cyprus. The master was unable to leave Rhodes, but he increased his forces in Cyprus during June and July until they numbered eighty Hospitallers, twenty other horsemen, and two hundred foot. These played a leading part in Henry's restoration, and in 1312 the Hospital secured the Templars' lucrative lands in Cyprus, which proved an invaluable source of supplies in times of dearth at Rhodes.[8]

The Convent and its hospital were moved to Rhodes, where the fortifications were presumably intact. The indigenous population of Rhodes had been reduced to perhaps some ten thousand Greeks. Chapters-general held there in April 1311 and November 1314 passed numerous measures, including ambitious decisions to maintain five hundred horse and a thousand foot to defend the island. The Florentine, Genoese, and other businessmen to be found at Rhodes from the time of its conquest increased its wealth and its dependable Latin population, but colonists who would fight were also needed. In May 1313 the Hospital publicly offered lands captured from the Greeks and Turks, both in Rhodes and on the mainland, to be held in perpetuity with obligations of military service, to any Latins who would settle with their families. Different terms were advertised for nobles, freemen, and laborers, and for those who would maintain an armed galley or a *lignum armatum* and its crew. Some settlers were found; in 1316, for example, the Assanti family of Ischia was enfeoffed with the island of Nisyros, just south of Cos, with the obligation to maintain an armed galley. Later, in 1325, when the Hospital granted the *casale* of Lardos to Vignolo de' Vignoli's brother Fulk, to be held *in feudum nobile* by him and his heirs in perpetuity, Fulk was forbidden to alienate the property without permission and was obligated to serve with a Latin man-at-arms in defense of Rhodes or outside the island. On the whole, however, strictly feudal arrangements were rare, and during the fourteenth century uncultivated lands in Rhodes were being leased to both Latins and Greeks on non-feudal tenures in perpetual emphyteusis.[9]

The Genoese had provided galleys for Villaret in 1309, but they

8. G. Hill, *A History of Cyprus,* II (Cambridge, 1948), 228–262, 270–275; cf. below, pp. 345–347.

9. A. Luttrell, "Feudal Tenure and Latin Colonization at Rhodes: 1306–1415," *English Historical Review,* LXXXV (1970), 755–775.

lost their predominance at Rhodes when the Hospitallers enforced the papal prohibitions against trading in war materials with the Moslems, the importance of which Villaret had stressed in his crusading tract. The Hospital confiscated a Genoese galley, and in 1311 Antonio Spinola arrived from Genoa to demand its return, having incidentally captured Vignolo between Candia and Rhodes. Spinola and the Genoese, meeting a refusal, offered 50,000 florins to the Turks of Menteshe to attack Rhodes. Numerous merchants from Rhodes were arrested on the mainland, and Genoese and Turkish galleys seized Hospitaller vessels bound for Rhodes. In 1312, however, the Hospitaller fleet pursued twenty-three Turkish ships to Amorgos in the Cyclades; when the Turks landed, the Hospitallers burned their ships and destroyed or captured almost the entire force, themselves losing some fifty or more brethren and three hundred foot, a serious loss. Marino Sanudo Torsello, who was at Rhodes with Villaret, had high praise for the way in which the master curbed the power of Orkhan, emir of Menteshe, and incited the other emirs against him. The Hospitallers took Cos and occupied certain castles on the mainland. In May 1313 Villaret seized more Genoese ships, including two galleys, but later the Genoese presumably reached an agreement with him. A period of peace followed.[10]

The Venetians, traditionally anticlerical and opportunistic in crusading affairs, were always hostile to the Hospital, although there were usually Venetian traders at Rhodes and circumstances often forced the two powers into uneasy alliance. The Venetians, like the Genoese, protested against the enforcement of the papal restrictions on trade, and were angered when in about 1312 the Hospitallers seized Carpathos and the other islands between Rhodes and Crete from Andrew Cornaro. In 1312 and 1314 the Venetian government sequestered Hospitaller funds in transit at Venice, and even after the return of the occupied islands to the Venetians in 1316 there were continual incidents and quarrels.[11] Villaret, still far from secure at Rhodes and unable to rely on Genoese or Venetian support, carefully maintained close relations with James II of Aragon, ignoring papal instructions of 1312 that the Hospital should intervene against the Catalans in Greece.[12] In Aragon, Catalonia, and Valencia the fate of the lands of the Temple and of those of the Hospital was in the balance until 1317. Certain influential Catalan Hospitallers con-

10. Delaville Le Roulx, *Rhodes,* pp. 4–7, 10–11; Luttrell. "Feudal Tenure," pp. 755–757. No more is heard of Vignolo. Statistics concerning forces and losses should be treated with caution.

11. Luttrell, "Venice," pp. 196–197, 202.

12. See above, pp. 181–182.

ducted the negotiations which led to James's marriage in 1315 to a
Cypriote princess, Marie de Lusignan; the Hospital even guaranteed
the dowry, probably in the hope that the birth of a son would give to
Aragon the reversion of the crowns of Cyprus and Jerusalem and
thus permanently implicate Aragonese strength in an area where it
might support the Hospital. James however lost interest in the
Levant even before Marie died, childless, in 1322.[13]

Fulk of Villaret, once established at Rhodes, where he saw himself
as sovereign, fell into extravagance, corruption, and despotism. Ignoring the crusading projects proposed to him and neglecting the Hospital's debts and difficulties in Europe, he increased his own powers
and income. The leading conventual brethren were incensed by
actions such as the granting to the grandiose Albert of Schwarzburg, a Saxon noble, of the Hospital's Cypriote lands at half their
proper *responsiones*, and in 1317 they attempted to assassinate
Villaret. When he fled they besieged him in the castle at Lindos and
elected the draper, Maurice of Pagnac, as master. Both parties then
appealed to pope John XXII, who summoned them to Avignon. The
Convent had some legal right to replace a corrupt master, but Villaret
was popular in Europe, and early in 1319 John XXII quashed
Pagnac's election; Villaret was confirmed as master but was then
persuaded to resign. In June 1319 Hélion of Villeneuve became
master, being in effect appointed by the pope.[14] Papal intervention
in the Hospital's affairs had increased after the Convent's appeal to
the pope against the master in 1295. There was a general expansion
of papal powers at this time, and after 1312 the papacy could
threaten to take back the Templars' lands that it had granted to the
Hospital in that year. From 1317 on John XXII, usurping the
master's duties, acted with the best intentions to reduce the
Hospital's debts, prevent alienations of its lands, and enforce discipline.

In the Levant the Turks again became aggressive, but Albert of
Schwarzburg achieved a success against them in 1318, and on July
23, 1319, Schwarzburg, now grand preceptor and commanding
twenty-four vessels with eighty Hospitallers and other knights, plus a
galley and some six other vessels provided by Martin Zaccaria, the
Genoese lord of Chios, defeated a Turkish force from Altoluogo
(Ephesus) off the island of Chios; many Turks were killed and out of
ten galleys and eighteen other craft only six Turkish ships escaped.
Schwarzburg next captured the castle of Leros, an island just north

---

13. Luttrell, "Aragonese Crown," pp. 5–6.

14. "... fuit per papam creatus, cum consilio procerum domus": L. de Mas-Latrie,
"Notice sur les Archives de Malte à Cité-la-Valette," *Archives des missions scientifiques et
littéraires,* 1st ser., VI (1857), 29. Villaret died in retirement in 1327.

of Cos, in which there were some two thousand Greeks who had slain the Hospitallers' garrison there and gone over to Andronicus; leaving a new garrison, he returned with numerous captives to Rhodes. Again in 1320, with four galleys and twenty lighter craft aided by six Genoese galleys, Schwarzburg inflicted severe losses on a Turkish force of eighty vessels and a large army preparing to attack Rhodes. After this, although there were often frightening reports of preparations against Rhodes, as for instance in 1325, no serious attack was made upon the island for over a century, and the Hospitallers were more free to intervene elsewhere. In 1319 and 1320 the pope instructed that Maurice of Pagnac, now preceptor in Cilicia, was to urge the kings of Cilician Armenia and Cyprus to respect their truce; he was also to reside on and defend the Hospital's Cilician lands if they were returned by king Ōshin, who had seized them, probably because of the Hospital's earlier support of king Henry of Cyprus. During the next few years, while Cilician Armenia was being ravaged by Mongol, Turkish, and Mamluk forces, Pagnac did provide some troops for its defense.[15]

At this point certain weaknesses limiting the Hospital's contribution to the crusading movement became increasingly evident to contemporaries. Once it was no longer necessary to defend Rhodes itself, the Hospitallers' lack of clear objectives and of a vigorous policy of their own was exposed. This weakness was due partly to the Hospital's dependence on the popes, who mostly failed to provide effective leadership, and partly to the corruption and disorganization to be found in many of the European priories, which prevented the Hospitallers from mobilizing their full resources at Rhodes. From the west the occupation of Rhodes looked at the time like an act of self-preservation or of self-aggrandizement which promised little crusading activity; subsequently the Hospitallers seemed to have transferred the defensive attitudes acquired in their Syrian castle to Rhodes, where they appeared to be defending only themselves.

The Hospital, while still in debt, faced heavy expenses for the fortification of Rhodes and the upkeep of the Convent, its mercenaries, and its hospital, and for costly imports of food, horses, and armaments. The Hospital possessed vessels used for transport from Europe and could summon Rhodian mariners into service, but the brethren often came from the petty landed nobility and many were French; probably few were interested in naval affairs. At times the Hospital had to rely on Sicilian, Provençal, Venetian, or, especially,

15. Luttrell, "Cilician Armenia" [forthcoming].

Genoese shipping, and the Venetians in particular were reluctant to help. Throughout the century the Hospitallers could seldom provide more than three or four galleys for an expedition, plus one or two retained to guard Rhodes.[16] Genuine debts and difficulties were ignored, even by an experienced man such as Marino Sanudo Torsello, whose crusading projects envisaged the exploitation of Latin seapower and the prohibition of all trade with Moslems through the maintenance of a blockade to be enforced by ten galleys, two of them to be provided by the Hospital. In about 1323 Sanudo claimed that, since the defense of Rhodes was costing less, the Hospitallers' Cypriote and Armenian incomes could be used to support 150 armed horsemen to defend Cilicia. In 1329 Sanudo expressed surprise that despite an annual income from the *responsiones* alone of 180,000 florins, of which some 20,000 came from Cyprus, the Hospitallers were unable to provide even two or three galleys for a small campaign; he also accused them of harboring pirates at Rhodes. [17] Papal crusading plans of 1323 theoretically involved a Hospitaller contribution of a thousand men-at-arms.[18]

Villeneuve, well aware of the serious problems in the west, remained in Europe from 1319 until 1332. There were rulers who seized the Hospitallers' lands and incomes, demanded their services, sought to control nominations to priories, and prevented men and money from leaving for Rhodes. The brethren themselves often failed to pay their *responsiones,* alienated the Hospital's lands, and refused to go to the Convent in the Levant. The master attacked these deficiencies in chapters-general held in Provence and, with papal coöperation, continued the struggle to gain effective control of the Templars' lands. Except in Portugal, Castile, and Valencia, a considerable number of these properties were secured, after much negotiation and litigation with kings, bishops, and nobles who claimed or had occupied them; in France, for example, the king demanded 200,000 livres for their transfer. These lands certainly enriched the Hospital, but their assimilation involved administrative problems, and the new priories of Catalonia, Aquitaine, Toulouse, and Champagne were created.[19] Some of the lands were sold to meet the huge debts

16. E. Rossi, *Storia della marina dell' Ordine di S. Giovanni di Gerusalemme, di Rodi e di Malta* (Rome and Milan, 1926), pp. 10–17; A. Luttrell, "The *Servitudo Marina* at Rhodes: 1306–1462," *Zeitschrift für Neogräzistik* [forthcoming].

17. Sanudo, in *Gesta Dei per Francos,* ed. J. Bongars, II (Hanover, 1611), 5–7, 31, 313–316.

18. Finke, *Acta aragonensia,* I (Berlin, 1908), 494–496.

19. A. Luttrell, "La Corona de Aragón y las Órdenes militares durante el siglo XIV," *VIII Congreso de Historia de la Corona de Aragón,* III (Valencia, 1970), 67–77; "The Hospitallers of Rhodes in Portugal: 1291–1415," *Congreso Luso-Espanhol de Estudos medievais* (Porto [forthcoming]).

incurred by Villaret between 1306 and 1310. In 1320 the Hospital owed over 500,000 florins, mainly to the pope's Florentine bankers, the Bardi and Peruzzi, but Villeneuve raised the *responsiones*, levied special subsidies, and had liquidated the debt by about 1335.[20] A visitor to Rhodes described the master as "a very old and stingy man, who amassed infinite treasures, built much in Rhodes, and freed the Hospital of incredible debts."[21]

Hospitallers moved back and forth between Europe and the Convent, although, despite regulations to the contrary, some acquired priories and preceptories without serving at Rhodes; such men often cared mainly for the wealth and social position the Hospital offered. Others served predominantly in the Levant, where they garrisoned castles and governed the populations of Rhodes and the lesser islands, the senior brethren sharing the higher offices of the Convent. There were reported to be four hundred Hospitallers at Rhodes in 1345, with a small garrison at Cos; their fighting force also included mercenaries and local levies. At Rhodes the brethren lived in a reserved quarter around the castle, the *collachium,* separated by a fortified wall from the rest of the city or *borgo.* Some Hospitallers had their own houses, while others lived in the *auberge* or hospice of their priory or nation; they included Italians, some Germans, and a few Englishmen and Spaniards, but the French-speaking group was the largest. In theory the details of their daily life and discipline, their religious exercises and military training, were regulated by the statutes. Some of the rules were harsh or trivial, but probably many brethren, served by their slaves in the semi-oriental society of Rhodes, lived comfortably in the Frankish town with its classical foundations or in the hilltop castles which looked out over the sea.

When Hélion of Villeneuve died in 1346 Rhodes possessed a strong castle and defensive landward fortifications, and his successor Dieudonné of Gozon built walls to the seaward side and a mole to improve the harbor. Rhodes was in part a Latin town, where notaries, clerics, doctors, scribes, soldiers, businessmen, and pilgrims from Italy and farther west lived in houses built in a western style. An English visitor of 1345 wrote: "Within the castle walls are an archbishop and his metropolitan church, and the dwellings of the many citizens are like those of distinguished men. There are money-

20. Luttrell, "Interessi fiorentini nell' economia e nella politica dei Cavalieri Ospedalieri di Rodi nel trecento," *Annali della Scuola Normale Superiore di Pisa: lettere, storia e filosofia,* 2nd ser., XXVIII (1959), 317–320; and documents in C. Tipton, "The 1330 Chapter General of the Knights Hospitallers at Montpellier," *Traditio,* XXIV (1968), 293–308. There are no regular statistics for the amounts of money reaching Rhodes.

21. Ludolph of Suchem, *De itinere Terrae Sanctae liber,* ed. F. Deycks (Stuttgart, 1851), p. 27.

ers, armorers, and all the artificers necessary to a city or royal castle. Below the castle is the house of the hospital, a mother, nurse, doctor, protector, and handmaiden to all the infirm." The considerable Greek population retained its Orthodox religion, and its relations with the Hospitallers, whom the Greeks probably regarded as protectors, were remarkably good. Rhodes was a port of call for merchantmen, and even for corsairs; in 1341 the master had to dispossess Ligorio Assanti of his half of the fief of Nisyros, which had become a "den of robbers," for his pirateering had involved the Hospital in trouble with king Hugh IV of Cyprus.[22] The Hospitallers themselves profitably traded large quantities of European cloth in the Levant, and marketed in France and Italy the lucrative sugar crop from their estates in Cyprus and Rhodes; they even sent ships to trade in the luxury markets at Alexandria.[23]

The master's chancery at Rhodes was developed into an efficient office with a proper archive, while Latin lawyers manned the judicial courts. Though seldom intellectuals, the Hospitallers placed some importance on education, and they sought to reduce their reliance on expensive lawyers by setting up an unofficial canon law *studium* at Paris; thereafter trained brethren could act as procurators at the papal curia and in the civil service at Rhodes. Hospitaller theologians and classicists were extremely rare, but one wealthy master, Juan Fernández de Heredia, patronized important historical compilations and translations.[24] At Rhodes, and in certain houses in the priories, the brethren maintained the ancient tradition of care for travelers, the sick, and the aged.[25]

22. Ludolph of Suchem (1336–1341), pp. 27–29, and the anonymous Englishman (1345) in Golubovich, *Biblioteca bio-bibliografica,* IV (1923), 444–445. Cf. G. Sommi Picenardi, *Itinéraire d'un chevalier de Saint-Jean de Jérusalem dans l'île de Rhodes* (Lille, 1900), and A. Gabriel, *La Cité de Rhodes, 1310–1522* (2 vols., Paris, 1921–1923). An almost completely unnoticed fourteenth-century text of town regulations *(capitula Rodi)* is in P. Ewald, "Reise nach Spanien im Winter von 1878 auf 1879," *Neues Archiv,* VI (1881), 265–269.

23. A. Luttrell, "Actividades económicas de los Hospitalarios de Rodas en el Mediterráneo occidental durante el siglo XIV," *VI Congreso de Historia de la Corona de Aragón* (Madrid, 1959), pp. 175–183.

24. In addition to Luttrell, "Historical Activities," XXIV, 126–129, see his "Notes on the Chancery of the Hospitallers of Rhodes: 1314–1332," *Byzantion,* XL (1970), 408–420; "Fourteenth-Century Hospitaller Lawyers," *Traditio,* XXI (1965), 449–456; "Jean and Simon de Hesdin: Hospitallers, Theologians, Classicists," *Recherches de théologie ancienne et médiévale,* XXXI (1964), 137–140; "Greek Histories Translated and Compiled for Juan Fernández de Heredia, Master of Rhodes, 1377–1396," *Speculum,* XXXV (1960), 401–407, with postscript in "Coluccio Salutati's Letter to Juan Fernández de Heredia," *Italia medioevale et umanistica,* XIII (1970), 63–71.

25. General considerations in A. Luttrell, "The Hospitallers' Hospice of Santa Caterina at Venice: 1358–1451," *Studi veneziani,* XII (1970), 369–383.

After their defeat of the Turks in 1320 the Hospitallers were inactive for over a decade. Their closest enemies were the Turks of the emirate of Menteshe, based on the port of Palatia (Miletus) on the mainland north of Rhodes, but Umur Pasha, emir of Aydin, whose strong fleet sailed from Altoluogo farther north to make damaging incursions in the Aegean and on mainland Greece, was a more dangerous foe. In 1327 the Venetians were sufficiently worried to decide on negotiations with the Byzantines, with Martin Zaccaria of Chios, and with the Hospitallers, in a fruitless attempt to prevent Umur from capturing the port of Smyrna. In 1329 the Venetians and Greeks were ready to arm if the Hospitallers gave the lead, but the Hospital could not produce even a few galleys. The Hospital also failed to take action when in August 1332 pope John XXII encouraged it to occupy the castles of Sechin and Antiochia Parva on the Cilician coast, which the Armenians were unable to defend.

At the time when Villeneuve finally reached Rhodes in 1332 Umur was attacking Gallipoli and Euboea. On September 6 at Rhodes, Greek and Venetian envoys finally agreed that a Christian fleet, to include four galleys from Rhodes, should assemble in April 1333, but an insurrection in Crete delayed the project. In March 1334 the pope and the kings of France and Cyprus joined the league; the Hospitallers' contribution was raised to ten galleys, at least some of which they did supply. The papal and French contingents, having revictualed at Rhodes, joined the fleet, which won limited naval successes in the autumn of 1334 but broke up leaving the Turks basically as strong as ever. The Hospitallers continued minor operations in the Aegean, and together with the Venetian Nicholas Sanudo, duke of the Archipelago, they occupied Lesbos, only to be evicted by the Genoese. The campaign of 1335, for which the Hospital had agreed to provide six galleys, eight transports, and two hundred men-at-arms, was abandoned.[26]

The recapture of Cos in about 1337 strengthened the Hospitallers' position, while they also held a small but strong castle somewhere on the mainland.[27] Encouraged by the pope and free of major debts, the Hospitallers had at last begun to make Rhodes a center of

---

26. Delaville Le Roulx, *Rhodes,* pp. 86–90; Lemerle, *Aydin,* pp. 54–61, 89–100, 108, 142, correcting serious errors and providing some evidence for an unsuccessful Hospitaller-Cypriote attack on Smyrna late in 1334. See also A. Laiou, "Marino Sanudo Torsello, Byzantium and the Turks: the Background to the Anti-Turkish League of 1332–1334," *Speculum,* XLV (1970), 374–392.

27. Ludolph of Suchem, pp. 27–28; Malta, cod. 280, folios 39^v, 43^r. The story of Cos, lost to the Turks before 1319, is obscure (Delaville Le Roulx, *Rhodes,* pp. 4, 8, 24, 99).

genuine crusading activity when John XXII died in December 1334. At first Benedict XII continued his predecessor's policy, but though the new pope had funds available he was pacific, economical, and somewhat unenthusiastic about the crusade. In any case, from 1336 onward Benedict's hands were tied by the great Anglo-French war and numerous concomitant struggles which precluded any major expedition, and he refused to declare an official crusade when, in effect, that meant granting papal crusading taxes for secular purposes, in particular to the French king. Meanwhile from about 1335, when its debts were extinguished, to about 1343, when it had a credit of some 360,000 florins with the Florentine banks of Bardi, Peruzzi, and Acciajuoli, the Hospital continued the payments it had long been making to them. Thus papal discouragement of any crusading effort by the Hospitallers prevented expenditures which would have increased the growing difficulties of these three houses, which, at least until 1339, were also the pope's own bankers. In May 1336 when Cilicia was threatened by the Mamluks, Benedict canceled all support for an expedition there. In June the Venetians suggested that although Benedict had refused financial aid, they and the Hospitallers should equip a fleet at their own expense; the fleet assembled but did nothing of note. [28] Thereafter the crusade was abandoned, although in 1341 the Cypriote king and the Hospital both appealed for papal aid, and negotiations for a new league were opened with Venice.[29]

Pope Clement VI, elected in 1342, was perhaps unjust in threatening the Hospitallers that he would found a new order with their possessions if they did not abandon their idle ways and contribute to the upkeep of a Latin fleet, but it was Clement's vigorous diplomacy which secured action against Umur of Aydin. The Hospitallers, faced with a demand for six galleys, increased their *responsiones* to finance the squadron which joined the Venetian, Cypriote, and papal forces in 1344. After a minor naval victory north of Euboea, the Latins attacked Smyrna, where Umur was preparing a large fleet for a new campaign; they surprised Umur and captured the port and its fortress on October 28, a great if lucky success.[30] Then during an assault in January 1345 on the upper citadel, which was never captured, the papal legate Henry of Asti, the papal captain Martin Zaccaria, and the Venetian leader Peter Zeno were killed; thereafter, the Latins

---

28. For this interpretation of Benedict's policy see Luttrell, "Interessi fiorentini," pp. 318–319, and "The Crusade," pp. 133–134; see also F. Giunta, "Benedetto XII e la crociata," *Anuario de estudios medievales,* III (1966), 215–234.

29. Hill, *Cyprus,* II, 299.

30. On the capture of Smyrna see above, pp. 11–12.

were besieged in the lower fortress. The Hospital played a leading role in the defense, and on May 1, 1345, the pope named a Hospitaller, John of Biandrate, prior of Lombardy, as *capitaneus armatae generalis*. In December a Hospitaller galley was among the six which met Humbert, the dauphin of Viennois, at Negroponte, and in the summer of 1346 the Hospital participated in his unsuccessful expedition to Smyrna;[31] talk of a truce followed, while Humbert wintered at Rhodes before returning to France in 1347. Around the end of April the Hospital's fleet, supported by other Latin forces, destroyed over a hundred Turkish vessels at Imbros near the mouth of the Dardanelles.

Success at Imbros did little to relieve Smyrna. In April 1347 the new master, Dieudonné of Gozon, specifically forbade the Hospitallers to assume responsibility for its defense; for while the Genoese were occupying Chios for their own advantage, the Venetians, quarreling bitterly with the Hospital over customs duties at Rhodes and persistently calling for action against Umur, were reluctant to make any contribution toward the defense of Smyrna, where they could expect only limited profits. After Clement VI had sanctioned truce negotiations in November 1346, the Hospitallers realistically took the lead in reaching an agreement that, in return for trading concessions at Smyrna and Altoluogo, the Latin powers would raze the harbor fortress at Smyrna. The pope vetoed this arrangement in February 1348, but after Umur was killed by chance while attacking the walls of Smyrna in May, a peace favorable to the Latins was agreed upon with Umur's brother Khiḍr on August 18. Clement and the Venetians again opposed the settlement and, when envoys from Venice, Cyprus, and Rhodes finally met at Avignon in May 1350 to ratify it, they were instead persuaded to form a new league. On August 11 the Hospitallers agreed to contribute 3,000 florins annually toward the cost of maintaining the garrison at Smyrna, and to provide three galleys for a fleet to defend Christian shipping. Then war between Genoa and Venice wrecked the new coalition, and Clement formally dissolved it in September 1351.[32]

After Villeneuve's death in 1346 the Hospitallers' lack of clear purpose again became evident. On papal instructions they sent some assistance to Cilician Armenia in 1347, but they ignored further orders to intervene there in 1351.[33] The Hospitallers' difficulties in

31. On Humbert's crusade see above, pp. 12–13.

32. Lemerle, *Aydin,* pp. 180–203, 226–235; Luttrell, "Venice," pp. 203–205; see also J. Gay, *Le Pape Clément VI et les affaires d'Orient, 1342–1352* (Paris, 1904).

33. Luttrell, "Cilician Armenia" [forthcoming]; this amends the standard accounts (e.g. in Gay, *Clément VI,* pp. 146–149). The Hospitallers did not retake Ayas (Lajazzo) in 1347.

Europe increased their reluctance to assume responsibilities. They lost heavily, more than 360,000 florins, when their Florentine bankers went bankrupt between 1343 and 1346,[34] and though the great plague of 1348 probably killed comparatively few Hospitallers, it certainly brought falling rents and increased indiscipline in its aftermath.[35] In view of the economic difficulties of supporting all who wished to serve at Rhodes, a *passagium* of a hundred brethren which was planned in April 1351 had subsequently to be limited to those who could come properly armed and horsed.[36] As usual, these difficulties were not appreciated in the west: Petrarch wrote, "Rhodes, shield of the faith, lies unwounded, inglorious,"[37] and in 1354 pope Innocent VI, reviving old accusations, reminded the Hospitallers that they had been endowed to fight the "infidel," and threatened that if they remained inactive he would transfer the Convent to the mainland, presumably to Smyrna, and use the Templars' lands to found a new order. In fact, the rather undistinguished masters who succeeded Villeneuve[38] only occasionally opposed the directions of the popes or their legates, and in 1356 an assembly of Hospitallers summoned to Avignon had to accept disciplinary and administrative reforms proposed by Innocent VI, who instructed that they be inserted in the statutes.

Acceptance of the Hospital's immobility at Rhodes and of defensive campaigns which mainly benefited Genoese and Venetian commerce was not complete. The Hospitallers occupied the castle of Carystus on Euboea for a period in 1351, despite the Venetians' protests at such an invasion of their sphere of interest.[39] The Hospitallers perhaps realized that Greece, where they had long possessed minor estates, offered far greater resources in agricultural produce and manpower than Rhodes, which was so expensive to occupy. The defense of the Morea against the ravages of the Turks was an increasingly serious problem, and during 1356 and 1357 Innocent VI sponsored secret plans to establish the Hospital some-

34. Luttrell, "Interessi fiorentini," pp. 318–319.
35. Luttrell, "Los Hospitalarios en Aragón y la peste negra," *Anuario de estudios medievales,* III (1966), 499–514; cf. the socio-economic analyses of Hospitaller statistics in G. Duby, "La Seigneurie et l'économie paysanne: Alpes du Sud, 1338," *Études rurales,* II (1961), 5–36, and J. Glénisson, "L'Enquête pontificale de 1373 sur les possessions des Hospitaliers de Saint-Jean-de-Jérusalem," *Bibliothèque de l'École des chartes,* CXXIX (1971), 83–111.
36. Malta, cod. 318, folios 13^V, 103^V.
37. *Le Familiari,* ed. V. Rossi, III (Florence, 1937), 148–153.
38. Dieudonné of Gozon was followed by Peter of Corneillan (1353–1355), Roger de Pins (1355–1365), Raymond Bérenger (1365–1374), and Robert of Juilly (1374–1377).
39. Luttrell, "Venice," p. 208.

where in the principality of Achaea, possibly at Corinth. The Angevin rulers of Achaea rejected the idea and entrusted Corinth to Nicholas Acciajuoli in 1358. The project was abandoned if not forgotten; it may have met opposition at Rhodes, but it indicated some awareness that the brethren might be more effectively and honorably employed.[40]

After Umur's death the Turks of Altoluogo and Palatia were less dangerous, but a sporadic piratical conflict continued at sea. With peace between Venice and Genoa, the league to defend Smyrna was revived in 1356; that autumn the Hospital's galleys lay ready, but the Venetian preparations were delayed and there was no significant action. In June and July 1358 a hundred Hospitallers were summoned to Rhodes, and in 1359 the pope appointed the Florentine Hospitaller Nicholas Benedetti as captain of Smyrna for eight years. Benedetti was to fortify the town with walls and towers and to maintain 150 Latin mercenaries and two galleys; he received a papal license to send one ship and two galleys to trade at Alexandria to finance these measures, while he and his brothers, who were granted rights of succession during his eight-year tenure, were to retain any territory they might capture from the Moslems. Probably in 1359, a fleet which included a Rhodian contingent under Raymond Bérenger, preceptor of Cos, burned thirty-five Turkish ships off Megara in Greece. Late in 1359 the Gascon Carmelite Peter Thomas, newly appointed as papal legate, visited Smyrna, where he organized the defenses and forced the Turks of Altoluogo to pay tribute. From 1363 until 1371 the captain of Smyrna was Peter Racanelli, an important Genoese of Chios, and the pope and the Hospital were sharing the cost of Smyrna's defense, 6,000 florins yearly.

In Byzantium itself, civil war had weakened resistance to the Turks. Innocent VI had made it clear that the price of Latin assistance was Greek submission in matters of faith, and in 1353 he had instructed the Hospitallers and others to help John VI Cantacuzenus in such circumstances. In 1354 the Ottoman Turks captured Gallipoli, establishing themselves in Europe; in 1357 John V Palaeologus

---

40. Documents referring obscurely to a *negotium principatus Achaye* (Archivio Segreto Vaticano, Reg. Vat. 238, folios 64^r–65^v; 239, folios 74^v–75^r) were used, but inaccurately, by Bosio. Later scholars, notably K. Hopf, K. Herquet, and J. Delaville Le Roulx, misled by Bosio and by each other, have produced wildly fantastic interpretations of this *negotium;* [H.] Zeininger de Borja, "Les Hospitaliers de Saint-Jean de Jérusalem en Grèce continentale," *Rivista araldica,* LVII (1959), 297–300, unfortunately followed them in these, as in various other errors (cf. below, p. 303, note 53).

submitted to the Roman church;[41] and in 1359 Peter Thomas arrived at Constantinople, accompanied by Venetian and Rhodian galleys. He failed to cement the union between the churches, but with Greek assistance the Latin forces destroyed the Ottoman fort at Lampsacus opposite Gallipoli in the Dardanelles; fifty Hospitallers fought a notable rearguard action in the withdrawal from the fort. The legate then sailed to Smyrna, and early in 1360 he lay ill at Rhodes. He went from there to Cyprus, abandoning the Latin league; two Hospitaller galleys were laid up at Rhodes and the Venetians were left to oppose the Ottomans alone. At the very moment when seapower had been used effectively against the Ottomans, who, unlike the Turks of Aydin and the emirates south of Smyrna, had no fleet and were therefore vulnerable, Peter Thomas, more interested in converting heretics than in defending the Balkans, turned Latin strength to another sphere centered on Cyprus. Demotica and Adrianople fell to the Ottomans in 1361.[42]

Peter de Lusignan, king of Cyprus from 1359, his chancellor Philip of Mézières, and Peter Thomas were jointly responsible for the diversion to the southern Levant of the limited political and financial support the papacy could provide. The Hospitallers were accustomed to participate in Cypriote affairs, and were probably more sympathetic to the French elements in Cyprus and to their own ancient chivalric ideal, the recovery of Jerusalem, than to Venetian commercial interests in Romania or to the Greeks, with whom coöperation was so difficult. The Hospital provided four galleys and some troops for the Cypriote campaign which captured Adalia from the emir of Tekke in August 1361, and when Peter de Lusignan visited Rhodes in 1362 on his way westward to organize a crusade, the Hospital gave a written promise of assistance. The king returned in 1365 and during August and September he assembled his forces at Rhodes, where the emirs of Altoluogo and Palatia hastened to offer him tribute through the master's mediation. After intensive preaching by Peter Thomas, a fleet of over 150 galleys sailed for an unannounced destination on October 4; the Hospital provided four galleys, some transport vessels, and a hundred brethren under the admiral, Ferlino of Airasca, prior of Lombardy. This force in fact made for Alexandria. There the Hospitallers' unexpected appearance

41. Cf. above, pp. 69–70, for a somewhat different interpretation.
42. To Luttrell, "Venice," pp. 205–206, add details in O. Halecki, *Un Empereur de Byzance à Rome: Vingt ans de travail pour l'union des églises et pour la défense de l'empire d'Orient, 1355–1375* (Warsaw, 1930), pp. 9–30, 60–77; J. Smet, *The Life of Saint Peter Thomas by Philippe de Mézières* (Rome, 1954), pp. 84–90, 206–212. See also above, pp. 72–73.

in the defenders' rear assured a successful landing, and they further distinguished themselves in the storming of the city, which was sacked with incredible destruction. Many crusaders, including Ferlino, maintained that resistance against the sultan's forces would be impossible, and so the fleet left for Cyprus with its plunder.[43]

The Venetians, infuriated by the ruin of their commercial position in Egypt, wrecked serious hopes of further action by spreading rumors of a peace, with the result that in 1366 an expedition led by Amadeo VI of Savoy sailed not toward Cyprus and the southern Levant but to Romania.[44] Early in 1366 the master, alarmed by Turkish and Mamluk preparations, summoned a hundred Hospitallers, together with all available money, to Rhodes; he arranged for the purchase of horses and arms in Italy. During 1366 and 1367 Peter of Cyprus, assisted by four galleys and other craft from Rhodes, attacked the Turks in Cilicia. In June 1367 Peter was in Rhodes, and in September he was pillaging the Syrian coast as far as Ayas (Lajazzo); the turcopolier of the Hospital was killed in fighting at Tripoli. King Peter's assassination in 1369 deprived the crusade of strong leadership, but in the autumn eight galleys representing Rhodes, Cyprus, Genoa, and Venice sailed to Alexandria to threaten the sultan, with whom negotiations were still dragging on. A general peace closed a crusading epoch in mid-1370, while in Cyprus a period of strife followed the accession of the fifteen-year-old Peter II.[45] In 1371 pope Gregory XI named a Hospitaller, Bertrand Flote, as the young king's guardian and appointed the master to a council of regency. Yet the Hospital was powerless to prevent a successful Genoese uprising against the Lusignans in 1373. The master, Raymond Bérenger, twice visited Cyprus to mediate, and died there in February 1374. When in April 1374 Peter II's uncle, John de Lusignan, arrived at Rhodes seeking protection but followed by Genoese galleys, the Hospitallers had to insist that he leave the island. Furthermore, the Hospital apparently did nothing to prevent the collapse of the Armenian kingdom in Cilicia before Mamluk and Turkish forces in 1375.[46]

The Hospitallers' ineffectiveness in the Levant was rooted in cor-

43. See below, pp. 356–357; Hill, *Cyprus,* II, 318–323, 329–334; and Smet, *Peter Thomas,* pp. 103, 125–140; see also F. Boehlke, *Pierre de Thomas: Scholar, Diplomat, and Crusader* (Philadelphia, 1966). The documents confirm the number of 100 Hospitallers given by Philip of Mézières; this included two Englishmen, the turcopolier William Middleton and Robert Hales, later prior of England (Malta, cod. 319, folios 171^r–172^r, 316^r).

44. On Amadeo VI's crusade see above, pp. 74–77.

45. See below, pp. 361–366.

46. Hill, *Cyprus,* II, 339, 344, 347–354, 373–379, 389–390, 402–403, 410–411.

ruption and indiscipline in Europe. Philip of Mézières complained that the brethren served four or five years at Rhodes in order to get a good preceptory or priory, and then returned to Europe: *c'est une moquerie ou grant derision.*[47] The blame lay partly with the popes, whose attempts to reform the Hospital achieved little but who increasingly interfered with nominations to offices and other business. Innocent VI had pretentious schemes for the reform of the vices he denounced, yet he disrupted the Hospital's whole European organization by overruling legitimate complaints from the Convent, and he abused his papal powers by providing his ambitious and experienced Aragonese favorite Juan Fernández de Heredia both to the priory of Castile and Leon and to the Hospital's richest priory, that of St. Gilles in Provence. Fernández de Heredia had obtained the castellany of Amposta (as the priory of Aragon was called) in 1346 through the favor of Peter IV of Aragon, and for many years he exemplified those unscrupulous brethren who scarcely visited Rhodes but controlled extensive Hospitaller possessions in the west. His own administrative and political talents enabled him to extract great wealth from the Hospital, and to enrich his kinsmen and illegitimate children.[48] Even so he was outdone in grandiosity, refractoriness, and personal immorality by Álvaro Gonçalves Pereira, prior of Portugal. The Iberian priories, notably those of Castile and Portugal, were especially difficult to discipline, but they were not the only ones which fell into arrears with their *responsiones* or failed to pay them in full.[49]

Capable brethren were not always employed to the Hospital's profit; in 1340, for example, every province in the Papal States was governed by a Hospitaller. The masters were well-intentioned but many were old men, and some had little experience in the east; Dieudonné of Gozon and Raymond Bérenger both tried to resign. The Convent attempted to resist Innocent VI but was powerless when, for example, he appointed a committee of cardinals to whitewash Fernández de Heredia's blatant transgressions; subsequently Raymond Bérenger and pope Urban V did manage to strip him of part of his power. The struggle for men and money conducted

47. Philip of Mézières, *Le Songe du vieil pèlerin,* ed. G. Coopland, I (Cambridge, 1969), 259–260.

48. Details and references in Luttrell, "Aragonese Crown," pp. 13–19; "Juan Fernández de Heredia at Avignon: 1351–1367," in *El Cardenal Albornoz y el Colegio de España,* ed. E. Verdera y Tuells, I (Bologna, 1972), 289–316.

49. While the administrative documents used extensively in Delaville Le Roulx, *Rhodes,* naturally tend to reflect the troubles which provoked them, the surviving accounts do modify this picture of widespread corruption; see J. Nisbet, "Treasury Records of the Knights of St. John in Rhodes," *Melita historica,* II, no. 2 (1957), 95–104.

against endless indifference and corruption seems to have exhausted most masters, and the Hospital's lack of gifted leaders and of firm and positive direction was enhanced by the predominance of feeble or distracted popes who usually counted on the Hospital to take part in their ineffective Levantine campaigns but whose meddling in Hospitaller affairs was of doubtful value. Many of the brethren themselves knew the Levant well enough to realize the futility of small amphibious expeditions which might make minor coastal gains but certainly lacked the sustained strength to conserve them; it was difficult enough to garrison Smyrna.

While further chances of crusading activity based on Cyprus faded, it became clear that the Latins must support the Greeks in Romania. Amadeo VI of Savoy took Gallipoli from the Ottomans in 1366 but was unable to hold it; John V Palaeologus submitted to the pope anew in 1369 but could not persuade his Greek subjects to coöperate with the Latins; and in 1371 Serbian resistance was crushed by the Turks at Chernomen on the Maritsa river. Latins as well as Greeks were in danger and the new pope, Gregory XI, was determined to use the Hospitallers, almost the only reliable military force available, to oppose the Ottomans. In 1373 he ordered episcopal inquests into the state of every preceptory in Europe, while expressing his intention of providing a Latin fleet to operate against the Turks in the Dardanelles and the Aegean. In 1374, despite the Hospitallers' marked reluctance, he made them wholly responsible for the defense of Smyrna, revoking the captaincy of Ottobono Cattaneo, a Genoese of Rhodes appointed in 1371, who had grossly neglected his duties. He also sent two Hospitallers, Bertrand Flote and Hesso Schlegelholtz, to Constantinople to prepare for a *passagium* of Hospitallers *ad partes Romanie;* this expedition was to be organized and commanded by Juan Fernández de Heredia, who had returned to papal favor and now secured wide powers as the master's lieutenant in the west. Preparations moved slowly. Late in 1375 some four hundred Hospitallers, each with a squire, were summoned for the *passagium;* the French priories were to provide 125 brethren, the Italian 108, the Spanish and Portuguese 73, the English and Irish 38, the German and Bohemian 32, the Hungarian 17, and the preceptories of the Morea and of the duchy of Athens two each. Hospitaller lands were to be sold or rented, and 24,500 florins were borrowed from the Alberti of Florence; Gregory supported these arrangements and ordered that the money raised should be kept in Europe, not sent to Rhodes.

On August 10, 1376, the master, Robert of Juilly, wrote of a *passagium ad partes ducatus Athenarum,* presumably intended to defend the Catalans of Thebes and Athens against the Turks; the Catalans, in fact, were so weak that in 1374 they were unable to prevent Nerio Acciajuoli of Corinth from seizing Megara.[50] These plans had to be changed when hopes of ecclesiastical union and military coöperation with the Greeks were ruined by a new war between Genoa and Venice, and by the intervention of both parties, and also of the Turks, in increasing civil strife within Byzantium. The *passagium* was further delayed while Gregory XI left Avignon late in 1376 and sailed slowly to Rome, with a fleet commanded by Fernández de Heredia. The pope continued to encourage elaborate preparations for the expedition, the destination of which was changed during the summer from the Aegean to the Adriatic. In about June 1377 the principality of Achaea was leased by the Hospital for five years from queen Joanna I of Naples, and a Hospitaller, Daniel del Carretto, was sent as bailie and took over the government of the Latin Morea.[51] Negotiations with Maddalena de' Buondelmonti (the widow of Leonard I Tocco, duke of Leucadia and count of Cephalonia), who was acting as regent for her two sons, were completed in October; from Maddalena the Hospitallers acquired Vonitsa, a port on the Gulf of Arta in Epirus which for some years had been subject to attacks from the Albanian forces of Ghin Boua Spata, lord of Arta, and which provided a gateway into northern Greece. Robert of Juilly died on July 27, 1377, and on October 24 Gregory XI, having previously reserved the provision *pro hac vice,* appointed Fernández de Heredia in his place. In response to vigorous protests from the Convent, Gregory had to promise that the Hospital's privileges would not again be flouted by such a provision.

The new master left Naples with the *passagium* around the beginning of 1378, accompanied by Francis and Esau de' Buondelmonti, Maddalena's brothers, and by various other Florentines who helped with financial, transport, and supply problems, apparently in the hope of commercial advantage. By April a rather small force of Hospitallers, which included the admiral, Palamedo Giovanni, and the priors of Venice, Pisa, and Capua, was at Vonitsa. There they delayed, apparently because the new pope Urban VI, elected on April 8, failed to send the necessary reinforcements. By summer, when the expedition advanced inland and attacked the walls of Arta with siege engines, Ghin Boua Spata had been given time to collect

---

50. See above, pp. 211–212.
51. See above, pp. 147–148, where the summer of 1376 is considered more likely.

an army which included Thomas Preljubovich, the Serbian despot of Ianina. The Hospitallers were ambushed, probably in August; some were killed and others, including Fernández de Heredia, were captured.[52] The Hospital's first major operation of its own since the conquest of Rhodes ended in military disaster.

Vonitsa was evacuated by the Hospitallers, though it remained in Latin hands, while Lepanto (Naupactus) and various fortresses in the Morea were garrisoned with Latin mercenaries; the Hospital also hired 150 members of the Navarrese companies who came into Greece from Durazzo in Albania under the command of John de Urtubia, Mahiot of Coquerel, and others. Though the master was free by the spring of 1379 and reached Rhodes in July, the Hospital gradually lost control in Greece. It had to borrow heavily; Lepanto passed to Ghin Boua Spata; and the Hospital was forced to pawn its possessions in the Catalan duchy of Athens to Nerio Acciajuoli. Certain individual Hospitallers joined with Nerio and the Navarrese in attacks on the Catalan duchy; the Catalans even lost Thebes to the Navarrese, probably in the spring of 1379. By 1381 the Navarrese were established in the Morea, where the Hospitaller commanders Bertrand Flote and Hesso Schlegelholtz, unable to control them, were forced to buy them off. Early in 1381, faced with the Navarrese, with problems at Rhodes, with the expenses of the *passagium* and the master's ransom, and with the crises both in Latin Greece and in the Hospital itself which had followed the election in September 1378 of Clement VII as a rival pope, the Hospitallers abandoned their expensive commitments in the principality of Achaea and handed its government back to queen Joanna's officials.[53]

52. See above, pp. 216–217. In 1386 Esau de' Buondelmonti married Thomas Preljubovich's widow Angelina, and became ruler of Ianina.

53. The standard versions of this Greek intervention, such as Delaville Le Roulx, *Rhodes,* pp. 199–211, and Zeininger, "Grèce continentale," pp. 393–396, repeat earlier errors of fact and interpretation. See R. J. Loenertz, "Hospitaliers et Navarrais en Grèce, 1376–1383: Régestes et documents," *Orientalia Christiana periodica,* XXII (1956), 319–360, reprinted in his *Byzantina et Franco-Graeca* (Rome, 1970), pp. 329–369; background studies in G. Dennis, *The Reign of Manuel II Palaeologus in Thessalonica, 1382–1387* (Rome, 1960), pp. 26–46; A. Eszer, *Das abenteuerliche Leben des Johannes Laskaris Kalopheros* (Wiesbaden, 1969), pp. 54–79; and above, chapter IV. Further details, amendments, and references are in A. Luttrell, "The Principality of Achaea in 1377," *Byzantinische Zeitschrift,* LVII (1964), 340–343; "Intrigue, Schism, and Violence among the Hospitallers of Rhodes: 1377–1384," *Speculum,* XLI (1966), 30–37; "Aldobrando Baroncelli in Greece: 1378–1382," *Orientalia Christiana periodica,* XXXVI (1970), 273–300; "La Corona de Aragón y la Grecia catalana: 1379–1394," *Anuario de estudios medievales,* VI (1969), 219–252; and "Le Compagnie navarresi in Grecia: 1376–1404" [forthcoming]. Much remains obscure, but there is no evidence to support the accepted allegations that these Greek schemes, or those of 1356–1357, sprang from Fernández de Heredia's ambitions, or that he had any particular interest in or obsession with Greece before he went there in 1378 (cf. Luttrell,

At Rhodes too there were difficulties. The chapters-general of 1370 and 1373 had taken steps, under papal pressure, to curb the overpowerful French brethren, to end their quarrels with the Italians over preceptories in Angevin Italy and Hungary, and to ensure a greater equality among the *langues* or nations at the Convent, especially in the election of masters. The provision to the mastership in 1377 of the powerful Aragonese, who for so many years had defied the master and Convent, was a further threat to the French monopoly. The French priors dominated the chapter-general which met at Rhodes in February 1379; they elected the grand preceptor Bertrand Flote to act as the lieutenant of the captive master, and then attempted to secure direction of the Hospital by enacting that the Convent was to be associated with all the master's decisions and to control his appointments to offices, his grants of land, and similar matters.

Fernández de Heredia's assumption of power when he reached Rhodes in July was probably facilitated by his firm stand in favor of the Avignonese pope Clement VII, whom the French brethren supported. The Hospitallers were among the few Levantine adherents of Clement, who on May 10, 1381, nominated Bertrand Flote as papal collector in Romania. There were difficulties with the garrisons at Smyrna and elsewhere, in raising supplies and paying mercenaries, and in disciplining brethren in the islands; late in February 1382 some sixty brethren were sent back or licensed to return to their priories, the reason given being that the Hospital could not afford to maintain them in the Levant. A dramatic manifestation of petty troubles at Rhodes occurred in the Conventual church on November 2, 1381, when a Gascon Hospitaller, Bertrin of Gagnac, who had been sentenced to the loss of his habit for crimes which included the embezzlement of money at Cos, attempted to knife the master, and was cut down by Palamedo Giovanni and Hesso Schlegelholtz. Thenceforth Fernández de Heredia placed special reliance on non-French brethren such as those two, and in particular on the Italian Dominic de Alamania. The master departed for the west on April 9, 1382, leaving the marshal Peter of Culan in command at Rhodes, but before he sailed, the Convent expressed its distrust of him by restricting his powers and sending commissioners to supervise his actions.

After Juan Fernández de Heredia became master he showed in-

"Greek Histories," pp. 401–402). The western chroniclers were confused and ill-informed on the Arta campaign, but see Laonicus Chalcocondylas, *Historiarum demonstrationes,* ed. E. Darkó, I (Budapest, 1922), 197–199, and the Chronicle of Ianina, in S. Cirac Estopañan,

creasing concern for the Hospital's interests, and resided almost uninterruptedly at Avignon, where he could best serve the Hospital, until his death as a very old man in 1396. He had certainly been the legitimate master, but in March 1381 the Roman pope Urban VI opened an inquiry into the Hospital which led in April 1383 to his nominating a fellow Neapolitan, Richard Caracciolo, prior of Capua, as "anti-master." Caracciolo held several "chapters-general" at Naples and elsewhere in Italy and received some support from English, Gascon, German, and Italian brethren, but even the Italians were far from unanimous in their adherence, while the Hospitallers from Urbanist England continued to send their *responsiones* via Venice to Clementist Rhodes. In 1384 Caracciolo's agent, a Piedmontese Hospitaller named Robaud Vaignon, conducted complex conspiracies with a secret Urbanist sympathizer, George of Ceva, preceptor of Cyprus, and then attempted to win over some of the English, German, and Italian brethren at Rhodes. One of these, Buffilo Panizzatti, preceptor of Bari, denounced Vaignon, who was sent to Avignon where he confessed under torture. Caracciolo's activities faded out after this and his followers dwindled; on his death in 1395 no new appointment was made and in 1410, following the Council of Pisa, the Romanist faction was almost completely reassimilated into the Hospital. That the schism among the Hospitallers ended before that in the church was a tribute to the brethren's restraint; both parties had refrained from actions likely to perpetuate a division in the Hospital.[54]

As serious a result of the schism as the defection of some brethren was the nonpayment of their *responsiones* by others. Despite these difficulties, the master's vast experience and ruthless financial abilities roughly maintained the Hospital's income, which by 1392 stood at some 45,000 florins annually.[55] Insofar as was possible Fernández de Heredia called assemblies, reformed the administration of the priories, and punished recalcitrant brethren; at one point the Hospital owed him 75,000 florins which he had lent it. The money was badly needed, for while Ottoman power continued to grow neither pope showed any real interest in the Levant, which was largely left to defend itself. From 1384 onwards the master flirted with the strate-

Byzancio y España: El Legado de la basilissa María y de los déspotas Thomas y Esaú de Joannina, I (Barcelona, 1943), 143–146 (placing the Arta ambush before the end of August).

54. Luttrell, "Intrigue, Schism, and Violence," pp. 33–48; see also C. Tipton, "The English Hospitallers during the Great Schism," *Studies in Medieval and Renaissance History,* IV (1967), 91–124.

55. Delaville Le Roulx, *Rhodes,* p. 382; Nisbet, "Treasury Records," pp. 102–104.

gically sound idea of renewed intervention in Greece. In about 1385 he negotiated with the Navarrese in the Morea; in 1386 he purchased the Angevin claim to the principality of Achaea; and in 1389 he actually appointed Dominic de Alamania as governor there, empowering him to raise 15,000 ducats.[56] Such schemes however were beyond the Hospital's resources, especially in view of the anarchy then reigning in Greece, and they were dropped when the danger to Smyrna increased after 1389.

The garrison at Smyrna was a minor irritant to the Ottomans, who maintained just sufficient pressure on it to ensure the expenditure of the Christians' energies there without provoking them to a desperate resistance or to alliance with the emirates. For the Hospital, the loss of Smyrna would have been politically disastrous in Europe, and in 1381 the defenses were strengthened and certain unreliable mercenaries expelled. The danger grew when an earthquake seriously damaged the walls in 1389. In that year, in which the vigorous young Bayazid I became the Ottoman ruler, the Hospitallers decided to strengthen Cos and to join the Latins of Cyprus, Chios, Lesbos, and Pera in a defensive naval union which functioned against the Turks for some years. From 1390 on the master was planning a *passagium* in response to appeals from Rhodes, but it was unable to leave until 1394. In 1392 Bayazid was preventing the exportation of food from the mainland, so provisions grew scarce at Rhodes, where a number of brethren died of plague. Negotiations were opened but broke down when the Turks demanded the right to trade slaves at Rhodes. Bayazid then turned his aggression toward the Balkans, and the Christians responded with a major crusade. In 1396 a contingent of Hospitallers sailed into the Black Sea and up the Danube. They fought valiantly in the terrible Christian defeat at Nicopolis, and escaped by sea.[57]

Juan Fernández de Heredia died shortly before the battle of Nicopolis and the leader of the Hospital's forces there, Philibert of Naillac, prior of Auvergne, returned to Rhodes to find himself elected master. He was a distinguished French noble who enjoyed the support of king Charles VI of France and duke Philip of Burgundy. During 1397 the Hospitallers helped to negotiate and finance the ransom of prisoners taken at Nicopolis, many of whom were entertained at Rhodes. One of these, the French marshal Boucicault, returned with six ships to the Levant, and in the autumn of 1399,

56. Luttrell, "Grecia catalana," pp. 242–248.
57. On the crusade of Nicopolis see above, pp. 21–25.

together with the Venetians and two galleys from Rhodes, he brought a respite to besieged Constantinople, winning minor successes against the Turks in and around the Dardanelles. The Christian naval union preserved a spasmodic existence until 1402, while the Venetians alternated proposals for a Christian league and negotiations with the Turks.[58]

After Nicopolis the Greeks faced disaster. Emperor Manuel II had visited Rhodes in 1390 and secured two ships to assist him. In 1396 the Hospital opened negotiations with the Greeks. The Ottomans controlled most of Greece north of the Gulf of Corinth, and after the Venetians had refused to defend the isthmus in April 1397, the Turks invaded the Morea. They captured Argos on June 3 but were unable to occupy all the lands within their grasp, and after ravaging the Morea they withdrew. Corinth was a strategic and defensible base and the Hospitallers, responding once again to the idea of intervention in Greece, occupied it in the second half of 1397.[59] They bound themselves to defend the despotate, which did enjoy a period of peace until early in 1399, when the Morea was again threatened by Ottoman armies. Manuel Palaeologus then left to seek aid in the west, while the Hospitallers prepared to help his brother, the despot Theodore.

In July 1399 Naillac sent Eli of Fossat, the captain at Corinth, to open abortive negotiations with Theodore for the acquisition of Megara, to the north of Corinth, while another Hospitaller, Gerard of Le Puy, went to Peter de Saint Superan, the Navarrese prince of Achaea, who by November had agreed to help resist the Turks and rebuild the Hexamilion wall across the isthmus at Corinth. The Hospitallers were anxious to make further acquisitions, and in February 1400 an impressive embassy, including the priors of Venice, England, Aquitaine, and Toulouse, and Dominic de Alamania, was dispatched with a credit of 60,000 ducats and powers to purchase the whole Greek despotate. Theodore apparently temporized, and in November new envoys were commissioned, with instructions either to purchase further territories in the Morea or to resign those already obtained. Peter de Saint Superan allowed the Turks to pillage part of the Morea, but in mid-1401 the Hospitallers were again negotiating with him for a new league. The territories acquired in the despotate probably included Mistra, Theodore's capital (which at one point he

58. Luttrell, "Venice," pp. 209–211; F. Thiriet, *Régestes des délibérations du Sénat de Venise concernant la Romanie*, I (Paris and The Hague, 1958), nos. 739, 813, 949; II (1959), nos. 981, 988, 1007, 1042.

59. On the Morea in 1397 see above, p. 159.

abandoned), as well as Kalavryta, held by May 1400. Theodore received 43,000 ducats for the castellanies of Corinth and Kalavryta, and reserved the right to repurchase his lands at will. The Hospitallers defended Corinth, but despite their attempts to conciliate the populace, they were Latins and aroused the old resentments; at Mistra Theodore had to intervene to pacify an uprising against them. In May 1402 the Hospitallers were prepared for Theodore to demand the repurchase of his lands. The brethren were, however, clearly an obstacle to Bayazid, who, with Timur's armies advancing against him, offered Theodore peace on condition that the Hospitallers leave Greece.[60]

In July 1402 the Ottomans were decisively defeated by Timur at Ankara. Smyrna, garrisoned by only two hundred knights under an Aragonese Hospitaller, Íñigo of Alfaro, was in serious danger. The admiral, Buffilo Panizzatti, was sent to strengthen the fortifications there, while Dominic de Alamania went to Chios to prevent the Genoese allying with Timur. Smyrna had resisted Ottoman assaults and now rejected Timur's offer to accept tribute. His troops attacked with siege-engines, mined the walls, blocked the harbor entrance with stones, and took Smyrna by assault during December after nearly fifteen days of valiant resistance against odds. Some Hospitallers escaped by sea, but Timur's army massacred large numbers of Christian refugees and razed Smyrna to the ground.[61] Timur's campaign temporarily checked Ottoman expansion; it also ended the strain on the Hospitallers' resources involved in defending Smyrna, and it led to the Hospital's withdrawal from mainland Greece.

In 1403 the Hospitallers were arranging for a renewal of the treaty of 1370 with Egypt. General agreement had been reached by April, but in June the French marshal Boucicault arrived at Rhodes with the Genoese fleet, intending to attack Alexandria. Boucicault was also involved in Genoese quarrels in Cyprus, where three Genoese galleys, inappropriately commanded by the Hospitaller preceptor of Genoa, had arrived in 1402. Naillac diverted Boucicault to a temporarily successful attack on the Turks at Alaya,[62] and himself sailed to

60. These events, and especially their chronology, remain obscure. Many errors of Delaville Le Roulx and others are corrected in Loenertz, *Byzantina et Franco-Graeca*, p. 248, note 5, and pp. 254–265. See also Malta, cod. 330, folios 118^v–119^r, 120^v, 122^v–123^r, 125^v–126^r, 126^v; cod. 331, folios 162^r, 162^v, 163^r, 174^r; cod. 332, folios 160^v–164^r; cod. 334, folios 147^r–148^r. Cf. above, pp. 160–161, and on leagues and relations with Manuel in 1390 and from 1396 to 1404, see J. Barker, *Manuel II Palaeologus (1391–1425): A Study in Late Byzantine Statesmanship* (New Brunswick, 1969), pp. 76–77, 146, 168–169, 171 note 84, 204 and note 5, 224, 232–233, 259, 482–485.

61. Delaville Le Roulx, *Rhodes*, pp. 283–286; on Dominic's mission, see N. Iorga, *Notes et extraits pour servir à l'histoire des croisades au XVe siècle*, I (Paris, 1899), 135–136.

62. Piloti had a story that the Hospital agreed to pay Boucicault 40,000 ducats for Alaya

Cyprus, where he arranged a treaty settling the differences between king Janus and the Genoese.[63] Boucicault was now free to sail to Alexandria but was foiled by contrary winds; the Venetians had, in any case, betrayed his plans. In August Boucicault attacked Tripoli, and Naillac and the Hospitallers distinguished themselves in the fighting there. Then, after sacking Beirut, he sailed via Rhodes for Genoa, fighting a sea-battle with the Venetians off Modon in October. The presence of a Hospitaller galley at this battle emphasized the difficulty of ensuring the complete neutrality of all the brethren, and caused protracted quarrels with Venice. Meanwhile the Egyptians as well as the Christians were suffering from the interruption of trade. Despite Boucicault's aggression, an Egyptian envoy came to Rhodes and on October 27, 1403, concluded a treaty by which the Hospital was to be allowed to maintain consuls at Jerusalem, Ramla, and Damietta, to administer its hospices and various shrines in and around Jerusalem, and to control the pilgrim traffic. In 1407 the Hospitallers accepted a project of Boucicault for a new attack on Egypt, but they failed to secure support for it from Janus of Cyprus. During 1411 the prior of Toulouse was killed when some Hospitaller galleys attacked Makri. In general, however, a period of more peaceful relations followed the accord of 1403.

As a result of the Ottomans' defeat at Ankara in July 1402, the Hospitallers' presence in the Morea was less essential and even less welcome than earlier, but they planned nonetheless to remain. In April 1403 a small force was preparing to leave Rhodes for Glarentsa, hoping to win control of the principality of Achaea, where Peter de Saint Superan had died in November 1402, and to attack Theodore, who had broken his pacts with the Hospital. Early in 1403, however, Antonio Acciajuoli had captured Athens from the Venetians, and on June 7 the men of Athens, Thebes, and Megara, and their Turkish allies, attacked the Hospitallers at Corinth. At about the same time the Christian powers were making a treaty with the Ottomans; by it the Hospitallers were to have the county of Salona and its castle of Zeitounion north of the Gulf of Corinth. At peace with the Turks and under attack by Greeks and Latins alike, the Hospital left the Morea. Negotiations over the repayment of monies received by Theodore began in March or earlier, and Corinth was evacuated on June 4, 1404, but Theodore occupied Salona and refused to hand it over. The Hospital retained latent interests in Greece; in 1405 it proposed to fortify Tenedos at the mouth of the Dardanelles at its

---

if it were conquered; see *Traité d'Emmanuel Piloti sur le passage en Terre Sainte (1420),* ed. P. H. Dopp (Louvain and Paris, 1958), pp. 193–194.

    63. See below, pp. 370–371.

own expense, while a proposal made soon after to the Palaeologi for a thirty-year alliance against the Turks and a suggestion of November 1408 for a league with Centurione II Zaccaria, prince of Achaea, met no effective response.[64]

Following their treaties with the Ottomans and the Mamluks, the Hospitallers reverted to the predominantly defensive strategy which they had modified after Nicopolis. The Christians failed to exploit Ottoman weaknesses and the quarrels among Bayazid's sons; the Venetians, who possessed real naval strength, were not convinced of the need for all-out war against the Turks and remained hostile to the Hospital. All being relatively calm at Rhodes, Naillac apparently lost interest in the Levant. In February 1409 he sailed for the west, where he became a prominent figure in the election of a third pope, Alexander V, at the Council of Pisa. Naillac was technically "deposed" from the mastership by Benedict XIII, successor to Clement VII, for taking the Hospitallers, including a number of Urbanists, over to Alexander's obedience. Like his predecessor, Naillac remained in Europe reconciling the quarrels and complications among the Hospitallers which had arisen out of the schism, and working to end the schism itself. Naillac did not return to Rhodes until 1420, and for one eighteen-month period he was apparently simply lingering in his native province. When Alexander V's successor, John XXIII, began disposing of the Hospital's benefices, it was the Conventual brethren who stopped him by threatening, in 1412, to abandon Rhodes.

After the loss of Smyrna the Hospital increasingly strengthened the defenses of Rhodes, a process partly dictated by the growth of Turkish seapower. The Hospitallers started to rebuild the walls at Smyrna, but the Ottoman ruler Mehmed I pulled them down again, and so, some time before 1408, the Hospitallers began to construct the new castle of St. Peter at Bodrum, a rocky mainland site opposite Cos town. Rhodes itself was strengthened by the construction of a great tower to guard the port. Throughout the archipelago there were fortified villages, such as Lindos, Polakia, and Cattavia on Rhodes, in which the population could take refuge, but many of the island's castles, including Pheraclos, Aphandou, and Archangelos, were in ruins. The lesser islands formed part of Rhodes's defensive system

64. For details concerning Greece, see above, pp. 161–162; G. Dennis, in *Orientalia Christiana periodica*, XXVI (1960), 43–44; Iorga, *Notes*, I, 106–109; Luttrell, "Venice," p. 211; Malta, cod. 333, folios 115ʳ–118ʳ, 120ᵛ, 121ᵛ, 124ᵛ–127ʳ, 129ʳ; cod. 334, folios 146ᵛ–149ᵛ, 153ᵛ; cod. 337, folios 125ʳ–125ᵛ. Here again Delaville Le Roulx's errors have misled all authors; the account given here is to be regarded as tentative and the date of the

and supplied it with food and wine; Cos was especially fertile. To the east of Rhodes, Castellorizzo was a garrisoned lookout post; to the north, the fortresses at Bodrum and Cos guarded the approaches to Rhodes. Unlike many of the modest defenses elsewhere in the archipelago, these two castles enclosed no town but were powerful isolated strongholds, partly surrounded by water. At Cos the preceptor had to maintain twenty-five Hospitallers, ten Latin men-at-arms, a hundred turcopoles, a doctor, and an apothecary, together with a ship with twenty banks of rowers.[65]

In fact, while the Latin possessions in the Levant gradually shrank, Rhodes grew stronger and, as a result, more important as a well-placed commercial entrepôt, a base for merchants of many nations, particularly for the Florentines and Catalans, who had no Levantine colony of their own.[66] Although in 1399 there were on Rhodes at least sixty-three brethren of the *langue* of Provence alone, and in 1409 there were thirty-three brethren of the *langue* of Auvergne there,[67] the Convent had become less exclusively French; Naillac's lieutenants at Rhodes between 1409 and 1420 were, successively, the Italian Dominic de Alamania, the German Hesso Schlegelholtz, a Frenchman, the marshal Lucius of Vallins, and a Catalan, the draper Anton Fluvian, who became master in 1421. In view of the Italian mercantile rivalries in the Levant the comparative paucity of Italians in the Convent was probably fortunate, but some became leading figures in the business community. The Florentine John Corsini possessed town and country property in Rhodes and lent money to the Hospital in the time of Juan Fernández de Heredia,[68] while Dragonet Clavelli, a citizen of Rhodes, became a leading moneylender and held both the Rhodian *casale* of Lardos and the island of Nisyros in fief. The Hospital needed such men to provide wealth and credit at Rhodes.

---

treaty with the Ottomans is uncertain. There seems to be no evidence that the Hospital ever held Salona, as often maintained.

65. Descriptions in "Relation du pèlerinage à Jérusalem de Nicolas de Martoni, notaire italien, 1394–1395," ed. E. Legrand, *Revue de l'Orient latin*, III (1895), 582–586, 638–645; Ruy González de Clavijo (1403), in F. López Estrada, *Embajada a Tamorlán* (Madrid, 1943), pp. 18–24; *Description des îles de l'Archipel par Christophe Buondelmonti*, ed. E. Legrand (Paris, 1897), pp. 25–33, 62–67, 181–189, 218–222; G. Gerola, "I Monumenti medioevali delle tredici Sporadi," *Annuario delle R. Scuola archeologica di Atene*, I (1914), 169–356; II (1916), 1–101; A. Maiuri, "I Castelli dei Cavalieri di Rodi a Cos e a Budrúm (Alicarnasso)," *ibid.*, IV–V (1921–1922), 275–343.

66. A. Luttrell, "Aragoneses y Catalanes en Rodas: 1350–1430," *VII Congreso de Historia de la Corona de Aragón*, II (Barcelona, 1962), 383–390. For the end of Catalan and Florentine rule in Greece see above, chapter VII.

67. Malta, cod. 330, folios 36[r]–38[r]; cod. 339, folios 233[v]–235[r].

68. Luttrell, "Interessi fiorentini," pp. 325–326.

From 1410 onward the brethren, periodically short of money and of food, attempted little crusading activity. Rhodes became instead a center of piracy directed against Christians and Moslems alike. Thus in 1412 when a Hospitaller vessel seized a Turkish ship in the waters of Mytilene, the Rhodian crew was imprisoned and tortured by James Gattilusio, lord of Lesbos, while the Turks of Palatia attacked the castle of Bodrum and the Hospital's island of Syme. In 1413 the Hospitallers were alarmed by rumors of an impending Ottoman naval assault on Rhodes and began to form a defensive alliance. At this time a group of Catalans discharged at Rhodes some merchandise captured in a raid at Alexandria, and in the following years the Catalan corsair Nicholas Samper used Rhodes as a base, involving the Hospital in quarrels with his Venetian and Genoese victims. When the Ottomans solicited aid against the Turks of Altoluogo and the other emirates in April 1415, the Hospital instructed the captain of its "guard galley" off Chios to act in concert with the Genoese there. There were also proposals for Venetian participation in a general defensive league against the Turks. In January 1417 the Venetians hoped to include a Rhodian galley in a union to attack the Turks in the Aegean. Yet when Naillac finally returned to Rhodes in 1420, there was still peace there.[69]

At the time of Naillac's death in 1421, a century after the last serious attack on Rhodes in 1320, Ottoman and Mamluk seapower were still relatively undeveloped and the brethren at Rhodes, as yet in no real danger, seemed demoralized and inactive. Throughout this period the Hospital suffered from a lack of resources. It could seldom count on a powerful ally, and was limited by the commercial self-interest and mutual quarrels of Venice and Genoa, by the intolerance of Greeks and Latins, by the ineffectiveness of papal crusading policy, and more fundamentally by the indifference of Latin Christendom to the problems of its own defense. The Hospitallers at Rhodes could rarely sustain a decisive role in crusading affairs or make the most of their opportunities. The old accusations against them, especially those of corruption in the priories, continued to be repeated, not without some justification. For example, one such critic, the Cretan merchant Manuel Piloti, who spent some time in Florence, may have known of the visit there in 1431 of a Hospitaller who conducted a mass sale of papal indulgences intended to finance the defense of Rhodes, dining and debauching himself spectacularly on the proceeds.[70]

69. Piloti, *Traité*, p. 234; Thiriet, *Régestes*, II, nos. 1589, 1635, 1648, 1690, 1764.
70. Piloti, *Traité*, pp. 216–217; Iorga, *Notes*, II, 299–301. In 1423 the Venetian senate

Granted its weaknesses, the Hospital had some claims to success, and if it played no very decisive part in Levantine affairs, it did overcome considerable difficulties. The Hospital's establishment at Rhodes, the absorption of the Templars' properties, the fortification and defense of the Rhodian archipelago, indeed its own very survival, were real if somewhat unspectacular achievements, without which later successes would have been impossible. The Hospital always acknowledged its subordination to the papacy, but at Rhodes it enjoyed many attributes of independence, passing laws, minting money, and sending ambassadors. The master's powers were not limited to Rhodes. In the west, *oultremer* to the brethren, he had extensive jurisdictions, and in extreme cases the Hospital's subjects made the long journey to Rhodes to appeal to the master. The brethren participated, usually with distinction, in most crusading enterprises and were seldom responsible when these were strategically misconceived. They had played a leading part in the capture of Smyrna in 1344 and in its defense until 1402, and in the period of crisis between the battles of Nicopolis in 1396 and Ankara in 1402 they had successfully defended Corinth, perhaps saving the Morea for Christendom for another sixty years. The Hospitallers provided a permanent and reliable military force to which their experience and discipline gave a value more than commensurate with its limited size. Their presence at Rhodes provided an element of stability in the Christian east.

---

gave favorable consideration to an approach from the Hospitallers, who wished to exchange Rhodes, which they claimed to find too difficult to defend, for a territory of equal value in Greece, preferably Euboea; nothing, however, came of this (Iorga, *Notes,* I, 338).

IX

THE HOSPITALLERS AT
RHODES, 1421–1523

The deaths in 1421 of the grand master Philibert of Naillac and his mighty adversary sultan Mehmed I provide a convenient pause midway in the history of the Knights Hospitaller at Rhodes. The military order of St. John of Jerusalem by then had been for over a

The sources for the history of the Hospitallers in Rhodes are more numerous and detailed for the period after 1421, and especially from about 1450 on, than for the earlier period, but they remain largely unpublished. Many such documents are preserved in the Archives of the Order of St. John, Royal Malta Library (cited as Malta); some of these are published in S. Pauli, *Codice diplomatico del sacro militare ordine Gerosolimitano* . . . (2 vols., Lucca, 1733–1737), while documents on particular subjects are scattered through such works as M. Barbaro di San Giorgio, *Storia della costituzione del sovrano militare ordine di Malta* (Rome, 1927).

The situation is different with respect to scholarly secondary literature: though much has been published on the Jem episode and the great sieges of 1480 and 1522, there is as yet no satisfactory general history comparable to J. Delaville Le Roulx's *Les Hospitaliers à Rhodes jusqu'à la mort de Philibert de Naillac: 1310–1421* (Paris, 1913), and recourse must still be had to G. Bosio, *Dell' Istoria della sacra religione ed ill. militia di San Giovanni Gierosolimitano,* II (2nd ed., Rome, 1629), which utilizes the Malta archives, and R. Vertot, *Histoire des chevaliers hospitaliers de St.-Jean de Jérusalem* (Paris, 1726). To the excellent recent bibliography by J. Mizzi, cited in the bibliographical note to chapter VIII, should be added F. de Hellwald, *Bibliographie méthodique de l'ordre souverain de St.-Jean de Jérusalem* (Rome, 1865); E. Rossi, *Aggiunta alla "Bibliographie . . ."* de Ferdinand de Hellwald (Rome, 1924), and A. Fumagalli, *Bibliografia rodia* (Florence, 1937). See also N. Iorga, "Rhodes sous les Hospitaliers," *Revue historique du sud-est européen,* VIII (1931), 32–51 78–113, 169–187; R. Valentini, "L'Egeo dopo la caduta di Constantinopoli nella relazioni dei Gran Maestri di Rodi," *Bullettino dell' Istituto storico italiano per il medio evo e Archivio Muratoriano,* LI (1936), 137–168; G. Bottarelli, *Storia politica e militare del sovrano militare ordine di San Giovanni* . . . , I (Malta, 1940), 305–358; and C. Marinescu, "L'Île de Rhodes au XVe siècle et l'Ordre de Saint-Jean de Jérusalem d'après des documents inédits," *Miscellanea Giovanni Mercati,* V (Studi e testi, no. 125, 1946), 382–401. More recent studies include those among the publications of Anthony Luttrell, cited in chapter VIII, which extend past 1421, as well as relevant portions of Robert Schwoebel, *The Shadow of the Crescent: The Renaissance Image of the Turk (1453–1517)* (Nieuwkoop, 1967), especially pp. 119–131, 182–184, and appertinent footnotes.

Guidebooks and descriptions of Rhodes under the Hospitallers start with V. M. Coronelli, *Isola di Rodi* (Venice, 1688); later ones of value include B. Rottiers, *Description des monumens de Rhodes* (Brussels, 1828); V. Guirin, *Voyage dans l'île de Rhodes* (Rhodes,

century a principal Christian bulwark in the eastern Mediterranean against the Mamluk rulers of Egypt and Syria, against the Turkish emirates which had succeeded the Selchükids of Rūm, and increasingly against the rising power of the Ottomans, who had started as a

1856); E. Billiotti and Abbé Cottret, *L'Ile de Rhodes* (Rhodes, 1881); C. Torr, *Rhodes in Modern Times* (Rhodes, 1881; rev. ed. Cambridge, 1887); G. Sommi Picenardi, *Itinéraire d'un chevalier de St.-Jean de Jérusalem dans l'île de Rhodes* (Lille, 1900); Baron F. de Belabre, *Rhodes of the Knights* (Oxford, 1908); G. Gerola, "I Monumenti medioevali delle tredici Sporadi," in *Annuario della R. Scuola archeologica di Atene*, I–II (1914–1916; publ. separately, Bergamo, 1914–1915); A. Gabriel, *La Cité de Rhodes MCCCX–MDXII:* I, *Architecture civile et religieuse* (Paris, 1923); II, *Topographie, architecture militaire* (Paris, 1921); A. Maiuri, *Rodi* (Rome, 1923); Maiuri, "I Castelli dei Cavalieri di Rodi a Cos e a Budrúm (Alicarnasso)," in *Annuario della R. Scuola archeologica di Atene*, IV–V (1921–1922); H. Balducci, *Architettura turca a Rodi* (Milan, 1932), which treats also of the Hospitallers; and G. Jacopi, *Rodi* (Bergamo, 1933).

On the siege of 1444 see L. Nicolau d'Olwer, "Un Témoignage catalan du siège de Rhodes en 1444," *Estudis universitaris catalans*, XII (1927), 376–387, and C. Marinescu ["Marinesco"], "Du Nouveau sur *Tirant lo Blanch*," *Estudis romànics*, IV (1953–1954), 137–203. On the siege of 1480 see G. Caoursin, *Obsidionis Rhodiae urbis descriptio* (Venice, 1480; several times reprinted, and translated together with other writings of the same author). The reprint made at Ulm in 1486 is noteworthy; cf. Hellwald, *op. cit.*, p. 49. A recent translation by E. Mizzi appears in his *Le Guerre de Rodi: Relazioni di diversi autori sui due grandi assedi di Rodi, 1480–1522* (Turin, 1934). An account sent by grand master Peter of Aubusson to emperor Frederick III was published by M. Freher, in *Scriptorum rerum germanicarum*, II (1602). Another account, by the Frenchman Mary Dupuis, is in the appendix of Vertot's *Histoire*, pp. 598–616. Two accounts by German pilgrims were published by Iorga in his *Notes et extraits pour servir à l'histoire des croisades au XVe siècle*, V (Paris, 1915), 64 ff. An account by Giacomo de Curti is found in translation in Mizzi, *Le Guerre di Rodi;* an account by Bernard of Breydenbach, *De Rhodiae urbis obsidione* (Mainz, 1486), is discussed in H. W. Davies, *Bernhard von Breydenbach and his Journey to the Holy Land, 1483–4* (London, 1911). See also, now, E. Brockman, *The Two Sieges of Rhodes: 1480–1522* (London, 1969).

On the siege of 1522 see Jacobus Fontanus (Jacob Fonteyn), *De bello Rhodio libri tres* (Rome, 1525; often reprinted and translated, e.g. in Mizzi, *Le Guerre di Rodi*); Th. Guichard, *Oratio habita coram Clementem VII P.M. in qua Rhodiorum expugnationis et deditionis summa continetur* (Rome, 1523); J. Bourbon (le Bâtard), *Relation de la grande et merveilleuse et très cruelle expugnation de la noble cité de Rhodes* (Paris, 1527; also in Vertot, *Histoire;* translated in Mizzi, *Le Guerre de Rodi*); M. Tercier, ed., "Mémoire sur la prise de la ville et de l'île de Rhodes en 1522 par Soliman II," in *Mémoirs de l'Académie des inscriptions et belles-lettres*, XXVI (1759), an extract from an account in Arabic by the sultan's physician; and P. Baudin, *Le Siège de Rhodes: Chronique du XVIe siècle* (Constantinople, 1871). Turkish sources are covered in E. Rossi, *Assedio e conquista di Rodi nel 1522 secondo le relazioni edite e inedite dei Turchi* (Rome, 1927), and Rossi, "Nuove ricerche sulle fonti turche relative all' assedio di Rodi nel 1522," *Rivista di studi orientali*, XV (1934), 97–102.

For the affair of Jem Sultan see L. Thuasne, *Djem-Sultan* (Paris, 1892); G. Zippel, "Un Pretendente ottomano alla corte dei Papi: il Turchetto," in *Nuova antologia*, Nov. 1, 1912; Arm. Sakisian, "Djem Sultan et les fresques de Pinturicchio," *Revue d'art*, 1925, pp. 81–91; F. Cognasso, "Il Sultano Djem alla corte di Alessandro VI," *Papoli*, II (Milan, 1942), 96–103; A. Refiq, *Jem Sultan* (Istanbul, 1924); "Cem Sultan" in *İslâm Ansiklopedisi*, III (Istanbul, 1944), 69–81; and F. Babinger, *Mahomet II, le conquerant . . . (1432–1481)* (Paris, 1954). Hospital activities are covered by H. Karl Zwehl, *Nachrichten üiber die Armen-*

local emirate in Bithynia, but had expanded rapidly at the expense of the other emirates and the waning Byzantine empire.[1] The order, which had held castles in the Holy Land as fiefs from the kings of Jerusalem until 1291, and which had been the guest of the king of Cyprus from 1291 to 1306, had become at Rhodes an independent state, recognized as such by the pope, and by many states, Christian and Moslem. Subject to constitutional limitations on his power, its grand master was lord of Rhodes and its dependent islands, treating with other heads of state, sending ambassadors, coining money, naming consuls, and, at least in theory, controlling the men and property of the order throughout Latin Europe.

When Anton Fluvian (1421–1437) succeeded Philibert of Naillac as grand master, a treaty negotiated in 1403 between the Hospital and the Mamluk sultan (known as the "soldan of Babylon") Faraj still governed relations between Rhodes and Egypt. Its terms, which were in French, give a clear picture of the scope of the order's activities in the eastern Mediterranean in the early fifteenth century.[2] It provided that: (1) the peace of 1370, concluded after the sack in 1365 of Alexandria, should be observed; (2) the order might maintain a hospital at Jerusalem and a consul at Ramla, to help all pilgrims visiting Jerusalem; (3) Hospitallers and their suites might freely traverse the sultan's lands, on horse or on foot, without impediment or tribute; (4) pilgrims visiting the Holy Sepulcher or the monastery of St. Catherine at Sinai should pay no dues other than those—precisely enumerated—prevailing before the capture of Alexandria; (5) brethren assigned to the hospital might enlarge the building for the better accommodation of pilgrims, and make repairs at the Holy Sepulcher and other holy places to prevent the ruin of those churches; (6) the

---

und *Krankenfürsorge des Ordens vom Hospital des Heiligen Johannes* (Rome, 1911), and *Über die Caritas im Johanniter-Malteser-orden seit seiner Gründung* (Essen, 1929). On the Hospitaller navy, see C. Manfroni, *Storia della marina italiana dalla caduta di Costantinopoli alla battaglia di Lepanto* (Rome, 1897); A. Guglielmotti, *Storia della marina pontificia* (10 vols., Rome, 1886–1893); and E. Rossi, *Storia della marina dell' ordine di San Giovanni di Gerusalemme, di Rodi e di Malta* (Rome, 1926). Reviews and periodicals which have published articles of importance on the Hospitallers at Rhodes include *Annuario della R. Scuola archeologica di Atene* (1914 on); *Clara Rhodos,* organ of the Istituto FERT di Rodi (1928–1941); and *Rivista illustrata del sovrano militare ordine di Malta* (Rome, 1937–1943), now the *Annales [Revue] de l'Ordre.*

This chapter was translated from the Italian by the late Theodore F. Jones, and edited by Harry W. Hazard after Professor Rossi's death.

1. See above, chapter VIII; cf. Paul Wittek, *Das Fürstentum Mentesche* (Istanbul, 1934) and *The Rise of the Ottoman Empire* (London, 1938; Royal Asiatic Society Monographs, no. 23). A chapter on the Ottomans is planned for volume V of this work (in preparation).

2. Malta, cod. 332, fol. 170, published in Pauli, *Codice diplomatico,* II, 108–110.

order might station a consul at Damietta, (7) ransom Christians from slavery, and (8) buy victuals free of duty; and (9) its vassals in Damietta, Alexandria, Jaffa, Beirut, Damascus, and Tripoli should pay the usual customs duties and no more. The parties promised to give each other three months' notice of any warlike activities, so that Christians or Moslems living in each other's territories might have time to remove themselves and their goods without hindrance. Although the terms of this treaty were not always observed, it is important because the order appears in it as guarantor and representative of the other Christian states, assuming in the Holy Land the role of protector of all pilgrims and maintainer of the holy places, a role later to be assumed by the Franciscans. The principal source of trouble with Egypt was the incessant piratical activity based on Rhodes and directed chiefly at Egyptian and Syrian merchant shipping.

Relations of the Hospital with its other Moslem neighbors were rather less amiable than with Egypt. The Selchükid sultanate of Rūm had collapsed, and by 1300 a number of small emirates had arisen on its ruins. Of these emirates, those which had seacoasts, and thus faced the increasingly seafaring Hospitallers, included—moving clockwise from the remnant of Cilician Armenia—Tekke (ancient Pamphylia) with the port of Adalia, Menteshe (ancient Caria) with the port of Palatia (Miletus), and Aydin (ancient Lydia) with the ports of Smyrna, until its capture by the Latins in 1344, and Altoluogo (Ephesus). All these had sheltered Turkish pirates, whose suppression was one of the Hospitallers' principal functions; all (except Smyrna) had fallen to the Ottoman ruler Bayazid I about 1390; all had been reëstablished by Timur after his victories at Ankara and Smyrna in 1402; all were again in danger in 1421 from the revived Ottoman state. This aggressive power was the enemy of all within its reach, Moslem and Christian alike. Now that the brief respite following Bayazid's defeat at Ankara was past, the Ottomans were once again the chief threat to the order's future at Rhodes, though not immediately recognized as such.[3]

In 1426 the new Ottoman sultan, Murad II (1421–1451), put an end to the quasi-independent emirates of Aydin, Menteshe, and Tekke, and again directly faced the Hospitallers at Bodrum, Cos, and Rhodes. In the same year, the Mamluk sultan Barsbey invaded Cyprus, laid waste the Hospital's commandery at Kolossi, and took king Janus prisoner.[4] The king was ransomed for 120,000 scudi, and

3. Valentini, "L'Egeo," pp. 137–139.
4. See below, chapter XI.

agreed to pay tribute. The order, which had joined in the defense of the island, and had contributed 15,000 florins for the ransoming of the king, renewed its truce with Egypt in 1428.[5] The remainder of Fluvian's tenure was comparatively uneventful; Catalan-Aragonese influence increased markedly. At his death in 1437 he bequeathed a legacy to the order for the reconstruction of the huge new hospital at Rhodes, which was further enlarged by his successor John of Lastic (1437–1454) and by Peter of Aubusson (1476–1503); it is now an archeological museum, and one of the finest monuments of the order on the island.

The structure of the order at Rhodes under Lastic, in 1447, was based on a division into seven *langues:* (1) Provence, whose chief (*pilier*) held the post of grand preceptor or grand commander; (2) Auvergne, under the marshal; (3) France, under the hospitaller; (4) Italy, under the admiral; (5) Spain, under the draper; (6) England, under the turcopolier; and (7) Germany, under the grand bailiff. In 1462 the *langue* of Spain was split into that of Aragon and Navarre (still called Spain), under the draper, and that of Castile and Portugal, under the chancellor; the number of *langues* remained at eight for the rest of the order's stay at Rhodes. The grand master was elected for life by the Convent of the order, and governed with the advice of his council, including the chiefs of· the seven (or eight) *langues.* The Hospitallers living in Rhodes or its dependent islands formed the Convent, but many stayed in the west at the various priories and commanderies, under the obligation of coming to Rhodes when summoned by the Convent.[6] While the order was at Rhodes, the office of admiral became so important that it rivaled that of marshal, the commander of the land forces.[7] The Hospital's ships were repaired, and sometimes built, in the arsenal (*tersenal*) at Rhodes, but more commonly were constructed at Genoa or Marseilles. Terms of service (*carovane*) on the ships were obligatory for the Hospitallers, while the crews were usually recruited at Rhodes.

The hospital activity for the sick and for pilgrims journeying to the Holy Sepulcher, which at its beginning in Jerusalem had been the principal mission of the order, had dwindled to secondary impor-

---

5. Bosio, *Istoria,* II, 146.

6. On this subject, see J. Delaville Le Roulx, *Les Hospitaliers en Terre Sainte et à Chypre (1100–1310)* (Paris, 1904), pp. 285–434, and R. Valentini's article, "Un Capitolo generale degli Ospitalieri . . . tenuto in Vaticano nel 1446," *Archivio storico di Malta,* VII (1936), 133–168.

7. See Rossi, *Storia della marina, passim,* and now A. Luttrell, "The *Servitudo Marina* at Rhodes: 1306–1462," *Zeitschrift für Neogräzistik* [forthcoming].

tance, both because the knights were busy fighting on land and at sea, and because the new situation in the Levant had reduced the number of pilgrims to the Holy Land, and not all who did come stopped at Rhodes on their way. The order did maintain the huge hospital at Rhodes, which it rebuilt after 1437 with Fluvian's legacy, and the smaller hospital of St. Catherine, built in 1392 by Dominic de Alamania, an Italian knight, and modernized in 1516 by Constant Oberti. The grand master continued to appear in chancery acts as "servus pauperum Christi et custos Hospitalis Hierusalem." Additional hospital activity was carried on in the priories and commanderies of western Europe, and brethren were still occasionally mentioned as serving in the hospital at Jerusalem; their hospice at Ramla did not pass to the Franciscans until 1514.[8]

In 1440, while John of Lastic was grand master, Rhodes was threatened by an Egyptian fleet of eighteen galleys, dispatched by sultan Jakmak az̧-Z̧āhir. After having devastated the little island of Castellorizzo[9] they approached Rhodes and anchored at Sandy Point. John of Lastic described the events in a letter written on November 6, 1440, to John de Villaragut, prior of Aragon and castellan of Amposta. The fleet of the order, composed of seven galleys, four other ships, and six lesser craft, attacked the Egyptian fleet, which resisted without moving, making much use of cannon and Greek fire. During the following night the Egyptians moved toward the coast of Turkey, and the next day formed their order of battle near the coast, above a sandy bottom where the Rhodian galleys could not maneuver. Nevertheless, the Hospitallers, commanded by their marshal, attacked the enemy, superior in number, pushing among them "not unlike a few bears amidst swarms of bees." There were heavy losses on both sides, until night divided the contestants. The next day the Egyptian fleet turned on Cos, devastating especially the property of the Hospitallers, and carrying off many Christian slaves. The grand master added that he had learned that the sultan, angry at his defeat, planned another expedition against Rhodes, thinking that if he could control it he would be able to reduce to submission the rest of eastern Christendom.[10]

8. See Girolamo Golubovich, ed., *Biblioteca bio-bibliografica della Terra Santa e dell' Oriente francescano,* IV (Quaracchi, 1923), 17, and A. Luttrell, "The Hospitallers' Hospice . . . at Venice: 1358–1451," *Studi veneziani,* XII (1970), 369–383.

9. Castellorizzo was destroyed by the Mamluks in 1444, and definitively lost by the order in 1450, having been occupied by the fleet of Alfonso V of Aragon, king of Naples, as authorized by a brief of pope Nicholas V (Marinescu, *Misc. Mercati,* V, 392–393).

10. Malta, cod. 354, fol. 103, published in Pauli, *Codice diplomatico,* II, 121–123. Cf. Bosio, *Istoria,* II, 158–159.

While the grand master welcomed Burgundian and Catalan reinforcements, and continued to strengthen the fortifications on
Rhodes, he did not neglect diplomacy. In 1442 he charged John
Marsanach, lieutenant of the grand commander of Cyprus, with
negotiations, and in 1443 John Delfino, grand squire of the order.
But in response an Egyptian fleet reached Rhodes, in August 1444,
besieged the fortress for forty days, and was repulsed.[11] In 1445
peace was restored. In an act of April 2, 1446, mention is made of
the sultan of Egypt, "with whom we are at peace;"[12] and in a decree
of March 6, 1448, to all Christians living "in the provinces, countries,
cities, lands, and places of the most potent lord sultan, with whom
we have good peace," it is made known that they can come to
Rhodes freely to carry on commerce, paying only the dues to which
other Christian merchants are held.[13]

When in 1448 Ibrāhīm Tāj-ad-Dīn, the emir of Karaman, took the
Cilician castle of Corycus, formerly belonging to the king of Cyprus,
John of Lastic wrote to the "most illustrious king of the Moors, and,
like Alexander in his time, great soldan of Babylon" Jakmak aẓ-
Ẓāhir, asking his intervention in obtaining the return of the castle,
and in stopping Karaman from injuring Cyprus, as it was tributary to
the sultan.[14] In 1451 Ibrāhīm besieged Alaya (Candeloro or Scandelore, now Alanya), the emir of which, Lûtfi Bey, was allied with
Cyprus and Rhodes.[15] The grand master sent the order's galleys to
attack Karaman, until the latter raised the siege of Alaya. By the
middle of the fifteenth century, apprehensions in Rhodes had increased because the Hospitallers distrusted the Egyptians, and were
disturbed by the Ottoman Turks. In 1449 watch was being kept day
and night, and guards stationed on the heights were to light fires to
give warning of the approach of ships "of enemies, both Turks and
Moors, or of any other nation, Christian or infidel, which may be
enemies of our order."[16] On July 20, 1450, John of Lastic read "ad

11. Bosio, *Istoria*, II, 162. On the four Egyptian attacks between 1439 and 1444, see
Marinescu, *Misc. Mercati*, V, 386–387, Valentini, "L'Egeo," p. 138, and Schwoebel, *Shadow
of the Crescent*, p. 84, as well as the Olwer article cited in the bibliographical note.
12. Malta, cod. 359, fol. 220.
13. Malta, cod. 365, fol. 176. This decree was renewed by grand master James of Milly in
1455.
14. Malta, cod. 360, fol. 225. On Alfonso V's attempt to assist the Hospital's truce efforts
see Marinescu, *Misc. Mercati*, V, 389–390.
15. Bosio, *Istoria*, II, 181.
16. Malta, cod. 361, fol. 362: "ordinationi . . . del 27.5.1449." Those guilty of negligence
in signaling were threatened with the loss of beard and hair.

clangorem sive pulsationem bucinarum" in the porch of the customs-house of Rhodes in the presence of an ambassador sent by "Morat-bey Grande Turcho," a proclamation in accordance with which "good, true, and loyal peace" being confirmed with Murad, the people of Rhodes were absolutely forbidden to receive or deal in slaves or goods taken from Turkish ships, or to privateer against the Turks, "under penalty of loss of life and property."[17]

With the accession in 1451 of the son and successor of Murad II, young Mehmed II (known as the Conqueror [Fātiḥ] after his capture of Constantinople, two years later), the situation of Christian hold-ings in the Levant became more critical. The order, like the other states, sent an ambassador, Peter Zinotto, to congratulate the new sultan and to renew, on December 25, 1452, the peace made with his father. The fall of Constantinople on May 29, 1453, after a short and desperate siege, caused acute alarm at Rhodes. The order was im-poverished; the island was sparsely manned. John of Lastic, in inform-ing the prior of Auvergne, and urging the Hospitallers in the west to come to the defense of Rhodes, said he was ready to meet martyr-dom for the defense of the faith. "Et si casus se offerat, pro salute animarum nostrarum martirium sumere, vitamque aeternam adipisci valeamus."[18] The Hospitallers could well say of their city, "Civitas nostra Rhodi communis et libera est omnibus nacionibus Christian-orum."[19]

Mehmed II asked Rhodes to pay 2,000 ducats as tribute in 1454, a humiliation to which the neighboring islands of Lesbos and Chios were subjected; as his final act of defiance, John of Lastic refused. Under his successor, James of Milly (1454–1461), a Turkish fleet laid waste the Hospitallers' islands of Syme, Nisyros, and Cos (1455), and sacked the village of Archangelos on the island of Rhodes itself; in 1456 it took Chios,[20] while plague and famine swept Rhodes. The king of Cyprus, John II de Lusignan, died in 1458. His heiress was his daughter, princess Charlotte, widow of John of Portugal, duke of Coimbra, and affianced to Louis of Savoy. A natural son of John II, called James the Bastard, hoped to succeed his father, and took

17. Malta, cod. 362, fol. 193. Valentini's description ("L'Egeo," p. 144) of this truce as an alliance is inaccurate.

18. Pauli, *Codice diplomatico*, II, 131. Cf. Bottarelli, *Storia politica e militare*, I (1940), 206, and Valentini, "L'Egeo," p. 138.

19. Iorga, *Notes et extraits*, III, 498.

20. Valentini, "L'Egeo," pp. 150–151; Marinescu, in *Misc. Mercati*, V, 395–400, with details of the order's precarious financial situation.

refuge with the sultan of Egypt, al-Ashraf Inal. There he turned Moslem, and with the sultan's aid landed on Cyprus, on August 18, 1460, just as Louis of Savoy arrived to assume the scepter. Queen Charlotte fled to Rhodes; Louis was besieged in the castle of Kyrenia, and resisted for some time with the help of the Hospitallers; then he retired to Piedmont. During these events the order sought to help Charlotte, the legitimate heiress, and at the same time to protect its own vast and lucrative interests in Cyprus.[21]   John Delfino, sent in 1459 to negotiate with sultan Inal, was thrown into prison, where he died before he could be freed.

At this time the order was repeatedly at odds with Venice for detaining Venetian ships. In 1460 the sequestration, the sale of goods, and the arrest of Saracen travelers on two Venetian ships bound for Egypt led to a punitive expedition by the Venetian captain-general, Alvise Loredan. He put troops ashore on Rhodes, and laid waste various villages until the order released the prisoners. Again in 1464, because of a similar incident involving two Venetian ships in Syrian waters, Venice mounted a naval demonstration at Rhodes until the prisoners were released and their merchandise returned.

In 1462 the Ottoman Turks renewed their truce with Rhodes; the order still refused to pay "tribute" but offered a "gift" to the sultan as a sign of friendship, without incurring the obligation of stated renewal.[22]   In the same year, on November 16, 1462, the Turks occupied Lesbos, and the last of the Gattilusi, Nicholas II, was strangled at Constantinople. Preparations for the crusade planned by Pius II were started by the Hospitallers, but the death of the pope at Ancona on August 15, 1464, delayed the enterprise.

In 1464, and again in 1466, Mehmed II renewed his demand for tribute; as the order did not comply, a complete rupture resulted. The order strengthened the fortifications of Rhodes; in 1464 the fort of St. Nicholas, defending the Mandraki (the later Port of Galleys) was rebuilt. When the Turks laid siege to Euboea (Negroponte), a Venetian possession, and conquered it, on July 12, 1470, two galleys commanded by John of Cardona, bailiff of Majorca, coöperated with the Venetian fleet in an attempt to save the island. The Christian league, initiated by pope Paul II, and backed by Sixtus IV, brought

21. On the death of James the Bastard in 1473, the rule of Cyprus was taken over by his widow, Catherine Cornaro, of Venice, and in 1489 passed directly to Venice, which kept it until 1571. See chapter XI, below.

22. Bosio, *Istoria,* II, 212. The grand master was (Peter) Raymond Zacosta (1461–1467). In 1466 there were 300 knights, 30 chaplains, and 20 sergeants stationed on Rhodes.

together in 1471–1472 the forces of Venice, of the pope, of Ferdinand of Aragon, king of Naples, and of Rhodes. The grand master, Giovanni Battista Orsini (1467–1476), contributed two galleys commanded by James of Vandenberg, bailiff of Brandenburg. The fleet of the league in 1472 attacked and devastated Smyrna, and then turned to the south and sacked Adalia, Seleucia (Silifke), and Corycus.[23] The commander entered into relations with Uzun Ḥasan, the "White Sheep" (Ak-koyunlu) Turkoman ruler of eastern Anatolia and western Persia, an enemy of the Turks. The defeat of Uzun Ḥasan in the battle of Kara Hisar (or Bashkent, in the mountains north of Erzinjan), on August 2, 1473, laid low the hopes of the league, which accomplished nothing more.

When Orsini died, his successor Peter of Aubusson (1476–1503) took care to strengthen the fortifications, to attract knights and volunteers from the west, and to stock the city with provisions in case of attack. Mehmed II was busy in Albania, in Hungary, and in Wallachia, and was raiding in Venetia as far as the Piave valley (1477). Relations between the Turks and the Hospitallers were those of prudent waiting on both sides; but there was no doubt that Rhodes would soon be attacked. Meanwhile peace was restored with Egypt; the text of the treaty[24] was drawn up in Italian, translated into Greek, and thence into Arabic. The customary commercial clauses were included, and a *fondaco* of Rhodes at Alexandria was mentioned. The Hospitallers would be permitted to go freely to the Holy Sepulcher in Jerusalem, and to the monastery of St. Catherine in Sinai. There was no longer any mention, however, of the hospice and hospital of the order in Jerusalem. A truce concluded in 1478 by Aubusson with abū-'Amr 'Uthmān, the Ḥafṣid ruler of Tunisia, through the mediation of John Philo of Rhodes, is evidence of the extent of the commercial interests of Rhodes at that time. The agreement concerns reciprocal customs duties, and permission for Rhodes to take annually from Tunis and its dependencies 30,000 *moggie* of corn.[25]

A son of Mehmed II by the name of Jem was governor of Caria, in

23. The commander of the papal fleet was cardinal Oliver Carafa. In the sack of Adalia (Satalia), the chains of the harbor were carried away and hung in St. Peter's at Rome, with the following inscription: "Smyrnam ubi Oliverius Card./Neap. Carafa Xysti IV Pontificiae/Classis dux vi occupasset in/Sataliae urbis Asiae portum/vi quoq. irrupit ferreamq./hanc catenam inde extraxit/et supra valvas huius basilicae/suspendit."

24. Malta, cod. 75, fols. 156–159. Cf. Bosio, *Istoria*, II, 299.

25. Malta, cod. 75, fol. 171. The Ottoman conquest of Constantinople may have prevented Rhodes from obtaining corn from the Black Sea ports.

the region still called Menteshe; in the correspondence of the order surviving in the *Libri Conciliorum* he is called "Prince Jem Sultan, son of the Grand Turk." To keep the Hospitallers quiet, Jem, evidently with his father's approval, negotiated with them at length from February 1478 to April 1479. His emissary was a renegade Greek named Dimitri Sofiano. Jem offered peace to the Hospitallers. Aubusson responded affably and diplomatically, remarking that if he were to make peace, he must inform "his holiness the pope, and the most serene Christian kings and princes," from whom he held garrison duty in honor of the Catholic faith; meanwhile he prepared a truce limited to the waters between Rhodes and the Turkish coast, in order to favor commerce. These negotiations led to nothing but a provisional truce; a real peace could not be concluded.[26]

On December 4, 1479, a Turkish squadron cruised before Rhodes, and landed troops which devastated villages and attacked the island of Telos (Piskopi). From that moment Rhodes and the Hospitallers' other islands were practically besieged. On May 23, 1480, a large Turkish fleet appeared and began to land forces on the island.[27] There were three thousand janissaries and an uncertain number of soldiers, collected at Marmaris (Fisco) and then ferried over to Rhodes.[28] Compared with the enemy, which had picked troops, and great siege guns able to throw stone balls weighing over 1,400 pounds, the defenders were in very small numbers—only a few more than three hundred knights, about the same number of sergeants, and not more than three to four thousand soldiers from France and Italy, including a detachment led by Benedict della Scala of Verona.

Mesih Pasha, who commanded the Ottoman forces, first tried to overpower the defenses of the fort of St. Nicholas, which protected the entrance to the Mandraki. He succeeded in dismantling it, and

26. Bosio, *Istoria*, II, 306–307. On the Ottoman conquest of Euboea and Lemnos in 1479 see Schwoebel, *Shadow of the Crescent*, pp. 121–122.

27. For Christian and Turkish accounts of the siege, consult the bibliographical note. In the archives of the order at Malta there is, it appears, no chronicle of the siege, but only actions taken on May 21, 1480, when the attack was imminent, and deliberations made after the siege, as for example on August 7, 1480, a reward given to a person who had distinguished himself for valor. G. Caoursin, vice-chancellor of the order, afterward wrote and had printed a famous account of the siege. The following notation made by him (Malta, cod. 76, fol. 35) deserves citation: "Quia civitas Rhodi obsidebatur per Turcos et summo conatu oppugnabatur, in tanta rerum perturbacione ac formidine peracta in scriptis non sunt redacta. Sed, habita victoria, historia est edita per Guillelmum Caoursin Rhodiorum Vice-cancellarium. Quae per orbem impressorum arte est divulgata, quapropter in hoc spacio nihil est registratum. Ita est: G. Caoursin, Rhodiorum Vicecancellarius."

28. Khoja Sa'd-ad-Dīn in the Turkish chronicle, *Tāj at-tawārīkh* (Istanbul, 1863), p. 573, gives the figures of 3,000 janissaries and 4,000 *azabs* (marines), who left Constantinople with him, and an uncertain number of soldiers coming from Rumelia and Anatolia. Modern Turkish historians accept the figure of 100 to 160 ships, and 70,000 to 100,000 soldiers.

attempted to put assault troops on it from a raft, but the valor of the knights and the effectiveness of their artillery stopped this under-taking. Then Mesih Pasha concentrated his forces on the eastern side of the city, at the bay of Acandia. The perimeter of the walls was shared by the eight *langues* of the order; the Acandia front, entrusted to the Italian *langue,* was the site of the bitterest fighting. At certain points the Turks, after demolishing the walls with gunfire and mines, were able to mount the parapet and begin a decisive attack. Aubus-son, more than once wounded, encouraged the defenders, who suc-ceeded in repelling the attack. Thirty-five hundred Turks are said to have fallen on July 27–28, in the climax of the battle.

Informed of the grave losses and of the difficulties of the enter-prise, sultan Mehmed II, who in these same months was engaged in an expedition led by Ahmed Pasha against Otranto in Apulia (cap-tured on August 18, 1480),[29] ordered Mesih Pasha to bring the ships back to Constantinople and to send home the Anatolian troops. On August 17, 1480, the siege was raised, and two ships sent by Ferdinand of Naples entered the harbor with reinforcements.[30] The Hospitallers, exultant over their success, set to work to repair the walls and strengthen those parts which had proved to be weakest. At the point where the melee had been the most violent, a church was built and dedicated to Our Lady of Victory.

On April 27, 1481,[31] the Ottoman sultan Mehmed II died, while with a large army near Scutari, perhaps planning a new enterprise toward the west. His death caused a fratricidal war for the succession between his two sons, Bayazid and Jem. Bayazid was governor at Amasya, and Jem at Konya (Iconium), both in Anatolia. Bayazid II was the elder, and knew of his father's death first. He reached Constantinople on May 21, and took over the government. But Jem reached Brusa, and proclaimed himself sultan on May 28. He sent a deputation to his brother, proposing that they divide the empire, one to govern Anatolia, the other Rumelia (European Turkey). Bayazid refused the proposal, and sent his army against his brother. Jem fled to Syria and thence to Cairo, where Ka'itbey, the Mamluk sultan, gave him shelter. Then Bayazid got in touch with the Hospitallers to

29. Otranto was liberated on September 10, 1481.

30. G. M. Monti, *La Espansione mediterranea del Mezzogiorno d'Italia e della Sicilia* (Bologna, 1942), pp. 185–186. "Mesih Pasha" has often been identified with the renegade Manuel Palaeologus, son of Thomas (of Achaea).

31. European sources give different dates; the most generally accepted is May 3. But the late author of this chapter considered 27 Safar 886 = April 27, 1481, more probable. The news of Mehmed's death was kept secret for several days.

renew the peace, and charged the *subashi* of Petsona[32] to negotiate with the knights. He sent them an emissary, one Hajjī Ibrāhīm, who on November 26, 1481, concluded a truce with the knights valid for six months. Traffic and commerce between Rhodes and the Anatolian coast as far as Palatia were to be allowed. The order sent its own ambassador, Mosco, to the subashi to treat for a real peace with the sultan, but one "without any sort or form of tribute between the sultan and the most reverend grand master." In case peace could not be made, and the sultan chose to disavow the truce, three months' notice was to be given, so that the Turks in Rhodes, and the Rhodians in Turkey, could return to their homes with their property.[33]

Shortly before this Jem Sultan, after a brief residence in Cairo and a pilgrimage to Mecca, had reappeared in Anatolia, laid siege to Konya and Ankara, and then retired to southern Anatolia, pursued by his brother's troops. To avoid being taken prisoner, he turned to the Hospitallers, with whom he had been in touch a few years previously. The archives of the order contain a letter, dated July 12, 1482,[34] and directed to Jem Sultan, in which he was advised of preparations being made to bring him to Rhodes, and of orders given to Dominic Álvaro de Stúñiga, captain-general of the galleys, to bring to Rhodes "Zam Soldan, son of Mahumet, formerly Grand Turk." He went on board a ship of the order of July 20 at Anamur,[35] and nine days later arrived in Rhodes.

His stay in Rhodes lasted little more than a month. On August 22, 1482, he signed with the grand master a perpetual treaty of peace, for himself and his heirs, pledging himself, when he had conquered the throne, to grant freedom of commerce in Turkey to the order and its subjects, and to pay expenses contracted in his favor to the amount of 150,000 gold scudi. He gave permission to the order to treat in his name with Bayazid, and expressed his willingness meanwhile to go to "France" (western Europe). He was probably afraid of being pursued even to Rhodes by his brother, and was probably also persuaded by the order, which, if it got rid of Jem but kept him in the west, could use him as a hostage in treating with Bayazid. Jem Sultan sailed from Rhodes on September 1, 1482, and arrived on October 16 at the Savoyard port of Villefranche. He spent

32. In Turkish, Pechin, capital of the territory which until 1426 constituted the emirate of Menteshe (Caria). A *subashi* was a subordinate official, commanding a district.

33. Malta, cod. 76, fol. 70.

34. Malta, cod. 76, fols. 93 ff.; published in Pauli, *Codice diplomatico,* II, 411–412.

35. For a discussion of the date of sailing, in contrast with that found in Thuasne, *Djem-Sultan* (Paris, 1892), cf. Ismail Hamdi Danişmend, *Izahli Osmanti tarihi kronolojisi* (Istanbul, 1947), p. 372.

four months in Nice, and was then sent to Chambéry in Savoy, and thence to other castles of the order in Dauphiné, Provence, and Auvergne.[36]

The day after Jem Sultan left Rhodes, instructions were given to the ambassadors charged with treating for peace with Bayazid II. Peace between "the most illustrious, excellent, and potent great lord Bayazid Sultan, and the most reverend lord Peter of Aubusson, grand master of Rhodes, and the noble religion of Jerusalem" was signed on December 2, 1482.[37] It was agreed that full liberty of commerce should exist for both parties, and that fugitive Christian slaves might be received at the castle of St. Peter at Bodrum in Anatolia. At the same time it was agreed that the order would assume custody of Jem Sultan (Zyzumus in the Latin text), receiving in return 35,000 Venetian ducats a year for the cost of maintenance of the unfortunate prince. As proof of his gratitude toward the Hospitallers, who kept Jem in golden imprisonment in France, and resisted the demands of various sovereigns who wanted him as a tool against the Turks, Bayazid sent to Rhodes on April 20, 1484, an ambassador bringing as a gift the right hand of St. John the Baptist, patron of the order.[38]

After the victorious repulse of the siege of 1480, and the lucky consequences of the consignment of Jem to the Hospitallers, the situation at Rhodes had greatly improved. The importance of the order had increased even in Turkish eyes. While up to 1480 the Turks

36. The rest of Jem's adventures belong rather to the history of Europe than to that of the Hospitallers. Many Christian states intrigued to get hold of him: the Aragonese king Ferdinand I of Naples, Matthias Corvinus of Hungary, and Charles VIII of France. In 1489 pope Innocent VIII managed to get custody of him. The Turkish prince, leaving Toulon on a Hospitaller ship, reached Civitavecchia on March 6, 1489, and going up the Tiber from Ostia to Porta Portese, entered Rome on March 13, was received by the pope, and was lodged in the Castel Sant' Angelo. Bayazid II negotiated with Innocent VIII, and promised to pay the pope 40,000 ducats a year for his brother's expenses; in 1492 he sent to the pope as a gift a relic believed to be "the lance which pierced Christ on the cross." To the new pope, Alexander VI (1492–1503), Bayazid proposed that Jem be poisoned and thus disposed of finally. But at that time Charles VIII, invading Italy, persuaded the pope to transfer Jem to his custody. Charles took him on the road to Naples; at Capua Jem sickened and died, on February 25, 1495, not without suspicion of poison. His body was embalmed and, after long insistence by Bayazid directed to the king of Naples, was sent in 1499 to Turkey and buried in Brusa. Jem Sultan's residence in Rome is commemorated in a picture by Pinturicchio: the *Disputa di Santa Caterina,* in the Borgia apartments of the Vatican. It is said that Jem is represented in the person of the knight on the right of the picture. Cf. articles by Zippel, Cognassa, and Sakisian, cited in the bibliographical note.

37. Italian and Greek text, in Malta, cod. 76, fols. 101–102. Cf. Greek text in Pauli, *Codice diplomatico,* II, 419–420.

38. The hand was kept at Rhodes until 1522 in a casket of gold and ivory made for the grand master Aubusson, and then taken to Malta, where it remained until 1798.

had claimed an act of vassalage at the payment of the tribute, now it was the knights who received a sort of tribute from the Turks in the guise of an annual payment for Jem's upkeep. The grand master Aubusson was carrying on a policy of acquiring prestige, with evident results both in the Levant and in Europe. In 1484 he reconfirmed the peace with the Mamluk sultan of Egypt, after having obtained compensation for breaches of the peace by Egypt; Ka'itbey on this occasion sent him a gift of 3,000 *arādib* of corn.[39]

In 1486 he intervened with Bayazid II in favor of the Mahona of Chios, which was involved in a contest with the Turks over damages inflicted by a Chian corsair on Turkish shipping, and was threatened with reprisals by the sultan. The grand master succeeded in turning the Turkish threat away from Chios, and getting the damages allegedly owed by the Mahona reduced. In 1489, by transferring Jem to Innocent VIII as a hostage, Aubusson got a cardinal's hat, which he received at Rhodes with solemn ceremony on July 29. At the same time, the pope gave to the order the possessions of the knightly orders of the Holy Sepulcher and of St. Lazarus, which had been dissolved.

But the worries of the order had not ceased, and the general situation was becoming worse. Rhodes was gravely injured by successive earthquakes in March, May, October, and December, 1481, which added ruins to those of the siege (and of previous quakes). A huge work of restoration and repair was needed, at enormous cost. The order could expect little help from western Europe, because of the disturbances there caused by the hostility between Charles VIII of France and the Aragonese king of Naples, and by the ill-fated policy of pope Alexander VI. And after Jem Sultan died on the road to Naples in 1495, the order could expect little consideration from the Turks.

On March 1, 1496, Paul di Saloma, of the priory of Messina, was sent to Sicily to collect "armed ships of any nation or condition, the owners and captains of which have the will and holy wish to injure infidels of any sort," offering them a welcome at Rhodes and liberty to "sell those goods captured, but from infidels only, not from Christians."[40] In a letter dated September 10, 1496,[41] the grand master and council, having learned that the "Grand Turk, enemy of the Christians and especially of our order, whose function it is in this portion of the Levant to resist his most insolent power," was build-

---

39. Bosio, *Istoria,* II, 394. *Arādib* is the plural of Arabic *irdabb.*

40. Malta, cod. 392, fol. 174.

41. Malta, cod. 392, fols. 118 ff. Cf., on folios 120 and 122 of the same volume, letters on the same subject.

ing great ships of two to three thousand tons, and many galleys, wishing to revenge the defeat which his father suffered under the walls of Rhodes, ordered Boniface de' Scarampi, commander of Savona, Brasco de Salvago of Genoa, and Fabrizio del Carretto, of the priory of Lombardy, to do their utmost to bring to Rhodes two galleys, with crews and material for the equipping of ships: "400 pieces of cotton cloth, 200 for sails for galleys, and 200 for ships, 300 oars, and ropes and hawsers for two galleys." Fabrizio del Carretto and Philip Provana were to command the ships.

Documents from the order's archives reveal the great interest taken by the grand master Aubusson at the end of the fifteenth century in the strengthening of his navy. Turkish corsairs increased their activities in the Aegean islands, and even among the Hospitallers' possessions. A Turkish pirate named Kemal Re'is became famous in these years for his pitiless chase of Christians on the sea.[42]

Nevertheless, Bayazid II was at that time not planning to attack Rhodes. In 1498 the truce between the Turks and the knights was confirmed, with the usual guarantees of freedom of commerce which were in practice constantly violated. Turkish preparations were directed rather against Venice, and threatened the Adriatic after the Turkish conquest of Lepanto in 1499. In 1501 a Christian league was organized, the participants being Venice, France, Spain, Portugal, the pope, and Rhodes. The Hospitallers agreed to supply four armed galleys, to be commanded by the admiral (of the *langue* of Italy), the turcopolier (of the *langue* of England), the prior of St. Gilles (of the *langue* of Provence), and the castellan of Amposta (of the *langue* of Aragon). The grand master, cardinal Peter of Aubusson, had been named by the pope to be captain-general of the league. A great fleet, composed of Venetian ships commanded by Benedict Pesaro, seven papal galleys under the bishop of Paphos, James Pesaro (brother of the Venetian commander), five galleys under the command of the Hospitaller Fabrizio del Carretto, and three galleys from Rhodes, besides the "great ship" and the "bark" of the order, all under the command of the admiral, Louis of Scalenghe, gathered at Cerigo in the summer of 1502. The grand master asked that part of the fleet be sent to Rhodian waters, where Turkish vessels had devastated the island of Chalce, but Benedict and James thought it better to use the whole fleet in attacking Santa Maura (Leucas), in the Ionian islands. Santa Maura was captured August 29, 1502, after a week's siege in which the Hospitallers distinguished themselves. For his part, the

---

42. Cf. H. A. von Burski, *Kemāl Re'is: Ein Beitrag zur Geschichte der türkischen Flotte* (Bonn, 1928).

grand master hastily armed a galley which captured many Turkish corsairs operating in Rhodian waters; some were killed, others were put to work excavating the moats of Rhodes.[43]

In 1503, when Venice made peace with the Turks, Rhodes was isolated. On July 3 of that year the grand master Peter of Aubusson died; his successor, Emery of Amboise, prior of France, was elected at once by the Convent, but did not arrive in Rhodes until 1504. Meanwhile his lieutenant, Guy of Blanchefort, prior of Auvergne, appointed captains for the three galleys of the order, which were called *Petronilla, Victoriosa,* and *Catherineta* (or *Catherinella*). He sent the galleys against a squadron of Turkish corsairs which had ravaged Rhodes itself in August 1503, and then gone toward Makri (Fethiye) on the mainland. Eight Turkish ships were sunk, and two captured, with much booty, but in the fight one Rhodian galley was burned.

For their part, the knights repaid with acts of piracy the continued incursions of Turkish corsairs. In 1504 it happened that one Kemal Beg, a *kapiji-bashi* (messenger or quartermaster) of Kurkut Chelebi, Bayazid II's son and governor of southern Anatolia, was captured by a boat commanded by Guy Borel Valdiviessa e Maldonato. Kemal was taken as a slave to Rhodes; but on the night of July 20 he succeeded with twelve other slaves in eluding the vigilance of his guards. He tried to escape on a Spanish ship, but fell into the sea and was drowned. Kurkut, from his residence in Laodicea, wrote the knights several letters in Greek demanding the liberation of his *kapiji-bashi* and threatening to inform the "lord Chonochiari."[44] The order replied, explaining what had happened, and expressing its regret at Kemal Beg's death; but, referring to the threats, it added that the order, for its part, had to complain of the continued attacks by "Cortogoli and his companion corsairs" and of devastations made by the Turks in the neighborhood of the castle of St. Peter. Finally, on July 28, 1504, the order sent this dry response to the son of the sultan: "Most illustrious sir, we are good and peaceful friends of the lord Chonochiari, and of your own most illustrious lordship, and we are always ready to do everything that is just and honest and due to good friends; and to this purpose we are on this island, by order of the most serene Christian princes, from whom we have favor and

---

43. Malta, cod. 79, fol. 83. Titian was commissioned by James Pesaro to paint an altarpiece commemorating this victory; see E. Panofsky, *Problems in Titian, Mostly Icono-graphic* (New York, 1969), pp. 178–179 and fig. 16.

44. I.e., his father Bayazid II. *Chonochiari,* which often occurs in Venetian and Rhodian documents of this period, is a European corruption of the Persian *khunkār, khudāvand-gār* (emperor), one of the titles of the Ottoman sultans.

help because we are their sons; and except them we know no other superior, and to God and then to them we have to answer for our affairs, and we hope in God that while we do justice, his aid will not fail us."[45]

These and other incidents,[46] however, did not cause a complete break in the truce with the Turks. In 1507, in giving permission to a certain Nidio de' Moralli to arm a brigantine at Cos, the order forbade him to molest Venetian ships, or to break the truce with the Turks within the stated confines (*limites induciarum*), that is to say, on the stretch of sea comprised between Palatia and Adalia, and in the channel of Chios.

The relations of the order with Egypt were ambivalent, from the time when, around 1505, sultan Kansuh al-Ghūrī, although fearing the Turks, had drawn closer to them and received from them provisions of war, and especially timber, for the ships with which he intended to dispute with the Portuguese the control of the Red Sea. Kansuh received help even from the Venetians, whose trade in spices was ruined by Portuguese colonial expansion. In fear of being handed over to Bayazid, a son[47] of Jem Sultan had fled from Cairo to Rhodes. This also could well be a motive for the Ottoman sultan's breaking the truce with Rhodes. However, no Turkish attack on Rhodes occurred yet. Instead, there were many naval successes of the knights at this time over the Egyptians. In 1506 near Cos the Hospitallers captured seven Egyptian ships which had come to devastate the island. In 1507 near Crete they captured a large merchant ship, called the "Gran Nave Mogarbina," chiefly employed in carrying spices from Alexandria to Tunis to supply the whole Maghrib. The ship was towed to Rhodes; in it were goods of great value, spices, cloths, and carpets, and travelers for whose ransom the Egyptians paid heavily. In the same year three Saracen ships were captured off Cyprus.

In 1510 the Egyptian sultan Kansuh sent his fleet to load timber in the ports of the Gulf of Alexandretta, which belonged to the Turks. The order learned of this, and on August 6 the grand master Amboise ordered Andrew do Amaral, the chancellor's lieutenant, and Philip Villiers de l'Isle Adam, the seneschal, the two commanders of the order's fleet, to sail toward the gulf, avoiding Cyprus (in order to keep the voyage secret), and, when the Egyptian fleet appeared, to

45. Malta, cod. 80, fols. 85–92. For "Cortogoli" see below.
46. In 1505 Kemal Re'is attacked the islands of Nisyros, Telos, and Syme, and in 1506, Leros.
47. Probably named Murad; he was killed at Rhodes, together with his two sons, after the Turkish conquest, in January 1523. Cf. Rossi, *Assedio e conquista,* p. 42, note 2.

attack it, and to fight "discreetly like wise and experienced men, and bravely like knights and gentlemen assigned to the defense of the holy faith."[48] The attack succeeded; when the two fleets met, on August 23, 1510, near Alexandretta (Iskenderun), the Egyptian fleet was thrown into confusion. Eleven cargo ships and four battle galleys were captured, in good condition; the other Egyptian ships were burned.[49]

Great changes took place in the next few years. Bayazid II died on May 26, 1512; on the whole he had maintained good relations with the knights. His son and successor Selim I (1512–1520) was more warlike, and, as we shall see, aggravated the threat to Rhodes. The grand master Emery of Amboise died in 1512. Guy of Blanchefort was elected his successor, but he was in France, and died before he reached Rhodes. His successor was Fabrizio del Carretto, *pilier* of the *langue* of Italy, and admiral, a man of great valor, who had distinguished himself in the defense of the fort of St. Nicholas against the Turks in 1480. Leo X (1513–1521) was pope, and well disposed toward the order, but the struggle between Charles V and Francis I prevented Europe from giving effective help to the order when the moment of peril arrived.[50]

Selim first got rid of his brothers, and then began his conquests in 1514 by defeating Ismā'īl, the Ṣafavid shah of Persia. The shah was for Selim an enemy to be feared on the eastern front, and one who had combined with Christian states to the sultan's loss. Compelled after the battle of Chaldiran (fought on August 23, 1514) to sue for peace with the Turks, shah Ismā'īl still cherished plans for revenge. He wrote to Rhodes in 1515, asking that the Hospitallers hand over to him Murad, the son of Jem Sultan, whom he evidently planned to use to stir up trouble for the sultan. The latter, meanwhile, was preparing a great enterprise which was to increase tremendously the territory of the Turks, and to assure the Ottoman empire of the control of the Levant for three centuries to come: the occupation of Syria, of Egypt, and of Arabia. Selim left Constantinople on June 5, 1516, and at Marj Dābiq near Aleppo defeated the Mamluk sultan of Syria and Egypt, Kansuh, who was killed in the battle (August 24, 1516). Just before the war began, Kansuh had negotiated with the

48. Malta, cod. 400, fol. 224.

49. An account of the battle written by the grand master to the doge of Venice, Leonard Loredan, is published in Marino Sanudo, *Diarii*, X, cols. 570–571. Another account is in Pauli, *Codice diplomatico*, II, 174.

50. On conditions in Europe and the Levant see K. M. Setton, "Pope Leo and the Turkish Peril," *Proceedings of the American Philosophical Society*, CXIII (1969), 367–414; reprinted in his *Europe and the Levant in the Middle Ages and the Renaissance* (London, 1974), no. IX.

knights a renewal of the peace. In the terms discussed, beyond the usual clauses relative to freedom of trade, and the freeing of Rhodian slaves in Egypt, was a request that merchants from Rhodes should be permitted to build booths at "Le Brulle" (Burlus) in the Nile delta, where timber for Egypt was sold. Kansuh could not complete the negotiations because of the outbreak of the war in which he was killed. The treaty was, however, signed on November 3, 1516, by his successor, Tumanbey II, and ratified at Rhodes on November 16.[51]

But only a few months later, Tumanbey was also defeated by Selim, and hanged at Cairo on April 13, 1517; Egypt became part of the Turkish empire. Up to the end, the Mamluk sultan had asked for help from Rhodes; and it seems that he obtained a certain amount of artillery from the knights during the winter of 1516–1517.[52] But Rhodes had plenty to do in providing for its own defense.

Rhodes at the end of the fifteenth century and the beginning of the sixteenth, during the masterships of Aubusson, Amboise, and Fabrizio del Carretto, was a unique concentration of force and power, art and grace. The siege of 1522, although it partly breached the walls, did not materially injure the aspect of the island, and the Turks did not touch the fortress, the *auberges* of the *langues*, the buildings of the castellany, or the magnificent hospital—indeed, in places they repaired the walls—and they left almost intact the coats of arms, the gateways, and the inscriptions. It is therefore not difficult for those who today visit Rhodes, restored with loving care by Italian archaeologists between 1912 and 1940, to imagine the city as it was before the siege of 1522. Passing along the quiet Street of the Knights, visiting the restored castellany, standing before the Sea Gate or that of St. Catherine, and the towers of the port, traversing the walls flanked by bulwarks and deep moats, the visitor can have the illusion of seeing alive again the Rhodes of four and a half centuries ago. One notable element of Rhodes of the knights is, however, lacking: the churches and chapels which the Turks changed into mosques or demolished, causing the destruction of many works of art. In the ground-plans and portals of some mosques the original style of knightly Rhodes survives. Grave damage was done by the explosion of a powder magazine in 1856, which destroyed the grand master's palace and the church of St. John, the campanile of which had already been lost in the siege of 1522.[53] The Gothic style of

51. Malta, cod. 405, fol. 215; cf. Bosio, *Historia,* II, 513.
52. Sanudo, *Diarii,* XXIII, cols. 554, 595.
53. The Roman Catholic church of St. John, rebuilt during the Italian occupation, has been transformed by the Greeks into the Orthodox cathedral (1947); on the architecture see volume IV of this work, chapter VI, section B.

the Trecento and Quattrocento prevails in the larger buildings, such as the palaces of the *langues* on the Street of the Knights, and the big hospital, but there are also monuments in Byzantine and in Renaissance style. Even the defensive works of the walled city show the meeting and fusion of medieval elements of fortification with the perfected technique of the sixteenth-century engineering of Basilio della Scala.

Letters and arts flourished at Rhodes. Latin and Italian were the official languages of the order, for the use of French diminished at the beginning of the fifteenth century. Many merchants and artisans, especially Italian, French, and Catalan, settled there. The bankers who often made loans to the Hospitallers, such as the Bardi and the Peruzzi in the earlier years, had banks and storehouses at Rhodes.[54] Commerce fluctuated with political change; the order often had to break off all relations with the Levantine states. However, it maintained almost constant commercial ties with Alexandria in Egypt (where it had, as we have seen, a consul and a *fondaco*), and with Turkey, the Aegean islands, Crete, the Morea, and even Tunisia.

Among scholars who visited Rhodes we may remember the Florentine Christopher Buondelmonti, who studied Greek there at the beginning of the fifteenth century, Sabba of Castiglione, a member of the order, who lived in Rhodes between 1500 and 1508 (and who, as a good humanist and archaeologist, gathered a collection of antiquities for Isabella d'Este Gonzaga), William Caoursin, a layman, but vice-chancellor (secretary) of the order (we have referred above to his history of the siege of 1480), and Bartholomew Poliziano, Aubusson's secretary, and later Caoursin's successor as vice-chancellor until 1522, just before the siege. Byzantine literature also flourished in Rhodes under the Hospitallers. Manuel Georgillas composed a poem on the pestilence (*thanatikon*) in Rhodes during 1498–1499. To the period of the knights have been ascribed most of the popular love songs known as *Rhodiaka erotika poiemata*.[55]

It was clear that the next Turkish move would be directed against Rhodes, the nearest Christian possession to the coast of Asia, and halfway between Constantinople and recently conquered Egypt. Grand master Fabrizio del Carretto hastened the work of fortifica-

54. See Wilhelm Heyd, *Histoire du commerce du Levant au moyen-âge*, trans. Furcy Raynaud, 2 vols. (Leipzig, 1885–1886; repr. Amsterdam, 1967), and Yves Renouard, *Les Relations des papes d'Avignon et des compagnies commerciales et bancaires de 1316 à 1378* (Paris, 1941).

55. Cf. Tryphon E. Euangelides, *Rhodiaka* (Rhodes, 1917). On the cultural aspect of Hospitaller Rhodes in general see A. Luttrell, "The Hospitallers' Historical Activities: (2) 1400–1530," *Annales de l'Ordre souverain militaire de Malte*, XXV (1967), 145–150.

tion; in 1520 he brought to Rhodes the engineer and architect Basilio della Scala of Vicenza, who reinforced the walls, the moats, and the towers according to the new rules of Italian military engineering, based on the increased attacking force of the new artillery. In his work of renovation, which harmonized strength with beauty, he had the collaboration of the Sicilian Matthew Gioeno.

Selim I did not have the time to conduct a campaign against Rhodes. He died in 1520, leaving on the throne his young son Suleiman, who began his reign by conquering Belgrade in August 1521. As Selim had in 1516 announced to the grand master of Rhodes his victory over the Mamluks, so Suleiman, as he sent from Belgrade to all his dependents and to other heads of state his "letters of victory" (fethname), did not forget the ruler of Rhodes. The grand master was now Philip Villiers de l'Isle Adam, who had succeeded Fabrizio del Carretto on January 22, 1521. It was a letter of courtesy,[56] according to the usage of the Ottoman chancery, but it gave warning to the Hospitallers. Indeed, Suleiman, who knew that the Christian states were involved in the war between Charles V and Francis I, concluded a new treaty with Venice, on December 1, 1521, which practically assured him of Venetian neutrality; in the spring of 1522 he began preparations for an attack on Rhodes.

In Rhodes at the time were only two hundred and ninety knights, fifteen *donati,* and about three hundred sergeants (*frères sergents d'armes*), in all about six hundred forming the Convent of the order; besides them there were five hundred Genoese sailors and fifty Venetian sailors, four hundred soldiers recruited in Crete unknown to the Venetian authorities, and a few thousand Rhodian citizens under arms. In all, the defenders numbered perhaps about seventy-five hundred. In July 1522 there arrived from Crete, in defiance of a ban by Venice, the military engineer Gabriel Tadino of Martinengo; as soon as he arrived he asked for and received the habit of a knight, and he played a most useful and valiant role during the siege.

The Turkish armada, composed of more than four hundred ships, part galleys and part transports, with forty thousand rowers, mostly Christian slaves, and twenty thousand marines (*azabs*), reached Rhodes on June 24, 1522; part of it anchored off the eastern shore, and part went to Marmaris (Fisco on medieval maps), to ferry over to the island the land army with which Suleiman had crossed Anatolia.

---

56. It is not probable that it contained threats; it was a simple announcement of victory. For the correspondence between Suleiman and the grand master, cf. Rossi, *Assedio e conquista,* p. 28.

With the Turkish fleet was the corsair Muṣliḥ-ad-Dīn Kurd-Oghlu, who had long been a feared adversary of the Rhodian navy. By July 28 the whole Turkish force, with the sultan, had landed on the island, and on that day the siege began. From various contemporary Turkish and Christian sources one could estimate that the Turks, together with reinforcements from Syria and Egypt, amounted to about two hundred thousand, but this is, as usual, much exaggerated. The élite of the army consisted of ten thousand janissaries, the most effective and warlike infantry of the time. Sultan Suleiman, who surveyed the operation from a height of land, had given the supreme command to his second vizir, Mustafa Pasha. The Turks, who had vast experience in such operations, had brought with them much heavy artillery, and had learned how to protect their batteries with trenches and platforms, and how to use mines under the walls of the fortress. But many of the mines failed because of Martinengo's countermines.

As in 1480, each of the eight *langues* had its own post of combat on the walls and parapets. In the section overlooking the east harbor (the later Port of Commerce) were the men of Castile; farther east, opposite the bay of Acandia, those of Italy, and then in order those of Provence, England, "Spain" (Aragon), Auvergne, Germany, and France (guarding the Mandraki). The main Turkish attack did not come from the side of the sea, as had occurred in 1480. That side had made a good resistance in 1480, and had recently been heavily reinforced. Now the Turks attacked on the land side, especially against the posts of Italy, England, and Aragon. Between England and Aragon was the tower, or bulwark, of St. Mary, which was severely battered by Turkish cannon in repeated attacks in August and September. On September 4 the Turks succeeded in undermining and destroying a great part of the bulwark of England, and in penetrating to the last defenses; but a counterattack led by the grand master in person repulsed the assailants, who on that day lost more than two thousand men. On September 9 a formidable attack was made at the same spot, but repulsed with the loss of three thousand Turks. On September 13 the walls of the *langue* of Italy, protected by the Carretto bulwark, were vigorously but unsuccessfully attacked. Another assault on September 17 brought great losses on both sides. A general attack, launched on September 24, against the posts of Italy, Provence, England, and Aragon, preceded by the explosion of mines under their bulwarks, cost the Turks thousands of lives.

Early in October Suleiman replaced Mustafa Pasha by Ahmed

Pasha, beylerbey of Rumeli, and had the attack renewed with vigor. Meanwhile in the city the courage of the defenders did not flag: knights, sergeants, soldiers, sailors, and Rhodian citizens. Even the women of Rhodes performed prodigies in aiding the wounded, in bringing up ammunition, and in throwing rocks, pitch, sulphur, and burning bitumen.[57]

Aid from the west did not come. Early in October a small ship sent to ask help from Christian princes returned with the news that in Naples and Messina forces were gathering to help Rhodes. But the hope was vain. A few ships which left England, Spain, and France never reached the island. The defenders remained alone to oppose the overwhelming enemy, and to face their destiny. At the end of October the grand chancellor of the order, Andrew do Amaral of the *langue* of Portugal (and Castile), was accused of committing the blackest treason by sending to the enemy by bow-shot dispatches which told of the precarious state of the defense and urged the Turks to continue their attack. He was tried and put to death.[58]

In November the Turks renewed their assaults against the posts of Aragon and Italy; they got across the moats and made breaches in the inner curtains, but still they did not crush the defense. Suleiman was impressed by his great losses, by the approach of winter,[59] and by the probability that pope Hadrian VI and emperor Charles V, if successful in Italy, would send reinforcements to Rhodes. The sultan, therefore, proposed to the grand master that the Hospitallers surrender.[60] The first proposal was indignantly rejected, but then the grand master yielded to the prayers of the severely tried citizens and the urging of his wisest advisers. On December 9 he called together the council of the order, and it voted to accept the terms offered. On December 11 two messengers of the order went to the Turkish camp, and on the next day were received by the sultan.

The sultan said that if the city surrendered, the Hospitallers and the inhabitants would have permission to leave, and take their property with them; if it did not surrender, the attack would con-

---

57. For accounts of the siege see the bibliographical note. A good modern account is that by Gottardo Bottarelli, *Storia politica e militare del . . . ordine di San Giovanni*, I, 305–358; cf. the brief account of Albergo di Rouan in Z. Tsirpanlis, *Dodekanesiaka*, II (1967), 63–64.

58. See E. Brockman, "Rhodes–1522: d'Amaral–Martyr or Traitor?" *Annales de l'Ordre . . . de Malte*, XXIV (1966), 18–25.

59. From October 25, heavy rainfall began. Even in November rain impeded the attack. Cf. Rossi, *Assedio e conquista*, p. 20, and Bottarelli, *op. cit.*, I, 345.

60. Turkish sources say that the proposal for surrender came from the grand master. But Christian accounts (cf. Bosio, *Istoria*, II, 582) show with certainty that Suleiman made an offer in November and renewed it on December 10.

tinue until all the defenders and citizens were killed. He gave them three days to reply. The grand master requested an extension of the truce, in order to discuss in greater detail guarantees for the people of the island. Suleiman was angered by this request, either because he thought it concealed a wish to gain time, or because of the arrival, on December 14, of a ship from Crete, with a few Hospitallers and Venetian volunteers aboard who had slipped through the Venetian blockade; he therefore renewed the assault. On December 17 a final attack on the walls of the post of Aragon brought considerable gains to the Turks. On the next day the grand master surrendered, and the terms were defined on December 20. The knights had twelve days to leave Rhodes. The inhabitants were guaranteed security of person, of property, and of religion, and were exempted for five years from the levy of boys to enter the corps of janissaries.[61] However, on December 24 and 25 a few Turkish units entered the fortress, and sacked it briefly, until halted.

On December 25, the grand master appeared at Suleiman's *divan,* accompanied by his generals and ministers; he was treated with honor and respect. Suleiman himself entered the city[62] on December 27, and returned old Villiers de l'Isle Adam's visit at the grand master's palace.

On January 1, 1523, after visiting Suleiman, the grand master embarked on the galley *Santa Maria.* The rest of the knights left on the galleys *Santa Caterina* and *San Giovanni,* the "great ship" of Rhodes, one galleon, and one bark. Shortly thereafter the island of Cos and the castle of St. Peter at Bodrum in Anatolia surrendered; the other islands had been occupied during the siege.

Having left Rhodes, the grand master, with the surviving Hospitallers and many Rhodian citizens who wished to follow him, stopped in Crete, and arrived at Messina in Sicily on March 1. Thence he went

61. Christian accounts speak also of a promise not to profane the churches; this is not probable, for the sultan would not have agreed to such an engagement. The fact is that the churches were turned into mosques; on Friday, January 2, 1523, Suleiman made his ritual prayer in the former church of St. John. For the Turkish celebrations after the conquest, see Rossi, "Nuove ricerche," *Rivista di studi orientali,* XV (1934), 97–102.

62. A tradition has it that Suleiman entered by St. Athanasius's gate, beside St. Mary's tower, and that he had it closed so that no one else could pass through the gate where he had made his victorious entrance. In support of this tradition, some historians and archeologists cite an inscription in Persian on the exterior of the bastion in front of St. Mary's tower. But a careful reading of this inscription proves that it only records that in 937 A.H. (A.D. 1530/1) this bastion was repaired at Suleiman's orders (and it is known that this section of the wall was badly ruined in the siege of 1522). No mention of the gate is made in the inscription. The question is clarified by E. Rossi, "L'Iscrizione ottomana in persiano sul bastione della Torre di S. Maria a Rodi," in *Ann. della R. Scuola arch. di Atene,* VIII (1929), 341–344.

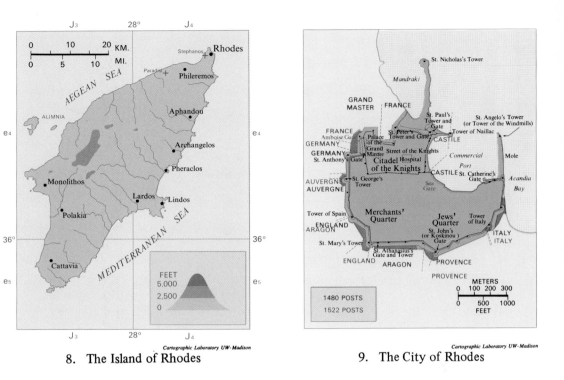

8. The Island of Rhodes

Map labels (Island of Rhodes):
J3 28° J4
0 10 20 KM.
0 5 10 MI.
AEGEAN SEA
Stephanos
Rhodes
Paradisi
Phileremos
ALIMNIA
e4
Aphandou
Archangelos
Pheraclos
Monolithos
Lardos
Lindos
Polakia
Cattavia
MEDITERRANEAN SEA
36°
e5
FEET
5,000
2,500
0
J3 28° J4
Cartographic Laboratory UW-Madison

9. The City of Rhodes

Map labels (City of Rhodes):
St. Nicholas's Tower
Mandraki
GRAND MASTER FRANCE
St. Paul's Tower and Gate
St. Angelo's Tower (or Tower of the Windmills)
FRANCE
GERMANY
Amboise Gate
Palace of the Grand Master
St. Peter's Tower and Gate
Tower of Naillac
CASTILE
St. Anthony's Gate
Street of the Knights
Citadel of the Knights
Hospital
Commercial Port
Mole
GERMANY
AUVERGNE
St. George's Tower
Sea Gate
CASTILE St. Catherine's Gate
Acandia Bay
AUVERGNE
Merchants' Quarter
Jews' Quarter
Tower of Spain
St. John's (or Koskinou) Gate
Tower of Italy
ENGLAND
ARAGON
ITALY
ITALY
St. Mary's Tower
St. Athanasius's Gate and Tower
ENGLAND ARAGON
PROVENCE
PROVENCE
1480 POSTS
1522 POSTS
METERS
0 100 200 300
0 500 1000
FEET
Cartographic Laboratory UW-Madison

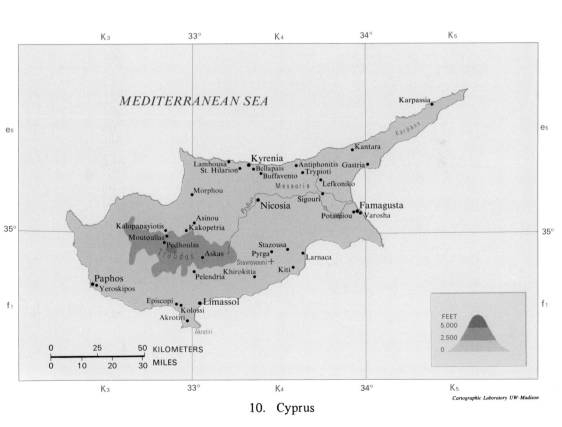

10. Cyprus

Map labels (Cyprus):
K3 33° K4 34° K5
MEDITERRANEAN SEA
Karpassia
Karpass
e5
Kantara
Kyrenia
Lambousa
St. Hilarion
Bellapais
Antiphonitis Gastria
Buffavento
Trypioti
Mesaoria
Lefkoniko
Morphou
Sigouri
Pedios
Nicosia
Famagusta
Asinou
Potamiou Varosha
Kalopanayiotis
Kakopetria
Moutoullas
Pedhoulas
Troodos
Askas
Stazousa
Pyrga
Stavrovouni
Larnaca
Paphos
Pelendria
Khirokitia
Kiti
Yeroskipos
Episcopi
Kolossi
Limassol
Akrotiri
Akrotiri
35°
FEET
5,000
2,500
0
0 25 50 KILOMETERS
0 10 20 30 MILES
K3 33° K4 34° K5
Cartographic Laboratory UW-Madison

to Civitavecchia, and met pope Hadrian VI in August 1523. At the end of 1523 he began to treat with Charles V for the cession of the islands of Malta and Gozo as a new residence for the order. Negotiations with the new pope, Clement VII, were protracted for several years, because of various judicial and political questions, including objections by the Maltese, and hesitation by the knights to assume the obligation imposed upon them to take over the defense of Tripoli as well as the Maltese islands. The act of cession was finally signed by Charles V on March 24, 1530, at Castelfranco, and the grand master took up his residence at Malta on October 26, 1530. During those years, Villiers de l'Isle Adam had cherished the hope of reconquering Rhodes. A conspiracy of Rhodian citizens who remained faithful to the order had been organized in Rhodes, and the Hospitaller Antonio Bosio had entered into communication with them, to plan an outbreak in Rhodes to coincide with a projected naval attack from the west. But in 1529 Bosio, who had gone to Rhodes, told the grand master that the plot had failed, having been repressed by the Turks. And so the order hastened its negotiations for the cession of Malta, Gozo, and Tripoli; held the latter from 1530 to 1551, when it was captured by the Turks; and defended Malta heroically in the great siege of 1565.[63]

Memories of Rhodes followed the order to its new seat in Malta. There were built in Malta churches and palaces with the same names as those in Rhodes: the churches of St. John, St. Catherine, and Our Lady of Victory, and the auberges of the *langues*. In Malta are preserved an important part of the archives of the order relating to the Rhodian period, when it was in fact what it purported to be, an eastern bulwark of Latin Christendom against the Ottoman menace.

63. Cf. R. Valentini, "I Cavalieri di S. Giovanni da Rodi a Malta: Trattative diplomatiche," *Archivium melitense,* IX (1935), 137–237.

X

THE KINGDOM OF CYPRUS
1291–1369

The steps taken at Acre in 1285 to overcome the Angevin party's opposition to the recognition of the Cypriote king Henry II as king of Jerusalem have been called "the one brilliant exploit of a long and

The standard bibliographical reference work is C. D. Cobham, *Bibliography of Cyprus,* (6th ed. by G. Jeffery, Nicosia, 1929). The sources in Cobham's *Excerpta Cypria: Materials for a History of Cyprus* (2nd ed., Cambridge, 1908) are complemented by T. A. H. Mogabgab's *Supplementary Excerpts on Cyprus* (3 parts, Nicosia, 1941–1945); see also L. de Mas Latrie, ed., *Nouvelles preuves de l'histoire de Chypre* (Bibliothèque de l'École des chartes, XXXII, XXXIV, XXXV; Paris, 1871–1874), which continues the collection of source materials in vols. II and III of his *Histoire de l'île de Chypre sous le règne des... Lusignan* (3 vols., Paris, 1852–1861).

Individual chroniclers include Badr-ad-Dīn al-'Ainī, "Account of the Conquest of Cyprus (1424–1426)," trans. M. M. Ziada and John L. LaMonte in *Annuaire de l'Institut de philologie et d'histoire orientales et slaves,* VII (1939–1944), 241–264; Francesco Amadi and Diomedes Strambaldi, *Chroniques de Chypre,* ed. R. de Mas Latrie (Collection des documents inédits sur l'histoire de France, 2 vols., Paris, 1891–1893); Florio Bustron, *Chronique de l'île de Chypre,* ed. R. de Mas Latrie (*ibid.,* Mélanges historiques, no. 5, Paris, 1886); Giorgio Bustron, Χρονικὸν Κύπρου, in K. N. Sathas, ed., Μεσαιωνικὴ Βιβλιοθήκη, II (Venice, 1873); Khalīl az-Ẓāhirī, *Zubdat kashf al-mamālik* (ed. P. Ravaisse, Paris, 1894; extracts trans. in Mogabgab's and Mas Latrie's collections, cited above); Jean Froissart, *Chroniques de France...* (many editions and translations available); Gianfrancesco Loredano ("Henri Giblet") *Historie de' re' Lusignani* (Bologna, 1647; French trans., 2 vols., Paris, 1732); Estienne de Lusignan, *Chorograffia et breve historia universale dell' isola de Cipro...* (Bologna, 1573; French trans., Paris, 1580); Leontius Machaeras, *Recital concerning the Sweet Land of Cyprus, entitled "Chronicle"* (ed. and trans. R. M. Dawkins, 2 vols., Oxford, 1932); Guillaume de Machaut, *La Prise d'Alexandrie ou chronique du roi Pierre Ier de Lusignan* (ed. L. de Mas Latrie, Société de l'Orient latin, série historique, no. 1, Geneva, 1877); Philippe de Mézières, *Songe du vieil pèlerin* (portions publ. by L. de Mas Latrie in *Histoire,* II, 116 ff.); *idem, Vita S. Petri Thomasii,* in *Acta Sanctorum* (Jan. 29) and ed. J. Smet (Textus et studia historica Carmelitana, no. 2, Rome, 1954); Enguerran[d] de Monstrelet, *Chronique* (ed. L. Douet d'Arcq, 6 vols., Paris, 1857–1862); and Pero Tafur, *Travels and Adventures, 1435–1439* (trans. M. Letts, London, 1926).

Modern historical treatments start with J. P. Reinhard, *Vollständige Geschichte des Königreiches Cypern* (2 vols., Erlangen, 1766–1768) and D. Jauna, *Histoire génerale des roïaumes de Chypre... comprenant les croisades et... l'empire ottoman* (2 vols., Leyden, 1785), followed by L. de Mas Latrie's *Des Relations politiques et commerciales de l'Asie Mineure avec l'île de Chypre...* (Bibliothèque de l'École des chartes, VI–VII = 2nd ser.,

otherwise unhappy reign."[1] But over his kingdom of Jerusalem, of which he proved to be the last *de facto* sovereign, Henry's reign lasted only six years. From his succession to the throne of Cyprus as an epileptic boy of fourteen, on May 20, 1285, upon the premature death of his elder brother John I, until his own death in 1324 Henry's life was beset with troubles. The first major disaster he had to face was the fall of Acre on May 18, 1291.

This landmark in history denoted the end of Frankish rule in Syria, even though the Templars held out at Tortosa (Antaradus, now Ṭarṭūs) until August 3, at Château Pèlerin (Athlith) until August 14,

---

I–II, 1844–1845) and *Histoire de l'île de Chypre* (cited above). Mas Latrie had previously published the first numismatic and sigillographic material, *Notice sur les monnaies et les sceaux des rois de Chypre* ... (Bibliothèque de l'École des chartes, V, 1843–1844); other studies are those by E. de Rozière, "Numismatique des rois latins de Chypre," in L. F. J. de Saulcy, ed., *Numismatique des croisades* (Paris, 1847), pp. 73–112, Gustave Schlumberger, *Numismatique de l'Orient latin* (Paris, 1878, suppl. 1882; repr. Graz, 1954) and *Sigillographie de l'Orient latin* (with F. Chalandon and A. Blanchet, Paris, 1943). In 1869 E. Dulaurier's "Fin de règne de Léon V ... d'Arménie" appeared in *RHC, Arm.,* I; Karl Herquet published *Charlotta von Lusignan und Caterina Cornaro, Königinnen von Cypern* (Regensburg, 1870) and *Cyprische Königsgestalten des Hauses Lusignan* (Halle, 1881); between these appeared William Stubbs, *The Medieval Kingdoms of Cyprus and Armenia* (Oxford, 1878); Mas Latrie added *L'Île de Chypre, sa situation présente et ses souvenirs du moyen-âge* (Paris, 1879), "Généalogie des rois de Chypre de la maison de Lusignan," *Archivio veneto,* XXI (1881), 309–359 (chart at end), and "Histoire des archevêques latins de l'île de Chypre," *Archives de l'Orient latin,* II (1884), 207–328; later ecclesiastical studies are J. Hackett, *History of the Orthodox Church of Cyprus* ... *(A.D. 45–1878)* (London, 1901) and L. Bréhier, *L'Église et l'Orient au moyen âge* (2nd ed., Paris, 1907). In 1886 there appeared I. J. Herzsohn's dissertation (Bonn) "Der Überfall Alexandriens durch Peter I. ... aus einer arabischen Quelle ... dargestellt." N. Iorga (Jorga) published *Philippe de Mézières (1327–1405) et la croisade au XIVe siècle* (Bibliothèque de l'École des hautes études, no. 110, Paris, 1896) and *Notes et extraits pour servir à l'histoire des croisades au XVe siècle* (3 vols. in *Revue de l'Orient latin,* IV–VIII, 1896–1901, and separately, Paris, 1899–1902; vols. IV–VI, Bucharest, 1915–1916). Art and architecture are treated in Camille Enlart, *L'Art gothique et de la Renaissance en Chypre* (2 vols., Paris, 1899) and more narrowly in Herbert F. Cook, *The Portrait of Caterina Cornaro by Giorgione* ... (London, 1915).

Other twentieth-century works of value include E. Oberhummer, *Die Insel Cypern,* I (Munich, 1903; no more publ.); K. J. Basmadjian, "Les Lusignans [sic] ... au trône de la Petite Arménie," *Journal asiatique,* CLXVIII (= 10th ser., vol. VII; 1906), 520–524; J. Delaville Le Roulx, *Les Hospitaliers en Terre Sainte et à Chypre (1100–1310)* (Paris, 1904); J. Billioud, "De la Date de la perte de Chypre par la branche légitime des Lusignan (1464)," *Le Moyen âge,* XXXIV (= 2nd ser., vol. XXV, 1923), 66–71; M. M. Ziada, "The Mamluk Conquest of Cyprus in the Fifteenth Century," *Bulletin of the Faculty of Arts of the University of Egypt,* I–II (Cairo, 1933–1934); and Sir George Hill's magistral *A History of Cyprus* (4 vols., Cambridge, 1940–1952), vols. II and III. Since Sir Harry Luke's death, Basmadjian's tables have been superseded by those of Count W. H. Rüdt-Collenberg, *The Rupenides, Hethumides, and Lusignans: the Structure of the Armeno-Cilician Dynastics* (Lisbon, 1963). This chapter and the next were edited after the author's death by Harry W. Hazard.

1. Stubbs, *Mediaeval Kingdoms of Cyprus and Armenia,* p. 28.

and on the islet of Ruad (Aradus), opposite Tortosa, until 1303.[2] It is true that the fall of Acre was a disaster to the crusading movement in general rather than to the kingdom of Cyprus in particular. No doubt the latter became somewhat congested, with the Templars and the Hospitallers, the ecclesiastics and baronage of Jerusalem, flocking to Cyprus together with the lesser refugees, who tended to be a drain on the island's resources. On the other hand, Cyprus was able to absorb a substantial part of the Syrian trade of Genoa and Venice, while its monarch, relieved of his mainland preoccupations as king of Jerusalem, could concentrate on the problems of his island realm, which were not wanting.

A futile attack by the galleys of pope Nicholas IV and king Henry on the Karamanian coast of Alaya ("Scandelore" or Candeloro) stung the Mamluk sultan al-Ashraf Khalīl into threatening that "Cyprus, Cyprus, Cyprus" should bear the brunt of his reprisals. This danger was removed by al-Ashraf's assassination in December 1293; and the growing Venetian and Genoese commercial activities in the island brought to it increasing wealth, though at the cost of the trading and other privileges which these republics exacted; those privileges were to become a canker that would eventually destroy the integrity of the kingdom. Meanwhile Genoa and Venice carried their mutual hostilities into Cypriote waters and even onto Cypriote soil, as when in 1294 a Venetian fleet destroyed the battlements of the Genoese fort at Limassol.

In 1300 Henry, in conjunction with the Templars and the Hospitallers, equipped an expedition against Egypt and Syria which accomplished little more than a series of marauding raids. Accompanying the expedition was one of the king's brothers, Amalric, titular lord of Tyre, who later in the same year was on Ruad at the head of a small force designed to take part with an army of Ghazan, the Persian Il-khan, in combined operations against the Saracens. The Mongols, who failed to arrive until February 1301, contented themselves with raiding northern Syria as far as Homs and then went home, whereupon Amalric and his men returned to Cyprus, their purpose unfulfilled.

It would have been better for Cyprus, and especially for king Henry, had Amalric never come back. For this disloyal prince, upon whom his brother had conferred the dignities (now purely nominal) of lord of Tyre and constable of the kingdom of Jerusalem, gradually

---

2. René Grousset, *Histoire des croisades et du royaume franc de Jérusalem,* III (Paris, repr. 1948), 763; cf. vol. II of this work, p. 598.

formed the design of ousting Henry from power and taking his place, in effect if not in form. To this end he enlisted the support of another brother, Aimery, constable of Cyprus, many of the leading members of the powerful Ibelin clan including his (and Henry's) brother-in-law Balian of Ibelin, prince of Galilee, and Philip of Ibelin, count of Jaffa, the ill-fated last grand master of the Templars, Jacques de Molay, and a majority of the high court. Loyal to the king—although Ibelins—were his mother queen Isabel and her brother Philip, the seneschal, together with "many others who did not consent to this evil deed." Amalric was married to an Armenian princess, also named Isabel, daughter of Leon III and sister of Hetoum II, Ṭoros III, and Ōshin, kings of Cilician Armenia, and he could count on the support of his Armenian connections on the mainland. Ṭoros was doubly his brother-in-law, for he had married Margaret de Lusignan, a sister of Amalric and king Henry.

The reasons alleged for Henry's supersession were his malady, his apathy in the face of Saracen and Genoese aggression, his failure to support his relatives on the throne of Cilician Armenia against the Moslems, general maladministration, his inaccessibility to those seeking justice, and so on. But the overwhelming balance of opinion of the chroniclers and historians of Amalric's usurpation supports the king against his accusers;[3] the evidence is convincing that Amalric was impelled by no loftier motives than personal ambition. If he contented himself with the titles of governor and regent *(gubernator et rector)* of Cyprus, it may well have been because he feared to alienate opinion at home and abroad (the papal curia, for example, was on Henry's side) by proceeding to the extreme lengths of deposing, and even putting to death, the anointed king.

By April 26, 1306, the plans of the lord of Tyre had come to maturity after six months of preparation. That evening the rebel leaders went to the palace, where the king was lying sick, and read to him a declaration to the effect that the barons, convinced that the public weal required the government to be taken out of his hands, had entrusted it to his brother Amalric as governor and regent; the declaration included an undertaking to meet all the king's needs from the revenues of the kingdom. Henry, who had hitherto disbelieved warnings of his brother's impending treachery, vigorously and indignantly protested but could do no more; the towns and castles were already in the hands of the usurper, whose men also took possession

3. Hill, *History of Cyprus,* II, 217–218.

of the estates and revenues of the royal domain. Three days later the masters of the Temple and the Hospital appeared as mediators and embarked on negotiations, lasting as many weeks, for an agreement between the helpless king and his opponents. This agreement, assuring certain revenues to Henry, the queen-mother, and others, and an establishment for the king, was confirmed in 1307 by a charter, sealed (though never signed) by the king and approved by the high court. Amalric's *coup d'état* not only had been successful but had secured a measure of legality, obtained from the king under duress.

Despite this agreement the king's position steadily deteriorated: Amalric took every opportunity to remove Henry's friends to a safe distance, and early in 1308 extorted from him under threats against his personal liberty a written patent appointing the lord of Tyre governor of the kingdom for life. But Henry, deeply aggrieved at his ill-treatment, to which was now added the removal from his custody of his much-loved nephew (and eventual successor) Hugh, declined to accept the homage of those who had received from Amalric grants which involved feudal service to the crown, and his refusal caused embarrassment to the usurper. Amalric was further exasperated by fear that the expected *passagium* through Cyprus of participants in the new crusade ordered by pope Clement V and the king of France would reveal to the world the unsoundness of his position.

During 1309 he continued to put increasingly heavy pressure on the king to make full submission, but Henry refused to yield more than he had done already. Finally, at the end of January 1310, Amalric and his brother Aimery the constable forced their way at night into the king's chamber and, despite the vehement protests of the queen-mother—made, according to Amadi, in a mixture of French, Greek and Arabic—and of the king's sisters, put him on a horse (he refusing to touch the saddle-bow or take the reins) and sent him under escort to Famagusta. As he was being led away, Henry warned his brother that he would "last but a short time in the kingdom of Cyprus, having laid his foundations in bad ground." He was to prove a true prophet. A few days later Henry was transported to the Cilician port of Ayas (Lajazzo) and placed in the custody of Amalric's brother-in-law and supporter, the shifty Ōshin, king of Cilician Armenia. The queen-mother remained in Cyprus under close guard.

The next phase of this sorry story was inaugurated with the arrival in Cyprus early in March 1310 of a papal nuncio, canon Raymond de Pins, charged by the pope and the king of France with the task of reconciling Amalric and king Henry. The nuncio made it clear to Amalric that opinion in Europe was against him, but the lord of Tyre, while willing to increase the king's allowance and permit Henry, after agreeing to his conditions, to return to Cyprus, declared that he would never surrender the governorship. So the nuncio next proceeded to Cilicia to convey these terms to the king and actually induced him to accept them, an achievement rather difficult to understand after Henry's stubborn defense of his rights through four perilous years. The explanation may be that the close and harsh confinement to which he was being subjected in the Cilician fortress of Lampron had now caused him to abandon all hope.

At all events, by the end of March the nuncio was back in Cyprus with Henry's agreement and presented it to Amalric for confirmation. But the governor delayed affixing his signature, possibly owing to preoccupation with the arraignment of the Templars, which had already been initiated in Paris in 1307 and now opened, so far as the members of the order in Cyprus were concerned, in April 1310, a few days after the nuncio's return. He was destined never to sign it at all because on June 5 he was murdered in the palace by his favorite, Simon de Montolif, who then escaped from Nicosia, was believed to have made his way on board some ship, and was never heard of again. While the motives for this deed have remained obscure, they have not been traced to any organized conspiracy by adherents of the king, whom Amalric had been able either to banish or to keep in subjection.

Nevertheless, with the usurper dead, the loyalists lifted up their heads and, rallying round the queen, took immediate steps to recall the people's allegiance to their lawful ruler. The constable Aimery indeed, backed by the murdered man's widow Isabel, titular lady of Tyre, quickly secured from the high court the nomination as governor in Amalric's place. But he was unable to maintain himself for long in the face of the strong sentiment in Henry's favor that was manifested by the knights and the towns. Limassol and Paphos declared for Henry, and one Aygue de Bessan was chosen as captain of the army and lieutenant of the king for the whole of Cyprus.

Negotiations were now opened with king Ōshin to secure Henry's return from Cilicia. For by June 13 the king had been proclaimed in Nicosia; the chancery had returned to the palace; and the constable with his henchman the prince of Galilee had come to terms with the queen, in consideration of her undertaking to do her best to secure pardons or amnesties for those who made their submission. Throughout the tortuous actions which followed on the part of the lady Isabel, the constable, the prince of Galilee, and their dwindling band of supporters, the queen-mother played a part of statesmanlike moderation so that Henry might return to a united rather than a divided kingdom.

These tortuous actions need not be described in detail. They amounted to delaying tactics on the part of Isabel, the constable, and the prince, aided and abetted by king Ōshin in Cilicia, in the hope that the situation might somehow be reversed in their favor or that, failing this, there might at least be assured the safety of Isabel and her children. But, although they contrived to postpone Henry's return for some weeks, they were unable ultimately to prevent it. By the beginning of August an agreement had been concluded with Ōshin providing for Henry's departure for Cyprus simultaneously with the return of the lady of Tyre and her children to Cilicia.

To the end there was bad faith on the part of the Armenians, who, after Isabel had actually landed at Ayas, tried to seize the boat in which Henry was being conveyed to his galley. The attempt was foiled by the vigilance of the Cypriotes, and the king, safely aboard, was visited by Isabel's son Hughet, who made his submission, offered his services, and was well received. Thereupon Isabel herself decided to follow suit and, "throwing herself at Henry's feet begged for pardon, assuring him that he would learn in time that her guilt was less than was imputed to her, and offering to swear allegiance. Then she opened a box and handed to Henry the crown, scepter, ring, and seals which her husband had seized from the Franciscans, with whom they had been deposited. She begged the king to punish the authors of her husband's death. The king replied briefly—for the fleet was ready to sail—accepting her excuse so far as she personally was concerned; but place and time were not suitable for him to receive her oath. He regretted that her husband had died with such a sin upon his soul, and promised to do his best to purchase his absolution."[4] On August 27, 1310, after nearly seven months of exile and four years and four months of exclusion from the exercise of his authority, Henry landed at Famagusta, where his return was celebrated with three days of rejoicing. In Nicosia, where he was greeted "as though he had risen from the dead," the festivities were even more prolonged.

The period of Amalric's usurpation (1306–1310) saw two events of an importance in crusading history far transcending the confines of the kingdom of Cyprus. One was the inquisition by pope Clement V,

4. Hill, *History of Cyprus,* II, 260.

acting at the instigation of Philip IV of France, into the affairs of the Knights Templar, which was to culminate in that order's dissolution in 1312; the other was the acquisition of the island of Rhodes by the Knights Hospitaller, operating from Cyprus, which had been their temporary headquarters since the fall of Acre.[5]

During the four years of his governorship Amalric struck coins of two distinctive types, both now of the greatest rarity. The earlier type retained Henry's name on the obverse, combined with Amalric's on the reverse, which bears the legend *Amalricus Gubernator Cipri.* The second type, reflecting the deterioration of Henry's position, omits all mention of him. The obverse bears the inscription *Amalricus Tirensis Dominus Cipri Gubernator et Rector,* surrounding the Lusignan lion in two concentric circles; on the reverse the words *Ierusalem et Cipri Regis Filius* encompass a shield impaling the arms of Jerusalem and Cyprus. The *gros* and *demi-gros* of the second type are from the artistic point of view among the handsomest examples of the Lusignan coinage.

Necessarily the first concern of the restored king Henry, thirty-nine years old on his return from dispossession and exile, was to secure the persons of Amalric's principal supporters. Some of these complied with his command to give themselves up, others had to be sought out: the king's brother Aimery the constable, Balian of Ibelin, titular prince of Galilee, Philip of Ibelin, titular count of Jaffa, with other disloyal knights, made submission and public confession of their treason and threw themselves on the royal mercy. They were not immediately put to death, although this might have proved a more clement fate: they were committed to rigorous confinement in the castles of Kyrenia and the more inaccessible Buffavento. The Ibelins perished in Kyrenia in 1316, the constable probably about the same time.

Toward his sister-in-law Isabel, the usurper Amalric's widow, on the other hand, Henry showed more leniency than was characteristic of the age. Nine weeks after his restoration he allowed her and three of her sons to reënter Cyprus and in the following year, 1311, to return with her family and household to Cilicia. She might have done better to remain where she was, for she ultimately met her death (in 1323) in an Armenian prison at the instance of the regent of her own country, Ōshin of Corycus.

Three major matters of external importance engaged Henry's attention after his restoration, in addition to the local one of striving to

5. See above, pp. 278–283.

rehabilitate the economy of the royal domain and the kingdom in general, seriously dislocated by Amalric's intrusion. The war against the Saracens was of course an ever-present preoccupation of the rulers of Cyprus, however urgent might be their more immediate problems, even when no military or naval operations were in progress; and on crusading policy Henry's envoys presented to pope Clement V a reasoned statement recommending "Cyprus rather than Armenia as a base, Egypt rather than Armenia or Syria as the objective."[6] Such had in fact been the opinion a little earlier of Edward I of England, who had ruled that Egypt must be the first point of attack, followed by Palestine and Constantinople in that order; and such was the policy to be adopted in due course by Henry's great-nephew Peter I.

The second matter concerned the arraignment of the Knights Templar. Their trial, resumed after a temporary interruption caused by Amalric's murder, resulted in their being cleared of the charges brought against them, an outcome unwelcome to pope Clement V, and still more so to his patron, Philip IV of France, who was intent on the order's dissolution. A new trial, ordered in 1311 to be held in Nicosia, produced the desired result; the properties of the Temple in Cyprus, including the historic commandery of Kolossi near Limassol, were allotted to the Knights Hospitaller.

A third difficulty involved the Genoese, already troublesome in the first period of Henry's reign not only by reason of the preponderating influence derived from their hold on the island's commerce but by the manner in which they made free of Cypriote territorial waters, and even the mainland of Cyprus, in their perennial hostile encounters with their rivals the Venetians. Now, in 1312, although Genoa was officially at peace with the kingdom, three Genoese galleys made a piratical raid on the district of Paphos, followed in 1316 by a more extended one with a force of eleven galleys. Henry had the spirit to retaliate by imprisoning all the Genoese of Nicosia and keeping them in confinement until 1320, when a truce between the two states was negotiated through the mediation of pope John XXII.

On the morning of March 31, 1324, Henry was found dead in his bed, after having been out hawking the previous day. Dante's reference to him in the *Paradiso* (XIX, 145–148),

> In earnest of this day, e'en now are heard
> Wailings and groans in Famagosta's streets
> And Nicosia's, grudging at their beast
> Who keepeth even footing with the rest,

6. Hill, *History of Cyprus,* II, 278.

may reasonably be ascribed to anti-French prejudice. Henry, physically handicapped by his epilepsy, grossly ill-used by two of his brothers and their supporters among his own subjects, was for his day not a bad man and not a bad king; we may well feel able to accept the verdict that "as so often happens after an unquiet reign, he outlived all his enemies and died rather regretted than not. . . . When he had been able to exercise independent authority he had used it well; he had welcomed the refugees from Acre and fortified Famagosta; he contributed largely to the judicial decisions which formed the supplement to the Assizes, and he established a strong judicature in Cyprus."[7] One may commend the tenacity with which he endured his sufferings at the hands of his enemies, "which would have been remarkable even in one who was not the victim of physical infirmity."[8] He had worn the crown of Cyprus for just under thirty-nine years.

Henry had married, in 1317, a Catalan princess, Constance, daughter of Frederick II, king of Sicily. He was probably impotent and the marriage was childless. He was therefore succeeded—since Amalric's sons were debarred on account of their father's treason—by his favorite nephew Hugh, son of his brother Guy, who had been constable of the kingdom until his death in 1302 or 1303, when he was followed in that office by the disloyal brother Aimery. The wise, patient, sorely tried queen-mother, Isabel of Ibelin, who had seen her family so bitterly and tragically torn asunder, survived king Henry by only a few weeks. His widow Constance married Leon V of Armenia.

Hugh IV and his consort, Alice of Ibelin, his second wife, were crowned as the sovereigns of Cyprus in Nicosia cathedral two weeks after the new king's accession; a month later the royal couple established the precedent of being crowned as sovereigns of the kingdom of Jerusalem in the cathedral of Famagusta, the city nearest to the lost mainland. The early years of the reign saw negotiations for treaties with Genoa and with Venice designed to stabilize the troubled relations between Cyprus and the two powerful and rival maritime republics, each with its close commercial interests in the kingdom. Other foreign cities and communities, such as Montpellier, Florence, and the Catalans, also developed their activities in this island so blessed by nature and geography; and it was toward the middle of the fourteenth century, that is to say in the time of Hugh IV, that Famagusta, its principal port—busy, wealthy, and cosmopolitan—attained its position of eminence among the *échelles* of the

---

7. Stubbs, *Mediaeval Kingdoms*, p. 33.
8. Hill, *History of Cyprus*, II, 284.

Levant. The Westphalian priest Ludolph of Suchem, visiting the island in 1349, is eloquent regarding the splendor of its nobles and its merchants. "In Cyprus," he says,

the princes, nobles, barons and knights are the richest in the world. . . . I knew a certain Count of Japhe [Jaffa] who had more than 500 hounds, and every two dogs have their own servant to guard and bathe and anoint them, for so must dogs be tended there. A certain nobleman has ten or eleven falconers with special pay and allowances. . . . Moreover there are very rich merchants, a thing not to be wondered at, for Cyprus is the farthest of Christian lands, so that all ships and all wares, . . . must needs come first from Cyprus, and in no wise can they pass it by, and pilgrims from every country journeying to the lands over sea must touch at Cyprus.[9]

He speaks of the daughter of a citizen of Famagusta, the jewels of whose headdress at her betrothal were "more precious than all the ornaments of the queen of France."

Five years earlier an anonymous Englishman had broken in Cyprus his journey to the Holy Land. He, too, marvels at Famagusta's luxury: "there reside in it merchants of Venice, Genoa, Catalonia, and Saracens from the Soldan's dominions, dwelling in palaces which are there called *loggias,* living in the style of counts and barons; they have abundance of gold and silver."[10] This observant traveler also outlines revealingly the characteristics of Hugh IV. The king, he says, "is a man of great kindness towards the gentle and of severity towards the perverse Greeks; nevertheless he rules the people of his realm with justice, without looking upon them too benignly." After an account of the monarch's delight in hunting the moufflon (the wild sheep of Cyprus), he continues: "the king is rightly called peaceful."

In his word "peaceful" he strikes the keynote of the reign, which differed from those of Hugh's predecessors and successors alike in its relative freedom from warlike operations. Hugh was above all a prudent ruler, who, while fully alive to the potential danger to his country from the Selchükid Turks, avoided (unlike his son and successor Peter I) unnecessary adventures. He agreed, it is true, to contribute six galleys to an expedition sent against the Selchükids in 1334 by a league in which Venice and France were the other partners, under the auspices of pope John XXII. An expedition

9. Cobham, *Excerpta Cypria,* pp. 19 ff.

10. The MS. of the record of this journey, preserved in Corpus Christi College, Cambridge, is published in the original Latin in G. Golubovich, ed., *Biblioteca bio-bibliografica della Terra Santa e dell' Oriente francescano,* IV (Quaracchi, 1923), 435–460. The passages relating to Cyprus are translated into English by Sir H. Luke in *Kypriaka Chronika,* II (1924), and republished by Mogabgab, *Supplementary Excerpts on Cyprus,* part II (1943).

planned by the same partners on a larger scale for the following year was rendered abortive by the preoccupation of Philip VI of France with a threatened invasion of his country by Edward III of England. But negotiations for a resumption of such activities were kept alive and resulted in the formation, in 1343, of a new league composed of the pope, the Hospitallers, Venice, and Cyprus. In 1344 the expedition dispatched by this alliance against the Selchükids captured the city of Smyrna, which remained in Christian hands until recaptured by Timur the Lame in 1402.[11] Hugh took no personal part in this or any other campaign, but he continued to contribute in ships and money to the patrolling of the Turkish coasts. Under his cautious rule his kingdom reached the zenith of its prosperity as the exporter to the west of its valuable products such as barley, wine, cane sugar, silk, and cotton, and as an important entrepot for the stuffs and spices of the farther east.

Though king Hugh thus governed his realm with wisdom, his character can scarcely be called an attractive one. Even to members of his own family he was capable of showing sustained cruelty, as to his son-in-law Ferdinand of Majorca, whom he pursued with vindictive hatred. When his sons Peter and John, titular prince of Antioch, determined to travel to the west in defiance of their father's objections and succeeded in leaving the country with the help of an amenable knight, one John Lombard, Hugh had the knight hanged after the amputation of a hand and a foot. When the young princes were eventually caught off the coast of Sicily and brought back home, the incensed monarch incarcerated them in Kyrenia, where they remained until released at the pope's intercession. On the other hand, he was a patron of scholars and artists, and Boccaccio dedicated to him his *Genealogy of the Gods,* written at the king's request.[12]

Hugh IV died in 1359 after a successful reign of thirty-five years. He had become reconciled with Peter, the eldest surviving son, whom he had caused to be crowned king of Cyprus in his own lifetime, in 1358. He took this step, no doubt, in the hope of avoiding a disputed succession, which nevertheless occurred. For the eldest of all his sons, Guy, titular prince of Galilee, had died in 1343, leaving a son Hugh, who claimed to be the rightful successor to his grandfather. In modern practice his claim would have been valid, and it was in fact supported by the pope and the king of France; Peter rejected it on

---

11. See also above, pp. 294–308.

12. See G. Boccaccio, *Genealogie deorum gentilium libri,* ed. V. Romano (2 vols., Bari, 1951), I, 1, and cf. II, 784–785.

the grounds that in accordance with the Assizes of Jerusalem a surviving son had the prior right over the son of a deceased elder brother. Later, young Hugh's claims were settled by a grant of a pension and, in 1365, the title prince of Galilee, and he became reconciled with his uncle, whom he accompanied on his western journeys and on the expedition against Alexandria.

Peter I was not only the most spectacular monarch of his house; he is one of the most spectacular figures in late medieval history. If his father had guided the Lusignan kingdom to material prosperity, the son brought it to the height of its reputation on the international stage. Devoted to the crusading ideal from the days before his first coronation and accession, when he bore the title of count of Tripoli, he became in pursuit of that ideal one of the most persistent knights-errant of his century. Brave and chivalrous, passionate and sensual, he not only could win the acclaim of a François Villon; he could inspire the personal devotion of a Peter Thomas, who is venerated as a saint by the Carmelites, and a Philip of Mézières. Until the final failure of his hopes, combined with domestic trouble, turned disappointment to despair and an idealist into a capricious and irresponsible tyrant, Peter had earned the approval of some of the leading spirits of his age. Jean Froissart, William of Machaut, and Philip of Mézières chronicle his remarkable activities; Petrarch and Chaucer award him praise.

Already by 1347, when still in his teens, the young count of Tripoli had founded his Order of the Sword as the embodiment of his compelling passion for the recovery of the holy places. He believed himself to have been divinely entrusted with this mission, in a vision vouchsafed to him in the mountain monastery of Stavro-vouni near Larnaca, a shrine famous for the relic of a piece of the True Cross embedded in pieces of the crosses of the two thieves, which had been brought to it by the empress Helena. The motto he gave to his order was *c'est pour loyauté maintenir,* and the inspiration of its emblem was not only daily before him but daily before his subjects. For on his coinage he caused to be placed in his hand the sword instead of the scepter held by his predecessors and his successors; heraldically, too, it supported his arms.

Peter was just thirty years old on his accession and had already been married for six years to his second wife, Eleanor of Aragon, a princess of physical attractions but of a jealous and vindictive temper. The pair were crowned for the kingdom of Jerusalem in Famagusta by the papal legate Peter Thomas, who was to become the king's trusted adviser and devoted friend. The reign began with the usual complicated dealings with the Genoese and the Venetians, but its major interest here lies in the king's preoccupation with his intended crusade, his indefatigable efforts to bring it about, and his actual achievement. The achievement was ephemeral in its results, but that the ruler of a small island state of limited resources, situated on the very confines of the enemy's territories, should have been able to bring his plans for a crusade to any sort of fruition, and that moreover in the second half of the fourteenth century, was a remarkable tribute to his unflagging zeal, his persistence in the face of discouragement, and his sense of vocation. In the matter of the crusade he was a dedicated man.

His first stroke was accomplished quite early in his reign, when the citizens of the fortress of Corycus on the Karamanian coast, rightly doubting the ability of their own sovereigns of the tottering kingdom of Cilician Armenia to protect them against the Turks, offered their town to Peter. A similar offer made previously to Hugh IV had been declined by that cautious monarch, but Peter accepted with alacrity the gift of a valuable base on the mainland of Anatolia. It was to remain in the possession of the Cypriote kingdom until lost in 1448 under the feeble John II. Fortified by the control of this foothold, Peter's next objective was the important walled Turkish city of Adalia ("Satalia," now Antalya), against which he assembled at Famagusta an expedition whose vessels, great and small, numbered one hundred and twenty. It was an appreciable force and included four galleys contributed by the master of the Hospitallers, Roger de Pins, two by pope Innocent VI, every craft that Peter himself could muster, and several privateers. The operation was completely successful. Adalia was taken by storm on August 24, 1361, not to be recovered by the Turks until 1373, when Cyprus was, as we shall see, heavily embroiled with Genoa.

Now began Peter's most difficult task, one requiring the utmost efforts that diplomacy, persuasiveness, a handsome presence, and an engaging personality could jointly contribute. The task was to induce the rulers of the west to combine in launching a major crusade against the heart of the Saracen power, that is to say, an expedition compared with which the attacks hitherto made on the Turkish coast would amount to no more than preliminary skirmishes. In October 1362 the king sailed from Paphos accompanied by his young son and heir, the future Peter II; Hugh de Lusignan, his nephew and former competitor for the throne; Philip of Mézières (1327–1405), chancellor of the kingdom (who in his later years was to describe his experiences in his *Songe du vieil pèlerin*); the legate, Peter Thomas; and a considerable retinue. It is to Peter's additional credit that he undertook his incessant journeys despite the sea-sickness from which he suffered acutely.

Landing in Venice, where, as next in Genoa, he spent some weeks, Peter then made for the papal court at Avignon. Here the party was warmly received by the new pope, Urban V, as by John II, king of France (but not, as often alleged, by the Danish monarch, Waldemar III). On April 12, 1363, a *passagium generale* was formally proclaimed by the pope, to be undertaken within two years under the command of the king of France. This all-important decision secured, and the pension of the young prince Hugh finally and satisfactorily settled, Peter and his following continued their way northward through Brabant and Flanders, being welcomed, notably in Brussels and Bruges, with lavish entertainment. In October they crossed the Channel to enlist the aid of the kings of England and Scotland. Jean Froissart, to whom we are primarily indebted for our detailed knowledge of Peter's wanderings, describes the king's visit to London, where he was well received by Edward III and queen Philippa. Edward gave him a ship named the *Katharine;* Philippa tendered him handsome presents; like royal visitors of a later age, he was entertained, according to a persistent tradition of the City of London, at a civic banquet, together with four brother kings. Edward offered his royal guest a tournament (for Peter excelled at jousting), but in the matter of the more serious business at hand excused himself from participating in the projected crusade on the ground of age, suggesting that this might be a task more suited to his sons. But he made it clear to the dismayed Peter that if he recovered his kingdom of Jerusalem, "he would be expected to hand over to Edward the Kingdom of Cyprus which Richard Lion Heart had given to his predecessor."[13]

In February 1364 the party returned to France, and in Angoulême Peter sought out Edward the Black Prince, who followed his father's example in giving an evasive answer to the appeal to take the cross. In May he was present at the funeral of his intended leader John II at St. Denis and twelve days later at the coronation of John's successor Charles V in Rheims. The pontifical mass on this occasion was sung to the music of William of Machaut (*c.* 1300–1377), the foremost French musician of his century and the poet who subsequently commemorated Peter's exploits in his epic *La prise d'Alexandrie ou chronique du roi Pierre I de Lusignan.*

----

13. Hill, *History of Cyprus,* II, 326. On Waldemar see Iorga, *Philippe de Mézières,* pp. 162–163.

Hitherto Peter had been unable to meet the emperor, Charles IV. For this purpose he now made his way through Germany to Prague, where Charles was then in residence in the Hradčany. Here the visitor was received with all the traditional pomp of the Holy Roman empire and by processions of the entire clergy. But the emperor assured Peter that he was in no position to support his guest's plan without the aid of others; he proposed a conference between himself and Peter with king Casimir III of Poland (whose granddaughter Elizabeth the emperor had recently married) and king Louis I of Hungary to consider the possibility of combined action. Cracow was designated as the venue of the meeting, and Peter, unwilling to miss any opportunity to advance his plans, agreed to this lengthening of his already formidable itinerary. The conference was held as arranged and Peter gave a brilliant account of himself at the tourneys held in Cracow, as elsewhere, in his honor. But in other respects it produced little more than vague promises and expressions of good will. Somewhat disheartened, Peter now turned southwest to Vienna, to be received with distinction by duke Rudolph IV of Austria, and from Vienna made his way across the Alps back to Venice. He reached Venice in November 1364 and there continued to organize the collection of the force brought into being by his two years of arduous traveling and pleading. That a force had been promised and raised at all was due to his initiative and his impassioned advocacy at the courts of Christendom, but his odyssey had been a heavy drain on the financial resources of his little kingdom. He sailed for Rhodes, where the expedition was due to assemble, on June 27, 1365.

It will be remembered that Edward I of England had held that in any major operation against the Saracens, Egypt must be the first point of attack, a policy later endorsed in the memorial presented to pope Clement V by the envoys of Peter's great-uncle, the Cypriote king Henry II. The fleet gathered in Rhodes for the great assault numbered 165 vessels of all sizes, including 31 galleys, and to this total Cyprus had contributed no fewer than 108. Not yet, however, was its objective communicated to the armada as a whole. Peter shared the views of his great-uncle and the English king, and the objective he had decided upon was Alexandria, the greatest port of the Mamluk sultan's realm and the gateway to Cairo, his capital. It was one of the richest cities of the Mediterranean, a consideration of realistic importance to the leader of a heterogeneous body of men, of whom some, at all events, had been induced to join by the sordid lure of loot. But he felt it necessary to keep secret to the last possible moment plans that would not commend themselves to all his partners. Venice in particular was sensitive as regards antagonizing the sultan, as it was the republic's policy to keep on good terms with him in order to safeguard its commercial activities in his dominions. [14] That it supported Peter's crusade to the extent it did may have been out of gratitude for Peter's helpfulness in connection with a revolt against the Venetians in Crete.

Attempts had been made, not without success, to delude the enemy into expecting the attack to be made on the crusaders' traditional objective, the Syrian coast. Alexandria was therefore taken by surprise when the fleet entered its harbor on October 9, 1365. The sultan, Sha'bān, was a boy; the governor, who had been on the pilgrimage, was still on his way back; many of the townsfolk, taking the visit to be a friendly one, at first came out prepared to trade. An opening assault was partially successful, yet some of the invaders were in favor, even then, of abandoning an enterprise of which they had never wholly approved. It required all Peter's determination to induce the half-hearted among his followers to persevere with the attack. During hand-to-hand skirmishes the king nearly lost his life and had to fight his way out of a band of Saracens who had managed to surround him; his nephew Hugh also displayed conspicuous gallantry and won the title prince of Galilee on the field of battle. By October 10 the Christians were within the walls and the city, for the time being, was theirs, to be pillaged, laid waste, and finally burned. Defenders and townspeople were indiscriminately slaughtered, irrespective of age and sex. William of Machaut estimated the slain among the Saracen troops and the Alexandrians at twenty thousand, no doubt an exaggerated figure, but not exaggerated was the destruction. Alexandria was reduced almost to ashes; movable objects of loot filled seventy of the attacking ships; five thousand of the population were put on board others to be taken away as captives. Alexandria's sack, which continued for three days, was complete.

It was Peter's plan to strengthen the captured city's fortifications and to use it as the advanced base for the recapture of the Holy Land, ultimate goal of the crusade. But a council of war which now assembled to consider the next step was overwhelmingly in favor of evacuation, notwithstanding the king's pleas, backed by Philip of Mézières and the pope's legate, Peter Thomas, for holding fast. The majority argued successfully that the captured city would be un-

14. The rulers of Venice must have known that the attack was to be made against Egypt, for they had exacted an undertaking from Peter not to land in the sultan's territories before the end of October, and complained bitterly that he had done so three weeks early.

tenable against the sultan's relieving army, already on the march, but many, particularly among the northern knights, were preoccupied with getting safely away with their loot. The decision was a bitter blow to Peter, turning his joy in victory to grief at its ephemeral result. Petrarch in a letter to Boccaccio[15] well sums up the situation in the following words:

> The conquest of Alexandria by the king of Cyprus, a great and memorable achievement, would have afforded a powerful basis for the increase of our religion had the spirit shown in its taking been equaled in the holding of it. He, indeed, it is reputed, was not lacking in it but rather his company, collected mainly from the transalpine races who always excel at the beginning rather than the end of things. These men, having followed a pious king not from piety but from greed, deserted him in the middle of his glorious undertaking, departing with their spoils to frustrate his pious vow while satisfying their own avarice.

Peter and his faithful followers were the last to return to their ships, embarking about October 16 as the sultan's troops from Cairo were actually entering the ravaged city. The retreating expedition sailed to Limassol and there dispersed, and Peter saw his kingdom again for the first time in three years, during which time his brother John, titular prince of Antioch, had exercised the regency. Philip of Mézières records that during the sad homecoming journey the legate composed an *oratio tragica* intended for the pope and the emperor; to Peter's loss and that of Cyprus this saintly man, the king's good genius, died in Famagusta the following January.

When the west became aware of what had happened in Alexandria, sympathy with Peter was such that the king of France, the count of Savoy, and famous warriors like Bertrand du Guesclin wished to take the cross so that they might help the king of Cyprus to retrieve the situation. These intentions were frustrated by the equivocal action of Venice, which, ever placing her oriental trade above other considerations, put about the false news that Peter had made his peace with the sultan.

Negotiations did indeed take place on pope Urban's advice between Peter and the sultan's powerful emir, Yelbogha al-Khaṣṣikī. Peter returned those of the Alexandrian captives whom the "transalpines" had not carried away into the west, and embassies were exchanged with fluctuating but in the end negative results. Meanwhile, his zeal not extinguished by his disappointments, he sent an expedition, foiled by a storm, against Beirut, relieved Corycus from an attack by the Turks, and secured Adalia against a discontented garrison. In

15. *Senilia,* book VIII, *ep.* 8 (July 20, 1367); cf. Hill, *History of Cyprus,* II, 335, note 3.

September and October 1367 he carried out powerful raids—with an international force of 7,000 fighting men and some 150 ships— against Tripoli, Tortosa, and Valania on the Syrian coast, and against Ayas in Cilicia, the last-named in aid of Constantine V, the hard-pressed king of Armenia, who had arranged to meet him there but failed to keep the appointment.

Nevertheless Peter knew well that these operations, irritating though they were to the enemy, brought him little or no nearer to his primary goal, the recovery of the Holy Land. This, he realized, could be achieved only by another *passagium generale,* which meant that he would have to go once more on his travels if there were to be any hope of bringing such an undertaking into being. So again this sanguine, indefatigable knight-errant set out on his self-imposed task, which proved on this occasion to be a fruitless one. Traveling by way of Rhodes and Naples, where he was entertained respectively by the master Raymond Bérenger and queen Joanna, he reached Rome in the early spring of 1368, to learn that his friend and supporter, the pope, had come to the inevitable conclusion (forced upon him not only by the Venetians, who were bent upon making their peace with the sultan, but by the circumstances of the time) that an effective crusade in the then state of Christendom was out of the question; it seemed to have become an anachronism. Urban V had always wished Peter well—he would refer to him in the parlance of the time as an "athlete of Christ"—and the king was forced to admit that he was right. Reluctantly but inevitably he agreed to accept the mediation of Venice and of Genoa, and wrote to Cyprus to his brother the regent that on the advice of the pope and the two republics he had consented to peace if the sultan would accept his terms. A copy of these was enclosed in the letter to prince John. In the event, the negotiations broke down, but Peter learned of their failure only on his return to Cyprus.

In the meantime he began his preparations for the homeward journey, to be made from Venice. Traveling northward through Florence and Bologna, where he was in the company of Froissart (presenting to him twenty ducats on their parting at Ferrara), he reached Venice in August and sailed for Cyprus on September 23 with a suite of five hundred persons. Before leaving Italy he was offered by the barons of Cilician Armenia, and appears to have accepted, the crown of that distressed country, already once offered to him tentatively on his first voyage; at all events there exists a coin of his in the Armenian series.

When Peter reached home he was just thirty-nine years old and had become one of the most acclaimed figures in Christendom. He was to live barely three more months, the most lamentable months of his life. For during his absence he had received reports not only of the unfaithfulness of his wife, queen Eleanor, with John of Morphou, titular count of Edessa ("Rochas"), but of Eleanor's ill-treatment of one of his two favorite mistresses, Joan l'Aleman, whom the queen had tried to cause to miscarry the king's child. It was a sad homecoming for the king, already suffering disappointment at the frustration of his plans, and that disappointment turned to bitterness when the barons of the high court refused him justice against the queen and John of Morphou. In clearing the couple they wished no doubt to save Eleanor's honor as well as to spare the island the wrath of Aragon-Catalonia, but equally to vex the king, whom they had grown to hate for his insistence on his costly wars and his alleged preference for the knights from the west. Peter for his part now became a capricious and cruel tyrant, imprisoning those who opposed his wishes in a tower which, in common with his daughter and a favorite mule, he called Margaret.

The end of this sorry tale is best told in the account by Leontius Machaeras of the last hour of Peter's life:

And on Wednesday the seventeenth of January 1369 after Christ very early all the knights in company with the prince [John] and his brother [James (I)] came to the king's lodging . . . . And they dismounted at the pavement and went up the stairs and went to the *loggia* with all those who had been at the prison. Then the prince knocks gently at the door. Of the ushers, it was the day of Gilet de Cornalie; he opened, and when the king's brothers went in, they all went in together. The king heard the stir and got up from the bed and says: "Who are these who have come?" The Lady Echive de Scandelion his mistress, who was sleeping with him, said to him: "Who can it be but your brothers?" And the lady covered herself with her coat and went out into the *loggia* and down into the between-room, where saddles for tournaments were stored; and they shut the trapdoor. When the prince saw that the Lady Echive who was at the king's side, had gone away, he went into the king's room, and greeted the king: and the constable did not go in, nor did the prince wish to go in, but the knights, who had another plan in their minds, forced him to go in. Then he says to the king: "Sir, a good day to you." And the king said to him "Good day to you, my good brother." And the prince said to him: "We worked all last night and have written down our opinion, and we have brought it to you for you to see." The king was naked in his shirt and wanted to dress, and he was ashamed to dress before his brother, and he says to him: "My princely brother, go outside for a little for me to dress, and I will look at what you have written." The prince went out. Then the Lord of Arsuf pushed in, holding in his hand a dagger like a little sword, as was usual at this time, and by him was Sir Henry de Giblet. And when the prince had gone out, the king put on his clothes to dress himself; and he had put on one sleeve (of his coat) and had turned his head to put on the other, when he sees the knights in his room: and he says to them: "Faithless traitors, what are you doing at this hour in my room, attacking me?" And there were there, Sir Philip d'Ibelin, the Lord of Arsuf, and Sir Henry de Giblet and Sir John de Gaurelle; these three went in at once and drew their swords and gave him each one of them three of four wounds: and the king cried out: "Help, mercy, for the love of God!" And immediately Sir John Gorap, the steward of the court, pushed his way in, and found him in a faint: and he draws his sword and cut off his head, saying: "You wished today to cut off my head, and I will cut off yours, and your threat shall fall upon your own self." And thus the knights came in one after the other, and they all laid their swords (upon him) because of their oath.[16]

Peter I had raised his island realm to the height of its reputation with friend and foe alike. The murder by an infuriated baronage of the outstanding Lusignan monarch and one of the most conspicuous figures of his age put a premature and pitiful end to a career of glorious promise not wholly unfulfilled. Chaucer is more generous to Peter than is Dante to his great-uncle Henry. His judgment in *The Monkes Tale* on the luckless monarch is kindly to his faults, does not withhold credit for his performance, and is alive to the significance of Cyprus, through Peter, to the western world:

> O worthy Petro, king of Cypre, also,
> That Alisaundre wan by heigh maistrye,
> Ful many a hethen wroghtestow ful wo,
> Of which thyn owene liges hadde envye,
> And, for no thing but for thy chivalrye,
> They in thy bedde han slayn thee by the morwe.
> Thus can fortune hir wheel governe and gye,
> And out of Ioye bringe men to sorwe.[17]

16. Machaeras, *Recital* (ed. and trans. Dawkins), pp. 264–269.
17. Walter W. Skeat, ed., *The Complete Works of Geoffrey Chaucer,* IV (Oxford, 1894), 256, lines 401–408.

XI

THE KINGDOM OF CYPRUS
1369–1489

The murdered Peter I was succeeded on the throne of Cyprus by his only son, another Peter, then a lad of fourteen commonly known by the diminutive form of the name, Perrin. Of the new king's two surviving uncles, John, titular prince of Antioch, was constable of Cyprus, while James was constable of Jerusalem and subsequently his nephew's successor on the throne as James I. The former, as the elder, became regent of the kingdom, as he had been before when his brother had been absent from the realm. But until Peter II came to marry, the most powerful influence on him, as in the affairs of the kingdom at large, was that of his mother, queen Eleanor. This passionate and tenacious woman was actuated by a single motive, that of avenging, despite his (and her own) notorious infidelities, her husband's murder; and she was prepared to employ for her purpose any instrument that came to hand. Her immediate objective in 1369 was to retain control over the young king.

In the first few months of the new reign the late king's practice of raiding the Mamluk sultan's dominions was maintained, and on July 10, 1369, Alexandria was once more entered by a Cypriote squadron, commanded by John of Morphou, titular count of Edessa ("Rochas"), who had taken part in the ephemeral capture of that city by Peter I in 1365. But in September of the following year peace between Cyprus, Genoa, and Venice on the one hand and the sultan on the other was agreed to in Famagusta, and a brief lull in warlike operations ensued, to be followed by hostilities of an entirely different kind. These were not only to overshadow and darken the remainder of the reign of Peter II; they were to compromise irremediably the kingdom's very existence. They resulted from no crusading activities or aspirations; they arose from a cause as seemingly trivial as a dispute over protocol at one of the king's coronations.

For bibliography, see preceding chapter.

361

Despite the regent's endeavors, successful up to a point, to delay his nephew's coronations, Peter II received the crown of Cyprus in the cathedral of Nicosia in January 1372, and in the following October that of Jerusalem—continuing the precedent set by his grandfather, Hugh IV, and followed by his father—in the cathedral of Famagusta, the Cypriote town geographically nearest to the lost kingdom. It had become the established practice, when the king mounted his horse on leaving the cathedral after the ceremony, for the representatives of Genoa and Venice to lead the king's mount, one on either side, the Genoese on the right, the Venetian on the left. Between these two Italian communities in Famagusta, which were based on their respective loggias, there existed a chronic state of feud, and it required no great provocation for the tension between them to find an outlet in mutual violence. One such episode had occurred as recently as 1368, in the last year of Peter I, and the memory of it was therefore still fresh. But on this occasion the provocation, given the importance which the age attached to matters of international precedence, was anything but slight. The Venetian, perhaps deriving confidence from the presence in Famagusta of a more than normally large number of his compatriots, usurped the position of the Genoese by seizing the right-hand rein of the king's bridle, and there ensued a bloody affray which was momentarily suppressed by the regent but broke out again with increased violence at the subsequent coronation banquet. The Genoese consul, a member of the great house of Doria, seems to have reacted very intemperately, even for an aggrieved party. He armed his nationals, who attacked the Venetians, and the regent's forces had to intervene once more to restore order. To make matters worse, the people of Famagusta, who hated the privileged and arrogant Genoese, sided with the Venetians, sacked the shops and houses of the Genoese, killed a number of them, and destroyed their loggia.

Negotiations to compose the situation were now set on foot between the Cypriote authorities and the Genoese podestà and might have achieved a settlement but for three unforeseen factors. First, despite the release and pardon of the Genoese who had been arrested for their part in the disturbances, and despite royal proclamations to the effect that no one should injure a Genoese on pain of losing his right hand and that the Genoese in Cyprus should remain in the full enjoyment of their customary rights and privileges, a large number of the Genoese merchants of Famagusta left the island secretly with their treasure before the Cypriote authorities could stop them.

Secondly, the queen-mother saw in the situation a favorable opportunity to pursue her vendetta against those guilty of her husband's murder, much of the responsibility for which she imputed to her brother-in-law the regent. In this cause she now prepared to enlist the aid of Genoa, to whom any additional excuse for forcible intervention in Cyprus was welcome, little recking that in so doing she might be undermining the foundations of her son's kingdom. Thirdly, reports of the affair reached Genoa in forms so exaggerated as to destroy any prospect of moderation on the part of the republic.

The king and the regent, in the hope of averting Genoese reprisals, sent emissaries to pope Gregory XI at Avignon with a statement of their case. They did not know that queen Eleanor was appealing to the pope in the contrary sense through her father, the infante Peter of Aragon, since his wife's death a Franciscan friar. Eleanor represented that, although her son had now been crowned, the regent John continued to withhold from him the control of the public revenues; she did not shrink from the unpatriotic course of begging Gregory to allow the Genoese to come to Cyprus to exact vengeance for the murder of Peter I and to establish the young king in his full powers. She can hardly have been unaware that these were matters of indifference to the Genoese, whose designs in and on Cyprus were not concerned with internal dynastic disputes within the Lusignan family.

The pope, to do him justice, besought the doge of Genoa, Dominic Campofregoso, to refrain from attacking a Christian country with which he should, on the contrary, be united against the "infidel." Later, however, after hearing the representations of a Genoese embassy, he abandoned his original acceptance of the Cypriote contention that the Genoese were liable, under the treaty of 1365, to pay a fine of 100,000 ducats for breaking the peace. It is strange how a dispute originating in the act of a Venetian official should now have resolved itself into one exclusively between Genoa and Cyprus, with Venice completely aloof. Indeed, when in 1373 the king appealed for Venetian support against the imminent Genoese invasion, Venice, preoccupied with the war of Chioggia, professed herself unable to offer anything more substantial than sympathy.

A Genoese squadron of seven galleys sailed against Cyprus in March 1373, and appeared off Famagusta in May. There was some pretense by the Genoese of preliminary discussions on an ultimatum which their commander was to present, but they did not seriously pursue them; on May 12 the invaders attempted a night landing, which was repelled. Even now the king behaved with remarkable forbearance, ordering, to the dismay of the people of Famagusta, that no one should attack the Genoese on pain of death. He hoped that the efforts for a peaceful solution which the pope was continuing to make might yet succeed, possibly reinforced by the support of the Knights Hospitaller of St. John at Rhodes, whose master, Raymond Bérenger, had been expressly forbidden by Gregory to help the Genoese. In June an emissary sent by Raymond to Cyprus to act as mediator obtained from the Genoese a clear statement of their terms. These comprised the surrender of those responsible for the Genoese casualties in the coronation day affray or a fine of 50,000 ducats, the payment of 100,000 ducats for the breach of the treaty of 1365, and the payment of two like sums for the losses of the Genoese merchants and for the costs of the expedition respectively. To these conditions was added perhaps the most onerous one of all: the cession of a stronghold in which the Genoese merchants would be able to live in safety.

Such terms were clearly unacceptable, and the Cypriotes had now to face the fact that they were at war with a powerful foe already on their soil. The Genoese ships circumnavigated the island on a raiding cruise, burnt Limassol, and took the castle of Paphos, which they held against a relieving expedition led by John, the king's uncle. At the beginning of October the Genoese were reinforced by no fewer than thirty-six ships, more than five times the number composing the original expeditionary force. Hastily Nicosia was put into a state of defense and—this has a modern sound—a blackout was imposed and all males over fifteen were registered and assigned to definite duties; in twenty days of incessant labor the fortifications were strengthened and there were rigged up 133 fighting platforms for the crossbowmen and archers. This accomplished, the king, with his mother, his two uncles, and a force of some two thousand men made a forced march to Famagusta and, driving the Genoese back to their galleys, established themselves within the city. Here, however, they were invested and immobilized by a considerable part of the Genoese forces, which were estimated to total fourteen thousand men, until John, with the king's consent, proposed a parley to the besiegers. The proposal was accepted, and it was agreed that a conference of five negotiators on each side, each party to be protected by twelve guards, should take place in the castle, which was situated on one of the corners of the sea side of the walled city. By a treacherous ruse, connivance in which has been attributed to John of Morphou, the Genoese took advantage of the opening of the sea gate for the conference to swarm into the castle, and seized the king and his people. John of Antioch, helped by his cook, effected his escape in the disguise of a kitchen-boy, while the king's younger uncle, James, had already made his way back to Nicosia in a previous, successful sortie. To these circumstances the royal uncles no doubt owed their lives, for the Genoese now beheaded, to the queen's unbounded satisfaction, a number of the regicides, alleging that in so doing they were executing the judgment of the king. But the king was in truth far from being in a position to give directions to the Genoese; he himself was in a most perilous position, completely at the mercy of the Genoese admiral (and later doge), Peter Campofregoso, who forced him to write under duress a series of instructions to his uncles to act apparently in accordance with his wishes but in reality in accordance with those of the Genoese. He was no more than a helpless tool in the hands of the enemy. The queen played a complicated and equivocal part, sometimes appearing to pursue the interests of the invaders, sometimes the true interests of her son. But always she had before her the paramount aim of contriving the death of John of Antioch, and set her tortuous course accordingly.

His brother James, whose loyalty to his nephew was not in doubt, deemed it in the best interests of the kingdom to concentrate on holding the important northern fortress of Kyrenia, where he made a stand against assault by land and sea so successful as finally to bring the war to an end by leading the Genoese to agree to terms. In the meantime these had first looted, then occupied the inland capital, Nicosia, and were making free of the island in general except for the fortresses of St. Hilarion ("Dieudamour," held by John of Antioch), Buffavento and Kantara in the northern range of mountains, and the city of Kyrenia itself. Yet by March 1374 something like stalemate had been reached. Although the Genoese had plundered the island bare and had contrived to possess themselves of a forced loan of one million ducats imposed on the kingdom by the king's council to sustain its defense, they were finding the prolonged campaign a heavy drain on their resources. They decided, therefore, to take advantage of their favorable situation to impose a final settlement, to which end they now played their trump card, the control they exercised over the captive king, to its fullest advantage. Their most effective adversary in Cyprus was James, and him they determined to get into their power and to hold as a hostage in Genoa for the fulfillment of the terms they would impose on the kingdom. They therefore forced Peter to send his uncle written orders to hand over his command at Kyrenia to the knight Luke d'Antiaume and to proceed to the west to protest—this was the pretext given—against what the Genoese had done in Cyprus. He was to take with him his wife, Heloise of Brunswick, and infant daughter. The orders did not mention that his destination was in fact a Genoese prison.

James had few illusions as to what was in store for him and, in complying with the king's instructions, was at pains to exact an oath from Luke d'Antiaume and his men to hold Kyrenia for the king in the face of whatever commands they might receive to the contrary, for such commands could be extorted from the king under duress. He set sail in April 1374, but it was not until October 21 of that year that the peace treaty was signed in the royal palace of Nicosia. Its terms were onerous indeed. In the first place Cyprus was saddled with an annual tribute in perpetuity of 40,000 gold florins. Next, 90,000 gold florins were to be paid by December 1, that is, within less than six weeks, toward the upkeep of the Genoese forces in the island. An indemnity of no less than 2,012,400 gold florins, a deliberately crippling amount, was to be paid over a period of twelve years. Until this indemnity had been liquidated in full, Famagusta with its port and suburbs was to remain in the hands and under the jurisdiction of the Genoese, and then restored only if satisfactory security were forthcoming for the continued payment of the tribute of 40,000 florins. Nicosia and the other parts of the island in Genoese hands, other than Famagusta, would be returned to the king only when the 90,000 florins had been paid over. The Genoese were to live freely on the island under their own consul and in the enjoyment of all their former privileges. If any of the terms of the treaty should be contravened by the Cypriotes, Famagusta would pass completely into Genoese possession and the kingdom would be hypothecated. Meanwhile, as a guarantee of compliance, the king was to surrender his uncle James, the two sons of his uncle John, and a number of knights as hostages to be held in Genoa.

While the island was still prostrate under this disaster, the indefatigable queen Eleanor achieved her ambition. In 1375, the year following the peace, she inveigled John of Antioch from St. Hilarion to Nicosia, and at a banquet in the palace, in the very room in which Peter I had been murdered, suddenly uncovered a dish containing Peter's bloodstained shirt. This was the signal for the death of the former regent.

It was now time for the king to marry. At the end of 1372, when war with Genoa was looming, the emperor John V Palaeologus had made an abortive offer of the hand of his daughter Irene. But it was not until 1376 that Peter II was betrothed, to Valentina, daughter of Bernabò Visconti, lord of Milan, an alliance which resulted in the participation of Cyprus in the pact concluded in 1377 between Milan and Venice against Genoa, and in a desultory and ineffective Venetian attack on Famagusta in 1378. In the same year 1378 was celebrated the king's marriage, which, although it was to remain childless save for a daughter who died in infancy, had one result of importance to the kingdom, the final departure from its shores of the fiery Spanish queen-mother. It was scarcely to be expected that a woman of Eleanor's temperament would accommodate herself to the presence of a daughter-in-law, and soon the young queen persuaded her husband to send his mother back to her own country. Eleanor left Cyprus in 1380, but she survived until 1417, when she died in Barcelona.

Peter II died in 1382 at the early age of twenty-eight. He had become very obese; the lad who had begun his career as Perrin ended it with the unattractive sobriquet of Peter the Fat. On his coins he reverted to the practice of earlier reigns by holding the scepter in his right hand in place of the sword—emblem of his order of chivalry— borne by his father Peter I.

When the king's uncle James set sail in April 1374 with his wife and infant daughter on the "mission to the west" trumped up by the Genoese, he was quickly overtaken by two Genoese galleys, which accompanied him, despite his protests, to his first port of call, Rhodes. Here his little daughter died, and here he remained until ten more Genoese galleys arrived with the hostages taken under the treaty, whereupon the fleet with its prisoners proceeded to Genoa. On arrival, contrary to the undertakings they had given and contrary to usage in such cases, the Genoese placed him in close confinement. His wife, it is true, was left at liberty but without means of support, so that she had to eke out a meager living with her needle. Later, possibly in reprisal for the abortive attack by Peter II and the Venetians on Famagusta in 1378, they increased the rigors of his imprisonment to the extent of hanging him in a cage in one of the towers of the prison with his feet in stocks, and placed him on a diet of bread and water, treatment generally reserved for the lowest and most desperate of malefactors. After a while he was released from the cage but still confined in the tower, where his dauntless wife was permitted to join him. It was during this period of his imprisonment that Heloise gave birth to her eldest son, to whom—with singular magnanimity—the royal pair gave the name of Janus, the mythical founder of their country's arch-enemy, Genoa, the place of their incarceration.

The death without issue of Peter II made his sole surviving uncle the lawful successor to the two crowns, but for the succession to become effective the approval of the high court, the whole body of the baronage, was still necessary. The high court duly confirmed the captive James in his rights and appointed a council of regency under the turcopolier John of Brie as regent to administer the kingdom pending the return of the new monarch. James and Heloise were conditionally set free and sent to Cyprus, but, by the time they reached Larnaca, two members of the council of regency, the brothers Perot and Wilmot de Montolif, had sought for their own purposes to have James's recognition annulled in favor of Marietta, one of the two unmarried daughters of Peter I, on the plea that the conditions which Genoa would exact for his definitive release would place an intolerable burden on the kingdom. It was a specious plea, which for a while prevailed, and the luckless royal couple were not allowed to land. Later the high court thought better of the matter, reverted to its original decision, and proclaimed James king.

Genoa's terms for James's release, embodied before his departure in a new treaty of February 19, 1383 (that of 1374 having been broken by the Cypro-Venetian attack on Famagusta in 1378), were certainly harsh. They included the transfer—no longer merely the pledge—of Famagusta with a zone of two leagues around it, the pledging of Kyrenia, and the payment by the new king of 852,000 florins in instalments until 1394. All ships trading to Cyprus, except those coming from Turkey, were obliged to call at Famagusta. The two sons of John of Antioch and the knights held as hostages under the treaty of 1374 were allowed to return to Cyprus, but with great inhumanity the little prince Janus, now the heir apparent, was held in Genoa as a hostage for the punctual fulfillment of these conditions. James did not reach Cyprus until April 23, 1385, when he was accorded an enthusiastic welcome by the populace. In the following month he received the Cypriote crown in the cathedral of Nicosia; four years later he was crowned king of Jerusalem, again in Nicosia since Famagusta was in the possession of the Genoese. Shortly after his first coronation the Montolif brothers, who had already been placed under arrest by the regency, were executed.

After prolonged negotiations, continuing from 1386 to 1391, the severity of the financial clauses of the Genoese treaty was to some degree mitigated, largely through the successful diplomacy of James's admiral and plenipotentiary, Peter de Cafran. Prince Janus was now allowed to return to Cyprus, which he reached in October 1392. Even so, the king, in order to meet his obligations, had to impose on the country most drastic taxation, which diminished his earlier popularity. A severe outbreak of the plague in 1392 added to the country's afflictions; on the other hand, the occupation of Genoa by France in 1396 reduced for a while the pressure from that quarter. In 1398 there was concluded between James and the French king, Charles VI, a treaty of friendship which gave the former at least a measure of moral support.

There was a close relationship, established by much intermarriage, between the Lusignan kings of Cyprus and the royal house of Armenia, the Heṭoumids.[1] Almost all the Heṭoumids after Leon III (1269–1289) were descended through female lines from Aimery of Lusignan, king of Jerusalem and Cyprus. Guy de Lusignan, grandson of Hugh III, became king as Constantine III (1342–1344). His nephew Leon VI, who was king of Cilician Armenia briefly in 1363–1364, was exiled, and ascended the throne for the second time in 1374, was also a Lusignan, being the illegitimate son of a grandson in the male line of Hugh III of Cyprus. The effective reign of the last *de jure* and *de facto* Armenian king was a brief one, for in 1375 Leon lost his sole remaining castle to the Mamluks and was taken into captivity in Cairo. When he died, an honored refugee, without issue in Paris in 1393, his second cousin James as next of kin assumed the crown of Armenia (which in 1368 had been offered to his brother Peter I, who accepted it and styled himself king, but never visited his new realm) in addition to the two he already wore. Thenceforth until the end of the kingdom he and his successors on the Cypriote throne styled themselves kings or queens of Jerusalem, Cyprus, and Armenia, and quartered the Armenian lion with their arms. It was, however, an empty dignity, for there was never again to be an independent Armenia of any sort until the proclamation of the Armenian Republic at Erivan on May 28, 1918.

James died, when still in middle age, in 1398, having had no fewer than eleven children by his queen, the devoted Heloise of Brunswick, who survived until 1422. Despite the vicissitudes, hardships, turmoils, and dangers by which his life had been beset, he left behind him a reputation for hospitality and for a love of architecture and

1. For full, reliable genealogies see the study by Count W. H. Rüdt-Collenberg, *The Rupenides, Hethumides, and Lusignans* (Paris, 1963).

sport, especially hunting and falconry. There exists correspondence between him and Richard II of England, in which James informs Richard that all friends of his are welcome in Cyprus.

Janus, the king born in captivity, was about twenty-four years old when he succeeded his father. Fourteen months after his accession he received the three crowns in a combined ceremony in Nicosia cathedral, and before 1401 had married as his first wife Heloise, another daughter of Bernabò Visconti of Milan and sister of the queen of his cousin, Peter II. It was natural that the circumstances of his birth and upbringing should have implanted in the new ruler an obsession: to expel the Genoese intruders from the country and its principal port and to restore the integrity of his realm. And it was not, perhaps, to be wondered at that youthful zeal should have outrun discretion. He decided to attempt the capture of Famagusta with the assistance of a mercenary fleet of thirteen Catalan galleys, possibly with the secret coöperation or at least the connivance of the Genoese commander, one Antonio Guarco, who had stood sponsor for Janus at his christening in Genoa and was well disposed toward him. Contemporary interpretations of Guarco's attitude and acts are contradictory. The Venetians alleged that Guarco was a rebel against his own government and—this not very convincingly—that Janus's attack on Famagusta was directed not against Genoa but against the disloyal Guarco. Genoa manifested its belief by superseding Guarco and mobilizing a fleet under its famous and combative French governor, John le Meingre, marshal Boucicault.

An attempt by Janus to enter Famagusta on Easter Sunday, 1402, was foiled, and the arrival in the autumn of an advance squadron of the Genoese fleet forced him to raise its siege for the time being. His efforts to enlist the active coöperation of Venice were unsuccessful; nevertheless, when the marshal himself sailed for Cyprus in April 1403, a strong Venetian naval force kept close watch on his movements. Since the king's ill success had not caused him to lose heart, but rather had reinforced his determination to recover the key to his kingdom when an opportunity should recur, the marshal planned a general attack on the island. But the grand master of the Hospitallers, Philibert of Naillac, now intervened as mediator, as had his predecessor in the reign of Peter II, proceeded in person from Rhodes to Cyprus, and persuaded Janus to come to terms. A new treaty of peace and commerce between Genoa and Cyprus was signed in Nicosia on July 7, 1403; included among the parties were the Old and the New Mahone of Cyprus, those successive Genoese financial corporations which financed and received the profits derived from the expeditions against the kingdom, and which were subsequently merged into the Bank of St. George. The terms continued the usual sordid extortion of the uttermost denier from long-suffering Cyprus. An indemnity of 150,000 ducats was imposed to cover the cost of the expedition, and as security for 80,000 ducats of this sum Janus had to pledge the property of himself and his successors. The balance was guaranteed by the crown jewels and plate, which were handed over to the grand master to be held in pawn by the Order of St. John.

The peace proved to be no more than a truce. Hostilities of an intermittent kind were resumed in 1404, and the combatants now began for the first time in the history of Cyprus to use cannon, which both sides obtained from Venice. A new treaty, with conditions of the usual type, was concluded in 1410. To add to the country's miseries, the plague raged for a year from 1409, to be followed for the ensuing three years by invasions of locusts, which have continued intermittently to scourge the island into the twentieth century. About 1407 the king's first wife died, and a more cheerful note is struck by his second marriage—by proxy in 1409, in person in 1411—to Charlotte of Bourbon, who bore him six children and died in 1422.

Another death must be chronicled before we come to the most humiliating event of the reign and the turning point of the later history of the Lusignan kingdom of Cyprus. The noble-minded Philip of Mézières, devoted follower, chancellor, and inspiration of Peter I, died in France in 1405 at the age of seventy-eight. "The old pilgrim," as he called himself, had accompanied Peter I on his missions to the courts of the west and was present with him at the capture of Alexandria, the withdrawal from which was a bitter blow to him. Although he never returned to Cyprus after the murder of his sovereign and friend, he never abandoned his title of chancellor, nor did he ever abandon his dream of another crusade. In 1384, in his retirement in France, he devised a new order of chivalry, the Order of the Passion, intended, like Peter's Order of the Sword, to give new life to the crusading spirit. Although he was by birth a Frenchman, history will always link this great idealist's name with that of Cyprus.

Since the accord arrived at with Egypt in September 1370, in the second year of the reign of Peter II, Cyprus and the Mamluk sultanate had remained officially at peace. But there had been much unofficial raiding on both sides, less on the part of the Egyptians than on that of the Cypriotes, who carried out their forays not only with privateers but even with the king's galleys. In November 1414, sultan Shaikh al-Mu'aiyad reached an understanding with Janus to put an end to these irritations, and for about a decade the pact was observed. Then there were fresh provocations on the Cypriote side, to which the new sultan, Barsbey, replied with an effective raid on Limassol. Janus, in retaliation, light-heartedly launched a raid on the Syrian coast. This foolish act provoked, in 1425, an organized attack on Cyprus on the part of Barsbey, whose troops made ready in the first instance to invest Famagusta. But, according to the Moslem chroniclers (the Christians remaining silent on the subject), the Genoese governor assured the Moslems that he was their friend and hoisted the sultan's flag over the castle. During the greater part of August the Moslems successfully, despite the opposition of the king's forces, ravaged the south coast of the island between Larnaca and Limassol, sacking the former city and burning the latter. At the end of the month, having amassed an adequate quantity of prisoners and booty, they returned to Egypt. The sale of the prisoners took several days and fetched 18,800 dinars.[2]

This expedition revealed to Barsbey the weakness of the kingdom's defenses and convinced him that a full-scale operation could be undertaken with success, although he was aware that Janus was now seeking to enlist what help he could from the Christian powers, even, in his plight, from Genoa. The Genoese replied that they would gladly have aided had circumstances made this possible. In effect, apparently, they were doing precisely the reverse and, notably through one Benedict Pallavicini, a Genoese merchant then in Egypt, were encouraging the sultan in his ambitions, hoping thereby to forestall any future attacks by the king on Famagusta.[3] On July 1, 1426, a powerful expedition of some 180 vessels, carrying a force of cavalry and infantry estimated at a total of five thousand men, landed on the south coast of Cyprus, just west of the Akrotiri peninsula. On July 3 Janus left Nicosia for the south to meet it with a force of sixteen hundred knights and four thousand foot, and received a message from the invader (who that day had taken the newly repaired castle of Limassol), summoning him "to sit on the sultan's carpet," that is to say, to acknowledge Barsbey as his superior, and to discuss terms of surrender. The summons was ignored and the emissary who bore the message was tortured and put to death, according to some accounts by burning.[4]

2. Ziada and LaMonte, trans., "Bedr ed-Dîn al-'Aini's Account of the Conquest of Cyprus (1424–1426)," *Annuaire de l'Institut de philologie et d'histoire orientales et slaves,* VII (1939–1944), 241–264.

3. Mas Latrie, *L'Île de Chypre,* p. 328, and see Hill, *History of Cyprus,* II, 475.

4. See Ziada, *The Mamluk Conquest of Cyprus,* and al-'Aini's "Account."

On Friday, July 5, the king took up his position at Khirokitia, a small village and commandery of the Hospitallers in what is now the Larnaca district, and on the following Sunday, the disastrous 7th, the two armies came face to face. The Cypriote army was not in good shape. The commissariat arrangements were faulty; the soldiers were undisciplined; morale had been impaired by the news of the loss of Limassol. The Moslems were the first to attack, and after the initial major clash the king withdrew, preparatory to taking the offensive in his turn; but when the infantry saw another wave of enemy troops approaching, they took to flight. The king and a group of his knights, including his brother Henry, titular prince of Galilee, performed prodigies of valor in trying to rally their disorganized troops, but without avail. Janus's horse fell under him three times, and his second mount could not stand up to his weight, for he was a heavy man. It was at this moment that he was attacked by two foemen who did not know who he was. One of them wounded him in the face with a lance, whereupon he cried out in Arabic: "I am the king," while his identity was also made known by the Catalan knight Carceran Suarez, who had joined his service, was to share his captivity, and later was to become admiral and then constable of Cyprus; thereupon Janus was taken alive. The estimates of the number of Christians killed, among them Henry of Galilee, range from one to six thousand, and the rout of the army was complete. The king was removed to the coast with his feet tied together and sent by sea to Larnaca. A part of the insignificant Cypriote fleet, together with two pilgrim ships present, engaged the overwhelmingly superior enemy naval force, and the pilgrim ships were captured, the pilgrims meeting with a cruel fate, according to the Christian chroniclers. The captive king was then compelled on pain of death to order his galleys and other craft to withdraw.

Nicosia was aghast at the news of the disaster. Cardinal Hugh de Lusignan, archbishop of Nicosia, another of the king's brothers, realizing that it was impossible to defend the capital, sent the treasure to Kyrenia and then followed with members of the royal family. On July 11 the Mamluk commander, the emir Taghrîberdi al-Maḥmūdī, entered the defenseless city and took up his residence in the royal palace. Although the population were promised their safety and ordered to go about their business as usual, the sight of the riches in the palace and elsewhere was too much for the soldiery. Houses and churches were pillaged, men killed, women raped, the city put to the sack.[5] The palace was destroyed by fire with many of

5. Al-'Ainī places the responsibility for these acts on reinforcements under the emir

the records, and it was with great difficulty that Taghrîberdi himself was extricated from the flames. Worse would have befallen Nicosia but for the recall after three days of the expedition to Larnaca, for which reason, no doubt, Kyrenia was left alone. But the invaders drove thousands of captive men, women, and children to the coast and, when a week later they reëmbarked for home, took them as prisoners to Egypt. They also sacked the hill-top shrine of Stavrovouni, famous for its wonder-working cross.

Early in August Taghrîberdi made his triumphal entry into Cairo with his prisoners and booty. King Janus, bareheaded, barefoot, his feet shackled, his standard reversed and dragging on the ground before him, was made to ride bareback in the conqueror's train and on several occasions to kiss the ground. Thereafter, the public humiliation over, his treatment improved, possibly because the sultan's heart was touched by some verses addressed to him by the captive monarch, more probably by reason of the latter's willingness to acquiesce in the sultan's terms. These comprised a ransom of 200,000 ducats, half payable before release, an annual tribute of 5,000 ducats, and the acknowledgment of the sultan's suzerainty.

Financially, these conditions imposed by a Moslem victor compared not unfavorably with the extortions habitually practised on Cyprus by Christian Genoa, but the recognition by the proud kingdom of the Lusignans of a Mamluk sultan as suzerain was a disgrace hard indeed to bear. Pope Martin V and the other Christian potentates and states, including the Knights Hospitaller and Venice, took counsel to help to find the ransom, while even the Genoese must have felt that they had overreached themselves in encouraging the sultan, for they were now profuse in their expressions of horror at the disaster and of their conviction that a repetition must at all costs be prevented. Thanks to the pope, who authorized the sale of indulgences for the purpose, and to other well-wishers, including a member of the Cypriote noble family of Podocataro, the king's ransom was raised, while Martin also allocated monies from the church dues of Italy, Piedmont, and Savoy toward the ransom of the other Cypriote captives and ordered the English, French, and Spanish churches to contribute the hundredth penny of their revenues to the same purpose. A treaty was then signed between the sultan and Janus to establish the terms of the latter's release, but it included a clause whereby the sultan bound himself to defend, in

Taghrîbermîsh, who arrived on July 12 and were unaware of the promise of safety given by Taghrîberdi. But he adds that "they committed wrong in doing all that as such things were unlawful after the proclamation of safety and security."

certain eventualities, his "viceroy in Cyprus," a galling reminder of Janus's new and ignominious status.[6]

Meanwhile in Nicosia and the country districts the temporary absence of authority produced a state of chaos in which brigandage flourished and no man's life was safe. The Greek peasantry of the Mesaoria plain acclaimed one of their number, a certain Alexius, as "king" and set him up in the big village of Lefkoniko; an Italian condottiere named Sforza established himself at the other end of the island with some Spanish troops under his command. To stem the anarchy, the knights and burgesses acknowledged archbishop Hugh as regent, and control was reëstablished. Sforza was slain and the peasant "king" Alexius caught, although he was not hanged until May 12, 1427, the very day on which the liberated Janus touched at Paphos on his return home.

The unfortunate monarch had been in captivity for eight months before he came back, "may God disgrace him, to the seat of his appointment," as al-'Ainī has it with emphasis on the subordinate position now occupied by the king of Cyprus. His experiences and humiliations left their permanent mark on him, and Machaeras states that he never laughed again. Physically he was a large and powerful man, but in 1431 he suffered a stroke, which left him paralyzed until a second stroke killed him at the end of June of the following year, when he was about fifty-eight years old. Janus was a man of many good qualities and some scholarship, but he was impetuous and without foresight, too apt to be influenced by the last person he had seen. We read without surprise that he died poor.

John, titular prince of Antioch, Janus's son and successor, was promptly acknowledged by the baronage, but, being only seventeen years of age, began his reign under the regency of his cousin Peter de Lusignan, titular count of Tripoli. (Peter was the son of Peter I's daughter Marietta and of James, the son of the constable John of Antioch, brother of Peter I and James I.) His uncle, the experienced cardinal Hugh, who had governed Cyprus during Janus's imprisonment in Egypt, was now out of the island as bishop of Palestrina and later of Tusculum (although retaining the see of Nicosia), but remained until his death in 1442 vigorously and effectively engaged in various diplomatic activities on behalf of his nephew's realm, for which purpose the procuration to act abroad on behalf of the kingdom which Janus had given him on his return from Egypt was

6. Ziada, *Mamluk Conquest,* II, 39.

renewed by John II. The new king received the three crowns in Nicosia cathedral in August 1432, and one of the first acts of his government was to send an embassy to the sultan of Egypt to announce his accession and to acknowledge the political and financial obligations accepted by Janus. Intermittently during the early years of the reign there were rumors of another Egyptian expedition against Cyprus, but no such attack was launched.

It was belief in the substance of these rumors that now led Genoa to adopt a more friendly attitude in political matters, although on the financial plane she showed herself as exacting as ever toward the exhausted kingdom. Yet despite this slackening of political pressure John, with astonishing inconsequence, in 1441 made an unsuccessful attempt to capture Famagusta. In 1447 Genoa, feeling unable any longer to administer Famagusta directly, transferred the government of that dependency to the Office of the Bank of St. George. To Cyprus this change brought no advantage but rather the reverse, while with Venice the relations of the harassed kingdom were also by no means easy, although the questions at issue with the Venetians included no major canker like that of Famagusta.

On the Moslem front the situation was even more uneasy. In 1444 only the intervention of the Hospitallers prevented an invasion of the island by Lûtfi Bey, the emir of Alaya ("Scandelore"), while the emir of Karaman, Ibrāhīm, despite the continued good offices of the Hospital, was even less amenable. In 1448 Corycus on the Cilician coast fell into his hands, and with it Cyprus lost the last of the overseas territorial acquisitions of Peter I. Overshadowing these more immediate dangers was the ever-growing menace of the Ottoman Turks, soon to culminate in their capture of Constantinople.

Meanwhile, in July 1440, the young king's proxy marriage (1437) to Amadea (or Medea) of Montferrat was resolemnized; the bride, though a Latin, had the blood of the Palaeologi in her veins. Within a little more than two months of this wedding the bride was dead, together with most of her suite, and some of the accounts mention rumors of poison. Be that as it might, John proceeded in 1442 to marry a full-blooded Palaeologina in the person of Helena, daughter of Theodore II, despot of the Morea, and granddaughter of the Byzantine emperor Manuel II; this alliance resulted in a marked departure from the policy hitherto pursued by the Frankish rulers of Cyprus toward the church of their Orthodox subjects, as embodied in the *Bulla Cypria* of 1260.

A Greek princess would naturally resent the subjection of the Greek-speaking and Orthodox native population of Cyprus to the foreign church of a foreign dynasty, and would use her influence to redress so far as she could the balance in favor of her Cypriote coreligionists. It was therefore unreasonable of Aeneas Sylvius Piccolomini (Pope Pius II) to ascribe to unrighteousness the fact that Helena was "hostile to the Latin rite and an enemy of the Roman church."[7] When, however, he calls her "a skilled and shrewd woman, well versed in Greek duplicity," he is on surer ground, for she was all that and more. She was in fact an ambitious, unscrupulous, determined, and vindictive termagant, whose chronic ill health served only to exacerbate the violence of her disposition. When we read that in her passionate hatred of her husband's mistress Marietta (or Maria) of Patras, the mother of the future James II and a fellow Greek, she bit off her rival's nose, we are reminded of the days of queen Eleanor. Quickly and completely she dominated and intimidated her feeble, indolent, hedonistic, and self-indulgent husband, so much so that according to two chroniclers[8] she actually obtained from the high court recognition as regent, and this despite the fact that John was at no time declared incapable of governing. She had brought to Cyprus in her train a number of greedy compatriots, including her foster-mother and the latter's son Thomas; and this Thomas she caused her husband to knight, endow with valuable estates, and appoint chamberlain of the kingdom.

John and Helena had two daughters, Cleopatra, who died in infancy, and the subsequent queen Charlotte, but no son; and it was inevitable that some eyes should turn towards James, the king's son by Marietta of Patras, then growing up a youth of outstanding parts: handsome, of good address, high-spirited, and determined. His father adored the lad, but Helena presciently saw in him a potential menace to the rights of succession of her daughter Charlotte.[9] About 1453 John caused the thirteen-year-old boy to be elected to the vacant archbishopric of Nicosia and begged pope Nicholas V to confirm the appointment, being instigated, according to Aeneas Sylvius, by Helena, who hoped that by being side-tracked into a miter James would be disqualified from the crown. The pope's reply was a refusal, consistently maintained; nevertheless, the king placed his son in possession of the temporalities of the see and housed him, with his mother, now known as *Komomytene* ("the Crop-nosed"), in the

---

7. *Commentarii,* book VII (Frankfurt, 1614), p. 176; cf. trans. by F. A. Gragg (with notes by L. C. Gabel; *Smith College Studies in History,* vols. XXII, XXV, XXX, XXXV, XLIII, 1937–1957), XXXV (Northampton, Mass., 1951), 480.

8. Florio Bustron, ed. Mas Latrie, p. 372; Loredano, *Historie de' re' Lusignani,* II, 175.

9. James was born in 1440 or 1441, Charlotte about 1443.

archiepiscopal palace. Probably James never received more than minor orders.[10]

Those who desired the ultimate succession of the young princess Charlotte were now concerned with the question of her marriage, and the choice of bridegroom (according to Genoese reports that of the queen against the wishes of the king) fell on John of Coimbra, grandson of John I, king of Portugal, who arrived in the island in 1456; on his marriage he received the titles of prince of Antioch and regent. If the Portuguese prince was indeed the queen's candidate, he was to prove a disappointment to her, for he used such authority as he had to counteract her pro-Orthodox policy and the influence of her foster-brother, the chamberlain Thomas. At first he and his bride lived with the king and queen under the same roof, but the situation in the palace became so strained that he soon removed himself and Charlotte to the house of the ex-regent Peter of Tripoli, who was Charlotte's godfather. In the summer of 1457, the year following his marriage, John of Coimbra died, poisoned, it was freely said, by his enemy the chamberlain with the connivance of the queen. Whatever may have been the truth with regard to these suspicions—and there can be no doubt that her son-in-law's disappearance was more than welcome to Helena—they were certainly shared by Charlotte herself, who in her distress appealed to her half-brother James, for whom she seems originally to have entertained considerable affection. James, still no more than sixteen or seventeen years old, rose to the occasion with the precocious vigor that characterized him (although it may be doubted if he did so solely to oblige his half-sister), appeared in Thomas's house with two Sicilian ruffians, and had the hated chamberlain dispatched by them before his eyes.

The king was now in a quandary for, much as he loved his son, he dared not face the wrath of the enraged queen if he left the murder of her foster-brother unpunished. So he deprived James of the revenues of the archiepiscopal see, and the young man found it opportune to leave the kingdom. He made his way to Rhodes, where the grand master, James of Milly, and the knights, at that time friendly to so prominent an opponent of the Greek queen although later to side actively with Charlotte against him, received him well and gave him shelter for some five or six months. At the end of this period James, accompanied by the Augustinian friar William Goneme, who was to remain his devoted adherent and to become for a time archbishop of Nicosia, returned to Cyprus with a flotilla of four vessels equipped in Rhodes. Landing secretly in Kyrenia, he and

10. Herquet, *Charlotta,* p. 103; Hill, *History of Cyprus,* III, 531.

his men forced their way into the capital, where they sacked the houses of the viscount of Nicosia, James Gurri, a supporter of the queen, and his brother Thomas, and slew the former. Taking their plunder with them, he and his followers then fortified themselves in the archbishop's palace.

The king could do no less in the face of this act of open aggression than to charge James before the high court, but this body, well aware of John's feelings toward his son which his fear of the queen forced him to conceal, accepted James's plea that he had attacked not the king but his own personal enemies and asked no more than to be allowed to serve the king in security and in the enjoyment of the archiepiscopal revenues which the king had given him. The court agreed to his reinstatement provided the men he had brought with him from Rhodes returned to their ships and left the island. This condition accepted and fulfilled, James appeared before the king, who took him to the queen's sickroom and for her benefit made a show of upbraiding him for his rebellious conduct. James then repaired to the archbishop's palace and not only took into favor the brother of the murdered viscount, Thomas Gurri, whose house he had looted, but placed him in charge of all his property.

In the midst of these violent happenings the question of Charlotte's remarriage was exercising the minds of the strife-torn court. The king's eldest sister, Anna, who bore a bad reputation for everything except her looks, had married Louis, count of Geneva, younger son of Amadeo VIII, duke of Savoy, whom (his elder brother having predeceased his father) he succeeded on the throne of that duchy. A proposal to marry this couple's younger son, another Louis, count of Geneva, to Charlotte had been mooted before Charlotte's betrothal to John of Coimbra, and was now revived. The proposal was strongly opposed by queen Helena on canonical grounds because of the Orthodox church's prohibition of the marriage of first cousins. But it was supported by the king, and also, with vigor, by the Genoese in Cyprus and their sympathizers there, because of the close relations subsisting between the duchy and the Genoese republic. Despite the protests of the queen, who on this occasion, at least, failed to get her way, the negotiations went forward and were still in progress when the constantly ailing Helena died on April 11, 1458. Nor did John II himself live to see the conclusion of the marriage, for on July 26 he followed his tempestuous wife to the grave, aged only forty-four.

Under John II the crown of Cyprus, which at times had shone with glory and was still to recover, through James II, a momentary flicker of its former luster, touched the nadir of its reputation. John has rightly been called "the weakest and most insignificant" of his house.[11] The judgment of one of the acutest minds among John's contemporaries is even more emphatic. Aeneas Sylvius Piccolomini became pope in the year of John's death, and although the accounts in his writings on Cyprus of events in previous reigns are hopelessly garbled—he is unaware, for example, of the very existence of Peter II and supposes James I to have been the immediate successor of Peter I—and although allowance has to be made for a strong, if natural, anti-Orthodox and anti-Greek bias, we cannot ignore the opinion of a man who was not only a brilliant man of letters and statesman but as pope played a considerable part in the political vicissitudes of John's children Charlotte and James. John, says Pius, "was brought up among women and when he was grown to manhood showed himself to be more a woman than a man. . . . He . . . was content if he could have his fill of banqueting and revelry. In this way the entire island came into the power of the Greeks. The person most influential with the queen was her nurse, and the nurse was under the influence of her son, who thus became supreme [in the realm since] he ruled his mother, his mother ruled the queen, and the queen the king. . . . [John] was more corrupt than [his wife]. In face and form he appeared worthy to wear a crown, but his heart was as base and cowardly as his person was fair."[12]

John II must indeed have been, to judge from the composite picture resulting from the descriptions of his contemporaries, a creature of unusual contradictions: tall and handsome but effeminate; of a lively spirit and gracious manners, yet lethargic and ready to yield his responsibilities to others; physically fit and fond of hunting, yet sunk in sloth and dissipation; hen-pecked by his wife to the degree of ignominy, yet a doting father to the bastard she hated. However we may judge him today, it cannot be doubted that by his weaknesses he quickened the tempo of the dissolution of his kingdom.

The constable Carceran Suarez, the Catalan knight who had shared Janus's captivity in Egypt, took the royal ring from the hand of the dead John II and sent it to Charlotte, whom her half-brother James and the barons forthwith acclaimed as queen. By now the majority of the high court were definitely hostile to James, but his half-sister sought to befriend him and to give him a part to play in the affairs of

11. Herquet, *Charlotta,* p. 95.
12. *Commentarii,* trans. Gragg, XXXV, 480–482. Cf. his *De Bello Cyprio,* in Mogabgab, *Supplementary Excerpts,* part II, pp. 76–86.

state. Thus, after the king's funeral, she asked him to organize the dispatch of a galley to the west to announce John's demise to the Christian rulers. James agreed and set up a recruiting office for the purpose in his palace, which his enemies promptly closed. This rebuff was followed by another. James was making it a practice to visit the queen each morning after he had heard mass in Hagia Sophia. One day, as he was about to enter the palace with his attendants, he was stopped and informed that it was the order of the queen and the high court that in future he must approach the palace alone. Indignant, he sent a message to Charlotte to ask if this was indeed her order, and received the oracular reply that once the high court had taken such a decision it must be regarded as hers also.

Then followed the third and heaviest affront. As archbishop, or at least as archbishop-elect,[13] James expected to officiate at Charlotte's coronation, due to take place after the customary forty days of mourning for the late king. On the eve of the coronation the seneschal appeared before him with an order from the queen and the high court confining him to his palace on the following day. Once again, although deeply aggrieved, James acquiesced, saying that if desired he was prepared to remove himself a distance of six miles from the city. Charlotte was crowned by bishop Peter of Limassol, but it was regarded as ominous that on her return from Hagia Sophia to the palace her horse shied and the crown fell from her head.

These misunderstandings, if such they were, make a sorry story. Clearly the lonely little orphaned and widowed queen had wanted to be on terms of both family affection and political coöperation with her only near relative; equally clearly, the high court were determined to prevent this. James's true feelings at the beginning of his half-sister's brief, unhappy reign are less easy to fathom. After the coronation, when relations between the two degenerated into an open breach and James decided once more to withdraw from the kingdom, he wrote the queen a letter which, if correctly given by Florio Bustron, our only authority for it, afforded an explanation of his conduct which was at least not inconsistent with the facts. He stated that he had always wished to serve her but that she had preferred to be guided by those who were his enemies and, if she would but realize it, hers also. He was willing to continue peaceably as archbishop in the enjoyment of her favor, but her evil counselors were making this impossible. After continuing in this strain, he concludes by assuring her that he will not cease to love her as a

13. In Latin *postulatus,* whence the appellation "Apostoles" by which James was commonly called by Greeks and many others, including the half-Greek, Greek-speaking Charlotte.

brother, and would do more for her honor than their joint enemies whose advice she was accepting.

The letter has not carried any more conviction with historians than it did (or was allowed to do) with the queen. Except in Venice, James had in the west what today would be called a "bad press." The popes, with the exception of the Venetian Paul II (1464–1471), were strong partisans of Charlotte, as were now the Hospitallers. Genoa was his enemy. The fact that he chose (as we shall see) to seek support from the sultan of Egypt, the enemy of his faith, against his rightful queen, made anything he was to say in self-defense suspect to his contemporaries other than the Venetians. And indeed it may well be that he had decided from the very outset to supplant his half-sister as soon as he could, and that his immediate acknowledgment of her as queen, his early efforts to serve her, and his protestations of loyalty were all parts of a preconceived plan to mask his real aims. On the other hand it seems not beyond the bounds of possibility given James's character—a strange blend of ungovernable violence with impulsive generosity more than bordering on quixotism (witness his attitude to Thomas Gurri)—that the better side of his nature might have prevailed had not the enmity of the high court driven him to rebellion and civil war.

James made his way with the faithful Goneme not to the west, as was supposed in Cyprus and as he maintained in an unsuccessful apologia submitted to Pius II in 1461 had been his original intention, but to Cairo, where his attractive and virile personality, handsome appearance, gallant bearing, and persuasive eloquence made a highly favorable impression upon sultan Inal and his court. He at once acknowledged the sultan's suzerainty over Cyprus and sought his support to secure the kingdom on the ground, particularly convincing to a Moslem audience, that a male claimant to a throne must clearly take precedence over a female. In the meantime the anxiously awaited Louis of Savoy had at last arrived in Cyprus and on October 7, 1459, was married to Charlotte in Hagia Sophia and was crowned with the three crowns.[14] He proved to be a poor creature, devout indeed but with a chilly manner and unhealthy, uninspiring, and unenterprising. He lacked all his wife's determination and persistence; what was more disastrous, he had no qualities wherewith to counteract the powerful personal appeal of his rival, James.

Owing to Louis's tardy appearance on the scene, James had been able to steal a march on the embassy which Charlotte now sent to the sultan with the usual tribute. To make matters worse, most of

14. Hill, *History of Cyprus,* III, 554, and cf. note 4 there.

the embassy members perished in Cairo of the plague, which necessitated the dispatch of a supplementary mission. The latter proceeded to offer the sultan, apart from the recognition of his suzerainty, the doubling of the tribute of 5,000 ducats, the reimbursement of the sultan's expenses on behalf of James, and an annual pension to James of 10,000 ducats. Inal and his emirs were inclined, despite their personal sympathy for James, to accept this offer, and a day was appointed for the presentation to the queen through Peter Podocataro, her envoy, of robes of honor, which would symbolize her recognition on the part of the sultan. The resourceful Goneme now saved the situation for the already despairing James by spending the night before the ceremony in bribing the emirs. On the morrow, as the robes were about to be presented, the Mamluk soldiery raised an outcry against preference being given to a woman over a man, placed on the shoulders of James, who was present, the robe intended for the queen, and shouted "Long live king James." The sultan accepted the situation and gave orders for a fleet to be prepared to conduct James to his kingdom; Pius II makes the unsupported statement than Inal's decision was also influenced by strong advice from the Ottoman sultan Mehmed II. Be that as it might, sultan Inal was as good as his word, mobilizing a naval force said to have consisted of eighty ships, great and small (which seems large for such a purpose); by September 1460 James was again in Cyprus, on this occasion as a successful invader and its master-to-be.

The news created consternation among the loyalists in Cyprus. Charlotte and Louis, concentrating on the defense of Kyrenia as constituting their lifeline to the west, fortified themselves in that stronghold and perforce left Nicosia unprotected. Before the end of the month the capital was in James's hands, although he made no headway with the siege of Kyrenia. An attempt by bishop Antonio of Limassol to reconcile Charlotte and James having come to nought, efforts were now set on foot in the west to organize relief for the hard-pressed queen. Her cause was upheld especially by Pius II and James of Milly, grand master of the Hospitallers, both of whom saw in success for James yet another victory for the hosts of Islam, more menacing than ever since the fall of Constantinople. The duke of Savoy raised what money he could for the support of his son and daughter-in-law, but nothing really effective came of all this. James continued to extend his sway over the island (apart from Kyrenia), even having the energy to spare for hostilities on another front by embarking, in 1461, on a preliminary attack on Genoese Famagusta.

Charlotte, determined to leave no stone unturned, went to Rhodes, probably at the beginning of 1461, obtained some ships, and returned to Kyrenia, but was again in Rhodes (where she was to spend a large part of the next thirteen years as the guest of the friendly Hospitallers) in May of the same year in the expectation of reinforcements wherewith to raise the siege and drive James out of the island. Her plans were held up by the illness, and the death in August, of her supporter, the grand master James of Milly. As his successor Peter Raymond Zacosta was then in Spain and the knights could undertake little without him, she decided to plead her cause in the west, first at the court of her well-wisher Pius II, then at that of her father-in-law, the duke of Savoy. Louis left Kyrenia shortly after his wife and followed her to Savoy. In Rome Charlotte was kindly received by the pope, who promised her a shipload of corn and wine and helped her on her northward journey, but said that she would have to rely on France and Savoy for troops. These, however, were not forthcoming, and in 1462 she returned to Rhodes "in worse condition," as Louis subsequently complained to his brother, Amadeo IX, "than she left." It is not clear whether she ever set foot in her kingdom again; the only tangible result of her indefatigable and courageous exertions was to prolong the resistance of Kyrenia until the autumn of 1464.[15] In other respects, too, the poor lady was dogged by misfortune, for in a pathetic letter written to her husband from Rhodes in September 1464, either just before the fall of Kyrenia or before the news had reached her, she says that "God wished in his mercy to console me with a dear son, but a malevolent fate has taken him from me."[16] After another desperate appeal for speedy help she ends her letter by saying that if this is not forthcoming, it would be better for them both to enter religious orders than to live shamefully on the charity of others.

Even before Kyrenia had fallen, the redoubtable James had, in January 1464, retaken Famagusta from the Genoese, so that with Kyrenia also in his hands a king of Cyprus was master of the whole island for the first time in ninety years.[17] Thenceforth Charlotte and Louis were no more than its *de jure* sovereigns, but it was not until 1485, long after both James II and James III—and Louis also[18] — were dead, that the indomitable Charlotte finally abandoned hope and brought herself to resign her rights. As far back as 1462, before

15. Hill, *History of Cyprus,* III, 618–620, discusses the date in a lengthy note.

16. Charlotte's only child, not otherwise mentioned, must have been stillborn or have died shortly after birth.

17. James II dated his reign from 1460, the year of his recognition as king by the sultan and his successful invasion of Cyprus from Egypt, but the loss of Kyrenia in 1464 marks the end of Charlotte's *de facto* reign, with the loss of her last foothold.

18. He died, ineffective to the last, in 1482.

returning from Savoy to Rhodes, she had concluded with her father-in-law, duke Louis, and her aunt Anna, his duchess, an agreement which included certain dispositions regarding the succession to the Cypriote crown. Of these dispositions the one ultimately to become operative was the provision that if both Charlotte and Louis died without issue, the three crowns would revert to the duchess Anna, as the daughter of king Janus, and her heirs. On February 25, 1485, in Rome, where she had been living under the protection of popes Sixtus IV and Innocent VIII more or less regularly since 1475, except for the expedition to Egypt referred to below, Charlotte made formal cession of her crowns to the house of Savoy in the person of the then reigning duke, Anna's grandson Charles I.[19] She retained the royal style for her lifetime but conceded its simultaneous use to duke Charles. It was by virtue of the agreements of 1462 and 1485 that the heads of the house of Savoy continued successively as dukes, kings of Sardinia, and kings of Italy to bear the titles of kings of Jerusalem, Cyprus, and Armenia until the abdication of Humbert II, last of the dynasty, in 1946.

Charlotte, who devoted the rest of her life and means to good works, died in Rome, apparently of some gouty trouble, on July 16, 1487, aged about forty-four, after a life of sorrow, fruitless wanderings, unflaggingly courageous and sanguine striving, and constant frustration. Innocent VIII gave her a royal funeral in St. Peter's where her unadorned tomb may be seen to this day in the crypt, not far from that of Pius X. "A more pathetic figure than Charlotte's never crossed the stage of Cypriote history. Married and widowed when she was barely fourteen, united again when she was but sixteen to a poor-spirited and ineffectual husband, despoiled by her own brother of everything when she was barely twenty, she fought tenaciously for her rights for over twenty years."[20] Charlotte had her mother's fixity of purpose without her mother's unattractive qualities; throughout her troubled life her upright character shone with a clear light. As with her mother, her best language was Greek, which she spoke, according to Pius II, with "torrential" rapidity; her French was definitely shaky. Unlike her mother, however, she was a loyal adherent of the church of Rome and a devoted servant of the holy see. Both Charlotte and Louis struck coins, not jointly but in separate issues. Charlotte is the only Lusignan sovereign other than James II not to be represented on the silver coinage sitting crowned and sceptered on the *banc royal;* the obverse of her *gros* (and

19. Venice rejected the validity of this cession on the legalistic ground that the suzerain of Cyprus was the sultan of Egypt, who had legally bestowed the kingdom on James.

20. Hill, *History of Cyprus,* III, 613.

demi-gros) bears instead a crowned shield with her arms. The coins of Louis follow broadly the normal Lusignan pattern.

James's expulsion of the Genoese from Famagusta while still contending with Charlotte for the crown was certainly an achievement of considerable magnitude. And it was no fault of his that the reintegration with the kingdom of its principal port and commercial center came too late to heal the wounds which this canker had been inflicting on the country in the course of the last three generations. Moreover, although he did not realize it, what Genoa had failed to accomplish in Cyprus was to be completed in full measure by Venice.

With James now fully in the saddle, consideration had to be given to the question of his marriage. Venice had not yet formulated her plan of finding him a Venetian queen but had already constituted herself his mentor in this as in other matters. In 1466 she suggested to him through his envoy, the invaluable Goneme, now archbishop of Nicosia, the princess Zoe (later Sophia), daughter of the ex-despot of the Morea, Thomas Palaeologus, and niece of the last Byzantine emperor, Constantine XI. Already in the reign of Pius II there had been talk of his marriage to this lady, but James would not take her without the pope's recognition of himself as king and permission for his coronation, and these demands Pius, in his consistent championship of Charlotte as the lawful sovereign, flatly refused. It was not until the pontificate of Pius's successor, the Venetian Paul II, who was prepared to be amenable to his country's policy in Cyprus, that both James as king, and his nominee Goneme as archbishop, received papal recognition.[21] Nevertheless, the alliance with the Palaeologina again failed to materialize; and Zoe in the event marrying Ivan III, grand duke of Muscovy, brought the double-headed eagle of Byzantium as her dowry to the future empire of the Romanovs.

By 1467 we find James acknowledging himself as "the son of Venice," and the relationship was soon to be converted into something less figurative. A branch of the distinguished Venetian patrician family of Cornaro (Corner, in the Venetian dialect) had long held an important Cypriote fief at Episcopi in the district of Limassol, while Mark Cornaro of the so-called Ca' Grande branch of the family had been a party to Cypriote affairs in the reign of John II as Venetian envoy to the emir of Karaman, as well as in other matters, and was a personal friend of James. Mark's brother Andrew, long resident in

21. But under Paul's successors Sixtus IV and Innocent VIII, the Vatican reverted, as we have seen, to the support of Charlotte. Goneme's recognition by Paul II came in 1467, although James had nominated him archbishop in 1460, when about to leave Egypt on his invasion of Cyprus. In 1456 the archiepiscopal see was granted *in commendam* to cardinal Isidore of Kiev.

Cyprus and originally a partisan of Charlotte, had gone over to James and been granted the dignity of auditor of the kingdom. It was Mark's daughter Catherine, the date of whose birth is given as April 30, 1454, whom the signoria now designated to share James's throne. It is interesting to note that Catherine, too, had Greek blood in her veins, for the maternal grandfather of her mother, Florence Crispo of Naxos, was John Comnenus, emperor of Trebizond. In July 1468 Catherine, being then in her fifteenth year, was married to James by proxy, the ceremony being held in Venice in the ducal palace with exceptional pomp and circumstance in the presence of the doge, Christopher Moro. The greatest possible importance was given to the event; the bride received from her gratified country the surname of "Veneta" and was formally adopted as "the daughter of St. Mark." No such distinction had previously been accorded, and its grant evoked from the Savoyard bishop Louis of Turin the sardonic comment that he had not known the Evangelist to have been married. With almost indecent haste her compatriots at once styled Catherine queen of Cyprus and gave her precedence as such.

It was not, however, with the object of honoring her "daughter" with yet another title that Venice went to the length of legally adopting Catherine; there was much more behind the step than this. It was done because, if Catherine were to survive both James and any heir they might have—an improbable contingency, it might be supposed, but the one that actually occurred—it could be claimed that the rights of Catherine as "daughter of Venice" passed at her death by law to the republic.[22] It was therefore with genuine alarm that the signoria became aware before long that the prize, pursued with such ingenious forethought, might yet elude their grasp. For Ferdinand I of Naples and Sicily, no friend of Venice, now appeared on the Cypriote scene, seeking to detach James from what may already be described as Venetian tutelage by the offer of a bride from his own house. Venice reacted with energy and speed. In the summer of 1469 she dispatched a special envoy to James in the person of one Dominic Gradenigo to remonstrate, to exhort, and even to warn. For included in the envoy's representations was the veiled threat that if James failed to proceed with the marriage Venice might yet find herself obliged to consider the restoration of Charlotte, then conveniently at hand in Rhodes. Gradenigo up to a point was highly successful. He had arrived in Nicosia in September; on October 4, on behalf of doge Christopher Moro, who had invested him in anticipation with the necessary powers, he formally took James II and his

---

22. For the legal aspect of this point cf. Hill, *History of Cyprus,* III, 635.

kingdom under the protection of the republic, which bound itself to defend him and his descendants, his subjects, and his territory, against all states except his suzerain, the sultan of Egypt. Venetian goods in Cyprus were made duty free.

Even so, it was not until 1472 that James sent galleys to Venice to fetch his bride. Catherine, eighteen and by all accounts plump and comely, was escorted to her ship by doge Nicholas Tron and sailed for Cyprus in November. She was married on arrival in Famagusta and subsequently crowned in Nicosia. But if the preliminaries to her wedding were protracted, her actual married life was brief. At the end of the following June or the beginning of July, James was out hunting near Famagusta with the queen's uncle Andrew and her cousin Mark Bembo when sudden and violent pains with dysenteric symptoms compelled him to abandon the chase. During the next few days the affliction grew steadily worse, and on July 6 he died, in the thirty-third year of his age according to the epitaph subsequently set up by Catherine. His anxiously awaited posthumous heir was born one month and twenty-two days later, on August 28.

James's abrupt death at so early an age and at the height of his exceptional physical vigor naturally gave rise to the suspicion of poison, a suspicion directed to more than one quarter. Venice had an obvious motive, since James's disappearance was the first and most important stage in the elimination of his dynasty (now hanging on the single, slight thread of Catherine's unborn child) and the reversion of the kingdom to the republic. Secondly, the king's numerous immoralities and the violence of his conduct had, as in the case of his great-great-uncle Peter I, gravely affronted a considerable number of his subjects. A third hypothesis, emanating from Venetian sources, which implicated Charlotte and her supporters, is not to be taken seriously. As regards the former two the motive, indeed, was there but proof is absent.

The dying king was able before he expired to make a will, in which he bequeathed the crown and lordship over Cyprus to Catherine and made the child she was expecting his heir. If the child should die, the inheritance was to pass to his natural children Eugene, John, and Charlotte (or Charla) in that order, and, failing them, to his nearest relative of the house of Lusignan.[23] He referred to a great treasure

---

23. This was James's second cousin Charles or Clarion de Lusignan, grandson of the Henry of Galilee who fell at Khirokitia. Clarion, who never swerved from his loyalty to Charlotte, for which reason James deprived him of twenty-four estates, represented the only surviving legitimate branch of this once-numerous family and would according to modern practice have been the next heir to the throne after Charlotte. He was the great-grandfather of James de Lusignan, the historian, who became a Dominican and is better known as Estienne de Lusignan, his name in religion.

which he had laboriously amassed, and he directed that the slaves manning his galleys should be freed, "car ie les ay assez tourmenté."[24] He appointed a council of regency of seven nobles, including the queen's uncle Andrew, but two of the members were Catalans and members of the Spanish party now growing in influence at court in opposition to the designs of Venice.

James was a prince of some power, who owed his achievements to outstanding personal qualities, a forceful and resolute character, already manifested in his teens, a persuasive eloquence, a charm of manner that could win affection, and an impetuous generosity. The other side of his nature reveals an equally impetuous violence and the capacity to inspire not only love but hatred. He seems to have observed loyally his obligations to the sultans of Egypt, who had helped him to win his crown. But he seems to have been lacking in perception as to whither his dependence on Venice was leading the kingdom. He was an exceptionally fine horseman, and it may be this accomplishment that led him, alone of the Lusignan kings, to be represented on horseback on his attractive silver *gros*. His *demi-gros*, showing his head crowned, is also unique as the only example of portraiture in the Lusignan coinage.

Catherine was allowed to succeed peacefully and on August 28, as has been said, gave birth to a son in Famagusta, which she had not left since her husband's last illness. In September the child was baptized with his father's name and acclaimed as James III, and a few weeks later underwent some form of coronation. According to Lusignan the infant was produced in public on important occasions and made to signify that the council of regency were acting in his name by the raising of his hand in assent to their measures. But two days or so before his first birthday the little James III died, and although once more there was talk of poison and suspicion again fell upon both Venice and the supporters of Charlotte, there seems no reason to believe that the baby did not die a natural death. Catherine, in a letter to the doge, Nicholas Marcello, writes that he succumbed to a fever, and elsewhere she complains bitterly that she would not have lost him if she had not been forced to remain in Famagusta.[25] Nevertheless, the child's death was another windfall for Venice, since the legitimate line of the illegitimate James II was now extinct.[26]

24. Hill, *History of Cyprus,* III, 653, quoting Estienne de Lusignan.

25. This city can be unpleasantly hot in the summer months and in those days was also unhealthy at that season of the year.

26. There exists a silver *gros* struck during the brief joint reign of Catherine and James III, bearing the names of both.

Brief as was the titular reign of the infant king, it witnessed one event important intrinsically and even more so in its consequences, the narration of which must be preceded by a word about the Catalan party at the Cypriote court and its objectives. The leaders of this party in the government were the regents John Tafur, titular count of Tripoli, and John Pérez Fabregues, titular count of Jaffa and count of Karpass, together with the latter's brother Louis Pérez Fabregues, an ardent supporter of James II whose appointment to the archbishopric of Nicosia (resigned by Goneme in 1469) not even the opposition of Venice had been able to prevent. A third regent of Spanish origin, Peter Davila, while suspect to Venice, probably without justification, was trusted by Catherine, who made him constable. John Pérez de Fabregues died in October 1473, and the leadership of the party passed to his brother the archbishop. The party aimed at the prevention of the kingdom's absorption by Venice and therefore at the maintenance of its independent existence, and they looked to Ferdinand of Naples to direct their policy. This monarch's first scheme was to marry his natural son Alonzo to Charla, natural daughter of James II, a proposal which had actually secured James's approval before he died. It also secured the approval of Charlotte, who, after the contract for the marriage had been made (much against Catherine's wishes) in November 1473, following the murders to be related below, actually adopted Alonzo and sent him to Egypt, where she hoped to induce sultan Ka'itbey to place her and the young couple in possession of the island. She herself followed him to Cairo in 1478, bravely risking threatened interception by Venetian galleys. The scheme was wrecked by Charla's death in 1480 at the age of twelve in Padua, where she and her brothers Eugene and John were being held in Venetian custody. To that extent, therefore, there was fusion between the interests of the Catalans and those of the supporters of Charlotte, a fusion which was dissolved when Ferdinand proceeded after Charla's death to entertain the idea of marrying Alonzo to the widowed Catherine.

To return to the events in Cyprus in 1473, the Catalans decided that the principal local obstacles to the success of their plans were the queen's uncle Andrew and certain other Venetian members of her entourage. On November 13 the archbishop and his supporters, including the Sicilian Rizzo di Marino, who was one of the regents and chamberlain, appeared armed in Famagusta. Rizzo killed Andrew Cornaro with his own hand and attempted to stab the queen's physician, one Gabriel Gentile, in her very chamber and in her presence, actually finishing him off outside; a companion dispatched

Catherine's cousin Mark Bembo. The Catalans then assumed complete control of the queen, taking, according to a Venetian account, her treasure-chest, jewels, and seal-ring and going to the length, according to a report made to the duke of Milan, of removing the infant James III from his mother's custody to that of his grandmother, Marietta of Patras.[27] But they failed to secure Kyrenia and the northern castles.

Venice took characteristically energetic measures to redress the situation, in the first instance by means of instructions to her captain-general at sea, Peter Mocenigo,[28] then operating against the Ottoman sultan off the Karamanian coast. By the time Mocenigo arrived in Cyprus at the beginning of February 1474, to help the queen and to reëstablish Venetian hegemony, the Catalan coup had collapsed and its leaders, including the archbishop and Rizzo, had escaped in a Neapolitan galley. But Venice was determined to take this opportunity to establish her control over the kingdom once and for all, subject only to the Egyptian tribute;[29] for she did not wish to see her dispositions, present and future, against the Turks embarrassed by possible disagreement with the Mamluks. In March 1474, after receiving reports from Mocenigo, the senate appointed two Venetian nobles as "counselors" to the queen, and another Venetian as *provveditore*, to have supreme command of the troops. These three Venetian officials were in effect to govern Cyprus on behalf of Venice, leaving to the queen no more than the nominal dignity and the mere appearance of taking a part in the affairs of state. It was laid down that the counselors were always to reside wherever the queen might be. It was also decided that the castle and city of Famagusta were to be garrisoned by Venetian forces.

When the news of the death of James III reached Venice, the senate, possibly realizing something of Catherine's distress, the incessant difficulties since her accession, and her humiliating position in the face of her own subjects, sent her father, Mark Cornaro, to be with her and to act unofficially as her adviser in conjunction and in harmony with the official trio. From Catherine's point of view, if not perhaps from that of the republic, the step was a helpful one, for the counselors had been interpreting their instructions all too literally. In two confidential letters to the doge Catherine complained that she

27. Marietta of Patras, together with the three bastard children of her son James II, was removed to Venetian territory in 1476. She died in 1503 at what must have been an advanced age, seeing that James was born about 1440.

28. He became doge at the end of 1474.

29. Venice saw to it that the tribute was paid, at least intermittently.

was not allowed by them to take even ten ducats from her own revenues; not allowed to receive letters addressed to her by her subjects or others, nor to send letters, except with their approval; and not allowed to dine or to hear mass in public, but had to have her meals alone in her chamber served by two maids and to hear mass in a room, unseen; and that she had been grossly abused, brow-beaten, and threatened if she demurred at signing a document of which she disapproved.

From supplementary instructions now sent by Venice to the counselors and repeated in 1479, we learn that they had been in the habit of placing so harsh a construction on their orders as actually to insist on living in the queen's apartments, and that this practice of theirs was to cease. Catherine was in fact a prisoner in all but name and the counselors her warders; if the Catalans had chastised her with whips, her own compatriots chastised her with scorpions. Here was indeed a contrast with the honors showered by the republic on its "daughter" at her betrothal, and the daughter was finding her treatment a heavy strain on her genuine love for her mother country. She never ceases to protest that she has always been a good Venetian.

Not unnaturally there was friction between Mark and the counselors, and Mark returned to Venice. Thenceforth, what remained of Catherine's so-called reign was an anticlimax from the point of view of the kingdom, for it was merely the prelude to Venetian annexation. Two factors decided the republic not to allow Catherine to live out her life in Cyprus in the enjoyment of her nominal sovereignty. Venice had continued to tolerate the island's make-believe independence after the death of James III solely because of its anxiety not to disturb relations with Egypt. Now, however, the growing menace of the Turks on the one hand, and on the other king Ferdinand's plan to marry Catherine to his son Alonzo, a plan which the signoria suspected Catherine of favoring, induced the Venetians to accelerate their moves. The Ottoman threat required that Cyprus should be placed in a proper state of defense, which could best be done under direct Venetian rule, while, were Catherine really to marry Alonzo, there was danger that Cyprus might slip at the last moment from the Venetian into the Neapolitan orbit. At the end of October 1488, the council of ten ordered Francis Priuli, then captain-general, to Cyprus to persuade the queen to leave the island and return to Venice, where she would be treated as a queen and assured the continuance of her existing civil list of 8,000 ducats. This she was to be urged to do for the sake of Cyprus, so that the island could be made safe from the Turks. Priuli was further instructed that should Catherine refuse, she was to be warned that she would incur the signoria's displeasure and be regarded as a rebel; in the last resort, she was to be removed by force. As an afterthought the council, preferring not to use extreme measures if these could be avoided, sent Catherine's brother George after Priuli to reinforce the captain-general's official persuasions. For if Catherine were to prove contumacious, the result would be disastrous for the Cornari, and it appears that this argument finally induced the bitterly reluctant queen to accept the ultimatum. "Are not my lords of Venice content," she asked, "to have their island when I am dead, that they would deprive me thus soon of what my husband left me?"

No time was lost by the Venetians in implementing the assent thus wrung from the queen. With somewhat heartless cynicism they staged, on February 26, 1489, a ceremony in Famagusta whereat the queen was made to hand to the captain-general the standard of St. Mark to be flown thenceforth in place of her own; "and thus," wrote cardinal Peter Bembo, her kinsman, "was the kingdom of Cyprus reduced to a province." When Catherine arrived in Venice the following June, her reception matched in splendor the functions attending her betrothal and her departure for Cyprus as a bride. The republic now granted its "daughter" the little lordship of Asolo at the foot of the Dolomites, where the former queen spent her time pleasantly enough as a patron of art and of scholars of the Renaissance. She died in Venice on July 9, 1510, aged fifty-six.

Catherine had not Charlotte's depth of character, nor was her lot on the whole, despite the sorrows, loneliness, and mortifications of her fifteen years of widowhood in Cyprus, as tragic as that of her consistently ill-starred sister-in-law and rival. Nor, again, were the rights for which she put up such struggle as she could to be compared in weight with those for which Charlotte fought with such admirable tenacity of purpose. Yet Catherine was of a kindly, affectionate, and—fortunately for herself—forgiving disposition, and she contrived in very unpropitious circumstances to render herself genuinely loved by her subjects. When the time came for her to make her final, compulsory exit from her kingdom, she effected it with dignity and a good grace.

The recorded history of medieval Cyprus is concerned mainly with an intruding ruling house and caste alien in blood, religion, and language to the people of the country, and with the rulers' dynastic quarrels, their diplomacy, their international relationships, and their wars, as well as with the designs upon the island of foreign powers in the Moslem east and, even more, in the Christian west. We hear little enough, except in parentheses, so to speak, of the Cypriotes themselves and of how they fared under their foreign rulers and feudal lords; in the minds of the western chroniclers they seemed scarcely to exist. It was taken for granted that the peasantry, who were largely synonymous with the Cypriote people,[30] were there to produce the crops and their share—in manpower and taxes—of the sinews of war, but without any say in the country's affairs. Indeed, the lowest of the three classes into which they were divided consisted of serfs. On the ecclesiastical side we know more, for the records contain full details of the subjection of the ancient autocephalous church of Cyprus to the Latin church of its rulers.

While it is unlikely that the Cypriote peasantry under the Lusignan kingdom were politically worse off, despite their passive role, than the peasantry of other Near Eastern countries during the same period, it is not surprising that by the end of the Venetian occupation they had come to conceive, albeit more on religious than political grounds, a profound hatred of the Latin xenocracy. Venice, it is true, maintained as the basis of the island's legal system the Assizes of Jerusalem, to which the people were accustomed, and caused them to be translated from French into the Venetian dialect by the chronicler Florio Bustron.[31] But when in 1571 the Turks displaced the Venetians they would be welcomed by the Cypriotes as liberators from the detested Latin yoke. It was the barrier of religion rather than that of language that prevented any fusion between the Cypriote people and the French and other Latin stocks in Cyprus during all the centuries of their presence beside them. That the language difficulty had to some extent, at least, been overcome in the later period of Lusignan rule we may infer from the statement of the Cypriote chronicler Leontius Machaeras that "we write both French and Greek in such a way that no one in the world can say what our language is." But the two churches—the intruding and dispossessing, the indigenous and dispossessed—stood rigidly apart.

The status and dignity of a kingdom conferred on Cyprus by the Lusignan dynasty were slow to disappear. When Peter Bembo wrote of Catherine's abdication ceremony that a kingdom was thus reduced to a province, he stated a fact but not the theory. Venice took very

30. Only a few Cypriote families, prominent among them the Podocataros, the Synkletikos, and the Sozomenos, made their way into the nobility of the kingdom, and they were probably descended from the old Byzantine aristocarcy.

31. F. Bustron's original holograph translation, made at the direction of doge Andrew Gritti and "the illustrious lords rectors of this kingdom of Cyprus" in 1531, was in the possession of the late author of this chapter.

seriously the circumstance that she was now possessed of a kingdom, and on the strength of that circumstance claimed and exacted[32] a higher diplomatic precedence than she had enjoyed before. And such had been the island's international prestige under the Lusignan kings that it would continue to be dignified unofficially with the royal style long after the Lusignans—and the Venetians, too, for that matter—had vanished from the scene.[33]

32. E.g. from the pope, the Porte, and Bavaria.

33. Consular officers of several continental European states prolonged even into the nineteenth century the habit of heading their dispatches *dal Regno di Cipro* ("from the kingdom of Cyprus"): H. C. Luke, *Cyprus under the Turks* (Oxford, 1921), p. 3.

XII

THE SPANISH
AND PORTUGUESE
RECONCONQUEST, 1095–1492

When pope Urban II in 1095 proclaimed the crusade for the recovery of the Holy Land, the struggle against Islam in the Iberian peninsula was already almost four centuries old, and yet another four would pass before, in the year of the discovery of America, the "Catholic Kings" at Granada could raise the cross and the banner of Castile over the highest tower of the Alhambra, ending forever an Islamic dominion that dated from the Visigothic catastrophe of 711−714. In this eight-hundred-year chronicle of Christian-Moslem confrontation and cultural interpenetration, the Council of Clermont (which several Spanish bishops attended) represents no merely fortuitous midpoint, for the last years of the eleventh century witnessed a profound transformation in the nature, tempo, and course of the

Basic sources and secondary works relating to each stage of the reconquest (1095–1492) are cited below at appropriate points of the text. Down to 1250 the chief Latin general chronicles are those of Rodrigo of Toledo (Rodrigo Ximénes de Rada), *Historia gothica* (ed. A. Schott, *Hispaniae illustratae*, 4 vols., Frankfurt, 1603–1608, II, 25–194); Lucas of Tuy, *Chronicon mundi* (*ibid.*, IV, 1–116); and Alfonso X, *Estoria de España* (ed. R. Menéndez Pidal, *Primera crónica general,* 2 vols., Madrid, 1906). Other narratives are collected in *Las Crónicas latinas de la Reconquista* (ed. A. Huici Miranda, 2 vols., Valencia, 1913). On the Portuguese side, see the sole *Scriptores* volume of *Portugaliae monumenta historica* (Lisbon, 1956); *Crónicas dos sete primeiros reis de Portugal* (ed. C. da Silva Tarouca, 3 vols., Lisbon, 1952); and *Fontes medievais da história de Portugal* (ed. A. Pimenta, Lisbon, 1948). For papal correspondence, see P. Kehr, *Papsturkunden in Spanien:* I. *Catalanien* (Abhandlungen der Akademie der Wissenschaften in Göttingen, philolog.-hist. Klasse, XVIII, 2, 1926), II. *Navarra und Aragon* (*ibid.*, XXII, 1928); and C. Erdmann, *Papsturkunden in Portugal* (*ibid.*, XX, 1927).

For general primary narratives of Moslem authorship relating to post-1095 Iberia, the only collection is *Colección de crónicas árabes de la Reconquista* (ed. A. Huici, 4 vols, Tetuán, 1952–1955), which includes Ibn-'Idhārī al-Marrākushī, *Kitāb al-bayān al-mughrib* (vols. II–III); and the anonymous *Al-hulal al-maushīyah* (vol. I). See also Ibn-abī-Zar' al-Fāsī, *Raud al-qirtās* (Fr. tr. A. Beaumier, Paris, 1860; Sp. tr. A. Huici, Valencia, 1918); Ahmad ibn-Muhammad al-Makkarī, *Kitāb nafh at-tīb* (tr. P. de Gayangos, *The History of the*

Spanish and Portuguese reconquest brought about by the confluence of three great movements of historical change.

The first of these was the accelerating internal growth and expansive thrust of the Iberian Christian peoples, whose principal foci were in 1095 temporarily aligned as the united kingdoms of Leon and Castile, with the former including a county of Portugal on the verge

Mohammedan Dynasties in Spain, 2 vols., London, 1840–1843, II); and Ibn-Khaldūn, *Kitāb al-'ibar* (tr. W. McG. de Slane, *Histoire des Berbères,* 3 vols., Algiers, 1852–1856; Iberian sections, Sp. tr. by O. Machado, in *Cuadernos de historia de España,* IV, VI–VIII, 1946–1947). Numerous Moslem sources are extracted in C. Sánchez Albornoz, *La España musulmana* (2 vols., Buenos Aires, 1946).

Aside from the collaborative *La Reconquista española y la repoblación del país* (Saragossa, 1951), A. Huici Miranda, *Las Grandes batallas de la Reconquista durante las invasiones africanas* (Madrid, 1956), and J. Goñi Gaztambide, *Historia de la Bula de la Cruzada en España* (Vitoria, 1958), reconquest history has to be pieced together from pertinent sections of general works or numerous specialized studies. In the former category the most useful are (i) for Spain: P. Aguado Bleye, *Manual de historia española* (9th ed., 3 vols., Madrid, 1963–1964), I–II; A. Ballesteros y Beretta, *Historia de España* (2nd ed., 11 vols., Barcelona, 1943–1956), II–III; L. García de Valdeavellano, *Historia de España* (4th ed., Madrid, 1968), I, part 2 (to 1212); and R. Menéndez Pidal, ed., *Historia de España* (Madrid, 1935–), vols. XIV–XVII available (14th–15th centuries); (ii) for the Crown of Aragon: J. Zurita, *Anales de la Corona de Aragón* (6 vols., Saragossa, 1562–1580); J. M. Lacarra, "Aragón en el pasado," in J. M. Casas Torres, J. M. Lacarra, and F. Estapé Rodríguez, *Aragón, cuatro ensayos* (2 vols., Saragossa, 1960), pp. 125–304; and F. Soldevila, *Història de Catalunya* (2nd ed., 3 vols., Barcelona, 1962), I; and (iii) for Portugal: A. Herculano, *História de Portugal* (9th ed., 8 vols., Lisbon, n.d.); F. de Almeida, *História de Portugal* (6 vols., Coimbra, 1922–1929), I–II; *História de Portugal* (ed. D. Peres, 8 vols., Barcelos, 1928–1935), II; L. Gonzaga de Azevedo, *História de Portugal* (6 vols., Lisbon, 1935–1944); and H. Livermore, *A History of Portugal* (Cambridge, 1947). See also the encyclopedic *Diccionario de historia de España* (ed. G. Bleiberg, 2nd ed., 3 vols., Madrid, 1968–1969) and *Dicionário de história de Portugal* (ed. J. Serrão, 4 vols., Lisbon, 1963–1971). On the Moslem side, H. Terrasse, *Histoire du Maroc* (2 vols., Casablanca, 1949–1950), and Ch. A. Julien, *Histoire de l'Afrique du nord* (2nd ed., Paris, 1951–1952; trans. John Petrie as *History of North Africa,* London and New York, 1970), treat Iberian affairs; and the *Encyclopaedia of Islam* (Leyden, 1930–1942; 2nd ed., Leyden and London, 1960–) contains many relevant entries. Pending appearance of a general history of Moslem Spain after 1100, see I. de las Cagigas, *Minorías étnico-religiosas de la edad media española* (4 vols., Madrid, 1947–1949), III–IV.

Reconquest treaties are calendared, with reference to published texts, in J. López Oliván, *Repertorio diplomático español* (Madrid, 1944). On institutional, military, and social organization, consult L. García de Valdeavellano, *Historia de las instituciones españolas* (Madrid, 1968) and H. de Gama Barros, *História da administração pública em Portugal nos séculos XII a XV* (2nd ed., 11 vols., Lisbon, 1945–1954). On ecclesiastical aspects, Goñi Gaztambide, *op. cit.,* is indispensable for papal and conciliar topics. Cf. also A. de J. da Costa, "Cruzada, Bula da," *Dicionário de história de Portugal, I,* 755–757.

On the debate over the significance of the reconquest in Iberian history may be cited: J. A. Maravall, *El Concepto de España en la edad media* (Madrid, 1954), chapter 5; A. Castro, *La Realidad de la historia de España* (4th ed., Mexico City, 1971; Eng. tr., based on a previous edition, *The Structure of Spanish History,* Princeton, 1954), chapters 5–8; C. Sánchez Albornoz, *España: un enigma histórico* (2nd ed., 2 vols., Buenos Aires, 1962), especially II, 9 ff.; and C. Erdmann, "Der Kreuzzugsgedanke in Portugal," *Historische Zeitschrift,* CXLI (1929–1930), 23–53.

of moving towards national autonomy; the similarly linked monar-
chies of Aragon and Navarre; and the foremost Catalan counties of
Barcelona and Urgel. The Leonese-Castilian sovereigns Ferdinand I
(1035/1038–1065) and Alfonso VI (1065/1072–1109) had attempted to construct a pan-Iberian federation of both Christian and
Moslem states based upon the ancient doctrine that the rulers of
Leon, as authentic heirs of the Visigothic kings, were both *reges* and
imperatores Hispaniae (or *Hispaniarum*), entitled to exercise an imperial hegemony over all other peninsular princes.[1] But this thesis
met with considerable opposition from the other Christian states, so
that in the year of Clermont it was plain that Christian unity would
remain a precarious ideal and that the reconquest, conceptually the
liberation of the peninsula from Islam but in practice much more a
contest for immediate secular prizes, would be fought by independent, often hostile, powers. Nevertheless, despite such disunity,
Christian Iberia's increasing population and resources, maturing political, social, and economic institutions, tightening religious, cultural,
and commercial ties with trans-Pyrenean Europe, and growing confidence that the reconquest was no longer a mere struggle for
survival—all created strong pressures to gain lands and spoils, power,
prestige, and satisfaction of religious ideals, across the open frontier
to the south.

Under Alfonso VI indeed, especially after Toledo's capitulation
(1085), the reconquest had seemed destined to a quick success, with
the Moorish principalities of al-Andalus (Moslem Spain) all being
reduced to vassalage as the prelude to complete absorption. Instead
Iberian Christendom—and this is the second fundamental change
affecting the reconquest of the late eleventh century—was to be
drawn into a protracted conflict with the three successive North
African Berber empires of the Murābiṭs, the Muwaḥḥids, and the
Marīnids. From the start, the Murābiṭ intrusion of Yūsuf ibn-Tāshfīn
(1061–1106), commencing in 1086, set the pattern: replacement of
weak, divided Hispano-Moslem "Taifa" (from Arabic *mulūk aṭ-
ṭawā'if*) kingdoms by an aggressive imperial power based on the
opposite side of the Strait of Gibraltar and possessing abundant
manpower reserves in the fighting tribes of the Maghrib and the
Sahara. Insofar as this meant Africanization of al-Andalus and of the
Islamic counter-reconquest, it rekindled in the peninsula, under Moroccan leadership incarnating Murābiṭ reformist fervor, the ideal of
the holy war (*jihād*) against the Christians; and, to the extent that

1. R. Menéndez Pidal, *El Imperio hispánico y los Cinco Reinos* (Madrid, 1950).

this inevitably provoked corresponding Christian militancy, what had been a kind of limited Spanish civil war now tended to become for both sides a perceptibly grimmer clash of alien peoples and sharply divergent religious, cultural, and political ideologies. It is important to observe, however, that this never ruled out, particularly among the Hispano-Moslems, frequent alliances of Christians and Moors for the purpose of warring upon one another's coreligionists.

Finally, the third new factor after 1095 is the trans-Pyrenean crusading movement, which thenceforth gave the Iberian reconquest its character as the western theater of Catholic Europe's war against Islam, greatly magnifying the peninsular movement's religious objectives and overtones and inspiring increased foreign ecclesiastical and military intervention below the Pyrenees. After Clermont the spreading view that recovery of Spain and Portugal from the Moors was a stage on the road to the Holy Sepulcher began to find expression in numerous innovations: preaching of the crusade in advance of certain campaigns; concessions of episcopal indulgences to fighters in or financial supporters of such ventures; appearance of prelates and priests on the battlefield as commanders of troops or as combatants; formation of religious military confraternities and eventually (as nowhere else in the west except the Baltic) of native military orders patterned after those of the Holy Land; and conciliar, royal, and municipal enactments regarding the religious status and legal rights of reconquest participants.

The thesis that it was primarily the monks of Cluny who converted the reconquest into an Iberian crusade merits little credence. Rather, it was the papacy which played a leading role not only in this process but in the whole development of the reconquest throughout the rest of the Middle Ages. From Urban II's time on, innumerable bulls of indulgence, like the acts of the First Lateran Council of 1123, equated in importance and spiritual privileges anti-Moorish combat in Spain with that against the Saracens of Palestine, while they prohibited (not always successfully) Spaniards and Portuguese from enlisting in eastern expeditions, on the grounds of prior need for their services at home;[2] and the popes, not infrequently under royal pressure, conceded peninsular monarchs tenths or other fractions of their kingdoms' ecclesiastical revenues as reconquest subsidies or exhorted them, with limited success, to abandon wars against one another in favor of united action against the common "infidel" foe.

---

2. See A. Sánchez Candeira, "Las Cruzadas en la historiografía española de la época," *Hispania,* XX (1960), 325–367, and bibliography cited there.

Foreign military and naval intervention likewise brought the crusade in all its fullness into the peninsula, whether this took the form of French, Italian, or northern European fighters arriving for this purpose, or of amphibious expeditions lending a hand on their way to the east.[3] While small numbers of such alien crusaders appeared as late as 1492, this was essentially a phenomenon of the twelfth and early thirteenth centuries, the importance of which should not be exaggerated. Foreign collaboration varied widely even in this period according to region and decade, being most prominent in Aragon, the kingdom which excelled in exploiting the use of the crusade in advancing its reconquest policies, and in Portugal, the way station between the northern Atlantic and the Mediterranean. But such external aid, although decisive in a limited number of campaigns or sieges, neither inspired nor dominated reconquest military planning or the conduct of operations. What made it particularly welcome, until in the later twelfth century the Iberian kingdoms caught up with certain more advanced trans-Pyrenean resources and techniques for warfare, was its three-fold contribution: ships for transport, for blockading and attacking fortified ports, and for engaging enemy fleets; heavy mailed cavalry trained in shock combat tactics, and, in contrast with the light-armed though more mobile horsemen typical of peninsular armies, capable of using massed weight, momentum, and relative invulnerability to smash enemy lines of battle; and improved engines of war and superior ballistic and mining expertise, of manifest utility in a struggle that so often centered about sieges of well-fortified towns and castles.

Revived Iberian Christian vigor, Africanization of the Islamic antagonist, the impact of the European crusade—these form the dynamic triad taking the Spanish and Portuguese reconquest after 1095 into new stages of dramatically intensified conflict and long-deferred fulfillment.

In 1086 the Ṣanhājī Berber chieftain Yūsuf ibn-Tāshfīn, responding to the appeal of leading Taifa princes alarmed by Alfonso VI's annexation of the kingdom of Toledo to Leon-Castile, had landed a North African army in al-Andalus and inflicted a smashing defeat

3. P. Boissonnade, *Du Nouveau sur la Chanson de Roland* (Paris, 1923), pp. 3–68; M. Defourneaux, *Les Français en Espagne aux XIe et XIIe siècles* (Paris, 1949); F. Kurth, "Der Anteil niederdeutscher Kreuzfahrer an den Kämpfen der Portugiesen gegen die Mauren," *Mittheilungen des Instituts für österreichische Geschichtskunde,* Ergänzungsband, VIII (1911), 131–159; H. A. R. Gibb, "English Crusaders in Portugal," in *Chapters in Anglo-Portuguese Relations* (ed. E. Prestage, Watford, 1935), pp. 1–23; A. H. de Oliveira Marques, *Hansa e Portugal na idade media* (Lisbon, 1959), pp. 35–45.

upon the king-emperor at Zallaca, north of Badajoz.[4] The immediate consequences of this Murābiṭ victory should not be over-estimated: Toledo remained firmly in Christian hands; in 1089 Alfonso could still optimistically plant a strong garrison at Aledo in distant Murcia and successfully throw back Yūsuf's counter-attack upon this projected base; and he could take under his protection two Taifa kings who now feared the ferocious Berbers even more than the Christians, 'Abd-Allāh of Granada and al-Mutawakkil of Badajoz, receiving from the latter the key lower Tagus strongholds of Santarem, Sintra (Cintra), and Lisbon. In 1094 his virtually independent vassal, the Cid Rodrigo Díaz of Vivar, after overrunning the northern half of the kingdom of Valencia and seizing its rich capital city, was able to defeat at Llano de Cuarte a Murābiṭ-Andalusian army sent against him.

Indeed, for Spain as a whole about 1090 the frontier belt separating Christian and Moorish territories had not yet been forced northward because of Zallaca. Starting at the Atlantic on the northern

4. Among narrative sources on the Christian side, in addition to Rodrigo of Toledo, Lucas of Tuy, and the *Primera crónica general*, there are the *Anales toledanos*, I and II (ed. H. Flórez, *España sagrada*, XXIII, 381–409); *Chronica Adefonsi imperatoris* (ed. Luis Sánchez Belda, Madrid, 1950); *Gesta comitum Barcinonensium* (ed. L. Barrau-Dihigo and J. Massó Torrents, Barcelona, 1925); J. M. Lacarra, "Documentos para el estudio de la reconquista y repoblación del valle del Ebro," *Estudios de edad media de la Corona de Aragón*, II (1946), 469–574; III (1947–1948), 499–727; V (1952), 511–668; *Liber Maiolichinus* (ed. C. Calisse, Rome, 1904; Fonti per la storia d'Italia); Laurentius Veronensis, *De bello balearico*, in *PL*, CLXIII, cols. 513–576; *Chronicon conimbricense* and *Chronica Gothorum* (Portugaliae monumenta historica, *SS*, I; Pimenta, *Fontes*, pp. 1–47). Cf. also *Documentos medievais portugueses: Documentos régios*, I, vols. I–II (ed. R. Pinto de Azevedo, Lisbon, 1958–1962).

On the Second Crusade's Iberian interventions, see *De expugnatione Lyxbonensi* (Portugaliae monumenta historica, *SS*, I; ed. C. W. David, *De expugnatione Lyxbonensi: The Conquest of Lisbon*, Columbia University Records of Civilization, XXIV, New York, 1936); the supplementary texts of Lisbon in Pimenta, *Fontes*, pp. 107–146; *Poema de Almería* (ed. Sánchez Belda, *Chronica Adefonsi imperatoris*, pp. 165–206; and Caffaro di Caschifellone, *Ystoria captionis Almarie et Turtuose*, in *Annali genovesi*, I (ed. L. T. Belgrano and C. Imperiale, Genoa, 1890; Fonti per la storia d'Italia, XI), 79–89.

On the secondary level, see R. Menéndez Pidal, *La España del Cid* (6th ed., Madrid, 1967); D. Peres, *Como nasceu Portugal* (5th ed., Porto, 1959); J. M. Lacarra, "La Reconquista y repoblación del valle del Ebro," in *Reconquista española*, pp. 39–83; A. Ubieto Arteta, *Colección diplomática de Pedro I de Aragón y Navarra* (Saragossa, 1951), Introduction, pp. 17–208; and J. González, "Reconquista y repoblación de Castilla, León, Extremadura y Andalucía (siglos XI a XIII)," in *Reconquista española*, pp. 163–181. On the wars of Murābiṭ al-Andalus, see A. Huici, "Los Banū Hūd de Zaragoza, Alfonso I el Batallador y los Almorávides," *Estudios de edad media de la Corona de Aragón*, VII (1962), 7–32; *idem*, "Contribución al estudio de la dinastía almorávide: El gobierno de Tāšfīn ben 'Alī ben Yūsuf en el Andalus," *Études d'orientalisme dédiées à la mémoire de Lévi-Provençal* (2 vols., Paris, 1962), pp. 605–621; and F. Codera y Zaidín, *Decadencia y desaparición de los Almorávides en España* (Saragossa, 1899).

bank of the Tagus estuary, it ran north toward the Mondego river, struck east below Coimbra, followed the middle Tagus past Talavera and Toledo almost to Molina de Aragón, and turned north to flank the Hūdid Taifa kingdom of Saragossa. This long border of Leon-Castile, reaching halfway down the peninsula to the approaches to the Guadiana plains and the gates of Andalusia, stood far in advance of its counterpart in eastern Spain, where Saragossa and Lerida still penned the Aragonese and Catalans close to the Pyrenees, barring access to the middle Ebro valley; even on the Mediterranean coast the county of Barcelona did not yet cross the Llobregat river just below its capital.

What actually did change the post-Zallacan situation drastically in the Moslems' favor was Yūsuf ibn-Tāshfīn's decision, following two further crossings to Spain (1089, 1090), to depose the Taifa kings, annex their territories to his Maghribin domains, and assume permanent military responsibility for throwing back the continuing Christian offensives in the Tagus and upper Ebro valleys and near the Cid's Valencia. The shuttling of African garrisons across the strait and progressive Murābiṭ occupation of Granada, Seville, and other Taifa capitals speedily provoked violent reaction all along the reconquest frontier, with grave setbacks for the Christian cause. In 1093 Alfonso VI's Burgundian son-in-law count Raymond suffered a defeat by which Santarem, Lisbon, and Sintra were lost and the Leonese-Castilian southwest exposed to imminent invasion, compelling the king-emperor to place all the Portuguese territory below the Minho in the hands of count Henry, the Burgundian husband of his illegitimate daughter Teresa (1094/1095). Alfonso himself lost the battle of Consuegra (1097); the death of the Cid, defeated at Jativa (1099), forced abandonment of Valencia by 1102; and, to cap these misfortunes, an attack upon Moslem-held Uclés in 1108 resulted in the death of the imperial heir-designate, Sancho (or Sanchuelo), Alfonso VI's half-Moorish son by Zaida, the widowed daughter-in-law of the late king al-Mu'tamid of Seville. This last event adversely affected the reconquest for years, since in 1109 it brought to the Leonese-Castilian throne the infanta Urraca, count Raymond's widow, and her second husband king Alfonso I of Aragon-Navarre. The early breakdown of this unfortunate marriage was followed by years of destructive war among the partisans of each estranged spouse, of the queen-empress's young son by count Raymond, Alfonso Raimúndez (the future Alfonso VII), and of count Henry and Teresa of Portugal. Only the failure of the Murābiṭs to launch major offensives, and sturdy resistance along the middle Tagus by veteran border fighters and the urban militias of the newly colonized towns and castles, averted disaster on the frontier.

It was in Urraca's troubled reign (1109–1126) that Leon-Castile, for the first time since the days of Ferdinand I, lost the leadership of the reconquest, which passed eastward to Aragon, a state which had existed only since 1035 but whose rulers had long been pressing the anti-Moorish war against the Taifas of Lerida and Saragossa. King Ramiro I (1035–1063) had died fighting the allied Saragossans and Castilians at Graus in an effort to move down the Cinca valley to the Ebro. Sancho Ramírez I (1063–1094), fearing imperial Leonese-Castilian domination, had tried the radical expedient of enlisting papal, French, and Catalan collaboration for a kind of proto-crusade; and when this failed at Barbastro (1064-1065), he made Aragon a fief of the papacy (1068) so as to give his kingdom's independence a papal shield. In 1076 Sancho further strengthened himself by becoming king of Navarre. Fighting continuously against the Moors on the line of the Cinca river, he took Estada (1087) and Monzón (1089) and built the fortress of El Castellar threatening Saragossa; but in 1094, when besieging Huesca, he was fatally wounded by an arrow. His son Peter I (1094–1104), who defeated a Saragossan-Castilian relief force at Alcoraz and then compelled Huesca to surrender (1096), also regained Barbastro of bloody memory (1100). In 1101 Peter took the cross, the first Iberian sovereign to do so, enlisted French knights for an attack on Saragossa, and in his last years was constructing just outside the latter city, as a prelude to its investment, a fortress significantly called Juslibol (i.e., *Deus le veult,* the war cry of Clermont).

When Alfonso the Warrior (*el Batallador,* 1104–1134) came to the Aragonese-Navarrese throne, he naturally continued this expansionist policy by occupying additional towns and territories on the left bank of the Ebro in the Cinco Villas district above Saragossa, and elsewhere. Plunged from 1110 into the troubles with Urraca and the Leonese-Castilian civil wars, the king came home in 1117 still clinging to the imperial title, the symbol of leadership in the reconquest, that his marriage had brought him. Thus Hispanic imperial tradition, familial pursuit of the reconquest in association with the papacy and the crusading movement, and a warlike, religious temperament all entered into his career as a *reconquistador.*

After leading the Aragonese-Navarrese forces across the Ebro to take Belchite, Alfonso I pushed preparations for an authentic crusade against Saragossa. A council held at Toulouse in January 1118 and attended by the archbishops of Arles and Auch as well as numerous other French, Navarrese, and Aragonese prelates, called upon the nobles of the Midi and Spain to take the *via de Hispania* to the Holy Land; and in the first such papal summons since Clermont Gelasius II promised remission of sins to those joining the Iberian crusade. On this basis a large army of Aragonese, Navarrese, Catalan, and south French fighters was assembled, including various noble veterans of the First Crusade, among them viscount Gaston of Béarn, who brought to the banks of the Ebro the siege machines and military engineers that had won him fame in 1099 at the capture of Jerusalem. After seven months of fiercely contested assaults, Saragossa capitulated (December 18, 1118) on the usual Iberian terms permitting those who wished to do so to leave with their movables.[5] The crusade then moved on to recover during the following year Tudela, Tarazona, Borja, Rueda, Épila, and other towns across the Ebro. When in 1120 the long-delayed Murābiṭ counterthrust finally came, it was thrown back at Cutanda, southeast of Daroca.

Alfonso the Warrior's next move was to occupy the plains country of the Jiloca and Jalón basins south of the great river, where he took such places as Calatayud and Daroca, and settled Aragonese, Navarrese, Catalan, and French colonists in towns that were given the added protection of the semi-military, semi-religious confraternities organized in Saragossa, Belchite, Daroca, Monreal del Campo, and other frontier danger points. In 1125–1126 he led a mobile army down past Valencia, Denia, Murcia, and Guadix all the way to Granada; when a promised Mozarab uprising failed to occur, he devastated the countryside of Cordova, defeated the Murābiṭ army near Lucena, and returned north with thousands of Mozarab settlers for his Ebro colonies. Thereafter Alfonso took Molina de Aragón, vainly besieged Valencia (1129), and secured Mequinenza at the junction of the Cinca and the Ebro (1133); but the next year the Murābiṭs crushed the royal army at Fraga, and Alfonso I died childless a few weeks later (July 17, 1134), bequeathing his kingdoms to the Palestinian orders of the Temple, Hospital, and Holy Sepulcher.

Meanwhile, to the east of Aragon-Navarre old Christian rivalries had long complicated the plans of the counts of Barcelona and Urgel to penetrate the Moorish borderlands extending from Lerida and Fraga down the Ebro to Tortosa and the sea. In 1093, for example, the Barcelonese count Berenguer Raymond II (1076–1096) had been

---

5. J. M. Lacarra, "La Conquista de Zaragoza por Alfonso I (18 diciembre 1118)," *Al-Andalus*, XII (1947), 65–96, and *Vida de Alfonso el Batallador* (Saragossa, 1971), pp. 59–77.

compelled to take up arms against a combined force of Leonese-Castilian and Aragonese-Navarrese troops and Genoese and Pisan naval squadrons which intended to assault Tortosa. By the time of count Raymond Berenguer III (1096–1131), the Barcelonese, despite stiff Moorish resistance along the Mediterranean coast, were at last driving their southern frontier beyond the Llobregat into the Panadés and the valleys of the Gayá and Francolí rivers. Count Raymond's particular goal here was the deserted site of the old Romano-Visigothic metropolitan see of Tarragona, at the mouth of the Francolí, which he hoped to restore as the head of an independent Catalan church by subordinating to it Barcelona and other Spanish March dioceses dependent since the early reconquest upon the archbishopric of Narbonne. Urban II not only gave this project his approval in 1089 but accepted Tarragona as a papal fief from the count, although three decades were to pass before the plan could be put into execution.

An important Catalan advance occurred in 1106, when the former Leonese counselor of Alfonso VI, count Peter Ansúrez, acting as guardian of the young count Ermengol VI of Urgel, captured the city of Balaguer. In reaction both to this loss and to Raymond Berenguer III's incursions around Tarragona, Murābiṭ forces struck north along the Mediterranean, devastating the Panadés and menacing Barcelona itself for the first time since the dark days of al-Manṣūr a century before. But this situation must have improved by 1114. When a fleet from Pisa arrived at Barcelona and solicited Catalan assistance in conquering the Baleares, which Gregory VII had assigned as a papal fief to Pisa (1085) and whose conquest Paschal II had just urged again in a bull of 1113, count Raymond readily agreed to command the expedition. A combined force of Catalan, Pisan, and south French crusaders sailed to Ibiza and occupied Majorca for a few months in 1114–1115, before being driven out by Murābiṭ troops who annexed this former Taifa kingdom to the North African empire.

Undaunted, Raymond Berenguer III continued to push south and west of Barcelona, in spite of a serious defeat on the Segre at Corbins, near Lerida (1124), while Catalan nobles and peasants poured irresistibly into the fertile farmlands of the so-called New Catalonia that stretched from Balaguer down the middle Francolí and through the district of Montblanch to the ruins of Tarragona and the sea. In 1118 Gelasius II had raised bishop Oleguer of Barcelona to the dignity of archbishop of Tarragona and entrusted to him the political administration of the papal fief, which embraced the city and its countryside. Soon afterward the new archbishop entered into a feudal contract with a Norman crusading nobleman famed for his exploits at the recent siege of Saragossa, Robert Bordet, who along with the title of *princeps* was given responsibility for the defense, colonization, and government of the district, although details remain obscure; Oleguer himself set about restoring the ancient metropolitan church and its province.

On the opposite side of the peninsula, in the county of Portugal, no counterpart to this active reconquest in Catalonia and Aragon can be discovered in the first third of the twelfth century. Bounded on the south by Coimbra and that city's ring of protective fortresses (like Soure) that guarded the rim of the Mondego valley, the county was a true frontier marchland, remote enough from Leon to be thrown upon its own resources—a fact that reinforced the strongly regionalist outlook of its nobles and peasants and found further expression in the plans of its comital dynasty to reduce Leonese-Castilian political control to a minimum. Count Henry (1094/1095–1112) seems to have been content to remain on the defensive along the Mondego and in the shelter of the sierras of Lousã and Estrêla. Although defeated at Malagón in 1100, when aiding Alfonso VI against the Murābiṭs, he rated the Moorish danger so low as to leave the peninsula in 1103, ostensibly to participate in the Holy Roman emperor Henry IV's projected crusade of that year. But there is no evidence that the Portuguese ruler actually went beyond Rome, where bishop Gerald of Braga was then pressing for restoration of his see's metropolitan rank as a way of taking the Portuguese dioceses out from under the authority of Leonese-Castilian Toledo.

On his return home in 1104 and thenceforth until he died, Henry ignored the reconquest to plunge into the troubled political waters of Alfonso VI's last years and Urraca's Aragonese marriage. Similarly, his widow and successor Teresa (1112–1128), engrossed in expanding the county across the Minho into Galicia rather than southwards, made no response when a Murābiṭ army swept through lower Beira, took the guardian fortresses of Coimbra, and briefly occupied that frontier bastion (1116). This paralysis can doubtless be attributed also to the widening schism within the Portuguese baronage and hierarchy between her own partisans and those rallying around her young son Afonso Henriques. At the battle of São Mamede (1128), where the two factions crossed swords, the Portuguese county passed from the defeated Teresa into the power of her son and his supporters, but Afonso Henriques was for some years too preoccupied with internal affairs, further Galician interventions, and wars aimed at preventing Alfonso VII of Leon-Castile's exercise of authority over Portugal, to pursue the reconquest.

By 1135, after fifty years of warfare against the Murābiṭs and their Hispano-Moslem auxiliaries, it can be seen that in the western and eastern halves of the peninsula the reconquest had so far followed a course quite the reverse of that between Ferdinand I's reign and the fall of Toledo. In the west, the frontier line had changed little from where it lay at Alfonso VI's death: in Portugal it still ran along the Mondego, in Leon it clung closely to the central sierras, and only in Castile, between Talavera and Toledo, did it yet extend below the southern edge of the Tagus basin. By contrast, in the once-diminutive eastern sectors notable progress had been registered: the Moorish kingdom of Saragossa, with its incomparable capital, had been won; great tracts on both sides of the middle Ebro were now in Aragon-ese-Navarrese possession; and the Catalans had marched from the Llobregat to the Francolí. Now the picture was about to change again into one of vigorous advance all across the peninsula from sea to sea, in part because of rapid Murābiṭ decline in Africa and therefore in Spain, in part by reason of the emergence in Christian Iberia of new political and military leadership that would take prompt advantage of the enemy's growing weakness.

At Alfonso the Warrior's death in 1134 Navarre again became an independent kingdom, but cut off by its more powerful neighbors from direct contact with the Moslem frontier, it thenceforth exercised decreasing influence upon the reconquest. Aragon, after Ramiro II's brief reign (1134–1137), joined with Raymond Berenguer IV's Barcelonese county to establish the powerful federation known as the Crown of Aragon. Alfonso VII, who had ruled Leon-Castile since his mother Urraca's death in 1126, having been formally crowned emperor in 1135, and protected on both his flanks by the peace treaties of Tuy with Afonso Henriques (1137) and of Carrión with Raymond Berenguer IV (1140), could turn his energies and those of his subjects back to the pursuit of the old imperial objective of the liberation of Spain. In Portugal also count Afonso, so soon to be a king, turned south toward the great prizes awaiting him on the Tagus and beyond.

All this helps explain why by 1140 there developed an uncoördinated but simultaneous three-pronged Portuguese, Leonese-Castilian, and Aragonese-Catalan offensive. In Portugal, as a preliminary, count Afonso Henriques began construction in 1135 of a powerful new base at Leiria, below Coimbra, which attracted and survived determined Moorish attacks in 1137 and 1140. At the same time military and colonizing activities to the southeast of Coimbra achieved Portuguese occupation of the valleys of the Ocreza, Nabão, and middle Zêzere rivers. Above all, in 1139 the count won a semi-legendary battle, reputedly against five Moslem princes, at Ourique, a site located perhaps above the Tagus but possibly, in this epoch of long-range raids into al-Andalus, near the town of that name in lower Alentejo, where Portuguese tradition places it. Whatever its military significance, this famous victory seems to lie behind Afonso's assumption in 1140 of the royal title, a step acknowledged by Alfonso VII in the treaty of Zamora (1143) on condition that the new kingdom of Portugal remain within the Hispanic empire. Thus it is as king Afonso I that in this same year he attacked the strongly fortified port of Lisbon, with the help of seventy ships carrying French crusaders to the east. This attack, like several others mounted in 1142 and afterward without such foreign collaboration, failed to take the key citadel of the Tagus estuary; but this need not detract from the very substantial achievement of the Portuguese in repeatedly deploying their armies on the north bank of the great river where Murābiṭ power had theretofore been unchallenged.

Alfonso VII was even more successful. In 1139 he captured the strategic fortress city of Oreja across the Tagus and afterward led various destructive expeditions across the marchlands *(extremaduras)* fringing both Leon and Castile. In 1142 he took Coria in the Leonese *extremadura* (still so called) and then rode northeast to Salamanca for a conference with Peter the Venerable of Cluny at which the abbey's annual Hispanic stipend of 2,000 gold dinars was re-funded. The Burgundian abbot's famous journey to Spain and commissioning of the first Latin translation of the Koran for his "intellectual crusade" against Islam thus belong in the optimistic context of Murābiṭ decline and Christian military success.[6] The king-emperor indeed was now to venture far beyond the Tagus basin: on long raids *(entradas)* in 1143 and 1144 he boldly crossed the Sierra Morena to invade Andalusia itself. Here Alfonso could take advantage of the spreading Hispano-Moslem revolts against Murābiṭ governors that were producing a new set of independent regional caudillos, the "Second Taifas," and promote political chaos at Cordova and elsewhere, with the help of such Moorish allies as Aḥmad ibn-Yūsuf Ibn-Hūd (self-styled Saif-ad-Daulah or Sword of the State, whence his Romance name Zafadola) at Saragossa and Ḥamdīn ibn-Muḥammad, Ibn-Ḥamdīn at Cordova. Above all, he gained control of the key pass across the Sierra Morena, Muradal, the medieval prede-

6. J. Kritzeck, *Peter the Venerable and Islam* (Princeton, 1964).

cessor of modern Despeñaperros, and with this principal gateway between southern Castile and Andalusia in his hands, he conquered Baeza, Úbeda, and other places in upper Andalusia. In 1146, when Alfonso was besieging Cordova, Genoese envoys arrived in the Leonese-Castilian camp and plans were concerted for an early joint land and naval attack upon Almeria. Then in January 1147 the king-emperor took the invaluable castle of Old Calatrava north of Muradal in La Mancha, commanding the point where the trunk highway south from Toledo to Andalusia crossed the Guadiana river.

Simultaneously in the east, where Raymond Berenguer IV (1137–1162) as ruler of the newly federated Crown of Aragon had inherited the active reconquest plans of both Alfonso the Warrior and the Barcelonese counts, the Murābiṭ war was also being pressed. By 1141 the last few remaining Moorish outposts north of the Ebro in the Cinca and Alcanadre valleys had been wiped out, and Catalan frontier fighters were penetrating across the Francolí below Tarragona. Raymond himself was negotiating with Genoa for an invasion of the Baleares when, in 1147, he was persuaded instead to collaborate in the international attack upon Almeria and hastened south with his army to join Alfonso VII on Moorish soil.

In the fifth decade of the century, therefore, the reconquest was advancing vigorously in all three sectors when Eugenius III's summons to the Second Crusade (December 1145) accelerated the Iberian offensive by bringing into the Murābiṭ war sizable contingents of foreign crusaders whose ultimate destination was the Holy Land.[7] The contribution of these warriors to the success of the sieges of Lisbon and Almeria (1147) and Tortosa (1148) has already been described in an earlier volume of this work, but now it needs to be considered in its reconquest context as auxiliary to the already successful Iberian exploitation of the crumbling Murābiṭ power. How much in 1145–1148 the pope may have been inspired to call for the Second Crusade by the good news from Spain (as well, of course, as by the shock of Edessa's fall), and how far correspondence with peninsular monarchs may have prepared the way for foreign intervention in the three sieges, is not altogether clear. In May 1145 Eugenius granted partial remission of penance to those giving aid to the Templars fighting in Spain; his crusading bull *Divina dispositione* in its revised version of April 6, 1147, recognized Spain as a crusade

7. See volume I of this work, chapter XV; G. Constable, "The Second Crusade as Seen by Contemporaries," *Traditio*, IX (1953), 213–279; David, *De expugnatione Lyxbonensi*, pp. 3–26.

theater; another bull of this year exhorted the Genoese to lend all possible assistance against Almeria; and on June 22, 1148, he promulgated another crusade bull for Raymond Berenguer's Tortosa campaign.

Be that as it may, the combined efforts of Iberians and crusaders proved militarily fruitful. In Portugal king Afonso I, in the spring of 1147, had slipped south from Coimbra for a surprise assault on Santarem, the Murābiṭ stronghold which guarded the head of the Tagus estuary as Lisbon did its mouth. In mid-March the Portuguese, escalading the walls at night and overcoming the resolute Moorish garrison, made themselves masters of the city, and were already marching to do the same at Lisbon when news came of the arrival at Oporto of the Anglo-Flemish-German expeditionaries of the Second Crusade. Persuaded in the king's name by bishop Peter Pitões of Oporto to join the royal army, the crusaders unquestionably made it possible for Afonso to take Lisbon, for its stubborn defense of some four months (June 28–October 23/24) against the combined Portuguese and crusader resources, including the northerners' heavy siege machines and poliorcetic skills, makes it certain that the city was still too strong to be taken by Afonso's men alone. The narrow limits, however, within which such collaboration was possible are illumined by the incompatibility in outlook evinced by trans-Pyrenean crusaders and Iberian *reconquistadores.* One instance is the constant breaking out in the crusader camp of misunderstanding and bitter suspicion because of the primarily secular attitude with which the Portuguese approached fighting the Moslems; the other, the implacably hostile ideas the northerners entertained of how to treat Lisbon's surrendered inhabitants, in contrast to the typically Iberian respect for capitulation terms and readiness to accept the vanquished as fellow-subjects under the king.

The siege of Almeria, between August and October 1147, by three kings—Alfonso VII, Raymond Berenguer IV, and García Ramírez of Navarre—and a combination of Genoese seamen and Leonese-Castilian, Aragonese-Catalan, and south French land units, can be explained, as far as the Italians are concerned, in terms of the city's commercial importance and its use as a base for Moorish attacks on Christian shipping in the western Mediterranean. But from Alfonso VII's standpoint, the selection of Almeria for assault can be seen as related both to his already extensive conquests and raids below Muradal and hopes of occupying all Andalusia, and to the continuance of the policy followed by Ferdinand I, Alfonso VI, and the Cid of securing a Mediterranean window for the Leonese-Castilian state.

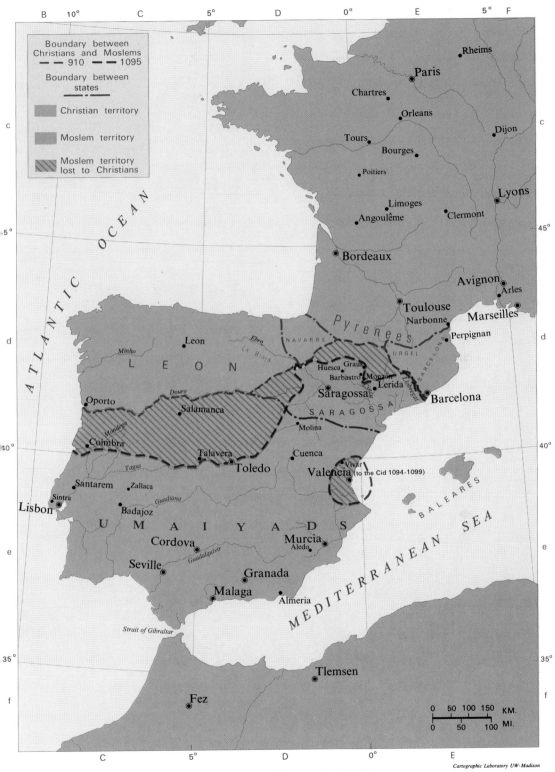

11. Spain and Portugal to 1095

Here no doubt the blockading Italian fleet, the few French noble participants, and the troops of Alfonso VII and Raymond Berenguer IV share the laurels; and it is indicative of the better spirit that prevailed here than at Lisbon that after Almeria's fall king Raymond contracted for an assault of his own upon Tortosa with the Genoese ships and also with some of the Anglo-Flemish-German veterans of the siege of Lisbon. Thus Tortosa's capture in December 1148 was a joint operation; on the other hand, the Aragonese and Catalans (assisted by troops of count Ermengol VI of Urgel) then went on without foreign support to besiege simultaneously in 1149 both Lerida and Mequinenza, taking both towns and clearing the whole line of the Segre river to its junction with the Ebro. The reconquest in Catalonia proper was now virtually complete.

The capture of these five urban centers in 1147–1149 constituted a new highwater mark in reconquest history, portending an immediate end to the Murābiṭ war and even, as in 1085, the possible total extinction of Islamic power in the peninsula. The rise of the Muwaḥḥid empire in Africa and its expansion across the strait was soon to crush this hope and embroil Christian Iberia in a new epoch of savage warfare.

In North Africa, by the middle of the twelfth century, the Maṣmūdah Berber reform movement of the Muwaḥḥids, founded by the Mahdī Muḥammad ibn-'Abd-Allāh, Ibn-Tūmart (c. 1080–1128 or 1130), had largely overthrown the Murābiṭ empire and firmly established itself at Marrakesh under the caliph 'Abd-al-Mu'min ibn-'Alī (1130–1163).[8] As early as 1146 Muwaḥḥid troops were disembark-

8. To Rodrigo of Toledo, Lucas of Tuy, and the *Primera crónica general* can be added on the Muwaḥḥid epoch *Anales toledanos,* III (ed. A. C. Floriano, *Cuadernos de historia de España,* XLIII–XLIV, 1967, 154–187); and *Crónica latina de los reyes de Castilla* (ed. M. D. Cabanes Pecourt, Valencia, 1964). Moslem primary sources include those cited above and: 'Abd-al-Malik ibn-Ṣāhib aṣ-Ṣalāt, *Al-mann bi'l-imāmah* (extracts in Sp. tr. in M. Antuña, "Campañas de los Almohades," as cited below); abū-Muḥammad 'Abd-al-Wāḥid al-Marrākushī, *Kitāb al-mu'jib fī talkhīs akhbār al-Maghrib* (ed. Huici, *Colección de crónicas árabes,* IV); and É. Lévi-Provençal, "Un Recueil de lettres officielles almohades," *Hespéris,* XVIII (1941), 1–70.

Important secondary studies are: A. Huici, *Historia política del imperio almohade* (2 vols., Tetuán, 1956–1957); M. M. Antuña, "Campañas de los Almohades en España," *Religión y cultura,* XXIX (1935), 53–67, 327–343; XXX (1935), 347–373; J. González, *Regesta de Fernando II* (Madrid, 1943); *idem, Alfonso IX* (2 vols., Madrid, 1944); *idem, El Reino de Castilla en la época de Alfonso VIII* (3 vols., Madrid, 1960); A. Huici, "Los Almohades en Portugal," *Anais,* 2nd series, V (1954), 9–51; *idem,* "Las Campañas de Ya'qūb al-Manṣūr en 1190 y 1191," *ibid.,* pp. 55–74; and M. Gual Camarena, "Precedentes de la Reconquista valenciana," *Estudios medievales,* V (Valencia, 1952), 167–246. Cf. also J. Gautier-Dalché, "Islam et chrétienté en Espagne au XIIᵉ siècle: Contribution à l'étude de la notion de frontière," *Hespéris,* XLVI (1959), 183–217.

ing in al-Andalus to take over Spanish Islam, commencing with Seville, a process in which it became evident that their chief opponents were not the helpless Murābiṭ governors but the new Hispano-Moslem caudillos of the Second Taifas who had sprung up during the last years of Murābiṭ dominion. Foremost among these was the redoutable Muḥammad ibn-Sa‘d, Ibn-Mardanīsh (1152–1172), *el Rey Lobo* or the Wolf-King, as the Christians called him, who made himself ruler of Murcia and Valencia and for many years fought to expel the Muwaḥḥids and conquer all al-Andalus. In this he was aided by his able general and father-in-law Ibn-Hamushk, by large bodies of Christian mercenaries, and by the friendship of Raymond Berenguer IV and Alfonso VII, who saw him as a shield against the new Maghribin imperialism. In 1159 Ibn-Mardanīsh besieged Jaen, Cordova, and Seville without success; in 1161 he captured Granada; and thereafter his mixed Moorish-Christian armies overcame the Muwaḥḥid forces in three battles before the exasperated caliph ‘Abd-al-Mu’min himself crossed the strait and defeated him near his capital of Murcia. Even then, Ibn-Mardanīsh managed to retain control over most of southeastern Spain, his big realm of Murcia-Valencia serving as a protective buffer between Aragon-Catalonia and Muwaḥḥid Andalusia until his death in 1172.

Islamic civil war in al-Andalus and Muwaḥḥid attempts to suppress continuing opposition in the Maghrib encouraged Christian hopes of maintaining the momentum of the reconquest. In 1151 the emperor Alfonso VII and king Raymond Berenguer IV optimistically drew up at Tudellén the first of the great partition pacts of reconquest diplomatic history which allotted zones of future occupation in Moslem Spain to particular Christian states. In this covenant of January 27, 1151, Alfonso VII, acting on the premise that he held title as Hispanic emperor to all territory recovered from the Moors, conceded the Aragonese-Catalan crown the right to reconquer and hold in fief of him the entire southeast from the limits of the old kingdom of Tortosa down through the realms of Valencia, Denia, and Murcia (except the castles of Lorca and Vera) all the way to Castilian-held Almeria. This encouraged Raymond Berenguer, after eliminating the last Moorish outposts in Catalonia in the sierra of Prades and at Miravet (1152–1153), to look hungrily towards Valencia, although for the time being his and the king-emperor's friendship pacts with Ibn-Mardanīsh restrained him from open aggression. Alfonso VII, on the other hand, continued his war in Andalusia, vainly besieging Cordova (1150), repulsing the first ominous Muwaḥḥid effort to recover Almeria, and in 1155 capturing Andújar and trying also for Jaen and Guadix, the vital stations on the overland route from Muradal to his Mediterranean port.

Meanwhile, in the Portuguese sector king Afonso I moved on from Lisbon across the Tagus to seize Almada and Palmela, which gave him control of the strategic peninsula between the Tagus and the Sado. Lisbon's new English bishop, Gilbert of Hastings, was sent back to his island home to recruit crusaders for the next target along the coast, the regional Moorish capital of Alcácer do Sal. Strengthened by foreign auxiliaries the Portuguese attacked this stronghold in 1151 or 1152, again in 1154, and a third time in 1157, being joined in this last year by a crusader fleet en route to Palestine under the count of Flanders, Thierry of Alsace. But it was not until 1158 that, unaided, they were successful. Allying himself with various anti-Muwaḥḥid chieftains in the south, king Afonso was also able to occupy Évora and Beja far down in Alentejo, and thus to threaten the whole Moslem position in the lower Guadiana valley and Algarve.

Before long, however, as the Muwaḥḥid caliphate firmly established itself throughout the Maghrib and moved to enlarge its territorial base on the Spanish side of the strait, its resistance to further Christian expansion became formidable. In the summer of 1157, in fact, Muwaḥḥid sea and land forces closed in on Almeria; in spite of Alfonso VII's stout defense the precious port had to be abandoned to the enemy. Even worse, the Berber army drove the Leonese and Castilians back across Andalusia, recovering all the Baeza-Úbeda region Alfonso had held for over a decade, and streamed through the Muradal pass to invade southern New Castile. During this retreat the king-emperor died at Fresneda (August 21, 1157); and his will compounded the disaster by assigning Leon and the imperial title to one son, Ferdinand II, and Castile to another, Sancho III, a splitting of the Hispanic empire that resulted in seventy years of interstate rivalry and seriously impeded the reconquest until in 1230 Ferdinand III reunited the two kingdoms permanently.

The earlier Muwaḥḥid caliphs—'Abd-al-Mu'min, Yūsuf I (1163–1184), Ya'qūb al-Manṣūr (1184–1199), and Muḥammad an-Nāṣir (1199–1213)—ruled a stronger, better organized, more enduring empire on both sides of the strait than had the Murābiṭs; and between 1150 and 1212 great African armies, not infrequently led by the caliph in person, crossed into Spain on numerous occasions. But for all their power the lords of Marrakesh could not field sufficient forces to cope at any given time with more than two of the three sectors of the Iberian frontier—west, center, and east—so that after 1150 the reconquest tended to advance in at least one of these subdivisions, even when halted or in retreat in the other two. This becomes evident as early as the death of Alfonso VII. Sancho III (1157–1158), his successor in Castile, reigned only a single year, during which Muwaḥḥid incursions above Muradal forced him to replace the Templar garrison at battered Old Calatrava by a religious military confraternity; this, organized by the Navarrese Cistercian abbot of Fitero, Raymond, and one of his monks, the veteran frontier warrior Diego Velázquez, swiftly developed into the first native Iberian military order, that of Calatrava. Sancho also negotiated with his brother Ferdinand II of Leon the treaty of Sahagún (May 23, 1158) which projected southward into al-Andalus the demarcation line between their kingdoms and, by assigning Leon not only Extremadura and western Andalusia but also Alentejo and Algarve, seemed to deny any future to the Portuguese reconquest.

King Afonso I's subjects, however, ignored this pact and indeed took advantage of the fact that the Muwaḥḥids were concentrating their attacks upon Castile and Ibn-Mardanīsh to overrun much of the Alentejan-Extremaduran region through which the modern Spanish-Portuguese boundary now runs. Here a talented military commander, Gerald the Fearless *(Geraldo sem Pavor),* often called the Portuguese Cid, who like Rodrigo Díaz belonged to the large class of aristocratic soldiers-of-fortune that the reconquest produced in every stage of its history, assembled a private army *(mesnada)* with which he seized most of the leading fortified Moorish towns in the area. Having perfected techniques of nocturnal surprise in wintry or stormy weather, stealthy escalading of walls by picked commando-like troops, cutting down of sentries and opening of town gates to the larger force stationed without, Gerald made himself lord of Serpa, Évora, Cáceres, Montánchez, Trujillo, and other citadels. By about 1165 he seemed to be on the point of carrying the Portuguese banner so far east in the basin of the lower Guadiana as to confine Leon's southern expansion to the Transierra district just below the Tagus. This thoroughly alarmed Ferdinand II, who proceeded to take Alcántara from the Moors, thus assuring himself safe passage across the famous trans-Tagan bridge (1166), and then entered into a military alliance with caliph Yūsuf so that both might coöperate against their common Portuguese foe.

This did not deter Gerald from getting possession in 1169 of the city of Badajoz, except for its *alcazaba* where the garrison took refuge. Caliph, king-emperor, and Afonso I of Portugal all rushed to the Guadiana city; in one of the more remarkable episodes of the reconquest the Leonese army drove the Portuguese from Badajoz, relieved the Moorish garrison, and took prisoner both the wounded king Afonso and the fearless Gerald. The two captives purchased their release by surrendering many of Gerald's captured towns either to Ferdinand II or to Yūsuf; the latter was now free to march off to the east, where in 1171 he decisively defeated Ibn-Mardanīsh and, after the latter's death in 1172, annexed Murcia and Valencia to his domains. With the caliphal army now so remote, Gerald the Fearless escaladed and took Beja in lower Alentejo (1172), amid renewed fighting among Portuguese, Leonese, and Moors throughout the Guadiana valley; but after quarreling with his king, apparently over whether to hold or raze Beja, Gerald in anger went over to the Muwaḥḥid side and accompanied the caliph to Morocco. Here he was given the governorship of Sūs, only to be put to death some time later when seized correspondence revealed he was proposing to turn this district over to king Afonso as a base for Portuguese invasion of the Maghrib.

During the long minorities of Alfonso II (1162–1196) in Aragon-Catalonia and of Alfonso VIII (1158–1214) in Castile, when conspiracies and wars among noble factions seeking to dominate each kingdom left the Moorish frontier largely unguarded save for the border nobility and the militias of adjacent towns, the Muwaḥḥids were too busy quelling a rebellion at Tunis and too torn between the military demands of the Maghrib and Spain to take advantage of this situation. By the 1170's it was too late. In 1169, even before the defeat and death of Ibn-Mardanīsh, Alfonso II was moving into the northern reaches of the Valencian kingdom, annexing Caspe, Alcañiz, and Guadalaviar, founding Teruel (1171)—thenceforth the major bastion of lower Aragon—and leading armies south as far as Valencia and Jativa (1172). In 1177 he went all the way to Murcia; but this had the effect of arousing Alfonso VIII who, in spite of the treaty of Tudellén, regarded this kingdom as falling within his sphere of future reconquest. The result, on March 20, 1179, was the new partition treaty of Cazorla, which restricted the Aragonese-Catalans territorially, although it relieved them of doing homage to the emperor for their southeastern acquisitions. The utmost limits of their permissible reconquest were now shifted from the southern to the northern boundary of the kingdom of Murcia, along a line from Biar, near Villena, to the sea at Calpe (in modern Alicante province), thus reserving Murcia for Castile.

Castile, in the years preceding the Cazorla settlement, had been experiencing extreme danger and scoring two notable successes. In 1172, determined to punish Alfonso VIII and the Castilians for their southern raids, Yūsuf mustered in Andalusia an army of Africans and Hispano-Moslems whose numbers contemporary sources reckon at 100,000. With this large host he crossed the Muradal, throwing out detachments to assail smaller Castilian settlements north of the Sierra Morena, and headed for the Tagus valley where he proceeded to besiege Huete, a Castilian frontier stronghold between Moslem Cuenca and the Tagus. The town was completely surrounded, its water supply was cut, and, with the caliph himself watching from before his red tent pitched on an adjoining hill, the Muwaḥḥid soldiers to the accompaniment of rolling drums and wild battle-cries tried to storm Huete. The garrison, commanded by count Nuño Manríquez, resisted stubbornly; an extraordinary mid-July rainfall relieved—miraculously, it was believed—the thirst of the besieged; and rations ran short in the Moorish camp, so that on the news of Alfonso VIII's approach with the royal army the caliph gave orders to retreat southward. This sorry failure the caliph could not repair, although remaining several years in Spain and launching various lesser offensives against Castile. Alfonso VIII in turn, with the help of Alfonso II of Aragon, placed Cuenca under siege in 1177; and after nine months received the surrender of this base on the mountainous rim of the New Castilian tableland, invaluable for further advances toward the south and east.

Over a quarter of a century had now elapsed since the Muwaḥḥid counteroffensive had become the chief barrier to reconquest advance. Although the years 1150–1177 had seen the Moslems recover Almeria and upper Andalusia, halt Portuguese penetration of Alentejo and Extremadura, invade Castile as far as Huete, and launch scores of destructive raids in all directions, this had slowed, but in no sense reversed, the insistent southern encroachments of the Christians. By 1180 the struggle had long assumed the shape of a gigantic duel in which each combatant could deal the other heavy blows but not mortal wounds; though this was partly due to their rough equality in effective strength—a parity intermittently upset by the landing of huge armies from Morocco—it was imposed even more by the special geographic conditions of the arena over which much of the conflict raged.

On the western and eastern flanks of the long frontier zone the duelists were in more or less continuous contact, but in the vast center they were separated by the bleak, thinly populated plateaux and steppelands of the southern half of the Iberian tableland (meseta), across which each side had to travel to strike its opponent.

In this epoch reconquest warfare was noteworthy for sieges and innumerable skirmishes but few pitched battles. Especially characteristic were the long-range cavalry incursions *(cabalgadas, correduras)* of fast-moving raiders and the larger invasions or penetrations *(entradas, algaras)* of horsemen *(caballeros, jinetes)*, infantry *(peones)*, and archers under the banner of free-lance nobles, frontier officials, frontier towns, or, when the king himself led the campaign, the full royal host *(hueste)* of the kingdom. Royal law codes, notably the *Siete Partidas* of Alfonso X, and Spanish and Portuguese municipal legislation of the twelfth and thirteenth centuries preserve a vivid picture of such bands and armies marching across the plains country of the Guadiana basin between the Tagus and the Sierra Morena on their way to attack unsuspecting towns or castles, throwing forward a column of highly mobile raiders (the *algara* proper) while the remaining troops of the *alzaga* constructed a fortified encampment in which the returning horsemen with their booty, livestock, and ransomable captives could find shelter against the inevitable counter-raid. Particularly do the town law codes *(fueros, forais)* contain for the frontier urban militias, upon which kings were becoming increasingly dependent, detailed regulations on the service obligations of their noble and non-noble citizens *(vecinos)*, the arms and other equipment required, the command structure, booty division, and compensation for wounds, and the terms of employment of spies and scouts. Adoption of Arabic military terminology and of such ruses as the feigned cavalry retreat *(rebato, torna fuye)* shows that enemy techniques and tactics influenced this Christian frontier warfare, while numerous royal, municipal, and papal condemnations of supplying the Moors with weapons, foodstuffs, or other strategic materiel such as horses make it plain that a lively contraband trade existed.[9]

9. Cf. *Las Siete Partidas,* Partida II (ed. M. M. Rivadeneyra, *Los Códigos españoles concordados y anotados,* 2nd ed., 12 vols., Madrid, 1872–1873, II); *Fuero de Cuenca* (ed. R. de Ureña y Smenjaud, Madrid, 1935), *passim;* A. Palomeque Torres, "Contribución al estudio del ejército en los estados de la Reconquista," *Anuario de historia del derecho español,* XV (1944), 205–351; C. Pescador, "La Caballería popular en León y Castilla," *Cuadernos de historia de España,* XXXIII–XXXIV (1961), 101–238; XXXV–XXXVI (1962), 56–201; XXXVII–XXXVIII (1963), 88–198; XXXIX–XL (1964), 169–260; J. Oliver Asín, "Origen árabe de rebato, arrobda y sus homónimos: Contribución al estudio de la historia medieval de la táctica militar y de su léxico peninsular," *Boletín de la R. Academia española,* XV (1928), 347–395, 496–542; J. F. Powers, "The Origins and Development of Municipal Military Service in the Leonese and Castilian Reconquest, 800–1250," *Traditio,* XXVI (1970), 91–111; and E. Lourie, "A Society Organized for War: Medieval Spain," *Past and Present,* no. 35 (December, 1966), 54–76. Consult, on castles, C. Sarthou Carreres, *Castillos de España* (3rd ed., Madrid, 1952); on routes across the southern Meseta, M. Criado de Val, *Teoría de Castilla la Nueva* (Madrid, 1960); and, on tribute and booty, H. Grassotti,

On the defensive side, to keep guard over border castles and towns, and to form the first line of resistance against serious attacks across the frontier, there were developed, in addition to the municipal militias, two types of standing armed forces: professional fighters and soldiers-of-fortune who lived off the spoils of forays and skirmishes; and the knights and sergeants of the military orders, both Palestinian and Iberian, whose rules show them sleeping clothed with weapons at their side, ready for instant action. Mimesis of the Templars and Hospitallers, present in the peninsular kingdoms from the 1120's, seems a far more likely inspiration for the Iberian groups than, as often contended, the Moslem *ribāṭ* and its *jihād* combatants.[10] We have already mentioned the religio-military confraternities springing up in the Ebro valley in the days of Alfonso the Warrior. Leon, Castile, and Portugal produced similar societies in the twelfth century in the *fratres* of Avila, Segovia, Salamanca, Évora, and other towns.

The first true Iberian military order, that of Calatrava, was founded in 1158, as noted above, by the Navarrese Cistercians of Fitero; granted approval of its rule in 1164 by Alexander III, it speedily acquired lands, castles, and commanderies in Aragon, Leon, and Portugal as well as in Castile, with its headquarters first at Old, then at New, Calatrava. From the castle given it in 1211 by Afonso II, the Portuguese branch took the name the Order of Avis. In Leonese Extremadura the Order of St. James (Santiago) arose in 1170 from the *Fratres de Caceres,* with the support of Ferdinand II and of the Compostelan archbishop Peter Gudestéiz, who was eager to recover

---

"Para la Historia del botín y de las parias en León y Castilla," *Cuadernos de historia de España,* XXXIX–XL (1964), 43–132.

10. In the debate over the historical genesis of the reconquest military orders, mimesis of the Islamic *ribāṭ* is argued by Oliver Asín, *op. cit.,* pp. 540–542; Castro, *Realidad histórica,* chapter 7; and M. Cocheril, "Essai sur l'origine des ordres militaires dans la péninsule ibérique," *Collectanea Ordinis Cisterciensium Reformatorum,* XX (1958), 346–361; XXI (1959), 228–250, 302–329; for the thesis of Christian origin based upon Holy Land precedent, see especially D. Lomax, *La Orden de Santiago (1170–1275)* (Madrid, 1965), pp. 1–8. On the Iberian military confraternities, consult P. Rassow, "La Cofradía de Belchite," *Anuario de historia del derecho español,* III (1926), 200–226. Also of prime value are Lomax, *op. cit.* (the one full-length scientific study of a single order); *idem,* "Las Milicias cistercienses en el reino de León," *Hispania,* XXIII (1963), 29–42; José-Luis Martín, "Orígenes de la Orden Militar de Santiago (1170–1195)," *Anuario de estudios medievales,* IV (1967), 571–590; J. F. O'Callaghan, "The Foundation of the Order of Alcántara, 1176–1218," *Catholic Historical Review,* XLVII (1961–1962), 471–486; S. A. García Larragueta, *El Gran Priorato de Navarra de la Orden de San Juan de Jerusalén, siglos XII–XIII* (2 vols., Pamplona, 1957); and A. J. Forey, "The Order of Mountjoy," *Speculum,* XLVI (1971), 250–266, and *The Templars in the Corona de Aragón* (London, 1973). On the Portuguese orders, Gama Barros, *História da administração em Portugal,* II, 291–340, is unsuperseded, though dated.

his Moslem-occupied suffraganates between the Tagus and the Guadiana. Quickly spreading into Alfonso VIII's Castile as well as Portugal and Aragon, Santiago administered its rapidly expanding patrimonies from Uclés in Castile and San Marcos in the city of Leon. By 1176 a third major order, primarily Leonese, that of St. Julian of Pereiro, which from 1218 became known as Alcántara, had come into existence; and in this same decade there was founded the relatively short-lived Order of Montegaudio (1175), active primarily in Aragon. Later royal foundations of still other military orders, such as those of St. George of Alfama in the Crown of Aragon (by Peter II in 1201) and Alfonso X's ephemeral Santa María de España, or those replacing the abolished Templars—the Order of Montesa in Aragon (by James II in 1317) and the Order of Christ in Portugal (by king Dinís in 1319)—make it clear how indispensable a role these increasingly aristocratic corporations played in the reconquest for the rest of the Middle Ages.

The anti-Muwaḥḥid reconquest, by reason of the emphasis both sides gave to raids aimed at seizing persons as well as livestock and movable property, led to a strong interest in the redemption of Christian captives from Moorish hands. Procedures for ransoming now became institutionalized in the hands of professional redemption agents *(alfaqueques, exeas),* whose methods and responsibilities the royal and municipal law codes defined; gifts to the church for redemptionist purposes multiplied; and such new organizations as the Order of Santiago or king Alfonso II of Aragon's Hospital of the Holy Redeemer at Teruel (by 1188) devoted part of their incomes *ad redimendos captivos.* Two new religious orders also took shape specifically for this purpose: that of the Most Holy Trinity, founded in France in 1198 by St. John of Matha, which early became active below the Pyrenees; and the Order of St. Mary of Mercy, which (by 1218 or 1223) grew out of the redemptionist work of St. Peter Nolasco at Barcelona. Trinitarians and Mercedarians, not only in Spain but in Morocco, Tlemsen, and Tunis, now labored to secure the release of thousands from Moslem captivity, often at great risk or even by substitution of their own persons.[11]

The appearance of these military and redemptorist orders manifestly reflected heightening religious and crusading fervor in the struggle against the Muwaḥḥid caliphate. This is further indicated by what few details are known about the propagation in the mid-twelfth

11. M. Heimbucher, *Die Orden und Kongregationen der katholischen Kirche* (3rd ed., Munich, 1965), pp. 448–455, 571–576; G. Vázquez Núñez, *Manual de historia de la Orden de Nuestra Señora de la Merced* (Toledo, 1931).

century of the cults of St. James the Moorslayer *(Santiago Mata-moros*—a guise in which, contrary to frequent asseveration, the Apostle had not previously appeared) and of his firmly anti-Leonese-Castilian counterpart in the Crown of Aragon, St. George.[12] Along with these warrior saints viewed as patrons of the reconquest, the Virgin Mary also was considered a champion of Hispanic liberation from the Islamic yoke. Popular preaching of the crusade, constant papal encouragement of the anti-Muwaḥḥid war, and the ferocity of the fighting itself were so intensifying the ideological and emotional dynamics of the conflict that by the thirteenth century the Riojan poet Gonzalo of Berceo could depict the Moors as responsible for the Crucifixion.

By 1180 strenuous efforts to break the prevailing deadlock in the long war can be discerned on the part of both Muwaḥḥids and Christians. The caliphal fleet from Ceuta struck repeatedly at Lisbon in king Afonso I's last years, until driven off by his capable admiral Fuas Roupinho. In 1183 caliph Yūsuf himself, assembling another huge Maghribin-Andalusian host, marched across Alentejo to strike at Santarem. In a bitterly contested siege the Portuguese garrison not only held out but succeeded in penetrating the enemy camp, and in desperate hand-to-hand fighting broke through the caliph's Negro bodyguard and mortally wounded Yūsuf, who died as the shattered Moorish army retreated southward.

Two years after this resounding triumph the aged Afonso I was succeeded by his son Sancho I (1185–1211), and he and the new caliph Ya'qūb resumed the war in the western sector. For several years, however, the new Muwaḥḥid sovereign was busy in Africa shoring up his disputed authority there, so that in 1189, the year of the Third Crusade, the Portuguese were able to strike another heavy blow. They organized a seaborne expedition and, with the support of twelve thousand Frisians and Danes who had arrived in Lisbon that spring, sailed around Cape St. Vincent to the south coast of Algarve, where they stormed the large castle of Alvor. Here, contrary to peninsular practice, the northern crusaders barbarously slaughtered some six thousand prisoners of war. In mid-July, when a second fleet, this time laden with Germans, Englishmen, and Flemings, put in at the Tagus on its way east, Sancho I took his army overland to join the crusader fleet in an assault on Silves, the chief town of

12. C. Sánchez Albornoz, *España: un enigma,* I, 268, 273–287; A. Canellas López, "Leyenda, culto y patronazgo en Aragón del señor San Jorge, mártir y caballero," *J. Zurita Cuadernos de Historia,* nos. 19–20 (1966–1967), 7–22.

central Algarve. After a siege fought in midsummer heat amid the usual exacerbation of feelings between Iberians and crusaders, the city fell in early September. The Portuguese king this time succeeded in preventing a general slaughter of the vanquished.[13]

Santarem, Alvor, and Silves were impressive successes but Ya'qūb, destined to be remembered in Maghribin annals as al-Manṣūr (the Conqueror), was now ready to reply in kind. In 1190 he dispatched an army of Andalusians to invest Silves, while he himself invaded Portugal, devastating the countryside, and in Ribatejo, well north of Lisbon, destroying to its foundations the powerful base of Tôrres Novas, although a similar attempt there to wipe out the Templar stronghold of Tomar failed. In 1191 he recovered Alcácer do Sal, which had been in Portuguese hands since 1158; then, after receiving in the same year the surrender of Silves, and judging Portugal sufficiently punished, he turned to harass Alfonso VIII of Castile.

Castile in the 1180's, like Portugal, was the scene of furious strokes and counterstrokes. In 1182, while Muwaḥḥid attention was focused on the imminent siege of Santarem, Alfonso VIII invaded Andalusia, besieged Cordova and Écija, and dared place a garrison in the castle of Setefilla, on the Guadalquivir above Seville. When the Moors, unable to take this potential base for raiders, tried a diversionary invasion of the Tagus valley, they accomplished little except to cause Ferdinand II of Leon to break off his old friendship with the Muwaḥḥids; in 1184 both kings joined in pressing the war at Cáceres and Alarcón, respectively, a policy continued after Alfonso IX ascended the Leonese throne in 1188.

This promising Leonese-Castilian coöperation, however, in 1195 met with disastrous consequences. That year caliph Ya'qūb was again in Spain, preparing to march north with the customary large force of Berber, Arab, Negro, and Andalusian troops. Alfonso VIII, unwisely failing to wait as planned for the arrival of Alfonso IX and the Leonese army, hastened south to engage the enemy as soon as possible. At Alarcos, southwest of Ciudad Real, on July 19, 1195, he led his army of nobles and urban militiamen into the largest battle the Guadiana plains had seen in many years. The heavy mass of some seven or eight thousand Castilian armored cavalrymen drove back the Muwaḥḥid center but failed to break through; in the savage hand-to-hand encounter the far more numerous Moslems surrounded the Christian army on both flanks and in the rear. From the crushing

13. *Narratio de itinere navali peregrinorum Hierosolymam tendentium et Silvam capien-tium, A.D. 1189* (ed. C. W. David, *Proceedings of the American Philosophical Society,* LXXXI, 1939, no. 5, pp. 591–678).

defeat that followed, Alfonso VIII barely escaped with his life and found refuge in Toledo.[14]

Alarcos was an impressive victory by a great Moslem commander, but it was destined to be Islam's last major triumph in the peninsula. It halted reconquest advance for a decade and a half but, just as after Zallaca in 1086, a decisive full-scale invasion of Castile did not ensue, only destructive raids around Talavera and Toledo (1196, 1197). Castilian determination to resume the offensive at the earliest opportunity remained unshaken. Peter II of Aragon-Catalonia (1196–1213), furthermore, supported Alfonso in this crisis by reconquering the rugged highland district of Rincón de Ademuz in the Iberian cordillera, thus relieving pressure on Castile from the east.

Following Ya'qūb al-Manṣūr's death in 1199, his much less able successor Muḥammad an-Nāṣir (1199–1213) was content to maintain a truce with Alfonso, so that the Castilian monarch was relatively free to commence preparations for an international crusade to regain the initiative lost at Alarcos. During the next decade Castile strengthened its border fortresses, built up its army, and tightened its ties with the other peninsular kingdoms. By 1210 these preparations were rapidly maturing when, in anticipation of early resumption of large-scale hostilities, the Muwaḥḥids moved a large army across the strait, marched north of Muradal, and captured the castle of Salvatierra, then the seat of the Order of Calatrava and a major base for *entradas* into Andalusia (1211). In this year, as in early 1212, Innocent III, who shared Alfonso's conviction that the great crisis of the reconquest was at hand and that all possible European assistance should be given Christendom's Iberian defenders, addressed bulls and letters to Spain and France, calling upon the Iberian kings to coöperate in the forthcoming crusade, to which as usual he extended the Holy Land indulgence, and urging the French and Provençal hierarchies to preach the cross and raise recruits.

With this papal backing, an international army now commenced to muster at Toledo, at its core the full Castilian royal *hueste* of nobles, town militias, members of military orders, and mercenaries. From the other peninsular kingdoms came king Peter II of Aragon, with some three thousand knights and a strong force of crossbowmen; numerous Portuguese and a smaller band of Leonese, permitted to serve by their kings, who themselves remained aloof; and, joining later, king Sancho VII of Navarre with two hundred retainers. Over

14. González, *Alfonso VIII,* I, 952–970; Huici, *Grandes batallas,* pp. 137–216; Terrasse, *Histoire du Maroc,* I, 327–328. On papal reconquest policy during this period, cf. H. Roscher, *Papst Innocenz III. und die Kreuzzüge* (Göttingen, 1969).

the Pyrenees streamed thousands of south French knights and other crusaders, mounted and on foot, whom the Castilians had to restrain by force from massacring Toledo's Jewish community.

On June 20, 1212, this Christian army, the greatest the reconquest had ever seen, moved south to meet the even larger Muwaḥḥid host commanded personally by caliph Muḥammad an-Nāṣir. During the crossing of the Guadiana plains the summer heat, shortage of rations, and a bout of hard fighting around Old Calatrava that yielded little spoil proved too much for the trans-Pyrenean crusaders; on July 3 they ignominiously quit the crusade and returned home. The Iberians, however, veterans of plains warfare, pushed on resolutely, retook Alarcos of unhappy memory, and, skirting Moslem-held Salvatierra, reached the foot of Muradal on July 12, to find the pass already blocked and the high ground about the defile occupied by detachments of the enormous Muwaḥḥid army already visible in the distance. A local rustic, it is said, pointed out an alternate route by which the Christians in long slow column descended into the plains (navas) on the Andalusian side of the Sierra Morena, where the greatest battle of all reconquest history, Las Navas de Tolosa, was to be joined.

On both the 14th and the 15th the Moslems deployed for battle in three lines, the great central mass of horse and foot screened by a vanguard of light-armed Berbers, Arabs, and bands of archers. Muḥammad an-Nāṣir stationed himself with the rearguard, surrounded by his Negro bodyguard and the massed banners and drums, where, seated on his shield before his red tent, clad in the black cloak of his predecessor 'Abd-al-Mu'min, sword and Koran in hand, he could direct his commanders. The Christians, however, carefully observing the enemy order of battle, refused to engage on either day. But on the 16th, at dawn, they drew up in battle array in three lines, their left wing under king Peter II of Aragon, their right under king Sancho VII of Navarre, and the center under Alfonso VIII, who remained with his rearguard, behind the second line of Castilian nobles and the military orders. In contrast with Alarcos, the less experienced municipal militias were distributed in all three lines of each division and reinforced by cavalry. The Christian vanguard began the attack, crashing through the Arab and Berber skirmishers, and with the second line closed with the main body of the Muwaḥḥid troops.

Sanguinary but indecisive fighting raged for hours, but when the caliph ordered his reserves into the struggle, the weary Christian center and flanks fell back. At this critical juncture Alfonso VIII, resolved to conquer or die, threw himself and the strong rearguard into the attack, while Peter II and Sancho VII rallied the wings. In the face of this general Christian counterassault the Moslems, commencing reputedly with the Andalusian contingents but soon continuing with the Berbers and Arabs, began to give way. As confusion and panic spread, the Christians broke through to the area of the red tent, cutting down the fiercely resisting Negro guards. Muḥammad an-Nāṣir barely managed to escape on horseback, and his whole immense army streamed rearward, hotly pursued by the Christian cavalry with immense slaughter while the infantry fell upon the rich spoils of the Muwaḥḥid camp.[15]

Thus on July 16, 1212, was Alarcos avenged at Las Navas de Tolosa. With no help other than the encouragement of Innocent III, the Iberians had shattered the full might of the Muwaḥḥid caliphate, dealing it a blow from which neither in Spain nor in Africa was it destined to recover. For the first time since 1150, the road to the reconquest of Andalusia, Algarve, and the southeast at last lay open.

As so often in reconquest history, the fruits of victory were slow to be harvested.[16] Although after Las Navas Alfonso VIII quickly seized New Calatrava and other fortresses above the Sierra Morena, and Baeza and Úbeda in Andalusia, his efforts were cut short by death in 1214; and under the regency for his son Henry I (1214–1217) and during the early reign of Ferdinand III (the son of Alfonso VIII's daughter Berengaria by Alfonso IX of Leon), internal dissensions halted Castilian advance. Similar disorders swept Aragon during the minority of James I, after his father Peter II, who had fought so valiantly at Las Navas, died in the battle of Muret (1213) while supporting the Albigensians against Simon of Montfort and his crusaders.

15. González, I, 981–1057; Huici, pp. 219–327; F. Lot, *L'Art militaire et les armées au moyen âge* (2 vols., Paris, 1946), II, 276–292 (often inaccurate and tendentious).
16. The Castilian chronicles listed above (note 8) cover wholly or in part the Fernandine reconquest of Andalusia. But little publication of the indispensable royal and municipal charters has yet taken place. James I's reconquest is much better documented by A. Huici, *Colección diplomática de Jaime I el Conquistador* (3 vols., Valencia, 1916–1922), and by three major royal chronicles: (i) the *Crónica de Jaime I,* ascribed to the king himself but more likely the work of a royal secretary enjoying James's collaboration (ed. M. de Aguiló, *Chronica, o commentaris . . . del rey En Jaume primier,* Barcelona, 1873; Eng. tr. by J. Forster, *The Chronicle of James I, King of Aragon, surnamed the Conqueror,* 2 vols., London, 1883); (ii) Bernat Desclot, *Crónica del rey En Pere e dels seus antecessors passats* (ed. M. Coll Alentorn, *Crónica de Bernat Desclot,* 5 vols., Barcelona, 1949–1951; Eng. tr. by F. L. Critchlow, *Chronicle of the Reign of King Pedro III of Aragon,* 2 vols., Princeton, 1928–1934); and (iii) Ramón Muntaner, *Chronica, o descripció dels fets e hazanyes del Ynclit rey Don Jaume primer* (2 vols., Barcelona, 1927–1951). See now, for all these works,

To the west, however, the fight against the Moslems actively continued. The Portuguese, eager to throw back the Muwaḥḥids below Palmela, welcomed in July 1217 the arrival of a fleet of some two hundred ships of the Fifth Crusade. Approximately half of these, carrying mostly German crusaders under the command of counts George of Wied and William of Holland, were persuaded to join Afonso II's army in a sea and land assault on Alcácer do Sal. A combined northern and Portuguese squadron blockaded the mouth of the Sado during the two months' siege; the Portuguese, with Leonese aid, turned back a Moorish relief column; and on October 18, 1217, Alcácer capitulated, so that after half a century the frontier could once more sweep eastward from the Atlantic into Alentejo.

In Leon also Alfonso IX was moving vigorously toward reconquering Extremadura from weakening Muwaḥḥid hands. In 1218–1219 his forces, among whom the military orders took a prominent role, besieged Cáceres, at first without success; but by 1221 they managed to capture Valencia de Alcántara, the city's chief protective fortress to the north, and in 1227 Cáceres capitulated. In 1230, just before Alfonso's death in September, the Leonese took possession of some other Extremaduran towns, including Montánchez, Mérida, and Badajoz, so that the Leonese reconquest was now firmly anchored all along the Guadiana from Mérida to Badajoz and south across the prized pasturelands of southern Extremadura to the slopes of the Sierra Morena.

By 1230, furthermore, both Castile and Aragon-Catalonia, free from their dark years of minorities and internal disorders, were in the capable hands of two of the foremost kings in reconquest annals, Ferdinand III (1217–1252) and James I the Conqueror (el Conquis-

---

Ferran Soldevilla, ed., *Jaume I, Bernat Desclot, Ramon Muntaner, Pere III: Les quatres grans cròniques* (Barcelona, 1971).

The most informative modern works are, for Andalusia, J. González, "Las Conquistas de Fernando III en Andalucía," *Hispania*, VI (1946), 515–631; *idem, Repartimiento de Sevilla* (2 vols., Madrid, 1951); and M. Ballesteros, "La Conquista de Jaén por Fernando III el Santo," *Cuadernos de historia de España*, XX (1953), 63–138; and for Murcia, A. Ballesteros, "La Reconquista de Murcia," *Boletín de la R. Academia de la historia,* CXI (1942), 133–150. On James I's achievements, see J. Miret y Sans, *Itinerari de Jaume I "el Conqueridor"* (Barcelona, 1918); Ch. de Tourtoulon, *Jacme Ier le Conquérant* (2 vols., Montpellier, 1863); Soldevila, *Història de Catalunya,* I, pp. 272–304; J. M. Font y Rius, "La Reconquista y repoblación de Levante y Murcia," in *Reconquista española,* pp. 85–126; J. E. Martínez Ferrando, ed., *Història del país valencià* (Barcelona, 1965), I, 253–333; and R. I. Burns, *The Crusader Kingdom of Valencia* (2 vols., Cambridge, Mass., 1967). For papal correspondence, and ecclesiastical restoration in the reconquered territories, cf., in addition to Goñi Gaztambide, *Bula de la Cruzada,* D. Mansilla Reoyo, *Iglesia castellano-leonesa y curia romana en los tiempos del rey San Fernando* (Madrid, 1945), pp. 34–90.

tador, 1213–1276). In Castile as far back as 1224 king Ferdinand had begun to take advantage of the civil strife in al-Andalus and the appearance of the caudillos of the Third Taifas. When in that year the governor of Baeza, 'Abd-Allāh ibn-Muḥammad ibn-'Umar ibn-'Abd-al-Mu'min, "al-Baiyāsī," declared himself caliph and threw Moslem Spain into political chaos, he appealed to the Castilian monarch for military assistance. Ferdinand, hopeful of resuming the reconquest where Alfonso VIII had left off, lost no time in fishing these troubled waters. In 1224 he captured Quesada and devastated adjacent districts in the Guadalquivir valley; in 1225 at Las Navas de Tolosa he made a pact with al-Baiyāsī under which the latter accepted Castilian vassalage and recognized that kingdom's rights to Martos, Andújar, Jaen, and other places (except Baeza) that might be recovered from his enemies. On this basis Ferdinand III's troops entered Andalusia, captured Priego and Loja, devastated the environs of Jaen and Granada, and compelled the latter city, under threat of immediate siege, to release all Christians it held captive. When in 1226 al-Baiyāsī was murdered by partisans of the caliph 'Abd-Allāh al-'Ādil (1224–1227) and his brother Idrīs, the governor of Cordova and Granada, the Castilians quickly occupied Baeza.

When Idrīs proclaimed himself the true caliph at Seville in 1227 and prepared to invade Morocco, Ferdinand agreed to provide troops for his army in return for the concession of ten Andalusian frontier fortresses, the right to build Christian churches in Marrakesh, and assurance of the personal safety there of all converted Moslems. With the help of these Castilian expeditionaries—like the alliance itself suggesting that so soon after Las Navas Castile had hopes of carrying the reconquest across the Strait of Gibraltar—Idrīs was successful in Morocco, but in 1228, during his absence from al-Andalus, another Hispano-Moslem caudillo, Muḥammad ibn-Yūsuf Ibn-Hūd, raised the black flag of the 'Abbāsids against the Muwaḥḥid caliphate, and was widely accepted throughout al-Andalus. This allowed Ferdinand III, posing as a defender of Idrīs, to besiege Jaen and devastate as far as the fertile Vega plain outside Granada, returning home with rich spoils and numerous captives.

In the midst of these events, in 1230, on the death of his father Alfonso IX, Ferdinand inherited the Leonese crown. The two states, separated and often at war since 1157, were now definitively reunited in what is commonly styled the kingdom of Castile, a reunion which made possible coördination of Christian efforts all along the reconquest frontier from Extremadura to Andalusia. In 1231 archbishop Rodrigo of Toledo reoccupied Quesada and various castles;

one of the latter, Cazorla, the Toletan church was to retain as the capital of a new border march to the east of Jaen, the Adelantamiento of Cazorla. In 1233 Ferdinand himself retook Úbeda; Ibn-Hūd, menaced by such other caudillos as Muḥammad ibn-Yūsuf Ibn-Naṣr, al-Aḥmar, was soon driven to make peace with Castile at the cost of surrendering various border fortresses. Disorder in Andalusia allowed the Leonese, particularly the military orders of Alcántara and Santiago, to strike hard blows in Extremadura, where in 1233 Trujillo fell, in 1234 Santa Cruz, Medellín, and Alange, and in 1235 Magacela.

By 1236 the civil wars in al-Andalus produced a major Islamic catastrophe, the loss of Cordova. Here in 1235 a Cordovan faction offered to help the Castilian nobles stationed at Andújar to take over the city's Ajarquía quarter, outside the walled Medina *(al-madīnah)* proper; when the plot succeeded and the Christians found themselves under attack from the city's garrison, they appealed to their king. Strong Castilian forces soon came up, invested Cordova, and on June 29, 1236, when it was on the verge of starvation and without hope of relief, the old Umaiyad capital surrendered. Ferdinand III's solemn entry into the fallen city, preceded by the affixing of the cross and the royal standard to the minaret of the famed caliphal mosque, can be taken as inaugurating the rapid downfall of Islamic power in Andalusia and Murcia. The fertile Cordovan countryside also now passed into Castilian power; and Ibn-Hūd, unable to retain his own kingdom of Murcia against the efforts of al-Aḥmar and the new Moroccan caliph, 'Abd-al-Wāḥid II ar-Rashīd, to overthrow him, had to purchase Castilian help by placing a number of Murcian towns, including the capital, under tribute to Castile and allowing Castilian garrisons to occupy their *alcázars.*

Ibn-Hūd died in 1238, leaving al-Aḥmar (1232–1273) as the chief Taifa ruler in al-Andalus, but this prince, who by 1237 had established his capital at Granada and—as Muḥammad I—founded the Naṣrid dynasty there, was not strong enough either to dominate all Moslem Spain or to hold back the steady Castilian infiltration all along its northern edges. When in 1244 he raided the environs of Andújar and Martos, Ferdinand III retaliated by first besieging and taking Arjona, and then going on to invest Jaen, one of the largest and best fortified of the Andalusian cities. During the long, difficult siege, which lasted from August 1245 to April 1246, al-Aḥmar tried without success to relieve the city. Finally, confronted with revolt in Granada itself, and desperate for peace with Castile, he agreed to allow Jaen's surrender, to become Ferdinand's tributary vassal, and, on summons, to attend the Castilian Cortes and serve with his troops in Castile's wars. It is this pact of Jaen in 1246 that ensured exclusion of Granada from the main Christian reconquest of al-Andalus, allowing this kingdom, under the Naṣrid dynasty descended from al-Aḥmar, to maintain itself to 1492 as a viable Moslem state.

The fall of Jaen in 1246 underscored the vulnerability of Seville, the economic and cultural center of Andalusia and, under both Murābiṭs and Muwaḥḥids, the chief Maghribin military base in Spain. It was against Seville that Ferdinand III next turned, in full awareness of the city's formidable defenses of walls, the protective encirclement of the Guadalquivir, and the outlying belt of guardian fortresses. Fortunately for Castile, in 1246 Seville was politically isolated: her citizens had refused allegiance to Marrakesh and driven out an extortionate governor sent them by king Yaḥyâ I of Ḥafṣid Tunisia, whose protection they had earlier solicited. In 1246 Ferdinand's warriors began by raiding Carmona on the Cordova-Seville highway and by storming the stronghold of Alcalá de Guadaira southeast of Seville. During the winter of 1246–1247 Raymond Boniface of Burgos was ordered to bring south ships from the ports of Cantabria, and the royal summons went out to towns and nobles for the convocation of the *hueste.* The summer of 1247 saw Castilian armies drive down the Carmona and Lora roads toward Seville, capture smaller towns en route, ravage all the countryside, and establish a fortified encampment at Tablada in preparation for a formal siege.

During the course of 1247 the city's walls were completely surrounded, the sallies of the besieged were repulsed, and under Raymond Boniface the first Castilian royal fleet to participate in a major reconquest enterprise moved up the Guadalquivir in the face of violent harassment from both banks. Throughout the winter of 1247–1248 the siege was vigorously pressed, with especially savage fighting by spring in the suburb of Macarena, at the powerful fortress of Triana located on the west side of the river and connected with the city by a pontoon bridge, and further down the Guadalquivir at Aznalfarache. As reinforcements poured in from all over Castile, Ferdinand moved his camp closer to the walls, while the fleet severed the pontoon bridge, isolating Triana. By autumn, Seville was completely cut off on the land and river sides, battered by catapults, and running short of provisions for the winter; on November 23, 1248, it capitulated. Once the city was emptied of inhabitants under the terms of surrender, the division of lands and properties *(reparto, repartimiento)* among the victors was drawn up, the royal entry took place, the chief mosque was consecrated as the cathedral, and Christian settlers moved in, so that Hispano-Moslem Seville now became a major Castilian city, the kingdom's chief military and naval base for Andalusia and the waters of the strait. On the morrow of his victory, without further fighting, Ferdinand also received the capitulation of other western Andalusian towns—Sanlúcar de Barrameda, Jerez de la Frontera, Puerto de Santa María, Cadiz (probably), Medina Sidonia, and Arcos, as well as Alcalá del Río north of Seville.

On the east coast the Aragonese-Catalan monarchy of James I was enjoying a no less spectacular series of reconquest triumphs. Once the bleak years of his minority were over, the young king revived the traditional expansion toward the southeast. In 1225 he mounted an abortive attack on the port of Peñiscola down the coast from Tortosa. By 1228 he was ready to undertake a major national effort, the reconquest of the Baleares, a project the Catalan Cortes greeted with enthusiasm and the concession of an extraordinary subsidy. An assembly of western Catalans and Aragonese at Lerida, however, refused support (even though the cardinal-legate Thomas de Episcopo affixed the cross to the royal mantle in their presence) on the grounds that the crusade should be directed not toward the islands, in which they had no commercial interest, but against the old Aragonese goal of Valencia. James's army, therefore, aside from a few Aragonese and south French combatants, was a predominantly Catalan one, and the occupation of the Baleares in 1229 a truly Catalan enterprise, demonstrating the principality's new naval strength as well as the effectiveness of its *almogàvers* (Castilian, *almogávares*) and other land troops.

On September 5, 1229, James's fleet of some 155 heavy ships and many lighter vessels, carrying a reputed fifteen hundred knights and fifteen thousand foot, sailed from Salou for Majorca. Disembarking at night on the north coast, the expeditionaries routed the Moslems from the nearby heights, and drove quickly south to the capital, Palma. The city held out resolutely for over three months, but the crusaders, after rejecting the governor Ibn-Yaḥyâ's offer to negotiate out of desire to avenge their fallen comrades, stormed the city on December 31 and slaughtered a large part of its population. The reconquest of the rest of the island took another fourteen months; and James, who had meanwhile returned to the mainland, twice had to come back to Majorca to continue the campaign, once in 1231 when a rumored Ḥafṣid expedition from Tunis failed to materialize, again in 1232 as Moorish resistance flared up in the hills. Many Moors were allowed to retain their lands, but the new Catalan colonial population now coming in ensured the establishment of that stock, language, and institutions. The Moslems of Minorca, threatened with large-scale invasion, surrendered in 1232; and in 1235, with royal approval, the archbishop-elect of Tarragona, William de Montgrín, the infante Peter of Portugal, and various Catalan magnates overran Ibiza and Formentera, both these islands becoming archiepiscopal fiefs of the church of Tarragona.

James I's second great triumph, the annexation of the old Moorish kingdom of Valencia, was a much more truly national enterprise. In this the Aragonese were predominant but the Catalans made significant contributions of money, men, and, above all, the ships required for provisioning the king's army, making landings, and blockading the coast. In 1232, fresh from his insular victories, king James stirred up general enthusiasm for a Valencian campaign, which Gregory IX proclaimed an authentic crusade. This turned out to be a much more formidable business than that of the Baleares; extending with pauses and truces over a period of thirteen years, it can be divided into three stages. In the first, 1232–1235, after Ares in the northwest was taken by the municipal army of Teruel, and Morella by the *ricohombre* Blasco of Alagón, the king himself, in a two-month siege, captured the important coastal town of Burriana (1233), which was to serve as a supply depot for foodstuffs brought from Catalonia; this victory was followed by the surrender of outflanked Peñíscola and other neighboring centers, while the Templars and Hospitallers, respectively, took over Chisvert and Cervera. By 1235, in short, the whole northern sector of the Valencian kingdom, roughly the modern province of Castellón, was in Christian possession.

The second phase of the Valencian reconquest, 1236–1238, saw operations focus upon the central zone and the capital. In 1236 James's army established a permanent base not far from Valencia city, on the hill known as Pueyo de la Cebolla or Puig de Santa María, where the Valencian king Ziyān ibn-Ṣa'd Ibn-Mardanīsh had recently destroyed a castle he had despaired of holding. As rebuilt by the Aragonese and provided with a strong garrison under the king's uncle Bernard William, this became the object of repeated Moorish onslaughts, but even after his kinsman fell in its defense king James refused to give up this strategic outpost. Returning to Valencia in 1238 with a larger army than ever, one that included a few English and French knights and archbishop Peter of Narbonne, he proceeded to place the capital, crowded as it was with refugees from smaller towns and the countryside, under tight investment by land and sea. Throughout the summer the siege machines battered the walls and houses; the defenders' frequent sallies were thrown back and hunger steadily sapped their ability to hold out. All hope of external succor vanished when a Ḥafṣid squadron of eighteen ships sent by king Yaḥyâ of Tunis failed to enter Valencia's harbor or to effect a landing at Peñíscola, so that on September 28, 1238, king Ziyān agreed to terms under which all who wished were given protected escort with their movables to his other cities of Cullera and Denia. The victors then proceeded to occupy Valencia and carry out the usual *repartimiento* of houses and lands within and outside the walls. Over the next few months Moorish sovereignty also ceased in various towns and castles below Valencia; by the end of 1238 the Aragonese frontier stood at the line of the river Júcar.

In the third and terminal phase of the Valencian war, 1239–1245, the Conqueror's warriors crossed the Júcar to annex the kingdom's southern sector, but at this point Ferdinand III of Castile, who had recently reconquered Cordova and was moving towards Jaen, and whose son the infante Alfonso (X) was engaged in occupying the kingdom of Murcia, intervened to impose a more precise demarcation of the zones of Castilian and Aragonese-Catalan reconquest as laid down in 1179 by the treaty of Cazorla. In the new partition treaty of Almizra (1244) the two kings reaffirmed the Cazorla line based on Biar with only slight modifications; what is significant is that with James I pressing south, once again the kingdom of Murcia, which lay just beyond that of Valencia, was recognized as reserved to Castile. Soon afterward, Alcira fell to the Conqueror; in 1248 his men took Jativa; and in 1253 they reached the castle of Biar on the line of the Cazorla-Almizra treaties. This is often mistakenly taken as the termination of the Aragonese-Catalan reconquest, in favor of the Crown of Aragon's expansion towards Sicily, the eastern Mediterranean, Sardinia, and Italy, but, as we shall see, the attempts to secure parts of Murcia and of the kingdom of Granada, and the policies followed in the eastern Maghrib as a zone of potential Christian penetration, prove that the reconquest ideal remained very much alive in the eastern Spanish realms.

Finally, in these same stirring years the Portuguese reconquest came to a climax. Sancho II (1223–1245, d. 1248) gained Elvas after several tries (1230) and even crossed the Guadiana to take Moura and Serpa (1232). In a sweep south of Évora, Aljustrel fell in 1234 and was given to the Order of Santiago, a principal agency in the whole reconquest of Alentejo; and Moorish districts along both sides of the Guadiana to its mouth, along with the Algarvan coastal towns of Cacela and Tavira (1239), surrendered to Sancho. In 1240–1241 the king had high hopes of a crusade against Silves. This did not materialize and Sancho was soon distracted by internal problems, so that the full occupation of Algarve awaited the reign of Afonso III (1248–1278). This king quickly took Faro (1249), Silves, and other towns, and since Portuguese power now extended all across Algarve and beyond the Guadiana into lands subsequently lost to Castile, it can be said that by 1250 the Portuguese reconquest, territorially speaking, had attained its long-hoped-for goals.

By 1252, then, the year of Ferdinand III's death, the consequences of Las Navas de Tolosa were patent. Muwaḥḥid dominion in the peninsula—to say nothing of Africa—had collapsed completely in the course of the Hispano-Moslem civil wars, and the victories between 1220 and 1250 of Alfonso IX, Ferdinand III, James I, Sancho II, and Afonso III had wrested from Islam Extremadura, Algarve, Andalusia (except the kingdoms of Granada and Niebla), Murcia, Valencia, and the Baleares. Most of the peninsula was now in Christian hands, yet the reconquest as an ideal, as an immediate factor in foreign relations with Islamic states, and as still—for Castile—territorially incomplete, was by no means over, as succeeding rulers in all three Christian kingdoms rapidly discovered.

After 1250 the elimination of Muwaḥḥid power from the peninsula and the drastic contraction of al-Andalus to Granada and the tiny kingdom of Niebla brought about radical changes in the theaters and modes of operation of the Iberian reconquest.[17] Castile alone now possessed a contiguous land frontier with the Moors, in Murcia and Andalusia; this imposed upon it not only the defense of a long border district, in which fighting always simmered and sporadically boiled over into active warfare, but the far more difficult task of preventing the intrusion into Spain of the foremost North African successor state to the Muwaḥḥids, the Marīnid sultanate with its capital at Fez. Furthermore, Castile, Aragon, and Portugal all still

17. With Alfonso X commence the Castilian royal chronicles; for this epoch see those of Alfonso X, Sancho IV, Ferdinand IV, and Alfonso XI, in *Crónicas de los reyes de Castilla* (ed. C. Rosell, 3 vols., Madrid, 1875–1878; Biblioteca de autores españoles, LXVI, LXVIII, LXX), I. The edition of Ferdinand IV's chronicle by A. de Benavides, *Memorias de D. Fernando IV de Castilla* (2 vols., Madrid, 1860), is superseded, but vol. II consists entirely of valuable supplementary documents.

On Alfonso X, cf. A. Ballesteros-Beretta, *Alfonso el Sabio* (Barcelona-Madrid, 1963); on Sancho IV, M. Gaibrois de Ballesteros, *Historia del reinado de Sancho IV de Castilla* (3 vols., Madrid, 1922–1928). Useful on the Marīnid and Ḥafṣid relations with Spain are Terrasse, *Histoire du Maroc*, II, 32–56, 95–99; and R. Brunschvig, *La Berbérie orientale sous les Ḥafṣides des origines à la fin du XVe siècle* (2 vols., Paris, 1940–1947; Publications de l'Institut d' études orientales d'Alger, VIII, XI), especially vol. I.

had a sea frontier with the Maghribin Mediterranean and Atlantic waters that constituted an area of attacks upon their shores and shipping, an avenue of communication with the post-Muwaḥḥid kingdoms at Tunis, Tlemsen, and Fez of potential value as the prelude to military occupation, and—again primarily for Castile—the first line of defense against debarkation of Marīnid troops in Spain. It was above all the control of this maritime frontier, rather than the elimination of Granada, which dominated the active pursuit of the reconquest between 1250 and 1350, and gave greater importance than previously to seapower and naval actions. The shores and waters of the extreme western Mediterranean leading to the Strait of Gibraltar became the principal arena of Christian-Moorish confrontation, and Tarifa, Algeciras, and Gibraltar, rather than the more remote, mountain-ringed Granadan harbors of Malaga, Vélez-Málaga, and Almeria, as the indispensable bridgeheads for Marīnid invasion of the Andalusian heartland, became the chief objects of Maghribin-Castilian conflict.[18]

Of the four Castilian reigns that span the century 1250–1350, the first, that of Alfonso X the Learned (el Sabio, 1252–1284), has been regarded unfavorably (except on the cultural side) by historians, who see it given over down to 1273 to the king's utopian quest for the Holy Roman imperial title and thereafter plunged into disarray by the succession struggles between Alfonso's second son Sancho (the later Sancho IV) and the infantes de la Cerda, the two sons of the king's eldest son Ferdinand, who in 1275 was killed by the Moors. In reconquest annals, however, Alfonso X's reign is especially notable as the first in Castilian history to confront the triple problem of Granada, Marīnid Africa, and the strait, and in its initial years it scored some significant gains, among them the formation of Castile's new Andalusian fleet, based on the Guadalquivir at Seville and Sanlúcar de Barrameda, and commanded by the thenceforth high-ranking royal official, the admiral (almirante) of Castile. On land Alfonso, already well-blooded in frontier fighting as his father Ferdinand III's lieutenant in the annexation of Andalusia and as himself the reconquistador of Murcia, clearly aimed at pursuing his father's goals in Spain and Africa. Beginning with reimposition of royal control over the rebellious Moslem towns below Seville of Jerez de la Frontera, Lebrija, Arcos de la Frontera, Medina Sidonia, and others,

18. A. Canellas, "Aragón y la empresa del Estrecho en el siglo XIV," *Estudios de edad media de la Corona de Aragón,* II (1946), 7–73; and Ch. E. Dufourcq, "La Question de Ceuta au XIIIᵉ siècle," *Hespéris,* XLII (1955), 67–127. On Castilian naval aspects, cf. F. Pérez Embid, "El Almirantazgo de Castilla, hasta las Capitulaciones de Santa Fe," *Anuario de estudios americanos,* I (1944), 1–170.

and the pacification of parts of eastern Algarve which he returned to his son-in-law Afonso III of Portugal, the Castilian monarch went on in 1262 to annex the small Moorish kingdom of Niebla, and apparently the town of Cadiz also, although the latter may have previously acknowledged Fernandine suzerainty.

In 1260 Alfonso sent a crusading fleet to attack Atlantic Morocco, the first tentative counterblow to the Murābiṭ-Muwaḥḥid invasions of Spain. After extensive preparations and with strong papal encouragement the Castilians sailed from Seville in September, surprised the port of Salé—perhaps with some idea of striking thence towards Arzila or even Marrakesh, then still feebly held by a Muwaḥḥid caliph—and three weeks later returned laden with spoils and captives. While indubitably ephemeral, this African crusade of Alfonso X was no mere isolated venture: preceding by a decade king Louis IX of France's Tunisian crusade, it continued Ferdinand III's known interest in getting a foothold in Africa, embodied Castilian hopes, strong all through the thirteenth century, of carrying the reconquest to the principal enemy's homeland, and was the authentic forerunner of the landings by the Portuguese at Ceuta (1415) and by the Castilians themselves at Melilla (1497) and Oran (1505).[19]

In 1264, with the encouragement of king Muḥammad II of Granada (1273–1302), the Mudejars (or subjugated Moors of Andalusia and Murcia) rose in a formidable revolt against Castilian rule, but by 1266 they were finally suppressed, in Andalusia by Alfonso X, and in Murcia by his father-in-law, James I of Aragon, who then restored this territory to Castile. Many of these rebels were expelled to Granada or North Africa, their place being taken by Christian colonists.

Alfonso's reconquest record after this date is less impressive. After failing to prevent the hostile Granadans from repeatedly violating their truces and vassalage pacts with Castile, he was confronted in 1275 with the formation of a dangerous military alliance between Muḥammad II of Granada and the Marīnid ruler Ya'qūb ibn-'Abd-al-Haqq (1258–1286), under the terms of which, in return for promised early dispatch of his troops to Spain, the sultan received the cession of the extreme western zone of the Naṣrid kingdom, comprising the fortified ports of Gibraltar, Algeciras, and Tarifa. This in effect reëstablished African power in Spain, providing the bases required for landing troops and supplies for an Andalusian war against Castile;

19. A. Ballesteros, "La Toma de Salé en tiempos de Alfonso el Sabio," *Al-Andalus,* VIII (1943), 89–196; Ch. E. Dufourcq, "Un Projet castillan du XIIIe siècle: La 'Croisade d'Afrique'," *Revue d'histoire et de civilisation du Maghreb,* I (1966), 26–51.

12. Spain and Portugal, 1095–1150

13. Spain and Portugal, 1150–1250

14. Spain and Portugal, 1250–1350

15. Spain and Portugal, 1350–1492

and since, unlike their Murābiṭ and Muwaḥḥid predecessors, the Marīnids were no reformist zealots, it seems evident that Ya'qūb saw championship of a *jihād* to recover the lost realms in al-Andalus primarily as a means of strengthening the somewhat precarious position of his dynasty against his Maghribin enemies. In any case, in 1275 and again in 1278, he proceeded to bring into the peninsula large African armies, the first seen there since Las Navas, armies which behaved with extraordinary ruthlessness; on both occasions Alfonso X, embroiled in succession problems, proved unable to halt the invaders. After he failed to capture Algeciras, at a time when his son, the infante Sancho, was raising most of the kingdom in revolt against him, the harassed Castilian monarch was actually driven in his last year to form a coalition with the caliph that permitted the Marīnid warriors to stream through Seville northwards as far as Toledo, no doubt stirring grim recollections there of days when that city still served as Castile's bastion in the frontier wars of the Guadiana plains.

Sancho IV (1284–1295) faced the same Marīnid-Granadan menace throughout his reign but much more successfully, for when Ya'qūb returned to Spain once more in 1285, put Jerez under siege, and captured Sanlúcar de Barrameda, thus shutting off Seville's access to the sea, the Castilian army drove back the enemy so decisively that the defeated sultan hastily returned to Fez. A peace, negotiated in 1285, was several times renewed, and this permitted Sancho IV to quell a new uprising of Alfonso and Ferdinand, the infantes de la Cerda, while never losing sight of plans to gain control of the strait. In 1291, when another Marīnid war was imminent, Sancho concluded a new reconquest partition agreement with James II of Aragon, which for the first time envisaged the division of North Africa into Castilian and Aragonese zones, showing how firmly rooted was the concept of extending the Christian advance southward beyond the peninsula into the Maghrib itself. By the treaty of Monteagudo (November 29, 1291) the Moulouya river, which enters the Mediterranean not far from the present Moroccan-Algerian boundary, was taken as the dividing line, everything to the west falling in Castile's sphere of penetration and possible future conquest, all to the east in Aragon's. In 1292 the Castilians captured the fortified port of Tarifa, where king Sancho placed a strong garrison under the command of the magnate Alfonso Pérez de Guzmán, immortalized in Castilian annals as Guzmán the Good *(el Bueno)* for his refusal to surrender the fortress as the alternative to the execution of his son.

Tarifa still held firm for Castile, as did Algeciras for the Marīnids, when Sancho's death left the kingdom to the young Ferdinand IV (1295–1312). While the new ruler's capable mother Maria de Molina tried to fend off noble conspiracies on behalf of the infantes de la Cerda, James II of Aragon took the opportunity to seize, contrary to the treaties of Cazorla and Almizra, the old Moorish kingdom of Murcia. Although in 1304 he returned most of this to Castile, he was able to annex permanently to the Crown of Aragon its northern portion in the Vinalapó and Segura basins, with the cities of Alicante, Elche, and Orihuela, or roughly the modern province of Alicante. Castilian weakness during Ferdinand IV's minority also encouraged Muḥammad II of Granada to try for Tarifa; his army sacked Quesada, defeated a Castilian force at Alcaudete, southwest of Jaen, and devastated the environs of Jaen itself, but the valiant Guzmán *el Bueno* once more held Tarifa safely for his king. The next Naṣrid ruler, Muḥammad III (1302–1309), was even more ambitious; although recognizing Castile's title to Tarifa in 1304, he showed himself highly belligerent toward Ferdinand IV throughout a reign that brought almost continuous war to Andalusia. In 1306 Muḥammad, exploiting political disorders in Morocco, occupied Ceuta, another instance—this time Moorish—of peninsular ambitions in the Maghrib.

By 1309 all this had led to the formation of a Christian-Moorish triple alliance against Granada: first, Ferdinand IV and James II at Alcalá de Henares agreed upon a total reconquest and partition of the Naṣrid kingdom, by which the Aragonese crown was to retain one-sixth of its area, comprising the city and kingdom of Almeria; then they were joined by the Marīnid sultan ʿĀmir (1307–1308), who sought to recover Ceuta. This was a year filled with fighting: ʿĀmir quickly regained Ceuta and then switched to the Granadan side; Ferdinand IV's siege of Algeciras and James II's of Almeria both proved failures; and Guzmán *el Bueno* succeeded in taking Gibraltar for Castile, although not long thereafter he died while invading Granada. An uneasy peace was arranged in 1310, but Ferdinand IV was preparing for a new Granadan war when in 1312 death overtook him.

The reign of Alfonso XI of Castile (1312–1350) also began with a long regency filled with factional disorders and civil wars, during which the young king's uncle, the infante Peter, acting as coregent with his grandmother Maria de Molina, twice took Christian armies to the gates of a Granada riven by civil war (1316–1317, 1319), and captured the border stronghold of Tiscar. But in the latter year the

Castilian army, under Peter and his uncle and coregent the infante John, was surprised in the Vega of Granada by troops of king Ismāʿīl I (1314–1325), and cut to pieces in a disastrous battle in which both princes died.

In 1325 Alfonso XI finally reached his majority and, rampant aristocratic violence notwithstanding, moved to avenge the defeat of 1319 by attacking Granada in 1327 and forcing Muḥammad IV (1325–1333) to sue for peace. But in 1333 a combined Granadan-Marīnid column retook Gibraltar from the Castilians, and this encouraged the sultan at Fez, ʿAlī (1331–1351), to muster over the next several years a large Marīnid army for crossing the strait and striking a major blow against Castilian Andalusia. The admiral of Castile, Jofre Tenorio, commanding a fleet into which a number of Catalan ships had been incorporated with the approval of Alfonso IV of Aragon (1327–1336), attempted to turn back the two hundred vessels of the Marīnid expedition; in a spirited engagement off Gibraltar the Castilians were defeated and their admiral killed (1340).

This victory ensured Marīnid control of the strait, so that in June 1340 ʿAlī and his ally king Yūsuf I of Granada (1333–1354) were able to concentrate large forces against Tarifa, where the garrison put up its traditional vigorous defense. At the same time, in October, Alfonso XI, along with king Afonso IV of Portugal (1325–1357), and supported at sea by an Aragonese-Catalan and Portuguese naval squadron, marched towards Tarifa with the royal *hueste,* which papal concession of a crusade bull had helped him to raise. Arriving near the city, the king slipped orders into Tarifa for the beleaguered garrison to sally forth and attack the Moslems during the coming battle. On October 30 the Christian army, much inferior in size to that of its foes, drew up in order of battle on the bank of the Salado river near Tarifa, and was soon in close combat with the Marīnid-Granadan host. At the height of the fighting the Tarifa garrison, as planned, fell upon the Moslem rear; this proved decisive in winning for the Castilians the battle of the river Salado, the largest such encounter fought in the reconquest since Las Navas de Tolosa a century before.[20]

Although this victory is often taken as marking the end of Marīnid ability to land large armies on Iberian soil, this was not immediately apparent. It was not until 1344, at the end of a two-year siege, that Algeciras finally capitulated, once Alfonso had defeated a relief army

20. Huici, *Grandes batallas,* pp. 331–387.

of Maghribins and Granadans in the battle of the Palmones river (1343). The Castilian monarch moved next to recover Gibraltar, the last remaining African bridgehead; but internal conditions in his kingdom kept him from besieging the fortress of the Rock until 1349–1350, at which time he died in the plague that swept through his camp and made the campaign a failure. Nevertheless, Alfonso XI's victories and his capture of Algeciras did make virtually impossible further large-scale troop debarkations from Morocco. African auxiliaries would still appear in the future in the service of Granadan kings but the days of Berber dominion on peninsular soil were gone forever, and in its next phase the Castilian reconquest would center above all upon the continuing problem of the kingdom of Granada.

Castile so overshadows reconquest history from the mid-thirteenth century that it is important to recognize that both Portugal and Aragon-Catalonia also continued to participate in the pursuit of and to retain consciousness of the anti-Moorish war. The Portuguese, stimulated by the expanding trade of their western and southern coastal cities with Andalusia and the Maghrib, obliged to protect their merchant shipping against attack by Barbary pirates or war navies, and determined to secure a sphere of interest in western Morocco in an era when Castile and Aragon were partitioning the Maghrib at the line of the Moulouya without reference to Lisbon, never lost sight of reconquest goals. Portuguese knights in considerable number fought in the Castilian campaigns against the Marīnids; king Afonso IV himself joined Alfonso XI for the crucial battle of the Salado; the Portuguese church, the military orders, the many exhortatory papal communications, stressed the urgency of the anti-Moorish effort; and it has been argued with some cogency that in the thirteenth and fourteenth centuries, when their peninsular frontier had closed, the Portuguese exhibited greater crusading fervor than ever before.

So too in Aragon-Catalonia reconquest values and objectives remained very much alive after 1250.[21] The rulers sought to acquire Murcia and at least eastern Granada, they deployed powerful war fleets against the Maghrib, and they repeatedly contributed indispensable ships and troops in anti-Marīnid and anti-Granadan alliances with Castile. The already noted treaties of Monteagudo (1291) and Alcalá (1309), evincing James II's reconquest goals in Africa as in the

---

21. For prolongation of the Aragonese reconquest into North Africa, see, above all, the admirable work, with extensive bibliography, of Ch. E. Dufourcq, *L'Espagne catalane et le Maghrib aux XIIIe et XIVe siècles* (Paris, 1966); also A. Giménez Soler, *La Corona de Aragón y Granada* (Barcelona, 1908), and A. Masiá de Ros, *La Corona de Aragón y los estados del norte de Africa* (Barcelona, 1951).

peninsula, attest the not always justly appreciated policy of this ruler, who in his long reign (1291–1327) helped materially to stabilize the whole peninsular confrontation with Islam during the series of Castilian minorities and civil wars that continued down to Alfonso XI's majority in 1325. Under James II the Aragonese crown's manifold ties with, above all, Ḥafṣid Tunisia, but also with other Islamic states from Morocco to Egypt, reached their peak in exchanges of embassies, pacts of friendship and military assistance, recruitment of hardy Catalan border fighters, the famous *almogàvers,* for service in North African militias,[22] and the intensive commercial penetration of the Barcelonese mercantile community, which in return for Catalan textiles imported into Europe African grain and the gold, ivory, and spices transported from the Sudan by the trans-Saharan caravan trade. This was the period also of the plantation of Christian churches and missions in the Maghrib, the trend that so attracted the new mendicant orders, and stirred the imagination of that remarkable theoretician of the crusades and the reconquest, the Majorcan Raymond Lull (1232–1315), whose *Liber de fine* and other works envisage, on the one hand, coördination of an eastern and an Iberian assault upon Islam and, on the other, the peaceful conversion of North African Moslems through missionaries trained in the Arabic language and Islamic thought.[23]

The period after 1350 often tends to be passed over as if it were of minimal significance in reconquest history.[24] In fact, it possesses high interest both in itself and as the historical connection between the anti-Moorish wars of Alfonso XI and those of the "Catholic Kings," Ferdinand and Isabella *(los Reyes Católicos).* The key fact explaining the astonishing prolongation of the reconquest to the end

22. F. Soldevila, *Els Almogàvers* (Barcelona, 1952); J. Alemany, "Milicias cristianas al servicio de los sultanes musulmanes del Almagreb," *Homenaje a Codera* (Saragossa, 1904), pp. 133–169.

23. Cf. A. S. Atiya, *The Crusade in the Later Middle Ages* (2nd ed., New York, 1965), pp. 74–94; E. A. Peers, *Ramon Lull: a Biography* (London, 1929), *passim* but especially pp. 316–341 on Lull's *Liber de fine* and *Liber de acquisitione Terrae Sanctae.*

24. The fifteenth-century Castilian chronicles contain abundant material on reconquest warfare along the Granadan frontier. See especially Pedro López de Ayala, *Crónica del rey Don Enrique, tercero de Castilla é de León* (ed. C. Rosell, *Crónicas de los reyes de Castilla,* II, 161–271); Álvaro García de Santa María, *Crónica de Don Juan II de Castilla* (Colección de documentos inéditos para la historia de España, vols. XCIX–C, Madrid, 1891); and the four chronicles edited by J. de M. Carriazo in the Colección de crónicas españolas (9 vols., Madrid, 1940–1946): *Crónica de Don Álvaro de Luna; Crónica del halconero de Juan II, Pedro Carrillo de Huete; Refundición de la Crónica del halconero por el obispo don Lope Barrientos;* and *Crónica del condestable Miguel Lucas de Iranzo.* The last-cited narrative has also been edited by P. de Gayangos in *Memorial histórico español,* VIII (Madrid, 1855), pp. 1–521. See further Alonso de Palencia, *Crónica de Enrique IV* (tr.

of the Middle Ages is of course the stubborn survival of the kingdom of Granada.[25] Solidly ensconced in the Sierra Nevada and outlying ranges of the Baetic Cordillera, the Naṣrid commonwealth was a formidable military nut to crack. Its interior could be reached only through a limited number of passes and twisting mountain roads, readily commanded by castles or walled towns and ideal for ambuscades. The few good harbors along its rockbound coast—Malaga, Vélez-Málaga, Almeria—gave no easy access to the interior. The relatively dense population, in part descended from refugees of previous fallbacks, possessed naturally warlike inclinations, hatred of the ancestral Christian enemy, a fierce love of independence, and a deep awareness that they were defending the last free Islamic homeland in the peninsula. Granada's rulers, usually capable or served by sagacious counselors, suffered constant harassment from dynastic and aristocratic factionalism and from recurrent uprisings in the Albaicín quarter of Granada city aimed at seizing the magnificent fortified palace of the Alhambra, but their armies generally managed to hold the long border against Castile and reduce Christian penetrations from the level of projected conquest to merely destructive raids.

Late medieval Castile long lacked the prerequisites for the conquest of this highly compartmentalized mountain massif which, as the ultimately successful ten-year Granadan war of Ferdinand and Isabella showed, demanded strong leadership and national persistence in the multiple campaigns and sieges of a costly war of attrition. Between Peter I (1350–1369) and Henry IV (1454–1474) a dismal succession of minorities, regencies, weak rulers, and spreading intra-aristocratic and anti-royal strife kept Castilian society in a state of constant civil violence and disorder, drastically weakening the monarchy's traditional authority, leadership, and ability to mobilize its military and financial resources or stir the popular enthusiasm necessary for the Granadan struggle. In consequence, for much of the time

---

A. Paz y Melia, 4 vols., Madrid, 1904–1908), and Diego Enríquez del Castillo, *Crónica del rey Don Enrique el Cuarto* (ed. Rosell, *Crónicas de los reyes de Castilla,* III).

Disappointingly brief treatment is given the reconquest, 1350–1475, by L. Suárez Fernández in Menéndez Pidal, *Historia de España,* XIV, 373–375; XV, 33–41, 225–227; but this scholar's *Juan II y la frontera de Granada* (Valladolid, 1954) is fundamental; cf. also Emilio Mitre Fernández, "De la Toma de Algeciras a la campagna de Antequera," *Hispania,* XXIII (1972), 77–122.

25. See M. Á. Ladero Quesada, *Granada, historia de un país islámico, 1232–1571* (Madrid, 1969); and on Castilian frontier literature and attitude toward the Granadans, M. S. Carrasco Urgoiti, *El Moro de Granada en la literatura (del siglo XV al XX)* (Madrid, 1956), pp. 19–46.

after 1350 the Iberian reconquest, as a predominantly Castilian enterprise, assumed two main forms: a roughly stabilized confrontation along a Castilian-Granadan border zone of endemic petty hostilities, and an intermittent full-scale war bringing kings and armies into serious combat. Together these two modes of conflict come to be known as the *Guerra de Granada* or *Guerra del Moro,* centering on what chroniclers and official documents call *la Frontera,* the borderland of daring deeds, violence, raids, and depredations commemorated in Castilian story and heroic balladry (the *romances fronterizos*).

In the fourteenth and fifteenth centuries Castile's reconquest frontier with Granada consisted of the southern districts of the former Moorish kingdoms of Seville, Cordova, and Jaen; the March *(Adelantamiento)* of Cazorla, controlled by the archbishops of Toledo; and the kingdom of Murcia. Not a line but a border zone, the frontier was the product of the fortuitous distribution of lands, castles, and towns held by each side in the mid-thirteenth century. After 1350 it began in the west just above Gibraltar (still in Moorish hands), and ran northward near Castellar de la Frontera and Jimena de la Frontera along the Serranía of Ronda to Morón de la Frontera. From there it continued eastward above Cañete la Real, Teba, and Antequera before turning northeastward again past Cambíl and Huelma (southeast of Jaen) to Quesada, whence it descended eastward past Huéscar toward the Mediterranean below Lorca, leaving Vélez Blanco, Vélez Rubio, Huércal-Overa, and Vera on the Granadan side.

Wardens *(adelantados),* frontier alcaldes,[26] and the garrisons of castles represented the royal authority on the frontier, but in large part defense against Moorish incursions or even major invasions rested with the so-called borderers *(fronteros),* the great Andalusian nobles such as the Guzmán dukes of Medina Sidonia, the Ponce de León marquises of Cadiz, and the counts of Cabra, Arcos, and the like. Their private armies of vassals and dependents joined the municipal militias and the knights of the military orders to hold the frontier, no matter how weak Castile's central government was.[27] But whenever, as intermittently occurred, the frontier's relative, uneasy peace broke down, either because one side had taken a castle or town by surprise,

---

26. J. de M. Carriazo, "Un Alcalde entre los cristianos y los moros en la frontera de Granada," *Al-Andalus,* XIII (1948), 35–96; J. Torres Fontes, "El Alcalde entre moros y cristianos del reino de Murcia," *Hispania,* XX (1960), 55–80.

27. M. Jiménez de la Espada, *La Guerra del Moro a fines del siglo XV* (2nd ed., Madrid, 1940); J. Moreno de Guerra y Alonso, *Bandos en Jerez: Los del Puesto de Abajo* (Madrid, 1929); M. Góngora, *Los Grupos de conquistadores en Tierra Firme, 1509–1530* (Santiago, Chile, 1962), pp. 91–94.

inflicting damage too serious for the enemy to accept, or because Castile or Granada failed to renew the usual two- or three-year truce, then the reconquest became an active effort to weaken and ultimately to destroy the Granadan state through annual ravaging *(tala)* and progressive annexation of its towns and territories.

For really large campaigns the crown was heavily dependent upon the Andalusians and Murcians, whose principal cities—Seville, Cordova, Jaen, Murcia, Lorca—were the bases for all such frontier operations, and whose noble retinues, urban militias, and military commanderies made up the bulk of the royal army. Such troops for the most part were willing to serve only short terms while being fed and paid at royal expense; and aside from the knights of the military orders, and such Castilian, Portuguese, and Aragonese volunteers as came to fight the "infidel," it is often difficult to visualize an army like this as a crusading host, however much its members prized the spiritual privileges secured for them by the king in papal crusade bulls. On the other hand, at times the crusading spirit burned high, and served to attract a thin trickle of extra-peninsular crusaders who found their way in this epoch to the Granadan frontier, like Sir James Douglas and other Scottish nobles who, while transporting the heart of king Robert Bruce for burial in Jerusalem, died in Spain in 1330 fighting the Moors; or Chaucer's knight, who presumably fought with Alfonso XI in 1344: "in Gernade [Granada] at the seege eek hadde he be/of Algezir [Algeciras] and riden in Belmarye [Banū Marīn, Morocco? Marīnid Andalusia?]." Castilian and foreign knights brought to this war, as indeed the Granadan Moors did also, much of the pageantry, color, and chivalric mores of late medieval aristocratic life: contemporary narratives abound in vivid scenes of military drama and heroism in this stage of the reconquest.

Warfare on the Granadan frontier, as the infante John Manuel points out in the illuminating military science sections of his *Libro de los estados* (written 1327–1332), differed in important respects from that fought by Castile against Christian enemies.[28] This he attributes in part to the special difficulties created by the very broken terrain, long waterless stretches, and scant foraging possibilities of the Granadan kingdom, in part to the fact that the Moors, shunning armor, continued to depend upon highly mobile light

---

28. Infante don Juan Manuel, *Libro de los estados* (ed. P. de Gayangos, Bibl. aut. esp., LI, Madrid, 1884), chapters 70–79 (pp. 319–326); I. I. Macdonald, *Don Fernando de Antequera* (Oxford, 1948), pp. 34–45; J. Torres Fontes, "La Caballería de alarde murciana en el siglo XV," *Anuario de historia del derecho español*, XXXVIII (1968), 31–86; M. A. Ladero Quesada, *Castilla y la conquista del reino de Granada* (Valladolid, 1967), pp. 11–17; Lourie, *op. cit.*, pp. 69–76.

cavalry *(jinetes)* and infantry in an essentially guerrilla-type war. The Granadans commonly avoided engagements with the heavy Castilian armored horse in its closed battle formations; when such encounters occurred, they used their traditional tactics of the *torna fuye,* making feigned or real thrusts *(puntas)* of wildly shouting horsemen against the Christian ranks to throw them into panic or disorder. Of course, ever since the twelfth century the Castilians had also possessed *jinetes,* riding in light saddles with short stirrups, and frontier conditions in Andalusia reinforced the indispensability of such troops as well as of the heavy cavalry.

Although it was apparently the Granadan Moors who in the mid-fourteenth century first introduced gunpowder into the reconquest, the Christians quickly discovered its utility for mines, wall-breachings, and cannon, so that the Castilian army's train came to include lombards and other artillery along with the older siege engines. In sieges Christian superiority was great; and on the battlefield the dense bodies of Castilian armored horse and well-equipped infantry were rarely defeated in regular combat. But for both sides so much of the war of Granada was fought off the battlefields, in cavalry raids, in the destruction of crops, livestock, and villages, and in surprises, ambuscades, and small-scale melees, that Moorish inferiority in numbers or materiel counted less and the fortunes of war were more equal than might be supposed.

It is against this background of the Granadan frontier, and the abiding consciousness in the minds of the Castilian people of the reconquest as an ultimate objective, that the reigns of the six kings between Alfonso XI and Ferdinand and Isabella prove more significant for reconquest history than is often recognized. To be sure, under Peter I (1350–1369), dubbed by his enemies "the Cruel" and accused of undue pro-Moorish and pro-Jewish sympathies, a coalition of rebel Castilians and of French barons drawn to Castile by the expansion of the Hundred Years' War below the Pyrenees, and seeking to depose the king in favor of his illegitimate half-brother, count Henry of Trastámara, kept the kingdom in an uproar until Peter's defeat and murder. This gave the throne to the new Trastámara dynasty, but neither in Henry II's time (1369–1379) nor during the long minority and weak rule of John I (1379–1390), was there much interest in Granada except for renewal of truces.

The same paralysis marks the first decade of Henry III's reign (1390–1406), so that between 1350 and 1400 the reconquest, at least on the part of the crown, can be said to have reached its nadir for the entire period since 1095. Yet at the opening of the fifteenth century the pattern abruptly changed when midway through his reign Henry III displayed clear signs of an intention to resume the reconquest on a scale unknown since Alfonso XI. The causes of this new offensive policy have been little studied, but surely they include Henry's own crusading proclivities, the even stronger convictions of his brother, the infante Ferdinand, increased royal military strength due to the new system of annual musters ordered by the Cortes of Guadalajara in 1390, and the intensifying social and religious tensions throughout Castile in the epoch of the Great Schism and the conciliar movement, which found expression in the drive to substitute uniformity of belief for traditional peninsular tri-fideism, the spread of Observantism in the monastic orders, the popular preaching of Vincent Ferrer and other mendicants, and the anti-Jewish pogroms of 1391. No doubt also the landing of the Portuguese at Ceuta (1415), carrying the reconquest into Morocco, aroused the Castilian monarchy to renewed consideration of its own Granadan and African expansionist possibilities. Finally, by 1400 there seems also to have been increased Granadan bellicosity; whether this was caused by a royal shunting of Naṣrid faction-torn nobility into a common anti-Christian enterprise or by a reaction to growing Castilian pressures, remains unclear. In 1401, a large Moorish *algara* crossed the border; five years later king Muḥammad VII invaded Murcia and Jaen, in violation of the prevailing truce, but his troops were repulsed at Vera, Lorca, and Caravaca. In Andalusia, however, they took Ayamonte, near Setenil, and ravaged widely until the *adelantado de la frontera* Peter Manrique defeated them near Quesada in the battle of Los Collejares (October 1406).

In 1406, therefore, the Cortes of Castile at Toledo supported Henry III's proposal for a Granadan war, but the king's grave illness and early death meant that the leadership of this project and the regency for the young John II (1406–1454) passed into the hands of the infante Ferdinand.[29] The scope of the revived reconquest is noteworthy: the Cortes promised a grant *(servicio)* of 45,000,000 maravedís, on condition that it be matched by a similar amount from the royal treasury; these funds were to be used for commissioning a naval squadron of thirty galleys and other ships to patrol the Granadan coast, and for raising an army optimistically set at four thousand Castilian and fifteen hundred Andalusian horse, sixteen thousand lances, fifty thousand foot, and sufficient artillery.

29. Macdonald, *Ferdinand de Antequera,* chapters 2–5.

With violence flaming along the frontier as both sides sensed the approach of a general conflict, Ferdinand marched south towards the Serranía of Ronda while the Granadans attacked Lucena in order to draw him back. Naṣrid hopes of obtaining supplies from North Africa were cut short when on August 26, 1506, the Castilian fleet defeated the Marīnid navy. By September the Castilian army, carrying in its midst the crusading sword of St. Ferdinand III, moved in the direction of Ronda, and stormed the frontier strongpoint of Zahara; but after this achievement the reluctance of the nobles to tackle a long Rondan siege with winter approaching led the infante to substitute the smaller but strategically valuable town of Setenil. This siege, however, during which detachments of the army recovered Ayamonte and gained Cañete la Real, Priego, and other places, proved unsuccessful, and on October 25, 1407, it had to be abandoned, in part, perhaps, because of aristocratic recalcitrance.

Undaunted, Ferdinand all through 1408 and 1409 made careful preparations for a second campaign in the Granadan west, possibly aimed at Ronda or Malaga as an ultimate objective, but having for its secret immediate target the border fortress-city of Antequera, which dominated the Guadalhorce valley. Once again the royal *hueste,* with its long train of siege engines and artillery, rolled across the frontier in the spring of 1410, surrounding Antequera, setting up five great encampments *(reales)* on various sides of the town, and seizing control of the nearby sierras and the routes to Granada city. King Yūsuf III (1408–1417) sent a large army of relief under his brothers Sīdī 'Alī and Sīdī Aḥmad, but the Castilians repulsed this decisively in the battle of Boca del Asno and proceeded to tighten the siege through ever greater use of catapults and cannon, a huge movable tower *(bastida),* and attempts at escalading, notwithstanding the ferocious resistance of the embattled Antequerans. A big assault in late June was thrown back with heavy Castilian casualties, but the isolated defenders were gradually worn down, and a new all-out attack commencing on September 16 forced them to capitulate within a week, giving to the weary Castilians their most important reconquest victory since Alfonso XI's capture of Algeciras in 1344, and to Ferdinand the proud sobriquet "of Antequera."

The Antequeran campaign was the infante's last anti-Moorish enterprise; in 1412 by the famed Compromise of Caspe he became king of Aragon and left Castile. As a *reconquistador* Ferdinand of Antequera's name is unquestionably the most important between Alfonso XI and the Catholic Kings for three reasons: his campaigns of 1407 and 1410 revived the reconquest spirit in Castile; at Antequera he brought about the first really major change of the frontier in Castile's favor since Algeciras; and his strategy of attacking the Naṣrids in the west so as to cut off the Ronda and Malaga sectors before closing in on Granada city was the one eventually adopted by Ferdinand and Isabella.

The infante's departure for his eastern throne, leaving the Castile of John II to fall under the sway of the powerful magnate Álvaro de Luna, led to some years of uneasy peace, but in 1430 the monarchy resumed the war against Granada. After a Castilian contingent had seized Jimena de la Frontera above Gibraltar (1431), drawing Granadan attention to the west, Álvaro de Luna invaded the Vega of Granada; here he and the king fought and won the modest battle of La Higueruela, just outside the capital (July 1, 1431). Thereafter it was left to the men of the frontier to press the attack: in Murcia the adelantado Fajardo gained Vélez Blanco and Vélez Rubio, opposite Lorca; in the west, although the count of Niebla died in a vain attempt to win Gibraltar, the Castilians took Huelma southeast of Jaen and raided widely around Ronda and Malaga. Pope Eugenius IV, seeking to secure John II's backing in his quarrel with the Council of Basel, vehemently encouraged the Castilian crusade, granting it the usual indulgence and forbidding—as the popes so often did—all sale of foodstuffs and strategic materials to the Moors.

During the years 1446–1447 the rival Granadan monarchs Muḥammad X (1445–1447) and Muḥammad IX (1419–1427, 1429–1445, 1447–1453) recovered the two Vélezes and other frontier strongholds except Antequera, thus wiping out most of the Christian gains since 1410. In 1448, indeed, the able Muḥammad IX took his troops so close to Jaen, Baena, and even Seville that John II, facing in addition the prospect of a Granadan-Navarrese alliance against Castile, made peace on the basis of conceding the Moorish gains. This did not prevent the Naṣrid from invading Murcia in 1452, but here he suffered a grave defeat at the hands of Fajardo *el Bravo* in the battle of Alporchones (March 7).

Two years later Henry IV (1454–1474) became king of Castile. This much maligned monarch, who was to spend most of his reign in desperate efforts to keep himself on the throne in the face of vicious baronial revolutions and to safeguard the successsion of his daughter Joanna against his half-brother Alfonso and later his half-sister Isabella, manifested in his early happier years a striking determination to avenge the setbacks under John II. In 1455 Henry made three separate *entradas* into the Naṣrid kingdom, the first to the Vega of Granada, the second to the environs of Archidona, the third once again, by way of Moclín and Íllora, to the Granadan Vega. In 1456 he occupied Estepona on the coast, and led his army toward Malaga. These campaigns, however, resulted in no permanent gains, possibly because the nobles' rancor kept Henry from venturing on extended sieges or pitched battles; instead they afforded an opportunity to the anti-royalist faction to charge that the king was in secret collusion with the Moors, a charge that lost nothing in plausibility when Henry crossed over to Portuguese-held Ceuta to confer with Marīnid envoys. The fact is, however, that the war continued, with the Granadans invading Andalusia all the way to Jaen, which they attacked. In 1462, furthermore, two Andalusian magnates, the count of Arcos and the duke of Medina Sidonia, captured Gibraltar, returning the Rock to Castile for the first time since 1333. This notable triumph had no sequel; Henry IV and his nobles disappeared into the chaotic civil wars then convulsing Castile, and the reconquest received no further royal attention until the ultimate victors in the fratricidal struggle, Isabella and her husband Ferdinand of Aragon, revived the national enterprise and the liberation of the peninsula from Islam entered its final phase.

The persistence of reconquest outlook and activity in this period on the part of the Aragonese-Catalans and the Portuguese has been much less investigated than for Castile. Yet both these adjoining kingdoms were acquiring extensive overseas territories and the continuity of such expansion with previous reconquest efforts can be taken as certain, although the relative importance of this factor alongside others of demographic, economic, dynastic, and geopolitical character in the full European context of the rise of the Ottoman Turks and late medieval crusade ideology and projects is still to be determined. Aragon, to be sure, was primarily engaged in acquiring in the central Mediterranean territories already Christianized: Sicily (from 1282), Sardinia (from 1323), and Naples (by 1443). But the anti-Turkish wars of the Catalan *almogàvers* in the east from 1303 on all through the fourteenth century, and Aragonese efforts to control the island of Jerba near Tripoli and collect tribute from the rulers of Tunisia, testify to the eastern Spanish kingdom's unbroken adhesion to the struggle against the "infidel" wherever he was to be found.

As for Portugal in 1350–1475, an abundant literature exists, relating to the genesis of the overseas conquests and discoveries that followed the advent of John I (1385–1433) of the Avis dynasty, and his sons Peter and Henry the Navigator (d. 1460).[30] Excessive debate

30. Key documents for the reconquest background of Portuguese African expansion can be found in *Monumenta henricina* (10 vols., Lisbon, 1960–). Continuity in terms of papal

on the relative weight to be assigned economic and political as against crusading and chivalric factors has tended to obscure the undeniable significance of the continuing thrust of the reconquest experience. As late as 1341–1344, when the Franciscan bishop of Silves, Álvaro Pais, dedicated his *Speculum regum* to Alfonso XI of Castile (who with Portuguese help had just triumphed at the Salado) and called upon that sovereign as the successor of the old Visigothic kings to smite the Moslems in Africa and restore to Christendom this once Visigothic land, the Portuguese may have hoped for Spanish collaboration in an invasion of the Maghrib. But Marīnid attacks upon Algarve in 1354/1355 and other years and upon the growing Portuguese trade and shipping in the strait, and a new interest from 1341 in the penetration of the Canaries, where Castilian rivalry soon developed, pointed them towards more positive, independent action, so that the house of Avis, just as it provided the nation with dynamic, capable, and ambitious leadership, also assumed the mantle of the reconquest.

The Portuguese landing in 1415 at Ceuta and capture of this notorious debarkation point for invasions of Iberia, and John's interest in joining Castile for an attack upon Granada—a project slow to die out and long encouraged by the popes—were followed in 1437 by the first, abortive crusade against Tangier; and, under Afonso V the African (*o Africano,* 1438–1481), by the seizures of Arzila (1458) and of Alcácer-Seghir and Tangier (1471). In these successes the crusading combatants, their contemporaries and chroniclers, and the ever-sympathetic popes foresaw the conscious extension to Africa not merely of the crusade in general but of the peninsular reconquest in particular. Thus across the strait in the so-called other Algarve, Christian expansion was once again forcing back the frontiers of Islam, and renewing the achievements of the twelfth and thirteenth centuries.

On the death of king Henry IV of Castile in 1474 in the midst of civil war, his half-sister Isabella and her husband, the infante Ferdinand of Aragon, seized power and, at the battle of Toro (1476),

---

outlook and support is treated at length in A. J. Dias Dinís, "Antecedentes da expansão ultramarina portuguesa: Os diplomas pontifícios dos séculos XII a XV," *Revista portuguesa de história,* X (1962), 1–118, and Ch. M. de Witte, "Les Bulles pontificales et l'expansion portugaise au XVe siècle," *Revue d'histoire ecclésiastique,* XLVIII (1953), 683–718; XLIX (1954), 438–461; LI (1956), 413–453, 809–836; LIII (1958), 5–46, 443–471. For discussion (with recent bibliography) of the crusade interpretation of Prince Henry's North African ventures, as defended by Joaquim Bensaúde and others, and of the relevant economic and other factors in Portuguese expansion into the Maghrib, see V. Magalhães Godinho, *A Economia dos descobrimentos henriquinos* (Lisbon, 1962).

defeated the aristocratic partisans of the infanta Joanna (whom Isabelline supporters decried as illegitimate and without claim to the throne) and her intended consort, Afonso V of Portugal, who had invaded Castile with a Portuguese army.[31] This victory, and Ferdinand's accession to the Aragonese throne three years later, made possible the new dual monarchy of Spain, insuring the replacement of late medieval Castile's weak government and divided society by a reorganized state of vastly increased authority, resources, and popular support which could impose controls upon nobility, military orders, and towns, reform and reinvigorate the church, and against the rising Ottoman Turkish threat in the Mediterranean pursue a program of resolute counterattack. It is then no surprise to find that, as an indispensable element in their program of cementing the yet fragile Castilian-Aragonese union and moving towards complete unification of all the peninsula, Isabella and Ferdinand early took up the cause of the reconquest, fulfillment of which promised so many religious, political, and economic rewards.

If we can trust the chroniclers, the Catholic Kings—to anticipate the honorific title conferred upon Isabella and Ferdinand by Alexander VI in 1494, following the fall of Granada—planned from the very start of their reign to annex the Naṣrid kingdom. Certainly the queen's pious, crusading temperament and strongly Castilian outlook must have made her eager to pursue without delay the reconquest objectives of her predecessors; she may well have insisted upon the destruction of Granada before agreeing to divert Castile's resources to her husband's more strictly Aragonese objectives along the Pyrenees and in Italy. Both rulers were fully aware of the latest outbreak of intra-dynastic strife in Granada, where king abū-l-Ḥasan ʿAlī (Muley Hacén, 1464–1485) and his brother abū-ʿAbd-Allāh Muḥammad az-Zaghall (the Valiant, 1485–1489) were busy trying to sup-

---

31. The four chief Castilian narratives are Diego de Valera, *Crónica de los Reyes Católicos* (ed. J. de M. Carriazo, Madrid, 1927; Col. crón. esp.); Fernando del Pulgar, *Crónica de los Reyes Católicos* (ed. Carriazo, Madrid, 1943; Col. crón. esp.); Alfonso de Palencia, *Narratio belli adversus Granatenses* (Sp. tr. by A. Paz y Melia, Madrid, 1909); and Andrés Bernáldez, *Memorias del reinado de los Reyes Católicos* (ed. M. Gómez-Moreno and J. de M. Carriazo, Madrid, 1962).

The classic accounts of Washington Irving, *A Chronicle of the Conquest of Granada* (2 vols., Philadelphia, 1829) and W. H. Prescott, *History of the Reign of Ferdinand and Isabella the Catholic* (3 vols., Boston, 1838), still the fullest in English and of value as based upon the chronicles, require extensive supplementation from recent works drawing upon neglected archival documentation. Of these the most valuable are J. de M. Carriazo, "Historia de la guerra de Granada," in Menéndez Pidal, ed., *Historia de España,* XVII, vol. I (Madrid, 1969), 385–914; A. de la Torre, *Los Reyes Católicos y Granada* (Madrid, 1946); and especially the two studies of M. Á. Ladero Quesada, particularly illuminating on military organization and financing, *Milicia y economía en la guerra de Granada* (Valladolid, 1964), and *Castilla y la conquista del reino de Granada* (Valladolid, 1967).

press the spreading revolt led by the king's elder son abū-'Abd-Allāh (Boabdil) Muḥammad XII (1482–1492), but for some years Afonso V's invasion and problems of internal reorganization led the new sovereigns to renew in 1475 and again in 1478 the standing truce with the Moorish state. However, the fact that the Spaniards failed to renew once more in 1481, and that abū-l-Ḥasan took advantage of Christian aristocratic feuding along his border to launch destructive raids into Murcia and Andalusia, suggests that both sides were aware of graver conflict in the offing. Yet the incidents that actually touched off the war were not of the royal doing and seem to have forced the monarchs' hands.

At the turn of the year 1481–1482 a Moorish contingent from Ronda surprised and occupied the Castilian border fortress of Zahara. In immediate riposte to this bold challenge, the Andalusian *fronteros,* led by count Rodrigo Ponce de León of Cadiz, slipped over the frontier all the way to the Vega of Granada, where in February 1482 they seized the unsuspecting castle of Alhama, only twenty miles from the capital astride the trunk Malaga highway, overcame its fierce resistance, and proceeded to hold it against massive counterattack. This Naṣrid loss, the most serious since Antequera (1410) and a direct threat to Granada city, abū-l-Ḥasan could not possibly accept. On the other hand, the Catholic Kings found themselves with a *fait accompli:* to reinforce and provision isolated Alhama and retain it meant engaging at once in a full-scale Granadan war. Isabella and Ferdinand were in the north at Medina del Campo when the news reached them. They did not hesitate: Alhama was to be held, and orders went out immediately to the frontier officers and Andalusian nobles to do everything possible pending the king's arrival. This royal decision, and the selection of Cordova as a base for mustering an army to move against Granada, mark the commencement of the definitive war to wrest all remaining Spanish soil from Islamic sovereignty.

Commencing thus in early 1482 with the thenceforth standing imperative of bringing through to Alhama supplies and sufficient men to beat off repeated assaults, the Granadan war of the Catholic Kings lasted approximately ten years, until the final capitulation terms were ratified on November 25, 1491, and the city formally surrendered in the first days of January 1492. Inevitably, it was a war of attrition in which the far stronger Spaniards took the offensive, a war of sieges, spring campaigns, occasional pitched battles, and piecemeal conquests. It was a war essentially Castilian, waged, as so often in the past, by nobles, military orders, and municipal militias, although the supreme commander was king Ferdinand of Aragon, and small numbers of Aragonese nobles, foreign volunteers, and Swiss and other mercenaries from abroad participated.

With all the frontier from Jimena de la Frontera to Lorca seething with forays and skirmishes, in July 1482 Ferdinand invested Loja with an army of some eighteen thousand horse and foot, but after suffering heavy casualties inflicted by Moorish sallies from the besieged city, he had to abandon this poorly planned affair. The next year, with the king in the north, the marquis (as he now was) of Cadiz, Rodrigo Ponce de León, and the master of Santiago, Alfonso de Cárdenas, moved south to attack Malaga, but as their army was making its way without due caution through the Ajarquía or rugged sierra country north of that city, it was surprised by king abū-l-Ḥasan and az-Zaghall, and routed with heavy loss. Boabdil, in rebellion against his father, had seized the Alhambra and, to strengthen his claim to the royal title, in this same year assaulted the Andalusian border town of Lucena, with the help of his father-in-law 'Alī-Atar ('Alī al-'Aṭṭār), but a strong Castilian relief column drove off the Granadans and forced them into a battle near Lucena in which 'Alī-Atar was killed and Boabdil himself taken prisoner.

Abū-l-Ḥasan took advantage of his son's misfortune to regain Granada, while Boabdil, in order to secure his freedom, had to submit to an agreement with the Catholic Kings. In the pact of Cordova, signed on August 24, 1483, he promised, in exchange for his release and a two-year truce, to become a vassal of Castile, pay an annual tribute of 12,000 doblas, release Christian captives, provide on demand seven hundred *lanzas* (mounted nobles with attendant warriors) to the Castilian army, and allow Spanish troops to cross his dominions in order to make war on abū-l-Ḥasan. The latter clause meant little, since Boabdil, having lost Granada city, controlled only the eastern section of the kingdom, which he ruled from Guadix; and even here, in 1485, he lost Almeria to his uncle az-Zaghall. Meanwhile, in 1483 the marquis of Cadiz recovered Zahara; and Ferdinand himself in 1484, using lombards and other ox-drawn guns to breach the walls, secured the surrender of Álora (June 18) and Setenil (September 21).

After the death of abū-l-Ḥasan in 1485, king Ferdinand launched a major campaign, ostensibly to take Malaga and cut off the western third of the Granadan state. The big royal army, after gaining Coín and Cártama on its march south, reached the port city but then swung back westward to attack Ronda. After an artillery barrage had breached its walls and set houses afire, Ronda capitulated, being accorded such generous terms that various smaller towns of the Serranía of Ronda, and Marbella down on the coast, did likewise. By this campaign the Castilians acquired their first significant portion of Granadan territory, although the severe mauling of count Diego Fernández of Cabra at Moclín this same summer showed that the Moors still had plenty of fight. In 1486 king Ferdinand set out again, this time with an artillery train estimated at two thousand wagons, to besiege Loja once more. Boabdil, contrary to his pact, had made a short-lived peace with az-Zaghall, his rival in the claim to the late abū-l-Ḥasan's throne, and was present in the city to take charge of its defense. When Loja fell, he again became a Castilian prisoner but was quickly released as a valuable instrument for promoting Granada's dynastic strife and self-destruction.

The campaign of the next year, 1487, turned out to be the longest, most costly, and in the end most productive of the war. Ferdinand's army struck first at Vélez-Málaga, and notwithstanding az-Zaghall's sacrifice in leaving Granada city to fall into Boabdil's hands while he himself patriotically sought to succor the besieged town, Vélez-Málaga was lost. The Castilians now pushed on to Malaga, the Naṣrid kingdom's second city, which the capture of Vélez-Málaga had cut off from any easy connection with the capital. The long, bloody Malagan siege, lasting 103 days between May 7 and August 18, 1487, is the grimmest episode of the whole war, chiefly because the Malagueños, who would have capitulated early, were compelled to leave their city's defense in the hands of a fanatical garrison of Spanish Christian renegades and North African Ghumārah led by one Aḥmad "el-Zegrí" (ath-Thaghrī, the borderer). This redoubtable commander, controlling Malaga's *alcazaba* or citadel and the nearby stronghold of Gibralfaro, brutally suppressed all efforts of the starving townsmen to negotiate with the enemy, so that week after week attacks and counterattacks, escalades, bombardments and minings continued with great loss of life on both sides. Az-Zaghall's effort to relieve the battered city failed, as did (narrowly) an attempted assassination of king Ferdinand. Finally, on terms of unconditional surrender, Malaga fell, to be given the harshest treatment of any captured city—complete enslavement of its surviving inhabitants—as a stern warning to others. During the course of this siege Boabdil had again installed himself in Granada, so that az-Zaghall, unable to relieve Malaga, had to take refuge in Almeria, while his unworthy nephew in the Alhambra made a new pact with the Catholic Kings, promising to surrender Granada city and its fortresses as soon as circumstances permitted.

The western half of the kingdom, from Ronda to Vélez-Málaga, was now in the possession of the Catholic Kings, so they could turn next to the east, to deal with az-Zaghall and his supporters in Almeria, Guadix, Baza, and other towns. 1488 was largely a year of minor combats and preparations. Then in 1489 there took place the memorable siege of Baza by a Castilian army set at thirteen thousand cavalry and forty thousand infantry, fighting under the eyes of Isabella and Ferdinand. Baza's governor, Yaḥyâ an-Naiyār (Cid Hiaya), proved an expert and resolute commander; az-Zaghall was able to slip an additional ten thousand picked men into the city through the Castilian lines; and foodstuffs were ample. Much of the protracted hand-to-hand fighting took place outside the walls, in the *huerta* or fertile garden, orchard, and olive area around the city, which the besiegers finally laid waste. At last az-Zaghall, despairing of bringing succor, authorized Baza's capitulation. Yaḥyâ an-Naiyār, taken into the service of the Catholic Kings, then negotiated az-Zaghall's own submission and the surrender of Almeria, which was followed by that of Guadix. Thus by 1490, another year of minor operations, what had been the eastern third of the Granadan kingdom had been reconquered; only the city and Vega of Granada, ruled by the passive Boabdil, remained to be secured.

Boabdil, despite his pacts of vassalage and the hopeless military situation after 1490, was much too fearful of popular uprising and his own overthrow to surrender the capital, so the Catholic Kings devoted the winter of 1490–1491 to making preparations for a full-scale siege. In the spring of 1491, the Castilian army occupied the Vega, completely surrounded the city and, after the accidental burning of its first camp, built a permanent military base, which was named Santa Fe, within sight of Granada's walls. The siege of 1491 has no real importance as a military operation; although hard fighting occasionally broke out outside the walls and exchanges of arrows and shots were frequent, the commanders on both sides knew the outcome was certain and deliberately kept hostilities at a low level while negotiations proceeded for Granada's surrender. These parleys, carried on by emissaries of the Catholic Kings and of Boabdil, were conducted in great secrecy so as not to stir revolt against their feeble monarch on the part of his undiscouraged subjects. The terms of capitulation, agreed upon by November 25, provided, as usual, for the evacuation within three years of those wishing to leave for Africa, and for those choosing to remain, the free practice of Islam, the use of Arabic and of Moorish dress and customs, the administration of justice under Moslem law before Moslem judges, and full property rights. All remaining fortresses and artillery in the kingdom were to be turned over, and Boabdil was to become lord of a small territory in the Alpujarras on the southern slopes of the Sierra Nevada.

Although the end of March had been fixed for actual surrender of the city, Boabdil's concern over his fate, as news of his submission spread, led him to fix January 2, 1492, as the day of Christian occupation. On this date were set in train the last events in the long drama of the reconquest: the installation of the new Christian garrison and its *alcaide,* Íñigo López de Mendoza, count of Tendilla; the raising of the cross and the royal banner of Castile over the Alhambra's highest tower; the departure of the fallen Boabdil for the seigneury in the Alpujarras that he soon exchanged for exile in Africa; and, on Epiphany, January 6, in an atmosphere of high religious and national exaltation, the solemn entry of the Catholic Kings into the city of Granada and through the gates of the Naṣrid palace of the Alhambra.

The fall of the small Naṣrid kingdom of Granada eight centuries after Ṭāriq ibn-Ziyād's landing at Gibraltar, and 400 years after Zallaca and Clermont, signalizes the formal close of the reconquest, but of course this does not mean the end of the Moorish problem or of Iberian territorial expansion toward the south and Africa. After 1492 numerous Moslems or imperfectly Christianized Moriscos continued to live as Spanish subjects in Granada, Andalusia, Murcia, Aragon, and Valencia, and in this story there are other chapters: the collapse by 1499–1500 of the so-called capitulations of Santa Fe made with Boabdil, the royal pragmatic of 1502 compelling conversion or expulsion of the Castilian Moors, the revolts of the Moriscos in 1506 and 1568–1570, the problem of clandestine Moorish collaboration with the Turks, and the final Morisco expulsion in 1609. We have already noted the Portuguese renewal of the reconquest in Morocco from 1415 on, and can now observe how at the very time of the Granadan war other commanders of the Catholic Kings were engaged in the conquest, Christianization, and colonization of the Canary islands, which Spaniards regarded as a continuation of the peninsular reconquest.[32] Even more directly, the debarkations of Spanish troops in North Africa—at Melilla in 1497 under Peter

32. Cf. R. B. Merriman, *The Rise of the Spanish Empire in the Old World and the New* (4 vols., New York, 1918–1934), II, chapters 16, 18; F. Pérez Embid, *Los Descubrimientos en el Atlántico y la rivalidad castellano-portuguesa hasta el Tratado de Tordesillas* (Seville, 1948; Publicaciones de la Escuela de estudios hispano-americanos, series 2, no. 6).

Estopiñán, at Mers-el-Kebir, Oran, Bugia, and Algiers in 1505–1510 under the direction of the cardinal-regent Francis Jiménez de Cisneros and the conquistador Peter Navarro, and in 1535 the capture of Tunis by Charles V—represent the continuing thrust of the motives and objectives of the medieval reconquest, the plan to acquire new Granadas in the Maghrib.

Thus 1492 marks a beginning as well as an end. Yet more fundamental still is the continuing impact upon Spaniards and Portuguese of convictions, values, institutions, practices, and goals shaped in the medieval centuries and surviving into the new age of overseas expansion after 1492 for both Iberian peoples. A distinguished authority has declared the anti-Moorish struggle of the Middle Ages the key to Spanish (and, we may add, Portuguese) history insofar as it gave it a unique character forged in the confrontation, military and cultural, with the alien dynamisms of Islam and Africa. The persistence for so long of an open frontier of war and conquest runs centrally through medieval Iberian experience, imposing its sense of danger and struggle, and its prizes of prestige, power, booty, and land as the rewards of individual and collective effort. To it can be traced in great measure such characteristics of medieval Iberian society as its high degree of mobility, the widespread preference for pastoralism over sedentary crop-farming, the predominance of walled towns and castles over dispersed village communities, the familiarity with techniques of planting cities and castles, churches and monasteries, in one countryside after another. No less surely the reconquest deepened religious feeling, the sense of championship of the faith on the rim of Christendom, and here the convergence with the crusade is strong.

From 1095 on the Iberian reconquest was unmistakably, with papal collaboration, the western theater of the crusading movement, holding firm the door of Christendom against the mighty blows of African Islam, tying down for centuries forces that might well have retarded, if not shattered, the emergent civilization of the awakening medieval west. Yet at the same time the Iberian reconquest was an undeniably autochthonous process, a testing ground of institutions and ideas, of nation-building and colonization, that like the other important elements of medieval Iberian history affected all three of its constituent religio-ethnic communities, not only Christians and Moors but—an aspect historians have yet to explore—the Jews, who appear as royal officials and administrators, financiers and redeemers of captives, combat warriors and colonists, and intermediaries of cultural exchange. Christians knew the Moor as a fierce, implacable foe but realized that, once the question of political supremacy was settled, he would become a fellow subject under the king; we need only cite the vast contrast in attitudes, for example, between the French *Chanson de Roland* and the Castilian *Cantar del Cid,* or between the late crusade ideal and the rejection of it in favor of peaceful conversion by so eminent a mid-fifteenth-century thinker as cardinal John of Segovia, to appreciate the extent to which acceptance of human coexistence (*convivencia*) as well as enmity toward external dominion colors the history of the reconquest.[33]

To be sure, between 1095 and 1492 many fluctuations in national and religious purpose can be discerned: the bitter drives for survival against the Murābiṭ, Muwaḥḥid, and Marīnid might in the twelfth and thirteenth centuries, the loss of momentum after 1350, and the revival of effort in the fifteenth century that carried over into the Turkish and Reformation wars, and the great overseas conquests, colonizations, and missionary enterprises of the early modern age. Yet the impulses and methods, the skills in warfare and in the creation of new societies that Spaniards displayed in the Caribbean, Mexico, and Peru, and Portuguese in the Atlantic islands, Africa, Asia, and the Brazilian captaincies, all are deeply rooted in the reconquest past and the long medieval confrontation with Islam.

33. D. Cabanelas Rodríguez, *Juan de Segovia y el problema islámico* (Madrid, 1952).

XIII
MOSLEM NORTH AFRICA
1049–1394

Toward the end of the fourteenth Christian or eighth Islamic century, abū-Zaid 'Abd-ar-Raḥmān ibn-Muḥammad, of the Banū-Khaldūn, snatched a few months from a remarkably full life to write a "Book of Examples," *Kitāb al-'ibar.* The latest date in the portion concerning his native North Africa falls in A.H. 796, or A.D. 1394,

The principal source, Ibn-Khaldūn's *Kitab al-'ibar,* has been published in full (7 vols.) at Būlāq, A.H. 1284 (A.D. 1867/8, reprinted 1971); the North African portions (vols. 6–7), ed. MacGuckin de Slane as *Histoire des Berbères* (2 vols., Algiers, 1847–1851), were translated by de Slane, also as *Histoire des Berbères* (4 vols., Algiers, 1852–1856; reprinted almost unaltered as "edited by Paul Casanova," Paris, 1925–1956, and again 1968–1969). For additional information, consult Carl Brockelmann, *Geschichte der arabischen Literatur* (2nd ed., 2 vols., Leyden, 1943–1949, with 3 supplemental vols. [cited as sI, sII, sIII], Leyden, 1937–1942), II, 314, 679; sII, 342.

The most important other chroniclers, in roughly chronological order, are the following; for each author the best edition and translation of his complete work or the relevant portion thereof will be cited, with reference to Brockelmann for further information:

Al-Bakrī (abū-'Ubaid 'Abd-Allāh ibn-'Abd-al-'Azīz), *Kitāb al-masālik wa-l-mamālik;* North African portion ed. de Slane as *Description de l'Afrique septentrionale* (2nd ed., Algiers, 1910) and trans. de Slane (2nd ed., Algiers, 1913); both were reprinted together (Paris, 1965): Brockelmann, I, 627; sI, 875; sIII, 1242.

Al-Idrīsī (abū-'Abd-Allāh Muḥammad ibn-Muḥammad), *Nuzhat al-mushtāq fī ikhtirāq al-āfāq;* North African and Spanish portions ed. and trans. by Reinhart Dozy and Michael Jan de Goeje as *Description de l'Afrique et de l'Espagne* (Leyden, 1866): Brockelmann, I, 628; sI, 876; sIII, 1242.

Anonymous, *Kitāb al-istibṣār fī 'ajā'ib al-amṣār;* North African portion ed. Alfred von Kremer as "Description de l'Afrique . . . ," *Sitzungsberichte der Kaiserlich-Königlichen Akademie der Wissenschaften (Wien), Philosophisch-historische Classe,* VIII (1852), 389–428, and trans. Edmond Fagnan as "L'Afrique septentrionale au XIIe siècle . . . ," *Recueil des notices et mémoires de la Société archéologique de Constantine,* XXXIII (1899): Brockelmann, sI, 879.

As-Sam'ānī ('Abd-al-Karīm ibn-Muḥammad), *Kitāb al-ansāb fī ma'rifat al-aṣḥāb;* selection ed. and trans. Évariste Lévi-Provençal as "La Généalogie des Almohades et l'organisation du parti" in his *Documents inédits d'histoire almohade* (Paris, 1928), pp. 25–74: Brockelmann, I, 401; sI, 564.

'Abd-al-Wāḥid al-Marrākushī (abū-Muḥammad . . . ibn-'Alī), *Kitāb al-mu'jib fī talkhīs akhbār al-Maghrib:* ed. Dozy as *The History of the Almohades* (2nd ed., Leyden, 1881; repr.

which will serve admirably as a terminus for the crusading period there, especially since the final crusade in this area occurred in 1390. If this choice serves to stress the importance of Ibn-Khaldūn among the multitude of medieval North African historians, nothing could be more appropriate. Any chronicle of this place and period must be in

1968); trans. Fagnan as *Histoire des Almohades* (Algiers, 1893; from *Revue africaine*): Brockelmann, I, 392; sI, 555.

Ibn-al-Athīr (abū-l-Ḥasan 'Alī ibn-Muḥammad), *Kitāb al-kāmil fī-t-ta'rīkh;* ed. Carl Johann Tornberg as *Chronicon* . . . (14 vols., Leyden, 1851–1876; repr. Beirut, 1965–); North African and Spanish portions trans. Fagnan as *Annales du Maghreb et de l'Espagne* (Algiers, 1901; from *Revue africaine*): Brockelmann, I, 422; sI, 587, 969.

Ibn-'Idhārī (al-Marrākushī), *Kitāb al-bayān al-mughrib fī akhbār mulūk al-Andalus wa-l-Maghrib;* portion ed. Dozy as *Histoire de l'Afrique et de l'Espagne* (2 vols., Leyden, 1848–1851) and trans. Fagnan (2 vols., Algiers, 1901–1904); balance ed. Lévi-Provençal as *Histoire de l'Espagne musulmane au XIème siècle* (Paris, 1930); rev. ed. by G. S. Colin and Lévi-Provençal (2nd ed., 2 vols., Leyden, 1948–1951, with 3rd vol. ed. A. Huici Miranda, Tetuan, 1960), all trans. Huici Miranda (2 vols., Tetuan, 1953–1954; 3rd vol., Valencia, 1963): Brockelmann, I, 411; sI, 577.

Al-Baidhaq (Abū-Bakr ibn-'Alī), *Ta'rīkh al-Muwaḥḥidīn;* ed. and trans. Lévi-Provençal as "L'Histoire des Almohades," in his *Documents inédits d'histoire almohade* (Paris, 1928), pp. 75–224: Brockelmann, sI, 554, 967.

Ibn-abī-Zar' (abū-l-Ḥasan 'Alī ibn-'Abd-Allāh), *Kitāb al-anīs al-muṭrib bi-rauḍ al-qirṭās fī akhbār mulūk al-Maghrib wa-ta'rīkh madīnat Fās;* ed. and trans. Tornberg as *Annales regum Mauritaniae* (Uppsala, 1843–1845); trans. Auguste Beaumier as *Roudh el-Kartas: Histoire des souverains du Maghreb . . . et annales de la ville de Fès* (Paris, 1860): Brockelmann, II, 312; sII, 339.

Ibn-Faḍl-Allāh al-'Umarī (abū-l-'Abbās Aḥmad ibn-Yaḥyâ), *Masālik al-abṣār fī mamālik al-amṣār;* Moroccan portion ed. M. Gaudefroy-Demombynes as "Quelques passages relatifs au Maroc," *Mémorial Henri Basset,* I (Paris, 1928), 269–280; North African portion trans. *idem* as *L'Afrique moins l'Égypte* (Paris, 1927): Brockelmann, II, 177; sII, 175; sIII, 1261.

Ibn-al-Khaṭīb (Lisān-ad-Dīn abū-'Abd-Allāh Muḥammad ibn-'Abd-Allāh), *Ta'rīkh al-Maghrib al-'Arabī* (Casablanca, 1964) and several other works in scattered editions and translations: Brockelmann, II, 337, 679; sII, 397; sIII, 1279.

Yaḥyâ ibn-Khaldūn (abū-Zakarīyā' Yaḥyâ ibn-Muḥammad), *Bughyat ar-rūwād fī dhikr al-mulūk min Banī 'Abd al-Wād;* ed. and trans. Alfred Bel as *Histoire des Beni 'Abd el-Wād* (2 vols., Algiers, 1904–1913): Brockelmann, II, 312; sII, 340.

Later Arabic historians of significance include Ibn-Qunfudh al-Qusanṭīnī (abū-l-'Abbās Aḥmad ibn-al-Ḥasan), *Al-Fārisīyah fī mabādi ad-daulah al-Ḥafṣīyah;* selections ed. and trans. Auguste Cherbonneau under various titles in *Journal asiatique,* 4:XII (1848), 239–252; 4:XIII (1849), 187–205; 4:XVII (1851), 52–77; 4:XX (1852), 211–238: Brockelmann, II, 313; sII, 341.

Ibn-al-Aḥmar (abū-l-Walīd Ismā'īl ibn-Yūsuf), *An-nafḥah an-nisrīnīyah wa-l-lamḥah al-Marīnīyah;* Moroccan portion ed. and trans. Ghaoutsi Bouali and Georges Marçais as "Histoire des Benî Merîn, rois de Fâs," *Bulletin de correspondance africaine,* LV (1917), 1–107; Algerian portion ed. Lévi-Provençal as "Deux nouveaux manuscrits . . . ," *Journal asiatique,* CCIII (1923), 231–255, and trans. Dozy as "Histoire des Benou-Ziyan de Tlemcen," *Journal asiatique,* 4:III (1844), 382–416: Brockelmann, II, 313; sII, 340.

Az-Zarkashī (abū-'Abd-Allāh Muḥammad ibn-Ibrāhīm), *Ta'rīkh ad-daulatain al-Muwaḥḥidīyah wa-l-Ḥafṣīyah* (Tunis, A.H. 1289 [A.D. 1872/3]); trans. Fagnan as *Chronique des Almohades et des Hafçides* (Constantine, 1895): Brockelmann, II, 606; sII, 677.

Ibn-abī-Dīnār (abū-'Abd-Allāh Muḥammad ibn-abī-l-Qāsim), *Al-mu'nis fī akhbār Ifrīqiyah* essentials a reworking of his narrative, amplified and occasionally corrected from other medieval Arabic sources. Direct historical evidence is limited to a few letters and official documents, supplemented by numismatic and epigraphic data of considerable value.

In the study of medieval history by modern scholars, North Africa has been a neglected stepchild between Egypt and Spain.[1] In the

wa-Tūnis (Tunis, A.H. 1286 [A.D. 1869/70] and 1350 [1931/2], repr. 1967); trans. Edmond Pellissier and Gaston Rémusat as *Histoire de l'Afrique* (Paris, 1845): Brockelmann, II, 607; sII, 682.

The best collections of letters and official documents are still Louis de Mas Latrie, *Traités de paix et de commerce et documents divers concernant les relations de l'Afrique septentrionale au moyen âge* (Paris, 1866; repr. New York, 1964); Lévi-Provençal, "Un Recueil de lettres officielles almohades," *Hespéris*, XXVIII (1941), 1–80; Mariano Gaspar y Remiro, *Correspondencia diplomática entre Granáda y Fez, siglo XIV* (Granada, 1916, from *Revista del Centro de estudios históricos de Granáda y su reino*); Lévi-Provençal, "Lettres d'Ibn Tumart et de 'Abd al-Mu'min," in his *Documents inédits d'histoire almohade* (Paris, 1928), pp. 1–24; and Silvestre de Sacy, "Pièces diplomatiques tirées des archives de la république de Gènes," *Notices et extraits,* XI-1 (1827), 1–96. Important individual items are Gaudefroy-Demombynes, "Une Lettre de Saladin au calife almohade," *Mélanges René Basset,* II (Paris, 1925), 279–304; Eugène Tisserant and Gaston Wiet, "Une Lettre de l'Almohade Murtad'â au pape Innocent IV," *Hespéris*, VI (1926), 27–53; de Sacy, "Mémoire sur le traité fait entre le roi de Tunis et Philippe-le-Hardi, en 1270 . . . ," and "Mémoire sur une correspondance de l'empereur de Maroc Yakoub, fils d'Abd-alhakk, avec Philippe-le-Hardi . . . ," *Mémoires de l'Académie des inscriptions et belles-lettres,* IX (1831), 488–506; and Julián Ribera, "Tratado de paz . . . entre Fernando I . . . rey de Nápoles y Abuámer Otmán rey de Tunez [1477]," *Centenario Michele Amari,* II (Palermo, 1910), 373–386.

The numismatic literature on Moslem North Africa is extensive; a complete bibliography and corpus of coins will be found in H. W. Hazard, *The Numismatic History of Late Medieval North Africa* (New York, 1952), with "Additions and Supplementary Notes" in the American Numismatic Society's *Museum Notes,* XII (New York, 1966), 195–221. For coins struck in medieval North Africa by Christian invaders, see H. H. Abdulwahab, "Deux dinars normands de Mahdia [1151, 1157]," *Revue tunisienne,* n.s., I (1930), 215–218, and G. Hannezo, "Monnaies d'or frappées à Tunis en 1270 par Charles Ier d'Anjou," *Revue tunisienne,* XXVII (1920), 44–45, as well as earlier articles noted there.

For epigraphy, consult especially Combe, Sauvaget, and Wiet, *Répertoire chronologique d'épigraphie arabe* (Cairo, 1931–); Gabriel Colin, *Corpus des inscriptions arabes et turques de l'Algérie: Département d'Alger* (Paris, 1901); Gustave Mercier, *Corpus . . . : Département de Constantine* (Paris, 1902); Octave Houdas and René Basset, "Épigraphie tunisienne," *Bulletin de correspondance africaine,* I (1882), 161–200; Gustave Mercier, "Inscriptions arabes de Bougie," *Bulletin de la Société d'archéologie de Constantine,* 1901, pp. 167–169; C. Brosselard, "Mémoire épigraphique et historique sur les tombeaux des émirs Beni-Zeiyân," *Journal asiatique,* 7:VII (1876), 5–197; Alfred Bel, "Inscriptions arabes de Fès," *Journal asiatique,* 11:IX (1917), 303–329; 11:X (1917), 81–170, 215–267; 11:XII (1918), 189–276, 337–399; 11:XIII (1919), 5–96; 11:XIV (1919), 467–479; and Henri Basset and Lévi-Provençal, "Chella, une nécropole mérinide," *Hespéris,* II (1922), 1–92, 255–316, 385–425.

1. Comparatively, of course, for much valuable work has been done, first by French scholars, and more recently by Spaniards and North Africans as well. The best general histories of medieval North Africa are Ernest Mercier's *Histoire de l'Afrique septentrionale* (3 vols., Paris, 1888–1891) and Charles A. Julien's *Histoire de l'Afrique du nord* (2nd ed., 2 vols., Paris, 1951–1952; rev. ed. 1966–), trans. John Petrie (New York, 1970).

English language, for example, there is no complete scholarly history of North Africa between the Arab conquest of the seventh century and the Turkish conquest of the sixteenth, nor a single translation of more than a few pages of any of the Arabic historians named in the bibliographical note.

This neglect does not signify any presumptive unimportance of North Africa, either relative or absolute. The southern coast of the Mediterranean played, during the crusading period, a larger role in human history than at any time after the fall of Carthage, larger than at any subsequent time until the brief struggle in 1942–1943 between the Allied and Axis military forces. Morocco, for instance, supplied two Berber waves which successively within a century's span swept over Spain, postponing and endangering the Christian reconquest.[2] Tunisia, where the Fāṭimids of Egypt had originated, provided the most logical and powerful claimant to the caliphate when the Fāṭimids, and their 'Abbāsid rivals, collapsed within the period of the crusades. Finally, it was with North Africa that Sicily maintained the continuous commercial and sporadic military contacts which made the island realm a center for transmission of Islamic culture to western Europe second only to Andalusia, and far more important than Constantinople, Frankish Greece, Cyprus, or the crusader principalities on the eastern shore of the Mediterranean.

For our purposes, as for those of all medieval Moslems, "North Africa" extends from about 25 degrees east longitude, the western boundary of Egypt then and now, westward between the desert and the Mediterranean in a gradually widening strip which reaches its greatest breadth near the Atlantic Ocean. This area has always been geographically and historically a single unit, clearly demarcated from Egypt to the east and from the Sahara and Sudan to the south; during these three and a half centuries continuous contacts were maintained with both, but on a smaller scale and with less effect than those with Spain and Sicily. This two-thousand-mile sweep includes part or all of the modern regions of Cyrenaica, Tripolitania, Tunisia, Algeria, and Morocco; from 1160 to 1230 under the Muwaḥḥids and briefly about 1347 and in 1357 under the Marīnids they were, except Cyrenaica, subject to the rule of a single monarch, a historical phenomenon which had not occurred since Roman times and has not since been repeated.

If the closing date adopted, 1394, is partly historiographical and

2. See above, chapter XII.

partly historical in import, the reasons for opening with 1049 are wholly historical, for within a decade the political, economic, and religious circumstances of both Tunisia and Morocco were to be profoundly altered. In 1049 Tunisia was visibly prosperous and peaceful, adjectives which would be inapplicable for over a century thereafter.[3] Agriculture was flourishing, with wheat along the north coast, olives along the east coast around Sfax and Susa, dates on the palms of the Jerid, gardens and fruit orchards everywhere, even cotton and sugar cane. Salt was obtained from the great deposits west of Kairawan, fish from the Mediterranean and the inlet of Bizerte; camels, horses, and sheep abounded in the less fertile desert and highland zones. Manufactures included cloth of cotton and of wool, some of it extremely rich or delicate, excellent pottery and glass, and competent metalwork. A thriving commerce was conducted overland with Fāṭimid Egypt, with the Sudan, with Algeria and Morocco; it was rivaled by sea-borne trade with Fāṭimid Sicily and with Andalusia, and with such Christian ports as Genoa and Pisa. Cities prospered, from semi-independent Gabes in the south, with its fair-sized Christian remnant, to the holy city of Kairawan in the center, full of scholars and orthodox theologians, past the ornate palaces in its suburb Ṣabrah, where excises and other highly productive imposts were collected and added to the royal treasury, to Mahdia, the strongly fortified port, and Tunis in the north.

The predominantly Berber population participated contentedly in this prosperity, considering their lives and property secure under a strong and competent government which was itself composed of serious-minded Ṣanhājah Berbers who shared the Sunnite tendencies of the large majority of their subjects. The small Christian, Jewish, Khārijite (heretical), and Arab minorities had no bitter grievances which might have threatened the dominant Berbers.

The temporal power was firmly in the hands of the Zīrid dynasty, which had no internecine rivalries to contend with, and whose nominal allegiance to the Shī'ite Fāṭimid caliph at Cairo, Ma'add al-Mustanṣir, rested lightly on them. Relations with the Ḥammādids of eastern Algeria had been placed on a peaceful basis by the treaty of 1042/3, and raids by Zanātah Berber tribesmen had been firmly repulsed in 1029 and 1035/6. The current ruler, fourth Zīrid to govern Tunisia in a direct line of descent, was al-Mu'izz ibn-Bādīs, a

---

3. Material on Tunisia and eastern Algeria has been carefully compared with the descriptive analysis in George Marçais's excellent *La Berbérie musulmane et l'Orient au moyen âge* (Paris, 1946).

strong, shrewd, popular man of Sunnite leanings and confident temperament. He had ruled ably since 1016, and the mob killing of some Shī'ite soldiers soon after his accession to power had not precipitated any open break with Cairo.

His father's cousin, al-Qā'id ibn-Ḥammād, maintained a similar regime in eastern Algeria, with his capital at the fortified mountain town called Qal'at Banī-Ḥammād. His reign, commencing in 1028, had been marked by skillful diplomacy, including the buying off of Zanātah raiders in 1038/9 and the negotiating of the treaty with al-Mu'izz to terminate a two-year siege. His realm, which his father Ḥammād ibn-Bulukkīn had detached from the Zīrid holdings in 1014 and in which the Fāṭimid suzerainty and the Shī'ite theology had been simultaneously renounced, was in most respects a less brilliant counterpart of Tunisia. Eastern Algeria in 1049 was prosperous, its capital was a fine city, its culture and scholarship and manufactures and commerce were adequate, its Berber citizens were content, yet in none of these did it succeed in rivaling its eastern neighbor.

By comparison with Tunisia and eastern Algeria under their Ṣanhā-jah Berber rulers, Morocco and western Algeria were turbulent and disorganized in 1049, but the contenders for power were all local chieftains. The situation during the tenth century, when the Spanish Umaiyads, the Tunisian Fāṭimids, and the Moroccan Idrīsids had intrigued for Berber support, had been resolved by the Fāṭimids' move eastward and the extinction of both the other contending dynasties. Even the successors of the Umaiyads, the Ḥammūdids of Malaga and Ceuta, held only the one toehold in Africa, and were too occupied with intradynastic warfare to think of expanding their holdings. Relieved of external pressure, the Berbers followed their ancient pattern of pastoral nomadism, small-scale cultivation of grains, and urban commerce. Petty warfare between tribes and strug-gles for tribal leadership occupied their attentions as in pre-Islamic days, and the whole region formed a cultural backwater and, to change the metaphor, a power vacuum susceptible to conquest from within or without. Like Morocco in the west, Tripolitania and Cyrenaica in the east were in fact held by local chieftains, some of whom governed the few towns, like Tripoli, while others led nomads who combined a pastoral life with sporadic raiding.

The first breach in this peaceful picture resulted from al-Mu'izz's Sunnite proclivities. He had gradually, for nearly a decade, abated his recognition of Fāṭimid suzerainty by denying the Shī'ite caliph in various implicit ways, becoming increasingly bolder as his defiant gestures went unpunished. Finally, relying on the leagues of desert between Egypt and Tunisia, al-Muʻizz in 1049 removed the name of Maʻadd from the coinage and the Friday invocation, thus formally renouncing allegiance to the Shīʻite.[4] He went further, placing a Sunnite legend on his coins and mentioning in public prayer the ʻAbbāsid caliph, al-Qāʼim, who responded with a diploma of investiture. Needless to say, this was a mere formal approbation, as no effective power was wielded in North Africa by any ʻAbbāsid after Hārūn ar-Rashīd.

Resenting this insurrection on both personal and religious grounds, Maʻadd at Cairo, counseled by his vizir al-Yazūrī, hit upon one of the most overwhelmingly effective revenges on record. It happened that in the fringes of the desert east of the Nile there were large groups of nomad Arabs who were disturbing the Fāṭimid's subjects by raids and similar incivilities. By the simple device—ingenious but unoriginal—of bestowing upon their leaders the titular governorship of all North Africa, he persuaded them to attack al-Muʻizz on his behalf.

This swarm of locusts, consisting of the great tribes Banū-Hilāl and Banū-Sulaim with their hangers-on, descended on Tripolitania and Tunisia during 1052, occupied Tripoli, defeated the Zīrid army in battle, besieged al-Muʻizz in Kairawan, and ravaged the countryside. Since this last phrase occurs frequently in history, further comment is necessary in this instance: North Africa, and particularly Tunisia, had been one of the most fertile areas of the known world, the granary of the Roman empire; the Arabs, scorning all cultivators of the soil, systematically devastated the whole province so that famine became endemic and agriculture has even today, over nine hundred years later, not been restored to its ancient level.

Al-Muʻizz tried every possible method of preserving his kingdom; he fought battles, he married his daughters to the least hostile chieftains, he bribed and threatened, he urged the Arabs to attack Algeria, which they cheerfully did, but nothing succeeded. He was forced to slip out of his capital to take refuge in the strongly fortified port of Mahdia, while the Arabs looted Kairawan with unusual thoroughness. The historians do not mention it, but al-Muʻizz and his son Tamīm, who succeeded him in 1062, apparently went to the extreme of attempting to propitiate the Fāṭimid Maʻadd, as the Sunnite coins give way between 1057/8 and 1065 to Shīʻite

---

4. Although the Arab historians differ on this date, it is firmly established by numismatic evidence (Hazard, *Numismatic History*, pp. 52–56, 90–94). It is noteworthy that the Hammādids, who had renounced Shīʻism and Fāṭimid allegiance in 1014, resumed them following the Zīrid rupture and derived some momentary benefit from their opportunism (*ibid.*, pp. 56–57, 94–96).

gold struck at Mahdia in the name of Ma'add. However, if there was such an attempt, it failed, and it is very unlikely that Ma'add could have recalled the voracious horde he had sent against Tunisia.[5]

The other cities of Tunisia reached separate agreements with the invaders, after the first murderous pillaging, and set up tiny sovereignties under Arab or Berber nobles or adventurers. It is not too far-fetched to compare their status in 1049 to that of provincial towns of the Roman empire at its height, and in 1059 to that of the same towns after the barbarian invasions, so shattered was the entire political and economic structure.

The Ḥammādids of eastern Algeria were slightly less hard hit. It is true they were defeated in battle by the Arabs, and their countryside was stripped, but the assault was weaker and less persistent, and a *modus vivendi* was soon reached by which the Berbers held the towns and paid tribute to the invaders. In partial recompense, Algeria inherited some of the commerce and culture which fled ravaged Tunisia. Scholars, artisans, and merchants moved to Qal'at Banī-Ḥammād and, when Arab impositions made that inland stronghold untenable, they accompanied the Ḥammādids to the new capital at Bugia in 1069, and again, definitively, in 1104. Yet the net effect of the Arab incursion on eastern Algeria was to decrease its prosperity in agriculture and commerce and to eliminate personal security for ruler and citizen alike.

This relatively unsatisfactory pattern became stabilized for the whole region between Egypt and Algiers, with land commerce totally prevented by roving marauders, with agriculture drastically curtailed, and with civilization isolated in fortified towns paying tribute to the nomads. Among the permanent effects of the Arab invasion must also be included the increase in the proportion of pastoral nomads to sedentary cultivators, the displacement of Berber nomads—chiefly Zanātah—by the newcomers, the diffusion of the Arabic language in rural areas, the movement of whatever culture survived northward to the ports or mountain towns such as Constantine, and the seaward orientation of Berber commercial activity and military prowess.[6]

Morocco meanwhile was undergoing a sharply contrasting series of events. An ascetic religious reformer, 'Abd-Allāh ibn-Yāsīn, of the Kazūlī tribe, had appeared in the desert fringes and secured support

5. The invaders, ironically enough, were admired by later generations as the epitome of Arab chivalry, and inspired a popular ballad-cycle, *Sirat abī Zaid wa-Banī Hilāl* (for editions see Brockelmann, II, 74; sII, 64).

6. For further details consult Marçais, *op. cit.,* and *Les Arabes en Berbérie du XIe au XIVe siècle* (Constantine, 1913).

among the Lamtūnah Berbers. Since religious movements in Islam usually develop political and military aspects, he appointed a Lamtūnī named Yaḥyâ ibn-'Umar to command his well-disciplined and fanatically determined forces. Yaḥyâ was succeeded in 1056 by his brother Abū-Bakr, generally considered the first Murābiṭ ("outpost," corrupted through Spanish to Almoravid) ruler. With Sijilmasa as a base conquests were made rapidly in all directions. The veil-wearing precursors of the modern Tuareg (*Ṭawāriq*) mustered a rapid striking force which defeated local rivals piecemeal, and then recruited among their victims with the ancient and irresistable Moroccan dual appeal to religious fanaticism and the desire for loot. In 1061 Abū-Bakr turned his attack southward, leaving his cousin Yūsuf ibn-Tāshfīn as his lieutenant in northern Morocco. Although most Arabic historians considered Yūsuf absolutely independent thereafter, his name did not replace that of Abū-Bakr on Murābiṭ coins until after the latter died in 1087 while fighting Negro tribes far to the south. In the intervening quarter-century Abū-Bakr had consolidated Murābiṭ power in southern Morocco, destroyed the remnants of the great Negro empire of Ghana, and spread his version of Islam over several degrees of latitude and longitude; nor had Yūsuf been idle, as he had conquered western Algeria and all northern Morocco, including Ceuta (then under Saqaut the Barghawāṭī), and had responded to Andalusian pleas for aid with the resounding victory of Zallaca in October of 1086,[7] after which he had returned to Africa.

It is frequently asserted, possibly correctly, that it was after this triumph over the Spanish Christians that Yūsuf, nominally deferring to the 'Abbāsid caliph as his spiritual superior, assumed the title *amīr al-muslimīn,* but his coins never go beyond the simple *amīr,* which he used after Abū-Bakr's death in 1087. For nearly twenty years more Yūsuf reigned as sole sovereign of the Murābiṭs, almost attaining the age of one hundred lunar years, with apparently undiminished vigor, for within this period fell his conquest of half the Iberian peninsula from his former Moslem allies and his Christian foes alike. At his death in 1106 his pious son 'Alī inherited an extensive, firmly controlled, prosperous empire including half Spain, half Algeria, and all Morocco.

'Alī's thirty-seven-year reign was uniquely fortunate for its time and place in having no history. Nothing happened, beyond a few border skirmishes, to mar his generation's enjoyment and easy-going exploitation of their warrior fathers' conquests—nothing, that is, beyond a typically Berber theological-military revolt among the hill

7. See above, p. 401.

tribes of the High Atlas, instigated by one Muḥammad Ibn-Tūmart, of the Harghī tribe, who proclaimed himself the Mahdī, or divinely guided leader, about 1121 and died seven (or nine) years later after rallying considerable support to his Muwaḥḥid ("unitarian," corrupted through Spanish to Almohad) anti-anthropomorphic dogmas and anti-Murābiṭ politics.

Ibn-Tūmart's successor, who was proclaimed in 1130, was a faithful disciple, 'Abd-al-Mu'min ibn-'Alī, of the Kūmī tribe, who by missionary zeal and military force converted the neighboring Berbers, cracked the imposing Murābiṭ façade, and eliminated 'Alī's young and incompetent successors Tāshfīn, Ibrāhīm, and Isḥāq. The conquest of Marrakesh in 1147 was followed by Muwaḥḥid acquisition of the whole Murābiṭ empire on both sides of the Strait of Gibraltar. The powerful military machine included many former Murābiṭ troops as well as Maṣmūdah Berber mountain nomads in great numbers.

Even before completing operations in Spain, 'Abd-al-Mu'min turned his forces eastward against eastern Algeria, still shared by Ḥammādids in the towns and, in the rural areas, Arabs who dominated the local Berbers. Neither group could resist the Muwaḥḥid onslaught of 1152. The ninth Ḥammādid, Yaḥyâ ibn-al-'Azīz, hastily surrendered Bugia, Algiers, Constantine, and his other meager holdings, while the Arabs were defeated and either scattered, deported to Morocco, or enrolled in the Muwaḥḥid forces in Spain.

Among those who acclaimed 'Abd-al-Mu'min in eastern Algeria was al-Ḥasan ibn-'Alī, eighth and last Zīrid ruler in Tunisia. Like his father and grandfather before him, he had exercised authority over little more than the port of Mahdia. The Zīrids had adjusted their policies as well as possible to their restricted status for nearly a century, developing a sea-borne trade to replace the vanished African commerce. Their position opposite Sicily had led them to intervene several times in unsuccessful efforts to prevent the Christian reconquest: in 1026 while sailing against the Byzantines a Zīrid fleet had been shipwrecked off Pantelleria; the same fate frustrated the expedition of 1052 against the Normans; a final thrust in 1068 landed but withdrew without accomplishing much. In 1075 a truce was negotiated between Tamīm of Mahdia and Roger I of Sicily, and peaceful trade flourished for many years between their realms.

Tamīm had meanwhile actively encouraged piracy against other Christian territories, and the inevitable reprisal occurred in 1087. Genoa and Pisa combined forces, with the papal blessing, and took Mahdia, pillaging it and levying heavy tribute before retiring. This brief foray, eight years before Urban's promulgation of the idea at Clermont, was the first crusading effort by Christians in North Africa, but its success failed to halt the organized and highly profitable Zīrid piracy, which was seconded by Ḥammādid corsairs based on Bugia. A second Italian assault, in 1104, was unsuccessful.

The real threat was to come from Norman Sicily, in retaliation for the 1122 sacking of Nicotera in Calabria by Moroccans transported on Zīrid ships. An attack on Mahdia in 1123 failed, as did a Ḥammādid combined land and sea operation in 1135. The Normans took the island of Jerba in 1135; in 1143 they took Sfax after unsuccessfully attacking Tripoli. Consecutive years witnessed punitive raids on other pirate lairs, culminating in the pillage of Tripoli in 1146. Finally, in 1148, Mahdia itself was stormed, and al-Ḥasan fled to the Arabs and then to his Ḥammādid relative and rival, who imprisoned him. He persuaded 'Abd-al-Mu'min that the honor of Islam, of which the Muwaḥḥid claimed to be *amīr al-mu'minīn* ("commander of the faithful"), required that the accursed "infidel" be expelled from his North African footholds. 'Abd-al-Mu'min delayed action for several years in order to consolidate his administration, appointing his many sons governors of the far-flung cities and provinces of Andalusia and Morocco, as well as the newly-won Numidia, always with experienced Muwaḥḥid counselors to assist them. In 1159 the army moved eastward, and within two years conquered all Tunisia and Tripolitania. The local chieftains were besieged if they hesitated to accept the inevitable incorporation into the Muwaḥḥid domain. The Christians too underwent siege, but were finally, in return for concessions and promises of friendship, permitted to sail to Sicily in January 1160. Their brief tenure of the African coast, marked by tolerance and an attempt by Roger II of Sicily to restore prosperity, was not only the lone extended occupation of North African soil by European Christians between 1049 and 1394 but the sole such occupation between 700 and 1400.[8]

By the time of 'Abd-al-Mu'min's death in 1163, his realm reached from Barca in Cyrenaica to the Atlantic, including all North Africa and half Spain. This was no loosely held aggregation of regions paying nominal allegiance to a titular overlord, but a cohesive, pacified, centrally controlled empire which professed adherence to the doctrines of Ibn-Tūmart and demonstrated its loyal submission to 'Abd-al-Mu'min and his sons by paying regular tribute to his representatives, who in turn forwarded the immense sums to Marra-

---

8. On the Normans in North Africa to 1160 see volume II of this work, pp. 30–31.

kesh. The size of this tribute reflected the return of prosperity to the eastern provinces, as well as the unified development of Morocco and Andalusia. The Tunisian Arabs, like those of Algeria, were broken as military threats to the central government by being dispersed or deported to Morocco, while their warriors were inducted into the Muwaḥḥid forces, often being sent to Spain for frontier defense. Agriculture was revived, land-borne commerce was encouraged and protected, cities were rebuilt and fortified. The new Muwaḥḥid empire represented the apogee of Berber power, exercised under the aegis of a purely Berber version of Islam, militant and virile, strict and intolerant, in which Jews and Christians were forcibly converted, and in which for the first time women were severely secluded.

Under 'Abd-al-Mu'min's son and successor Yūsuf, North Africa experienced twenty-one years of unbroken prosperity. From 1163 to 1184 there were no serious invasions, few important revolts or rivalries, no catastrophic interruptions of any kind. Commercial relations were inaugurated with Genoa and Pisa, and a fortunate generation began to repair the previous century's ravages, while those whose tastes were warlike subdued several minor disturbances and added Almeria and Murcia to Yūsuf's Iberian holdings. In 1184 he was killed while besieging Santarem, and his mantle fell on his son Ya'qūb.

While Ya'qūb's accession was dutifully accepted throughout his father's realm, it was considered as an opportunity by adventurers from an unexpected quarter. Majorca, or Mallorca, largest of the Balearic islands, was ruled by descendants of the last Murābiṭ governor in Spain. He and his heirs were known, after a female ancestor, as the Banū-Ghāniyah, and they were firmly established in their island stronghold. In the November following Ya'qūb's enthronement the current Ibn-Ghāniyah, 'Alī ibn-Isḥāq, left Majorca to his brother Ṭalḥah and sailed with several relations and kindred spirits to Bugia, which was taken by surprise, as were two relatives of the caliph, later ransomed. Leaving his brother Yaḥyâ to govern Bugia, 'Alī took Algiers and Miliana, attacked Qal'at Banī-Ḥammād, and besieged Constantine. Pursuit and retaliation were prompt and vigorous. Miliana expelled its new ruler, Algiers and Bugia were retaken by the Muwaḥḥid fleet, the siege of Constantine was raised. Ibn-Ghāniyah, moving rapidly, assaulted Tozeur, took Gafsa, and joined with an Armenian former slave of Saladin named Karakush, leading a band of Ghuzz Turkomans, to take Tripoli. Ya'qūb in person defeated the combined rebels in battle, retook Gafsa, and left Tunisia well garrisoned. Nevertheless, the Banū-Ghāniyah and their disreputable Arab allies continued smash-and-grab raids, disrupting agriculture and commerce from Tripolitania to Algeria.

In 1190 Saladin of Egypt sent 'Abd-ar-Raḥmān of the Banū-Munqidh to Ya'qūb to ask for naval aid to intercept the supply ships of the crusaders at Acre. Ibn-Khaldūn says the Aiyūbid forwarded a rich present to the Muwaḥḥid, who regretted his inability to aid but later reconsidered and sent 180 ships, which prevented the Christians from landing in Syria. Al-Maqqarī, writing about 1630, says that Ya'qūb was so offended by Saladin's failure to accord him the caliphal title *amīr al-mu'minīn* that he declined to grant help. Gaudefroy-Demombynes concludes that aid was withheld for three reasons: because Ya'qūb needed his ships for Spanish waters, because he did not wish to anger the French, and because he was irritated by Saladin's connections with the Banū-Ghāniyah. The truth is probably that a small flotilla was sent as a gesture, but that it played no significant role in the Syrian fighting. Two letters embodying this request and dated 1189 and 1190 appear to be apocryphal.[9]

Ya'qūb had other problems, of which the most urgent was the Christian counter-attack in Spain culminating in the taking of Silves. In 1195 he crossed to Andalusia and at Alarcos defeated the Spanish Christians decisively. This led him to adopt the sobriquet al-Manṣūr (the victorious, by the help of Allāh), by which he is known to Arab historians. He then returned to Africa, where he died in 1199.

His son Muḥammad, an-Nāṣir, was faced with the same problems, the increasing Christian pressure in Spain and the insolent brigandage of the Banū-Ghāniyah in Tunisia. They took Mahdia in 1202 and Tunis in 1203, at which time they held all Tunisia and pronounced the Friday prayer in the name of the 'Abbāsid caliph. The only fixed policies attributable to the Banū-Ghāniyah are extortion and devastation, at both of which they excelled. An all-out effort by an-Nāṣir, his fleet, and his highly effective general abū-Muḥammad ibn-abī-Ḥafṣ finally trapped and exterminated the raiders, restoring to the Muwaḥḥids their considerably damaged eastern provinces. An-Nāṣir then turned his attention to Spain, but was decisively beaten by the Christians in 1212 at Las Navas de Tolosa, the real turning point in the struggle for the peninsula.[10]

After an-Nāṣir's death in 1213 his son Yūsuf II, al-Mustanṣir, reigned rather tranquilly for eleven years, but after he was killed by a cow in 1224, the Muwaḥḥid strength was dissipated in internal

9. For these letters, and the exchange between Saladin and Ya'qūb, see Gaudefroy-Demombynes's article in *Mélanges René Basset,* II, 279–304.
10. On the reconquest of Spain and Portugal see chapter XII, above.

rivalries. Between 1224 and 1236 there were six major claimants to the Muwaḥḥid caliphate, and, while they scrambled for power and executed one another, the empire fell apart. Andalusia was detached by Ibn-Hūd and Ibn-Naṣr, who established dynasties at Murcia (in 1228) and Granada (in 1232). Thenceforth, except for a brief reversion about 1237, Muwaḥḥid power did not extend into Spain. Likewise the governor of Tunisia, Yaḥyâ, son of the general and governor abū-Muḥammad ibn-abī-Ḥafṣ, in 1230 seized the occasion to disown the contending factions in Morocco and set up an independent state, ostensibly predicated on a return to the original Muwaḥḥid doctrines promulgated by the Mahdī. As the first Ḥafṣid monarch Yaḥyâ made good his revolt, but his neighbor on the west was less fortunate. Western Algeria was under the governorship of Yaghmurāsan ibn-Ziyān, of the Zanātah Berber Banū-'Abd-al-Wād. He set himself up as an independent sovereign at Tlemsen in 1236, but lost his capital to the Ḥafṣid emir in 1242/3 and had to accept a subservient status, the first but not the last Ziyānid to do so. Even within Morocco the Muwaḥḥid dominance was severely challenged. Ceuta in the far north broke away in 1232, while in the vicinity of Fez the Zanātah Berber Banū-Marīn were becoming menacingly aggressive.

The survivor of the Muwaḥḥid free-for-all, 'Abd-al-Wāḥid ibn-Idrīs, ar-Rashīd, strove to rebuild his shattered heritage, but the difficulties proved insuperable. Seville and Granada in Spain, Ceuta (which had been taken in 1235 by a Genoese fleet and ransomed for 400,000 dinars) and Sijilmasa in Morocco recognized his suzerainty for brief periods, but only Fez and Marrakesh remained in his possession at his death in 1242. His brother 'Alī, as-Sa'īd, spent six hectic years in subduing the Marīnids, and was killed attacking the Ziyānids in Tlemsen in 1248. A distant cousin, 'Umar ibn-Isḥāq, al-Murtaḍâ, took up the losing battle and for eighteen years fought Ziyānids, Marīnids, and local rivals. He was executed by another distant cousin, Idrīs II ibn-Muḥammad, known as Abū-Dabbūs, who won the throne with Marīnid aid, refused to share the spoils, and was killed by the fifth Marīnid, Ya'qūb ibn-'Abd-al-Ḥaqq, in 1269. With him ended the only dynasty to rule North Africa as a whole for any extensive period of time, and the last to exert any great influence in Spain.

Thus at the very moment when Louis IX of France was planning his crusade against North Africa, the last vestige of a power which might have coördinated African opposition to him was eliminated. For the balance of the crusading period, and until the Turkish conquest in the sixteenth century, Morocco under the Marīnids and their successors the Waṭṭāsids, western Algeria under the Ziyānids, and Tunisia and eastern Algeria—with Tripolitania and occasionally Cyrenaica as unwieldy appendages—under the Ḥafṣids would go their mutually hostile ways.

In Morocco the Marīnids had gradually taken over all the Muwaḥḥid holdings, but without the strong religious motivation which had made their predecessors so formidable a foe in their early years. Ya'qūb spent the years before 1270 in acquiring firm control of northern and central Morocco, and was finally secure enough at home to contemplate foreign adventures.

Yaghmurāsan the Ziyānid was still alive and active at Tlemsen in western Algeria. He had snatched Sijilmasa from the debris of the Muwaḥḥid realm, and had tentatively attacked the Marīnid Ya'qūb, had been repulsed, and had negotiated a truce. When he had once thrown off his fealty to the Ḥafṣids, he paid little further attention to his eastern neighbor, and neither he nor Ya'qūb participated at all in repelling the crusade. In fact, a private and bloody quarrel was to occupy their full attention throughout its brief course.

In Tunisia Yaḥyâ I the Ḥafṣid had constructed a firm and secure state, had expanded it to include Bugia and Constantine, and later Algiers, had been acknowledged suzerain by Ibn-Mardanīsh at Valencia when that skillful intriguer was in unusually desperate straits, had taken Tlemsen and made Yaghmurāsan his vassal, and had been fleetingly proclaimed in such widely separated cities as Seville, Denia, Jerez, and Almería in Spain, and Ceuta, Tangier, Sijilmasa, and Meknes in Morocco. These distant proclamations, like the Naṣrid, Marīnid, and Ziyānid acknowledgments of fealty, were merely transitory but flattering testimonials to his renown; his merit lay in his administrative achievements within his own greatly enlarged and firmly held borders. The state he bequeathed in 1249 to his son Muḥammad I was by far the most stable and prosperous of the three successor states.

Relations with Christian powers had also become regular and fruitful.[11] Yaḥyâ had inherited commercial accords with Pisa, Genoa, Venice, and Sicily, and he renewed them all as definite treaties; Marseilles, Narbonne, Montpellier, and Barcelona began to compete for the rich Tunisian trade, all of which was carried in Christian vessels. During his reign the primacy of Pisa gave way to a Sicilian preponderance which approached monopoly. Excellent relations

---

11. The best modern discussion is Robert Brunschvig's *La Berbérie orientale sous les Ḥafṣides . . .* (2 vols., Paris, 1940–1947), I, 27–37.

were established with Aragon, whose king, James I, went so far as to have his Genoese agent Nicholas Cigala request—unsuccessfully—from pope Innocent IV an assurance that French king Louis IX's 1248 crusade to Egypt would not attack Tunisia, a strange foreshadowing of the events of 1270.

Yaḥyâ refused to adopt any title beyond the simple *amīr,* and at first Muḥammad imitated his father's modesty, but early in 1253[12] he was proclaimed *amīr al-mu'minīn* and assumed the epithet al-Mustanṣir. After the extinction of the 'Abbāsid caliphate by the Mongols in 1258, he was the foremost ruler of Islam, and his claim to caliphal dignity was recognized as valid by the authorities at Mecca in 1259. By 1270 he had expelled two local rivals, had been acknowledged as suzerain by Naṣrids, Ziyānids, and Marīnids, and had made a notable record for orderly administration and development of Tunisia. He had recently returned from an armed patrol of his remoter territories, during which he had punished fractious nomads and restored order. He was on excellent diplomatic and commercial terms with the Italian cities and Aragon, and his relations with France and Sicily were far from hostile. This is the state which was represented to aspiring crusaders as an easy and rich conquest; this is the ruler who was depicted to pious Christians as a timid potential convert.

Louis IX, his motivations for crusading in general and for crusading to Tunis in 1270 in particular, his finances, his military dispositions, and the consequences of his death have been carefully analyzed in a previous volume.[13] The Moslems' reaction to this onslaught is of equal interest; their accounts differ in several important points from the familiar European narratives.

Charles of Anjou is known to have had several strong motives for deflecting the crusade to Tunis—reluctance to leave turbulent Sicily for any long period or at any great distance; the desire to punish al-Mustanṣir for furnishing troops to the Hohenstaufens Manfred and Conradin, and for sheltering Frederick of Castile, who had commanded these troops in Sicily; the need to collect sums previously paid by the Ḥafṣids for navigational and commercial privileges, often miscalled "tribute"; and his friendship with Baybars of Egypt, the logical target. He is, consequently, usually blamed[14] for manufac-

---

12. This date, wrongly given by Ibn-Khaldūn as October 1249, one month after Muḥammad's accession, is established by az-Zarkashī and confirmed by the quantity of coins on which he is termed merely *amīr* (Hazard, *Numismatic History,* pp. 74, 162–163). Al-'Umarī is of course even more incorrect in ascribing these events to the period after the "victory" over the crusaders in 1270.

13. See volume II of this work, chapter XIV.

14. An important group of modern historians tend to absolve Charles on the grounds that his real interest was the attacking of the Byzantine empire after peacefully negotiating with

turing more respectable and speciously attractive reasons for duping his saintly brother Louis—that al-Mustanṣir was an ally of the Egyptian Mamlūk rulers, that he could cut the supply line and retreat of a crusade to Egypt, that he encouraged piracy, and that he and his realm could easily be converted to Christianity.[15] Yet Charles is scarcely mentioned by the Moslem historians.

These authors, in their innocence of the intricacies of European political and dynastic affairs, blame Louis alone for the disastrous decision, and do not credit him with pious or even sensible motives. One anecdote, reported by Ibn-abī-Dīnār, ascribes the invasion to Louis's resentment at a slurring reference to him by al-Mustanṣir as "the one who was captured by such as they," indicating his Turkish bodyguard and recalling the fiasco at Damietta.

The better-informed Ibn-Khaldūn gives a circumstantial account in which European traders, unsatisfied creditors of a Tunisian merchant who had been executed several years earlier, complained to Louis and assured him that Tunis, weakened by a recent famine, could easily be captured. Although Berber rulers did often attack one another on equally flimsy pretexts, our knowledge of Louis's character and of the magnitude of his enterprise leads inevitably to the conclusion that in this instance the Moslem chroniclers were ill-informed. Nevertheless, Ibn-Khaldūn had extraordinarily accurate information on the methods by which crusaders were recruited and financial support was provided and on the identity of their leaders, but he erred in ascribing this data to Ibn-al-Athīr, who had died in 1234.

A more serious contradiction concerns the diplomatic preliminaries to the assault. Ibn-Khaldūn's account conflicts with the European version, according to which the decision to attack Tunisia, in spite of its previous satisfactory commercial and diplomatic relations with France, was not publicly announced until the fleet rendezvous at Cagliari in July of 1270. The Arabic historian, on the other hand, asserts that Louis's plans were known throughout North Africa as far as Egypt, whose envoy recited taunting verses recalling the French king's previous captivity and ransoming. Al-Mustanṣir sent an embassy to ascertain Louis's intentions and to propose "conditions of

Tunisia for the resumption of payments; see Brunschvig, *Berbérie orientale,* I, 58. Apparently, however, Charles wanted no crusade at all, but when confronted with Louis's determination he could not decently avoid participation; he therefore decided that his interests would be better served, or less damaged, by diverting the crusade from his potential Egyptian ally to his recalcitrant Tunisian "debtor," but arranged to delay military operations in favor of extended negotiations, from which he emerged the sole beneficiary.

15. Brunschvig (*Berbérie orientale,* I, 57) suggests that the incomprehensible delusion obsessing Louis was caused by over-optimistic Franciscan and Dominican missionaries.

peace sufficiently advantageous to quell his warlike ardor." Ibn-Khaldūn adds, not as fact but as hearsay, that the ambassadors took 80,000 pieces of gold to buy Louis off, but that the latter accepted the gold and then announced that the expedition would nevertheless be aimed at Tunisia, because al-Mustanṣir had frequently broken the treaty between them. The envoys, being dismissed, returned to Africa and informed the caliph of the situation, leading him to strengthen the measures of defense he had commenced on first learning of Louis's preparations.

This narrative contains four essential features: Tunisian knowledge of the destination of the crusade, the Ḥafṣid peace feelers, Louis's public declaration of his plans, and the episode of the gold. It is clear that the Moslems were well aware that extensive preparations were being made by Louis for a crusade; even in the absence of definite knowledge of its destination al-Mustanṣir would have been criminally remiss if he had neglected the obvious precautions for defending his realm which he certainly took, and which will be discussed in more detail below. The peace mission sent by al-Mustanṣir to France fits the circumstances very plausibly,[16] and may well have taken a small but royal gift; Louis's answers would not have been reassuring and the envoys on their return would probably have advised their caliph to look to his defenses. On the third point, however, the Moslems are clearly in error. It can be stated categorically that Louis did not announce publicly his intention of attacking Tunisia and his pretexts for so doing. At most, he might have alleged, in his reply to the envoys, instances of Ḥafṣid treaty-breaching, but the final decision was not generally known until July of 1270, so much is certain. The incident of the 80,000 dinars is assigned by Mercier,[17] with apparent plausibility, to the period immediately following the appearance of the fleet off Carthage, a last desperate attempt to purchase immunity. His assertion that Louis's nature was too chivalrous to permit him to retain the gold and deny the peace plea may be doubted in view of that saintly monarch's infinite capacity for rationalization and self-deception in a pious cause, as well as of the contemporary concept that no Christian need observe any code of ethics in dealing with the "infidel." But the utter silence of the French sources on this matter suggests that the only gold actually paid was the authenticated reparations collected by Charles of Anjou.

In general, Ibn-Khaldūn was poorly informed on the motivations of

16. Geoffrey of Beaulieu indicates that a Ḥafṣid embassy visited Paris in October 1269, but does not specify its mission (*RHGF*, XX [Paris, 1840], 20–23).

17. *Histoire de l'Afrique septentrionale*, II, 198–199.

the crusade but well informed on Louis's preparations. He was wrong in asserting that the Tunisians knew they were the destined target, right in that they had strong and well-founded suspicions. He was probably correct in his account of the embassy, except in his report of Louis's response. And he may have narrated accurately his hearsay on the gold but ascribed it to the wrong occasion. In addition, he is our best source on al-Mustanṣir's plans and preparations for repelling the crusaders.

The first steps were the strengthening of city walls and especially the repairing of breaches facing seaward, the accumulating of reserve stocks of grain and other necessities, and the prohibiting of free access by Christian merchants to the inland portions of his realm. Further precautions, taken when his suspicions were confirmed by the return empty-handed of his embassy, concerned the recruitment of defenders. He requested contingents from western Algeria and Morocco, which were too involved in fighting each other to accede to his demands, and from Egypt, whose Mamlūk sultan Baybars ordered the garrison of Cyrenaica to proceed immediately to his assistance. He enlisted a splendid volunteer corps from among the refugee Spanish Moslems within his borders. Contingents were requisitioned from all his provinces, and swarms of Arabs joined him for the interval before the autumnal date-ripening. The garrisons and citizens of the coastal cities were armed and alerted, and his own court and household troops were made the mobile nucleus of his forces.

When the hostile fleet appeared off Carthage, al-Mustanṣir's councillors were divided over the best strategy. One group wanted to prevent a landing; others argued that it was desirable for the French to commit their troops to an attack on such a strongly fortified position rather than to sail away and seek a softer spot elsewhere. The caliph, to his later regret, adopted this latter course and the landing was effected without strong opposition on July 18, 1270.

There is no reason to repeat here in detail the actual events of the crusade—the skirmishes and inaction pending the arrival of Charles of Anjou, the dysentery that decimated the French, the death of Louis on August 25, the belated arrival of Charles, the further skirmishes, the treaty signed November 1, the coming on November 10 of Edward, prince of Wales, with the English and Scottish contingents, the evacuation on November 18, and the storm which sank several ships, allegedly including the one bearing the gold paid to Charles by al-Mustanṣir. The Moslem accounts do not differ significantly from the European except to exaggerate the number of crusaders (40,000 knights, 100,000 archers, and a million foot-soldiers according to

Ibn-abī-Zar', reduced by Ibn-Khaldūn to 6,000 knights and 30,000 men, whereas Strayer estimates the true total as about 10,000) and to display uncertainty on the cause of Louis's death (Ibn-Khaldūn hesitates between fever and an arrow-wound but dismisses the tale, accepted by al-Maqrīzī, that it was caused by his avarice in grasping a jeweled sword-hilt which had been coated with poison).

The results of the crusade, so disastrous in the eyes of European chroniclers, appeared as a victory to the Moslems. Al-Mustanṣir announced to his subjects and his fellow sovereigns that he had succeeded in repelling a sacrilegious invasion of Moslem soil and had concluded an advantageous treaty; he successfully invited them to contribute to the indemnity, which he said was ten mule-loads of silver, though the treaty specifies 210,000 ounces of gold. To prevent a recurrence of the incident he ordered the walls of Carthage razed, and North Africa's first true crusade passed into history with far less effect on the victims than on the aggressors.

The death of Muḥammad al-Mustanṣir in 1277 led to dynastic complications which became involved with Aragonese politics and finally produced another crusade. Muḥammad's son Yaḥyâ II was acclaimed caliph with the epithet al-Wāthiq (he who trusts in Allāh); he continued on good terms with the Italian cities, with Angevin Sicily, and with James I of Majorca, antagonizing Peter III of Aragon,[18] brother and rival of James and enemy of Charles of Anjou. Peter conspired with Ibrāhīm, a son of Yaḥyâ I who was in exile in Spain, and in 1279 gave him military and naval support in overthrowing his ineffectual nephew. Ibrāhīm forebore to assume caliphal dignities, contenting himself with his father's title al-amīr. Peter, who had hoped to add a quasi-vassal Tunisia to the ring of allies he was erecting around Sicily, was disappointed by Ibrāhīm's independence and lack of subservience, and cast about for another potential sultan who would be more amenable to control. He found such a one in the governor of Constantine, Abū-Bakr ibn-Mūsâ, of the Kūmī tribe, usually called Ibn-al-Wazīr, and agreed to support this man's ambition to overthrow the Ḥafṣid by landing troops at Collo in April of 1282.

Peter then announced a crusade against the Saracens and made

18. Peter's complex African ties are summarized by Brunschvig, *Berbérie orientale,* I, 74–83, relying chiefly on Christian sources, as the Arab historians neglect the overseas ramifications of Ḥafṣid family dissensions. See also C. E. Dufourcq, "La Couronne d'Aragonne et les Hafsides . . . ," *Analecta sacra tarraconensis,* XXV (1952), 51–113, and *idem, L'Espagne catalane et le Maghrib . . . de . . . (1212) à . . . (1331)* (Paris, 1966), as well as E. Solal, ". . . L'Expédition de Pierre III d'Aragon à Collo (1282)," *Revue africaine,* CI (1957), 247–271.

ostentatious preparations, but his plans were upset by the premature massacre of the French in Sicily on March 30. He arrived at Collo on June 28 only to find that Ibn-al-Wazīr's revolt, starting on schedule, had already been suppressed by Ibrāhīm's energetic son 'Abd-al-'Azīz, governor of Bugia. He nevertheless stayed there several weeks, engaged in desultory fighting and looting, until he was ready, late in August, to accede to the request of the Sicilian insurgents to lead them against the hated Angevins. He then departed, with the "crusaders" he had presumably planned all along to use in Sicily, to eject Charles and establish a Catalan hegemony in the central Mediterranean, leaving North Africa almost undisturbed by his brief sojourn.[19]

The next territory invaded by Christians was the island of Jerba, seized in 1284 as a fief by Roger de Lluria, Peter's Italian admiral.[20] It later passed to some dissident Catalans from the Grand Company's Greek holdings and as an alternately Christian and Moslem outlaw state would remain a pirate haunt and a source of unrest in the central Mediterranean until the Turkish conquest.

Meanwhile the North African mainland had resumed its tripartite Berber existence untroubled by further crusading incursions. Marīnid strength in Morocco increased steadily, enabling the sultans to impose their will on western Algeria and on Andalusia. For seven decades, from 1270 to 1340, the Berber Marīnids were involved in Spanish Moslem affairs, holding various fortified towns, meddling in the Naṣrid succession, sending unruly nobles as "volunteers of the faith" to hold the frontier against Christian attempts at reconquest, and occasionally crossing to participate in person in the "holy war" (*jihād*) by looting small towns or ravaging Spanish fields and orchards. Despite the encomiums offered by Moslem chroniclers these Marīnid sultans accomplished little in Spain, and their definitive expulsion in 1340 following 'Alī ibn-'Uthmān's catastrophic defeat at Tarifa merely deflected their ambitions eastward, but it was decisive in assuring the Spanish that no third Berber wave would overrun the reconquered territories and again delay and endanger the final Christian triumph.

The steady interchange of persons and ideas between Andalusia and Morocco which had started under the Murābiṭs and continued

19. Ibn-Khaldūn correctly links the Aragonese arrival to Ibn-al-Wazīr's revolt, but implies that Peter did not land and states that the crusade had no effect.

20. On this early Roger de Lluria (Loria, in southern Italy) see volume II of this work, p. 264. On the Catalan Grand Company see chapter VI, above.

without serious interruption for two and a half centuries, from 1090 to 1340, and which was to persist for two and a half more as a one-way flow southward until the final expulsion of the Moriscos in 1609, served to strengthen and broaden Moroccan culture immeasurably by exposing it to the influence of the advanced civilization developed by Moslems and Jews in Spain.

The rivalry between the Zanātah dynasties of western Algeria and Morocco was too heavily weighted in favor of the Marīnids. They besieged the Ziyānid capital, Tlemsen, at every opportunity, even building a rival city, Manṣūrah, adjacent to it so that the sieges might be conducted in comfort. Between 1271 and 1337 these efforts numbered eleven, one of which lasted eight years and was on the point of success when the Marīnid sultan, Yūsuf ibn-Ya'qūb, was assassinated, and the last of which did succeed, resulting in the temporary suppression of Ziyānid rule. The victor, 'Alī, after his setback in Spain in 1340, moved eastward against Ḥafṣid Tunisia and took the capital, but his dream of reëstablishing a North African empire comparable to the Muwaḥḥids' was shattered by the nomad Arabs, who overwhelmed his Berber army near Kairawan in 1348 and sent him fleeing back to Morocco, where his son Fāris had assumed control. A brief Ziyānid revival was stopped by Fāris in 1352, but the second attempt, in 1359, proved permanent, though the new Ziyānid ruler, Mūsâ II ibn-Yūsuf, repeatedly lost his capital to Marīnid armies, regaining it on their departure.

The result of this one-sided struggle was that Morocco and western Algeria came to differ sharply by 1394. Morocco had grown strong and prosperous, despite constant intradynastic struggles for the throne in which each contender intrigued and bid for Berber and Arab support. Before 1358 these contests were adequately controlled by a series of strong sultans—Ya'qūb, Yūsuf, 'Uthmān, 'Alī, and Fāris—but after 1358 the accumulated wealth and power were dissipated by a free-for-all from which no single victor emerged to rebuild the nation. In the last thirty-six years of the crusading period fifteen sultans or major contenders emerged, and their fruitless warfare so weakened the country that its ports were doomed to fall easy victims in the fifteenth and sixteenth centuries to Spanish and Portuguese attacks, first merely raids, like that at Tetuan in 1399, then actual conquests, commencing with Ceuta in 1415.

Western Algeria was a perpetual battleground. Aside from the Marīnid invasions there were incessant battles between Arab and Berber tribes and a running contest between Ziyānids and Ḥafṣids for the possession of Algiers. In general the Ziyānids ruled only the

capital city of Tlemsen, exercising occasional control over the hinterland by alliances with one group of nomads against another, or by
bribery. Tlemsen became a commercial center whose prosperity
attracted Christian and Moslem merchants and was reflected in
architectural and cultural eminence, but political and personal security was never attained. The rural economy became predominantly
pastoral, and the only cities to rival Tlemsen were the ports of
Algiers, Tenes, and Oran. Nominal Ḥafṣid suzerainty was disowned
by ʿUthmān ibn-Yaghmurāsan before 1300, and he and his successors
constantly invited attack by intervening in Ḥafṣid and Marīnid rebellions and by invading eastern Algeria. After the interregnal years of
1337–1348 and 1352–1359 Mūsâ II spent his thirty-year reign in
eluding the attacks of Marīnid invaders and their Ziyānid puppets, as
well as of his son ʿAbd-ar-Raḥmān II, who succeeded him in 1389
after two years of open rebellion. The new ruler had to repay
Marīnid favors by acknowledging the suzerainty of the reigning
sultan, Aḥmad ibn-Ibrāhīm, and the crusading period closed with a
murderous scramble for the succession among his brothers, six of
whom were to rule briefly—as were two sons and a nephew—between
1393 and 1431, when a seventh brother, Aḥmād, would succeed in
establishing himself for a thirty-one-year period.

Thus despite their differences the two Zanātah dynasties were
stricken by the same fatal malady, intradynastic contentions for
power in which each candidate sought nomad and urban support by
unremitting intrigue in which neighboring rulers meddled opportu-
nistically. In each case the result was to atomize the realm into
confederations whose ephemeral ties were based on momentary
self-interest or personal pique, thus rendering the ports helpless
against impending Christian assaults and preventing the interior from
being developed in an orderly manner. From this century of strife
stemmed the great weakness which would become manifest after
1400; from being a vital and prosperous competitor in the commercial and military affairs of the Mediterranean this region then
commenced its long decline, accelerated during Turkish and Sharīfian
rule, to its recent subordinate position.

These observations on Morocco and western Algeria apply almost
unaltered to eastern Algeria, Tunisia, and Tripolitania, theoretically a
single Ḥafṣid realm, but subject to countless palace revolutions,
provincial secessions, and nomad uprisings, all serving to weaken the
state and diminish its prosperity, as well as to render it incapable of
resisting eventual Christian and Turkish onslaughts. The 120-year
intermission between the Tunisian crusades of 1270 and 1390 is

historically divisible into four rather unequal portions.[21] The fratricidal warfare which had started after al-Mustanṣir's death in 1277 continued until 1318, with such added complications as the two-year reign of the audacious impostor, Aḥmad ibn-Marzūq, who impersonated the murdered son of al-Wāthiq. The characteristics of this period include the fragmentation of the Ḥafṣid realm into emirates—ruled from Tunis, Bugia, Constantine, and Tripoli—and tribal domains in the smaller cities and the interior, the concession to the Arab nomads of ever-increasing privileges and immunities, and the gradual subordination of Moslems to Christians in Mediterranean power politics, marked by favorable treaties for Italians and Catalans and regular payments to Aragon from Tunisian customs receipts.

This dismal situation was improved by Abū-Bakr II ibn-Yaḥyâ, emir of Bugia, who in 1318 conquered Tunis; he spent fourteen years suppressing revolts, repelling invasions, and restoring order, and then ruled fourteen years longer over a Ḥafṣid state which had been strengthened internally and externally, though he could not avoid recognizing the preponderant military power of his Marīnid son-in-law ʿAlī. The next quarter-century, from Abū-Bakr's death in 1346 to 1370, was compounded of the same fragmentation and internecine warfare as the first, with the added menace of Marīnid invasions, culminating in the short-lived conquests of Tunisia by ʿAlī in 1347 and by his son Fāris in 1357; Tripoli was sacked by the Genoese in 1355. The last twenty years, during which the Ḥafṣid territory was united under Aḥmad II ibn-Muḥammad, who in 1370 succeeded in eliminating his opponents and reorganizing the realm, were comparable to Abū-Bakr's reign but were more prosperous and more independent because of the Marīnid collapse.

Throughout the whole period commercial and diplomatic relations were maintained with the Italian cities—Genoa and Venice, and Pisa until its eclipse in 1325—as well as with Marseilles, and with Aragon-Catalonia and its associated powers in Majorca and Sicily. These relations, described in numerous letters and treaties in Italian and Catalan archives, involved consulates, mutual indemnity for corsairs' activities, safety and freedom of worship for Christian merchants resident in North Africa, ransoming of prisoners, payment of "tribute" during periods of weakness, and occasional naval aid against the Ziyānids. During Aḥmad's reign, however, a great increase in governmentally-approved piracy led to sharp protests and threats from Europe's maritime powers.

21. Brunschvig, *Berbérie orientale,* I, 83–198, gives a thoughtful, detailed account of Ḥafṣid political history between the crusades, an account on which I have not hesitated to draw.

The political situation within North Africa in 1390 can be summarized thus: Ḥafṣid Tunisia, Tripolitania, and Numidia were stable and well governed under Aḥmad; western Algeria under the Ziyānid 'Abd-ar-Raḥmān II was experiencing a brilliant but turbulent reaction after Mūsâ's long and adventurous reign; Morocco under Aḥmad the Marīnid was enjoying a short interlude of relative calm between fratricidal combats. Dealings with Moslem powers were amicable; Naṣrid Granada, Mamlūk Egypt (which controlled Cyrenaica), and the Sudan were important commercially but not politically. The deterioration in Tunisian relations with France and Italy was offset by an improvement in those with Aragon following the death in 1387 of Peter IV, who had dreamt of conquering Tunisia, as had his predecessors in 1282 and 1314.

The 1390 crusade was conceived by Catalonia's rival for maritime leadership, Genoa, as a secular enterprise to suppress the pirates based on Mahdia.[22] In 1388 the same city had sent a fleet to retake the notorious island of Jerba from its Moslem proprietors, for the same eminently practical reason. There was little essential difference in the "Barbary corsairs" under the twelfth-century Zīrids, the fourteenth-century Ḥafṣids, and the eighteenth-century beys and deys, or in the suppressive measures adopted respectively by Normans of Sicily, by Genoese, and by European and American mercantile powers. In order to secure French support the Genoese late in 1389 sent envoys to king Charles VI with instructions to depict the proposed expedition as his sacred duty, to which he should contribute a commander and an army while Genoa would supply galleys and six thousand archers, as well as all necessary provisions.

Charles VI assented without enthusiasm, permitting up to fifteen thousand of his knights and squires to participate at their own expense. His maternal uncle Louis II, duke of Bourbon, volunteered to command and was so designated. The crusading host included, besides the numerous French, contingents from England, Burgundy, Hainault, and Flanders, and a few Catalans to keep a sharp eye on Genoese schemes. The combined host met at a tiny island off the east coast of Tunisia and confirmed the selection of Mahdia as the object of attack. This had been the Genoese destination throughout,

22. The standard modern accounts, drawn almost entirely from European sources, are Léon Mirot, "Une Expédition française en Tunisie au XIVe siècle: Le siège de Mahdia (1390)," *Revue des études historiques,* XCVII (1931), 357–406, and Aziz S. Atiya, *The Crusade in the Later Middle Ages* (London, 1938), pp. 398–454, despite such minor errors as dating the Genoese embassy in November 1390 and twice calling Aḥmad "Abū-Bakr." See also chapter I, above.

and presumably they convinced the genuine crusaders and the duke
of Bourbon by recalling its repeated capture by Christians in 1087
and 1148.

A landing was made, apparently unopposed, late in July 1390, on
the isthmus which connects Mahdia with the mainland, and a complete sea and land blockade was instituted, effectively isolating
Mahdia—called Auffricque (Africa) by the medieval Christians—for
the duration of the crusade. The tactical position of the crusaders
was excellent, as their flanks were covered by their fleet, their front
was on the alert against sallies from the beleaguered town and
repulsed the only such effort with ease, and their rear was protected
by palisades against the Saracen cavalry. Provisions were ample, and
were brought daily from the galleys offshore. The composition of
their forces was good, with a relatively small force of trained fight-
ing-men, mostly knights and archers, and apparently without horses.
Discipline and morale were high; this crusade was unique in that it
paid its own way in Europe and thus did not alienate the populace.
The strategic position was less admirable, for the crusaders' siege
equipment for taking so strongly fortified a city proved hopelessly
inadequate, and so they had to rely on blockade, against which
ample supplies of food and water had been laid up in Mahdia.

The Moslems' situation was also not unfavorable. Mahdia, besides
being well fortified and well provisioned, was well garrisoned. Large
contingents of cavalry were available to harass the crusaders, although Arabic histories do not confirm Christian assertions that the
rulers of Tlemsen and Bugia brought sixty thousand cavalry to
reinforce the Tunisians commanded by Aḥmad's brother and sons.
Other Christian estimates of the enemy as comprising about forty
thousand Tunisians are probably still much too high. Avoiding battle,
they skirmished constantly, wearing down the invaders, who also
suffered from the inevitable onslaughts of sickness, heat, and shortage of fresh water.

A determined assault on Mahdia having been repelled, both Tunisians and Genoese were willing to negotiate, and a tentative agreement is said to have been reached by which a ten-year truce would be
proclaimed and substantial payments would be made by Aḥmad to
the doge and commune of Genoa.[23] Although Louis had asserted
that the purpose of the crusade was to conquer rather than to extort

23. Or to Louis and the commune of Genoa, as the chronicler's statement "au duc et
commune de Gênes" is susceptible of either interpretation, and in fact Mirot adopts the
former and Atiya the latter, while the Arabic sources mention no such payment, and none
seems ever to have been made.

gold, he and his nobles ratified these terms and raised the siege after having maintained it about two months. On the return journey the crusaders were persuaded to further Genoese interests in Sardinia by replacing the Catalan garrisons of Cagliari and Ogliastra with Genoese; in Terracina, which was captured and "entrusted to the Genoese;" and in Piombino, where a long-standing dispute was settled. The crusaders then returned home triumphant, having accomplished much for Genoa but nothing which might be construed as a legitimate crusading purpose.

The effects on Europe of this expedition were minor. Genoa's treaty with Tunisia was soon matched, except for the payments, which were never collected, by similar treaties with Pisa, Venice, and Sicily. The enthusiasm of the returning nobles helped recruit the major crusade directed at Nicopolis in 1396, which in turn by its catastrophic defeat helped to discredit the anachronistic crusading idea still further.[24] In historical perspective it was the last of a series of attacks directed at Tunisia by pious crusaders in the misguided belief that success would weaken the Moslem position in the Egypt-Palestine-Syria region; it was midway in a long series of practical expeditions to suppress piracy. Future Christian attacks were to be of a different type, Spanish and Portuguese efforts to make permanent secular conquests. The effect on North Africa was insignificant. Mahdia was scarcely damaged and quickly repaired; the military power of the Ḥafṣids was not perceptibly diminished; any gold paid was not enough to affect the economy adversely; piracy was not suppressed.

During the final four years between 1390 and the end of Ibn-Khaldūn's narrative all three Berber rulers were replaced. Aḥmad the Ḥafṣid died in 1394 and was succeeded by his son 'Abd-al-'Azīz, who had distinguished himself against the crusaders and whose forty-year reign would further enhance Ḥafṣid power and prosperity. The dynasty was not to be definitively overthrown until 1574. The Ziyānid 'Abd-ar-Raḥmān II died in 1393, and his death precipitated a long period of struggles from which the dynasty was to recover slowly, surviving until 1556. The similar warfare in Morocco following the death of Aḥmad the Marīnid in 1393 was to prove fatal to that dynasty, once the strongest of the Muwaḥḥids' inheritors. In 1465 they were to give way to the Waṭṭāsids, who had actually exercised power since 1420, only one generation after the end of the crusading period, and the Waṭṭāsids themselves would predecease the neighboring dynasties, their final overthrow coming in 1554.

24. See chapter I, above.

The astonishing ability of these Berber dynasties, so weak and so lacking in family loyalty or theological endorsement, to retain the thrones of their turbulent nations for two or three centuries has a fourfold explanation. No external aggressor sufficiently powerful to subdue them had arisen, for France, Spain, and the Ottoman empire were all engaged in consolidating their realms and eliminating neighboring enemies, and Egypt had served as a shield against the Mongols who twice overran most of the central Islamic world. No new religious movement had swept over the Berbers and united them in opposition to the existing governments, as had the Fāṭimid, Murābiṭ, and Muwaḥḥid dogmas, and indeed North African Moslems had become less susceptible to religious motivations simultaneously with their European Christian foes. No adequate intellectual or emotional challenge had developed to shake the universal popular acceptance of the dynastic concept, so that every rebellious tribe or clique sought, and easily found, a dissident member of the ruling house to serve as their figurehead, to be crowned or cast aside as fortune and policy dictated; in the sixteenth century the Spaniards and Turks would likewise find subservient Ḥafṣid and Ziyānid puppet princes to lend a spurious aura of legitimacy to the rival invading factions.

To these three negative reasons must be added one more positive: within each dynasty there occasionally appeared capable rulers who would succeed in eliminating rivals, subduing nomad revolts, repelling invasions, and creating stable and prosperous regimes. A series of such men among the Marīnids ruled from 1258 to 1358; a similar series of Ḥafṣid sultans held power from 1370 to 1488; the Ziyānids produced several capable individuals like Yaghmurāsan rather than a consecutive series of strong reigns, but were relatively strongest late in the fifteenth century.

The outstanding characteristic of the political history of late medieval North Africa can thus be identified as the extraordinary importance of the ruler's personal ability. The political tensions between Arabs and Berbers, urban merchants and pastoral nomads, indigenous nobles and refugees from Andalusia, theologians and courtiers, could be resolved by a skillful and determined sultan, but would severely penalize incompetence or indecision. The resources of each state were sufficient to repel invasions and maintain the integrity of the realm only if properly exploited by a single intelligence; if misused or dissipated by internal rivalries they proved inadequate. This emphasis on individual capability contrasts sharply with the Byzantine and Ottoman empires and with Mamlūk Egypt, whose institutions and administration were effective in minimizing the harm a weak ruler or a contest for the throne could do the state.

During the entire 345-year period Morocco can be seen to have reached its maximum power on three occasions, under the Murābiṭs about 1100, the Muwaḥḥids about 1180, and the Marīnids about 1350, and to have started immediately thereafter on its rapid and permanent decline. Tunisia after its initial devastation had experienced several alternations of prosperity and instability, as well as occasional ephemeral invasions, but finished at its strongest. Algeria, divided and disputed, had never rivaled its neighbors, as it was destined to do in modern times. North Africa as a whole, however, was by 1394 far less powerful in relation to either Europe or the Moslem Near East than it had been in 1049, because of its failure to share in their progress.

XIV
THE MAMLUK SULTANS
1291–1517

To divide the history of the Mamluk empire at 1291, the year of the decisive victory at Acre over the last crusaders on the Palestine littoral, is convenient, and perhaps as sound as any such choice can be, though chronologically this date demarcates two periods of most uneven length within the span (1250–1517) of Mamluk hegemony in the Near East.[1] The reason for the somewhat arbitrary choice, however, is of course Egypt's relationship to the crusades, which after 1291 went into a rather drastic decline both in and outside Europe, so that many years were to elapse before a crusading expedition on the old scale would be recorded in Mamluk annals.

The succumbing of the last strongholds of the crusaders in Syria was a momentous event, for both Europe and the Near East. It was the final termination of the "debate of the world" according to Gibbon, as well as to some later historians. Yet plenty of wars were to take place in the Near East and southeastern Europe, including several crusades and counter-crusades, while a vast diverse literature,

The Arabic chronicles of al-Maqrīzī (*Kitāb as-sulūk li ma'rifat duwal al-mulūk,* ed. M. M. Ziada [Cairo, 1956–]) and abū-l-Mahāsin Ibn-Taghrī-Birdī (*An-nujūm az-zāhirah fī mulūk Miṣr wa-l-Qāhirah,* ed. by the staff of the National Library in Cairo [11 vols., 1929–1950], portions ed. [1909–1936] and trans. [1954–1957] by W. Popper at Berkeley), used for the writer's chapter on the Mamluk sultans to 1293, which appeared in volume II of this work (pp. 735–758), remain primary source material for the period after 1291. To these must be added the chronicle of Ibn-Iyās, *Badā'i' az-zuhūr fī waqā'i' ad-duhūr* (Būlāq and Istanbul), for the last decades of Mamluk history and beyond. Modern works in European languages include those by G. Wiet, A. N. Poliak, and P. K. Hitti cited in volume II (p. 735), as well as C. Huart, *Histoire des Arabes* (2 vols., Paris, 1912–1913), and G. Wiet, *L'Égypte arabe de la conquête arabe à la conquête ottomane, 642–1517* (2nd ed., Paris, 1946). This chapter was edited after the author's death by Harry W. Hazard.

1. On the final days of the Latin states in Syria, see volume II of this work, pp. 595–598, 753–755. The Moslem chroniclers divide the Mamluk period into a Turkish (*Daulat al-Utrūk,* 1250–1382) and a Circassian (*Daulat al-Jarkas,* 1382–1517) phase.

486

suggesting ways and means of resuscitating the old crusading flame, was debated in various European courts.[2]

For the Mamluk sultanate itself, the fall of Acre was no more than another major step toward the eventual elimination of the militant, "infidel" Frank from the world of Islam. In December 1293, after destroying the other crusading strongholds in Syria, al-Ashraf Khalīl, the victor of Acre, was brutally murdered, less than three years after he had been hailed in Cairo as a liberator. As Khalīl left only a daughter, no recourse was necessary to the usual Mamluk tragi-comedy of installing a son of the deceased sultan on the throne, until the most acceptable among the Mamluk oligarchy was ready to usurp it. Yet the Mamluk leaders proceeded to set up Khalīl's step-brother, an-Nāṣir Muḥammad, a boy eight years of age, whom they later twice deposed, but then twice reinstalled, alternately with three other sultans from the powerful Mamluk ranks, all in less than twenty years. Such strange caprice reflects the sheer in-ability of the Mamluk emirs to leave any one of themselves in the sultanate for long undisturbed, once a chance to oust him pre-sented itself.

It was in the year 1310 that an-Nāṣir began his third reign, in an ugly frame of mind, understandable after the vicissitudes of the previous seventeen years. Whatever kindly traits he might have devel-oped in his youth had been soured and embittered by his unhappy experiences, when he was used as a mere pawn in the Mamluk game of making and unmaking sultans at pleasure. "Though only in his twenty-fifth year," wrote Lane-Poole, "he was already a cynic, a double dealer, and thirsty to revenge the miseries of his boyhood and youth, and to free himself entirely from the interference of the powerful emirs. He managed it by trickery and deceit,"[3] with a technique of delaying action to strike down an enemy until the latter was least expecting it.[4] Yet he proved himself to be an able and calculating administrator. He was especially interested in the eco-nomic development of the Mamluk empire, preferring a commercial treaty to a pitched battle, a devious diplomatic success to a victori-ous campaign, a thoroughbred horse to a huge sum of money, and an architectural gem of a palace to amassed gold. In some respects he could be likened to Louis XI, king of France in the fifteenth century,

2. See A. S. Atiya, *The Crusade in the Later Middle Ages* (London, 1938), pp. 29–230, and above, chapter I.

3. S. Lane-Poole, *A History of Egypt in the Middle Ages* (London, 1914), p. 306.

4. Al-Maqrīzī, *As-sulūk* (ed. Ziada), II, part 2.

despite vast differences in background, outlook, and institutional environment.

An-Nāṣir Muḥammad ruled with a velvet-gloved but iron hand until his death in 1341, and his uninterrupted third reign might well be considered the Indian summer of the whole Baḥrī Mamluk period, especially in Egypt. This remarkable reign should not be judged merely by its length, but by its general prosperity, the absence of great wars, wide patronage of learned men, high prestige in Europe and Asia, and extraordinary luxuriance in every aspect of court life in Cairo. In his enthusiasm for architecture, art, and art objects, an-Nāṣir Muḥammad had no rival, and his Mamluk emirs vainly emulated his aesthetic tastes. This brilliance continued in an afterglow even under his puppet successors, for the next forty-nine years, during which the court remained as refined and lavish as ever, and exquisite mosques and palaces were built, thanks to vast revenues from international trade, and to improved methods in agriculture, which had been introduced into Egypt and Syria by an-Nāṣir Muḥammad himself.

Of the twelve Baḥrī successors of an-Nāṣir Muḥammad, eight were his sons, two his grandsons, and two his great-grandsons. It looked as if some hereditary principle was being progressively established, to supplant the time-honored method of keeping the son of a deceased sultan only as long as was expedient for Mamluk manipulations. These descendants of an-Nāṣir Muḥammad, not unlike the later Merovingians of early medieval France, and for the same reasons, rapidly succeeded one another on the throne of the Mamluk empire, but can not be said to have ruled. The reins of power were in the hands of the Mamluk emirs and their barrack factions of al-Baḥrīyah[5] and al-Burjīyah,[6] until the leader of the latter party, Barkuk by name, removed the last of the line of an-Nāṣir Muḥammad in 1390, and became the first sultan of the Burjī, or Circassian, Mamluk dynasty.

Three events of varied importance and significance took place during those forty-nine years. First was the pestilence, known as the Black Death, which, coupled with cattle murrain and fruit disease, played havoc with the population of Egypt and the entire Near East from 1348 to 1350, causing appalling loss of life everywhere. Secondly, after a long respite from crusading warfare, a considerable

5. See volume II of this work, p. 738.
6. The word "Burjī" means "of the citadel" of Cairo, where sultan Kalavun had quartered a section of his Mamluks, mostly Circassians.

fleet consisting of Cypriote, Rhodian, Venetian, and Genoese ships, carrying an army with discordant loyalties, attacked Alexandria in the autumn of 1365. It was led by Peter I de Lusignan, king of Cyprus, and founder of the Order of the Sword for the delivery of Jerusalem. Alexandria was seized, sacked, and plundered for about a week, during which neither Moslem, nor Jew, nor Christian was spared. The fleet sailed away with about five thousand men and women of all three creeds, and, according to a Moslem eye-witness account, seventy of the crusading ships were full to the brim with rich plunder.[7] Lengthy peace negotiations ensued, which were interrupted, now and again, by Cypriote naval raids on the coasts of Syria and Egypt. These raids were intended to bring pressure upon the sultan, until peace was made between Cyprus and the Mamluk sultanate, in 1370, with the mediation of the Italian republics of Genoa and Venice.[8] The third event concerned the Christian kingdom of Lesser Armenia, in Cilicia. This kingdom seldom failed to give valuable support to the crusaders in the east, even against the Byzantine empire, and was thus a constant target of Mamluk invasion in the thirteenth century. After the fall of Acre it became the next objective of the Mamluk sultans, and its towns, such as Adana, Tarsus, Mamistra, and Sis, the capital, were destroyed one after the other by Mamluk armies. It was finally conquered in 1375 by the emir of Aleppo in the name of sultan Sha'bān, and the country was divided among feudal lords. Its last king, Leon VI, was carried off as a prisoner of war to the citadel of Cairo, where he remained in captivity until his ransom was paid by the church, in 1382.[9]

A threat of greater magnitude than the new Burjī dynasty could easily withstand was ominously brewing in the heart of west Central Asia. Barkuk was put severely to the test, in the closing years of the fourteenth century, when the terrible Timur Lenk (Tamerlane), fresh from his stupendous conquests in India, appeared to be intent upon another bout of destruction, threatening the inhabitants of both Syria and Egypt with extermination, after having marched roughshod through Mesopotamia and sacked Baghdad. Sultan Barkuk was not found wanting in courage but rose valiantly to the impending menace, showing a firm defiance of the vituperations of the approaching invader, despite an unfavorable political situation inside the Mamluk

7. See Atiya, *op cit.,* pp. 341, 347, 349–369, and above, pp. 15–18.
8. *Ibid.,* pp. 371–376.
9. *Ibid.,* pp. 11, 15; cf. C. Toumanoff, "Armenia and Georgia," in *Cambridge Medieval History,* IV-1 (1966), 637.

empire because of the recent change of dynasty. First, Barkuk joined the northern princes, including the Ottoman Bayazid I and the Turkish "Mongol" Toktamîsh of the eastern Kîpchaks and the Golden Horde on the Volga, in a general league of resistance. He even had sufficient hardihood to give refuge, in Cairo, to the expelled sultan of Baghdad, Aḥmad the Jalāyirid. When eventually Timur sent an embassy to Egypt, to open negotiations for peace on terms of virtual Mongol supremacy, Barkuk executed the envoys, in imitation perhaps of sultan Kutuz in like circumstances on the eve of the battle of 'Ain Jālūt.[10] Mamluk troups were then mustered in great numbers at Bira on the Euphrates, scene of several previous Mamluk victories over the Mongols. Timur was then fully occupied in Georgia, far to the north, against Toktamîsh, the most formidable of his enemies, and Barkuk died in June 1399, before proving his prowess against the Mongols.

Faraj, the eldest of Barkuk's three surviving sons, immediately succeeded to the throne. His mother was a Greek, as was the mother of his commander-in-chief (atabek) Taghrîberdi, the father of the historian abū-l-Maḥāsin. Sultan Faraj was only thirteen years old, but he had to step quickly into his father's shoes, and march to Syria at the close of 1400 to check the fearful Timur, who had swooped southward, sacked Aleppo, and seemed about to seize Damascus. A fierce battle raged north of Damascus, where the Mamlùk army was repulsed after some initial success, and sultan Faraj withdrew in haste to Cairo, leaving his army to its fate. Damascus surrendered on terms, which the historian Ibn-Khaldūn was instrumental in extracting from the usually unyielding Timur. Nevertheless, the Syrian capital was subjected to Mongol ferocity, and the whole of Syria was savagely ruined. Sultan Faraj, who certainly was too young to be any match for the situation, lived in mortal fear of Timur's next move in this campaign of devastation. But the Mongols were diverted, luckily for Faraj, toward Asia Minor, where Timur utterly defeated the Ottoman army at the battle of Ankara in 1402. The Ottoman power seemed, at the time, to be irreparably broken, especially as sultan Bayazid I had been captured and was thereafter dragged in the conqueror's train. Faraj, who had already taken to drinking and other unworthy pursuits, meekly consented to the terms demanded of him by Timur's envoys in 1403, and even agreed to strike coins in the conqueror's name, as proof of his subservience. Timur, however,

10. See volume II of this work, p. 745. Although Timur's hordes are referred to as Mongols for convenience, they were chiefly Turkish, though Timur claimed descent from Genghis Khan; see below, p. 544.

never went beyond Damascus in Syria, nor did his control over Egypt exceed obsequious personal protestations of the boy sultan.

These humiliating proceedings on the part of Faraj, however, cost him any chance of continuing to hold the throne. This was at best tenuous, in view of the inveterate Mamluk attitude toward sons of deceased sultans. It was solely because of the protracted struggle for power among the leading emirs, in both Egypt and Syria, that Faraj was left to his immoralities for a number of years, though his reign was interrupted by the brief sultanate of 'Abd-al-'Azīz al-Manṣūr (1405–1406). Finally he was deposed and executed, in May 1412, on substantiated charges of notorious debauchery and uxoricide. One of the two most powerful emirs, called Shaikh, after fighting so long and so violently for the throne, was ultimately able to succeed; he was a drunkard, notorious for his excesses, yet he built himself a beautiful mosque.

For the next ten years Cairo witnessed nine stormy reigns, three of which ended within the span of 1421. The year 1422 might well, therefore, be considered the beginning of established rule, being the year in which Barsbey—the strongest, though not the best, of the Circassian Mamluk dynasty—came to the throne. Needless to say, sultan Barsbey achieved the throne at the consummation of the usual Mamluk drama following a royal demise. He had witnessed the installation and brief reign (January-August 1421) of a minor sultan, Aḥmad son of Shaikh, with a leading emir named Tatar acting as regent. This had been followed by the still briefer reign of Tatar himself (August–November 1421), who was succeeded in turn by his own infant son Muḥammad, under the joint regency of two rising emirs, Barsbey and Janibek aṣ-Ṣūfī. Almost equally brief was the duration of this reign (November 1421–April 1422); the child was dethroned as usual to make room for Barsbey.

It is to be remarked, however, that despite this chronic feature of Mamluk Circassian rule in Egypt, the internal history of the country, reign after reign, was so singularly consistent that a full study of the main outline of the policy of any one sultan suffices to give a good picture of them all. Thus a sultan would signalize his accession by rewarding the emirs of the faction, or factions, upon whose shoulders he had climbed to the throne. This would entail, besides the succession largess, a series of sometimes wholesale dismissals of lukewarm or disgruntled emirs from office, to find room for the others; this in turn would lead to disaffection or rebellion, which usually lasted for many years. On his accession, too, the sultan would seek to render his position secure by purchasing new slaves and enrolling them in his private army corps, the sulṭānīyah Mamluks. These new recruits (known as the *jilbān* or *ajlab*), unlike the disciplined youngsters of the previous Mamluk dynasty, were mostly adults at time of purchase, and soon became unruly pests and a public nuisance, even to the sultan himself. Their perpetual conflicts with the factions of the older Mamluks, their street fights, and their unbridled license often produced a reign of terror, and Egypt suffered grievously indeed at their ruthless hands. As a foreign soldiery, of course, neither they nor the older corps of the army had any compassion for the afflicted populace, and so debauched were these domineering slaves that even Barsbey, the strongest of the Circassian sultans, was powerless to restrain them. Moreover, the government as a whole was corrupt, and justice was sold to the highest bidder.

Yet in spite of constant conspiracy at every succession, with all the chaos it produced afterward, and notwithstanding the violence of Mamluk factions and the incurable corruption of the government, the Circassian sultans contrived not only to preserve the power of Egypt, but even to enlarge its dominions and greatly extend its foreign trade in the Red and Mediterranean seas. They continued to hold Syria as far as Melitene, and maintained a less stringent suzerainty over the Hejaz, and over the congeries of beduin tribes and Turkoman clans in Syria and along the Syrian frontier. They stood up dauntlessly to the threats and vituperations of Timur's son Shāh Rūkh, who considered himself the most powerful Moslem monarch of his time. They conquered Cyprus in 1426 with a fleet of galleys built at the port of Būlāq, recently risen from the Nile; similar attempts upon Rhodes were successfully repelled by the valiant Knights Hospitaller of the Order of St. John of Jerusalem.[11] They fought several campaigns in Asia Minor, where for a time they secured the submission of the proud emir of Karaman. They even braved the wrath of the terrible Mehmed II, the Ottoman sultan, and during the reign of his successor, Bayazid II, they defeated the Turkish armies three times in the course of a prolonged campaign lasting from 1486 to 1491. They drew up trade agreements with most countries of southern and southwestern Europe as far as Brittany, and when they launched their naval campaign against the Portuguese in India, the Venetian republic gave them moral support and all the guidance possible. Its own prosperity was then at stake, for its vast commerce with Europe depended largely on uninterrupted supplies of oriental produce, from the markets of Damascus and Alexandria.

11. See above, pp. 317–318, 372–375.

It would seem impossible to associate these achievements with a system of government at the head of which the reigning sultan, however strong or adroit, was in reality at the mercy of a factious oligarchy of envious emirs, who held all the military commands and governorships as well as the court offices, and each of whom was a veritable sultan in miniature. But the explanations of this strange anomaly are not far to seek: first, infamous as was their government, and apparently suicidal as were their mutual jealousies, the Mamluks from the sultan downward were a splendid soldiery, evidently possessed of the faculty of collective self-preservation. They knew how to keep their own quarrels to themselves, and invited neither the Egyptians, nor the beduins of the provinces, nor least of all the forces of a foreign neighbor, to intervene in their private dissensions.[12] A few rebellious emirs did break the rule by seeking refuge abroad, stirring up border troubles for the ruling sultan with the aid of foreign adventurers, but on the whole the princes of the surrounding countries refused to give countenance to such emirs, and preferred to live in peace with the occupants of the Mamluk throne.

Moreover, though the government was corrupt, and offices were sold or farmed, the sultan had at his disposal a highly developed administrative machinery, which had the virtue of continuity, and which went on working independently in spite of surrounding turmoil. Even the troubles of the reign of a minor or a feeble sultan made no great inroads on its efficiency, especially as its functionaries were Egyptians or Syrians of all creeds, who had no interest in the jealousies and petty rivalries of their quarrelsome masters. Thirdly, the mass of the Egyptian population was docile and peace-loving. Indeed, the Egyptians gave their foreign masters no serious trouble, but were reconciled to cultivating the land, paying the oppressive taxes, and manufacturing the magnificent robes and other articles of luxury which the sultan and the emirs required. Thus not only were they a positive asset and a source of revenue, but their docility enabled the sultans to embark upon schemes of foreign war and aggression. Not so docile were the law-breaking beduins of the provinces, who constituted a real danger to Mamluk rule, although, like the Egyptians themselves, they contributed to the ranks of the militia, which often accompanied the Mamluk army on foreign military expeditions. Fourthly, besides the immense revenues which the sultan drew from the various sources of taxation, his coffers were continually overflowing with vast sums of money that poured in through the customs stations between Jidda and Alexandria on the

12. Ibn-Iyās, *Badā'i' az-zuhūr*, II, 39.

main high road of Indo-European commerce. Thus alongside the disruptive tendencies, for which the military oligarchy was responsible, the Mamluk sultanate possessed many elements of stability, which supplied it with considerable resources in money, men, and material, and made it a power to be reckoned with in southern Europe and the Near East.

It has already been remarked that every adult Burjī Mamluk sultan began his career as a slave. Sultan Barsbey was originally bought by a governor of Melitene named Dukmak, by whom he was presented as a gift to sultan Barkuk, first ruler of the Circassian line. Barsbey was thus enrolled among the Mamluks of the latter, and after his enfranchisement began to work his way up from rank to rank until he became governor of Tripoli, and some time afterward *dawatdar* (private secretary) to sultan Tatar in Cairo. Tatar died soon afterward, having designated his minor son Muḥammad for the succession, with Barsbey as *lala* (tutor), and the emir Janibek aṣ-Ṣūfī as regent. Barsbey was determined to become sultan, and after disposing of Janibek, whom he threw into prison with other enemies and doubtful friends, he deposed his benefactor's son, and ascended the throne in April 1422. Having thus completely extinguished his opponents, Barsbey felt so secure as to dispense with the distribution of the customary accession largess to the royal Mamluks, but then began, nevertheless, to play for popularity. First he ordered that persons approaching his person should only kiss his hand, or merely bow, instead of performing the elaborate genuflection and the kissing of the ground as theretofore. Then he issued an edict depriving all non-Moslem government officials of their posts, but it was soon discovered that some of the departments could not be operated without them, and the order was simply left in abeyance.

For the next year and a half quiet prevailed throughout the Mamluk empire, except for the rebellions of the governors of Safad and Behesni in Syria, who were soon routed and replaced. But in August 1423 Barsbey and his empire shook with the news of the escape of the sultan's arch-rival Janibek aṣ-Ṣūfī from his prison in Alexandria. Barsbey arrested and banished many suspected partisans of the vanished emir, and began to suspect many of his own friends, but neither persecution nor search could produce the dangerous rival; it was not till 1435 that his whereabouts became known. Even then the sultan was unable to seize him, for he had taken refuge with Turkoman enemies beyond the border.

Shortly after the escape of Janibek, Barsbey found himself confronted with a menacing variety of external problems, including the rebellion of the governor of Damascus, the depredations of Frankish pirates on the Mediterranean coast of Egypt, and the denying of allegiance by the sharīf of Mecca, Ḥasan ibn-ʿAjlān. First he sent an expedition with a new governor for Damascus, named Sudun; as soon as the news reached him that the rebel was defeated and incarcerated in the citadel of the Syrian capital, he turned his attention to the other two problems. He resolved to put down the Frankish pirates by depriving them of their base, the island of Cyprus, and after two successful expeditions, he vigorously prosecuted his efforts to obtain permanent control of the island.[13] A strong army from Egypt and Syria, supported by a formidable fleet from both countries, was dispatched in 1426. Limassol, Larnaca, and Nicosia, the capital, were seized, and the king of Cyprus, Janus de Lusignan, was taken prisoner. He was brought in triumph to the citadel of Cairo, but eventually released for a high ransom, after becoming a tributary vassal of the Mamluk sultanate. Two years earlier Ḥasan ibn-ʿAjlān, the sharīf of Mecca, was subdued and the supremacy of Egypt over the holy city and its seaport Jidda was restored. Ḥasan himself traveled to Cairo, in the company of the pilgrim caravan and the army that had been sent against him. There he assured Barsbey of his allegiance to the Mamluk throne, and consented to pay an annual tribute of 30,000 dinars; he was kept in Cairo as an honored hostage until the first instalment was paid.

Before the Mamluk army had left Mecca a convoy of Indian merchant shipping had sailed into the port of Jidda, after its captain had been assured by the Mamluk general in command that it would be accorded all facilities for trade, now that the port had come under the benign authority of Mamluk rule. Until then Aden in the Yemen had been the first Red Sea port for all Indian trade, but driven thence by oppressive treatment and eccentric exactions, oriental merchants suddenly found a better emporium at Jidda. A special office was created in Cairo, and its holder, the *shadd* (inspector) of Jidda, repaired there annually to receive the immense customs duties that were willingly paid at the rate of ten percent ad valorem on all imports. Not content with this new source of revenue, Barsbey assumed a monopoly of many sorts of commerce including all eastern spices and such home-produced articles as sugar—measures which caused prices to become prohibitive even to European merchants, who were always ready to buy the luxuries of the east. This

13. See above, pp. 372–375.

led to complaints and reprisals by the Venetian republic, as well as by the kingdoms of Castile and Aragon-Catalonia.

Besides interfering with trade Barsbey meddled with the coinage, altering the rate of exchange of gold and silver to his own advantage, and putting foreign money out of circulation so that he might buy it cheaply and then readmit it, to the extreme annoyance and loss of the merchants, native and foreign. The population, too, were galled by the sultan's rapacious methods of making money to satisfy his unbounded extravagance. The high price of sugar was most resented, because it was widely used as a remedy against the recurrent plague. But when the monopoly was extended to such necessities as meat and grain, and the free sale of cattle was forbidden, the resulting shortages led to famine in many parts of Egypt. Still worse were the outrages of the uncontrolled and wayward Mamluk soldiery, who mishandled the people and treated the women so insolently that the latter had to be forbidden to appear in the streets.

In Syria the system of monopolies brought similar hardships to both merchants and common people, but the country remained free from rebellious governors, and the people were at least spared the troublesome outrages of the soldiery. Since 1429, however, the Syrian roads had witnessed several military operations directed against the Turkomans. In the background was Shāh Rūkh, who was exasperated by the flat refusal of the sultan to allow him to share in the clothing of the Ka'bah in Mecca. He therefore supported Kara Yoluk, chief of the White Sheep Turkomans, against whose forces Barsbey had to fight continually, and even marched in person in 1432. The princes of the Dhū-l-Qadr, who were the sultan's vassals, were also a source of trouble, as they had given harbor to Barsbey's bitter enemy, the escaped Janibek. In the end, however, Barsbey was victorious: Kara Yoluk was killed in 1435 in a battle with the chief of another Turkoman tribe called the Black Sheep, Janibek was slain, and the Dhū-l-Qadr were finally subdued.

Barsbey did not long survive a success which the historian al-Maqrīzī thought to have been totally undeserved.[14] He died unregretted in June 1438, after he had appointed his fourteen-year-old son Yūsuf as his successor, and an emir named Jakmak as regent. Barsbey had been a stern ruler, and the outward tranquillity of both Egypt and Syria was no proof of corresponding prosperity. His conquest of Cyprus had pleased his Mamluks, and his monopolies had filled their pockets with ill-gotten gain, but the people had suffered during the

14. Al-Maqrīzī, *As-sulūk* (Brit. Mus. MS.), IV, fol. 200B.

sixteen years of his reign, and Egypt was often in a state of famine even in years of plenty.

Yūsuf, the new sultan, occupied the throne for but ninety-four days, during which the regent Jakmak gathered all power into his hands; he was ultimately proclaimed sultan in September 1438, after his nomination to the dignity by a blundering and impetuous emir named Kirkmas, who had been plotting to obtain the sultanate for himself. The deposed Yūsuf was imprisoned at the citadel in Cairo, and Kirkmas was given the office of atabek, which Jakmak had held with the regency. Kirkmas accepted the office without apparent demur, but, unable to dissimulate longer, he seized the first opportunity which offered itself to besiege the sultan at the citadel. He was defeated, however, and after his surrender Jakmak sent him in chains to Alexandria, where he was condemned to death by the doctors of law, and publicly beheaded with a blunt sword, in December 1438. The Mamluks who had supported him in the rebellion were now seized in great numbers; some of them were imprisoned and others were banished to distant oases in Upper Egypt. Thus all opposition in Cairo was completely quelled, but soon afterward Jakmak was faced by a joint rebellion of the governors of Aleppo and Damascus, who had declared for the deposed Yūsuf only to further their own ends. Jakmak decided to march in person at the head of an expedition against them, but before he had made preparations, young Yūsuf escaped from the citadel disguised as a scullion. Jakmak was greatly disconcerted, especially as the news reached him from Upper Egypt that a part of the troops he had dispatched against the beduins there had been won over by Yūsuf's supporters. Eventually, however, Jakmak triumphed over all his difficulties, and emerged unscathed. Yūsuf was discovered in April 1439; contrary to all expectations the sultan treated him well, sending him to Alexandria, where he was kept under a mild form of custody which did not prevent him from indulging in pious studies. In the course of the following month the governors of Damascus and Aleppo were finally defeated and put to death, with many of their followers. Shortly before the arrest of Yūsuf trouble among the troops in Upper Egypt had vanished.

Like his predecessor Barsbey, sultan Jakmak wished to chastise the Christians, whose freebooters had begun again, in spite of the subjugation of Cyprus, to despoil the Egyptian and Syrian coasts. He therefore sent an expedition against Rhodes, in August 1440, but the troops returned empty-handed, as the resistance offered by the Knights of St. John, who had been well prepared, was too strong for them. The attempt was renewed with greater preparations in 1443 and 1444, but with the same result. Finally giving up the design as hopeless, Jakmak made peace with the doughty grand master of the order, John of Lastic, whose envoy to Cairo was assisted in his negotiations by an agent of Jacques Coeur, the great French merchant. For the rest of his reign Jakmak sought no quarrel with any Christian power, and though he continued the system of monopolies on oriental merchandise, his treatment of Frankish merchants, who were irked most by these restrictions, was honorable and straightforward.

Toward the Moslem countries around, Jakmak pursued a wise policy of friendliness and accommodation. Against the advice of his unbending emirs, he allowed Shāh Rūkh to send a covering for the sacred Ka'bah in 1443, thus ending, without loss of rights or prestige, a controversy which had been the source of arrogant correspondence during the reign of Barsbey. He was also on the best of terms with the Ottoman sultan Murad II, as well as the princes of Asia Minor, whom he allied to his interests by marrying two widowed ladies of their kin at the beginning of his reign.

In his domestic policy Jakmak was not quite as successful, because of the unbridled outrages of the Mamluk soldiery, whose savage treatment of obnoxious emirs and administrators fills many a page in the contemporary chronicles. Unable to restrain them from molesting women on festive days, the sultan was compelled to forbid the pretty Cairenes from enjoying an outing even on such rare occasions. Nor was Jakmak able to put a stop to the rampant mismanagement of the trade monopolies. But on the whole his government was mild and benevolent, especially when compared with that of his greedy predecessor. His personal character, moreover, was exemplary; he observed the laws of the Koran scrupulously, touched no forbidden food, prohibited wines, and suppressed profane music. He loathed gaudy apparel, and for pious reasons he ordained that his courtiers and emirs should wear short clothes and clip their long mustaches. Indeed, through his example the morals of the court improved, and many religious buildings were raised in Cairo by the leading emirs, in imitation of the sultan's zeal for repairing old mosques or founding new ones.[15] His orthodoxy induced him to persecute Jews and Christians, and to enforce the old sumptuary distinctions regarding the size of turbans for non-Moslems. But he was liberal to the learned, and thought no price too high for a beautiful book. He died at the age of about eighty, in February 1453, after a long illness

15. Abū-l-Maḥāsin, *An-nujūm,* VII (Berkeley, 1926–1929), 245–247.

which he bravely suffered for a year. And despite his simple life, he left but a trifling fortune for his only remaining son 'Uthmān.

Shortly before he breathed his last, sultan Jakmak took the unprecedented step of abdicating the throne, and though he had privately intimated that he wished his son to be appointed his successor, he refrained from giving official voice to his parental predilection, and left the 'Abbāsid caliph and the qadis and the assembled emirs, all of whom he had especially summoned to his sick bed, to make the choice themselves. "The question rests entirely with you, as regards whom you would elevate to the sultanate," he assured the assembly, knowing that they could not possibly turn his son aside.[16] 'Uthmān was accordingly nominated to succeed, and homage was done to him at once.

'Uthmān was about nineteen years old at the time of his accession, and was therefore no infant, but he fared worse than previous younger sons of sultans elevated to the throne, and his reign, which lasted but six weeks and one day, was shorter than that of any former youth. The cause of his downfall was that he had rashly alienated all but the party of his father's Mamluks, and had thus roused the indignation of every other faction. He was consequently besieged at the Cairene citadel, in March 1453, and after seven days of fierce fighting with the forces of the atabek Inal, around whom the malcontents had rallied, he was forced to surrender. He had been deposed two days before, with the full consent of the same caliph who had officiated at his accession ceremony, and on the morrow of his surrender he was sent in fetters to Alexandria by the new sultan Inal.

Elevated to the sultanate at the advanced age of seventy-three, and so uneducated that he could not even write his own name, Inal nevertheless was able to maintain himself on the throne for nearly eight years. He was an easy-going, pliable old man, whose policy was to meet the exacting demands of his own Mamluks (jilbān) with as much financial indulgence as he could afford. Some of the leading emirs, moreover, were bound to his interests by a series of marriages, one of which was the marriage of his eldest son Aḥmad, who became sultan after him, to a daughter of his grand *dawatdar* (chief private secretary).[17] Inal's good nature and pliability, however, were responsible for the shamelessness and turbulence of his Mamluks, whose

16. *Ibid.*, VII, 240–241.
17. Ibn-Iyās, *Badā'i' az-zuhūr*, II, 41, 43, 64.

violent excesses and disorders covered the length of an otherwise beneficial reign. At first the sultan was able to temporize with them, but on the eve of a punitive expedition against the beduins of the province of Beheira, in June 1455, they refused to march until camels were provided. These not being granted, they rose in armed rebellion around the citadel, and were joined by older Mamluks, who had previously persuaded the caliph al-Qā'im to support them in an endeavor to restore the deposed 'Uthmān. This, however, displeased the *jilbān* and decided them to return to their master, so that eventually the outbreak was quelled, and the caliph was sent to Alexandria as a prisoner, after being divested of the title "commander of the faithful." A handful of the older Mamluks were banished to Syria or thrown into the dungeons of the tower of the citadel, but the *jilbān* were given the camels for which they had clamored, and shortly afterwards marched with the punitive expedition.

In December 1456 Inal was again confronted with the open rebellion of his spoiled *jilbān;* this time the source of the trouble was a series of exorbitant demands which they had put forth with defiance, but which the sultan had completely refused to concede. The Mamluks were equally adamant, and when Inal came out of the citadel to admonish them in person, they pelted him with a shower of stones. Strangely, however, the sultan gave way to all their demands a few days after, much to the disgust of the chronicler abū-l-Maḥāsin, who observed with bitterness that such weak-kneed indulgence could not but sap all sense of decency from the *jilbān,* and tempt them to worse acts of violence.[18] The remark was justified to the full; during the remaining five years of Inal's reign the *jilbān* became all-powerful. They had several officials dismissed and changed at pleasure; and neither sultan nor magistrate dared rebuke them for their organized robberies and arson, their lynch-law and incendiarism. In 1460, a terrible plague broke out, but the calamity failed to check the wild atrocities of the *jilbān,* who not only attacked the passing biers, but ravaged the property of the dead and the dying.

Amidst the reigning chaos, and in the teeth of strong opposition, however, sultan Inal finally carried through a reform of the currency, in 1458. The debased silver coinage which his predecessors had struck was gradually withdrawn from circulation, and improved coins were issued. Money forgers and counterfeiters were visited with harsh penalties, and on one occasion the sultan beheaded ten of them

18. Abū-l-Maḥāsin, *An-nujūm,* VII, 477.

without much ado.[19] In foreign politics, too, Inal was both fortunate and successful. He was on the best of terms with the Ottoman
sultan Mehmed II, to whom he sent a special embassy to offer
congratulations on the conquest of Constantinople; rather than dis-
please the great conqueror, he turned a deaf ear to the complaints of
emir Ibrāhīm of Karaman against Ottoman aggression. In consequence Ibrāhīm made war on Mamluk territory, and captured
several fortified places in Cilicia, but he was driven out, and forced to
make peace in 1458. Shortly afterward sultan Inal was also involved
in European politics by taking sides in the succession dispute in
Cyprus, which had been tributary to Egypt since the reign of Barsbey. Inal championed the cause of the bastard James, archbishop of
Nicosia, who came to Egypt and applied for military aid against his
half-sister, queen Charlotte de Lusignan.[20] James returned to Cyprus
with an Egyptian army, and with its help occupied the capital
Nicosia, but the campaign dragged on for a few more years, and the
issue was not decided in the lifetime of sultan Inal, who died in
February 1461. He left a family of four, two daughters and two sons,
by a single wife, who (strange exception in Mamluk history) had not
even one rival, but his life was less edifying in other respects.

Only one day before his death, sultan Inal abdicated the throne in
favor of his elder son Aḥmad. During his father's reign, Aḥmad had
filled more than one responsible office, and had wielded considerable
influence and power behind the scenes. He was thirty years old at his
accession, and by age and experience he was well qualified for the
sultanate. But he was too enthusiastic for reform, and in his brave
attempts to check the outbursts of Mamluk violence in Cairo, and the
irregularities of absentee governors in Syria, he alienated most of the
leaders of his father's party, and displeased as well the older factions,
all of whom joined in a conspiracy to dethrone him. A majority
were in favor of a governor of Damascus, named Janim, as sultan,
and immediately sent to him an invitation to come to Cairo, but
other Mamluks preferred the atabek Khushkadam; their leader Janibey dexterously persuaded the former party to agree to the appointment of the atabek as a stop-gap sultan until their nominee arrived.
With this agreement the citadel was attacked in June 1461, and after
an unequal battle which lasted for three days, sultan Aḥmad gave up
resistance and surrendered himself. He was deposed on the same day,
and immediately afterward Khushkadam was proclaimed sultan.

19. Ibn-Iyās, *Badā'i' az-zuhūr*, II, 56–57, 71.
20. See above, pp. 382–383.

Aḥmad was eventually sent to Alexandria, where he remained in prison for a while, but he was released later, and spent his remaining years in peaceful retirement.

Unlike previous Mamluk sovereigns of the Burjī dynasty, who were Turks or Circassians, sultan Khushkadam was by origin a Greek. The first problem of his reign arose out of the very circumstances of his elevation to the sultanate, for no sooner had the ceremonies of his accession been concluded than the emir Janim, responding to the summons of his friends, arrived in the vicinity of Cairo to claim the throne. Khushkadam was seriously perturbed, but, with the aid of Janibey, he was able to prevent Janim from entering Cairo, and even to send him back to Syria, as governor of Damascus again. Not content with this stroke of fortune, Khushkadam arrested and imprisoned many Mamluk leaders in Cairo, a measure which raised a rebellion that nearly cost him the throne. He now determined to do away with Janim, but the latter got wind of what was in store for him, and fled from Damascus to Edessa in the territory of the White Sheep Turkomans. Khushkadam dreaded Janim's return at the head of an army to avenge himself, and an expedition was consequently prepared to pursue him, but tidings of his death in 1462 rendered its march unnecessary.

Unnatural though it might seem, Khushkadam's next step was to turn upon Janibey, to whose acumen and skill he owed not only his elevation to the throne, but the power to remain there. Janibey had been powerful enough as Mamluk leader, but when he had put Khushkadam so much in his debt, the sultan began to see in his old friend a dangerous foe, and he resolved to get rid of him. And so one day in August 1463, as Janibey was entering the citadel, he was set upon by the *jilbān,* who stabbed him to death with their spears, and then dashed out his brains with a heavy stone. Other leaders of Mamluk parties were arrested and imprisoned or banished. The sultan now felt secure, and during the remaining years of his reign he adopted toward the leaderless Mamluk factions a policy of playing off one corps against another, thus nullifying their power and opposition. This left the field free for the riotous debauchery of his own Mamluks, who murdered and ravished and plundered just as they pleased. Meanwhile the sultan enriched himself by several unrighteous means; official posts were openly sold, and innocent persons were given over to their enemies to be scourged, tortured, or executed without trial so long as the sultan's palm had previously been greased with fat gold. Worse still was the practice of the crafty Greek of calling in state upon some wealthy grandee, and handsomely fleecing the unlucky host before the visit was ceremoniously over.

In the field of foreign politics Khushkadam's reign is to be remembered as the one in which began the struggle between the Egyptian and the Ottoman sultanates, which finally led to the incorporation of Egypt and its dependencies in the Ottoman empire. The dispute began in 1463 with a struggle over the succession in the principality of Karaman, where the two sultans favored rival claimants, and the Ottoman sultan Mehmed II supported the claim of his candidate by force of arms, obtaining as the price of his assistance several towns where only recently the suzerainty of the Egyptian sultan had been acknowledged. Open war did not, however, break out between the two states in Khushkadam's time. In Cyprus Khushkadam continued the policy inaugurated by his predecessor Inal, and sent several expeditions to the island, partly to support king James II, but mainly to be rid of the remaining dangerous Mamluk factions.

Toward the close of the reign beduin tribes caused terror and disorder not only in Upper Egypt and Syria, but in northern Arabia, where they plundered even the pilgrim caravans. While preparations were being made for the dispatch of the necessary troops, Khushkadam was seized with dysentery and rapidly became powerless. Yet he managed somehow to send an expedition to Arabia in August 1467, but when the order went out to the troops designed for Upper Egypt, the commanding general politely refused to march, preferring to tarry in Cairo to watch the impending turn of events.[21] At last Khushkadam died in October 1467, leaving two sons, of whom the elder was called Manṣūr.[22]

For the next four months or so Cairo was the scene of unceasing intrigue and intermittent strife among contending factions, for during that short interval two more sultans began and terminated their rule. It should be noted first, however, that contrary to previous Mamluk usage, sultan Khushkadam had not named his son to succeed him, nor had any leading emir even troubled to learn the last wishes of the dying man upon the question. A few hours before the Greek's death the leading emirs held a meeting at which the head of the Khushkadamite party, named Khairbek, with the support of another faction leader, Timurbogha, secured the succession for the atabek Yelbey, who was known by the sobriquet of al-Majnūn (the lunatic). Yelbey was proclaimed sultan on the same day, with Timurbogha in the atabekship, almost immediately after the burial of Khushkadam.

21. Abū-l-Mahāsin, An-nujūm, VII, 826, note e.
22. Ibn-Iyās, Badā'i' az-zuhūr, II, 82.

His reign lasted for nearly two months, in the course of which he soon realized that Khairbek had helped him to the sultanate only to use him as a stepping-stone to the throne. In consequence he began to plot against the formidable Khairbek, and waged war upon him, but he was foiled in his design, and paid for his temerity by being deposed and imprisoned.

With the support of Khairbek and his powerful party, the atabek Timurbogha was elevated to the throne, in December 1467, but his reign also did not exceed two months. In sharp contrast to his niggardly and unlettered predecessor, however, Timurbogha, who was also Greek by origin, was not only a munificent man, but a lover of learning and the arts, and a past master in horsemanship, lance-play, and marksmanship. Had he possessed the means of gratifying the incessant demands of the factions around him, he might have held the throne for the remaining years of his lifetime. But the treasury was empty, and without gold he was unable to win over many followers. He was deposed in January 1468 by Khairbek, who deemed the moment opportune for becoming sultan himself. Khairbek, however, had not reckoned beforehand with the forces of the new atabek Ka'itbey, and as a result of this oversight found himself besieged at the citadel before he was even proclaimed sultan. Then a battle took place between the besiegers and the besieged; it resulted in the victory of Ka'itbey, who accepted the sultanate after some apparent hesitation. Khairbek was sent in fetters to Alexandria, while with cheerful resignation Timurbogha bowed to the accomplished fact, and retired into private life to Damietta; he was not held prisoner, but was left at liberty and accompanied by some of his retinue.

Ka'itbey was proclaimed sultan in January 1468; his reign, which lasted for nearly twenty-nine years, was phenomenal, for it was not only the longest, but the most successful and warlike of the Circassian line. Much of this reign was spent in struggles with Shāhsuvār, vassal chief of the Dhū-l-Qadr Turkomans, who was ultimately vanquished and put to death in Cairo, and with Uzun Ḥasan (Ḥasan the Long), formidable prince of the White Sheep, who had been masquerading as the sultan's loyal vassal during the prolonged campaign against Shāhsuvār. Moreover, in 1482 Ka'itbey offended the new Ottoman sultan Bayazid II by entertaining his rival brother Jem in Cairo, and supplying him with means for a fruitless rising in Anatolia. Because of this, and also the unjustifiable intercepting of an Indian embassy to the Ottoman court by the agents of Ka'itbey, Bayazid II declared war against Egypt in 1486, having flatly refused to listen to any talk of peace. One Ottoman army seized Adana, Tarsus, and other places within Mamluk territory in Cilicia, and another army besieged the outlying town of Melitene, but the Egyptian forces operated with success against both armies and drove them away with heavy losses. Adana and Tarsus were regained by the Ottomans two years later, only to be lost again after a battle with the Egyptians, in the field of Agha Chayrî, and in 1489 the emir Izbek inflicted a further severe defeat on the considerable forces of Bayazid II at Caesarea in Anatolia. Peace was not brought about until 1491, and Ka'itbey showed a wise moderation in proposing it first to the Ottoman court.

Despite his preoccupation with the campaigns of his first twenty-three years, Ka'itbey was able to exercise diplomatic sternness with the reigning queen of Cyprus, the Venetian Catherine Cornaro, who had not been punctual in paying the annual tribute due to him as overlord of the island. Ka'itbey threatened her with war if she did not dispatch the tribute for 1478, but the Venetian republic, which had a stake in the matter, persuaded the queen to avoid the sultan's anger, and the tribute duly arrived. However, the sultan's threats were not always effective; in 1487 he endeavored to assist the Moslem ruler of Granada abū-'Abd-Allāh (Boabdil) by threatening king Ferdinand of Spain with the destruction of Jerusalem, and the annihilation of all Egyptian and Syrian Christians, if Spanish hostilities against the Moslem kingdom did not cease, but king Ferdinand refused to be cowed, and went on undismayed with his successful campaign.

In domestic politics during the reign of Ka'itbey, the sultan's conduct of affairs differed in many respects from that of all other Circassian rulers, before or after him. He treated deposed sultans and descendants of former sultans with constant magnanimity and honor, and frequently invited them to play polo tournaments with him in Cairo, in royal colors. He allowed them to make the pilgrimage to Mecca, and even permitted them to visit Cairo in his absence without any suspicion or fear of conspiracy. Contrary to previous custom, too, he not only frequently left the citadel for riding and hunting excursions, but performed the pilgrimage to Mecca, visited Hebron, Jerusalem, Alexandria, and Damietta, and once made a great tour of inspection to Aleppo and to the banks of the Euphrates, the frontier of the empire. And wherever he went, it must be recorded to his credit, sultan Ka'itbey left splendid traces of his progress in good roads, bridges, mosques, schools, fortifications, or other pious or necessary works. Of these constructions the great medieval fort of Alexandria deserves special mention.

Ka'itbey could not have succeeded in the spheres of foreign and domestic politics to such an extent had he been a bad leader of men, or an incompetent weakling. Besides tact and courage, he possessed experience and knowledge of the world, and he lacked neither insight, nor energy, nor decision. His strong character dominated the immense numbers of his own Mamluks, whom he skillfully bound by self-interest to himself. They became really devoted to him, and with their unstinted aid he was able to deal, effectively and at will, with the other Mamluk factions. There were the usual outbursts from time to time, but party was so cleverly balanced against party that the government was uncommonly safe.

For his campaigns and his buildings Ka'itbey required considerable means, which he could raise only by persistent mulcting and arbitrary levies, in the absence of a regulated system of taxation. Such extraordinary contributions were necessary for the wars in which he was obliged to engage. Not only was all real estate once taxed to the amount of seven months' rental, but a very burdensome tax was levied on the sale of corn.[23] Rich Jews and Christians were correspondingly squeezed, and many high officials of the administration were remorselessly tortured, scourged, or flogged, sometimes by the sultan in person, to extort their ill-gotten treasure. On several occasions Ka'itbey stooped to the method of calling in state upon notables of the provinces, receiving from them rich gifts which were not always voluntary.

The last five years of Ka'itbey's reign were free from troubles abroad, but they were dismally clouded at home by an exceptionally virulent plague which swept over Egypt in 1492. It carried off more than 200,000 of the population, killed a third of the Mamluks, and bereaved the sultan himself of a daughter and her slave-mother in one day.[24] The plague was followed, two years later, by scarcity and cattle disease, while to add to the general misery a long-pent-up quarrel among the Mamluk factions broke out in 1495. The aged sultan, who was then about eighty-five years old, displayed his standard at the citadel gate, assembled his men, and without bloodshed quelled the riot for the moment, but the intrigues and jealousies between the ringleaders, Kansuh Khamsmi'ah and Akberdi, continued.[25] In the following year the contest was about to break out

23. The tax on corn belonged to the latter part of the reign; see *ibid.*, II, 291.
24. *Ibid.*, II, 274.
25. The name Kansuh occurs frequently in the next few pages, denoting three different men. The sobriquet Khamsmi'ah (five hundred) is applied to this Kansuh, to distinguish him

again, when the sultan, overcome by years, illness, and worry, breathed his last on July 28, 1496. The emirs and officials of the court and the entire army attended his funeral, mourning the loss of one who for more than a quarter of a century had ruled them well, and had raised the prestige of the Mamluk empire to a great height abroad.

Within the next five years Cairo witnessed five turbulent reigns, the first of which was that of Muḥammad, the fourteen-year-old only son of Ka'itbey by a freed concubine. Muḥammad was solemnly proclaimed sultan the day before his father's death, but, contrary to what was generally asserted, Ka'itbey had no say in choosing him, for he had been completely unconscious when he was approached on the matter. Nor, presumably, would Ka'itbey have sanctioned the appointment of his son to the sultanate had he been able to voice his last wishes, for he knew that the hereditary principle had proved totally alien to the conceptions of the military oligarchy.

In the case of this Muḥammad the danger came from the emir Kansuh Khamsmi'ah, whose deadly antagonist Akberdi had secretly fled from Egypt, leaving him virtual ruler of the sultanate. But Kansuh could not feel safe as long as Akberdi's supporters were at large, especially as the young sultan was strongly inclined toward them and their leader. He therefore compelled Muḥammad to banish and imprison many of them, and on one occasion (January 1497) he caused some of their leaders to be drowned in the Nile. Thinking that the time had come to bid for the throne, he seized one of the gates of the citadel on the day following the drowning of the emirs, and immediately had himself recognized as sultan by the emirs of his faction, the caliph, and the qadis. But when he attempted to seize the citadel itself, he was repulsed by sultan Muḥammad's uncle, Kansuh al-Ashrafī, and after a "reign" of three days he sought safety in hiding. He made a second attempt the following February, but failed again, and fled with most of his faction to Palestine, where, together with many of his followers, he met his death at the hands of the emir Akberdi, who had been recalled by sultan Muḥammad to Cairo. Thus reinstated, Akberdi entered Cairo amid great rejoicing, but the surviving emirs of his old opponent's faction soon found a leader in Kansuh al-Ashrafī, and Akberdi had to fly again to Syria in July 1497, this time never to return.

Meanwhile sultan Muḥammad had been declared of age, and the

---

from both Kansuh Khāl (uncle) al-Ashrafī and Kansuh al-Ghūrī (also found as Qanṣauh al-Ghaurī). All three men became sultans.

reins of government were formally entrusted to him. But the new
burdens of responsibility failed to check, or even modify, his earlier
puerile cruelties, dissipation, and lewdness. He now began to live a
life of wild libertinism; male and female singers were his companions
in night orgies on the Nile, and during the day he was often found in
the company of the scum of the capital. With his slaves and comrades
he paraded the streets, attacked men as they passed, and entered
houses in the dark. On one occasion he attacked the house of an
official of the department of the privy purse with the intent of
seizing his wife, who was known to be a pretty woman.[26] And to
add to this reign of terror and immorality the Mamluk factions
committed untold barbarities, while organized bands of thieves
robbed many houses of their riches with impunity. Wearied at last by
such excesses, Kansuh plotted against his own nephew, and after an
extraordinary reign of about two years, the depraved Muḥammad
was finally murdered in October 1498, by the men of the emir
Tumanbey, his second private secretary.

Kansuh al-Ashrafī was proclaimed sultan two days later, with the
full support of his accomplice Tumanbey. He was about thirty years
of age at that time, but though on several occasions he proved to be
of a higher stamp than the typical run of Mamluks, and Cairo had a
much quieter time than usual during his sultanate, he was able to
hold the throne for only about twenty months. He lacked the power
of decision, and was wanting in both moral strength and funds,
without which it was impossible to cope with the chronic rapacity of
Mamluk demands. In Syria he was faced with the continued rebellion
of Akberdi, but fortunately for Kansuh, the veteran rebel came to
terms in May 1499, shortly after which he died a natural death, at
Aleppo. The sultan was soon confronted with another rebel in the
person of the governor of Aleppo, Kasruh, with whom the sultan's
old friend Tumanbey had entered into an agreement for the latter's
own ends. Kansuh was not unaware of the conspiracy, and accordingly victualed the citadel and fortified its walls, in preparation for a
siege. Meanwhile Tumanbey, who had been in Upper Egypt on a
punitive expedition, returned in June 1500, and before the end of
the month the citadel was stormed after three days of fierce fighting.
But the attackers failed to find sultan Kansuh, for he had escaped by
the women's gate (Bāb al-Harīm) in female disguise.

Cairo remained sultanless for two days after the escape of Kansuh,
owing to the difficulty of agreeing upon a suitable successor to the
throne. Tumanbey, who had caused the downfall of the sultan, and

26. Ibn-Iyās, *Badā'i' az-zuhūr*, II, 343–344.

was therefore the obvious candidate, cunningly waived his own claim
for the time being, and in the teeth of general opposition he secured
the succession for his senior in office, the atabek Janbalat. Kansuh,
still in hiding, was formally dethroned and the atabek was recognized
as sultan in his place, in June 1500. Ten days later the hapless
Kansuh was discovered, and eventually sent to the prison of Alexandria. But the new sultan was to remain on the throne only until
Tumanbey thought fit to unmask his designs. The chance presented
itself when Janbalat innocently sent him at the head of an expedition
for the suppression of the emir Kasruh, the rebel governor of Damascus. There Tumanbey joined forces with his old friend Kasruh, at
whose suggestion he had himself proclaimed sultan. Then he marched
back to Cairo, and with considerable forces advanced on the citadel,
which was captured in January 1501, after seven days' siege. On the
same day Janbalat was seized, and subsequently sent as a prisoner to
Alexandria where, contrary to the usual lot of deposed sultans, he
was beheaded by order of Tumanbey, called al-ʿĀdil (the Just).

As the accession ceremony at Damascus was not enough to legit-
imize his position, Tumanbey I was duly recognized, in January
1501, by the caliph, the qadis, and the emirs assembled. But the
esteem with which the new sultan had been regarded soon turned
into hatred and terror, as a result of the cruelties he perpetrated on
coming to the throne. Besides his barbarous treatment of one of the
chief qadis for his past loyalty to the deposed sultan, he treacherously caused the emir Kasruh, his right-hand man at Damascus and
Cairo, to be strangled and buried within a few hours in the stillness
of a wintry night.[27] Many other emirs were banished or even
drowned, while those who eluded arrest were ruthlessly hunted
down. At last the emirs were roused, and hearing a rumor that the
sultan was about to arrest a number of them, they attacked him in
the citadel, in April 1501. Tumanbey made but little resistance,
because all that he had at his disposal to put against the raging emirs
was a handful of his own Mamluks. Even these deserted him at the
critical hour, so that nothing was left for him but to fly and seek
concealment in the house of a friend.

Owing to the circumstances of the attempt to oust Tumanbey I,
the emirs had had no chance to decide upon whom the mantle of the
sultanate was to be conferred, with likely general consent. As a result
of the consequent haste, their first choice proved unacceptable to
most of the soldiery, and it was only after much deliberation that
another Kansuh, surnamed al-Ghūrī, was proclaimed sultan in April

27. *Ibid.*, II, 388–389.

1501.[28] Kansuh accepted the dangerous honor only after considerable hesitation, no doubt because of his fear of Mamluk fickleness
and caprice. He was then over sixty years of age, but still firm,
cunning, and vigorous, and he soon showed the emirs that he was not
to be overruled or browbeaten by any of them. By the simple
method of cajoling the secret supporters of the deposed Tumanbey I,
he succeeded in having the latter murdered with their connivance,
and thus rid himself of the ex-sultan without arousing the hostility of
his adherents. Like other sultans, however, al-Ghūrī had to face the
clamor of the Mamluks for the customary accession donative, but as
the treasury was empty and he himself was rapacious, he turned the
occasion to his own advantage, and under pretext of collecting funds
for the pressing largess, he resorted to a system of extortion and
heavy taxation, the extent of which had never been known in
Circassian annals. He levied ten months' rental at a stroke, laying not
only the lands and shops of Cairo under contribution, but also the
baths, water-wheels, mills, boats, beasts of burden, Jews, Christians,
and palace-servants down to the very doorkeeper. Even the waqfs or
pious endowments were pressed for the sum of a full year's returns,
and, further, he debased the coinage for his own benefit.[29] The
result was a handsome revenue with which, besides paying off the old
Mamluks, he bought a considerable number of new slaves in order to
create a new party, which was subsequently known as al-Ghūrīyah. It
is true, however, that he also spent a great portion of the extorted
money on strengthening the fortresses of Alexandria, Rosetta, and
Aleppo, on improving the pilgrim road to Mecca, and on building his
mosque and college in Cairo.

Yet in spite of continued extortion the country remained quiet,
and beyond a few military expeditions to quell beduin risings in
Egypt and Syria, there were few events to disturb the earlier years of
sultan al-Ghūrī's reign. But since the landing of the Portuguese in
India in 1498, and their establishment of the first European trade
colony on the west Indian coast in 1500, the immense trade which
had always poured into Egypt by way of Aden and Jidda had
gradually been diverted to the route around the Cape of Good Hope
to Europe. In consequence the excessively high cost of passing
through Egyptian ports, as well as the cost of overland transit to
Alexandria, were all avoided, and the profits of Indian trade now
went to the Portuguese. These vast losses to the Mamluk treasury
could not be tolerated by sultan al-Ghūrī, who was further infuriated

28. *Idem* (Paris MS.), fols. 117B–118B.
29. *Ibid.*, fols. 122B–123B.

by the attacks of the Portuguese upon Egyptian shipping in the Indian seas. At first, however, the sultan tried to obtain redress by peaceful means, although he might have been wiser if, as repeatedly advised by the Venetian republic, he had quickly resolved upon checking Portuguese aggression by naval force. His peace messenger reached Rome in 1504, and handed to pope Julius II a letter of complaint threatening to destroy the holy places in Palestine and Egypt, if king Manuel of Portugal did not cease from oppressing Moslem traders in India, and from conducting hostilities against Egyptian shipping. The mission failed in its object, and the sultan had, therefore, to equip a considerable fleet to fight the Portuguese in Indian waters. The first encounter took place in 1508 in the Indian harbor of Chaul, where the Mamluk fleet, in collaboration with a squadron from the Moslem state of Gujerat as well as several vessels from other Indian allies, defeated the Portuguese. But the next year the Portuguese had their revenge tenfold upon the Mamluk fleet at the battle of Diu, near Bombay, and the Mamluk carrying trade with India was doomed.

Only eight years after Diu the Mamluk empire itself was wiped out of existence by the Ottoman sultan Selim I. Since the peace of 1491 between sultans Ka'itbey and Bayazid II, Turco-Mamluk relations had been friendly, but with the accession of the warlike and ambitious Selim I in 1512, affairs assumed a serious turn. Thus, after defeating Isma'īl, the first shah of the new Ṣafavid dynasty of Persia, at the battle of Chaldiran in 1514, Selim I turned his eyes southward toward Syria and Egypt. He seized the border state of the Dhū-l-Qadr, then tributary to Egypt, though Turkey and Egypt were still at peace with each other. Then Selim I resolved to conquer Egypt, and with several trifling grievances against Kansuh al-Ghūrī as a pretext for war, he met the Mamluk army at the field of Marj Dābiq, north of Aleppo, in August 1516. The Mamluks were utterly defeated, and al-Ghūrī fell fighting. The superior numbers and the artillery of the Turks, aided by the treachery of the commander of the left wing of the Mamluk army, were responsible for the rout. After Marj Dābiq, Selim I's army advanced southward, and Syria passed quickly into the possession of the Ottomans, whose advent was in many places welcomed as meaning deliverance from the Mamluks.

In Cairo, when the news of the defeat and death of al-Ghūrī arrived, the emir Tumanbey, who had been left by al-Ghūrī to manage the government in his absence, was elected sultan, in October 1516. Tumanbey II accepted the office with real reluctance, and only after the emirs had pledged themselves to absolute and unswerving loyalty to him, in the presence of a saintly recluse named shaikh abū-Suʿūd. Meanwhile the Ottomans were advancing toward Egypt, and despite the desperate efforts which were made by Tumanbey II in preparation for the impending encounter with the Turk, the Mamluk army was defeated first near Gaza, and then at Raidānīyah outside Cairo. The latter battle was fought in January 1517, and on the next day Selim I was recognized as sultan of Egypt and Syria from the pulpits of Cairo. Tumanbey II continued the struggle for some months, but was finally vanquished and, after being captured, was executed in April 1517. With his death the proud empire of the Mamluks came to an end.

It was not until sultan Tumanbey II had breathed his last, as Ibn-Iyās, the eye-witness chronicler of the period, observed, that the Ottoman Selim I became undisputed master of Egypt and its numerous dependencies.[30] That Egypt should have thus changed hands was accepted by the chronicler with resignation, as the unalterable decree of fate, but it puzzled him deeply that it should at the same time sink into the position of a mere province of an empire, of which Cairo itself was not to be the capital. "The incredible thing was," he noted, "that Egypt became a governorship (*niyābah*), after its sultan had always been the greatest on earth; for he was the guardian of the two holy sanctuaries, and the holder of the kingdom of Egypt, of which . . . the accursed Pharaoh himself was justly proud. . . ." Ibn-Iyās lived long enough after 1517 not only to contemplate the unthinkable calamity taking place in Egypt, but to see Egypt going sadly into one of the darkest periods of her long history.

30. A chapter on the Ottomans is planned for volume V of this work, in preparation.

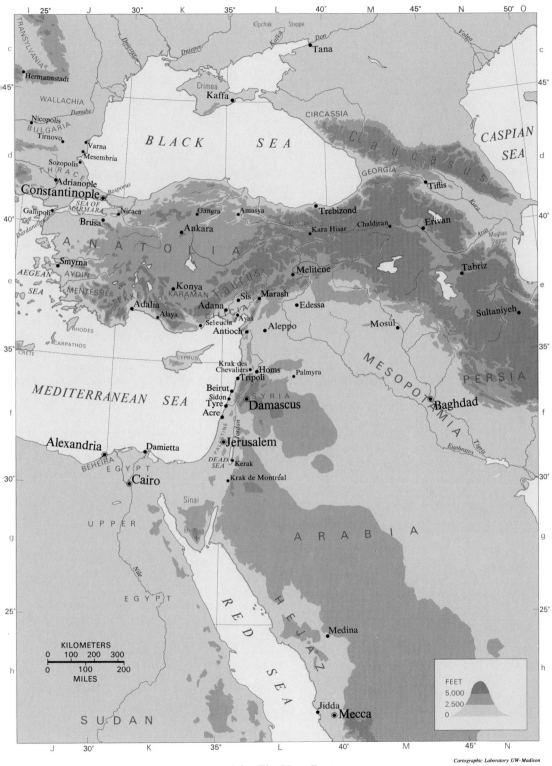

16. The Near East

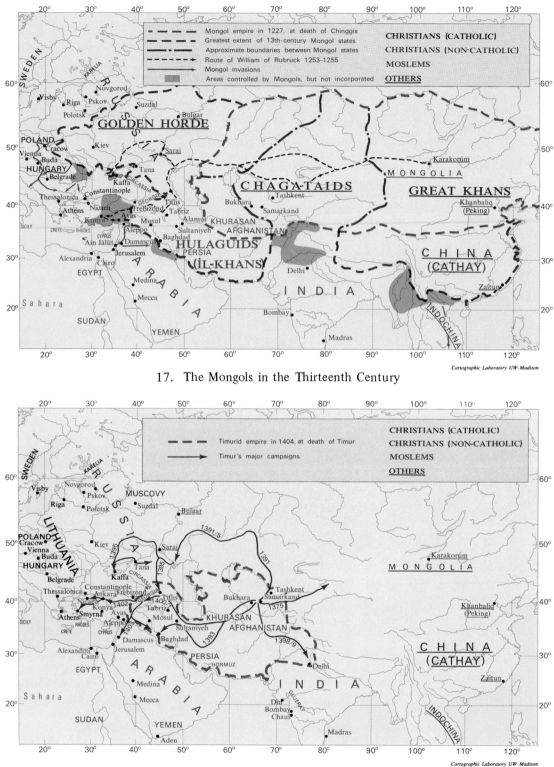

17. The Mongols in the Thirteenth Century

18. The Mongols in the Fifteenth Century

XV

THE MONGOLS AND WESTERN EUROPE

In this chapter an attempt will be made to give a succinct but comprehensive picture of the relations that existed between the Mongols and western Europe, with particular emphasis on their effect upon the crusades. To achieve this aim it will be necessary to start with the period of the Second Crusade, and thus to go over ground partially covered—from a different point of view—in previous volumes. An effort has been made to avoid needless duplication and, by relating this material to relevant parts of the chapters contributed to this volume by other historians, to reconstruct the links established for the first time in recorded history between the eastern and western borderlands of the Eurasian continent.

The number of relevant primary sources is so great that an enumeration would be both impracticable and superfluous. Evidence can be culled from innumerable western and Iranian sources of the 13th and 14th centuries. The footnotes will show which chronicles or other documents yielded the principal data used.

The following collections of sources were particularly useful: Girolamo Golubovich, *Bibliotheca bio-bibliografica della Terra Santa e dell' Oriente francescano* (vols. I–V, Quaracchi, 1906–1927); Anastasius van den Wyngaert, *Sinica franciscana*, I, *Itinera et relationes Fratrum Minorum saeculi XIII et XIV* (Quaracchi, 1929); *Recueil des historiens des croisades: Documents arméniens,* vol. II (Paris, 1906), which contains, among other sources, *La Flor des estoires de la terre d'Orient* by the Armenian Hayton, *Directorium ad passagium faciendum* by the Pseudo-Brocardus, *De modo Saracenos extirpandi* by William Adam, and *Les Gestes des Chiprois.* The appendix of Johannes Laurentius Mosheim, *Historia Tartarorum ecclesiastica* (Helmstadt, 1741) remains a useful collection of documents. There are no primary Mongol narrative sources of importance from the point of view of western-Mongol relations. Other Mongol documents, such as letters, will be quoted where necessary.

Denis Sinor, *Introduction à l'étude de l'Eurasie centrale* (Wiesbaden, 1963), contains an annotated bibliography of works dealing with Mongol history (pp. 294–319), with particular reference to relations with the west (pp. 314–318). The usefulness of Aziz S. Atiya, *The Crusade: Historiography and Bibliography* (Bloomington, Indiana, 1962), although considerable, is greatly reduced by the total inadequacy of its index. There is a good bibliography in Bertold Spuler, *Die Mongolen in Iran: Politik, Verwaltung und Kultur der Ilchanzeit* (2nd ed., Wiesbaden, 1965).

In the thirteenth century the immense military power of the Mongols was a decisive factor in Asian history, and hence could have exerted great influence on the Moslem-Christian confrontation. At that time no power capable of resisting a full-scale military onslaught by the Mongols existed anywhere in the world. Individual Mongol armies could sometimes be resisted, but only because they were operating without the full backing of Mongol power. It is highly doubtful whether the Great Khan Kubilai was even aware of the skirmishes which some of his lieutenants fought, and lost, in Anatolia. But it is certain that the forces which achieved the conquest of China and pushed far into Indochina could have conquered with much greater ease the small states of the Near East and even Byzantium.

It is important to bear in mind that from the very beginning of the

---

General works dealing with our subject include Giovanni Soranzo, *Il Papato, l'Europa cristiana e i Tartari: Un secolo di penetrazione occidentale in Asia* (Milan, 1930); A. C. Moule, *Christians in China before the year 1550* (London, 1930); Ilona Pálfy, *A Tatárok és a XIII. századi Europa* (Hefte des Collegium hungaricum in Wien, II; Budapest, 1928); and a number of articles, such as Denis Sinor, "Les Relations entre les Mongols et l'Europe jusqu'à la mort d'Arghoun et de Béla IV," *Cahiers d'histoire mondiale,* III (1956), 39–62; Jean Richard, "The Mongols and the Franks," *Journal of Asian History,* III (1969), 45–57; Luciano Petech, "Les Marchands italiens dans l'empire mongol," *Journal asiatique,* CCL (1962), 549–574; and J. B. Chabot, "Notes sur les relations du roi Argoun avec l'Occident," *ROL,* II (1894), 566–629.

Special mention is due to the following: Abel-Rémusat, "Mémoires sur les relations politiques des princes chrétiens et particulièrement des rois de France, avec les empereurs mongols," *Mémoires . . . de l'Académie des inscriptions et belles-lettres,* VI (1882), 396–469; VII (1824), 335–438, still unsurpassed in many respects; and Paul Pelliot, "Les Mongols et la papauté," *Revue de l'Orient chrétien,* XXIII (1922), 3–30; XXIV (1924), 225–335; XXVIII (1931), 3–84, not, as the title would suggest, a comprehensive account of the relations but a masterly elucidation of several problems pertaining to the subject.

Among general histories of the Mongols, C. d'Ohsson, *Histoire des Mongols depuis Tchinguiz khan jusqu'à Timour bey ou Tamerlan* (4 vols., The Hague and Amsterdam, 1834–1835; reprints available) remains unequaled. Avowedly or tacitly most later works rely on it, as does the massive compilation of Henry H. Howorth, *History of the Mongols from the 9th to 19th century* (5 vols., London, 1876–1927; reprint available). Both d'Ohsson and Howorth gave due share in their presentation to the Mongols' contacts with the west. General histories of the crusades or the crusader states pay scant attention to the Mongols, and if they do mention them, they usually copy d'Ohsson—or more recently Grousset—and add a few mistakes of their own. René Grousset, *Histoire des croisades et du royaume franc de Jérusalem* (3 vols., Paris, 1937–1948), and Jean Richard, *Le Royaume latin de Jérusalem* (Paris, 1953), are welcome exceptions.

For general background information on the Mongols of Iran, with whom we are mainly concerned in this chapter, there is in addition to Spuler, *Die Mongolen in Iran,* already mentioned, *The Saljuq and Mongol Periods,* edited by J. A. Boyle as vol. V of *The Cambridge History of Iran* (Cambridge, 1968). Sir Henry Yule, *Cathay and the Way Thither,* new edition revised by Henri Cordier (4 vols., Hakluyt Society, 1913–1916) contains a wealth of information relevant to our topic.

Mongol expansion, military operations in the west had a low priority in the eyes of the Mongol leaders. This is particularly true of the early military campaigns against the 'Abbāsids and the later ones against the Selchükids of Rūm. Thus the Mongol generals Jebe and Sübötei, pursuing the fleeing Khorezm-Shāh Muḥammad, did not turn toward Baghdad after his death in 1220, but embarked on a rather superfluous military campaign against Georgia and the peoples of the Kîpchak steppe. The caliph an-Nāṣir, well aware of the danger of being crushed in the fearful pincer of the advancing Mongol and Christian armies, asked for help that never came,[1] and indeed owing to the sudden northward push of Jebe and Sübötei was not even needed. The crushing defeat inflicted on the joint Russian and Kuman forces in the battle of the Kalka in 1223 makes it abundantly clear that it was well within the capabilities of the forces commanded by Jebe and Sübötei to achieve a victory over such forces as the caliph could have mustered against them. The fall of Baghdad at such an early date would have exerted a considerable influence on the crusades and would in itself have been an important victory. If no attempt was made at that time to conquer Baghdad, the reason must be sought in the east-oriented Mongol policy rather than in the short-sightedness of the Mongol rulers or in any presumed weakness of their forces. It is a revealing fact that the *Secret History of the Mongols,* a contemporary document of great importance, gives detailed descriptions of internal squabbles and of campaigns against China, while the militarily amazing western campaigns are dealt with in only a few lines.[2]

   In assessing the Mongol role in the crusades it must be borne in mind that neither the Christians nor the Moslems possessed a military capability even approaching that of the Mongol main army, and that in the order of Mongol priorities the Anatolian theater followed not only the East Asian but also that of Mongol involvement in eastern Europe. Thus the campaign which culminated in the devastation of Hungary in 1241–1242 was led by Batu—possibly the second most powerful man in the Mongol empire—assisted by an impressive array of princes, whereas we do not even know the name of the Mongol general who, at the same time, commanded the operations on Selchükid territory which led to the battle at Köse Dagh in 1243 and the subsequent collapse of the Selchükid state.

   1. See volume II of this work, p. 421.
   2. Erich Haenisch, *Die geheime Geschichte der Mongolen* (2nd ed., Leipzig, 1948), pp. 131–132.

Another aspect of Mongol involvement in the crusades deserves attention. It is well known that the line dividing friends from foes did not always coincide with that between Christians and Moslems. Yet, despite frequent internal dissensions in the ranks of both parties, the basic religious pattern remained, its outlines accentuated by racial and linguistic differences. At the time of the Mongols' appearance on the Anatolian horizon neither of the opposing camps, Christian or Moslem, had a distinct, undeniable advantage over the other, and the possibility of outside help was the most realistic hope each party could entertain. In the "long chronicle of greed, stupidity, treachery, duplicity, and incompetence"[3] so characteristic of the crusades, no single factor is more deserving of the last of these epithets than the obvious reluctance of each party to avail itself of Mongol power to achieve ultimate victory. Perhaps the most striking example of this unrealistic attitude is the permission given by the Franks of Acre to Kutuz to pass through their territory on his way to encounter—and defeat at 'Ain Jālūt on September 3, 1260[4]—the Mongol army led by the Christian Kitbogha. It is certain that a joint effort by Franks and Mongols could have checked Mamluk expansion. It would seem that for the Moslems and Christians of Outremer, accustomed to each other's presence, the Mongols were unwelcome intruders, spoil-sports as it were, bringing a new, disquieting dimension to the old, familiar conflict, breaking the pattern of what had become routine warfare. It is important to note that attempts to seek an alliance with the Mongols were made by princes of France or England rather than by the rulers of the Latin states, entangled as these were in dissensions that clouded not only the real issues but also the means to solve them. History might exonerate the Moslems, the ultimate victors in the conflict. In the seven centuries that have elapsed since that time, no circumstances have been discovered that would mitigate the political short-sightedness displayed by the crusaders.

From the middle of the twelfth century it was common belief in Europe that a Far Eastern Christian prince, fabulously rich and powerful, was to assist the crusaders by attacking the Moslems from the rear. The news spread through Otto of Freising, who made himself the mouthpiece of bishop Hugh of Jabala in a desperate appeal for western aid.[5] According to Otto, Hugh had reported that

3. See volume II of this work, p. xviii.
4. *Ibid.*, pp. 573–574.
5. See volume I of this work, p. 466.

"one John, king and priest, who dwells in the Extreme Orient beyond Persia and Armenia and is a Christian and a descendant of the Magi who are mentioned in the Gospel, fired by the example of his fathers who came to adore Christ in the cradle, was proposing to go to Jerusalem to help the crusaders."[6]

Whether the victory of the Kara-Kitai over the Selchükid Sanjar in 1141 was the historical impetus giving rise to the Prester John legend is of relatively little importance.[7] The theme of the story of a mighty potentate eager to help his western Christian brethren in conquering the Holy Land was so much in accordance with the general trends of medieval thought, it responded so completely to the material and moral expectations of the time, that it was given credence in all quarters. The objective evidence of the existence of Prester John, flimsy though it is in our eyes, was sufficient to induce pope Alexander III to write him a letter.[8]

The help expected from Prester John did not materialize in the middle of the twelfth century and yet, almost eighty years later, and for the sake of the same cause slightly remodeled, the legend came once again to the fore of political activities. After the fall of Damietta in November 1219, James of Vitry "preached publicly that David, king of the two Indies, hastened to the help of the Christians, bringing with him most ferocious peoples who will devour like beasts the sacrilegious Saracens."[9] James of Vitry's information was based on a report originally written in Arabic and then translated into French and finally into Latin, a *Relatio de Davide rege Tartarorum Christiano.*[10] The terrible distortion of proper names notwithstanding—they are often unrecognizable—the *Relatio* contains a summary but not altogether inaccurate report of the Mongol campaigns between 1218 and 1221. In it the deeds of Chinggis (Genghis Khan) are attributed to a king David, "who is usually called Prester John," a somewhat unexpected identification if we consider that the latter was thought of as an adult some eighty years earlier.

The Mongol conquest—known to Europe largely through James of Vitry and the legate Pelagius—raised considerable hopes, and in 1221 in an encyclical letter Honorius III announced in glowing terms to

---

6. Not a verbatim citation. The Latin text is given, with comments, in Friedrich Zarncke, "Der Priester Johannes," I, *Abhandlungen der Königl. sächsischen Gesellschaft der Wissenschaften, Phil.-Hist. Classe,* VII (1879), 848. The abstract here given relies on the English version of Sir Henry Yule, *The Book of Ser Marco Polo,* I (London, 1903), 233.

7. See volume II of this work, p. 669.

8. See Yule, *The Book of Ser Marco Polo,* I, 231.

9. Cited by Zarncke, "Der Priester Johannes," II, *Abhandlungen . . . ,* VIII (1876 [sic]), 9.

10. Zarncke, "Der Priester Johannes," II, 10.

the archbishops of Gaul and to the English clergy that king David, commonly called Prester John, a God-fearing man, offered battle to the shah (called *soldano Persidis*) of Persia, occupied his land, and was only ten days' journey from Baghdad.[11] It is perhaps not too far-fetched to suggest that these rumors, widely circulated since 1219, were a decisive factor in Pelagius's rejection of the extremely favorable peace offer made by al-Kāmil.[12] In 1221 the identification of king David with Prester John and of his people with the Mongols was generally accepted. The fact that in the winter of 1220–1221 the Mongols attacked Georgia was conveniently ignored by Pelagius, who urged the king of Georgia, George Lashen IV, to send a contingent to Damietta.

The true nature of the Mongol menace was first realized in eastern Europe in 1236 when an important campaign was launched against the peoples living in what is now the European part of Russia. In the autumn of 1237 the flourishing empire of the Bulghars of the Volga was destroyed, together with a number of Russian cities. Though these countries were distant and barely known in western Europe, their plight somewhat changed the thitherto rosy picture painted of the Mongols. In the year of 1238 people everywhere in Europe became aware of the danger presented by this strange and apparently ferocious people. As Philip Mouskes put it in his rhymed chronicle:

> Vint noviele que le Tatart
> Une gent de tiere lontainne –
> Jhesus lor doinst honte proçainne! –
> S'adrecierent parmi Rousie,
> Si l'ont praee et defroisie
> Et ne sai quante autre cité
> Dont pas ne me sont recordé
> Li non, ne recorder nes sai;
> Mais moult destruisent sans asai.[13]

This is not the place to recount, however briefly, the development of Hungarian-Mongol relations which culminated in 1241–1242 with the terrible devastation of Hungary. The collapse of Hungarian resistance took the west European powers by surprise, and emperor Frederick II, blaming the Hungarians for the defeat, tried to capitalize on it for his own benefit. He used the imminence of the Mongol peril to urge the union of all Christian princes under his own

---

11. *Annals of Dunstable*, ed. H. R. Luard, in *Annales monastici*, IV, 66; *Rerum britannicarum medii aevi scriptores* (Rolls Series, no. 36), p. 36.
12. See volume II of this work, p. 415.
13. *MGH, SS.*, XXVI, 815.

leadership. The harassed pope Gregory IX was unable to answer the desperate requests for help sent to him by king Bela IV of Hungary. The news of the Mongols' sudden withdrawal in the spring of 1242—for which no satisfactory explanation exists—was received with a sigh of relief in Europe, and the danger of a renewal of such an attack would probably have been disregarded had it not been for the far-sighted policies introduced by pope Innocent IV.

At this time the possibility of an alliance with the Mongols was completely lost from sight and attention was focused on the dangers of a renewed attack against Hungary. Only a few weeks after his election Innocent IV called upon Berthold, patriarch of Aquileia and an uncle of Bela IV, to induce the faithful in Germany to take up the cross against the Tatars,[14] and in the encyclical summoning the Council of Lyons the task of finding relief against the Tatars was assigned to the coming council. Innocent IV did not intend to indulge in idle discussions; by the time the council opened, three papal envoys were on their way to the Mongols.

Two pontifical letters, *Dei patris immensa* dated March 5 and *Cum non solum* dated March 13, 1245, were prepared with the intention of being carried to wherever the ruler of the Mongols could be found. Of the three missions, that of the Franciscan John of Pian del Carpine is by far the most important, partly because it was the only one to reach the Great Khan in Mongolia but also because there is a detailed written account of it. However, from our present point of view the mission is of relatively small importance, as Pian del Carpine followed a northern route via Russia, probably suggested by the Hungarians. The other two, on the whole unsuccessful, missions took the road through the Holy Land and are thus of more immediate interest for the crusades.

The mission led by the Dominican Ascelin is known in some detail through the description given by one of its members, Simon of Saint Quentin, author of a *Historia Tartarorum* now lost, but from which large passages were incorporated in the *Speculum historiale* of Vincent of Beauvais.[15] Ascelin took the southern route to the Mongols, which probably led him via Cyprus and Palestine—the country where Simon must have joined him—to Tiflis. Here another Dominican, Guiscard of Cremona, joined the party, which, after a journey that took about six weeks, reached the headquarters *in territorio Sitiens*

14. *MGH, Epist. saec. XIII,* II, doc. 2, pp. 3–4.
15. Simon of Saint Quentin, *Histoire des Tartares,* ed. Jean Richard, *Documents relatifs à l'histoire des croisades publiés par l'Académie des inscriptions et belles-lettres,* VIII (Paris, 1965).

castri of the Mongol commander Baiju on May 25, 1247. The meeting between Ascelin and Baiju was far from friendly, both being equally obdurate. Simon of Saint Quentin records with complacency various proposals made in Baiju's entourage. Some proposed putting only two of the envoys to death, others suggested flaying Ascelin and sending back to the pope his skin stuffed with straw.

Baiju, unwilling to accept the pope's message to the Great Khan, wanted the friars to continue their journey to Mongolia, but Ascelin sternly refused and, curiously enough, had his way. So with the help of Greek and Turkish interpreters and the collaboration of the friars themselves, the Latin message was put first into Persian and then into Mongolian. Baiju then dispatched the original and its Mongolian translation to Karakorum and took to writing an answer to the pope. The dispatch of this reply, and the departure of the friars, were delayed to allow Baiju to consider a missive sent by the Great Khan Güyük and transmitted through the hands of Eljigidei, one of his familiars. The instructions of Güyük to Baiju were uncompromising even by Mongol standards; they demanded nothing less than total submission of all peoples, and instructed Baiju to carry out this supremely simple order. Accordingly, Baiju's own letter sent to the pope was couched in terms equally harsh. It was this cheerless message that Ascelin and his companions brought back to the pope in the summer of 1248. However disappointing in its final result, Ascelin's mission had one redeeming feature, perhaps not fully appreciated at that time. With him to Lyons came two Mongol envoys, Aybeg and Sargis (the former probably a Turk, the latter a Christian), the first of their kind to have peaceful contacts with any west European power.

The second mission requiring mention here was led by the Dominican Andrew of Longjumeau. On his way to the Mongols he paid a visit first to aṣ-Ṣāliḥ Ismā'īl in Baalbek, then to al-Manṣūr of Homs, both of whom were at that time on friendly terms with the Franks. In a letter dated December 30, 1245, and addressed to the pope, al-Manṣūr states that "for various reasons we have given, we have advised the said friars [Andrew of Longjumeau and his companions] against continuing their journey to the Mongols."[16] It is likely that in his discussions with Andrew of Longjumeau al-Manṣūr did not mention the most cogent among the various reasons he had against their traveling to the Mongols: his fear that an alliance between them and the Christians might endanger his own situation.

In spite of al-Manṣūr's discouragement, Andrew of Longjumeau

---

16. Golubovich, *Biblioteca,* II, 335.

pursued his journey and in the neighborhood of Tabriz met a Mongol army. He also encountered the Nestorian Simeon, better known under his honorific appellation Rabban Ata, described as "vicarius Orientis." Rabban Ata, a familiar of the Great Khan Ögödei, had been sent to Cilician Armenia sometime between 1235 and 1240, and had exerted his not inconsiderable influence in favor of the Christians living under Mongol rule. Andrew of Longjumeau and Rabban Ata conferred for twenty days. When they parted, the Nestorian priest charged Andrew with a present, a stick of ebony, for the pope, and also with a letter in which he urged him to make peace with the emperor just when the most powerful king of the Tatars, "against whose power the whole Christian world cannot resist," contemplated attacking them. The letter also refers to a document of unspecified content which Rabban Ata himself had brought "from the heart of the Orient, namely from China."[17] Whether the word *Sin,* used in the text, refers to China proper or to Mongolia, the fact remains that through Rabban Ata and Andrew of Longjumeau a bridge of Christian solidarity was erected between east and west, spanning pagan Mongols and Moslem Mamluks. With all these messages in his charge, rich with the wealth of information acquired on a trip that lasted two years, sometime in the first half of 1247 Andrew of Longjumeau reached Lyons and reported to the pope.

Andrew of Longjumeau was the first of the papal envoys to return. His report was probably quite favorable when compared to those brought to the pope by Ascelin and by John of Pian del Carpine, who had met the Great Khan himself and returned with the alarming news that Güyük, supposedly favorable to Christians, "raised the flag against the church of God, the Roman empire and all Christian kingdoms and nations of the west."[18] Güyük's letter to Innocent IV corroborated the friar's account.[19] The peremptory tone of the Mongol letters received, the demand expressed in them that the pope should come personally and pay homage to the Great Khan, were not likely to enhance the pope's prestige had they become generally known. It is thus quite understandable that the two Mongol messengers, Aybeg and Sargis, were held virtually incommunicado, to the great chagrin of the chronicler Matthew Paris.[20] To all evidence the

17. On Rabban Ata and all pertinent questions see Pelliot, "Les Mongols et la papauté," II; on Andrew of Longjumeau see part III of the same article.

18. Wyngaert, *Sinica franciscana,* p. 94.

19. The letter has been preserved in Latin and Persian versions. The best study is by Pelliot, "Les Mongols et la papauté," pp. 11–28 (reference is to the pagination of the offprint and not of the periodical).

20. *Chronica majora,* ed. H. R. Luard (Rolls Series), V, 37. For other relevant data, see also J. J. Saunders, "Matthew Paris and the Mongols," in *Essays in Medieval History*

papal missions had achieved no other purpose than that of bringing back reliable, first-hand information on what Innocent IV must have considered a most dangerous foe. The pope's reply to Baiju's letter, *Viam agnoscere veritatis,* dated November 22, 1248, and probably carried back by Aybeg and Sargis, simply stated that Innocent IV had acted out of a sense of duty to let the true religion be known to the Mongols, and that he regretted the Mongols' perseverance in their errors and adjured them to cease their menaces.[21]

The projects to establish friendly contacts with the Mongols, abandoned by the pope, were immediately taken up by Louis IX. Despite the gloomy picture painted for him by John of Pian del Carpine, specially sent by the pope to dissuade the French king from approaching the Mongols, Louis IX decided to continue the endeavors initiated by Innocent IV. He was to succeed in no small measure, and it is in his lifetime, and partly owing to his efforts, that the relations between the Mongols and the Occident took a new course. Was the king of France prompted only by the political advantages he could expect from friendly relations with a power in the rear of the Moslems, or did he aim primarily at the conversion of the Mongols? Probably both thoughts were present in his mind. A concurrence of unexpected circumstances came to lend support to what the pope, by then, considered a hopeless enterprise.

In December 1248 two Mongol envoys presented themselves to Louis IX in Cyprus. They came on behalf of Eljigidei, whose letter they handed over to the king.[22] The ambassadors had Christian names, David and Mark respectively, and the message they delivered to Louis IX by letter and by word of mouth was truly astonishing. The general purport of their exposition was that Güyük and a number of Mongol dignitaries, among them Eljigidei himself, had been baptized, and that Eljigidei had been sent to the west by the Great Khan so that he might help the crusaders to reconquer the Holy Land. The Mongols were eager to enter into an alliance with the king of France, for their intention was to move on Baghdad, and the French, by attacking the sultan of Egypt at the same time, could prevent his coming to the help of the caliph. This was the century-old dream come true, and the fulfillment of a hope which in spite of repeated, bitter disappointments lingered in the hearts of the cru-

presented to Bertie Wilkinson, ed. T. A. Sandquist and M. R. Powicke (Toronto, 1969), pp. 116–132.

21. *Les Registres d'Innocent IV,* ed. É. Berger, II (Paris, 1887), no. 4682, pp. 113–114.

22. On all these events see d'Ohsson, *Histoire des Mongols,* II, 236 ff., and the very important comments of Pelliot, "Les Mongols et la papauté," pp. 151 ff.

saders set on their Danaidean task: the arrival of Prester John, the Christian potentate of the east, striking from the rear the Moslem forces.

All this was in such striking contrast to Mongol attitudes as experienced by the envoys of Innocent IV that the opinion was voiced that David and Mark were self-styled ambassadors and that their "embassy" was in fact an imposture.[23] It seems that this idea can now be discarded. Andrew of Longjumeau had met David in the Mongol camp he had visited, and it is certain that Eljigidei's letter transmitted to Louis IX by David was not a fake. In fact, this letter,[24] though insisting on Christian solidarity, does not contain any blatantly false statements. These came only by word of mouth from the two ambassadors eager for the success of their mission. After a year spent in Anatolia, Eljigidei must have acquired a sufficient insight into the political and military conditions prevailing there to be aware of the advantages an alliance with the Franks could represent. One is probably entitled to the view that David and Mark were sent to Louis IX by Eljigidei acting on his own initiative. This policy of rapprochement was destined to fail. Between March 27 and April 28, 1248, about a month before David and Mark set out on their mission, Güyük had died, and Eljigidei, the man who took upon himself to gain the confidence of Louis IX, was soon to lose his own life in the struggles which followed the passing of his sovereign.

David and Mark were again received by Louis IX on January 25, 1249, and two days later they sailed from Nicosia in the company of three Dominicans—Andrew of Longjumeau and his brother Guy, and John of Carcassonne. The king sent with them, records Joinville, "a chapel which he had caused to be fashioned all in scarlet; and in order to draw the Tartars to our faith, he had caused all our faith to be imaged in the chapel: the Annunciation of the angel, the Nativity, the baptism that God was baptised withal, and all the Passion, and the Ascension, and the coming of the Holy Ghost; and with the chapel he sent also cups, books and all things needful for the chanting of the mass."[25]

By the time the party reached Eljigidei—the political situation within the empire having considerably changed—he found it wiser not to negotiate personally with the envoys but to send them on to

---

23. Güyük himself called David an impostor, but this does not necessarily mean that he really acted in bad faith; the Great Khan had valid reasons to repudiate the policy of which David was a representative. Wyngaert, *Sinica franciscana,* p. 308.

24. For the text, see Pelliot, "Les Mongols et la papauté," pp. 160–164.

25. *Memoirs of the Crusades,* translated by Sir Frank Marzials (1908; repr. New York and London, 1955), p. 253.

Güyük's widow, the regent Oghul Kaimîsh. Terrible tensions were building up in the struggle for Güyük's succession. At the time Louis's ambassadors reached the Mongol headquarters deep in Inner Asia, somewhere near the river Imil, Oghul Kaimîsh was still regent but the *quriltay*, the general assembly to elect the new Great Khan, had already been convened and Möngke, protégé of the powerful Batu, was a strongly favored candidate. There was no love lost between him and Oghul Kaimîsh, who endeavored to ensure the succession either for her son or for Siremün, Ögödei's grandson. She was to be judged very severely by Möngke: "as to the affairs of war and peace and the welfare and happiness of a great realm," he would write to Louis IX, "what could this woman, who was viler than a dog, know about them?"[26]

In her precarious situation Oghul Kaimîsh tried to make the most out of the French embassy, which she presented to her subjects, as one "suing for mercy." She also sent a letter to Louis IX which her own ambassadors, attached to the returning French, carried back to Caesarea, where they met the king, probably in April 1251. The content of this letter is known only through a paraphrase given by Joinville.[27] It was an ultimatum in typical Mongol style, enjoining Louis IX to submit and send yearly tribute lest he and his people be destroyed like so many others before him.

For the French king the result of this embassy was a bitter disappointment. While his ambassadors were en route he was sorely tried by illness, captivity, and all the sorrow and concern of a most difficult political situation. Perhaps in the darkest moments of affliction Louis had the hopeful thought that the Mongols might wish to join forces with him against the common enemy. Now, although the worst of his ordeal was over, he had to realize the vanity of his hopes, his own loneliness. Soon Oghul Kaimîsh was to perish, and her death would create new opportunities, but there was nothing to portend this to Louis IX. So "you must know," as Joinville summed up the situation, "that it repented the king sorely that he had ever sent envoys to the great king of the Tartars."

It is generally, although mistakenly, assumed that approximately two years after the disappointment caused by Andrew of Long-jumeau's second mission, Louis IX deemed it worthwhile to make a fresh attempt to establish relations with the Mongols. The responsibility for the fabulous journey undertaken by the Franciscan William

26. The words were said by Möngke to Rubruck. The translation is that of W. W. Rockhill, *The Journey of William of Rubruck to the Eastern Parts of the World, 1253–55* (London, 1900), p. 250.

27. See translation by Marzials, pp. 258–259.

of Rubruck is often attributed to the French king. This is not the place to refute in detail this widespread misapprehension; suffice it to say that the moving force behind the decision to make yet another attempt to establish friendly relations with the Mongols was Rubruck's own missionary zeal.

Rubruck believed the rumors then current in certain circles that Sartak, son of Batu, had been converted to Christianity, and he felt that with the help of a protector so powerful, proselytism in the Mongol empire was a real possibility. There is no evidence to suggest that Rubruck worked for, or even envisaged the concluding of, a military alliance between the crusaders and the Mongols. "I have nothing to say on the part of any man . . . I have only to speak the words of God,"[28] declared Rubruck at Möngke's court. Because of the missionary character of Rubruck's journey a detailed examination of its multifaceted importance lies outside the scope of the present volume. The letter of Möngke which Rubruck had to carry, rather reluctantly, to Louis IX was yet another version of the by then customary orders of submission. The friendly, one might even say warm, reception accorded to the missionary Rubruck had in no way altered Möngke's uncompromising attitude toward foreign powers, in this instance toward the west.

It seems certain that by the mid-1250's contacts between westerners and Mongols had multiplied and that among the former not everyone was as indifferent as Rubruck to the political implications of such contacts. Thus we know that Baldwin of Hainault, a knight in the service of emperor Baldwin II, had preceded Rubruck to Karakorum, although unfortunately nothing is known of his journey. Baldwin had married a Kuman princess and through her had excellent contacts with leaders of the western parts of the Mongol empire. He obviously used his influence to boost French prestige: when Rubruck was asked by Sartak's entourage who was the greatest lord among the Franks and he replied that it was Frederick II, he was rebuked by Sartak, who, referring to Baldwin's judgment, thought that this honor should belong to Louis IX.[29]

It is worth noting that both Pian del Carpine and Rubruck, the only early travelers known to have reached Mongolia, used the northern route, the one leading through Kuman territories. The role of the Kumans, acting as intermediaries between the Mongols on the one side and the Latins and Hungarians on the other, must have been a very important one; it has not yet been sufficiently examined. The

28. Translation by Rockhill, p. 226.
29. On Baldwin of Hainault see *ibid.*, p. 102.

Kumans lived in territories under either Mongol or Hungarian control and had many personal contacts with the Latins of the Levant. Sometime before 1254 Bela IV, king of Hungary, married his son, the future Stephen V, to a Kuman princess, and a few years later Berke, khan of the Golden Horde, made him an offer of alliance against the western powers. While rejecting this offer Bela IV was able to avert Mongol punitive action, a result that could be achieved only through constant vigilance and by keeping open the channels of communication.

In the south the principal champion of a rapprochement with the Mongols was Heṭoum I, king of Cilician Armenia, whose efforts in this direction have already been described.[30] The diplomatic activities of the Armenian king were directed principally toward the establishment of an alliance between the Christians and the Mongols of Iran, whom he quite rightly thought to be more interested in his project than were the Mongols ruling north of the Caucasus, the Golden Horde. The Great Khan Möngke, who received Rubruck, died in 1259; Batu, the strong man of the Golden Horde, had died in 1256. Things were rapidly changing within the Mongol empire, and these changes considerably affected the Mongols' relations with the west.

The Golden Horde—the westernmost part of the Mongol empire—had, from the time of its formation, always enjoyed an independence greater than that of the other parts of the empire. The principal reason for this was the exceptional status of Batu, its first ruler and the second most important person in the Mongol world. William of Rubruck quotes the Great Khan Möngke comparing himself and Batu to "two eyes in the head, which, though they are two, they have but one sight."[31] Under the rule of Batu's successor Berke (1257–1266), the Golden Horde gained greater autonomy, an evolution partially caused by Kubilai's ever-increasing engagements in distant China. Contacts between the Great Khan Kubilai and the il-khans of Iran were closer not only on account of the relatively shorter distance separating the two but also as a result of the maritime communications between China and Persia. Although very slow and fraught with dangers, the sea route was considered sufficiently convenient for Kökächin—a young lady consigned to Arghun but destined to become the wife of his son Ghazan—to be sent by ship to Persia in the company of Nicholas, Matthew, and Marco Polo.

30. See volume II of this work, pp. 652–654.
31. Wyngaert, *Sinica franciscana*, p. 299.

While links between the Mongols of Iran and those of East Asia were thus maintained and even strengthened, the Mongols of Russia under the leadership of Berke were not only becoming increasingly independent, but were also gradually sliding into an area of civilization which was to set them apart from their kin. Socially, linguistically, and religiously, the populations living on lands controlled by the rulers of the Golden Horde were mixed. The forest-dwelling Finno-Ugrians notwithstanding, the Mongol conquerors had found, in what is geographically known as European Russia, predominantly Slavic and Turkic populations—the former Christian, the latter Moslem. On the south Russian steppe the Mongols met with the Turkic tribal confederation of the Kïpchaks (Kumans, Polovtsy, etc.), while farther north they put an end to the Bulghar empire of the Volga, a Turkic state with century-old traditions of trade with both Baghdad and Egypt. For centuries prior to the Mongol conquest these very regions had constituted a manpower reservoir both of Byzantium and of the Aiyūbid sultans of Egypt. The Mamluk soldiery recruited among Kïpchak (Kuman) slaves gained increased importance under sultan aṣ-Ṣāliḥ Aiyūb, who organized them into an elite bodyguard. Many of the Kïpchak Turks were, to use modern terminology, political refugees, displaced by the conquering Mongols to whom, quite understandably, they were hostile. After 1250, when the first Mamluk dynasty was established, the Kïpchak Turks wielded decisive influence in Egypt and Syria as well as in south Russia, where they outnumbered the native Mongols. It is a fact of crucial importance that the Mamluks of Egypt and the "Mongols" of the Golden Horde were natural allies, not only because of historical tradition reaching far back into the times of the Volga-Bulghar empire, but simply because the ruling class in Egypt and an important and influential segment of the Golden Horde's society belonged, in fact, to the same ethnic group. The Turkic dialect spoken by the Mamluks was the same as that used by the majority of Berke's Turkic subjects, and to this day the Turkic populations of the middle Volga region speak Kïpchak-Turkic languages. Mamluk antipathy against the Mongols focused not on the Golden Horde but on the Mongols of Iran, while tension was building up between the two Mongol states.

Antagonism between the Golden Horde and the Mongols of Iran exerted so important an influence on events in Asia Minor, and hence on the crusades, that it may not be superfluous to examine here briefly its causes as well as its effects. Berke's conversion to Islam was an act of personal faith.[32] His attitudes were still much too

32. For the general background on Berke, see Bertold Spuler, *Die Goldene Horde: Die*

Mongol to allow for the persecution of other religions or for him to impose on his subjects his own religious beliefs. But his faith was sincere, and he was a reluctant partner in the campaign waged by his cousin Hulagu (Hülegü), which in 1258 culminated in the sack of Baghdad and the demise of the last 'Abbāsid caliph. Indeed, Berke's disapproval of these actions was so strong that he ordered his troops engaged in the campaign to join the Egyptian army. It is thus possible, though no documentation to this effect has come to light, that at the battle of 'Ain Jālūt contingents detached from Berke's army fought against the il-khanid Mongol forces of Kitbogha.[33] Tension between the successors of Batu and the il-khanids was not caused solely by religious differences; it continued to exist under Berke's successor Möngke Temür, who was no Moslem. As a matter of fact the final adoption of Islam by the khans of the Golden Horde came only during the rule of Jāni Beg (1342–1357), later than the conversion of the il-khanids to that religion.

As so often in history, subjective, personal feelings had their role to play. The first il-khan, Hulagu, was the brother of two successive Great Khans, Möngke and Kubilai, of whom Berke was a mere cousin. The relationship between Hulagu and Möngke was a very close one—Rashīd-ad-Dīn records the former's affliction on learning of the Great Khan's death[34] —whereas Berke was cast in the role of a poor relative. While it is always dangerous to speculate on motives, it seems probable that the personal sympathy linking Möngke to Hulagu was the principal factor in the former's decision to assign the Caucasus region to the latter. Berke's repeated attempts to wrest from Hulagu what he considered—not without reason—his rightful appanage, and to push south of the Caucasus, met with failure. The chasm separating the Golden Horde from the rest of the Mongol world was further widened after the death of Möngke, during the struggle for the succession from which Hulagu's candidate Kubilai emerged victorious against Berke's protégé Arïq Böge. Nor did tension cease with the deaths of the protagonists of this conflict (Hulagu in 1265 and Berke in 1266); it continued under their respective successors Abagha and Möngke Temür. The initiative was on the side of the ruler of the Golden Horde, and to defend the Caucasian border Abagha was compelled to create a system of fortifications

---

Mongolen in Russland, 1223–1502 (2nd ed., Wiesbaden, 1965), particularly pp. 33–52, 213–216.

33. See Klaus Lech, *Das mongolische Weltreich: Al-'Umari's Darstellung der mongolischen Reiche* (Wiesbaden, 1968), p. 313.

34. Étienne Quatremère, *Raschid-eldin: Histoire des Mongols de la Perse* (Paris, 1836), p. 341.

which consisted of palisades and moats and more or less followed the river Kura. It also incorporated the steppe of Mughan, a favorite resting place for migratory birds, who played their part in the defensive strategy of the il-khan: flushed by the enemy advancing through the steppe, the birds gave the alert to his forces.

Temporary lulls notwithstanding, the basic political interests of the Golden Horde on the one hand and of the il-khans on the other were so incompatible that both powers were permanently in search of allies who would enable them to outflank the other party. Looking for allies located on the northeastern flank of the Mongols of Iran, both Berke and Möngke Temür linked forces with Kaidu, a grandson of Ögödei. Kaidu had first rallied to Arïq Böge but after Kubilai's accession had established himself on his own account, and controlled a territory which probably centered on the Ili and Chu valleys and incorporated also the northern parts of present-day Afghanistan.[35] Thus the Mongols of Iran were all but encircled by a chain of alliances linking the Mamluks to the Golden Horde and this power to Kaidu. Contacts in the form of correspondence and exchange of embassies multiplied between the Golden Horde and the Mamluks. For geographical as well as for political reasons the European powers could not remain unaware of or indifferent to the creation of this north-south axis linking two powers established respectively on the banks of the Volga and the Nile.

Not unnaturally, Byzantium could not avoid being involved in the triangular relationship of the Mamluks and the two Mongol states. Recently installed in Constantinople, Michael VIII Palaeologus paid particular attention to his contacts with the Mongols. He maneuvered skillfully between the two antagonistic Mongol powers, both capable of helping him, both jealous of seeing the other's influence grow in Constantinople. With the Mongols of Iran, from whom only the weak Selchükid buffer states separated Byzantium, Michael VIII was compelled to seek a *modus vivendi* which would secure him a relatively peaceful southeastern border. Even before his accession to the throne, when still in Nicaea, he concluded an alliance with Hulagu which, despite passing tensions, remained effective even after the khan's death. Michael's illegitimate daughter Maria, betrothed to Hulagu, after her fiancé's death married Abagha, his son and successor.

Increased tension with the Golden Horde was the corollary of friendly relations with the il-khans. In 1265 Berke and his Bulghar

---

35. On these events, see W. Barthold, *Zwölf Vorlesungen über die Geschichte der Türken Mittelasiens* (Berlin, 1935), pp. 186–187.

allies attacked Byzantium's northern border. The Mongol armies were under the command of Noghay, a Chingisid prince himself and a perennial candidate for the throne of the Golden Horde. For many years he had been the *de facto* ruler of the south Russian steppe bordering on Byzantium, and in 1273 he was given for wife Euphrosyne, another of Michael's illegitimate daughters. The emperor was thus linked through family ties with the rulers of both the il-khanid state and the Golden Horde, and with skillful diplomacy secured peace for his country wedged between the contending Mongol states. Moreover, toward the end of his reign Michael Palaeologus succeeded in establishing friendly relations with the Mamluk sultan Kalavun.[36] The maritime road through the Bosporus, linking the Golden Horde to Egypt, was thus in the hands of a ruler on friendly terms with both of these powers. The result was an increased flow of commerce through Byzantine territory and the multiplication of diplomatic contacts between the Mamluks and the Golden Horde.[37]

The desperate situation of the Frankish possessions in the late 1260's prompted the west to seek outside help; Abagha (1265–1282), son-in-law of Michael VIII and well known for his Christian sympathies, was an obvious target for their political overtures. The initiative was shared by pope Clement IV and king James I of Aragon, already engaged in the preparation of his crusade. Their envoy James Alaric of Perpignan was well received by Abagha, probably in 1267, and returned to the west accompanied by two Mongol emissaries. Contacts between Clement IV and Abagha were apparently quite frequent. In one letter sent to the il-khan the pope complained that he had received a letter from him which no one could read, and he expressed his regrets that Abagha had not written in Latin as on previous occasions.[38] A safe-conduct issued by Abagha in 1267 or in 1279 for the benefit of envoys traveling to the pope has been preserved in the Vatican archives.[39] Abagha kept in touch with several European powers, and these contacts resulted in a number of projects of collaboration, all of which came to naught. The Aragonese crusade, which set sail under the leadership of James I but after his early return was led by his two bastard sons, failed to

36. A. A. Vasiliev, *History of the Byzantine Empire* (2nd ed., Madison, Wisc., 1958), p. 601.

37. The history of these diplomatic relations is treated in great detail in Salikh Zakirov, *Diplomaticheskie otnosheniya Zolotoy Ordy s Egiptom* (Moscow, 1966).

38. See d'Ohsson, *Histoire des Mongols*, III, 540.

39. Antoine Mostaert and Francis Woodman Cleaves, "Trois documents mongols des Archives secrètes vaticanes," *Harvard Journal of Asiatic Studies*, XV (1952), 419–506. The safe-conduct is examined on pp. 430–445.

achieve coördination with Abagha, who at the crucial time was engaged in defending Khurasan against the Chagataid prince Barak.[40] At the time of Louis's ill-fated Tunisian venture Abagha would have been ready and willing to attack Baybars. Such a coördination of eastern and western forces had been the plan of Clement IV; had it been realized, it could have redressed a balance already fatefuily tilted in favor of the Mamluks. But Louis IX failed to perceive the possibilities offered by an il-khanid alliance, and preferred to undertake the Tunisian expedition.

More perspicacious, Edward of England, as soon as he disembarked at Acre on May 9, 1271,[41] sought to obtain Abagha's help and dispatched a delegation of three to discuss the modalities of coöperation.[42] As a result of these negotiations an army of about ten thousand horsemen, part of the Mongol force stationed in Anatolia, invaded Syria, where it achieved some local successes but withdrew before engaging Baybars's principal army.[43] Although of limited importance, this first case of effective coöperation between Mongol and western forces justified, in Abagha's view, further efforts to strengthen his alliance with England. On his side Edward, after his accession to the throne, remembered his personal experiences, hopes, and disappointments and endeavored to maintain relations with Abagha and his second successor, Arghun (1284–1291).

The reign of Arghun marks the apogee of Mongol-western relations. It is interesting to note that it was the Buddhist Arghun—under his rule Buddhism was declared the official religion of the il-khanid state—who was more eager to establish friendly relations with the Christian princes than had been some of his half-Christian predecessors. Arghun's first embassy to the west was sent to pope Honorius IV in 1285 and carried a letter dated in May of that year still extant in a Latin translation.[44] In it, by way of *captatio benevolentiae,* Arghun pointed to the special favors accorded to Christians by

40. This is the correct form of this proper name, usually spelled Borak or Burak. See Paul Pelliot, *Notes sur l'histoire de la Horde d'Or* (Paris, 1949), p. 57.

41. See volume II of this work, p. 582.

42. See Grousset, *Histoire des croisades,* III, 659.

43. See volume II of this work, p. 582.

44. The Latin text has been published often, perhaps most recently by Chabot, "Notes sur les relations . . . ," pp. 570–571. The embassy which carried Arghun's letter included two westerners, a Thomas Banchrinus and an interpreter whose name is spelled Ase. The name is probably a distorted form of Jesus, and Ase was a Syrian Christian "versed in all tongues of the west" and probably also of the east. He was a valued adviser of the Great Khan Kubilai and by him was put in charge of the Office of Western Astronomy and Medicine. Ai-hsüeh, to use the Chinese form of his name, was obviously a widely traveled man, familiar with Tabriz and Rome as well as with Peking, where he died in 1320. Ase's life exemplifies well that of a distinguished scholar and civil servant in the multi- and supra-

himself and his ancestors, with the notable exception of his predecessor Aḥmad (1282–1284), who adopted Islam and who was dethroned by Arghun. The truthfulness of Arghun's message was confirmed by some Franciscan and Dominican monks, recently returned from Outremer. Neither here nor in his later correspondence with the west is there any mention of Arghun's own conversion to Buddhism. In replying to exhortations that he should become a Christian Arghun's main argument was—as in his letter of May 14, 1290, to pope Nicholas IV[45] —that for anyone recognizing God Eternal and behaving properly, there was no need to join the church. In the same letter Arghun also pointed out that his subjects were free to adopt the religion of their choice.

Arghun's boldest attempt to establish an alliance with the western powers was his dispatch of the Nestorian monk Rabban Mar Ṣaumā on a mission to which the il-khan attached considerable importance.[46] A native of China but an Uighur by birth, Rabban Ṣaumā was appointed in 1280 visitor-general of the Nestorian church in Mongol territories. Thoroughly familiar with the internal conditions of the Mongol empire and himself a Christian, he was ideally suited for the task. He left early in 1287 and reached Rome on June 23 of that year, some two months after the death of Honorius IV, at a time of a papal interregnum. He was received with signs of great respect by the cardinals, whose eagerness to discuss religious questions he countered by affirming the political character of his mission. From Rome, by way of Tuscany and Genoa, he went to Paris, where he was received by Philip IV the Fair, and thence to Bordeaux to meet king Edward I. The king of England, a champion of long standing of an alliance with the Mongols, received Rabban Ṣaumā and his companions well and treated them generously. It is unlikely that he seriously envisaged effective armed coöperation with the Mongols, since his interest focused on other matters, and since he was probably quite realistic about the future of the whole crusading enter

national Mongol empire. Scores of similar men, whose names, however, have not been preserved, must have had similar destinies, traveling widely and carrying "from where the sun rises" to "where the sun sets" ideas, objects, scientific knowledge, and technological skill. On Ase/Ai-hsüeh, cf. Moule, *Christians,* pp. 107, 228–229.

45. Mostaert and Cleaves, "Trois documents," pp. 450–452.

46. The description of this journey is included in a Syriac text of which several translations exist. The best English version is by Sir E. A. Wallis Budge, *The Monks of Ḵûblâi Khân, Emperor of China* (London, 1928), but the scholarly apparatus accompanying the French translation cannot be dispensed with: J. B. Chabot, "Histoire de Mar Jabalaha III, patriarche des Nestoriens (1281–1317), et du moine Rabban Çauma, ambassadeur du roi Argoun en Occident (1287)," *ROL,* I (1893), 567–610; II (1894), 73–142, 235–304; and in book form (Paris, 1895). More up-to-date is N. V. Pigulevskaya, *Istoriya mar Yabalakhi III i rabban Saumy* (Moscow, 1958).

prise. From Bordeaux Rabban Ṣaumā proceeded to Genoa, where he spent most of the winter of 1287–1288. The choice of this city for such a long stay has not, it seems, awakened the curiosity of scholars, and yet it could hardly have been fortuitous. Its explanation lies in the close commercial and diplomatic ties linking Genoa to the il-khans and in the fact that many Genoese were actually in the latter's service. In Rabban Ṣaumā's own party there was at least one of them, Thomas Anfossi, a member of a distinguished Genoese family of bankers.[47]

On February 20, 1288, pope Nicholas IV was elected and Rabban Ṣaumā hastened to Rome to terminate a diplomatic mission unduly protracted because of the vacancy on the papal throne. In April of that same year Rabban Ṣaumā was on his way back to Arghun, carrying with him several papal letters and accompanied by a number of Italians and Frenchmen. It seems certain that his party was joined by that of Gobert of Helleville, ambassador to Arghun of Philip IV, which included the clergymen Robert of Senlis and William of Bruyères and a crossbowman, and whose expenses were paid for by the Templars, more anxious than most to see an alliance with the Mongols concluded.[48] By that time a whole colony of westerners was firmly ensconced in Tabriz. It included merchants, mainly from Venice and Genoa,[49] and missionaries from the great mendicant orders. Dominican presence is attested there in the 1250's,[50] and Franciscans were active in Tabriz by 1286–1287, if not earlier.[51] One can surmise that the lobbying power of such a strong western colony was considerable, its involvement in Arghun's endeavor to establish friendly relations with the west great. European names appear again and again among those listed as having taken part in the embassies traveling to and from the court of the il-khan. In their understandable eagerness to achieve their aim, these westerners were sometimes less than candid, and were quite willing to distort or even invent facts. From one of the letters sent by Nicholas IV to Arghun and dated April 2, 1288, it appears that the pope had been led to believe that Arghun intended to receive baptism in Jerusalem once this city had been delivered from the Moslems.[52]

47. Petech, "Les Marchands italiens . . . ," p. 561.

48. See Moule, *Christians in China,* p. 109.

49. Petech, "Les Marchands italiens . . . ," p. 561.

50. See Bertold Altaner, *Die Dominikanermission des 13. Jahrhunderts* (Habelschwerdt, 1924), p. 140.

51. See Odolphus van der Vat, *Die Anfänge der Franziskanermissionen und ihre Weiterentwicklung im nahen Orient und in den mohammedanischen Ländern während des 13. Jahrhunderts* (Werl in Westf., 1934), p. 131.

52. See Moule, *Christians in China,* p. 114.

Misunderstandings, intentional or not, combined with insufficient linguistic ability of interpreters and translators, certainly had their share in the painfully slow process of harmonizing western and il-khanid interests. Arghun's next ambassador, the Genoese Buscarel de' Ghisolfi, brought to Philip the Fair a firm proposal for a joint military undertaking. The offer, still extant in the French national archives, was written in Mongolian and dated the summer of 1289.[53] In it Arghun, planning far ahead, notified the French king of his intention to set out on a campaign against the Mamluks in 1290, so as to reach Damascus on the fifteenth day of the first spring moon in 1291. Arghun urged Philip IV to send his own army in time, and stated that, following the victory of the allies, Jerusalem would become a French possession. Technical details were dealt with in a separate memorandum prepared by Buscarel and written in French.[54] Among the points covered it is interesting to note Arghun's offer to provide the French king with twenty to thirty thousand horses, either free of charge or at a reasonable price. Buscarel brought letters and messages not only to Philip IV but also to pope Nicholas IV and to king Edward I. He arrived in London on January 5, 1290, and spent thirteen days at the court and a total of twenty days in England, where he was well entertained. Edward, as it appears from his reply to Arghun, declared himself willing to undertake a joint campaign with the Mongol ruler, subject only to the pope's approval. It is difficult to ascertain whether Buscarel himself returned to Arghun or whether he prolonged his stay in the west. In December 1290 he was certainly in Italy, as his name appears in papal letters recommending yet another of Arghun's embassies to Edward I.[55]

That spring of 1291, which should have witnessed the triumph of the Mongol-western alliance and the recovery from the Moslems of the city of Jerusalem, saw the fall of Acre and the death, on March 10, of Arghun. The il-khan succumbed to a long illness which, one may assume, would in any event have prevented him from fulfilling his pledge. So neither the il-khans nor the kings of France or England were present with anything but token forces when the sultan al-Ashraf Khalīl liquidated the last remnants of Frankish presence in Outremer.[56]

53. The best edition is Antoine Mostaert and Francis Woodman Cleaves, *Les Lettres de 1289 et 1305 des ilkhan Arγun et Öljeitü à Philippe le Bel* (Scripta Mongolica Monograph Series, I; Cambridge, Mass., 1962).

54. Texte in Rémusat, "Mémoires . . . ," pp. 430–432 and on pp. 610–613 of J. B. Chabot, "Notes sur les relations du roi Argoun avec l'Occident," *ROL*, II (1894), 566–643.

55. Chabot, "Notes . . . ," pp. 617–618.

56. See volume II of this work, p. 595.

Emboldened by his success, al-Ashraf Khalīl declared a holy war against the Mongols, now ruled by Arghun's brother Gaikhatu (1291–1295). Hostilities led to the capture of Hromgla by Mamluk forces but did not develop into a full-scale war. Gaikhatu and al-Ashraf Khalīl, equally dissolute, were soon to meet violent deaths at the hands of their own subjects. Baidu, Gaikhatu's cousin and successor, ruled but a few months. He was put to death on October 4, 1295, by the followers of Arghun's son Ghazan, the next ruler of the Mongols of Iran.

Ghazan (1295–1304), probably the most gifted il-khanid ruler, came to power committed to a program of Islamization. His accession to power was marked by excesses committed against Christians. Nevertheless, in religious matters he proved to be fairly moderate. His own religious feelings, whether sincere or dictated by political expediency, did not cloud his political judgment, and he rightly recognized the Mamluks as his principal external enemies. Several small-scale clashes and betrayals, in both camps, eventually led to Ghazan's invasion of Syria. On December 22, 1299, a few miles north of Homs the Mongols inflicted a crushing defeat on the Mamluks. Homs and Damascus soon surrendered, and by the end of January 1300 there were no Mamluk forces left in Syria.

In Europe, Ghazan's success gave rise to over-optimistic expectations. News was abroad to the effect that Ghazan had conquered the whole of the Holy Land and even Cairo, that he had given back their former holdings to the Templars and the Hospitallers and was to entrust the Dominicans with the guard of the Holy Sepulcher. It was even rumored that Ghazan had coins struck with a representation of the Holy Sepulcher on them and the legend *In nomine Patris, Filii, et Sancti Spiritus,* and that his standards carried the sign of the cross.[57] Some sources ascribed the deliverance of the Holy Land to the joint action of the Tatars and the kings of Greece, Cyprus, and Armenia.[58] The part attributed to western help might have been exaggerated, but it had some basis in reality. In 1300–1301 a Cypriote flotilla dispatched by Henry II de Lusignan, with the help of Templars and Hospitallers, attacked Rosetta,[59] where some skirmishes took place. Coördination of Mongol and Cypriote action was achieved through Zolus Bofeti, commonly referred to as Isol the Pisan, a man of some status in Ghazan's entourage and his ambas-

57. See Reinhold Röhricht, "Études sur les derniers temps du royaume de Jérusalem," *AOL,* I (1881; repr. Brussels, 1964), 649.
58. See the references assembled in Pálfy, *A Tatárok,* p. 58.
59. "Les Gestes de Chiprois," *RHC, Arm.,* II, 848, par. 615.

sador to Henry II. Isol the Pisan was, astonishing as it may seem, Öljeitü's godfather—for Ghazan's brother was baptized—and participated in the naval expedition just mentioned.[60] Isol was not the only Italian to bask in the reflected glory of Ghazan's victories. In 1300 in St. John Lateran, Boniface VIII received the Florentine Guiscard Bastari, ambassador of the il-khan, accompanied by a retinue of one hundred men, all clad in Tatar garments.[61] For reasons that today cannot be determined, Ghazan did not try to consolidate his hold on Syria, which by the end of May 1300 was again in Mamluk hands. The evacuation of Syria was certainly not due to a lack of interest on the part of Ghazan. He returned there in the fall of the same year and then, in February 1301, without having engaged in any major battle, he once again retraced his steps. It is possible that Ghazan did not feel strong enough to engage the Mamluks single-handed. Be that as it may, he sought to secure European collaboration for the projected campaign, and did his best to keep up the friendly relations which had been established by his predecessors.

Ghazan sent several embassies to the pope, to Philip IV, and to Edward I. Members of an embassy received by Boniface VIII in 1302 were said to have been baptized in Rome and given a golden crown to be carried from the pope to Ghazan "for the forgiveness of his sins and because he had reintroduced Christian worship in the Holy Land."[62] In April 1302 Ghazan sent a letter to Boniface VIII in which, referring to previous correspondence, he urged the pope to prepare his troops for an attack on the Mamluks, and to keep the date agreed upon for this operation. The letter, still extant in its original Mongolian version, was brought to the pope by three envoys with Moslem personal names. It mentions Buscarel de' Ghisolfi, who is referred to as having been attached to a previous embassy. The clever Genoese had weathered well the troubled years that followed the rule of his former master, Arghun, to whom he was so devoted that he named his son Argone after him. Buscarel's name appears also in a letter written by Edward I and dated March 12, 1302. In it the king, replying to a request made by Ghazan and transmitted by Buscarel, expressed his regrets at not being able to pay due attention to matters involving the Holy Land, and blamed this on wars raging within Christendom. The counter-embassy carrying Edward's reply

60. Petech, "Les Marchands . . . ," p. 567. The exact identity of Isol the Pisan has now been established by Jean Richard, "Isol le Pisan: Un aventurier franc gouverneur d'une province mongole?" *Central Asiatic Journal*, XIV (1970), 186–194.

61. Petech, "Les Marchands . . . ," p. 566.

62. See Röhricht, "Études . . . ," p. 651.

included Geoffrey of Langles and Nicholas of Chartres, traveling presumably in the company of Buscarel.[63] In 1303, at Eastertime, Mongol ambassadors visited Paris, repeating the by then usual offer of alliance.[64] Ghazan also kept in touch with James II of Aragon, who in May 1300, expressing his joy over the alleged recovery of the Holy Sepulcher, made what seemed a generous offer of help.[65] Ghazan maintained friendly relations too with Andronicus II. The alliance, more profitable to the harassed Byzantine emperor than to Ghazan, was to have been sealed by the marriage of the il-khan with a bastard daughter of Andronicus, but the project came to naught because of Ghazan's death.

Öljeitü, Ghazan's brother and successor (1304–1316) followed the same friendly policy toward the western powers. In a letter written in the summer of 1305 to Philip the Fair the il-khan recalled, perhaps not without some exaggeration, the friendly relations that according to him had always existed between his ancestors and the Franks, and offered in very general terms an alliance against those who would wish to destroy international understanding. "Verily," reads Öljeitü's letter, "what is better than concord?"[66] A contemporary Italian paraphrase written on the back of the Mongolian original leads us to believe that more precise information, and perhaps also some concrete proposals, were to be transmitted by word of mouth through the ambassadors carrying the letter. It has been suggested that Öljeitü envisaged an all-embracing alliance with a view to securing peace for the world.[67] According to other opinions, behind the general terms of the letter the specific purpose of an alliance against the Mamluks must be seen. This is a distinct possibility, yet there seems to be no evident reason why such a concrete proposal should have remained unmentioned in the original Mongolian letter as well as in its Italian paraphrase. In all probability the letter was intended as a general gesture of goodwill toward the west, written at a time when there was a temporary lull in the internecine warfare which for almost half a century had so much weakened the Mongol empire. To this newly won internal peace Öljeitü refers in his letter to Philip IV. No answer by the French king to Öljeitü's letter has come to light, but it seems likely that, if sent, such a letter was couched in very general terms.

63. Moule, *Christians in China,* p. 123.
64. *Continuatio chronici Guillelmi de Nangiaco,* in *RHGF,* XX, 588.
65. See Soranzo, *Il Papato,* p. 333.
66. See Mostaert and Cleaves, *Les Lettres,* pp. 55–85.
67. In a not very convincing but often quoted article: W. Kotwicz, "Les Mongols, promoteurs de l'idée de paix universelle au début du XIVe siècle," *La Pologne au VIIe Congrès international des sciences historiques* (Warsaw, 1933), I, 199–204.

Once more we find that one of the "Mongol" ambassadors was an Italian, Thomas Ugi of Siena, who with his companions visited and was well received in a number of European courts, including that of England. Edward II had already replaced his father, who died on July 7, 1307. The king of England is known to have sent at least two letters to Öljeitü. From the first of these, written in Northampton on October 16, 1307,[68] it is possible to conclude that Edward II had before him a letter essentially identical to that received by Philip IV. Edward's second letter, dated from Langley on November 30, 1307,[69] is a rather surprising document and clearly shows that whoever transmitted Öljeitü's letter to the king deliberately distorted some of the basic political realities of the il-khanid empire. Edward's letter is a venomous attack on "the abominable sect of Mohammed," which Öljeitü is asked to extirpate, thus completing the task already undertaken to this effect. It is inconceivable that, had Edward II been informed that Öljeitü was a pious Moslem, he would have committed a diplomatic gaffe of such magnitude. Suspicion is easily cast on Thomas, but in his dealings with the pope he certainly did not give the impression that Öljeitü was a Christian. In a letter written by Clement V in Poitiers and dated March 1, 1308, no anti-Moslem references are made.[70] Instead, the pope acknowledges Öljeitü's very concrete offer of help. If one can believe the facts referred to in Clement's reply—that is, if these are not the product of Thomas's misapplied zeal and imagination—Öljeitü had offered 200,000 horses and 200,000 loads of corn to be put at the disposal of the Christian armies when these disembarked in Cilician Armenia, where they would be joined for the purposes of an attack against the Mamluks by an army of 100,000 horsemen led by the il-khan.

The interest shown by Clement V in establishing a military alliance with the Mongols was quite genuine. He had commissioned the Armenian Heṭoum, known as the historian "Hayton," nephew of king Heṭoum I of Cilician Armenia, to prepare a memorandum on the feasibility and desirability of an alliance with the Mongols. Hayton presented his work, which constitutes Book IV of his *La Flor des estoires de la terre d'orient*,[71] to the pope in August 1307, well before the time of Clement's reply to Öljeitü's real or imaginary offer. Hayton, as could naturally be expected of a member of the Armenian royal family, was a vigorous advocate of a Mongol alliance

---

68. Th. Rymer, *Foedera*, I (1816), 8.

69. *Ibid.*, p. 18.

70. *Regestum Clementis Papae V*, annus tertius (Rome, 1886), no. 3549, pp. 331–332; cf. d'Ohsson, *Histoire des Mongols*, IV, 595–597.

71. *RHC, Arm.*, II, 220–253; Latin version on pp. 340–363.

and in general of a western presence in Outremer. Outlining plans to reconquer the Holy Land Hayton states: "As for me, who know quite well the Tatars' intentions, I firmly believe that they would willingly, without any dispute and without asking for taxes or any other type of vassalage, hand over all the cities and the land conquered to the Christians, since because of the great heat obtaining there during the summer, the Tatars would not stay in those regions, and would readily agree that the Christians should receive and hold them. For the Tatars do not wage war against the sultan of Egypt for territorial gains—since the whole of Asia is already subject to them— but because the sultan is their principal enemy who has done them more wrong than anyone else."[72]

Clement V was not the only western statesman to envisage seriously the possibility of regaining Outremer with the help of the Mongols. James II of Aragon also established contacts with Öljeitü and, probably in 1307, sent his ambassador Peter Desportes to the il-khan. In his letter the Aragonese king tried to clarify the conditions under which his army to be sent overseas could be supplied, and also asked that Christians should have free access to the holy places.[73] The general tone of this letter makes it quite clear that other missives must have preceded it. Neither these nor further correspondence between James II and Öljeitü have come to light. It would be most interesting to have additional information on James's political conceptions concerning the Mongols, particularly in view of his dealings with their arch-enemy, the Mamluks. In the correspondence of James II with the sultan Muhammad an-Nāṣir there seems to be no reference to the Mongols.[74] It is possible, even likely, that James's approach to Öljeitü was prompted by the sudden deterioration of his relations with the sultan. Between 1306 and 1314 diplomatic contacts between Aragon and Egypt were suspended.

A word should be said on the gradual increase in commercial relations between the il-khanid empire and the west, particularly marked during the reign of Öljeitü. Trade was almost entirely in the hands of Italian merchants, but their effect on the issues here examined was small, manifest mainly in the broadening of western knowledge of the internal conditions of the il-khanid state and also of China, which for many merchants remained the most desirable

72. *RHC, Arm.,* II, 245, 357.

73. Rémusat, "Mémoires . . . ," pp. 402–403.

74. This remark is based on the correspondence published by Aziz S. Atiya, *Egypt and Aragon: Embassies and Diplomatic Correspondence between 1300 and 1330 A.D.* (Abhandlungen für die Kunde des Morgenlandes, XXIII, 7; Leipzig, 1938).

market. Most of the time commercial activities remained apolitical, and it can safely be stated that the greatest influence trade exerted was toward the maintenance of peace. The trade routes had to be kept open, and to ensure this, commercial treaties and consular agreements linked some of the Italian republics to the Mongol states. There was even machinery to settle private commercial litigations, as is shown by the case of one Hajjī Sulaimān Tabī, a citizen of Tabriz, who in 1322 was awarded an indemnity of 4,000 bezants to be paid by Venice for damages caused, so it seems, by unruly Venetians.[75]

Many of the trade links survived the fall of the il-khans and continued even to the time of Timur. Development of maritime links notwithstanding, the transcontinental trade routes remained the fastest and most reliable way to reach East Asia. This is expressly stated by John of Monte Corvino, well acquainted with the sea-route: "As for the road hither [to China] I may tell you that the way through the land of the Goths [Crimea], subject to the emperor of the northern Tatars, is the shortest and safest; and by it the friars might come along with letter-carriers in five or six months. The other route again is very long and very dangerous, involving two sea-voyages . . . . And it is possible that it might take more than two years to accomplish the journey that way. But, on the other hand, the first-mentioned route has not been open for a considerable time, on account of wars that have been going on."[76] John of Monte Corvino was unduly pessimistic; the overland road was still practicable in 1338, when it was used both by the envoys of the Great Khan Toghan Temür on their way to Avignon and by the counter-embassy headed by John de' Marignolli.[77] The "heavenly horse" presented by this embassy, which caused a considerable sensation in the Sino-Mongol court, could hardly have survived transportation by sea.[78]

In his letter dated November 30, 1307, and already referred to, Edward II recommended some missionaries to Öljeitü, among them the Dominican William, bishop of Lydda. As this city was *in partibus infidelium,* and no longer under Latin jurisdiction, William was only

75. See Petech, "Les Marchands . . . ," p. 568. The standard work on trade remains W. Heyd, *Histoire du commerce du Levant au moyen âge,* trans. Furcy Raynaud (2 vols., Leipzig, 1885–1886, reprints available). It should be stated emphatically that in this chapter only a few cursory remarks are made on both commercial and missionary activities.

76. Yule, *Cathay,* III, 48.

77. Yule, *Cathay,* III, 179–183.

78. On the destinies of the "heavenly horse," see Yule, *Cathay,* III, 177–269; Moule, *Christians,* pp. 252–264; and, most recently, Herbert Franke, "Die Gesandtschaft des Johann von Marignola im Spiegel der chinesichen Literatur," in *Asien: Tradition und Fortschritt: Festschrift für Horst Hammitzsch,* ed. Lydia Brüll and Ulrich Kemper (Wiesbaden, 1970), pp. 117–134.

its titular bishop, and his principal aim was proselytism among the Moslems living in il-khanid territory.[79] We have mentioned earlier the presence of Dominican and Franciscan missionaries in Tabriz. At the end of the thirteenth century the Franciscans had a fairly strong foothold in the il-khanid state, but there seems to be no reason to believe that their activity was anything but spiritual. They do not seem to have made efforts to bring about a military alliance between the west and the Mongols.

If the Franciscans were not involved in the pursuit of an illusory alliance to recover Syria, they certainly took advantage of the opening up of Asia to widen their missionary field. The earliest and most successful effort was made in the territories controlled by the Golden Horde, to which they had easy access through Hungary and through the Kuman contacts. In the il-khanid state the missionaries availed themselves of the links existing with China to expand their field of activity. The formidable friar John of Monte Corvino was sent to the east about the year 1280 and must have lived some time in Persia before returning to Rome in 1289. The information John was able to provide on conditions prevalent in the Mongol empire was sufficiently detailed to cause pope Nicholas IV to send him back to Arghun so that he should proceed further to China. Among the letters given to the Franciscan there was one for Arghun, and another dated July 13, 1289, addressed personally to the Great Khan Kubilai, whose name was known to the pope.[80] The texts of these missives make it sufficiently clear that, while illusions on the willingness of the Mongol rulers to embrace Christianity might have persisted, information available on the internal conditions and basic geography of the Mongol empire was quite up-to-date and reliable.

John of Monte Corvino left Tabriz in 1291, never to return; he was to die as the first Catholic archbishop of Peking. His departure, however, did not spell the end of Franciscan and Dominican activities in Persia. The Friars Minor had three vicariates established within the Mongol empire: of the north (*vicaria aquilonis*) situated on the territory of the Golden Horde; of Cathay; and of the east, with centers in Constantinople, Trebizond, and Tabriz. It is interesting to note that the pope, well aware of the fact that the principal seat of Mongol power was in distant China, subordinated to the archdiocese of Khanbaliq (Peking) all the priests active within the

---

79. See Jean Richard, "La Papauté et les missions catholiques en Orient au moyen âge," *Mélanges d'archéologie et d'histoire publiés par l'École française de Rome*, années 1941–1946, pp. 239–266, especially p. 262.
80. Moule, *Christians*, pp. 168–171.

Mongol empire, even those working in lands as close to the west as the Crimea or Persia. It was only in 1318 that John XXII created a new archiepiscopal see *in imperio Tartarorum,* that of Sulṭānīyeh, the new capital city of the il-khans. Its first incumbent, the Dominican Francis of Perugia, was succeeded in 1323 by William Adam, a vigorous advocate of a new offensive against the Mamluks.[81]

In 1317, shortly after Öljeitü's death, William Adam submitted a voluminous memorandum, *De modo Sarracenos extirpandi,*[82] to cardinal Raymond William of Farges, a nephew of Clement V. In Adam's view the reconquest of Constantinople by the Latins was a prerequisite to any successful military operation against the Mamluks, but in his plans to extirpate the latter, the Mongols were assigned a considerable part. Adam's project consisted in a blockade of Egypt to be achieved through two distinct undertakings. The first of these would be to have a Christian fleet stop the flow of supplies from the Golden Horde to Egypt. William Adam was fully cognizant of the ties between those whom he called the northern Mongols and Egypt, *inter hos duos amicicia est tam grandis,* and he voiced the opinion that this alliance was directed against the Mongols of Persia. His second proposal was to block the southern maritime route leading to Egypt, which by geographical necessity would involve the coöperation of the Mongols of Persia. The idea of establishing a fleet manned by western, preferably Genoese, sailors in the Indian Ocean and the Persian Gulf was not new. William Adam himself supported his suggestion by recalling that in 1291 two Genoese galleys built on il-khanid territory had descended the Euphrates toward the Indian Ocean. The expedition failed, he said, not for navigational reasons but because the Genoese seamen, embroiled in political strife, killed one another. While according to Bar Hebraeus at one time some nine hundred Genoese seamen were employed by Arghun, it is not known what did ultimately prevent the creation of a Mongol fleet, manned by Genoese, on the Indian Ocean. In 1324 the Dominican Jordan of Sévérac still deplored the absence of such a fleet: "If our lord the pope would but establish a couple of galleys on this sea [the Indian

---

81. In 1318 William Adam, together with some of his fellow Dominicans, was appointed suffragan of Sulṭānīyeh. Afterward, for a short while, he was bishop of Smyrna, and on October 6, 1322, he was nominated to the see of Sulṭānīyeh. Two years later, on October 26, 1324, he was transferred to the archiepiscopal see of Antivari. William Adam's pastoral zeal was not on a par with his other preoccupations. On January 25, 1337, pope Benedict XII had to remind the absentee archbishop of Antivari in no uncertain terms of his duties. This is the last secure date we have on his life; he probably died soon after but certainly before December 1341, when a successor was appointed to the archiepiscopal see he had held. See *RHC, Arm.,* II, pp. CLXXVII–CLXXXIX.

82. *RHC, Arm.,* II, 519–555.

Ocean] what a gain it would be! And what damage and destruction to the Sultan of Alexandria!"[83] The idea was taken up later by the Portuguese, in altered circumstances, using Persian bases in their operations against the Turks.

Possibly the last detailed plan for a crusade involving Mongol help was that set forth in the *Directorium ad passagium faciendum* prepared in 1332 for Philip VI of France. Its author, William Adam or (more probably) Raymond Étienne, advocated an attack upon the Turks as a preparatory move to an assault on Egypt. The memorandum gives in a nutshell the history of the antagonism between the il-khans and the Mamluks and concludes that the Mongols of Persia will certainly be ready to ally themselves with the Christians.

In this assumption the author of the *Directorium* was completely mistaken. By the time his memorandum was submitted to the king of France, an alliance of the il-khanid state with the west directed against the Mamluks had become inconceivable. Ending a feud that had lasted all too long, a peace treaty was concluded in 1323 between the Mamluk sultan an-Nāṣir and Öljeitü's son and successor Abū-Saʿīd. In spite of some sensitive issues the treaty was honored by both parties until the il-khan's death in 1335. As we have seen, peace with the Mamluks did not entail on the part of Abū-Saʿīd the severing of all relations with the west or the interdiction of missionary activities in il-khanid territories. But it cannot be cause for surprise that a letter addressed to Abū-Saʿīd by pope John XXII and dated July 12, 1322, remained, as far as we know, unanswered. In it the pope, in terms that recall those of Öljeitü in his letter to Philip the Fair, encouraged the il-khan to follow the example set by his ancestors in sending embassies to the pope and renewing friendship with the king of France.[85]

Within a few years after Abū-Saʿīd's death the Mongol empire of Persia collapsed in a *bellum omnium contra omnes.* But the power vacuum created by the disappearance of this remarkable state, a unique bridge between east and west, was soon to be filled. Over the smoldering ruins of the il-khanids' Mongol state rose the pale crescent of Turkish Ottoman power.

As the whole crusading pattern changed to meet this powerful

83. Yule, *Cathay*, III, 80. Further interesting data can be found in Jean Richard, "Les Navigations des Occidentaux sur l'océan indien et la mer caspienne (XIIᵉ-XVᵉ siècles)," in *Sociétés et compagnies de commerce en Orient et dans l'océan indien,* ed. Michel Mollat, *Bibliothèque générale de l'École pratique des hautes études, VIᵉ Section* (Paris, 1970), pp. 353–363.

84. *RHC, Arm.*, II, 368–517.

85. Mosheim, *Historia,* appendix no. 61, pp. 145–146.

threat, a new conqueror claiming Chinggisid descent made his bid for the domination of the Near East. In Anatolia, Timur's conquests culminated in his victory at Ankara in 1402 over Bayazid I, and the ejection of the Hospitallers from Smyrna. Ephemeral as the incident was from the Inner Asian point of view, it was of major importance to western Europe and Constantinople, as has been pointed out in previous chapters of this volume. So in effect, though unwittingly and without any collaboration, a turkicized Mongol ruler—the Moslem Timur rather than a Christian "Prester John"—did assist Christendom by attacking the primary Turkish and Moslem foe from the rear, and by leaving a Timurid state in Iran to divide subsequent Ottoman military efforts between two distant frontiers.

XVI

THE GERMAN CRUSADE
ON THE BALTIC

B y the German crusade on the Baltic is meant the medieval expansion beyond the Elbe-Saale frontier to the shores of Lake Peipus. It is not historically possible to separate crusades from expansion and colonization in this area. It would not make sense, for example, to consider the Crusade of 1147 against the Wends without reviewing the history of the Slavic trans-Elbean lands since the days of Otto the Great, nor to separate the crusades of bishop Albert from the expansion of the German aristocracy and bourgeoisie into Livonia. It would likewise lead to a faulty understanding of the history of the Teutonic Knights in Prussia if an attempt were made to separate crusades against the Prussians from colonization and settlement. The campaigns to subject the Slavs and other Baltic peoples coincided with the campaigns to convert them. To some princes it made little difference whether they became converts so long as they became subjects; to some churchmen the reverse was true, but ordinarily it was realized that both went together. There could be no subjection without conversion, no conversion without subjection, and no permanence in either without German settlement.

An introductory bibliography on the history of the Teutonic Order is Rudolf ten Haaf, *Kurze Bibliographie zur Geschichte des Deutschen Ordens, 1198–1561* (Kitzingen am Main, 1949). The chronicles of Helmold of Bosau, Arnold of Lübeck, and Henry of Livonia will be found in *MGH, SS.,* XXI, pp. 1–99 (Helmold); XXI, pp. 100–250 (Arnold); and XXIII, pp. 231–332 (Henry). The narrative sources for early Livonian and Prussian history will be found in *Scriptores rerum livonicarum,* vols. I and II (Riga, 1848, 1853), and *Scriptores rerum prussicarum,* vols. I–V (Leipzig, 1861–1874). The documents of the archives of the Teutonic Order formerly at Königsberg and now at Goslar have been listed and described, with (if published) place of imprint indicated, by Erich Joachim and Walther Hubatsch, *Regesta historico-diplomatica Ordinis S. Mariae Theutonicorum, 1198–1525* (Göttingen, 1948). The author has incorporated into the text extensive quotations from Helmold's *Chronicle of the Slavs* and Henry of Livonia's *Chronicle.* The translator of the former is F. J. Tschan, *The Chronicle of the Slavs by Helmold, Priest of Bosau* (Columbia Records of Civilization, no. 31; New York, 1935), and of the latter, James Brundage, *The Chronicle of*

Obviously we have here to do with an early phase of the displacement of peoples and power responsible for the central and eastern Europe of today. It is this which makes the German Baltic crusade of such intense and even tragic interest. It is not necessary, in order to give it this meaning, to transfer to these medieval centuries the precise notions of national and ethnic conflict with which we have become only too familiar. The German state of the Middle Ages was not national. The German crusade was not directed by German kings or emperors. The peoples against whom it was directed had no national political organization. This was no conflict between anything that could be called national states. The crusade was directed by German princes, secular and ecclesiastical, against Slavic, Baltic, and Finnic tribes headed by native chieftains. There was not in the mind of any German participant the concept of a German nation fighting against a Slavic people, or in that of any Slavic, Baltic, or Finnic defender the notion of protecting his own from a Germanic "race."

Henry of Livonia (Madison, Wisc., 1961). The following are brief general accounts of the German expansion eastward, helpful in the writing of this chapter: A. Bruce-Boswell, "Poland, 1050–1303," *The Cambridge Medieval History,* VI (1936), 447–463; Hermann Aubin, "The Lands East of the Elbe . . . ," *The Cambridge Economic History,* I (1966), ch. VII-4; G. Barraclough, *The Origins of Modern Germany* (Oxford, 1947), chap. 10; A. Bilmanis, *A History of Latvia* (Princeton, 1951), parts I–II; K. Hampe, *Der Zug nach dem Osten* (4th ed., Leipzig, 1939); and R. Kötzschke, *Geschichte der ostdeutschen Kolonisation* (Leipzig, 1937). Kötzschke has also published a useful collection of source material: *Quellen zur Geschichte der ostdeutschen Kolonisation im 12. bis 14. Jahrhundert* (Leipzig-Berlin, 1931). More detailed accounts will be found in A. Hauck, *Kirchengeschichte Deutschlands,* vol. IV, chap. 7; K. Lohmeyer, *Geschichte von Ost- und Westpreussen,* vol. I (Gotha, 1881); E. Seraphim, *Geschichte Liv-, Esth-, und Curlands,* 3 vols. (Reval, 1897–1904); and J. W. Thompson, *Feudal Germany* (Chicago, 1928). Other helpful works are E. Caspar, *Hermann von Salza und die Gründung des Deutschordensstaates in Preussen* (Tübingen, 1924); C. Krollmann, *Politische Geschichte des Deutschen Ordens* (Königsberg, 1932); E. Maschke, *Der Deutsche Ordensstaat, Gestalten seiner grossen Meister* (Hamburg, 1935); M. Ammann, *Kirchenpolitische Wandlungen im Ostbaltikum bis zum Tode Alexander Newski* (Rome, 1936); K. Forstreuter, *Preussen und Russland im Mittelalter* (Königsberg and Berlin, 1938); H. G. V. Rundstedt, *Die Hanse und der Deutsche Orden in Preussen bis . . . 1410* (Weimar, 1937); and W. Werminghoff, *Der Deutsche Orden und die Stände in Preussen bis . . . 1466* (Munich and Leipzig, 1912). There is much important literature in such journals as *Altpreussische Monatsschrift, Altpreussiche Forschungen, Zeitschrift der Altertumsgesellschaft Prussia,* and *Zeitschrift des Westpreussischen Geschichtsvereins,* in which see, for example, C. Krollmann, "Die Herkunft der deutschen Ansiedler in Preussen," LIV (1912), 1–103; O. Zippel, "Die Kolonisation des Ordenlandes Preussens bis zum Jahre 1309," in *Altpreussiche Monatschrift,* LVIII (1921), 176–213, 239–279; and A. Werminghoff, "Der Hochmeister des Deutschen Ordens und das Reich bis zum Jahre 1525," *Historische Zeitschrift,* CX (1913), 473–518.

The author of this chapter wished to express his gratitude to the Research Council of the University of Nebraska for a semester's leave with pay to work on this and another chapter of this work. This chapter was edited after the author's death by Harry W. Hazard.

It is, however, possible to go too far in denying this crusade certain aspects of a national character, for the factor of nationality, though not of a national state, was present. The "crusade" lasted some six centuries or more. During this long period original ideas changed and others became prominent. In the later Middle Ages the concept of a common Germanic people emerged, superseding the earlier idea of separate German tribes. What to the German chronicler Helmold is the work of Frisians, Hollanders, Flemings, and especially Saxons in trans-Elbia is for Henry of Livonia, only a couple of generations later, the work of Germans in Livonia. It would be strange if after centuries of influx Germans from different regions had given no recognition to their common experience of settling a frontier land. The Livonian Brothers of the Sword and the Teutonic Knights were German orders. They pursued a Germanic policy with respect to recruitment and the use of the Prussian dialect by Germans. The order precipitated among Lithuanians and Poles some feeling of common nationality under their princes and kings. It is impossible not to feel in the speeches which Helmold puts into the mouths of desperate and disillusioned Slavic princes an appeal to a common Slavic people threatened with extinction.

If then the crusade on the Baltic was not a fully national or ethnic movement as we understand it, that is not to say that it did not possess embryonic aspects of nationalism. It was an aggressive movement of German Christians against pagan Slavs and other Baltic peoples. Subsequent national historians did not hesitate to interpret it as a national and ethnic conflict. Very few German historians who have touched upon the subject have been able to avoid regarding it as an extraordinary accomplishment of a very advanced people against inferior natives. It was inevitably a popular theme with Nazi historians. But a slight acquaintance with the historical literature of the other side reveals feelings of deep national hatred for the Germans and an unwillingness, often carried to absurd lengths, to recognize that anything the Germans did could be considered honest or praiseworthy.

Better than nation, people, or even nationality as a touchstone by which to interpret this crusade is the simple notion of the expansion of a comparatively advanced civilization into an undeveloped area held by primitive tribes. The civilization is, of course, early western, in its feudal Christian stage. The mediators are the Germans. The fact that the Slavs remained pagan had long injected the idea of superior and inferior into the relationship between Germans and Slavs. When

Fredegar treats of the history of Samo, a Frankish merchant who in 623 became a Slavic king, he introduces the incident of Sichar, a Merovingian envoy come to Samo's court to seek compensation for the robbery and murder of Frankish merchants by Samo's Slavic subjects. "As is the heathenish and proud way of a bad people," says the chronicler, Samo "made nothing good." The Frankish envoy then "roared out to Samo that he and his people would be made slaves" to his king and that "it is not possible that Christians, God's servants, should become friendly with dogs." Sturmi, a disciple of St. Boniface, seeking in the Thuringian wilderness a proper site for a Benedictine monastery, found "the road whereby traders came from Thuringia to Mainz, and the spot where it crosses the river Fulda. There he found a great multitude of Slavonians, who had plunged in for the sake of washing, and were swimming up and down the stream. His beast, fearing these naked bodies, began to tremble, and the man of God himself loathed the stench that proceeded from them." The stinking pagan? The stinking Slav? The stinking pagan Slav?

Thietmar, a bishop and historian serving at the frontier post of Merseburg in the early eleventh century, refers to his future Slavic parishioners as "greedy dogs." In Helmold's chronicle there are many evidences of this point of view. "With incautious and insulting words," friends of bishop Wago of Oldenburg advised him not to marry his sister to the Abodrite prince Billug, for it was "not right that a most beautiful virgin should be united with an uncultured and boorish man." In a similar case the Saxon margrave Dietrich opposed the marriage of the Slavic prince Mistivoi to a niece of duke Bernard I of Saxony, "vociferating that a kinswoman of the duke should not be given to a dog." This prince "called together all the Slavs and made known to them the insult that had been offered him, and that in the language of the Saxons, the Slavs are called dogs." Helmold can also say that "there has been inborn in the Slavic race a cruelty that knows no satiety," and can attribute to Slavs atrocities ascribed to the Turks by pope Urban at Clermont to initiate the First Crusade. Henry of Livonia reveals the same attitude toward the Livonians as that held by the Germans opening up that country.

Thus the feeling of Germanic superiority over inferior Slavic and Baltic peoples was not based solely upon the difference between Christian and pagan. It was grounded also in the differences in cultural level between west and east. The crusades to the Near East have ordinarily been interpreted as an early stage of western imperialism, the aggressive expansion to the eastern Mediterranean of the western feudal state (Latin kingdom of Jerusalem, Latin empire of Constantinople), the western Latin church, and the early capitalism of the western, especially Italian, town. It would be difficult to maintain, however, that this marked the penetration of a superior civilization into an inferior one. This difficulty is not present in the German crusade on the Baltic. We have here an early chapter in German imperialism involving the expansion of the German state, the German church, and the Germanic people. For the Baltic peoples this expansion meant a loss of independence and of religion. For some of them it meant extermination, for others deportation or assimilation by the dominant Germans. For the free non-German peasant it meant ultimately the loss of his freedom.

The German conqueror and settler who moved into this area brought with him the higher civilization of the west, for his own use and, when they were converted and subjected, for Slavs and Balts. He brought western Christianity with its highly organized secular and regular branches, its stone churches, elaborate services, music, art, tradition of learning, and its, for the most part German, clergy. The new converts, to be sure, built their new churches with their own labor, and paid tithes to maintain them. The acceptance of a Christian instead of a pagan way of life obliged them to abandon— reluctantly—many cherished practices and customs. The Germans also brought the western territorial state and feudal institutions, German law, the German town, a superior military, industrial, and mining technology, superior arts and crafts, and even a superior specialized agriculture, using an iron rather than a wooden plow. These advantages of a higher civilization had to be paid for by forced labor, military service, and new taxes, and, except for a very few, by the loss of freedom itself.

The cost of this superior western civilization was so high that the Baltic peoples refused to pay. It had to be imposed upon them by conquest, crusade, and German settlement. The Baltic peoples would be made to pay for new freedom for the Germans with the loss of their own. They resisted, accordingly, with utmost determination, as few peoples have resisted, the loss of their independence, religion, primitive customs, and personal freedom. From the days of Charlemagne to those of Otto I, the Baltic Slavs had been to the Germans a pest along the frontier, an uneasy source of tribute, or ready victims of raids to collect booty. Otto I, one of the few German kings and emperors able to devote much attention to the Elbe-Saale frontier, had planned actually to incorporate into Germany all the Slavic peoples between the Elbe and the Oder, by means of a systematic subdivision of the country into military districts controlled from strongpoints (*Burgwärde*), and by the creation of five new marches on this frontier, one each for the northern and middle Elbe, and for Merseburg, Meissen, and Zeitz.

This military and political organization was accompanied by a complete ecclesiastical organization for a region that was as yet in no sense Christian: new bishoprics at Havelberg, Brandenburg, and Oldenburg, and a new archbishopric at Magdeburg with additional suffragans at Merseburg, Meissen, and Zeitz. Such thoroughgoing plans for subjection the Wends resisted at what they thought their first good opportunity, in 983, after the defeat in 982 of German military might in Calabria. As a result of bloody revolts against the Saxon nobility and the clergy of a German God (Jesus was *theutonicus deus* to the Slavs), whatever Christianity there had been on the middle and lower Elbe ceased to exist in the years following 983. Bishop Dodilo of Brandenburg had in fact been choked to death as early as 980. The bishopric of Merseburg had ultimately to be dissolved. The bishops of Zeitz finally decided that their see was too open to Slav attack and in 1032 moved back a little closer to the German frontier at Naumburg. One bishop of Meissen refused to be buried there because he was afraid of having his grave torn open by the Slavs. At Havelberg, Brandenburg, and Oldenburg the sees were maintained, but the bishops were unable to stay in or even get to them. The first bishop of Havelberg, Udo, lived in Magdeburg the life of a canon of the cathedral church. After the murder of Dodilo of Brandenburg, bishops of this see are difficult to trace.

Helmold says frankly of duke Bernard II of Saxony at the time of the second major Slavic revolt, in 1018: "through his avarice [he] cruelly oppressed the nation of the Winuli, and sheerly drove it into paganism." The Slavs, he explains, "still immature in the faith," were pursued by the margrave Dietrich of Wettin and duke Bernard with such villainy and cruelty that they were forced into apostasy and "finally threw off the yoke of servitude, and had to take up arms in defense of their freedom." The revolt crystalized in Rethra, the sanctuary of the Slavic god Redigast and the religious center of the Pomeranian Slavs. It was led by that Mistivoi whom a Saxon margrave had called a dog. Helmold describes what happened: The Slavs first wasted "the whole of Nordalbingia with fire and sword. Then, roving about the rest of Slavia, they burned all the churches and destroyed them even to the ground. They murdered the priests and the other ministers of the churches with diverse tortures, and left not a vestige of Christianity beyond the Elbe. At Hamburg, then and later, many clerics and citizens were led off into captivity and many more were put to death through hatred of Christianity. The old men of the Slavs . . . tell how Oldenburg had been a city most populous with Christians. There sixty priests (the rest had been slaughtered like cattle) were kept as objects of derision." The oldest of them, "named Oddar . . . and others were martyred in this manner. After the skin of their heads had been cut in the form of a cross, the brain of each was laid bare with an iron. With hands tied behind their backs, the confessors of God were then dragged through one Slavic town after another until they died. . . . Many deeds of this kind, which for lack of written records are now regarded as fables, are remembered as having been done at this time in the several provinces of the Slavs and Nordalbingians. In fine, there were so many martyrs in Slavia that they can hardly be enumerated in a book. All the Slavs who dwelt between the Elbe and Oder and who had practised the Christian religion . . . during the whole time of the reigns of the Ottos, in this manner cut themselves off from the body of Christ and of the church with which they had before been united." Thus, as Helmold puts it is another place, "a country teeming with men and churches was reduced to a vast solitude."

After another start had been made by the Saxon dukes and church, the Slavs rose once more in 1066, led by a Rugian chief named Kruto. Helmold describes the general situation preceding the revolt as follows: "In those days there was a firm peace in Slavia because Conrad, who succeeded the pious Henry in the empire, wore down the Winithi [Wends] in successive wars. Nevertheless, the Christian religion and the service of the house of God made little headway, since it was hindered by the avarice of the duke and of the Saxons, who in their rapacity let nothing remain either for the churches or for the priests." The man who precipitated this revolt was the lordly archbishop Adalbert of Hamburg-Bremen, whose vision swept from Greenland to the eastern Baltic, conjuring up plans for a patriarchate of the north. He had as a helper in the Slavic mission Gottschalk, a grandson of Billug, the leader of the rebellion of 983, and himself a rebel leader about 1028, who however now thought to make his people Christian. The results of their combined efforts were monasteries in Mecklenburg, Lübeck, Oldenburg, Lenzen, and Ratzeburg, the reinvigoration of the Oldenburg bishopric, and two new bishoprics: Ratzeburg for the Polabians and Mecklenburg for the Abodrites. It was possible, Adalbert thought, that the whole Wendish region might soon become solidly Christian. Helmold again attributes the ruin of these plans to the "insatiable greed of the Saxons who . . . are ever more intent upon increasing the tribute than upon winning souls for the Lord. Through the perseverance of the priests Christianity would long ago have grown in the esteem of Slavia if the avarice of the Saxons had not stood in the way."

When the Slavic reaction came, Gottschalk was put to death at Lenzen and together with him the priest Eppo, "who was immolated on the altar." The monk Ansver, and with him others, were stoned at Ratzeburg. The aged bishop John, "who had out of his love for roving come from Ireland to Saxony," was taken with other Christians at Mecklenburg "and held for a triumph. And because he confessed Christ he was beaten with rods, and then was led in mockery through one city of the Slavs after another. Since he could not be turned from the profession of Christ his hands and feet were lopped off, and his body was thrown into the road. His head, however, the barbarians cut off, fixed on a spear, and offered to their god Redigast in token of their victory." Gottschalk's widow Sigrid, "the daughter of the king of the Danes," with other women, "was sent naked out of Mecklenburg. . . . When the Slavs had achieved victory they ravaged the whole of the region of Hamburg with fire and sword. . . . The stronghold of Hamburg was razed to the ground . . ." and Schleswig, "a city of the Transalbingians situated on the frontier of the Danish kingdom . . . , was utterly destroyed by a surprise raid of the barbarians. . . . And so all the Slavs who were sworn to a general conspiracy lapsed again into paganism after they had killed those who persisted in the faith. . . . . And the see of Oldenburg was vacant for eighty-four years."

The Germans were led finally to realize that Wend territory would never be permanently German or Christian so long as it remained Slavic. Only through German settlement would the area become a part of the civilization of the west. At the beginning of the twelfth century Dutchmen and Flemings inaugurated the eastward movement. But it took one more effort on the part of the Germans before they were convinced that colonization was a better method than conquest to reduce the area. This was the crusade of 1147 against the Wends,[1] which arose when Bernard of Clairvaux could not, for all his

---

1. See volume I of this work, pp. 479, 492–495, for an account of this crusade, which Albert Hauck called "das törichtste Unternehmen, das das zwölfte Jahrhundert kennt."

rhetorical gifts, induce the Saxon princes to go to the Holy Land. They had their own little private war against pagan Slavs at home. When the suggestion arose that the fight against the Wends might be a part of the larger undertaking, raising it to the dignity of a war against all non-Christian peoples, and destined to topple the devil from his throne, Bernard took up the notion with enthusiasm and gave the movement its slogan, "either the Wends or their religion are to be wiped out." The crusading army gathered around Magdeburg and the lower Elbe. Czechs, Poles, and Swabians joined the Saxon army, and a Danish fleet was also there to support it. Here was an army the like of which had never faced the Wends before. It was dominated by the grasping, unscrupulous, and cruel duke of the Saxons, Henry the Lion, of whom Helmold says that in all his various expeditions "no mention was made of Christianity, but only of money." When the leader of the Slavs, Niklot, was unable to prevent the launching of the crusade, he led his people against Lübeck. "That day were slain there three hundred or more men." Eastern Holstein, and especially those regions that had been settled by the "Westphalians, Hollanders, and other foreign peoples, [were] consumed by the devouring flames." The crusading armies drew up against Dobin and then Demmin, neither of which they were able to take. The Germans suddenly realized then that they had been victimized by crusading oratory, and that they were actually devastating what they regarded as their own land. Helmold makes the "vassals of our duke and of the margrave Albert" say before Dobin, "Is not the land we are devastating our land, and the people we are fighting our people? Why are we, then, found to be our own enemies and the destroyers of our own [countries]? Does not this loss fall back on our lords?" Finally, "when our men were weary, an agreement was made to the effect that the Slavs were to embrace Christianity. . . . Thus, that grand expedition broke up with slight gain. The Slavs immediately afterward became worse."

At this moment, then, under the leadership of such Saxon princes as Conrad the Great of Wettin, margrave of Meissen, Adolf of Schauenburg, count of Holstein, Albert the Bear, the Ascanian margrave of Brandenburg, and Henry the Lion, duke of Saxony, there began what Karl Lamprecht has called "the one great accomplishment of our German people during the Middle Ages," that trek eastward which was in the course of about two centuries first of all to transform Holstein, Mecklenburg, Brandenburg, and Pomerania into German lands, and then to move into Silesia, Bohemia, Poland, the Baltic lands, and Prussia. Helmold is the chronicler of the first surge eastward. He includes in his work the summons of count Adolf of Holstein to prospective colonists to come to Wagria and receive the benefits of its rich land:

"As the land was without inhabitants," count Adolf sent messengers into all the regions roundabout, "to Flanders and Holland, to Utrecht, Westphalia, and Frisia," proclaiming that all who were oppressed by want of land should go thither with their families; there they would receive the best of soils, rich in fruits and abounding in fish and flesh, and blessed with fine pastures. And to the Holsteiners and Sturmarians he said: "Have you not subjugated the land of the Slavs and bought it with the blood of your fathers and brothers? Why, then, are you the last to enter into possession of it? Be the first to go over into a delectable land and inhabit it and partake of its delights, for the best of it is due you who have wrested it from the hands of the enemy." And when he had said this there arose a countless multitude from many regions with their families and all that they possessed, and they came into the territory of the Wagrians to count Adolf to receive the lands which he had promised them. In a series of somewhat melancholy summaries he quite clearly describes what was going on at the time he finished his work (1172):

All the country of the Slavs, beginning at the Eider . . . and extending between the Baltic Sea and the Elbe river in a most lengthy sweep to Schwerin, a region once feared for its ambuscades and almost deserted, was now through the help of God all made, as it were, into one colony of Saxons. And cities and villages grew up there and churches were built and the number of ministers of Christ multiplied.

All the land of the Abodrites [Obotrites], and the neighboring regions which belong to the realm of the Abodrites, had been wholly reduced to a solitude through unremitting warfare. . . . If there were any last remnants of Slavs remaining, they were, on account of the want of grain and the desolation of the fields, so reduced by hunger that they had to flee together to the Pomeranians, and to the Danes, who, showing them no mercy, sold them to the Poles, Sorbs, and Bohemians.

The work of God thus increased in the land of Wagria and the count and the bishop [of Oldenburg] coöperated one with the other. About this time the count rebuilt the stronghold at Plön and made there a city and market place. The Slavs who lived in the villages round about withdrew, and Saxons came and dwelt there; and the Slavs, little by little, failed in the land.

The tithes in the land of the Slavs increased because Germans came from their lands to dwell in the spacious country, rich in grain, smiling in the fullness of pasture lands, abounding with fish and flesh and all good things.

At that time Albert, the margrave, whose by-name is the Bear, held eastern Slavia. By the favor of God he also prospered splendidly in the portion of his lot. . . . In the end, as the Slavs gradually decreased in number, he sent to Utrecht, and to places lying on the Rhine, to those, moreover, who live by the ocean and suffer the violence of the sea—to wit, Hollanders, Zeelanders, Flem-

19. The Baltic Littoral and Hinterland

Cartographic Laboratory UW-Madison

ings—and he brought large numbers of them, and had them live in the strong-holds and villages of the Slavs. . . .

Now, because God gave plentiful aid and victory to our duke and to the other princes, the Slavs have been everywhere crushed and driven out. A people strong and without number have come from the bounds of the ocean, and taken possession of the territories of the Slavs. They have built cities and churches and have grown in riches beyond all estimation.

Some three centuries and more of stubborn and rather successful resistance had finally exhausted and decimated the trans-Elbean Slavs. At the beginning of the twelfth century they were in no position to resist further the German prince, prelate, peasant, merchant, and worker who brought them, at a price, the advantages of the German adaptation of the higher civilization of the west. To the Oder at least it was no longer necessary to push this movement by the sword. Slavic princes in Pomerania and Silesia welcomed the more efficient and hard-working German colonists. Assimilation took the place of extermination by war. If, however, the Slavs were no longer to be slaughtered, they were expected to become Christian, politically docile, and, if they did not wish to lose their holdings, efficient hard-working peasants. The Germanized Slav, the *Conradus Slavus* and *Elizabeth Slava,* appear soon in the official documents. But German dominance meant, if not the total, at least the partial extermination of a people, and with assimilation the almost complete disappearance of the Slavic culture, such as it was. It is not enough, therefore, merely to listen to the hopeful songs of the colonists singing "to the eastland we shall ride." It is necessary also to try to see the faces and understand the hearts of the Slav peasants as they watch these new colonists crowd in and threaten with extinction, if no longer themselves, then their way of life. One can at least listen to the sentiments of Slavic leaders who do not like what is going on.

Helmold heard the reply of prince Pribislav to bishop Gerald of Oldenburg when, of the Slavs assembled in the market place of Lübeck, he demanded that they "give up their idols and worship the one God who is in heaven." He said, "How shall we, ensnared by so many evils, enter upon this way? . . . The people whom you see are your people, and . . . it will be reasonable for you to pity us. Your princes rage against us with such severity that, because of the taxes and most burdensome services, death is better for us than life. Behold, this year we, the inhabitants of this tiny place, have paid the duke in all a thousand marks, so many hundred besides to the count, and yet we are not through, but every day we are outdone and oppressed even to the point of exhaustion. How, therefore, shall we, for whom flight is a matter of daily consideration, be free to build churches for this new religion and to receive baptism? Were there but a place to which we could flee! On crossing the Trave, behold, like ruin is there; on coming to the Peene, it is not less there. What remains, therefore, but to leave the land and take to the sea and live with the waves?"

"You all know," says another Pribislav to a group of his fellow-countrymen, "what great calamities and what oppression have come upon our people through the violent might which the duke has exerted against us. He has taken from us the inheritance of our fathers and settled foreigners in all its bounds—Flemings and Hollanders, Saxons and Westphalians, and diverse folk. . . . No one save me is left who thinks of the good of our nation or wishes to raise up its ruins. Again pluck up your courage, therefore, O men who are the remnants of the Slavic race, [and] resume your daring spirit!"

Twenty-eight years after Helmold finished his chronicle, in the early spring of 1200, a fleet of twenty-three ships set out from a north German port on a journey across the pirate-infested Baltic to the mouth of the Düna. There were crusaders aboard and merchants, clerics, and artisans. The expedition had been organized and was directed by a vigorous, young, and tough-minded former member of the cathedral chapter at Bremen, a scion of the noble Lower Saxon family of Appeldern, and a nephew of archbishop Hartwig of Hamburg-Bremen. He was the recently consecrated bishop of Livonia, Albert von Buxhövden. The purpose of the expedition was to retrieve the fortunes of those Germans who had first penetrated the Düna valley.

For something like sixteen years two bishops had labored to introduce Christianity to the Livs, only to leave them unimpressed, resentful, and indeed, violent. The first of these was Meinhard, an old gray-haired Augustinian monk from the missionary house of Segeberg in Holstein. He had been inspired to join a group of Lübeck merchants who were about to explore the possibility of tapping the resources of the Russian interior by means of the establishment of a direct route up the valley of the Düna, thus avoiding Visby. Meinhard preached the advantages of Christian baptism to the Livs as they approached the stalls of German merchants. He had no appreciable success until, after an attack on Livonia by the Lithuanians, he informed his prospective converts that there was no reason why they should live in open villages, quite unprotected from the ravages of their neighbors except by their shadowy groves and dark forests. The acceptance of Christianity could bring them the stone fortifications of the west. The impression made by this proposal led to the erection of stone forts upriver at Üxküll and Holm after stonemasons had been imported from Gotland. Yet Meinhard found his labors unrewarded. He did not enjoy the taunts of the natives when they charged that he was too concerned about the prices of goods at Visby, and he longed to return home with those merchants who had brought him. The Livs would not let him go, since, they said, he might bring back an army. He was obliged to end his life in this Baltic no-man's-land.

His successor, Berthold, the abbot of Loccum, a Cistercian monastery near Bremen, came to Livonia on his first trip without an army. There were soon conspiracies to burn, kill, or drown him. The Livs charged him with coming because he was poor. When he returned from Germany a second time, he brought with him a Saxon army. When the Livonians asked him the cause of it, he said that now he was prepared to deal with "dogs" who had returned "to their vomit." The Livs asked him to send his army back to Saxony, and to instruct them with "words and not with blows." They soon learned what it meant to their fields when the Saxons foraged for food for their horses. The bishop himself rode a horse, and, in a battle which ensued over these difficulties, "two of the Livonians surrounded him, a third, Ymaut by name, pierced him from the back with a lance, and others tore him to pieces."

The Livs near Üxküll and Holm now had their fields of ripening grain ravaged by "horses, fire, and sword." They learned that when, to forestall these consequences, they received a priest into their forts, they must pay a "measure of grain" from each plow[2] to cover his expenses. When the Saxon army withdrew after what it regarded as a general pacification, leaving the clerics and one ship of merchants behind, those Livs who had received baptism, concluding that this Christianity which had been so easily imposed with water could be as easily washed off, rushed to submerge themselves in the Düna, and cast the symbol of their impending subjection after the departing German ships. Together with it they threw what they thought to be an image of the hostile Saxon God, which they had discovered in a neighboring forest. There followed attacks upon the remaining clergy, and the following spring those who survived departed for home upon threat of death. The Livs decided then to make a clean sweep of it by destroying the merchants also, but the latter "took thought for their lives" and "gave gifts to important Livs." This was the situation that Albert set out to retrieve.

2. A measure of land; for different views on its size, see Brundage, *op. cit.*, p. 33, note 22.

He had calculated well how the manifold resources of the west were to be used for the conquest and occupation that must accompany the formal baptism of the inhabitants. The conquest was to be entrusted to crusaders annually recruited from the west, and to a standing army composed of the bishop's retainers, and of a new military order, the Brothers of the Militia of Christ, better known as the Livonian Brothers of the Sword. The occupation was to be carried out not only by the Brothers in that part of the conquered territory turned over to them to rule, but by the rapid organization of both the secular administration and the regular branches of the church, for which, in the case of the latter, Albert utilized the experience of the Cistercians and the Premonstratensians in the Slavic territory beyond the Elbe and the Saale. The land was, moreover, to be held by strategically located garrisons of episcopal vassals and their retainers, recruited from the Saxon nobility. The secular administration was to be in the hands of advocates of the bishop, located in the chief native villages. The powerful commercial interests behind the conquest and the occupation were to be safeguarded by the creation of a permanent urban colony at the mouth of the Düna, recruited from the north German cities, a colony whose militia would supplement the permanent military establishment and act as the capital city of the enterprise. The whole plan was conceived in a form to satisfy the ambition of the bishop and his numerous relatives. What was to be established on the Baltic was the kind of ecclesiastical principality that German bishops had had their hearts set on for centuries. Albert, as an independent bishop in Livonia, preferably even as an archbishop, was to transform a group of primitive communities of Finnic and Baltic peoples into a western church-state, a theocracy in miniature.

It cannot be said that the bishop did not labor strenuously to carry out his plans. Riga was founded in the year after his arrival, and pilgrims were set to work to raise its walls to a height capable of withstanding the hatred of the peoples in whose midst it was set. The episcopal see was moved from Üxküll to Riga and provided with a Premonstratensian chapter. From the tower of the new cathedral the bells celebrated the widening and tightening of the German grip on the land. When a fire destroyed them and the old town, bigger and better bells were cast, and the circumference of the city was enlarged. The Brothers of the Militia came in 1202, and three years later the Brothers of St. Bernard at Dünamünde. It was Albert's task, meanwhile, to organize further the support of this enterprise in the west by a personally conducted recruiting and publicity campaign.

Almost every year he returned to Germany, often bearing with him prize exhibits of converted natives, or the hostage children of defeated tribes, to bring back an army of pilgrims, knights for the order, and men to administer the new posts opening up in the ecclesiastical and secular administration. He preached up and down the highways and byways, says Henry of Livonia, and traveled through the counties and to the castles. He had, moreover, to conduct the foreign affairs of his principality. By 1207 he had arranged to become a prince of the empire, holding Livonia in fief. At the Fourth Lateran Council he managed to have the bishopric of Riga exempted from the authority of the archbishop of Hamburg-Bremen, and put directly under Rome.

By this date the conquest had proceeded with such vigor and the occupation launched with such severity that the Livs and Letts, confessing their inability to withstand them, bowed with sullenness and hatred to the inevitable new regime. By this date also had begun the incredibly vicious campaign against the Esths; participants included not only the crusaders from Germany—for whom, often, a memorable experience of their pilgrimage had to be created—but also the bishop and his men, the abbot and his men, the Knights, the Rigans, and levies of the now baptized Livs and Letts. In this war, after the booty had been taken, terms of peace were to be had only upon the promise of baptism and the surrender of boys and girls as hostages. The priests who accompanied these armies were ready to begin their mass baptisms immediately upon the cessation of the slaughter. Henry describes how, after taking the fortress of the Selonians, a tribe of Letts, "the abbot and the provost, with the other priests, ascended to them in the fort, instructed them in the beginnings of the faith, sprinkled the fort with holy water, and raised the banner of Blessed Mary over it."

The relentless pressure of Albert's machine of conquest and occupation inspired fear and terror, hatred and scorn, in the minds and hearts of the natives. It induced them to seek every means to escape it. They were prompt to prepare conspiracies to murder advocates, priests, and the heads of the garrisons. Conrad of Meiendorf had to be installed in the fort at Üxküll by an army of crusaders. In order to supply his garrison with food, the ripened grain of the neighboring Livonian fields was cut down with sickle and sword and stored to the very roofs of the fort. The conspiracies were answered with campaigns of revenge driving the Livs and their families into the forests. When caught in their own forts they often, in the stress of a moment of victory, returned to their own gods, giving thanks with sacrificial animals, whose carcasses they threw down from the walls into the face of the bishop. When the leaders of a rebellion were captured, their severed heads were sent to the bishop, to his great satisfaction, we are assured.

In his reduction of the Esths, Albert used the levies of baptized Livs and Letts to open the way. German troops, priests, and merchants accompanied and followed them. Henry describes the villages in Estonia before these invasions as beautiful, prosperous, and well populated. The Rigans, he relates, were urged to participate by the reminder that even before Riga was built a merchant caravan on its way up the Düna to Pskov was waylaid by some Esths and plundered of goods worth over a thousand silver marks. No priestly embassy had ever been able to make this loss good. The campaigns into the various regions of Estonia finally reduced it to a wasteland and brought in their wake famine and plague. The accounts of them make sickening reading. "Moving into Sakala," begins one, "the Christian army found the men, women, and little children in their homes in all the villages and localities. From morning until night the men killed those whom they found, the women as well as the children. They killed three hundred of the more prominent and leading men of the province and innumerable others until their hands and arms, because of excessive slaughter of the people, tired and failed them. All the villages were colored with the abundant blood of the pagans. On the following day they returned and collected much spoil in all the villages, oxen, cattle, and a great many little girls. They led them all back with them into their lands."

On another campaign "they killed a great many people in the villages and took others captive. They got much loot and took back with them the women and young girls, leaving the villages deserted. Having made a great slaughter, and started a huge conflagration, they returned home." Subsequently a priest was sent to negotiate peace, and to ask about that thousand marks' worth of pilfered goods. "The Esths rushed at him with swords and lances." On another day "the army, having separated into all the roads and villages, killed many of the people in every place and took the women and boys captive. In the days following they laid waste everything and burned everything they found. They took both horses and oxen. Indeed, they took four thousand oxen and cows, not counting the horses and other flocks, and captives which were innumerable. Many of the pagans who had escaped into the woods and onto the ice of the sea froze to death. . . . When the Esths refused Christianity they seized all the captives, cut them down, and cast them into a trench." At moments of greatest fury both sides burned and buried alive. The attacks were sometimes made in regular relays. "Upon returning home the army met on the road other Letts going into Ungannia. What they had left these took, what they had neglected these seized; whoever had escaped from the first were killed by these. Those provinces and villages not reached by them were reached by these; . . . when these returned they came across other Letts on the way. What had been left undone by the former was really completed by the latter, and they, upon their return, came across a fourth army moving into Estonia." During another "summer nine different expeditions and armies were sent into Estonia. It was left desolate and deserted and no men or provisions could be found any more." What had formerly been a "fertile, great, and populous country was laid waste and burned by our men. . . . They killed here and there until, completely worn out, they and their horses with them, they could kill no more. And so with great joy they returned to Livonia, blessing God for the vengeance granted us against the pagans." The Esths "bewailed and wept. . . . . Estonia weeping for her sons could not be comforted. . . . And so God caused their pride to subside and humbled the arrogance of the strong." And in the camps of the Christians at night there were games "with great clamor and striking of shields."

The German and Christian domination in these Estonian lands was set up over a waste of slaughtered natives and burned-out villages. By 1217 (battle of Fellin, September 26) Sakala had been won; by 1224, the region of Ungannia (Dorpat, Tartu). Before Albert's death, the Esths on the island of Ösel had been subdued. The Germans, however, were not able to extend their control over all of Estonia, for the Danes from Reval (Tallinn) maintained their claims in this region. Both the Brothers and the bishop competed for their favor and support, with the result that under papal auspices a settlement was reached leaving Reval with the provinces of Wierland and Harrien to the Danes. These they would hold until 1346, when they sold out to the Teutonic Order.

The piecemeal nature of the conquest and occupation made impossible effective concerted resistance. It was inevitable, however, that both Liv and Esth should appeal to what Henry calls the "little and great kings of the Russians" to come to their rescue. Before the Germans arrived Russian princes had imposed tribute upon isolated groups—the Düna Livs, for example, and certain of the Letts. They had even introduced Greek Orthodox Christianity into the neighborhood of Lettish Tholowa, but on the whole, as one of the princes said to Albert, it was not the custom of the Russians to impose their religion upon the conquered; they imposed tribute only. As the German power grew, and the resistance of the Livs and Esths became more desperate, these princes realized that access to the Baltic was being denied them. Their last chance to thwart these unpleasant neighbors and to keep open the opportunities for tribute was to establish themselves as allies of the rebellious natives. They began to appreciate also the value of extending Greek Christianity and made some efforts to baptize. Of the danger of the expansion of the Greek church into Livonia even Innocent III was aware. Thus the struggle between German and native developed into a conflict between German and Russian and between Latin and Greek Christianity for the possession of this part of the Baltic littoral. The Mongol invasions helped to preclude effective Russian intervention, itself limited by the difficulties of coöperation among the Russian princes themselves. Of the neighboring Russian principalities, Albert was able to destroy one, Kokenhusen (1208), and reduce another to vassalage, Gertsike (1209). The neighboring princes of Polotsk, Pskov, and Novgorod, however, were ultimately beyond his reach. Nor could he prevent the raids of the Lithuanians, now helping and now attacking the Russians, now helping and now attacking the Balts.

It was the superior military technology of the west which established the Germans in Livonia and Estonia, and checked the Lithuanians and Russians. It was the brilliant glitter of their arms that the Lithuanians abhorred, says the chronicler. It was, moreover, the new stone fortifications, hitherto unknown in this area. Albert sent stonemasons to help a Russian prince strengthen his castle. It was in addition the siege machinery—the ballista, the paterell, and those little engines called hedgehogs and swine. The word machine is used so often by Henry that one cannot avoid thinking of a technological revolution. The natives and Russians could not deal with the episcopal forts and the castles of the Brothers. The Esths, remarks Henry, had never seen such things and had not protected their homes against attacks of this kind. The Russians, he remarks, were ignorant of the art of the ballista, being used to bows. It took some time for them to learn. When at first they wounded and killed their own men with the new machines, the Germans smiled. "The Russians," says Henry, "made a little machine, in the fashion of the Germans, but not understanding the art of hurling stones they injured a great many of their men by hurling them into their backs." But they did learn. When Russians were introduced into the Estonian forts at Dorpat and Fellin, "they built paterells and machines to counter the machines of the Christians in all the forts, teaching each other the ballistarian art, and dividing the ballistas of the Brothers of the Militia, of which among themselves they had seized a great many." The Esths in the Reval neighborhood learned the art from the Danes. "When the Danes besieged the island of Ösel, certain of the Öselians went to the Esths along the coast of the mainland to study the art of the paterell or of the machine which the Danes had given them. And they returned to Ösel and began to build machines, and taught others. And each one of them built his own machine."

Albert was thus a champion of Latin Christianity against paganism and Greek Christianity, and a defender of German—primarily Saxon—against Russian interests. The struggle was essentially between the Saxon nobility and church and a disunited array of primitive Finnic, Baltic, Russian, and Lithuanian peoples. It has already been suggested that the larger category into which this conflict fits is the expansion of a comparatively advanced, vigorous, and prosperous western civilization, carried by Germans, into the undeveloped regions of northeastern Europe. It is the impingement of a "higher" upon a "lower," a "superior" upon an "inferior" civilization, in many respects an unpleasant incident in the "march of progress." That these German representatives of the west felt very superior to the Baltic peoples is only too obvious from their chronicler. There was no question in their minds as to their right to impose by force the disciplinary institutions of their church. The mentality and practices of the Baltic pagans were, of course, an object of curiosity, but more especially of that scorn which western Christians had felt from time immemorial. Resistance to baptism was considered to be only pagan pride and arrogance, and any return to their own gods, sheer apostasy. These pagans sacrificed animals and an occasional Christian to their gods, cremated their dead with heavy feasting and drinking, and thought it possible to interpret the will of the gods by setting a fat priest upon a fat cow, or by seeing whether a horse raised his left or right front foot. It was infuriating to a German to watch the profanation of Christian churches by wild carousals of victorious pagans with their woman captives, or the impudence of that Lithuanian warrior who rode into a church on his horse, and finding nothing to carry away, exploded with a simple "Bah!"

The material superiority of the west has been alluded to. Its feudal civilization, as adapted by the Saxons, themselves once hardened by the Carolingian conversion, moved into the east. It was first of all military, the knowledge of strategy and tactics, how to direct the levies of militarily inexperienced peoples, how to build, defend, and besiege stone castles with what the natives regarded as new-fangled military machines. The pagans knew so little about cement that they thought they could pull down one of these forts. There came too the civil as well as the military institutions of the Saxon west. Among these were the municipal institutions of an expanding urban economy, the knowledge of how to build, govern, and protect a town so as to make it prosperous. Because of all this activity such pagan pursuits as piracy and highway robbery were intolerable. To the morality of the established commercial practices of the western merchants these peoples were indifferent.

From the west was imported as well a higher and literate culture—the new ecclesiastical architecture, for example, and the impressive splendor of the new Christian service. There was also the new Christian drama, and those new musical instruments which the Germans brought along. On one occasion, when the Lettish fort at Beverin was being attacked by the Esths, the Letts had a priest with them, possibly Henry of Livonia, who kept up constant prayer during the course of the battle. It was going so well that individual Letts ran into the fort from time to time to join their priest in praising "the Christian God who was fighting for them." Finally, in sheer exaltation, the priest climbed to the top of the walls and sang with a "musical instrument." He managed to stop the battle, for "the barbarians hearing the sweet song and the sharp sound of the instrument" stood still in amazement, for "they had never heard such an instrument in their land." They saw the Germans enter battle with the beating of drums "stirring up the souls of their men." They heard them also, in their camps after a fine day of slaughter and collecting booty, give vent to their "great exultation" with Christian games, to the accompaniment of "drums, pipes, and musical instruments." The Germans brought also new standards of cleanliness, for the Russians were offensively indifferent to the rules of sanitation. When the Germans were about to occupy the recently abandoned fort at Kokenhusen they found that "because of the lack of cleanliness on the part of the former inhabitants, it was filled with worms and snakes, and had to be thoroughly cleaned before they would enter it."

At a moment, then, when the German empire was in chaos, and the papacy too preoccupied with other important matters to be able to direct what was going on in the Baltic area, expanding western civilization, adding the fervid impulse of the crusader to the attraction of an undeveloped area, entered Livonia in the theocratic form given it by a Saxon bishop. Although his plans had to be modified to accord with the intense ambitions of the Brothers, the Danes, and the papacy, and although, after his death, Livonia fell into the hands of the Teutonic Knights, Albert had succeeded, after some twenty-five years of conquest and occupation, in laying the foundation for German control upon the sands of human misery, exploitation, and widespread devastation.

The methods pursued by Albert in setting up his ecclesiastical state in Livonia made an overwhelming impression upon his contemporaries who were confronted in Prussia with the identical problem of how to convert the heathen—upon, that is, bishop Christian (1215–1245) and his competitors, the Teutonic Knights. The earlier medieval centuries had established the tradition that Christianity was to be spread, under the guidance of the papacy, by the peaceful persuasion of native kings and chieftains, not imposed as a condition of peace by the sword. Pope Gregory the Great, Augustine of Canterbury, and the Anglo-Saxon mission to the continent had illustrated the effectiveness of this method. It taught that the state was to be the helper, and the church the director. In conversion, religious and not political or economic motives were to prevail. The missionary himself was to be, in Alcuin's phrase, the *praedicator pietatis* and not the *exactor decimarum*. The acceptance of Christianity was to bring with it a new freedom under the church.

The supporters of this point of view saw clearly the hypocrisy of preaching the liberation of the soul from heathen bondage when this liberation by force brought serfdom and the tithe. Albert and the Brothers of the Sword had been reminded of these things by the papal legate William of Savoy, bishop of Modena. The same point of view was constantly emphasized by Rome in its direction of the Prussian venture. But the impact of this advice was fatally limited by the fact that Innocent III and his successors, however interested in mitigating the effects of conversion associated with conquest, were unwilling to see the new conquests escape the control of papal theocracy. The liberty of the new Christian was to be enjoyed within the boundaries of a papal state. Nor were they willing to go so far as to risk the exclusion from their ecclesiastical empire of the new Baltic states by taking extreme measures against those whose methods they criticized. It was not easy to insist upon the peaceful persuasion of the Baltic heathen when the use of force, in the form of crusades, had already been promoted in the case of the Moslem and the Albigensian heretic. Without serious opposition from the papacy, Albert had been able to abandon the earlier missionary tradition for that established by Charlemagne with his conquest of the pagan Saxons, and by Bernard of Clairvaux, in sanctioning the application of crusading methods to suppress and Christianize the Slavs south of the Baltic.

Bishop Christian was himself a Cistercian monk, possibly the abbot, of the Polish monastery of Lekno. The failure of all previous missionary efforts in Prussia, together with the successful inauguration of the Livonian mission, inspired him to work among the Prussians. The early successes of his mission brought him the support of such Polish princes as duke Conrad of Masovia and bishop Goslav of Plock. He had first conceived of his mission as the peaceful persuasion of Prussian princes. He had extraordinary notions about founding schools to train Prussians in the conversion of their own people and to educate young girls, whom Prussian custom considered worthless. He had brought some of his noble converts to Rome to be baptized. He had indeed even been endowed by them with land along the Vistula. By Innocent III in 1215 he was ordained the bishop of Prussia and his Polish supporters endowed the new bishopric extensively in the area of Kulm. When the Prussians became aware, however, that Christianization might lead to Polish conquests and when, accordingly, the results of Christian's missionary endeavors were threatened with extinction, he made the mistake of resorting to a crusade in order to protect Prussian Christians from the attacks of their pagan kinsmen. In vain did he seek to control and restrain the mainly Polish crusaders by securing from Rome a privilege obliging them to respect his episcopal authority, to secure his permission before crossing into Prussia, and to refrain from reducing Christian Prussians to subjects. In vain did he urge, in imitating Albert further, the formation of a new German military order, founded upon the example of the Livonian Brothers of the Sword, the Knights of Dobrzyn. The Prussians answered these steps by attacks upon the Polish frontier. Christian could maintain himself neither in Prussia nor in Kulmerland, which, together with Masovia and Kujavia, was overrun and laid waste. It was under these circumstances that Conrad of Masovia was persuaded to offer the Teutonic Knights, recently expelled from eastern Hungary, Kulmerland in return for their undertaking the defense of his frontiers by a crusade against the Prussians.

The grand master of the Teutonic Order at this time was the able Hermann of Salza, who knew precisely the conditions under which he would introduce the Knights into Prussia. These had little concern with Christian's plans for converting Prussians, or for the political needs or ambitions of Polish princes. If there were to be crusades they would have to advance the interests of the Teutonic Order, and the interests of the Teutonic Order had to do with the establishment, under empire and papacy, of an autonomous monastic state, tolerating no competition from other monastic orders or the secular church. If the Knights could get such terms, they would march into Prussia.

The Order of German Knights of the Hospital of Saint Mary at Jerusalem was but ten years old when Hermann of Salza was elected its fourth grand master in 1209. It was the product of the frustrated hopes of those German crusaders who had joined Frederick I Barbarossa on the Third Crusade and of those who had associated themselves with the crusade of Henry VI. The early German hospital at Jerusalem, lost in 1187, was reorganized as a field hospital before the walls of Acre when the sad remnants of Barbarossa's army, under his son duke Frederick of Swabia, joined the other troops of the west in the siege of the city. It was organized with the help of German merchants from Bremen and Lübeck, moved into the city after its fall, and provided with the rule of the Hospitallers.[3] As such it existed until 1198, when another group of German crusaders, among whom were such men from northern Germany as landgrave Hermann of Thuringia, margrave Conrad of Landsberg, and margrave Dietrich of Meissen, undertook before returning to Germany, upon the news of the death of Henry VI, to transform the German hospital into a German military order by supplying it with knights, clergy, serving brothers, and the rule of the Templars. The new order was approved by Innocent III in the following year, and was provided by Honorius III with no fewer than 113 papal privileges, making it the equal of the older orders. Meanwhile it had become richly endowed in Palestine, Cilician Armenia, Greece, and Europe, up indeed to the very borders of Prussia. Its regional organization in Germany centered in the *Ballei* (bailiwick) of Thuringia. Its earliest foundation had been at Halle, in that northern Germany whose interests had turned eastward centuries ago, and which at the moment was cut off from the east by the expansion into northern Germany of king Waldemar II of Denmark. From this region (Langensalza) Hermann, called "the Bismarck of the thirteenth century" and "the greatest German statesman of the Middle Ages," may well have come.

The European career of the Teutonic Order was opened up by the invitation (1211) of Andrew II, king of Hungary, to occupy territory in Transylvania (the Burzenland), in modern Rumania, where the Knights were to protect his frontier from the raids of the heathen

---

3. A chapter in volume V of this work (in preparation) will treat the Teutonic Knights in the Holy Land, to 1291. On the crusades of Barbarossa and Henry VI see volume II, chapter III.

Kumans. It must be assumed that in accepting this invitation Hermann was aware of what bishop Albert was accomplishing in Livonia, and that he wished to guide his order in Hungary by this example. Nor can there be any doubt that Hermann profited from the experience in Hungary when about to introduce the order into Prussia. In any case he knew how to take advantage of his friendship with Honorius III to secure for the order in Hungary what it was never intended by Andrew to have. Privileges from Rome exempted it from the local ecclesiastical jurisdiction of the bishop of Siebenbürgen and took its landed endowment into the proprietorship of St. Peter and under the special protection of the holy see. The order moreover seems to have violated the privileges granted by Andrew and to have increased its holdings illegally. It also introduced German colonists into the region. Hermann's Hungarian program called, therefore, for the founding, under the papacy, of an autonomous German monastic state, not limited to the defense of a frontier. These steps made the order unwelcome in Hungary. The king, once aware of the implications of the new foundation, abrogated its privileges, ordered it to leave Hungary, and when it resisted, expelled it by force (1225).

This experience did not put an end to Hermann's plans for the future establishment of the Teutonic Knights in Europe. It only made him more careful in negotiating the conditions of any such establishment. The invitation from duke Conrad of Masovia followed hard upon the expulsion from Hungary and offered to the Knights a similar mission, the defense of an endangered frontier against pagans. It was followed by five years of negotiations with the duke, conducted from Halle. During this period Hermann, as an intimate advisor of emperor Frederick II, conducted important business with the papacy, and at the same time was in close touch with the situation in northern Germany. When king Waldemar of Denmark was taken prisoner by his vassal count Henry of Schwerin (1223), it was Hermann of Salza who was sent to negotiate terms of release that would help to remove the Danish obstacle to the expansion of northern Germany eastward. When the north German princes at Bornhöved (1227) removed this obstacle, Hermann utilized the situation for his order. In the previous year he had supported the efforts of the Lübeckers to raise their city, quite essential to the overseas expansion of the Germans, to the status of a free imperial city.

He was, of course, well acquainted with what bishop Albert had accomplished in Livonia by this date, and of the way in which it had been done. He knew the eagerness and capacity of the north German nobility, and peasantry, to participate as entrepreneurs and colonists in a second Baltic venture in Prussia. This knowledge, combined with the outcome of the invitation to Hungary, convinced him of the great possibilities which Prussia offered. His position at the imperial and papal courts made it possible for him to get what he wanted. The political ambitions of a petty Polish prince, unable to provide for the protection of his own borders, would not be permitted to thwart the order even if his invitation were accepted. Nor would the ecclesiastical ambitions of a local Prussian bishop, with idealistic notions about how a new area should be Christianized, be permitted to interfere with conquest. If the Knights were to go into Prussia it must be with outside help to be sure, but with no outside interference. This is what would distinguish them from the Livonian Brothers of the Sword. Conquest would establish under emperor and pope a new Christian state open to German enterprise. Its government would follow the example of Frederick II, rather than that of the feudal kingdom of Jerusalem. In this state, the Livonian dualism between order and bishop would be avoided. Prussian bishops would be subordinated to, and even come from the ranks of, the Knights themselves.

The way was provided for the realization of such a program in the years following Conrad's invitation. In the very next year (1226) Hermann received from Frederick II, in the Golden Bull of Rimini, the full authority of an imperial prince (*Reichsfürst*) for Kulmerland and all Prussia that should be conquered by the Knights. In 1234, after the conquest had been begun, the territory then held by the Knights was taken into the proprietorship of St. Peter and under the special protection of the holy see. It was returned to the Knights as a papal fief owing an annual rent. Meanwhile, by 1230, hastened by the formation of the Knights of Dobrzyn, negotiations with Conrad and Christian had gone far enough to permit, under the above conditions, the dispatch of Hermann Balke with seven knights across the Vistula at Nessau to begin the conquest. In a document—if it is not a forgery—then prepared in Italy for Conrad to sign, the original terms of his invitation were reformulated in terms freeing the order from any Polish interference. Christian was persuaded to abandon his temporal holdings in Kulmerland in exchange for a guarantee of his episcopal rights in the Prussian territory to be conquered. In this the good bishop was to be disappointed. In 1233 he was captured by the Prussians and held for six years. This convenient circumstance the Knights did not undertake to modify by exchanging notable Prussian prisoners for Christian. The papal grant of Prussia as a fief of the order (1234) ignored him. Two years later the papal legate William of

Modena was instructed to take over the ecclesiastical organization of Prussia.

When Christian was finally released, he protested the violation of his rights, and complained that the Knights were more interested in making subjects than Christians, and that they were driving the Prussians back into heathendom. For protests of this sort it was too late. They postponed until 1243 the ecclesiastical organization of Prussia, but they did not change the nature of the conquest nor alter the proposed subordination of the secular church to the order. Christian had in fact been abandoned by the papacy as well as by the order. As compensation for the loss of his position as missionary bishop of all Prussia, he was offered, in fact ordered, to take one of the four bishoprics into which Prussia was to be divided. But this, until his death (1245), the embittered and disillusioned missionary could not be persuaded to do. After conquest and forcible conversion Hermann of Salza in Prussia no less than Albert of Riga in Livonia meant to establish a little Baltic theocracy, but monastic rather than episcopal.

The conquest of Prussia by the Knights began in 1230, the year following Albert's death, and lasted for the rest of the thirteenth century, for only by its close may Prussia be said to have been completely subdued. It was accompanied by the consummation of Albert's plans for the conquest of Livonia. In 1237 the surviving Livonian Brothers of the Sword, after a serious defeat by the Lithuanians at Saule (1236), were formally received into the Teutonic Order, which two years earlier had incorporated the Dobrzyn Brothers. Yet despite the union the history of the Livonian branch of the order with its own *Landmeister* was still a separate history. In both areas primitive tribes with no common political organization were obliged hopelessly to protect their lives, farms, tribal independence, and religion against the superior might of the west, and a fanaticism compounded of crusading zeal and contempt for the un-Christian and uncivilized. Prussia, like Livonia and trans-Elbia before it, was a new area to be opened to western German enterprise. No less than the Livonian Brothers could the Teutonic Knights manage this conquest alone. Indeed, the two areas competed for the aid of the aristocracy and burghers of northern Germany. This aid took the form of crusades, promoted from Rome and recruited by the respective agents of the orders.

The spiritual rewards which these crusaders sought, no less glittering than the rewards to be sought in the Holy Land, and more easily procured, were less tangible than the material rewards which successful conquest would bring. The north German aristocracy which participated in these crusades had become successful colonizers of Slavic trans-Elbia. It had been well established that without colonization mere conquest and superficial Christianization were impermanent. There were huge landed estates to be had in Prussia, in return for support without which the Knights could not hope to hold the area. The German burghers who participated in these crusades, the counterparts of those Venetians, Genoese, and Pisans who crusaded to Syria, comprehended well the economic possibilities of opening up the Baltic and its hinterland as a market for a vigorous young western industry, and importing therefrom the raw products and surplus of an improved agriculture. Prussia then, like Livonia, was confronted not only by the highly organized Christianity of the west, but by new political, economic, and social forces breaking through the restrictions of a feudal society. The Prussians were able to withstand this combination no better than other primitive peoples inhabiting the southern Baltic shore. They, too, were victims of the German expansion of the west.

The strategy of the Knights for the conquest of Prussia was well conceived, and the military power developed was extraordinary. The strategy involved the protection of all advances by forts and castles, built by the forced labor of conquered Prussians in accordance with principles of military architecture imported from Syria. Alongside these strongholds urban settlements of German burghers were immediately founded, and in some areas German nobles were granted, on feudal tenure, large holdings. From these well fortified centers the conquest of the surrounding territory followed, making use again of enforced Prussian military service. Accompanying these crusading armies were Dominican priests who performed the wholesale baptisms required as a condition of peace. The general plan involved going down the right bank of the Vistula from Kulmerland as a base to the Frisches Haff and along its shores and that of the Kurisches Haff to meet the advance from Livonia, thus opening up contact by sea with Lübeck and the German homeland. Thence the conquest was to proceed into the interior.

After clearing Kulmerland of the Prussians, the Knights advanced from the castles of Thorn (1231) and Kulm (1232) down the Vistula with the help of the crusading army of burgrave Burchard of Magdeburg. In the territory of the Pomeranians they built Marienwerder (1233). In the fall of 1233 with the help of an army of crusaders led by Polish and Pomeranian nobles, including duke Conrad of Masovia, his son Casimir of Kujavia, duke Vladislav Odonicz of Great Poland, duke Henry of Silesia and Cracow, and duke Svantopelk of eastern Pomerania and his brother Sambor, the Knights won a victory over the next pagan group to the east—confusingly called the Pomesanians—and built Burg Rheden further to protect Kulmerland. With Henry of Breslau came the first burghers from Silesia and Breslau for Thorn and Kulm, and one of the first sovereign acts of the Knights was to grant them the *Kulmer Handfeste* (1233), a charter of self-government based upon the law of Magdeburg. With the help of the crusading army of Henry, the margrave of Meissen, all Pomesania (between Marienwerder and Elbing) was occupied. The advance then continued down the Nogat to Lake Drausen, and finally (1236) to the shores of the Frisches Haff, where in 1237 the castle of Elbing was built and immediately supplied with an urban community from Lübeck. These crusades left such Germans as Bernard of Kamenz, John von Pak, and Frederick of Zerbst with large holdings in Pomesania, Kulmerland, and the Elbing area. The campaign against Varmians and Natangians along the southern shores of the Frisches Haff to the Pregel was supported by the castle at Balga (1239), from which an advance was made into the interior against Pogesanians, Varmians, and Bartens. With the help of duke Otto of Brunswick, a grandson of Henry the Lion, castles were built in the midst of these peoples, Kreuzburg in Natangia, Bartenstein and Rössel among the Bartens (1241), Braunsberg in Ermland, and Heilsberg in Pogesania (1241). This further advance left Dietrich of Depenow (Tiefenau) from Hanover with a huge estate near Marienwerder.

The determination of the Knights to deprive duke Svantopelk of eastern Pomerania of control of the navigation of the Vistula delta led to war. The whole conquered territory except Pomesania was now lost by the order in the first Prussian revolt (1240). In the south only the castles of Thorn, Kulm, and Rheden were able to withstand the rebels; in the north only Elbing and Balga. The peace of Christburg (1249) with the Prussians was made under papal mediation. Peace with Svantopelk (1253) brought control of the navigation of the lower Vistula. Meanwhile, while the revolt was being suppressed, expansion continued. In 1246 Lübeckers were crusading in Samland, taking home natives to be baptized in Germany, and leaving behind in Braunsberg and Frauenburg the important Fleming and Baysen families. By 1252 the Livonian branch had advanced southward down the coast to Memel. In 1254 an impressive crusading force under king Ottokar II of Bohemia, Rudolph of Hapsburg, and Otto of Brandenberg carried the advance into Samland, where in honor of Ottokar Königsberg was built (1254).

While the Pogesanians, Varmians, Bartens, Natangians, and Samlanders were being incorporated into the order's state, a second revolt broke out in 1260. It was precipitated when the Lithuanians seriously defeated the Livonian branch of the order at Durben in Samogitia (Samaiten, September 20, 1260). It was again only the Pomesanians who remained aloof from a merciless attack upon the Christians. On this occasion the Prussians were well organized under native leaders such as Glande (Samland), Herkus Monte (Natangia), Glappe (Ermland), Auttume (Pogesania), and Diwane (Bartens). The Knights held out only in the strongholds of Thorn, Kulm, Elbing, Christburg, Balga, and Königsberg. Braunsberg and Heilsberg were starved out and burned; Kreuzberg and Bartenstein were taken. The revolters were assisted by the still pagan and unconquered Nadravians, Schalavians, and Sudavians of the south and east, and these in turn by the Lithuanians. New crusades enabled the Knights ruthlessly to put down this revolt. They were led by duke Albert I of Brunswick and landgrave Albert of Thuringia (1264–1265), margrave Otto of Brandenburg (1266), king Ottokar of Bohemia (1267), and margrave Dietrich of Landsberg (1272). After the Nadravians, Schalavians, and Sudavians had been virtually exterminated, deported, or driven into Lithuania, and over half of Prussia had been turned into a wilderness, the revolt came to an end (1283). Thereafter there were but sporadic outbursts, notably a revolt in Samland in 1295 under the leadership of Naudote.

The ferocity with which the revolt of 1260 was suppressed marked the final escape of the order from the limitations which the papacy had tried to put upon subjection and conversion of the Prussians. The treaty of Christburg in 1249 had sought to establish the principle that a voluntary return to Christianity would bring the Prussians, under the immediate but mild suzerainty of the order, a guarantee of the liberties they had formerly enjoyed, and the new Christian freedom of citizenship in a large papal community. The treaty was made with the rebelling Pomesanians, Pogesanians, Varmians, Natangians, and Bartens as a group and as equal partners in the negotiation. They were guaranteed their personal freedom and their property. The conditions under which the latter was to be bought, sold, and inherited were precisely regulated. They were to engage in no further conspiracies against the order. The pagan burial and marriage customs to be abandoned were enumerated and the new Christian obligations, including tithes and participation in crusades, prescribed.

The Prussians were promised that they could become clergy and even, if of noble birth, members of the order. It was made clear, however, that to abandon the newly accepted cult would entail loss of property with severe punishment and even deportation.

The peace of Christburg had made it possible for the crusades against the still remaining heathen Prussians to go on. When the revolt of 1260 was suppressed, the order had abandoned all pretense of dealing mildly with the natives. They were treated as apostates and rebels, despisers of Christianity and traitors. The original plans for an *Ordensstaat* could now be carried out. The dreams of missionaries and popes could be forgotten as unrealistic. In suppressing the revolt the Knights repeated bishop Albert's Livonian and Estonian horrors and evoked similar retaliatory Prussian reprisals. There were slaughter, murder, burnings alive, human sacrifice to pagan gods, devastation, extermination, and deportation. Samland was reduced to a desert; the Pogesanians were wiped out; the Nadravians, Schalavians, and Sudavians were driven into Lithuania and deported into Samland and elsewhere—a wilderness was created into which new colonists might move, and conditions evolved under which the Prussians as a people were in time to disappear. This time the rebelling Prussians could have peace only by surrendering their freedom. The order made treaties with individuals and separate groups whom it treated according to their recent behavior. Those who had remained loyal to the order—these were for the most part the Prussian nobility—were established as landowners under German law, intermediate between the German nobility and the peasantry. Those Prussians who had persisted in the revolt lost their freedom. They were made virtual serfs on the estates of Germans, Prussians, high churchmen, and the order. By the end of the thirteenth century, reconstruction in the form of large-scale German colonization and Germanization was ready to begin.

The Prussian and Livonian conquests were completed together. A temporary settlement of the German-Russian issue was made at the same time. Before Albert of Livonia's death, attempts had been made to bring the Kurs and the Zemgals into the western Christian fold. The Kurs had taken advantage of the order's defeat at Saule to revolt, and the Zemgals had revolted the year before the order's defeat at Durben (1260). Both were put down after fierce repressions. Peace with the Kurs was not established until 1267, and only after the foundation of a castle at Goldingen. Mitau (1265) was used as a fortified center against the Zemgals, who were not actually crushed until 1290, and then driven into Samogitia rather than subjected.

The union of the Livonian Brothers with the Teutonic Knights had given great impetus to plans for expansion against the Russian principalities. After 1237, the Germans had moved north and south of Lake Peipus, northeastward into Watland, Ingria, and possibly Karelia, establishing a fort at Kaporje, and southeastward, capturing Irboska (Izborsk) and then Pskov (1240). This eastward expansion against Novgorod had been cut short, however, when Alexander Nevski of Suzdal retook Kaporje (1241), Irboska, and Pskov (1242), and on April 5, 1242, had set a limit to further expansion in this direction by defeating the order in the bloody battle on Lake Peipus.

This setback had not put an end, however, to papal dreams looking to a union of the Russian church with western Christianity and a common struggle against the Mongols led by the Teutonic Knights. The papacy had been much encouraged when the Lithuanian prince Mindoug had become a Christian (about 1251), in order to ward off attacks of the order upon his country. It had promptly taken Lithuania under its special protection, provided it with a bishop, and had bishop Heidenric of Kulm crown the new Christian prince-king. It had moreover set up a new archbishopric of Prussia (1245), which it entrusted to an ambitious prelate from the Bremen chapter, Albert Sürbeer, who was also made a papal legate for Russia and Galicia. In return for union with the western church the Russian princes were offered assistance against the Mongols.[4] Indeed, in 1260 the papacy had gone so far as to give the Prussian master command of a campaign against these pagan invaders, and the order was to have all lands taken from resisting Russians and Mongols. But the actual character of the Baltic crusade at the moment, and the theocratic pretensions of Rome, did not attract the Lithuanian or Russian princes. The defeat of the order at Durben had led Mindoug to return to paganism (1262) and to ally with Alexander Nevski against the Germans, but the alliance did not work well; in any event, both princes died the following year. Further plans of the western church for incorporating the Russians came to nothing.

In Prussia the German branch of the order continued to expand westward. It took unprincipled advantage of the dispute between the dukes of Great Poland and the margraves of Brandenburg over eastern Pomerania to acquire this whole area with its important city of Danzig (1308–1310). The subsequent acquisition of the Werder region from the duchess of Kujavia cut off all immediate hope of

---

4. On the Mongols and the papacy see above, chapter XV.

Poland for access to the sea. The purchase of the Neumark from Brandenburg (1402) would help to strengthen the western approach to Prussia, at the cost of precipitating war with Poland-Lithuania.

The early stages of the conquest in both Livonia and Prussia had brought German noble and bourgeois colonists into these lands. Bishops and cathedral chapters, in addition to military orders, had been set up as the over-all directors of this movement. When the actual conquest was over (about 1290) a heavy stream of peasant colonization began, but only to Prussia, where for sixty years peasants—chiefly from Silesia, Lower Saxony, Westphalia, Meissen, and the Elbe-Saale area—poured in in sufficient numbers to form some fourteen hundred village settlements with a total population estimated at 150,000. For as long as the German towns at home were unable to absorb the surplus rural population, this stream continued populating trans-Elbia more heavily, as well as colonizing Prussia. When the German towns in the late fifteenth century began to absorb the surplus, the Teutonic Knights would find it necessary to encourage Polish peasants from Masovia to come into the wilderness of southern and eastern Prussia and the Masovian lake district, and to bring Lithuanian peasants into the area about Memel. In addition to colonization from Germany proper there was, of course, a good deal of internal movement from older to newer colonial areas. In Livonia, however, the Germans formed a thin upper crust of aliens unsupported by peasant colonization from home. Thus Prussia was actually Germanized while Livonia was not.

The peasant colonization of Prussia was a movement carefully planned by the central authorities of the order and turned over to the individual commanderies (sing. *Komturei*) for execution. To bring in the German peasant, their commanders, as well as German landlords, bishops, and chapters, employed a special type of professional developed by this eastern frontier, the locator, or colonizing agent. For a price, the locator guaranteed to bring in and to set up a peasant village. He recruited the peasants, surveyed the village fields, allocated the plots, and organized the government of the village community. For this service he received an allotment of village land larger than the peasant's (usually one-tenth of the whole), the position of village judge and overseer (*Schulze*), and often the ownership of the mill or inn. The ordinary Prussian village set up by the locator consisted of about sixty hides of forty-two acres each to provide for a population of some eighteen or twenty peasant families. Each peasant held from two to three hides, with the remainder going to the locator and the church.

The German peasant moving eastward to Prussia with his superior agriculture escaped the limitations of the manorial system at home. He moved out to an area where he was unquestionably a free man, cultivating a larger amount of land on a rental basis only, and free to leave his holding as and when he saw fit. He colonized more thickly where the Prussians had been wiped out or diminished by warfare. Yet there was turned over to him land to drain and forest to cut down, hard work that he was willing and able to do. Prussians who had remained loyal in the course of the thirteenth-century revolts were given land and status equivalent to those accorded the German immigrant (the so-called large and small Prussian freemen), and in rare instances their peasant communities might profit from an extension to them of German law. For the most part the Prussian peasant was unfree and held his much smaller plots of land by rent and labor services. He was in fact reduced to an agricultural proletariat that would be unable to survive the wars of the fifteenth century. After 1400, when the Prussians and Germans were about equal in number, the former were to be gradually absorbed into the German immigrant mass.

In 1309, when eastern Pomerania was being incorporated into the order's lands, the grand master Siegfried of Feuchtwangen moved the center of the order's administration from Venice, where it had been since 1291, to Marienburg in Prussia. For about a century after this date the order continued to expand its holdings by purchase, if not by the conquest of pagan peoples. It perfected an efficient administration of the lands, the like of which is hard to find in fourteenth-century Europe, and the purpose of which was chiefly to build up its own economic and political power, rather than to nourish neophyte natives in the faith, or even to expand this faith. If indeed the combination of Christian monk and knight was originally incompatible and unfortunate, a century of conquest made it more so, and, except in superficial aspects, transformed the order from a religious into a political and economic institution, in effect a state, and thus prepared for its collapse in competition with the other states of the Baltic area.

Christian Europe never failed to concern itself with the propriety of conquering pagans and imposing Christianity upon them. The enemies of the order did not permit it to. When it became obvious, in the cases of Samogitia and Lithuania, that even this justification for the European support of the order was a sham, the moral basis for its position disappeared. It became clear also that however efficient its political administration it really did not know how to govern, for it succeeded only in antagonizing those very Germans whom it encour-

aged to come into the area. It remained indeed an institution of the
German aristocracy, organized to provide for a small number of its
younger sons, living as the political, economic, and social elite of a
state composed of natives and German colonists. It was accordingly
repudiated by both its external and its internal enemies. Prussian,
Baltic, and German, these hostile forces were well established by the
end of the fourteenth century.

The sovereign powers granted to the order by the empire were in
the hands of the grand master, resident at Marienburg and elected to
his office for life by a chapter-general of the order. He shared his
authority with a deputy, the grand commander (*Grosskomtur*), and
with the heads of the chief departments, the military (*Ordensmar-
schall*), the hospital (*Spittler*), the commissary (*Trapier*), and the
treasury (*Tressler*). Together these five formed the council of the
grand master. The local administration was in the hands of provincial
masters (*Landmeister* of, for example, Greece, Italy, Germany, Prussia, and Livonia) and, in some cases, of regional commanders (*Land-
komtur*, as of Kulm). The ordinary unit of administration was the
commandery (*Komturei*) governed by a commander (*Komtur*) and a
convent consisting of at least twelve brothers. More remote commanderies were governed by advocates (*Vögte*) without convents;
within the commandery the *Waldamt* contained the forest lands
available for colonization. The trade of the order was in the charge of
the two chief agents (*Gross-Schäffer*) at Marienburg and Königsberg.
There were also masters of the mint and directors of the post. The
whole business of the order was soon reduced to written reports
centering in the chancery at Marienburg and still preserved in remarkable archives. In Prussia the order shared its sovereignty over the land
with four bishops (Kulm, Pomesania, Ermland, and Samland) and
they with their respective chapters. Of these only Ermland was not
incorporated into the order; that is, its chapter was not composed of
priests of the order and its bishops, therefore, were not necessarily
members of the order. In Livonia, on the contrary, there were no
incorporated bishoprics, and the Livonian branch never quite succeeded in overcoming the preponderance of the bishops which Albert
had originally impressed upon the Livonian settlement. Hence the
interminable feud between the archbishops of Riga and the order, a
feud leading to constant open warfare, and at one point to the pagan
Lithuanian defense of the archbishop and city of Riga against the
Knights. The archbishop's Livonian suffragans were Dorpat, Leal-
Ösel, and Kurland. The bishop of Reval was, until 1346, a suffragan
of Lund, in Sweden.

The chief cities of Prussia and Livonia were members of the Hanse, and as such enjoyed its privileges in northern and western Europe, carrying western goods not only to Prussia and Livonia, but to Silesia, Poland, Bohemia, Hungary, Lithuania, and Russia, and carrying from these through the Baltic ports to the west the raw materials, timber, timber products, and furs of these countries. The order, itself treated as a virtual member of the Hanse, was a major source of its security, but as the sovereign of the Prussian and Livonian Hanse cities it often found itself at odds with them. This position became more delicate when, on the authority of a falsified papal privilege, the order itself engaged in trade on its own behalf, and therefore in competition with its own towns and other members of the League. This trade was centered in the *Gross-Schäfferei* in Marienburg and Königsberg, the former specializing in the export of grain and the latter managing the order's monopoly in amber. The order carried on its large and lucrative trade through an extensive organization within and without Prussia. Such a practice, however, caused fundamental discontent on the part of the Prussian and Livonian towns which found themselves discriminated against by their own rulers, the order, on behalf of the latter's trade. The grain from the order's depots could by exception go to the west when that of the towns could not. Indeed, the order went so far as to take over for itself the income (*Pfundzoll*) collected by the towns to pay for their participation in the Scandinavian wars of the Hanseatic League. Not only did the order use its grain surplus (in part the payment of its native and German subjects) to engage in an extensive and forbidden trade, but it employed its monetary surplus (in part the taxes of its subjects) in banking operations and the purchase of rents.

Like many another important Englishman and European of his day, Chaucer's "parfit gentil Knyght . . . hadde reysed in Lettow" as well as in "Pruce" and "Ruce." By the end of the thirteenth century the completed conquest of Prussia, Kurland, and Zemgalia brought the Knights into direct contact with the last remaining pagans in this area, the Lithuanian tribes of Samogitia and the Lithuanians themselves. If the two branches of the order were to be able to coöperate with each other effectively inside Prussia and Livonia or against Lithuania, it was necessary that the Samogitian gap between Prussia and Livonia be closed. This the order was never able to do for any long period and indeed never tried very seriously to do. It preferred to keep this pagan neighbor as some justification for its existence as a crusading order and to expand against Christian neighbors (eastern Pomerania, Werder, Danish Estonia, Gotland, Neumark). After a desperate peasant revolt, the Danes in 1346 sold Harrien and Wier-land to the Knights.

The order was in no position to think of conquering or colonizing the powerful Lithuanian state of the fourteenth century. But across the wilderness separating Prussia from Lithuania, operating from fortified centers on the Niemen and Memel, it could conduct raids into Lithuania and thus act as host to a western chivalry anxious at this late date to fight the pagan and to gain knighthood as a reward. Thus there came to be organized from Livonia, and more numerously from Prussia, the notorious Lithuanian raids, a belated caricature of the western crusading spirit. There were two regular Prussian raids annually in summer and winter. They were initiated with elaborate festivities which the Knights prepared in Marienburg for their most distinguished guests. For his "Tanz mit den Heiden" in 1377 duke Albert of Austria came with two thousand knights and his own poet. The raids provoked furious counter-raids across the Livonian and Prussian borders, raids making the colonization of the Prussian wilderness practically impossible. The real spirit behind the raids is revealed by the fact that the order did not stop them when the Lithuanians became Christian.

The latter event was a condition for the dynastic union of Poland-Lithuania formed by the marriage of the Lithuanian grand duke Jagiello to the Polish queen Jadwiga in Cracow (February 1386) and the coronation of Jagiello as Vladislav II, king of Poland, on March 4 of the same year. A further condition of this union was that Jagiello should undertake to recover for the Polish crown eastern Pomerania and Kulmerland. A halt was thus called to further German expansion eastward, both in theory by removing the justification of crusading war against the heathen and in practice by uniting to recover from the Knights lands not completely colonized. German colonization had penetrated the towns but only barely touched the countryside of eastern Pomerania. In Kulmerland large elements of the Polish nobility and peasantry had maintained themselves. Thus the advance of the Knights as the instrument of German rather than Christian expansion precipitated a kind of national reaction among those who had suffered from this expansion and who were cut off from future expansion to the Baltic, the Russian princes of Novgorod and the Polish-Lithuanian nobility. The order had reached the limit of its power.

If the dynastic union of Poland-Lithuania of 1386 was an external threat to the order, the formation of the Lizard League (*Eidechsen-*

gesellschaft, 1397) was an internal one. It was organized among the nobility of Kulmerland by George of Wirsberg, the commander of Rheden, and Nicholas of Renys, to defend the local privileges of the region against the order's encroachments. From the beginning it was friendly to Poland. It envied the independence of the Polish nobility with respect to both taxation and justice. These events obliged the order to prepare for war by forming alliances with west Pomeranian and east German princes able to furnish the aid of mercenary troops. In a war against Christians, the order could not expect sufficient crusading aid from the west. The acquisition of Samogitia from the new grand duke of Poland, Vitold, in 1398 and of the Neumark in 1402 helped to bring on the war. The abandonment of Gotland (taken in 1398 from the Mecklenburg pirates) to Sweden in 1407 meant a conservation of resources for the oncoming struggle. A revolt in Samogitia helped to precipitate it. When it came (1409), bringing a motley army of Poles, Lithuanians, Samogitians, Czechs, Russians, Galicians, Mongols, and Cossacks down the right bank of the Vistula, it was more than the order could withstand.

The main battle came near Tannenberg, at Grünwald, on July 15, 1410. What promised to be a brilliant German victory turned out to be a disastrous defeat, what Treitschke calls "the first signal victory gained by the Slavs over our nation." In the course of the battle the contingent from Kulmerland under Nicholas of Renys deserted, and when it was over, the grand master Ulrich of Jungingen, the chief officials of the order, many of the commanders, and some two hundred of the order's eight hundred knights lay dead on the field. From Tannenberg the troops of Vladislav and Vitold swept on to Marienburg, hoping to engulf the order in total disaster. Yet an eight weeks' siege of the order's chief fortress could not break the defense of the commander and future grand master Henry of Plauen. The Polish army withdrew, permitting the order to retake most of the territory and towns originally lost. The treaty which ended the war (the first treaty of Thorn, February 1, 1411) was thus, on the face of it, not disastrous for the order, though it lost Samogitia and Sudavia to Lithuania for the lifetimes of Vladislav and Vitold, while the Dobrzyn area and a large war indemnity went to Poland. Those Prussian towns which had sought to make separate peaces with the enemy were harshly treated. The burgomasters of Thorn and Danzig, together with Nicholas of Renys, were beheaded.

Tannenberg was, however, much more serious for the order than the first treaty of Thorn reveals. It obliged all classes in Prussia—the nobility, the bourgeoisie, and the Prussian and German peasantry—to answer the question of whether they were willing to pay the cost of restoring to the order sufficient power to withstand future attacks. For Tannenberg had not settled the political issues between the order and its neighbors. Their promise to Prussia was war, continuous war, until the order should be so weakened that it could not thwart the Baltic ambitions of its enemies. The economic consequences of Tannenberg were serious enough. The order's treasury was exhausted, and so to pay the huge war indemnity new and unpopular taxation was necessary. Indeed, the grand masters immediately resorted to a debasement of the coinage. After 1410 the foreign trade of the *Gross-Schäfferei* at Marienburg and Königsberg was ruined. The campaigns of 1409–1410 had devastated the order's estates, with the result that a surprisingly large percentage of them became and remained uncultivated. Indeed, after 1410 the population of Prussia declined.

The economic consequences of war hurt the order's subjects no less than itself. They could avoid constant war for the future either by means of an accommodation with Poland-Lithuania or by restoring to the order its former strength. The order had not built up in Prussia, among either Prussians or Germans, the loyalty necessary to call forth this support. To an important section among all classes in Prussia the order's sway had become an alien occupation by relatively few squabbling German aristocrats for whom it was worth sacrificing nothing. Indeed, since Prussia no longer needed the order, it was worth sacrificing much to get rid of it.

In the years following Tannenberg, therefore, the order had its last chance to win over its subjects by removing the sources of complaint that had created the *Eidechsengesellschaft.* It failed to do so. The Prussian towns had come to look upon the freedom of the Hanse towns in much the same way as the Prussian nobility looked upon the independence of the Polish nobility. The order had not learned how to associate the nobility and townsmen with itself in the government of Prussia. It did not learn how to do this in the first half of the fifteenth century, in spite of constant demands and many attempts. The representatives of the Prussian nobility and towns, in their almost regular meetings, kept demanding that the grand master share his authority with some kind of *Landesrat,* and that he permit some kind of appeal from the arbitrary violence of the order's officials and the arbitrary appropriation of income from the towns (*Pfundzoll*) for the order's treasury. The very condition of the order itself inspired no respect. The constant deposition or resignation of the grand masters; the outrageous insubordination of lesser officials, leading to conspiracy and murder; the flagrant importation into the order of the tribal disputes of the German aristocracy, between Swabians and Franconians, for example, or Rhinelanders and West-phalians; and finally the separatism in the order, the desire of the Livonian branch and the German bailiwicks to free themselves from the grand master—all this pointed to serious incompetence. The chief purpose of the Knights had in fact long since disappeared, and the order itself was constantly assailed before councils of the church (Constance) and the imperial and papal courts.

Under these circumstances it is not surprising that the spirit of revolt contained in the earlier Lizard League grew after 1410. Under the leadership of men like John Czegenberg and Hans von Baysen and supported by towns like Danzig and Thorn, it took final shape in the powerful Prussian League, formed on March 14, 1440, at Marien-werder by some fifty-three nobles and eighteen towns of western Prussia. The efforts of this League to come to terms with the order after 1440 were unavailing. The order sought rather to have it dissolved by both emperor Frederick III and pope Nicholas V. When the imperial decision for dissolution was made (December 1453), the League chose rather to fight and started the civil war that was to cost the order its independence, or as Treitschke has put it, to bring about "this unnatural state of affairs that Slavs should rule Germans." After occupying most of the order's fortifications, the League sent Hans von Baysen to Cracow to negotiate terms of surrendering Prussia to king Casimir IV of Poland. The Polish declaration of war against the order came on February 22, 1454. The document incor-porating Prussia into Poland was completed on March 6, and three days later Hans von Baysen was made the governor of Polish Prussia.

The final struggle between the order and Poland and the Prussian League lasted until 1466 (the Thirteen Years' War). It was largely an unedifying struggle between the mercenary forces of each side. With no money to pay the wages of its troops (Danzig supplied most of the money for the troops of the League), the order was obliged to turn over its towns instead, and Polish-Prussian League victories were won by buying these towns from the order's mercenaries. Thus on June 4, 1457, after the grand master Ludwig von Erlichshausen had been removed on the previous day never to return, Marienburg was delivered to Poland for a very high price. The taxes which Prussian towns such as Danzig, Thorn, and Königsberg levied on their citizens caused furious revolts of protest. When the end came (second treaty of Thorn, October 19, 1466) the order lost to Poland Kulmerland and eastern Pomerania, including Thorn, Kulm, Danzig, Marienburg, the town of Elbing, and the bishopric of Ermland. The rest of Prussia, including the important sections of the commanderies of Christburg, Elbing (without the town of Elbing), Osterode, Balga, Brandenburg, Königsberg, Ragnit, and Memel, were to be retained by the grand master as a fief held of the king of Poland. It was provided also that half of the order must thenceforth consist of Poles. The second treaty of Thorn thus separated what was called in the 1930's the Polish Corridor to the Baltic, the less heavily German-colonized West Prussia, from Germanized East Prussia.

The second treaty of Thorn for all intents established the independence of the Livonian and German branches of the order. In Prussia after this date the grand masters were able to undertake the colonization of the wilderness with the aid of Polish and Lithuanian peasants, but they were unable to prevent the deterioration of the status of both the German and Prussian free peasants to a position of virtual serfdom. Unable to pay in cash the mercenaries they had brought to Prussia, the Knights had to reimburse them with lands, and thus enlarged the original class of noble colonists with further members of the aristocracy from which these mercenaries came. Through its policy of selling to the nobility lands it could not cultivate, the order lost its predominant position as a landholder in a state now largely agricultural. The flight of the peasants to the remaining towns—in an effort to escape the pressure of an aristocracy struggling to restore the ruined economy by creating large commercially managed estates—was stopped only by binding the peasant to the soil and then imposing upon him additional labor services. The order thus deepened the hatred of the peasantry.

It would finally attempt to save itself by associating the grand mastership with the petty dynasties of Germany. In 1498 the Wettiner Frederick of Saxony would be elected grand master, to be succeeded in 1511 by the Hohenzollern Albert of Brandenburg-Ansbach. Albert would bring the order in Prussia to an end in 1525 by transforming it into a hereditary duchy of Prussia, to be held by the Hohenzollerns as fiefs of the Polish crown. The dissolution would take the form of a treaty with king Sigismund I of Poland, and it would not be made until Albert, after consulting with Martin Luther in 1523, decided, together with many of the Knights, to become Lutheran. The Prussian knights would offer little resistance to this transformation; as administrators of property formerly belonging to the order they would join the ranks of the Prussian Junker aristocracy.

The Livonian branch of the order would manage to prolong its

existence until 1561, because of the energy of its provincial master
Walter of Plettenberg (1499–1535) in saving Livonia from Russia. It
was to end like the Prussian branch. The last master of Livonia,
Gotthard Kettler, would be permitted to transform Kurland and
Zemgalia into a secular duchy of Courland with its capital at Mitau,
to be held by Kettler and his family under the suzerainty of Poland-
Lithuania. The remainder of Livonia would be incorporated into
Poland-Lithuania as the principality of Transdaugava. Its extent,
however, would by then have been reduced by neighboring states
struggling for that control of the Baltic which the order had failed to
establish: by a Denmark which had acquired the estates of the bishop
of Ösel; by a Sweden which had taken Reval; and by a Russia which
had taken Dorpat and eastern Estonia.

XVII

THE CRUSADES
AGAINST THE HUSSITES

The Hussite wars, which lasted throughout much of the third and fourth decades of the fifteenth century, had many aspects, but primarily they were the violent expressions of a great revolution, one of the first in the chain of European revolutions which produced decisive changes in the structural character of European societies. This first great upheaval also had the aspect of a civil war in which

The series of Hussite wars, one important aspect of the Hussite revolution, is probably the greatest event in Czech history and has therefore been an object of a vast literature in Czech historiography. It has also been treated to some extent in other languages, especially in German, in French, and, more recently, also in English. In Czech the first modern substantial treatment came from the pen of the greatest of 19th-century Czech historians, František Palacký, in vol. II, parts 1–3, of his *History of Bohemia* (in several Czech editions and a German one in 1851); it is still valuable. This is even more true of Palacký's basic source publications, such as *Urkundliche Beiträge zur Geschichte des Hussitenkrieges* (2 vols., Prague, 1873; repr. Osnabrück, 1966), giving letters and documents in German and Latin, and *Archiv český*, especially the early volumes published by Palacký between 1840 and 1872, containing only Czech material. Of later Czech publications the most important are the fourth volume of V. V. Tomek's huge *Dějepis města Prahy [History of the city of Prague]* (2 vols., Prague, 1899), in fact more a Bohemian than merely a Prague history; as well as the same author's *Jan Žižka* (Prague, 1879; also in German translation); some of the large literature specifically on Žižka will be mentioned in the footnotes. In the 20th century the main publications in Czech are O. Frankenberger, *Naše velká armáda [Our great army]*, relating only to the events of the Hussite Wars (3 vols., Prague, 1921); J. Pekař, *Žižka a jeho doba [Žižka and his time]*, a work that goes beyond the personality of Žižka and touches upon the whole Hussite Revolution (4 vols., Prague, 1927–1933); R. Urbánek, *Lipany a konec polních vojsk [Lipany and the end of the field armies]* (Prague, 1934); a number of works by Jos. Macek, especially *Husitské revoluční hnutí [The Hussite revolutionary movement]* (Prague, 1952; translated into many languages, including English), *Tábor v husitském revolučním hnutí* (2 vols., Prague, 1955–1956), and *Prokop Veliký [Prokop the Great]* (Prague, 1953); and finally F. M. Bartoš, *Husitská revoluce [Hussite revolution]* (2 vols., České dějiny, part II, vols. 7 and 8; Prague, 1965–1966).

In other languages the most important contributions on the Hussite wars in the 19th century were in German. For the crusades, and especially for the role of emperor Sigismund, the first (to some extent still valuable) is J. Aschbach, *Geschichte Kaiser Sigmunds,* vol. IV (Hamburg, 1845). Far more valuable, and still highly valued by Czech historiography, is F. v. Bezold, *König Sigmund und die Reichskriege gegen die Hussiten* (3 vols., Munich, 1872,

the people of Bohemia and Moravia, the majority Czechs, a minority Germans, were involved. To some extent the term "civil war" could also be used in relation to the other dependencies of the Crown of St. Wenceslas, the duchies of Upper and Lower Silesia and the margraviates of Upper and Lower Lusatia. Their ethnic composition, however, was overwhelmingly non-Czech, with a German majority and a Slavic minority—Polish and Lusatian Sorb. On the whole these northern dependencies belong among the countries whose rulers would try to intervene, for political and religious reasons, in Bohemian events.

1875, and 1877). No other work has presented the material as clearly and objectively, although Bezold did not as yet have all today's source material at his disposal; e.g., *Deutsche Reichstagsakten,* vols. VIII and IX (Munich, 1867–1886; repr. Göttingen; cited as *RTA*). Excellent also is Bezold's more ideological work *Zur Geschichte des Hussitenthums* (Munich, 1874). In the framework of later German history the work of A. Bachmann, *Geschichte Böhmens,* vol. II (Gotha, 1905; mainly chapters 4–6, pp. 142–342) is of some value, but since then few contributions were made in German until the important production by F. Seibt, *Hussitica: Zur Struktur einer Revolution* (Cologne and Graz, 1965), and his concise but highly reliable contribution, "Die Zeit der Luxemburger und der Hussitischen Revolution," in vol. I of the *Handbuch der Geschichte der böhmischen Länder,* ed. K. Bosl (Stuttgart, 1967). In French the most valuable work is Ernest Denis, *Hus et la guerre des Hussites* (Paris, 1878). In English the history of Hussitism, with special emphasis upon the religious background and the influence of the papacy, was first presented in a careful treatment by Bishop Mandel Creighton, *A History of the Papacy from the Great Schism to the Sack of Rome* (London, 1899), vol. II, especially chapters III to VI (pp. 171–321). A more popular treatment was Count [F. H. H. V. von] Lützow's *The Hussite Wars* (London, 1914). In 1955 appeared *John Žižka and the Hussite Revolution* by the present author (Princeton; repr. New York, 1969), which puts its emphasis, in the phase from 1419 to 1424, on political and military events, whereas H. Kaminsky's valuable work *A History of the Hussite Revolution* (Berkeley and Los Angeles, 1967) puts its emphasis on ideological and to some extent sociological issues and accordingly begins with the prehistory of the Hussite wars, also ending in 1424. The huge bibliography on Hussitism and Wyclifism before the wars cannot be mentioned here, but will be found in the bibliographies of some of the listed works, including the two mentioned last.

In addition to the original source works mentioned in relation to Palacký, a few other basic source works should be mentioned. There are the contemporary chronicles called "Staří letopisové čeští" (Old Czech Annalists), published in three versions, first by Palacký (reprinted by Charvát in 1941, and completed by publishing in 1945 parts which had been eliminated by Nazi censorship); the *Vratislavský rukopis* (Breslau edition) published by F. Šimek (Prague, 1937); and the *Křižovnický rukopis* published by M. Kaňák and F. Šimek (Prague, 1959); the last two are somewhat more thoroughly exact than the combined versions of Palacký. Of the greatest importance is the "Chronicle of Lawrence [Vavřinec] of Březová," without which our knowledge of the Hussite revolution, especially during the early phases, would be far more scanty; see J. Goll, ed., *Fontes rerum Bohemicarum,* V (Prague, 1893), 327–541. In the same publication, the "Chronicle of Bartošek of Drahonice" (pp. 589–628) is valuable. Of considerable importance also, as a contemporary report of the history of Sigismund, is the account by his financial counselor and biographer Eberhart Windecke, published by W. Altmann under the title *Denkwürdigkeiten zur Geschichte des Zeitalters Kaiser Sigmunds* (Berlin, 1893). For further original sources and secondary works see the bibliographies in the works by H. Kaminsky and F. G. Heymann mentioned above.

But the Hussite wars were not only among the first of the great European revolutions, and as such a step across the threshold of the modern period; they can also be considered an important late medieval event: almost the last of the great crusades in the traditional form of a war proclaimed by the papacy and meant to save Christendom from the dangers of eastern invaders or European heretics. There were, it is true, some still later crusading attempts, such as the catastrophic campaign of Varna of 1444,[1] the successful defense of Belgrade in 1456, and the abortive crusade planned for 1464 by pope Pius II. But the Hungarian and Roman king Sigismund, the official "sword-bearer" in the crusades against the Hussites, had seldom paraded as a crusader in his many collisions with the Turks after his early and disastrous defeat at Nicopolis in 1396. Similarly, the "second Hussite wars" of 1468 and later, fought against the Czech king George of Poděbrady by several of his neighbors, did not, though strongly supported by the papacy, take the official form of a sequence of crusades, characteristic of the campaigns directed against Bohemia in the years 1420, 1421, 1422, 1427, and 1431.

It is impossible, within the framework of this chapter, to discuss in any detail the origins of the Hussite revolution.[2] Elements of Czech nationalism directed against the strong position of the Germans, especially in the cities and monasteries of Bohemia and Moravia; mass dissatisfaction with the dominating and wealthy representatives of the church; and the movement for a far-reaching religious reform— these three motive forces, often combined with one another, occasionally colliding, can probably be considered the main causes leading to the revolution.[3] This ideological and political development had already gone quite far by July 6, 1415, when John Hus, for some years the most influential and most popular leader of the reform movement, was burned at the stake in Constance.

Hus had already, in 1412, come out against an enterprise officially termed a crusade: the campaign of pope John XXIII against king Ladislas of Naples. The financing of this "crusade" was partly based on the sale of indulgences, and against this Hus had inveighed even more strongly, thus antagonizing the Roman papacy.[4] Pope John,

---

1. A chapter on the crusade of Varna is planned for volume V of this work, in preparation.

2. The history of these origins is presented most thoroughly in Howard Kaminsky's *A History of the Hussite Revolution* (cited as *Revolution*).

3. But see Seibt's questioning of these three motive elements in his *Hussitica*, pp. 5–6, 183 ff.

4. M. Spinka, *John Hus, a Biography*, (Princeton, 1968), pp. 132 ff.

indeed, was deposed on May 29, 1415, by the same council that was to have Hus burned so soon afterward. But Odo Colonna, who in 1417 was to replace John and his two rival popes, Gregory XII and Benedict XIII, and thus as pope Martin V effectively put an end to the Great Schism, was as determined to fight the ideas of Wyclif and Hus as his predecessors had been.[5] Accordingly, early in 1418 he explicitly charged cardinal John Dominici with the preparations for a crusade.

Sigismund, at this stage, was not yet decided. Having taken from his older brother Wenceslas IV the dignity of "king of the Romans," he had long had his eyes also upon the kingdom of Bohemia, which Wenceslas had retained. During the years between 1415 and 1419 he tried to gain more influence on the Bohemian situation, but found himself in a difficult position. Hus had been executed in spite of the safe-conduct issued in his favor by Sigismund, and a large part of the Czech people, including many of the great lords, considered the king responsible for this. As early as September 1415 a passionate declaration in defense of Hus and his reforming ideas was signed by 452 prominent members of the Czech nobility, lords as well as knights. In response, the leaders of the Council of Constance put some pressure on Sigismund to act immediately, using force against this dangerously growing religious rebellion in the center of Europe; indeed, this seems to have been the origin of the idea of a great crusade against the Czech "heretics." Among the most active of the Catholic Czech prelates trying to suppress the rebellious movement in Bohemia was John "the Iron" (Jan Železný), bishop of Litomyšl, whom the council tried to make its legate to Bohemia. Sigismund was not yet willing to undertake any militant enterprise himself. Instead, he tried to persuade his brother Wenceslas to take vigorous action. For a time he had little success, since neither Wenceslas nor his queen Sophia was willing to take a strong position against the steadily growing reform movement. Above all, the statement of Prague University in March 1417 upholding the right of laymen to receive communion under both kinds, not only the bread but also the wine, made a vast impression,[6] even though it went directly against the decisions of the Council of Constance.

During the early months of 1419, however, Wenceslas, partly under the pressure of his brother Sigismund, came to believe that his royal position would be in danger if he permitted the Hussite deviations,

---

5. Bartoš, *Husitská revoluce*, I, 48–49.
6. Kaminsky, *Revolution*, p. 266.

and especially the usage of the chalice, to become general. To prove his orthodoxy Wenceslas took the important but dangerous step of ejecting the Hussites (or "Utraquists") from all but one or two churches in Prague.[7] This act of religious-political reaction led immediately to the open outbreak of a militant upheaval. One of the most vigorous of the revolutionary leaders, the former Premonstratensian monk John Želivský, on July 30 led a crowd of his followers to the city hall of the New Town of Prague, whose administration had only recently, on the king's order, been taken away from Hussites and put into the hands of reliable Catholics. What began as a parley turned into a bloody struggle in which most of the members of the city council were killed by being thrown out of the windows—the first "defenestration of Prague."[8] This open act of rebellion infuriated king Wenceslas so much that he suffered a sequence of strokes, culminating in his death on August 16. The heir to his Bohemian kingdom, on the basis of normal dynastic succession, would be none other than Sigismund of Hungary, king of the Romans.

Sigismund, obviously, would do everything in his power to realize this claim. As a good orthodox Catholic he could hardly avoid trying to lead the people of Bohemia back toward orthodoxy. There was strong antagonism against him as the man considered responsible for the deaths of John Hus and his friend Jerome of Prague, although he repeatedly denied any such responsibility. But he was not without support among the Czech nobility, including even some men who had disapproved of the way in which he had handled the trial of Hus at Constance but who felt that they ought to be loyal to their "natural" king. An even more solid basis of support for Sigismund existed in a number of cities, not only those which, like Cheb, Kadaň, Chomutov, and Ústí in northwestern Bohemia, or Jihlava, Znojmo, Brno, and Olomouc in Moravia, were essentially German in character, but also cities in central Bohemia with a mixed population such as Kutná Hora, east of Prague, Bohemia's greatest center of silver mining and one of the main sources of regular income for the crown. Even if Sigismund had had no other important reason to march, as soon as possible, toward the very center of Bohemia, the chance of increasing his income from the Kutná Hora silver mines would have been of considerable interest to this ruler who was almost always in financial difficulties. And Sigismund was advised to do just that by some of the leading Catholic barons.

7. *Ibid.*, pp. 267–268.
8. Kaminsky, "The Prague Insurrection of 30 July 1419," *Medievalia et humanistica,* XVII (1966), 106–126.

Yet he decided otherwise, partly under the influence of his Hungarian advisers. Having left Germany at the beginning of 1419 and arrived in Hungary in February and at Buda in August, he was now involved in renewed trouble with the Turks. They had gained a rather firm foothold in Bosnia and had invaded Hapsburg (Habsburg) territories such as Styria. It seemed to him urgent first to safeguard Hungary, especially since, at the time when he learned of Wenceslas's death, the Hungarian nobility had already made preparations for defense against the Ottomans. Whether there was—as is frequently assumed—a battle near Nish in Serbia is somewhat doubtful.[9] However, it seems that Hungarian war preparations resulted temporarily in a reduction in Turkish activity, probably even in an armistice. Thereupon Sigismund finally decided in favor of establishing control over his new realm. In mid-December he arrived at Brno in Moravia, to which a diet of the estates of the Bohemian crown had been summoned. It was to be followed, in January 1420, by a Reichstag of the Holy Roman empire, to be held—somewhat unusually—also within the borders of the Bohemian realm, in Breslau, the leading city of Silesia.

It was high time if Sigismund wanted to gain the throne of Bohemia. The situation there was complex: splits had occurred not only between the Catholics and the party of reform, but also between two wings of the Hussites. In Prague, as well as in some regions south of it, a really revolutionary, radical movement, later generally called Taborite, had become more and more active and widespread, while other, more conservative groups, without giving up the claim for lay access to the chalice, were reluctant to deviate strongly from the Roman creed and ritual. Among the latter were some of the Utraquist masters at the University, as well as some prominent members of the high nobility, among whom the leading figure was the lord high burgrave Čeněk of Wartenberg, the chief official of the kingdom.[10] He had been one of the 452 signatories of the protest note sent to Constance after Hus's execution, and in the following years he had done everything in his power to arrange for the ordination of Utraquist priests on his own estates and elsewhere in Bohemia.

The queen-dowager Sophia—whom Sigismund had, upon learning of his brother's death, appointed regent of the kingdom—had, still in

---

9. Aschbach, *Kaiser Sigmund,* II, 404–412.
10. Pekař, *Žižka a jeho doba,* III, 43 ff., and Bartoš, *Husitská revoluce,* I, 38 ff.

August 1419, in close coöperation with Čeněk, summoned a diet in Prague. With the agreement of all three estates (lords, gentry, and royal cities), the diet had formulated certain demands to which they insisted Sigismund accede before he would be accepted as king of Bohemia.[11] Among these demands was that for the freedom within the kingdom of communion under both kinds (*sub utraque specie*, hence the term "Utraquists" for its proponents). Moreover, the king must agree to intercede with the pope for the freedom of Hussite worship, and urge him to desist from any further denunciation of the Czech nation as heretical. Finally, he was required to promise to help toward reforms in the church, particularly regarding simony, and to disregard all papal bulls against Bohemia until a final accommodation between Sigismund and the Bohemian estates had been achieved. The king was also asked to avoid giving any offices to people (mostly Germans) who had been exiled under king Wenceslas, nor should foreigners, especially Germans, be given any administrative offices in the cities of Bohemia wherever Czechs were available. Sigismund never directly answered these demands.

During the months from August to December 1419 the leadership in Prague had undergone some weakening, primarily because John Žižka, formerly the captain of king Wenceslas's palace guard but soon the most active and most successful military leader of the revolutionary wing in Prague, had left the city. He had been in conflict with the city authorities ever since the latter had returned the great Vyšehrad castle, earlier occupied by Žižka's troups, to the royalists. For some time Žižka had occupied the city of Pilsen, but he had eventually been forced to evacuate this important western center as well. Early in 1420 he established himself in the newly built fortress-town of Hradiště, thenceforth called Tábor. This new revolutionary center in the south of the country was, for a long time, to play a nearly decisive role in the Hussite movement.[12]

For Sigismund the existence of a radical wing seemed, in a way, to be a considerable advantage. Its hostility not only to him as king but also to the whole institution of the Catholic church would strengthen the support that he could expect from Rome. But he was not satisfied with struggling against radicalism. He was determined also to destroy those less radical deviations which might make his situation difficult. And in executing this policy he immediately aroused great

---

11. *Archiv český*, III, 206–208; also Bartoš, *op. cit.*, pp. 72 ff., and Heymann, *John Žižka and the Hussite Revolution*, pp. 70 ff. (cited as *Žižka*).

12. Heymann, *Žižka*, pp. 87–88, 94 ff.; Kaminsky, *Revolution*, pp. 334 ff.; and especially Macek, *Tábor v husitském revolučním hnutí*, in both volumes.

hostility. While he hoped to split the Czech Utraquists, his harshness tended in fact to unite them.

At first he seemed to be doing well, concluding a compact with Čeněk of Wartenberg, whose control of the Hradčany, the main castle largely dominating the left bank of the Vltava (Moldau) river, gave the king a potentially strong position in relation to the city. For a time it seemed that not only Čeněk but also other leading barons, including lord Ulrich of Rosenberg, who had formerly been Čeněk's ward and was to play a most important role later, could enjoy access to the chalice as well as the benevolent understanding of the king. This tolerance seemingly prevailed also at the December (1419) diet of the Bohemian estates at Brno.[13] To this assembly the city of Prague sent representatives, who asked forgiveness for earlier acts of resistance and promised to do homage, but requested the right to defend publicly their understanding of the faith, especially the chalice for the laity. Sigismund's answer was harsh. He demanded, before anything else, the complete removal of all recent structures for military defense. On their embassy's return, the majority of the people of Prague felt that they had no choice but to obey the king. If he had immediately gone on to Prague, even with his relatively modest army, he would have had a chance of gaining an easy and perhaps decisive victory.

Sigismund, however, against the advice of the Czech Catholic nobles, decided that he would not go to Prague until he had held the Reichstag in Breslau and could afterward approach the Bohemian capital with a truly large and powerful army. It was a fateful decision, but one which he made rather too early. While in Brno he had seemed to be willing, especially in his discussions with the nobility, to consider the issue of the chalice as an open question. Immediately upon his arrival in Breslau his whole attitude changed.[14] In a substantial correspondence with some of the German cities in Bohemia and Lusatia during February and March the king urged preparation for war against the "heretics."[15] Finally, on March 17, 1420, the papal legate, Ferdinand, bishop of Lucena, read from the pulpit the text of the bull *Omnium plasmatoris domini,* [16] which solemnly proclaimed a crusade with the task of exterminating all "Wyclifites, Hussites, other heretics, and those favoring, accept-

---

13. Heymann, *Žižka,* pp. 105–107.

14. For the main events at the Breslau Reichstag, see *RTA,* vol. VII.

15. Palacký, *Urkundliche Beiträge zur Geschichte der Hussitenkriege,* I, 15 ff. and later (cited as *U.B.*).

16. *U.B.,* I, 17–18.

ing, and defending such heresies," with the usual addition that men
fighting this war for the cross would thereby expiate all their sins.
The bull was dated March 1 and had been sent from Florence (where
pope Martin at this time had taken refuge)[17] directly to Breslau
upon the request of Sigismund. The king added, in several specific
orders, the command that the armies entering Bohemia should kill
anyone practising such heresy and not immediately recanting.[18]
Sigismund's intentions had been expressed even earlier (on March 6)
when he ordered the public execution of twenty-three guild members
of Breslau who had, in July 1418, rebelled against the patrician city
council.[19] Another victim of an especially cruel public execution
was a Prague citizen called Krása who refused to recant his support
of the teachings of Hus.[20]

These actions were carefully watched at Prague, as well as by the
one leading Czech nobleman from whom Sigismund had expected
support as long as he himself and his family were not prevented from
taking communion under both kinds: Čeněk of Wartenberg. The
baron was treated, by the king, with extreme friendliness,[21] but as
soon as he left Breslau he joined in a solemn declaration which the
councillors of the Old and the New Town[22] had issued after a
meeting on April 3,[23] making it clear that Bohemia's capital no
longer considered meek surrender to Sigismund's demands desirable.
On the contrary, Prague strengthened its defenses, and sent a message
to all cities of the kingdom condemning the crusading bull as "a vile
and venomous serpent's egg hatched by this church who had long
before shown herself to be not a mother but a vicious stepmother to
the Czech people." Besides joining with the Prague Hussites, radicals
as well as moderates, in their opposition to Sigismund's Breslau
policy, Čeněk added the considerable power of the Hradčany castle.
Having renounced all fealty to Sigismund, he sent out on April 20 a
manifesto to all Bohemians and Moravians in which the king was
characterized as "the great enemy of the Czech kingdom and nation
who wants cruelly to exterminate it."[24] In consequence, three days

17. Creighton, *The Papacy,* II, 138 ff.
18. *U.B.,* I, 24–25, 28–29.
19. There is no proof that the rebellion of 1418 had any connection with events in
Bohemia. For details see Bartoš, *Husitská revoluce,* I, 85–86, and the sources cited in his
note 88.
20. Lawrence of Březová, "Kronika husitská," ed. Goll, in vol. V of *Fontes rerum
Bohemicarum* (Prague, 1893), pp. 358–359 (cited as Březová).
21. Windecke, *Denkwürdigkeiten zur Geschichte Kaiser Sigismunds,* ed. Altmann (Berlin,
1893), pp. 130–131 (cited as Altmann, *Windecke*).
22. Březová, p. 363.
23. Heymann, *Žižka,* pp. 112–113.
24. *Archiv český,* III, 210.

later a majority of the lords and knights sent their challenge to the king. This, surely, was not the development which Sigismund, by his crusading policy, had intended and expected.

He did not, however, give up his attempts to divide the Hussite population of Bohemia. He hoped that he could still gain support among the high nobility, and astonishingly enough after a very short time won over Čeněk, as well as his young friend Ulrich of Rosenberg.[25] Thereby Sigismund regained not only the Hradčany castle but also a much greater freedom of action. At the head of an army of about 20,000 men he had meanwhile moved, early in May (1420), to Hradec Králové, an important, thoroughly Czech and Hussite city which however did not at this stage dare to resist. From there he went on to Kutná Hora, where the patricians and the German miners as well as many refugees, mainly Catholic clerics, greeted him enthusiastically. Meanwhile, temporarily protected by an armistice between the city and the royalist barons, including Čeněk, another Prague embassy went to Kutná Hora.[26] Its reception by Sigismund was largely a repetition of what had happened five months earlier in Brno: the Prague representatives promised surrender and even willingness to make some breaches in the walls provided they could retain access to the chalice. The king, angrily, went one step farther than he had at Brno: not only must all barricades and fortifications be removed, but the people of Prague must surrender all their weapons to the royalist garrisons of the Hradčany and Vyšehrad castles, thus leaving themselves completely defenseless.

The report given by the members of the Prague city embassy upon their return home made it clear that, unless a totally hopeless unconditional surrender (and with it the loss of access to the chalice) was decided upon, the only alternative was armed resistance to the king. There was a united decision for the latter, but it was clear that Prague had to secure support from other parts of the kingdom. This came from more than one region, but none as strong and effective as that sent by the fortress-town of Tábor, some 9,000 men (perhaps including noncombatants) led by John Žižka. Without him and his army the fate of Prague, and with it of Hussite Bohemia, might have been quite different.

The crusading army which Sigismund led to Prague was large and included contingents from many countries. One of our best informed

---

25. Heymann, *Žižka*, pp. 117–118; Pekař, *Žižka a jeho doba*, III, 43 ff.; and Březová, pp. 365 ff.

26. Heymann, *Žižka*, pp. 120–121, and also the sources cited there in note 27.

sources, the chronicle of the Prague city secretary Lawrence of Březová,[27] names among the members of the crusading army various German-speaking groups, all the ethnic groups of the kingdom of Hungary, other southeastern peoples like Bulgarians, Serbians, and Wallachians, several representatives of the Slavic east like Poles, Russians, and Ruthenians, and finally from the west the Dutch, Swiss, English, French, Aragonese, and other Spaniards. (The omission of Italians was certainly a slip.) Březová's claim that this army grew to 150,000 men is surely much exaggerated; on this issue a source from Sigismund's camp, the chronicle of his financial adviser and biographer Eberhart Wendecke, speaks of 80,000, still a rather high figure though perhaps not quite impossible. In any case even this, for medieval times, enormous army would have had difficulties in conquering a strongly fortified city like Prague, with a population of some 40,000 inhabitants (the emigration of Germans and anti-Hussites was roughly offset by the addition of the troops of the Czech allies). The history of the later Middle Ages shows hardly any examples, with the remarkable exception of Constantinople, of the conquest of great, well-defended cities. But the very size of the population—and 40,000 was, for the time, a large population—could have its disadvantages, if the aggressor succeeded in maintaining a truly effective siege which would prevent the city from being sufficiently supplied, particularly with food.

The situation of Prague was dangerous. The two great castles were in the hands of the royalists, and attempts of the Hussites to conquer the Hradčany before the crusading army established itself outside the city had failed. The Hradčany dominated the accesses to the west and southwest, the Vyšehrad those to the southeast, while the main body of the crusaders' army had built a large tent city to the north across the Vltava on what today is called the Letná. Prague, therefore, was open to the outside world only as long as the roads to the rich valley of the upper Elbe were free. In the neighborhood of Prague they were dominated by a longish hill east of the city, called the Vítkov, whose southern slopes were covered with vineyards. If this hill could be occupied and upheld by the crusaders, it would indeed make the siege effective. Sigismund planned the occupation of the Vítkov as his first and most promising stroke, but Žižka anticipated the king's intentions and acted accordingly.[28] He ordered the building of a small but well situated bulwark consisting

---

27. Březová, pp. 383–384; also other sources given in detail in Heymann, *Žižka,* pp. 136 ff.

28. See, on the battle on the Vítkov, *ibid.,* chapter 9 (pp. 136–147).

of two wooden forts, whose main purpose was to keep the defenders in constant readiness and to warn Žižka's Taborite army in case of an attack.

This offensive strike did indeed occur, on July 14 (1420), when several thousand troops, largely cavalry from Meissen and Thuringia, as well as some from Hungary, crossed the Vltava river at its eastern-most point and attacked the Vítkov hill from the east, at its least steep slope. While they occupied part of the fortifications, Žižka with his Taborite soldiers climbed the southern slope and made a surprise flank attack. The crusaders fled after a number of them, apparently about five hundred, had been killed. Žižka followed up his victory by building stronger fortifications on the hill.

The defeat on the Vítkov was, in itself, only a limited one. Most of the crusaders' army had not seen action and might still have been used in renewed assaults. However, the Czech Catholic lords in Sigismund's entourage tried to convince him that, after the failure of the Vítkov battle, he would have a better chance of winning Prague by political means. They persuaded him not to bombard the city with heavy artillery, as he had planned, and assured him that within one month Prague would be in his hands. When the king expressed doubts, they promised him that as a first step he would be crowned by archbishop Conrad in St. Vitus's cathedral on the Hradčany. In Sigismund's eyes this seemed to be a substantial success: the official coronation which, traditionally and in the eyes of the high nobility, would make him legally the king of Bohemia. The coronation took place on July 28, 1420.

This, however, soon proved to be the only success that Sigismund would achieve during this phase of the crusading war against the Hussites. The general morale deteriorated rapidly. The crusaders did, whenever they had a chance, catch and kill people who were sus-pected of being heretics, regardless of their age and sex, whereas the Czechs were, with rare exceptions, careful to spare the lives of women and children all through the Hussite wars. However, since the killing and burning took place in the crusaders' camp within sight of the Praguers, who were separated from the enemy only by the limited width of the Vltava river, the Czechs decided to burn sixteen German prisoners within view of the enemy. In the crusaders' en-campment, during an unusually hot summer, epidemics killed men and horses in large numbers. The German princes and their soldiers became even more impatient, and the suspicion spread that the king was in secret agreement with the Hussites.

For Sigismund the situation became doubly difficult. His cash reserves for the payment of the German and Hungarian mercenaries had already been exhausted, and his earlier expectation of getting money or precious metals from the hoped-for conquest of Prague was soon completely disappointed. To deal with the danger of open rebellion among the soldiers he recklessly confiscated all the precious metals and jewelry to be found in the cathedral of St. Vitus and in other churches on the Hradčany,[29] which barely sufficed to pay his debts. By the end of July the German princes returned to their lands, and Sigismund himself raised the siege and went, with his now limited army of about 16,000 men, to Kutná Hora. His only significant military enterprise in the following weeks was a strong attempt to relieve the Vyšehrad castle, to which the Praguers had laid siege in September, since in royal hands it could still have military as well as, perhaps, political influence. However, the king, as usual, was late in his movements, waiting for troops expected from royalist nobles of Moravia. On November 1 a battle took place between Sigismund's army and a Hussite army[30] led by lord Hynek Krušina of Lichtenburg, the military leader of a growing brotherhood in eastern Bohemia called Orebites (after Mount Horeb), whose structure was rather similar to that of Tábor. Krušina had been asked to take over the leadership of the Prague forces when the Taborites under Žižka had left for the south in late August; Tábor sent only a small contingent to help in this struggle near Prague. The battle was won by the Hussites, with even heavier royalist losses than at the battle on the Vítkov, especially among the Moravian nobles.

Meanwhile the Taborites had made considerable gains in southern and western Bohemia, and had weakened especially the position of Ulrich of Rosenberg, Sigismund's strongest ally in Bohemia, who was forced to conclude an armistice on terms dictated by Žižka. At the beginning of 1421 the king made another attempt to regain a broader basis in Bohemia, especially in the west where he received some German support. However, when the combined armies of Tábor and Prague approached, he did not dare risk another battle. He moved eastward, making a wide detour through northern Bohemia, and in March he left Bohemia and Moravia altogether. For some time minor fights occurred, skirmishes between Hussites and Catholic Bohemians and invasions from neighboring territories, including Silesia and Lusatia, both dependencies of the Bohemian crown.

On the whole, however, with Sigismund out of the country and even the offshoots of the first great crusade withering in utter failure,

29. Březová, p. 396.
30. Heymann, *Žižka*, pp. 175–180, with a source bibliography in note 22 on p. 178.

the position of the Hussites was enormously strengthened. The surrender of the Vyšehrad was followed, a few months later, by that of the Hradčany. Prague had been able to hold out with the two great castles still in enemy hands, so its defenses were now even stronger. The royalist party, realizing this, and seeing Žižka and the Taborites still active, especially in southern and western Bohemia, hardly dared to show itself. It was characteristic that Čeněk of Wartenberg, concerned for his rich possessions and no longer expecting the king to win out, turned back, for the second time, to the Hussites.[31] He was not the only leading baron to do this, but it was perhaps of even greater significance that Conrad of Vechta, the German-born archbishop of Prague, who only recently had crowned Sigismund king of Bohemia, joined the Hussite side and declared his adherence to the "Four Articles of Prague."

These articles were increasingly the unifying basic charter of the revolutionaries.[32] They demanded freedom of preaching, the offering of the chalice to laymen, the restriction of the priesthood to its religious duties without any power or wealth, and the proper punishment of all public mortal sins. The Four Articles were also solemnly confirmed by a great diet which was held at Čáslav in early June 1421 and which, through the strong representation of the estates of Bohemia and Moravia, had all the characteristics of a national assembly.[33] This meeting deposed Sigismund, claiming that he had "never been accepted as king," and that he was a "notorious despiser of the sacred truths proven from the Scriptures" and "the deadly enemy of the honor and the people of the Czech nation." The assembly also appointed a regency council of twenty men representing the three estates, including especially the cities of Prague and Tábor.

The council was given only a limited time for operation since there was already a strong hope that grand duke Alexander Vitold of Lithuania, a cousin of king Vladislav II (Władysław, in Polish) Jagiello of Poland, would accept the crown of Bohemia, which was offered to him in repeated negotiations. The seeming willingness of Vitold, not completely shared by Vladislav, was largely a reaction to the fact that at the Reichstag of Breslau king Sigismund had, in arbitrating between Poland-Lithuania and the order of Teutonic Knights over the fate of the province of Samogitia, decided essentially in favor of the Knights. For a rather long time Sigismund was considered an

31. *Ibid.*, p. 217, and Březová, p. 483.

32. Heymann, *Žižka*, chapter 10 (pp. 148–163), and Bartoš, *Do čtyř artykulu* (Prague, 1926).

33. Heymann, "The National Assembly of Čáslav," *Medievalia et humanistica*, VIII (1954), 32–55; also in *Žižka*, pp. 220–240; and cf. Seibt, *Hussitica*, pp. 167–176.

enemy by the two Jagiellon princes, who were therefore willing to help his opponents, yet they tried not to annoy the pope, claiming that their real goal was to lead the Czech schismatics back to proper Roman orthodoxy.[34]

Pope Martin, however, did not believe that such a peaceable solution of the Hussite movement was either possible or desirable. From the beginning he had been convinced that the only way to deal with the "Wiclefistae et Hussitae" was to destroy them. Originally there was hardly any difference in this respect between the pope and Sigismund; again and again the Hussite spokesmen, in as wide a representation as that at the diet of Čáslav, accused the king of having the complete destruction of the whole nation as his goal. Since eventually he wanted to rule over the Czechs, have them work for him, and tax them, we may doubt that he really planned such a total annihilation. In fact, under the influence of the Czech barons in his entourage, he had refused to go as far in his attack upon Prague as the German princes had demanded. As a result, a lack of confidence in Sigismund's determination to destroy the "heresy" developed steadily in several circles in the empire, even among some of the German electors. There was also in Rome, if not exactly suspicion of Sigismund's orthodoxy and devotion to the church of Rome, then at least doubt as to his true intentions. From then on the holy see, far from giving up the idea of an effective crusade, strengthened the propaganda for this policy.

It cannot be denied that Martin V himself was a strong personality with a clear consciousness of what he considered to be his sacred duty.[35] His many briefs written to those involved in the intended crusades—king Sigismund, the electors, king Vladislav of Poland, grand duke Vitold of Lithuania, the grand master of the Teutonic Knights, Michael Küchenmeister of Sternberg, duke Albert of Austria, and a good many others—are generally impressive.[36] He also chose, as his helpers and especially as his legates, men of a rather high caliber, such as bishop Ferdinand of Lucena, who had accompanied Sigismund as legate during the whole phase of the 1420 crusade. He was present at the siege of Prague, and during the last phase, shortly

---

34. J. Goll, *Čechy a Prusy ve středověku,* (Prague, 1897), pp. 151 ff.

35. Pastor, *Geschichte der Päpste,* I (7th ed., Freiburg, 1925), 223–224, 290 ff.; also Creighton, *A History of the Papacy,* II, 135 ff., 163.

36. These can be found in the Vatican Archives. Few have been published, but 511 are calendared in K. A. Fink, "Die politische Korrespondenz Martins V. nach den Brevenregistern," *Quellen und Forschungen, Preussisches historisches Institut,* XXVI (Rome, 1935–1936), 172–244.

before the battle on the Vítkov, he was involved in an attempt to discuss the Four Articles with some of the leading masters of the University, especially the very nearly orthodox John Přibram, with the purpose of convincing the more moderate Utraquist theologians that they ought to return to the orthodox faith.[37] It may be that this action, even though it ended in complete deadlock, annoyed the pope, and it seems that he also held his legate at least partially responsible for the whole pitiful failure of the first crusade. He decided to replace bishop Ferdinand as legate to the empire with a man of more diplomatic experience and a higher clerical rank, cardinal Branda of Castiglione.[38]

The fact that, after the failure of the 1420 crusade, another campaign was started at a relatively early date was due largely to the energy of Branda, and to the considerable influence he managed to gain, especially upon the German prince-electors. Sigismund had to appear eager for renewed action, if for no other reason than to prove that the rumor of his secret understanding with the heretics was wrong, as in fact it was. At the end of November 1420 the king sent out letters to princes and cities suggesting the holding of a Reichstag, which after many difficulties met in April 1421 at Nuremberg, but in Sigismund's absence and with little success. The initiative slipped, with the strong support of the legate, ever more clearly into the hands of the Rhenish electors—the three archbishops of Mainz, Trier, and Cologne, and the palsgrave Louis of Wittelsbach—who on April 23 concluded a union directed against the Hussites and promising support for the king in his actions,[39] subject, however, to a prior understanding based on the consensus of the four electors. A subsequent meeting of the electors at Wesel in May tried, with rather limited success, to gain promises of military support from the imperial cities, a procedure which was repeated with greater results at Mainz in June. Finally, in July, the planning that had begun at the previous meetings was set down in detail at a conference at Boppard on the Rhine. By this time a powerful alliance had been created which could put considerable pressure on Sigismund. While the king did not take part personally in any of the negotiations, he sent to Mainz and Boppard, as his special representative with far-reaching powers, his chancellor George, bishop of Passau. The bishop expressed to the electors the full agreement of the king, as well as his

37. See, on this, Pekař, *Žižka*, III, 69–72, and Heymann, *Žižka*, pp. 157–163.
38. See, on him, Pastor, *Geschichte der Päpste*, I, 283 ff., and Bartoš, *Husitská revoluce*, I, 148.
39. *RTA*, VIII, 28 ff.

promise to coöperate fully with the German princes so as to make the new crusade as effective and powerful as possible.

There was a prelude to the crusade proper: an invasion on the part of Frederick of Wettin, margrave of Meissen, into northern Bohemia, where a Hussite army led by John Želivský was trying to conquer the Catholic and ethnically German city of Most. The collision of the two armies on August 5 (1421) led, for the first time, to a painful defeat of the Hussites,[40] and might have helped toward the success of the crusade if there had been sufficient coöperation among their opponents. The Meissen army left Bohemia when they were informed that a Hussite force was approaching, led by Žižka, although the Taborite general had recently lost his eyesight. Meanwhile the far larger German army had crossed the Bohemian border in the region of Cheb in late August. The total number was alleged to be at least 125,000 men, as usual an exaggeration.[41] After considerable destruction and indiscriminate killing of all Czechs except small children,[42] detachments of the army occupied the towns of Kadaň and Chomutov. The main body, however, moved eastward in the direction of Prague, but stopped about September 10 to besiege the city of Žatec. The expectation was clearly that Sigismund with his predominately Hungarian troops was about to start his own invasion of Bohemia, thus forcing the Czechs to defend themselves in several regions of their country at the same time. He procrastinated, to the bitter disappointment of the German forces and their leaders, the princes and bishops. The siege of Žatec, though it was a far smaller city, began to resemble the siege of Prague the year before.[43] After enduring three weeks of siege and several ineffective assaults, the Žatec garrison undertook a successful sortie. Early in October the news came that a strong Czech army, again with Žižka as one of the leaders, was on its way to attack the besiegers of Žatec. The result was, strangely enough, a frantic retreat from Žatec, during which the Czech garrison pursued the Germans and inflicted considerable losses upon them. The German princes, who had done little to stop the stampede, blamed Sigismund's absence for this second debacle, whereas the king on his part was most disappointed and angry to hear of the retreat when he finally invaded Moravia in October, only a short time after the German crusading army had left Bohemia.[44]

40. Heymann, *Žižka*, pp. 248–253, with contemporary sources in notes 12 and 13.
41. See, *ibid.*, p. 273, note 20.
42. See the report from Nuremberg to Ulm, *U.B.*, I, no. 134, p. 144.
43. Heymann, *Žižka*, pp. 274 ff.
44. *U.B.*, I, 159–163.

There is no doubt that Sigismund favored the strategy of combined operations from west and east, but he wanted to have an army of overwhelming strength, and this took more time than he had originally expected. He might have been wiser if, under these circumstances, he had stopped the whole campaign and replanned it for the next year, but he had, by then, spent a good deal of money on the enterprise. So he decided to invade the kingdom with an army which was still very strong, and not to worry about the lateness of the season.[45] Though he maintained the role of supreme commander, he left many of the decisions, and especially the tactical details, to the Florentine condottiere Philip Scolari (created by Sigismund count of Ozora), usually called Pipo Spano, who had proved his gifts as a general repeatedly in fights with the Turks, and who was in command of the Hungarian troops. Among them, as usual, light cavalry was to play an important role. It was Pipo Spano who, still in the first half of October (1421), entered Moravia, joining up in its northern region with a small army raised by John "the Iron," the vigorous anti-Hussite bishop of Olomouc (formerly of Litomyšl), and soon afterward also with troops from Silesia and Lusatia led by bishop Conrad of Breslau and some other Silesian princes.

Sigismund himself, who had entered Moravia on October 16, moved very slowly, gaining some additional strength through the arrival of Austrian troops under his son-in-law Albert of Hapsburg. It appears that at this stage the king had altogether an army of about fifty thousand, almost one third of whom consisted of Hungarian cavalry. He might have had a good chance now, since even after the withdrawal of the German crusaders in the west the situation of the Hussites was far from good. The Taborites under Žižka were engaged in a difficult struggle with the royalists organized in the so-called "Landfrieden" of Pilsen, while the Prague forces, at the time commanded by a young and inexperienced squire called John Hvězda of Vícemilice who had been made captain-general by Želivský, had limited strength and would hardly have been able to deal with an army the size of Pipo Spano's.

But Sigismund, far from acting fast, tried first to establish his position in Moravia by political means. He summoned a diet at which a majority of the Moravian nobility, including those who had taken part in the assembly of Čáslav, renounced their previous actions.[46] They were also forced to condemn the Four Articles as heresy and to

45. See, for this whole exciting campaign, *ibid.*, chapter 18 (pp. 286–306), with references to the main sources.
46. *U.B.*, I, 166–171.

swear never to adhere to them again. Sigismund did not gain anything by this policy, since nothing was so apt to unite the Hussites as a renewed attack upon the Four Articles. Moreover, the king spent almost four weeks in Moravia, mainly in Brno and Jihlava, both Catholic and mostly German cities, before he finally entered Bohemia. His first goal, understandably, was Kutná Hora. This city had previously joined the Hussites within the Prague league of cities, but the German-Catholic majority of the city's population hoped to be liberated by the king, who had managed to form strong contacts with the leading Germans within the city. The royalist army, however, took another twenty days to march from Jihlava to the region of Kutná Hora (a distance of less than fifty miles), still expecting more reinforcements. En route, the crusading army, especially the Hungarians, committed as much destruction, killing, and raping among the Czech people as possible.[47]

The events from late October to mid-December 1421, as Sigismund's activities became known throughout Bohemia, were bound to unite the Hussites, as always happened when their land and faith seemed in real danger. Just as they had done at the time of the 1420 crusade, the Praguers asked for help from the Taborites, and again Žižka responded promptly. The enthusiasm of his reception in Prague established his position as commander-in-chief of all Hussite troops. Again the old soldier anticipated the king's intentions, and marched with his combined forces—the field armies of Taborites and Orebites and the troops and militias of Prague and of the cities under its suzerainty—toward Kutná Hora.[48] When the royal army approached from the west on December 21 Žižka stationed his own troops outside the gates, and there was a prolonged fight which does not seem to have had any important consequences. Žižka was not aware that in the meantime the Kutnohorian Germans, in an understanding with the royalists, had planned a massacre of all Hussite Czechs in the city, after which they opened the gates to such royalist troops as had been able to approach the city at nightfall. By this bloody maneuver, planned and directed by Pipo Spano, the Czech army found itself suddenly surrounded. The situation looked nearly hopeless, but Žižka managed, by using his guns as field artillery,[49] to

47. Březová, pp. 531–532.

48. See, on the battle of Kutná Hora, in addition to the general sources J. Durdík, *Husitské vojenství* (Prague, 1953), pp. 145–148, and Heymann, "Kutná Hora–Malešov, Dva problemy topografie Žižkových bitev [Two problems of the topography of Žižka's battles]," *Československý časopis historický*, no. 9 (1961), pp. 75–81.

49. This is the first case of the use of field artillery which can be proved from the sources. See Heymann, *Žižka*, pp. 294–296, which cites the sources.

force a breach in the enemy lines and to escape from the iron ring. There was no pursuit; Sigismund was, at the moment, satisfied with having gained Bohemia's second most important city, and was even so sure of himself that he sent a Polish nobleman as an emissary to Prague demanding its surrender. He was not successful.

Meanwhile the king, who had established his headquarters in Kutná Hora and was feeling close to victory, had to find quarters for his army. It was an early and cold winter and he could not expect his soldiers to camp in the open. There was not enough space for the army in Kutná Hora, and so its contingents were distributed among the villages in the region roundabout, with a somewhat stronger unit established at the large village of Nebovidy halfway between Kutná Hora and Kolín.

It was at Kolín that Žižka had halted after his retreat and planned his further steps, including a good deal of additional recruiting, especially in the Orebite region, where he was very popular. In early January 1422 his numerical strength was no longer so inferior to that of the royalists, and he had his troops together whereas the royalists were dispersed. On January 6 Žižka began his own offensive, striking first at the royalist troops at Nebovidy. Completely unprepared, they could not resist long, and soon were in headlong flight. Žižka's army, in hot pursuit, approached Kutná Hora. Sigismund, seeing himself in danger of being surrounded there, decided to leave immediately, and since the Bohemian and Moravian barons whom he asked to defend the precious city refused, he ordered that it be evacuated and put to the torch. Before the order could be obeyed Žižka's army arrived. While the fleeing German Catholics tried to keep up with the king's army, the Czech inhabitants returned. In the further retreat southeastward Sigismund's reassembled army made an attempt, on January 8, to stand up to the Czechs at the little town of Habry, but this battle, again, ended with a complete defeat of the royal troops. The next stop was at the city of Německý Brod, on the Sázava river near the Moravian border. Here another attempt at resistance was made by the king's army; it was sufficient to cover his own retreat, freeing him from personal danger,[50] but after a short siege the Hussites took and burned Německý Brod. The royalist army, having lost several

50. The "Old Annalists" (in Palacký's edition, see the most recent issue, "Staří letopisové čeští," in *Dílo Frant. Palackého,* II [Prague, 1941], 61) reports that no fewer than 548 Hungarian soldiers drowned when attempting to cross the Sázava river by riding across the current. This was taken as a fact by most historians, including the present writer (*Žižka,* pp. 301–302). At a later visit to this neighborhood I became rather doubtful about it, since the Sázava river below Německý Brod (now Havlíčkův Brod) appeared to me too narrow and too shallow to play the role of a Berezina.

thousand men and nearly all its ample materiel, no longer existed. Sigismund went first to Brno, where he could reasonably feel safe, and soon afterward returned to Hungary. It was the greatest defeat he had suffered since the catastrophe of Nicopolis a quarter of a century before.

Žižka's victory over Sigismund, after the failure of the first part of the 1421 crusade in western Bohemia, not only had great military significance; it also influenced the political situation. Ever since the spring of 1420, there had been negotiations between the Hussites and king Vladislav of Poland and grand duke Vitold of Lithuania, concerning the possibility that one of them might accept the crown of St. Wenceslas.[51] Vladislav had never actually contemplated such a step, even though he felt bitter about Sigismund's decision against him and in favor of the Teutonic order. Vitold, on the other hand, seriously considered the offer to become king of Bohemia, although he was unwilling to approve the Four Articles, which the Czechs asked him to accept and protect. The Bohemian estates had actually elected (or, as it was called, "postulated") him at a diet held at Kutná Hora in August 1421, when the situation of Hussite Bohemia did not seem promising. A second crusade was imminent, as everybody knew. The fate of the first crusade had not convinced most observers that the second, too, would be a total failure. On the contrary, the pope, his legate, king Sigismund, and the German princes had all been optimistic about the outcome of the impending invasion. Vitold was cautious enough not to burden himself with the military, political, and theological dangers which close coöperation with the "heretics" would entail.

Vladislav went even further, offering Sigismund Polish support against the Czechs if Sigismund would revise his Breslau award. However, this possibility disappeared when a Czech embassy sent to Poland and Lithuania was arrested by the duke of Ratibor and extradited to Sigismund, to the extreme anger of Vitold himself and of a large number of the Polish and Lithuanian gentry.[52] Above all, the second crusade, both the early western part involving the electors and the later part directed by Sigismund himself, left little doubt of Hussite Bohemia's ability to withstand even a large-scale invasion. Vitold now took a step which he had been considering for some time. He declared, in a letter to pope Martin dated March 5, 1422,[53]

---

51. About this and the ensuing diplomatic developments see Bartoš, *Husitská revoluce*, I, 177 ff., and Heymann, *Žižka*, pp. 165–166, 269 ff., 319 ff.

52. *Ibid.*, pp. 320–321, and the documents cited there in notes 6–8.

53. *U.B.*, I, 186 ff.

that from then on he would take the Czechs under his protection in order to lead the schismatics back to the church of Rome, and that for this purpose he was going to send his nephew Sigismund (son of) Korybut to Bohemia as his representative. He did so, but prince Korybut was much less prudent than the grand duke, claiming the country as Vitold's, and presenting himself as the regent representing the "postulated king."

As was to be expected, Sigismund considered this a particularly nasty way of depriving him of his legitimate crown, and he complained bitterly to the pope, feeling that the holy see had not been diligent enough to prevent this step. The pope reacted very strongly with a whole range of letters to Vladislav, to Vitold, to archbishop Nicholas Tramba of Gniezno (Gnesen), and to Sigismund, protesting to the latter his innocence regarding Vitold's step. At the same time the pope again urged the king, directly and through cardinal Branda, to deal with the heretics by means of another, a third, crusade.[54] It was hardly possible for Sigismund not to agree to this plan. But he had been sufficiently burned to avoid any personal involvement this time. He did go so far as to attend a Reichstag which he had summoned to Regensburg, but which the electors, in considerable disagreement with him, had convened in Nuremberg, supported again by the papal legate cardinal Branda.[55] The latter tried his best to concentrate all efforts upon another crusade, but serious difficulty arose from the fact that king Vladislav of Poland had become involved, in mid-July, in another war with the Teutonic Knights. The electors wrote to the king of Poland, demanding that he and his cousin Vitold recall prince Korybut from Bohemia, cease altogether any support to the "heretics," and instead of war against the Teutonic Knights help wage war against the Czechs.[56] Sigismund, who had long encouraged the order to military action against Poland, went farther, and made them the somewhat astonishing promise to lead Hungarian and Silesian troops against the Poles.

The elector least willing to play this game was Frederick of Hohenzollern, margrave of Brandenburg, who had for some time established close ties with the house of Jagiello. He hoped to make this friendship even warmer and politically more promising by a marriage of his son Frederick to Jadwiga, a daughter of Vladislav, who was, at that time, still without a male heir. This approach to Poland was one of the reasons for the bitter feeling of disappointment and even hatred

54. *U.B.,* I, 194–196, 199–214, and *RTA,* VIII, 119–121.
55. *RTA,* VIII, 122 ff., 125 ff., 140 ff.
56. Aschbach, *Geschichte Kaiser Sigmunds,* III, 155–156, notes 25 ff.

which Sigismund, once the warm friend and protector of the Hohen-zollern prince, now harbored toward Frederick. He also held him, perhaps not quite without justification, responsible for the steadily growing distrust and opposition to him among the majority of the electors.[57] But just for this reason, and surely remembering what had happened two decades earlier to his brother Wenceslas at the hand of the electors, Sigismund felt all the more bound to reëstablish, if only on the surface, a tolerable relationship with Frederick of Brandenburg.

Suggestions from some princes that the Germans and Hungarians begin open war against Poland were rejected not only by Frederick and others of his colleagues but above all by cardinal Branda, who never tired of asking for the immediate organization of another crusade against the Hussites. Pope Martin supported him by ordering the German clergy to tax themselves.[58] The hope of financing the whole campaign by the so-called "hundredth penny" met strong resistance among the cities, and instead the diet decided for a so-called taxation "according to the most equal and best," which left a good many principalities and cities more or less free from taxation. Even so the crusading army, while weaker than the preceding one, was respectable, and it was put under the command of an experienced and gifted soldier, Frederick of Brandenburg. On September 4, 1422, in Nuremberg's St. Sebaldus church, Branda presented Sigismund with a banner personally blessed by the pope, and the king passed it on to the generalissimo—with whom he had, at least superficially, reëstablished the old friendship—while a detailed written instruction gave Frederick a great deal of power.[59]

Crusading armies were to enter Bohemia from the north as well as the west.[60] The first was that of William of Meissen, who early in October (1422) succeeded in conquering the city of Chomutov. Lusatian and Silesian forces were to strengthen this army. Toward the middle of October forces immediately under Frederick's command, particularly troops from Brandenburg and from the bishoprics of Würzburg and Bamberg, crossed the border from Tirschenreuth, joining near Tachov with Bohemian Catholics (the "Landfrieden" of Pilsen) as well as the troops of the city of Cheb. Additional forces

---

57. This whole issue is treated well and in considerable detail by Erich Brandenburg in his early book, *König Sigmund und Kurfürst Friedrich I von Brandenburg* (Berlin, 1891), especially in chapter VII, pp. 119 ff.

58. *RTA*, VIII, 181–182.

59. See *RTA*, VIII, 184, and *U.B.*, I, 236 ff. Other sources are given in Bezold, *König Sigmund*, I, 96, 97, note 5.

60. See, for what follows, Heymann, *Žižka*, especially pp. 347–353, notes 21 to 31, with bibliography. The most detailed treatment is in Bezold, *König Sigmund*, I, 90–130.

from German cities, chiefly the armies of the electors of the Palatinate and of Cologne, were to join the western army. Among the
immediate goals was the relief of the Catholic garrison of the great
castle of Karlstein, the only strong fortress in central Bohemia to
have been held by the royalists since the beginning of the struggle.
The castle had been put under siege by Korybut fairly soon after he
had, as Vitold's representative, taken over the regency of Bohemia.

This third crusade, while weaker in manpower than the second, had
at least one advantage at its very beginning: a growing disagreement
within the Hussite camp. Korybut had, in Prague as well as in some
other cities, established a government which intended to eliminate all
the more radical elements. This, of course, was desired by the two
rulers to whom he was, to some extent, responsible, and who tried to
maintain a satisfactory relationship with the papacy. A Bohemia
ruled by the more radical elements, especially by the Taborites and
their adherents in Prague, would never agree to a compromise with
Rome, one of the hopes nourished by Vitold as well as by Korybut,
who at this time seems to have dreamed of a future as king of
Bohemia. The radicals were soon displeased with Korybut's policy,
and on September 30 two of the leading figures of Tábor, lord
Bohuslav of Švamberg and the former captain John Hvězda of
Vícemilice, having established contact with radicals inside the capital,
undertook to enter Prague with their modest forces and to replace
the city government which Korybut had installed with men formerly
led by John Želivský, who had been killed by his enemies the
previous March.[61] The Taborite invasion, apparently undertaken
against the wishes of Žižka, was a total failure, but caused Korybut
to take some of his Czech and Polish forces away from Karlstein,
partly to secure his position in Prague, partly to be stronger in case a
direct combat should result from the crusading invasion. With their
weakened forces the Czechs nevertheless undertook, on October 22,
a full-scale assault which ended in total failure, leading to considerable losses and strengthening the morale of the defenders.

Meanwhile the crusading army achieved very little, largely because
some of the potentially strongest forces, such as those of bishop
John of Würzburg, refused any action, and advised Frederick to give
up an enterprise they considered hopeless. Frederick made an enormous effort to keep the crusading army together,[62] and at least was
able, for a time, to prevent William of Meissen from pulling his forces
out of Bohemian territory. The whole situation can be explained only by

---

61. Heymann, *Žižka,* pp. 344–347.
62. See his correspondence in *U.B.,* I, 238 ff., 260 ff., and II, 499 ff.

the fear that the experience of the first two crusades had left among so many participants. Frederick, as a result, decided to concentrate his still shrinking forces upon the relief of Karlstein, while he and Korybut conducted negotiations for a prolonged truce. The prince sent a substantial embassy led by archbishop Conrad of Prague and a number of high nobles, but the Czechs were not willing to include in the truce Sigismund and the princes and cities of Lusatia and Silesia. Hence Frederick broke off negotiations and returned to Tachov in order to undertake action to relieve Karlstein, only to be informed that in the meantime (on November 8) an armistice had been signed between the Hussites and Karlstein. The chance of a real military collision shrank, as neither side was eager for a battle. Apart from some minor skirmishes (the "daily war") nothing of significance occurred, and before the end of 1422 the third crusade had, as it were, evaporated. While Frederick of Brandenburg had not been able to cover himself with glory, he did, at least, return home without having suffered a smashing defeat. It was the only one of the crusades of this war that did not end with such a catastrophe.

Even so, Hussite Bohemia was, for a longer time than before, left alone; not completely—there were repeated minor attacks across the borders—but to the extent that no powerful strike comparable to the earlier expeditions occurred for a number of years. It could almost be said that this relative safety from invasion jeopardized the Hussite movement. As long as they were under fire from outside, with specific attacks against the political-religious program of the Four Articles, the Hussites, or at least the center and the left wing, tended to coöperate. As soon as they felt fairly safe they began to fight against one another; early in August 1423 such a conflict turned into a civil war among the leading groups of Hussites. The Hussite right, no longer willing to tolerate an increasingly revolutionary development, went so far as to ally itself with Roman Catholic royalists in order to reëstablish, as far as possible, the former feudal structure. A good many among the more conservative masters of the University supported this course, most clearly expressed by the diet of St. Gall, which took place in Prague in October 1423.[63]

But there were differences even within the more radical camp which resulted in John Žižka's leaving his place as commander of the Taborites and establishing himself in eastern Bohemia at the head of the somewhat less radical brotherhood of Orebites.[64] The most

---

63. Heymann, *Žižka*, pp. 395–398 (and the main source in *Archiv český*, III, 240 ff.).

64. Pekař, *Žižka*, III, 193 ff. and (with considerably differing understanding) Heymann, *Žižka*, chapter 22.

important clash between Hussites was the battle of Malešov (June 7, 1424), in which Žižka destroyed a fairly strong army based on a coalition of Praguers, mainly of the Old Town, and some more or less counter-revolutionary members of the nobility.[65] By this victory Žižka established, more solidly than before, his leading role in the Orebite brotherhood, which soon joined up again with Tábor. The dominating position of the two brotherhoods, based on a large number of Czech-Hussite cities, was by and large maintained for the next ten years. No radical change resulted from the return in June 1424 of prince Korybut, who had been recalled by Vitold early in 1423, nor even from the death of Žižka from the plague on October 11, 1424.

The most gifted and influential of the political and military leaders of this new phase was a Taborite priest called Prokop the Great (or the Bald), a worthy successor to Žižka who changed the strategy of the Hussites.[66] From the earlier, essentially defensive actions against the invaders he moved toward a policy of invading the neighboring territories from which previous crusading campaigns had started.

While on the Catholic side the activity of king Sigismund as well as of the German electors and princes was weaker than before, the holy see tried hard to keep the struggle against the "heretics" going. Cardinal Branda had done his best, but the pope felt that even this was not good enough, especially as the legate, at seventy-five, was beginning to weaken physically. In his place Martin V appointed, after a short interim filled by cardinal Jordan Orsini, a man whom he had quite recently (in May 1427) raised to the rank of cardinal: Henry Beaufort, a half-brother of the late king Henry IV of England. The new legate tried to revive the crusading movement by being present at the diets and eventually also in the field. But before there was an effective reawakening of the movement the Czech Hussites and their German neighbors fought a climactic battle which was not technically part of the crusades, the battle of Ústi.[67]

This city, together with a few other places in northern Bohemia, had been pledged by Sigismund to Frederick of Wettin, since 1423

---

65. Heymann, *Žižka*, pp. 409–415, and Frankenberger, *Naše velká armáda*, II, 79 ff.

66. See on him Urbánek, *Lipany;* Macek, *Prokop Veliký*; Bartoš, *Prokop Veliký* (Brno, 1934); and briefly, in English, Heymann, *Žižka*, pp. 457–471.

67. Probably no other battle of this war has received so much attention and literary treatment. We shall name only H. Ermisch, "Zur Geschichte der Schlacht bei Aussig," in *Neues Archiv für Sächsische Geschichte und Altertumskunde,* XLVII (1926), 5–34; E. Kroker, "Sachsen und die Hussitenkriege," *ibid.,* XXI (1900), 1–28; Bezold, *König Sigmund,* II, 81–86; R. Jecht, "Der Oberlausitzer Hussitenkrieg," *Neues Lausitzer Magazin,* LXXVI (1910), 138 ff.; O. Frankenberger, *Naše velká armáda,* II, 115–130; and J. Durdík, *Husitské vojenství,* pp. 152–156.

the elector of Saxony, and had therefore been occupied by Saxon troops. But in June 1426 a strong Hussite army began to besiege Ústí, and the Saxon rulers, with the elector's wife Catherine especially active, sent a large army to raise the siege and safeguard Saxony's possession of this important Elbe town. The Saxon army—until then considered among the best—was certainly larger than the Hussite army of about 24,000 men, under the overall command of Korybut, with Prokop commanding the Taborite forces. Apparently none of the previous battles fought between Germans and Czechs had resulted in losses as catastrophic as the battle of Ústí, even though the assertion, made by German chroniclers, that the German dead numbered 15,000 was probably much exaggerated. Prokop, after the victory, tried to convince the other commanders that this was the right moment to enter Saxony in "hot pursuit" and reduce that country's war-mindedness, but as yet without success.

Even so it seemed likely, in the eyes of the Germans, that the terrible heretics would not wait long before crossing the border. If the idea of destroying the "heresy" was not to be given up for good, preparation for a new crusade could not long be postponed. Modest invasions of Silesia and Austria were undertaken by Czech-Hussite troops in the winter of 1426–1427, and in March 1427 a Taborite army under Prokop defeated an Austrian army, causing it heavy losses, at the Austrian town of Zwettl,[68] midway between Budweis and Vienna. It seemed increasingly doubtful whether the margraviate of Moravia, solemnly presented to duke Albert by his father-in-law Sigismund, could be maintained in Hapsburg hands. In addition, some vague possibilities for an understanding between the Catholic powers and the conservative Hussite elements, rather strongly represented by some of the masters of Prague University and some nobles, collapsed when negotiations with Rome secretly conducted by Korybut were discovered in April 1427. The more determined Utraquists, with John Rokycana at their head, undertook to prevent what seemed to them pure treason.[69] The prominent conservatives, among them the masters at the University who had supported a policy of compromise or even submission, were banished from Prague, and Korybut not only lost his already somewhat enfeebled position as regent but was even imprisoned for several months.

It was not, however, this development which led to the final decision for a fourth crusade. This had already been decided upon at the very beginning of the year, at a rather remarkable meeting at

68. Macek, *Prokop Veliký*, pp. 52–53.
69. Bartoš, *Husitská revoluce*, II, 19–22.

Bamberg of members of the lesser nobility, mainly Franconian, who concluded a solemn alliance against the Hussites.[70] The more detailed arrangements were made at a Reichstag convened at Frankfurt am Main in late April and May (1427).[71] The Reichstag accepted a military ordinance which, in some of its points, showed a remarkable similarity to the type of ordinance issued by Žižka in 1423.[72] The crusade was to be organized in four separate armies, the first containing troops from the Rhineland, Alsace, Swabia, Franconia, and Bavaria; the second from Saxony; the third from the princes and cities of Silesia; and the fourth from the Hapsburg lands and the archbishopric of Salzburg.[73] If all those armies had really been put into the field, they would have formed a powerful force, one which the Czechs would not have found it easy to defeat. But as in the preceding crusades much of the planning remained on paper.

The impending campaign was to be led by the princes, under Frederick of Brandenburg,[74] whose bitter struggle with Sigismund had been terminated early in 1426.[75] Frederick, at this stage, considered a combination of military with diplomatic means, aimed at splitting the Hussite camp. Correspondence exists which shows that suggestions were made to Frederick by some unknown agent, possibly one of the Czech royalists.[76] He was urged to write letters to the cities of Prague, Žatec, and Louny, and also to a number of prominent moderates, trying to win them over to a measure of political rapprochement. This, however, was to go hand in hand with the invasion, to be concentrated upon the town of Slaný, whose supposedly easy conquest would drive the Prague people toward fast and bloodless surrender.

It was odd enough, after the previous campaigns, to assume that such an easy success could be expected, yet to some extent the Brandenburg elector did, indeed, follow the advice. His letter to Prague has survived, together with the answer, while of the correspondence with Žatec only the answer remains.[77] In any case the

70. Bezold, *König Sigmund,* II, 95–97, and *RTA,* IX, 11–14.

71. *RTA,* IX, 41–44.

72. See *U.B.,* I, 503–509, and Žižka's military ordinance, translated into English in Heymann, *Žižka,* pp. 492–497.

73. *RTA,* IX, 41–44.

74. *RTA,* IX, 136–138.

75. See Brandenburg, *König Sigmund und Friedrich I,* pp. 195–200.

76. Published first by Bezold, *König Sigmund,* II, Appendices, pp. 161–163. It is only a draft but the fact that many of its recommendations were followed by Frederick indicate that the letter was indeed received by him.

77. See *U.B.,* I, Frederick's letter, pp. 516–518, as well as the answers of the cities on pp. 519–520 and 522–523.

correspondence emphasized not only the sadness and horrors of the war (which the crusaders were just about to renew) but also the close relationship between the elector and the Bohemian capital as well as the Bohemian king. The Praguers, in their answer, acknowledged Frederick's warm feelings for the city, but also declared that specific proposals for peace had to be submitted to the estates of the realm.

The whole procedure—an urgent call for peace at the moment of starting a massive invasion—is, of course, strange, though not unique. It can hardly be doubted that some prominent men among the more conservative Hussites would have been willing to make very far-reaching concessions—indeed, almost any short of surrendering their insistence upon access to the chalice for laymen. These men had supported prince Korybut in the months preceding the events of the previous April, and their political goals had not radically changed as a result of Korybut's fall and imprisonment. But it was surely a mistake to assume that they would become more amenable under the threat of imminent invasion. On the contrary, past experience showed that the considerable internal differences, occasionally even amounting to civil war, temporarily lost their power as soon as foreign attacks, especially those taking the form of crusades and thereby exposing the country to German and Hungarian armies, threatened the very existence of Hussite Bohemia. This, indeed, would also be the result of the 1427 invasion. There was, as always, a measure of coöperation between the established royalists, such as the Pilsen "Landfrieden," and the crusaders, and a few Hussites went over to the Catholic side, but the majority even of the more conservative Hussites did nothing to support the enemy, and the most important units—the brotherhoods and the city of Prague—were sufficiently willing and well prepared to stand up to the crusaders. They may not have expected that their task would be quite so easy.[78]

Of the four great armies that were supposed to invade Bohemia in July 1427 from the north, the northwest, the southwest, and the south, only two ever appeared, and they were weaker than had been expected.[79] One, led by Otto, archibishop-elector of Trier, with

78. Of the detailed treatments of the 1427 crusade Bezold's is still one of the best: *König Sigmund*, II, 109–122. A later monograph by Georg Juritsch, oddly titled *Der dritte Kreuzzug gegen die Hussiten* (Vienna and Prague, 1900), did not add much to it, but he had the *Reichstagsakten* at his disposal. Among the Czech treatments the best is that by V. V. Tomek, *Dějepis města Prahy*, IV, chapter 14, pp. 366 ff., especially valuable for the political background. The most recent treatment, rather concise, is Bartoš's *Husitská Revoluce*, II, 23–24.

79. See Altmann, *Windecke*, pp. 221–227, and Juritsch, *op. cit.*, pp. 24–25. The com-

additions from the dukes of Bavaria and from Franconian and Swabian cities, crossed the mountains near the still-royalist border city of Tachov and moved eastward toward Stříbro, a town that had been part of the Pilsen "Landfrieden" but had been conquered, with very little resistance, by Taborite troops in September 1426.[80] This town, midway between Tachov and Pilsen on the old highway leading from Nuremberg to Prague, had considerable strategic value for the Hussites, since their capture of it established them in the rear of the forces of Pilsen and the Pilsen "Landfrieden." Some of the leaders of the allied crusaders, with Otto at the head, considered that a quick reconquest of Stříbro would be valuable, and hence decided to concentrate their forces first upon the siege of this small but strategically important place. This decision was made, however, without the knowledge of Frederick of Brandenburg and young Frederick (II) of Saxony (the Saxon elector was ill, but his son and early successor by the same name took over in his father's place). The siege took a long time, and so gave the "heretics" an excellent opportunity for the preparation of their counter-measures.

Frederick of Brandenburg was highly dissatisfied with this strategic decision made without his agreement, and with the consequent delay in marching in the direction of Prague. He sent most of his troops and those of Saxony to Stříbro but himself went to Tachov, claiming illness. Meanwhile, apparently, little was done to compel the early surrender of Stříbro. The crusaders had a rather large number of siege guns at their disposal, but seem to have made very inadequate use of them.[81] And word soon reached the crusaders that a Hussite army was approaching.

What followed was an extraordinary combination of confusion, disorganization, cowardice, and stupidity in the arrangements made by the leaders of the crusade. A trustworthy, though in some details not quite unprejudiced, report was presented to king Sigismund by Frederick of Brandenburg, who should have been the supreme leader but had not really played this role, largely because he was aware of the difficulties, and hence had not taken steps similar to those which had helped prevent any major catastrophe during the 1422 crusade. Frederick's letter, sent from Plassenburg, his castle at the western-

---

bined size of the crusading armies is presented by Bartošek of Drahonice (ed. Goll, *Fontes rerum Bohemicarum*, V, 596) as 80,000 horse and as many infantry, probably an exaggeration.

80. *RTA*, IX, 51–54.

81. See Juritsch, *op. cit.*, pp. 36–38, with the sources, especially "Chronicon veteris collegiati Pragensis" in *Fontes rerum Austriacarum*, VI, 89. Cf. Hans Rosenblüt in *Volkslieder der Deutschen*, I, 295 ff.

most point in his Franconian principality of Bayreuth, was dated
August 24, rather late after the painful events which had begun on
the 3rd or 4th and concluded on the 14th of that month.[82]

In his report Frederick described the first stages of the invasion and
strongly criticized the decision to besiege Stříbro. He then explained
that, having reluctantly joined the southern army, he had fallen ill
and had to seek help from the physicians at Tachov. Meanwhile a
reconnaisance force of cavalry had reported on August 2 that the
Hussite army was approaching in great strength. This led the German
princes to move the siege artillery away from the vicinity of Stříbro
to a hill in the neighborhood where the crusaders would be better
positioned to resist the expected Czech attack. A second order, to
burn the tents of the previous encampment, seems to indicate that a
degree of panic had already infected the commanders, but according
to Frederick's letter it was this step that caused the panic reaction:
"In view of such conflagration," he writes, "a misunderstanding
arose among the common people and the wagon drivers, so that part
of them drove hither and thither and struck at one another, and thus
the army got as far as Tachov, where I and the cardinal of England
were staying, and we were much shocked, as is easy to understand.
Thus all those of us in command and the cardinal got together to
consult, and decided to move up to a mountain near Tachov and
from there to approach the enemy. When we therefore [on the
following morning, August 4] went up to the mountain and looked
for our troops, many of the people had left during the preceding
night, riding on horseback or walking or driving on those wagons that
should have been used to construct a *Wagenburg* [wagon fortress], as
had been planned and ordered; and so many had left and the army
had become so small that the advice was given to the cardinal and the
other princes by most of those present that no attempt ought to be
made to engage the enemy without a *Wagenburg*."

It seems from our other sources[83] that at least two of the leaders
disagreed: cardinal Henry Beaufort and young Frederick, the son of
the elector of Saxony. Both wanted, even with the totally inadequate
forces still at their disposal, to mount an active resistance against the
Hussites. Both offered to fight in the first row of warriors, and could
only with some effort on the part of more experienced men, among
them almost certainly Frederick of Brandenburg, be dissuaded from
what would at this stage have been a totally hopeless enterprise.
Nevertheless the cardinal, believing deeply in the righteousness of the

82. *U.B.,* I, 539–542; *RTA,* IX, 66–68.
83. Juritsch, *op. cit.,* p. 42, note 5.

crusade and desperate in the face of defeat, tried to save his cause by displaying the papal banner. As none of the former leaders was willing to renew the enterprise without much of an army, the cardinal decided to pass the banner on to John, the young palsgrave of Neumarkt, but this gesture had no influence upon the ensuing events, as the palsgrave could not collect even a small army. Nor is there any reason to assume—as Frederick of Brandenburg claimed toward the end of his report to the king[84] —that the chances of this crusade for success would have been much better if only "der Cardinal von Engellant" had arrived sooner at the main theater of war.

In fact the slaughter of the crusaders had just begun at the time when the German armies started their headlong flight from the region around Tachov across the mountain forests of Bohemia's western border to the safer region of the Upper Palatinate. The losses that the crusaders suffered during their hasty retreat remain unknown. The only source which attempts an estimate, the Augsburg chronicle,[85] presents the obviously impossible figure of 100,000 dead. All we can guess is that the losses, both in men and in materiel, were heavy, until their flight had taken the crusading troops over into Germany.

There was no further pursuit beyond the border on the part of the Hussites. Their army, led again by Prokop but including also, in addition to the Taborite troops, those of the Orebites (since Žižka's death called "Orphans") and of Prague, found a more immediately challenging object to attack: the strong border city and fortress of Tachov. It had seemed unconquerable, since it had, six years earlier, successfully resisted even the great Žižka, who had conquered so many towns.[86] Now, apart from its largely German and exclusively Catholic population, it had been strengthened by a number of crusaders, who may have felt safer there than in continued flight westward, or have stayed there with the purpose of resisting the enemy. The Hussites acted more effectively than the German army had only a few days earlier when they besieged Stříbro. Prokop used not only siege artillery but also incendiary missiles, and ordered his forces to dig holes in the base of the walls.[87] After less than a week the city's defenses collapsed. Urgent calls for help, sent to Frederick of Brandenburg (then at Wunsiedel near Bayreuth) and to other princes, either were ignored or arrived too late.[88] Three days after

---

84. *U.B.*, I, 542.
85. *Chroniken der deutschen Städte*, V-2, 92.
86. See Heymann, *Žižka*, p. 202.
87. Bartošek of Drahonice, in *Fontes rerum Bohemicarum*, V, 597.
88. *U.B.*, I, 542.

the city's fall, on August 14 (1427), the Hussites also gained the strong castle with its recently reinforced garrison.

With the conquest of Tachov, the second-strongest royalist position in western Bohemia—after Pilsen—had fallen. This region had been a convenient base for crusading invasions from the western border toward the center of Bohemia. Apart from Sigismund's personal invasions from Hungary via Moravia in 1420 and 1421, and some other invasions from Silesia and Saxony, all the main crusading forces had advanced from Franconia into the western territories of Bohemia. Tachov, in its central position between Cheb in the north and Domažlice in the south, had been considered a particularly valuable point of operation for any further crusades and also for the minor military enterprises called "daily war" in which the Catholic circles of the Pilsen "Landfrieden" had often engaged. Thenceforth this base was lost, and Hussite Bohemia had correspondingly gained. Its leaders did not, at this time, consider an invasion of Germany, even though German fear of such an attack was growing, especially in the most exposed cities of Franconia.[89] Some Silesian forces which had been intended to strengthen the crusade by an invasion of northwestern Bohemia halted as soon as they were informed of the fate of Tachov.[90]

To the Hussites, or at least to the more determined among them, the victory gave tremendous satisfaction, even though a somewhat half-hearted attempt at attacking Pilsen did not succeed.[91] On the other side there was a small but not insignificant clique which had, in coöperation with prince Korybut and probably also with Frederick of Brandenburg, worked for an arrangement going far toward capitulation.[92] To them, of course, the fate of the crusade was anything but happy, but they hoped that a sudden coup in Prague might change the whole situation and might also free Korybut. The resulting enterprise was led by two prominent Utraquist leaders, Hynek of Kolstein and John Smiřický, and was supported by two old Czech servants of king Sigismund, John Městecký of Opočno and Půta of Častolovice. Their attack, however, proved a total failure when their limited force, some six hundred horse, reached the center of Prague and tried to gain the support of the people with the slogan "holy peace." The masses of the Utraquist people, largely under the influ-

89. See, for example, *Chroniken der deutschen Städte,* I, 374.
90. Tomek, *Dějepis Prahy,* IV, 387.
91. *Ibid.,* IV, 388.
92. The main sources are the "Old Annalists" ("Staří letopisové") *Dílo F. Palackého,* ed. Charvát (Prague 1941), II, 77 ff., and "Kronika Bartoška z Drahonic," *Fontes rerum Bohemicarum,* V, 597 ff.; see also Tomek, *Dějepis Prahy,* IV, 389 ff.

ence of John Rokycana, the successor as theological leader of Jacobellus of Stříbro,[93] stood unanimously against the invaders, whom they considered traitors. Some of them, including Hynek of Kolstein, were killed, others imprisoned. But so as to forestall similar developments in the future, Korybut was released from his imprisonment, in the justified expectation that he would leave Bohemia and return to Poland. There he maintained, despite his imprisonment, his generally favorable attitude toward the Hussites.

The defeat of the conservative party among the Hussites, with their strong base among members of the high nobility as well as among the less radical Hussite masters at the University, had a liberating effect upon the whole foreign and military policy of the standard-bearers of the revolution. This was true especially of the two strong brotherhoods—the Taborites under Prokop the Great and the "Orphans" under another Prokop, "the Short"—but also of the majority of the people in the New Town of Prague. The main leader of this coalition, Prokop the Great, had, as mentioned before, already tried to capitalize on the great victory of Ústí in 1426 by an invasion of Saxony. The purely defensive strategy which had been ordained at the beginning of the war by the masters of the University was finally abandoned in 1427, and offensives into enemy territory now became a systematic policy. The reasons were obvious: in spite of the long series of victories over the invading armies of the crusaders the country of Bohemia had suffered grave damage. The enemies, whether crusaders or other invaders from Hungary, Austria, Saxony, or Silesia, had always done their worst to destroy houses and fields, villages and small towns, had killed Czechs, often with little regard to their religion, age, or sex, and had thereby also reduced the number of productive hands. Occasionally, too, destruction resulted from internal strife between Hussites and Catholics or even between more conservative and more radical Hussites. Therefore it seemed to be most urgent to shift the theater of war from the suffering lands of Bohemia to those of her hostile neighbors.

The Hussite leaders could well assume that the morale of their enemies would decline when the latter had to fight on their own soil. As long as the crusaders could decide when, where, and how the war should be conducted there would not be any great pressure toward serious consideration of compromise and peace: even though the first few crusades had been utter failures, it was still possible to claim that

93. See Heymann, "John Rokycana," in *Church History,* XXVIII (1959), 240–280.

the defeats represented a divine punishment which would sooner or later, with God's help, turn into victory. If, however, as the Hussites could hope, future battles could be won in the countries of the enemy, the impression upon their inhabitants would be infinitely greater. After so many years of military success the Hussite claim that God had been and remained on their side could no longer be considered an empty boast. What was even more dangerous in the eyes of the church and the German princes was that with Czech armies marching almost at will through the countries surrounding Bohemia, the "heretical poison" might infect some of the masses of the people in Germany and elsewhere. All these considerations strengthened the determination, especially of the more active brotherhoods, to mount a steady sequence of campaigns into the neighboring lands. They would, of course, not use the term "crusade" for these enterprises. Instead they called them "spanilé jízdy" (something like "beautiful, noble rides").[94] In the eyes of the neighbors who until recently had felt quite safe these rides were anything but beautiful. The usual defeat of the Catholics, and especially the vast destruction wrought by the Hussite armies, resulted in a bitter reaction on the part of the victims. There was, of course, hatred for the "heretics," but also a considerable degree of disappointment and of accusations against those who presumably had the responsibility for providing protection.[95] These attacks were directed against many of the rulers, from Sigismund down to the various temporal and ecclesiastical princes. But the relationship between the king and the princes was bad enough to lead to mutual accusations of secret coöperation with the "heretics." Sigismund himself was, in 1427 and the spring of 1428, engaged in a struggle with the Turks over northern Serbia. He seemed, for a short time, to be successful in establishing a strong fortress near the Danubian port city of Golubats, where however in late May 1428 he suffered one of his worst defeats, barely escaping with his life and forfeiting Hungary's strong claim to suzerainty over Serbia.[96]

In this situation the king seemed to have very nearly forgotten the urgent problems of Bohemia and the empire. It was by no means the Hussite movement alone with which he would have to deal. Just when the Holy Roman empire was for the first time exposed to dangerous Hussite attacks, the realm was also the theater of a

94. The term is used as the heading of the relevant chapter of Bartoš, *Husitská revoluce*, II, 46–76, and of that of Macek, *Prokop Veliký*, pp. 65–122.

95. See, for example, *U.B.*, I, 551 ff., 581–582.

96. Aschbach, *Geschichte Kaiser Sigmunds*, II, 269–279.

number of grim civil wars.[97] There was a repeated bloody struggle between palsgrave Louis of Wittelsbach and margrave Bernard of Baden, in which duke Charles of Lorraine and a number of cities—Strassburg, Basel, Freiburg, and others—were also involved. Another war was being waged between archbishop Conrad of Mainz and landgrave Louis of Hesse; archbishop Dietrich of Cologne, bishop John of Würzburg, and prince-abbot John of Fulda, as well as a number of lay princes, were drawn into this struggle. Margrave-elector Frederick of Brandenburg—still trying to maintain his close friendship with Poland and at the same time under continuous pressure from the holy see—had had, up to the summer of 1427, difficulty in defending the Brandenburg province called Ückermark against attacks by the dukes of Mecklenburg and Pomerania, though eventually he maintained his position.

Perhaps of even more significance were the rebellions in a considerable number of German cities. It is especially noteworthy that the majority of these cities were the seats of bishops and archbishops, such as Mainz, Cologne, Magdeburg, Speyer, Strassburg, Constance, Würzburg, and Bamberg, or, in the case of Erfurt, a city dependent on the archbishop of Mainz. While in some of them the rebellions were, as in earlier times, directed mainly against the patricians, the majority displayed a special hatred for the clergy and above all for the bishops, some of whom had been the allies of the patrician families. It is not easy to decide to what extent these developments reflect a direct influence from the Hussites, with their antagonism against leading clerical figures such as the newly promoted cardinal John "the Iron" of Olomouc. In some regions where the Hussite armies had not only begun to invade repeatedly but had also tried to establish contacts with the local population—as was, for instance, true in some corners of Silesia—there is little doubt that there had been some direct influence.[98] There were also attempts at broadcasting leaflets over territories quite distant from Bohemia. In any case the worry that such an influence might spread contributed to a changed attitude on the part of those who until recently had taken it for granted that the only proper policy was to destroy the "heresy"—and the "heretics"—by force. This was true also in the case of Sigismund, who wanted at least a prolonged truce which would enable him to go to Rome to be crowned emperor. A measure of willingness toward compromise could also be found on the other

97. See, for example, for what follows, J. Gustav Droysen, *Geschichte der preussischen Politik,* I (Berlin, 1855), 504–507.

98. See *U.B.,* II, 175 (no. 712) and 181–183 (nos. 719 and 720).

side, including the most powerful leader of Hussite militancy, Prokop the Great. One hope was, on both sides, the expectation of a new church council.

Some feelers from the side of the king were answered by a positive reaction at a diet called early in January 1429 to Český Brod. The result was that the Hussite leaders, including Prokop, accepted Sigismund's invitation to meet him and some of the German princes at Bratislava (Pressburg) in western Hungary. The very fact of such a meeting seemed remarkable—it could hardly have been imaginable as long as John Žižka still led the Hussite armies. Prokop, though probably just as determined to fight for the basic ideas of Hussitism as long as necessary, was less rigid in his tactics.[99] He was cautious enough, however, to demand, in addition to a normal safe-conduct, some very high-ranking hostages, including two Silesian princes. The Hussite representatives arrived, accompanied by a strong retinue with two hundred horse, on April 3, led by Prokop the Great as leader of the Taborites, Peter Payne ("Master English") as speaker for the brotherhood of "Orphans," and lord Menhart of Hradec as representative of the less radical Hussites, especially in Prague; Menhart appears to have been used by both sides as a go-between. Among the Catholics there were cardinal John of Olomouc, long the most "iron" among the Czech orthodox clergy, lord Ulrich of Rosenberg, Sigismund's most faithful and powerful Czech noble, and a considerable number of German princes (including Albert of Austria), Hungarian and German ecclesiastical princes and nobles, and representatives of universities, among them four doctors of Paris and one or two from Vienna.

The king had just returned from a short visit to Poland, where he had tried, with some temporary success, to split Vitold of Lithuania from his cousin Vladislav by offering the grand duke a royal crown.[100] If this had succeeded it would indeed have led to a considerable weakening of Poland, the only potential ally (at least temporarily) of the Hussite Czechs. This, of course, was one of Sigismund's aims, but old Vitold was to die before the promised crown could be put on his head.

Back in Bratislava the negotiations began on April 4 (1429). The discussion started with a speech by the king, who tried to convince the Hussite representatives that they were in deep error—a claim

99. See Heymann, Žižka, p. 458. For the sources regarding the Bratislava meeting the most complete bibliography is to be found in Bartoš, Husitská revoluce, II, 46, note 1. For the most important single source see U.B., II, 22–26.

100. See Aschbach, op. cit., III, 319-327, and Paweł Jasiencia, Polska Jagiellonów (Warsaw, 1964), pp. 136–137.

which the Hussites naturally refused to admit—and that consequently they should be willing to be taught in the true faith. This would be done best by the priests and teachers expected at the impending Council of Basel. Until then Sigismund urged a complete truce on both sides, and the return of estates taken over by the Hussites during the war. After a largely negative short answer on the part of Prokop, the main speech on the side of the Hussites was delivered by Peter Payne, the former Lollard who had often undertaken important diplomatic missions for the Hussite cause. [101] He tried to convince the king and his Catholic associates that it was quite possible for them to follow the truth of God and still to accept the demands of the Hussites for a far-reaching reform, a step which would make Sigismund fully acceptable to the Hussites as ruler of Bohemia. The speech, teeming with quotations from the bible, was, of course, far too doctrinaire a presentation of the Hussite position to be acceptable to the king. Sigismund's immediate reaction seems to have been utterly negative, to judge from letters which he wrote to some of the leading German princes right after the meeting: since the negotiations had been totally unsuccessful a new crusade must immediately be prepared, with all strength, for that very summer. [102]

In fact, plans for the supposed great invasion of Bohemia did not get beyond rather vague discussion. The king had, it seems, not completely written off the possibility of a rapprochement based on the forthcoming ecumenical council. Without it his chances of regaining the throne of Bohemia seemed hopeless, and even his position as ruler of the Holy Roman empire would be steadily weakened, unless he could obtain the Roman imperial coronation in the near future. But he also had to counteract the constantly increasing rumors that he was ready meekly to accept the Hussite "heresy." It was a difficult position, but Sigismund was shrewd enough to play the game.

At this stage the problem, quite apart from defending his prestige as a good, orthodox protector of the Roman church, was to devise an arrangement which would convince the Hussites that they would be accepted at Basel without too many difficulties, and especially without abandoning their own religious convictions and rituals. As yet the Hussites, and especially Prokop, were quite unwilling to conclude the truce which the king had tried to gain rather cheaply for the

101. The text is printed in Bartoš's book *M. Petr Payne, diplomat husitské revoluce* (Prague, 1956), pp. 51–73.

102. *U.B.,* II, 27–35 (nos. 575–577); cf. Altmann, *Windecke,* pp. 261–263.

period up to the opening of the council in Basel. But after some hesitation the Czech representatives did, at least, agree to present the issue to another diet which was to be convened in Prague and to which Sigismund was invited to send representatives. In fact there were two such meetings, one at the end of May 1429, on which Prokop reported in person to the king, and a second, again in Prague, in mid-August. [103] The outcome was that both brotherhoods, Taborites as well as "Orphans," refused to accept the truce, as did the New Town of Prague. The future participation of Hussite Bohemia in the Council of Basel was not completely excluded, but the conditions for such participation were still uncertain, and in view of what had happened to Hus and Jerome of Prague fourteen years earlier at the Council of Constance it was obvious that the Hussites would want very strict guarantees.

Meanwhile the military initiative remained in the hands of the brotherhoods under Prokop's leadership. From the fall of 1429 through the early months of 1430 the "beautiful rides" reached the climax of their power.[104] The first offensive was directed against Saxony-Meissen and Upper as well as Lower Lusatia. Soon afterward, in mid-December, this was followed by the most tremendous of all these enterprises: Prokop organized five armies under his command, the total strength being reported as 40,000 infantry, 4,000 cavalry, and 3,000 battle wagons, perhaps the greatest single military force that the Hussites had assembled during the whole long war. Again the first target was the territory of Saxony-Meissen, and even though Frederick II of Saxony, with support from other princes, mobilized a still larger army, the one collision, near Grimma, ended as usual with the flight of the defenders. Avoiding the strongest cities but conquering a number of smaller towns, the offensive turned toward Leipzig, where Frederick ordered the burning of all the suburbs. In many cases the towns occupied were found to be empty of men, since the Germans had long since realized that the Hussites were careful not to harm women and children. From the region of Leipzig the Czech army made a sharp turn south, conquering Altenburg and Plauen and then crossing over into Franconia, attacking the Bayreuth lands of the Hohenzollerns and of the bishopric of Bamberg, and threatening the neighboring Upper Palatinate. Returning from the meeting at Bratislava to deal with this terrific attack, Frederick of Brandenburg tried to mount an effective defense, but it was already too late, and

---

103. Tomek, *Dějepis Prahy,* IV, 425 ff.
104. See, for this whole phase, Bezold, *König Sigmund,* III, 26 ff.; Macek, *Prokop Veliký,* pp. 86 ff.; and Grünhagen, *Die Hussitenkämpfe der Schlesier* (Breslau, 1872), pp. 178 ff.

the two important towns in his possession, Kulmbach and Bayreuth, were conquered without much resistance. The next target was Bamberg, whose bishop Frederick had left the city with almost no means of defense. In fact part of the city's population anticipated the expected destruction and plundering by doing it themselves.

The strong city of Nuremberg now seemed in danger, but before the Hussite forces penetrated that far south an unexpected development took place. Frederick of Brandenburg learned that at least a provisional understanding with the Czechs was possible. He met on February 11, 1430, with the Czech commanders at the castle of Beheimstein, three miles from Nuremberg, and there a temporary truce was concluded. [105] It provided that Frederick himself, the city of Nuremberg, the palsgrave John, and several other princes would pay the Hussites a total indemnity of over 30,000 guilders, but this was secondary to the political arrangement, which appeared to be of decisive importance. The Hussites were to be invited to a great public religious discussion with the leading scholars of the six German archdioceses, and would have the right to present in detail and in full freedom the Four Articles, orally and in writing. They would also have the right to worship in their way—with communion under both kinds—in Nuremberg, as well as in the places through which they would travel, without trouble and without having an interdict imposed upon those towns. Finally, even if no final understanding were to be achieved, the Czech representatives would, under a reliable safe-conduct, be allowed to return to Bohemia. [106]

It is obvious that these arrangements and promises would not, with such far-reaching concessions, commend themselves to the Catholic establishment in Rome, in Germany, or at the court of Sigismund. The change from a policy of utter, merciless annihilation to a careful effort to achieve mutual understanding was too rapid and radical to be acceptable. True, the promise of concessions had been the only way to avoid a dreadful catastrophe, and this was emphasized in all the many letters sent out by Frederick, especially through the city council of Nuremberg. [107] On the other hand, none of these letters outlined frankly the decisive concessions regarding Czech participation in the promised Nuremberg meeting. Frederick had obviously exceeded the special authority which the king, in August 1428, had conferred on him: the permission to accept the submission of any

---

105. See *U.B.*, II, 109–129, Bezold, *König Sigmund*, III, 41 ff., and Bartoš, *Husitská revoluce*, II, 66 ff.

106. For the drafted texts, see Bezold, *op. cit.*, III, Appendix, pp. 165 ff.

107. *U.B.*, II, 111–114, 120–122, and Bezold, *op. cit.*, III, 49–50, 54–55. See also *RTA*, IX, 382–385 (no. 292).

Hussites who offered their obedience to the church and to Sigismund. [108] No such intention could, of course, be assumed on the part of the Hussites, especially the more radical ones who had directed the outcome of the Prague diets and the military conduct of the "beautiful rides." Indeed, the cautious and apologetic letters sent out by Frederick indicate that either from the beginning, or at least from soon after the negotiations leading to the armistice of Beheimstein, Frederick had doubts as to whether he would be able to carry through those far-reaching promises, which had been taken very seriously by the Hussite leadership. It would, however, be wrong to assume that Frederick had meant to deceive the Hussites. The fact that he continued to meet the Czech leaders at their encampments, not once but repeatedly, [109] that he made serious preparations for the reception of the Hussite delegation in Nuremberg, and that he energetically enforced the indemnity payments (though these were not very large) [110] indicates that he meant to do his best, and his Czech enemies never accused him of an attempt to cheat them.

Even so there was considerable disappointment on both sides, resulting in an immediate decision by both to resume the military initiative and offensive. The Hussites were already active toward the end of March (1430). The "Orphans," under Prokop the Short, went into Moravia and Slovakia, and met a Hungarian army sent out upon Sigismund's orders near the city of Trnava. Though the Czech losses were considerable, those of the enemy were three times as large. [111] Of greater significance were the enterprises of the Taborites in Silesia, especially noteworthy since the Czechs received some strong support from Poland. [112] This was largely the result of Sigismund's attempt, mentioned earlier, to split Lithuania from Poland by giving grand duke Vitold the crown for a Lithuanian kingship, against the energetic protests of king Vladislav Jagiello. In consequence the Polish king no longer took, as he had sometimes done, Sigismund's side against the Hussites. Prince Korybut, in spite of the difficulties he had had in Prague, now helped the Czechs in Silesia and established a strong military center through the conquest and occupation of the city of Gliwice, while some other important cities, including Brzeg, were taken by a combined Czech-Polish army led by the

108. *U.B.,* I, 637.
109. *U.B.,* II, 135, in a well-informed report to the grand master of the Teutonic Knights, Paul of Russdorf.
110. Bezold, *op. cit.,* III, 45, note 3.
111. Altmann, *Windecke,* p. 280, claiming 2,000 dead Czechs and "well six thousand Christians, may God have mercy on us."
112. Bartoš, *Husitská revoluce,* II, 71–72, 75–76.

Polish Hussite Dobeslav Puchala. The Hussites, who had experienced nothing but grim hatred from the Silesians and especially from the (mostly German) cities, now occasionally succeeded in gaining some Silesian adherents, including duke Bolko of Opole, who fully took the side of the Czech reform. An effort to gain the understanding and friendship of the citizens of Namslau, a little east of Breslau, appears to have failed, whereas another town, Bernstadt, accepted the Hussite recommendations completely and consequently were, as being piously devoted to the truth of God, taken under the full protection of the Hussite armies. [113]

The renewed military successes of the Hussites, the support they had recently received from Vladislav, the beginnings of serious doubts as to the heretical character of the Czechs and God's impending help against them—all these developments made it clear that a decisive change in the attitudes and actions of the Catholic world was necessary. Either crusading invasions would now have to be organized and carried out with a far stronger and more decisive effort, or else reconciliation would have to be tried; for this the earlier attempts at Bratislava and, more hopefully, at Beheimstein would point the direction, and the expected Council of Basel would provide an opportunity. But this, to succeed, would require a readiness to make concessions which only a few princes, especially Frederick of Brandenburg, and cities, such as Nuremberg, were willing to make; and pope Martin was implacably opposed.

The mood that spread to some regions far from the Hussite war is shown by a remarkable letter sent, it appears, "To the Bohemian Heretics" by Joan of Arc. The Maid of Orleans had at this time (early 1430) reached the peak of her dramatic career and had recently received noble rank from king Charles VII. The letter threatens the Bohemian "heretics" with military destruction if they persist in their "terrible blindness." [114] Whether or not Joan of Arc had, at any time, seriously considered acting against the Hussites, she was not to have an opportunity to do so. Soon afterward, in late May, she fell into the hands of the Burgundians, and one of the most determined enemies of the Czech "heretics," the cardinal and papal legate Henry Beaufort, bishop of Winchester, became one of Joan's jailers when the English accused and finally burned her—as a heretic—in 1431.

Strong pressure from Rome continued. To be sure that another

---

113. *U.B.,* II, 181–182.

114. See *U.B.,* II, 132, and Bartoš, *Husitská revoluce,* II, 74. The question of whether this letter is genuine is still not definitely solved.

crusade would be started under the supervision of a trusted prelate, Martin V appointed as his legate the young Julian Cesarini, who earlier had served as assistant to the legate Branda and had only recently been promoted to cardinal. [115] In addition, the pope entrusted Cesarini with opening the session of the council and directing it, but this authority was contained in one letter while another one gave Cesarini the right to dissolve the council or transfer it to another place, an expression of the pope's displeasure with its very calling. Martin V, however, died on February 20, 1431. On March 12 the Venetian cardinal Gabriel Condulmer was elected and took the name Eugenius IV. The new pontiff inherited from his predecessor a strong reluctance to permit a council to accomplish the necessary reforms. Cesarini retained his position as legate and considered his first duty to be the support of the plans for another crusade. Therefore he took part in the great Reichstag which had begun at Nuremberg in early February and lasted through nearly all of March. [116]

Hardly any of the numerous diets of the Holy Roman empire during the previous twelve years had boasted so magnificent a representation, especially of electors and other princes. It was one of the few assemblies to which king Sigismund himself found his way, as did some Czech Catholic nobles. The general consensus was that this time, largely through the efforts of Cesarini, the crusaders' preparations were far greater than ever before and were bound to be successful. On paper, indeed, the strength of the crusading army appeared most impressive, [117] for the princes had come to the conclusion that a concentrated crusading effort should be made, although the cities, at one time supported by Sigismund, preferred the "daily war" as the best way to exhaust and defeat the Hussite enemy.

In addition to planning for the fifth crusade itself an attempt was made by the king and some of the princes to establish a solid "Landfrieden," a domestic peace settlement to make sure that existing feuds were eliminated and new ones prevented, thus strengthen-

115. On Cesarini see, among other sources, Pastor, *Geschichte der Päpste,* I (5th edition, Freiburg, 1925), 278–280, and for bibliographical information note 7 on p. 279; also Creighton, *The Papacy,* II, 194 ff., and Bartoš's article "Manifesty Nuncia Cesariniho" in *Sborník prací věnovaných J. B. Novákovi* (Prague, 1932), pp. 178–188.

116. See, on this Reichstag, *U.B.,* II, 194–204; Bezold's careful discussion in *König Sigmund,* III, 89–118; and above all the very complete presentation of all available sources in *RTA,* IX, 493–628.

117. See *RTA,* IX, 517–535, which seems to permit the conclusion that with the coöperation of the cities some 33,000 men would be mobilized, with the use of artillery and battle wagons in a way which appeared to follow the Hussite example quite closely. The Hussite example can also be found in the military ordinance ("Heeresordnung") on pp. 536–540. See also, on all these arrangements, Bezold, *König Sigmund,* II, 110 ff.

ing the sources for the crusade. But the decision of the Reichstag, like so many others, remained essentially a paper decision, all the more so as it was given the limited duration of only twenty months. [118]

During the later phase of the Nuremberg Reichstag another meeting had begun which was meant to improve the situation of Hussite Bohemia: a conference with king Vladislav Jagiello of Poland. The two West Slav nations had recently drawn closer together, almost concluding a formal alliance. It seems absurd that Vladislav, himself born a heathen and converted to the Catholic religion only in his late thirties, should have received from Martin V encouragement in dealing with the Czech "heretics." [119] The pope, indeed, had expressed his dislike of Sigismund's scheme of a separate Lithuanian kingdom with Vitold as king. Martin had, by that time, lost most of his confidence in the genuineness of the intentions of the king of the Romans to continue the old struggle with the Hussites. If Sigismund could not be trusted, perhaps, was the papal assumption, Vladislav could be more successful in destroying the Hussites by force, a goal fully supported by Zbigniev Oleśnicki, the bishop of Cracow, Poland's first cardinal and a highly influential counselor of the king. But the pope's letters did not eliminate the possibility that Vladislav might, again more successfully than Sigismund, be able to lead the Hussites "back into the arms of holy church." [120] With that aim Vladislav, at prince Korybut's suggestion, declared his readiness to receive at his castle in Cracow a number of the leading Hussites, including especially Prokop the Great and William Kostka of Postupice, a man who had long had close friends in Poland, had taken part in the great battle of Grünwald, near Tannenberg, in 1410, had been Korybut's chief adviser during his regency in 1422–1423 and again in 1424–1427, and had played an especially important role in directing the policy of the Old Town of Prague. On the Polish side the Hussites received their strongest support from a group led by John Szafraniec, the lord chancellor, while bishop Oleśnicki tried, not without success, to limit the readiness of the king to help the Hussites. [121] While Vladislav was willing to support the safe-conduct for the Czechs if they should accept an invitation to the Basel council, he hardly deviated from the demand presented at Bratislava by Sigismund—that

118. *RTA,* IX, 497, 508, 511–512.

119. Bezold, *op. cit.,* III, 81 ff.

120. See J. Macůrek, ed., *Češi a Poláci v minulosti,* I (Prague, 1964), 136 ff., and J. Caro, *Geschichte Polens,* IV (Gotha, 1875), 43 ff., especially, on p. 46, the king's letter to his brother Švidrigello.

121. See Jan Długosz, *Opera omnia,* publ. Alexander Przezdziecki, XIII (Cracow, 1877), 437 ff., 462 ff. On the battle near Tannenberg see above, chapter XVI, p. 581.

the Hussites should, in advance, promise to submit to the theological decisions of the council. On the whole, therefore, the meeting had, in spite of a thorough presentation of the Four Articles by Peter Payne, less value to the Hussites than they had expected. To submit in advance to the decisions of the council was in any case unthinkable, as it would have made it easy to destroy all the elements of even the least radical demands for reform, and especially the Four Articles. The meeting in Cracow thus ended without any real improvement.[122]

The same was true when the Hussites, clearly eager to end the wars, offered to attend another conference with Sigismund. The meeting took place in late May (1431), this time in Cheb, which, though originally a free German city, had been pledged more than a century earlier to the crown of Bohemia.[123] Sigismund was accompanied by Frederick of Brandenburg, and the Hussites were represented by a number of prominent priests and knights (but none of the lords). Again the Czechs suggested that all Christian churches, including those of the east, be invited, and that the Czechs receive complete freedom in presenting their views without being forced to accept the council's decision in advance. The king, on his own, might have agreed to some of the Hussite demands, since he was eager to gain the long-desired and often-postponed imperial crown, and was, as king of Hungary, deeply involved in struggles with Venice. Having learned by now that the chances of a military conquest of Bohemia were remote, he would probably have been ready to make at least some of the concessions which he had refused at Bratislava.

At this moment, however, the Council of Basel—from which people on both sides had expected progress toward peace—intervened in just the opposite direction: to put all possible effort into the next, the fifth, the greatest crusade, which would have to achieve what the earlier ones had so shamefully failed to. This, above all, was the firm conviction of cardinal Cesarini. The papal legate, who was reconfirmed very soon in his position by Eugenius IV, had left the official opening of the council to two of his assistants. He himself, after the decisions of Nuremberg which he had influenced so decisively, had spent several weeks on an expedition down the Rhine, all the way to the Netherlands, and had received firm promises of participation in the crusade, not only from the many Rhenish bishops and archbishops, but even from duke Philip the Good of Bur-

---

122. Długosz, *op. cit.*, pp. 472 ff.
123. For the sources see Bartoš, *Husitská revoluce*, II, 84–85, and Bezold, *König Sigmund*, III, 123–128.

gundy, who, of course, never seriously intended to fulfill his promise. [124] Cesarini's feverish activity in the west had prevented him from taking part in the meeting at Cheb, but he had sent as leader of the Basel delegation the Dominican John Stoikovich of Ragusa (Dubrovnik), an active and determined enemy of Hussitism. His presence, if nothing else, doomed the Cheb conference to total failure. [125] The next step, it was now utterly clear, would be a crusade, and the general mood, expressed not only by the Basel delegation but also, it appears, by Sigismund and Frederick, was to proceed as energetically as possible. At once the Hussites, whose main parties—Taborites, "Orphans," and the more conservative Prague masters led by John Rokycana—had only recently been involved in rather harshly antagonistic religious discussions, [126] began to prepare for the expected invasion.

The center for the mobilization of the crusade was again Nuremberg, with the same solemn ceremonies used on June 29, 1431, as had been employed in the same city and the same church (St. Sebaldus) in 1422, except that the papal legate then had been Cesarini's friend and mentor cardinal Branda. Again Frederick of Brandenburg was appointed commander-in-chief by Sigismund, who had promised to participate in the crusade but had changed his mind, supposedly because he had had a painful accident. [127] The appointment of Frederick [128] was similar to earlier ones but gave him a still stronger position as the only commander-in-chief, which had not in fact been the case in 1427, as well as more freedom to negotiate with the enemy. It is not likely that he undertook the task with great pleasure, but it was hardly possible for him to refuse. He must have had some serious misgivings when he found that the participation of the German princes as well as the cities would be by no means as extensive as had been assumed during the later phase of the spring meeting of the Reichstag at Nuremberg.

If Frederick began to look at the whole enterprise with little enthusiasm, the same was not true for the cardinal-legate Cesarini. But even he was shocked when at the last moment he was informed that the firmly promised army of duke Philip of Burgundy was not available, and that palsgrave Louis of Wittelsbach also had his army engaged in other fields. Nevertheless he managed to convince himself

124. Bezold, *op. cit.,* III, 129–130.
125. *Ibid.,* III, 127.
126. Bartoš, *Husitská revoluce,* II, 81–82.
127. *U.B.,* II, 276.
128. *U.B.,* II, 218–221.

and some others that the crusading army was adequate to achieve—with the help of God—the final cleansing from the country of the sickness of heresy. He also, to do his utmost, wrote letters to those princes and cities whom he considered tardy, claiming that most of the others had followed his urging, so that now huge armies were marching east and would soon cross the Bohemian borders. [129]

In fact, by mid-July of 1431 the main contingents of the crusaders from western and central Germany had passed Nuremberg on the way to Weiden or to one or two other places near the Bohemian border. [130] Among the main princely troops there were those of the electors of Brandenburg and Saxony, of the archbishop-electors of Mainz and Cologne, and of count Louis of Württemberg, as well as of some of the greater cities such as Frankfurt, Nuremberg, Basel, Strassburg, Cologne, Aachen, and some of the Swabian towns. Somewhat farther south, but intended to maintain contact with these troops, were the Bavarian dukes with considerable forces. This army was directly under Frederick of Brandenburg's command and was accompanied by the legate; it was meant to attack Bohemia from the west. There were two other army groups, one, consisting mainly of the Silesians and Lusatians, coming from the north, and a second, stronger, based on Austria and commanded by duke Albert, Sigismund's son-in-law. Altogether, therefore, the forces of the crusaders were not insignificant, though the often accepted figure of 40,000 cavalry and 90,000 infantry is probably exaggerated. [131] All these armies, put in motion with reasonable coördination, would probably have been at least as strong as any of the earlier crusades. In one respect the planning of the fifth crusade seems to have been better than that of the earlier ones: for the first time the strategy of the crusaders appeared to be coördinated, with the three principal units supposedly attacking from west, north, and southeast simultaneously. [132] In earlier attempts this had never been accomplished,

129. *U.B.*, II, 226–227, where the city council of Nuremberg defends itself against such reproaches.

130. The most detailed and up-to-date treatment of the military aspects of this crusade is the chapter "Bitva u Domažlic" (Battle of Domažlice) by Urbánek, in the collection of earlier works published under the title *Z husitského věku* (Prague, 1957), pp. 135–157, with a fairly complete bibliography on this final crusading conflict on the last two pages.

131. The basis here is the Czech royalist (Catholic) captain Bartošek of Drahonice, whose "Kronika" was published by J. Goll in vol. V of *Fontes rerum Bohemicarum*, pp. 589–628, with the report on the 1431 crusade on pp. 604 ff. Palacký (German ed. of 1851, vol. 3, II, p. 541) accepted Bartošek's statement, followed by others. O. Frankenberger (*Naše velká armáda*, III, 89) thinks that the crusaders were numerically weaker than the Czech armies—an almost certainly wrong assumption. See also Bezold, *König Sigmund*, III, 144, and Urbánek, *Lipany*, p. 138.

132. See Sigismund's letter to Ulrich of Rosenberg in *Archiv český*, I, 33, and the report

especially in the case of the 1421 crusade, when Sigismund's strong invasion from the southeast had started only after the western forces had been driven out by the Hussites. This time hopes were strengthened when it was learned that the Hussite armies, apparently somewhat frightened, had pulled back from the border regions to the center of Bohemia and were thereby giving the invaders more freedom of movement. In the event, the Hussite strategy turned out to be highly effective.

Shortly before the crusaders crossed Bohemia's border the two sides exchanged, as it were, manifestoes trying to explain their positions. The first, dated July 21, 1431, came from the Hussites, [133] who tried, by referring to their meetings at Bratislava, Beheimstein, and Cheb, to prove that they had done their best to achieve understanding. They would do so again, but would not submit themselves to one-sided and arbitrary decisions on the part of the bishops and prelates at Basel, men who, it was claimed, all had reason to subject themselves to those badly needed reforms that had been formulated by the Four Articles of Prague. If the attempt were to be made again to subject the Czech people to the old ways by force, they would know how to defend themselves. This declaration sounds almost like an answer to a manifesto directed to the whole population of the kingdom of Bohemia by cardinal Cesarini which, however, was sent out only on July 26 from Weiden, just before crossing into Bohemia.[134] The legate's statements sound quite devoted to the hope of a return of the Czech kingdom to the old, great church of Christ. Repeatedly he emphasized the readiness of the crusaders to embrace all those that would rejoin the church of Rome, promising that no harm would ever be done to those who belonged or returned to the loving mother church. The reasoning presented by Cesarini, though impressively styled and probably quite honestly meant, contained few if any new arguments and certainly none which could convince the Hussites. One, indeed, of the legate's assurances proved immediately to be utterly wrong—the assurance that the crusading army was coming not to do any damage to the people of Bohemia but to bring peace and happiness. The early phases of the crusading campaign proved the exact opposite.

---

of Kilian von der Mosel to the grand master of the Teutonic Knights in *U.B.*, II, 233, 238–239.

133. *U.B.*, II, 228–231.

134. There is an authentic publication by Bartoš in his contribution to *Sborník prací věnovaných J. B. Novákovi* (Prague, 1932), pp. 188–191, correcting the date which was assumed, by Palacký and others, to have been July 5.

The crusaders, who had concentrated their forces in and around Weiden, crossed the mountain forests into Bohemia on August 1 and seemed to be headed for Pilsen, which would have given them a strong base for further penetration in the direction of Prague and the center of Bohemia. The first town of significance in their way was Tachov, which the Hussites had taken near the end of the 1427 crusade, and which since then had remained an important Hussite fortress near the border. The legate suggested that the place should be surprised by a sudden onslaught, but the army commanders, probably including Frederick of Brandenburg, decided against this, arguing that the troops had to have a day of rest. The result was that the next day the town appeared well prepared for defense against the crusaders. Immediate assault, therefore, seemed out of the question, [135] but the commanders of the crusading troops hoped in the end to gain the city by besieging it. Hence a large part of the army remained for about a week in the same neighborhood, with only relatively short marches undertaken by smaller units, mostly in a northeasterly direction, as far as Teplá and Bezdružice. Their main purpose, as no enemy armies were as yet visible, was to burn and destroy as many places as possible and kill their Czech inhabitants. In the town of Brod not a stone was left standing, and all the inhabitants were killed; some two hundred villages in the same region between the border and Pilsen suffered similarly. This reckless destruction and mass killing, often done without regard to the religious beliefs of the people involved, was surely the exact opposite of what cardinal Cesarini had promised, but even if he had wanted to prevent or limit these activities, he would have had no effective influence upon the masses of the crusaders. After all, their attitude, inflamed by the Roman propaganda, had been characteristic from the beginning of the Hussite wars, as is fully confirmed by German Catholic sources. [136]

While the crusaders gained little or no profit by keeping the bulk of the western army near Tachov, it is not clear why after a lost week the army began to move—first, it seems, eastward via Kladruby in the direction of Pilsen, and then rather suddenly taking a sharp turn in a southerly direction, passing Horšovský Týn and then stopping before

135. Supposedly also upon the protest of "duke John of Bavaria," who claimed the city as his own heritage which should not be destroyed. See Kilian's report to the Teutonic grand master, *U.B.*, II, 237–239, with valuable details on the further events. "Duke John" was actually the Wittelsbach palsgrave of Neumarkt; see, with other works, Benno Hubensteiner, *Regententafel*, V (Munich, 1967), 382.

136. *U.B.*, II, 240, 241. For additional proofs see Piccolomini, *Bohemian History*, chapter 48, and Bezold, *König Sigmund*, III, 148.

the gates of Domažlice. This town had, almost alone in the western border region, early joined the active Hussite cities belonging to the Taborite brotherhood, and had been especially loyal to John Žižka; [137] it was certainly a stronger bulwark of Hussitism than Tachov. At the same time, by staying so close to the western border, the crusaders lost any chance of joining up with the other two strong armies, the Silesian-Lusatian in the northeast and the Austrian in the southeast; it began to be clear that the planned coöperation of the three main army groups would not materialize. Perhaps it was understandable that the Lusatian troops tried to regain the city of Löbau, as well as some other places which the Hussites had gained in a short but effective offensive during May. Indeed, the Lusatians, perhaps because they (and the Silesians) fought on their own soil, were the only crusaders who had any success. [138]

Of far greater significance were the activities of duke Albert with his Austrian forces. This army was probably better organized than any of the others, and until quite recently the duke had given reason to his allies in the west to expect that he would join them soon. In fact he made not a single move in this direction. Instead of marching toward the northwest he led his troops—some 14,000 men—northeast into the eastern part of Moravia. The purpose is rather obvious: while he had a not unjustified doubt as to the efficacy of the crusading armies now in the west, his foremost interest was not so much the general destruction of heresy, although he was an orthodox Catholic. Rather, he wanted to use this opportunity to strengthen his position in Moravia, which his father-in-law, as king of Bohemia and of the Romans, had given him in 1423 by enfeoffing him as margrave of Moravia—a very substantial increase in his possessions. This position, of course, had never been acknowledged by the Hussite Czechs, and various parts of the country had changed hands several times. The leading cities, however—especially Olomouc as the residence of cardinal John "the Iron," as well as Brno, Znojmo, and Jihlava, all inhabited predominantly by Germans—had accepted the Hapsburg prince. Now Albert decided to establish his hold more firmly, in the expectation that the main Hussite forces, which at other times would have reacted against him, would be busy in the defense of the Bohemian west. From Laa, south of the border, his army crossed the Dyje (Thaya) river into Moravia, easily took the small town of Kyjov, and killed, as a Catholic source claims, most of the defenders. Then,

---

137. See his letter to Domažlice, Appendix IV, in Heymann, *Žižka,* p. 488, and pp. 205 and 276 in the text.

138. *U.B.,* II, 245–246.

crossing the Morava river near Kroměříž, he besieged Přerov south-east of Olomouc, but, because Moravian Hussites were approaching, soon gave up the siege. The Hussites, however, were not strong enough to deal with him. Besides some struggles with a Moravian Hussite sect called "the temperate ones,"[139] it appears that the duke, though these were supposed to be his own subjects, burned some five hundred villages (probably an exaggeration), killing most of the inhabitants.[140]

Meanwhile one looks in vain for any reasonable strategy on the part of the main army in western Bohemia. The lack of it, and of even minimal discipline among the crusading soldiery, is somewhat astonishing, since the crusading army was numerically much stronger than the Hussite army with which the German leaders, and especially Frederick of Brandenburg, had to cope. What were the causes that weakened the supreme commander to such an extent? In 1427, during the fourth crusade, he was subject to severe restrictions from other leaders as well as hampered by poor health, but the 1422 crusade had at least shown him to be a man of determination and clarity of purpose. In 1431 on the contrary, he seems to have been quite unclear as to his goals, and the results were correspondingly negative. It appears obvious that he had no confidence at all in the possibility of victory over the "heretics."

The bulk of Hussite military forces had, in the meantime, been assembled in the very center of the country, near the town of Beroun, less than forty miles west of Prague and a little over fifty east of Pilsen. It seems that at first, with the news of another great crusading army's having invaded Bohemia, at least a few war-weary nobles, including some well-known knights who had at earlier times firmly fought against king Sigismund and his anti-Hussite policy, refused to participate in the defense of the country and its religious reform.[141] Yet the three main groups, Taborites, "Orphans," and Praguers, could be mobilized fast and effectively under the supreme leadership of Prokop the Great. The total number of the troops under Prokop's command is sometimes given as 40,000, sometimes as 55,000, with some 3,000 war wagons.[142] If the second figure were

139. "Qui Mediocres vocantur." See Bartošek of Drahonice in *Fontes rerum Bohemicarum,* V, 604–605.

140. *Ibid.,* see also Piccolomini's *Bohemian History,* last pages of chapter 48; Rudolf Dvorák, *Dějiny markrabství Moravského* (Brno, 1906), p. 166; and T. Pešina, *Mars Moravicus* (Prague, 1677), pp. 562–563 and later.

141. See *U.B.,* II, 235.

142. See Bezold, *König Sigmund,* III, 149, note 3, and Frankenberger, *Naše velká armáda,* III, 89–90.

correct—which seems a little doubtful—then it would certainly have to include those Polish troops who had come to help the Czechs. [143] Their leader was, as in earlier times, prince Korybut, who had, with the support of the pro-Hussite members of the *szlachta* (gentry), put together an army which supposedly was 8,000 men strong. The assumption that this help was given directly upon the order of Vladislav is highly doubtful, [144] but the Polish king, still angry with Sigismund, does not seem to have taken any direct measures to prevent the support which his nephew gave to the "heretics."

It is quite clear that the main Czech military effort was, as before, made by the brotherhoods, and that the specific credit belongs to the priest-general Prokop the Great. Starting from Beroun on August 11 or 12, [145] the Czech army went west at great speed, apparently bypassing Pilsen to the south, and stopping first for a short rest at Chotěšov. Early on August 14, having ascertained the position of the enemy, who had burned some of the suburbs of Domažlice, the Czech army, organized in three corps, approached the crusaders, who, astonishingly, had made few if any preparations for meeting the army of the "heretics." Above all, no attempt had been made to employ the rich supply of war wagons which, if properly used, could have created a very strong mobile fortress. [146] In fact these instruments of technical progress in the history of late medieval war, which had helped the armies of Žižka and Prokop so much, functioned in the hands of the crusaders almost as impediments.

Meanwhile the only at all substantial effort made by the crusaders was the attempt to conquer Domažlice. The suburbs had been burned down, and according to some sources the besiegers had tried to persuade the defenders to surrender—a suggestion which was not accepted, since the Hussite army was not far away. The whole siege can, in any case, not have lasted long, probably not more than three or four days. [147]

Early on August 14 (1431) the Hussite army, organized in its three divisions, moved on from Chotěšov, went southwest via Stod, bypassed in its main body Horšovský Týn to the east, and then marched

143. See, for the background, J. Macůrek, ed., *Češi a Poláci v minulosti,* pp. 137 ff.

144. Altmann, *Windecke,* p. 317.

145. See the "Old Annalists," e.g. *Staré letopisy české z rukopisu křižovnického,* ed. Simek and Kaňák, pp. 100–102, and *Archiv český*, VI, 424.

146. The war-wagons and their handling, originally invented and used by Žižka, had by this time ceased to be a new or secret weapon, and occasionally their use by the enemies of Hussitism is emphasized. See, for example, Sigismund's letter to Ulrich of Rosenberg in *Archiv český,* I, 33.

147. Bartoš, *Husitská revoluce,* II, 91 and note 45.

almost directly south,[148]   getting close to the old, strong castle of Ryžmberk (Riesenberg), quite near to Domažlice. Presumably Frederick had sent out reconnaissance patrols who warned him before the Hussites arrived near enough to be seen or heard. He ordered the forces which were directly under his command (especially the Brandenburg troops) to establish a defensive position on a hill, near the road from Domažlice to Kdyně. While the main body of war wagons had, it seems, been put up on the hill for defense against Hussite attack, he had ordered other wagons, used mostly for supply purposes, to be placed behind the war wagons, probably to protect and save them in case a retreat should be necessary. [149] This information, however, did not reach the neighboring army groups, nor their commanders, among them Frederick II of Saxony and cardinal-legate Cesarini, who, at the head of some Italian troops, had taken his own position with the Saxon army.

The Czech forces, it is generally assumed, attacked with their famous song "Ye who are the warriors of God," [150] a song which had encouraged the Hussites and frightened their enemies more than once before. The details of the ensuing battle are not altogether clear. It is, however, obvious that the general mood among the masses of crusaders was almost from the beginning totally defeatist as soon as they had to deal with a strong, well-organized army instead of the helpless peasants who so far had been their victims. [151] The sudden movement of the wagons in the direction of the border forests was noticed by the Saxon elector and the papal legate, who had climbed another hill to ascertain the military situation. Cardinal Cesarini angrily protested, jumping to the erroneous conclusion that Frederick of Brandenburg had intended to betray the purpose of the crusade (the cardinal did not maintain this painful suspicion). Frederick apparently tried to maintain discipline, even during the retreat which he must have considered inevitable. But his army, demoralized, had already begun to dissolve, and a determination to escape from any fight was steadily growing among the masses. There

148. Urbánek, *Z husitského věku*, pp. 148 ff.

149. See "Staří letopisové čeští," *Dílo Palackého*, ed. Charvát, II, 83, and the addition in *Censura*, 1945, pp. 15–16 (also valuable for what follows).

150. See Bezold, *König Sigmund*, III, 151 and footnote. The text is given in literal translation in Heymann, *Žižka*, pp. 497–498.

151. John of Segovia, "Historia gestorum synodi Basiliensis," in *Monumenta conciliorum saec.*, XV, 2 (1873). See also, for what follows, the letters in *U.B.*, II, 237 ff. and 240–241; Altmann, *Windecke*'s report on pp. 311, 317, and 340; *Staří letopisové čeští*, as cited in note 145, above; and Bartošek of Drahonice, *Fontes rerum Bohemicarum*, V, 604–605. For later presentations see Urbánek, *Z husitského věku*, pp. 148 ff., and Bartoš, *Husitská revoluce*, II, 90 ff.

were a few exceptions, the most impressive being the two hundred
Italians who had joined the crusade with the papal legate. Near the
entrance into the border forests a lone attempt was made, mainly
upon the repeated urging of Cesarini, to stop the wild flight by the
hurried construction of a wagon-fortress, a procedure that the more
experienced of the German and Austrian soldiers had begun to learn
from the Hussites. But the Czech forces were following too closely
after their enemies, and soon penetrated the crusaders' position. Of
the defenders, especially the Italians, hardly anybody escaped alive,
while many others were taken prisoners. [152] Cesarini himself escaped
only with difficulty, having changed his clothes because he was in
danger not only from the "heretics" but even from the crusaders,
many of whom held him responsible for the terrible disaster.

After this episode not the slightest attempt was made to resist the
frightening enemy. Whereas at first the German troops had tried to
use wagons for fast travel by keeping to the few existing roads across
the mountainous forests, a steadily growing number now looked for,
and sometimes found, forest trails on which they might have a better
chance to escape with their lives. The Czech soldiers, having again
easily defeated a numerically superior army, were in an ecstasy,
which was further increased when, on seizing all sorts of war materiel, they also gained large quantities of wine, which they consumed
that night. [153]

The actual losses of Catholic soldiers of the fifth and last crusade
have never been clearly established, either from Czech or from
German sources. We cannot even be sure whether the victims were
numbered in hundreds or in thousands. The first reports emerging
from the nearby German cities, such as Nuremberg, claimed that the
loss of life was rather small, and thus did not give the recipients even
a partial idea of the pitiful collapse of the great crusading army. [154]
At most there was an admission that much of the war materiel had
been lost. Somewhat more accurate was a report sent by the council
of the town of Cheb, expressing deep pessimism, since there was now

152. See Bartoš, *op. cit.,* II, 92, and the other sources quoted in his note 138.

153. It is rather odd that, especially at this phase, some information has come to us by
way of two works of poetry. One, from the side of the crusaders, is written by the German
poet and occasional war reporter Hans Rosenplüt, in a poem called "Von der Hussenflucht,"
in Liliencron, *Historische Volkslieder der Deutschen.* The other is by the town secretary of
Prague, Lawrence of Březová, author of the "Kronika husitská," who wrote a long,
triumphant Latin poem published by Goll in *Fontes rerum Bohemicarum,* V, 543–563, and
republished by Hrdina and Ryba, with Czech translation as *Piseň o vítězství u Domažlic*
(Prague, 1951).

154. *U.B.,* II, 241, 243.

hardly any chance of eliminating, by military means, the danger that the heretics presented to "us poor people." [155]

Among those who had not been present at the great disaster, the man with the fewest illusions was probably Sigismund, king of the Romans. He had, in the last weeks before the decisive battle, still received optimistic reports. They came from, among others, his close friend and supporter, lord Ulrich of Rosenberg, [156] and the king, on the last day of July 1431, thanked him warmly for this promising (and in some details quite wrong) information, and urged him to give support to Frederick of Brandenburg and his forces. He probably did not consider a miraculous victory completely impossible, but he can hardly have expected it to be likely. A few weeks later when, still dwelling at Nuremberg and busy preparing for his long journey to Rome, he was informed of the events of August 14, he wrote two remarkable letters, one to Frederick of Brandenburg, the other to Ulrich. The former is somewhat difficult to evaluate. [157] There is no outspoken reproach to the man who, if anybody, might have been held responsible for the defeat. The king presents a picture which seems to be the direct echo of a report sent to him by Frederick himself. "The army," he writes, "as you know well, has regrettably broken off its position in Bohemia and has returned home without much damage to the people, by the grace of God." The situation, he continues, "cannot be simply left as it is. Christianity and the neighboring countries [next to Bohemia] must not be allowed to remain totally hopeless, nor must the heretics further remain so delighted and strengthened." He informs Frederick that he has already called a meeting of the Reichstag at Frankfurt for October 16 with the purpose of organizing a "daily war." Specifically, he urges him to prepare for further possible invasions by the heretics across the forests (of the lands west of Bohemia), a measure which anyhow would be very much in the interest of Frederick and his Franconian lands if—which was doubtful in view of the recent fights in Franconia—the margrave and his friends could deal effectively with Hussite invaders.

Two days later Sigismund wrote to Ulrich of Rosenberg. This letter seems to express the king's feelings more genuinely. Ulrich appears to have given him a much clearer idea of the defeat at Domažlice and the way in which the German princes and their armies were thrown

155. *Ibid.,* II, 242.
156. B. Rynešová, *Listář a listinář Oldřicha z Rožmberka,* I (Prague, 1929), 125 ff.
157. *U.B.,* II, 243–245.

out of Bohemia. [158] There is no claim that the armies had returned to Germany nearly undiminished; obviously the Czech-royalist magnate knew better. The king simply expressed his deep sadness about what had happened. He had, he says, discussed the whole development with the German princes and the papal legate, but none of them had made it fully clear what had caused the catastrophe, except perhaps what Ulrich had already written to him: that it was their sins which had been punished. This, indeed, had long been the only acceptable explanation for the painful fact that God, throughout those twelve years, had always withheld his blessings from those who had tried to eliminate the "heresy."

The old expectation—that before long God would change his mind and help the papal party—was less and less maintained by princes, nobles, and even clerics in Germany and elsewhere. Frederick of Brandenburg, a thoughtful man, had been one of the first among these skeptics. Now the question why God had withheld his help in five great crusades became a subject of doubt even in the mind of cardinal Cesarini. From what he had seen with his own eyes the chances for military successes, even on a modest level, seemed to have vanished. On the other hand the Council of Basel, he began to feel, might lead to some solution, and this was now his chief responsibility. The council had been opened, with as yet sparse participation, on July 23, 1431, just one week before the crusaders had invaded Bohemia. Now, on September 9, the legate himself joined the council. His was not an easy task.

The final chapters of the Hussite wars are no longer part of the history of anti-Hussite crusades in the strict sense. No real attempt was made by the Catholics to build another such army, let alone to send it into the Bohemian lands; even the "daily war" was tending to disappear. Yet the war as such was not quite finished: especially the Taborites and the "Orphans" continued fighting in neighboring lands after the victory of Domažlice. In Silesia Prokop the Great relieved one of the strongest Hussite positions, Niemcza, which had for some time been under siege. After that he turned south toward Moravia, where the Hussite field armies drove duke Albert of Austria out. For some time the rural regions, as well as many of the castles belonging to Hussite nobility, could be considered Czech dependencies. Yet a number of cities, lightly fortified and strengthened with additional Austrian troops, maintained loyalty to the Hapsburg prince. The Hussites continued marching into the northern regions of Hungary

---

158. Again the letter to which Sigismund specifically refers has not been preserved. See Ryněšová, *op. cit.*, I, 127–128.

(today's Slovakia), but some struggle between the two brotherhoods led to Prokop's returning to Bohemia and, as a result, to a painful defeat of some "Orphan" troops by combined Austrian and Hungarian forces. [159] On the whole, however, the Hussites, in the fall and winter of 1431, could feel stronger than at any time before.

For the other side, especially the Germans, all hopes were now pinned on Basel. While some members of the council still looked for a military solution, the majority began to hope for a constructive diplomatic settlement. In many ways this was, at this stage, the most important issue with which the council had to deal. It was Cesarini who played the leading role, since the earlier expectation that Sigismund, on his way to Italy, would spend some time at Basel was not fulfilled. [160] If the king had personally contributed to the early work of the council, pope Eugenius IV would probably have been less tempted to try to throttle it. One of the main reasons was the pope's unwillingness to permit negotiations (and, of course, a compromise) with the Hussites. But if Eugenius had been successful all chance for peace would have been killed. At this stage of the prolonged struggle between pope and council not only the overwhelming majority of the members of the council but many of the leading prelates of Italy and France fought against the pope. [161] The struggle went on for a long time. In the main it was Cesarini's stubborn fight for its survival and the support by king Sigismund which eventually forced the pope to tolerate its continuance.

At an early date, on October 10, the council, mainly directed by Cesarini, sent a warm and open invitation to the Hussites, and after some difficulties the issues were given a fairly thorough discussion at Cheb between representatives of the council and of the Hussites. Above all, the certain safety of the Hussites, as well as their complete freedom to speak out and express their views, had to be guaranteed, and indeed were by the representatives of the council. The result was that a strongly representative Hussite embassy arrived in Basel on January 4, 1433, and was received with great politeness, especially

159. Bartošek of Drahonice, *Fontes rerum Bohemicarum*, V, 605–606.

160. Aschbach, *Geschichte Kaiser Sigmunds*, III, 384–385.

161. The most recent treatment of Eugenius's fight with the Council of Basel is presented by J. Gill in his book *Eugenius IV, Pope of Christian Union* (London, 1961), especially in chapter 3 (pp. 39–68). A considerably older, but more detailed and still highly valuable, treatment is that by Creighton in *A History of the Papacy*, II, chapter VI. A shorter treatment is in Pastor, *Geschichte der Päpste* (5th ed.), I, 299–305. Among the basic sources there are especially Raynaldus, *Annales ecclesiastici,* vol. IX, and Mansi, *Monumenta conciliorum generalium,* vol. II (Vienna, 1873). The difficulties between Eugenius and Sigismund (mainly before his imperial coronation by the pope) are treated in detail by Aschbach, *Geschichte Kaiser Sigmunds,* III, 17–106. For the decisive letter of Cesarini to the pope see the partial translation in Creighton, *op. cit.,* II, 204–207.

by Cesarini. [162] It could hardly be expected that mutual understanding would be easy. Repeatedly it looked as if the negotiations would fail. The demand for a general truce was refused by Prokop the Great—still the dominant personality among the Czech leaders—since this would eliminate the only strong pressure which could be exerted upon the council. In almost all issues he was supported by the leading figure among the Utraquist clergy, John Rokycana. Both also tried to gain a concession which the council refused to grant: the rule that in all parts of Bohemia and Moravia communion under both kinds should be obligatory. For the Czechs it would mean the prevention of regional struggles within the realm. But in the eyes of the members of the council it would have meant forcing the principles of Utraquism upon those cities that had maintained the orthodox Catholic ritual, such as Pilsen, and on the surrounding royalist castles whose owners were considered as the "Landfrieden" of Pilsen. Apart from one of the most impressive "beautiful rides"—the successful march of the "Orphan" army, supporting its Polish ally in a war against the Teutonic Knights and getting as far as the West Prussian Baltic coast [163] —the armies of the brotherhoods hoped to enforce religious unity in Bohemia by besieging and conquering Pilsen. Since the Hussite demand could not be accepted by the council, the more determined Hussites decided to impose this change by military means.

The enterprise against Pilsen, first limited to the Taborite field army under Prokop the Great, later also strengthened by "Orphans," proved a failure. [164] An attempt to seize provisions in neighboring Bavaria resulted in serious losses, and as the great priest-general was held responsible, some of his soldiers—many of them no longer devoted fighters for God—exploded in a mutiny and even kept Prokop under arrest for a short time, after which he left the army and settled in the New Town of Prague. This led to a considerable weakening of the military strength of the Taborites. In military terms this loss of power by the brotherhoods and their cities turned out to be the beginning of the end. In 1424 Žižka had defeated an army consisting of many nobles and of citizens of the Old Town of Prague. For ten years the fairly radical Taborite brotherhood, the somewhat

162. The history of the Hussite Czechs at Basel is well presented by Tomek, *Dějepis Prahy,* IV, 541–587, 689–713; by Bartoš, *Husitská revoluce,* II, 120–162, 187–196; and in English by the concise but lively and excellent treatment of E. F. Jacob under the title "The Bohemians at the Council of Basel, 1433," in R. W. Seton-Watson's collection of articles called *Prague Essays* on the occasion of the 600th anniversary of the Caroline University of Prague (Oxford, 1949).

163. Macek, *Husité na Baltu a ve Velkopolsku* (Prague, 1952).

164. Macek, *Prokop Veliký,* pp. 176 ff.

more moderate "Orphans," and to some extent the inhabitants of the New Town of Prague had maintained most of the ideas and policies of the original revolution. All attempts at a counter-revolution had so far ended in a fiasco. Now, finally, an alliance of the majority of the high nobility, some of the knights, and the people of the Old Town of Prague combined for action against the brotherhoods. The first step was the rapid conquest of the New Town. Prokop the Great, having barely escaped, decided to take the initiative to save the brotherhoods and the freedom of the many cities which had joined them in the course of time. He was welcomed back by the masses of the Taborite army, which now pulled away from Pilsen and was soon joined by Prokop the Short with his "Orphans." Even so, with about 18,000 men, they were weaker than the army of the League of Lords, which had grown to about 25,000. A battle fought on May 30, 1434, at Lipany, about thirty miles east of Prague, ended with the total defeat of the field armies of the brotherhoods, with both Prokops falling in the fight.[165]

From then on the role of the brotherhoods and their cities, though not completely eliminated, was considerably reduced. Essentially this was the end of the Hussite revolution, though by no means of the Hussite reformation. Radicalism, in its various aspects, was no longer dominant, and in Basel hopes were strong that most of the Hussite demands for reform would be essentially reduced. It is difficult to decide to what extent this turned out to be true. The death, especially, of Prokop the Great certainly was a gain for those masters of the University who had always wanted to go back as far as possible toward Roman orthodoxy, and in this sense one could perhaps say that the "moderate" armies of the lords and of Old Prague had done the very work which the crusades had never achieved.

But this is only partially true, particularly because the final arrangement, based on the four so-called Compacts, had already, before the battle of Lipany, become the basis of a possible understanding, and also because of the dominant role played by John Rokycana, definitely the true leader of the Utraquist reformation, who had not lost his influence upon the further negotiations with the council. [166] It was another two years until the Compacts which were the final result of the negotiations were signed by both sides and

165. For the origins, the source, and the results of the battle of Lipany see the second part of Urbánek, *Lipany*; cf. Macek, *Prokop Veliký*, pp. 183–191, and Bartoš, *Husitská revoluce*, II, 163–174.

166. The role of Rokycana, together with that of Peter Payne, is remarkably well presented by E. F. Jacob, *op. cit.*

endorsed by emperor Sigismund, [167] in the Moravian city of Jihlava on July 5, 1436. True, they were a compromise, considerably weaker than the original Four Articles of Prague for which the Hussites had fought so hard. [168] Above all, the wording was such that they could be understood in very different ways, and those different interpretations were to cause difficulties from the first moment after the signing of the Compacts, even between such relatively moderate men as John Rokycana on the side of the Hussites and bishop Philibert of Coutances of the council. "Neither side," writes Creighton, "abandoned their convictions, and the peace which had been proclaimed affected only the outward aspect of affairs. The Bohemians remained the victors. They had re-entered the Church on condition that they were allowed an exceptional position." [169]

The immediate winner was Sigismund, who after many years of fierce antagonism had in the end repeatedly supported the Czechs against the council, since he realized that only thereby could he regain the crown of St. Wenceslas. But once on his throne in Prague he expected, slowly but definitely, to destroy the religious autonomy of Utraquism. Thus it was characteristic that he first promised to support the election of John Rokycana as archbishop of Prague and then cautiously urged the council in the opposite direction.[170]

A dangerous struggle might have broken out if Sigismund's rule, from August 1436 to his death in December 1437, had not been so short and had not been followed by another very short reign, that of his son-in-law Albert of Hapsburg, from June 1438 to October 1439. He had great difficulty in establishing his position in Bohemia as well as in Hungary. In the following period of interregnum, the Utraquist church, in spite of certain difficulties and weaknesses, established its position as an essentially autonomous national church under the leadership of Rokycana.[171]

This position became even stronger when, in the years from 1448

167. See Aschbach, *Geschichte Kaiser Sigmunds*, IV, 251–253, 293–305. Sigismund was crowned by the pope in Rome in May 1433.

168. The most thorough study of the Compacts is presented in vol. I of Urbánek, *Věk Poděbradský* (České dějiny, III, 1; Prague 1915), chapter 2. Cf. Tomek, *Dějepis Prahy*, IV, 617–628, 676–687, 704–711. See also O. Odložilik, *The Hussite King* (New Brunswick, 1965), pp. 5–13, and Heymann, *George of Bohemia* (Princeton, 1965), pp. 6–12.

169. *A History of the Papacy*, II, 291.

170. For the whole issue see Urbánek, *Lipany*, I, 120 ff.

171. See F. Hrejsa, *Dějiny Křest'anství v Československu*, III (Prague, 1948), 31–89; and in English, Heymann, "The Hussite-Utraquist Church in the 15th and 16th Centuries," *Archiv für Reformationsgeschichte*, LII (1961), 1–16, and, on Rokycana, Heymann, "John Rokycana, Church Reformer between Hus and Luther," *Church History*, XXVIII (1959), 240–280.

to 1452, George of Kunštat and Poděbrady, a firm believer in Utraquism as it was understood and shaped by Rokycana, gained the position of regent for Albert's posthumous son Ladislas and then, soon after the young king's early death in 1457, was elected king. [172] As a matter of principle and political wisdom George did his best to ensure that Catholicism and Utraquism might live peacefully with each other, a policy of determined tolerance based on the existence of the Compacts. For some time it also seemed as if his relation to the holy see was a good one, but later pope Pius II (Aeneas Silvius Piccolomini) tried to force him to give up, with the Compacts, the substance of Utraquism. Pius himself did not go beyond political and legal pressure, steadily harsher in his last years, when he still hoped to lead a crusade against the Turks, until he died in 1464.

Pius's successor Paul II, however, went farther, making use of the political antagonism of a clique of lords who disliked the king's strength, and of the ambitions of George's son-in-law, the Hungarian king Matthias Corvinus. The result was a war which was at least presented, by papal bull, as a crusade and in various aspects looked like one. [173] Matthias was a much better general and a far more dangerous enemy than his predecessor Sigismund had been. Yet, in spite of Matthias's temporary gains, he was unable to accomplish the intended extermination of Hussitism. King George was unshakable in the defense of his basic policy. There were some desperately difficult phases, especially in the fall of 1468. [174] Yet George managed to turn the tide, to prove his strength in standing up to his enemies, and even to conclude peace and friendship with a number of them, including emperor Frederick III. But in March 1471, as the result of illness, he died, to be succeeded by Vladislav II (Władysław), the oldest son of king Casimir IV of Poland. George's heroic defense of his country and of the freedom of Utraquism led, in the final outcome, to the survival of the Hussite-Utraquist reformation down to the time when it became one of the branches of the Reformation of the sixteenth century. The "second Hussite war," with its occasional aspects of a crusade, turned out to be as ineffective as had been the long, more painful, more solemnly organized series of five crusades which, in the years from 1420 to 1431, had ended almost every time in such utter disaster.

172. For the following see the two recent works in English on George by Odložilik and Heymann cited in note 168, above.

173. For these attempted crusades see Odložilik, *op. cit.,* pp. 194 ff., 208–209, and Heymann, *George of Bohemia,* pp. 420 ff., 437 ff., 460–461, 490–491.

174. Palacký (in second Czech ed., part 4, II, 475 ff.) called it eight horrible weeks. In fact the hard time lasted longer.

20. Bohemia and its Neighbors

21. The Eastern Mediterranean

XVIII
THE AFTERMATH
OF THE CRUSADES

The revival of the crusade as an international movement in the fourteenth century had ended with the disaster of Nicopolis in 1396; the massacre of the flower of the western chivalry by the Turks in Bulgaria had disheartened the princes of Europe in their intermittent struggle for the deliverance of the east.[1] Moreover, the internal conditions of European nations, both political and religious, had already become less and less favorable for united action under the banner of the cross. Nevertheless, in the face of imminent danger during the fifteenth century, some measure of defense had to be undertaken to arrest Ottoman progress. The Orthodox principalities of the Balkans were overrun by the irresistible Turkish armies, and the kingdom of Hungary was increasingly becoming the bulwark of European Christendom. Though western Europe would send occasional reinforcements to the east, the people of east Central Europe and the Balkans had to shoulder the main burden of the mortal strife against the Turks. Thus in the fifteenth century, two movements ran in parallel lines—both heroic and both hopeless: the Hungarian crusade and the defense of Constantinople. In the meantime, desperate attempts were made to convert the Greeks to Catholicism and thus rouse the monarchs of the west to save the tottering Byzantine empire from final downfall. But all this was futile, for western assistance to the east remained insignificant and relatively ineffective.

Apart from the papal curia, the court of Burgundy became the chief center of crusading propaganda after the tragedy of Nicopolis, in which Burgundian nobles were the principal victims. While they wanted to avenge themselves for past humiliation at the hands of the Turks, most enthusiasts for the cause turned their eyes from the thrones of Europe to the duke of Burgundy as the richest prince in Europe who might lead a successful crusade. Philip the Good aspired

1. See above, chapter I.

647

to that honor, but, to avoid another calamity, he preferred to proceed with greater caution than before and gauge the strength and methods of his enemy in order to deal with him effectively. Accordingly, his choice fell upon Gilbert of Lannoy to visit the east and record his observations on its condition for the use of his benefactor. Lannoy was not a complete stranger to the east. In 1401, as a young man, he had undertaken a pilgrimage to the Holy Land in the train of John of Warchin, a noble of Hainault. The pilgrims then visited the monastery of St. Catherine on Mount Sinai and the ancient Coptic churches in Old Cairo; they returned, after nearly two years' peregrinations in the Near East, by way of Constantinople, Rhodes, Cyprus, and Turkey. Lannoy was therefore singularly fitted for the mission with which the duke entrusted him; the kings of England and France also approved of the proposed voyage. He remained in the east from 1420 to 1423 and collected a great mass of original information on the countries beyond the sea, describing his journey and registering his observations and experiences in a work entitled *Voyages et ambassades.*[2] Lannoy's route to the east is interesting and instructive. Traveling overland through Germany, Prussia, Poland, and Russia to the Genoese colony of Kaffa in the Crimea, he sailed on the Black Sea to Constantinople, where he made his first contact with emperor Manuel II Palaeologus. Then he crossed the Mediterranean by way of Cyprus and Crete to the city of Alexandria, whence he traveled to Rosetta and sailed up the Nile to Cairo. From the capital of Egypt, he repeated the pilgrimage to the monastery of St. Catherine on Mount Sinai, and further visited the ancient Coptic monasteries of St. Anthony and St. Paul in the eastern desert by the Red Sea. Finally he returned home by way of Damietta, Rhodes, and Venice.

The rest of Lannoy's work contains much descriptive material of the highest importance for the fifteenth-century traveler, the pilgrim, and the crusader. His account of Alexandria with its two harbors, its hostels, walls, and fortifications, and its numerous internal organizations and local government provides a fine specimen of the author's treatment of his subject-matter. He reports the existence of large beautiful hostels for the Venetians, Genoese, and Catalans, and mentions that the smaller dormitories of the merchants of Ancona, Naples, Palermo, Marseilles, and Constantinople were relatively empty at the time of his sojourn in Alexandria. He further gives a detailed statement about the Mamluks and their numbers, status, and

2. Ed. Charles Potvin in *Oeuvres* . . . (Louvain, 1878).

methods of recruitment and the countries of their origin. He devotes much attention to their military education, their tactics and strategy, war ruses, and implements of war. He was struck by the centralization of authority throughout Syria and Egypt in the hands of the sultan of "Babylon," though that title was not hereditary. Lannoy's description of the river Nile with its periodic inundation is illuminating, and his notes on the land of Prester John to the south are interesting. He says that the sultan does not allow Christians to go to India by way of Upper Egypt and the Red Sea for fear that they may contact Prester John and persuade him to deflect the course of the Nile from Egypt.

The particulars on the roads and towns of the Holy Land are very much in the nature of a travel guide, which Lannoy compiled mainly for the benefit of Christian pilgrims to Jerusalem. Nevertheless, he assured the European Christians that the holy city is not invulnerable, with its low walls and poor castles. Turkey is represented in his work by some reflections on the position of Gallipoli. This peninsula is employed by the Turkish armies as a landing place and a strong military base in Europe. It should be wrested from Ottoman hands in order to serve as a strategic point for intercepting the passage of Turkish soldiers into Greece.

Lannoy's attention was devoted primarily to Egypt and the Holy Land, though he did not overlook Turkey altogether. This position is clearly reversed in the work of Bertrandon of La Broquière, who also acted for the duke of Burgundy in his eastern embassy of 1432–1439. He left Venice on a pilgrim ship and landed at Jaffa after touching several seaports in the Morea as well as the islands of Corfu, Rhodes, and Cyprus. Then he went to Jerusalem and, like his predecessor Lannoy, paid a hurried visit to St. Catherine's monastery on Mount Sinai. Unlike him, however, Bertrandon did not take the western road to Egypt, but preferred to retrace his steps to the Holy Land and proceed north toward Cilicia and Anatolia. While in Damascus, he met the renowned French merchant adventurer Jacques Coeur, as well as a Genoese from Kaffa commissioned by sultan Barsbey of Egypt to purchase more slaves for his Mamluk ranks. After wandering through Asia Minor, he ultimately reached the Turkish capital Brusa, a great emporium noted in particular for its trade in Christian slaves. There he spent ten days as a guest in the Florentine hostel, which enabled him to carry out at his leisure his work of reconnaissance among the Turks. Then he crossed the Bosporus to the city of Constantinople, which he found in a lamentable condition, with an impotent emperor (John VIII) who was tributary to the sultan. He left Byzantium in the company of a Milanese ambassador to the Grand Turk, Benedict Folco of Forli, and both went together to see Murad II at Adrianople.

Bertrandon's wanderings in Macedonia, Bulgaria, Serbia, Albania, and Bosnia revealed that the Balkans were completely under the Ottoman yoke except Constantinople, which was a doomed city. He makes the poignant remark that the Turks were more friendly towards the Latins than were the Greeks. Further, he gives a useful account of the Turkish armies and their armor as well as their administrative and military systems. On the whole, the information embodied in Bertrandon's work *Le Voyage d'outremer*[3] ranks high among the contemporary sources for the political, social, economic, and military conditions of the Turks in the fifteenth century. After his final return to Burgundy by the land route across Europe, he reported on his mission to duke Philip, then at the abbey of Pothières in the Côte d'Or. He presented his august master with a set of oriental robes and a Latin rendering of the Koran (Qur'ān) made by the chaplain of the Venetian consul at Damascus. The duke accepted the robes, but passed the Koran to his learned consultant, bishop John Germain, chancellor of the Order of the Golden Fleece.

At a later date, in the year 1452, only a few months before the final collapse of Byzantium, duke Philip commanded the same John Germain to submit his recommendations on the subject of the crusade to Charles VII of France. These the bishop formulated in *Le Discours du voyage d'oultremer,*[4] which proved to be of great interest in spite of the fact that it was derived mainly from the written accounts of others at his disposal. On reviewing the state of Europe and the rest of the world, he found that though many countries remained within the pale of Christian governance, Islam still ruled supreme in Granada, Africa, and the Holy Land. Moreover, Moslem forces were still expanding in many other areas. The Latin kingdom of Cyprus had become tributary to Egypt, and in the last decade the Mamluk sultan had started to send his naval armament against the island of Rhodes. In eastern Europe, the Turks had seized the Balkans and begun their ruthless attacks on Hungary. Nevertheless, the situation was not utterly without hope. When weighed more closely, the balance of current events in the Orient and the Occident

3. Ed. Charles Schéfer in *Recueil de voyages . . . depuis le XIIIe jusqu'à la fin du XIVe siècle,* XII (Paris, 1892).

4. Ed. Schéfer in *Revue de l'Orient latin,* III (1895), 303–342.

tended to be more favorable to the Christians than to the Moslems, if only they would set their hearts on the enterprise. Despite all their might, the Mamluks were divided among themselves, and some of their greater emirs were in discord with the sultan. The lord of Damascus had even allied himself with Timur against his own suzerain in Cairo. On the Turkish side, Germain found that the Ottoman hold on the Balkans was still precarious, though their raids had been carried farther into Hungary. The great gulf which had separated the eastern and western Christians had been temporarily bridged by Eugenius IV at the Council of Ferrara-Florence in 1438–1439.[5] The time was now ripe, he felt, for united action between Orthodox and Catholic, while there was no real love between the Turk and the Egyptian in the Islamic empire. The Florentine accord would bring with it 200,000 combatants from Cilician Armenia and 50,000 from Georgia for the aid of the crusading host, in addition to other reinforcements from the empires of Constantinople and Trebizond, from the "Jacobites of Ethiopia," Russia, and "Prester John of India." The Discourse ended with an exhortation to the king of France, whom Germain implored to follow in the steps of Godfrey of Bouillon and the great St. Louis. But the king was in the throes of the last phase of the Hundred Years' War, and the expulsion of the English from France left him no time and means to be devoted to an uncertain cause in the distant east.

In the meantime, another propagandist of a different type emerged in the person of Manuel Piloti, a Latin native of Crete, who had spent thirty-five years in the east and witnessed some of the most stirring events in the Islamic wars in the Levant. In 1396 he had seen the two hundred slaves presented by Bayazid I to sultan Barkuk of Egypt from among the captives of the battle of Nicopolis, and records that they had to abjure their faith. Then he had watched the downfall of Cyprus and the captivity of king Janus with six thousand men and women of position in 1426.[6] Piloti was moved by these and other catastrophes to espouse the cause of the defense of the oppressed Christian principalities in the eastern Mediterranean. He wanted to put his long experience in the realm of the Moslems at the disposal of the Latins of the west to ensure a successful crusade for the recovery of the Holy Land. Accordingly, he composed a treatise entitled *De modo, progressu, ordine ac diligenti providentia habendis in passagio*

5. See above, p. 94, and Joseph Gill, *The Council of Florence* (Cambridge, 1959).
6. See above, p. 374, and Sir George Hill, *A History of Cyprus*, II (Cambridge, 1948), 485.

Christianorum pro conquesta Terrae Sanctae,[7] to be submitted to pope Eugenius IV. In this work, Piloti resuscitated the idea that a permanent conquest of the Holy Land should begin by the invasion of Egypt. Without seizing Alexandria and Cairo in the first instance, all Latin victories in Syria and Palestine would remain empty. The task of winning Egypt would be made easier by the depopulation of Alexandria and by the customary practice of the sultan, who butchered his emirs on the least suspicion of treachery. The author then outlined the Mamluk power and methods of war for the benefit of the crusader. Unlike most propagandists, he repudiated the crusade as an act of vindictiveness aimed at the extermination of the Moslems. The victorious leaders of Christendom, on the contrary, should treat their new subjects with love and leniency in order to win them over to Christianity. In this respect, his work recalls the thesis of earlier propagandists like Peter the Venerable in the twelfth century and Raymond Lull toward the end of the thirteenth and the beginning of the fourteenth. A propagandist document of considerable weight, the *De modo* must also be regarded as a worthy complement to Marino Sanudo Torsello's *Secreta fidelium crucis* (1321)[8] as a source for the history of medieval commerce in the Levant.

While propagandists were thus busy discussing the possibilities of an eastern reconquest, the Ottomans proceeded firmly with the task of consolidating their territorial gains in Europe; their troops were already mustered in the environs of Constantinople. The situation became critical for the isolated city; and in the summer of 1397 Manuel II Palaeologus dispatched his ambassador Theodore Cantacuzenus to implore Charles VI for immediate help. After some procrastination, the French king consented to contribute 400 knights, 400 squires, and a number of archers under the command of marshal Boucicault; the expedition started from Aigues-Mortes on June 26, 1399. Arriving at the island of Chios, the French squadron awaited in vain a promised reinforcement from Venice and from the Knights of Rhodes, and had to sail alone through the hazardous waters of the Dardanelles and Sea of Marmara to Constantinople. Perhaps the only achievement of the French was in helping to raise the maritime blockade of the capital. Otherwise, Boucicault realized the hopelessness of the position and decided to retrace his steps to

7. Ed. Baron de Reiffenberg, *Monument pour servir à l'histoire de Namur . . . ,* IV (Brussels, 1846), 312–419.
8. See above, p. 10.

the west, with emperor Manuel, in December of the same year to beg for more substantial relief. The marshal of France left behind him John of Châteaumorand with a hundred knights. During his "mendicant pilgrimage" to the west, the emperor was well received at Venice, Paris, and London.[9] He was given generous promises but failed to secure any concrete result. Relief finally came from an unexpected direction when Timur defeated the Ottomans in the memorable battle of Ankara on July 28, 1402, and carried Bayazid into captivity. This stunning event postponed the fate of the tottering Greek empire for half a century; as soon as the news reached Manuel, he hastened back to his metropolis in order to readjust his policy and cope with the fresh circumstances.

Although the moment was most propitious for a *passagium generale,* the west was not sufficiently responsive to a call for united action on a large scale and thus lost its only possible chance for saving the empire. Even when the indefatigable Boucicault decided to resume fighting in the east after his appointment by Charles VI as governor of Genoa, his campaign was deflected from European Turkey. First, he found it expedient to defend the interests of his commune in Cyprus, where the Genoese colony of Famagusta was beleaguered by king Janus from the land side and by Catalan galleys from the sea. He succeeded in relieving the city, and a treaty of peace was signed between Genoa and Cyprus in July 1403.[10] Next, as soon as he regained his liberty of action, he headed for Alexandria, but its impregnable fortifications proved to be too strong for his modest contingent. So he sailed to the Syrian coast, where he stormed and pillaged the towns of Tripoli and Beirut, but attempted in vain to seize Sidon and Latakia. Finally, he was forced to retire to Famagusta, always pursued by the Venetian galleys, which betrayed his movements to the Moslems; it appears that most of the booty which he collected in Beirut consisted of Venetian merchandise. His campaign led in the end to the outbreak of open warfare between Venice and Genoa. After heavy fighting at Modon in October 1403, Boucicault returned to Genoa without ever reaching Constantinople, and the burden of the defense of the empire and of eastern Europe fell again on the Hungarians and the impotent Greeks.

With the regeneration of Ottoman power under Murad II (1421–1451), the Turks resumed their pressure on the imperial city, and the emperors renewed their efforts at the papal curia for a crusade. The

9. On all this, see above, chapter III.
10. See above, pp. 370–371.

pontiff seized the opportunity to insist on the conversion of the Greeks to Roman obedience. The Greek delegation, headed by emperor John VIII and patriarch Joseph II, was received with honor by pope Eugenius IV and his cardinals at Ferrara in March 1438. Prolonged discussions took place between the two parties, who moved to Florence on February 26, 1439. The Greeks were at a disadvantage, and eventually John VIII and Joseph II (before his death on June 10), together with a multitude of eastern Orthodox prelates, gave way to the Latins in regard to doctrinal differences and to the primacy of Rome, "saving the privileges and rights of the eastern patriarchs." The bull "Laetentur coeli" of July 6, 1439, was the official proclamation whereby Constantinople was reconciled to the Roman see. In return, Eugenius signed a treaty in which he agreed to reinforce the defense of Byzantium with two galleys and three hundred men annually, and to increase his contribution to twenty galleys for six months or ten for a year in case of imminent danger. He further promised to promote the cause of holy war at the courts of Europe. But the unionist movement was evidently a matter of diplomacy and not of faith, and as such, it was foredoomed. Neither was the pope able to carry out his promises and reanimate the crusading spirit among Catholic princes, nor were the Greeks able to forgive and forget the sins of the Latins in the Fourth Crusade and after. Finally, the Greek patriarchs Philotheus of Alexandria, Dorotheus of Antioch, and Joachim of Jerusalem allegedly condemned the Ferrara-Florence compromise and accused their colleague in Constantinople of heresy; their resolutions were supposedly issued in a common encyclical in 1443.[11]

In spite of the hopelessness of the situation in western Europe for the crusade, the reign of Murad II brought Ottoman rule in the Balkans almost to the edge of disaster. This was due mainly to the heroic career of John Hunyadi, the regent of Hungary and voivode of Transylvania, who led the Hungarian crusade with varying fortunes against the Turks. In 1438, Murad had already crossed the Danube and invaded Transylvania as far as the gates of the strong town of Hermannstadt (now Sibiu). Meanwhile, his westerly irruption into Serbia was arrested before Belgrade. At this moment Hunyadi appeared on the scene and succeeded in forming a coalition with two other outstanding eastern leaders: king Vladislav III of Poland

11. Doubt has been cast on the authenticity of this condemnation by Joseph Gill, "The Condemnation of the Council of Florence by the Three Oriental Patriarchs in 1443," *Personalities of the Council of Florence, and other Essays* (Oxford, 1964), pp. 213–221. On the council in general see above, pp. 92–95, and Gill, *The Council of Florence.*

(1434–1444), who also became king (László IV) of Hungary in 1440, and George Brankovich, despot of Serbia (1427–1456). At the beginning, each of the three coalition members conducted hostilities against the Turks separately within his own realm and according to his means. In 1442, Murad attempted another invasion of Transylvania, and was again beaten at Hermannstadt. The Turks are said to have left behind them 20,000 slain in the field of battle. In his fury, the sultan made a third attempt which met with the same fate, and Hunyadi seized 5,000 Ottoman prisoners and 200 standards. Hitherto on the defensive, the voivode was encouraged by the arrival of Latin crusaders under cardinal Julian Cesarini in 1443 to take the offensive south of the Danube. Both king Vladislav and prince George Brankovich joined the crusade, and John Hunyadi, advancing into Serbia, was able to rout the Turks at Nish and pursue them until he made his triumphant entry into Sofia. The Albanians, who were Murad's sworn vassals, were emboldened by these successes and rejected Turkish suzerainty in order to help their coreligionists under their local leader George Castriota, better known as Scanderbeg. Murad, concerned about his European frontiers and at war with Karaman in Anatolia, negotiated an agreement at Adrianople in June 1444 which was ratified by Vladislav and Hunyadi at Szeged in July. By its terms, George Brankovich was reinstated in Serbia, the sultan paid 60,000 ducats as a ransom for one of his sons-in-law, and a ten-year truce was declared (but not kept). Immediately afterward, Murad decided to abdicate and retire to Anatolia.

Cardinal Cesarini protested in vain against the conclusion of the treaty, more especially as the news from the west assured him that reinforcements from France and elsewhere were underway. A fresh embassy from emperor John VIII arrived at Chalon-sur-Saône to implore Philip the Good for help. The duke responded by equipping a flotilla of four galleys under the command of Geoffrey of Thoisy and Martin Alphonse, whom he ordered to sail to Constantinople immediately. On their way east, they assisted the Hospitallers in warding off the Egyptian attack of 1444 on Rhodes. Pope Eugenius IV also sent a similar fleet for the same purpose under the command of his nephew Francis Condulmer. Meanwhile, cardinal Cesarini persuaded Vladislav and Hunyadi to break the truce, alleging that a treaty concluded with an infidel was void and could not bind Christians. He further promised Hunyadi the crown of Bulgaria after its deliverance from the Ottoman yoke. In the end, the treaty was actually broken when the crusaders overran Bulgaria and besieged the important coastal town of Varna by land and by sea (November

1444). The Christian leaders had been counting on the old sultan's abdication and the dispersal of his troops in Asia Minor. A great victory was within sight when Murad unexpectedly emerged from his retreat at the head of 40,000 men, whom the Genoese had transported to the shores of Europe for a substantial price. At first the fighting dragged on and the issue remained in the balance. Then the death of the king of Hungary and that of the apostolic legate deprived the crusade of two of its leaders, and Hunyadi was left alone in an exposed position to face the rising tide of the Turks. On November 10, he had no choice but to take to flight to save the remnant of his troops from extermination.[12]

In the following year, Murad's victorious armies resumed their ravaging campaigns in the Balkans and the Morea. Only the valiant Albanian mountaineer Scanderbeg stood up in defiance to the invader. The sultan himself marched against the dauntless rebel in 1447 without avail. The Albanian opposition on the one hand, and the threatening attacks to which Constantinople was steadily subjected on the other, decided Hunyadi to renew hostilities with the enemy. In 1448, the Hungarian regent crossed the Danube at the Iron Gate with 24,000 men and invaded Serbia. He found Murad waiting for him with a much larger army. The two adversaries met again on the field of Kossovo, with the odds definitely against Hunyadi. Not only was the number of the Turkish hordes far too great for the Christians, but Hunyadi's followers included 10,000 Wallachians whose loyalty to Hungary had always been doubtful. Moreover, Hunyadi imprudently overlooked the desirability of concerted action with Scanderbeg and his indomitable Albanians. In the second battle of Kossovo the Hungarians fought heroically, and the German and Bohemian infantry in the center used the fearful new hand-guns, but neither valor nor even gunpowder and missiles availed against the immense Ottoman battalions. The janissaries in the Turkish center and the timariot cavalry on the wings also proved their intrepidity. The ruthless fray was sustained for three days without interruption (October 17–19, 1448). As soon as the ammunition of the Christians was exhausted, the Turks began to mow them down, and Hunyadi's losses were irreparable. Perhaps a quarter of the Turks were slain, but Murad won the day and repelled the last serious attempt to save Byzantium.

---

12. A chapter on the crusade of Varna, and events leading up to it, is planned for volume V of this work, in preparation. On the preliminaries see G. Ostrogorsky, "The Palaeologi," *Cambridge Medieval History,* IV-1 (1966), 381–384.

With the failure of the Hungarian crusade, the imperial city was virtually abandoned to its fate.[13] Even the ruling class within its walls recognized in some way or other the suzerainty of the sultans. When John VIII died in 1448, his brothers Constantine and Demetrius disputed the succession to the imperial throne; the sultan approved the selection of Constantine Dragases as emperor. On Murad's death in 1451, his son and successor Mehmed II (1451–1481) was destined to obliterate the last traces of the eastern Roman empire within the next two years.

The downfall of Constantinople, long foreseen by its contemporaries, was deferred by the Turks only until they had completed all their preparations. On the Byzantine side, the position of the city was worse than ever. It was impoverished and depopulated. Whole districts were in ruins, and the population in those latter days was estimated at 45,000–50,000. The walls built by Theodosius II, and constantly repaired, nevertheless betrayed signs of old age and debility in several places. The emperor became unpopular with his subjects since he, like his immediate predecessors, declared union with the Roman see in the church of Hagia Sophia, in the hope that the west might come to his relief. The fury of the Greeks found a strong leader in the person of their future patriarch Gennadius, alias George Scholarius, a monk of the convent of the Pantocrator. Certain members of the community, like Lucas Notaras, a high dignitary and admiral of the fleet, went so far as to say that they would rather see the Turkish turban than the papal tiara in Constantinople. Constantine's army of defense could not have exceeded 8,000 for the whole length of the immense walls. Of these, the *Chronicon maius*, falsely attributed to the Greek chronicler Sphrantzes, tells us, 4,973 were Byzantine soldiers, while the rest were Genoese and foreign volunteers and mercenaries. Their war materiel was continuously depleted without hope of any substantial help from outside.

On the Turkish side, the picture was totally different. Although Mehmed II was only nineteen on his accession to the throne, he had already gained considerable experience in both civil and military administration during his father's reign. Since 1444, he had either ruled alone or shared the affairs of state with the old sultan. It was obvious from the beginning that he had set his mind wholly on the capture of Constantinople. To ensure a free passage for his troops from Asia to Europe, he constructed in 1452 a great fortress (Rumeli

---

13. On the last years of Constantinople see above, pp. 101–103, and Steven Runciman, *The Fall of Constantinople, 1453* (Cambridge, 1965).

Hisar) on the European shore and at the narrowest point of the Bosporus facing an older one (Anadolu Hisar) previously founded by sultan Bayazid. Then he concentrated on investing the city with all his might. It is difficult to estimate with precision the number of his forces marshaled outside the walls, given as 160,000 or more men; we must assume that reinforcements continued to pour in from Anatolia to replace the dead and the wounded after the beginning of fighting. The sultan was conscious that nothing could be done without a maritime blockade to complete the siege circle from the sea. For this purpose, he collected 140 ships including twelve great galleys. But we must not exaggerate the strength of the nascent Turkish sea power, and we must remember that that fleet was shut out of the Golden Horn by the famous chain until a late stage in the ensuing assaults. Still more important was Mehmed's stress on the importance of the artillery and the use of gunpowder. He hired Christian renegades to manufacture the finest cannon of the age for him. One of them, a Hungarian named Urban, foundered seventy pieces including a giant super-bombard capable of casting balls of stone weighing 800 pounds. It was drawn from Adrianople to the siege by sixty oxen in forty-two days. However, it turned out to be a failure as it exploded and killed its maker when it was fired. Other more successful pieces comprised eleven cannon casting 500-pound stone balls, and over fifty of smaller caliber casting 200-pound stone balls. Undoubtedly, Ottoman artillery was a decisive factor in paving the way for storming the city of Constantine.

In Europe, two propagandists spoke out for a *passagium generale,* with little or no effect. John Germain, on behalf of the duke of Burgundy, read his famous "Discourse on the Crusade" to Charles VII in 1452, and Aeneas Sylvius Piccolomini, then bishop of Siena, representing emperor Frederick III, delivered an eloquent oration on the same subject before the pope and the cardinals. Both were dismissed with only promises. This was time not for negotiations, but for immediate action. When six Venetian merchant galleys arrived in the Bosporus from Candia, they were requisitioned for the defense, and the republic of St. Mark could but register its approval. Gabriel Trevisan, the Venetian commander, and his mariners were thus employed by the Byzantine emperor, and this represents the only real contribution from Venice. When the commune received the still more alarming news of the position in the east during February 1453, the senate issued orders to James Loredan to lead five more galleys for the relief of the city. The fleet arrived in the waters of Negroponte one day after the fall of Constantinople. Perhaps the most serious reinforcement was that which voluntarily came from the island of Chios under a member of the Giustiniani families named John William Longo, thitherto known as a pirate in the Archipelago. He arrived with seven hundred men at Constantinople on January 29, 1453, and the emperor readily accepted his services and promised him the island of Lesbos.

The last great siege of Byzantium was officially inaugurated on April 6. The Turkish direct attacks and the heavy bombardment of the walls took a serious turn from April 11. Then on April 20, three Genoese galleys with men and munitions from pope Nicholas V succeeded in forcing their way into the Golden Horn. This prompted Mehmed II to devise an unprecedented war ruse to occupy the Golden Horn and deprive the city of its sole outlet to the Genoese colony of Pera. On April 22, his men rolled seventy light ships overland from the Bosporus behind Pera and Galata to the inner harbor of the Golden Horn. This gigantic engineering feat commenced at dawn, by the use of greased planks on the road and sheer manpower. Havoc ensued among the Christian mariners when they suddenly discovered the Turks in their midst. Taken unawares, these Christians took to flight, and the siege was extended to all the sea walls. Continuous bombardment was concentrated on a land sector that appeared to be weak, between the gate of Adrianople (Edirnekapî) and the civil gate of St. Romanus (Topkapî). A breach in one of the lateral towers of the latter gate was valiantly defended and somewhat repaired, but the remaining debris filled the moat and provided the Turks with a direct bridge across to the city walls.

Intermittent sallies and unremitting bombardment were unexpectedly suspended on May 28. Like the calm which precedes the storm, this ominous tranquillity proved to be the prelude to the end. At midnight of May 28–29 a sudden mass assault was launched on the walls by land and sea. Mehmed II's aim was to dissipate the defense on all sides to screen his greater concentration on the most vulnerable northwestern point, where the wall was extensively dilapidated; the plan worked. To make matters worse, Giustiniani was wounded and withdrew from the walls. Later, he and his men deserted the city and took to the sea. This demoralized the Greeks at a most critical moment, for it was during these maneuvers that a janissary detachment filtered into the city enceinte through the undefended Circus gate (Kerkoporta) exactly at dawn and surprised the imperial formations from the rear at the gate of St. Romanus. Constantine Dragases drew his sword and joined in the last fighting to die an honorable death, and his body was lost in the increasing pile of those who fell in the fray. Resistance soon ceased and the sack of the city commenced, to last for three full and fearful days. The depleted population was either massacred or reduced to slavery. Late in the afternoon of May 29, Mehmed II made his triumphant entry through the gate of St. Romanus and went straight to say his prayers in the converted mosque of Aya Sofia. An old empire had passed out of the picture, and a new one came into being. Constantinople, hitherto a declining city, received fresh vigor and gradually rose to the status of the greater cities of Europe. When Selim I annexed Egypt in 1517, Cairo sank into a secondary position, and Constantinople, now called Istanbul, became the metropolis of the Islamic world.[14]

The fall of Constantinople in 1453, like the fall of Jerusalem in 1187 and of Acre in 1291, was received with great bitterness by the bewildered west. Constantine Dragases' brother Thomas, who had ruled the Morea, ultimately took refuge in Rome in 1461, bringing with him the head of St. Andrew the Apostle. Aeneas Sylvius Piccolomini, renowned for his crusading zeal, had become pope as Pius II, and he undertook to lead a crusade. On June 18, 1464, he took the cross himself at St. Peter's in order to set an example to all the Catholic monarchs of the west, who displayed utter indifference to the crusading cause. Even duke Philip, who had sworn to follow the pontiff with 6,000 men, asked for a year's respite and blamed Louis XI, perhaps rightly, for the change in his attitude. A dying man, Pius II was determined to inaugurate the expedition nevertheless. He actually set out, but died on August 14 at Ancona, to be buried with his project at the Vatican. His successor, Paul II (1464–1471), apparently diverted the crusading funds to Venice and Hungary for use in their wars with the Turks.

Nevertheless, the idea of the crusade continued to haunt the imagination of western princes until the seventeenth century. Henry V of England, on his deathbed in 1422, had made a solemn vow to undertake the holy war on his return to health. Joan of Arc in the same period had dreamt of a similar enterprise, but the circumstances of the Hundred Years' War had made the realization of her project an impossibility. During the pontificate of Innocent VIII (1484–1492), the flight of Bayazid II's brother and rival Jem to the west resuscitated plans for war against the Turks and for inciting rebellion among the supporters of the refugee, but this, too, came to nothing. The reconquest of Jerusalem was discussed in 1515 by pope Leo X and king Francis I of France, but their project went no further. Emperor

---

14. On the Ottoman conquest of Egypt see above, pp. 511–512.

Charles V (1519—1556) later espoused the cause; he demonstrated his pious intentions by granting the island of Malta in 1530 to the Knights of St. John of Jerusalem after their expulsion from Rhodes, and by the descent of his forces on Tunis in 1535, on Algiers in 1541, and on Mahdia in 1550 for the suppression of the activities of the Barbary corsairs. As a result, his antagonist, Francis I, adopted an opposite policy by allying himself in 1536 with sultan Suleiman I "the Magnificent" (1520—1566) to secure his maritime assistance against the emperor. Viewed from another angle this Franco-Turkish treaty may be regarded as the beginning of the supremacy of French influence in the Levant, characteristic of modern times, and as a landmark in the development of the "capitulations" in the Ottoman empire.

The anti-Turkish policy was, however, prolonged in Spain by Philip II (1556—1598), who delegated his half-brother, Don John of Austria, to command the Spanish fleet and join the Venetians in their naval struggle against the Turks in the Levant. The combined armada numbered 208 against 250 Ottoman galleys when the memorable battle of Lepanto was fought between them on October 7, 1571. Eighty Turkish galleys foundered, 130 were captured, and 40 managed to escape within the short span of three hours. Though Turkish naval expansion in the Mediterranean was seriously curtailed after Lepanto, the Christians' dissensions prevented them from reaping the full benefit of their great victory. The Spaniards wanted to direct the fleet toward North Africa, while the Venetians hoped to retake Cyprus. In the end, Venice came to terms with the Turks by relinquishing Cyprus to its fate and even by paying a heavy indemnity of 300,000 ducats to the sultan in March 1573. Don John descended alone on Tunisia in the same year, and was expelled from it in 1574. Peace pourparlers between Spain and Turkey were begun in 1581 and completed in 1585.

By land, the Turkish conquests and Christian defeats continued until the seventeenth century. When George Castriota (Scanderbeg) died in 1468, Albania was conquered and assimilated into the Ottoman empire. In 1521, Belgrade succumbed; in 1522 Rhodes was captured. Still more staggering was the rout of the Hungarians in the battle of Mohács on August 29—30, 1526. King Louis of Hungary was killed in the field, and his death precipitated the fall of his kingdom. Then the first siege of Vienna occurred in September 1529 and was raised on October 16. This was only the forerunner of repeated assaults on the Austrian capital, and the Turkish tide would not definitively recede until the failure of the siege of 1683, when

John Sobieski, king of Poland, saved the city from imminent destruction.

In the Levant, there was little or no activity aimed specifically at the deliverance of Jerusalem, although numerous European leaders kept proclaiming new projects for this purpose. It may be surprising to know that people like Cardinal Richelieu (1585–1642) and Father Joseph (1577–1638), the famous French diplomat, found time to ruminate on the salvation of the Holy Land. Perhaps the only person of the time who not only entertained this idea but actually did some preliminary work toward its realization was Ferdinand I de' Medici, grand duke of Tuscany, who managed to land in Cyprus and make contact with some discontented Asian chieftains for joint action against sultan Ahmed I (1603–1617). These attempts in the years 1607–1608 had no positive result, and Ferdinand himself died on February 7, 1609. A propagandist document of the same year, composed by an Italian priest residing in Cairo, John Dominelli, describes a fresh plan for an effective campaign against the Turks to save "the most Holy Sepulcher and the holy places of Jerusalem." [15] The writer argues that the sultan was involved in war on several fronts in Europe and Asia, his men suffered from disaffection, and the Christians under the Turkish yoke were ready for insurrection, while the garrisons in Egypt and the Holy Land were depleted. The times were, on the whole, most suitable for a successful campaign against the Ottomans, but Father Dominelli was oblivious of the circumstances in Europe which had rendered the crusade an anachronistic dream.

It becomes evident from the march of events that the most enduring result of the crusades was the vehement reaction of the Islamic polity to the continued aggression of western Christendom against Moslem territory for three centuries. The momentum gained by the Moslem powers while defending their own ground ultimately swung the pendulum in the opposite direction, and the assailed became the assailant; the outlying Christian states in the Levant became an easy prey to inroads from Egypt and Turkey. This movement, which has been described as the "counter-crusade," was, indeed, a counterfoil to the crusade in almost every aspect of its history. Just as there was propaganda in Europe for holy war, there was also propaganda among the peoples of Islam for the repulsion of Christian incursions. Expeditions conducted under the banner of the cross gave rise to

---

15. See N. Iorga, "Un Projet relatif à la conquête de Jérusalem, 1609," *Revue de l'Orient latin*, II (1894), 183–189.

anti-crusades from the Islamic states. Both were not merely armed struggles, but also conflicts of faith and of ideals. Both aimed at the deliverance of the Holy Land from the yoke of an "infidel" usurper. Both started with words of conviction in the form of propaganda, and ended in a mortal struggle for supremacy.

The history of the counter-crusade offers the scholar immense opportunities for original research.[16] Its literature compares miserably with the gigantic output on the crusades, despite the comparability of the two great movements. As a matter of fact, the counter-crusade had begun at the time of the Second Crusade with the rise of the house of Zengi at Mosul during the twelfth century. Then it had become a serious menace in Saladin's reign, with the fall of Jerusalem in 1187. Finally, the thirteenth century had seen the total eclipse of Latin dominion on the Asian mainland in 1291. Afterward, the Moslem battalions become an irresistible force in annihilating the eastern Christian principalities within their reach. This offensive outlived the Middle Ages and reached its zenith with the Turks in the sixteenth century.

The great mass of Moslem propagandist treatises, mostly unpublished, may be divided into three categories, all working up to the same ultimate aim of evoking lively interest in the Holy Land and of urging the community of the faithful to take arms in its defense. The first category comprises the books of pilgrimages (*kutub az-ziyārāt*), whose authors elaborate the thesis that pilgrimage, one of the pillars of Islam, is not confined to Mecca and Medina. Good Moslems are also expected to visit the tombs of the earlier prophets of the two other monotheistic religions, Judaism and Christianity. Mohammed did not denounce either; what Islam discredited was the alleged interpolations or elements of corruption by subsequent generations in the original holy texts. All Moslems were therefore bound by their religion to keep these shrines from being polluted by the "infidel" crusader.

The second category includes the books of virtues (*kutub al-faḍā'il*). A considerable number of tracts were written to enumerate the virtues of the Holy Land and of all the Islamic countries in such persuasive style as to inflame the zeal of the faithful against Christian aggression. Some of these books are devoted to such key towns of the Islamic empire as Aleppo, Alexandria, Cairo, and Damascus.

The third category, which is by far the most important, consists of books on holy war (*kutub al-jihād*), which may be further subdivided

16. On the counter-crusade and its literature see E. Sivan, *L'Islam et la croisade* (Paris, 1968).

into two sections or sets of treatises. One set deals with the principle of Moslem holy warfare, which well-nigh attained the status of a sixth pillar of the faith. This placed all able-bodied Moslems under the obligation of fighting non-Moslems until the whole world became converted or subdued to Islam. Apart from a multitude of tracts specially written on this subject, all authors in the field of Islamic jurisprudence (al-fiqh) devote considerable parts of their study to a full discussion of the tenets of holy war. The other set of treatises speaks of the more practical issues of the eastern art of war. Some authors tackle the equestrian art, others describe the implements of war and their usage, and still others discuss the technique of fighting and the order of battle. These books are intended for the initiation of the ranks as well as the edification of the generals who led the Moslem forces. The size of this literature leaves no room for doubt as to the existence of an elaborate system of war which helps to account for the brilliant victories of the Islamic armies in both Asia and Europe.[17]

The outcome of these varied exhortations and expositions was a regular anti-crusading movement from Egypt and Turkey, the two great Islamic powers in the Levant. The Egyptian counter-crusade chose Cilician Armenia as its primary target; its conquest was accomplished during the sultanate of al-Ashraf Sha'bān (1363–1376). After a bitter struggle, the emir of Aleppo stormed the Armenian capital Sis in 1375, and left it in ruins after leveling its fortifications to the ground and seizing the last of the kings of Armenia, Leon VI of the house of Lusignan, who was carried in chains to the citadel of Cairo. After seven years of imprisonment, Leon was released on payment of a heavy ransom by Venice and the papacy, to spend the remainder of his years wandering in Europe until his death, childless, in Paris in 1393.[18]

The next Egyptian counter-crusade was undertaken by sultan Barsbey's fleet against the Latin kingdom of Cyprus. The Mamluks could not forget the sack of Alexandria by Peter I de Lusignan in 1365, and they were determined to avenge themselves on the island kingdom. After assembling and fitting out suitable galleys for the enterprise, they launched naval expeditions to Cyprus in the years 1424, 1425, and 1426. The Cypriote army was routed and king Janus was seized in the battle of Khirokitia on July 7, 1426. Nicosia was

17. For examples of the first two categories of Moslem propagandist literature see section V of the bibliography of Atiya, *The Crusade in the Later Middle Ages* (pp. 545–546); on the third category see section IV (pp. 544–545).

18. See above, p. 489. A chapter on the later rulers of Cilician Armenia is planned for volume V of this work, in preparation.

pillaged, and the king and his retinue were, like Leon VI, led in chains to the Cairo citadel. In the following year, they managed to regain their freedom through the intercession of the Genoese and Venetian consuls on payment of a ransom of 200,000 ducats and an annual tribute of 5,000 ducats. The king was, furthermore, constrained to swear an oath of fealty to the sultan; Cyprus thus became tributary to Egypt.[19]

The downfall of Cyprus whetted the appetite of the Mamluks to purge the waters of the Levant of all traces of Latin domination. Accordingly, the next stage of their counter-crusade was directed against the Knights Hospitaller stationed in Rhodes.[20] They mounted three naval campaigns against the island fortress in 1440, 1443, and 1444. Here they confronted a defense stiffer than that of Cyprus. The Knights of St. John formed a regular standing body of chivalry under one leadership ready for any emergency at any time. Moreover, they had developed an elaborate system of espionage covering many countries, including Egypt, and were therefore forewarned of the details of the coming Mamluk attacks on them. The Egyptians used Syria and southern Anatolia as bases to revictual their fleet before attacking Rhodes, assisted by some of the Turkish emirs of Asia Minor. Nevertheless, they failed to achieve their aim. Though they occupied the knights' little isolated island of Castellorizzo off the southern Anatolian coast, the main stronghold of Rhodes remained intact. The third campaign ended in disaster. The Mamluks lost 300 killed and 500 wounded, while most of the Christian renegades who accompanied the Moslem army deserted the Egyptians and fled to the other side; the survivors raised the siege of Rhodes and returned to Egypt just in time to escape the austerity of winter. The fate of the island was therefore deferred until 1522, when Suleiman I expelled the order during the reign of the grand master Philip Villiers de l'Isle Adam. When emperor Charles V granted them Malta in 1530, they established there a small buffer state against the Ottomans and the Barbary corsairs. They distinguished themselves in the fighting which took place between May 19 and September 12, 1565, under the grand master John of La Valette.

The expulsion of the Hospitallers from Rhodes was but a minor chapter in the story of the Moslem counter-crusade from Turkey. When the Ottomans swept over the Balkans and into east Central Europe, they were, in a sense, anti-crusading. They had fought and routed the crusaders at Nicopolis in 1396, and at Varna in 1444.

19. See above, pp. 373–375.
20. See above, chapter IX.

Their victorious career had reached a peak in the capture of Constantinople in 1453. The downfall of the Mamluks in Syria and Egypt in 1517 had transferred all Islamic authority in the Levant to Istanbul. Turkish aggrandizement in the west was arrested only at Belgrade in 1456, outside the gates of Vienna in 1529, and in the waters of Lepanto in 1571. It was only then that the counter-crusade came to a standstill, and men's minds turned to the new "eastern question" instead of the old cause of the crusade.

The ascendancy of Turkey on the one hand, and the downfall of Egypt on the other, led to the deflection of the eastern trade from the great emporia of the Mamluk empire. In fact, the exchange of trade between east and west, which had received its greatest stimulus from the movement of the crusade, suffered its severest blow from the Ottomanization of the Near East. The immediate result of this position was a new burst of energy in search of India and Cathay by way of the ocean rather than the Mediterranean. In 1486, Bartholomew Díaz rounded the Cape of Good Hope; in 1492, Vasco da Gama reaped the fruit of his predecessor's achievement by reaching the shores of India. In 1492, also, Christopher Columbus discovered a whole new world in his attempt to reach Cathay by the western sea route. Thus new vistas and immense possibilities were opened up by the age of discoveries, and crusading ideas were all but drowned out in the tumult of imminent changes and the dawn of a modern era.

IMPORTANT DATES
AND EVENTS

1049		Zīrids of Tunisia disown Fāṭimid suzerainty and Shī'ite faith
1052		Arab raiders from Egypt devastate Tripolitania and Tunisia
1054	July 20	Schism precipitated by patriarch Cerularius and cardinal Humbert
1056		Abū-Bakr founds Murābiṭ dynasty at Sijilmasa in Morocco
1064–1065		Great German pilgrimage to Jerusalem
1066		Slavic revolt against Saxon domination and conversion efforts
1071	August 26	Selchükid Turks defeat Byzantines at Manzikert
1072		Normans under Robert Guiscard take Palermo from the Moslems
1081	April	Accession of Alexius I Comnenus as Byzantine emperor
1085	May 25	Alfonso VI of Castile and Leon conquers Toledo from the Moors
1086	October 23	Murābiṭs under Yūsuf defeat Spanish under Alfonso at Zallaca
1087		Abū-Bakr dies after destroying Ghana; Yūsuf is Murābiṭ ruler
1087–1090 or 1091		Pilgrimage of count Robert I of Flanders to Jerusalem
1087	August 6	Genoese and Pisan fleets sack Mahdia as reprisal for piracy
1089	late summer	Fāṭimids of Egypt acquire Acre, Tyre, and Jerusalem
1090		Assassins establish headquarters at Alamut in Persia
1091		Normans under Roger I complete conquest of Moslem Sicily
1094	June 15	Rodrigo Díaz, the Cid (dies 1099), seizes Valencia (lost 1102)
1095	November 27	Pope Urban II preaches the crusade at the Council of Clermont
1096	October 21	People's crusade annihilated near Nicaea by Selchükid Turks
1096	November	The First Crusade: the first armies reach Constantinople
1097	June 19	Nicaea surrendered to Byzantines by Selchükid Turks
1097	July 1	Crusaders defeat Turks under Kîlîj Arslan I at Dorylaeum
1098	March 10	Baldwin of Boulogne assumes rule of Edessa, with title of count
1098	June 3	Crusaders take Antioch; Bohemond of Taranto becomes prince
1099	July 15	The First Crusade ends with conquest of Jerusalem from Fāṭimids
1099	July 22	Godfrey of Bouillon elected Advocate of the Holy Sepulcher
1100	July 18	Godfrey of Bouillon dies, amid accusations of poisoning
1100	December 25	Baldwin I crowned king of Jerusalem at Bethlehem
1101	late March	Tancred regent of Antioch for captured Bohemond
1101	August–Sept.	Crusade of 1101 defeated piecemeal in Anatolia by the Turks
1103	early May	Bohemond freed by Turks, resumes rule over Antioch
1104	summer	Byzantines regain Cilicia from crusaders and Armenians
1105	February 28	Raymond of St. Gilles dies when besieging Tripoli
1106	September 2	Yūsuf ibn-Tāshfīn dies; son 'Alī Murābiṭ ruler (to 1143)
1107–1110		Crusade of Norwegians under king Sigurd "Jorsalfar"
1107	autumn	Bohemond's anti-Greek "crusade" takes Avlona, besieges Durazzo
1108	September	Bohemond's expedition collapses (he dies in Italy in March 1111)
1109	July 12	Tripoli falls to crusaders; Bertram assumes title of its count
1112	December 12	Tancred dies; Roger of Salerno regent of Antioch
1113		Hospitallers granted protection by bull of pope Paschal II
1115		Baldwin I builds Krak de Montréal south of the Dead Sea
1118	April 2	Baldwin I dies; Baldwin II of Le Bourg, count of Edessa, succeeds

1118	August 15	Alexius I Comnenus dies; his son John becomes Byzantine emperor
1118	December 18	Saragossa surrenders to Alfonso I of Aragon-Navarre
1119	June 28	Roger of Antioch killed by Īl-Ghazi near Darb Sarmadā
1119	Aug. or Sept.	Baldwin II installs Joscelin of Courtenay as count of Edessa
1123	April 18	Baldwin II captured by Turks (freed August 29, 1124)
1124	July 7	Tyre falls to Frankish army and Venetian fleet
1128	June 18	Zengi, governor of Mosul, enters Aleppo
1130	February	Bohemond II of Antioch killed in Cilicia by Turks
1130		'Abd-al-Mu'min founds Muwaḥḥid caliphal dynasty, Murābits wane
1131	August 21	Baldwin II of Jerusalem dies, leaving no son
1131	September 14	Baldwin's son-in-law Fulk of Anjou crowned king of Jerusalem
1132 or 1133		Assassins purchase al-Qadmūs, first foothold in Syria
1134	July 17	Alfonso I of Aragon dies after defeat by Murābits at Fraga
1135		Alfonso VII of Castile-Leon crowned emperor of Spain, Portugal
1137		Byzantine emperor John Comnenus invades Cilicia, besieges Antioch
1137		Aragon and Catalonia (Barcelona) unite as the Crown of Aragon
1138	May	Byzantine emperor John Comnenus takes Antioch but withdraws
1139		Count Afonso Henriques of Portugal defeats Moors at Ourique
1140		Afonso Henriques assumes title king Afonso I of Portugal
1142		Fulk's vassal Pagan builds Kerak (Krak of Moab) in Transjordan
1143	April 8	John Comnenus dies; his son Manuel I Byzantine emperor
1143	November 10	Fulk of Anjou, king of Jerusalem, dies
1143	December 25	Fulk's widow Melisend and son Baldwin III are crowned
1144	Dec. 24–26	Zengi captures Edessa, kills Franks and destroys their churches
1145	December 1	The Second Crusade: pope Eugenius III issues the crusade bull
1146	March 31	Bernard, abbot of Clairvaux, preaches the crusade at Vézelay
1146	September 14	Zengi killed; sons Saif-ad-Dīn Ghāzī (Mosul), Nūr-ad-Dīn (Aleppo)
1147	July–September	German expedition against the Wends accomplishes little
1147	Sept.–Oct.	Second Crusade: Conrad III and Louis VII arrive at Constantinople
1147	October	Almeria taken by Spanish, Lisbon by Portuguese and English
1147	October	Conrad III and the German crusaders defeated near Dorylaeum
1148	January	Louis VII and the French crusaders defeated near Cadmus
1148	July 24–28	The Second Crusade fails to take Damascus, and collapses
1148		Mahdia taken by Sicilians (retaken January 1160 by Muwaḥḥids)
1148	December	Tortosa captured by Aragonese, Catalans, crusaders, and Genoese
1149	June 29	Army of Antioch defeated by Nūr-ad-Dīn near Inab
1151	January 27	Alfonso VII, Raymond Berenguer IV allocate spheres at Tudellén
1151 (or 1152) spring		Baldwin III breaks with Melisend, assumes full royal authority
1152		Raymond II of Tripoli killed by Assassins
1153	spring	Reginald of Châtillon marries Constance of Antioch, becomes prince
1153	August 22	Ascalon surrenders to Baldwin III, king of Jerusalem
1154	April 25	Damascus submits to Nūr-ad-Dīn
1157	August 21	Alfonso VII dies after losing Almeria to Muwaḥḥids
1162	August 8	Raymond Berenguer IV dies after career of reconquest (from 1137)
1163	February 10	Baldwin III dies; brother Amalric crowned king (February 18)
1163	May	'Abd-al-Mu'min dies; son Yūsuf I is Muwaḥḥid caliph
1163–1169		Amalric leads five expeditions against Fāṭimid Egypt
1169	March 23	Saladin succeeds his uncle Shīrkūh as vizir of Egypt
1171	September 10	Saladin, at Nūr-ad-Dīn's order, proclaims 'Abbāsid caliphs in Egypt
1171	September 13	The last Fāṭimid caliph, al-'Āḍid, dies
1172	summer	Muwaḥḥids under Yūsuf I fail to take Huete, retreat
1174	May 15	Nūr-ad-Dīn dies; Saladin occupies Damascus (October 28)
1174	July 11	Amalric dies; leper son Baldwin IV crowned king (July 15)
1175	May	'Abbāsid caliph formally invests Saladin with Egypt and Syria

1176	September 17	Selchükid Turks defeat the Byzantines at Myriokephalon
1178		Castilians, with Aragonese aid, take Cuenca after 9-month siege
1179	March 20	Castile and Aragon-Catalonia sign new partition treaty at Cazorla
1180	September 24	Manuel I Comnenus dies; son Alexius II is emperor
1182–1183	February	Reginald of Châtillon, lord of Kerak, raids Red Sea ports
1183		Yūsuf I fails to take Santarem, dies (1184); son Ya'qūb is caliph
1183	November 20	Baldwin IV ill; child-nephew Baldwin V crowned king
1185	March 16	Baldwin IV of Jerusalem dies of leprosy
1186	late summer	Baldwin V dies; mother Sibyl and Guy of Lusignan crowned jointly
1187	July 4	Saladin defeats Franks at Hattin, captures Guy, executes Reginald
1187	October 2	Jerusalem surrenders to Saladin, followed by most of Palestine
1188	March 27	Emperor Frederick I Barbarossa takes the cross at Mainz
1189	August 27	Guy of Lusignan besieges Acre; Pisan fleet blockades it
1189	September 6	English crusaders aid Portuguese to recapture Silves (lost 1191)
1190	May 18	German crusaders defeat Selchükid Turks, take Konya
1190	June 10	Frederick I drowns in Cilicia; army proceeds to Antioch, disbands
1191	May 6–June 5	Richard I conquers Cyprus on way to Syria for the Third Crusade
1191	July 12	Acre surrenders to combined armies of Philip II and Richard I
1192	April 28	Conrad of Montferrat is killed at Tyre by Assassins
1192	May	Guy of Lusignan buys Cyprus from Templars, founds dynasty
1192	October 9	Richard I sails from Acre, ending the Third Crusade
1193	March 4	Saladin dies; Aiyūbid and Zengid princes struggle for provinces
1194	April	Guy of Lusignan dies; brother Aimery inherits Cyprus
1195	July 19	Alfonso VIII of Castile defeated at Alarcos by Ya'qūb, Muwaḥḥid
1197	September	Aimery crowned king of Cyprus and (October) of Jerusalem
1197	September 28	Emperor Henry VI dies, causing collapse of new German crusade
1198	January 8	Innocent III elected pope, declares (1199) first "political" crusade
1199		Ya'qūb dies; son Muḥammad an-Nāṣir Muwaḥḥid caliph (dies 1213)
1199	late November	French counts at Écry take the cross for the Fourth Crusade
1200	spring	Albert von Buxhövden leads German fleet to conquer Latvia
1200	August 4	Saladin's brother al-'Ādil proclaimed sultan of Egypt and Syria
1202	October 1	Crusaders sail on Venetian ships to attack Zara
1203	July 6	French and Venetian crusaders begin siege of Constantinople
1204	April 13	Constantinople is taken by Latins, sacked; the Fourth Crusade ends
1204	May 9	Baldwin of Flanders elected Latin emperor by the crusaders
1204	October	Byzantine empire is partitioned among the crusaders
1205		Geoffrey of Villehardouin, William of Champlitte conquer Morea
1205	April 1	Aimery dies, leaving Cyprus and Jerusalem under separate regencies
1205	April 14	Baldwin I captured by Bulgarians; brother Henry is regent
1206	August 20	Henry becomes emperor after death of his brother Baldwin I
1207		Deaths of Ioannitsa and Boniface disrupt Bulgaria and Thessalonica
1208	January 14	Murder of Peter of Castelnau touches off Albigensian Crusade
1208	spring	Theodore I Lascaris crowned Greek emperor at Nicaea
1209	May	Geoffrey I becomes prince of Achaea, founds Villehardouin dynasty
1210	October 3	John of Brienne and wife Mary crowned rulers of Jerusalem
1211		Andrew II of Hungary invites Teutonic Knights to Transylvania
1212	spring–August	Children's Crusade from France and Germany collapses in Italy
1212	July 16	Peter II of Aragon defeats Muwaḥḥids at Las Navas de Tolosa
1213	September 12	Peter II killed as Simon of Montfort wins battle of Muret
1215	November	The Fourth Lateran Council considers Albigensians, a Fifth Crusade
1216	June 11	Henry of Hainault dies; Peter of Courtenay Latin emperor-elect
1217–1218		Andrew II and Hungarians on the Fifth Crusade accomplish nothing
1217	October 18	Alcácer do Sal falls to Portuguese, German crusaders, and Leonese
1218	January 10	Hugh I of Cyprus dies; infant son Henry I under regency

1218	June 25	Simon of Montfort killed while besieging Toulouse
1219	early	Peter of Courtenay dies in captivity; son Robert Latin emperor
1219	November 5	Damietta abandoned to crusaders by its Egyptian garrison
1220	November 22	Frederick II crowned Holy Roman emperor by pope Honorius III
1221	August 30	Crusaders surrender to Aiyūbids, evacuate Damietta (September 8)
1222	August	Theodore I Lascaris dies; son-in-law John Ducas Vatatzes emperor
1223		Mongols under Jebe rout Russians and Kumans at the Kalka
1224	autumn	Thessalonica falls to Theodore of Epirus, who assumes the purple
1225	November 9	Frederick II marries Isabel of Brienne, claims throne of Jerusalem
1226	early June	Louis VIII of France leads "crusade" against Languedoc
1226	November 8	Louis VIII dies; son Louis IX is king, under regency
1227		Chinggis (Genghis Khan) dies; son Ögödei rules (dies 1242)
1227	September 29	Frederick II excommunicated by Gregory IX (to August 28, 1230)
1228	January (?)	Robert of Courtenay dies; brother Baldwin II under regency
1229	February 18	Frederick II gains Jerusalem by treaty with al-Kāmil, Aiyūbid
1229	April 12	Peace of Paris ends the Albigensian Crusade
1229	(about)	Geoffrey I of Villehardouin dies; son Geoffrey II prince of Achaea
1230		Yahyâ I independent in Tunisia; establishes Hafsid dynasty
1230		Teutonic Knights under Hermann of Salza start conquest of Prussia
1230	April	John Asen of Bulgaria defeats Theodore of Epirus at Klokotnitsa
1230	September 24	Ferdinand III permanently reunites Castile and Leon
1231	September	Baldwin II marries Mary of Brienne; her father John is co-emperor
1232–April 1233		Civil war between Frederick II's forces and Cypriote lords
1232–1237		Muhammad I al-Ahmar establishes Nasrids at Granada (to 1492)
1235		Ceuta taken by Genoese fleet, ransomed for 400,000 dinars
1236	June 29	Cordova surrenders to Castilians under Ferdinand III
1237	March 23	John of Brienne dies, leaving Baldwin II sole Latin emperor
1238	March 9	Al-Kāmil's death touches off struggle among Aiyūbid princes
1238	September 28	Valencia surrenders to James I of Aragon-Catalonia
1239	November 13	Crusaders defeated near Gaza; Jerusalem surrenders (December 7)
1240–1249		Prussian revolt against Teutonic Knights almost succeeds
1241–1242		Mongols under Batu devastate Hungary, withdraw eastward
1242	April 5	Alexander Nevski defeats Teutonic Knights on Lake Peipus
1243	July 2	Mongols defeat Selchükid Turks at Köse Dagh
1244	August 23	Jerusalem sacked by Khorezmian Turks (never regained by Franks)
1245	June 28	Council of Lyons considers Latin empire, "deposes" Frederick II
1246		Güyük chosen to succeed his father Ögödei, dies 1248
1246	summer	Geoffrey II of Villehardouin dies; brother William prince of Achaea
1247–1248		Andrew, Ascelin, John of Pian del Carpine report on Mongols
1248	August 25	Louis IX of France sails to Cyprus, winters there preparing crusade
1248	November 23	Seville taken by Ferdinand III after a long siege
1249	June 5	French crusaders land in Egypt, capture Damietta (June 6)
1249–1250		Capture of Faro, Silves, and Algarve ends Portuguese reconquest
1250	April 6	Louis IX and the crusaders surrender to the Egyptians at Mansūrah
1250	May 2	Mamluks kill Aiyūbid sultan Tūrān-Shāh; his widow rules
1250	May 6	Crusaders surrender Damietta, ransom Louis IX and other leaders
1250	July 30	Aybeg marries sultan's widow, is first Mamluk sultan of Egypt
1250	December 13	Frederick II dies; son Conrad IV (king of Jerusalem) succeeds him
1253	January 18	Henry I of Cyprus dies; his infant son Hugh II king under regency
1253		Hafsid ruler (from 1249) Muhammad I assumes caliphal title
1253–1255		William of Rubruck, Franciscan, travels to Karakorum and back
1254	April 24	Louis IX sails for France after strengthening Palestine defense
1254	May 21	Conrad IV of Jerusalem dies, leaving infant son Conradin as heir
1254	November 3	John Ducas Vatatzes dies; son Theodore II Lascaris is emperor

1255		Civil war splits Frankish Greece
1256	December 20	Mongols under Hulagu take Alamut, end Assassins' sway in Persia
1256		Batu, khan of the Golden Horde, dies
1257		Berke succeeds his brother Batu as khan (to 1266)
1258	February	Mongols under Hulagu sack Baghdad, kill last 'Abbāsid caliph
1258	August	Theodore II dies; Michael VIII Palaeologus seizes Nicaean throne
1259	summer	Michael VIII defeats Franks at Pelagonia, captures leaders
1260	winter	Mongols devastate Aleppo (January 24), take Damascus (March 1)
1260		Kubilai succeeds brother Möngke (1251–1259) as Mongol ruler
1260	September 3	Mamluk army under Baybars routs Mongols at 'Ain Jālūt
1261	July 25	Greeks reconquer Constantinople, ending Latin empire
1265	February 8	Hulagu dies; his son Abagha establishes il-khanid dynasty in Iran
1266	February 26	Charles of Anjou defeats Manfred at Benevento, wins Sicily
1266	Aug.–Sept.	Mamluks led by Kalavun devastate Cilician Armenia
1267	May 24	William of Villehardouin is vassal of Charles of Anjou for Achaea
1267	December 5	Hugh II of Lusignan dies; cousin Hugh III "de Lusignan" king
1268	May 18	Antioch is overwhelmed and sacked by Mamluks under Baybars
1268	August 23	Charles of Anjou and William of Achaea defeat Conradin at Tagliacozzo
1268	October 29	Conradin is executed, extinguishing Hohenstaufen line
1269	September 24	Hugh III of Cyprus crowned king of Jerusalem at Tyre
1270	July 18	Louis IX and French crusaders attack Carthage in Ḥafṣid Tunisia
1270	August 25	Louis IX dies; Charles of Anjou arranges treaty, sails (November 18)
1270–1272		Edward [I] of England leads crusade to Tunisia and Palestine
1271	April 8	Baybars takes Krak de Chevaliers from Hospitallers after siege
1273	July 9	Last Assassin stronghold in Syria falls to the Mamluks
1274	July 6	Union of the Greek and Roman churches proclaimed at Lyons
1276	January 10	Pope Gregory X dies, ending plans for joint Latin-Greek crusade
1277	April 18	Mamluks under Baybars defeat Mongols at Albistan
1277	July 1	Baybars dies; Kalavun soon becomes sultan (1279–1290)
1278	May 1	William of Villehardouin dies; Achaea reverts to Charles of Anjou
1280–1289		John of Monte Corvino makes missionary voyage to Persia
1281	April	Michael VIII and Greek army defeat Angevin invaders at Berat
1281	late October	Mamluks under Kalavun rout invading Mongols near Homs
1282	March 30	Angevin garrison in Sicily is massacred (the Sicilian Vespers)
1282	June 28	Peter III of Aragon "crusades" to Collo, sails to Sicily (August)
1282	December 11	Michael VIII Palaeologus dies; son Andronicus II Byzantine emperor
1283		Prussian revolt (started 1260) suppressed by Teutonic Knights
1284	March 4	Hugh III de Lusignan dies; son John I king of Jerusalem and Cyprus
1285	January 7	Charles of Anjou dies; succeeded by son Charles II (Naples, Achaea)
1285	May 20	John I de Lusignan of Cyprus dies; brother Henry II succeeds him
1286	August 15	Henry II of Cyprus is crowned king of Jerusalem at Tyre
1287	June 23	Rabban Ṣaumā, envoy of il-khanid Arghun, reaches Rome
1290	Nov. or Dec.	Kalavun dies while marching on Acre; son al-Ashrāf Khalīl sultan
1291	May 18	Mamluks under Khalīl take Acre, ending the kingdom of Jerusalem
1291	May–August	The remaining Frankish towns in Syria surrender to the Mamluks
1293	December 13	Murder of Khalīl touches off struggle among Mamluks for throne
1293	end	John of Villiers dies; Odo de Pins master of the Hospital, in Cyprus
1296	winter	Odo de Pins dies; William of Villaret elected master of the Hospital
1299	December 22	Ghazan's il-khanid Mongol army crushes Mamluks near Homs
1302	August 31	Treaty of Caltabellotta (Aragonese of Sicily, Angevins of Naples)
1303	August 18	Roger de Flor and the Catalan Company sack Ceos
1304		Benedict Zaccaria, a Genoese, seizes Chios from the Byzantines
1305	April	Roger de Flor is killed in Constantinople by Michael (IX)'s men
1305		William of Villaret dies; his nephew Fulk is master of the Hospital

1306–1310		Hospitallers under Fulk of Villaret conquer Rhodes from the Greeks
1307	November 17	Mongol Bilarghu kills Armenian rulers, crippling Cilician kingdom
1307–1312		Templars suppressed by Philip IV of France and pope Clement V
1308	early	Catherine of Courtenay dies; daughter Catherine of Valois "empress"
1308–1310		Teutonic Knights gain possession of eastern Pomerania
1309	May 6	Charles II of Anjou dies; son Robert the Wise king of Naples
1309		Headquarters of Teutonic Knights moved to Marienburg in Prussia
1310	June 5	Amalric de Lusignan, usurper of Cyprus, assassinated; Henry II freed
1311	March 15	Catalans overwhelm Franks at the Cephissus, kill Walter of Brienne
1312	early	Catalan Company accepts suzerainty of Frederick II of Sicily
1313	July 29	Several dynastic marriages affect France, Italy, Burgundy, Greece
1314	November 29	Philip IV of France dies; son Louis X, grandson John I rule briefly
1315 or 1316		Raymond Lull, missionary, stoned to death near Bugia in Algeria
1316	July 5	Louis of Burgundy defeats Ferdinand at Manolada; both soon die
1317	January 9	Philip V succeeds infant nephew John I as king of France
1317		Alfonso Fadrique vicar-general of duchy of Athens (to 1330)
1318–1319		Alfonso Fadrique takes Thessaly from Greeks as duchy of Neopatras
1319	June 9	Catalans (Athens), Venetians (Negroponte), Euboeans make peace
1319		Hélion of Villeneuve replaces Fulk as master of Hospital
1320	summer	Andronicus Asen wins much of Frankish Morea for the Byzantines
1321		Mahaut of Hainault imprisoned by Robert of Naples, dies 1331
1322	January 2	Charles IV succeeds brother Philip V as king of France (dies 1328)
1322	January 5	John of Gravina becomes prince of Achaea (to 1333)
1324	March 31	Henry II de Lusignan dies; nephew Hugh IV king of Cyprus
1325–1326		John of Gravina leads Angevin army through the Morea in vain
1326	November (?)	Osman dies; son Orkhan becomes Ottoman ruler
1328		Andronicus II deposed by his grandson Andronicus III, dies 1332
1328	January 17	Louis IV the Bavarian crowned Holy Roman emperor (dies 1347)
1328	February 1	Philip VI of Valois establishes Valois line as kings of France
1331–1332		Walter VI of Brienne leads futile expedition against the Catalans
1331	December 26	Philip I of Taranto dies; son Robert is lord of Albania
1332–1334		Papacy, Venice, Hospital, Cyprus, Greeks in anti-Turkish coalition
1333		John of Gravina to Albania, Robert of Taranto prince of Achaea
1337	June 24–25	Frederick II dies; son Peter II becomes king of Sicily
1338	August 22	William II of Randazzo dies; brother John is duke of Athens
1338–1341		Catherine of Valois, son Robert, Nicholas Acciajuoli in the Morea
1340	October 30	Castilians, Catalan and Portuguese fleets, rout Moors near Tarifa
1341	June 15	Andronicus III dies; civil war of John V and John VI Cantacuzenus
1341		Sultan an-Nāṣir Muḥammad dies after interrupted 48-year reign
1343	January 20	Robert dies; granddaughter Joanna I queen of Naples under regency
1343	August 31	Clement VI forms Holy League with Venice, Cyprus, Hospitallers
1344		Algeciras surrenders to Alfonso XI of Castile after 2-year siege
1344	October 28	Smyrna taken by league from Umur Pasha, emir of Aydin
1345–1347		Humbert II of Viennois leads fruitless crusade to the Aegean
1346		Danes sell northern Estonia to the Teutonic Knights
1346		Hélion dies; Dieudonné of Gozon master of the Hospital
1346	October 4–5	Catherine of Valois dies; Robert of Taranto titular Latin emperor
1348	April 3	John of Randazzo dies; son Frederick I is duke of Athens
1348–1350		Black Death (plague) batters Europe and Levant, killing 1 in 3
1349		Il-khanid dynasty in Iran overthrown, leaving power vacuum
1350	August 12	Philip VI dies; his son John II is king of France
1352	February 13	Venetian and Aragonese fleets defeat Genoese near Constantinople
1353		Dieudonné of Gozon dies; Peter of Corneillan master of the Hospital
1354		Ottoman Turks under Orkhan capture Gallipoli from Byzantines

1354	November	John VI Cantacuzenus forced to abdicate by John V and Genoese
1355		Peter of Corneillan dies; Roger de Pins master of the Hospital
1355	April 5	Charles V of Luxemburg crowned Holy Roman emperor
1355	July 11	Frederick I of Athens dies; Frederick II (III of Sicily) becomes duke
1355	December 20	Stephen Dushan of Serbia dies
1359	October 10	Hugh IV de Lusignan dies; son Peter I king of Cyprus
1361	August 24	Peter I captures Adalia from Turks of Tekke (lost 1373)
1362		James of Florence killed in China, ending Catholic missions
1362		Orkhan dies; his son Murad I becomes Ottoman ruler
1362		Roger de Lluria seizes Thebes, kills Peter de Pou and others
1362–1365		Peter I of Cyprus tours western Europe to promote crusade
1363		Turks slaughter Hungarians and Serbs besieging Adrianople
1364	April 8	John II dies; son Charles V becomes king of France
1364	September 10	Robert of Taranto dies; his brother Philip becomes prince of Achaea
1365		Roger de Pins dies; Raymond Bérenger is master of the Hospital
1365	October 10–16	Crusaders under Peter I sack Alexandria, sail with loot and captives
1366	August–Dec.	Crusade under Amadeo VI of Savoy in Thrace and Bulgaria
1367	January 2	"Articles of Thebes" adopted (considered May 18 by Frederick III)
1368		Charles Topia takes Durazzo and Albania from the Angevins
1369	January 17	Peter I de Lusignan murdered; son Peter II king of Cyprus
1369		John V visits Rome, accepts Catholicism (October), goes to Venice
1370–1371		Enghien brothers fail to regain Athenian duchy from Catalans
1371	September 26	Serbs crushed by Ottoman Turks at Chernomen, on the Maritsa
1372	November	Nerio Acciajuoli recognized as lord of Corinth by pope Gregory XI
1373	November 25	Philip II of Taranto dies; Joanna I of Naples rules Achaea
1373–1374		Genoese invasion devastates Cyprus, undermines Lusignans' rule
1374	February 16	Raymond Bérenger dies; Robert of Juilly master of the Hospital
1375	April	Louis Fadrique vicar-general of Athens (to 1381, dies 1382)
1375		Armenian kingdom of Cilicia overthrown by Mamluks and Turks
1376 or 1377		Joanna of Naples leases Achaea to the Hospitallers (to 1381)
1377	July 27	Frederick III dies, leaving Athens and Neopatras to daughter Maria
1377	July 27	Robert of Juilly dies; Juan Fernández de Heredia master (Oct. 24)
1378–1417		Great Schism between popes of Rome and Avignon splits Catholics
1378	August (?)	Heredia captured at Arta by Ghin Boua Spata (released May 1379)
1379	May or June	John de Urtubia and Navarrese (and Gascon) Company seize Thebes
1379	summer	Peter IV of Aragon establishes suzerainty over the Catalan duchies
1380	May 20	"Articles of Athens" adopted (considered September 1 by Peter IV)
1380	September 16	Charles V dies; son Charles VI king of France
1381	September 2	Joanna captured by Charles of Durazzo (killed May 22, 1382)
1382		Peace of Turin ends war between Venice and Genoa over Tenedos
1382	October 3	Peter II de Lusignan dies; uncle James I king of Cyprus
1383		Richard Caracciolo anti-master of Hospital (to 1395) in Great Schism
1383	July 7	James of Les Baux, last titular Latin emperor, dies
1385	April 23	James I reaches Cyprus after 9-year captivity in Genoa
1386	February 18	Jagiello (Vladislav II) of Lithuania marries Jadwiga of Poland
1386		Charles III of Naples and Achaea dies; succeeded by son Ladislas
1386–1391		Amadeo of Savoy, lord of Pinerolo, fails to win Achaea
1387	January 5	Peter IV dies; son John is king of Aragon and duke of Athens
1388	May 2	Nerio Acciajuoli takes Acropolis, ending Catalan rule in Athens
1389	June 15	Serbs crushed at Kossovo by Turks under Murad I, who is killed
1390		Last Baḥrī Mamluk sultan replaced by Barkuk, first Burjī
1390	July–Sept.	French, Genoese crusaders under Louis of Bourbon attack Mahdia
1391	February 16	John V Palaeologus dies; son Manuel II Byzantine emperor
1392–1394		Thessaly overrun by Turks, becomes fief under Evrenos Beg

1393	July 17	Bulgarians lose Tirnovo to Ottoman Turks under Bayazid I
1394	September 25	Nerio Acciajuoli dies, leaving chaos in Attica; Turkish raids
1396		Heredia dies at Avignon; Philibert of Naillac master of the Hospital
1396		Navarrese leader Peter of St. Superan prince of Achaea (dies 1402)
1396	September 25	Burgundian and Hungarian crusaders slain at Nicopolis by Bayazid I
1397	June 3	Argos taken and sacked by Ottoman Turks, population enslaved
1397		Lizard League of nobles and Polish towns opposes Teutonic Knights
1398	September 9	James I de Lusignan dies; son Janus becomes king of Cyprus
1399–1402		Manuel II tours western Europe seeking aid against the Turks
1400–1401		Timur's hordes sack Aleppo and Damascus, devastate Syria
1402	summer	Antonio I Acciajuoli takes Athens and (early 1403) the Acropolis
1402	July 28	Bayazid I defeated and captured by Timur at Ankara (dies 1403)
1402	December	Timur takes Smyrna from the Hospitallers, razes defenses
1403–1413		Civil war among Bayazid's sons Suleiman, Isa, Mehmed, and Musa
1404	April 20	Ladislas of Naples names Centurione II Zaccaria prince of Achaea
1405	February 19	Timur dies at Samarkand, after restoring Anatolian emirates (1403)
1406		Suleiman rules in Europe, Mehmed in Anatolia, Musa fights, Isa dead
1407 (?)		Hospitallers build castle at Bodrum on Anatolian mainland
1410		Suleiman defeated (killed 1411) by Musa, who rules Ottoman Europe
1410	July 15	Poles and allies defeat Teutonic Knights near Tannenberg
1410	September	Antequera taken by Ferdinand of Castile (king of Aragon 1412)
1413	July 10	Mehmed I defeats brother Musa, becomes sole Ottoman sultan
1415		Portuguese take Ceuta in Morocco
1415	July 6	John Hus, Czech reformer, burned at stake in Constance
1417	November 11	Odo Colonna's election as pope Martin V ends Great Schism
1419	July 30	"Defenestration of Prague," led by John Želivský
1420	May–November	First anti-Hussite crusade, led by emperor Sigismund, fails
1421	May 4	Mehmed I dies; son Murad II becomes Ottoman sultan
1421		Philibert of Naillac dies; Anton Fluvian master of the Hospital
1421	June	"Four Articles of Prague" adopted; second anti-Hussite crusade fails
1422	April	Barsbey becomes Mamluk sultan after series of short reigns
1422	fall	Third anti-Hussite crusade, led by Frederick of Brandenburg, fails
1422	October 21	Charles VI dies; son Charles VII king of France (crowned 1429)
1423–1430		Venetians rule Thessalonica until its capture by Murad II
1424	June 7	Hussite civil war ends in John Žižka's victory at Malešov
1424	October 11	John Žižka dies of plague; Prokop leads brotherhoods
1425	July 21	Manuel II Palaeologus dies; son John VIII Byzantine emperor
1425	August	Mamluk fleet ravages southern Cyprus, burns Limassol
1426	July 7	Barsbey's Mamluks defeat Cypriotes at Khirokitia, capture Janus
1426	summer	Hussites under Prokop smash Saxon army at Ústí
1427	May 12	Janus returns to Cyprus as vassal of Mamluk sultan Barsbey
1427	July–August	Fourth anti-Hussite crusade fails; Hussites take Tachov
1429–1430		Hussite "beautiful rides" raid Saxony-Meissen and Lusatia
1430	February 11	Frederick of Brandenburg and Hussites accept short-lived truce
1430		Centurione II Zaccaria, last Latin prince of Achaea, dispossessed
1431	May 30	Joan of Arc burned at stake as a heretic by English
1431	June–August	Fifth anti-Hussite crusade fails, during Council of Basel
1432	June 28 or 29	Janus de Lusignan dies; son John II king of Cyprus
1432		Centurione II Zaccaria dies; Thomas Palaeologus rules the Morea
1433	January 4	Hussite representatives address the Council of Basel
1433	May 31	Sigismund is crowned Holy Roman emperor by Eugenius IV
1434	May 30	Czech lords and Praguers defeat Hussite brotherhoods at Lipany
1434		Antonio I Acciajuoli dies; duchy of Athens fatally weakened
1436	July 5	Sigismund signs "Four Compacts" with Hussites led by Rokycana

1437	October 29	Anton Fluvian dies; John of Lastic elected master of the Hospital
1437	December 9	Sigismund dies, succeeded by son-in-law Albert of Hapsburg
1438	June	Barsbey dies; succeeded by son Yūsuf (94 days), then Jakmak
1439	July 6	Union of Greek and Latin churches decreed at Council of Florence
1440	March 14	Prussian League of nobles and towns opposes Teutonic Knights
1440	summer	Rhodes attacked by Mamluk fleet, which devastates Cos
1442		Ottoman invasion of Transylvania repelled by John Hunyadi
1444	Aug.–Sept.	Rhodes attacked by Mamluk fleet; 40-day siege fails
1444	November 10	Murad II annihilates Hungarian and Slavic crusaders at Varna
1446		Murad II devastates the Morea
1448	October 17–19	Hunyadi defeated at Kossovo by Ottoman Turks under Murad II
1448	October 31	John VIII dies; brother Constantine XI last Byzantine emperor
1451		Antonello de Caupena, Catalan, leaves Aegina to Venice (lost 1537)
1451	February 3	Murad II dies; son Mehmed II (the Conqueror) Ottoman sultan
1452	March 19	Frederick III, Hapsburg, crowned Holy Roman emperor (dies 1493)
1452	December 12	Union of Greek and Latin churches proclaimed in Constantinople
1453	February	Jakmak dies; succeeded by son 'Uthmān (43 days), then Inal
1453	May 29	Mehmed II takes Constantinople, ending Byzantine empire
1453	October	Hundred Years' War (1337 on) between France and England ends
1454	February 22	Poland (and Prussia) declare war on Teutonic Knights
1454		John of Lastic dies; James of Milly master of the Hospital
1456	June 4	Athens annexed by Ottomans, ending Florentine duchy, Latin rule
1456	June-July	Hunyadi prevents Mehmed II from capturing Belgrade
1457	June 4	Teutonic Knights' unpaid mercenaries sell Marienburg to Poles
1458	July 26	John II de Lusignan dies; daughter Charlotte queen of Cyprus
1460		Mehmed II expels Greeks, completing conquest of the Morea
1460	September 18	James de Lusignan invades Cyprus as vassal of Mamluk sultan Inal
1461	February 26	Inal dies; succeeded by son Aḥmad (to June), then Khushkadam
1461	July 22	Charles VII dies; son Louis XI becomes king of France
1461	August 17	James of Milly dies; Peter Raymond Zacosta grand master
1462		Gibraltar retaken by Castilians (Moorish since 1333)
1462	November 16	Turks occupy Lesbos, ending sway of Gattilusi family
1464	summer	James II takes Kyrenia, becomes king of Cyprus
1465		Marīnid dynasty overthrown by Waṭṭāsids (established 1420)
1466	October 19	Treaty of Thorn ends 13-year war of Poles to oust Teutonic Knights
1467		Zacosta dies; Giovanni Battista Orsini grand master of the Hospital
1467	October	Khushkadam dies; after two short reigns Ka'itbey sultan (Jan. 1468)
1468	January 17	Scanderbeg dies; Albania soon absorbed into Ottoman empire
1470	July 12	Negroponte (Euboea) lost by Venice to the Ottoman Turks
1471	August 28	Tangier (and Alcácer-Saghir) taken by Portuguese (to 1661)
1473	July 6	James II dies, leaving widow Catherine and unborn son James III
1473	August 2	Uzun Ḥasan, pro-Latin Turkoman, defeated by Turks at Kara Hisar
1474	August 26	James III dies in infancy; Catherine Cornaro queen of Cyprus
1476		Orsini dies; Peter of Aubusson grand master of the Hospital
1479	December	Ottoman fleet attacks Rhodes and Telos
1480	May 23–Aug. 17	Major Ottoman assault on Rhodes repulsed by Hospitallers
1480	August 18	Otranto captured by Turks (retaken summer 1481)
1481	April 27	Mehmed II dies; son Bayazid II Ottoman sultan (May 20)
1482	July 29	Jem, brother of Bayazid II, lands in Rhodes (leaves September 1)
1483	August 30	Louis XI dies; son Charles VIII king of France (dies 1498)
1486		Bartholomew Díaz rounds Cape of Good Hope
1486–1491		Mamluk armies defeat Ottomans thrice in extended campaign
1487	August 18	Spanish take Malaga after bloody 103-day siege, enslave Moors
1489	February 26	Catherine Cornaro forced to cede Cyprus to Venice (lost 1571)

1489		Baza, Almeria, and Guadix surrendered to Spanish by Naṣrids
1490	April 4	Matthias Corvinus of Hungary, son of John Hunyadi, dies
1492	January 2	Granada surrendered by Boabdil to Ferdinand and Isabella
1492		Vasco da Gama reaches India; Columbus discovers America
1492		Egypt swept by plague, with over 200,000 deaths
1494		Ferdinand and Isabella acclaimed "the Catholic Kings" by pope
1496	July 28	Ka'itbey dies; series of short reigns ensues (to 1501)
1501	April	Kansuh al-Ghūrī Mamluk sultan (killed August 1516)
1502	August 29	Leucas captured by fleets of Hospitallers and Italian cities
1503	July 3	Peter of Aubusson dies; Emery of Amboise grand master
1505–1510		Castilians attack Oran, Bugia, and Algiers
1506		Morisco revolt crushed by Spanish
1508		Mamluk fleet defeats Portuguese at Chaul, near Bombay
1509		Portuguese fleet decisively defeats Mamluks at Diu, near Bombay
1510	August 23	Hospitaller fleet defeats Egyptians near Alexandretta
1512	May 26	Bayazid II dies; son Selim I (the Grim) Ottoman sultan
1512		Emery dies; Guy of Blanchefort elected grand master
1513		Guy dies; Fabrizio del Carretto grand master of the Hospital
1514	August 23	Selim I defeats shah Ismā'īl of Persia at Chaldiran
1515	January 1	Francis I (dies 1547) establishes Angoulême line of French kings
1516	August 24	Selim defeats the Mamluks at Marj Dābiq, conquers Syria
1517	January 22–23	Selim defeats the Mamluks at Raidaniyah, rules Egypt
1517	April 14	Tumanbey II, last Mamluk sultan, hanged at Cairo
1520	September 30	Selim I dies; son Suleiman I (the Magnificent) Ottoman sultan
1521	January 22	Fabrizio dies; Philip Villiers de l'Isle Adam grand master
1521	August 30	Suleiman I takes Belgrade
1522	December 18	Rhodes falls to Suleiman after 6-month siege
1523	January 1	Hospitallers leave Rhodes; Cos and Bodrum surrender to Turks
1525		Teutonic Knights' holdings transformed into duchy of Prussia
1526	August 29–30	Turks overwhelm Hungarians at Mohács, kill king Louis
1529	Sept. 26–Oct.	Vienna successfully withstands siege by Suleiman I
1530	March 24	Emperor Charles V grants Malta and Tripoli to Hospitallers
1534		Villiers de l'Isle Adam dies
1535	July	Charles V captures Tunis as step against Barbary pirates
1536		Francis I of France and Suleiman I allies against Charles V
1541		Fleet of Charles V defeated at Algiers in effort to suppress piracy
1550	September 8	Mahdia taken by Andrea Doria to suppress Dragut's piracy
1551	August 14	Hospitallers surrender Tripoli to Ottomans
1554		Waṭṭāsid dynasty of Morocco supplanted by Sharifian
1556		Ziyānid dynasty of western Algeria overthrown by Turks
1558	September 21	Charles V of Spain, Holy Roman emperor 1530–1556, dies
1561		Livonian branch of Teutonic Knights secularized as duchy
1565	May–Sept. 12	Hospitallers successfully repulse Ottoman siege of Malta
1566	September 5–6	Suleiman I dies; Ottoman decline begins under Selim II (the Fat)
1568–1570		Morisco revolt crushed by Spanish
1571	October 7	Spanish and Venetian fleets defeat Turks at Lepanto

GAZETTEER
AND NOTE ON MAPS

This gazetteer has been prepared to fill a variety of functions. Every relevant place name found in the text or on the maps is here alphabetized and identified, variant spellings and equivalent names in other languages are supplied, and the map location is indicated. Thus it not only serves as an index to the maps, and a supplement to them, but is itself a source for reference on matters of historical geography and changing nomenclature. Names originating in Arabic, Turkish, Persian, or Armenian have been carefully transliterated according to the systems described in the prefatory note on transliteration and nomenclature.

In the gazetteer, alphabetization is by the first capital letter of the form used in maps and text, disregarding such lower-case prefixes as *al-* and such geographical words as Cape, Gulf, Lake, Mount, and the like. The designation "classical" may mean Greek, Latin, biblical, or other ancient usage, and the designation "medieval" generally means that the name in question was in common use among speakers of various languages during the crusades, or appears in contemporary sources.

The maps themselves fall into three groups: ten locational, five historical, and six combined. On the locational and combined maps may be found nearly every place name occurring in the text, except a few whose exact locations are unknown, a few outside the regions mapped, several in areas overcrowded with names, some of minimal importance or common knowledge, and many which occur only in the names of crusaders or other persons. The maps of Western Europe, Central Europe, and the Near East are revised versions of similar maps appearing in volumes I and II, while those of the Straits and Aegean, Frankish Greece, and Cyprus have been revised from volume II. Locational maps of Rhodes, the Baltic area, Bohemia and its neighbors, and the Eastern Mediterranean have been added. The five new maps of Spain and Portugal combine the locational and historical functions, as does the plan of the city of Rhodes. The historical series shows the changing fortunes of the crusaders and their Christian rivals and Moslem enemies in the Levant as of 1300, 1400, and 1500, and of the Mongols and their Christian and Moslem opponents in the 13th and 15th centuries.

All maps for this volume have been designed and prepared in the University of Wisconsin Cartographic Laboratory under the direction of Randall P. Sale, assisted by Michael L. Czechanski and Carleton Cox. Base information was compiled from U.S.A.F. Jet Navigation Charts at a scale of 1:2,000,000. Historical data have been supplied by Dr. Harry W. Hazard (who also compiled the gazetteer) from such standard works as Sprüner-Menke, Stieler, Andree, and Baedeker for Europe, Lévi-Provençal for Moslem Spain, Rubió i Lluch and Bon for Frankish Greece, and Honigmann, Dussaud, Deschamps, Cahen, and LeStrange for the Near East. Additional information was found in *The Encyclopaedia of Islām* (old and new editions) and *İslâm Ansiklopedisi,* in Yāqūt and other Arabic sources, in *The Columbia Lippincott Gazetteer of the World,* on Michelin and Hallweg road maps, and of course in the text of this volume.

Aachen (German), Aix-la-Chapelle (French): city—F2b5: 1, 2.
Abū-Ghosh: village—see Qaryat al-'Inab.
Abyssinia: region—see Ethiopia.
Acarnania (classical), Akarnanía (modern Greek): district of western Greece—I1e2: 4.
Achaea (Latin), Akhaïa (modern Greek): district of northern Morea—I2e2: 4.
Achrida: town—see Ochrida.
Acre; Ptolemaïs (classical), Saint John or Saint Jean d'Acre (medieval), 'Akkā (Arabic), 'Akko (Israeli): city, port—L1f3: 16, 21.
Acrocorinth; Acrocorinthus (Latin), Akrokórinthos (modern Greek): rock dominating Corinth—I3e3: 4.
Acropolis: hill in Athens (I4e3: 4).
Adalia or Satalia (medieval), Attalia (classical), Antalya (Turkish): port—K1e4: 2, 16, 21.
Adana (classical, Armenian, Turkish): city—L1e3: 16, 21.
Aden; 'Adan (Arabic): port in southern Arabia—18.
Aderno; Adernò (medieval Italian), Adrano (modern Italian): town—G5e3: 2.
Adramyttium (Latin), Edremit (Turkish): town—J3e1: 3.
Adrianople; Hadrianopolis (classical), Edirne (Turkish): city—J2d4: 2, 3, 16.
Adriatic Sea; Hadria or Mare Hadriaticum (Latin)—GHd: 1, 2, 4.
Aegean Sea; Aigaion Pelagos (classical Greek), Mare Aegaeum (Latin), Ege Denizi (Turkish)—IJde: 2, 3, 4, 8, 16.
Aegina (Latin), Engia (medieval Italian), Ekine (Turkish), Aíyina (modern Greek): island—I4e3: 4.
Aegium: town—see Vostitsa.
Aetolia (Latin), Aitolía (modern Greek): district of central Greece—I2e2: 4.
Afāmiyah: town—see Apamea.
Afántos, or Afándos: town—see Aphandou.
Afghanistan: region, now nation, east of northern Persia—17, 18.
Agha Chayri (Turkish): plain between Adana and Tarsus (L1e4: 21).
Agosta (medieval), Augusta (classical, modern Italian): port—H1e3: 2.

Aigaion Pelagos—see Aegean Sea.

Aigues-Mortes (French): port 15 miles east of Montpellier (E4d2: 13).

'Ain Jālūt (Arabic: well of Goliath), Well of Harod (medieval), 'En Harod (Israeli): village—L1f3: 17, 21.

'Ain Zarbâ, or 'Ain Zarbah: town—see Anazarba.

Airasca (Italian): village 13 miles SW of Turin (F3c5: 1).

Aitolía: district—see Aetolia.

Aix-la-Chapelle: city—see Aachen.

Aíyina: island—see Aegina.

Aíyion: town—see Vostitsa.

Ajarquía (Spanish): district north of Malaga (D1e4: 1).

Ajarquía (Spanish): quarter of Cordova (D1e3: 1).

'Ajlūn (Arabic): town—L1f3: 21.

Akarnanía: district—see Acarnania.

Akche Hisar: town—see Kroia.

Akhaía: district—see Achaea.

'Akkā, or 'Akko: city—see Acre.

Akova or Matagrifon (medieval: kill-Greek), Ákovos (modern Greek): castle—I2e3: 4.

Akritochóri: castle—see Grisi.

Akrokórinthos: rock—see Acrocorinth.

Akrotiri; Akrotíri (modern Greek): peninsula, and town—K3f1: 10.

Alagón (Spanish): town—D4d4: 13.

'Ala'iyah, or Alanya: port—see Alaya.

Alamannia: region—see Germany.

Alamut; Alamūt (Persian, Arabic): fortress—17.

Alange, Alanje, or Alhange (Spanish): town 10 miles SE of Mérida (C4e2: 13).

Alarcón (Spanish): village—D3e1: 13.

Alarcos (Spanish), al-Arak or al-Ark (Arabic): battlefield—D2e2: 13.

Alashehir: town—see Philadelphia.

Alaya; Scandelore or Candeloro (medieval), 'Ala'iyah or 'Alāyā (Arabic), Alanya (Turkish): port—K2e4: 2, 16, 21.

Alba (Italian): town—F4d1: 1.

Albaicín (Spanish): quarter of Granada (D2e3: 1).

Albania; Shqipni or Shqipri (Albanian): region NW of Epirus—HId: 2, 4.

Albūr: fortress—see Alvor.

Alcácer do Sal (Portuguese), al-Qaṣr or Qaṣr Abī-Dānis (Arabic): town—C2e2: 13.

Alcácer-Seghir (Spanish), al-Qaṣr aṣ-Ṣaghīr (Arabic: the small castle): town—C5e5: 15.

Alcalá de Chisvert: town—see Chisvert.

Alcalá de Guadaira (Spanish): fortress, now town, 8 miles SE of Seville (C5e3: 1).

Alcalá de Henares (Spanish), al-Qal‘ah (Arabic: the fort): town—D2d5: 14.

Alcalá del Río (Spanish): fortress, now town, 9 miles north of Seville (C5e3: 1).

Alcanadre (Spanish): river NW of Fraga (E1d4: 12).

Alcañiz (Spanish): town—D5d4: 13.

Alcántara (Spanish), al-Qanṭarah or Qanṭarat as-Saif (Arabic: the bridge of the sword): town—C4e1: 13.

Alcaudete (Spanish): town—D1e3: 14.

Alcira (Spanish), Jazīrat Shuqr (Arabic): town—D5e1: 13.

Alcoraz (Spanish): village about 20 miles SW of Huesca (D5d3: 1).

Aledo (Spanish): village—D4e3: 11.

Alentejo (Portuguese): region of southern Portugal—Ce: 12, 13.

Aleppo; Ḥalab (Arabic), Haleb (Turkish): city—L3e4: 16, 17, 18, 21.
Alessio: town—see Lesh.
Alexandretta; İskenderun (Turkish): port—L2e4: 21.
Alexandretta, Gulf of; Sinus Issicus (classical), İskenderun Körfezi (Turkish)—
    L1e4: 21.
Alexandria (classical), al-Iskandarīyah (Arabic): city, port—J5f4: 2, 16, 17, 18,
    21.
Alfama (Spanish): castle on coast ENE of Tortosa (E1d5: 1).
Alfaro (Spanish): town—D4d3: 15.
Alfiós: river—see Alpheus.
Algarve (Portuguese), Ukshūnubah, Gharb al-Andalus, or al-Gharb (Arabic: the
    west): region of southern Portugal—Ce: 13, 14, 15.
Algeciras (Spanish), al-Jazīrah al-Khaḍrā' (Arabic: the green peninsula): port—
    C5e4: 14.
Algeria; al-Jazā'ir (Arabic): region between Morocco and Tunisia—DEFef: 1.
Alghero (Italian): port—F4d5: 1.
Algiers; al-Jazā'ir (Arabic): city—E4e4: 1.
Alhama de Granada (Spanish), al-Ḥāmmah (Arabic): town 24 miles SW of
    Granada (D2e3: 1).
Alhange: town—see Alange.
Aliákmon: river—see Haliacmon.
Alicante (Spanish), Laqant (Arabic): port—D5e2: 14.
Alignan-du-Vent (French): village—E4d2: 15.
Alimnia; Limonia (medieval Italian), Liman (Turkish), Alímnia (modern Greek):
    island—J3e4: 3, 8.
Alivérion: town—see Haliveri.
Aljustrel (Portuguese): town—C2e3: 13.
Allemania: region—see Germany.
Alma Daghï: range—see Amanus.
Almada (Portuguese), al-Ma'din (Arabic): town—C1e2: 13.
Almagro: castle—see Calatrava, New.
Almenara (Spanish): town—D5e1: 15.
Almeria; Almería (Spanish), al-Marīyah (Arabic): city, port—D3e4: 1, 11–15.
Almizra or Campet de Mirra (Spanish): village—D5e2: 13.
Almuradiel: pass—see Muradal.
Álora (Spanish): town—D1e4: 15.
Alpheus or Alpheios (classical), Charbon (medieval), Alfiós (modern Greek):
    river—I2e3: 4.
Alporchones (Spanish): battlefield 6 miles ESE of Lorca (D4e3: 13).
Alps: mountain range—FGc: 1, 2, 20.
Alpujarras (Spanish): district of southern Spain—D2e4: 15.
Alsace (French), Alsatia (classical), Elsass (German): region west of the upper
    Rhine—Fc: 1, 2.
Alsh: town—see Elche.
Alt Rahden: battlefield—see Saule.
Altenburg (German): town—G3b5: 20.
Altoluogo: town—see Ephesus.
Altwied: town—see Wied.
Alvor (Portuguese), Albūr (Arabic): fortress, now town—C2e3: 13.
Amalfi (Italian): port—G5d5: 2.
Amanus (classical), Gavur, Alma, or Elma Daghï (Turkish): mountain range—
    L2e4: 21.
Amasya (Turkish), Amasia (classical): town—L1d5: 16.
Amboise (French): town—E2c3: 15.

Ambracia: town—see Arta.

Ambracian Gulf—see Arta, Gulf of.

Ammōkhostos: port—see Famagusta.

Amorgos; Murgo (medieval Italian), Yamurgi (Turkish), Amorgós (modern Greek): island—J1e4: 3.

Amphissa, or Amfíssa :town—see Salona.

Amposta (Spanish): town—E1d5: 15.

Ampurias (Spanish), Emporium (classical), Anbūrish (Arabic): town, now unimportant—E4d3: 14.

Amvrakikós Kólpos—see Arta, Gulf of.

Amwās: village—see Emmaus.

Amyūn (Arabic): town 20 miles south of Tripoli (L1f1: 21).

Anadolu Hisar (Turkish): fortress on Bosporus—J5d4: 3.

Anamur (Turkish): town—K3e4: 21.

Anatolia; Rūm (medieval Arabic), Anadolu (Turkish): region south of the Black Sea—JKLde: 2, 3, 16.

Anazarba; Anazarbus (classical), Anavarza (Armenian), 'Ain Zarbâ or 'Ain Zarbah (Arabic): town, now abandoned—L1e3: 21.

Anbūrish: town—see Ampurias.

Ancona (Italian): port—G4d2: 1, 2.

Ancyra: city—see Ankara.

Andalusia; al-Andalus (Arabic), Andalucía (Spanish): region of southern Spain—CDe: 1.

Andimachia; Antimacheia (classical Greek), Antimachia (Italian), Andimákhia (modern Greek): town 12 miles west of Narangia (J3e4: 3).

Andravida, or Andreville (medieval), Andravídha (modern Greek): town—I2e3: 4.

Andria (Italian): town—H2d4: 2.

Andros; Andro (medieval Italian), Andria (Turkish), Ándros (modern Greek): island—I5e3: 3.

Androusa; Ithomē (classical Greek), Druges (medieval), Androúsa (modern Greek): town—I2e3: 4.

Andújar (Spanish), Andūjar or Andūshar (Arabic): town—D1e2: 13.

Angoulême (French): town—E1c5: 1, 11–15.

Anjou (French): region of NW France—D5c3: 1, 12–15.

Ankara (Turkish), Ancyra (classical), Angora (medieval): city—K3e1: 16, 18.

Ansbach (German): town—G1c1: 2.

Antakya, or Anṭākiyah: city—see Antioch.

Antalya: port—see Adalia.

Antalya, Gulf of—see Pamphylia Bay.

Antaradus, or Anṭarṭūs: port—see Tortosa.

Antebarium: port—see Antivari.

Antequera (Spanish), Anticaria or Antiquaria (classical), Antaqīrah (Arabic): town—D1e3: 14, 15.

Antimacheia, or Antimachia: town—see Andimachia.

Antioch; Antiochia (classical), Anṭākiyah (Arabic), Antakya (Turkish): city—L2e4: 16, 21.

Antiochia Parva or Antiochia ad Cragum (classical): town, now abandoned—K3e4: 21.

Antiphonitis; Antifonítis (modern Greek): monastery—K4e5: 10.

Antiquaria: town—see Antequera.

Antivari (Italian), Antebarium (Latin), Bar (Serbian): port—H5d3: 2.

Apamea (classical), Afāmiyah or Qal'at al-Muḍīq (Arabic); town, now unimportant—L2e5: 21.

Apanokastro; Apanókastron (modern Greek): castle on Naxos—J1e3: 3.

Aphandou or Aphantos (medieval Greek), Afántos or Afándos (modern Greek): town—J4e4: 8.

Apolakkía: town—see Polakia.

Apollonia: town—see Sozopolis.

Apollonia-Suzusa: town—see Arsuf.

Apulia (classical), Puglia or Puglie (Italian): region of SE Italy—Hd: 2.

Aqaba, Gulf of; Khalīj al-'Aqabah (Arabic)—Kg: 21.

Aquileia (classical, Italian): town—G4c5: 2.

Aquitaine (French), Aquitania (classical): region of western France—Dcd: 1, 12—15.

Arabia (classical), Jazīrat al-'Arab (Arabic): peninsular region east of the Red Sea—LMNgh: 16, 17, 18.

Arachova; Arákhova (modern Greek): village—I3e3: 4.

Aradus: island—see Ruad.

Aragon; Aragón (Spanish), Araghūn (Arabic): region of NE Spain—DEd: 1, 12—15.

al-Arak: battlefield—see Alarcos.

Aras (Turkish), Araxes (classical): river—N5e1: 16.

Arcadia (classical), Mesaréa (medieval Greek), Arkadhía (modern Greek): district of northern Morea—I2e3: 4.

Arcadia (medieval), Cyparissia (classical), Kiparissía (modern Greek): town—I2e3: 4.

Archangelos; Arkhángelos (modern Greek): town—J4e4: 8.

Archidona (Spanish), Urshudhūnah (Arabic): town 26 miles north of Malaga (D1e4: 1).

Archipelago (from Greek Aigaion Pelagos): islands of the Aegean Sea (IJde: 3).

Arcila: port—see Arzila.

Arcos de la Frontera (Spanish), Arkush (Arabic): town—C5e4: 13, 14, 15.

Ardeal: region—see Transylvania.

Arelas: town—see Arles.

Arenós (Catalan): village, possibly Areños, 45 miles NNE of Carrión (D1d3: 12).

Ares del Maestre (Spanish): village—D5d5: 13.

Arezzo (Italian), Arretium (classical): town—G2d2: 2.

Argolid or Argolis (classical), Argolís (modern Greek): district of eastern Morea—I3e3: 4.

Argos; Árgos (modern Greek): town—I3e3: 2, 4.

Arīhā: town—see Jericho.

al-'Arīmah: village—see Aryma.

Arjona (Spanish), Arjūnah (Arabic): town 19 miles NW of Jaen (D2e3: 1).

al-Ark: battlefield—see Alarcos.

Arkadhía: district—see Arcadia.

Arkhángelos: town—see Archangelos.

Arkush: town—see Arcos de la Frontera.

Arles (French), Arelas (classical): town—E5d2: 1, 11, 12.

Armena: castle—see Larmena.

Aroánia: mountain—see Chelmos.

Arretium: town—see Arezzo.

Arsuf; Apollonia-Sozusa (classical), Arsur (medieval), Arsūf (Arabic): town, now unimportant—K5f3: 21.

Arta; Ambracia (classical), Narda (Turkish), Árta (modern Greek): town—I1e1: 2, 4.

Arta, Gulf of, or Ambracian Gulf; Amvrakikós Kólpos (modern Greek)—Ie: 4.

Artois (French): district of northern France—E3b5: 1, 13.

Arwād: island—see Ruad.

Aryma (medieval), al-'Arīmah (Arabic): village—L2f1: 21.

Arzila; Zilis (classical), Arcila (Spanish), Aṣīlah (Arabic): port—C4e5: 14, 15.

Asar Tepe: castle—see Sechin.

Ascalon; Ashkelon (classical), 'Asqalān (Arabic); port, now unimportant, near modern Ashqelon—K5f4: 21.

Ashṭabūnah: town—see Estepona.

al-'Āṣī: river—see Orontes.

Asia Minor (classical): region equivalent to western Anatolia (JKde: 16).

Aṣīlah: port—see Arzila.

Asinou; Asínou (modern Greek): village—K3e5: 10.

Askas (Greek): village—K4f1: 10.

Asolo (Italian): village 27 miles north of Padua (G2c5: 2).

'Asqalān: port—see Ascalon.

Assailly (French): village—E5c5: 15.

Asterode: town—see Osterode.

Asti (Italian), Hasta (classical): town—F4d1: 1.

Astypalaea (classical), Stampalia (Italian), Ustrapalia (Turkish), Astipálaia (modern Greek): island—J2e4: 3.

al-Athārib (Arabic), Cerep (medieval): fortress 25 miles west of Aleppo (L3e4: 21).

Athens; Athēnai (classical Greek), Cetines or Satines (medieval), Athínai (modern Greek): city—I4e3: 2, 4, 17, 18.

Athlith, or 'Atlīṭ: castle—see Château Pèlerin.

Athos, Mount; Áyion Óros (modern Greek): monastery—I5d5: 3, 4.

Atlantic Ocean—1.

Atlas, High: mountain range—Cf: 1.

al-Aṭrūn: village—see Latrun.

Attalia: port—see Adalia.

Attica (Latin), Attikē (classical Greek), Attikí (modern Greek): district of eastern Greece—I4e3: 3, 4.

Aubusson (French): town—E3c5: 15.

Auch (French): town—E1d2: 12.

Augsburg (German): city—G1c2: 1, 2.

Augusta: port—see Agosta.

Aulnay-de-Saintonge (French): village—D5c4: 14.

Aulon: port—see Avlona.

Aussig: town—see Ústí nad Labem.

Austria; Ostmark (German): region east of Bavaria, smaller than modern nation—GHc: 1, 2, 20.

Autremencourt (French): village—E4c1: 14.

Auvergne (French): region of southern France—Ecd: 1, 12, 14, 15.

al-Auwalī (Arabic: the nearer): river—L1f2: 21.

Auxerre (French): town—E4c3: 1, 13.

Aversa (Italian): town—G5d5: 2.

Avesnes-sur-Helpe (French): town 40 miles SSE of Tournai (E4b5: 1).

Avignon (French), Avenio (classical): city—E5d2: 1, 11–15.

Avila; Avela (classical), Ávila de los Caballeros (Spanish): town—D1d5: 13.

Avis (medieval), Aviz (Portuguese): town—C3e1: 13.

Avlona (medieval), Aulon (classical), Valona (Italina), Vlonë or Vlorë (Albanian): port—H5d5: 2, 4.

Ayamonte or Aymonte (Spanish): castle near Olvera, 7 miles NW of Setenil (C5e4: 15).

Ayas (medieval), Lajazzo (Italian), Yumurtalik (Turkish): port—L1e4: 16, 17, 18, 21.

Ayasoluk: town—see Ephesus.
Aydin; Aydïn (Turkish): district of western Anatolia, equivalent to classical Lydia—Je: 2, 3, 16.
Ayerbe or Ayerve (Spanish): town—D5d3: 15.
Ayion Óros: monastery—see Athos, Mount.
Ayios Ilárion: castle—see Saint Hilarion.
Aymonte: castle—see Ayamonte.
Ayrivank: city—see Erivan.
al-'Azarïyah: abbey—see Bethany.
Aznalfarache (Spanish): suburb just south of Seville (C5e3: 1).
Azov: port—see Tana.

Baalbek; Heliopolis (classical), Ba'labakk (Arabic): town—L2f1: 21.
Bāb al-Ajal: fort—see Le Destroit.
Babylon: city—see Cairo.
Badajoz (Spanish), Batalyaus (Arabic): town—C4e2: 1, 11–15.
Baden (German): district of SW Germany—Fc: 1, 2.
Baena (Spanish), Baiyānah (Arabic): town—D1e3: 15.
Baetic Cordillera; Cordillera Penibética (Spanish): mountain range south of the Guadalquivir (De: 1).
Baeza (Spanish), Baiyāsah (Arabic): town—D2e3: 12, 13.
Baghdad; Baghdād (Arabic): city—M5f2: 16, 17, 18.
Baghrās (Arabic), Pagrae (classical), Gaston (medieval), Baghra (Turkish): town—L2e4: 21.
al-Bahr al-Ahmar—see Red Sea.
Bahr Lūt—see Dead Sea.
Bairūt: port—see Beirut.
Bait Jibrīn or Jibrīl: town—see Beth Gibelin.
Bait Lahm: town—see Bethlehem.
Baiyānah: town—see Baena.
Baiyāsah: town—see Baeza.
Bājah: town—see Beja.
Ba'labakk: town—see Baalbek.
Balaguer (Spanish): town 15 miles NE of Lerida (E1d4: 1).
Balansiyah: city—see Valencia.
Balarm: city—see Palermo.
Balātunus or Qal'at al-Mahalbah (Arabic): village 13 miles east of Latakia (L1e5: 21).
Bâle: city—see Basel.
Baleares (Spanish): island group—Ede: 1, 11–15.
Balga (German): fort—H5b1: 19.
Balkans: peninsular region east of the Adriatic Sea (GHd: 2).
Ballānah: town—see Villena.
Balmāllah: town—see Palmela.
Baltic Sea—HIab: 1, 2, 19, 20.
Bamberg (German): city—G1c1: 2.
Banï-Zart: port—see Bizerte.
Banishkulah: town—see Peñíscola.
Bāniyās: port—see Valania.
Banyas; Paneas or Caesarea Philippi (classical), Belinas (medieval), Bāniyās (Arabic): town—L1f2: 21.
Bar: port—see Antivari.
Bar (French): town, now Bar-le-Duc—F1c2: 15.
Bara: island—see Paros.

Barbary: the coast of North Africa.

Barbastro (Spanish), Barbashtrū (Arabic): town—E1d3: 11, 12.

Barca (classical), Barce (Italian), Barqah (Arabic): town—I1f3: 2.

Barcelona (Spanish), Barcino (classical), Barshilūnah (Arabic); city, port—E3d4: 1, 11–15.

Barcelona: county—Ed: 11, 12.

Bari (Italian), Barium (classical): port—H2d4: 2.

Barletta (Italian): port—H2d4: 2.

Barqah: region—see Cyrenaica.

Barqah: town—see Barca.

Barshilūnah: city—see Barcelona.

Bartenland (German): district of NE Poland—Ib: 20.

Bartenstein (German), Bartoszyce (Polish): town—I1b1: 19.

Basel (German), Basle or Bâle (French): city—F3c3: 1, 2.

Bashkent: battlefield—see Kara Hisar.

Basilicata: region—see Lucania.

Basilicata: town—see Vasilicata.

Bastah: town—see Baza.

Batalyaus: town—see Badajoz.

Batnos: island—see Patmos.

al-Batrūn: town—see Botron.

Bavaria; Bayern (German): region of southern Germany—Gc: 1, 2, 20.

Bayreuth (German): town—G2c1: 2, 20.

Baza (Spanish), Bastah (Arabic): town—D3e3: 15.

Béarn (French): district of SW France—Dd: 12.

Beaufort: castle (in Syria)—see Belfort.

Beaufort (French), Leuctrum (classical), Léftro (modern Greek): castle—I3e4: 4.

Beaulieu-sur-Dordogne (French: town—E2d1: 15.

Beaumont-le-Roger (French): town—E1c1: 15.

Beauvais (French): town—E3c1: 1, 15.

Beauvoir: castle (in Palestine)—see Belvoir.

Beauvoir or Belvedere (French), Pontikókastron (modern Greek): castle—I2e3: 4.

Bechin: town—see Petsona.

Beersheba (classical), Bīr as-Sab' (Arabic), Be'er Sheva' (Israeli): town—K5f4: 21.

Beheimstein (German): castle 3 miles from Nuremberg (G2c1: 2).

Beheira; al-Buḥairah (Arabic): region of NW Egypt—Jf: 16.

Behesni; Behesnou (Armenian), Besni (modern Turkish): fortress, now town—L3e3: 21.

Beira (Portuguese): region of central Portugal—Cd: 12.

Beirut; Berytus (classical), Bairūt (Arabic): port—L1f2: 16, 21.

Beja (Portuguese), Bājah (Arabic): town—C3e2: 1, 13.

Belchite (Spanish): town—D5d4: 12.

Belen Boghazi: pass—see Syrian Gates.

Belfort or Beaufort (medieval), Shaqīf Arnūn or Qal'at ash-Shaqīf (Arabic: fort of the rock): castle—L1f2: 21.

Belgrade; Beograd (Serbian: white town): city—I1d1: 2, 17, 18.

Belhacem (medieval), Qal'at Abū-l-Ḥasan (Arabic): village 6 miles ENE of Sidon (L1f2: 21).

Belinas: town—see Banyas.

Bellagrada: town—see Berat.

Bellapais or Bella Paise (medieval): monastery—K4e5: 10.

Belmont (French): abbey and castle 8 miles SSW of Tripoli (L1f1: 21).

Belmont: castle at Qaryat al-'Inab.

Belvedere: castle—see Beauvoir.

Belvoir or Beauvoir (medieval), Kaukab al-Hawā' (Arabic: star of the sky): castle—13 miles SSW of Tiberias (L1f3: 21).

Benevento (Italian), Beneventum (Latin): town—G5d4: 2.

Beograd: city—see Belgrade.

Berat; Pulcheriopolis (classical), Bellagrada (medieval): town—H5d5: 2, 4.

Beraun: town—see Beroun.

Berceo (Spanish): village—D3d3: 13.

Berezina (Russian): river—K1b3: 19.

Berezó: town—see Březová nad Bradlom.

Bernstadt (German), Bierutów (Polish): town—H3b4: 20.

Beroun (Czech), Beraun (German): town—G5c1: 20.

Berytus: port—see Beirut.

Besni: town—see Behesni.

Beth Gibelin (medieval), Betogabri or Eleutheropolis (classical), Bait Jibrīn or Bait Jibrīl (Arabic), Bet Guvrin (Israeli): town, now village—K5f4: 21.

Bethany; al-'Āzarīyah (Arabic), 'Eizariya (Israeli): abbey and fort 2 miles ESE of Jerusalem (L1f4: 21).

Bethlehem; Ephrata (classical), Bait Laḥm (Arabic: house of flesh): town—L1f4: 21.

Beverin: fortress—J1a3: 19.

Beyoghlu: port—see Pera.

Bezdružice (Czech), Weseritz (German): village—G3c1: 20.

Biandrate (Italian): village 8 miles west of Novara (F4c5: 1).

Biar (Spanish): town—D5e2: 13.

Bierutów: town—see Bernstadt.

Bīghū: town—see Priego de Córdoba.

al-Bijāyah: port—see Bugia.

Bīr as-Sab': town—see Beersheba.

Bira; al-Bīrah (Arabic), Bir (Armenian), Birejik (Turkish): town—L3e3: 21.

Birgu or Vittoriosa (Maltese): town—G5e5: 2.

Bischofteinitz: town—see Horšovský Týn.

Bistritsa: river—see Haliacmon.

Bithynia (classical): region of NW Anatolia—Jde: 3.

Bitsibardi (medieval Greek), Isova (medieval), Trypētē (classical Greek), Tripití (modern Greek): village 10 miles ESE of Olympia (I2e3: 4).

Bivar: town—see Vivar.

Bizerte; Hippo Zarytus (classical), Banī-Zart (Arabic): port—F5e3: 1.

Black Sea—JKLd: 2, 3, 16.

Blanche Garde (medieval), at-Tall aṣ-Ṣāfiyah (Arabic: the glittering hill): castle 14 miles SSE of Ramla (K5f4: 21).

Blanquefort or Blanchefort (French): town 6 miles NNW of Bordeaux (D5d1: 1)

Blgariya: region—see Bulgaria.

Boca del Asno (Spanish): battlefield 5 miles ESE of Antequera (D1e3: 14).

Bodonitsa or Boudonitsa (medieval), Pharygae (classical), Mendhenítsa (modern Greek): village—I3e2: 4.

Bodrum or Budrum (Turkish), Halicarnassus (classical), Petroúnion (modern Greek): town—J3e3: 3.

Boeotia (Latin), Boiōtia (classical Greek), Voiotía (modern Greek): district of eastern Greece—I4e2: 4.

Bohemia; Čechy (Czech): region north of Austria—GHbc: 1, 2, 20.

Boiano or Boyano (Italian): town 29 miles NW of Benevento (G5d4: 2).

Boixols: town—see Boxolis.

Bokhārā: city—see Bukhara.

Bolgar, or Bolgary: town—see Bulgar.

Bologna (Italian): city—G2d1: 1, 2.

Bombay: city and port on west coast of India—17, 18.

Boppard (German): town—F3b5: 1, 2.

Bordeaux (French), Burdigala (classical): city, port—D5d1: 1, 11–15.

Borja (Spanish), Borgia (Italian): town—D4d4: 12.

Bornhöved (Danish, German): town 24 miles NW of Lübeck (G1b2: 1).

Borysthenes: river—see Dnieper.

Bosau (German): town—G1b1: 20.

Bosnia; Bosna (Serbian, Turkish): region west of Serbia—Hd: 2.

Bosporus (classical), Karadeniz Boghazi (Turkish: Black Sea strait)—J5d4: 3, 16.

Bosra; Bostra (classical), Buṣrâ (Arabic): town—L2f3: 21.

Botron (medieval), Botrys (classical), al-Batrūn (Arabic): town—L1f1: 21.

Boudonitsa: village—see Bodonitsa.

Bougie: port—see Bugia.

Bouillon (French): town—F1c1: 1, 12.

Boulogne-sur-Mer (French): port—E2b5: 1.

Bourbon-l'Archambault (French): town—E4c4: 15.

Bourges (French): town—E3c3: 1, 11–15.

Bourgogne: region—see Burgundy.

Bourzey (medieval), Qal'at Barzah (Arabic): castle—L2e5: 21.

Boxolis or Boixols (Spanish): town—E2d3: 15.

Boyano: town—see Boiano.

Bozjaada: island—see Tenedos.

Brabant (French, Flemish): district east of Flanders—E5b4: 1, 2.

Braga (Portuguese), Brāqarah (Arabic): town—C2d4: 1, 12.

Brandenburg (German): district of northern Germany—Gb: 1, 2, 20.

Brasil: region—see Brazil.

Braşov: district—see Burzenland.

Bratislava (Slovakian), Pressburg (German), Pozsony (Hungarian): city—H3c2: 2, 20.

Braunsberg (German), Braniewo (Polish): town—H5b1: 19.

Braunschweig: city—see Brunswick.

Brazil; Brasil (Portuguese): region in South America—not in area mapped.

Breidenbach or Breydenbach (German): town 54 miles NNW of Frankfurt (F4b5: 1).

Breiz: region—see Brittany.

Bremen (German): city, port—F4b2: 1, 2.

Brenthē: castle—see Karytaina.

Breslau (German), Wrocław (Polish): city—H3b4: 2, 20.

Bretagne: region—see Brittany.

Breydenbach: town—see Breidenbach.

Březová nad Bradlom (Slovakian), Berezó (Hungarian): town—H3c2: 20.

Brie (French): district SE of Paris—E3c2: 15.

Brieg: town—see Brzeg.

Brienne-la-Vieille (French): village—E5c2: 14.

Brindisi (Italian), Brundisium (Latin): port—H3d5: 2.

Brittany; Bretagne (French), Breiz (Breton): region of NW France—Dc: 1, 12–15.

Brno (Czech), Brünn (German): city—H2c1: 2, 20.

Brod (Czech), Bruck (German): village 4 miles NNE of Tachov (G3c1: 20).

Bruges (French), Brugge (Flemish): port, now city, 24 miles NW of Ghent (E4b4: 1).

Brunswick; Braunschweig (German): city—G1b3: 1, 2.

Brusa (medieval), Prusa (classical), Bursa (Turkish): city—J5d5: 2, 3, 16.

Brussels; Brussel (Flemish), Bruxelles (French): city 50 miles ESE of Ghent (E4b4: 1).

Brüx: town—see Most.

Bruyères (French): town 30 miles SW of Strassburg (F3c2: 1).

Brzeg (Polish), Brieg (German): town—H3b5: 20.

Buda (Hungarian), Ofen (German): city, now part of Budapest—H5c3: 2, 17, 18, 20.

Budrum: town—see Bodrum.

Budweis (German), České Budějovice (Czech): town—G5c2: 1, 2, 20.

Buffavento (medieval): castle—K4e5: 10.

Bugia; Saldae (classical), al-Bijāyah (Arabic), Bougie (French): port—F1e4: 1.

al-Buḥairah: region—see Beheira.

Buḥairat Ṭabarīyah—see Tiberias, Lake.

Bukhara; Bokhārā (Persian), Bukhārā (Arabic): city—17, 18.

Būlāq (Arabic): suburb NW of Cairo (K2f5: 21).

Bulgar or Bolgar; Bolgary (Russian, formerly Uspenskoye): town, now village, near the Volga—17, 18.

Bulgaria; Blgariya (Bulgarian): region south of the lower Danube—IJd: 2, 3, 16.

Bullis: town—see Canina.

Bulunyās: port—see Valania.

Burdigala: city—see Bordeaux.

Burg Rheden (German): fortress—H5b2: 19.

Burgos (Spanish), Burghush (Arabic): city—D2d3: 1, 13.

Burgundy; Bourgogne (French): region of eastern France—EFc: 1, 13, 14, 15.

Burj Ṣāfīthā: castle—see Chastel-Blanc.

Burlus or Burullus (Arabic), Le Brulle (medieval): town—K1f4: 21.

Burriana (Spanish), Burīyānah (Arabic): town—D5e1: 13.

Bursa: city—see Brusa.

Burtuqāl: city—see Oporto.

Burzenland (German), Braşov (Rumanian): district of SE Transylvania—IJc: 2.

Buṣrā: town—see Bosra.

Byblos: town—see Jubail.

Byllis: town—see Canina.

Byzantium: city—see Constantinople.

Cabra (Spanish), Qabrah (Arabic): town—D1e3: 15.

Cacela (Portuguese), Qasṭallat Darrāj (Arabic): town—C3e3: 13.

Cáceres (Spanish): town—C4e1: 13.

Cadiz: Gadir (Phoenician), Gades (Latin), Cádiz (Spanish), Qādis (Arabic): port—C4e4: 1, 13, 14, 15.

Caesaraugusta: city—see Saragossa.

Caesarea ad Argaeum or Caesarea Mazaca (classical), Kayseri (Turkish): city 120 miles NW of Marash (L2e3: 16).

Caesarea Maritima or Palestinae (classical), Qaisārīyah (Arabic), Sedot Yam (Israeli): port, now unimportant—K5f3: 21.

Caesarea Philippi: town—see Banyas.

Caffa: port—see Kaffa.

Cagliari (Italian), Caralis (classical): port—F5e1: 1, 2.

Caiffa or Caiphas: port—see Haifa.

Cairo; al-Qāhirah (Arabic): city—K2f5: 2, 16, 17, 18, 21.

Calabria (Italian): region of SW Italy—He: 2.

Calais (French): port—E2b5: 1.

Calatayud (Spanish), Qal'at Aiyūb (Arabic): town—D4d4: 12.
Calatrava, New; Almagro (Spanish): castle, now town—D2e2: 13.
Calatrava, Old; Qal'at Rabāḥ (Arabic): fortress—D2e1: 12, 13.
Calchi: island—see Chalce.
Calino: island—see Calymnos.
Callipolis: town—see Gallipoli.
Calpe (Spanish), Qalb (Arabic): town—E1e2: 13.
Caltabellotta (Italian): town—G4e3: 2.
Calycadnus (classical), Saleph (medieval), Selef or Gök(-Su) (Turkish): river—
    K5e4: 21.
Calymnos; Calymna (Latin), Calino (Italian), Gelmez (Turkish), Kálimnos (mod-
    ern Greek): island—J2e4: 3.
Cambaluc: city—see Khanbaliq.
Cambíl (Spanish): town—D2e3: 14.
Campet de Mirra: village—see Almizra.
Campus Stellae: town—see Compostela.
Canary Islands; Islas Canarias (Spanish): island group west of Morocco—not in
    area mapped.
Candeloro: port—see Alaya.
Candia: island—see Crete.
Candia (medieval), Heracleum (Latin), Iráklion (modern Greek): port—J1e5: 2.
Cañete la Real (Spanish): town—C5e4: 14.
Canina (medieval), Bullis or Byllis (classical), Kanine (Albanian): town, now
    unimportant—H5d5: 4.
Cantabria (Spanish): region of northern Spain—CDd: 13.
Canterbury: town—E2b4: 1.
Capsa: town—see Gafsa.
Capua (Italian): town—G5d4: 2.
Caralis: port—see Cagliari.
Caravaca (Spanish), Qarabākah (Arabic): town—D4e2: 15.
Carcassonne (French): town—E3d2: 14.
Carchi: island—see Chalce.
Cárdenas (Spanish): village—D3d3: 15.
Cardona (Spanish): town—E2d4: 15.
Caria: region—see Menteshe.
Caribbean Sea—not in area mapped.
Carinola (Italian): town 14 miles WNW of Capua (G5d4: 2).
Carmel, Mount; Jabal Mār Ilyās (Arabic: Mount St. Elias), Karmel (Israeli):
    south of Haifa (K5f3: 21).
Carmona (Spanish), Qarmūnah (Arabic): town—C5e5: 13.
Carpathos; Scarpanto (Italian), Kerpe (Turkish), Kárpathos (modern Greek):
    island—J3e5: 2, 16.
Carretto (Italian): village near Cáiro Montenotte, 12 miles NW of Savona (F4d1:
    1).
Carrión de los Condes (Spanish): town—D1d3: 12.
Cártama (Spanish): town 10 miles west of Malaga (D1e4: 1).
Carthage; Carthago (Latin): town—G1e4: 1, 2.
Carystus (Latin), Káristos (modern Greek): town—I5e2: 3, 4.
Čáslav (Czech), Czaslau (German): town—H1c1: 20.
Caspe (Spanish): town—D5d4: 13, 15.
Caspian Sea—NOde: 16.
Cassandra; Pallene (classical), Kassándra (modern Greek): peninsula—I4e1: 4.
Cassandrea or Potidaea (classical), Cassandria (medieval Greek), Potídhaia (mod-
    ern Greek): town—I4d5: 4.

Castel Basso: castle—see Katokastro.

Castel de Fer: castle—see Siderokastron.

Castel del Monte (Italian): fortress 10 miles south of Andria (H2d4: 2).

Castel Sant' Angelo (Italian): castle in Rome (G3d4: 2).

Castelfranco Veneto (Italian): town 18 miles NNE of Padua (G2c5: 2).

Castell dell' Uovo (Italian): fortress in Naples (G5d5: 2).

Castellar de la Frontera (Spanish): village—C5e4: 14.

Castellón de la Plana (Spanish): town—D5e1: 13.

Castellorizzo; Megista (classical), Meis (Turkish), Kastellórizo (modern Greek), Castelrosso (Italian): island—J5e4: 3, 21.

Castiglione d' Olona (Italian): town 38 miles NW of Milan (F5c5: 1).

Castiglione della Stiviere (Italian): town 28 miles NE of Cremona (G1c5: 2).

Castile; Castilla (Spanish), Qashtālah (Arabic): region of north central Spain—Dd: 1, 12, 15.

Castilla la Nueva: region—see New Castile.

Castilla la Vieja: region—see Old Castile.

Častolovice (Czech), Castolowitz (German): town—H2b5: 20.

Catalonia; Cataluña (Spanish), Catalunya (Catalan): region of NE Spain—Ed: 1, 13, 14, 15.

Catania (Italian), Catana or Catina (Latin): city, port—H1e3: 2.

Cathay: region—see China.

Cattavia; Kattaviá (modern Greek): town—J3e5: 8.

Caucasus; Kavkaz (Russian): mountain range—MNd: 16.

Cazorla (Spanish): town—D3e3: 13, 15.

Čechy: region—see Bohemia.

Cefalù (Italian), Cephaloedium (Latin): town—G5e2: 2.

Celje: town—see Cilly.

Cenchreae (classical): port, now unimportant—I4e3: 4.

Ceos; Keōs (classical Greek, Tziá (medieval Greek), Zea (Italian), Morted (Turkish), Kéa (modern Greek): island—I5e3: 3, 4.

Cephalonia; Kephallēnia (classical Greek), Kephallōnia (medieval Greek), Kefallinía (modern Greek): island—I1e2: 4.

Cephissus (Latin), Kēphisos (classical Greek), Kifissós (modern Greek): stream—I4e2: 4.

Cépoy: town—see Chepoix.

Cerep: fortress—see al-Athārib.

Cerigo (Italian), Cythera (Latin), Kythēra (classical Greek), Kíthira (modern Greek): island—I3e4: 4.

Cerines: town—see Kyrenia.

Cervera del Maestre (Spanish): town—E1d5: 13.

Česke Budějovice: town—see Budweis.

Český Brod (Czech): town 20 miles east of Prague (G5b5: 1).

Cetines: city—see Athens.

Ceuta (Spanish), Septa (classical), Sabtah (Arabic): port—C5e5: 1, 13, 14, 15.

Ceva (Italian): town 24 miles WNW of Savona (F4d1: 1).

Ceylon; Taprobane (classical), Lanka (Sanskrit), Serendib (medieval): island south of India, now Sri Lanka—not in area mapped.

Chaeronea (classical), Kapraina (medieval), Khairónia or Kherónia (modern Greek): town, now village, 4 miles NNW of Livadia (I3e2: 4).

Chalandritsa (medieval), Khalandrítsa (modern Greek): town—I2e2: 4.

Chalce or Khalkē (classical), Carchi or Calchi (Italian), Herke (Turkish), Khálki (modern Greek): island—J3e4: 3.

Chalcidice (Latin), Khalkidikē (classical Greek), Khalkidhikí (modern Greek): peninsula—I4d5: 4.

Chalcis: town—see Negroponte.
Chaldiran: battlefield—M4d5: 16.
Chalon-sur-Saône (French): town—E5c4: 15.
Chambéry (French): town—F1c5: 1.
Champagne (French): region of NE France—EFc: 1, 12–15.
Champlitte-et-le-Prélot (French): town—F1c3: 13.
Chanakkale Boghazï: strait—see Dardanelles.
Chankïrï: town—see Gangra.
Charbon: river—see Alpheus.
Charny (French): town—E4c3: 15.
Chartres (French): town—E2c2: 1, 11–15.
Chastel-Blanc (medieval), Burj Ṣāfīthā (Arabic): castle—L2f1: 21.
Chastel-Rouge (medieval), Qal'at Yaḥmur (Arabic): fortress—L1f1: 21.
Château Pèlerin or Athlith (medieval), 'Atlīt (Arabic), 'Atlit (Israeli): castle—K5f3: 21.
Châteaumorand (French): village 8 miles east of Lapalisse (E4c4: 15).
Châtillon-sur-Loing (French): town, now part of Châtillon-Coligny—E3c3: 14.
Chaul: port on west coast of India—17, 18.
Chaumont-en-Bassigny (French): town—F1c2: 14.
Cheb (Czech), Eger (German): town—G3b5: 20.
Chełmńo: town—see Kulm.
Chelmos, Mount; Aroánia or Khelmós (modern Greek)—I3e3: 4.
Chepoix (French), Cépoy (medieval): town—E3c1: 13.
Chernomen; Črnomen (Bulgarian), Chirmen, Chermen, or Sïrf Sïndïgï (Turkish: destruction of the Serbs), Orménion (modern Greek): battlefield—J2d4: 3.
Chi: city—see Khanbaliq.
Chiarenza: town—see Glarentsa.
Chieri (Italian): town 8 miles SE of Turin (F3c5: 1).
China; Cathay (medieval): region of eastern Asia—17, 18.
Chioggia (Italian): port—G3c5: 2.
Chios; Scio (Italian), Khíos (modern Greek), Sakïz (Turkish): island—J1e2: 3.
Chirmen: battlefield—see Chernomen.
Chisvert, or Alcalá de Chisvert (Spanish): town—E1d5: 13.
Chomutov (Czech), Komutau (German): town—G4b5: 20.
Chotĕšov (Czech): village—G4c1: 20.
Christburg (German), Dzierzgoń (Polish): fortress, now town—H5b2: 19.
Chrysoceras: bay—see Golden Horn.
Chrysopolis: port—see Scutari.
Chu (Russian): river in Turkestan—17, 18.
Chudskoye Ozero—see Peipus, Lake.
Chungtu: city—see Khanbaliq.
Cilicia (classical): region of southern Anatolia—KLe: 16, 21.
Cilly; Celje (Slovene): town—H1c4: 2, 20.
Cinca (Spanish), Nahr az-Zaitūn (Arabic: river of the olive trees): river—E1d4: 11, 12.
Cinco Villas (Spanish): district NW of Saragossa (D5d4: 1).
Cintra: town—see Sintra.
Circassia: region north of western Caucasus—Md: 16, 17, 18.
Cirta: town—see Constantine.
Cisneros (Spanish): town—D1d3: 1.
Citó: town—see Zeitounion.
Ciudad Real (Spanish: royal city): town, originally Villa Real, 6 miles WSW of Carrión (D1d3: 12).
Civitavecchia (Italian: old city): port—G2d3: 2.

Clairvaux (French): abbey—E5c2: 12.

Clarence: town—see Glarentsa.

Clermont (French), Khelōnatas (classical Greek), Khloumoutsi (medieval Greek): castle—I2e3: 4.

Clermont (French): town, now part of Clermont-Ferrand—E4c5: 1, 11–15.

Clermont de l'Oise (French): town—E3c1: 15.

Cluny (French): abbey—E5c4: 12.

Coimbra (Portuguese), Qulumrīyah (Arabic): town—C2d5: 1, 11, 12.

Coín (Spanish): town 19 miles west of Malaga (D1e4: 1).

Coliat (medieval), al-Qulai'ah (Arabic: the small fort): fortress—L2f1: 21.

Collo: port—F2e3: 1.

Colmenar de Oreja: town—see Oreja.

Cologne (French), Colonia Agrippinensis (Latin), Köln (German): city—F2b5: 1, 2.

Como (Italian): town—F5c5: 1.

Compostela or Santiago de Compostela (Spanish), Campus Stellae (Latin), Shant Yāqūb (Arabic): town—C2d3: 1, 13.

Conigliera (Italian): islet—G2e5: 2.

Conques (French): abbey—E3d1: 15.

Constance (French), Konstanz (German): town—F5c3: 1, 2.

Constantine (French), Cirta (classical), Qusanṭinah (Arabic): town—F2e4: 1.

Constantinople; Byzantium or Constantinopolis (classical), İstanbul (Turkish): city, port—J4d4: 2, 3, 16, 17, 18.

Consuegra (Spanish): town—D2e1: 12.

Conversano (Italian): town—H3d5: 2.

Conza (Italian): village 19 miles wsw of Melfi (H1d5: 2).

Copais, Lake; Kōpais Limnē (classical Greek): lake, now filled in—I4e2: 4.

Coquerel (French): village in Normandy, either 7 miles SE of Abbeville or 13 miles NW of Évreux (E2c1: 1).

Corbins (Spanish): village 7 miles NE of Lerida (E1d4: 1).

Cordillera Penibética—see Baetic Cordillera.

Cordova; Córdoba (Spanish), Qurṭubah (Arabic): city—D1e3: 1, 11–15.

Corfu; Corcyra (Latin), Kerkyra (classical Greek), Corfù (Italian), Kérkira (modern Greek): island—H5e1: 2, 4.

Coria (Spanish), Qūriyah (Arabic): town—C4e1: 12.

Corinth; Korinthos (classical Greek), Kórinthos (modern Greek): city—I3e3: 2, 4.

Corinth, Gulf of; Korinthiakós Kólpos (modern Greek)—I3e2: 4.

Corinth, Isthmus of: land connection between Morea and central Greece (I3e3: 4).

Corinthia (classical), Korinthía (modern Greek): district of NE Morea—I3e3: 4.

Corneillan (French): village—D5d2: 15.

Cornellá de Llobregat (Spanish), Cornellà (Catalan): town—E3d4: 15.

Coron; Korōnē (medieval Greek), Koróni (modern Greek): town—I2e4: 2, 4.

Corsica; Cyrnus (classical), Corse (French): island—Fd: 1, 2.

Corycus (classical), Gorigos (Armenian), Le Courc (medieval), Korgos (Turkish): port—K5e4: 21.

Cos; Kós (Greek), Lango or Stanchio (medieval Italian), Stankoi (Turkish): island—J3e4: 3.

Côte d'Or (French: gold ridge or coast): district of east central France—E5c3: 1, 14, 15.

Coucy-le-Château (French): village—E4c1: 15.

Courland: district—see Kurland.

Courtenay (French): town—E4c2: 13.

Coustouges (French): village—E3d3: 15.
Coutances (French): town—D4c1: 14.
Cracow; Cracovia (Latin), Kraków (Polish): city—H5b5: 2, 17, 18, 20.
Crambusa (medieval): islet—K1e4: 21.
Crécy-en-Ponthieu (French): town—E2b5: 15.
Cremona (Italian): town—G1c5: 1, 2.
Crete; Candia (medieval Italian), Krētē (medieval Greek), Kandia (Turkish), Kríti
    (modern Greek): island—IJe: 2, 16, 17, 18.
Crimea; Krym (Russian): peninsula—K4c5: 2, 16.
Črnomen: battlefield—see Chernomen.
Croia: town—see Kroia.
Cuarte, Llano de (Spanish): plain 10 miles west of Valencia (D5e1: 1).
Cuenca (Spanish), Qūnkah (Arabic): town—D3d5: 1, 11–15.
Culan or Culant (French): village—E3c4: 15.
Cullera (Spanish): town—D5e1: 13.
Cursat (medieval), Quṣair (Arabic: little castle): castle—L2e4: 21.
Cutanda (Spanish): town—D4d5: 12.
Cyclades (classical), Kikládhes (modern Greek): island group—IJe: 3.
Cyllene: town—see Glarentsa.
Cyllene, Mount; Kyllēnē (medieval Greek), Killíni (modern Greek)—I3e3: 4.
Cymru: region—see Wales.
Cynaetha: town—see Kalavryta.
Cyparissia: town—see Arcadia.
Cyprus or Kypros (classical), Kípros (modern Greek), Kíbrĭs (Turkish): island—
    Kef: 16, 17, 18, 21.
Cyrenaica (classical), Barqah (Arabic): region between Tripolitania and northern
    Egypt—If: 2.
Cyrnus: island—see Corsica.
Cyrus: river—see Kura.
Cythera: island—see Cerigo.
Czaslau: town—see Čáslav.

Dalmatia; Dalmacija (Croatian): region east of the Adriatic Sea, equivalent to
    classical Illyria—Hd: 2.
Damala (medieval), Troezen (Latin), Troizēn (classical Greek), Troizén (modern
    Greek): town, now unimportant—I4e3: 4.
Damascus (classical), Dimashq or ash-Sha'm (Arabic: the left): city—L2f2: 16,
    17, 18, 21.
Damietta; Dimyāṭ (Arabic): port—K2f4: 16, 21.
Dampierre; Le Vieil Dampierre (French): village—E5c2: 15.
Dāniyah: port—see Denia.
Danmark: region—see Denmark.
Danube; Donau (German), Duna (Hungarian), Dunav (Serbian, Bulgarian),
    Dunărea (Rumanian): river—J5c5: 1, 2, 16, 20.
Danzig (German), Gdańsk (Polish): city, port—H4b1: 19, 20.
Daphne; Daphnē (classical Greek), Dhafní (modern Greek): monastery 5 miles
    WNW of Athens (I4e3: 4).
Dardanelles; Hellespontus (classical), Chanakkale Boghazĭ (Turkish): strait—
    J2d5: 3, 16.
Daroca (Spanish), Darauqah (Arabic): town—D4d4: 12.
Darsous: town—see Tarsus.
Darum or Daron (classical), ad-Dārum (Arabic): town—K5f4: 21.
Daugava: river—see Düna.
Daugavgrīva: port—see Dünamünde.

Dauphiné: district—see Viennois.
Daviá: town—see Tabia.
Dead Sea; Baḥr Lūṭ (Arabic: sea of Lot), Yam Hamelah (Israeli)—L1f4: 16, 21.
Degir Menlik: island—see Melos.
Delhi; Dillī (Hindi), Dihlī or Dehlī (Persian): city in NW India—17, 18.
Demetsana: town—see Dimitsana.
Demmin (Slavic, German): town—G4b2: 20.
Demotica; Dēmotika (medieval Greek), Dhidhimótikhon (modern Greek): town—J2d4: 3.
Denia (Spanish), Dāniyah (Arabic): port—E1e2: 1, 12, 13.
Denmark; Danmark (Danish): region, then including the southern part of Sweden—FGHab: 1, 2.
Depenow: village—see Tiefenau.
Ðerdap: gorge—see Iron Gate.
Dertosa: town—see Tortosa.
Despeñaperros (Spanish): pass, superseding Muradal (D2e2: 12).
Deutschland: region—see Germany.
Dhafní: monastery—see Daphne.
Dhidhimótikhon: town—see Demotica.
Dhimitsána: town—see Dimitsana.
Dhístos: village—see Dystos.
Dhodhekánisoi: island group—see Dodecanese.
Dhomokós: town—see Domokos.
Dieudamour: castle—see Saint Hilarion.
Dihlī, or Dilli: city—see Delhi.
Dijlah, or Dijle: river—see Tigris.
Dijon (French): city—F1c3: 1, 2, 11—15.
Dimashq: city—see Damascus.
Dimitsana; Demetsana (medieval Greek), Dhimitsána (modern Greek): town 7 miles north of Karytaina (I3e3: 4).
Dimyāṭ: port—see Damietta.
Diu: port on Diu island off west coast of India—17, 18.
Dnieper; Borysthenes (classical), Dnepr (Russian): river—K3c4: 2, 16.
Dniester; Tyras (classical), Dnestr (Russian), Nistru (Rumanian): river—K1c4: 2, 16.
Dobin (Slavic): town, now unimportant—G2b2: 20.
Dobrzyn; Dobrzyń nad Wisłą (Polish): town—H5b3: 19.
Dodecanese; Dōdekanēsos (medieval Greek: 12 islands), Dhodhekánisoi (modern Greek): island group—Je: 2, 3.
Dolomites; Dolomiti (Italian): mountain range—G2c4: 1, 2.
Domažlice (Czech), Taus (German): town—G3c1: 20.
Domokos; Thaumacia (classical), Dhomokós (modern Greek): town—I3e1: 4.
Don; Tanaïs (classical): river—L5c3: 16.
Donau: river—see Danube.
Doornijk: town—see Tournai.
Dorpat (German), Tartu (Estonian): city—J2a2: 19.
Douro (Portuguese), Duero (Spanish), Duwīruh (Arabic): river—C2d4: 1, 11—15.
Drahonice (Czech): village near Březnice, 30 miles ESE of Pilsen (G4c1: 20).
Draj: port—see Durazzo.
Dramelay: village—see Trémolay.
Drausen, Lake; Jezioro Drużno (Polish)—H5b1: 19.
Druges: town—see Androusa.
Dubrovnik: port—see Ragusa.
Duero: river—see Douro.

Duna, Dunărea, or Dunav: river—see Danube.
Düna (German), Dvina (Russian), Daugava (Lettish): river—I5a3: 19.
Dünamünde (German), Daugavgrïva (Lettish): port—I5a3: 19.
Durazzo (Italian), Epidamnus or Dyrrachium (classical), Draj (Turkish), Durrës (Albanian): port—H5d4: 2, 4.
Durben (German), Durbe (Lettish): village—I2a4: 19.
Duwïruh: river—see Douro.
Dvina: river—see Düna.
Dyje (Czech), Thaya (German): river—H2c2: 20.
Dyrrachium: port—see Durazzo.
Dystos (medieval Greek), Dhístos (modern Greek): village—I5e2: 4.
Dzierzgón: fortress—see Christburg.

East Indies or Malay Archipelago: island group SE of Asia—not in area mapped.
Ebro (Spanish), Ibruh (Arabic): river—E1d5: 1, 11⁻15.
Echinades (Greek): island group—I1e2: 4.
Écija (Spanish), Istijjah (Arabic): town—C5e3: 13.
Edessa; Roucha or Rochas (medieval), ar-Ruhā' (Arabic), Urfa (Turkish): city—L4e3: 16.
Edingen: town—see Enghien.
Edirne: city—see Adrianople.
Edremit: town—see Adramyttium.
Eesti: region—see Estonia.
Ege Denizi—see Aegean Sea.
Eger: town—see Cheb.
Egripos: island—see Euboea.
Egypt; Miṣr (Arabic): region of NE Africa—Kfg: 2, 16, 17, 18, 21.
Egypt, Upper: region along the Nile south of Cairo—Kg: 16.
Eider (German): river—G1b1: 1, 2.
Eire: island—see Ireland.
'Eizariya: abbey—see Bethany.
Ekine: island—see Aegina.
El Castellar (Spanish): fortress 4 miles NW of Saragossa (D5d4: 1).
El Puerto: port—see Puerto de Santa María.
Elbasan (medieval, Albanian): town—I1d4: 4.
Elbe (German), Labe (Czech): river—F5b2: 1, 2, 20.
Elbing (German), Elbląg (Polish): town—H5b1: 19.
Elche (Spanish), Alsh (Arabic): town—D5e2: 14.
Eleutheropolis: town—see Beth Gibelin.
Elis; Ēlis or Ēleia (classical Greek), Ilía (modern Greek): district of NW Morea—I2e3: 4.
Elis: town—see Palaeopolis.
Elma Daghï: range—see Amanus.
Elsass: region—see Alsace.
Elvas (Portuguese): town—C3e2: 13.
Ely: town—E1b3: 1.
Emel: river—see Imil.
Emesa: city—see Homs.
Emmaus; Nicopolis (classical), Amwās (Arabic), Imwas (Israeli): village, not biblical Emmaus, 9 miles WNW of Jerusalem (L1f4: 21).
Emporium: town—see Ampurias.
Enghien (French), Edingen (Flemish): town—E5b5: 1.
Engia: island—see Aegina.
England: region—DEb: 1.

Epaktos: port—see Naupactus.
Epeiros: region—see Epirus.
Ephesus (classical), Altoluogo (medieval), Ayasoluk (Turkish): town, now un-
    important—J3e3: 3.
Ephrata: town—see Bethlehem.
Epidamnus: port—see Durazzo.
Epidaurus (classical), Palaiá Epídhavros (modern Greek): town—I4e3: 4.
Epila (Spanish): town—D4d4: 12.
Epirus; Epeiros (classical Greek: mainland), Ípiros (modern Greek): region west
    of Thessaly—I1e1: 2, 4.
Episcopi; Episkopí (modern Greek): town—K3f1: 10.
Erdély: region—see Transylvania.
Erfurt (German): city—G2b5: 1, 2, 20.
Erivan; Ayrivank (East Armenian), Yerevan (modern Armenian): city—M5d5:
    16.
Ermland (German), Warmja or Varmia (Polish): district inland from Frisches
    Haff—HIb: 20.
Escandelion: castle—see Scandelion.
Eskihisar: town—see Laodicea ad Lycum.
España: region—see Spain.
Estada (Spanish): village 6 miles ENE of Barbastro (E1d3: 11).
Estanor: port—see Pera.
Este (Italian): town—G2c5: 2.
Estepona (Spanish), Ashṭabūnah (Arabic): town—C5e4: 15.
Estir: castle—see Stiris.
Estives: city—see Thebes.
Estonia; Estland (German), Eesti (Estonian): region—IJa: 19.
Estrêla, Serra da (Portuguese): mountain range NW of the Zêzere (Ce: 12).
Esztergom: town—see Gran.
Ethiopia or Abyssinia; Ityopya (Amharic): region of east central Africa—not in
    area mapped.
Eu (French): town—E2b5: 15.
Euboea (classical), Evripos (medieval Greek), Egripos (Turkish), Negroponte
    (Italian), Évvoia (modern Greek): island—I5e2: 3, 4.
Euphrates (classical), al-Furāt (Arabic), Firat Nehri (Turkish): river—N4f5: 16,
    21.
Évora (Portuguese), Yāburah (Arabic): town—C3e2: 1, 13.
Évreux (French): town—E2c1: 1, 13.
Evros: river—see Maritsa.
Évvoia, or Evripos: island—see Euboea.
Extremadura (Spanish): region of western Spain—Cde: 12, 13.
Eynihal: town—see Myra.

Famagusta; Ammōkhostos (classical Greek), Famagosta (medieval Italian):
    port—K4e5: 10, 21.
Farges-en-Septaine (French): village 12 miles east of Bourges (E3c3: 1).
Faro (Portuguese), Santa Maria do Algarve (medieval), Shantamarīyat al-Gharb
    (Arabic): port—C3e3: 13.
Fársala: town—see Pharsala.
Fās: city—see Fez.
Feke: town—see Vahka.
Fellin (medieval), Viljandi (Estonian): town—J1a2: 19.
Feodosiya: port—see Kaffa.
Feraklos: village—see Pheraclos.

Ferrara (Italian): city—G2d1: 2.
Fetenli: port—see Pteleum.
Fethiye: port—see Makri.
Feuchtwangen (German): town 40 miles w sw of Nuremberg (G2c1: 1).
Fez; Fās (Arabic): city—D1f1: 1, 11—15.
Fília: district—see Triphylia.
Filibe: city—see Philippopolis.
Filírimos: castle—see Phileremos.
Filistīn: region—see Palestine.
Fīrat Nehri: river—see Euphrates.
Fisco: port—see Marmaris.
Fitero (Spanish): abbey, now town—D4d3: 13.
Flanders; Vlaanderen (Flemish): region of northern France and Belgium—Eb: 1.
Florence; Firenze (Italian): city—G2d2: 1, 2.
Fokís: district—see Phocis.
Fontainebleau (French): town—E3c2: 15.
Forli; Forlì (Italian): town—G3d1: 2.
Formentera (Spanish): island—E2e2: 13.
Fossanova (Italian): convent, and village, 10 miles NNW of Terracina (G4d4: 2).
Fossat (French): chateau near Estissac, 12 miles west of Troyes (E5c2: 1).
Foucherolles (French): village—E3c2: 14.
Fraga (Spanish), Ifrāghah (Arabic): town—E1d4: 12.
France: region, smaller than modern nation—DEFbcd: 12, 13, 15.
Francolí (Spanish): river—E2d4: 12.
Franconia; Franken (German): region of western Germany—FGbc: 1, 2.
Frankfurt am Main (German): city—F4b5: 1, 2.
Frauenburg (German), Frombork (Polish): fortress, now village—H5b1: 19.
Freiburg im Breisgau (German): city—F3c2: 1.
Freising (German): town—G2c2: 20.
Fresneda or La Fresneda (Spanish): town—E1d5: 13.
Frisches Haff (German), Zalew Wiślany (Polish: Vistual lagoon), Vislinskiy Zaliv
   (Russian): lagoon—HIb: 19, 20.
Frisia (classical), Friesland (Dutch, German): region—Fb: 1, 2.
Frombork: fortress—see Frauenburg.
Fulda (German): river—F5b4: 1, 2.
Fulda (German): town—F5b5: 1, 2.
al-Fūrat: river—see Euphrates.

Gabala: port—see Jabala.
Gabes; Tacapae (classical), Qābis (Arabic): port—G1f2: 1, 2.
Gadir, or Gades: port—see Cadiz.
Gadres: town—see Gaza.
Gaeta (Italian): port—G4d4: 2.
Gafsa; Capsa (classical), Qafṣah (Arabic): town—F4f1: 1, 2.
Gagnac (French): village 4 miles south of Beaulieu (E2d1: 15).
Galata (medieval), Sycae (classical): southern part of Pera (J4d4: 3).
Galaxidi; Oeanthea (Latin), Galaxeidion (medieval Greek), Galaxídhion (modern
   Greek): town—I3e2: 4.
Galicia; Galich (Russian), Halicz (Polish): region of NW Ukraine and SE Poland,
   larger than modern Polish province—Ibc: 2.
Galicia (Spanish), Jillīqiyah (Arabic): region of NW Spain—Cd: 12.
Galilee; Hagalil (Israeli): region of northern Palestine—L1f3: 21.
Galilee, Sea of—see Tiberias, Lake.
Gallia: region—see Gaul.

Gallipoli: peninsula—J2d5: 3.

Gallipoli; Callipolis (classical), Gelibolu (Turkish): town—J2d5: 2, 3, 16.

Gand: city—see Ghent.

Gangra or Germanicopolis (classical), Chankĭrĭ (Turkish): town—K4d5: 16.

Gardiki (medieval), Gardhíki or Kókkala (modern Greek): castle—I3e3: 4.

Gardiki (medieval), Pelinnaeon or Larissa Kremastē (ancient Greek): castle—I3e2: 4.

Gascony; Gascogne (French): region of SW France—Dd: 1, 12–15.

Gaston: town—see Baghrās.

Gastouni; Gastounē (medieval Greek), Gastogne (medieval), Gastoúni (modern Greek): town—I2e3: 4.

Gastria; Gastriá (modern Greek): village—K4e5: 10.

Gath (classical): ruined ancient town, near modern Qiryat Gat, 14 miles ESE of Ascalon (K5f4: 21).

Gâtineau (French): village 6 miles NNW of Matha (D5c5: 13).

Gaul; Gallia (Latin): ancient region roughly equivalent to France.

Gavur Daghĭ: range—see Amanus.

Gayá (Spanish): river—E2d4: 12.

Gaya: town—see Kyjov.

Gaza; Gadres (medieval), Ghazzah (Arabic); town—K5f4: 21.

Gdańsk: port—see Danzig.

Gedein: town—see Kdyně.

Gelibolu: town—see Gallipoli.

Gelmez: island—see Calymnos.

Geneva; Genava (Latin), Genève (French), Genf (German): city—F2c4: 1, 2.

Genoa; Genua (Latin), Genova (Italian): city, port—F4d1: 1, 2.

Gent: city—see Ghent.

Georgia; Sakartvelo (Georgian): region south of the western Caucasus—MNd: 16, 17, 18.

Gerace (Italian): town—H2e2: 2.

Geraki: fief—see Nivelet.

Geraki (medieval), Geronthrae (classical), Yeráki (modern Greek): town—I3e4: 4.

Germanicia: town—see Marash.

Germanicopolis: town—see Gangra.

Germany; Alamannia or Allemania (medieval), Deutschland (German): region of north central Europe (FGbc: 2).

Gertsike (Lettish): town—J1a4: 19.

Ghana (medieval): empire north of the Niger, not equivalent to modern nation— not in area mapped.

al-Gharb, or Gharb al-Andalus: region—see Algarve.

Gharnāṭah: city—see Granada.

Ghaudesh: island—see Gozo.

Ghazzah: town—see Gaza.

Ghent; Gand (French), Gent (Flemish): city, port—E4b4: 1.

Gibelet: town—see Jubail.

Gibralfaro (Spanish): fort near Malaga (D1e4: 1).

Gibraltar; Jibraltar (Spanish), Jabal Ṭāriq (Arabic): rock—C5e4: 1, 13, 14, 15.

Gibraltar, Strait of; az-Zuqāq (Arabic)—C5e5: 1, 11–15.

Giovinazzo (Italian): town 11 miles NNW of Bari (H2d4: 2).

Gitonis: town—see Zeitounion.

Glarentsa, Chiarenza, or Clarence (medieval), Cyllene (Latin), Kyllēnē (classical Greek), Killíni (modern Greek): town—I2e3: 4.

Gliwice (Polish), Gleiwitz (German): city—H4b5: 20.

Gniezno (Polish), Gnesen (German): town—H3b3: 20.

Gök-Su: river—see Calycadnus.

Golden Horn; Chrysoceras (classical), Halich (Turkish): bay between Constantinople and Pera (J4d4: 3).

Goldenstein: castle—see Kolstein.

Goldingen (German), Kuldīga (Lettish): town—I2a4: 19.

Golubats; Golubac (Serbian): village—I2d1: 2.

Good Hope, Cape of: southern tip of Africa—not in area mapped.

Gorigos: port—see Corycus.

Gortys: district—see Skorta.

Goslar (German): town—G1b4: 1, 2.

Gotland (Swedish): island—H4a3: 19.

Gozo; Ghaudesh (Maltese): island—G5e4: 2.

Gozon (French): chateau near St. Rome-de-Tarn, 27 miles SE of Rodez (E3d1: 14).

Gran (German), Esztergom (Hungarian): town 27 miles NW of Buda (H5c3: 20).

Granada (Spanish), Ighranāṭah or Gharnāṭah (Arabic): city—D2e3: 1, 11—15.

Granada: kingdon—CDe: 12—15.

Graus (Spanish): town—E1d3: 11.

Graville (French): village, now part of Graville-Sainte Honorine, 20 miles west of Jumièges (E1c1: 1).

Gravina (Italian): town—H2d5: 2.

Greece; Hellas (Greek): region, smaller than modern nation (Ide: 4).

Greenland; Grønland (Danish): island—not in area mapped.

Gríllos: village—see Moundritsa.

Grimaldi (Italian): town—H2e1: 2.

Grimma (German): town—G3b4: 20.

Grisi (medieval), Grízi or Akritochóri (modern Greek): castle—I2e4: 4.

Grønland: island—see Greenland.

Grubenhagen (German): castle—F5b4: 1.

Grünwald or Grünfelde (German), Grunwald (Polish): village—I1b2: 19.

Guadalajara (Spanish), Madīnat al-Faraj or Wādī-l-Ḥijārah (Arabic: river of the stones): town—D2d5: 15.

Guadalaviar (Spanish), al-Wādī al-Abyaḍ (Arabic: the white river): village—D4d5: 13.

Guadalhorce (Spanish): river—D1e4: 15.

Guadalquivir (Spanish), al-Wādī al-Kabīr (Arabic: the great river): river—C4e4: 1, 11—15.

Guadiana (Spanish, Portuguese), Wādī Ānah (Arabic): river—C3e3: 1, 11—15.

Guadix (Spanish), Wādī Āsh (Arabic): town—D2e3: 12, 13, 15.

Gujerat or Gujarat: district of western India—18.

Guzmán (Spanish): village—D2d4: 14.

Gymno (medieval), Yimnón (modern Greek): village—I4e2: 4.

Ḥabrūn: town—see Hebron.

Habry (Czech): town—H1c1: 20.

Habsburg: castle—see Hapsburg.

Haddeby: town—see Schleswig.

Hadria, or Mare Hadriaticum—see Adriatic Sea.

Hadrianopolis: city—see Adrianople.

Hadrumetum: port—see Susa.

Hagalil: region—see Galilee.

Haifa; Caiphas or Caiffa (medieval), Haifā (Arabic): port—L1f3: 21.

Hainault; Hainaut (French), Henegouwen (Flemish): district east of Artois—EFb: 1, 2.

Halab, or Haleb: city—see Aleppo.

Haliacmon (classical), Bistritsa (Macedonian), Aliákmon (modern Greek): river—
I3d5: 4.
Halicarnassus: town—see Bodrum.
Halich: bay—see Golden Horn.
Halicz: region—see Galicia.
Haliveri (medieval), Alivérion (modern Greek): town—I5e2: 4.
Halle an der Saale (German): city—G2b4: 20.
Ham (French): town—E3c1: 15.
Hambroeck (medieval): village, probably Hambrücken, 12 miles SE of Speyer
(F4c1: 1).
Hamburg (German): city, port—G1b2: 1, 2.
al-Ḥāmmah: town—see Alhama de Granada.
Hanover; Hannover (German): city—F5b3: 1, 2.
Hapsburg; Habsburg (German): castle—F4c3: 1.
al-Ḥaram ash-Sharīf: Temple district in Jerusalem (L1f4: 21).
Ḥārim (Arabic), Harenc (medieval): town—L2e4: 21.
Harod, Well of, or ‘En Ḥarod: village—see ‘Ain Jālūt.
Harrien (medieval), Harju (Estonian): district of western Estonia—Ia: 19.
Hasta: town—see Asti.
Hastings: port—E1b5: 1.
Hattin, Horns of; Ḥaṭṭīn or Ḥiṭṭīn (Arabic): hill battlefield—L1f3: 21.
Havelberg (German): town—G3b3: 20.
Havlíckův Brod: town—see Německý Brod.
Hebron; Ḥabrūn or Khalīl (Arabic), Saint Abraham (medieval): town—L1f4: 21.
Hebrus: river—see Maritsa.
Heilsberg (German), Lidzbark Warmiński (Polish): town—I1b1: 19.
Hejaz; al-Hijāz (Arabic): region of western Arabia—Lgh: 16.
Heliopolis: town—see Baalbek.
Hellas: region—see Greece.
Hellespontus: strait—see Dardanelles.
Helleville (French): village—D4c1: 14.
Helly (French): château near Créquy, 25 miles SE of Boulogne (E2b5: 1).
Henegouwen: district—see Hainault.
Heraclea: castle—see Siderokastron.
Heracleum: port—see Candia.
Heredia (Spanish): village—D3d3: 15.
Herke: island—see Chalce.
Hermannstadt (German), Nagyszeben (Hungarian), Sibiu (Rumanian): town—
I5c5: 2, 16.
Hesse; Hessen (German): district of NW Germany—Fb: 1, 2.
Hexamilion (Greek): wall across isthmus of Corinth—I3e3: 4.
Hibernia: island—see Ireland.
Hierosolyma: city—see Jerusalem.
al-Ḥijāz: region—see Hejaz.
Ḥimṣ: city—see Homs.
Hippo Zarytus: port—see Bizerte.
Hisarlik: village—see Troy.
Ḥiṣn al-Akrad: fortress—see Krak des Chevaliers.
Hispalis: city—see Seville.
Hispania: region—see Spain.
Ḥiṭṭīn: battlefield—see Hattin, Horns of.
Hohenzollern (German): castle 45 miles east of Freiburg (F3c2: 1).
Holland (Dutch): region north of Brabant—Eb: 1, 2.
Holm or Kirchholm (German): town, now unimportant—I5a4: 19.

Holstein (German): region south of Denmark—FGb: 1, 2.

Holy Roman Empire—12–15.

Homs; Emesa (classical), Ḥimṣ (Arabic): city—L2f1: 16, 21.

Horeb, Mount—see Sinai, Mount.

Hormuz; Hormōz (Persian): island in Persian Gulf—17, 18.

Horšovský Týn or Horšuv Týn (Czech), Bischofteinitz (German): town—G3c1: 20.

Hradčany (Czech): castle across the Vltava, west of Prague (G5b5: 20).

Hradec Králové (Czech), Königgrätz (German): town—H1b5: 20.

Hradiště: town—see Tábor.

Hromgla; Qal'at ar-Rūm (Arabic: fort of Rome), Ranculat (medieval), Hromgla (Armenian), Rum Kalesi (Turkish): fortress, now town—L3e3: 21.

Huelma (Spanish): town—D2e3: 14, 15.

Huércal-Overa (Spanish): town—D4e3: 14.

Huesca (Spanish), Osca (classical), Washqah (Arabic): town—D5d3: 1, 11, 12.

Huéscar (Spanish): town—D3e3: 14, 15.

Huete (Spanish), Wabdhah (Arabic): town—D3d5: 13.

Hungary; Magyarország (Hungarian): region of central Europe—HIc: 2, 17, 18, 20.

Huntingdon: town—D5b3: 1.

Hypatē: town—see Neopatras.

Ianina or Janina (medieval), Ioánnina (modern Greek): town—I1e1: 4.

Ibelin (medieval), Jabneel or Jamnia (classical), Yabnâ (Arabic), Yavne (Israeli): village 7 miles SW of Ramla (K5f4: 21).

Iberian peninsula: Spain and Portugal (CDEde: 1).

Ibiza or Iviza (Spanish), Yābisah (Arabic): island—Ee: 12, 13.

Ibruh: river—see Ebro.

Iconium: city—see Konya.

Ifrāghah: town—see Fraga.

Ifrīqiyah: region—see Tunisia.

Ighranāṭah: city—see Granada.

Iglau: town—see Jihlava.

Ikškile: village—see Üxküll.

Ilan-kale (Turkish): castle 10 miles N E of Mamistra (L1e4: 21).

Île de France (French): region around Paris—Ec: 1, 12–15.

Ilerda: town—see Lerida.

Ileros: island—see Leros.

Ili (Russian): river in Siberia—17, 18.

Ilía: district—see Elis.

Iliaki: island—see Telos.

Ilis: town—see Palaeopolis.

Ilium: city—see Troy.

Illora (Spanish): town 17 miles W N W of Granada (D2e3: 1).

Imbros; Lembro (medieval Italian), İmroz (Turkish): island—J1d5: 3.

Imil, Emel, or Yemel (Russian): river in Siberia—17, 18.

Imwas: village—see Emmaus.

India: region of southern Asia—17, 18.

Indian Ocean—17, 18.

Indochina: peninsular region of SE Asia—17, 18.

Ingria; Ingermanland (German), Inkeri (Estonian): district N E of Lake Peipus—Ja: 19.

İnjirli: island—see Nisyros.

Ioánnina: town—see Ianina.

Ionian Islands: island group from Corfu to Zante (HIe: 4).
Ipáti: town—see Neopatras.
Ípiros: region—see Epirus.
al-'Iqab: battlefield—see Las Navas de Tolosa.
Iráklion: port—see Candia.
Irān: region—see Persia.
Iraq; al-'Irāq (Arabic): modern nation, approximately equivalent to Mesopotamia.
Irboska (Estonian), Izborsk (Russian, now Novo-Izborsk): town, now village—J3a3: 19.
Ireland; Hibernia (Latin), Eire (Gaelic): island—Cb: 1.
Iron Gate; Đerdap (Serbian), Porṭile de Fier (Rumanian): gorge in the Danube—I3d1: 2.
Ischia (Italian): island—G4d5: 2.
Ishbīliyah: city—see Seville.
al-Iskandarīyah: city—see Alexandria.
İskenderun: port—see Alexandretta.
İskenderun Körfezi, or Issicus, Sinus: see Alexandretta, Gulf of.
Isova: village—see Bitsibardi.
Israel: modern nation, controlling Palestine and Sinai.
İstanbul: city—see Constantinople.
İstendil: island—see Tenos.
Istijjah: town—see Écija.
Istria (Italian), Istra (Croatian, Slovenian): peninsula—Gc: 2.
Italy; Italia (Italian): peninsular region, now a nation (FGHde: 2).
Ithomē: town—see Androusa.
Itil: river—see Volga.
Ityopya: region—see Ethiopia.
Iviza: island—see Ibiza.
Izborsk: town—see Irboska.
İzmir: city—see Smyrna.
İznik: town—see Nicaea.

Jabal aṭ- Ṭūr—see Olives, Mount of, and Tabor, Mount.
Jabal Mār Ilyās—see Carmel, Mount.
Jabal Mūsâ—see Sinai, Mount.
Jabal Tābūr—see Tabor, Mount.
Jabal Ṭāriq: rock—see Gibraltar.
Jabala; Gabala (classical), Jabalah (Arabic): port—Lle5: 21.
Jabneel: village—see Ibelin.
Jacob's Well: village, now abandoned, 2 miles ESE of Nablus (L1f3: 21).
Jaen; Jaén (Spanish), Jaiyān (Arabic): city—D2e3; 1, 12, 13, 14, 15.
Jaffa; Joppa (medieval), Yāfā (Arabic), Yafo (Israeli): port, now joined to Tel Aviv—K5f3: 21.
Jalón (Spanish), Shalūn (Arabic): river—D4d4: 12.
Jamnia: village—see Ibelin.
Janina: town—see Ianina.
Jarbah: island—see Jerba.
al-Jarīd: district—see Jerid.
Jativa; Játiva or Játiba (Spanish), Shāṭibah (Arabic): town—D5e2: 12. 13.
Java: island of East Indies—not in area mapped.
al-Jazā'ir: nation, city—see Algeria, Algiers.
al-Jazīrah al-Khaḍrā': port—see Algeciras.
Jazīrat al-'Arab: region—see Arabia.

Jazīrat Shuqr: town—see Alcira.

Jehoshaphat (classical): valley, possibly Kidron, but probably north of Jerusalem (L1f4: 21).

Jelgava: town—see Mitau.

Jerba; Meninx (classical), Jarbah (Arabic): island—G1f2: 1, 2.

Jerez de la Frontera, or Xeres (Spanish), Sharīsh (Arabic): town—C4e4: 13, 14.

Jericho; Arīḥā or ar-Rīḥā (Arabic): town, now village—L1f4: 21.

Jerid; al-Jarīd (Arabic): district around Tozeur—F4f2: 1.

Jerusalem; Hierosolyma (classical), al-Quds (Arabic: the holy), Yerushalayim (Israeli): city—L1f4: 16, 17, 18, 21.

Jibraltar: rock—see Gibraltar.

Jidda; Jiddah (Arabic): city, port—L5h4: 16.

Jihlava (Czech), Iglau (German): town—H1c1: 20.

Jillīqiyah: region—see Galicia.

Jiloca (Spanish): river—D4d4: 12.

Jimena de la Frontera (Spanish): town—C5e4: 14, 15.

Jisr ash-Shughūr (Arabic): bridge, now town—L2e5: 21.

Joinville (French): town—F1c2: 13.

Jonvelle (French): village 28 miles ENE of Langres (F1c3: 1).

Joppa: port—see Jaffa.

Jordan; al-Urdunīyah (Arabic): modern nation, controlling area east of the Jordan and Dead Sea.

Jordan; al-Urdunn (Arabic): river—L1f4: 16, 21.

Jubail (Arabic: small mountain), Byblos (classical), Gibelet (medieval): town—L1f1: 21.

Júcar (Spanish), Shuqr (Arabic): river—D5e1: 13.

Juilly (French): village 21 miles NE of Paris (E3c2: 1).

Jumièges (French): village—E1c1: 13.

Jungingen (German): castle 46 miles NNW of Constance (F5c2: 1).

Juslibol (Spanish): fort near Saragossa (D5d4: 1).

Kadaň (Czech), Kaaden (German): town—G4b5: 20.

Kaffa or Caffa (medieval), Theodosia (classical), Feodosiya (Russian): port—L1c5: 16, 17, 18.

Kairawan; al-Qairawān (Arabic): city—G1e5: 1, 2.

Kakopetria; Kakopetriá (modern Greek): town—K3f1: 10.

Kalamata (medieval), Pharae (classical), Kalámai (modern Greek): town—I3e3: 4.

Kalavryta (medieval), Cynaetha (classical), Kalávrita (modern Greek): town—I3e2: 4.

Kálimnos: island—see Calymnos.

Kaliningrad: city—see Königsberg.

Kalka (Russian): river—L2c4: 16.

Kalopanayiotis; Kalopanayiótis (modern Greek): town—K3f1: 10.

Kamenz (German): town—G5b4: 20.

Kandia: island—see Crete.

Kangurlan: town—see Sultaniyeh.

Kanine: town—see Canina.

Kanīsat al-Ghurāb—see Saint Vincent, Cape.

Kanizsay (Hungarian): town, now Nagykanizsa—H2c4: 2, 20.

Kantara; Kantára (modern Greek), al-Qanṭarah (Arabic: the bridge): town—K4e5: 10.

Kaporje (Estonian): town, now abandoned—J4a1: 19.

Kapraina: town—see Chaeronea.

Kara Hisar or Bashkent (Turkish): battlefield—L5e1: 16.

Karadeniz Boghazï: strait—see Bosporus.

al-Karak: fortress—see Kerak.

Karakorum (Turkish): town in Mongolia, now unimportant—17, 18.

Karaman (Turkish): region of south central Anatolia—Ke: 16.

Karelia; Karjala (Finnish): district of SE Finland—not in area mapped.

Káristos: town—see Carystus.

Karítaina: castle—see Karytaina.

Karlstein (German), Karlštejn or Karlův Týn (Czech): village 15 miles SW of Prague (G5b5: 1).

Karmel: mountain—see Carmel.

Karpass: peninsular district—K5e5: 10.

Kárpathos: island—see Carpathos.

Karytaina (medieval), Brenthē (classical Greek), Karítaina (modern Greek): castle, now village—I3e3: 4.

Kassándra: peninsula—see Cassandra.

Kastellórizo: island—see Castellorizzo.

Katakolon; Katákolon (modern Greek): town—I2e3: 4.

Katokastro; Castel Basso (medieval Italian), Katókastron (modern Greek): castle on Andros—I5e3: 3.

Kattaviá: town—see Cattavia.

Katzenellenbogen or Katzenelnbogen (German): town 12 miles ENE of Boppard (F3b5: 1).

Kaukab al-Hawā': castle—see Belvoir.

Kavkaz: range—see Caucasus.

Kayseri: city—see Caesarea.

Kdyně or Nová Kdyně (Czech), Gedein or Neugedein (German): town—G4c1: 20.

Keōs or Kéa: island—see Ceos.

Kephallēnia, Kephallōnia, or Keffalinía: island—see Cephalonia.

Kēphisos: stream—see Cephissus.

Kerak; Kir-hareseth (classical), Krak des Moabites or Krak of Moab (medieval), al-Karak (Arabic): fortress, now town—L1f4: 16, 21.

Kerkyra, or Kérkira: island—see Corfu.

Kerpe: island—see Carpathos.

Kerýnia: town—see Kyrenia.

Khairónia: town—see Chaeronea.

Khalandrítsa: town—see Chalandritsa.

Khalīj-i-Fars, or Khalīj al-'Ajam—see Persian Gulf.

Khalīl: town—see Hebron.

Khalkē, or Khálki: island—see Chalce.

Khalkidikē, or Khalkidhikí: peninsula—see Chalcidice.

Khalkís: town—see Negroponte.

Khanbaliq (Mongolian), Chi, Yenking, or Chungtu (classical Chinese), Cambaluc (medieval), Peking (Chinese): city—17, 18.

Khelmós: mountain—see Chelmos.

Khelōnatas: castle—see Clermont.

Kherónia: town—see Chaeronea.

Khíos: island—see Chios.

Khirbat al-Mafjar (Arabic): village 14 miles NE of Jerusalem (L1f4: 21).

Khirokitia; Khirokitía or Khoirokitía (modern Greek): battlefield—K4f1: 10.

Khloumoutsi: castle—see Clermont.

Khurasan; Khorāsān (Persian): region of NE Persia—17, 18.

Kíbris: island—see Cyprus.

Kidron: valley SE of Jerusalem (L1f4: 21).

Kiev (Russian): city—K1b5: 2.
Kifissós: stream—see Cephissus.
Kikládhes: island group—see Cyclades.
Killíni: mountain—see Cyllene.
Killíni: town—see Glarentsa.
Kióni: village—see Zaraca.
Kiparissía: town—see Arcadia.
Kïpchak steppe: region of southern Russia—Lc: 16.
Kípros: island—see Cyprus.
Kir-hareseth: fortress—see Kerak.
Kirchholm: town—see Holm.
Kíthira: island—see Cerigo.
Kiti; Kíti (modern Greek): village—K4f1: 10.
Kladruby (Czech): village—G3c1: 20.
Klaipéda: port—see Memel.
Kocha Papasi: island—see Lipsos.
Kokenhusen (German), Koknese (Lettish): town—J1a4: 19.
Kókkala: castle—see Gardiki.
Kolín (Czech): town—H1b5: 20.
Köln: city—see Cologne.
Kolossi (medieval), Kolóssi (modern Greek): fortress—K3f1: 10.
Kolstein or Goldenstein (German): castle—H2b5: 20.
Koluri: island—see Salamis.
Komutau: town—see Chomutov.
Königgrätz: town—see Hradec Králové.
Königsberg (German): city, now part of Kaliningrad—I1b1: 19, 20.
Konstanz: town—see Constance.
Konya (Turkish), Iconium (medieval): city—K3e3: 16, 17, 18.
Kōpais Limnē—see Copais, Lake.
Korgos: port—see Corycus.
Korinthía: district—see Corinthia.
Korinthiakós Kólpos—see Corinth, Gulf of.
Kórinthos: city—see Corinth.
Korōnē, or Koróni: town—see Coron.
Kós: island—see Cos.
Kós: town—see Narangia.
Köse Dagh (Turkish): peak—L3d5: 16.
Kossovo; Kosovo Polje (Serbian: field of blackbirds): battlefield—I2d3: 2.
Koulourē: island—see Salamis.
Kozan: town—see Sis.
Krak de Montréal (medieval), ash-Shaubak (Arabic): fortress, now village—L1f5:
    16, 21.
Krak des Chevaliers (medieval), Ḥiṣn al-Akrād (Arabic: stronghold of the Kurds):
    fortress—L2f1: 16, 21.
Krak of Moab: fortress—see Kerak.
Kraków: city—see Cracow.
Krētē, or Kríti: island—see Crete.
Kreuzburg (German), Slavskoye (Russian): town—I1b1: 19.
Kroia; Croia (Italian), Akche Hisar (Turkish), Krujë (Albanian): town—H5d4: 4.
Kroměříž (Czech), Kremsier (German): town—H3c1: 20.
Krym: peninsula—see Crimea.
Kujavia (medieval), Kujawy (Polish): district of north central Poland—Hb: 19,
    20.
Kuldīga: town—see Goldingen.
Kulm (German), Chełmńo (Polish): town—H4b2: 19.

Kulmbach (German): town—G2b5: 1, 2, 20.
Kulmerland (German): district of northern Poland—Hb: 20.
Kunštát (Czech), Kunstadt (German): town—H2c1: 20.
Kura; Cyrus (classical): river—N5e1: 16.
Kurisches Haff (German), Kuršiu Įlanka (Lithuanian), Kurskiy Zaliv (Russian): lagoon—Ia: 19.
Kurland (German), Courland (medieval), Kurzeme (Lettish): district of western Latvia—Ia: 19.
Kutná Hora (Czech), Kuttenberg (German): town—H1c1: 20.
Kwidzyń: town—see Marienwerder.
Kyjov (Czech), Gaya (German): town—H3c1: 20.
Kyllēnē: mountain—see Cyllene.
Kyllēnē: town—see Glarentsa.
Kypros: island—see Cyprus.
Kyrenia; Cerines (medieval), Kerýnia (modern Greek): town—K4e5: 10.
Kythēra: island—see Cerigo.

L'Assebebe: fortress—see Subaibah.
L'Isle Adam (French): town 10 miles NNW of Paris (E3c2: 1).
La Bastide-de-Sérou (French): village—E2d3: 14.
La Broquère or La Broquière (French): village—E1d2: 15.
La Cava (Spanish): town—E1d5: 12.
La Fresneda: town—see Fresneda.
La Glisière: castle—see Vlesiri.
La Higueruela (Spanish): battlefield 6 miles NW of Granada (D2e3: 1).
La Mancha (Spanish): region of central Spain—De: 12.
La Marche: district—see Marche.
La Palisse: town—see Lapalisse.
La Portelle: pass—see Syrian Gates.
La Rioja (Spanish): district of north central Spain—Dd: 13.
La Roche-sur-Ognon (French): castle in Burgundy (Fc: 1) on upper Ognon river.
La Rochechenard (French): village, probably Rochechinard, 15 miles east of Romans (F1c5: 1).
La Sola: town—see Salona.
La Tour-du-Pin (French): town—F1c5: 14.
La Valette-du-Var (French): suburb 3 miles ENE of Toulon (F1d2: 1).
La Vega: plain—see Vega.
Laa an der Thaya (German): town—H2c2: 20.
Labe: river—see Elbe.
Lablah: town—see Niebla.
Lacedaemon: town—see Sparta.
Laconia (classical), Lakōnia or Lakōnikē (medieval Greek), Lakonía (modern Greek): district of SE Morea—I3e4: 4.
al-Lādhiqīyah: port—see Latakia.
Lajazzo: port—see Ayas.
Lakedaimon: town—see Sparta.
Lambousa; Lámbousa (modern Greek): village—K4e5: 10.
Lamía: town—see Zeitounion.
Lamia, Gulf of, or Malian Gulf; Maliakós Kólpos (modern Greek): bay east of Zeitounion (Lamia, I3e2: 4).
Lampron (Armenian), Namrun (Turkish): fortress—K5e3: 21.
Lampsacus (classical), Lapseki (Turkish): village—J2d5: 3.
Lancaster: city—D3b1: 1.
Landsberg (German): town—G3b4: 20.

Langensalza (German): town—G1b4: 2.

Langles (French): village near Saint Martin de Villeréal, 55 miles NW of Montauban (E2d1: 15).

Langley: town, now an eastern suburb of Slough, 21 miles west of London (D5b4: 1).

Lango: island—see Cos.

Langres (French): town—F1c3: 13.

Lanka: island—see Ceylon.

Lannoy (French): town 9 miles NW of Tournai (E4b5: 1).

Laodicea ad Lycum (classical), Eskihisar (Turkish): town, now abandoned in favor of Denizli—J5e3: 3.

Laodicea ad Mare: port—see Latakia.

Lapalisse or La Palisse (French): town—E4c4: 15.

Lapater: town—see Neopatras.

Lapseki: village—see Lampsacus.

Laqant: port—see Alicante.

Lardos (Greek): village—J4e4: 8.

Lāridah: town—see Lerida.

Larissa (medieval), Lárisa (modern Greek): castle on hill west of Argos (I3e3: 4).

Larissa Kremastē: castle—see Gardiki.

Larmena (medieval), Armena (medieval Greek): castle—I5e2: 4.

Larnaca; Lárnaka (modern Greek): town—K4f1: 10.

Las: castle—see Passava.

Las Navas de Tolosa (Spanish), al-'Iqab or al-'Uqab (Arabic): battlefield—D2e2: 13.

Lastic (French): village near Saint Flour, 39 miles west of Le Puy (E4c5: 15).

Latakia; Laodicea ad Mare (classical), al-Lādhiqīyah (Arabic): port—L1e5: 21.

Latrun; al-Aṭrūn (Arabic), Le Toron des Chevaliers (medieval); village 10 miles SE of Ramla (K5f4: 21).

Laun: town—see Louny.

Lauraqah: town—see Lorca.

Lauria: town—see Lluria.

Lausanne (French): city—F2c4: 1, 2.

Laushah: town—see Loja.

Lausitz: region—see Lusatia.

Le Brulle: town—see Burlus.

Le Courc: port—see Corycus.

Le Destroit or Pierre Encise (medieval French), Bāb al-Ajal (Arabic): fort guarding rock cleft 1 mile east of Château Pèlerin (K5f3: 21).

Le Grand Mayne or Le Grand Magne (medieval): castle, probably at Maina but possibly at Porto Kaio (I3e4: 4).

Le Petit Mayne (medieval French): castle, possibly at Mikrománi, 6 miles WNW of Kalamata (I3e3: 4).

Le Puy-en-Velay (French): town—E4c5: 15.

Le Toron des Chevaliers: village—see Latrun.

Le Vieil Dampierre: village—see Dampierre.

Leal (German), Lihula (Estonian): fort, now village—I4a2: 19.

Lebadea: town—see Livadia.

Lebrija (Spanish): town—C4e4: 14.

Lecce (Italian): town—H4d5: 2.

Lechaina: town—see Lichina.

Lechonia: village—see Liconia.

Lefkoniko; Lefkonikó (modern Greek): town—K4e5: 10.

Léftro: castle—see Beaufort.

Leghorn; Livorno (Italian): port—G1d2: 2.
Leipsos: island—see Lipsos.
Leipzig (German), Lipsk (Slavic): city—G3b4: 1, 2, 20.
Leiria (Portuguese): town—C2e1: 12.
Leitomischl: town—see Litomyšl.
Lekhainá: town—see Lichina.
Lekhónia: village—see Liconia.
Lembro: island—see Imbros.
Lemesós: port—see Limassol.
Lenzen (German): town—G2b2: 20.
Leon; León (Spanish), Liyūn (Arabic): city—C5d3: 1, 11–15.
Leon; León (Spanish): region of northern Spain—Cd: 1, 11–15.
Leondari (medieval Greek), Leontárion (modern Greek): village 3 miles SE of Veligosti (I3e3: 4).
Leontes: river—see Litani.
Lepanto: port—see Naupactus.
Lerida; Ilerda (classical), Lérida (Spanish), Lāridah (Arabic): town—E1d4: 1, 11, 12, 13.
Leros; Lero (Italian), İleros (Turkish), Léros (modern Greek): island—J2e3: 3.
Les Baux (French): town, now village—E5d2: 15.
Les Vaux (French): not identified, among several of the name.
Lesbos (classical), Mytilēnē (medieval Greek), Metelino (medieval Italian), Midülü (Turkish), Lésvos (modern Greek): island—J2e1: 3.
Lesh (Albanian), Lissus (classical), Alessio (Italian): town—H5d4: 4.
Lesparre (French): town, now part of Lesparre-Médoc—D5c5: 14.
Letná (Czech): hill north of Prague, across the Vltava (G5b5: 20).
Leucas or Leukas (classical), Leucadia or Santa Maura (medieval), Levkás (modern Greek): island—I1e2: 2, 4.
Leuctrum: castle—see Beaufort.
Levádhia: town—see Livadia.
Levkōsia: city—see Nicosia.
Li Vaux Moysi (medieval), al-Wu'airah or Wādī Mūsâ (Arabic: the valley of Moses): town—L1f5: 21.
Lichina or Lechaina; Lekhainá (modern Greek): town—I2e3: 4.
Lichtenburg (on Zornstein): castle in Moravia or Bohemia, location uncertain.
Liconia or Lechonia (medieval), Lekhónia (modern Greek): village—I4e1: 4.
Lidhoríkion: town—see Loidoriki.
Lidzbark Warmiński: town—see Heilsberg.
Lietuva: region—see Lithuania.
Ligoúrion: village—see Lygourio.
Lihula: fort—see Leal.
Limassol; Nemesos (medieval Greek), Lemesós (modern Greek): port—K4f1: 10, 21.
Limoges (French): city—E2c5: 1, 11–15.
Limonia, or Liman: island—see Alimnia.
Lindos; Líndhos (modern Greek): town—J4e4: 8.
Lipany (Czech): battlefield—G5b5: 20.
Lipsk: city—see Leipzig.
Lipsos; Leipsos (classical), Lipso or Lisso (Italian), Kocha Papasi (Turkish), Lipsoí (modern Greek): island—J2e3: 3.
Lisbon; Lisboa (Portuguese), Ushbūnah (Arabic): city, port—C1e2: 1, 11–15.
Lissus: town—see Lesh.
Listrina (medieval): fief in mountains SE of Vostitsa (I3e2: 4).
Litani; Leontes (classical), al-Līṭānī (Arabic): river—L1f2: 21.

Lithuania; Lietuva (Lithuanian): region east of Poland, larger than modern state—IJab: 2, 18, 19.

Litomyšl (Czech), Leitomischl (German): town—H2c1: 20.

Livadia; Lebadea (classical), Levádhia (modern Greek): town—I3e2: 4.

Livadostro or Rivadostia (medieval): port, now abandoned—I4e2: 4.

Livonia; Livland (German): district of southern Estonia and northern Latvia—IJa: 19.

Livorno: port—see Leghorn.

Liyūn: city—see Leon.

Llobregat (Catalan): river—E3d4: 11, 12.

Lluria or Loria (medieval), Lauria (Italian), Lloria (Catalan): town—H1d5: 2.

Löbau (German), Lubawa (Polish), Lubije (Czech): town—H5b2: 19.

Loccum (German): monastery, now town—F5b3: 1.

Locris (classical): district of central Greece—I3e2: 4.

Lod: town—see Lydda.

Loidoriki (medieval), Lidhoríkion (modern Greek): town—I3e2: 4.

Loire (French): river—D3c3: 1.

Loja (Spanish), Laushah (Arabic): town—D1e3: 13, 15.

Lombardy; Lombardia (Italian): region of NW Italy—FGcd: 1, 2.

London: city, port—D5b4: 1.

Longjumeau (French): town 11 miles SSW of Paris (E3c2: 1).

Lor (French): village—E5c1: 14.

Lora del Río (Spanish): town—C5e3: 13.

Lorca (Spanish), Lauraqah (Arabic): town—D4e3: 13, 14, 15.

Loria: town—see Lluria.

Lorraine (French), Lothringen (German): region of eastern France—Fc: 1, 2.

Los Collejares (Spanish): battlefield 6 miles SW of Quesada (D2e3: 13).

Louny (Czech), Laun (German): town—G4b5: 20.

Lousã, Serra da (Portuguese): mountain range SE of Coimbra (C2d5: 1).

Lubawa, or Lubije: town—see Löbau.

Lübeck (German): city, port—G1b2: 1, 2, 20.

Lucania (medieval), Basilicata (modern Italian): region of southern Italy—Hd: 2.

Lucca (Italian): town—G1d2: 2.

Lucena (Spanish): town—D1e3: 12, 15.

Lucerne (French), Luzern (German): town—F4c3: 1, 2.

al-Ludd: town—see Lydda.

Luna (Spanish): town—D5d3: 15.

Lund (Swedish): city—G4a5: 1, 2.

Lusatia (medieval), Lausitz (German), Łużyca (Polish): region of eastern Germany and SW Poland—GHb: 2, 20.

Lusatia, Lower; Niederlausitz (German): NE Lusatia (H1b3: 20).

Lusatia, Upper; Oberlausitz (German): SW Lusatia (G5b4: 20).

Lusignan (French): town—E1c4: 14.

Luzern: town—see Lucerne.

Łużyca: region—see Lusatia.

Lychnidus: town—see Ochrida.

Lydda; Saint George (medieval), al-Ludd (Arabic), Lod (Israeli): town—K5f4:21.

Lydia: district—see Aydin.

Lygourio (medieval), Ligoúrion (modern Greek): village—I4e3: 4.

Lyons; Lyon (French): city—E5c5: 1, 11–15.

Macarena (Spanish): suburb of Seville (C5e3: 1).

Macedonia (classical), Makedhonía (modern Greek), Makedonija (Serbian): region east of Albania—Id: 2, 3, 4.

Machault or Machaut (French): village 22 miles ENE of Rheims (E5c1: 1).
Madallīn: town—see Medellín.
al-Ma'din: town—see Almada.
al-Madīnah: city—see Medina.
Madīnat al-Farāj: town—see Guadalajara.
Madras: city, port on east coast of India—17, 18.
Magacela (Spanish), Umm Ghazālah (Arabic): town 33 miles east of Mérida (C4e2: 13).
Magdeburg (German): city—G2b3: 1, 2, 20.
al-Maghrib: region—see North Africa.
al-Maghrib al-Aqṣā: region—see Morocco.
Magyarország: region—see Hungary.
Mahdia; al-Mahdīyah (Arabic): city, port—G2e5: 1, 2.
Maina; Máni (modern Greek): castle—I3e4: 4.
Maina; Mainē (medieval Greek), Máni (modern Greek): peninsular district—I3e4: 4.
Mainz (German), Mayence (French): city—F4b5: 1, 2.
Maisy (French): village, probably Mézilles, 38 miles west of Noyers (E4c3: 1).
al-Majah: village—see Modin.
Majorca; Mallorca (Spanish), Mayūrqah (Arabic): island—Ee: 12, 13.
Makedhonía, or Makedonija: region—see Macedonia.
Makkah: city—see Mecca.
Makri (medieval), Fethiye (Turkish): port—J5e4: 3.
Makryplagi (medieval), Makripláyi (modern Greek): pass—I3e3: 4.
Malabar: coastal region of western India—17, 18.
Malaga; Malaca (classical), Málaga (Spanish), Mālaqah (Arabic): city, port—D1e4: 1, 11—15.
Malagón (Spanish): town—D2e1: 12.
Malatia, or Malatya: city—see Melitene.
Malbork: fortress—see Marienburg.
Malešov (Czech): battlefield 4 miles SSW of Kutná Hora (H1c1: 20).
Malian Gulf, or Maliakós Kólpos—see Lamia, Gulf of.
Malīlah: port—see Melilla.
Mallorca: island—see Majorca.
Malta; Melita (classical), Mālițah (Arabic): island—G5e5: 2.
Malvasia: fortress—see Monemvasia.
Malwīyah: river—see Moulouya.
Mamistra (medieval), Mopsuestia (classical), Msis (Armenian), Misis (Turkish): town—L1e4: 21.
Mandria (medieval): fief south of the Alpheus (Ie: 4), possibly Moundritsa.
Máni: castle, district—see Maina.
Manolada (medieval): battlefield—I2e2: 4.
Manṣūrah (Arabic): fort adjacent to Tlemsen (D4f1: 1).
Mantua: Mantova (Italian): city 80 miles WSW of Venice (G3c5: 2).
Marash (Armenian, Turkish), Germanicia (classical), Mar'ash (Arabic): town—L2e3: 16, 21.
Marbella (Spanish), Marballah (Arabic): town 30 miles SW of Malaga (D1e4: 1).
March: river—see Morava.
Marche; La Marche (French): district of NW France—E2c4: 1, 12—15.
Margat (medieval), al-Marqab (Arabic: the watch-tower): fortress—L1e5: 21.
Māridah: town—see Mérida.
Marienburg (German), Malbork (Polish): fortress, now town—H5b1: 2, 19, 20.
Marienwerder (German), Kwidzyń (Poland): town—H4b2: 19, 20.
Maritsa; Hebrus (Latin), Evros (medieval Greek), Merich (Turkish): river—J2d5: 3.

al-Marīyah: city—see Almeria.

Marj Dābiq (Arabic): plain—L3e4: 21.

Marmara, Sea of; Propontis (classical), Marmara Denizi (Turkish)—J4d5: 3, 16.

Marmaris (Turkish), Fisco (medieval): port—J4e4: 3.

al-Marqab: fortress—see Margat.

Marrakesh; Marrākush (Arabic): city—C2f4: 1.

al-Marsâ al-Kabīr: port—see Mers-el-Kebir.

Marseilles; Massalia (classical Greek), Massilia (Latin), Marseille (French): city, port—F1d2: 1, 11—15.

Martinengo (Italian): town 29 miles east of Milan (F5c5: 1).

Martoni (Italian): village near Carinola, 14 miles W NW of Capua (G5d4: 2).

Martos (Spanish): town—D2e3: 13.

Masovia (medieval), Mazowsze (Polish): region of east central Poland—HIb: 19, 20.

Massa (Italian): town—G1d1: 2.

Massalia, or Massilia: city—see Marseilles.

Matagrifon: castle—see Akova.

Matha (French): town—D5c5: 13.

Maurūr: town—see Morón de la Frontera.

al-Mauṣil: city—see Mosul.

Mayence: city—see Mainz.

Mayūrqah: island—see Majorca.

Mazowsze: region—see Masovia.

Mecca; Makkah (Arabic): city—L5h4: 16, 17, 18.

Mecklenburg (German): district of northern Germany—Gb: 20.

Medellín (Spanish): Madallīn (Arabic): town 21 miles east of Mérida (C5e2: 13).

Medina; al-Madīnah (Arabic: the city): city—L5h1: 16, 17, 18.

Medina del Campo (Spanish): town—D1d4: 15.

Medina Sidonia (Spanish), Shadhūnah (Arabic): town—C5e4: 13, 14, 15.

Mediterranean Sea—D/Ldef.

Megalopolis (classical Greek), Megalópolis (modern Greek): town 8 miles SSE of Karytaina (I3e3: 4).

Megara; Mégara (modern Greek): town—I4e3: 4.

Megarid: district around Megara—I4e2: 4.

Megista, or Meis: island—see Castellorizzo.

Meiendorf or Megendorf (German): village 8 miles NE of Hamburg (G1b2: 1).

Meissen (German): town—G4b4: 1, 2, 20.

Meknes; Miknāsah (Arabic): city—C5f2: 1.

Melfi (Italian): town—H1d5: 2.

Melilla; Malīlah, now Mlīlyah (Arabic), Tāmlīlt (Berber: the white): port—D3e5: 15.

Melita: island—see Malta.

Melitene (classical), Melden (Armenian), Malatia (medieval), Malatya (Turkish): city—L4e2: 16.

Melos; Mēlos (classical Greek), Milo (medieval Italian), Degir Menlik (Turkish), Mílos (modern Greek) : island—I5e4 :3, 4.

Memel (German), Klaipéda (Lithuanian): port—I2a5: 19.

Memel: river—see Niemen.

Mendhenítsa: village—see Bodonitsa.

Mendoza (Spanish): village 11 miles W SW of Heredia (D3d3: 15).

Meng-ku: region—see Mongolia.

Meninx: island—see Jerba.

Menorca: island—see Minorca.

Menteshe (medieval), Mughla (modern Turkish): region of western Anatolia, equivalent to classical Caria—Je: 2, 3, 16.

Mequinenza (Spanish): town 11 miles SW of Lerida (E1d4: 1).

Mercato San Severino: town—see San Severino Rota.

Merich: river—see Maritsa.

Mérida (Spanish), Māridah (Arabic): town—C4e2: 13.

Mers-el-Kebir; al-Marsâ al-Kabîr (Arabic: the great port): port—D5e5: 15.

Merseburg (German): city—G2b4: 20.

Mesaoria; Mesaréa (modern Greek): plain around Lefkoniko—K4e5: 10.

Mesaréa: district—see Arcadia.

Mesembria (medieval), Misivri (Turkish), Nesebar (Bulgarian): town—J3d3: 2, 3, 16.

Mesopotamia (classical): region between the Euphrates and the Tigris—LMef: 16.

Messenia; Messēnē (medieval Greek), Messíni (modern Greek): district of SW Morea—I2e4: 4.

Messina (Italian): port, city—H1e2: 2.

Město Teplá: town—see Teplá.

Mestre (Italian): town 5 miles NW of Venice (G3c5: 2).

Metelino: island—see Lesbos.

Methocya (medieval): castle near Stiris (I3e2: 4).

Methōnē, or Methóni: port—see Modon.

Mexico; México (Spanish): region of North America—not in area mapped.

Mézières (French): town, now attached to Charleville—E5c1: 15.

Midi (French): southern France (DEd: 1).

Midülü: island—see Lesbos.

Mies: town—see Stříbro.

Miknāsah: city—see Meknes.

Míkonos, or Micone: island—see Myconos.

Milan; Milano (Italian): city—F5c5: 1, 2.

Miletus: port—see Palatia.

Miliana; Milyānah (Arabic): town—E3e4: 1.

Milly (French): village—E5c1: 15.

Mílos, or Milo: island—see Melos.

Minho (Portuguese), Miño (Spanish), Minyuh (Arabic): river—C2d3: 1, 11–15.

Minōa: fortress—see Monemvasia.

Minorca; Menorca (Spanish), Minurqah (Arabic): island—Ede: 12, 13.

Miravet (Spanish): village—E1d4: 12, 13.

Misis: town—see Mamistra.

Misivri: town—see Mesembria.

Miṣr: region—see Egypt.

Mistra; Myzithra (medieval Greek), Mistrás (modern Greek): town—I3e3: 2, 4.

Mistretta (Italian): town—G5e3: 2.

Mitau (German), Jelgava (Lettish): town—I4a4: 19.

Mitopoli (Greek): village 7 miles SW of Chalandritsa (I2e2: 4).

Mitylēnē, or Mitilíni: island—see Mytilene.

Mlilyah: port—see Melilla.

Moclín (Spanish): town, now village, 15 miles NW of Granada (D2e3: 1).

Modena (Italian): town—G1d1: 2.

Modin; al-Majah (Arabic), Modi'im (Israeli): village, now abandoned, 7 miles east of Ramla (K5f4: 21).

Modon (medieval), Methōnē (medieval Greek), Methóni (modern Greek): port—I2e4: 2, 4.

Mohács (Hungarian): town—H4c5: 2.

Mokene: island—see Myconos.

Molay (French): village 22 miles ESE of Langres (F1c3: 1).

Moldau: river—see Vltava.

Molina de Aragón (Spanish): town—D4d5: 11, 12.

Molines (medieval), Myloi (medieval Greek): fief near Niklena, 5 miles NE of Navarino (I2e4: 4).

Moncada y Reixach (Spanish): town—E3d4: 15.

Mondego (Portuguese), Mundīq (Arabic): river—C2d5: 11, 12.

Monemvasia; Minōa (classical Greek), Malvasia (medieval), Monemvásia (modern Greek): fortress, now town—I4e4: 4.

Monferrato: district—see Montferrat.

Mongolia; Meng-ku (Chinese): region north of China—17, 18.

Monolithos; Monólithos (modern Greek): town—J3e4: 8.

Monreal del Campo (Spanish): town—D4d5: 12.

Monreale (Italian): town—G4e2: 2.

Mont Escové (medieval), Pendeskouphi (medieval Greek): fortress 2 miles SW of Corinth (I3e3: 4).

Montaigu -sur-Champeix or Montaigut-le-Blanc (French): castle—E4c5: 14.

Montánchez (Spanish), Munt Antash (Arabic): town—C4e1: 13.

Montauban (French): town—E2d1: 15.

Montblanch (Spanish, from French): town 19 miles NNW of Tarragona (E2d4: 12).

Monte Cassino (Italian): abbey—G4d4: 2.

Monte Corvino or Montecorvino Rovella (Italian): town 11 miles ENE of Salerno (G5d5: 2).

Monteagudo de las Vicarías (Spanish): village—D3d4: 14.

Monteil-au-Vicomte (French): village—E2c5: 15.

Montferrat (French), Monferrato (Italian): district of NW Italy—F4c5: 1.

Montfort (French), Starkenberg (German), Qal'at al-Qurain (Arabic): castle—L1f2: 21.

Montfort-l'Amaury (French): town—E2c2: 13.

Montmirel (French): village near Canisy, 15 miles ENE of Coutances (D4c1: 1).

Montona (Italian), Motovun (Croatian): town—G4c5: 2.

Montpellier (French): town—E4d2: 13.

Montréal (medieval): fief surrounding Krak de Montréal (L1f5: 21).

Monzón (Spanish): town—E1d4: 11.

Mopsuestia: town—see Mamistra.

Morava (Czech), March (German): river—H2c2: 20.

Moravia; Morava (Czech): region SE of Bohemia—Hc: 2, 20.

Morea (medieval), Peloponnesus (Latin), Peloponnēsos or Moreas (medieval Greek), Pelopónnisos (modern Greek): peninsular region of southern Greece—Ie: 2, 4.

Morella (Spanish): town—D5d5: 13.

Morena, Sierra (Spanish): mountain range—CDe: 12, 13.

Morocco; al-Maghrib al-Aqṣâ (Arabic: the farthest west): region of NW Africa—CDef: 1.

Morón de la Frontera (Spanish), Qalb or Maurūr (Arabic): town—C5e3: 14, 15.

Morphou; Mórphou (modern Greek): town—K3e5: 10.

Morted: island—see Ceos.

Moscow; Moskva (Russian): city in Muscovy (17, 18).

Moselle (French), Mosel (German): river—F3b5: 1, 2.

Most (Czech), Brüx (German): town—G4b5: 20.

Mosul; al-Mauṣil (Arabic), Musul (Turkish): city—M4e4: 16, 17, 18.

Motovun: town—see Montona.

Mouchli (medieval Greek), Palaió Moúchli (modern Greek): mountain fortress—I3e3: 4.

Moulki; Moúlki (modern Greek): village 15 miles ESE of Livadia (I3e2: 4).

Moulouya; Malwīyah (Arabic): river—D3e5: 14.
Moundritsa (medieval), Gríllos (modern Greek): village 5 miles SSE of Olympia (I2e3: 4).
Moura (Portuguese): town—C3e2: 13.
Moutoullas; Moutoullás (modern Greek): village—K3f1: 10.
Msailha (medieval), Musailah (Arabic): castle 2 miles NE of Botron (L1f1: 21).
Msis: town—see Mamistra.
Mughan steppe; Muganskaya (Russian): region south of the lower Aras—Ne: 16.
Mughla: region—see Menteshe.
Mundīq: river—see Mondego.
Munt Atash: town—see Montánchez.
Munychia (classical): port adjoining Piraeus on SE, now included in it (I4e3: 4).
Muradal (medieval), Almuradiel (Spanish): pass—D2e2: 12, 13.
Murcia (Spanish), Mursiyah (Arabic): city, port—D4e3: 1, 11–15.
Murcia: kingdom—De: 12–15.
Muret (French): town—E2d2: 13.
Murgo: island—see Amorgos.
Muro Lucano (Italian): town—H1d5: 2.
Musailah: castle—see Msailha.
Muscovy: region around Moscow—17, 18.
Musul: city—see Mosul.
Myconos; Micone (medieval Italian), Mokene (Turkish), Míkonos (modern Greek): island—J1e3: 3.
Myloi: fief—see Molines.
Myra (classical), Eynihal (Turkish): town, now abandoned for Finike—J5e4: 3, 21.
Mytilēnē: island—see Lesbos.
Mytilene; Mytilēnē (classical Greek), Mitylēnē (medieval Greek), Mitilíni (modern Greek): town—J2e1: 3.
Myzithra: town—see Mistra.

Nabão (Portuguese): river—C2e1: 12.
Nablus; Shechem or Neapolis (classical), Nābulus (Arabic): town—L1f3: 21.
Nadravia (medieval): district of East Prussia—Iab: 19.
Nagykanizsa: town—see Kanizsay.
Nagyszeben: town—see Hermannstadt.
Nagyszombat: town—see Trnava.
Naillac (French): chateau at Le Blanc, 35 miles east of Poitiers (E1c4: 1).
Naissus: town—see Nish.
Naksa: island—see Naxos.
Namrun: fortress—see Lampron.
Namslau (German), Namysłów (Polish): town—H3b4: 20.
Naples; Napoli (Italian): city, port—G5d5: 2.
Narangia (medieval), Kós (modern Greek): town—J3e4: 3.
Narbonne (French): town—E4d2: 1, 11, 12, 13.
Narda: town—see Arta.
an-Nāṣirah: town—see Nazareth.
Natangia (medieval): district of East Prussia—Ib: 20.
Naumburg an der Saale (German): city—G2b4: 20.
Naupactus (classical), Lepanto (Italian), Epaktos (medieval Greek), Návpaktos (modern Greek): port—I2e2: 4.
Nauplia (classical), Návplion (modern Greek): port—I3e3: 4.
Navarino, Old Navarino, or Zonklon (medieval), Pylos (ancient Greek): port, now superseded by New Navarino—I2e4: 4.

Navarino, New (medieval), Neokastron (medieval Greek: new castle), Pílos (modern Greek): port—I2e4: 4.

Navarre; Navarra (Spanish): region of northern Spain—Dd: 1, 11–15.

Návpaktos: port—see Naupactus.

Návplion: port—see Nauplia.

Naxos; Nicosia (medieval Italian), Naksa (Turkish), Náxos (modern Greek): island—J1e3: 3.

Nazareth; an-Nāṣirah (Arabic): town—L1f3: 21.

Néa Epídhavros: town—see Piada.

Neapolis: town—see Nablus.

Nebovidy (Czech): village 3 miles NW of Kutná Hora (H1c1: 20).

Nederland: nation—see Netherlands.

Negroponte: island—see Euboea.

Negroponte (medieval Italian: black bridge), Chalcis (classical), Khalkís (modern Greek): town—I4e2: 2, 4.

Neman: town—see Ragnit.

Německý Brod, now Havlíčkův Brod (Czech): town—H1c1: 20.

Nemesos: port—see Limassol.

Nemunas, or Neman: river—see Niemen.

Neokastron: port—see Navarino, New.

Neopatras or Lapater (medieval), Hypatē (classical Greek), Ipáti (modern Greek): town—I3e2: 4.

Nesebar: town—see Mesembria.

Nessau (German): village—H4b3: 19.

Netherlands; Nederland (Dutch): modern nation, larger than medieval Holland (Eb: 1).

Neumark (German), Nowe Miasto Lubawskie (Polish): town—H5b2: 19.

Neumarkt in der Oberpfalz (German): town—G2c1: 20.

Nevada, Sierra (Spanish): Shulair (Arabic): mountain range—De: 15.

Nevers (French): town—E4c4: 15.

New Castile; Castilla la Nueva (Spanish): region of central Spain—Dde: 13, 14.

Nicaea (classical), İznik (Turkish): town—J5d5: 2, 3, 16, 17, 18.

Nice (French), Nizza (Italian): port, city—F3d2: 1, 2.

Nicopolis (classical), Nikopol (Bulgarian): town—I5d2: 2, 16.

Nicopolis: village—see Emmaus.

Nicosia; Levkōsia (medieval Greek), Nicosía (modern Greek): city—K4e5: 10, 21.

Nicosia: island—see Naxos.

Nicotera (Italian): town—H1e2: 2.

Niebla (Spanish), Lablah (Arabic): town—C4e3: 13, 14, 15.

Niederlausitz: district—see Lusatia, Lower.

Niederschlesien: region—see Silesia, Lower.

Niemcza (Polish), Nimptsch (German): town—H2b5: 20.

Niemen (Polish), Nemunas (Lithuanian), Memel (German), Neman (Russian): river flowing into Kurisches Haff (Ia: 19).

Nikopol: town—see Nicopolis.

Nile; Baḥr an-Nīl (Arabic): river—K3f4: 2, 16, 21.

Niort (French): town—D5c4: 14.

Nish (Turkish, Serbian), Naissus or Nissa (classical): town—I2d2: 2.

Nistru: river—see Dniester.

Nisyros; Nisiro (Italian), İnjirli (Turkish), Nísiros (modern Greek): island—J3e4: 3.

Nivelet (medieval): fief in Messenia assigned to lord of Geraki after Geraki itself (I3e4: 4) was lost.

Nizza: port—see Nice.
Nogaret (French): village—E3d2: 15.
Nogat (German, Polish): river—H5b1: 19, 20.
Nola (Italian): town—G5d5: 2.
Nordalbingia (medieval): district east of Hamburg (G1b2: 1).
Norge: region—see Norway.
Normandy; Normandie (French): region of northern France—DEc: 1, 12—15.
North Africa; al-Maghrib (Arabic: the west): region from Morocco to Cyrenaica, north of the Sahara.
North Sea—DEFab: 1, 2.
Northampton: town—D5b3: 1.
Norway; Norge (Norwegian): region west of Sweden—17, 18.
Novara (Italian): town—F4c5: 1.
Novgorod (Russian: new city): city in northern Russia—17, 18.
Nowe Miasto Lubawskie: town—see Neumark.
Noyers or Noyer (French): village—E4c3: 14.
Numidia (classical): region west and south of Tunisia (Fef: 1).
Nuremberg; Nürnberg (German): city—G2c1: 1, 2, 20.

Oberlausitz: district—see Lusatia, Upper.
Oberpfalz: region—see Palatinate, Upper.
Oberschlesien: region—see Silesia, Upper.
Ochrida or Prima Justiniana (medieval), Lychnidus or Achrida (classical), Ohrid (Serbian): town—I1d4: 4.
Ocreza or Ribeira da Ocreza (Portuguese): river—C2e2: 12.
Oder (German), Odra (Czech, Polish): river—G5b2: 1, 2, 20.
Oea: city—see Tripoli.
Oeanthea: town—see Galaxidi.
Ofen: city—see Buda.
Ogliastra (Italian): islet—F5e1: 1.
Ohrid: town—see Ochrida.
Old Castile; Castilla la Vieja (Spanish): region of northern Spain—CDd: 13, 14.
Oldenburg (German): city—F4b2: 1.
Olena; Ōlena (medieval Greek): town, now abandoned—I2e3: 4.
Olives, Mount of, or Olivet; Jabal aṭ-Ṭūr (Arabic): hill east of Jerusalem (L1f4: 21).
Olomouc (Czech), Olmütz (German): town—H3c1: 20.
Olympia (classical): ruined city—I2e3: 4.
Opočno (Czech): town—H2b5: 20.
Opole (Polish), Oppeln (German): town—H3b5: 20.
Oporto; Porto or Pôrto (Portuguese), Burṭuqāl (Arabic): city, port—C2d4: 1, 11—15.
Oran; Wahrān (Arabic): port—D5e5: 15.
Oreja or Colmenar de Oreja (Spanish): town—D2d5: 12.
Oreus (Latin), Ōreos (medieval Greek), Oreoí (modern Greek): town—I4e2: 4.
Orihuela (Spanish), Ūriyūlah (Arabic): town—D5e2: 14.
Orleans; Orléans (French): town—E2c3: 1, 11—15.
Orménion: battlefield—see Chernomen.
Orontes (classical), al-ʿĀṣī (Arabic): river—L1e4: 21.
Oropus (Latin), Ōrōpos (medieval Greek), Oropós (modern Greek): town, now village—I4e2: 4.
Orsova; Orṣova (Rumanian); town—I3d1: 2.
Oryakhovo: town—see Rahova.
Osca: town—see Huesca.

Ösel (German), Saare Maa (Estonian): island–I3a2: 19.
Osterode or Asterode (German), Ostróda (Polish): town–H5b2: 19.
Ostia (Italian): port, now village–G3d4: 2.
Ostmark: nation–see Austria.
Otranto (Italian): town–H4d5: 2.
Ourique (Portuguese): town–C2e3: 12.
Ozora (Hungarian): town–H4c4: 2, 20.

Padua; Padova (Italian): city–G2c5: 1, 2.
Pagasitikós Kólpos–see Volos, Gulf of.
Pagnac (French): village near Verneuil, 7 miles WNW of Limoges (E2c5: 1).
Pagrae: town–see Baghras.
Palaeopolis (medieval Greek), Ēlis (classical Greek), Ílis (modern Greek): town, now village, 7 miles east of Andravida (I2e3: 4).
Palaestina: region–see Palestine.
Palaiofánaro: town–see Phanaro.
Palaiokastrítsa: castle–see Sant' Angelo.
Palaiókastron Áyios Yeóryios: castle–see Saint George.
Palatia (medieval), Miletus (classical): port, now abandoned–J3e3: 3.
Palatinate; Pfalz (German): region of western Germany–Fc: 1, 2.
Palatinate, Upper; Oberpfalz (German): region of southern Germany–Gc: 2, 20.
Palermo (Italian), Balarm (Arabic): city, port–G4e2: 2.
Palestine; Palaestina (classical), Filistin (Arabic): region west of the Jordan–KLf: 16.
Palestrina (Italian): town–G3d4: 2.
Paliri (medieval): castle on Naxos–J1e3: 3.
Pallene: peninsula–see Cassandra.
Palma de Mallorca (Spanish): city, port–E3e1: 13.
Palmela (Portuguese), Balmāllah (Arabic): town–C2e2: 13.
Palmones (Spanish): stream north of Algeciras (C5e4: 14).
Palmyra or Tadmor (classical), Tadmur, now Tudmur (Arabic): caravan town–L4f1: 16, 21.
Pamphilon (medieval), Uzunköprü (Turkish): town–J2d4: 3.
Pamphylia: region–see Tekke.
Pamphylia Bay, or Gulf of Antalya–K2e4: 21.
Panadés (Spanish): district WSW of Barcelona–E2d4: 12.
Paneas: town–see Banyas.
Pantelleria (Italian): island–G3e4: 2.
Paphos; Páphos (modern Greek): town–K3f1: 10.
Paradisi, Mount; Paradísi (modern Greek)–J4e4: 8.
Paris (French): city–E3c2: 1, 11–15.
Paros; Paro (medieval Italian), Bara (Turkish), Páros (modern Greek): island–J1e3: 3.
Passau (German); town–G4c2: 1, 2, 20.
Passava or Passavant (medieval), Las (medieval Greek): castle–I3e4: 4.
Patmos; Patmo (Italian), Batnos (Turkish), Pátmos (modern Greek): island–J2e3: 3.
Patras (medieval), Pátrai (modern Greek): port, city–I2e2: 2, 4.
Pau (Spanish): village–E4d3: 15.
Pavia (Italian): town–F5c5: 1.
Pechin: town–see Petsona.
Pēdēma: village–see Pidhima.
Pedhoulas; Pedoulás or Pedhoulás (modern Greek): town–K3f1: 10.
Pedias; Pediás (modern Greek): river–K3e5: 10.

Peene (German): river—G4b2: 20.

Peipus, Lake; Peipsi Järv (Estonian), Chudskoye Ozero (Russian)—J3a2: 19.

Peking: city—see Khanbaliq.

Pelagonia (classical): district of NW Macedonia—I2d4: 4.

Pelendria; Peléndria (modern Greek): town—K3f1: 10.

Pelinnaeon: castle—see Gardiki.

Pelion, Mount; Pílion (modern Greek)—I4e1: 4.

Peloponnesus, Pelopónnisos: peninsula—see Morea.

Pendeskouphi: fortress—see Mont Escové.

Peñíscola (Spanish), Banishkulah (Arabic): town—E1d5: 13.

Pera or Estanor (medieval), Beyoghlu (Turkish): port east of the Golden Horn—J4d4: 3.

Peralta (Spanish): village—E2d4: 15.

Pereiro (Portuguese): village near Pinhel, 75 miles west of Salamanca (C5d5: 1).

Perigord; Périgord (French): district south of Limoges—E1c5: 1, 15.

Perpignan (French): town—E3d3: 11.

Persia; Īrān (Persian): region of SW Asia—NOef: 16, 17, 18.

Persian Gulf; Khalīj-i-Fars (Persian), Khalīj al-'Ajam (Arabic)—17, 18.

Peru; Perú (Spanish): region in South America—not in area mapped.

Perugia (Italian): town—G3d2: 1, 2.

Pesaro (Italian): town—G3d2: 2.

Pescia (Italian): town 9 miles ENE of Lucca (G1d2: 2).

Petite Mahomerie: fortress—see al-Qubaibah.

Petra Deserti (classical): ancient city 2 miles WSW of Wādī Mūsâ ("Li Vaux Moysi," L1f5: 21).

Petrela; Petrelë (Albanian): town—H5d4: 4.

Petroúnion: town—see Bodrum.

Petsona (medieval), Pechin or Bechin (Turkish): town, now abandoned—J3e3: 3.

Pfalz: region—see Palatinate.

Phanari (medieval Greek): town, now abandoned, 9 miles NW of Damala (I4e3: 4).

Phanaro (medieval Greek), Palaiofánaro (modern Greek): village 4 miles east of Olympia (I2e3: 4).

Pharae: town—see Kalamata.

Pharsala (medieval Greek), Fársala (modern Greek): town—I3e1: 4.

Pharygae: village—see Bodonitsa.

Pheraclos; Feraklos (modern Greek): castle, now village—J4e4: 8.

Philadelphia (classical), Alashehir (Turkish): town—J4e2: 3.

Phileremos; Filírimos (modern Greek): hilltop castle—J4e4: 8.

Philippopolis (classical), Filibe (Turkish), Plovdiv (Bulgarian): city—I5d3: 3.

Phlious: village—see Polyphengos.

Phocaea (classical): town, now abandoned for Focha—J2e2: 3.

Phocis (classical), Fokís (modern Greek): district north and west of Lake Copais—I3e2: 4.

Piada; Piádha or Néa Epídhavros (modern Greek: New Epidaurus): town—I4e3: 4.

Pian del Carpine or Piano della Magione (Italina), Planocarpino (medieval): village 9 miles WNW of Perugia (G3d2: 2).

Piave (Italian): river—G3c5: 1, 2.

Picotin (medieval): battlefield near Palaeopolis, possibly Boukhioti.

Pidhima; Pēdēma (medieval Greek), Pídhima (modern Greek): village—I3e3: 4.

Piedmont; Piemonte (Italian): region of NW Italy—Fcd: 1.

Pierre Encise: fort—see Le Destroit.

Pili; Pyli (classical), Pilí (modern Greek): town—J3e4: 3.

Pílion: mountain—see Pelion.
Pílos: port—see Navarino, New.
Pilsen (German), Plzeň (Czech): city—G4c1: 1, 2, 20.
Pinerolo (Italian): town—F3d1: 1.
Piombino (Italian): town—G1d3: 2.
Piraeus (classical), Piraiévs (modern Greek): port—I4e3: 4.
Pirineos: range—see Pyrenees.
Pisa (Italian): port, now city—G1d2: 1, 2.
Piscopi: island—see Telos.
Plaimpied (French): village—E3c3: 12.
Planocarpino: village—see Pian del Carpine.
Plassenburg (German): castle 2 miles NE of Kulmbach (G2b5: 1).
Platamon or Platamona (medieval), Platámon (modern Greek): port, now village—I3e1: 4.
Plauen im Vogtland (German): town—G3b5: 20.
Pleskau: city—see Pskov.
Plettenberg (German): town—F3b4: 1.
Plock; Płock (Polish): town—H5b3: 19.
Plön (German): town—G1b1: 2.
Plovdiv: city—see Philippopolis.
Plžen: city—see Pilsen.
Poděbrady (Czech), Podiebrad (German): town—H1b5: 20.
Pogesania (medieval): district of East Prussia—HIb: 20.
Poggibonsi (Italian): town 14 miles NW of Siena (G2d2: 2).
Poggio a Caiano (Italian): town 10 miles WNW of Florence (G2d2: 2).
Poitiers (French): town—E1c4: 1, 11.
Polabia (medieval): district of northern Germany—G1b2: 20.
Polakia or Polacchia (medieval), Apolakkiá (modern Greek): town—J3e4: 8.
Poland; Polska (Polish): region east of Germany—HIb: 2, 17, 18, 19, 20.
Polotsk (Russian): town—J4a5: 2, 17, 18, 19.
Polyphengos (medieval), Phlious (classical Greek): village, now abandoned—I3e3: 4.
Pomerania; Pommern (German): region of NE Germany—GHb: 1, 2, 19, 20.
Pomerelia; Pommerellen (German), Pomorze (Polish): district of northern Poland—Hb: 2, 19, 20.
Pomesania (medieval): district of northern Poland—Hb: 20.
Pontikókastron: castle—see Beauvoir.
Pordenone (Italian): town 28 miles WSW of Udine (G4c4: 2).
Port-de-Jonc (French): castle at Navarino (I2e4: 4).
Porțile de Fier: gorge—see Iron Gate.
Porto, or Pôrto: city—see Oporto.
Porto Kaio; Pórto Káyio (modern Greek): village—I3e4: 4.
Portugal: region, now nation—Cde: 1, 12–15.
Postupice (Czech): town—G5c1: 20.
Potamiou; Potamioú (modern Greek): village—K4e5: 10.
Pothières (French): abbey—E5c3: 15.
Potidaea, or Potídhaia: town—see Cassandrea.
Pozsony: city—see Bratislava.
Prades, Sierra de (Spanish): mountain range—Ed: 13.
Prague; Praha (Czech): city—G5b5: 1, 2, 20.
Prato in Toscana (Italian): town 12 miles NW of Florence (G2d2: 2).
Pregel (German), Pregolya (Russian): river—I1b1: 19, 20.
Přerov (Czech), Prerau (German): town—H3c1: 20.
Pressburg: city—see Bratislava.

Preussen: region—see Prussia.

Priego de Córdoba (Spanish), Bīghū (Arabic): town—D1e3: 13, 15.

Prima Justiniana: see—see Ochrida.

Propontis—see Marmara, Sea of.

Propylaea (Greek): castle on the Acropolis, in Athens (I4e3: 4).

Provence (French): region of SE France—EFd: 1, 2, 12—15.

Prusa: city—see Brusa.

Prussia; Preussen (German), Prusy (Polish): region of NE Germany—HIab: 2, 20.

Pskov (Russian), Pleskau (German): city—J4a3: 17, 18, 19.

Pteleum or Pteleon (classical), Fetenli (medieval), Pteleón (modern Greek): port—I3e1: 4.

Ptolemaïs: city—see Acre.

Puerto de Santa María or El Puerto (Spanish): port 6 miles NE of Cadiz (C4e4: 1).

Pueyo de la Cebolla or Puig de Santa María (Spanish): hill near Valencia (D5e1: 1).

Puglia, or Puglie: region—see Apulia.

Pulcheriopolis: town—see Berat.

Pylae: pass—see Thermopylae.

Pyli: town—see Pili.

Pylos: port—see Navarino.

Pyrenees; Pyrénées (French), Pirineos (Spanish): mountain range—DEd: 1, 11—15.

Pyrga; Pyrgá (modern Greek): town—K4f1: 10.

Qābis: port—see Gabes.

Qabrah: town—see Cabra.

Qādis: port—see Cadiz.

Qafṣah: town—see Gafsa.

al-Qāhirah: city—see Cairo.

Qaijātah, or Qaishātah: town—see Quesada.

al-Qairawān: city—see Kairawan.

Qaisārīyah: port—see Caesarea.

al-Qal'ah: town—see Alcalá de Henares.

Qal'at Abū-l-Ḥasan: village—see Belhacem.

Qal'at Aiyūb: town—see Calatayud.

Qal'at al-Mahalbah: village—see Balāṭunus.

Qal'at al-Muḍīq: town—see Apamea.

Qal'at al-Qurain: castle—see Montfort.

Qal'at ar-Rūm: fortress—see Hromgla.

Qal'at ash-Shaqīf: castle—see Belfort.

Qal'at Banī-Ḥammād (Arabic: fortress of the Ḥammādids): town, now abandoned—F1e5: 1.

Qal'at Barzah: castle—see Bourzey.

Qal'at Rabāḥ: fortress—see Calatrava, Old.

Qal'at Yaḥmur: fortress—see Chastel-Rouge.

Qalb: town (E Spain)—see Calpe.

Qalb: town (SW Spain)—see Morón de la Frontera.

al-Qanṭarah: town (Cyprus)—see Kantara.

al-Qanṭarah, or Qanṭarat as-Saif: town (Spain)—see Alcántara.

Qarabākah: town—see Caravaca.

Qarmūnah: town—see Carmona.

Qaryat al-'Inab or Abū-Ghosh (Arabic), Qiryat 'Anavim (Israeli): village 7 miles WNW of Jerusalem (L1f4: 21).

Qashtālah: region—see Castile.
al-Qaṣr, or Qaṣr Abī-Dānis: town—see Alcácer do Sal.
al-Qaṣr aṣ-Ṣaghīr: town—see Alcácer-Seghir.
Qaṣṭallat Darrāj: town—see Cacela.
al-Qubaibah (Arabic), Petite Mahomerie (medieval): fortress, now village, 7 miles
    NW of Jerusalem (L1f4: 21).
al-Quds: city—see Jerusalem.
Quesada (Spanish), Qaijātah or Qaishātah (Arabic): town—D2e3: 13, 14, 15.
al-Qulaiʻah: fortress—see Coliat.
Qulumrīyah: town—see Coimbra.
Qūnkah: town—see Cuenca.
Qūriyah: town—see Coria.
Qurṭubah: city—see Cordova.
Quṣair: castle—see Cursat.
Quṣanṭīnah: town—see Constantine.

Racibórz: town—see Ratibor.
Ragnit (German), Ragaine (Lithuanian), Neman (Russian): town—I3a5: 19.
Ragusa (medieval), Rhausium (classical), Dubrovnik (Serbian): port—H4d3: 2.
Rahova or Rakhovo (medieval), Oryakhovo (Rumanian): town—I4d2: 3.
Raidānīyah (Arabic): suburb of Cairo (K2f5: 16).
Ramatha (medieval): abbey 3 miles north of Lydda (K5f4: 21).
Ramla; Rama or Rames (medieval), ar-Ramlah (Arabic: the sandy): town—K5f4:
    21.
Ranculat: fortress—see Hromgla.
Randazzo (Italian): town—G5e3: 2.
Rangia: village—see Villeneuve.
Rans (French): village—F1c3: 13.
Rashīd: port—see Rosetta.
Ratibor (German), Racibórz (Polish): town—H4b5: 20.
Ratzeburg (German): town—G1b2: 20.
Ravenna (Italian): port, now town—G3d1: 2.
Red Sea; al-Baḥr al-Aḥmar (Arabic)—Lgh: 16.
Regensburg (German), Ratisbon (medieval): city—G3c1: 1, 2, 20.
Reims: city—see Rheims.
Renys (medieval): village, probably Renzin, 18 miles WSW of Marienburg
    (H5b1: 19).
Reszel: town—see Rössel.
Rethra (Slavic): sanctuary west of Lake Lucin, near Feldberg—G4b2: 20.
Reval (German), Tallinn (Estonian): city, port—I5a1: 19.
Rhausium: port—see Ragusa.
Rheims; Reims (French): city—E5c1: 1, 11–15.
Rhine; Rijn (Dutch), Rhin (French), Rhein (German): river—E5b4: 1, 2.
Rhineland: region of the middle Rhine (Fc: 1).
Rhodes; Rhodus (Latin), Rhodos (classical Greek), Ródhos (modern Greek):
    city, port—J4e4: 3, 8.
Rhodes; Rhodus (Latin), Rhodos (classical Greek), Rodos (Turkish), Rodi (Itali-
    an), Ródhos (modern Greek): island—Je: 2, 3, 16, 17, 18.
Ribatejo (Portuguese: banks of the Tagus): district of central Portugal—C2e1:
    13.
Ridefort (French): chateau, location unknown.
Riesenberg: castle—see Ryžmberk.
Riga; Rīga (Lettish): city—I5a4: 17, 18, 19.
ar-Rīḥā: town—see Jericho.

Rijn: river—see Rhine.
Rimini (Italian): town—G3d1: 2.
Rincón de Ademuz (Spanish): district of east central Spain—D4d5: 13.
Rivadostia: port—see Livadostro.
Rocaberti (Spanish): viscounty, location unknown.
Rocafort (Spanish): suburb NW of Valencia (D5e1: 1).
Rochas: city—see Edessa.
Rodez (French): town—E3d1: 14.
Ródhos, or Rodi: city, island—see Rhodes.
Rogoi (medieval): fort—I1e1: 4.
România: nation—see Rumania.
Romans-sur-Isère (French): town—F1c5: 14.
Rome; Roma (Italian): city—G3d4: 1, 2.
Ronda (Spanish), Rundah (Arabic): town—C5e4: 14, 15.
Rosenberg (German), Rožmberk nad Vltavou (Czech): castle, now village—
    G5c2: 20.
Rosetta; Rashīd (Arabic): port—K1f4: 21.
Rössel (German), Reszel (Polish): town—I2b1: 19.
Rossiya: region—see Russia.
Roucha: city—see Edessa.
Roviata (medieval): village—I2e3: 4.
Rožmberk nad Vltavou: castle—see Rosenberg.
Ruad; Aradus (classical), Arwād or Ruwād (Arabic): island—L1f1: 21.
Rubruck (Flemish), Rubrouck (French): village 7 miles NNE of St. Omer (E3b5:
    1).
Rueda (Spanish), Rūṭah (Arabic): village 2 miles NNE of Épila (D4d4: 12).
ar-Ruhā': city—see Edessa.
Rūm: region—see Anatolia.
Rum Kalesi: fortress—see Hromgla.
Rumania; România (Rumanian): modern nation north of Bulgaria (IJd: 2).
Rumeli Hisar (Turkish): fortress on Bosporus—J5d4: 3.
Rumelia; Rumeli (Turkish): Ottoman territory in Europe.
Rundah: town—see Ronda.
Russdorf (German): village, probably Roisdorf, 16 miles south of Cologne
    (F2b5: 1).
Russia; Rus (medieval), Rossiya (Russian): region of eastern Europe—JKab: 2,
    17, 18, 19.
Rūṭah: town—see Rueda.
Ruthenia (medieval): eastern Galicia, not equivalent to modern Czechoslovak
    province—IJc: 2.
Ruwād: island—see Ruad.
Ryžmberk (Czech), Riesenberg (German): castle 2 miles NNW of Kdyně (G4c1:
    20).

Saale (German): river—G2b4: 20.
Saare Maa: island—see Ösel.
Saaz: town—see Žatec.
Sabastīyah: village—see Sebastia.
Ṣabrah (Arabic): suburb of Kairawan (G1e5: 1).
Sabran (French): village—E5d1: 14.
Sabtah: port—see Ceuta.
Saccalia: district—see Sakala.
Sachsen: region—see Saxony.
Sacralias: battlefield—see Zallaca.

Sado (Portuguese), Shatūbar (Arabic): river—C2e2: 13.

Safad; Saphet (medieval), Ṣafad (Arabic), Tsefat (Israeli): town—L1f3: 21.

Safāqus: town—see Sfax.

Saffūriyah (Arabic), Sepphoris (classical), Sephorie (medieval), Tsippori (Israeli): village 5 miles NNW of Nazareth (L1f3: 21).

Ṣafītha (Arabic): village just west of Chastel-Blanc (L2f1: 21).

Sagitta: port—see Sidon.

Sagrajas: battlefield—see Zallaca.

Sahagún (Spanish): town—C5d3: 13.

Sahara; as-Ṣahrā' (Arabic): desert—DEFGfg: 1, 17, 18.

Ṣahyūn: castle—see Saone.

Ṣaidā': port—see Sidon.

Saint Abraham: town—see Hebron.

Saint Anatolia; Sant' Anatolia (Italian): village near Camerino, 33 miles east of Perugia (G3d2: 2).

Saint Aventin (French): village—E1d3: 15.

Saint Denis (French): town 7 miles north of Paris (E3c2: 1).

Saint George (medieval), Palaiókastron Áyios Yeóryios (modern Greek): castle—I3e3: 4.

Saint George: town—see Lydda.

Saint Germain-en-Laye (French): town—E3c2: 15.

Saint Gilles-du-Gard (French): town—E5d2: 12.

Saint Hilarion or Dieudamour (medieval), Áyios Ilárion (modern Greek): castle—K4e5: 10.

Saint John, or Saint Jean d'Acre: city—see Acre.

Saint Omer: castle on the Cadmea, above Thebes (I4e2: 4).

Saint Omer (French), Santaméri (modern Greek): castle—I2e3: 4.

Saint Omer (French): town—E3b5: 1.

Saint Peter: castle at Bodrum (J3e3: 3).

Saint Peter: castle at Smyrna (J3e2: 3).

Saint Quentin (French): town—E4c1: 1, 14.

Saint-Sauveur (French): abbey at Modon (I2e4: 4), and adjoining fief.

Saint Simeon (medieval), as-Suwaidīyah (Arabic), Süveydiye (Turkish): port—L1e4: 21.

Saint Superan (French), San Superano (Catalan): chateau, probably near Landiras, 19 miles SSE of Bordeaux (D5d1: 1).

Saint Vincent, Cape; Cabo de São Vicente (Portuguese), Kanīsat al-Ghurāb (Arabic): SW tip of Portugal—C2e3: 13.

Sakala or Saccalia (medieval): district of SW Estonia—IJa: 19.

Sakartvelo: region—see Georgia.

Sakız: island—see Chios.

Salā: port—see Salé.

Salado (Spanish): stream near Tarifa (C5e4: 14).

Salamanca (Spanish), Salmantiqah (Arabic): city—C5d5: 1, 11–15.

Salamis (classical), Koulourē (medieval Greek), Koluri (Turkish), Salamís (modern Greek): island—I4e3: 4.

Saldae: port—see Bugia.

Salé; Salā (Arabic): port—C4f1: 1, 14.

Saleph: river—see Calycadnus.

Salerno (Italian): port—G5d5: 2.

as-Ṣālihīyah (Arabic): suburb north of Damascus (L2f2: 21).

Salmantiqah: city—see Salamanca.

Salona or La Sola (medieval), Amphissa (classical Greek), Amfíssa (modern Greek): town—I3e2: 4.

Salonika: city—see Thessalonica.
Salonika, Gulf of—see Thermaic Gulf.
Salou (Spanish): port—E2d4: 13.
Salvatierra (medieval), Shalbaṭarrah (Arabic): castle—D2e2: 12, 13.
Salza: town—see Langensalza.
Salzburg (German): city—G4c3: 1, 2, 20.
Samaria: village—see Sebastia.
Samarkand; Samarqand (Persian, Arabic): city—17, 18.
Samland or Sambia (medieval): district of East Prussia—I1b1: 19, 20.
Sammūrah, or Ṣammūrah: town—see Zamora.
Samogitia (medieval), Zmudz (Polish), Samaiten (Lithuanian): district of western Lithuania—Ia: 19.
Samos; Samo (medieval Italian), Susam (Turkish), Sámos (modern Greek): island—J2e3: 3.
San Severino Rota (Italian): town, now Mercato San Severino, 8 miles north of Salerno (G5d5: 2).
San Superano: chateau—see Saint Superan.
Sanlúcar de Barrameda (Spanish): port—C4e4: 13, 14.
Sant' Anatolia: village—see Saint Anatolia.
Sant' Angelo (medieval), Palaiokastrítsa (modern Greek): castle on Corfu—H5e1: 4.
Santa Cruz de la Sierra (Spanish): village 9 miles south of Trujillo (C5e1: 13).
Santa Fe or Santafé (Spanish): town 7 miles west of Granada (D2e3: 1).
Santa Maria do Algarve: port—see Faro.
Santa Maura: island—see Leucas.
Santa Pau (Spanish): village—E3d3: 15.
Santaméri: castle—see Saint Omer.
Santarem; Santarém (Portuguese), Shantarīn (Arabic): city—C2e1: 1, 11, 12, 13.
Santiago de Compostela: town—see Compostela.
São Mamede de Aldão (Portuguese): battlefield—C2d4: 12.
São Vicente, Cabo de—see Saint Vincent, Cape.
Saone (medieval), Ṣahyūn or Ṣihyaun (Arabic): castle—L2e5: 21.
Saphet: town—see Safad.
Saragossa; Caesaraugusta (classical), Zaragoza (Spanish), Saraqusṭah (Arabic): city—D5d4: 1, 11—15.
Saragossa: kingdom—DEd: 11, 12.
Sarai; Sarāi (Persian, palace): town, now abandoned, near the Volga—17, 18.
Sardica: city—see Sofia.
Sardinia; Sardegna (Italian): island—Fde: 1, 2.
Sardis (classical): town, now abandoned—J4e2: 3.
Sarmadā (Arabic): village 40 miles west of Aleppo (L3e4: 21).
Saronic Gulf; Saronikós Kólpos (modern Greek)—I4e3: 4.
Sarvantikar; Sarouantikar (Armenian): fortress—L2e3: 21.
Satalia: port—see Adalia.
Satines: city—see Athens.
Saule (medieval and Latvian), Alt Rahden (German): battlefield—I5a4: 19.
Savona (Italian): port—F4d1: 1, 2.
Savoy; Savoie (French): region of SE France—F2c5: 1, 2.
Saxony; Sachsen (German): region of northern Germany—Gb: 1, 2, 20.
Sázava (Czech): river—G5c1: 20.
Scalenghe (Italian): village 10 miles east of Pinerolo (F3d1: 1).
Scandelion or Escandelion (medieval): castle—L1f2: 21.
Scandelore: port—see Alaya.

Scarpanto: island—see Carpathos.

Schachten (German): village, probably in Hesse (Fb: 1).

Schalavia (medieval): district of SW Lithuania—Ia: 19.

Schauenburg or Schaumburg (German): district of NW Germany south of Loccum (F5b3: 1).

Schlan: town—see Slaný.

Schlesien: region—see Silesia.

Schleswig or Haddeby (German), Slesvig (Danish): town—F5b1: 1, 2.

Schwaben: region—see Swabia.

Schwamberg: village—see Švamberg.

Schwarzburg (German): castle—G2b4: 20.

Schwerin (German): town—G2b2: 20.

Scio: island—see Chios.

Scotland: region north of England—CDa: 1.

Scutari (Italian), Chrysopolis (classical), Üsküdar (Turkish): port—J5d4: 3.

Scutari (Italian), Scodra (classical), Shkodër (Albanian): port—H5d3: 2.

Sebastia (medieval), Samaria (ancient), Sabasṭīyah (Arabic): village—L1f3: 21.

Sechin or Sequin (medieval), Syedra (classical), Asar Tepe (Turkish): castle—K3e4: 21.

Sedot Yam: port—see Caesarea.

Segeberg (German): monastery, now town of Bad Segeberg—G1b2: 2.

Segovia (Spanish), Shaqūbiyah (Arabic): town—D1d5: 13.

Segre (Spanish), Sègre (French), Shīqar (Arabic): river—E1d4: 12.

Segura (Spanish), Shaqūrah (Arabic): river—D5e2: 14.

Seine (French): river—E1c1: 1.

Self: river—see Calycadnus.

Seleucia Trachea (classical), Selevgia (Armenian), Silifke (Turkish): port, now town—K4e4: 16.

Selonia (medieval): district of central Latvia—Ja: 19.

Senlis (French): town—E3c1: 15.

Seo de Urgel: town—see Urgel.

Sepphoris, or Sephorie: village—see Saffūrīyah.

Septa: port—see Ceuta.

Sequin: castle—see Sechin.

Serbia; Srbija (Serbian): region east of Dalmatia—HId: 2.

Serendib: island—see Ceylon.

Serpa (Portuguese): town—C3e3: 13.

Serranía of Ronda: mountain range south of Ronda (C5e4: 14).

Serres (medieval), Sérrai (modern Greek): town—I4d4: 3, 4.

Servia; Sérvia (modern Greek): town—I2d5: 4.

Setefilla (Spanish): castle on the Guadalquivir north of Seville (C5e3: 1).

Setenil (Spanish): town—C5e4: 15.

Sévérac-le-Château (French): village—E4d1: 15.

Seville; Hispalis (classical), Sevilla (Spanish), Ishbīliyah (Arabic): city—C5e3: 1, 11–15.

Sfax; Safāqus (Arabic): town—G1f1: 1, 2.

Shadhūnah: town—see Medina Sidonia.

Shalbaṭarrah: castle—see Salvatierra.

Shalūn: river—see Jalón.

ash-Sha'm: city—see Damascus.

ash-Sha'm: region—see Syria.

Shant Yāqūb: town—see Compostela.

Shantamarīyat al-Gharb: port—see Faro.

Shantarīn: city—see Santarem.

Shaqīf Arnūn: castle—see Belfort.
Shaqīf Tīrūn: fortress—see Tyron.
Shaqūbiyah: town—see Segovia.
Shaqūrah: river—see Segura.
Sharīsh: town—see Jerez de la Frontera.
Shātibah: town—see Jativa.
Shatūbar: river—see Sado.
ash-Shaubak: fortress—see Krak de Montréal.
Shechem: town—see Nablus.
Shilb: town—see Silves.
Shintarah: town—see Sintra.
Shiqār: river—see Segre.
Shkodër: port—see Scutari.
Shqipni, or Shqipri: region—see Albania.
Shughr Baqās (Arabic): village, formerly forts of Baqās and ash-Shughr—L2e5: 21.
Shulair: range—see Nevada, Sierra.
Shuqr: river—see Júcar.
Sibiu: town—see Hermannstadt.
Sicily; Sicilia (Italian), Ṣiqillīyah (Arabic), Trinacria (medieval): island—Ge: 1, 2, 17, 18.
Sicyon: town—see Vasilicata.
Siderokastron (medieval), Heraclea (classical), Sidhirókastron (modern Greek): castle—I3e2: 4.
Siderokastron or Castel de Fer (medieval), Sidhirókastron (modern Greek): castle, now town—I2e3: 4.
Sidon; Ṣaidā' (Arabic), Sagitta (medieval): port—L1f2: 16, 21.
Siebenbürgen: region—see Transylvania.
Siena (Italian): town—G2d2: 1, 2.
Sigouri; Sígouri (modern Greek): castle—K4e5: 10.
Ṣihyaun: castle—see Saone.
Sijilmasa; Sijilmāsah (Arabic): city, now abandoned—D1f4: 1.
Sikión: town—see Vasilicata.
Silesia; Schlesien (German), Śląsk (Polish), Slezsko (Czech): region north of Moravia—Hb: 2.
Silesia, Lower; Niederschlesien (German): NW Silesia—Hb: 20.
Silesia, Upper; Oberschlesien (German): SE Silesia—Hb: 20.
Silifke: port—see Seleucia.
Silpius, Mount (classical), Ziyaret Daghï (Turkish): south of Antioch (L2e4: 21).
Silves (Portuguese), Shilb (Arabic): town—C2e3: 1, 13, 14.
Sími: island—see Syme.
Sinai; Sīnā' (Arabic): peninsula—Kfg: 16, 21.
Sinai, Mount, or Mount Horeb; Jabal Mūsâ (Arabic: mountain of Moses)—K4g2: 16, 21.
Sintra or Cintra (Portuguese), Shintarah (Arabic): town—C1e2: 1, 11.
Sinus Issicus—see Alexandretta, Gulf of.
Sion or Zion, Mount: hill south of Jerusalem (L1f4: 21).
Ṣiqillīyah: island—see Sicily.
Sïrf Sïndïgï: battlefield—see Chernomen.
Sis (Armenian, medieval), Kozan (Turkish): town—L1e3: 16, 21.
Skorta; Skortá (medieval Greek), Gortys (classical Greek): district of central Morea—I3e3: 4.
Ṣlaný (Czech), Schlan (German): town—G5b5: 20.
Śląsk, or Slezsko: region—see Silesia.

Slavia (medieval): region east of the Elbe—Gb: 20.

Slavskoye: town—see Kreuzburg.

Slesvig: town—see Schleswig.

Slovakia; Slovensko (Slovakian): region east of Moravia—HIc: 2, 20.

Smith, Mount—see Stephanos, Mount.

Smithfield, or Smoothfield: market quarter of London (D5b4: 1).

Smyrna (classical, medieval), İzmir (Turkish): city, port—J3e2: 2, 3, 16, 18.

Sofia; Sardica (classical), Sofiya (Bulgarian): city—I4d3: 3.

Solun: city—see Thessalonica.

Sorbia (medieval): district of north central Germany—G3b4: 20.

Soure (Portuguese): town—C2d5: 12.

Sozopolis (medieval), Apollonia (classical), Sozopol (Bulgarian): town—J3d3: 2, 3, 16.

Spain; Hispania (classical), España (Spanish): region south of the Pyrenees (CDEde: 1).

Sparta or Lacedaemon (Latin), Spartē or Lakedaimōn (classical Greek), Spárti (modern Greek): town—I3e3: 4.

Speroni (medieval): fief on coast NE of Glarentsa (I2e3: 4).

Speyer (German), Spire (French): town—F4c1: 1, 2.

Srbija: region—see Serbia.

Sri Lanka: island—see Ceylon.

Staab: town—see Stod.

Stalin: city—see Varna.

Stampalia: island—see Astypalaea.

Stanchio, or Stankoi: island—see Cos.

Starkenberg: castle—see Montfort.

Stavrovouni; Stavrovoúni (modern Greek): mountain—K4f1: 10.

Stazousa; Stázousa (modern Greek): village, now part of Kalokhorio—K4f1: 10.

Stębark: village—see Tánnenberg.

Steiermark: region—see Styria.

Stephanos, Mount, or Mount Smith—J4e4: 8.

Sternberg (German): town—G2b2: 20.

Stimfalía: village—see Stymphalia.

Stiris; Estir (medieval), Stíris (modern Greek): castle—I3e2: 4.

Stod (Czech), Staab (German): town—G4c1: 20.

Straits: see Bosporus, Dardanelles.

Strassburg (German), Strasbourg (French): city—F3c2: 1, 2.

Střibro (Czech), Mies (German): town—G3c1: 20.

Sturmaria (medieval): district north of Hamburg (G1b2: 1).

Stymphalia (classical), Stimfalía (modern Greek): village 1 mile SW of Zaraca (I3e3: 4).

Styria; Steiermark (German): region of southern Austria—HIc: 2, 20.

Subaibah (Arabic), L'Assebebe (medieval): fortress—L1f2: 21.

Suchem (German): parish, probably Sudheim, 65 miles WSW of Goslar (G1b4: 20).

Sudan; as-Sūdān (Arabic): region south of Egypt—Kh: 16, 17, 18.

Sudavia (medieval): district of NE Poland—Ib: 19.

Sultaniyeh; Kangurlan (Mongol), Sulṭānīyeh (Persian): town—N4e4: 16, 17, 18.

Sumatra: island of East Indies—not in area mapped.

Sumbeki: island—see Syme.

Ṣūr: port—see Tyre.

Sūriyah: region—see Syria.

Sūs (Arabic): region of western Morocco—Cf: 1.

Susa; Hadrumetum (classical), Sūsah (Arabic): port, city—G1e5: 1, 2.

Susam: island—see Samos.
as-Suwaidīyah, or Süveydiye: port—see Saint Simeon.
Suzdal (Russian): city in northern Russia—17, 18.
Švamberg (Czech), Schwamberg (German): village 17 miles ENE of Tachov (G3c1: 20).
Swabia; Schwaben (German): region of SW Germany—G1c2: 2, 20.
Sweden; Sverige (Swedish): region west of the Baltic Sea—GHa: 17, 18, 19.
Sycae: quarter—see Galata.
Syedra: castle—see Sechin.
Sykaminon (medieval Greek): town, now abandoned—I4e2: 4.
Syme; Symē (classical Greek), Simi (medieval Italian), Sumbeki (Turkish), Sími (modern Greek): island—J3e4: 3.
Syria (classical), ash-Sha'm or Sūriyah (Arabic): region—Lef: 16.
Syrian Gates; La Portelle (medieval), Tourn (Armenian), Belen Boghazǐ (Turkish): pass over the Amanus range—L2e4: 21.
Szegedin (Hungarian): city, now Szeged—I1c4: 2, 20.

Ṭabarīyah: town—see Tiberias.
Tabia or Tavia (medieval), Daviá (modern Greek): town—I3e3: 4.
Ṭabīrah: town—see Tavira.
Tablada (Spanish): suburb SSW of Seville (C5e3: 1).
Tábor (Czech): town, formerly Hradiště—G5c1: 20.
Tabor, Mount; Jabal Tābūr or Jabal aṭ-Ṭūr (Arabic), Tavor (Israeli): south of Tiberias (L1f3: 21).
Tabriz; Tabrīz (Persian): city—N2e2: 16, 17, 18.
Tacapae: port—see Gabes.
Tachov (Czech), Tachau (German): town—G3c1: 20.
Tadmor, or Tadmur: town—see Palmyra.
Tagus (classical), Tajo (Spanish), Tejo (Portuguese), Tājuh (Arabic): river—C1e2: 1, 11–15.
Talavera de la Reina (Spanish), Ṭalabīrah (Arabic): town—D1e1: 11, 12, 13.
Talay (French): village near Trézioux, 14 miles ESE of Clermont (E4c5: 1).
at-Tall aṣ-Ṣāfiyah: castle—see Blanche Garde.
Tall Ḥamdūn (Arabic), Tilhamdoun (Armenian), Toprakkale (Turkish): castle, now village 18 miles east of Adana (L1e3: 21).
Tallinn: city—see Reval.
Tāmlīlt: port—see Melilla.
Tana (medieval), Tanaïs (classical), Azov (Russian): port—L5c3: 16, 17, 18.
Tanaïs: river—see Don.
Tanas: town—see Tenes.
Tangier; Tingis (classical), Ṭanjah (Arabic): port—C5e5: 1, 15.
Tannenberg (German), Stębark (Polish): village—I1b2: 19.
Taprobane: island—see Ceylon.
Ṭarābulus: city—see Tripoli.
Taranto (Italian): port, city—H3d5: 2.
Tarazona de Aragón (Spanish), Ṭarasūnah (Arabic): town—D4d4: 12.
Tarifa (Spanish), Ṭarīf (Arabic): port—C5e4: 14.
Tarjāluh: town—see Trujillo.
Tarragona (Spanish), Ṭarrakūnah (Arabic): town—E2d4: 12, 13.
Tarsus (classical, Turkish), Darsous (Armenian): town—K5e4: 21.
Tartu: city—see Dorpat.
Ṭarṭūs: port—see Tortosa.
Tashkent; Binkāth or Tāshkand (Arabic): city—17, 18.
Ṭaṭwān: town—see Tetuan.

Ṭaudhah: town—see Tuy.

Taurus (classical), Toros Daghlari̊ (Turkish): mountain range—KLe: 16, 21.

Taus: town—see Domazlice.

Tavia: town—see Tabia.

Tavira (Portuguese), Ṭabīrah (Arabic): town—C3e3: 13.

Tavor—see Tabor, Mount.

Tbilisi: city—see Tiflis.

Teba (Spanish): town—D1e4: 14.

Tēganion: village—see Tigani.

Tejo: river—see Tagus.

Tekke (Turkish): region of sw Anatolia, equivalent to classical Pamphylia—JKe: 2, 16, 21.

Telos; Piscopi (medieval Italian), İliaki (Turkish), Tílos (modern Greek): island— J3e4: 3.

Tendilla (Spanish): town—D3d5: 15.

Tenedos; Tenedo (medieval Italian), Bozjaada (Turkish): island—J2e1: 3.

Tenes; Tanas (Arabic): town—E2e4: 1.

Tenos; Tēnos (classical Greek), Tine (medieval Italian), İstendil (Turkish), Tínos (modern Greek): island—J1e3: 3.

Teplá or Město Teplá (Czech), Tepl (German): town—G3c1: 20.

Ternovum: town—see Tirnovo.

Terracina (Italian): town—G4d4: 2.

Terre oultre le Jourdain: fief—see Montreal.

Teruel (Spanish): town—D4d5: 13.

Tetuan; Ṭaṭwān (Arabic): town—C5e5: 1.

Tevere: river—see Tiber.

Thabaria, or Tevarya: town—see Tiberias.

Thaumacia: town—see Domokos.

Thaya: river—see Dyje.

Thebes; Thēvai (classical Greek), Estives (medieval), Thívai (modern Greek): city—I4e2: 2, 4.

Theodosia: port—see Kaffa.

Thermaic Gulf, or Gulf of Salonika; Thermaïkós Kólpos (modern Greek)—I3d5: 4.

Thermopylae (classical), Pylae (medieval), Thermopílai (modern Greek): pass— I3e2: 4.

Thessalonica (medieval), Therma (classical), Solun (Macedonian), Salonika (Italian), Thessaloníki (modern Greek): city, port—I3d5: 2, 4.

Thessaly; Thessalia (classical), Vlachia (medieval), Thessalía (modern Greek): region of northern Greece—Ie: 2, 4.

Thēvai, or Thívai: city—see Thebes.

Thoisy-la-Berchère (French): village—E5c3: 15.

Tholowa or Tolowa (medieval): district of eastern Latvia—Ja: 19.

Thomokastron; Thomókastron (modern Greek): castle—I1e1: 4.

Thorn (German), Toruń (Polish): city—H4b2: 2, 19, 20.

Thrace; Thracia (Latin), Thrakē (classical Greek), Thráki (modern Greek), Trakya (Turkish): region south of Bulgaria—Jd: 2, 3, 16.

Thuringia; Thüringen (German): region of central Germany—Gb: 1, 2, 20.

Thymiana (Greek): village—J2e2: 3.

Tiber; Tevere (Italian): river—G3d4: 1, 2.

Tiberias; Thabaria (medieval), Ṭabarīyah (Arabic), Tevarya (Israeli): town— L1f3: 21.

Tiberias, Lake, or Sea of Galilee; Buḥairat Ṭabarīyah (Arabic), Yam Kinneret (Israeli)—L1f3: 21.

Tiefenau (German), Depenow (medieval): village—H4b2: 19.
Tiflis; Tiflis (Persian), Tbilisi (Georgian): city—M5d4: 16, 17, 18.
Tigani; Tēganion (classical Greek), Tigáni (modern Greek): village—I3e4: 4.
Tigris (classical), Dijlah (Arabic), Dijle (Turkish): river—N4f5: 16.
Tilbury: town, now part of Thurrock, 20 miles east of London (D5b4: 1).
Tilhamdoun: castle—see Tall Ḥamdūn.
Tilimsān: city—see Tlemsen.
Tílos: island—see Telos.
Tingis: port—see Tangier.
Tínos, or Tine: island—see Tenos.
Tintern: abbey—D3b4: 1.
Tirnovo; Ternovum (Latin), Trnovo (Bulgarian): town—J1d2: 2, 3, 16.
Tirschenreuth (German): town—G3c1: 20.
Tiscar (Spanish): village—D2e3: 14.
Tlemsen; Tilimsān (Arabic): city—D4f1: 1, 11–15.
Toledo (Spanish), Toletum (classical), Ṭulaiṭulah (Arabic): city—D1e1: 1, 11–15.
Tolowa: district—see Tholowa.
Tomar (Portuguese): town—C2e1: 13.
Toprakkale: castle—see Tall Ḥamdūn.
Torino: city—see Turin.
Toro (Spanish): town—C5d4: 15.
Toron (medieval): fortress—L1f2: 21.
Toros Daghlari: range—see Taurus.
Torre de' Passeri (Italian): town—G4d3: 2.
Tôrres Novas (Portuguese): town—C2e1: 13.
Tortosa; Antaradus (classical: opposite Aradus), Anṭarṭūs or Ṭarṭūs (Arabic): port—L1f1: 21.
Tortosa (Spanish), Dertosa (classical), Ṭurṭūshah (Arabic): town—E1d5: 1, 12, 13.
Toruń: city—see Thorn.
Toscana: region—see Tuscany.
Toulon (French): port, city—F1d2: 1, 15.
Toulouse (French): city—E2d2: 1, 11–15.
Toulouse: county—Ed: 12–14.
Tourn: pass—see Syrian Gates.
Tournai (French), Doornijk (Flemish): town—E4b5: 1.
Tours (French): city—E1c3: 1, 11–15.
Tozeur; Tuzar (Arabic): town—F4f2: 1, 2.
Trabzon: city—see Trebizond.
Trakya: region—see Thrace.
Trani (Italian): port—H2d4: 2.
Transierra (Spanish): district south of the Tagus (C5e1: 1).
Transylvania; Siebenbürgen (German), Erdély (Hungarian), Ardeal (Rumanian): region SE of Hungary—IJc: 2, 16.
Trapani (Italian): port—G3e2: 2.
Trastámara (Spanish): district of NW Spain—C2d3: 15.
Trave (German): river—G1b2: 2, 20.
Trebizond; Trapezus (classical), Trapezunt (medieval), Trabzon (Turkish): city, port—L5d5: 16, 17, 18.
Trémolay or Dramelay (French): village—F1c4: 14.
Triana (Spanish): fortress 1 mile west of Seville (C5e3: 1).
Trier (German), Trèves (French): city—F2c1: 1, 2.
Trikkala; Tricca (classical), Tríkkala (modern Greek): town—I2e1: 4.

Trinacria: island—see Sicily.

Triphylia (classical), Trifília or Fília (modern Greek): district of western Morea—I2e3: 4.

Tripití: village—see Bitsibardi.

Tripoli; Oea (classical), Ṭarābulus al-Gharb (Arabic): city, port—G4f3: 2.

Tripoli; Tripolis (classical), Ṭarābulus ash-Sha'm (Arabic): city, port—L1f1: 16, 21.

Tripolitania: region east of Tunisia—GHfg: 2.

Trnava (Slovakian), Tyrnau (German), Nagyszombat (Hungarian): town—H3c2: 20.

Trnovo: town—see Tirnovo.

Troezen, or Troizén: town—see Damala.

Troödos; Tróodos (modern Greek): mountain—K3f1: 10.

Troy; Ilium or Troia (classical): site of ancient city, at village of Hisarlik—J2e1: 3.

Troyes (French): town—E5c2: 1, 15.

Trujillo (Spanish), Tarjāluh (Arabic): town—C5e1: 13.

Trypētē: village—see Bitsibardi.

Tsefat: town—see Safad.

Tsinkiang: port—see Zaitun.

Tsippori: village—see Saffūriyah.

Tudela (Spanish), Tutela (classical), Tuṭīlah (Arabic): town—D4d3: 1, 12, 13.

Tudellén or Tudején (Spanish): castle near Fitero (D4d3: 13).

Tudmur: town—see Palmyra.

Ṭulaiṭulah: city—see Toledo.

Tunis; Tūnis (Arabic): city—G1e4: 1, 2.

Tunisia; Ifrīqiyah (Arabic): region of North Africa—FGef: 1, 2.

Turin; Torino (Italian): city—F3c5: 1, 2.

Turkey; Türkiye (Turkish): modern nation, holding Anatolia and parts of Thrace, Armenia, and Kurdistan.

Ṭurṭūshah: town—see Tortosa.

Tuscany; Toscana (Italian): region of central Italy—Gd: 1, 2.

Tusculum (Latin): town 12 miles SE of Rome (G3d4: 2), now abandoned for Frascati.

Tutela, or Tuṭīlah: town—see Tudela.

Tuy; Túy (Spanish), Ṭaudhah (Arabic): town—C2d3: 1, 12.

Tuzar: town—see Tozeur.

Tyras: river—see Dniester.

Tyre; Tyrus (classical), Ṣūr (Arabic): port—L1f2: 16, 21.

Tyrnau: town—see Trnava.

Tyron (medieval), Shaqīf Tīrūn (Arabic): cave fortress—L1f2: 21.

Tziá: island—see Ceos.

Úbeda (Spanish), Ubbadhah (Arabic): town—D2e2: 12, 13.

Uckermark (German): district of NE Germany—G4b2: 20.

Uclés (Spanish), Uqlīsh (Arabic): town—D3d5: 12, 13.

Udine (Italian): town—G4c4: 2, 20.

Ukshūnubah: region—see Algarve.

Umm Ghazālah: town—see Magacela.

Ungannia or Ugaunia (medieval): district of SE Estonia—Ja: 19.

al-'Uqab: battlefield—see Las Navas de Tolosa.

Uqlīsh: town—see Uclés.

al-Urdunīyah: nation—see Jordan.

al-Urdunn: river—see Jordan.

Urfa: city—see Edessa.
Urgel, or Seo de Urgel (Spanish): town—E2d3: 12.
Ūriyūlah: town—see Orihuela.
Urshudhūnah: town—see Archidona.
Urtubia (medieval), Urtubie (French): chateau—D4d2: 15.
Ushbūnah: city—see Lisbon.
Ụsk: town 9 miles west of Tintern (D3b4: 1).
Ụsküdar: port—see Scutari.
Ustí nad Labem (Czech), Aussig (German): town—G5b5: 20.
Ustrapalia: island—see Astypalaea.
Ụtrecht (Dutch): city—F1b3: 1, 2.
Ūxküll or Yxküll (medieval), Ikškile (Lettish): village—I5a4: 19.
Uzunköprü: town—see Pamphilon.

Vahka; Ṿahga (Armenian), Feke (Turkish): fortress, now town—L1e3: 21.
Val d'Ema (Italian): valley 3 miles SSW of Florence (G2d2: 2).
Valachia: region—see Wallachia.
Valania (medieval), Bulunyās (medieval Arabic), Bāniyās (modern Arabic): port—L1e5: 21.
Valencia (Spanish), Balansiyah (Arabic): city, port—D5e1: 1, 11–15.
Valencia: kingdom—De: 12, 13.
Valencia de Alcántara (Spanish): town—C3e1: 13.
Valenciennes (French): town 19 miles SSE of Tournai (E4b5: 1).
Vallins or Valines (French): village 10 miles east of Eu (E2b5: 1).
Valois (French): district NE of Paris—E4c1: 15.
Valona: port—see Avlona.
Vandenberg (German): castle, probably in Brandenburg (Gb: 20).
Varmia: district—see Ermland.
Varna (medieval): city, port, recently called Stalin—J3d2: 2, 3, 16.
Varosha or Varoshia; Varósha (modern Greek): suburb SE of Famagusta—K4e5: 10.
Vasilicata or Basilicata (medieval Greek), Sicyon (classical), Sikión (modern Greek): town—I3e3: 4.
Vechta (German): town—F4b3: 1, 2.
Vega; La Vega (Spanish): plain—De: 13, 14, 15.
Vélez Blanco (Spanish): town 3 miles NNW of Vélez Rubio (D3e3: 14).
Vélez-Málaga (Spanish): town—D1e4: 14, 15.
Vélez Rubio (Spanish): town—D3e3: 14.
Veligosti; Veligostē (medieval Greek): castle—I3e3: 4.
Velletri (Italian): town—G3d4: 2.
Venetia (classical), Veneto (Italian): region of NE Italy—Gc: 1, 2.
Venice; Venezia (Italian): city, port—G3c5: 1, 2.
Vera (Spanish): town—D4e3: 13, 14, 15.
Verona (Italian): city—G2c5: 2.
Veteranitsa (medieval Greek): castle—I3e2: 4.
Via Egnatia (medieval): road across Balkans from Durazzo to Constantinople—HIJd: 3, 4.
Vícemilice (Czech): village near Čáslav (H1c1: 20).
Vicenza (Italian): town—G2c5: 2.
Vich (Spanish): town—E3d4: 15.
Vidin (Bulgarian): town—I3d2: 2.
Vienna; Wien (German): city—H2c2: 2, 17, 18, 20.
Vienne (French): town—E5c5: 15.
Viennois (French): district of SE France now called Dauphiné—EFcd: 1, 15.
Viljandi: town—see Fellin.

Villa Real: town—see Ciudad Real.
Villaret (French): village near St. André-de-Majencoules, 45 miles west of Sabran (E5d1: 14).
Villefranche-sur-Mer (French), Villafranca (Italian): port—F3d2: 1.
Villehardouin (French): castle near Troyes (E5c2: 1).
Villena (Spanish), Ballānah (Arabic): town—D5e2: 13.
Villeneuve (French): town, probably Villeneuve-lès-Avignon, 1 mile NW of Avignon (E5d2: 1).
Villeneuve (French), Rangia (medieval): village on slope of Mt. Paradisi (J4e4: 8).
Villiers-le-Bel (French): town 10 miles NNE of Paris (E3c2: 1).
Vinalapó (Spanish): river—D5e2: 14.
Viru: district—see Wierland.
Visby or Wisby (Swedish): port—H4a3: 17, 18, 19.
Vislinsky Zaliv: lagoon—see Frisches Haff.
Vistula; Wisła (Polish), Weichsel (German): river—H4b1: 2, 19, 20.
Viterbo (Italian): town—G3d3: 2.
Vítkov (Czech): hill just east of Prague (G5b5: 20).
Vitry-en-Artois (French): village 26 miles SW of Tournai (E4b5: 1).
Vittoriosa: town—see Birgu.
Vivar or Bivar or Viver (Spanish): town—D5e1: 11.
Vlaanderen: region—see Flanders.
Vlachia: region—see Thessaly, Wallachia.
Vlesiri or La Glisière (medieval): castle, possibly at modern Besere, 6 miles NW of Olena (I2e3: 4).
Vlonë, or Vlorë: port—see Avlona.
Vltava (Czech), Moldau (German): river—G5b5: 20.
Voiotía: district—see Boeotia.
Volga (Russian), Itil (Tatar): river—N3c4: 16.
Volos, Gulf of; Pagasētikos Kolpos (classical and medieval Greek), Pagasitikós Kólpos (modern Greek)—I3e1: 4.
Volterra (Italian): town—G1d2: 2.
Vonitsa (medieval Greek), Vónitsa (modern Greek): town—I1e2: 4.
Vostitsa (medieval), Aegium (classical), Aíyion (modern Greek): town—I3e2: 4.
Vyšehrad (Czech): castle just south of Prague (G5b5: 20).

Wabdhah: town—see Huete.
al-Wādī al-Abyaḍ: town—see Guadalaviar.
al-Wādī al-Kabīr: river—see Guadalquivir.
Wādī Ānah: river—see Guadiana.
Wādī Ash: town—see Guadix.
Wādī-l-Hijārah: town—see Guadalajara.
Wādī Mūsâ: town—see Li Vaux Moysi.
Wagria (medieval): district north of Lübeck—Gb: 20.
Wahrān: port—see Oran.
Wales; Cymru (Welsh): region west of England—Db: 1.
Wallachia; Vlachia (medieval), Valachia (Rumanian): region north of Bulgaria—IJd: 2, 16.
Warchin (French): suburb 2 miles east of Tournai (E4b5: 1).
Warmja: district—see Ermland.
Wartenberg (German, Czech): castle—H1b5: 20.
Washqah: town—see Huesca.
Watland (medieval): district of northern Estonia—Ja: 19.
Wavrin (French): town 18 miles west of Tournai (E4b5: 1).
Weichsel: river—see Vistula.

Weiden (German): town—G3c1: 20.
Werder (German): district of northern Poland—Hb: 20.
Wesel (German): town—F2b4: 1, 2.
Weseritz: village—see Bezdružice.
Westminster: abbey and quarter in London (D5b4: 1).
Westphalia; Westfalen (German): region of NW Germany—Fb: 1, 2.
Wettin (German): town—G2b4: 20.
Wied or Altwied (German): town—F3b5: 1, 2.
Wien: city—see Vienna.
Wierland (medieval), Viru (Estonian): district of northern Estonia—IJa: 19.
Winchester: city—D4b4: 1.
Wirsberg (German): castle near Schiffenburg, 29 miles NNW of Frankfurt (F4b5: 1).
Wisby: port—see Visby.
Wisła: river—see Vistula.
Wittelsbach (German): castle 16 miles ENE of Augsburg (G1c2: 1).
Wrocław: city—see Breslau.
al-Wu'airah: town—see Li Vaux Moysi.
Wunsiedel (German): town—G2b5: 20.
Württemberg (German): region of SW Germany—Fc: 1, 2.
Würzburg (German): city—F5c1: 1, 2.

Xeres: town—see Jerez de la Frontera.

Yābisah: island—see Ibiza.
Yabnâ: village—see Ibelin.
Yāburah: town—see Évora.
Yāfā, or Yafo: port—see Jaffa.
Yam Hamelah—see Dead Sea.
Yam Kinneret—see Tiberias, Lake.
al-Yaman: region—see Yemen.
Yamurgi: island—see Amorgos.
Yavne: village—see Ibelin.
Yemel: river—see Imil.
Yemen; al-Yaman (Arabic): region of SW Arabia—17, 18.
Yenking: city—see Khanbaliq.
Yeráki: town—see Geraki.
Yerevan: city—see Erivan.
Yeroskipos; Yeroskípou (modern Greek): village—K3f1: 10.
Yerushalayim: city—see Jerusalem.
Yimnón: village—see Gymnos.
Yumurtalik: port—see Ayas.
Yxküll: village—see Üxküll.

Zacynthus, or Zákinthos: island—see Zante.
Zahara (Spanish): town 14 miles NW of Ronda (C5e4: 15).
Zaitun (medieval), Tsinkiang (Chinese): port—17, 18.
az-Zaitūn, Nahr: river—see Cinca.
Zalew Wíslany: lagoon—see Frisches Haff.
Zallaca; Sacralias or Sagrajas (Spanish), az-Zallāqah (Arabic): battlefield—C4e2: 11.
Zamora (Spanish), Sammūrah or Ṣammūrah (Arabic): town—C5d4: 1, 12.
Zante (Italian), Zacynthus (classical), Zákinthos (modern Greek): island—I1e3: 4.
Zaraca (classical), Kióni (modern Greek): village—I3e3: 4.

Zaragoza: city—see Saragossa.

Žatec (Czech), Saaz (German): town—G4b5: 20.

Zea: island—see Ceos.

Zeeland (Dutch: sealand): region at mouth of Rhine—Eb: 1.

Zeitounion; Lamia (classical), Gitonis or Citó (medieval), Zitouni (medieval Greek), Lamía (modern Greek): town—I3e2: 4.

Zeitz (German): town—G3b4: 20.

Zemgalia (medieval), Zemgale (Lettish): district of southern Latvia—Ia: 19.

Zerbst (German): town—G3b4: 20.

Zêzere (Portuguese): river—C2e1: 12.

Zilis: port—see Arzila.

Zitouni: town—see Zeitounion.

Ziyaret Daghî—see Silpius, Mount.

Zmudz: district—see Samogitia.

Znojmo (Czech), Znaim (German): town—H2c2: 20.

Zonklon: port—see Navarino.

az-Zuqāq—see Gibraltar, Strait of.

Zwettl (German): town—H1c2: 20.

INDEX

Aachen, 632, 678

Abagha, son of Hulagu; il-khan of Persia 1265–1282: 528–531, 671; wife of, *see* Maria Palaeologina (d. after 1308)

'Abbādids, Arab dynasty at Seville, *see* al-Mu'tamid 1069–1091, Zaida

'Abbāsids, Arab caliphal dynasty at Baghdad 749–1258: 426, 460, 465, 469, 472, 515, 528, 668, 671; *and see* Hārūn ar-Rashīd 786–809, al-Qā'im 1031–1075, an-Nāṣir 1180–1225, al-Musta'ṣim 1242–1258; at Cairo 1261–1519, *see* al-Qā'im 1451–1455, al-Mustamsik 1497–1517

'Abd-al-'Azīz I (abū-Fāris), son of Ibrāhīm I; Ḥafṣid ruler of Tunisia 1283–1283: 477

'Abd-al-'Azīz II (abū-Fāris), son of Aḥmad II; Ḥafṣid ruler of Tunisia 1394–1434: 482, 483

'Abd-al-'Azīz, al-Manṣūr, Mamluk sultan of Egypt and Syria 1405–1406: 491

'Abd-al-Mu'min (abū-Muḥammad) ibn-'Alī, Muwaḥḥid caliph of Morocco and Andalusia 1130–1163: 411–413, 423, 466–468, 668

'Abd-al-Wāḥid, al-Marrākushī, Arabic chronicler (d. after 1223), 458 note

'Abd-al-Wāḥid II (abū-Muḥammad), ar-Rashīd, son of Idrīs I; Muwaḥḥid caliph of Morocco 1232–1242: 427, 470

'Abd-Allāh (abū-Muḥammad), al-'Ādil, son of Ya'qūb; Muwaḥḥid caliph of Morocco and Andalusia 1224–1227: 426

'Abd-Allāh ibn-Buluggīn, Zīrid king of Granada 1073–1090 (d. 1095), 401

'Abd-Allāh (abū-Muḥammad) ibn-Muḥammad, al-Baiyāsī, Muwaḥḥid governor of Baeza (in 1224), "caliph" (d. 1226), 426

'Abd-Allāh ibn-Yāsīn, al-Kazūlī, founder of Murābiṭ sect (*fl.* 1056), 464

'Abd-ar-Raḥmān, Ibn-Munqidh, Egyptian envoy (in 1190), 469

'Abd-ar-Raḥmān II (abū-Tāshfīn), son of Mūsâ II; Ziyānid rebel 1387–1389, ruler in Algeria 1389–1393: 479, 481–483

Abodrites (Obotrites), Slavic people, 552, 554, *and see* Billug, Gottschalk, Niklot, Pribislav

Abū-Bakr ibn-Mūsâ, al-Kūmī ("Ibn-al-Wazīr"), Ḥafṣid governor of Constantine (in 1282), 476, 477

Abū-Bakr ibn-'Umar, al-Lamtūnī, brother of Yaḥyâ; Murābiṭ ruler of Morocco 1056–1087: 465, 667

Abū-Bakr II (abū-Yaḥyâ) ibn-Yaḥyâ (son of Ibrāhīm I), Ḥafṣid ruler of Tunisia 1310–1346: 480

Abū-Dabbūs (Muwaḥḥid), *see* Idrīs II

Abū-Sa'īd, son of Öljeitu; il-khan of Persia 1316–1335: 543

Acandia bay, 325, 336

Acarnania, 129, 147, 164, 678

Acciajuoli, Florentine banking family, 120, 123–127, 140, 141, 215, 224, 238, 255, 257, 267, 272, 274, 294, 296, *and see individual entries;* properties of, 148 note, 155, 158, 253

Acciajuoli, Angelo, brother of Nerio I; cardinal-priest (Roman) 1384–1397, Angevin vicar of Achaea 1394–1405, cardinal-bishop of Ostia 1397–1408: 156, 238, 239 note, 250, 255, 258, 267

Acciajuoli, Angelo, son of Nicholas; grand seneschal of Naples, count of Melfi 1365–1391: 140, 144, 257

Acciajuoli, Antonio, son of Donato; bishop of Cephalonia 1427–?1430: 270

Acciajuoli, Antonio I, bastard son of Nerio I and Maria Rendi; lord of Thebes 1394–1435, duke of Athens 1403–1435: 158, 224, 255, 256, 258, 263–271, 275, 277, 309, 674; wife of, *see* Maria (Melissena?, d. after 1435)

Acciajuoli, Antonio II, son of Francis (of Sykaminon); duke of Athens 1439?–1441: 270–273

Acciajuoli, Bartolommea, daughter of Nerio I; wife of Theodore I Palaeologus (m. by 1385), 238, 255–258

COMPOSED BY THE COMPOSING ROOM, GRAND RAPIDS, MICHIGAN
MANUFACTURED BY NORTH CENTRAL PUBLISHING CO., MINNEAPOLIS, MINNESOTA
TEXT IS SET IN PRESS ROMAN, DISPLAY LINES IN GARAMOND

ᵾᵾᵾ

Library of Congress Cataloging in Publication Data (Revised)
Setton, Kenneth Meyer, 1914–
A history of the Crusades.
Bibliographical footnotes.
CONTENTS: v. 1. The first hundred years, edited by
M. W. Baldwin.–v. 2. The later Crusades, 1189–1311,
edited by R. L. Wolff and H. W. Hazard.–v. 3. The
fourteenth and fifteenth centuries, edited by Harry W.
Hazard.
1. Crusades. I. Title.
D157.S482   940.1'8   68-9837
ISBN 0-299-06670-3   (v.3)

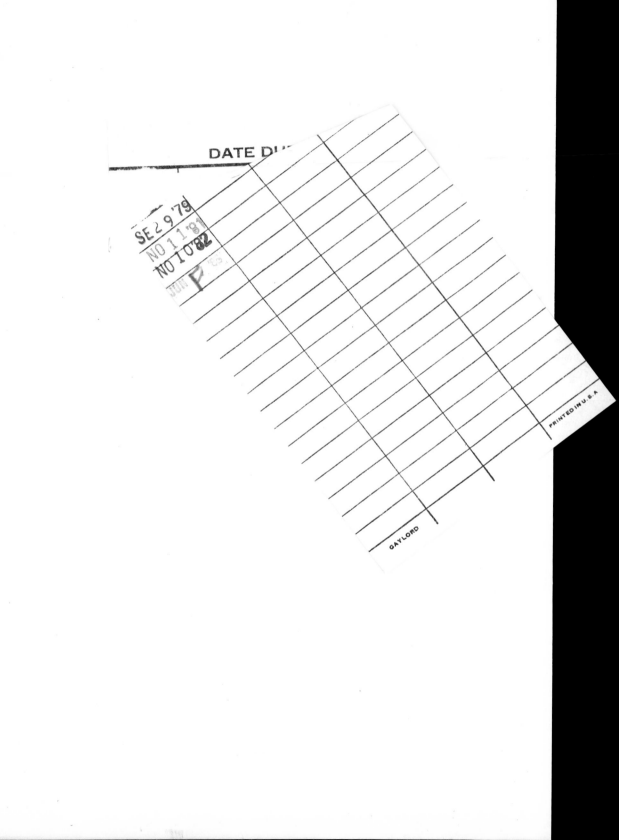

DATE DUE

SE 29 79
NO 11 '81
NO 10 82
JUN

GAYLORD

PRINTED IN U.S.A